TAX CONTROVERSIES:
STATUTES, REGULATIONS,
AND OTHER MATERIALS

TAX CONTROVERSIES: STATUTES, REGULATIONS, AND OTHER MATERIALS

Fourth Edition
2013

Leandra Lederman
William W. Oliver Professor of Tax Law
Indiana University Maurer School of Law, Bloomington

Stephen W. Mazza
Dean and Professor of Law
University of Kansas School of Law

LexisNexis®
Matthew Bender®

ISBN: 9780769847450

E-book ISBN: 9780327185536

NOTE TO USERS

To ensure that you are using the latest materials available in this area, please be sure to periodically check the LexisNexis Law School website for downloadable updates and supplements at www.lexisnexis.com/lawschool.

Editorial Offices

121 Chanlon Road, New Providence, NJ 07974

201 Mission St., San Francisco, CA 94105-1831 (415) 908-3200

www.lexisnexis.com

Summary Table of Contents

Table of Contents

Form 9465, Installment Agreement Request.
Form 12153, Request for a Collection Due
  Process or Equivalent Hearing.

Form 12510, Questionnaire for Requesting
  Spouse.

IRS Publication 1, Your Rights as a Taxpayer.
IRS Publication 5, Your Appeal Rights and How to Prepare a Protest If You Don't Agree.
IRS Publication 556, Examination of Returns, Appeal Rights, and Claims for Refund.
IRS Publication 594, The IRS Collection Process.
IRS Publication 947, Practice Before the IRS and Power of Attorney.
IRS Publication 971, Innocent Spouse Relief.

PART I

Internal Revenue Code (Selected Sections)

§ 1311. Correction of error.

(a) General rule. If a determination (as defined in section 1313 is described in one or more of the paragraphs of section 1312 and, on the date of the determination, correction of the effect of the error referred to in the applicable paragraph of section 1312 is prevented by the operation of any law or rule of law, other than this part and other than section 7122 (relating to compromises), then the effect of the error shall be corrected by an adjustment made in the amount and in the manner specified in section 1314.

(b) Conditions necessary for adjustment.

(1) Maintenance of an inconsistent position. Except in cases described in paragraphs (3)(B) and (4) of section 1312, an adjustment shall be made under this part only if –

(A) in case the amount of the adjustment would be credited or refunded in the same manner as an overpayment under section 1314, there is adopted in the determination a position maintained by the Secretary, or

(B) in case the amount of the adjustment would be assessed and collected in the same manner as a deficiency under section 1314, there is adopted in the determination a position maintained by the taxpayer with respect to whom the determination is made, and the position maintained by the Secretary in the case described in subparagraph (A) or maintained by the taxpayer in the case described in subparagraph (B) is inconsistent with the erroneous inclusion, exclusion, omission, allowance, disallowance, recognition, or nonrecognition, as the case may be.

(2) Correction not barred at time of erroneous action.

(A) Determination described in section 1312(3)(B). In the case of a determination described in section 1312(3)(B) (relating to certain exclusions from income), adjustment shall be made under this part only if assessment of a deficiency for the taxable year in which the item is includible or against the related taxpayer was not barred, by any law or rule of law, at the time the Secretary first maintained, in a notice of deficiency sent pursuant to section 6212 or before the Tax Court, that the item described in section 1312(3)(B) should be included in the gross income of the taxpayer for the taxable year to which the determination relates.

(B) Determination described in section 1312(4). In the case of a determination described in section 1312(4) (relating to disallowance of certain deductions and credits), adjustment shall be made under this part only if credit or refund of the overpayment attributable to the deduction or credit described in such section which should have been allowed to the taxpayer or related taxpayer was not barred, by any law or rule of law, at the time the taxpayer first maintained before the Secretary or before the Tax Court, in writing, that he was entitled to such deduction or credit for the taxable year to which the determination relates.

(3) Existence of relationship. In case the amount of the adjustment would be assessed and collected in the same manner as a deficiency (except for cases described in section

1312(3)(B), the adjustment shall not be made with respect to a related taxpayer unless he stands in such relationship to the taxpayer at the time the latter first maintains the inconsistent position in a return, claim for refund, or petition (or amended petition) to the Tax Court for the taxable year with respect to which the determination is made, or if such position is not so maintained, then at the time of the determination.

§ 1312. Circumstances of adjustment.

The circumstances under which the adjustment provided in section 1311 is authorized are as follows:

(1) Double inclusion of an item of gross income. The determination requires the inclusion in gross income of an item which was erroneously included in the gross income of the taxpayer for another taxable year or in the gross income of a related taxpayer.

(2) Double allowance of a deduction or credit. The determination allows a deduction or credit which was erroneously allowed to the taxpayer for another taxable year or to a related taxpayer.

(3) Double exclusion of an item of gross income.

(A) Items included in income. The determination requires the exclusion from gross income of an item included in a return filed by the taxpayer or with respect to which tax was paid and which was erroneously excluded or omitted from the gross income of the taxpayer for another taxable year, or from the gross income of a related taxpayer; or

(B) Items not included in income. The determination requires the exclusion from gross income of an item not included in a return filed by the taxpayer and with respect to which the tax was not paid but which is includible in the gross income of the taxpayer for another taxable year or in the gross income of a related taxpayer.

(4) Double disallowance of a deduction or credit. The determination disallows a deduction or credit which should have been allowed to, but was not allowed to, the taxpayer for another taxable year, or to a related taxpayer.

* * *

§ 1313. Definitions.

(a) Determination. For purposes of this part, the term 'determination' means –

(1) a decision by the Tax Court or a judgment, decree, or other order by any court of competent jurisdiction, which has become final;

(2) a closing agreement made under section 7121;

(3) a final disposition by the Secretary of a claim for refund. For purposes of this part, a claim for refund shall be deemed finally disposed of by the Secretary –

(A) as to items with respect to which the claim was allowed, on the date of allowance of refund or credit or on the date of mailing notice of disallowance (by reason of offsetting items) of the claim for refund, and

(B) as to items with respect to which the claim was disallowed, in whole or in part, or as to items applied by the Secretary in reduction of the refund or credit, on expiration of the time for instituting suit with respect thereto (unless suit is instituted before the expiration of such time); or

(4) under regulations prescribed by the Secretary, an agreement for purposes of this part, signed by the Secretary and by any person, relating to the liability of such person (or the person for whom he acts) in respect of a tax under this subtitle for any taxable period.

(b) Taxpayer. Notwithstanding section 7701(a)(14), the term 'taxpayer' means any person subject to a tax under the applicable revenue law.

* * *

§ 1314. Amount and method of adjustment.

(a) Ascertainment of amount of adjustment. In computing the amount of an adjustment under this part there shall first be ascertained the tax previously determined for the taxable year with respect to which the error was made. The amount of the tax previously determined shall be the excess of –

(1) the sum of –

(A) the amount shown as the tax by the taxpayer on his return (determined as provided in section 6211(b)(1), (3), and (4), (3), and (4)], relating to the definition of deficiency), if a return was made by the taxpayer and an amount was shown as the tax by the taxpayer thereon, plus

(B) the amounts previously assessed (or collected without assessment) as a deficiency over –

(2) the amount of rebates, as defined in section 6211(b)(2), made. There shall then be ascertained the increase or decrease in tax previously determined which results solely from the correct treatment of the item which was the subject of the error (with due regard given to the effect of the item in the computation of gross income, taxable income, and other matters under this subtitle. A similar computation shall be made for any other taxable year affected, or treated as affected, by a net operating loss deduction (as defined in section 172 or by a capital loss carryback or carryover (as defined in section 1212), determined with reference to the taxable year with respect to which the error was made. The amount so ascertained (together with any amounts wrongfully collected as additions to the tax or interest, as a result of such error) for each taxable year shall be the amount of the adjustment for that taxable year.

(b) Method of adjustment. The adjustment authorized in section 1311(a) shall be made by assessing and collecting, or refunding or crediting, the amount thereof in the same manner as if it were a deficiency determined by the Secretary with respect to the taxpayer as to whom the error was made or an overpayment claimed by such taxpayer, as the case may be, for the taxable year or years with respect to which an amount is ascertained under subsection (a), and as if on the date of the determination one year remained before the expiration of the periods of limitation upon assessment or filing claim for refund for such taxable year or years. If, as a result of a determination described in section 1313(a)(4), an adjustment has been made by the assessment and collection of a deficiency or the refund or credit of an overpayment, and subsequently such determination is altered or revoked, the amount of the adjustment ascertained under subsection (a) of this section shall be redetermined on the basis of such alteration or revocation and any overpayment or deficiency resulting from such redetermination shall be refunded or credited, or assessed and collected, as the case may be, as an adjustment under this part. In the case of an adjustment resulting from an increase or decrease in a net operating loss or net capital loss which is carried back to the year of adjustment, interest shall not be collected or paid for any period prior to the close of the taxable year in which the net operating loss or net capital loss arises.

(c) Adjustment unaffected by other items. The amount to be assessed and collected in the same manner as a deficiency, or to be refunded or credited in the same manner as an overpayment, under this part, shall not be diminished by any credit or set-off based upon any item other than the one which was the subject of the adjustment. The amount of the adjustment under this part, if paid, shall not be recovered by a claim or suit for refund or suit for erroneous refund based upon any item other than the one which was the subject of the adjustment.

* * *

§ 1372. Partnership rules to apply for fringe benefit purposes.

(a) General rule. For purposes of applying the provisions of this subtitle which relate to employee fringe benefits –

(1) the S corporation shall be treated as a partnership, and

(2) any 2-percent shareholder of the S corporation shall be treated as a partner of such partnership.

(b) 2-percent shareholder defined. For purposes of this section, the term "2-percent shareholder" means any person who owns (or is considered as owning within the meaning of section 318) on any day during the taxable year of the S corporation more than 2 percent of the outstanding stock of such corporation or stock possessing more than 2 percent of the total combined voting power of all stock of such corporation.

* * *

§ 6001. Notice or regulations requiring records, statements, and special returns.

Every person liable for any tax imposed by this title, or for the collection thereof, shall keep such records, render such statements, make such returns, and comply with such rules and regulations as the Secretary may from time to time prescribe. Whenever in the judgment of the Secretary it is necessary, he may require any person, by notice served upon such person or by regulations, to make such returns, render such statements, or keep such records, as the Secretary deems sufficient to show whether or not such person is liable for tax under this title. The only records which an employer shall be required to keep under this section in connection with charged tips shall be charge receipts, records necessary to comply with section 6053(c), and copies of statements furnished by employees under section 6053(a).

* * *

§ 6011. General requirement of return, statement, or list.

(a) General rule. When required by regulations prescribed by the Secretary any person made liable for any tax imposed by this title, or with respect to the collection thereof, shall make a return or statement according to the forms and regulations prescribed by the Secretary. Every person required to make a return or statement shall include therein the information required by such forms or regulations.

* * *

(f) Promotion of electronic filing.

(1) In general. The Secretary is authorized to promote the benefits of and encourage the use of electronic tax administration programs, as they become available, through the use of mass communications and other means.

(2) Incentives. The Secretary may implement procedures to provide for the payment of appropriate incentives for electronically filed returns.

* * *

§ 6012. Persons required to make returns of income.

(a) General rule. Returns with respect to income taxes under subtitle A shall be made by the following:

(1) (A) Every individual having for the taxable year gross income which equals or exceeds the exemption amount, except that a return shall not be required of an individual –

(i) who is not married (determined by applying section 7703), is not a surviving spouse (as defined in section 2(a)), is not a head of a household (as defined in section 2(b)), and for the taxable year has gross income of less than the sum of the exemption amount plus the basic standard deduction applicable to such an individual,

(ii) who is a head of a household (as so defined) and for the taxable year has gross income of less than the sum of the exemption amount plus the basic standard deduction applicable to such an individual,

(iii) who is a surviving spouse (as so defined) and for the taxable year has gross income of less than the sum of the exemption amount plus the basic standard deduction applicable to such an individual, or

(iv) who is entitled to make a joint return and whose gross income, when combined with the gross income of his spouse, is, for the taxable year, less than the sum of twice the exemption amount plus the basic standard deduction applicable to a joint return, but only if such individual and his spouse, at the close of the taxable year, had the same household as their home.

Clause (iv) shall not apply if for the taxable year such spouse makes a separate return or any other taxpayer is entitled to an exemption for such spouse under section 151(c).

(B) The amount specified in clause (i), (ii), or (iii) of subparagraph (A) shall be increased by the amount of 1 additional standard deduction (within the meaning of section 63(c)(3)) in the case of an individual entitled to such deduction by reason of section 63(f)(1)(A) (relating to individuals age 65 or more), and the amount specified in clause (iv) of subparagraph (A) shall be increased by the amount of the additional standard deduction for each additional standard deduction to which the individual or his spouse is entitled by reason of section 63(f)(1).

(C) The exception under subparagraph (A) shall not apply to any individual –

(i) who is described in section 63(c)(5) and who has –

(I) income (other than earned income) in excess of the sum of the amount in effect under section 63(c)(5)(A) plus the additional standard deduction (if any) to which the individual is entitled, or

(II) total gross income in excess of the standard deduction, or

(ii) for whom the standard deduction is zero under section 63(c)(6).

(D) For purposes of this subsection –

(i) The terms "standard deduction", "basic standard deduction" and "additional standard deduction" have the respective meanings given such terms by section 63(c).

(ii) The term "exemption amount" has the meaning given such term by section 151(d). In the case of an individual described in section 151(d)(2), the exemption amount shall be zero.

(2) Every corporation subject to taxation under subtitle A;

(3) Every estate the gross income of which for the taxable year is $600 or more;

(4) Every trust having for the taxable year any taxable income, or having gross income of $600 or over, regardless of the amount of taxable income;

(5) Every estate or trust of which any beneficiary is a nonresident alien;

(6) Every political organization (within the meaning of section 527(e)(1)), and every fund treated under section 527(g) as if it constituted a political organization, which has political organization taxable income (within the meaning of section 527(c)(1)) for the taxable year; and

(7) Every homeowners association (within the meaning of section 528(c)(1)) which has homeowners association taxable income (within the meaning of section 528(d)) for the taxable year[;]

(8) Every estate of an individual under chapter 7 or 11 of title 11 of the United States Code (relating to bankruptcy) the gross income of which for the taxable year is not less than the sum of the exemption amount plus the basic standard deduction under section 63(c)(2)(D).

(9) [Redesignated]

except that subject to such conditions, limitations, and exceptions and under such regulations as may be prescribed by the Secretary, nonresident alien individuals subject to the tax imposed by section 871 and foreign corporations subject to the tax imposed by section 881 may be exempted from the requirement of making returns under this section.

* * *

§ 6013. Joint returns of income tax by husband and wife.

(a) Joint returns. A husband and wife may make a single return jointly of income taxes under subtitle A, even though one of the spouses has neither gross income nor deductions, except as provided below:

(1) no joint return shall be made if either the husband or wife at any time during the taxable year is a nonresident alien;

(2) no joint return shall be made if the husband and wife have different taxable years; except that if such taxable years begin on the same day and end on different days because of the death of either or both, then the joint return may be made with respect to the taxable year of each. The above exception shall not apply if the surviving spouse remarries before the close of his taxable year, nor if the taxable year of either spouse is a fractional part of a year under section 443(a)(1);

* * *

(d) Special rules. For purposes of this section –

* * *

(3) if a joint return is made, the tax shall be computed on the aggregate income and the liability with respect to the tax shall be joint and several.

* * *

§ 6014. Income tax return--tax not computed by taxpayer.

(a) Election by taxpayer. An individual who does not itemize his deductions and who is not described in section 6012(a)(1)(C)(i), whose gross income is less than $10,000 and includes no income other than remuneration for services performed by him as an employee, dividends or interest, and whose gross income other than wages, as defined in section 3401(a), does not exceed $100, shall at his election not be required to show on the return the tax imposed by section 1. Such election shall be made by using the form prescribed for purposes of this section. In such case the tax shall be computed by the Secretary who shall mail to the taxpayer a notice stating the amount determined as payable.

* * *

§ 6015. Relief from joint and several liability on joint return.

* * *

(b) Procedures for relief from liability applicable to all joint filers.

(1) **In general.** Under procedures prescribed by the Secretary, if –

(A) a joint return has been made for a taxable year;

(B) on such return there is an understatement of tax attributable to erroneous items of one individual filing the joint return;

(C) the other individual filing the joint return establishes that in signing the return he or she did not know, and had no reason to know, that there was such understatement;

(D) taking into account all the facts and circumstances, it is inequitable to hold the other individual liable for the deficiency in tax for such taxable year attributable to such understatement; and

(E) the other individual elects (in such form as the Secretary may prescribe) the benefits of this subsection not later than the date which is 2 years after the date the Secretary has begun collection activities with respect to the individual making the election, then the other individual shall be relieved of liability for tax (including interest, penalties, and other amounts) for such taxable year to the extent such liability is attributable to such understatement.

(2) **Apportionment of relief.** If an individual who, but for paragraph (1)(C), would be relieved of liability under paragraph (1), establishes that in signing the return such individual did not know, and had no reason to know, the extent of such understatement, then such individual shall be relieved of liability for tax (including interest, penalties, and other amounts) for such taxable year to the extent that such liability is attributable to the portion of such understatement of which such individual did not know and had no reason to know.

(3) **Understatement.** For purposes of this subsection, the term "understatement" has the meaning given to such term by section 6662(d)(2)(A).

(c) Procedures to limit liability for taxpayers no longer married or taxpayers legally separated or not living together.

(1) **In general.** Except as provided in this subsection, if an individual who has made a joint return for any taxable year elects the application of this subsection, the individual's liability for any deficiency which is assessed with respect to the return shall not exceed the portion of such deficiency properly allocable to the individual under subsection (d).

(2) **Burden of proof.** Except as provided in subparagraph (A)(ii) or (C) of paragraph (3), each individual who elects the application of this subsection shall have the burden of proof with respect to establishing the portion of any deficiency allocable to such individual.

(3) **Election.**

(A) **Individuals eligible to make election.**

(i) **In general.** An individual shall only be eligible to elect the application of this subsection if –

(I) at the time such election is filed, such individual is no longer married to, or is legally separated from, the individual with whom such individual filed the joint return to which the election relates; or

(II) such individual was not a member of the same household as the individual with whom such joint return was filed at any time during the 12-month period ending on the date such election is filed.

(ii) Certain taxpayers ineligible to elect. If the Secretary demonstrates that assets were transferred between individuals filing a joint return as part of a fraudulent scheme by such individuals, an election under this subsection by either individual shall be invalid (and section 6013(d)(3) shall apply to the joint return).

(B) Time for election. An election under this subsection for any taxable year may be made at any time after a deficiency for such year is asserted but not later than 2 years after the date on which the Secretary has begun collection activities with respect to the individual making the election.

(C) Election not valid with respect to certain deficiencies. If the Secretary demonstrates that an individual making an election under this subsection had actual knowledge, at the time such individual signed the return, of any item giving rise to a deficiency (or portion thereof) which is not allocable to such individual under subsection (d), such election shall not apply to such deficiency (or portion). This subparagraph shall not apply where the individual with actual knowledge establishes that such individual signed the return under duress.

(4) Liability increased by reason of transfers of property to avoid tax.

(A) In general. Notwithstanding any other provision of this subsection, the portion of the deficiency for which the individual electing the application of this subsection is liable (without regard to this paragraph) shall be increased by the value of any disqualified asset transferred to the individual.

(B) Disqualified asset. For purposes of this paragraph –

(i) In general. The term "disqualified asset" means any property or right to property transferred to an individual making the election under this subsection with respect to a joint return by the other individual filing such joint return if the principal purpose of the transfer was the avoidance of tax or payment of tax.

(ii) Presumption.

(I) In general. For purposes of clause (i), except as provided in subclause (II), any transfer which is made after the date which is 1 year before the date on which the first letter of proposed deficiency which allows the taxpayer an opportunity for administrative review in the Internal Revenue Service Office of Appeals is sent shall be presumed to have as its principal purpose the avoidance of tax or payment of tax.

(II) Exceptions. Subclause (I) shall not apply to any transfer pursuant to a decree of divorce or separate maintenance or a written instrument incident to such a decree or to any transfer which an individual establishes did not have as its principal purpose the avoidance of tax or payment of tax.

(d) Allocation of deficiency. For purposes of subsection (c) –

(1) In general. The portion of any deficiency on a joint return allocated to an individual shall be the amount which bears the same ratio to such deficiency as the net amount of items taken into account in computing the deficiency and allocable to the individual under paragraph (3) bears to the net amount of all items taken into account in computing the deficiency.

(2) Separate treatment of certain items. If a deficiency (or portion thereof) is attributable to –

(A) the disallowance of a credit; or

(B) any tax (other than tax imposed by section 1 or 55) required to be included with the joint return; and such item is allocated to one individual under paragraph (3), such deficiency (or portion) shall be allocated to such individual. Any such item shall not be taken into account under paragraph (1).

(3) Allocation of items giving rise to the deficiency. For purposes of this subsection—

(A) In general. Except as provided in paragraphs (4) and (5), any item giving rise to a deficiency on a joint return shall be allocated to individuals filing the return in the same manner as it would have been allocated if the individuals had filed separate returns for the taxable year.

(B) Exception where other spouse benefits. Under rules prescribed by the Secretary, an item otherwise allocable to an individual under subparagraph (A) shall be allocated to the other individual filing the joint return to the extent the item gave rise to a tax benefit on the joint return to the other individual.

(C) Exception for fraud. The Secretary may provide for an allocation of any item in a manner not prescribed by subparagraph (A) if the Secretary establishes that such allocation is appropriate due to fraud of one or both individuals.

(4) Limitations on separate returns disregarded. If an item of deduction or credit is disallowed in its entirety solely because a separate return is filed, such disallowance shall be disregarded and the item shall be computed as if a joint return had been filed and then allocated between the spouses appropriately. A similar rule shall apply for purposes of section 86.

(5) Child's liability. If the liability of a child of a taxpayer is included on a joint return, such liability shall be disregarded in computing the separate liability of either spouse and such liability shall be allocated appropriately between the spouses.

(e) Petition for review by Tax Court.

(1) In general. In the case of an individual against whom a deficiency has been asserted and who elects to have subsection (b) or (c) apply, or in the case of an individual who requests equitable relief under subsection (f) –

(A) In general. In addition to any other remedy provided by law, the individual may petition the Tax Court (and the Tax Court shall have jurisdiction) to determine the appropriate relief available to the individual under this section if such petition is filed –

(i) at any time after the earlier of –

(I) the date the Secretary mails, by certified or registered mail to the taxpayer's last known address, notice of the Secretary's final determination of relief available to the individual, or

(II) the date which is 6 months after the date such election is filed or request is made with the Secretary, and

(ii) not later than the close of the 90th day after the date described in clause (i)(I).

(B) Restrictions applicable to collection of assessment.

(i) In general. Except as otherwise provided in section 6851 or 6861, no levy or proceeding in court shall be made, begun, or prosecuted against the individual making an election under subsection (b) or (c) or requesting equitable relief under subsection (f) for collection of any assessment to which such election or request relates until the close of the 90-day period referred to in subparagraph (A)(ii), or, if a petition has been filed with the Tax Court, until the decision of the Tax Court has become final. Rules similar to the rules of section 7485 shall apply with respect to the collection of such assessment.

(ii) Authority to enjoin collection actions. Notwithstanding the provisions of section 7421(a), the beginning of such levy or proceeding during the time the prohibition under clause (i) is in force may be enjoined by a proceeding in the proper court, including the Tax Court. The Tax Court shall have no jurisdiction under this subparagraph to enjoin any action or proceeding unless a timely petition has been filed under subparagraph (A) and then only in respect of the amount of the assessment to which the election under subsection (b) or (c) relates or to which the request under subsection (f) relates.

(2) Suspension of running of period of limitations. The running of the period of limitations in section 6502 on the collection of the assessment to which the petition under paragraph (1)(A) relates shall be suspended –

(A) for the period during which the Secretary is prohibited by paragraph (1)(B) from collecting by levy or a proceeding in court and for 60 days thereafter, and

(B) if a waiver under paragraph (5) is made, from the date the claim for relief was filed until 60 days after the waiver is filed with the Secretary.

(3) Limitation on tax court jurisdiction. If a suit for refund is begun by either individual filing the joint return pursuant to section 6532 –

(A) the Tax Court shall lose jurisdiction of the individual's action under this section to whatever extent jurisdiction is acquired by the district court or the United States Court of Federal Claims over the taxable years that are the subject of the suit for refund, and

(B) the court acquiring jurisdiction shall have jurisdiction over the petition filed under this subsection.

(4) Notice to other spouse. The Tax Court shall establish rules which provide the individual filing a joint return but not making the election under subsection (b) or (c) or the request for equitable relief under subsection (f) with adequate notice and an opportunity to become a party to a proceeding under either such subsection.

(5) Waiver. An individual who elects the application of subsection (b) or (c) or who requests equitable relief under subsection (f) (and who agrees with the Secretary's determination of relief) may waive in writing at any time the restrictions in paragraph (1)(B) with respect to collection of the outstanding assessment (whether or not a notice of the Secretary's final determination of relief has been mailed).

(f) Equitable relief. Under procedures prescribed by the Secretary, if –

(1) taking into account all the facts and circumstances, it is inequitable to hold the individual liable for any unpaid tax or any deficiency (or any portion of either); and

(2) relief is not available to such individual under subsection (b) or (c), the Secretary may relieve such individual of such liability.

(g) Credits and refunds.

(1) In general. Except as provided in paragraphs (2) and (3), notwithstanding any other law or rule of law (other than section 6511, 6512(b), 7121, or 7122), credit or refund shall be allowed or made to the extent attributable to the application of this section.

(2) Res judicata. In the case of any election under subsection (b) or (c) or of any request for equitable relief under subsection (f), if a decision of a court in any prior proceeding for the same taxable year has become final, such decision shall be conclusive except with respect to the qualification of the individual for relief which was not an issue in such proceeding. The exception contained in the preceding sentence shall not apply if the court determines that the individual participated meaningfully in such prior proceeding.

(3) Credit and refund not allowed under subsection (c). No credit or refund shall be allowed as a result of an election under subsection (c).

(h) Regulations. The Secretary shall prescribe such regulations as are necessary to carry out the provisions of this section, including –

(1) regulations providing methods for allocation of items other than the methods under subsection (d)(3); and

(2) regulations providing the opportunity for an individual to have notice of, and an opportunity to participate in, any administrative proceeding with respect to an election made under subsection (b) or (c) or a request for equitable relief made under subsection (f) by the other individual filing the joint return.

* * *

§ 6020. Returns prepared for or executed by Secretary.

(a) Preparation of return by Secretary. If any person shall fail to make a return required by this title or by regulations prescribed thereunder, but shall consent to disclose all information necessary for the preparation thereof, then, and in that case, the Secretary may prepare such return, which, being signed by such person, may be received by the Secretary as the return of such person.

(b) Execution of return by Secretary.

(1) Authority of Secretary to execute return. If any person fails to make any return required by any internal revenue law or regulation made thereunder at the time prescribed therefor, or makes, willfully or otherwise, a false or fraudulent return, the Secretary shall make such return from his own knowledge and from such information as he can obtain through testimony or otherwise.

(2) Status of returns. Any return so made and subscribed by the Secretary shall be prima facie good and sufficient for all legal purposes.

* * *

§ 6072. Time for filing income tax returns.

(a) General rule. In the case of returns under section 6012, 6013, 6017, or 6031 (relating to income tax under subtitle A), returns made on the basis of the calendar year shall be filed on or before the 15th day of April following the close of the calendar year and returns made on the basis of a fiscal year shall be filed on or before the 15th day of the fourth month following the close of the fiscal year, except as otherwise provided in the following subsections of this section.

(b) Returns of corporations. Returns of corporations under section 6012 made on the basis of the calendar year shall be filed on or before the 15th day of March following the close of the calendar year, and such returns made on the basis of a fiscal year shall be filed on or before the 15th day of the third month following the close of the fiscal year. Returns required for a taxable year by section 6011(e)(2) (relating to returns of a DISC) shall be filed on or before the fifteenth day of the ninth month following the close of the taxable year.

* * *

§ 6081. Extension of time for filing returns.

(a) General rule. The Secretary may grant a reasonable extension of time for filing any return, declaration, statement, or other document required by this title or by regulations. Except in the case of taxpayers who are abroad, no such extension shall be for more than 6 months.

(b) Automatic extension for corporation income tax returns. An extension of 3 months for the filing of the return of income taxes imposed by subtitle A shall be allowed any corporation if, in such manner and at such time as the Secretary may by regulations prescribe, there is filed on behalf of such corporation the form prescribed by the Secretary, and if such corporation pays, on or before the date prescribed for payment of the tax, the amount properly estimated as its tax; but this extension may be terminated at any time by the Secretary by mailing to the taxpayer notice of such termination at least 10 days prior to the date for termination fixed in such notice.

(c) Cross references. For time for performing certain acts postponed by reason of war, see section 7508, and by reason of Presidentially declared disaster or terroristic or military action, see section 7508A.

* * *

§ 6103. Confidentiality and disclosure of returns and return information.

(a) General rule. Returns and return information shall be confidential, and except as authorized by this title –

(1) no officer or employee of the United States,

(2) no officer or employee of any State, any local law enforcement agency receiving information under subsection (i)(7)(A), any local child support enforcement agency, or any local agency administering a program listed in subsection (l)(7)(D) who has or had access to returns or return information under this section or section 6104(c), and

(3) no other person (or officer or employee thereof) who has or had access to returns or return information under subsection (e)(1)(D)(iii), paragraph (6), (10), (12), (16), (19), (20), or (21) of subsection (l), paragraph (2) or (4)(B) of subsection (m), or subsection (n), shall disclose any return or return information obtained by him in any manner in connection with his service as such an officer or an employee or otherwise or under the provisions of this section. For purposes of this subsection, the term "officer or employee" includes a former officer or employee.

(b) Definitions. For purposes of this section –

(1) Return. The term "return" means any tax or information return, declaration of estimated tax, or claim for refund required by, or provided for or permitted under, the provisions of this title which is filed with the Secretary by, on behalf of, or with respect to any person, and any amendment or supplement thereto, including supporting schedules, attachments, or lists which are supplemental to, or part of, the return so filed.

(2) Return information. The term "return information" means –

(A) a taxpayer's identity, the nature, source, or amount of his income, payments, receipts, deductions, exemptions, credits, assets, liabilities, net worth, tax liability, tax withheld, deficiencies, overassessments, or tax payments, whether the taxpayer's return was, is being, or will be examined or subject to other investigation or processing, or any other data, received by, recorded by, prepared by, furnished to, or collected by the Secretary with respect to a return or with respect to the determination of the existence, or possible existence, of liability (or the amount thereof) of any person under this title for any tax, penalty, interest, fine, forfeiture, or other imposition, or offense,

(B) any part of any written determination or any background file document relating to such written determination (as such terms are defined in section 6110(b)) which is not open to public inspection under section 6110,

(C) any advance pricing agreement entered into by a taxpayer and the Secretary and any background information related to such agreement or any application for an advance pricing agreement, and

(D) any agreement under section 7121, and any similar agreement, and any background information related to such an agreement or request for such an agreement, but such term does not include data in a form which cannot be associated with, or otherwise identify, directly or indirectly, a particular taxpayer. Nothing in the preceding sentence, or in any other provision of law, shall be construed to require the disclosure of standards used or to be used for the selection of returns for examination, or data used or to be used for determining such standards, if the Secretary determines that such disclosure will seriously impair assessment, collection, or enforcement under the internal revenue laws.

(3) Taxpayer return information. The term "taxpayer return information" means return information as defined in paragraph (2) which is filed with, or furnished to, the Secretary by or on behalf of the taxpayer to whom such return information relates.

(4) Tax administration. The term "tax administration"–

(A) means –

(i) the administration, management, conduct, direction, and supervision of the execution and application of the internal revenue laws or related statutes (or equivalent laws and statutes of a State) and tax conventions to which the United States is a party, and

(ii) the development and formulation of Federal tax policy relating to existing or proposed internal revenue laws, related statutes, and tax conventions, and

(B) includes assessment, collection, enforcement, litigation, publication, and statistical gathering functions under such laws, statutes, or conventions.

(5) State.

(A) In general. The term "State" means –

(i) any of the 50 States, the District of Columbia, the Commonwealth of Puerto Rico, the Virgin Islands, Guam, American Samoa, and the Commonwealth of the Northern Mariana Islands,

(ii) for purposes of subsections (a)(2), (b)(4), (d)(1), (h)(4), and (p), any municipality –

(I) with a population in excess of 250,000 (as determined under the most recent decennial United States census data available),

(II) which imposes a tax on income or wages, and

(III) with which the Secretary (in his sole discretion) has entered into an agreement regarding disclosure, and

(iii) for purposes of subsections (a)(2), (b)(4), (d)(1), (h)(4), and (p), any governmental entity –

(I) which is formed and operated by a qualified group of municipalities, and

(II) with which the Secretary (in his sole discretion) has entered into an agreement regarding disclosure.

(B) Regional income tax agencies. For purposes of subparagraph (A)(iii) –

(i) Qualified group of municipalities. The term "qualified group of municipalities" means, with respect to any governmental entity, 2 or more municipalities –

(I) each of which imposes a tax on income or wages,

(II) each of which, under the authority of a State statute, administers the laws relating to the imposition of such taxes through such entity, and

(III) which collectively have a population in excess of 250,000 (as determined under the most recent decennial United States census data available).

(ii) References to State law, etc. For purposes of applying subparagraph (A)(iii) to the subsections referred to in such subparagraph, any reference in such subsections to State law, proceedings, or tax returns shall be treated as references to the law, proceedings, or tax returns, as the case may be, of the municipalities which form and operate the governmental entity referred to in such subparagraph.

(iii) Disclosure to contractors and other agents. Notwithstanding any other provision of this section, no return or return information shall be disclosed to any contractor or other agent of a governmental entity referred to in subparagraph (A)(iii) unless such entity, to the satisfaction of the Secretary –

(I) has requirements in effect which require each such contractor or other agent which would have access to returns or return information to provide safeguards (within the meaning of subsection (p)(4)) to protect the confidentiality of such returns or return information,

(II) agrees to conduct an on-site review every 3 years (or a mid-point review in the case of contracts or agreements of less than 3 years in duration) of each contractor or other agent to determine compliance with such requirements,

(III) submits the findings of the most recent review conducted under subclause (II) to the Secretary as part of the report required by subsection (p)(4)(E), and

(IV) certifies to the Secretary for the most recent annual period that such contractor or other agent is in compliance with all such requirements.

The certification required by subclause (IV) shall include the name and address of each contractor and other agent, a description of the contract or agreement with such contractor or other agent, and the duration of such contract or agreement. The requirements of this clause shall not apply to disclosures pursuant to subsection (n) for purposes of Federal tax administration and a rule similar to the rule of subsection (p)(8)(B) shall apply for purposes of this clause.

(c) Disclosure of returns and return information to designee of taxpayer. The Secretary may, subject to such requirements and conditions as he may prescribe by regulations, disclose the return of any taxpayer, or return information with respect to such taxpayer, to such person or persons as the taxpayer may designate in a request for or consent to such disclosure, or to any other person at the taxpayer's request to the extent necessary to comply with a request for information or assistance made by the taxpayer to such other person. However, return information shall not be disclosed to such person or persons if the Secretary determines that such disclosure would seriously impair Federal tax administration.

(d) Disclosure to State tax officials and State and local law enforcement agencies.

(1) In general. Returns and return information with respect to taxes imposed by chapters 1, 2, 6, 11, 12, 21, 23, 24, 31, 32, 44, 51, and 52 and subchapter D of chapter 36 shall be open to inspection by, or disclosure to, any State agency, body, or commission, or its legal representative, which is charged under the laws of such State with responsibility for the administration of State tax laws for the purpose of, and only to the extent necessary in, the administration of such laws, including any procedures with respect to locating any person who may be entitled to a refund. Such inspection shall be permitted, or such disclosure made, only upon written request by the head of such agency, body, or commission, and only to the representatives of such agency, body, or commission designated in such written request as the individuals who are to inspect or to receive the returns or return information on behalf of such agency, body, or commission. Such representatives shall not include any individual who is the chief executive officer of such State or who is neither an employee or legal representative of such agency, body, or commission nor a person described in subsection (n). However, such return information shall not be disclosed to the extent that the Secretary determines that such disclosure would identify a confidential informant or seriously impair any civil or criminal tax investigation.

(2) Disclosure to State audit agencies.

(A) In general. Any returns or return information obtained under paragraph (1) by any State agency, body, or commission may be open to inspection by, or disclosure to, officers and employees of the State audit agency for the purpose of, and only to the extent necessary in, making an audit of the State agency, body, or commission referred to in paragraph (1).

(B) State audit agency. For purposes of subparagraph (A), the term "State audit agency" means any State agency, body, or commission which is charged under the laws of the State with the responsibility of auditing State revenues and programs.

(3) Exception for reimbursement under section 7624. Nothing in this section shall be construed to prevent the Secretary from disclosing to any State or local law enforcement agency which may receive a payment under section 7624 the amount of the recovered taxes with respect to which such a payment may be made.

(4) Availability and use of death information.

(A) In general. No returns or return information may be disclosed under paragraph (1) to any agency, body, or commission of any State (or any legal representative thereof) during any period during which a contract meeting the requirements of subparagraph (B) is not in effect between such State and the Secretary of Health and Human Services.

(B) Contractual requirements. A contract meets the requirements of this subparagraph if –

(i) such contract requires the State to furnish the Secretary of Health and Human Services information concerning individuals with respect to whom death certificates (or equivalent documents maintained by the State or any subdivision thereof) have been officially filed with it, and

(ii) such contract does not include any restriction on the use of information obtained by such Secretary pursuant to such contract, except that such contract may provide that such information is only to be used by the Secretary (or any other Federal agency) for purposes of ensuring that Federal benefits or other payments are not erroneously paid to deceased individuals.

Any information obtained by the Secretary of Health and Human Services under such a contract shall be exempt from disclosure under section 552 of title 5, United States Code, and from the requirements of section 552a of such title 5.

(C) Special exception. The provisions of subparagraph (A) shall not apply to any State which on July 1, 1993, was not, pursuant to a contract, furnishing the Secretary of Health and Human Services information concerning individuals with respect to whom death certificates (or equivalent documents maintained by the State or any subdivision thereof) have been officially filed with it.

(5) Disclosure for combined employment tax reporting.

(A) In general. The Secretary may disclose taxpayer identity information and signatures to any agency, body, or commission of any State for the purpose of carrying out with such agency, body, or commission a combined Federal and State employment tax reporting program approved by the Secretary. Subsections (a)(2) and (p)(4) and sections 7213 and 7213A shall not apply with respect to disclosures or inspections made pursuant to this paragraph.

(B) Termination. The Secretary may not make any disclosure under this paragraph after December 31, 2007.

(6) Limitation on disclosure regarding regional income tax agencies treated as States. For purposes of paragraph (1), inspection by or disclosure to an entity described in subsection (b)(5)(A)(iii) shall be for the purpose of, and only to the extent necessary in, the administration of the laws of the member municipalities in such entity relating to the imposition of a tax on income or wages. Such entity may not redisclose any return or return information received pursuant to paragraph (1) to any such member municipality.

(e) Disclosure to persons having material interest.

(1) In general. The return of a person shall, upon written request, be open to inspection by or disclosure to –

(A) in the case of the return of an individual –

(i) that individual,

(ii) the spouse of that individual if the individual and such spouse have signified their consent to consider a gift reported on such return as made one-half by him and one-half by the spouse pursuant to the provisions of section 2513; or

(iii) the child of that individual (or such child's legal representative) to the extent necessary to comply with the provisions of section 1(g);

(B) in the case of an income tax return filed jointly, either of the individuals with respect to whom the return is filed;

(C) in the case of the return of a partnership, any person who was a member of such partnership during any part of the period covered by the return;

(D) in the case of the return of a corporation or a subsidiary thereof –

(i) any person designated by resolution of its board of directors or other similar governing body,

(ii) any officer or employee of such corporation upon written request signed by any principal officer and attested to by the secretary or other officer,

(iii) any bona fide shareholder of record owning 1 percent or more of the outstanding stock of such corporation,

(iv) if the corporation was an S corporation, any person who was a shareholder during any part of the period covered by such return during which an election under section 1362(a) was in effect, or

(v) if the corporation has been dissolved, any person authorized by applicable State law to act for the corporation or any person who the Secretary finds to have a material interest which will be affected by information contained therein;

(E) in the case of the return of an estate –

(i) the administrator, executor, or trustee of such estate, and

(ii) any heir at law, next of kin, or beneficiary under the will, of the decedent, but only if the Secretary finds that such heir at law, next of kin, or beneficiary has a material interest which will be affected by information contained therein; and

(F) in the case of the return of a trust –

(i) the trustee or trustees, jointly or separately, and

(ii) any beneficiary of such trust, but only if the Secretary finds that such beneficiary has a material interest which will be affected by information contained therein.

(2) Incompetency. If an individual described in paragraph (1) is legally incompetent, the applicable return shall, upon written request, be open to inspection by or disclosure to the committee, trustee, or guardian of his estate.

(3) Deceased individuals. The return of a decedent shall, upon written request, be open to inspection by or disclosure to –

(A) the administrator, executor, or trustee of his estate, and

(B) any heir at law, next of kin, or beneficiary under the will, of such decedent, or a donee of property, but only if the Secretary finds that such heir at law, next of kin, beneficiary, or donee has a material interest which will be affected by information contained therein.

(4) Title 11 cases and receivership proceedings. If –

(A) there is a trustee in a title 11 case in which the debtor is the person with respect to whom the return is filed, or

(B) substantially all of the property of the person with respect to whom the return is filed is in the hands of a receiver, such return or returns for prior years of such person shall, upon written request, be open to inspection by or disclosure to such trustee or receiver, but only if the Secretary finds that such trustee or receiver, in his fiduciary capacity, has a material interest which will be affected by information contained therein.

(5) Individual's title 11 case.

(A) In general. In any case to which section 1398 applies (determined without regard to section 1398(b)(1)), any return of the debtor for the taxable year in which the case commenced or any preceding taxable year shall, upon written request, be open to inspection by or disclosure to the trustee in such case.

(B) Return of estate available to debtor. Any return of an estate in a case to which section 1398 applies shall, upon written request, be open to inspection by or disclosure to the debtor in such case.

(C) Special rule for involuntary cases. In an involuntary case, no disclosure shall be made under subparagraph (A) until the order for relief has been entered by the court having jurisdiction of such case unless such court finds that such disclosure is appropriate for purposes of determining whether an order for relief should be entered.

(6) Attorney in fact. Any return to which this subsection applies shall, upon written request, also be open to inspection by or disclosure to the attorney in fact duly authorized in writing by any of the persons described in paragraph (1), (2), (3), (4), (5), (8), or (9) to inspect the return or receive the information on his behalf, subject to the conditions provided in such paragraphs.

(7) Return information. Return information with respect to any taxpayer may be open to inspection by or disclosure to any person authorized by this subsection to inspect any return of such taxpayer if the Secretary determines that such disclosure would not seriously impair Federal tax administration.

* * *

(h) Disclosure to certain Federal officers and employees for purposes of tax administration, etc.

(1) Department of the Treasury. Returns and return information shall, without written request, be open to inspection by or disclosure to officers and employees of the Department of the Treasury whose official duties require such inspection or disclosure for tax administration purposes.

(2) Department of Justice. In a matter involving tax administration, a return or return information shall be open to inspection by or disclosure to officers and employees of the Department of Justice (including United States attorneys) personally and directly engaged in, and solely for their use in, any proceeding before a Federal grand jury or preparation for any proceeding (or investigation which may result in such a proceeding) before a Federal grand jury or any Federal or State court, but only if –

(A) the taxpayer is or may be a party to the proceeding, or the proceeding arose out of, or in connection with, determining the taxpayer's civil or criminal liability, or the collection of such civil liability in respect of any tax imposed under this title;

(B) the treatment of an item reflected on such return is or may be related to the resolution of an issue in the proceeding or investigation; or

(C) such return or return information relates or may relate to a transactional relationship between a person who is or may be a party to the proceeding and the taxpayer which affects, or may affect, the resolution of an issue in such proceeding or investigation.

* * *

(4) Disclosure in judicial and administrative tax proceedings. A return or return information may be disclosed in a Federal or State judicial or administrative proceeding pertaining to tax administration, but only –

(A) if the taxpayer is a party to the proceeding, or the proceeding arose out of, or in connection with, determining the taxpayer's civil or criminal liability, or the collection of such civil liability, in respect of any tax imposed under this title;

(B) if the treatment of an item reflected on such return is directly related to the resolution of an issue in the proceeding;

(C) if such return or return information directly relates to a transactional relationship between a person who is a party to the proceeding and the taxpayer which directly affects the resolution of an issue in the proceeding; or

(D) to the extent required by order of a court pursuant to section 3500 of title 18, United States Code or rule 16 of the Federal Rules of Criminal Procedure, such court being authorized in the issuance of such order to give due consideration to congressional policy favoring the confidentiality of returns and return information as set forth in this title.

However, such return or return information shall not be disclosed as provided in subparagraph (A), (B), or (C) if the Secretary determines that such disclosure would identify a confidential informant or seriously impair a civil or criminal tax investigation.

(5) Withholding of tax from Social Security benefits. Upon written request of the payor agency, the Secretary may disclose available return information from the master files of the Internal Revenue Service with respect to the address and status of an individual as a nonresident alien or as a citizen or resident of the United States to the Social Security Administration or the Railroad Retirement Board (whichever is appropriate) for purposes of carrying out its responsibilities for withholding tax under section 1441 from social security benefits (as defined in section 86(d)).

(i) Disclosure to Federal officers or employees for administration of Federal laws not relating to tax administration.

(1) Disclosure of returns and return information for use in criminal investigations.

(A) In general. Except as provided in paragraph (6), any return or return information with respect to any specified taxable period or periods shall, pursuant to and upon the grant of an ex parte order by a Federal district court judge or magistrate under subparagraph (B), be open (but only to the extent necessary as provided in such order) to inspection by, or disclosure to, officers and employees of any Federal agency who are personally and directly engaged in –

(i) preparation for any judicial or administrative proceeding pertaining to the enforcement of a specifically designated Federal criminal statute (not involving tax administration) to which the United States or such agency is or may be a party,

(ii) any investigation which may result in such a proceeding, or

(iii) any Federal grand jury proceeding pertaining to enforcement of such a criminal statute to which the United States or such agency is or may be a party, solely for the use of such officers and employees in such preparation, investigation, or grand jury proceeding.

(B) Application for order. The Attorney General, the Deputy Attorney General, the Associate Attorney General, any Assistant Attorney General, any United States attorney, any special prosecutor appointed under section 593 of title 28, United States Code, or any attorney in charge of a criminal division organized crime strike force established pursuant to section 510 of title 28, United States Code, may authorize an application to a Federal district court judge or magistrate for the order referred to in subparagraph (A). Upon such application, such judge or magistrate may grant such order if he determines on the basis of the facts submitted by the applicant that –

(i) there is reasonable cause to believe, based upon information believed to be reliable, that a specific criminal act has been committed,

(ii) there is reasonable cause to believe that the return or return information is or may be relevant to a matter relating to the commission of such act, and

(iii) the return or return information is sought exclusively for use in a Federal criminal investigation or proceeding concerning such act, and the information sought to be disclosed cannot reasonably be obtained, under the circumstances, from another source.

(2) Disclosure of return information other than taxpayer return information for use in criminal investigations.

(A) In general. Except as provided in paragraph (6), upon receipt by the Secretary of a request which meets the requirements of subparagraph (B) from the head of any Federal agency or the Inspector General thereof, or, in the case of the Department of Justice, the Attorney General, the Deputy Attorney General, the Associate Attorney General, any Assistant Attorney General, the Director of the Federal Bureau of Investigation, the Administrator of the Drug Enforcement Administration, any United States attorney, any special prosecutor appointed under section 593 of title 28, United States Code, or any attorney in charge of a criminal division organized crime strike force established pursuant to section 510 of title 28, United States Code, the Secretary shall disclose return information (other than taxpayer return information) to officers and employees of such agency who are personally and directly engaged in –

(i) preparation for any judicial or administrative proceeding described in paragraph (1)(A)(i),

(ii) any investigation which may result in such a proceeding, or

(iii) any grand jury proceeding described in paragraph (1)(A)(iii), solely for the use of such officers and employees in such preparation, investigation, or grand jury proceeding.

(B) Requirements. A request meets the requirements of this subparagraph if the request is in writing and sets forth –

(i) the name and address of the taxpayer with respect to whom the requested return information relates;

(ii) the taxable period or periods to which such return information relates;

(iii) the statutory authority under which the proceeding or investigation described in subparagraph (A) is being conducted; and

(iv) the specific reason or reasons why such disclosure is, or may be, relevant to such proceeding or investigation.

(C) Taxpayer identity. For purposes of this paragraph, a taxpayer's identity shall not be treated as taxpayer return information.

* * *

(4) Use of certain disclosed returns and return information in judicial or administrative proceedings.

(A) Returns and taxpayer return information. Except as provided in subparagraph (C), any return or taxpayer return information obtained under paragraph (1) or (7)(C) may be disclosed in any judicial or administrative proceeding pertaining to enforcement of a specifically designated Federal criminal statute or related civil forfeiture (not involving tax administration) to which the United States or a Federal agency is a party –

(i) if the court finds that such return or taxpayer return information is probative of a matter in issue relevant in establishing the commission of a crime or the guilt or liability of a party, or

(ii) to the extent required by order of the court pursuant to section 3500 of title 18, United States Code, or rule 16 of the Federal Rules of Criminal Procedure.

(B) Return information (other than taxpayer return information). Except as provided in subparagraph (C), any return information (other than taxpayer return information) obtained under paragraph (1), (2), (3)(A) or (C), or (7) may be disclosed in any judicial or administrative proceeding pertaining to enforcement of a specifically designated Federal criminal statute or related civil forfeiture (not involving tax administration) to which the United States or a Federal agency is a party.

(C) Confidential informant; impairment of investigations. No return or return information shall be admitted into evidence under subparagraph (A)(i) or (B) if the Secretary determines and notifies the Attorney General or his delegate or the head of the Federal agency that such admission would identify a confidential informant or seriously impair a civil or criminal tax investigation.

(D) Consideration of confidentiality policy. In ruling upon the admissibility of returns or return information, and in the issuance of an order under subparagraph (A)(ii), the court shall give due consideration to congressional policy favoring the confidentiality of returns and return information as set forth in this title.

(E) Reversible error. The admission into evidence of any return or return information contrary to the provisions of this paragraph shall not, as such, constitute reversible error upon appeal of a judgment in the proceeding.

(j) Statistical use.

(1) Department of Commerce. Upon request in writing by the Secretary of Commerce, the Secretary shall furnish –

(A) such returns, or return information reflected thereon, to officers and employees of the Bureau of the Census, and

(B) such return information reflected on returns of corporations to officers and employees of the Bureau of Economic Analysis, as the Secretary may prescribe by regulation for the purpose of, but only to the extent necessary in, the structuring of censuses and national economic accounts and conducting related statistical activities authorized by law.

(2) Federal Trade Commission. Upon request in writing by the Chairman of the Federal Trade Commission, the Secretary shall furnish such return information reflected on any return of a corporation with respect to the tax imposed by chapter 1 to officers and employees of the Division of Financial Statistics of the Bureau of Economics of such commission as the Secretary may prescribe by regulation for the purpose of, but only to the extent necessary in, administration by such division of legally authorized economic surveys of corporations.

(3) Department of Treasury. Returns and return information shall be open to inspection by or disclosure to officers and employees of the Department of the Treasury whose official duties require such inspection or disclosure for the purpose of, but only to the extent necessary in, preparing economic or financial forecasts, projections, analyses, and statistical studies and conducting related activities. Such inspection or disclosure shall be permitted only upon written request which sets forth the specific reason or reasons why such inspection or disclosure is necessary and which is signed by the head of the bureau or office of the Department of the Treasury requesting the inspection or disclosure.

(k) Disclosure of certain returns and return information for tax administration purposes.

(1) Disclosure of accepted offers-in-compromise. Return information shall be disclosed to members of the general public to the extent necessary to permit inspection of any accepted offer-in-compromise under section 7122 relating to the liability for a tax imposed by this title.

(2) Disclosure of amount of outstanding lien. If a notice of lien has been filed pursuant to section 6323(f), the amount of the outstanding obligation secured by such lien may be disclosed to any person who furnishes satisfactory written evidence that he has a right in the property subject to such lien or intends to obtain a right in such property.

(3) Disclosure of return information to correct misstatements of fact. The Secretary may, but only following approval by the Joint Committee on Taxation, disclose such return information or any other information with respect to any specific taxpayer to the extent necessary for tax administration purposes to correct a misstatement of fact published or disclosed with respect to such taxpayer's return or any transaction of the taxpayer with the Internal Revenue Service.

(4) Disclosure to competent authority under tax convention. A return or return information may be disclosed to a competent authority of a foreign government which has an income tax or gift and estate tax convention, or other convention or bilateral agreement relating to the exchange of tax information, with the United States but only to the extent provided in, and subject to the terms and conditions of, such convention or bilateral agreement.

(5) State agencies regulating tax return preparers. Taxpayer identity information with respect to any tax return preparer, and information as to whether or not any penalty has been assessed against such tax return preparer under section 6694, 6695, or 7216, may be furnished to any agency, body, or commission lawfully charged under any State or local law with the licensing, registration, or regulation of tax return preparers. Such information may be furnished only upon written request by the head of such agency, body, or commission designating the officers or employees to whom such information is to be furnished. Information may be furnished and used under this paragraph only for purposes of the licensing, registration, or regulation of tax return preparers.

(6) Disclosure by certain officers and employees for investigative purposes. An internal revenue officer or employee and an officer or employee of the Office of Treasury Inspector General for Tax Administration may, in connection with his official duties relating to any audit, collection activity, or civil or criminal tax investigation or any other offense under the internal revenue laws, disclose return information to the extent that such disclosure is necessary in obtaining information, which is not otherwise reasonably available, with respect to the correct determination of tax, liability for tax, or the amount to be collected or with respect to the enforcement of any other provision of this title. Such disclosures shall be made only in such situations and under such conditions as the Secretary may prescribe by regulation.

(7) Disclosure of excise tax registration information. To the extent the Secretary determines that disclosure is necessary to permit the effective administration of subtitle D, the Secretary may disclose –

(A) the name, address, and registration number of each person who is registered under any provision of subtitle D (and, in the case of a registered terminal operator, the address of each terminal operated by such operator), and

(B) the registration status of any person.

(8) Levies on certain government payments.

(A) Disclosure of return information in levies on financial management service. In serving a notice of levy, or release of such levy, with respect to any applicable government payment, the Secretary may disclose to officers and employees of the Financial Management Service –

(i) return information, including taxpayer identity information,

(ii) the amount of any unpaid liability under this title (including penalties and interest), and

(iii) the type of tax and tax period to which such unpaid liability relates.

(B) Restriction on use of disclosed information. Return information disclosed under subparagraph (A) may be used by officers and employees of the Financial Management Service only for the purpose of, and to the extent necessary in, transferring levied funds in satisfaction of the levy, maintaining appropriate agency records in regard to such levy or the release thereof, notifying the taxpayer and the agency certifying such payment that the levy has been honored, or in the defense of any litigation ensuing from the honor of such levy.

(C) Applicable government payment. For purposes of this paragraph, the term 'applicable government payment' means –

(i) any Federal payment (other than a payment for which eligibility is based on the income or assets (or both) of a payee) certified to the Financial Management Service for disbursement, and

(ii) any other payment which is certified to the Financial Management Service for disbursement and which the Secretary designates by published notice.

(9) Disclosure of information to administer section 6311. The Secretary may disclose returns or return information to financial institutions and others to the extent the Secretary deems necessary for the administration of section 6311. Disclosures of information for purposes other than to accept payments by checks or money orders shall be made only to the extent authorized by written procedures promulgated by the Secretary.

(10) Disclosure of certain return information to certain prison officials.

(A) In general. Under such procedures as the Secretary may prescribe, the Secretary may disclose to the head of the Federal Bureau of Prisons and the head of any State agency charged with the responsibility for administration of prisons any return information with respect to individuals incarcerated in Federal or State prison whom the Secretary has determined may have filed or facilitated the filing of a false return to the extent that the Secretary determines that such disclosure is necessary to permit effective Federal tax administration.

(B) Restriction on redisclosure. Notwithstanding subsection (n), the head of the Federal Bureau of Prisons and the head of any State agency charged with the responsibility for administration of prisons may not disclose any information obtained under subparagraph (A) to any person other than an officer or employee of such Bureau or agency.

(C) Restriction on use of disclosed information. Return information received under this paragraph shall be used only for purposes of and to the extent necessary in taking administrative action to prevent the filing of false and fraudulent returns, including administrative actions to address possible violations of administrative rules and regulations of the prison facility.

(D) Termination. No disclosure may be made under this paragraph after December 31, 2011.

* * *

§6110. Public inspection of written determinations.

(a) General rule. Except as otherwise provided in this section, the text of any written determination and any background file document relating to such written determination shall be open to public inspection at such place as the Secretary may by regulations prescribe.

(b) Definitions. For purposes of this section –

(1) Written determination.

(A) In general. The term "written determination" means a ruling, determination letter, technical advice memorandum, or Chief Counsel advice.

(B) Exceptions. Such term shall not include any matter referred to in subparagraph (C) or (D) of section 6103(b)(2).

(2) Background file document. The term "background file document" with respect to a written determination includes the request for that written determination, any written material submitted in support of the request, and any communication (written or otherwise) between the Internal Revenue Service and persons outside the Internal Revenue Service in connection with such written determination (other than any communication between the Department of Justice and the Internal Revenue Service relating to a pending civil or criminal case or investigation) received before issuance of the written determination.

(3) Reference and general written determinations.

(A) Reference written determination. The term "reference written determination" means any written determination which has been determined by the Secretary to have significant reference value.

(B) General written determination. The term "general written determination" means any written determination other than a reference written determination.

(c) Exemptions from disclosure. Before making any written determination or background file document open or available to public inspection under subsection (a), the Secretary shall delete –

(1) the names, addresses, and other identifying details of the person to whom the written determination pertains and of any other person, other than a person with respect to whom a notation is made under subsection (d)(1), identified in the written determination or any background file document;

(2) information specifically authorized under criteria established by an Executive order to be kept secret in the interest of national defense or foreign policy, and which is in fact properly classified pursuant to such Executive order;

(3) information specifically exempted from disclosure by any statute (other than this title) which is applicable to the Internal Revenue Service;

(4) trade secrets and commercial or financial information obtained from a person and privileged or confidential;

(5) information the disclosure of which would constitute a clearly unwarranted invasion of personal privacy;

(6) information contained in or related to examination, operating, or condition reports prepared by, or on behalf of, or for use of an agency responsible for the regulation or supervision of financial institutions; and

(7) geological and geophysical information and data, including maps, concerning wells. The Secretary shall determine the appropriate extent of such deletions and, except in the case of intentional or willful disregard of this subsection, shall not be required to make such deletions (nor be liable for failure to make deletions) unless the Secretary has agreed to such deletions or has been ordered by a court (in a proceeding under subsection (f)(3)) to make such deletions.

(d) Procedures with regard to third party contacts.

(1) Notations. If, before the issuance of a written determination, the Internal Revenue Service receives any communication (written or otherwise) concerning such written determination, any request for such determination, or any other matter involving such written determination from a person other than an employee of the Internal Revenue Service or the person to whom such written determination pertains (or his authorized representative with regard to such written determination), the Internal Revenue Service shall indicate, on the written determination open to public inspection, the category of the person making such communication and the date of such communication.

(2) Exception. Paragraph (1) shall not apply to any communication made by the Chief of Staff of the Joint Committee on Taxation.

(3) Disclosure of identity. In the case of any written determination to which paragraph (1) applies, any person may file a petition in the United States Tax Court or file a complaint in the United States District Court for the District of Columbia for an order requiring that the identity of any person to whom the written determination pertains be disclosed. The court shall order disclosure of such identity if there is evidence in the record from which one could reasonably conclude that an impropriety occurred or undue influence was exercised with respect to such written determination by or on behalf of such person. The court may also direct the Secretary to disclose any portion of any other deletions made in accordance with subsection (c) where such disclosure is in the public interest. If a proceeding is commenced under this paragraph, the person whose identity is subject to being disclosed and the person about whom a notation is made under paragraph (1) shall be notified of the proceeding in accordance with the procedures described in subsection (f)(4)(B) and shall have the right to intervene in the proceeding (anonymously, if appropriate).

(4) Period in which to bring action. No proceeding shall be commenced under paragraph (3) unless a petition is filed before the expiration of 36 months after the first day that the written determination is open to public inspection.

(e) Background file documents. Whenever the Secretary makes a written determination open to public inspection under this section, he shall also make available to any person, but only upon the written request of that person, any background file document relating to the written determination.

(f) Resolution of disputes relating to disclosure.

(1) Notice of intention to disclose. Except as otherwise provided by subsection (i), the Secretary shall upon issuance of any written determination, or upon receipt of a request for a background file document, mail a notice of intention to disclose such determination or document to any person to whom the written determination pertains (or a successor in interest, executor, or other person authorized by law to act for or on behalf of such person).

(2) Administrative remedies. The Secretary shall prescribe regulations establishing administrative remedies with respect to –

(A) requests for additional disclosure of any written determination of any background file document, and

(B) requests to restrain disclosure.

(3) Action to restrain disclosure.

(A) Creation of remedy. Any person –

(i) to whom a written determination pertains (or a successor in interest, executor, or other person authorized by law to act for or on behalf of such person), or who has a direct interest in maintaining the confidentiality of any such written determination or background file document (or portion thereof),

(ii) who disagrees with any failure to make a deletion with respect to that portion of any written determination or any background file document which is to be open or available to public inspection, and

(iii) who has exhausted his administrative remedies as prescribed pursuant to paragraph (2), may, within 60 days after the mailing by the Secretary of a notice of intention to disclose any written determination or background file document under paragraph (1), together with the proposed deletions, file a petition in the United States Tax Court (anonymously, if appropriate) for a determination with respect to that portion of such written determination or background file document which is to be open to public inspection.

(B) Notice to certain persons. The Secretary shall notify any person to whom a written determination pertains (unless such person is the petitioner) of the filing of a petition under this paragraph with respect to such written determination or related background file document, and any such person may intervene (anonymously, if appropriate) in any proceeding conducted pursuant to this paragraph. The Secretary shall send such notice by registered or certified mail to the last known address of such person within 15 days after such petition is served on the Secretary. No person who has received such a notice may thereafter file any petition under this paragraph with respect to such written determination or background file document with respect to which such notice was received.

(4) Action to obtain additional disclosure.

(A) Creation of remedy. Any person who has exhausted the administrative remedies prescribed pursuant to paragraph (2) with respect to a request for disclosure may file a petition in the United States Tax Court or a complaint in the United States District Court for the District of Columbia for an order requiring that any written determination or background file document (or portion thereof) be made open or available to public inspection. Except where inconsistent with subparagraph (B), the provisions of subparagraphs (C), (D), (E), (F), and (G) of section 552(a)(4) of title 5, United States Code, shall apply to any proceeding under this paragraph. The Court shall examine the matter de novo and without regard to a decision of a court under paragraph (3) with respect to such written determination or background file document, and may examine the entire text of such written determination or background file document in order to determine whether such written determination or background file document or any part thereof shall be open or available to public inspection under this section. The burden of proof with respect to the issue of disclosure of any information shall be on the Secretary and any other person seeking to restrain disclosure.

(B) Intervention. If a proceeding is commenced under this paragraph with respect to any written determination or background file document, the Secretary shall, within 15 days after notice of the petition filed under subparagraph (A) is served on him, send notice of the commencement of such proceeding to all persons who are identified by name and address in such written determination or background file document. The Secretary shall send such notice by registered or certified mail to the last known address of such person. Any person to whom such determination or background file document pertains may intervene in the proceeding (anonymously, if appropriate). If such notice is sent, the Secretary shall not be required to defend the action and shall not be liable for public disclosure of the written determination or background file document (or any portion thereof) in accordance with the final decision of the court.

(5) Expedition of determination. The Tax Court shall make a decision with respect to any petition described in paragraph (3) at the earliest practicable date.

(6) Publicity of Tax Court proceedings. Notwithstanding sections 7458 and 7461, the Tax Court may, in order to preserve the anonymity, privacy, or confidentiality of any person under this section, provide by rules adopted under section 7453 that portions of hearings, testimony, evidence, and reports in connection with proceedings under this section may be closed to the public or to inspection by the public.

(g) Time for disclosure.

(1) In general. Except as otherwise provided in this section, the text of any written determination or any background file document (as modified under subsection (c)) shall be open or available to public inspection –

(A) no earlier than 75 days, and no later than 90 days, after the notice provided in subsection (f)(1) is mailed, or, if later,

(B) within 30 days after the date on which a court decision under subsection (f)(3) becomes final.

(2) Postponement by order of court. The court may extend the period referred to in paragraph (1)(B) for such time as the court finds necessary to allow the Secretary to comply with its decision.

(3) Postponement of disclosure for up to 90 days. At the written request of the person by whom or on whose behalf the request for the written determination was made, the period referred to in paragraph (1)(A) shall be extended (for not to exceed an additional 90 days) until the day which is 15 days after the date of the Secretary's determination that the transaction set forth in the written determination has been completed.

(4) Additional 180 days. If –

(A) the transaction set forth in the written determination is not completed during the period set forth in paragraph (3), and

(B) the person by whom or on whose behalf the request for the written determination was made establishes to the satisfaction of the Secretary that good cause exists for additional delay in opening the written determination to public inspection, the period referred to in paragraph (3) shall be further extended (for not to exceed an additional 180 days) until the day which is 15 days after the date of the Secretary's determination that the transaction set forth in the written determination has been completed.

(5) Special rules for certain written determinations, etc. Notwithstanding the provisions of paragraph (1), the Secretary shall not be required to make available to the public –

(A) any technical advice memorandum, any Chief Counsel advice, and any related background file document involving any matter which is the subject of a civil fraud or criminal investigation or jeopardy or termination assessment until after any action relating to such investigation or assessment is completed, or

(B) any general written determination and any related background file document that relates solely to approval of the Secretary of any adoption or change of –

(i) the funding method or plan year of a plan under section 412,

(ii) a taxpayer's annual accounting period under section 442,

(iii) a taxpayer's method of accounting under section 446(e), or

(iv) a partnership's or partner's taxable year under section 706, but the Secretary shall make any such written determination and related background file document available upon the written request of any person after the date on which (except for this subparagraph) such determination would be open to public inspection.

(h) Disclosure of prior written determinations and related background file documents.

(1) In general. Except as otherwise provided in this subsection, a written determination issued pursuant to a request made before November 1, 1976, and any background file document relating to such written determination shall be open or available to public inspection in accordance with this section.

(2) Time for disclosure. In the case of any written determination or background file document which is to be made open or available to public inspection under paragraph (1) –

(A) subsection (g) shall not apply, but

(B) such written determination or background file document shall be made open or available to public inspection at the earliest practicable date after funds for that purpose have been appropriated and made available to the Internal Revenue Service.

(3) Order of release. Any written determination or background file document described in paragraph (1) shall be open or available to public inspection in the following order starting with the most recent written determination in each category:

(A) reference written determinations issued under this title;

(B) general written determinations issued after July 4, 1967; and

(C) reference written determinations issued under the Internal Revenue Code of 1939 or corresponding provisions of prior law.

General written determinations not described in subparagraph (B) shall be open to public inspection on written request, but not until after the written determinations referred to in subparagraphs (A), (B), and (C) are open to public inspection.

(4) Notice that prior written determinations are open to public inspection. Notwithstanding the provisions of subsections (f)(1) and (f)(3)(A), not less than 90 days before making any portion of a written determination described in this subsection open to public inspection, the Secretary shall issue public notice in the Federal Register that such written determination is to be made open to public inspection. The person who received a written determination may, within 75 days after the date of publication of notice under this paragraph, file a petition in the United States Tax Court (anonymously, if appropriate) for a determination with respect to that portion of such written determination which is to be made open to public inspection. The provisions of subsections (f)(3)(B), (5), and (6) shall apply if such a petition is filed. If no petition is filed, the text of any written determination shall be open to public inspection no earlier than 90 days, and no later than 120 days, after notice is published in the Federal Register.

(5) Exclusion. Subsection (d) shall not apply to any written determination described in paragraph (1).

(i) Special rules for disclosure of Chief Counsel advice.

(1) Chief Counsel advice defined.

(A) In general. For purposes of this section, the term "Chief Counsel advice" means written advice or instruction, under whatever name or designation, prepared by any national office component of the Office of Chief Counsel which –

(i) is issued to field or service center employees of the Service or regional or district employees of the Office of Chief Counsel; and

(ii) conveys –

(I) any legal interpretation of a revenue provision;

(II) any Internal Revenue Service or Office of Chief Counsel position or policy concerning a revenue provision; or

(III) any legal interpretation of State law, foreign law, or other Federal law relating to the assessment or collection of any liability under a revenue provision.

(B) Revenue provision defined. For purposes of subparagraph (A), the term "revenue provision" means any existing or former internal revenue law, regulation, revenue ruling, revenue procedure, other published or unpublished guidance, or tax treaty, either in general or as applied to specific taxpayers or groups of specific taxpayers.

(2) Additional documents treated as Chief Counsel advice. The Secretary may by regulation provide that this section shall apply to any advice or instruction prepared and issued by the Office of Chief Counsel which is not described in paragraph (1).

(3) Deletions for Chief Counsel advice. In the case of Chief Counsel advice and related background file documents open to public inspection pursuant to this section –

(A) paragraphs (2) through (7) of subsection (c) shall not apply, but

(B) the Secretary may make deletions of material in accordance with subsections (b) and (c) of section 552 of title 5, United States Code, except that in applying subsection (b)(3) of such section, no statutory provision of this title shall be taken into account.

(4) Notice of intention to disclose.

(A) Nontaxpayer-specific Chief Counsel advice. In the case of Chief Counsel advice which is written without reference to a specific taxpayer or group of specific taxpayers –

(i) subsection (f)(1) shall not apply; and

(ii) the Secretary shall, within 60 days after the issuance of the Chief Counsel advice, complete any deletions described in subsection (c)(1) or paragraph (3) and make the Chief Counsel advice, as so edited, open for public inspection.

(B) Taxpayer-specific Chief Counsel advice. In the case of Chief Counsel advice which is written with respect to a specific taxpayer or group of specific taxpayers, the Secretary shall, within 60 days after the issuance of the Chief Counsel advice, mail the notice required by subsection (f)(1) to each such taxpayer. The notice shall include a copy of the Chief Counsel advice on which is indicated the information that the Secretary proposes to delete pursuant to subsection (c)(1). The Secretary may also delete from the copy of the text of the Chief Counsel advice any of the information described in paragraph (3), and shall delete the names, addresses, and other identifying details of taxpayers other than the person to whom the advice pertains, except that the Secretary shall not delete from the copy of the Chief Counsel advice that is furnished to the taxpayer any information of which that taxpayer was the source.

(j) Civil remedies.

(1) Civil action. Whenever the Secretary –

(A) fails to make deletions required in accordance with subsection (c), or

(B) fails to follow the procedures in subsection (g) or (i)(4)(B), the recipient of the written determination or any person identified in the written determination shall have as an exclusive civil remedy an action against the Secretary in the United States Claims Court [United States Court of Federal Claims], which shall have jurisdiction to hear any action under this paragraph.

(2) Damages. In any suit brought under the provisions of paragraph (1)(A) in which the Court determines that an employee of the Internal Revenue Service intentionally or willfully failed to delete in accordance with subsection (c), or in any suit brought under subparagraph (1)(B) in which the Court determines that an employee intentionally or willfully failed to act in accordance with subsection (g) or (i)(4)(B), the United States shall be liable to the person in an amount equal to the sum of –

(A) actual damages sustained by the person but in no case shall a person be entitled to receive less than the sum of $1,000, and

(B) the costs of the action together with reasonable attorney's fees as determined by the Court.

(k) Special provisions.

(1) Fees. The Secretary is authorized to assess actual costs –

(A) for duplication of any written determination or background file document made open or available to the public under this section, and

(B) incurred in searching for and making deletions required under subsection (c) or (i)(3) from any written determination or background file document which is available to public inspection only upon written request.

The Secretary shall furnish any written determination or background file document without charge or at a reduced charge if he determines that waiver or reduction of the fee is in the public interest because furnishing such determination or background file document can be considered as primarily benefiting the general public.

(2) Records disposal procedures. Nothing in this section shall prevent the Secretary from disposing of any general written determination or background file document described in subsection (b) in accordance with established records disposition procedures, but such disposal shall, except as provided in the following sentence, occur not earlier than 3 years after such written determination is first made open to public inspection. In the case of any general written determination described in subsection (h), the Secretary may dispose of such determination and any related background file document in accordance with such procedures but such disposal shall not occur earlier than 3 years after such written determination is first made open to public inspection if funds are appropriated for such purpose before January 20, 1979, or not earlier than January 20, 1979, if funds are not appropriated before such date. The Secretary shall not dispose of any reference written determinations and related background file documents.

(3) Precedential status. Unless the Secretary otherwise establishes by regulations, a written determination may not be used or cited as precedent. The preceding sentence shall not apply to change the precedential status (if any) of written determinations with regard to taxes imposed by subtitle D.

(l) Section not to apply. This section shall not apply to –

(1) any matter to which section 6104 or 6105 applies, or

(2) any –

(A) written determination issued pursuant to a request made before November 1, 1976, with respect to the exempt status under section 501(a) of an organization described in section 501(c) or (d), the status of an organization as a private foundation under section 509(a), or the status of an organization as an operating foundation under section 4942(j)(3),

(B) written determination described in subsection (g)(5)(B) issued pursuant to a request made before November 1, 1976,

(C) determination letter not otherwise described in subparagraph (A), (B), or (E) issued pursuant to a request made before November 1, 1976,

(D) background file document relating to any general written determination issued before July 5, 1967, or

(E) letter or other document described in section 6104(a)(1)(B)(iv) issued before September 2, 1974.

(m) Exclusive remedy. Except as otherwise provided in this title, or with respect to a discovery order made in connection with a judicial proceeding, the Secretary shall not be required by any Court to make any written determination or background file document open or available to public inspection, or to refrain from disclosure of any such documents.

* * *

§ 6112. Material advisors of reportable transactions must keep lists of advisees, etc.

(a) In general. Each material advisor (as defined in section 6111) with respect to any reportable transaction (as defined in section 6707A(c)) shall (whether or not required to file a return under section 6111 with respect to such transaction) maintain (in such manner as the Secretary may by regulations prescribe) a list –

(1) identifying each person with respect to whom such advisor acted as a material advisor with respect to such transaction, and

(2) containing such other information as the Secretary may by regulations require.

(b) Special rules.

(1) Availability for inspection; retention of information on list. Any person who is required to maintain a list under subsection (a) (or was required to maintain a list under subsection (a) as in effect before the enactment of the American Jobs Creation Act of 2004 [enacted Oct. 22, 2004]) –

(A) shall make such list available to the Secretary for inspection upon written request by the Secretary, and

(B) except as otherwise provided under regulations prescribed by the Secretary, shall retain any information which is required to be included on such list for 7 years.

(2) Lists which would be required to be maintained by 2 or more persons. The Secretary may prescribe regulations which provide that, in cases in which 2 or more persons are required under subsection (a) to maintain the same list (or portion thereof), only 1 person shall be required to maintain such list (or portion).

* * *

§ 6151. Time and place for paying tax shown on returns.

(a) General rule. Except as otherwise provided in this subchapter, when a return of tax is required under this title or regulations, the person required to make such return shall, without assessment or notice and demand from the Secretary, pay such tax to the internal revenue officer with whom the return is filed, and shall pay such tax at the time and place fixed for filing the return (determined without regard to any extension of time for filing the return).

(b) Exceptions.

(1) Income tax not computed by taxpayer. If the taxpayer elects under section 6014 not to show the tax on the return, the amount determined by the Secretary as payable shall be paid within 30 days after the mailing by the Secretary to the taxpayer of a notice stating such amount and making demand therefor.

(2) Use of Government depositaries. For authority of the Secretary to require payments to Government depositaries, see section 6302(c).

(c) Date fixed for payment of tax. In any case in which a tax is required to be paid on or before a certain date, or within a certain period, any reference in this title to the date fixed for payment of such tax shall be deemed a reference to the last day fixed for such payment (determined without regard to any extension of time for paying the tax).

* * *

§ 6159. Agreements for payment of tax liability in installments.

(a) Authorization of agreements. The Secretary is authorized to enter into written agreements with any taxpayer under which such taxpayer is allowed to make payment on any tax in installment payments if the Secretary determines that such agreement will facilitate full or partial collection of such liability.

(b) Extent to which agreements remain in effect.

(1) In general. Except as otherwise provided in this sub-section, any agreement entered into by the Secretary under subsection (a) shall remain in effect for the term of the agreement.

(2) Inadequate information or jeopardy. The Secretary may terminate any agreement entered into by the Secretary under subsection (a) if –

(A) information which the taxpayer provided to the Secretary prior to the date such agreement was entered into was inaccurate or incomplete, or

(B) the Secretary believes that collection of any tax to which an agreement under this section relates is in jeopardy.

(3) Subsequent change in financial conditions. If the Secretary makes a determination that the financial condition of a taxpayer with whom the Secretary has entered into an agreement under subsection (a) has significantly changed, the Secretary may alter, modify, or terminate such agreement.

(4) Failure to pay an installment or any other tax liability when due or to provide requested financial information. The Secretary may alter, modify, or terminate an agreement entered into by the Secretary under subsection (a) in the case of the failure of the taxpayer –

(A) to pay any installment at the time such installment payment is due under such agreement,

(B) to pay any other tax liability at the time such liability is due, or

(C) to provide a financial condition update as requested by the Secretary.

(5) Notice requirements. The Secretary may not take any action under paragraph (2), (3), or (4) unless –

   (A) a notice of such action is provided to the taxpayer not later than the day 30 days before the date of such action, and

   (B) such notice includes an explanation why the Secretary intends to take such action.

The preceding sentence shall not apply in any case in which the Secretary believes that collection of any tax to which an agreement under this section relates is in jeopardy.

(c) Secretary required to enter into installment agreements in certain cases. In the case of a liability for tax of an individual under subtitle A, the Secretary shall enter into an agreement to accept the full payment of such tax in installments if, as of the date the individual offers to enter into the agreement

   (1) the aggregate amount of such liability (determined without regard to interest, penalties, additions to the tax, and additional amounts) does not exceed $10,000;

   (2) the taxpayer (and, if such liability relates to a joint return, the taxpayer's spouse) has not, during any of the preceding 5 taxable years –

   (A) failed to file any return of tax imposed by subtitle A;

   (B) failed to pay any tax required to be shown on any such return; or

   (C) entered into an installment agreement under this section for payment of any tax imposed by subtitle A,

   (3) the Secretary determines that the taxpayer is financially unable to pay such liability in full when due (and the taxpayer submits such information as the Secretary may require to make such determination);

   (4) the agreement requires full payment of such liability within 3 years; and

   (5) the taxpayer agrees to comply with the provisions of this title for the period such agreement is in effect.

(d) Secretary required to review installment agreements for partial collection every two years. In the case of an agreement entered into by the Secretary under subsection (a) for partial collection of a tax liability, the Secretary shall review the agreement at least once every 2 years.

(e) Administrative review. The Secretary shall establish procedures for an independent administrative review of terminations of installment agreements under this section for taxpayers who request such a review.

(f) Cross reference. For rights to administrative review and appeal, see section 7122(e).

* * *

§ 6161. Extension of time for paying tax.

   (a) Amount determined by taxpayer on return.

(1) General rule. The Secretary, except as otherwise provided in this title, may extend the time for payment of the amount of the tax shown or required to be shown, on any return or declaration required under authority of this title (or any installment thereof), for a reasonable period not to exceed 6 months (12 months in the case of estate tax) from the date fixed for payment thereof. Such extension may exceed 6 months in the case of a taxpayer who is abroad.

(2) Estate tax. The Secretary may, for reasonable cause, extend the time for payment of –

    (A) any part of the amount determined by the executor as the tax imposed by chapter 11, or

    (B) any part of any installment under section 6166 (including any part of a deficiency prorated to any installment under such section), for a reasonable period not in excess of 10 years from the date prescribed by section 6151(a) for payment of the tax (or, in the case of an amount referred to in subparagraph (B), if later, not beyond the date which is 12 months after the due date for the last installment).

* * *

§ 6201. Assessment authority.

(a) Authority of Secretary. The Secretary is authorized and required to make the inquiries, determinations, and assessments of all taxes (including interest, additional amounts, additions to the tax, and assessable penalties) imposed by this title, or accruing under any former internal revenue law, which have not been duly paid by stamp at the time and in the manner provided by law. Such authority shall extend to and include the following:

    (1) Taxes shown on return. The Secretary shall assess all taxes determined by the taxpayer or by the Secretary as to which returns or lists are made under this title.

* * *

§ 6203. Method of assessment.

The assessment shall be made by recording the liability of the taxpayer in the office of the Secretary in accordance with rules or regulations prescribed by the Secretary. Upon request of the taxpayer, the Secretary shall furnish the taxpayer a copy of the record of the assessment.

* * *

§ 6211. Definition of a deficiency.

(a) In general. For purposes of this title in the case of income, estate, and gift taxes imposed by subtitles A and B and excise taxes imposed by chapters 41, 42, 43, and 44, the term "deficiency" means the amount by which the tax imposed by subtitle A or B, or chapter 41, 42, 43, or 44, exceeds the excess of –

(1) the sum of

(A) the amount shown as the tax by the taxpayer upon his return, if a return was made by the taxpayer and an amount was shown as the tax by the taxpayer thereon, plus

(B) the amounts previously assessed (or collected without assessment) as a deficiency, over –

(2) the amount of rebates, as defined in subsection (b)(2), made.

* * *

§ 6212. Notice of deficiency.

(a) In general. If the Secretary determines that there is a deficiency in respect of any tax imposed by subtitle A or B or chapter 41, 42, 43 or 44, he is authorized to send notice of such deficiency to the taxpayer by certified mail or registered mail. Such notice shall include a notice to the taxpayer of the taxpayer's right to contact a local office of the taxpayer advocate and the location and phone number of the appropriate office.

(b) Address for notice of deficiency.

(1) Income and gift taxes and certain excise taxes. In the absence of notice to the Secretary under section 6903 of the existence of a fiduciary relationship, notice of a deficiency in respect of a tax imposed by subtitle A, chapter 12, chapter 41, chapter 42, chapter 43, or chapter 44 if mailed to the taxpayer at his last known address, shall be sufficient for purposes of subtitle A, chapter 12, chapter 41, chapter 42, chapter 43, chapter 44, and this chapter even if such taxpayer is deceased, or is under a legal disability, or, in the case of a corporation, has terminated its existence.

(2) Joint income tax return. In the case of a joint income tax return filed by husband and wife, such notice of deficiency may be a single joint notice, except that if the Secretary has been notified by either spouse that separate residences have been established, then, in lieu of the single joint notice, a duplicate original of the joint notice shall be sent by certified mail or registered mail to each spouse at his last known address.

(3) Estate tax. In the absence of notice to the Secretary under section 6903 of the existence of a fiduciary relationship, notice of a deficiency in respect of a tax imposed by chapter 11, if addressed in the name of the decedent or other person subject to liability and mailed to his last known address, shall be sufficient for purposes of chapter 11 and of this chapter.

(c) Further deficiency letters restricted.

(1) General rule. If the Secretary has mailed to the taxpayer a notice of deficiency as provided in subsection (a), and the taxpayer files a petition with the Tax Court within the time prescribed in section 6213(a), the Secretary shall have no right to determine any additional deficiency of income tax for the same taxable year, of gift tax for the same calendar year, of estate tax in respect of the taxable estate of the same decedent, of chapter 41 tax for the same taxable year, of chapter 43 tax for the same taxable year, of chapter 44 tax for the same taxable year, of section 4940 tax for the same taxable year, or of chapter 42 tax (other than under section 4940) with respect to any act (or failure to act) to which such petition relates, except in the case of fraud, and except as provided in section 6214(a) (relating to assertion of greater deficiencies before the Tax Court), in section 6213(b)(1) (relating to mathematical or clerical errors), in section 6851 or 6852 (relating to termination assessments), or in section 6861(c) (relating to the making of jeopardy assessments).

(2) Cross references. For assessment as a deficiency notwithstanding the prohibition of further deficiency letters, in the case of –

(A) Deficiency attributable to change of treatment with respect to itemized deductions, see section 63(e)(3).

(B) Deficiency attributable to gain on involuntary conversion, see section 1033(a)(2)(C) and (D).

(C) [Repealed]

(D) Deficiency attributable to activities not engaged in for profit, see section 183(e)(4).

For provisions allowing determination of tax in title 11 cases, see section 505(a) of title 11 of the United States Code.

(d) Authority to rescind notice of deficiency with taxpayer's consent. The Secretary may, with the consent of the taxpayer, rescind any notice of deficiency mailed to the taxpayer. Any notice so rescinded shall not be treated as a notice of deficiency for purposes of subsection (c)(1) (relating to further deficiency letters restricted), section 6213(a) (relating to restrictions applicable to deficiencies; petition to Tax Court), and section 6512(a) (relating to limitations in case of petition to Tax Court), and the taxpayer shall have no right to file a petition with the Tax Court based on such notice. Nothing in this subsection shall affect any suspension of the running of any period of limitations during any period during which the rescinded notice was outstanding.

§ 6213. Restrictions applicable to deficiencies; petition to Tax Court.

(a) Time for filing petition and restriction on assessment. Within 90 days, or 150 days if the notice is addressed to a person outside the United States, after the notice of deficiency authorized in section 6212 is mailed (not counting Saturday, Sunday, or a legal holiday in the District of Columbia as the last day), the taxpayer may file a petition with the Tax Court for a redetermination of the deficiency. Except as otherwise provided in section 6851, 6852, or 6861 no assessment of a deficiency in respect of any tax imposed by subtitle A or B, chapter 41, 42, 43, or 44, and no levy or proceeding in court for its collection shall be made, begun, or prosecuted until such notice has been mailed to the taxpayer, nor until the expiration of such 90-day or 150-day period, as the case may be, nor, if a petition has been filed with the Tax Court, until the decision of the Tax Court has become final. Notwithstanding the provisions of section 7421(a), the making of such assessment or the beginning of such proceeding or levy during the time such prohibition is in force may be enjoined by a proceeding in the proper court, including the Tax Court, and a refund may be ordered by such court of any amount collected within the period during which the Secretary is prohibited from collecting by levy or through a proceeding in court under the provisions of this subsection. The Tax Court shall have no jurisdiction to enjoin any action or proceeding or order any refund under this subsection unless a timely petition for a redetermination of the deficiency has been filed and then only in respect of the deficiency that is the subject of such petition. Any petition filed with the Tax Court on or before the last date specified for filing such petition by the Secretary in the notice of deficiency shall be treated as timely filed.

(b) Exceptions to restrictions on assessment.

(1) Assessments arising out of mathematical or clerical errors. If the taxpayer is notified that, on account of a mathematical or clerical error appearing on the return, an amount of tax in excess of that shown on the return is due, and that an assessment of the tax has been or will be made on the basis of what would have been the correct amount of tax but for the mathematical or clerical error, such notice shall not be considered as a notice of deficiency for the purposes of subsection (a) (prohibiting assessment and collection until notice of the deficiency has been mailed), or of section 6212(c)(1) (restricting further deficiency letters), or of section 6512(a) (prohibiting credits or refunds after petition to the Tax Court), and the taxpayer shall have no right to file a petition with the Tax Court based on such notice, nor shall such assessment or collection be prohibited by the provisions of subsection (a) of this section. Each notice under this paragraph shall set forth the error alleged and an explanation thereof.

(2) Abatement of assessment of mathematical or clerical errors.

(A) Request for abatement. Notwithstanding section 6404(b), a taxpayer may file with the Secretary within 60 days after notice is sent under paragraph (1) a request for an abatement of any assessment specified in such notice, and upon receipt of such request, the Secretary shall abate the assessment. Any reassessment of the tax with respect to which an abatement is made under this subparagraph shall be subject to the deficiency procedures prescribed by this subchapter.

(B) Stay of collection. In the case of any assessment referred to in paragraph (1), notwithstanding paragraph (1), no levy or proceeding in court for the collection of such assessment shall be made, begun, or prosecuted during the period in which such assessment may be abated under this paragraph.

(3) Assessments arising out of tentative carryback or refund adjustments. If the Secretary determines that the amount applied, credited, or refunded under section 6411 is in excess of the overassessment attributable to the carryback or the amount described in section 1341(b)(1) with respect to which such amount was applied, credited, or refunded, he may assess without regard to the provisions of paragraph (2) the amount of the excess as a deficiency as if it were due to a mathematical or clerical error appearing on the return.

(4) Assessment of amount paid. Any amount paid as a tax or in respect of a tax may be assessed upon the receipt of such payment notwithstanding the provisions of subsection (a). In any case where such amount is paid after the mailing of a notice of deficiency under section 6212, such payment shall not deprive the Tax Court of jurisdiction over such deficiency determined under section 6211 without regard to such assessment.

(5) Certain orders of criminal restitution. If the taxpayer is notified that an assessment has been or will be made pursuant to section 6201(a)(4) –

(A) such notice shall not be considered as a notice of deficiency for the purposes of subsection (a) (prohibiting assessment and collection until notice of the deficiency has been mailed), section 6212(c)(1) (restricting further deficiency letters), or section 6512(a) (prohibiting credits or refunds after petition to the Tax Court), and

(B) subsection (a) shall not apply with respect to the amount of such assessment.

(c) Failure to file petition. If the taxpayer does not file a petition with the Tax Court within the time prescribed in subsection (a), the deficiency, notice of which has been mailed to the taxpayer, shall be assessed, and shall be paid upon notice and demand from the Secretary.

(d) Waiver of restrictions. The taxpayer shall at any time (whether or not a notice of deficiency has been issued) have the right, by a signed notice in writing filed with the Secretary, to waive the restrictions provided in subsection (a) on the assessment and collection of the whole or any part of the deficiency.

* * *

(g) Definitions. For purposes of this section –

(1) Return. The term "return" includes any return, statement, schedule, or list, and any amendment or supplement thereto, filed with respect to any tax imposed by subtitle A or B, or chapter 41, 42, 43, or 44.

(2) Mathematical or clerical error. The term "mathematical or clerical error" means –

(A) an error in addition, subtraction, multiplication, or division shown on any return,

(B) an incorrect use of any table provided by the Internal Revenue Service with respect to any return if such incorrect use is apparent from the existence of other information on the return,

(C) an entry on a return of an item which is inconsistent with another entry of the same or another item on such return,

(D) an omission of information which is required to be supplied on the return to substantiate an entry on the return,

(E) an entry on a return of a deduction or credit in an amount which exceeds a statutory limit imposed by subtitle A or B, or chapter 41, 42 43, or 44, if such limit is expressed –

(i) as a specified monetary amount, or

(ii) as a percentage, ratio, or fraction,
and if the items entering into the application of such limit appear on such return,

(F) an omission of a correct taxpayer identification number required under section 32 (relating to the earned income credit) to be included on a return,

(G) an entry on a return claiming the credit under section 32 with respect to net earnings from self-employment described in section 32(c)(2)(A) to the extent the tax imposed by section 1401 (relating to self-employment tax) on such net earnings has not been paid,

(H) an omission of a correct TIN required under section 21 (relating to expenses for household and dependent care services necessary for gainful employment) or section 151 (relating to allowance of deductions for personal exemptions),

(I) an omission of a correct TIN required under section 24(e) (relating to child tax credit) to be included on a return,

(J) an omission of a correct TIN required under section 25A(g)(1) (relating to higher education tuition and related expenses) to be included on a return,

(K) an omission of information required by section 32(k)(2) (relating to taxpayers making improper prior claims of earned income credit),

(L) the inclusion on a return of a TIN required to be included on the return under section 21, 24, 32, or 6428 if –

    (i) such TIN is of an individual whose age affects the amount of the credit under such section, and

    (ii) the computation of the credit on the return reflects the treatment of such individual as being of an age different from the individual's age based on such TIN,

(M) the entry on the return claiming the credit under section 32 with respect to a child if, according to the Federal Case Registry of Child Support Orders established under section 453(h) of the Social Security Act, the taxpayer is a noncustodial parent of such child,

(N) an omission of the reduction required under section 36A(c) with respect to the credit allowed under section 36A or an omission of the correct social security account number required under section 36A(d)(1)(B),

(O) an omission of any increase required under section 36(f) with respect to the recapture of a credit allowed under section 36, and

(P) an entry on a return claiming the credit under section 36 if –

    (i) the Secretary obtains information from the person issuing the TIN of the taxpayer that indicates that the taxpayer does not meet the age requirement of section 36(b)(4),

    (ii) information provided to the Secretary by the taxpayer on an income tax return for at least one of the 2 preceding taxable years is inconsistent with eligibility for such credit, or

    (iii) the taxpayer fails to attach to the return the form described in section 36(d)(4).

A taxpayer shall be treated as having omitted a correct TIN for purposes of the preceding sentence if information provided by the taxpayer on the return with respect to the individual whose TIN was provided differs from the information the Secretary obtains from the person issuing the TIN.

* * *

§ 6214. Determinations by Tax Court.

* * *

(b) Jurisdiction over other years and quarters. The Tax Court in redetermining a deficiency of income tax for any taxable year or of gift tax for any calendar year or calendar quarter shall consider such facts with relation to the taxes for other years or calendar quarters as may be necessary correctly to redetermine the amount of such deficiency, but in so doing shall have no jurisdiction to determine whether or not the tax for any other year or calendar quarter has been overpaid or underpaid. Notwithstanding the preceding sentence, the Tax Court may apply the doctrine of equitable recoupment to the same extent that it is available in civil tax cases before the district courts of the United States and the United States Court of Federal Claims.

* * *

§ 6221. Tax treatment determined at partnership level.

Except as otherwise provided in this subchapter, the tax treatment of any partnership item (and the applicability of any penalty, addition to tax, or additional amount which relates to an adjustment to a partnership item) shall be determined at the partnership level.

* * *

§ 6223. Notice to partners of proceedings.

(a) Secretary must give partners notice of beginning and completion of administrative proceedings. The Secretary shall mail to each partner whose name and address is furnished to the Secretary notice of –

(1) the beginning of an administrative proceeding at the partnership level with respect to a partnership item, and

(2) the final partnership administrative adjustment resulting from any such proceeding. A partner shall not be entitled to any notice under this subsection unless the Secretary has received (at least 30 days before it is mailed to the tax matters partner) sufficient information to enable the Secretary to determine that such partner is entitled to such notice and to provide such notice to such partner.

(b) Special rules for partnership with more than 100 partners.

(1) Partner with less than 1 percent interest. Except as provided in paragraph (2), subsection (a) shall not apply to a partner if –

(A) the partnership has more than 100 partners, and

(B) the partner has a less than 1 percent interest in the profits of the partnership.

(2) Secretary must give notice to notice group. If a group of partners in the aggregate having a 5 percent or more interest in the profits of a partnership so request and designate one of their members to receive the notice, the member so designated shall be treated as a partner to whom subsection (a) applies.

(c) Information base for Secretary's notices, etc. For purposes of this subchapter –

(1) Information on partnership return. Except as provided in paragraphs (2) and (3), the Secretary shall use the names, addresses, and profits interests shown on the partnership return.

(2) Use of additional information. The Secretary shall use additional information furnished to him by the tax matters partner or any other person in accordance with regulations prescribed by the Secretary.

(3) Special rule with respect to indirect partners. If any information furnished to the Secretary under paragraph (1) or (2) –

(A) shows that a person has a profits interest in the partnership by reason of ownership of an interest through 1 or more pass-thru partners, and

(B) contains the name, address, and profits interest of such person, then the Secretary shall use the name, address, and profits interest of such person with respect to such partnership interest (in lieu of the names, addresses, and profits interests of the pass-thru partners).

(d) Period for mailing notice.

(1) Notice of beginning of proceedings. The Secretary shall mail the notice specified in paragraph (1) of subsection (a) to each partner entitled to such notice not later than the 120th day before the day on which the notice specified in paragraph (2) of subsection (a) is mailed to the tax matters partner.

(2) Notice of final partnership administrative adjustment. The Secretary shall mail the notice specified in paragraph (2) of subsection (a) to each partner entitled to such notice not later than the 60th day after the day on which the notice specified in such paragraph (2) was mailed to the tax matters partner.

(e) Effect of Secretary's failure to provide notice.

(1) Application of subsection.

(A) In general. This subsection applies where the Secretary has failed to mail any notice specified in subsection (a) to a partner entitled to such notice within the period specified in subsection (d).

(B) Special rules for partnerships with more than 100 partners. For purposes of subparagraph (A), any partner described in paragraph (1) of subsection (b) shall be treated as entitled to notice specified in subsection (a). The Secretary may provide such notice –

(i) except as provided in clause (ii), by mailing notice to the tax matters partner, or

(ii) in the case of a member of a notice group which qualifies under paragraph (2) of subsection (b), by mailing notice to the partner designated for such purpose by the group.

(2) Proceedings finished. In any case to which this subsection applies, if at the time the Secretary mails the partner notice of the proceeding –

(A) the period within which a petition for review of a final partnership administrative adjustment under section 6226 may be filed has expired and no such petition has been filed, or

(B) the decision of a court in an action begun by such a petition has become final, the partner may elect to have such adjustment, such decision, or a settlement agreement described in paragraph (2) of section 6224(c) with respect to the partnership taxable year to which the adjustment relates apply to such partner. If the partner does not make an election under the preceding sentence, the partnership items of the partner for the partnership taxable year to which the proceeding relates shall be treated as nonpartnership items.

(3) Proceedings still going on. In any case to which this subsection applies, if paragraph (2) does not apply, the partner shall be a party to the proceeding unless such partner elects –

    (A) to have a settlement agreement described in paragraph (2) of section 6224(c) with respect to the partnership taxable year to which the proceeding relates apply to the partner, or

    (B) to have the partnership items of the partner for the partnership taxable year to which the proceeding relates treated as nonpartnership items.

(f) Only one notice of final partnership administrative adjustment. If the Secretary mails a notice of final partnership administrative adjustment for a partnership taxable year with respect to a partner, the Secretary may not mail another such notice to such partner with respect to the same taxable year of the same partnership in the absence of a showing of fraud, malfeasance, or misrepresentation of a material fact.

(g) Tax matters partner must keep partners informed of proceedings. To the extent and in the manner provided by regulations, the tax matters partner of a partnership shall keep each partner informed of all administrative and judicial proceedings for the adjustment at the partnership level of partnership items.

(h) Pass-thru partner required to forward notice.

    (1) In general. If a pass-thru partner receives a notice with respect to a partnership proceeding from the Secretary, the tax matters partner, or another pass-thru partner, the pass-thru partner shall, within 30 days of receiving that notice, forward a copy of that notice to the person or persons holding an interest (through the pass-thru partner) in the profits or losses of the partnership for the partnership taxable year to which the notice relates.

    (2) Partnership as pass-thru partner. In the case of a pass-thru partner which is a partnership, the tax matters partner of such partnership shall be responsible for forwarding copies of the notice to the partners of such partnership.

* * *

§ 6226. Judicial review of final partnership administrative adjustments.

(a) Petition by tax matters partner. Within 90 days after the day on which a notice of a final partnership administrative adjustment is mailed to the tax matters partner, the tax matters partner may file a petition for a readjustment of the partnership items for such taxable year with –

    (1) the Tax Court,

    (2) the district court of the United States for the district in which the partnership's principal place of business is located, or

    (3) the Claims Court [Court of Federal Claims].

(b) Petition by partner other than tax matters partner.

    (1) In general. If the tax matters partner does not file a readjustment petition under subsection (a) with respect to any final partnership administrative adjustment, any notice partner (and any 5-percent group) may, within 60 days after the close of the 90-day period set forth in subsection (a), file a petition for a readjustment of the partnership items for the taxable year involved with any of the courts described in subsection (a).

(2) Priority of the tax court action. If more than 1 action is brought under paragraph (1) with respect to any partnership for any partnership taxable year, the first such action brought in the Tax Court shall go forward.

(3) Priority outside the Tax Court. If more than 1 action is brought under paragraph (1) with respect to any partnership for any taxable year but no such action is brought in the Tax Court, the first such action brought shall go forward.

(4) Dismissal of other actions. If an action is brought under paragraph (1) in addition to the action which goes forward under paragraph (2) or (3), such action shall be dismissed.

(5) Treatment of premature petitions. If –

(A) a petition for a readjustment of partnership items for the taxable year involved is filed by a notice partner (or a 5-percent group) during the 90-day period described in subsection (a), and

(B) no action is brought under paragraph (1) during the 60-day period described therein with respect to such taxable year which is not dismissed,
such petition shall be treated for purposes of paragraph (1) as filed on the last day of such 60-day period.

(6) Tax matters partner may intervene. The tax matters partner may intervene in any action brought under this subsection.

* * *

§ 6227. Administrative adjustment requests.

(a) General rule. A partner may file a request for an administrative adjustment of partnership items for any partnership taxable year at any time which is –

(1) within 3 years after the later of –

(A) the date on which the partnership return for such year is filed, or

(B) the last day for filing the partnership return for such year (determined without regard to extensions), and

(2) before the mailing to the tax matters partner of a notice of final partnership administrative adjustment with respect to such taxable year.

* * *

§ 6228. Judicial review where administrative adjustment request is not allowed in full.

(a) Request on behalf of partnership.

(1) In general. If any part of an administrative adjustment request filed by the tax matters partner under subsection (c) of section 6227 is not allowed by the Secretary, the tax matters partner may file a petition for an adjustment with respect to the partnership items to which such part of the request relates with –

(A) the Tax Court,

(B) the district court of the United States for the district in which the principal place of business of the partnership is located, or

(C) the Claims Court [Court of Federal Claims].

(2) Period for filing petition.

(A) In general. A petition may be filed under paragraph (1) with respect to partnership items for a partnership taxable year only –

    (i) after the expiration of 6 months from the date of filing of the request under section 6227, and

    (ii) before the date which is 2 years after the date of such request.

(B) No petition after notice of beginning of administrative proceeding. No petition may be filed under paragraph (1) after the day the Secretary mails to the partnership a notice of the beginning of an administrative proceeding with respect to the partnership taxable year to which such request relates.

(C) Failure by secretary to issue timely notice of adjustment. If the Secretary –

    (i) mails the notice referred to in subparagraph (B) before the expiration of the 2-year period referred to in clause (ii) of subparagraph (A), and

    (ii) fails to mail a notice of final partnership administrative adjustment with respect to the partnership taxable year to which the request relates before the expiration of the period described in section 6229(a) (including any extension by agreement), subparagraph (B) shall cease to apply with respect to such request, and the 2-year period referred to in clause (ii) of subparagraph (A) shall not expire before the date 6 months after the expiration of the period described in section 6229(a) (including any extension by agreement).

(D) Extension of time. The 2-year period described in subparagraph (A)(ii) shall be extended for such period as may be agreed upon in writing between the tax matters partner and the Secretary

(3) Coordination with administrative adjustment.

(A) Administrative adjustment before filing of petition. No petition may be filed under this subsection after the Secretary mails to the tax matters partner a notice of final partnership administrative adjustment for the partnership taxable year to which the request under section 6227 relates.

(B) Administrative adjustment after filing but before hearing of petition. If the Secretary mails to the tax matters partner a notice of final partnership administrative adjustment for the partnership taxable year to which the request under section 6227 relates after the filing of a petition under this subsection but before the hearing of such petition, such petition shall be treated as an action brought under section 6226 with respect to that administrative adjustment, except that subsection (e) of section 6226 shall not apply.

(C) Notice must be before expiration of statute of limitations. A notice of final partnership administrative adjustment for the partnership taxable year shall be taken into account under subparagraphs (A) and (B) only if such notice is mailed before the expiration of the period prescribed by section 6229 for making assessments of tax attributable to partnership items for such taxable year.

(4) Partners treated as party to action.

(A) In general. If an action is brought by the tax matters partner under paragraph (1) with respect to any request for an adjustment of a partnership item for any taxable year –

(i) each person who was a partner in such partnership at any time during the partnership taxable year involved shall be treated as a party to such action, and

(ii) the court having jurisdiction of such action shall allow each such person to participate in the action.

(B) Partners must have interest in outcome. For purposes of subparagraph (A), rules similar to the rules of paragraph (1) of section 6226(d) shall apply.

(5) Scope of judicial review. Except in the case described in subparagraph (B) of paragraph (3), a court with which a petition is filed in accordance with this subsection shall have jurisdiction to determine only those partnership items to which the part of the request under section 6227 not allowed by the Secretary relates and those items with respect to which the Secretary asserts adjustments as offsets to the adjustments requested by the tax matters partner.

(6) Determination of court reviewable. Any determination by a court under this subsection shall have the force and effect of a decision of the Tax Court or a final judgment or decree of the district court or the Claims Court [Court of Federal Claims], as the case may be, and shall be reviewable as such. With respect to the partnership, only the tax matters partner, a notice partner, or a 5-percent group may seek review of a determination by a court under this subsection.

* * *

§ 6231. Definitions and special rules.

(a) Definitions. For purposes of this subchapter –

(1) Partnership.

(A) In general. Except as provided in subparagraph (B), the term "partnership" means any partnership required to file a return under section 6031(a).

(B) Exception for small partnerships.

(i) In general. The term 'partnership' shall not include any partnership having 10 or fewer partners each of whom is an individual (other than a nonresident alien), a C corporation, or an estate of a deceased partner. For purposes of the preceding sentence, a husband and wife (and their estates) shall be treated as 1 partner.

(ii) Election to have subchapter apply. A partnership (within the meaning of subparagraph (A)) may for any taxable year elect to have clause (i) not apply. Such election shall apply for such taxable year and all subsequent taxable years unless revoked with the consent of the Secretary.

(2) Partner. The term "partner" means –

    (A) a partner in the partnership, and

    (B) any other person whose income tax liability under subtitle A is determined in whole or in part by taking into account directly or indirectly partnership items of the partnership.

(3) Partnership item. The term "partnership item" means, with respect to a partnership, any item required to be taken into account for the partnership's taxable year under any provision of subtitle A to the extent regulations prescribed by the Secretary provide that, for purposes of this subtitle, such item is more appropriately determined at the partnership level than at the partner level.

(4) Nonpartnership item. The term "nonpartnership item" means an item which is (or is treated as) not a partnership item.

(5) Affected item. The term "affected item" means any item to the extent such item is affected by a partnership item.

(6) Computational adjustment. The term "computational adjustment" means the change in the tax liability of a partner which properly reflects the treatment under this subchapter of a partnership item. All adjustments required to apply the results of a proceeding with respect to a partnership under this subchapter to an indirect partner shall be treated as computational adjustments.

(7) Tax matters partner. The tax matters partner of any partnership is –

    (A) the general partner designated as the tax matters partner as provided in regulations, or

    (B) if there is no general partner who has been so designated, the general partner having the largest profits interest in the partnership at the close of the taxable year involved (or, where there is more than 1 such partner, the 1 of such partners whose name would appear first in an alphabetical listing).

If there is no general partner designated under subparagraph (A) and the Secretary determines that it is impracticable to apply subparagraph (B), the partner selected by the Secretary shall be treated as the tax matters partner. The Secretary shall, within 30 days of selecting a tax matters partner under the preceding sentence, notify all partners required to receive notice under section 6223(a) of the name and address of the person selected.

(8) Notice partner. The term "notice partner" means a partner who, at the time in question, would be entitled to notice under subsection (a) of section 6223 (determined without regard to subsections (b)(2) and (e)(1)(B) thereof).

(9) Pass-thru partner. The term "pass-thru partner" means a partnership, estate, trust, S corporation, nominee, or other similar person through whom other persons hold an interest in the partnership with respect to which proceedings under this subchapter are conducted.

(10) Indirect partner. The term "indirect partner" means a person holding an interest in a partnership through 1 or more pass-thru partners.

(11) 5-percent group. A 5-percent group is a group of partners who for the partnership taxable year involved had profits interests which aggregated 5 percent or more.

(12) Husband and wife. Except to the extent otherwise provided in regulations, a husband and wife who have a joint interest in a partnership shall be treated as 1 person.

* * *

§ 6240. Application of subchapter.

(a) General rule. This subchapter shall only apply to electing large partnerships and partners in such partnerships.

(b) Coordination with other partnership audit procedures.

(1) In general. Subchapter C of this chapter shall not apply to any electing large partnership other than in its capacity as a partner in another partnership which is not an electing large partnership.

(2) Treatment where partner in other partnership. If an electing large partnership is a partner in another partnership which is not an electing large partnership –

(A) subchapter C of this chapter shall apply to items of such electing large partnership which are partnership items with respect to such other partnership, but

(B) any adjustment under such subchapter C shall be taken into account in the manner provided by section 6242.

* * *

§ 6241. Partner's return must be consistent with partnership return.

(a) General rule. A partner of any electing large partnership shall, on the partner's return, treat each partnership item attributable to such partnership in a manner which is consistent with the treatment of such partnership item on the partnership return.

* * *

(c) Adjustments not to affect prior year of partners.

(1) In general. Except as provided in paragraph (2), subsections (a) and (b) shall apply without regard to any adjustment to the partnership item under part II.

(2) Certain changes in distributive share taken into account by partner.

(A) In general. To the extent that any adjustment under part II involves a change under section 704 in a partner's distributive share of the amount of any partnership item shown on the partnership return, such adjustment shall be taken into account in applying this title to such partner for the partner's taxable year for which such item was required to be taken into account.

(B) Coordination with deficiency procedures.

(i) In general. Subchapter B shall not apply to the assessment or collection of any underpayment of tax attributable to an adjustment referred to in subparagraph (A).

(ii) Adjustment not precluded. Notwithstanding any other law or rule of law, nothing in subchapter B (or in any proceeding under subchapter B) shall preclude the assessment or collection of any underpayment of tax (or the allowance of any credit or refund of any overpayment of tax) attributable to an adjustment referred to in subparagraph (A) and such assessment or collection or allowance (or any notice thereof) shall not preclude any notice, proceeding, or determination under subchapter B.

(C) Period of limitations. The period for –

(i) assessing any underpayment of tax, or

(ii) filing a claim for credit or refund of any overpayment of tax, attributable to an adjustment referred to in subparagraph (A) shall not expire before the close of the period prescribed by section 6248 for making adjustments with respect to the partnership taxable year involved.

(D) Tiered structures. If the partner referred to in subparagraph (A) is another partnership or an S corporation, the rules of this paragraph shall also apply to persons holding interests in such partnership or S corporation (as the case may be); except that, if such partner is an electing large partnership, the adjustment referred to in subparagraph (A) shall be taken into account in the manner provided by section 6242.

* * *

§ 6242. Procedures for taking partnership adjustments into account.

(a) Adjustments flow through to partners for year in which adjustment takes effect.

(1) In general. If any partnership adjustment with respect to any partnership item takes effect (within the meaning of subsection (d)(2)) during any partnership taxable year and if an election under paragraph (2) does not apply to such adjustment, such adjustment shall be taken into account in determining the amount of such item for the partnership taxable year in which such adjustment takes effect. In applying this title to any person who is (directly or indirectly) a partner in such partnership during such partnership taxable year, such adjustment shall be treated as an item actually arising during such taxable year.

(2) Partnership liable in certain cases. If –

(A) a partnership elects under this paragraph to not take an adjustment into account under paragraph (1),

(B) a partnership does not make such an election but in filing its return for any partnership taxable year fails to take fully into account any partnership adjustment as required under paragraph (1), or

(C) any partnership adjustment involves a reduction in a credit which exceeds the amount of such credit determined for the partnership taxable year in which the adjustment takes effect, the partnership shall pay to the Secretary an amount determined by applying the rules of subsection (b)(4) to the adjustments not so taken into account and any excess referred to in subparagraph (C).

(3) Offsetting adjustments taken into account. If a partnership adjustment requires another adjustment in a taxable year after the adjusted year and before the partnership taxable year in which such partnership adjustment takes effect, such other adjustment shall be taken into account under this subsection for the partnership taxable year in which such partnership adjustment takes effect.

(4) Coordination with part II. Amounts taken into account under this subsection for any partnership taxable year shall continue to be treated as adjustments for the adjusted year for purposes of determining whether such amounts may be readjusted under part II.

(b) Partnership liable for interest and penalties.

(1) In general. If a partnership adjustment takes effect during any partnership taxable year and such adjustment results in an imputed underpayment for the adjusted year, the partnership —

(A) shall pay to the Secretary interest computed under paragraph (2), and

(B) shall be liable for any penalty, addition to tax, or additional amount as provided in paragraph (3).

(2) Determination of amount of interest. The interest computed under this paragraph with respect to any partnership adjustment is the interest which would be determined under chapter 67 —

(A) on the imputed underpayment determined under paragraph (4) with respect to such adjustment,

(B) for the period beginning on the day after the return due date for the adjusted year and ending on the return due date for the partnership taxable year in which such adjustment takes effect (or, if earlier, in the case of any adjustment to which subsection (a)(2) applies, the date on which the payment under subsection (a)(2) is made).

Proper adjustments in the amount determined under the preceding sentence shall be made for adjustments required for partnership taxable years after the adjusted year and before the year in which the partnership adjustment takes effect by reason of such partnership adjustment.

(3) Penalties. A partnership shall be liable for any penalty, addition to tax, or additional amount for which it would have been liable if such partnership had been an individual subject to tax under chapter 1 for the adjusted year and the imputed underpayment determined under paragraph (4) were an actual underpayment (or understatement) for such year.

(4) Imputed underpayment. For purposes of this subsection, the imputed underpayment determined under this paragraph with respect to any partnership adjustment is the underpayment (if any) which would result —

(A) by netting all adjustments to items of income, gain, loss, or deduction and by treating any net increase in income as an underpayment equal to the amount of such net increase multiplied by the highest rate of tax in effect under section 1 or 11 for the adjusted year, and

(B) by taking adjustments to credits into account as increases or decreases (whichever is appropriate) in the amount of tax.

For purposes of the preceding sentence, any net decrease in a loss shall be treated as an increase in income and a similar rule shall apply to a net increase in a loss.

* * *

§ 6245. Secretarial authority.

(a) General rule. The Secretary is authorized and directed to make adjustments at the partnership level in any partnership item to the extent necessary to have such item be treated in the manner required.

(b) Notice of partnership adjustment.

(1) In general. If the Secretary determines that a partnership adjustment is required, the Secretary is authorized to send notice of such adjustment to the partnership by certified mail or registered mail. Such notice shall be sufficient if mailed to the partnership at its last known address even if the partnership has terminated its existence.

(2) Further notices restricted. If the Secretary mails a notice of a partnership adjustment to any partnership for any partnership taxable year and the partnership files a petition under section 6247 with respect to such notice, in the absence of a showing of fraud, malfeasance, or misrepresentation of a material fact, the Secretary shall not mail another such notice to such partnership with respect to such taxable year.

(3) Authority to rescind notice with partnership consent. The Secretary may, with the consent of the partnership, rescind any notice of a partnership adjustment mailed to such partnership. Any notice so rescinded shall not be treated as a notice of a partnership adjustment, for purposes of this section, section 6246, and section 6247, and the taxpayer shall have no right to bring a proceeding under section 6247 with respect to such notice. Nothing in this subsection shall affect any suspension of the running of any period of limitations during any period during which the rescinded notice was outstanding.

* * *

§ 6246. Restrictions on partnership adjustments.

(a) General rule. Except as otherwise provided in this chapter, no adjustment to any partnership item may be made (and no levy or proceeding in any court for the collection of any amount resulting from such adjustment may be made, begun or prosecuted) before –

(1) the close of the 90th day after the day on which a notice of a partnership adjustment was mailed to the partnership, and

(2) if a petition is filed under section 6247 with respect to such notice, the decision of the court has become final.

* * *

§ 6247. Judicial review of partnership adjustment.

(a) General rule. Within 90 days after the date on which a notice of a partnership adjustment is mailed to the partnership with respect to any partnership taxable year, the partnership may file a petition for a readjustment of the partnership items for such taxable year with –

(1) the Tax Court,

(2) the district court of the United States for the district in which the partnership's principal place of business is located, or

(3) the Claims Court.

(b) Jurisdictional requirement for bringing action in district court or Claims Court.

(1) In general. A readjustment petition under this section may be filed in a district court of the United States or the Claims Court only if the partnership filing the petition deposits with the Secretary, on or before the date the petition is filed, the amount for which the partnership would be liable under section 6242(b) (as of the date of the filing of the petition) if the partnership items were adjusted as provided by the notice of partnership adjustment. The court may by order provide that the jurisdictional requirements of this paragraph are satisfied where there has been a good faith attempt to satisfy such requirement and any shortfall of the amount required to be deposited is timely corrected.

(2) Interest payable. Any amount deposited under paragraph (1), while deposited, shall not be treated as a payment of tax for purposes of this title (other than chapter 67).
(c) Scope of judicial review. A court with which a petition is filed in accordance with this section shall have jurisdiction to determine all partnership items of the partnership for the partnership taxable year to which the notice of partnership adjustment relates and the proper allocation of such items among the partners (and the applicability of any penalty, addition to tax, or additional amount for which the partnership may be liable under section 6242(b)).
(d) Determination of court reviewable. Any determination by a court under this section shall have the force and effect of a decision of the Tax Court or a final judgment or decree of the district court or the Claims Court, as the case may be, and shall be reviewable as such. The date of any such determination shall be treated as being the date of the court's order entering the decision.

* * *

(e) Effect of decision dismissing action. If an action brought under this section is dismissed other than by reason of a rescission under section 6245(b)(3), the decision of the court dismissing the action shall be considered as its decision that the notice of partnership adjustment is correct, and an appropriate order shall be entered in the records of the court.

§ 6251. Administrative adjustment requests.

(a) General rule. A partnership may file a request for an administrative adjustment of partnership items for any partnership taxable year at any time which is –

(1) within 3 years after the later of –

(A) the date on which the partnership return for such year is filed, or

(B) the last day for filing the partnership return for such year (determined without regard to extensions), and

(2) before the mailing to the partnership of a notice of a partnership adjustment with respect to such taxable year.

(b) Secretarial action. If a partnership files an administrative adjustment request under subsection (a), the Secretary may allow any part of the requested adjustments.

(c) Special rule in case of extension under section 6248. If the period described in section 6248(a) is extended pursuant to an agreement under section 6248(b), the period prescribed by subsection (a)(1) shall not expire before the date 6 months after the expiration of the extension under section 6248(b).

* * *

§ 6255. Definitions and special rules.

(a) Definitions. For purposes of this subchapter –

(1) Electing large partnership. The term "electing large partnership" has the meaning given to such term by section 775.

(2) Partnership item. The term "partnership item" has the meaning given to such term by section 6231(a)(3).

(b) Partners bound by actions of partnership, etc.

(1) Designation of partner. Each electing large partnership shall designate (in the manner prescribed by the Secretary) a partner (or other person) who shall have the sole authority to act on behalf of such partnership under this subchapter. In any case in which such a designation is not in effect, the Secretary may select any partner as the partner with such authority.

(2) Binding effect. An electing large partnership and all partners of such partnership shall be bound –

(A) by actions taken under this subchapter by the partnership, and

(B) by any decision in a proceeding brought under this subchapter.

* * *

§ 6303. Notice and demand for tax.

(a) General rule. Where it is not otherwise provided by this title, the Secretary shall, as soon as practicable, and within 60 days, after the making of an assessment of a tax pursuant to section 6203, give notice to each person liable for the unpaid tax, stating the amount and demanding payment thereof. Such notice shall be left at the dwelling or usual place of business of such person, or shall be sent by mail to such person's last known address.

(b) Assessment prior to last date for payment. Except where the Secretary believes collection would be jeopardized by delay, if any tax is assessed prior to the last date prescribed for payment of such tax, payment of such tax shall not be demanded under subsection (a) until after such date.

* * *

§ 6306. Qualified tax collection contracts.

(a) In general. Nothing in any provision of law shall be construed to prevent the Secretary from entering into a qualified tax collection contract.

(b) Qualified tax collection contract. For purposes of this section, the term "qualified tax collection contract" means any contract which –

(1) is for the services of any person (other than an officer or employee of the Treasury Department) –

(A) to locate and contact any taxpayer specified by the Secretary,

(B) to request full payment from such taxpayer of an amount of Federal tax specified by the Secretary and, if such request cannot be met by the taxpayer, to offer the taxpayer an installment agreement providing for full payment of such amount during a period not to exceed 5 years, and

(C) to obtain financial information specified by the Secretary with respect to such taxpayer,

(2) prohibits each person providing such services under such contract from committing any act or omission which employees of the Internal Revenue Service are prohibited from committing in the performance of similar services,

(3) prohibits subcontractors from –

(A) having contacts with taxpayers,

(B) providing quality assurance services, and

(C) composing debt collection notices, and

(4) permits subcontractors to perform other services only with the approval of the Secretary.

(c) Fees. The Secretary may retain and use –

(1) an amount not in excess of 25 percent of the amount collected under any qualified tax collection contract for the costs of services performed under such contract, and

(2) an amount not in excess of 25 percent of such amount collected for collection enforcement activities of the Internal Revenue Service.

The Secretary shall keep adequate records regarding amounts so retained and used. The amount credited as paid by any taxpayer shall be determined without regard to this subsection.

* * *

(e) Application of Fair Debt Collection Practices Act. The provisions of the Fair Debt Collection Practices Act shall apply to any qualified tax collection contract, except to the extent superseded by section 6304, section 7602(c), or by any other provision of this title.

* * *

§ 6311. Payment of tax by commercially acceptable means.

(a) Authority to receive. It shall be lawful for the Secretary to receive for internal revenue taxes (or in payment for internal revenue stamps) any commercially acceptable means that the Secretary deems appropriate to the extent and under the conditions provided in regulations prescribed by the Secretary.

(b) Ultimate liability. If a check, money order, or other method of payment, including payment by credit card, debit card, or charge card so received is not duly paid, or is paid and subsequently charged back to the Secretary, the person by whom such check, or money order, or other method of payment has been tendered shall remain liable for the payment of the tax or for the stamps, and for all legal penalties and additions, to the same extent as if such check, money order, or other method of payment had not been tendered.

* * *

§ 6320. Notice and opportunity for hearing upon filing of notice of lien.

(a) Requirement of notice.

(1) In general. The Secretary shall notify in writing the person described in section 6321 of the filing of a notice of lien under section 6323.

(2) Time and method for notice. The notice required under paragraph (1) shall be –

(A) given in person;

(B) left at the dwelling or usual place of business of such person; or

(C) sent by certified or registered mail to such person's last known address, not more than 5 business days after the day of the filing of the notice of lien.

(3) Information included with notice. The notice required under paragraph (1) shall include in simple and nontechnical terms –

(A) the amount of unpaid tax;

(B) the right of the person to request a hearing during the 30-day period beginning on the day after the 5-day period described in paragraph (2);

(C) the administrative appeals available to the taxpayer with respect to such lien and the procedures relating to such appeals; and

(D) the provisions of this title and procedures relating to the release of liens on property.

(b) Right to fair hearing.

(1) In general. If the person requests a hearing in writing under subsection (a)(3)(B) and states the grounds for the requested hearing, such hearing shall be held by the Internal Revenue Service Office of Appeals.

(2) One hearing per period. A person shall be entitled to only one hearing under this section with respect to the taxable period to which the unpaid tax specified in subsection (a)(3)(A) relates.

(3) Impartial officer. The hearing under this subsection shall be conducted by an officer or employee who has had no prior involvement with respect to the unpaid tax specified in subsection (a)(3)(A) before the first hearing under this section or section 6330. A taxpayer may waive the requirement of this paragraph.

(4) Coordination with section 6330. To the extent practicable, a hearing under this section shall be held in conjunction with a hearing under section 6330.

(c) Conduct of hearing; review; suspensions. For purposes of this section, subsections (c), (d) (other than paragraph (2)(B) thereof), (e), and (g) of section 6330 shall apply.

* * *

§ 6321. Lien for taxes.

If any person liable to pay any tax neglects or refuses to pay the same after demand, the amount (including any interest, additional amount, addition to tax, or assessable penalty, together with any costs that may accrue in addition thereto) shall be a lien in favor of the United States upon all property and rights to property, whether real or personal, belonging to such person.

§ 6322. Period of lien.

Unless another date is specifically fixed by law, the lien imposed by section 6321 shall arise at the time the assessment is made and shall continue until the liability for the amount so assessed (or a judgment against the taxpayer arising out of such liability) is satisfied or becomes unenforceable by reason of lapse of time.

§ 6323. Validity and priority against certain persons.

(a) Purchasers, holders of security interests, mechanic's lienors, and judgment lien creditors. The lien imposed by section 6321 shall not be valid as against any purchaser, holder of a security interest, mechanic's lienor, or judgment lien creditor until notice thereof which meets the requirements of subsection (f) has been filed by the Secretary.

(b) Protection for certain interests even though notice filed. Even though notice of a lien imposed by section 6321 has been filed, such lien shall not be valid –

(1) Securities. With respect to a security (as defined in subsection (h)(4)) –

(A) as against a purchaser of such security who at the time of purchase did not have actual notice or knowledge of the existence of such lien; and

(B) as against a holder of a security interest in such security who, at the time such interest came into existence, did not have actual notice or knowledge of the existence of such lien.

(2) Motor vehicles. With respect to a motor vehicle (as defined in subsection (h)(3)), as against a purchaser of such motor vehicle, if –

(A) at the time of the purchase such purchaser did not have actual notice or knowledge of the existence of such lien, and

(B) before the purchaser obtains such notice or knowledge, he has acquired possession of such motor vehicle and has not thereafter relinquished possession of such motor vehicle to the seller or his agent.

(3) Personal property purchased at retail. With respect to tangible personal property purchased at retail, as against a purchaser in the ordinary course of the seller's trade or business, unless at the time of such purchase such purchaser intends such purchase to (or knows such purchase will) hinder, evade, or defeat the collection of any tax under this title.

(4) Personal property purchased in casual sale. With respect to household goods, personal effects, or other tangible personal property described in section 6334(a) purchased (not for resale) in a casual sale for less than $1,000, as against the purchaser, but only if such purchaser does not have actual notice or knowledge (A) of the existence of such lien, or (B) that this sale is one of a series of sales.

(5) Personal property subject to possessory lien. With respect to tangible personal property subject to a lien under local law securing the reasonable price of the repair or improvement of such property, as against a holder of such a lien, if such holder is, and has been, continuously in possession of such property from the time such lien arose.

(6) Real property tax and special assessment liens. With respect to real property, as against a holder of a lien upon such property, if such lien is entitled under local law to priority over security interests in such property which are prior in time, and such lien secures payment of –

(A) a tax of general application levied by any taxing authority based upon the value of such property;

(B) a special assessment imposed directly upon such property by any taxing authority, if such assessment is imposed for the purpose of defraying the cost of any public improvement; or

(C) charges for utilities or public services furnished to such property by the United States, a State or political subdivision thereof, or an instrumentality of any one or more of the foregoing.

(7) Residential property subject to a mechanic's lien for certain repairs and improvements. With respect to real property subject to a lien for repair or improvement of a personal residence (containing not more than four dwelling units) occupied by the owner of such residence, as against a mechanic's lienor, but only if the contract price on the contract with the owner is not more than $5,000.

(8) Attorneys' liens. With respect to a judgment or other amount in settlement of a claim or of a cause of action, as against an attorney who, under local law, holds a lien upon or a contract enforcible against such judgment or amount, to the extent of his reasonable compensation for obtaining such judgment or procuring such settlement, except that this paragraph shall not apply to any judgment or amount in settlement of a claim or of a cause of action against the United States to the extent that the United States offsets such judgment or amount against any liability of the taxpayer to the United States.

(9) Certain insurance contracts. With respect to a life insurance, endowment, or annuity contract, as against the organization which is the insurer under such contract, at any time –

(A) before such organization had actual notice or knowledge of the existence of such lien;

(B) after such organization had such notice or knowledge, with respect to advances required to be made automatically to maintain such contract in force under an agreement entered into before such organization had such notice or knowledge; or

(C) after satisfaction of a levy pursuant to section 6332(b), unless and until the Secretary delivers to such organization a notice, executed after the date of such satisfaction, of the existence of such lien.

(10) Deposit-secured loans. With respect to a savings deposit, share, or other account with an institution described in section 581 or 591, to the extent of any loan made by such institution without actual notice or knowledge of the existence of such lien, as against such institution, if such loan is secured by such account.

(c) Protection for certain commercial transactions financing agreements, etc.

(1) In general. To the extent provided in this subsection, even though notice of a lien imposed by section 6321 has been filed, such lien shall not be valid with respect to a security interest which came into existence after tax lien filing but which –

(A) is in qualified property covered by the terms of a written agreement entered into before tax lien filing and constituting –

(i) a commercial transactions financing agreement,

(ii) a real property construction or improvement financing agreement, or

(iii) an obligatory disbursement agreement, and

(B) is protected under local law against a judgment lien arising, as of the time of tax lien filing, out of an unsecured obligation.

(2) Commercial transactions financing agreement. For purposes of this subsection –

(A) Definition. The term "commercial transactions financing agreement" means an agreement (entered into by a person in the course of his trade or business) –

(i) to make loans to the taxpayer to be secured by commercial financing security acquired by the taxpayer in the ordinary course of his trade or business, or

(ii) to purchase commercial financing security (other than inventory) acquired by the taxpayer in the ordinary course of his trade or business;

but such an agreement shall be treated as coming within the term only to the extent that such loan or purchase is made before the 46th day after the date of tax lien filing or (if earlier) before the lender or purchaser had actual notice or knowledge of such tax lien filing.

(B) Limitation on Qualified Property. The term "qualified property", when used with respect to a commercial transactions financing agreement, includes only commercial financing security acquired by the taxpayer before the 46th day after the date of tax lien filing.

(C) Commercial Financing Security Defined. The term "commercial financing security" means (i) paper of a kind ordinarily arising in commercial transactions, (ii) accounts receivable, (iii) mortgages on real property, and (iv) inventory.

(D) Purchaser Treated as Acquiring Security Interest. A person who satisfies subparagraph (A) by reason of clause (ii) thereof shall be treated as having acquired a security interest in commercial financing security.

* * *

(f) Place for filing notice; form.

(1) Place for filing. The notice referred to in subsection (a) shall be filed –

(A) Under state laws.

(i) Real property. In the case of real property, in one office within the State (or the county, or other governmental subdivision), as designated by the laws of such State, in which the property subject to the lien is situated; and

(ii) Personal property. In the case of personal property, whether tangible or intangible, in one office within the State (or the county, or other governmental subdivision), as designated by the laws of such State, in which the property subject to the lien is situated, except that State law merely conforming to or reenacting Federal law establishing a national filing system does not constitute a second office for filing as designated by the laws of such State; or

(B) With clerk of district court. In the office of the clerk of the United States district court for the judicial district in which the property subject to the lien is situated, whenever the State has not by law designated one office which meets the requirements of subparagraph (A); or

(C) With recorder of deeds of the District of Columbia. In the office of the Recorder of Deeds of the District of Columbia, if the property subject to the lien is situated in the District of Columbia.

* * *

(h) Definitions. For purposes of this section and section 6324 –

(1) Security interest. The term "security interest" means any interest in property acquired by contract for the purpose of securing payment or performance of an obligation or indemnifying against loss or liability. A security interest exists at any time (A) if, at such time, the property is in existence and the interest has become protected under local law against a subsequent judgment lien arising out of an unsecured obligation, and (B) to the extent that, at such time, the holder has parted with money or money's worth.

(2) Mechanic's lienor. The term "mechanic's lienor" means any person who under local law has a lien on real property (or on the proceeds of a contract relating to real property) for services, labor, or materials furnished in connection with the construction or improvement of such property. For purposes of the preceding sentence, a person has a lien on the earliest date such lien becomes valid under local law against subsequent purchasers without actual notice, but not before he begins to furnish the services, labor, or materials.

(3) Motor vehicle. The term "motor vehicle" means a self-propelled vehicle which is registered for highway use under the laws of any State or foreign country.

(4) Security. The term "security" means any bond, debenture, note, or certificate or other evidence of indebtedness, issued by a corporation or a government or political subdivision thereof, with interest coupons or in registered form, share of stock, voting trust certificate, or any certificate of interest or participation in, certificate of deposit or receipt for, temporary or interim certificate for, or warrant or right to subscribe to or purchase, any of the foregoing; negotiable instrument; or money.

(5) Tax lien filing. The term "tax lien filing" means the filing of notice (referred to in subsection (a)) of the lien imposed by section 6321.

(6) Purchaser. The term "purchaser" means a person who, for adequate and full consideration in money or money's worth, acquires an interest (other than a lien or security interest) in property which is valid under local law against subsequent purchasers without actual notice. In applying the preceding sentence for purposes of subsection (a) of this section, and for purposes of section 6324 –

(A) a lease of property,

(B) a written executory contract to purchase or lease property,

(C) an option to purchase or lease property or any interest therein, or

(D) an option to renew or extend a lease of property, which is not a lien or security interest shall be treated as an interest in property.

* * *

(j) Withdrawal of notice in certain circumstances.

(1) In general. The Secretary may withdraw a notice of a lien filed under this section and this chapter shall be applied as if the withdrawn notice had not been filed, if the Secretary determines that –

(A) the filing of such notice was premature or otherwise not in accordance with administrative procedures of the Secretary,

(B) the taxpayer has entered into an agreement under section 6159 to satisfy the tax liability for which the lien was imposed by means of installment payments, unless such agreement provides otherwise,

(C) the withdrawal of such notice will facilitate the collection of the tax liability, or

(D) with the consent of the taxpayer or the National Taxpayer Advocate, the withdrawal of such notice would be in the best interests of the taxpayer (as determined by the National Taxpayer Advocate) and the United States.

Any such withdrawal shall be made by filing notice at the same office as the withdrawn notice. A copy of such notice of withdrawal shall be provided to the taxpayer.

(2) Notice to credit agencies, etc. Upon written request by the taxpayer with respect to whom a notice of a lien was withdrawn under paragraph (1), the Secretary shall promptly make reasonable efforts to notify credit reporting agencies, and any financial institution or creditor whose name and address is specified in such request, of the withdrawal of such notice. Any such request shall be in such form as the Secretary may prescribe.

* * *

§ 6325. Release of lien or discharge of property.

(a) Release of lien. Subject to such regulations as the Secretary may prescribe, the Secretary shall issue a certificate of release of any lien imposed with respect to any internal revenue tax not later than 30 days after the day on which –

(1) Liability satisfied or unenforceable. The Secretary finds that the liability for the amount assessed, together with all interest in respect thereof, has been fully satisfied or has become legally unenforceable; or

(2) Bond accepted. There is furnished to the Secretary and accepted by him a bond that is conditioned upon the payment of the amount assessed, together with all interest in respect thereof, within the time prescribed by law (including any extension of such time), and that is in accordance with such requirements relating to terms, conditions, and form of the bond and sureties thereon, as may be specified by such regulations.

(b) Discharge of property.

(1) Property double the amount of the liability. Subject to such regulations as the Secretary may prescribe, the Secretary may issue a certificate of discharge of any part of the property subject to any lien imposed under this chapter if the Secretary finds that the fair market value of that part of such property remaining subject to the lien is at least double the amount of the unsatisfied liability secured by such lien and the amount of all other liens upon such property which have priority over such lien.

(2) Part payment; interest of United States valueless. Subject to such regulations as the Secretary may prescribe, the Secretary may issue a certificate of discharge of any part of the property subject to the lien if –

(A) there is paid over to the Secretary in partial satisfaction of the liability secured by the lien an amount determined by the Secretary, which shall not be less than the value, as determined by the Secretary, of the interest of the United States in the part to be so discharged, or

(B) the Secretary determines at any time that the interest of the United States in the part to be so discharged has no value.

In determining the value of the interest of the United States in the part to be so discharged, the Secretary shall give consideration to the value of such part and to such liens thereon as have priority over the lien of the United States.

(3) Substitution of proceeds of sale. Subject to such regulations as the Secretary may prescribe, the Secretary may issue a certificate of discharge of any part of the property subject to the lien if such part of the property is sold and, pursuant to an agreement with the Secretary, the proceeds of such sale are to be held, as a fund subject to the liens and claims of the United States, in the same manner and with the same priority as such liens and claims had with respect to the discharged property.

(4) Right of substitution of value.

(A) In general. At the request of the owner of any property subject to any lien imposed by this chapter, the Secretary shall issue a certificate of discharge of such property if such owner –

(i) deposits with the Secretary an amount of money equal to the value of the interest of the United States (as determined by the Secretary) in the property; or

(ii) furnishes a bond acceptable to the Secretary in a like amount.

(B) Refund of deposit with interest and release of bond. The Secretary shall refund the amount so deposited (and shall pay interest at the overpayment rate under section 6621), and shall release such bond, to the extent that the Secretary determines that –

(i) the unsatisfied liability giving rise to the lien can be satisfied from a source other than such property; or

(ii) the value of the interest of the United States in the property is less than the Secretary's prior determination of such value.

(C) Use of deposit, etc., if action to contest lien not filed. If no action is filed under section 7426(a)(4) within the period prescribed therefor, the Secretary shall, within 60 days after the expiration of such period –

(i) apply the amount deposited, or collect on such bond, to the extent necessary to satisfy the unsatisfied liability secured by the lien; and

(ii) refund (with interest as described in subparagraph (B)) any portion of the amount deposited which is not used to satisfy such liability.

(D) Exception. Subparagraph (A) shall not apply if the owner of the property is the person whose unsatisfied liability gave rise to the lien.

* * *

§ 6326. Administrative appeal of liens.

(a) In general. In such form and at such time as the Secretary shall prescribe by regulations, any person shall be allowed to appeal to the Secretary after the filing of a notice of a lien under this subchapter on the property or the rights to property of such person for a release of such lien alleging an error in the filing of the notice of such lien.

(b) Certificate of release. If the Secretary determines that the filing of the notice of any lien was erroneous, the Secretary shall expeditiously (and, to the extent practicable, within 14 days after such determination) issue a certificate of release of such lien and shall include in such certificate a statement that such filing was erroneous.

* * *

§ 6330. Notice and opportunity for hearing before levy

(a) Requirement of notice before levy.

(1) In general. No levy may be made on any property or right to property of any person unless the Secretary has notified such person in writing of their right to a hearing under this section before such levy is made. Such notice shall be required only once for the taxable period to which the unpaid tax specified in paragraph (3)(A) relates.

(2) Time and method for notice. The notice required under paragraph (1) shall be –

(A) given in person;

(B) left at the dwelling or usual place of business of such person; or

(C) sent by certified or registered mail, return receipt requested, to such person's last known address;

not less than 30 days before the day of the first levy with respect to the amount of the unpaid tax for the taxable period.

(3) Information included with notice. The notice required under paragraph (1) shall include in simple and nontechnical terms –

(A) the amount of unpaid tax;

(B) the right of the person to request a hearing during the 30-day period under paragraph (2); and

(C) the proposed action by the Secretary and the rights of the person with respect to such action, including a brief statement which sets forth –

(i) the provisions of this title relating to levy and sale of property;

(ii) the procedures applicable to the levy and sale of property under this title;

(iii) the administrative appeals available to the taxpayer with respect to such levy and sale and the procedures relating to such appeals;

(iv) the alternatives available to taxpayers which could prevent levy on property (including installment agreements under section 6159); and

(v) the provisions of this title and procedures relating to redemption of property and release of liens on property.

(b) Right to fair hearing.

(1) In general. If the person requests a hearing in writing under subsection (a)(3)(B) and states the grounds for the requested hearing, such hearing shall be held by the Internal Revenue Service Office of Appeals.

(2) One hearing per period. A person shall be entitled to only one hearing under this section with respect to the taxable period to which the unpaid tax specified in subsection (a)(3)(A) relates.

(3) Impartial officer. The hearing under this subsection shall be conducted by an officer or employee who has had no prior involvement with respect to the unpaid tax specified in subsection (a)(3)(A) before the first hearing under this section or section 6320. A taxpayer may waive the requirement of this paragraph.

(c) Matters considered at hearing. In the case of any hearing conducted under this section –

(1) Requirement of investigation. The appeals officer shall at the hearing obtain verification from the Secretary that the requirements of any applicable law or administrative procedure have been met.

(2) Issues at hearing.

(A) In general. The person may raise at the hearing any relevant issue relating to the unpaid tax or the proposed levy, including –

(i) appropriate spousal defenses;

(ii) challenges to the appropriateness of collection actions; and

(iii) offers of collection alternatives, which may include the posting of a bond, the substitution of other assets, an installment agreement, or an offer-in-compromise.

(B) Underlying liability. The person may also raise at the hearing challenges to the existence or amount of the underlying tax liability for any tax period if the person did not receive any statutory notice of deficiency for such tax liability or did not otherwise have an opportunity to dispute such tax liability.

(3) Basis for the determination. The determination by an appeals officer under this subsection shall take into consideration –

(A) the verification presented under paragraph (1);

(B) the issues raised under paragraph (2); and

(C) whether any proposed collection action balances the need for the efficient collection of taxes with the legitimate concern of the person that any collection action be no more intrusive than necessary.

(4) Certain issues precluded. An issue may not be raised at the hearing if –

(A) (i) the issue was raised and considered at a previous hearing under section 6320 or in any other previous administrative or judicial proceeding; and

(ii) the person seeking to raise the issue participated meaningfully in such hearing or proceeding; or

(B) the issue meets the requirement of clause (i) or (ii) of section 6702(b)(2)(A).

This paragraph shall not apply to any issue with respect to which subsection (d)(2)(B) applies.

(d) Proceeding after hearing.

(1) Judicial review of determination. The person may, within 30 days of a determination under this section, appeal such determination to the Tax Court (and the Tax Court shall have jurisdiction with respect to such matter).

(2) Jurisdiction retained at IRS Office of Appeals. The Internal Revenue Service Office of Appeals shall retain jurisdiction with respect to any determination made under this section, including subsequent hearings requested by the person who requested the original hearing on issues regarding –

(A) collection actions taken or proposed with respect to such determination; and

(B) after the person has exhausted all administrative remedies, a change in circumstances with respect to such person which affects such determination.

(e) Suspension of collections and statute of limitations.

(1) In general. Except as provided in paragraph (2), if a hearing is requested under subsection (a)(3)(B), the levy actions which are the subject of the requested hearing and the running of any period of limitations under section 6502 (relating to collection after assessment), section 6531 (relating to criminal prosecutions), or section 6532 (relating to other suits) shall be suspended for the period during which such hearing, and appeals therein, are pending. In no event shall any such period expire before the 90th day after the day on which there is a final determination in such hearing. Notwithstanding the provisions of section 7421(a), the beginning of a levy or proceeding during the time the suspension under this paragraph is in force may be enjoined by a proceeding in the proper court, including the Tax Court. The Tax Court shall have no jurisdiction under this paragraph to enjoin any action or proceeding unless a timely appeal has been filed under subsection (d)(1) and then only in respect of the unpaid tax or proposed levy to which the determination being appealed relates.

(2) Levy upon appeal. Paragraph (1) shall not apply to a levy action while an appeal is pending if the underlying tax liability is not at issue in the appeal and the court determines that the Secretary has shown good cause not to suspend the levy.

(f) Exceptions. If –

(1) the Secretary has made a finding under the last sentence of section 6331(a) that the collection of tax is in jeopardy,

(2) the Secretary has served a levy on a State to collect a Federal tax liability from a State tax refund,

(3) the Secretary has served a disqualified employment tax levy, or

(4) the Secretary has served a Federal contractor levy,
this section shall not apply, except that the taxpayer shall be given the opportunity for the hearing described in this section within a reasonable period of time after the levy.

(g) Frivolous requests for hearing, etc. Notwithstanding any other provision of this section, if the Secretary determines that any portion of a request for a hearing under this section or section 6320 meets the requirement of clause (i) or (ii) of section 6702(b)(2)(A), then the Secretary may treat such portion as if it were never submitted and such portion shall not be subject to any further administrative or judicial review.

* * *

§ 6331. Levy and distraint.

(a) Authority of Secretary. If any person liable to pay any tax neglects or refuses to pay the same within 10 days after notice and demand, it shall be lawful for the Secretary to collect such tax (and such further sum as shall be sufficient to cover the expenses of the levy) by levy upon all property and rights to property (except such property as is exempt under section 6334) belonging to such person or on which there is a lien provided in this chapter for the payment of such tax. Levy may be made upon the accrued salary or wages of any officer, employee, or elected official, of the United States, the District of Columbia, or any agency or instrumentality of the United States or the District of Columbia, by serving a notice of levy on the employer (as defined in section 3401(d)) of such officer, employee, or elected official. If the Secretary makes a finding that the collection of such tax is in jeopardy, notice and demand for immediate payment of such tax may be made by the Secretary and, upon failure or refusal to pay such tax, collection thereof by levy shall be lawful without regard to the 10-day period provided in this section.

(b) Seizure and sale of property. The term "levy" as used in this title includes the power of distraint and seizure by any means. Except as otherwise provided in subsection (e), a levy shall extend only to property possessed and obligations existing at the time thereof. In any case in which the Secretary may levy upon property or rights to property, he may seize and sell such property or rights to property (whether real or personal, tangible or intangible).

(c) Successive seizures. Whenever any property or right to property upon which levy has been made by virtue of subsection (a) is not sufficient to satisfy the claim of the United States for which levy is made, the Secretary may, thereafter, and as often as may be necessary, proceed to levy in like manner upon any other property liable to levy of the person against whom such claim exists, until the amount due from him, together with all expenses, is fully paid.

(d) Requirement of notice before levy.

(1) In general. Levy may be made under subsection (a) upon the salary or wages or other property of any person with respect to any unpaid tax only after the Secretary has notified such person in writing of his intention to make such levy.

(2) 30-day requirement. The notice required under paragraph (1) shall be –

(A) given in person,

(B) left at the dwelling or usual place of business of such person, or

(C) sent by certified or registered mail to such person's last known address,
no less than 30 days before the day of the levy.

(3) Jeopardy. Paragraph (1) shall not apply to a levy if the Secretary has made a finding under the last sentence of subsection (a) that the collection of tax is in jeopardy.

(4) Information included with notice. The notice required under paragraph (1) shall include a brief statement which sets forth in simple and nontechnical terms –

(A) the provisions of this title relating to levy and sale of property,

(B) the procedures applicable to the levy and sale of property under this title,

(C) the administrative appeals available to the taxpayer with respect to such levy and sale and the procedures relating to such appeals,

(D) the alternatives available to taxpayers which could prevent levy on the property (including installment agreements under section 6159),

(E) the provisions of this title relating to redemption of property and release of liens on property, and

(F) the procedures applicable to the redemption of property and the release of a lien on property under this title.

(e) Continuing levy on salary and wages. The effect of a levy on salary or wages payable to or received by a taxpayer shall be continuous from the date such levy is first made until such levy is released under section 6343.

* * *

(i) No levy during pendency of proceedings for refund of divisible tax.

* * *

(5) Suspension of statute of limitations on collection. The period of limitations under section 6502 shall be suspended for the period during which the Secretary is prohibited under this subsection from making a levy.

* * *

(k) No levy while certain offers pending or installment agreement pending or in effect.

(1) Offer-in-compromise pending. No levy may be made under subsection (a) on the property or rights to property of any person with respect to any unpaid tax –

(A) during the period that an offer-in-compromise by such person under section 7122 of such unpaid tax is pending with the Secretary; and

(B) if such offer is rejected by the Secretary, during the 30 days thereafter (and, if an appeal of such rejection is filed within such 30 days, during the period that such appeal is pending).

For purposes of subparagraph (A), an offer is pending beginning on the date the Secretary accepts such offer for processing.

(2) Installment agreements. No levy may be made under subsection (a) on the property or rights to property of any person with respect to any unpaid tax –

(A) during the period that an offer by such person for an installment agreement under section 6159 for payment of such unpaid tax is pending with the Secretary;

(B) if such offer is rejected by the Secretary, during the 30 days thereafter (and, if an appeal of such rejection is filed within such 30 days, during the period that such appeal is pending);

(C) during the period that such an installment agreement for payment of such unpaid tax is in effect; and

(D) if such agreement is terminated by the Secretary, during the 30 days thereafter (and, if an appeal of such termination is filed within such 30 days, during the period that such appeal is pending).

(3) Certain rules to apply. Rules similar to the rules of –

(A) paragraphs (3) and (4) of subsection (i), and

(B) except in the case of paragraph (2)(C), paragraph (5) of subsection (i), shall apply for purposes of this subsection.

* * *

§ 6332. Surrender of property subject to levy.

(a) Requirement. Except as otherwise provided in this section, any person in possession of (or obligated with respect to) property or rights to property subject to levy upon which a levy has been made shall, upon demand of the Secretary, surrender such property or rights (or discharge such obligation) to the Secretary, except such part of the property or rights as is, at the time of such demand, subject to an attachment or execution under any judicial process.

* * *

(c) Special rule for banks. Any bank (as defined in section 408(n)) shall surrender (subject to an attachment or execution under judicial process) any deposits (including interest thereon) in such bank only after 21 days after service of levy.

(d) Enforcement of levy.

(1) Extent of personal liability. Any person who fails or refuses to surrender any property or rights to property, subject to levy, upon demand by the Secretary, shall be liable in his own person and estate to the United States in a sum equal to the value of the property or rights not so surrendered, but not exceeding the amount of taxes for the collection of which such levy has been made, together with costs and interest on such sum at the underpayment rate established under section 6621 from the date of such levy (or, in the case of a levy described in section 6331(d)(3), from the date such person would otherwise have been obligated to pay over such amounts to the taxpayer). Any amount (other than costs) recovered under this paragraph shall be credited against the tax liability for the collection of which such levy was made.

(2) Penalty for violation. In addition to the personal liability imposed by paragraph (1), if any person required to surrender property or rights to property fails or refuses to surrender such property or rights to property without reasonable cause, such person shall be liable for a penalty equal to 50 percent of the amount recoverable under paragraph (1). No part of such penalty shall be credited against the tax liability for the collection of which such levy was made.

(e) Effect of honoring levy. Any person in possession of (or obligated with respect to) property or rights to property subject to levy upon which a levy has been made who, upon demand by the Secretary, surrenders such property or rights to property (or discharges such obligation) to the Secretary (or who pays a liability under subsection (d)(1)) shall be discharged from any obligation or liability to the delinquent taxpayer and any other person with respect to such property or rights to property arising from such surrender or payment.

* * *

§ 6334. Property exempt from levy.

(a) Enumeration. There shall be exempt from levy –

(1) Wearing apparel and school books. Such items of wearing apparel and such school books as are necessary for the taxpayer or for members of his family;

(2) Fuel, provisions, furniture, and personal effects. So much of the fuel, provisions, furniture, and personal effects in the taxpayer's household, and of the arms for personal use, livestock, and poultry of the taxpayer, as does not exceed $6,250 in value;

(3) Books and tools of a trade, business, or profession. So many of the books and tools necessary for the trade, business, or profession of the taxpayer as do not exceed in the aggregate $3,125 in value;

(4) Unemployment benefits. Any amount payable to an individual with respect to his unemployment (including any portion thereof payable with respect to dependents) under an unemployment compensation law of the United States, of any State, or of the District of Columbia or of the Commonwealth of Puerto Rico.

(5) Undelivered mail. Mail, addressed to any person, which has not been delivered to the addressee.

(6) Certain annuity and pension payments. Annuity or pension payments under the Railroad Retirement Act, benefits under the Railroad Unemployment Insurance Act, special pension payments received by a person whose name has been entered on the Army, Navy, Air

Force, and Coast Guard Medal of Honor roll, and annuities based on retired or retainer pay under chapter 73 of title 10 of the United States Code.

(7) Workmen's compensation. Any amount payable to an individual as workmen's compensation (including any portion thereof payable with respect to dependents) under a workmen's compensation law of the United States, any State, the District of Columbia, or the Commonwealth of Puerto Rico.

(8) Judgments for support of minor children. If the taxpayer is required by judgment of a court of competent jurisdiction, entered prior to the date of levy, to contribute to the support of his minor children, so much of his salary, wages, or other income as is necessary to comply with such judgment.

(9) Minimum exemption for wages, salary, and other income. Any amount payable to or received by an individual as wages or salary for personal services, or as income derived from other sources, during any period, to the extent that the total of such amounts payable to or received by him during such period does not exceed the applicable exempt amount determined under subsection (d).

(10) Certain service-connected disability payments. Any amount payable to an individual as a service-connected (within the meaning of section 101(16) of title 38, United States Code) disability benefit under –

    (A) subchapter II, III, IV, V, or VI of chapter 11 of such title 38, or

    (B) chapter 13, 21, 23, 31, 32, 34, 35, 37, or 39 of such title 38.

(11) Certain public assistance payments. Any amount payable to an individual as a recipient of public assistance under –

    (A) title IV or title XVI (relating to supplemental security income for the aged, blind, and disabled) of the Social Security Act, or

    (B) State or local government public assistance or public welfare programs for which eligibility is determined by a needs or income test.

(12) Assistance under Job Training Partnership Act. Any amount payable to a participant under the Job Training Partnership Act from funds appropriated pursuant to such Act.

(13) Residences exempt in small deficiency cases and principal residences and certain business assets exempt in absence of certain approval or jeopardy.

    (A) Residences in small deficiency cases. If the amount of the levy does not exceed $5,000 –

        (i) any real property used as a residence by the taxpayer; or

        (ii) any real property of the taxpayer (other than real property which is rented) used by any other individual as a residence.

    (B) Principal residences and certain business assets. Except to the extent provided in subsection (e) –

        (i) the principal residence of the taxpayer (within the meaning of section 121); and

(ii) tangible personal property or real property (other than real property which is rented) used in the trade or business of an individual taxpayer.

* * *

(d) Exempt amount of wages, salary, or other income.

(1) Individuals on weekly basis. In the case of an individual who is paid or receives all of his wages, salary, and other income on a weekly basis, the amount of the wages, salary, and other income payable to or received by him during any week which is exempt from levy under subsection (a)(9) shall be the exempt amount.

(2) Exempt amount. For purposes of paragraph (1), the term "exempt amount" means an amount equal to –

(A) the sum of –

(i) the standard deduction, and

(ii) the aggregate amount of the deductions for personal exemptions allowed the taxpayer under section 151 in the taxable year in which such levy occurs, divided by

(B) 52.

Unless the taxpayer submits to the Secretary a written and properly verified statement specifying the facts necessary to determine the proper amount under subparagraph (A), subparagraph (A) shall be applied as if the taxpayer were a married individual filing a separate return with only 1 personal exemption.

(3) Individuals on basis other than weekly. In the case of any individual not described in paragraph (1), the amount of the wages, salary, and other income payable to or received by him during any applicable pay period or other fiscal period (as determined under regulations prescribed by the Secretary) which is exempt from levy under subsection (a)(9) shall be an amount (determined under such regulations) which as nearly as possible will result in the same total exemption from levy for such individual over a period of time as he would have under paragraph (1) if (during such period of time) he were paid or received such wages, salary, and other income on a regular weekly basis.

(e) Levy allowed on principal residences and certain business assets in certain circumstances.

(1) Principal residences.

(A) Approval required. A principal residence shall not be exempt from levy if a judge or magistrate of a district court of the United States approves (in writing) the levy of such residence.

(B) Jurisdiction. The district courts of the United States shall have exclusive jurisdiction to approve a levy under subparagraph (A).

(2) Certain business assets. Property (other than a principal residence) described in subsection (a)(13)(B) shall not be exempt from levy if –

(A) a district director or assistant district director of the Internal Revenue Service personally approves (in writing) the levy of such property; or

(B) the Secretary finds that the collection of tax is in jeopardy.

An official may not approve a levy under subparagraph (A) unless the official determines that the taxpayer's other assets subject to collection are insufficient to pay the amount due, together with expenses of the proceedings.

* * *

§ 6335. Sale of seized property.

(a) Notice of seizure. As soon as practicable after seizure of property, notice in writing shall be given by the Secretary to the owner of the property (or, in the case of personal property, the possessor thereof), or shall be left at his usual place of abode or business if he has such within the internal revenue district where the seizure is made. If the owner cannot be readily located, or has no dwelling or place of business within such district, the notice may be mailed to his last known address. Such notice shall specify the sum demanded and shall contain, in the case of personal property, an account of the property seized and, in the case of real property, a description with reasonable certainty of the property seized.

(b) Notice of sale. The Secretary shall as soon as practicable after the seizure of the property give notice to the owner, in the manner prescribed in subsection (a), and shall cause a notification to be published in some newspaper published or generally circulated within the county wherein such seizure is made, or, if there be no newspaper published or generally circulated in such county, shall post such notice at the post office nearest the place where the seizure is made, and in not less than two other public places. Such notice shall specify the property to be sold, and the time, place, manner, and conditions of the sale thereof. Whenever levy is made without regard to the 10-day period provided in section 6331(a), public notice of sale of the property seized shall not be made within such 10-day period unless section 6336 (relating to sale of perishable goods) is applicable.

(c) Sale of indivisible property. If any property liable to levy is not divisible, so as to enable the Secretary by sale of a part thereof to raise the whole amount of the tax and expenses, the whole of such property shall be sold.

(d) Time and place of sale. The time of sale shall not be less than 10 days nor more than 40 days from the time of giving public notice under subsection (b). The place of sale shall be within the county in which the property is seized, except by special order of the Secretary.

(e) Manner and conditions of sale.

(1) In general.

(A) Determinations relating to minimum price. Before the sale of property seized by levy, the Secretary shall determine –

(i) a minimum price below which such property shall not be sold (taking into account the expense of making the levy and conducting the sale), and

(ii) whether, on the basis of criteria prescribed by the Secretary, the purchase of such property by the United States at such minimum price would be in the best interest of the United States.

(B) Sale to highest bidder at or above minimum price. If, at the sale, one or more persons offer to purchase such property for not less than the amount of the minimum price, the property shall be declared sold to the highest bidder.

(C) Property deemed sold to United States at minimum price in certain cases. If no person offers the amount of the minimum price for such property at the sale and the Secretary has determined that the purchase of such property by the United States would be in the best interest of the United States, the property shall be declared to be sold to the United States at such minimum price.

(D) Release to owner in other cases. If, at the sale, the property is not declared sold under subparagraph (B) or (C), the property shall be released to the owner thereof and the expense of the levy and sale shall be added to the amount of tax for the collection of which the levy was made. Any property released under this subparagraph shall remain subject to any lien imposed by subchapter C.

(2) Additional rules applicable to sale. The Secretary shall by regulations prescribe the manner and other conditions of the sale of property seized by levy. If one or more alternative methods or conditions are permitted by regulations, the Secretary shall select the alternatives applicable to the sale. Such regulations shall provide:

(A) That the sale shall not be conducted in any manner other than –

(i) by public auction, or

(ii) by public sale under sealed bids.

(B) In the case of the seizure of several items of property, whether such items shall be offered separately, in groups, or in the aggregate; and whether such property shall be offered both separately (or in groups) and in the aggregate, and sold under whichever method produces the highest aggregate amount.

(C) Whether the announcement of the minimum price determined by the Secretary may be delayed until the receipt of the highest bid.

(D) Whether payment in full shall be required at the time of acceptance of a bid, or whether a part of such payment may be deferred for such period (not to exceed 1 month) as may be determined by the Secretary to be appropriate.

(E) The extent to which methods (including advertising) in addition to those prescribed in subsection (b) may be used in giving notice of the sale.

(F) Under what circumstances the Secretary may adjourn the sale from time to time (but such adjournments shall not be for a period to exceed in all 1 month).

(3) Payment of amount bid. If payment in full is required at the time of acceptance of a bid and is not then and there paid, the Secretary shall forthwith proceed to again sell the property in the manner provided in this subsection. If the conditions of the sale permit part of the payment to be deferred, and if such part is not paid within the prescribed period, suit may be instituted against the purchaser for the purchase price or such part thereof as has not been paid, together with interest at the rate of 6 percent per annum from the date of the sale; or, in the discretion of the Secretary, the sale may be declared by the Secretary to be null and void for failure to make full payment of the purchase price and the property may again be advertised and sold as provided in subsections (b) and (c) and this subsection. In the event of such readvertisement and sale any new purchaser shall receive such property or rights to property, free and clear of any claim or right of the former defaulting purchaser, of any nature whatsoever, and the amount paid upon the bid price by such defaulting purchaser shall be forfeited.

(4) Cross reference. For provision providing for civil damages for violation of paragraph (1)(A)(i), see section 7433.

(f) Right to request sale of seized property within 60 days. The owner of any property seized by levy may request that the Secretary sell such property within 60 days after such request (or within such longer period as may be specified by the owner). The Secretary shall comply with such request unless the Secretary determines (and notifies the owner within such period) that such compliance would not be in the best interests of the United States.

(g) Stay of sale of seized property pending Tax Court decision. For restrictions on sale of seized property pending Tax Court decision, see section 6863(b)(3).

* * *

§ 6337. Redemption of property.

(a) Before sale. Any person whose property has been levied upon shall have the right to pay the amount due, together with the expenses of the proceeding, if any, to the Secretary at any time prior to the sale thereof, and upon such payment the Secretary shall restore such property to him, and all further proceedings in connection with the levy on such property shall cease from the time of such payment.

(b) Redemption of real estate after sale.

(1) Period. The owners of any real property sold as provided in section 6335, their heirs, executors, or administrators, or any person having any interest therein, or a lien thereon, or any person in their behalf, shall be permitted to redeem the property sold, or any particular tract of such property, at any time within 180 days after the sale thereof.

(2) Price. Such property or tract of property shall be permitted to be redeemed upon payment to the purchaser, or in case he cannot be found in the county in which the property to be redeemed is situated, then to the Secretary, for the use of the purchaser, his heirs, or assigns, the amount paid by such purchaser and interest thereon at the rate of 20 percent per annum.

(c) Record. When any lands sold are redeemed as provided in this section, the Secretary shall cause entry of the fact to be made upon the record mentioned in section 6340, and such entry shall be evidence of such redemption.

* * *

§ 6343. Authority to release levy and return property.

(a) Release of levy and notice of release.

(1) In general. Under regulations prescribed by the Secretary, the Secretary shall release the levy upon all, or part of, the property or rights to property levied upon and shall promptly notify the person upon whom such levy was made (if any) that such levy has been released if –

    (A) the liability for which such levy was made is satisfied or becomes unenforceable by reason of lapse of time,

    (B) release of such levy will facilitate the collection of such liability,

    (C) the taxpayer has entered into an agreement under section 6159 to satisfy such liability by means of installment payments, unless such agreement provides otherwise,

    (D) the Secretary has determined that such levy is creating an economic hardship due to the financial condition of the taxpayer, or

    (E) the fair market value of the property exceeds such liability and release of the levy on a part of such property could be made without hindering the collection of such liability.

For purposes of subparagraph (C), the Secretary is not required to release such levy if such release would jeopardize the secured creditor status of the Secretary.

(2) Expedited determination on certain business property. In the case of any tangible personal property essential in carrying on the trade or business of the taxpayer, the Secretary shall provide for an expedited determination under paragraph (1) if levy on such tangible personal property would prevent the taxpayer from carrying on such trade or business.

(3) Subsequent levy. The release of levy on any property under paragraph (1) shall not prevent any subsequent levy on such property.

* * *

(d) Return of property in certain cases. If –

    (1) any property has been levied upon, and

    (2) the Secretary determines that –

        (A) the levy on such property was premature or otherwise not in accordance with administrative procedures of the Secretary,

        (B) the taxpayer has entered into an agreement under section 6159 to satisfy the tax liability for which the levy was imposed by means of installment payments, unless such agreement provides otherwise,

        (C) the return of such property will facilitate the collection of the tax liability, or

        (D) with the consent of the taxpayer or the National Taxpayer Advocate, the return of such property would be in the best interests of the taxpayer (as determined by the National Taxpayer Advocate) and the United States, the provisions of subsection (b) shall apply in the same manner as if such property had been wrongly levied upon, except that no interest shall be allowed under subsection (c).

* * *

§ 6401. Amounts treated as overpayments.

(a) Assessment and collection after limitation period. The term "overpayment" includes that part of the amount of the payment of any internal revenue tax which is assessed or collected after the expiration of the period of limitation properly applicable thereto.

(b) Excessive credits.

(1) In general. If the amount allowable as credits under subpart C of part IV of subchapter A of chapter 1 (relating to refundable credits) exceeds the tax imposed by subtitle A (reduced by the credits allowable under subparts A, B, D, G, H, I, and J of such part IV), the amount of such excess shall be considered an overpayment.

(2) Special rule for credit under section 33. For purposes of paragraph (1), any credit allowed under section 33 (relating to withholding of tax on nonresident aliens and on foreign corporations) for any taxable year shall be treated as a credit allowable under subpart C of part IV of subchapter A of chapter 1 only if an election under subsection (g) or (h) of section 6013 is in effect for such taxable year. The preceding sentence shall not apply to any credit so allowed by reason of section 1446.

(c) Rule where no tax liability. An amount paid as tax shall not be considered not to constitute an overpayment solely by reason of the fact that there was no tax liability in respect of which such amount was paid.

* * *

§ 6402. Authority to make credits or refunds.

(a) General rule. In the case of any overpayment, the Secretary, within the applicable period of limitations, may credit the amount of such overpayment, including any interest allowed thereon, against any liability in respect of an internal revenue tax on the part of the person who made the overpayment and shall, subject to subsections (c), (d), (e), and (f) refund any balance to such person.

* * *

§ 6404. Abatements.

(a) General rule. The Secretary is authorized to abate the unpaid portion of the assessment of any tax or any liability in respect thereof, which –

(1) is excessive in amount, or

(2) is assessed after the expiration of the period of limitation properly applicable thereto, or

(3) is erroneously or illegally assessed.

(b) No claim for abatement of income, estate, and gift taxes. No claim for abatement shall be filed by a taxpayer in respect of an assessment of any tax imposed under subtitle A or B.

(c) Small tax balances. The Secretary is authorized to abate the unpaid portion of the assessment of any tax, or any liability in respect thereof, if the Secretary determines under uniform rules prescribed by the Secretary that the administration and collection costs involved would not warrant collection of the amount due.

(d) Assessments attributable to certain mathematical errors by Internal Revenue Service. In the case of an assessment of any tax imposed by chapter 1 attributable in whole or in part to a mathematical error described in section 6213(g)(2)(A), if the return was prepared by an officer or employee of the Internal Revenue Service acting in his official capacity to provide assistance to taxpayers in the preparation of income tax returns, the Secretary is authorized to abate the assessment of all or any part of any interest on such deficiency for any period ending on or before the 30th day following the date of notice and demand by the Secretary for payment of the deficiency.

(e) Abatement of interest attributable to unreasonable errors and delays by Internal Revenue Service.

    (1) In general. In the case of any assessment of interest on –

      (A) any deficiency attributable in whole or in part to any unreasonable error or delay by an officer or employee of the Internal Revenue Service (acting in his official capacity) in performing a ministerial or managerial act, or

      (B) any payment of any tax described in section 6212(a) to the extent that any unreasonable error or delay in such payment is attributable to such an officer or employee being erroneous or dilatory in performing a ministerial or managerial act, the Secretary may abate the assessment of all or any part of such interest for any period. For purposes of the preceding sentence, an error or delay shall be taken into account only if no significant aspect of such error or delay can be attributed to the taxpayer involved, and after the Internal Revenue Service has contacted the taxpayer in writing with respect to such deficiency or payment.

    (2) Interest abated with respect to erroneous refund check. The Secretary shall abate the assessment of all interest on any erroneous refund under section 6602 until the date demand for repayment is made, unless –

      (A) the taxpayer (or a related party) has in any way caused such erroneous refund, or

      (B) such erroneous refund exceeds $50,000.

(f) Abatement of any penalty or addition to tax attributable to erroneous written advice by the Internal Revenue Service.

    (1) In general. The Secretary shall abate any portion of any penalty or addition to tax attributable to erroneous advice furnished to the taxpayer in writing by an officer or employee of the Internal Revenue Service, acting in such officer's or employee's official capacity.

    (2) Limitations. Paragraph (1) shall apply only if –

      (A) the written advice was reasonably relied upon by the taxpayer and was in response to a specific written request of the taxpayer, and

      (B) the portion of the penalty or addition to tax did not result from a failure by the taxpayer to provide adequate or accurate information.

(3) Initial regulations. Within 180 days after the date of the enactment of this subsection [enacted Nov. 10, 1988], the Secretary shall prescribe such initial regulations as may be necessary to carry out this subsection.

(g) Suspension of interest and certain penalties where Secretary fails to contact taxpayer.

(1) Suspension.

(A) In general. In the case of an individual who files a return of tax imposed by subtitle A for a taxable year on or before the due date for the return (including extensions), if the Secretary does not provide a notice to the taxpayer specifically stating the taxpayer's liability and the basis for the liability before the close of the 36-month period beginning on the later of –

(i) the date on which the return is filed; or

(ii) the due date of the return without regard to extensions, the Secretary shall suspend the imposition of any interest, penalty, addition to tax, or additional amount with respect to any failure relating to the return which is computed by reference to the period of time the failure continues to exist and which is properly allocable to the suspension period.

(B) Separate application. This paragraph shall be applied separately with respect to each item or adjustment.

If, after the return for a taxable year is filed, the taxpayer provides to the Secretary 1 or more signed written documents showing that the taxpayer owes an additional amount of tax for the taxable year, clause (i) shall be applied by substituting the date the last of the documents was provided for the date on which the return is filed.

(2) Exceptions. Paragraph (1) shall not apply to –

(A) any penalty imposed by section 6651;

(B) any interest, penalty, addition to tax, or additional amount in a case involving fraud;

(C) any interest, penalty, addition to tax, or additional amount with respect to any tax liability shown on the return;

(D) any interest, penalty, addition to tax, or additional amount with respect to any gross misstatement;

(E) any interest, penalty, addition to tax, or additional amount with respect to any reportable transaction with respect to which the requirement of section 6664(d)(2)(A) is not met and any listed transaction (as defined in 6707A(c)); or

(F) any criminal penalty.

(3) Suspension period. For purposes of this subsection, the term "suspension period" means the period –

(A) beginning on the day after the close of the 36-month period under paragraph (1); and

(B) ending on the date which is 21 days after the date on which notice described in paragraph (1)(A) is provided by the Secretary.

(h) Review of denial of request for abatement of interest.

(1) In general. The Tax Court shall have jurisdiction over any action brought by a taxpayer who meets the requirements referred to in section 7430(c)(4)(A)(ii) to determine whether the Secretary's failure to abate interest under this section was an abuse of discretion, and may order an abatement, if such action is brought within 180 days after the date of the mailing of the Secretary's final determination not to abate such interest.

(2) Special rules.

(A) Date of mailing. Rules similar to the rules of section 6213 shall apply for purposes of determining the date of the mailing referred to in paragraph (1).

(B) Relief. Rules similar to the rules of section 6512(b) shall apply for purposes of this subsection.

(C) Review. An order of the Tax Court under this subsection shall be reviewable in the same manner as a decision of the Tax Court, but only with respect to the matters determined in such order.

* * *

§ 6405. Reports of refunds and credits.

(a) By Treasury to Joint Committee. No refund or credit of any income, war profits, excess profits, estate, or gift tax, or any tax imposed with respect to public charities, private foundations, operators' trust funds, pension plans, or real estate investment trusts under chapter 41, 42, 43, or 44, in excess of $2,000,000 shall be made until after the expiration of 30 days from the date upon which a report giving the name of the person to whom the refund or credit is to be made, the amount of such refund or credit, and a summary of the facts and the decision of the Secretary, is submitted to the Joint Committee on Taxation.

* * *

§ 6501. Limitations on assessment and collection.

(a) General rule. Except as otherwise provided in this section, the amount of any tax imposed by this title shall be assessed within 3 years after the return was filed (whether or not such return was filed on or after the date prescribed) or, if the tax is payable by stamp, at any time after such tax became due and before the expiration of 3 years after the date on which any part of such tax was paid, and no proceeding in court without assessment for the collection of such tax shall be begun after the expiration of such period. For purposes of this chapter, the term "return" means the return required to be filed by the taxpayer (and does not include a return of any person from whom the taxpayer has received an item of income, gain, loss, deduction, or credit).

(b) Time return deemed filed.

(1) Early return. For purposes of this section, a return of tax imposed by this title, except tax imposed by chapter 3, 4, 21, or 24, filed before the last day prescribed by law or by regulations promulgated pursuant to law for the filing thereof, shall be considered as filed on such last day.

(2) Return of certain employment and withholding taxes. For purposes of this section, if a return of tax imposed by chapter 3, 4, 21, or 24 for any period ending with or within a calendar year is filed before April 15 of the succeeding calendar year, such return shall be considered filed on April 15 of such calendar year.

(3) Return executed by Secretary. Notwithstanding the provisions of paragraph (2) of section 6020(b), the execution of a return by the Secretary pursuant to the authority conferred by such section shall not start the running of the period of limitations on assessment and collection.

(4) Return of excise taxes. For purposes of this section, the filing of a return for a specified period on which an entry has been made with respect to a tax imposed under a provision of subtitle D (including a return on which an entry has been made showing no liability for such tax for such period) shall constitute the filing of a return of all amounts of such tax which, if properly paid, would be required to be reported on such return for such period.

(c) Exceptions.

(1) False return. In the case of a false or fraudulent return with the intent to evade tax, the tax may be assessed, or a proceeding in court for collection of such tax may be begun without assessment, at any time.

(2) Willful attempt to evade tax. In case of a willful attempt in any manner to defeat or evade tax imposed by this title (other than tax imposed by subtitle A or B), the tax may be assessed, or a proceeding in court for the collection of such tax may be begun without assessment, at any time.

(3) No return. In the case of failure to file a return, the tax may be assessed, or a proceeding in court for the collection of such tax may be begun without assessment, at any time.

(4) Extension by agreement.

(A) In general. Where, before the expiration of the time prescribed in this section for the assessment of any tax imposed by this title, except the estate tax provided in chapter 11, both the Secretary and the taxpayer have consented in writing to its assessment after such time, the tax may be assessed at any time prior to the expiration of the period agreed upon. The period so agreed upon may be extended by subsequent agreements in writing made before the expiration of the period previously agreed upon.

(B) Notice to taxpayer of right to refuse or limit extension. The Secretary shall notify the taxpayer of the taxpayer's right to refuse to extend the period of limitations, or to limit such extension to particular issues or to a particular period of time, on each occasion when the taxpayer is requested to provide such consent.

(5) Tax resulting from changes in certain income tax or estate tax credits. For special rules applicable in cases where the adjustment of certain taxes allowed as a credit against income taxes or estate taxes results in additional tax, see section 905(c) (relating to the foreign tax credit for income tax purposes) and section 2016 (relating to taxes of foreign countries, States, etc., claimed as credit against estate taxes).

* * *

(e) Substantial omission of items. Except as otherwise provided in subsection (c) –

(1) Income taxes. In the case of any tax imposed by subtitle A –

(A) General rule. If the taxpayer omits from gross income an amount properly includible therein and –

(i) such amount is in excess of 25 percent of the amount of gross income stated in the return, or

(ii) such amount –

(I) is attributable to one or more assets with respect to which information is required to be reported under section 6038D (or would be so required if such section were applied without regard to the dollar threshold specified in subsection (a) thereof and without regard to any exceptions provided pursuant to subsection (h)(1) thereof), and

(II) is in excess of $5,000, the tax may be assessed, or a proceeding in court for collection of such tax may be begun without assessment, at any time within 6 years after the return was filed.

(B) Determination of gross income. For purposes of subparagraph (A) –

(i) in the case of a trade or business, the term "gross income" means the total of the amounts received or accrued from the sale of goods or services (if such amounts are required to be shown on the return) prior to diminution by the cost of such sales or services; and

(ii) in determining the amount omitted from gross income, there shall not be taken into account any amount which is omitted from gross income stated in the return if such amount is disclosed in the return, or in a statement attached to the return, in a manner adequate to apprise the Secretary of the nature and amount of such item.

(C) Constructive dividends. If the taxpayer omits from gross income an amount properly includible therein under section 951(a), the tax may be assessed, or a proceeding in court for the collection of such tax may be done without assessing, at any time within 6 years after the return was filed.

(2) Estate and gift taxes. In the case of a return of estate tax under chapter 11 or a return of gift tax under chapter 12, if the taxpayer omits from the gross estate or from the total amount of the gifts made during the period for which the return was filed items includible in such gross estate or such total gifts, as the case may be, as exceed in amount 25 percent of the gross estate stated in the return or the total amount of gifts stated in the return, the tax may be assessed, or a proceeding in court for the collection of such tax may be begun without assessment, at any time within 6 years after the return was filed. In determining the items omitted from the gross estate or the total gifts, there shall not be taken into account any item which is omitted from the gross estate or from the total gifts stated in the return if such item is disclosed in the return, or in a statement attached to the return, in a manner adequate to apprise the Secretary of the nature and amount of such item.

* * *

§ 6502. Collection after assessment.

(a) Length of period. Where the assessment of any tax imposed by this title has been made within the period of limitation properly applicable thereto, such tax may be collected by levy or by a proceeding in court, but only if the levy is made or the proceeding begun –

(1) within 10 years after the assessment of the tax, or

(2) if –

(A) there is an installment agreement between the taxpayer and the Secretary, prior to the date which is 90 days after the expiration of any period for collection agreed upon in writing by the Secretary and the taxpayer at the time the installment agreement was entered into; or

(B) there is a release of levy under section 6343 after such 10-year period, prior to the expiration of any period for collection agreed upon in writing by the Secretary and the taxpayer before such release.

If a timely proceeding in court for the collection of a tax is commenced, the period during which such tax may be collected by levy shall be extended and shall not expire until the liability for the tax (or a judgment against the taxpayer arising from such liability) is satisfied or becomes unenforceable.

(b) Date when levy is considered made. The date on which a levy on property or rights to property is made shall be the date on which the notice of seizure provided in section 6335(a) is given.

§ 6503. Suspension of running of period of limitation.

(a) Issuance of statutory notice of deficiency.

(1) General rule. The running of the period of limitations provided in section 6501 or 6502 (or section 6229, but only with respect to a deficiency described in paragraph (2)(A) or (3) of section 6230(a)) on the making of assessments or the collection by levy or a proceeding in court, in respect of any deficiency as defined in section 6211 (relating to income, estate, gift and certain excise taxes), shall (after the mailing of a notice under section 6212(a)) be suspended for the period during which the Secretary is prohibited from making the assessment or from collecting by levy or a proceeding in court (and in any event, if a proceeding in respect of the deficiency is placed on the docket of the Tax Court, until the decision of the Tax Court becomes final), and for 60 days thereafter.

(2) Corporation joining in consolidated income tax return. If a notice under section 6212(a) in respect of a deficiency in tax imposed by subtitle A for any taxable year is mailed to a corporation, the suspension of the running of the period of limitations provided in paragraph (1) of this subsection shall apply in the case of corporations with which such corporation made a consolidated income tax return for such taxable year.

* * *

(j) Extension in case of certain summonses.

(1) In general. If any designated summons is issued by the Secretary to a corporation (or to any other person to whom the corporation has transferred records) with respect to any return of tax by such corporation for a taxable year (or other period) for which such corporation is being examined under the coordinated examination program (or any successor program) of the Internal Revenue Service, the running of any period of limitations provided in section 6501 on the assessment of such tax shall be suspended –

(A) during any judicial enforcement period –

(i) with respect to such summons, or

(ii) with respect to any other summons which is issued during the 30-day period which begins on the date on which such designated summons is issued and which relates to the same return as such designated summons, and

(B) if the court in any proceeding referred to in paragraph (3) requires any compliance with a summons referred to in subparagraph (A), during the 120-day period beginning with the 1st day after the close of the suspension under subparagraph (A).

If subparagraph (B) does not apply, such period shall in no event expire before the 60th day after the close of the suspension under subparagraph (A).

(2) Designated summons. For purposes of this subsection –

(A) In general. The term 'designated summons' means any summons issued for purposes of determining the amount of any tax imposed by this title if –

(i) the issuance of such summons is preceded by a review of such issuance by the regional counsel of the Office of Chief Counsel for the region in which the examination of the corporation is being conducted,

(ii) such summons is issued at least 60 days before the day on which the period prescribed in section 6501 for the assessment of such tax expires (determined with regard to extensions), and

(iii) such summons clearly states that it is a designated summons for purposes of this subsection.

(B) Limitation. A summons which relates to any return shall not be treated as a designated summons if a prior summons which relates to such return was treated as a designated summons for purposes of this subsection.

(3) Judicial enforcement period. For purposes of this subsection, the term 'judicial enforcement period' means, with respect to any summons, the period –

(A) which begins on the day on which a court proceeding with respect to such summons is brought, and

(B) which ends on the day on which there is a final resolution as to the summoned person's response to such summons.

* * *

§ 6511. Limitations on credit or refund.

(a) Period of limitation on filing claim. Claim for credit or refund of an overpayment of any tax imposed by this title in respect of which tax the taxpayer is required to file a return shall be filed by the taxpayer within 3 years from the time the return was filed or 2 years from the time the tax was paid, whichever of such periods expires the later, or if no return was filed by the taxpayer, within 2 years from the time the tax was paid. Claim for credit or refund of an overpayment of any tax imposed by this title which is required to be paid by means of a stamp shall be filed by the taxpayer within 3 years from the time the tax was paid.

(b) Limitation on allowance of credits and refunds.

(1) Filing of claim within prescribed period. No credit or refund shall be allowed or made after the expiration of the period of limitation prescribed in subsection (a) for the filing of a claim for credit or refund, unless a claim for credit or refund is filed by the taxpayer within such period.

(2) Limit on amount of credit or refund.

(A) Limit where claim filed within 3-year period. If the claim was filed by the taxpayer during the 3-year period prescribed in subsection (a), the amount of the credit or refund shall not exceed the portion of the tax paid within the period, immediately preceding the filing of the claim, equal to 3 years plus the period of any extension of time for filing the return. If the tax was required to be paid by means of a stamp, the amount of the credit or refund shall not exceed the portion of the tax paid within the 3 years immediately preceding the filing of the claim.

(B) Limit where claim not filed within 3-year period. If the claim was not filed within such 3-year period, the amount of the credit or refund shall not exceed the portion of the tax paid during the 2 years immediately preceding the filing of the claim.

(C) Limit if no claim filed. If no claim was filed, the credit or refund shall not exceed the amount which would be allowable under subparagraph (A) or (B), as the case may be, if claim was filed on the date the credit or refund is allowed.

(c) Special rules applicable in case of extension of time by agreement. If an agreement under the provisions of section 6501(c)(4) extending the period for assessment of a tax imposed by this title is made within the period prescribed in subsection (a) for the filing of a claim for credit or refund –

(1) Time for filing claim. The period for filing claim for credit or refund or for making credit or refund if no claim is filed, provided in subsections (a) and (b)(1), shall not expire prior to 6 months after the expiration of the period within which an assessment may be made pursuant to the agreement or any extension thereof under section 6501(c)(4).

(2) Limit on amount. If a claim is filed, or a credit or refund is allowed when no claim was filed, after the execution of the agreement and within 6 months after the expiration of the period within which an assessment may be made pursuant to the agreement or any extension thereof, the amount of the credit or refund shall not exceed the portion of the tax paid after the execution of the agreement and before the filing of the claim or the making of the credit or refund, as the case may be, plus the portion of the tax paid within the period which would be applicable under subsection (b)(2) if a claim had been filed on the date the agreement was executed.

(3) Claims not subject to special rule. This subsection shall not apply in the case of a claim filed, or credit or refund allowed if no claim is filed, either –

(A) prior to the execution of the agreement or

(B) more than 6 months after the expiration of the period within which an assessment may be made pursuant to the agreement or any extension thereof.

* * *

(h) Running of periods of limitation suspended while taxpayer is unable to manage financial affairs due to disability.

(1) In general. In the case of an individual, the running of the periods specified in subsections (a), (b), and (c) shall be suspended during any period of such individual's life that such individual is financially disabled.

(2) Financially disabled.

(A) In general. For purposes of paragraph (1), an individual is financially disabled if such individual is unable to manage his financial affairs by reason of a medically determinable physical or mental impairment of the individual which can be expected to result in death or which has lasted or can be expected to last for a continuous period of not less than 12 months. An individual shall not be considered to have such an impairment unless proof of the existence thereof is furnished in such form and manner as the Secretary may require.

(B) Exception where individual has guardian, etc. An individual shall not be treated as financially disabled during any period that such individual's spouse or any other person is authorized to act on behalf of such individual in financial matters.

* * *

§ 6512. Limitations in case of petition to Tax Court.

(a) Effect of petition to Tax Court. If the Secretary has mailed to the taxpayer a notice of deficiency under section 6212(a) (relating to deficiencies of income, estate, gift, and certain excise taxes) and if the taxpayer files a petition with the Tax Court within the time prescribed in section 6213(a) (or 7481(c) with respect to a determination of statutory interest or section 7481(d) solely with respect to a determination of estate tax by the Tax Court) no credit or refund of income tax for the same taxable year, of gift tax for the same calendar year or calendar quarter, of estate tax in respect of the taxable estate of the same decedent, or of tax imposed by chapter 41, 42, 43, or 44 with respect to any act (or failure to act) to which such petition relates in respect of which the Secretary has determined the deficiency shall be allowed or made and no suit by the taxpayer for the recovery of any part of the tax shall be instituted in any court except —

(1) As to overpayments determined by a decision of the Tax Court which has become final, and

(2) As to any amount collected in excess of an amount computed in accordance with the decision of the Tax Court which has become final, and

(3) As to any amount collected after the period of limitation upon the making of levy or beginning a proceeding in court for collection has expired; but in any such claim for credit or refund or in any such suit for refund the decision of the Tax Court which has become final, as to whether such period has expired before the notice of deficiency was mailed, shall be conclusive, and

(4) As to overpayments attributable to partnership items, in accordance with subchapter C of chapter 63, and

(5) As to any amount collected within the period during which the Secretary is prohibited from making the assessment or from collecting by levy or through a proceeding in court under the provisions of section 6213(a), and

(6) As to overpayments the Secretary is authorized to refund or credit pending appeal as provided in subsection (b).

(b) Overpayment determined by Tax Court.

(1) Jurisdiction to determine. Except as provided by paragraph (3) and by section 7463, if the Tax Court finds that there is no deficiency and further finds that the taxpayer has made an overpayment of income tax for the same taxable year, of gift tax for the same calendar year or calendar quarter, of estate tax in respect of the taxable estate of the same decedent, or of tax imposed by chapter 41, 42, 43, or 44 with respect to any act (or failure to act) to which such petition relates, in respect of which the Secretary determined the deficiency, or finds that there is a deficiency but that the taxpayer has made an overpayment of such tax, the Tax Court shall have jurisdiction to determine the amount of such overpayment, and such amount shall, when the decision of the Tax Court has become final, be credited or refunded to the taxpayer. If a notice of appeal in respect of the decision of the Tax Court is filed under section 7483, the Secretary is authorized to refund or credit the overpayment determined by the Tax Court to the extent the overpayment is not contested on appeal.

(2) Jurisdiction to enforce. If, after 120 days after a decision of the Tax Court has become final, the Secretary has failed to refund the overpayment determined by the Tax Court, together with the interest thereon as provided in subchapter B of chapter 67, then the Tax Court, upon motion by the taxpayer, shall have jurisdiction to order the refund of such overpayment and interest. An order of the Tax Court disposing of a motion under this paragraph shall be reviewable in the same manner as a decision of the Tax Court, but only with respect to the matters determined in such order.

(3) Limit on amount of credit or refund. No such credit or refund shall be allowed or made of any portion of the tax unless the Tax Court determines as part of its decision that such portion was paid –

(A) after the mailing of the notice of deficiency,

(B) within the period which would be applicable under section 6511(b)(2), (c), or (d), if on the date of the mailing of the notice of deficiency a claim had been filed (whether or not filed) stating the grounds upon which the Tax Court finds that there is an overpayment, or

(C) within the period which would be applicable under section 6511(b)(2), (c), or (d), in respect of any claim for refund filed within the applicable period specified in section 6511 and before the date of the mailing of the notice of deficiency –

(i) which had not been disallowed before that date,

(ii) which had been disallowed before that date and in respect of which a timely suit for refund could have been commenced as of that date, or

(iii) in respect of which a suit for refund had been commenced before that date and within the period specified in section 6532.

In the case of a credit or refund relating to an affected item (within the meaning of section 6231(a)(5)), the preceding sentence shall be applied by substituting the periods under sections 6229 and 6230(d) for the periods under section 6511(b)(2), (c), and (d).

In a case described in subparagraph (B) where the date of the mailing of the notice of deficiency is during the third year after the due date (with extensions) for filing the return of tax and no return was filed before such date, the applicable period under subsections (a) and (b)(2) of section 6511 shall be 3 years.

(4) Denial of jurisdiction regarding certain credits and reductions. The Tax Court shall have no jurisdiction under this subsection to restrain or review any credit or reduction made by the Secretary under section 6402.

* * *

§ 6513. Time return deemed filed and tax considered paid.

(a) Early return or advance payment of tax. For purposes of section 6511, any return filed before the last day prescribed for the filing thereof shall be considered as filed on such last day. For purposes of section 6511(b)(2) and (c) and section 6512, payment of any portion of the tax made before the last day prescribed for the payment of the tax shall be considered made on such last day. For purposes of this subsection, the last day prescribed for filing the return or paying the tax shall be determined without regard to any extension of time granted the taxpayer and without regard to any election to pay the tax in installments.

(b) Prepaid income tax. For purposes of section 6511 or 6512 –

(1) Any tax actually deducted and withheld at the source during any calendar year under chapter 24 shall, in respect of the recipient of the income, be deemed to have been paid by him on the 15th day of the fourth month following the close of his taxable year with respect to which such tax is allowable as a credit under section 31.

(2) Any amount paid as estimated income tax for any taxable year shall be deemed to have been paid on the last day prescribed for filing the return under section 6012 for such taxable year (determined without regard to any extension of time for filing such return).

(3) Any tax withheld at the source under chapter 3 or 4 shall, in respect of the recipient of the income, be deemed to have been paid by such recipient on the last day prescribed for filing the return under section 6012 for the taxable year (determined without regard to any extension of time for filing) with respect to which such tax is allowable as a credit under section 1462 or 1474(b). For this purpose, any exemption granted under section 6012 from the requirement of filing a return shall be disregarded.

* * *

§ 6532. Periods of limitation on suits.

(a) Suits by taxpayers for refund.

(1) General rule. No suit or proceeding under section 7422(a) for the recovery of any internal revenue tax, penalty, or other sum, shall be begun before the expiration of 6 months from the date of filing the claim required under such section unless the Secretary renders a decision thereon within that time, nor after the expiration of 2 years from the date of mailing by certified mail or registered mail by the Secretary to the taxpayer of a notice of the disallowance of the part of the claim to which the suit or proceeding relates.

(2) Extension of time. The 2-year period prescribed in paragraph (1) shall be extended for such period as may be agreed upon in writing between the taxpayer and the Secretary.

(3) Waiver of notice of disallowance. If any person files a written waiver of the requirement that he be mailed a notice of disallowance, the 2-year period prescribed in paragraph (1) shall begin on the date such waiver is filed.

(4) Reconsideration after mailing of notice. Any consideration, reconsideration, or action by the Secretary with respect to such claim following the mailing of a notice by certified mail or registered mail of disallowance shall not operate to extend the period within which suit may be begun.

(5) Cross reference. For substitution of 120-day period for the 6-month period contained in paragraph (1) in a title 11 case, see section 505(a)(2) of title 11 of the United States Code.

* * *

§ 6601. Interest on underpayment, nonpayment, or extensions of time for payment, of tax.

(a) General rule. If any amount of tax imposed by this title (whether required to be shown on a return, or to be paid by stamp or by some other method) is not paid on or before the last date prescribed for payment, interest on such amount at the underpayment rate established under section 6621 shall be paid for the period from such last date to the date paid.

(b) Last date prescribed for payment. For purposes of this section, the last date prescribed for payment of the tax shall be determined under chapter 62 with the application of the following rules:

(1) Extensions of time disregarded. The last date prescribed for payment shall be determined without regard to any extension of time for payment or any installment agreement entered into under section 6159.

(2) Installment payments. In the case of an election under section 6156(a) to pay the tax in installments –

(A) The date prescribed for payment of each installment of the tax shown on the return shall be determined under section 6156(b), and

(B) The last date prescribed for payment of the first installment shall be deemed the last date prescribed for payment of any portion of the tax not shown on the return.

(3) Jeopardy. The last date prescribed for payment shall be determined without regard to any notice and demand for payment issued, by reason of jeopardy (as provided in chapter 70), prior to the last date otherwise prescribed for such payment.

(4) Accumulated earnings tax. In the case of the tax imposed by section 531 for any taxable year, the last date prescribed for payment shall be deemed to be the due date (without regard to extensions) for the return of tax imposed by subtitle A for such taxable year.

(5) Last date for payment not otherwise prescribed. In the case of taxes payable by stamp and in all other cases in which the last date for payment is not otherwise prescribed, the last date for payment shall be deemed to be the date the liability for tax arises (and in no event shall be later than the date notice and demand for the tax is made by the Secretary).

(c) Suspension of interest in certain income, estate, gift, and certain excise tax cases. In the case of a deficiency as defined in section 6211 (relating to income, estate, gift and certain excise taxes), if a waiver of restrictions under section 6213(d) on the assessment of such deficiency has been filed, and if notice and demand by the Secretary for payment of such deficiency is not made within 30 days after the filing of such waiver, interest shall not be imposed on such deficiency for the period beginning immediately after such 30th day and ending with the date of notice and demand and interest shall not be imposed during such period on any interest with respect to such deficiency for any prior period. In the case of a settlement under section 6224(c) which results in the conversion of partnership items to nonpartnership items pursuant to section 6231(b)(1)(C), the preceding sentence shall apply to a computational adjustment resulting from such settlement in the same manner as if such adjustment were a deficiency and such settlement were a waiver referred to in the preceding sentence.

(d) Income tax reduced by carryback or adjustment for certain unused deductions.

(1) Net operating loss or capital loss carryback. If the amount of any tax imposed by subtitle A is reduced by reason of a carryback of a net operating loss or net capital loss such reduction in tax shall not affect the computation of interest under this section for the period ending with the filing date for the taxable year in which the net operating loss or net capital loss arises.

(2) Foreign tax credit carrybacks. If any credit allowed for any taxable year is increased by reason of a carryback of tax paid or accrued to foreign countries or possessions of the

United States, such increase shall not affect the computation of interest under this section for the period ending with the filing date for the taxable year in which such taxes were in fact paid or accrued, or, with respect to any portion of such credit carryback from a taxable year attributable to a net operating loss carryback or a capital loss carryback from a subsequent taxable year, such increase shall not affect the computation of interest under this section for the period ending with the filing date for such subsequent taxable year.

(3) Certain credit carrybacks.

(A) In general. If any credit allowed for any taxable year is increased by reason of a credit carryback, such increase shall not affect the computation of interest under this section for the period ending with the filing date for the taxable year in which the credit carryback arises, or, with respect to any portion of a credit carryback from a taxable year attributable to a net operating loss carryback, capital loss carryback, or other credit carryback from a subsequent taxable year, such increase shall not affect the computation of interest under this section for the period ending with the filing date for such subsequent taxable year.

(B) Credit carryback defined. For purposes of this paragraph, the term "credit carryback" has the meaning given such term by section 6511(d)(4)(C).

(4) Filing date. For purposes of this subsection, the term "filing date" has the meaning given to such term by section 6611(f)(4)(A).

(e) Applicable rules. Except as otherwise provided in this title –

(1) Interest treated as tax. Interest prescribed under this section on any tax shall be paid upon notice and demand, and shall be assessed, collected, and paid in the same manner as taxes. Any reference in this title (except subchapter B of chapter 63, relating to deficiency procedures) to any tax imposed by this title shall be deemed also to refer to interest imposed by this section on such tax.

(2) Interest on penalties, additional amounts, or additions to the tax.

(A) In general. Interest shall be imposed under subsection (a) in respect of any assessable penalty, additional amount, or addition to the tax (other than an addition to tax imposed under section 6651(a)(1) or 6653 or under part II of subchapter A of chapter 68) only if such assessable penalty, additional amount, or addition to the tax is not paid within 21 calendar days from the date of notice and demand therefor (10 business days if the amount for which such notice and demand is made equals or exceeds $100,000), and in such case interest shall be imposed only for the period from the date of the notice and demand to the date of payment.

(B) Interest on certain additions to tax. Interest shall be imposed under this section with respect to any addition to tax imposed by section 6651(a)(1) or 6653 or under part II of subchapter A of chapter 68 for the period which –

(i) begins on the date on which the return of the tax with respect to which such addition to tax is imposed is required to be filed (including any extensions), and

(ii) ends on the date of payment of such addition to tax.

(3) Payments made within specified period after notice and demand. If notice and demand is made for payment of any amount and if such amount is paid within 21 calendar days (10 business days if the amount for which such notice and demand is made equals or exceeds $100,000) after the date of such notice and demand, interest under this section on the amount so paid shall not be imposed for the period after the date of such notice and demand.

(f) Satisfaction by credits. If any portion of a tax is satisfied by credit of an overpayment, then no interest shall be imposed under this section on the portion of the tax so satisfied for any period during which, if the credit had not been made, interest would have been allowable with respect to such overpayment. The preceding sentence shall not apply to the extent that section 6621(d) applies.

(g) Limitation on assessment and collection. Interest prescribed under this section on any tax may be assessed and collected at any time during the period within which the tax to which such interest relates may be collected.

§ 6603. Deposits made to suspend running of interest on potential underpayments, etc.

(a) Authority to make deposits other than as payment of tax. A taxpayer may make a cash deposit with the Secretary which may be used by the Secretary to pay any tax imposed under subtitle A or B or chapter 41, 42, 43, or 44 which has not been assessed at the time of the deposit. Such a deposit shall be made in such manner as the Secretary shall prescribe.

(b) No interest imposed. To the extent that such deposit is used by the Secretary to pay tax, for purposes of section 6601 (relating to interest on underpayments), the tax shall be treated as paid when the deposit is made.

(c) Return of deposit. Except in a case where the Secretary determines that collection of tax is in jeopardy, the Secretary shall return to the taxpayer any amount of the deposit (to the extent not used for a payment of tax) which the taxpayer requests in writing.

(d) Payment of interest.

(1) In general. For purposes of section 6611 (relating to interest on overpayments), except as provided in paragraph (4), a deposit which is returned to a taxpayer shall be treated as a payment of tax for any period to the extent (and only to the extent) attributable to a disputable tax for such period. Under regulations prescribed by the Secretary, rules similar to the rules of section 6611(b)(2) shall apply.

(2) Disputable tax.

(A) In general. For purposes of this section, the term "disputable tax" means the amount of tax specified at the time of the deposit as the taxpayer's reasonable estimate of the maximum amount of any tax attributable to disputable items.

(B) Safe harbor based on 30-day letter. In the case of a taxpayer who has been issued a 30-day letter, the maximum amount of tax under subparagraph (A) shall not be less than the amount of the proposed deficiency specified in such letter.

(3) Other definitions. For purposes of paragraph (2) –

(A) Disputable item. The term "disputable item" means any item of income, gain, loss, deduction, or credit if the taxpayer –

(i) has a reasonable basis for its treatment of such item, and

(ii) reasonably believes that the Secretary also has a reasonable basis for disallowing the taxpayer's treatment of such item.

(B) 30-day letter. The term "30-day letter" means the first letter of proposed deficiency which allows the taxpayer an opportunity for administrative review in the Internal Revenue Service Office of Appeals.

(4) Rate of interest. The rate of interest under this subsection shall be the Federal short-term rate determined under section 6621(b), compounded daily.

(e) Use of deposits.

(1) Payment of tax. Except as otherwise provided by the taxpayer, deposits shall be treated as used for the payment of tax in the order deposited.

(2) Returns of deposits. Deposits shall be treated as returned to the taxpayer on a last-in, first-out basis.

* * *

§ 6611. Interest on overpayments.

(a) Rate. Interest shall be allowed and paid upon any overpayment in respect of any internal revenue tax at the overpayment rate established under section 6621.

(b) Period. Such interest shall be allowed and paid as follows:

(1) Credits. In the case of a credit, from the date of the overpayment to the due date of the amount against which the credit is taken.

(2) Refunds. In the case of a refund, from the date of the overpayment to a date (to be determined by the Secretary) preceding the date of the refund check by not more than 30 days, whether or not such refund check is accepted by the taxpayer after tender of such check to the taxpayer. The acceptance of such check shall be without prejudice to any right of the taxpayer to claim any additional overpayment and interest thereon.

(3) Late returns. Notwithstanding paragraph (1) or (2) in the case of a return of tax which is filed after the last date prescribed for filing such return (determined with regard to extensions), no interest shall be allowed or paid for any day before the date on which the return is filed.

* * *

(d) Advance payment of tax, payment of estimated tax, and credit for income tax withholding. The provisions of section 6513 (except the provisions of subsection (c) thereof), applicable in determining the date of payment of tax for purposes of determining the period of limitation on credit or refund, shall be applicable in determining the date of payment for purposes of subsection (a).

(e) Disallowance of interest on certain overpayments.

(1) Refunds within 45 days after return is filed. If any overpayment of tax imposed by this title is refunded within 45 days after the last day prescribed for filing the return of such tax (determined without regard to any extension of time for filing the return) or, in the case of a return filed after such last date, is refunded within 45 days after the date the return is filed, no interest shall be allowed under subsection (a) on such overpayment.

(2) Refunds after claim for credit or refund. If –

(A) the taxpayer files a claim for a credit or refund for any overpayment of tax imposed by this title, and

(B) such overpayment is refunded within 45 days after such claim is filed, no interest shall be allowed on such overpayment from the date the claim is filed until the day the refund is made.

(3) IRS initiated adjustments. If an adjustment initiated by the Secretary, results in a refund or credit of an overpayment, interest on such overpayment shall be computed by subtracting 45 days from the number of days interest would otherwise be allowed with respect to such overpayment.

(4) Certain withholding taxes. In the case of any overpayment resulting from tax deducted and withheld under chapter 3 or 4, paragraphs (1), (2), and (3) shall be applied by substituting "180 days" for "45 days" each place it appears.

* * *

§ 6621. Determination of rate of interest.

(a) General rule.

(1) Overpayment rate. The overpayment rate established under this section shall be the sum of –

(A) the Federal short-term rate determined under subsection (b), plus

(B) 3 percentage points (2 percentage points in the case of a corporation).

To the extent that an overpayment of tax by a corporation for any taxable period (as defined in subsection (c)(3), applied by substituting 'overpayment' for 'underpayment') exceeds $10,000, subparagraph (B) shall be applied by substituting "0.5 percentage point" for "2 percentage points".

(2) Underpayment rate. The underpayment rate established under this section shall be the sum of –

(A) the Federal short-term rate determined under subsection (b), plus

(B) 3 percentage points.

(b) Federal short-term rate. For purposes of this section –

(1) General rule. The Secretary shall determine the Federal short-term rate for the first month in each calendar quarter.

(2) Period during which rate applies.

(A) In general. Except as provided in subparagraph (B), the Federal short-term rate determined under paragraph (1) for any month shall apply during the first calendar quarter beginning after such month.

(B) Special rule for individual estimated tax. In determining the addition to tax under section 6654 for failure to pay estimated tax for any taxable year, the Federal short-term rate which applies during the 3rd month following such taxable year shall also apply during the first 15 days of the 4th month following such taxable year.

(3) Federal short-term rate. The federal short-term rate for any month shall be the Federal short-term rate determined during such month by the Secretary in accordance with section 1274(d). Any such rate shall be rounded to the nearest full percent (or, if a multiple of 1/2 of 1 percent, such rate shall be increased to the next highest full percent).

(c) Increase in underpayment rate for large corporate underpayments.

(1) In general. For purposes of determining the amount of interest payable under section 6601 on any large corporate underpayment for periods after the applicable date, paragraph (2) of subsection (a) shall be applied by substituting "5 percentage points" for "3 percentage points".

(2) Applicable date. For purposes of this subsection –

(A) In general. The applicable date is the 30th day after the earlier of –

(i) the date on which the 1st letter of proposed deficiency which allows the taxpayer an opportunity for administrative review in the Internal Revenue Service Office of Appeals is sent, or

(ii) the date on which the deficiency notice under section 6212 is sent.

The preceding sentence shall be applied without regard to any such letter or notice which is withdrawn by the Secretary.

(B) Special rules.

(i) Nondeficiency procedures. In the case of any underpayment of any tax imposed by this title to which the deficiency procedures do not apply, subparagraph (A) shall be applied by taking into account any letter or notice provided by the Secretary which notifies the taxpayer of the assessment or proposed assessment of the tax.

(ii) Exception where amounts paid in full. For purposes of subparagraph (A), a letter or notice shall be disregarded if, during the 30-day period beginning on the day on which it was sent, the taxpayer makes a payment equal to the amount shown as due in such letter or notice, as the case may be.

(iii) Exception for letters or notices involving small amounts. For purposes of this paragraph, any letter or notice shall be disregarded if the amount of the deficiency or proposed deficiency (or the assessment or proposed assessment) set forth in such letter or notice is not greater than $100,000 (determined by not taking into account any interest, penalties, or additions to tax).

(3) Large corporate underpayment. For purposes of this subsection –

(A) In general. The term "large corporate underpayment" means any underpayment of a tax by a C corporation for any taxable period if the amount of such underpayment for such period exceeds $100,000.

(B) Taxable period. For purposes of subparagraph (A), the term "taxable period" means –

(i) in the case of any tax imposed by subtitle A, the taxable year, or

(ii) in the case of any other tax, the period to which the underpayment relates.

(d) Elimination of interest on overlapping periods of tax overpayments and underpayments. To the extent that, for any period, interest is payable under subchapter A and allowable under subchapter B on equivalent underpayments and overpayments by the same taxpayer of tax imposed by this title, the net rate of interest under this section on such amounts shall be zero for such period.

§ 6622. Interest compounded daily.

(a) General rule. In computing the amount of any interest required to be paid under this title or sections 1961(c)(1) or 2411 of title 28, United States Code, by the Secretary or by the taxpayer, or any other amount determined by reference to such amount of interest, such interest and such amount shall be compounded daily.

(b) Exception for penalty for failure to file estimated tax. Subsection (a) shall not apply for purposes of computing the amount of any addition to tax under section 6654 or 6655.

* * *

§ 6631. Notice requirements.

The Secretary shall include with each notice to an individual taxpayer which includes an amount of interest required to be paid by such taxpayer under this title information with respect to the section of this title under which the interest is imposed and a computation of the interest.

* * *

§ 6651. Failure to file tax return or to pay tax.

(a) Addition to the tax. In case of failure –

(1) to file any return required under authority of subchapter A of chapter 61 (other than part III thereof), subchapter A of chapter 51 (relating to distilled spirits, wines, and beer), or of subchapter A of chapter 52 (relating to tobacco, cigars, cigarettes, and cigarette papers and tubes), or of subchapter A of chapter 53 (relating to machine guns and certain other firearms), on the date prescribed therefor (determined with regard to any extension of time for filing), unless it is shown that such failure is due to reasonable cause and not due to willful neglect, there shall be added to the amount required to be shown as tax on such return 5 percent of the amount of such tax if the failure is for not more than 1 month, with an additional 5 percent for each additional month or fraction thereof during which such failure continues, not exceeding 25 percent in the aggregate;

(2) to pay the amount shown as tax on any return specified in paragraph (1) on or before the date prescribed for payment of such tax (determined with regard to any extension of time for payment), unless it is shown that such failure is due to reasonable cause and not due to willful neglect, there shall be added to the amount shown as tax on such return 0.5 percent of the amount of such tax if the failure is for not more than 1 month, with an additional 0.5 percent for each additional month or fraction thereof during which such failure continues, not exceeding 25 percent in the aggregate; or

(3) to pay any amount in respect of any tax required to be shown on a return specified in paragraph (1) which is not so shown (including an assessment made pursuant to section 6213(b)) within 21 calendar days from the date of notice and demand therefor (10 business days if the amount for which such notice and demand is made equals or exceeds $100,000), unless it is shown that such failure is due to reasonable cause and not due to willful neglect, there shall be added to the amount of tax stated in such notice and demand 0.5 percent of the amount of such tax if the failure is for not more than 1 month, with an additional 0.5 percent for each additional month or fraction thereof during which such failure continues, not exceeding 25 percent in the aggregate.

In the case of a failure to file a return of tax imposed by chapter 1 within 60 days of the date prescribed for filing of such return (determined with regard to any extensions of time for filing), unless it is shown that such failure is due to reasonable cause and not due to willful neglect, the addition to tax under paragraph (1) shall not be less than the lesser of $135 or 100 percent of the amount required to be shown as tax on such return.

(b) Penalty imposed on net amount due. For purposes of –

(1) subsection (a)(1), the amount of tax required to be shown on the return shall be reduced by the amount of any part of the tax which is paid on or before the date prescribed for payment of the tax and by the amount of any credit against the tax which may be claimed on the return,

(2) subsection (a)(2), the amount of tax shown on the return shall, for purposes of computing the addition for any month, be reduced by the amount of any part of the tax which is paid on or before the beginning of such month and by the amount of any credit against the tax which may be claimed on the return, and

(3) subsection (a)(3), the amount of tax stated in the notice and demand shall, for the purpose of computing the addition for any month, be reduced by the amount of any part of the tax which is paid before the beginning of such month.

(c) Limitations and special rule.

(1) Additions under more than one paragraph. With respect to any return, the amount of the addition under paragraph (1) of subsection (a) shall be reduced by the amount of the addition under paragraph (2) of subsection (a) for any month (or fraction thereof) to which an addition to tax applies under both paragraphs (1) and (2). In any case described in the last sentence of subsection (a), the amount of the addition under paragraph (1) of subsection (a) shall not be reduced under the preceding sentence below the amount provided in such last sentence.

(2) Amount of tax shown more than amount required to be shown. If the amount required to be shown as tax on a return is less than the amount shown as tax on such return, subsections (a)(2) and (b)(2) shall be applied by substituting such lower amount.

(d) Increase in penalty for failure to pay tax in certain cases.

(1) In general. In the case of each month (or fraction thereof) beginning after the day described in paragraph (2) of this subsection, paragraphs (2) and (3) of subsection (a) shall be applied by substituting "1 percent" for "0.5 percent" each place it appears.

(2) Description. For purposes of paragraph (1), the day described in this paragraph is the earlier of –

(A) the day 10 days after the date on which notice is given under section 6331(d), or

(B) the day on which notice and demand for immediate payment is given under the last sentence of section 6331(a).

(e) Exception for estimated tax. This section shall not apply to any failure to pay any estimated tax required to be paid by section 6654 or 6655.

(f) Increase in penalty for fraudulent failure to file. If any failure to file any return is fraudulent, paragraph (1) of subsection (a) shall be applied –

(1) by substituting "15 percent" for "5 percent" each place it appears, and

(2) by substituting "75 percent" for "25 percent" .

(g) Treatment of returns prepared by Secretary under section 6020(b). In the case of any return made by the Secretary under section 6020(b) –

(1) such return shall be disregarded for purposes of determining the amount of the addition under paragraph (1) of subsection (a), but

(2) such return shall be treated as the return filed by the taxpayer for purposes of determining the amount of the addition under paragraphs (2) and (3) of subsection (a).

(h) Limitation on penalty on individual's failure to pay for months during period of installment agreement. In the case of an individual who files a return of tax on or before the due date for the return (including extensions), paragraphs (2) and (3) of subsection (a) shall each be applied by substituting "0.25" for "0.5" each place it appears for purposes of determining the addition to tax for any month during which an installment agreement under section 6159 is in effect for the payment of such tax.

* * *

§ 6654. Failure by individual to pay estimated income tax.

* * *

(d) Amount of required installments. For purposes of this section –

(1) Amount.

(A) In general. Except as provided in paragraph (2), the amount of any required installment shall be 25 percent of the required annual payment.

(B) Required annual payment. For purposes of subparagraph (A), the term 'required annual payment' means the lesser of –

(i) 90 percent of the tax shown on the return for the taxable year (or, if no return is filed, 90 percent of the tax for such year), or

(ii) 100 percent of the tax shown on the return of the individual for the preceding taxable year.

Clause (ii) shall not apply if the preceding taxable year was not a taxable year of 12 months or if the individual did not file a return for such preceding taxable year.

(C) Limitation on use of preceding year's tax.

(i) In general. If the adjusted gross income shown on the return of the individual for the preceding taxable year beginning in any calendar year exceeds $150,000, clause (ii) of subparagraph (B) shall be applied by substituting the applicable percentage for '100 percent'. For purposes of the preceding sentence, the applicable percentage shall be determined in accordance with the following table:

If the preceding taxable year begins in:	The applicable percentage is:
1998...............	105
1999...............	108.6
2000...............	110
2001...............	112
2002 or thereafter........	110

(ii) Separate returns. In the case of a married individual (within the meaning of section 7703) who files a separate return for the taxable year for which the amount of the installment is being determined, clause (i) shall be applied by substituting '$75,000' for '$150,000'.

(iii) Special rule. In the case of an estate or trust, adjusted gross income shall be determined as provided in section 67(e).

(D) Special rule for 2009.

(i) In general. Notwithstanding subparagraph (C), in the case of any taxable year beginning in 2009, clause (ii) of subparagraph (B) shall be applied to any qualified individual by substituting "90 percent" for "100 percent".

(ii) Qualified individual. For purposes of this subparagraph, the term "qualified individual" means any individual if –

(I) the adjusted gross income shown on the return of such individual for the preceding taxable year is less than $500,000, and

(II) such individual certifies that more than 50 percent of the gross income shown on the return of such individual for the preceding taxable year was income from a small business. A certification under subclause (II) shall be in such form and manner and filed at such time as the Secretary may by regulations prescribe.

(iii) Income from a small business. For purposes of clause (ii), income from a small business means, with respect to any individual, income from a trade or business the average number of employees of which was less than 500 employees for the calendar year ending with or within the preceding taxable year of the individual.

(iv) Separate returns. In the case of a married individual (within the meaning of section 7703) who files a separate return for the taxable year for which the amount of the installment is being determined, clause (ii)(I) shall be applied by substituting "$250,000" for "$500,000".

(v) Estates and trusts. In the case of an estate or trust, adjusted gross income shall be determined as provided in section 67(e).

(2) Lower required installment where annualized income installment is less than amount determined under paragraph (1).

(A) In general. In the case of any required installment, if the individual establishes that the annualized income installment is less than the amount determined under paragraph (1) –

(i) the amount of such required installment shall be the annualized income installment, and

(ii) any reduction in a required installment resulting from the application of this subparagraph shall be recaptured by increasing the amount of the next required installment determined under paragraph (1) by the amount of such reduction (and by increasing subsequent required installments to the extent that the reduction has not previously been recaptured under this clause).

(B) Determination of annualized income installment. In the case of any required installment, the annualized income installment is the excess (if any) of –

(i) an amount equal to the applicable percentage of the tax for the taxable year computed by placing on an annualized basis the taxable income, alternative minimum taxable income, and adjusted self-employment income for months in the taxable year ending before the due date for the installment, over

(ii) the aggregate amount of any prior required installments for the taxable year.

(C) Special rules. For purposes of this paragraph –

(i) Annualization. The taxable income, alternative minimum taxable income, and adjusted self-employment income shall be placed on an annualized basis under regulations prescribed by the Secretary.

(ii) Applicable percentage.

In the case of the following required installments:	The applicable percentage is:
1st	22.5
2nd	45
3rd	67.5
4th	90.

(iii) Adjusted self-employment income. The term "adjusted self-employment income" means self-employment income (as defined in section 1402(b)); except that section 1402(b) shall be applied by placing wages (within the meaning of section 1402(b)) for months in the taxable year ending before the due date for the installment on an annualized basis consistent with clause (i).

(D) Treatment of subpart F and section 936 income.

(i) In general. Any amounts required to be included in gross income under section 936(h) or 951(a) (and credits properly allocable thereto) shall be taken into account in computing any annualized income installment under subparagraph (B) in a manner similar to the manner under which partnership income inclusions (and credits properly allocable thereto) are taken into account.

(ii) Prior year safe harbor. If a taxpayer elects to have this clause apply to any taxable year –

(I) clause (i) shall not apply, and

(II) for purposes of computing any annualized income installment for such taxable year, the taxpayer shall be treated as having received ratably during such taxable year items of income and credit described in clause (i) in an amount equal to the amount of such items shown on the return of the taxpayer for the preceding taxable year (the second preceding taxable year in the case of the first and second required installments for such taxable year).

* * *

§6662. Imposition of accuracy-related penalty on underpayments.

(a) Imposition of penalty. If this section applies to any portion of an underpayment of tax required to be shown on a return, there shall be added to the tax an amount equal to 20 percent of the portion of the underpayment to which this section applies.

(b) Portion of underpayment to which section applies. This section shall apply to the portion of any underpayment which is attributable to 1 or more of the following:

(1) Negligence or disregard of rules or regulations.

(2) Any substantial understatement of income tax.

(3) Any substantial valuation misstatement under chapter 1.

(4) Any substantial overstatement of pension liabilities.

(5) Any substantial estate or gift tax valuation understatement.

(6) Any disallowance of claimed tax benefits by reason of a transaction lacking economic substance (within the meaning of section 7701(o)) or failing to meet the requirements of any similar rule of law.

(7) Any undisclosed foreign financial asset understatement.

This section shall not apply to any portion of an underpayment on which a penalty is imposed under section 6663. Except as provided in paragraph (1) or (2)(B) of section 6662A(e), this section shall not apply to the portion of any underpayment which is attributable to a reportable transaction understatement on which a penalty is imposed under section 6662A.

(c) Negligence. For purposes of this section, the term "negligence" includes any failure to make a reasonable attempt to comply with the provisions of this title, and the term 'disregard' includes any careless, reckless, or intentional disregard.

(d) Substantial understatement of income tax.

(1) Substantial understatement.—

(A) In general. For purposes of this section, there is a substantial understatement of income tax for any taxable year if the amount of the understatement for the taxable year exceeds the greater of—

(i) 10 percent of the tax required to be shown on the return for the taxable year, or

(ii) $ 5,000.

(B) Special rule for corporations. In the case of a corporation other than an S corporation or a personal holding company (as defined in section 542), there is a substantial understatement of income tax for any taxable year if the amount of the understatement for the taxable year exceeds the lesser of—

(i) 10 percent of the tax required to be shown on the return for the taxable year (or, if greater, $ 10,000), or

(ii) $ 10,000,000.

(2) Understatement.

(A) In general. For purposes of paragraph (1), the term 'understatement' means the excess of—

(i) the amount of the tax required to be shown on the return for the taxable year, over

(ii) the amount of the tax imposed which is shown on the return, reduced by any rebate (within the meaning of section 6211(b)(2)).

The excess under the preceding sentence shall be determined without regard to items to which section 6662A applies.

(B) Reduction for understatement due to position of taxpayer or disclosed item. The amount of the understatement under subparagraph (A) shall be reduced by that portion of the understatement which is attributable to—

(i) the tax treatment of any item by the taxpayer if there is or was substantial authority for such treatment, or

(ii) any item if—

(I) the relevant facts affecting the item's tax treatment are adequately disclosed in the return or in a statement attached to the return, and

(II) there is a reasonable basis for the tax treatment of such item by the taxpayer.

For purposes of clause (ii)(II), in no event shall a corporation be treated as having a reasonable basis for its tax treatment of an item attributable to a multiple-party financing transaction if such treatment does not clearly reflect the income of the corporation.

(C) Reduction not to apply to tax shelters.

(i) In general. Subparagraph (B) shall not apply to any item attributable to a tax shelter.

(ii) Tax shelter. For purposes of clause (i), the term "tax shelter" means—

(I) a partnership or other entity,

(II) any investment plan or arrangement, or

(III) any other plan or arrangement,

if a significant purpose of such partnership, entity, plan, or arrangement is the avoidance or evasion of Federal income tax.

(3) Secretarial list. The Secretary may prescribe a list of positions which the Secretary believes do not meet 1 or more of the standards specified in paragraph (2)(B)(i), section 6664(d)(2), and section 6694(a)(1). Such list (and any revisions thereof) shall be published in the Federal Register or the Internal Revenue Bulletin.

(e) Substantial valuation misstatement under chapter 1.

(2) Limitation. No penalty shall be imposed by reason of subsection (b)(3) unless the portion of the underpayment for the taxable year attributable to substantial valuation misstatements under chapter 1 exceeds $5,000 ($10,000 in the case of a corporation other than an S corporation or a personal holding company (as defined in section 542)).

(f) Substantial overstatement of pension liabilities.

(1) In general. For purposes of this section, there is a substantial overstatement of pension liabilities if the actuarial determination of the liabilities taken into account for purposes of computing the deduction under paragraph (1) or (2) of section 404(a) is 200 percent or more of the amount determined to be the correct amount of such liabilities.

(2) Limitation. No penalty shall be imposed by reason of subsection (b)(4) unless the portion of the underpayment for the taxable year attributable to substantial overstatements of pension liabilities exceeds $1,000.

* * *

(h) Increase in penalty in case of gross valuation misstatements.

(1) In general. To the extent that a portion of the underpayment to which this section applies is attributable to one or more gross valuation misstatements, subsection (a) shall be applied with respect to such portion by substituting '40 percent' for '20 percent'.

(2) Gross valuation misstatements. The term 'gross valuation misstatements' means –

(A) any substantial valuation misstatement under chapter 1 as determined under subsection (e) by substituting –

(i) in paragraph (1)(A), "200 percent" for "150 percent",

(ii) in paragraph (1)(B)(i) –

(I) "400 percent" for "200 percent", and

(II) "25 percent" for "50 percent", and

(iii) in paragraph (1)(B)(ii) –

(I) "$20,000,000" for "$5,000,000", and

(II) "20 percent" for "10 percent".

(B) any substantial overstatement of pension liabilities as determined under subsection (f) by substituting "400 percent" for "200 percent", and

(C) any substantial estate or gift tax valuation understatement as determined under subsection (g) by substituting "40 percent" for "65 percent".

* * *

§ 6662A. Imposition of accuracy-related penalty on understatements with respect to reportable transactions.

(a) Imposition of penalty. If a taxpayer has a reportable transaction understatement for any taxable year, there shall be added to the tax an amount equal to 20 percent of the amount of such understatement.

(b) Reportable transaction understatement. For purposes of this section –

(1) In general. The term "reportable transaction understatement" means the sum of –

(A) the product of –

(i) the amount of the increase (if any) in taxable income which results from a difference between the proper tax treatment of an item to which this section applies and the taxpayer's treatment of such item (as shown on the taxpayer's return of tax), and

(ii) the highest rate of tax imposed by section 1 (section 11 in the case of a taxpayer which is a corporation), and

(B) the amount of the decrease (if any) in the aggregate amount of credits determined under subtitle A which results from a difference between the taxpayer's treatment of an item to which this section applies (as shown on the taxpayer's return of tax) and the proper tax treatment of such item.

For purposes of subparagraph (A), any reduction of the excess of deductions allowed for the taxable year over gross income for such year, and any reduction in the amount of capital losses which would (without regard to section 1211) be allowed for such year, shall be treated as an increase in taxable income.

(2) Items to which section applies. This section shall apply to any item which is attributable to –

(A) any listed transaction, and

(B) any reportable transaction (other than a listed transaction) if a significant purpose of such transaction is the avoidance or evasion of Federal income tax.

(c) Higher penalty for nondisclosed listed and other avoidance transactions. Subsection (a) shall be applied by substituting "30 percent" for "20 percent" with respect to the portion of any reportable transaction understatement with respect to which the requirement of section 6664(d)(2)(A) is not met.

(d) Definitions of reportable and listed transactions. For purposes of this section, the terms "reportable transaction" and "listed transaction" have the respective meanings given to such terms by section 6707A(c).

* * *

§ 6663. Imposition of fraud penalty.

(a) Imposition of penalty. If any part of any underpayment of tax required to be shown on a return is due to fraud, there shall be added to the tax an amount equal to 75 percent of the portion of the underpayment which is attributable to fraud.

(b) Determination of portion attributable to fraud. If the Secretary establishes that any portion of an underpayment is attributable to fraud, the entire underpayment shall be treated as attributable to fraud, except with respect to any portion of the underpayment which the taxpayer establishes (by a preponderance of the evidence) is not attributable to fraud.

(c) Special rule for joint returns. In the case of a joint return, this section shall not apply with respect to a spouse unless some part of the underpayment is due to the fraud of such spouse.

* * *

§ 6664. Definitions and special rules.

(a) Underpayment. For purposes of this part, the term "underpayment" means the amount by which any tax imposed by this title exceeds the excess of –

(1) the sum of –

(A) the amount shown as the tax by the taxpayer on his return, plus

(B) amounts not so shown previously assessed (or collected without assessment), over

(2) the amount of rebates made.

For purposes of paragraph (2), the term "rebate" means so much of an abatement, credit, refund, or other repayment, as was made on the ground that the tax imposed was less than the excess of the amount specified in paragraph (1) over the rebates previously made.

(b) Penalties applicable only where return filed. The penalties provided in this part shall apply only in cases where a return of tax is filed (other than a return prepared by the Secretary under the authority of section 6020(b)).

(c) Reasonable cause exception for underpayments.

(1) In general. No penalty shall be imposed under section 6662 or 6663 with respect to any portion of an underpayment if it is shown that there was a reasonable cause for such portion and that the taxpayer acted in good faith with respect to such portion.

(2) Exception. Paragraph (1) shall not apply to any portion of an underpayment which is attributable to one or more transactions described in section 6662(b)(6).

(3) Special rule for certain valuation overstatements. In the case of any underpayment attributable to a substantial or gross valuation overstatement under chapter 1 with respect to charitable deduction property, paragraph (1) shall not apply. The preceding sentence shall not apply to a substantial valuation overstatement under chapter 1 if –

(A) the claimed value of the property was based on a qualified appraisal made by a qualified appraiser, and

(B) in addition to obtaining such appraisal, the taxpayer made a good faith investigation of the value of the contributed property.

(4) Definitions. For purposes of this subsection –

(A) Charitable deduction property. The term "charitable deduction property" means any property contributed by the taxpayer in a contribution for which a deduction was claimed under section 170. For purposes of paragraph (3), such term shall not include any securities for which (as of the date of the contribution) market quotations are readily available on an established securities market.

(B) Qualified appraisal. The term "qualified appraisal" has the meaning given such term by section 170(f)(11)(E)(i).

(C) Qualified appraiser. The term "qualified appraiser" has the meaning given such term by section 170(f)(11)(E)(ii).

(d) Reasonable cause exception for reportable transaction understatements.

(1) In general. No penalty shall be imposed under section 6662A with respect to any portion of a reportable transaction understatement if it is shown that there was a reasonable cause for such portion and that the taxpayer acted in good faith with respect to such portion.

(2) Exception. Paragraph (1) shall not apply to any portion of a reportable transaction understatement which is attributable to one or more transactions described in section 6662(b)(6).

(3) Special rules. Paragraph (1) shall not apply to any reportable transaction understatement unless –

(A) the relevant facts affecting the tax treatment of the item are adequately disclosed in accordance with the regulations prescribed under section 6011,

(B) there is or was substantial authority for such treatment, and

(C) the taxpayer reasonably believed that such treatment was more likely than not the proper treatment.

A taxpayer failing to adequately disclose in accordance with section 6011 shall be treated as meeting the requirements of subparagraph (A) if the penalty for such failure was rescinded under section 6707A(d).

(4) Rules relating to reasonable belief. For purposes of paragraph (3)(C) –

(A) In general. A taxpayer shall be treated as having a reasonable belief with respect to the tax treatment of an item only if such belief –

(i) is based on the facts and law that exist at the time the return of tax which includes such tax treatment is filed, and

(ii) relates solely to the taxpayer's chances of success on the merits of such treatment and does not take into account the possibility that a return will not be audited, such treatment will not be raised on audit, or such treatment will be resolved through settlement if it is raised.

(B) Certain opinions may not be relied upon.

(i) In general. An opinion of a tax advisor may not be relied upon to establish the reasonable belief of a taxpayer if –

(I) the tax advisor is described in clause (ii), or

(II) the opinion is described in clause (iii).

(ii) Disqualified tax advisors. A tax advisor is described in this clause if the tax advisor –

(I) is a material advisor (within the meaning of section 6111(b)(1)) and participates in the organization, management, promotion, or sale of the transaction or is related (within the meaning of section 267(b) or 707(b)(1)) to any person who so participates,

(II) is compensated directly or indirectly by a material advisor with respect to the transaction,

(III) has a fee arrangement with respect to the transaction which is contingent on all or part of the intended tax benefits from the transaction being sustained, or

(IV) as determined under regulations prescribed by the Secretary, has a disqualifying financial interest with respect to the transaction.

(iii) Disqualified opinions. For purposes of clause (i), an opinion is disqualified if the opinion –

(I) is based on unreasonable factual or legal assumptions (including assumptions as to future events),

(II) unreasonably relies on representations, statements, findings, or agreements of the taxpayer or any other person,

(III) does not identify and consider all relevant facts, or

(IV) fails to meet any other requirement as the Secretary may prescribe.

§ 6665. Applicable rules.

(a) Additions treated as tax. Except as otherwise provided in this title –

(1) the additions to the tax, additional amounts, and penalties provided by this chapter shall be paid upon notice and demand and shall be assessed, collected, and paid in the same manner as taxes; and

(2) any reference in this title to 'tax' imposed by this title shall be deemed also to refer to the additions to the tax, additional amounts, and penalties provided by this chapter.

(b) Procedure for assessing certain additions to tax. For purposes of subchapter B of chapter 63 (relating to deficiency procedures for income, estate, gift, and certain excise taxes), subsection (a) shall not apply to any addition to tax under section 6651, 6654, or 6655; except that it shall apply –

(1) in the case of an addition described in section 6651, to that portion of such addition which is attributable to a deficiency in tax described in section 6211; or

(2) to an addition described in section 6654 or 6655, if no return is filed for the taxable year.

* * *

§ 6671. Rules for application of assessable penalties.

(a) Penalty assessed as tax. The penalties and liabilities provided by this subchapter shall be paid upon notice and demand by the Secretary, and shall be assessed and collected in the same manner as taxes. Except as otherwise provided, any reference in this title to 'tax' imposed by this title shall be deemed also to refer to the penalties and liabilities provided by this subchapter.

(b) Person defined. The term 'person', as used in this subchapter, includes an officer or employee of a corporation, or a member or employee of a partnership, who as such officer, employee, or member is under a duty to perform the act in respect of which the violation occurs.

* * *

§ 6673. Sanctions and costs awarded by courts.

(a) Tax court proceedings.

(1) Procedures instituted primarily for delay, etc. Whenever it appears to the Tax Court that –

(A) proceedings before it have been instituted or maintained by the taxpayer primarily for delay,

(B) the taxpayer's position in such proceeding is frivolous or groundless, or

(C) the taxpayer unreasonably failed to pursue available administrative remedies, the Tax Court, in its decision, may require the taxpayer to pay to the United States a penalty not in excess of $25,000.

(2) Counsel's liability for excessive costs. Whenever it appears to the Tax Court that any attorney or other person admitted to practice before the Tax Court has multiplied the proceedings in any case unreasonably and vexatiously, the Tax Court may require –

(A) that such attorney or other person pay personally the excess costs, expenses, and attorneys' fees reasonably incurred because of such conduct, or

(B) if such attorney is appearing on behalf of the Commissioner of Internal Revenue, that the United States pay such excess costs, expenses, and attorneys' fees in the same manner as such an award by a district court.

(b) Proceedings in other courts.

(1) Claims under section 7433. Whenever it appears to the court that the taxpayer's position in the proceedings before the court instituted or maintained by such taxpayer under section 7433 is frivolous or groundless, the court may require the taxpayer to pay to the United States a penalty not in excess of $10,000.

(2) Collection of sanctions and costs. In any civil proceeding before any court (other than the Tax Court) which is brought by or against the United States in connection with the determination, collection, or refund of any tax, interest, or penalty under this title, any monetary sanctions, penalties, or costs awarded by the court to the United States may be assessed by the Secretary and, upon notice and demand, may be collected in the same manner as a tax.

(3) Sanctions and costs awarded by a court of appeals. In connection with any appeal from a proceeding in the Tax Court or a civil proceeding described in paragraph (2), an order of a United States Court of Appeals or the Supreme Court awarding monetary sanctions, penalties or court costs to the United States may be registered in a district court upon filing a certified copy of such order and shall be enforceable as other district court judgments. Any such sanctions, penalties, or costs may be assessed by the Secretary and, upon notice and demand, may be collected in the same manner as a tax.

* * *

§ 6676. Erroneous claim for refund or credit.

(a) Civil penalty. If a claim for refund or credit with respect to income tax (other than a claim for a refund or credit relating to the earned income credit under section 32) is made for an excessive amount, unless it is shown that the claim for such excessive amount has a reasonable basis, the person making such claim shall be liable for a penalty in an amount equal to 20 percent of the excessive amount.

(b) Excessive amount. For purposes of this section, the term "excessive amount" means in the case of any person the amount by which the amount of the claim for refund or credit for any taxable year exceeds the amount of such claim allowable under this title for such taxable year.

(c) Noneconomic substance transactions treated as lacking reasonable basis. For purposes of this section, any excessive amount which is attributable to any transaction described in section 6662(b)(6) shall not be treated as having a reasonable basis.

(d) Coordination with other penalties. This section shall not apply to any portion of the excessive amount of a claim for refund or credit which is subject to a penalty imposed under part II of subchapter A of chapter 68.

* * *

§ 6694. Understatement of taxpayer's liability by tax return preparer.

(a) Understatement due to unreasonable positions.

(1) In general. If a tax return preparer –

(A) prepares any return or claim of refund with respect to which any part of an understatement of liability is due to a position described in paragraph (2), and

(B) knew (or reasonably should have known) of the position, such tax return preparer shall pay a penalty with respect to each such return or claim in an amount equal to the greater of $1,000 or 50 percent of the income derived (or to be derived) by the tax return preparer with respect to the return or claim.

(2) Unreasonable position.

(A) In general. Except as otherwise provided in this paragraph, a position is described in this paragraph unless there is or was substantial authority for the position.

(B) Disclosed positions. If the position was disclosed as provided in section 6662(d)(2)(B)(ii)(I) and is not a position to which subparagraph (C) applies, the position is described in this paragraph unless there is a reasonable basis for the position.

(C) Tax shelters and reportable transactions. If the position is with respect to a tax shelter (as defined in section 6662(d)(2)(C)(ii)) or a reportable transaction to which section 6662A applies, the position is described in this paragraph unless it is reasonable to believe that the position would more likely than not be sustained on its merits.

(3) Reasonable cause exception. No penalty shall be imposed under this subsection if it is shown that there is reasonable cause for the understatement and the tax return preparer acted in good faith.

(b) Understatement due to willful or reckless conduct.

(1) In general. Any tax return preparer who prepares any return or claim for refund with respect to which any part of an understatement of liability is due to a conduct described in paragraph (2) shall pay a penalty with respect to each such return or claim in an amount equal to the greater of –

(A) $5,000, or

(B) 50 percent of the income derived (or to be derived) by the tax return preparer with respect to the return or claim.

(2) Willful or reckless conduct. Conduct described in this paragraph is conduct by the tax return preparer which is –

(A) a willful attempt in any manner to understate the liability for tax on the return or claim, or

(B) a reckless or intentional disregard of rules or regulations.

(3) Reduction in penalty. The amount of any penalty payable by any person by reason of this subsection for any return or claim for refund shall be reduced by the amount of the penalty paid by such person by reason of subsection (a).

* * *

§ 6695A. Substantial and gross valuation misstatements attributable to incorrect appraisals

(a) Imposition of penalty. If –

(1) a person prepares an appraisal of the value of property and such person knows, or reasonably should have known, that the appraisal would be used in connection with a return or a claim for refund, and

(2) the claimed value of the property on a return or claim for refund which is based on such appraisal results in a substantial valuation misstatement under chapter 1 (within the meaning of section 6662(e)), a substantial estate or gift tax valuation understatement (within the meaning of section 6662(g)), or a gross valuation misstatement (within the meaning of section 6662(h)), with respect to such property, then such person shall pay a penalty in the amount determined under subsection (b).

(b) Amount of penalty. The amount of the penalty imposed under subsection (a) on any person with respect to an appraisal shall be equal to the lesser of –

(1) the greater of –

(A) 10 percent of the amount of the underpayment (as defined in section 6664(a)) attributable to the misstatement described in subsection (a)(2), or

(B) $1,000, or

(2) 125 percent of the gross income received by the person described in subsection (a)(1) from the preparation of the appraisal.

(c) Exception. No penalty shall be imposed under subsection (a) if the person establishes to the satisfaction of the Secretary that the value established in the appraisal was more likely than not the proper value.

* * *

§ 6700. Promoting abusive tax shelters, etc.

(a) Imposition of penalty. Any person who –

(1) (A) organizes (or assists in the organization of) –

(i) a partnership or other entity,

(ii) any investment plan or arrangement, or

(iii) any other plan or arrangement, or

(B) participates (directly or indirectly) in the sale of any interest in an entity or plan or arrangement referred to in subparagraph (A), and

(2) makes or furnishes or causes another person to make or furnish (in connection with such organization or sale) –

(A) a statement with respect to the allowability of any deduction or credit, the excludability of any income, or the securing of any other tax benefit by reason of holding an interest in the entity or participating in the plan or arrangement which the person knows or has reason to know is false or fraudulent as to any material matter, or

(B) a gross valuation overstatement as to any material matter, shall pay, with respect to each activity described in paragraph (1), a penalty equal to the $1,000 or, if the person establishes that it is lesser, 100 percent of the gross income derived (or to be derived) by such person from such activity. For purposes of the preceding sentence, activities described in paragraph (1)(A) with respect to each entity or arrangement shall be treated as a separate activity and participation in each sale described in paragraph (1)(B) shall be so treated. Notwithstanding the first sentence, if an activity with respect to which a penalty imposed under this subsection involves a statement described in paragraph (2)(A), the amount of the penalty shall be equal to 50 percent of the gross income derived (or to be derived) from such activity by the person on which the penalty is imposed.

(b) Rules relating to penalty for gross valuation overstatements.

(1) Gross valuation overstatement defined. For purposes of this section, the term 'gross valuation overstatement' means any statement as to the value of any property or services if –

(A) the value so stated exceeds 200 percent of the amount determined to be the correct valuation, and

(B) the value of such property or services is directly related to the amount of any deduction or credit allowable under chapter 1 to any participant.

(2) Authority to waive. The Secretary may waive all or any part of the penalty provided by subsection (a) with respect to any gross valuation overstatement on a showing that there was a reasonable basis for the valuation and that such valuation was made in good faith.

(c) Penalty in addition to other penalties. The penalty imposed by this section shall be in addition to any other penalty provided by law.

* * *

§ 6702. Frivolous tax submissions.

(a) Civil penalty for frivolous tax returns. A person shall pay a penalty of $5,000 if –

(1) such person files what purports to be a return of a tax imposed by this title but which –

(A) does not contain information on which the substantial correctness of the self-assessment may be judged, or

(B) contains information that on its face indicates that the self-assessment is substantially incorrect, and

(2) the conduct referred to in paragraph (1) –

(A) is based on a position which the Secretary has identified as frivolous under subsection (c), or

(B) reflects a desire to delay or impede the administration of Federal tax laws.

(b) Civil penalty for specified frivolous submissions.

(1) Imposition of penalty. Except as provided in paragraph (3), any person who submits a specified frivolous submission shall pay a penalty of $5,000.

(2) Specified frivolous submission. For purposes of this section –

(A) Specified frivolous submission. The term "specified frivolous submission" means a specified submission if any portion of such submission –

(i) is based on a position which the Secretary has identified as frivolous under subsection (c), or

(ii) reflects a desire to delay or impede the administration of Federal tax laws.

(B) Specified submission. The term "specified submission" means –

(i) a request for a hearing under –

(I) section 6320 (relating to notice and opportunity for hearing upon filing of notice of lien), or

(II) section 6330 (relating to notice and opportunity for hearing before levy), and

(ii) an application under –

(I) section 6159 (relating to agreements for payment of tax liability in installments),

(II) section 7122 (relating to compromises), or

(III) section 7811 (relating to taxpayer assistance orders).

(3) Opportunity to withdraw submission. If the Secretary provides a person with notice that a submission is a specified frivolous submission and such person withdraws such submission within 30 days after such notice, the penalty imposed under paragraph (1) shall not apply with respect to such submission.

* * *

§ 6707. Failure to furnish information regarding reportable transactions.

(a) In general. If a person who is required to file a return under section 6111(a) with respect to any reportable transaction –

(1) fails to file such return on or before the date prescribed therefor, or

(2) files false or incomplete information with the Secretary with respect to such transaction, such person shall pay a penalty with respect to such return in the amount determined under subsection (b).

(b) Amount of penalty.

(1) In general. Except as provided in paragraph (2), the penalty imposed under subsection (a) with respect to any failure shall be $50,000.

(2) Listed transactions. The penalty imposed under subsection (a) with respect to any listed transaction shall be an amount equal to the greater of –

(A) $200,000, or

(B) 50 percent of the gross income derived by such person with respect to aid, assistance, or advice which is provided with respect to the listed transaction before the date the return is filed under section 6111.

Subparagraph (B) shall be applied by substituting "75 percent" for "50 percent" in the case of an intentional failure or act described in subsection (a).

(c) Rescission authority. The provisions of section 6707A(d) (relating to authority of Commissioner to rescind penalty) shall apply to any penalty imposed under this section.

(d) Reportable and listed transactions. For purposes of this section, the terms "reportable transaction" and "listed transaction" have the respective meanings given to such terms by section 6707A(c).

§ 6707A. Penalty for failure to include reportable transaction information with return.

(a) Imposition of penalty. Any person who fails to include on any return or statement any information with respect to a reportable transaction which is required under section 6011 to be included with such return or statement shall pay a penalty in the amount determined under subsection (b).

(b) Amount of penalty.

(1) In general. Except as otherwise provided in this subsection, the amount of the penalty under subsection (a) with respect to any reportable transaction shall be 75 percent of the decrease in tax shown on the return as a result of such transaction (or which would have resulted from such transaction if such transaction were respected for Federal tax purposes).

(2) Maximum penalty. The amount of the penalty under subsection (a) with respect to any reportable transaction shall not exceed –

(A) in the case of a listed transaction, $200,000 ($100,000 in the case of a natural person), or

(B) in the case of any other reportable transaction, $50,000 ($10,000 in the case of a natural person).

(3) Minimum penalty. The amount of the penalty under subsection (a) with respect to any transaction shall not be less than $10,000 ($5,000 in the case of a natural person).

(c) Definitions. For purposes of this section:

(1) Reportable transaction. The term "reportable transaction" means any transaction with respect to which information is required to be included with a return or statement because, as determined under regulations prescribed under section 6011, such transaction is of a type which the Secretary determines as having a potential for tax avoidance or evasion.

(2) Listed transaction. The term "listed transaction" means a reportable transaction which is the same as, or substantially similar to, a transaction specifically identified by the Secretary as a tax avoidance transaction for purposes of section 6011.

* * *

§ 6708. Failure to maintain lists of advisees with respect to reportable transactions.

(a) Imposition of penalty.

(1) In general. If any person who is required to maintain a list under section 6112(a) fails to make such list available upon written request to the Secretary in accordance with section 6112(b) within 20 business days after the date of such request, such person shall pay a penalty of $10,000 for each day of such failure after such 20th day.

(2) Reasonable cause exception. No penalty shall be imposed by paragraph (1) with respect to the failure on any day if such failure is due to reasonable cause.
(b) Penalty in addition to other penalties. The penalty imposed by this section shall be in addition to any other penalty provided by law.

* * *

§ 6721. Failure to file correct information returns.

(a) Imposition of penalty.

(1) In general. In the case of a failure described in paragraph (2) by any person with respect to an information return, such person shall pay a penalty of $100 for each return with respect to which such a failure occurs, but the total amount imposed on such person for all such failures during any calendar year shall not exceed $1,500,000.

(2) Failures subject to penalty. For purposes of paragraph (1), the failures described in this paragraph are –

(A) any failure to file an information return with the Secretary on or before the required filing date, and

(B) any failure to include all of the information required to be shown on the return or the inclusion of incorrect information.

(b) Reduction where correction in specified period.

(1) Correction within 30 days. If any failure described in subsection (a)(2) is corrected on or before the day 30 days after the required filing date –

(A) the penalty imposed by subsection (a) shall be $30 in lieu of $100, and

(B) the total amount imposed on the person for all such failures during any calendar year which are so corrected shall not exceed $250,000.

(2) Failures corrected on or before August 1. If any failure described in subsection (a)(2) is corrected after the 30th day referred to in paragraph (1) but on or before August 1 of the calendar year in which the required filing date occur –

(A) the penalty imposed by subsection (a) shall be $60 in lieu of $100, and

(B) the total amount imposed on the person for all such failures during the calendar year which are so corrected shall not exceed $500,000.

(c) Exception for de minimis failures to include all required information.

(1) In general. If –

(A) an information return is filed with the Secretary,

(B) there is a failure described in subsection (a)(2)(B) (determined after the application of section 6724(a)) with respect to such return, and

(C) such failure is corrected on or before August 1 of the calendar year in which the required filing date occurs, for purposes of this section, such return shall be treated as having been filed with all of the correct required information.

(2) Limitation. The number of information returns to which paragraph (1) applies for any calendar year shall not exceed the greater of –

(A) 10, or

(B) one-half of 1 percent of the total number of information returns required to be filed by the person during the calendar year.

* * *

§ 6722. Failure to furnish correct payee statements.

(a) Imposition of penalty.

(1) General rule. In the case of each failure described in paragraph (2) by any person with respect to a payee statement, such person shall pay a penalty of $100 for each statement with respect to which such a failure occurs, but the total amount imposed on such person for all such failures during any calendar year shall not exceed $1,500,000.

(2) Failures subject to penalty. For purposes of paragraph (1), the failures described in this paragraph are –

(A) any failure to furnish a payee statement on or before the date prescribed therefor to the person to whom such statement is required to be furnished, and

(B) any failure to include all of the information required to be shown on a payee statement or the inclusion of incorrect information.

(b) Reduction where correction in specified period.

(1) Correction within 30 days. If any failure described in subsection (a)(2) is corrected on or before the day 30 days after the required filing date –

(A) the penalty imposed by subsection (a) shall be $30 in lieu of $100, and

(B) the total amount imposed on the person for all such failures during any calendar year which are so corrected shall not exceed $250,000.

(2) Failures corrected on or before August 1. If any failure described in subsection (a)(2) is corrected after the 30th day referred to in paragraph (1) but on or before August 1 of the calendar year in which the required filing date occurs –

(A) the penalty imposed by subsection (a) shall be $60 in lieu of $100, and

(B) the total amount imposed on the person for all such failures during the calendar year which are so corrected shall not exceed $500,000.

(c) Exception for de minimis failures.

(1) In general. If –

(A) a payee statement is furnished to the person to whom such statement is required to be furnished,

(B) there is a failure described in subsection (a)(2)(B) (determined after the application of section 6724(a)) with respect to such statement, and

(C) such failure is corrected on or before August 1 of the calendar year in which the required filing date occurs, for purposes of this section, such statement shall be treated as having been furnished with all of the correct required information.

(2) Limitation. The number of payee statements to which paragraph (1) applies for any calendar year shall not exceed the greater of –

(A) 10, or

(B) one-half of 1 percent of the total number of payee statements required to be filed by the person during the calendar year.

* * *

§ 6724. Waiver; definitions and special rules.

(a) Reasonable cause waiver. No penalty shall be imposed under this part with respect to any failure if it is shown that such failure is due to reasonable cause and not to willful neglect.

(b) Payment of penalty. Any penalty imposed by this part shall be paid on notice and demand by the Secretary and in the same manner as tax.

* * *

§ 6851. Termination assessments of income tax.

(a) Authority for making.

(1) In general. If the Secretary finds that a taxpayer designs quickly to depart from the United States or to remove his property therefrom, or to conceal himself or his property therein, or to do any other act (including in the case of a corporation distributing all or a part of its assets in liquidation or otherwise) tending to prejudice or to render wholly or partially ineffectual proceedings to collect the income tax for the current or the immediately preceding taxable year unless such proceeding be brought without delay, the Secretary shall immediately make a determination of tax for the current taxable year or for the preceding taxable year, or both, as the case may be, and notwithstanding any other provision of law, such tax shall become immediately due and payable. The Secretary shall immediately assess the amount of the tax so determined (together with all interest, additional amounts, and additions to the tax provided by law) for the current taxable year or such preceding taxable year, or both, as the case may be, and shall cause notice of such determination and assessment to be given the taxpayer, together with a demand for immediate payment of such tax.

* * *

(4) This section inapplicable where section 6861 applies. This section shall not authorize any assessment of tax for the preceding taxable year which is made after the due date of the taxpayer's return for such taxable year (determined with regard to any extensions).

(b) Notice of deficiency. If an assessment of tax is made under the authority of subsection (a), the Secretary shall mail a notice under section 6212(a) for the taxpayer's full taxable year (determined without regard to any action taken under subsection (a)) with respect to which such assessment was made within 60 days after the later of (i) the due date of the taxpayer's return for such taxable year (determined with regard to any extensions), or (ii) the date such taxpayer files such return. Such deficiency may be in an amount greater or less than the amount assessed under subsection (a).

* * *

§ 6861. Jeopardy assessments of income, estate, gift, and certain excise taxes.

(a) Authority for making. If the Secretary believes that the assessment or collection of a deficiency, as defined in section 6211, will be jeopardized by delay, he shall, notwithstanding the provisions of section 6213(a), immediately assess such deficiency (together with all interest, additional amounts, and additions to the tax provided for by law), and notice and demand shall be made by the Secretary for the payment thereof.

(b) Deficiency letters. If the jeopardy assessment is made before any notice in respect of the tax to which the jeopardy assessment relates has been mailed under section 6212(a), then the

Secretary shall mail a notice under such subsection within 60 days after the making of the assessment.

* * *

§ 7121. Closing agreements.

(a) Authorization. The Secretary is authorized to enter into an agreement in writing with any person relating to the liability of such person (or of the person or estate for whom he acts) in respect of any internal revenue tax for any taxable period.

(b) Finality. If such agreement is approved by the Secretary (within such time as may be stated in such agreement, or later agreed to) such agreement shall be final and conclusive, and, except upon a showing of fraud or malfeasance, or misrepresentation of a material fact –

    (1) the case shall not be reopened as to the matters agreed upon or the agreement modified by any officer, employee, or agent of the United States, and

    (2) in any suit, action, or proceeding, such agreement, or any determination, assessment, collection, payment, abatement, refund, or credit made in accordance therewith, shall not be annulled, modified, set aside, or disregarded.

§ 7122. Compromises.

(a) Authorization. The Secretary may compromise any civil or criminal case arising under the internal revenue laws prior to reference to the Department of Justice for prosecution or defense; and the Attorney General or his delegate may compromise any such case after reference to the Department of Justice for prosecution or defense.

(b) Record. Whenever a compromise is made by the Secretary in any case, there shall be placed on file in the office of the Secretary the opinion of the General Counsel for the Department of the Treasury or his delegate, with his reasons therefor, with a statement of –

    (1) The amount of tax assessed,

    (2) The amount of interest, additional amount, addition to the tax, or assessable penalty, imposed by law on the person against whom the tax is assessed, and

    (3) The amount actually paid in accordance with the terms of the compromise.

Notwithstanding the foregoing provisions of this subsection, no such opinion shall be required with respect to the compromise of any civil case in which the unpaid amount of tax assessed (including any interest, additional amount, addition to the tax, or assessable penalty) is less than $50,000. However, such compromise shall be subject to continuing quality review by the Secretary.

(c) Rules for submission of offers-in-compromise.

    (1) Partial payment required with submission.

        (A) Lump-sum offers.

(i) In general. The submission of any lump-sum offer-in-compromise shall be accompanied by the payment of 20 percent of the amount of such offer.

(ii) Lump-sum offer-in-compromise. For purposes of this section, the term 'lump-sum offer-in-compromise' means any offer of payments made in 5 or fewer installments.

(B) Periodic payment offers.

(i) In general. The submission of any periodic payment offer-in-compromise shall be accompanied by the payment of the amount of the first proposed installment.

(ii) Failure to make installment during pendency of offer. Any failure to make an installment (other than the first installment) due under such offer-in-compromise during the period such offer is being evaluated by the Secretary may be treated by the Secretary as a withdrawal of such offer-in-compromise.

(2) Rules of application.

(A) Use of payment. The application of any payment made under this subsection to the assessed tax or other amounts imposed under this title with respect to such tax may be specified by the taxpayer.

(B) Application of user fee. In the case of any assessed tax or other amounts imposed under this title with respect to such tax which is the subject of an offer-in-compromise to which this subsection applies, such tax or other amounts shall be reduced by any user fee imposed under this title with respect to such offer-in-compromise.

(C) Waiver authority. The Secretary may issue regulations waiving any payment required under paragraph (1) in a manner consistent with the practices established in accordance with the requirements under subsection (d)(3).

(d) Standards for evaluation of offers.

(1) In general. The Secretary shall prescribe guidelines for officers and employees of the Internal Revenue Service to determine whether an offer-in-compromise is adequate and should be accepted to resolve a dispute.

(2) Allowances for basic living expenses.

(A) In general. In prescribing guidelines under paragraph (1), the Secretary shall develop and publish schedules of national and local allowances designed to provide that taxpayers entering into a compromise have an adequate means to provide for basic living expenses.

(B) Use of schedules. The guidelines shall provide that officers and employees of the Internal Revenue Service shall determine, on the basis of the facts and circumstances of each taxpayer, whether the use of the schedules published under subparagraph (A) is appropriate and shall not use the schedules to the extent such use would result in the taxpayer not having adequate means to provide for basic living expenses.

(3) Special rules relating to treatment of offers. The guidelines under paragraph (1) shall provide that –

(A) an officer or employee of the Internal Revenue Service shall not reject an offer-in-compromise from a low-income taxpayer solely on the basis of the amount of the offer,

(B) in the case of an offer-in-compromise which relates only to issues of liability of the taxpayer –

(i) such offer shall not be rejected solely because the Secretary is unable to locate the taxpayer's return or return information for verification of such liability; and

(ii) the taxpayer shall not be required to provide a financial statement, and

(C) any offer-in-compromise which does not meet the requirements of subparagraph (A)(i) or (B)(i), as the case may be, of subsection (c)(1) may be returned to the taxpayer as unprocessable.

(e) Administrative review. The Secretary shall establish procedures –

(1) for an independent administrative review of any rejection of a proposed offer-in-compromise or installment agreement made by a taxpayer under this section or section 6159 before such rejection is communicated to the taxpayer; and

(2) which allow a taxpayer to appeal any rejection of such offer or agreement to the Internal Revenue Service Office of Appeals.

(f) Deemed acceptance of offer not rejected within certain period. Any offer-in-compromise submitted under this section shall be deemed to be accepted by the Secretary if such offer is not rejected by the Secretary before the date which is 24 months after the date of the submission of such offer. For purposes of the preceding sentence, any period during which any tax liability which is the subject of such offer-in-compromise is in dispute in any judicial proceeding shall not be taken into account in determining the expiration of the 24-month period.

[(g)](f) Frivolous submissions, etc. Notwithstanding any other provision of this section, if the Secretary determines that any portion of an application for an offer-in-compromise or installment agreement submitted under this section or section 6159 meets the requirement of clause (i) or (ii) of section 6702(b)(2)(A), then the Secretary may treat such portion as if it were never submitted and such portion shall not be subject to any further administrative or judicial review.

§ 7123. Appeals dispute resolution procedures.

(a) Early referral to appeals procedures. The Secretary shall prescribe procedures by which any taxpayer may request early referral of 1 or more unresolved issues from the examination or collection division to the Internal Revenue Service Office of Appeals.

(b) Alternative dispute resolution procedures.

(1) Mediation. The Secretary shall prescribe procedures under which a taxpayer or the Internal Revenue Service Office of Appeals may request non-binding mediation on any issue unresolved at the conclusion of –

(A) appeals procedures; or

(B) unsuccessful attempts to enter into a closing agreement under section 7121 or a compromise under section 7122.

(2) Arbitration. The Secretary shall establish a pilot program under which a taxpayer and the Internal Revenue Service Office of Appeals may jointly request binding arbitration on any issue unresolved at the conclusion of –

    (A) appeals procedures; or

    (B) unsuccessful attempts to enter into a closing agreement under section 7121 or a compromise under section 7122.

§ 7210. Failure to obey summons.

Any person who, being duly summoned to appear to testify, or to appear and produce books, accounts, records, memoranda, or other papers, as required under sections 6420(e)(2), 6421(g)(2), 6427(j)(2), 7602, 7603, and 7604(b), neglects to appear or to produce such books, accounts, records, memoranda, or other papers, shall, upon conviction thereof, be fined not more than $1,000, or imprisoned not more than 1 year, or both, together with costs of prosecution.

* * *

§ 7213. Unauthorized disclosure of information.

(a) Returns and return information.

    (1) Federal employees and other persons. It shall be unlawful for any officer or employee of the United States or any person described in section 6103(n) (or an officer or employee of any such person), or any former officer or employee, willfully to disclose to any person, except as authorized in this title, any return or return information (as defined in section 6103(b)). Any violation of this paragraph shall be a felony punishable upon conviction by a fine in any amount not exceeding $5,000, or imprisonment of not more than 5 years, or both, together with the costs of prosecution, and if such offense is committed by any officer or employee of the United States, he shall, in addition to any other punishment, be dismissed from office or discharged from employment upon conviction for such offense.

    (2) State and other employees. It shall be unlawful for any person (not described in paragraph (1)) willfully to disclose to any person, except as authorized in this title, any return or return information (as defined in section 6103(b)) acquired by him or another person under subsection (d), (i)(3)(B)(i) or (7)(A)(ii), (l)(6), (7), (8), (9), (10), (12), (15), (16), (19), (20), or (21) or (m)(2), (4), (5), (6), or (7) of section 6103 or under section 6104(c). Any violation of this paragraph shall be a felony punishable by a fine in any amount not exceeding $5,000, or imprisonment of not more than 5 years, or both, together with the costs of prosecution.

    (3) Other persons. It shall be unlawful for any person to whom any return or return information (as defined in section 6103(b)) is disclosed in a manner unauthorized by this title thereafter willfully to print or publish in any manner not provided by law any such return or return information. Any violation of this paragraph shall be a felony punishable by a fine in any amount not exceeding $5,000, or imprisonment of not more than 5 years, or both, together with the costs of prosecution.

* * *

§ 7401. Authorization.

No civil action for the collection or recovery of taxes, or of any fine, penalty, or forfeiture, shall be commenced unless the Secretary authorizes or sanctions the proceedings and the Attorney General or his delegate directs that the action be commenced.

§ 7402. Jurisdiction of district courts.

* * *

(b) To enforce summons. If any person is summoned under the internal revenue laws to appear, to testify, or to produce books, papers, or other data, the district court of the United States for the district in which such person resides or may be found shall have jurisdiction by appropriate process to compel such attendance, testimony, or production of books, papers, or other data.

* * *

§ 7403. Action to enforce lien or to subject property to payment of tax.

(a) Filing. In any case where there has been a refusal or neglect to pay any tax, or to discharge any liability in respect thereof, whether or not levy has been made, the Attorney General or his delegate, at the request of the Secretary, may direct a civil action to be filed in a district court of the United States to enforce the lien of the United States under this title with respect to such tax or liability or to subject any property, of whatever nature, of the delinquent, or in which he has any right, title, or interest, to the payment of such tax or liability. For purposes of the preceding sentence, any acceleration of payment under section 6166(g) shall be treated as a neglect to pay tax.

(b) Parties. All persons having liens upon or claiming any interest in the property involved in such action shall be made parties thereto.

(c) Adjudication and decree. The court shall, after the parties have been duly notified of the action, proceed to adjudicate all matters involved therein and finally determine the merits of all claims to and liens upon the property, and, in all cases where a claim or interest of the United States therein is established, may decree a sale of such property, by the proper officer of the court, and a distribution of the proceeds of such sales according to the findings of the court in respect to the interests of the parties and of the United States. If the property is sold to satisfy a first lien held by the United States, the United States may bid at the sale such sum, not exceeding the amount of such lien with expenses of sale, as the Secretary directs.

(d) Receivership. In any such proceeding, at the instance of the United States, the court may appoint a receiver to enforce the lien, or, upon certification by the Secretary during the pendency of such proceedings that it is in the public interest, may appoint a receiver with all the powers of a receiver in equity.

* * *

§ 7405. Action for recovery of erroneous refunds.

(a) Refunds after limitation period. Any portion of a tax imposed by this title, refund of which is erroneously made, within the meaning of section 6514, may be recovered by civil action brought in the name of the United States.

(b) Refunds otherwise erroneous. Any portion of a tax imposed by this title which has been erroneously refunded (if such refund would not be considered as erroneous under section 6514) may be recovered by civil action brought in the name of the United States.

* * *

§ 7421. Prohibition of suits to restrain assessment or collection.

(a) Tax. Except as provided in sections 6015(e), 6212(a) and (c), 6213(a), 6225(b), 6246(b), 6330(e)(1), 6331(i), 6672(c), 6694(c), and 7426(a) and (b)(1), 7429(b), and 7436, no suit for the purpose of restraining the assessment or collection of any tax shall be maintained in any court by any person, whether or not such person is the person against whom such tax was assessed.

(b) Liability of transferee or fiduciary. No suit shall be maintained in any court for the purpose of restraining the assessment or collection (pursuant to the provisions of chapter 71) of –

(1) the amount of the liability, at law or in equity, of a transferee of property of a taxpayer in respect of any internal revenue tax, or

(2) the amount of the liability of a fiduciary under section 3713(b) of title 31, United States Code in respect of any such tax.

§ 7422. Civil actions for refund.

(a) No suit prior to filing claim for refund. No suit or proceeding shall be maintained in any court for the recovery of any internal revenue tax alleged to have been erroneously or illegally assessed or collected, or of any penalty claimed to have been collected without authority, or of any sum alleged to have been excessive or in any manner wrongfully collected, until a claim for refund or credit has been duly filed with the Secretary, according to the provisions of law in that regard, and the regulations of the Secretary established in pursuance thereof.

* * *

(e) Stay of proceedings. If the Secretary prior to the hearing of a suit brought by a taxpayer in a district court or the United States Claims Court [United States Court of Federal Claims] for the recovery of any income tax, estate tax, gift tax, or tax imposed by chapter 41, 42, 43, or 44 (or any penalty relating to such taxes) mails to the taxpayer a notice that a deficiency has been determined in respect of the tax which is the subject matter of taxpayer's suit, the proceedings in taxpayer's suit shall be stayed during the period of time in which the taxpayer may file a petition with the Tax Court for a redetermination of the asserted deficiency, and for 60 days thereafter. If the taxpayer files a petition with the Tax Court, the district court or the United States Claims Court [United States Court of Federal Claims], as the case may be, shall lose jurisdiction of taxpayer's suit to whatever extent jurisdiction is acquired by the Tax Court of the subject matter of taxpayer's suit for refund. If the taxpayer does not file a petition with the Tax Court for a redetermination of the asserted deficiency, the United States may counterclaim in the taxpayer's suit, or intervene in the event of a suit as described in subsection (c) (relating to suits against officers or employees of the United States), within the period of the stay of proceedings notwithstanding that the time for such pleading may have otherwise expired. The taxpayer shall have the burden of proof with respect to the issues raised by such counterclaim or intervention of the United States except as to the issue of whether the taxpayer has been guilty of fraud with intent to evade tax. This subsection shall not apply to a suit by a taxpayer which, prior to the date of enactment of this title [enacted Aug. 16, 1954], is commenced, instituted, or pending in a district court or the United States Claims Court [United States Court of Federal Claims] for the recovery of any income tax, estate tax, or gift tax (or any penalty relating to such taxes).

* * *

§ 7429. Review of jeopardy levy or assessment procedures.

(a) Administrative review.

(1) Administrative review.

(A) Prior approval required. No assessment may be made under section 6851(a), 6852(a), 6861(a), or 6862, and no levy may be made under section 6331(a) less than 30 days after notice and demand for payment is made, unless the Chief Counsel for the Internal Revenue Service (or such Counsel's delegate) personally approves (in writing) such assessment or levy.

(B) Information to taxpayer. Within 5 days after the day on which such an assessment or levy is made, the Secretary shall provide the taxpayer with a written statement of the information upon which the Secretary relied in making such assessment or levy.

(2) Request for review. Within 30 days after the day on which the taxpayer is furnished the written statement described in paragraph (1), or within 30 days after the last day of the period within which such statement is required to be furnished, the taxpayer may request the Secretary to review the action taken.

(3) Redetermination by Secretary. After a request for review is made under paragraph (2), the Secretary shall determine –

(A) whether or not –

(i) the making of the assessment under section 6851, 6861, or 6862, as the case may be, is reasonable under the circumstances, and

(ii) the amount so assessed or demanded as a result of the action taken under section 6851, 6861, or 6862 is appropriate under the circumstances, or

(B) whether or not the levy described in subsection (a)(1) is reasonable under the circumstances.

(b) Judicial review.

(1) Proceedings permitted. Within 90 days after the earlier of –

(A) the day the Secretary notifies the taxpayer of the Secretary's determination described in subsection (a)(3), or

(B) the 16th day after the request described in subsection (a)(2) was made, the taxpayer may bring a civil action against the United States for a determination under this subsection in the court with jurisdiction determined under paragraph (2).

(2) Jurisdiction for determination.

(A) In general. Except as provided in subparagraph (B), the district courts of the United States shall have exclusive jurisdiction over any civil action for a determination under this subsection.

(B) Tax court. If a petition for a redetermination of a deficiency under section 6213(a) has been timely filed with the Tax Court before the making of an assessment or levy that is subject to the review procedures of this section, and 1 or more of the taxes and taxable periods before the Tax Court because of such petition is also included in the written statement that is provided to the taxpayer under subsection (a), then the Tax Court also shall have jurisdiction over any civil action for a determination under this subsection with respect to all the taxes and taxable periods included in such written statement.

(3) Determination by court. Within 20 days after a proceeding is commenced under paragraph (1), the court shall determine –

(A) whether or not –

(i) the making of the assessment under section 6851, 6861, or 6862, as the case may be, is reasonable under the circumstances, and

(ii) the amount so assessed or demanded as a result of the action taken under section 6851, 6861, or 6862 is appropriate under the circumstances, or

(B) whether or not the levy described in subsection (a)(1) is reasonable under the circumstances.

If the court determines that proper service was not made on the United States or on the Secretary, as may be appropriate, within 5 days after the date of the commencement of the proceeding, then the running of the 20-day period set forth in the preceding sentence shall not begin before the day on which proper service was made on the United States or on the Secretary, as may be appropriate.

(4) Order of court. If the court determines that the making of such levy is unreasonable, that the making of such assessment is unreasonable, or that the amount assessed or demanded is inappropriate, then the court may order the Secretary to release such levy, to abate such assessment, to redetermine (in whole or in part) the amount assessed or demanded, or to take such other action as the court finds appropriate.

* * *

§ 7430. Awarding of costs and certain fees.

(a) **In general.** In any administrative or court proceeding which is brought by or against the United States in connection with the determination, collection, or refund of any tax, interest, or penalty under this title, the prevailing party may be awarded a judgment or a settlement for –

(1) reasonable administrative costs incurred in connection with such administrative proceeding within the Internal Revenue Service, and

(2) reasonable litigation costs incurred in connection with such court proceeding.

(b) **Limitations.**

(1) **Requirement that administrative remedies be exhausted.** A judgment for reasonable litigation costs shall not be awarded under subsection (a) in any court proceeding unless the court determines that the prevailing party has exhausted the administrative remedies available to such party within the Internal Revenue Service. Any failure to agree to an extension of the time for the assessment of any tax shall not be taken into account for purposes of determining whether the prevailing party meets the requirements of the preceding sentence.

(2) **Only costs allocable to the United States.** An award under subsection (a) shall be made only for reasonable litigation and administrative costs which are allocable to the United States and not to any other party.

(3) **Costs denied where party prevailing protracts proceedings.** No award for reasonable litigation and administrative costs may be made under subsection (a) with respect to any portion of the administrative or court proceeding during which the prevailing party has unreasonably protracted such proceeding.

(4) **Period for applying to IRS for administrative costs.** An award may be made under subsection (a) by the Internal Revenue Service for reasonable administrative costs only if the prevailing party files an application with the Internal Revenue Service for such costs before the 91st day after the date on which the final decision of the Internal Revenue Service as to the determination of the tax, interest, or penalty is mailed to such party.

(c) **Definitions.** For purposes of this section –

(1) **Reasonable litigation costs.** The term "reasonable litigation costs" includes –

(A) reasonable court costs, and

(B) based upon prevailing market rates for the kind or quality of services furnished –

(i) the reasonable expenses of expert witnesses in connection with a court proceeding, except that no expert witness shall be compensated at a rate in excess of the highest rate of compensation for expert witnesses paid by the United States,

(ii) the reasonable cost of any study, analysis, engineering report, test, or project which is found by the court to be necessary for the preparation of the party's case, and

(iii) reasonable fees paid or incurred for the services of attorneys in connection with the court proceeding, except that such fees shall not be in excess of $125 per hour unless the court determines that a special factor, such as the limited availability of qualified attorneys for such proceeding, the difficulty of the issues presented in the case, or the local availability of tax expertise, justifies a higher rate.

In the case of any calendar year beginning after 1996, the dollar amount referred to in clause (iii) shall be increased by an amount equal to such dollar amount multiplied by the cost-of-living adjustment determined under section 1(f)(3) for such calendar year, by substituting "calendar year 1995" for "calendar year 1992" in subparagraph (B) thereof. If any dollar amount after being increased under the preceding sentence is not a multiple of $10, such dollar amount shall be rounded to the nearest multiple of $10.

(2) Reasonable administrative costs. The term "reasonable administrative costs" means –

(A) any administrative fees or similar charges imposed by the Internal Revenue Service, and

(B) expenses, costs, and fees described in paragraph (1)(B), except that any determination made by the court under clause (ii) or (iii) thereof shall be made by the Internal Revenue Service in cases where the determination under paragraph (4)(C) of the awarding of reasonable administrative costs is made by the Internal Revenue Service.

Such term shall only include costs incurred on or after whichever of the following is the earliest: (i) the date of the receipt by the taxpayer of the notice of the decision of the Internal Revenue Service Office of Appeals; (ii) the date of the notice of deficiency; or (iii) the date on which the first letter of proposed deficiency which allows the taxpayer an opportunity for administrative review in the Internal Revenue Service Office of Appeals is sent.

(3) Attorneys' fees.

(A) In general. For purposes of paragraphs (1) and (2), fees for the services of an individual (whether or not an attorney) who is authorized to practice before the Tax Court or before the Internal Revenue Service shall be treated as fees for the services of an attorney.

(B) Pro bono services. The court may award reasonable attorneys' fees under subsection (a) in excess of the attorneys' fees paid or incurred if such fees are less than the reasonable attorneys' fees because an individual is representing the prevailing party for no fee or for a fee which (taking into account all the facts and circumstances) is no more than a nominal fee. This subparagraph shall apply only if such award is paid to such individual or such individual's employer.

(4) Prevailing party.

(A) In general. The term "prevailing party" means any party in any proceeding to which subsection (a) applies (other than the United States or any creditor of the taxpayer involved) –

(i) which –

(I) has substantially prevailed with respect to the amount in controversy, or

(II) has substantially prevailed with respect to the most significant issue or set of issues presented, and

(ii) which meets the requirements of the 1st sentence of section 2412(d)(1)(B) of title 28, United States Code (as in effect on October 22, 1986) except to the extent differing procedures are established by rule of court and meets the requirements of section 2412(d)(2)(B) of such title 28 (as so in effect).

(B) Exception if United States establishes that its position was substantially justified.

(i) General rule. A party shall not be treated as the prevailing party in a proceeding to which subsection (a) applies if the United States establishes that the position of the United States in the proceeding was substantially justified.

(ii) Presumption of no justification if Internal Revenue Service did not follow certain published guidance. For purposes of clause (i), the position of the United States shall be presumed not to be substantially justified if the Internal Revenue Service did not follow its applicable published guidance in the administrative proceeding. Such presumption may be rebutted.

(iii) Effect of losing on substantially similar issues. In determining for purposes of clause (i) whether the position of the United States was substantially justified, the court shall take into account whether the United States has lost in courts of appeal for other circuits on substantially similar issues.

(iv) Applicable published guidance. For purposes of clause (ii), the term "applicable published guidance" means –

(I) regulations, revenue rulings, revenue procedures, information releases, notices, and announcements, and

(II) any of the following which are issued to the taxpayer: private letter rulings, technical advice memoranda, and determination letters.

(C) Determination as to prevailing party. Any determination under this paragraph as to whether a party is a prevailing party shall be made by agreement of the parties or –

(i) in the case where the final determination with respect to the tax, interest, or penalty is made at the administrative level, by the Internal Revenue Service, or

(ii) in the case where such final determination is made by a court, the court.

(D) Special rules for applying net worth requirement. In applying the requirements of section 2412(d)(2)(B) of title 28, United States Code, for purposes of subparagraph (A)(ii) of this paragraph –

(i) the net worth limitation in clause (i) of such section shall apply to –

(I) an estate but shall be determined as of the date of the decedent's death, and

(II) a trust but shall be determined as of the last day of the taxable year involved in the proceeding, and

(ii) individuals filing a joint return shall be treated as separate individuals for purposes of clause (i) of such section.

(E) Special rules where judgment less than taxpayer's offer.

(i) In general. A party to a court proceeding meeting the requirements of subparagraph (A)(ii) shall be treated as the prevailing party if the liability of the taxpayer pursuant to the judgment in the proceeding (determined without regard to interest) is equal to or less than the liability of the taxpayer which would have been so determined if the United States had accepted a qualified offer of the party under subsection (g).

(ii) Exceptions. This subparagraph shall not apply to –

(I) any judgment issued pursuant to a settlement; or

(II) any proceeding in which the amount of tax liability is not in issue, including any declaratory judgment proceeding, any proceeding to enforce or quash any summons issued pursuant to this title, and any action to restrain disclosure under section 6110(f).

(iii) Special rules. If this subparagraph applies to any court proceeding –

(I) the determination under clause (i) shall be made by reference to the last qualified offer made with respect to the tax liability at issue in the proceeding; and

(II) reasonable administrative and litigation costs shall only include costs incurred on and after the date of such offer.

(iv) Coordination. This subparagraph shall not apply to a party which is a prevailing party under any other provision of this paragraph.

(5) Administrative proceedings. The term "administrative proceeding" means any procedure or other action before the Internal Revenue Service.

(6) Court proceedings. The term "court proceeding" means any civil action brought in a court of the United States (including the Tax Court and the United States Claims Court [United States Court of Federal Claims]).

(7) Position of United States. The term "position of the United States" means –

(A) the position taken by the United States in a judicial proceeding to which subsection (a) applies, and

(B) the position taken in an administrative proceeding to which subsection (a) applies as of the earlier of –

(i) the date of the receipt by the taxpayer of the notice of the decision of the Internal Revenue Service Office of Appeals, or

(ii) the date of the notice of deficiency.

* * *

(f) Right of appeal.

(1) Court proceedings. An order granting or denying (in whole or in part) an award for reasonable litigation or administrative costs under subsection (a) in a court proceeding, may be incorporated as a part of the decision or judgment in the court proceeding and shall be subject to appeal in the same manner as the decision or judgment.

(2) Administrative proceedings. A decision granting or denying (in whole or in part) an award for reasonable administrative costs under subsection (a) by the Internal Revenue Service shall be subject to the filing of a petition for review with the Tax Court under rules similar to the rules under section 7463 (without regard to the amount in dispute). If the Secretary sends by certified or registered mail a notice of such decision to the petitioner, no proceeding in the Tax Court may be initiated under this paragraph unless such petition is filed before the 91st day after the date of such mailing.

(3) Appeal of Tax Court decision. An order of the Tax Court disposing of a petition under paragraph (2) shall be reviewable in the same manner as a decision of the Tax Court, but only with respect to the matters determined in such order.

* * *

§7431. Civil damages for unauthorized inspection or disclosure of returns and return information.

(a) In general.

(1) Inspection or disclosure by employee of United States. If any officer or employee of the United States knowingly, or by reason of negligence, inspects or discloses any return or return information with respect to a taxpayer in violation of any provision of section 6103, such taxpayer may bring a civil action for damages against the United States in a district court of the United States.

(2) Inspection or disclosure by a person who is not an employee of United States. If any person who is not an officer or employee of the United States knowingly, or by reason of negligence, inspects or discloses any return or return information with respect to a taxpayer in violation of any provision of section 6103 or in violation of section 6104(c), such taxpayer may bring a civil action for damages against such person in a district court of the United States.

(b) Exceptions. No liability shall arise under this section with respect to any inspection or disclosure –

(1) which results from a good faith, but erroneous, interpretation of section 6103, or

(2) which is requested by the taxpayer.

(c) Damages. In any action brought under subsection (a), upon a finding of liability on the part of the defendant, the defendant shall be liable to the plaintiff in an amount equal to the sum of –

(1) the greater of –

(A) $1,000 for each act of unauthorized inspection or disclosure of a return or return information with respect to which such defendant is found liable, or

(B) the sum of –

(i) the actual damages sustained by the plaintiff as a result of such unauthorized inspection or disclosure, plus

(ii) in the case of a willful inspection or disclosure or an inspection or disclosure which is the result of gross negligence, punitive damages, plus

(2) the costs of the action, plus

(3) in the case of a plaintiff which is described in section 7430(c)(4)(A)(ii), reasonable attorney's fees, except that if the defendant is the United States, reasonable attorney's fees may be awarded only if the plaintiff is the prevailing party (as determined under section 7430(c)(4)).

(d) **Period for bringing action.** Notwithstanding any other provision of law, an action to enforce any liability created under this section may be brought, without regard to the amount in controversy, at any time within 2 years after the date of discovery by the plaintiff of the unauthorized inspection or disclosure.

(e) **Notification of unlawful inspection and disclosure.** If any person is criminally charged by indictment or information with inspection or disclosure of a taxpayer's return or return information in violation of –

(1) paragraph (1) or (2) of section 7213(a),

(2) section 7213A(a), or

(3) subparagraph (B) of section 1030(a)(2) of title 18, United States Code,
the Secretary shall notify such taxpayer as soon as practicable of such inspection or disclosure.

* * *

§ 7441. Status.

There is hereby established, under article I of the Constitution of the United States, a court of record to be known as the United States Tax Court. The members of the Tax Court shall be the chief judge and the judges of the Tax Court.

* * *

§ 7443. Membership.

(a) **Number.** The Tax Court shall be composed of 19 members.

(b) **Appointment.** Judges of the Tax Court shall be appointed by the President, by and with the advice and consent of the Senate, solely on the grounds of fitness to perform the duties of the office.

(c) **Salary.**

(1) Each judge shall receive salary at the same rate and in the same installments as judges of the district courts of the United States.

(2) For rate of salary and frequency of installment see section 135, title 28, United States Code, and section 5505, title 5, United States Code.

(d) Expenses for travel and subsistence. Judges of the Tax Court shall receive necessary traveling expenses, and expenses actually incurred for subsistence while traveling on duty and away from their designated stations, subject to the same limitations in amount as are now or may hereafter be applicable to the United States Court of International Trade.

(e) Term of office. The term of office of any judge of the Tax Court shall expire 15 years after he takes office.

* * *

§ 7443A. Special trial judges.

(a) Appointment. The chief judge may, from time to time, appoint special trial judges who shall proceed under such rules and regulations as may be promulgated by the Tax Court.

(b) Proceedings which may be assigned to special trial judges. The chief judge may assign

(1) any declaratory judgment proceeding,

(2) any proceeding under section 7463,

(3) any proceeding where neither the amount of the deficiency placed in dispute (within the meaning of section 7463) nor the amount of any claimed overpayment exceeds $50,000,

(4) any proceeding under section 6320 or 6330,

(5) any proceeding under section 7436(c),

(6) any proceeding under section 7623(b)(4), and

(7) any other proceeding which the chief judge may designate, to be heard by the special trial judges of the court.

(c) Authority to make court decision. The court may authorize a special trial judge to make the decision of the court with respect to any proceeding described in paragraph (1), (2), (3), (4), or (5) of subsection (b), subject to such conditions and review as the court may provide.

* * *

§ 7452. Representation of parties.

The Secretary shall be represented by the Chief Counsel for the Internal Revenue Service or his delegate in the same manner before the Tax Court as he has heretofore been represented in proceedings before such Court. The taxpayer shall continue to be represented in accordance with the rules of practice prescribed by the Court. No qualified person shall be denied admission to practice before the Tax Court because of his failure to be a member of any profession or calling.

§ 7453. Rules of practice, procedure, and evidence.

Except in the case of proceedings conducted under section 7436(c) or 7463, the proceedings of the Tax Court and its divisions shall be conducted in accordance with such rules of practice and procedure (other than rules of evidence) as the Tax Court may prescribe and in accordance with the rules of evidence applicable in trials without a jury in the United States District Court of the District of Columbia.

§ 7454. Burden of proof in fraud, foundation manager, and transferee cases.

(a) Fraud. In any proceeding involving the issue whether the petitioner has been guilty of fraud with intent to evade tax, the burden of proof in respect of such issue shall be upon the Secretary.

* * *

§ 7463. Disputes involving $50,000 or less.

(a) In general. In the case of any petition filed with the Tax Court for a redetermination of a deficiency where neither the amount of the deficiency placed in dispute, nor the amount of any claimed overpayment, exceeds –

(1) $50,000 for any one taxable year, in the case of the taxes imposed by subtitle A,

(2) $50,000, in the case of the tax imposed by chapter 11,

(3) $50,000 for any one calendar year, in the case of the tax imposed by chapter 12, or

(4) $50,000 for any 1 taxable period (or, if there is no taxable period, taxable event) in the case of any tax imposed by subtitle D which is described in section 6212(a) (relating to a notice of deficiency), at the option of the taxpayer concurred in by the Tax Court or a division thereof before the hearing of the case, proceedings in the case shall be conducted under this section. Notwithstanding the provisions of section 7453, such proceedings shall be conducted in accordance with such rules of evidence, practice, and procedure as the Tax Court may prescribe. A decision, together with a brief summary of the reasons therefor, in any such case shall satisfy the requirements of sections 7459(b) and 7460.

(b) Finality of decisions. A decision entered in any case in which the proceedings are conducted under this section shall not be reviewed in any other court and shall not be treated as a precedent for any other case.

* * *

(d) Discontinuance of proceedings. At any time before a decision entered in a case in which the proceedings are conducted under this section becomes final, the taxpayer or the Secretary may request that further proceedings under this section in such case be discontinued. The Tax Court, or the division thereof hearing such case, may, if it finds that (1) there are reasonable grounds for believing that the amount of the deficiency placed in dispute, or the amount of an overpayment, exceeds the applicable jurisdictional amount described in subsection (a), and (2) the amount of such excess is large enough to justify granting such request, discontinue further proceedings in such case under this section. Upon any such discontinuance, proceedings in such case shall be conducted in the same manner as cases to which the provisions of sections 6214(a) and 6512(b) apply.

* * *

(f) Additional cases in which proceedings may be conducted under this section. At the option of the taxpayer concurred in by the Tax Court or a division thereof before the hearing of the case, proceedings may be conducted under this section (in the same manner as a case described in subsection (a)) in the case of –

(1) a petition to the Tax Court under section 6015(e) in which the amount of relief sought does not exceed $50,000, and

(2) an appeal under section 6330(d)(1)(A) to the Tax Court of a determination in which the unpaid tax does not exceed $50,000.

* * *

§ 7481. Date when Tax Court decision becomes final.

(a) Reviewable decisions. Except as provided in subsections (b), (c), and (d), the decision of the Tax Court shall become final –

(1) Timely notice of appeal not filed. Upon the expiration of the time allowed for filing a notice of appeal, if no such notice has been duly filed within such time; or

(2) Decision affirmed or appeal dismissed.

(A) Petition for certiorari not filed on time. Upon the expiration of the time allowed for filing a petition for certiorari, if the decision of the Tax Court has been affirmed or the appeal dismissed by the United States Court of Appeals and no petition for certiorari has been duly filed; or

(B) Petition for certiorari denied. Upon the denial of a petition for certiorari, if the decision of the Tax Court has been affirmed or the appeal dismissed by the United States Court of Appeals; or

(C) After mandate of Supreme Court. Upon the expiration of 30 days from the date of issuance of the mandate of the Supreme Court, if such Court directs that the decision of the Tax Court be affirmed or the appeal dismissed.

(3) Decision modified or reversed.

(A) Upon mandate of Supreme Court. If the Supreme Court directs that the decision of the Tax Court be modified or reversed, the decision of the Tax Court rendered in accordance with the mandate of the Supreme Court shall become final upon the expiration of 30 days from the time it was rendered, unless within such 30 days either the Secretary or the taxpayer has instituted proceedings to have such decision corrected to accord with the mandate, in which event the decision of the Tax Court shall become final when so corrected.

(B) Upon mandate of the Court of Appeals. If the decision of the Tax Court is modified or reversed by the United States Court of Appeals, and if –

(i) the time allowed for filing a petition for certiorari has expired and no such petition has been duly filed, or

(ii) the petition for certiorari has been denied, or

(iii) the decision of the United States Court of Appeals has been affirmed by the Supreme Court, then the decision of the Tax Court rendered in accordance with the mandate of the United States Court of Appeals shall become final on the expiration of 30 days from the time such decision of the Tax Court was rendered, unless within such 30 days either the Secretary or the taxpayer has instituted proceedings to have such decision corrected so that it will accord with the mandate, in which event the decision of the Tax Court shall become final when so corrected.

(4) Rehearing. If the Supreme Court orders a rehearing; or if the case is remanded by the United States Court of Appeals to the Tax Court for a rehearing, and if –

(A) the time allowed for filing a petition for certiorari has expired and no such petition has been duly filed, or

(B) the petition for certiorari has been denied, or

(C) the decision of the United States Court of Appeals has been affirmed by the Supreme Court, then the decision of the Tax Court rendered upon such rehearing shall become final in the same manner as though no prior decision of the Tax Court has been rendered.

(5) Definition of "mandate." As used in this section, the term "mandate", in case a mandate has been recalled prior to the expiration of 30 days from the date of issuance thereof, means the final mandate.

* * *

(c) Jurisdiction over interest determinations.

(1) In general. Notwithstanding subsection (a), if, within 1 year after the date the decision of the Tax Court becomes final under subsection (a) in a case to which this subsection applies, the taxpayer files a motion in the Tax Court for a redetermination of the amount of interest involved, then the Tax Court may reopen the case solely to determine whether the taxpayer has made an overpayment of such interest or the Secretary has made an underpayment of such interest and the amount thereof.

(2) Cases to which this subsection applies. This subsection shall apply where –

(A) (i) an assessment has been made by the Secretary under section 6215 which includes interest as imposed by this title, and

(ii) the taxpayer has paid the entire amount of the deficiency plus interest claimed by the Secretary, and

(B) the Tax Court finds under section 6512(b) that the taxpayer has made an overpayment.

(3) Special rules. If the Tax Court determines under this subsection that the taxpayer has made an overpayment of interest or that the Secretary has made an underpayment of interest, then that determination shall be treated under section 6512(b)(1) as a determination of an overpayment of tax. An order of the Tax Court redetermining interest, when entered upon the records of the court, shall be reviewable in the same manner as a decision of the Tax Court.

* * *

§ 7482. Courts of review.

(a) Jurisdiction.

(1) In general. The United States Courts of Appeals (other than the United States Court of Appeals for the Federal Circuit) shall have exclusive jurisdiction to review the decisions of the Tax Court, except as provided in section 1254 of Title 28 of the United States Code, in the same manner and to the same extent as decisions of the district courts in civil actions tried without a jury; and the judgment of any such court shall be final, except that it shall be subject to review by the Supreme Court of the United States upon certiorari, in the manner provided in section 1254 of Title 28 of the United States Code.

(2) Interlocutory orders.

(A) In general. When any judge of the Tax Court includes in an interlocutory order a statement that a controlling question of law is involved with respect to which there is a substantial ground for difference of opinion and that an immediate appeal from that order may materially advance the ultimate termination of the litigation, the United States Court of Appeals may, in its discretion, permit an appeal to be taken from such order, if application is made to it within 10 days after the entry of such order. Neither the application for nor the granting of an appeal under this paragraph shall stay proceedings in the Tax Court, unless a stay is ordered by a judge of the Tax Court or by the United States Court of Appeals which has jurisdiction of the appeal or a judge of that court.

(B) Order treated as tax court decision. For purposes of subsections (b) and (c), an order described in this paragraph shall be treated as a decision of the Tax Court.

(C) Venue for review of subsequent proceedings. If a United States Court of Appeals permits an appeal to be taken from an order described in subparagraph (A), except as provided in subsection (b)(2), any subsequent review of the decision of the Tax Court in the proceeding shall be made by such Court of Appeals.

(3) Certain orders entered under section 6213(a). An order of the Tax Court which is entered under authority of section 6213(a) and which resolves a proceeding to restrain assessment or collection shall be treated as a decision of the Tax Court for purposes of this section and shall be subject to the same review by the United States Court of Appeals as a similar order of a district court.

(b) Venue.

(1) In general. Except as otherwise provided in paragraphs (2) and (3), such decisions may be reviewed by the United States court of appeals for the circuit in which is located –

(A) in the case of a petitioner seeking redetermination of tax liability other than a corporation, the legal residence of the petitioner,

(B) in the case of a corporation seeking redetermination of tax liability, the principal place of business or principal office or agency of the corporation, or, if it has no principal place of business or principal office or agency in any judicial circuit, then the office to which was made the return of the tax in respect of which the liability arises,

(C) in the case of a person seeking a declaratory decision under section 7476, the principal place of business, or principal office or agency of the employer,

(D) in the case of an organization seeking a declaratory decision under section 7428, the principal office or agency of the organization,

(E) in the case of a petition under section 6226, 6228(a), 6247, or 6252, the principal place of business of the partnership, or

(F) in the case of a petition under section 6234(c) –

(i) the legal residence of the petitioner if the petitioner is not a corporation, and

(ii) the place or office applicable under subparagraph (B) if the petitioner is a corporation.

If for any reason no subparagraph of the preceding sentence applies, then such decisions may be reviewed by the Court of Appeals for the District of Columbia. For purposes of this paragraph, the legal residence, principal place of business, or principal office or agency referred to herein shall be determined as of the time the petition seeking redetermination of tax liability was filed with the Tax Court or as of the time the petition seeking a declaratory decision under section 7428 or 7476, or the petition under section 6226, 6228(a), or 6234(c), was filed with the Tax Court.

(2) By agreement. Notwithstanding the provisions of paragraph (1), such decisions may be reviewed by any United States Court of Appeals which may be designated by the Secretary and the taxpayer by stipulation in writing.

(3) Declaratory judgment actions relating to status of certain governmental obligations. In the case of any decision of the Tax Court in a proceeding under section 7478, such decision may only be reviewed by the Court of Appeals for the District of Columbia.

(c) Powers.

(1) To affirm, modify, or reverse. Upon such review, such courts shall have power to affirm or, if the decision of the Tax Court is not in accordance with law, to modify or to reverse the decision of the Tax Court, with or without remanding the case for a rehearing, as justice may require.

* * *

§ 7491. Burden of proof.

(a) Burden shifts where taxpayer produces credible evidence.

(1) General rule. If, in any court proceeding, a taxpayer introduces credible evidence with respect to any factual issue relevant to ascertaining the liability of the taxpayer for any tax imposed by subtitle A or B, the Secretary shall have the burden of proof with respect to such issue.

(2) Limitations. Paragraph (1) shall apply with respect to an issue only if –

(A) the taxpayer has complied with the requirements under this title to substantiate any item;

(B) the taxpayer has maintained all records required under this title and has cooperated with reasonable requests by the Secretary for witnesses, information, documents, meetings, and interviews; and

(C) in the case of a partnership, corporation, or trust, the taxpayer is described in section 7430(c)(4)(A)(ii).

Subparagraph (C) shall not apply to any qualified revocable trust (as defined in section 645(b)(1)) with respect to liability for tax for any taxable year ending after the date of the decedent's death and before the applicable date (as defined in section 645(b)(2)).

(3) Coordination. Paragraph (1) shall not apply to any issue if any other provision of this title provides for a specific burden of proof with respect to such issue.

* * *

(c) Penalties. Notwithstanding any other provision of this title, the Secretary shall have the burden of production in any court proceeding with respect to the liability of any individual for any penalty, addition to tax, or additional amount imposed by this title.

§ 7502. Timely mailing treated as timely filing and paying.

(a) General rule.

(1) Date of delivery. If any return, claim, statement, or other document required to be filed, or any payment required to be made, within a prescribed period or on or before a prescribed date under authority of any provision of the internal revenue laws is, after such period or such date, delivered by United States mail to the agency, officer, or office with which such return, claim, statement, or other document is required to be filed, or to which such payment is required to be made, the date of the United States postmark stamped on the cover in which such return, claim, statement, or other document, or payment, is mailed shall be deemed to be the date of delivery or the date of payment, as the case may be.

(2) Mailing requirements. This subsection shall apply only if –

(A) the postmark date falls within the prescribed period or on or before the prescribed date –

(i) for the filing (including any extension granted for such filing) of the return, claim, statement, or other document, or

(ii) for making the payment (including any extension granted for making such payment), and

(B) the return, claim, statement, or other document, or payment was, within the time prescribed in subparagraph (A), deposited in the mail in the United States in an envelope or other appropriate wrapper, postage prepaid, properly addressed to the agency, officer, or office with which the return, claim, statement, or other document is required to be filed, or to which such payment is required to be made.

(b) Postmarks. This section shall apply in the case of postmarks not made by the United States Postal Service only if and to the extent provided by regulations prescribed by the Secretary.

(c) Registered and certified mailing; electronic filing.

(1) Registered mail. For purposes of this section, if any return, claim, statement, or other document, or payment, is sent by United States registered mail –

(A) such registration shall be prima facie evidence that the return, claim, statement, or other document was delivered to the agency, officer, or office to which addressed; and

(B) the date of registration shall be deemed the postmark date.

(2) Certified mail; electronic filing. The Secretary is authorized to provide by regulations the extent to which the provisions of paragraph (1) with respect to prima facie evidence of delivery and the postmark date shall apply to certified mail and electronic filing.

(d) Exceptions. This section shall not apply with respect to –

(1) the filing of a document in, or the making of a payment to, any court other than the Tax Court,

(2) currency or other medium of payment unless actually received and accounted for, or

(3) returns, claims, statements, or other documents, or payments, which are required under any provision of the internal revenue laws or the regulations thereunder to be delivered by any method other than by mailing.

(e) Mailing of deposits.

(1) Date of deposit. If any deposit required to be made (pursuant to regulations prescribed by the Secretary under section 6302(c)) on or before a prescribed date is, after such date, delivered by the United States mail to the bank, trust company, domestic building and loan association, or credit union authorized to receive such deposit, such deposit shall be deemed received by such bank, trust company, domestic building and loan association, or credit union on the date the deposit was mailed.

(2) Mailing requirements. Paragraph (1) shall apply only if the person required to make the deposit establishes that –

(A) the date of mailing falls on or before the second day before the prescribed date for making the deposit (including any extension of time granted for making such deposit), and

(B) the deposit was, on or before such second day, mailed in the United States in an envelope or other appropriate wrapper, postage prepaid, properly addressed to the bank, trust company, domestic building and loan association, or credit union authorized to receive such deposit.

In applying subsection (c) for purposes of this subsection, the term "payment" includes "deposit", and the reference to the postmark date refers to the date of mailing.

(3) No application to certain deposits. Paragraph (1) shall not apply with respect to any deposit of $20,000 or more by any person who is required to deposit any tax more than once a month.

(f) Treatment of private delivery services.

(1) In general. Any reference in this section to the United States mail shall be treated as including a reference to any designated delivery service, and any reference in this section to a postmark by the United States Postal Service shall be treated as including a reference to any date recorded or marked as described in paragraph (2)(C) by any designated delivery service.

(2) Designated delivery service. For purposes of this subsection, the term "designated delivery service" means any delivery service provided by a trade or business if such service is designated by the Secretary for purposes of this section. The Secretary may designate a delivery service under the preceding sentence only if the Secretary determines that such service –

(A) is available to the general public,

(B) is at least as timely and reliable on a regular basis as the United States mail,

(C) records electronically to its data base, kept in the regular course of its business, or marks on the cover in which any item referred to in this section is to be delivered, the date on which such item was given to such trade or business for delivery, and

(D) meets such other criteria as the Secretary may prescribe.

(3) Equivalents of registered and certified mail. The Secretary may provide a rule similar to the rule of paragraph (1) with respect to any service provided by a designated delivery service which is substantially equivalent to United States registered or certified mail.

§ 7503. Time for performance of acts where last day falls on Saturday, Sunday, or legal holiday.

When the last day prescribed under authority of the internal revenue laws for performing any act falls on Saturday, Sunday, or a legal holiday, the performance of such act shall be considered timely if it is performed on the next succeeding day which is not a Saturday, Sunday, or a legal holiday. For purposes of this section, the last day for the performance of any act shall be determined by including any authorized extension of time; the term "legal holiday" means a legal holiday in the District of Columbia; and in the case of any return, statement, or other document required to be filed, or any other act required under authority of the internal revenue laws to be performed, at any office of the Secretary or at any other office of the United States or any agency thereof, located outside the District of Columbia but within an internal revenue district, the term "legal holiday" also means a Statewide legal holiday in the State where such office is located.

* * *

§ 7521. Procedures involving taxpayer interviews.

(a) Recording of interviews.

(1) Recording by taxpayer. Any officer or employee of the Internal Revenue Service in connection with any in-person interview with any taxpayer relating to the determination or collection of any tax shall, upon advance request of such taxpayer, allow the taxpayer to make an audio recording of such interview at the taxpayer's own expense and with the taxpayer's own equipment.

(2) Recording by IRS officer or employee. An officer or employee of the Internal Revenue Service may record any interview described in paragraph (1) if such officer or employee –

(A) informs the taxpayer of such recording prior to the interview, and

(B) upon request of the taxpayer, provides the taxpayer with a transcript or copy of such recording but only if the taxpayer provides reimbursement for the cost of the transcription and reproduction of such transcript or copy.

* * *

§ 7522. Content of tax due, deficiency, and other notices.

(a) General rule. Any notice to which this section applies shall describe the basis for, and identify the amounts (if any) of, the tax due, interest, additional amounts, additions to the tax, and assessable penalties included in such notice. An inadequate description under the preceding sentence shall not invalidate such notice.

(b) Notices to which section applies. This section shall apply to –

(1) any tax due notice or deficiency notice described in section 6155, 6212, or 6303,

(2) any notice generated out of any information return matching program, and

(3) the 1st letter of proposed deficiency which allows the taxpayer an opportunity for administrative review in the Internal Revenue Service Office of Appeals.

* * *

§ 7525. Confidentiality privileges relating to taxpayer communications.

(a) Uniform application to taxpayer communications with federally authorized practitioners.

(1) General rule. With respect to tax advice, the same common law protections of confidentiality which apply to a communication between a taxpayer and an attorney shall also apply to a communication between a taxpayer and any federally authorized tax practitioner to the extent the communication would be considered a privileged communication if it were between a taxpayer and an attorney.

(2) Limitations. Paragraph (1) may only be asserted in –

(A) any noncriminal tax matter before the Internal Revenue Service; and

(B) any noncriminal tax proceeding in Federal court brought by or against the United States.

(3) Definitions. For purposes of this subsection –

(A) Federally authorized tax practitioner. The term "federally authorized tax practitioner" means any individual who is authorized under Federal law to practice before the Internal Revenue Service if such practice is subject to Federal regulation under section 330 of title 31, United States Code.

(B) Tax advice. The term "tax advice" means advice given by an individual with respect to a matter which is within the scope of the individual's authority to practice described in subparagraph (A).

(b) Section not to apply to communications regarding tax shelters. The privilege under subsection (a) shall not apply to any written communication which is –

(1) between a federally authorized tax practitioner and –

(A) any person,

(B) any director, officer, employee, agent, or representative of the person, or

(C) any other person holding a capital or profits interest in the person, and

(2) in connection with the promotion of the direct or indirect participation of the person in any tax shelter (as defined in section 6662(d)(2)(C)(ii)).

* * *

§7602. Examination of books and witnesses.

(a) Authority to summon, etc. For the purpose of ascertaining the correctness of any return, making a return where none has been made, determining the liability of any person for any internal revenue tax or the liability at law or in equity of any transferee or fiduciary of any person in respect of any internal revenue tax, or collecting any such liability, the Secretary is authorized –

(1) To examine any books, papers, records, or other data which may be relevant or material to such inquiry;

(2) To summon the person liable for tax or required to perform the act, or any officer or employee of such person, or any person having possession, custody, or care of books of account containing entries relating to the business of the person liable for tax or required to perform the act, or any other person the Secretary may deem proper, to appear before the Secretary at a time and place named in the summons and to produce such books, papers, records, or other data, and to give such testimony, under oath, as may be relevant or material to such inquiry; and

(3) To take such testimony of the person concerned, under oath, as may be relevant or material to such inquiry.

(b) Purpose may include inquiry into offense. The purposes for which the Secretary may take any action described in paragraph (1), (2), or (3) of subsection (a) include the purpose of inquiring into any offense connected with the administration or enforcement of the internal revenue laws.

(c) Notice of contact of third parties.

(1) General notice. An officer or employee of the Internal Revenue Service may not contact any person other than the taxpayer with respect to the determination or collection of the tax liability of such taxpayer without providing reasonable notice in advance to the taxpayer that contacts with persons other than the taxpayer may be made.

(2) Notice of specific contacts. The Secretary shall periodically provide to a taxpayer a record of persons contacted during such period by the Secretary with respect to the determination or collection of the tax liability of such taxpayer. Such record shall also be provided upon request of the taxpayer.

(3) Exceptions. This subsection shall not apply –

(A) to any contact which the taxpayer has authorized;

(B) if the Secretary determines for good cause shown that such notice would jeopardize collection of any tax or such notice may involve reprisal against any person; or

(C) with respect to any pending criminal investigation.

* * *

(e) Limitation on examination on unreported income. The Secretary shall not use financial status or economic reality examination techniques to determine the existence of unreported income of any taxpayer unless the Secretary has a reasonable indication that there is a likelihood of such unreported income.

§ 7603. Service of summons.

(a) In general. A summons issued under section 6420(e)(2), 6421(g)(2), 6427(j)(2) or 7602 shall be served by the Secretary, by an attested copy delivered in hand to the person to whom it is directed, or left at his last and usual place of abode; and the certificate of service signed by the person serving the summons shall be evidence of the facts it states on the hearing of an application for the enforcement of the summons. When the summons requires the production of books, papers, records, or other data, it shall be sufficient if such books, papers, records, or other data are described with reasonable certainty.

(b) Service by mail to third-party recordkeepers.

(1) In general. A summons referred to in subsection (a) for the production of books, papers, records, or other data by a third-party recordkeeper may also be served by certified or registered mail to the last known address of such recordkeeper.

(2) Third-party recordkeeper. For purposes of paragraph (1), the term "third-party recordkeeper" means –

(A) any mutual savings bank, cooperative bank, domestic building and loan association, or other savings institution chartered and supervised as a savings and loan or similar association under Federal or State law, any bank (as defined in section 581), or any credit union (within the meaning of section 501(c)(14)(A)),

(B) any consumer reporting agency (as defined under section 603(f) of the Fair Credit Reporting Act),

(C) any person extending credit through the use of credit cards or similar devices,

(D) any broker (as defined in section 3(a)(4) of the Securities Exchange Act of 1934),

(E) any attorney,

(F) any accountant,

(G) any barter exchange (as defined in section 6045(c)(3)),

(H) any regulated investment company (as defined in section 851) and any agent of such regulated investment company when acting as an agent thereof,

(I) any enrolled agent, and

(J) any owner or developer of a computer software source code (as defined in section 7612(d)(2)).

Subparagraph (J) shall apply only with respect to a summons requiring the production of the source code referred to in subparagraph (J) or the program and data described in section 7612(b)(1)(A)(ii) to which such source code relates.

§ 7604. Enforcement of summons.

(a) Jurisdiction of district court. If any person is summoned under the internal revenue laws to appear, to testify, or to produce books, papers, records, or other data, the United States district court for the district in which such person resides or is found shall have jurisdiction by appropriate process to compel such attendance, testimony, or production of books, papers, records, or other data.

(b) Enforcement. Whenever any person summoned under section 6420(e)(2), 6421(g)(2), 6427(j)(2) or 7602 neglects or refuses to obey such summons, or to produce books, papers, records, or other data, or to give testimony, as required, the Secretary may apply to the judge of the district court or to a United States commissioner for the district within which the person so summoned resides or is found for an attachment against him as for a contempt. It shall be the duty of the judge or commissioner to hear the application, and, if satisfactory proof is made, to issue an attachment, directed to some proper officer, for the arrest of such person, and upon his being brought before him to proceed to a hearing of the case; and upon such hearing the judge or the United States commissioner shall have power to make such order as he shall deem proper, not inconsistent with the law for the punishment of contempts, to enforce obedience to the requirements of the summons and to punish such person for his default or disobedience.

(c) Cross references.

(1) Authority to issue orders, processes, and judgments. For authority of district courts generally to enforce the provisions of this title, see section 7402.

(2) Penalties. For penalties applicable to violation of section 6420(e)(2), 6421(g)(2), 6427(j)(2), or 7602, see section 7210.

* * *

§ 7609. Special procedures for third-party summonses.

(a) Notice.

(1) In general. If any summons to which this section applies requires the giving of testimony on or relating to, the production of any portion of records made or kept on or relating to, or the production of any computer software source code (as defined in 7612(d)(2)) with respect to, any person (other than the person summoned) who is identified in the summons, then notice of the summons shall be given to any person so identified within 3 days of the day on which such service is made, but no later than the 23rd day before the day fixed in the summons as the day upon which such records are to be examined. Such notice shall be accompanied by a copy of the summons which has been served and shall contain an explanation of the right under subsection (b)(2) to bring a proceeding to quash the summons.

(2) Sufficiency of notice. Such notice shall be sufficient if, on or before such third day, such notice is served in the manner provided in section 7603 (relating to service of summons) upon the person entitled to notice, or is mailed by certified or registered mail to the last known address of such person, or, in the absence of a last known address, is left with the person summoned. If such notice is mailed, it shall be sufficient if mailed to the last known address of the person entitled to notice or, in the case of notice to the Secretary under section 6903 of the existence of a fiduciary relationship, to the last known address of the fiduciary of such person, even if such person or fiduciary is then deceased, under a legal disability, or no longer in existence.

(3) Nature of summons. Any summons to which this subsection applies (and any summons in aid of collection described in subsection (c)(2)(D) shall identify the taxpayer to whom the summons relates or the other person to whom the records pertain and shall provide such other information as will enable the person summoned to locate the records required under the summons.

(b) Right to intervene; right to proceeding to quash.

(1) Intervention. Notwithstanding any other law or rule of law, any person who is entitled to notice of a summons under subsection (a) shall have the right to intervene in any proceeding with respect to the enforcement of such summons under section 7604.

(2) Proceeding to quash.

(A) In general. Notwithstanding any other law or rule of law, any person who is entitled to notice of a summons under subsection (a) shall have the right to begin a proceeding to quash such summons not later than the 20th day after the day such notice is given in the manner provided in subsection (a)(2). In any such proceeding, the Secretary may seek to compel compliance with the summons.

(B) Requirement of notice to person summoned and to Secretary. If any person begins a proceeding under subparagraph (A) with respect to any summons, not later than the close of the 20-day period referred to in subparagraph (A) such person shall mail by registered or certified mail a copy of the petition to the person summoned and to such office as the Secretary may direct in the notice referred to in subsection (a)(1).

(C) Intervention; etc. Notwithstanding any other law or rule of law, the person summoned shall have the right to intervene in any proceeding under subparagraph (A). Such person shall be bound by the decision in such proceeding (whether or not the person intervenes in such proceeding).

(c) Summons to which section applies.

(1) In general. Except as provided in paragraph (2), this section shall apply to any summons issued under paragraph (2) of section 7602(a) or under section 6420(e)(2), 6421(g)(2), 6427(j)(2), or 7612.

(2) Exceptions. This section shall not apply to any summons –

(A) served on the person with respect to whose liability the summons is issued, or any officer or employee of such person;

(B) issued to determine whether or not records of the business transactions or affairs of an identified person have been made or kept;

(C) issued solely to determine the identity of any person having a numbered account (or similar arrangement) with a bank or other institution described in section 7603(b)(2)(A);

(D) issued in aid of the collection of –

(i) an assessment made or judgment rendered against the person with respect to whose liability the summons is issued; or

(ii) the liability at law or in equity of any transferee or fiduciary of any person referred to in clause (i); or

(E) (i) issued by a criminal investigator of the Internal Revenue Service in connection with the investigation of an offense connected with the administration or enforcement of the internal revenue laws; and

(ii) served on any person who is not a third-party recordkeeper (as defined in section 7603(b)).

(3) John doe and certain other summonses. Subsection (a) shall not apply to any summons described in subsection (f) or (g).

(4) Records. For purposes of this section, the term "records" includes books, papers, and other data.

* * *

§ 7612. Special procedures for summonses for computer software.

(a) General rule. For purposes of this title –

(1) except as provided in subsection (b), no summons may be issued under this title, and the Secretary may not begin any action under section 7604 to enforce any summons to produce or analyze any tax-related computer software source code; and

(2) any software and related materials which are provided to the Secretary under this title shall be subject to the safeguards under subsection (c).

(b) Circumstances under which computer software source code may be provided.

(1) In general. Subsection (a)(1) shall not apply to any portion, item, or component of tax-related computer software source code if –

(A) the Secretary is unable to otherwise reasonably ascertain the correctness of any item on a return from –

(i) the taxpayer's books, papers, records, or other data; or

(ii) the computer software executable code (and any modifications thereof) to which such source code relates and any associated data which, when executed, produces the output to ascertain the correctness of the item;

(B) the Secretary identifies with reasonable specificity the portion, item, or component of such source code needed to verify the correctness of such item on the return; and

(C) the Secretary determines that the need for the portion, item, or component of such source code with respect to such item outweighs the risks of unauthorized disclosure of trade secrets.

(2) Exceptions. Subsection (a)(1) shall not apply to –

(A) any inquiry into any offense connected with the administration or enforcement of the internal revenue laws;

(B) any tax-related computer software source code acquired or developed by the taxpayer or a related person primarily for internal use by the taxpayer or such person rather than for commercial distribution;

(C) any communications between the owner of the tax-related computer software source code and the taxpayer or related persons; or

(D) any tax-related computer software source code which is required to be provided or made available pursuant to any other provision of this title.

(3) Cooperation required. For purposes of paragraph (1), the Secretary shall be treated as meeting the requirements of subparagraphs (A) and (B) of such paragraph if –

(A) the Secretary determines that it is not feasible to determine the correctness of an item without access to the computer software executable code and associated data described in paragraph (1)(A)(ii);

(B) the Secretary makes a formal request to the taxpayer for such code and data and to the owner of the computer software source code for such executable code; and

(C) such code and data is not provided within 180 days of such request.

(4) Right to contest summons. In any proceeding brought under section 7604 to enforce a summons issued under the authority of this subsection, the court shall, at the request of any party, hold a hearing to determine whether the applicable requirements of this subsection have been met.

* * *

§ 7623. Expenses of detection of underpayments and fraud, etc.

(a) In general. The Secretary, under regulations prescribed by the Secretary, is authorized to pay such sums as he deems necessary for –

(1) detecting underpayments of tax, or

(2) detecting and bringing to trial and punishment persons guilty of violating the internal revenue laws or conniving at the same, in cases where such expenses are not otherwise provided for by law. Any amount payable under the preceding sentence shall be paid from the proceeds of amounts collected by reason of the information provided, and any amount so collected shall be available for such payments.

(b) Awards to whistleblowers.

(1) In general. If the Secretary proceeds with any administrative or judicial action described in subsection (a) based on information brought to the Secretary's attention by an individual, such individual shall, subject to paragraph (2), receive as an award at least 15 percent but not more than 30 percent of the collected proceeds (including penalties, interest, additions to tax, and additional amounts) resulting from the action (including any related actions) or from any settlement in response to such action. The determination of the amount of such award by the Whistleblower Office shall depend upon the extent to which the individual substantially contributed to such action.

(2) Award in case of less substantial contribution.

(A) In general. In the event the action described in paragraph (1) is one which the Whistleblower Office determines to be based principally on disclosures of specific allegations (other than information provided by the individual described in paragraph (1)) resulting from a judicial or administrative hearing, from a governmental report, hearing, audit, or investigation, or from the news media, the Whistleblower Office may award such sums as it considers appropriate, but in no case more than 10 percent of the collected proceeds (including penalties, interest, additions to tax, and additional amounts) resulting from the action (including any related actions) or from any settlement in response to such action, taking into account the significance of the individual's information and the role of such individual and any legal representative of such individual in contributing to such action.

(B) Nonapplication of paragraph where individual is original source of information. Subparagraph (A) shall not apply if the information resulting in the initiation of the action described in paragraph (1) was originally provided by the individual described in paragraph (1).

(3) Reduction in or denial of award. If the Whistleblower Office determines that the claim for an award under paragraph (1) or (2) is brought by an individual who planned and initiated the actions that led to the underpayment of tax or actions described in subsection (a)(2), then the Whistleblower Office may appropriately reduce such award. If such individual is convicted of criminal conduct arising from the role described in the preceding sentence, the Whistleblower Office shall deny any award.

(4) Appeal of award determination. Any determination regarding an award under paragraph (1), (2), or (3) may, within 30 days of such determination, be appealed to the Tax Court (and the Tax Court shall have jurisdiction with respect to such matter).

(5) Application of this subsection. This subsection shall apply with respect to any action —

(A) against any taxpayer, but in the case of any individual, only if such individual's gross income exceeds $200,000 for any taxable year subject to such action, and

(B) if the tax, penalties, interest, additions to tax, and additional amounts in dispute exceed $2,000,000.

(6) Additional rules.

(A) No contract necessary. No contract with the Internal Revenue Service is necessary for any individual to receive an award under this subsection.

(B) Representation. Any individual described in paragraph (1) or (2) may be represented by counsel.

(C) Submission of information. No award may be made under this subsection based on information submitted to the Secretary unless such information is submitted under penalty of perjury.

* * *

§ 7701. Definitions.

(a) When used in this title, where not otherwise distinctly expressed or manifestly incompatible with the intent thereof —

* * *

(36) Tax return preparer.

(A) In general. The term "tax return preparer" means any person who prepares for compensation, or who employs one or more persons to prepare for compensation, any return of tax imposed by this title or any claim for refund of tax imposed by this title. For purposes of the preceding sentence, the preparation of a substantial portion of a return or claim for refund shall be treated as if it were the preparation of such return or claim for refund.

(B) Exceptions. A person shall not be an "tax return preparer" merely because such person —

(i) furnishes typing, reproducing, or other mechanical assistance,

(ii) prepares a return or claim for refund of the employer (or of an officer or employee of the employer) by whom he is regularly and continuously employed,

(iii) prepares as a fiduciary a return or claim for refund for any person, or

(iv) prepares a claim for refund for a taxpayer in response to any notice of deficiency issued to such taxpayer or in response to any waiver of restriction after the commencement of an audit of such taxpayer or another taxpayer if a determination in such audit of such other taxpayer directly or indirectly affects the tax liability of such taxpayer.

* * *

§ 7805. Rules and regulations.

(a) Authorization. Except where such authority is expressly given by this title to any person other than an officer or employee of the Treasury Department, the Secretary shall prescribe all needful rules and regulations for the enforcement of this title, including all rules and regulations as may be necessary by reason of any alteration of law in relation to internal revenue.

(b) Retroactivity of regulations.

(1) In general. Except as otherwise provided in this subsection, no temporary, proposed, or final regulation relating to the internal revenue laws shall apply to any taxable period ending before the earliest of the following dates:

(A) The date on which such regulation is filed with the Federal Register.

(B) In the case of any final regulation, the date on which any proposed or temporary regulation to which such final regulation relates was filed with the Federal Register.

(C) The date on which any notice substantially describing the expected contents of any temporary, proposed, or final regulation is issued to the public.

(2) Exception for promptly issued regulations. Paragraph (1) shall not apply to regulations filed or issued within 18 months of the date of the enactment of the statutory provision to which the regulation relates.

(3) Prevention of abuse. The Secretary may provide that any regulation may take effect or apply retroactively to prevent abuse.

(4) Correction of procedural defects. The Secretary may provide that any regulation may apply retroactively to correct a procedural defect in the issuance of any prior regulation.

(5) Internal regulations. The limitation of paragraph (1) shall not apply to any regulation relating to internal Treasury Department policies, practices, or procedures.

(6) Congressional authorization. The limitation of paragraph (1) may be superseded by a legislative grant from Congress authorizing the Secretary to prescribe the effective date with respect to any regulation.

(7) Election to apply retroactively. The Secretary may provide for any taxpayer to elect to apply any regulation before the dates specified in paragraph (1).

(8) Application to rulings. The Secretary may prescribe the extent, if any, to which any ruling (including any judicial decision or any administrative determination other than by regulation) relating to the internal revenue laws shall be applied without retroactive effect.

* * *

(e) Temporary regulations.

(1) Issuance. Any temporary regulation issued by the Secretary shall also be issued as a proposed regulation.

(2) 3-Year duration. Any temporary regulation shall expire within 3 years after the date of issuance of such regulation.

* * *

§ 7811. Taxpayer Assistance Orders.

(a) Authority to issue.

(1) In general. Upon application filed by a taxpayer with the Office of the Taxpayer Advocate (in such form, manner, and at such time as the Secretary shall by regulations prescribe), the National Taxpayer Advocate may issue a Taxpayer Assistance Order if –

(A) the National Taxpayer Advocate determines the taxpayer is suffering or about to suffer a significant hardship as a result of the manner in which the internal revenue laws are being administered by the Secretary; or

(B) the taxpayer meets such other requirements as are set forth in regulations prescribed by the Secretary.

(2) Determination of hardship. For purposes of paragraph (1), a significant hardship shall include –

(A) an immediate threat of adverse action;

(B) a delay of more than 30 days in resolving taxpayer account problems;

(C) the incurring by the taxpayer of significant costs (including fees for professional representation) if relief is not granted; or

(D) irreparable injury to, or a long-term adverse impact on, the taxpayer if relief is not granted.

(3) Standard where administrative guidance not followed. In cases where any Internal Revenue Service employee is not following applicable published administrative guidance (including the Internal Revenue Manual), the National Taxpayer Advocate shall construe the factors taken into account in determining whether to issue a Taxpayer Assistance Order in the manner most favorable to the taxpayer.

(b) Terms of a Taxpayer Assistance Order. The terms of a Taxpayer Assistance Order may require the Secretary within a specified time period –

(1) to release property of the taxpayer levied upon, or

(2) to cease any action, take any action as permitted by law, or refrain from taking any action, with respect to the taxpayer under –

(A) chapter 64 (relating to collection),

(B) subchapter B of chapter 70 (relating to bankruptcy and receiverships),

(C) chapter 78 (relating to discovery of liability and enforcement of title), or

(D) any other provision of law which is specifically described by the National Taxpayer Advocate in such order.

PART II

Treasury and Internal Revenue Service Regulations
(Selected Sections)

REGULATIONS

Sec. 1.6001-1. Records.

(a) In general. Except as provided in paragraph (b) of this section, any person subject to tax under Subtitle A of the Code (including a qualified State individual income tax which is treated pursuant to section 6361(a) as if it were imposed by Chapter 1 of Subtitle A), or any person required to file a return of information with respect to income, shall keep such permanent books of account or records, including inventories, as are sufficient to establish the amount of gross income, deductions, credits, or other matters required to be shown by such person in any return of such tax or information.

(b) Farmers and wage-earners. Individuals deriving gross income from the business of farming, and individuals whose gross income includes salaries, wages, or similar compensation for personal services rendered, are required with respect to such income to keep such records as will enable the district director to determine the correct amount of income subject to the tax. It is not necessary, however, that with respect to such income individuals keep the books of account or records required by paragraph (a) of this section. For rules with respect to the records to be kept in substantiation of traveling and other business expenses of employees, see § 1.162-17.

* * *

Sec. 1.6011-1. General requirement of return, statement, or list.

(a) General rule. Every person subject to any tax, or required to collect any tax, under Subtitle A of the Code, shall make such returns or statements as are required by the regulations in this chapter. The return or statement shall include therein the information required by the applicable regulations or forms.

(b) Use of prescribed forms. Copies of the prescribed return forms will so far as possible be furnished taxpayers by district directors. A taxpayer will not be excused from making a return, however, by the fact that no return form has been furnished to him. Taxpayers not supplied with the proper forms should make application therefor to the district director in ample time to have their returns prepared, verified, and filed on or before the due date with the internal revenue office where such returns are required to be filed. Each taxpayer should carefully prepare his return and set forth fully and clearly the information required to be included therein. Returns which have not been so prepared will not be accepted as meeting the requirements of the Code. In the absence of a prescribed form, a statement made by a taxpayer disclosing his gross income and the deductions therefrom may be accepted as a tentative return, and, if filed within the prescribed time, the statement so made will relieve the taxpayer from liability for the addition to tax imposed for the delinquent filing of the return, provided that without unnecessary delay such a tentative return is supplemented by a return made on the proper form.

* * *

Sec. 1.6013-4. Applicable rules.

* * *

(d) Return signed under duress. If an individual asserts and establishes that he or she signed a return under duress, the return is not a joint return. The individual who signed such return under duress is not jointly and severally liable for the tax shown on the return or any deficiency in tax with respect to the return. The return is adjusted to reflect only the tax liability of the individual who voluntarily signed the return, and the liability is determined at the applicable rates in section 1(d) for married individuals filing separate returns. Section 6212 applies to the assessment of any deficiency in tax on such return.

* * *

Sec. 1.6015-1. Relief from joint and several liability on a joint return.

* * *

(h) Definitions –

* * *

(5) **Election or request.** A qualifying election under § 1.6015-2 or 1.6015-3, or request under § 1.6015-4, is the first timely claim for relief from joint and several liability for the tax year for which relief is sought. A qualifying election also includes a requesting spouse's second election to seek relief from joint and several liability for the same tax year under § 1.6015-3 when the additional qualifications of paragraphs (h)(5)(i) and (ii) of this section are met –

(i) The requesting spouse did not qualify for relief under § 1.6015-3 when the Internal Revenue Service considered the first election solely because the qualifications of § 1.6015-3(a) were not satisfied; and

(ii) At the time of the second election, the qualifications for relief under § 1.6015-3(a) are satisfied.

* * *

Sec. 1.6015-2. Relief from liability applicable to all qualifying joint filers.

* * *

(c) **Knowledge or reason to know.** A requesting spouse has knowledge or reason to know of an understatement if he or she actually knew of the understatement, or if a reasonable person in similar circumstances would have known of the understatement. For rules relating to a requesting spouse's actual knowledge, see § 1.6015-3(c)(2). All of the facts and circumstances are considered in determining whether a requesting spouse had reason to know of an understatement. The facts and circumstances that are considered include, but are not limited to, the nature of the erroneous item and the amount of the erroneous item relative to other items; the couple's financial situation; the requesting spouse's educational background and business experience; the extent of the requesting spouse's participation in the activity that resulted in the erroneous item; whether the requesting spouse failed to inquire, at or before the time the return was signed, about items on the return or omitted from the return that a reasonable person would question; and whether the erroneous item represented a departure from a recurring pattern reflected in prior years' returns (e.g., omitted income from an investment regularly reported on prior years' returns).

* * *

Sec. 1.6015-3. Allocation of deficiency for individuals who are no longer married, are legally separated, or are not members of the same household.

* * *

(c) Limitations — (1) No refunds. Relief under this section is only available for unpaid liabilities resulting from understatements of liability. Refunds are not authorized under this section.

(2) Actual knowledge — (i) In general. If, under section 6015(c)(3)(C), the Secretary demonstrates that, at the time the return was signed, the requesting spouse had actual knowledge of an erroneous item that is allocable to the nonrequesting spouse, the election to allocate the deficiency attributable to that item is invalid, and the requesting spouse remains liable for the portion of the deficiency attributable to that item. The Service, having both the burden of production and the burden of persuasion, must establish, by a preponderance of the evidence, that the requesting spouse had actual knowledge of the erroneous item in order to invalidate the election.

(A) Omitted income. In the case of omitted income, knowledge of the item includes knowledge of the receipt of the income. For example, assume W received $5,000 of dividend income from her investment in X Co. but did not report it on the joint return. H knew that W received $5,000 of dividend income from X Co. that year. H had actual knowledge of the erroneous item (i.e., $5,000 of unreported dividend income from X Co.), and no relief is available under this section for the deficiency attributable to the dividend income from X Co. This rule applies equally in situations where the other spouse has unreported income although the spouse does not have an actual receipt of cash (e.g., dividend reinvestment or a distributive share from a flow-through entity shown on Schedule K-1, "Partner's Share of Income, Credits, Deductions, etc.").

(B) Deduction or credit — (1) Erroneous deductions in general. In the case of an erroneous deduction or credit, knowledge of the item means knowledge of the facts that made the item not allowable as a deduction or credit.

(2) Fictitious or inflated deduction. If a deduction is fictitious or inflated, the IRS must establish that the requesting spouse actually knew that the expenditure was not incurred, or not incurred to that extent.

(ii) Partial knowledge. If a requesting spouse had actual knowledge of only a portion of an erroneous item, then relief is not available for that portion of the erroneous item. For example, if H knew that W received $1,000 of dividend income and did not know that W received an additional $4,000 of dividend income, relief would not be available for the portion of the deficiency attributable to the $1,000 of dividend income of which H had actual knowledge. A requesting spouse's actual knowledge of the proper tax treatment of an item is not relevant for purposes of demonstrating that the requesting spouse had actual knowledge of an erroneous item. For example, assume H did not know W's dividend income from X Co. was taxable, but knew that W received the dividend income. Relief is not available under this section. In addition, a requesting spouse's knowledge of how an erroneous item was treated on the tax return is not relevant to a determination of whether the requesting spouse had actual knowledge of the item. For example, assume that H knew of W's dividend income, but H failed to review the completed return and did not know that W omitted the dividend income from the return. Relief is not available under this section.

(iii) Knowledge of the source not sufficient. Knowledge of the source of an erroneous item is not sufficient to establish actual knowledge. For example, assume H knew that W owned X Co. stock, but H did not know that X Co. paid dividends to W that year. H's knowledge of W's ownership in X Co. is not sufficient to establish that H had actual knowledge of the dividend income from X Co. In addition, a requesting spouse's actual knowledge may not be inferred when the requesting spouse merely had reason to know of the erroneous item. Even if H's knowledge of W's ownership interest in X Co. indicates a reason to know of the dividend income, actual knowledge of such dividend income cannot be inferred from H's reason to know. Similarly, the IRS need not establish that a requesting spouse knew of the source of an erroneous item in order to establish that the requesting spouse had actual knowledge of the item itself. For example, assume H knew that W received $1,000, but he did not know the source of the $1,000. W and H omit the $1,000 from their joint return. H has actual knowledge of the item giving rise to the deficiency ($1,000), and relief is not available under this section.

(iv) Factors supporting actual knowledge. To demonstrate that a requesting spouse had actual knowledge of an erroneous item at the time the return was signed, the IRS may rely upon all of the facts and circumstances. One factor that may be relied upon in demonstrating that a requesting spouse had actual knowledge of an erroneous item is whether the requesting spouse made a deliberate effort to avoid learning about the item in order to be shielded from liability. This factor, together with all other facts and circumstances, may demonstrate that the requesting spouse had actual knowledge of the item, and the requesting spouse's election would be invalid with respect to that entire item. Another factor that may be relied upon in demonstrating that a requesting spouse had actual knowledge of an erroneous item is whether the requesting spouse and the nonrequesting spouse jointly owned the property that resulted in the erroneous item. Joint ownership is a factor supporting a finding that the requesting spouse had actual knowledge of an erroneous item. For purposes of this paragraph, a requesting spouse will not be considered to have had an ownership interest in an item based solely on the operation of community property law. Rather, a requesting spouse who resided in a community property state at the time the return was signed will be considered to have had an ownership interest in an item only if the requesting spouse's name appeared on the ownership documents, or there otherwise is an indication that the requesting spouse asserted dominion and control over the item. For example, assume H and W live in State A, a community property state. After their marriage, H opens a bank account in his name. Under the operation of the community property laws of State A, W owns 1/2 of the bank account. However, W does not have an ownership interest in the account for purposes of this paragraph (c)(2)(iv) because the account is not held in her name and there is no other indication that she asserted dominion and control over the item.

(v) Abuse exception. If the requesting spouse establishes that he or she was the victim of domestic abuse prior to the time the return was signed, and that, as a result of the prior abuse, the requesting spouse did not challenge the treatment of any items on the return for fear of the nonrequesting spouse's retaliation, the limitation on actual knowledge in this paragraph (c) will not apply. However, if the requesting spouse involuntarily executed the return, the requesting spouse may choose to establish that the return was signed under duress. In such a case, § 1.6013-4(d) applies.

* * *

(4) Examples. The following examples illustrate the rules in this paragraph (c):

Example 1. Actual knowledge of an erroneous item. (i) H and W file their 2001 joint Federal income tax return on April 15, 2002. On the return, H and W report W's self-employment income, but they do not report W's self-employment tax on that income. H and W divorce in July 2003. In August 2003, H and W receive a 30-day letter from the Internal Revenue Service proposing a deficiency with respect to W's unreported self-employment tax on the 2001 return. On November 4, 2003, H files an election to allocate the deficiency to W. The erroneous item is the self-employment income, and it is allocable to W. H knows that W earned income in 2001 as a self-employed musician, but he does not know that self-employment tax must be reported on and paid with a joint return.

(ii) H's election to allocate the deficiency to W is invalid because, at the time H signed the joint return, H had actual knowledge of W's self-employment income. The fact that H was unaware of the tax consequences of that income (i.e., that an individual is required to pay self-employment tax on that income) is not relevant.

Example 2. Actual knowledge not inferred from a requesting spouse's reason to know. (i) H has long been an avid gambler. H supports his gambling habit and keeps all of his gambling winnings in an individual bank account, held solely in his name. W knows about H's gambling habit and that he keeps a separate bank account, but she does not know whether he has any winnings because H does not tell her, and she does not otherwise know of H's bank account transactions. H and W file their 2001 joint Federal income tax return on April 15, 2002. On October 31, 2003, H and W receive a 30-day letter proposing a $100,000 deficiency relating to H's unreported gambling income. In February 2003, H and W divorce, and in March 2004, W files an election under section 6015(c) to allocate the $100,000 deficiency to H.

(ii) While W may have had reason to know of the gambling income because she knew of H's gambling habit and separate account, W did not have actual knowledge of the erroneous item (i.e., the gambling winnings). The Internal Revenue Service may not infer actual knowledge from W's reason to know of the income. Therefore, W's election to allocate the $100,000 deficiency to H is valid.

Example 3. Actual knowledge and failure to review return. (i) H and W are legally separated. In February 1999, W signs a blank joint Federal income tax return for 1998 and gives it to H to fill out. The return was timely filed on April 15, 1999. In September 2001, H and W receive a 30-day letter proposing a deficiency relating to $100,000 of unreported dividend income received by H with respect to stock of ABC Co. owned by H. W knew that H received the $100,000 dividend payment in August 1998, but she did not know whether H reported that payment on the joint return.

(ii) On January 30, 2002, W files an election to allocate the deficiency from the 1998 return to H. W claims she did not review the completed joint return, and therefore, she had no actual knowledge that there was an understatement of the dividend income. W's election to allocate the deficiency to H is invalid because she had actual knowledge of the erroneous item (dividend income from ABC Co.) at the time she signed the return. The fact that W signed a blank return is irrelevant. The result would be the same if W had not reviewed the completed return or if W had reviewed the completed return and had not noticed that the item was omitted.

Example 4. Actual knowledge of an erroneous item of income. (i) H and W are legally separated. In June 2004, a deficiency is proposed with respect to H's and W's 2002 joint Federal income tax return that is attributable to $30,000 of unreported income from H's plumbing business that should have been reported on a Schedule C. No Schedule C was attached to the return. At the time W signed the return, W knew that H had a plumbing business but did not know whether H received any income from the business. W's election to allocate to H the deficiency attributable to the $30,000 of unreported plumbing income is valid.

(ii) Assume the same facts as in paragraph (i) of this Example 5 except that, at the time W signed the return, W knew that H received $20,000 of plumbing income. W's election to allocate to H the deficiency attributable to the $20,000 of unreported plumbing income (of which W had actual knowledge) is invalid. W's election to allocate to H the deficiency attributable to the $10,000 of unreported plumbing income (of which W did not have actual knowledge) is valid.

(iii) Assume the same facts as in paragraph (i) of this Example 5 except that, at the time W signed the return, W did not know the exact amount of H's plumbing income. W did know, however, that H received at least $8,000 of plumbing income. W's election to allocate to H the deficiency attributable to $8,000 of unreported plumbing income (of which W had actual knowledge) is invalid. W's election to allocate to H the deficiency attributable to the remaining $22,000 of unreported plumbing income (of which W did not have actual knowledge) is valid.

(iv) Assume the same facts as in paragraph (i) of this Example 5 except that H reported $26,000 of plumbing income on the return and omitted $4,000 of plumbing income from the return. At the time W signed the return, W knew that H was a plumber, but she did not know that H earned more than $26,000 that year. W's election to allocate to H the deficiency attributable to the $4,000 of unreported plumbing income is valid because she did not have actual knowledge that H received plumbing income in excess of $26,000.

(v) Assume the same facts as in paragraph (i) of this Example 5 except that H reported only $20,000 of plumbing income on the return and omitted $10,000 of plumbing income from the return. At the time W signed the return, W knew that H earned at least $26,000 that year as a plumber. However, W did not know that, in reality, H earned $30,000 that year as a plumber. W's election to allocate to H the deficiency attributable to the $6,000 of unreported plumbing income (of which W had actual knowledge) is invalid. W's election to allocate to H the deficiency attributable to the $4,000 of unreported plumbing income (of which W did not have actual knowledge) is valid.

Example 5. Actual knowledge of a deduction that is an erroneous item. (i) H and W are legally separated. In February 2005, a deficiency is asserted with respect to their 2002 joint Federal income tax return. The deficiency is attributable to a disallowed $1,000 deduction for medical expenses H claimed he incurred. At the time W signed the return, W knew that H had not incurred any medical expenses. W's election to allocate to H the deficiency attributable to the disallowed medical expense deduction is invalid because W had actual knowledge that H had not incurred any medical expenses.

(ii) Assume the same facts as in paragraph (i) of this Example 6 except that, at the time W signed the return, W did not know whether H had incurred any medical expenses. W's election to allocate to H the deficiency attributable to the disallowed medical expense deduction is valid because she did not have actual knowledge that H had not incurred any medical expenses.

(iii) Assume the same facts as in paragraph (i) of this Example 6 except that the Internal Revenue Service disallowed $400 of the $1,000 medical expense deduction. At the time W signed the return, W knew that H had incurred some medical expenses but did not know the exact amount. W's election to allocate to H the deficiency attributable to the disallowed medical expense deduction is valid because she did not have actual knowledge that H had not incurred medical expenses (in excess of the floor amount under section 213(a)) of more than $600.

(iv) Assume the same facts as in paragraph (i) of this Example 6 except that H claims a medical expense deduction of $10,000 and the Internal Revenue Service disallows $9,600. At the time W signed the return, W knew H had incurred some medical expenses but did not know the exact amount. W also knew that H incurred medical expenses (in excess of the floor amount under section 213(a)) of no more than $1,000. W's election to allocate to H the deficiency attributable to the portion of the overstated deduction of which she had actual knowledge ($9,000) is invalid. W's election to allocate the deficiency attributable to the portion of the overstated deduction of which she had no knowledge ($600) is valid.

* * *

(d) Allocation — (1) In general. (i) An election to allocate a deficiency limits the requesting spouse's liability to that portion of the deficiency allocated to the requesting spouse pursuant to this section.

(ii) Only a requesting spouse may receive relief. A nonrequesting spouse who does not also elect relief under this section remains liable for the entire amount of the deficiency. Even if both spouses elect to allocate a deficiency under this section, there may be a portion of the deficiency that is not allocable, for which both spouses remain jointly and severally liable.

(2) Allocation of erroneous items. For purposes of allocating a deficiency under this section, erroneous items are generally allocated to the spouses as if separate returns were filed, subject to the following four exceptions:

(i) Benefit on the return. An erroneous item that would otherwise be allocated to the nonrequesting spouse is allocated to the requesting spouse to the extent that the requesting spouse received a tax benefit on the joint return.

(ii) Fraud. The Internal Revenue Service may allocate any item between the spouses if the Internal Revenue Service establishes that the allocation is appropriate due to fraud by one or both spouses.

(iii) Erroneous items of income. Erroneous items of income are allocated to the spouse who was the source of the income. Wage income is allocated to the spouse who performed the services producing such wages. Items of business or investment income are allocated to the spouse who owned the business or investment. If both spouses owned an interest in the business or investment, the erroneous item of income is generally allocated between the spouses in proportion to each spouse's ownership interest in the business or investment, subject to the limitations of paragraph (c) of this section. In the absence of clear and convincing evidence supporting a different allocation, an erroneous income item relating to an asset that the spouses owned jointly is generally allocated 50% to each spouse, subject to the limitations in paragraph (c) of this section and the exceptions in paragraph (c)(2)(iv) of this section. For rules regarding the effect of community property laws, see § 1.6015-1(f) and paragraph (c)(2)(iv) of this section.

(iv) Erroneous deduction items. Erroneous deductions related to a business or investment are allocated to the spouse who owned the business or investment. If both spouses owned an interest in the business or investment, an erroneous deduction item is generally allocated between the spouses in proportion to each spouse's ownership interest in the business or investment. In the absence of clear and convincing evidence supporting a different allocation, an erroneous deduction item relating to an asset that the spouses owned jointly is generally allocated 50% to each spouse, subject to the limitations in paragraph (c) of this section and the exceptions in paragraph (d)(4) of this section. Deduction items unrelated to a business or investment are also generally allocated 50% to each spouse, unless the evidence shows that a different allocation is appropriate.

(3) Burden of proof. Except for establishing actual knowledge under paragraph (c)(2) of this section, the requesting spouse must prove that all of the qualifications for making an election under this section are satisfied and that none of the limitations (including the limitation relating to transfers of disqualified assets) apply. The requesting spouse must also establish the proper allocation of the erroneous items.

(4) General allocation method — (i) Proportionate allocation. (A) The portion of a deficiency allocable to a spouse is the amount that bears the same ratio to the deficiency as the net amount of erroneous items allocable to the spouse bears to the net amount of all erroneous items. This calculation may be expressed as follows:

$$X = (\text{deficiency}) \times \frac{\text{net amount of erroneous items allocable to the spouse}}{\text{net amount of all erroneous items}}$$

where X = the portion of the deficiency allocable to the spouse.

(B) The proportionate allocation applies to any portion of the deficiency other than –

(1) Any portion of the deficiency attributable to erroneous items allocable to the nonrequesting spouse of which the requesting spouse had actual knowledge;

(2) Any portion of the deficiency attributable to separate treatment items (as defined in paragraph (d)(4)(ii) of this section);

(3) Any portion of the deficiency relating to the liability of a child (as defined in paragraph (d)(4)(iii) of this section) of the requesting spouse or nonrequesting spouse;

(4) Any portion of the deficiency attributable to alternative minimum tax under section 55;

(5) Any portion of the deficiency attributable to accuracy-related or fraud penalties;

(6) Any portion of the deficiency allocated pursuant to alternative allocation methods authorized under paragraph (d)(6) of this section.

(ii) Separate treatment items. Any portion of a deficiency that is attributable to an item allocable solely to one spouse and that results from the disallowance of a credit, or a tax or an addition to tax (other than tax imposed by section 1 or section 55) that is required to be included with a joint return (a separate treatment item) is allocated separately to that spouse. If such credit or tax is attributable in whole or in part to both spouses, then the IRS will determine on a case by case basis how such item will be allocated. Once the proportionate allocation is made, the liability for the requesting spouse's separate treatment items is added to the requesting spouse's share of the liability.

(iii) Child's liability. Any portion of a deficiency relating to the liability of a child of the requesting and nonrequesting spouse is allocated jointly to both spouses. For purposes of this paragraph, a child does not include the taxpayer's stepson or stepdaughter, unless such child was legally adopted by the taxpayer. If the child is the child of only one of the spouses, and the other spouse had not legally adopted such child, any portion of a deficiency relating to the liability of such child is allocated solely to the parent spouse.

(iv) Allocation of certain items — (A) Alternative minimum tax. Any portion of a deficiency relating to the alternative minimum tax under section 55 [26 USCS § 55] will be allocated appropriately.

(B) Accuracy-related and fraud penalties. Any accuracy-related or fraud penalties under section 6662 or 6663 are allocated to the spouse whose item generated the penalty.

(5) Examples. The following examples illustrate the rules of this paragraph (d). In each example, assume that the requesting spouse or spouses qualify to elect to allocate the deficiency, that any election is timely made, and that the deficiency remains unpaid. In addition, unless otherwise stated, assume that neither spouse has actual knowledge of the erroneous items allocable to the other spouse. The examples are as follows:

Example 1. Allocation of erroneous items. (i) H and W file a 2003 joint Federal income tax return on April 15, 2004. On April 28, 2006, a deficiency is assessed with respect to their 2003 return. Three erroneous items give rise to the deficiency –

(A) Unreported interest income, of which W had actual knowledge, from H's and W's joint bank account;

(B) A disallowed business expense deduction on H's Schedule C; and

(C) A disallowed Lifetime Learning Credit for W's post-secondary education, paid for by W.

(ii) H and W divorce in May 2006, and in September 2006, W timely elects to allocate the deficiency. The erroneous items are allocable as follows:

(A) The interest income would be allocated 1/2 to H and 1/2 to W, except that W has actual knowledge of it. Therefore, W's election to allocate the portion of the deficiency attributable to this item is invalid, and W remains jointly and severally liable for it.

(B) The business expense deduction is allocable to H.

(C) The Lifetime Learning Credit is allocable to W.

* * *

Sec. 1.6161-1. Extension of time for paying tax or deficiency.

(a) In general — (1) Tax shown or required to be shown on return. A reasonable extension of the time for payment of the amount of any tax imposed by Subtitle A of the Code and shown or required to be shown on any return, or for payment of the amount of any installment of such tax, may be granted by the district directors (including the Director of International Operations) at the request of the taxpayer. The period of such extension shall not be in excess of six months from the date fixed for payment of such tax or installment, except that if the taxpayer is abroad the period of the extension may be in excess of six months.

(2) Deficiency. The time for payment of any amount determined as a deficiency in respect of tax imposed by Chapter 1 of the Code, or for the payment of any part thereof, may, at the request of the taxpayer, be extended by the internal revenue officer to whom the tax is required to be paid for a period not to exceed 18 months from the date fixed for payment of the deficiency, as shown on the notice and demand, and, in exceptional cases, for a further period not in excess of 12 months. No extension of the time for payment of a deficiency shall be granted if the deficiency is due to negligence, to intentional disregard of rules and regulations, or to fraud with intent to evade tax.

(b) Undue hardship required for extension. An extension of the time for payment shall be granted only upon a satisfactory showing that payment on the due date of the amount with respect to which the extension is desired will result in an undue hardship. The extension will not be granted upon a general statement of hardship. The term "undue hardship" means more than an inconvenience to the taxpayer. It must appear that substantial financial loss, for example, loss due to the sale of property at a sacrifice price, will result to the taxpayer for making payment on the due date of the amount with respect to which the extension is desired. If a market exists, the sale of property at the current market price is not ordinarily considered as resulting in an undue hardship.

(c) Application for extension. An application for an extension of the time for payment of the tax shown or required to be shown on any return, or for the payment of any installment thereof, or for the payment of any amount determined as a deficiency shall be made on Form 1127 and shall be accompanied by evidence showing the undue hardship that would result to the taxpayer if the extension were refused. Such application shall also be accompanied by a statement of the assets and liabilities of the taxpayer and an itemized statement showing all receipts and disbursements for each of the 3 months immediately preceding the due date of the amount to which the application relates. The application, with supporting documents, must be filed on or before the date prescribed for payment of the amount with respect to which the extension is desired. If the tax is required to be paid to the Director of International Operations, such application must be filed with him, otherwise, the application must be filed with the applicable district director referred to in paragraph (a) or (b) of § 1.6091-2, regardless of whether the return is to be filed with, or tax is to be paid to, such district director. The application will be examined, and within 30 days, if possible, will be denied, granted, or tentatively granted subject to certain conditions of which the taxpayer will be notified. If an additional extension is desired, the request therefor must be made on or before the expiration of the period for which the prior extension is granted.

(d) Payment pursuant to extension. If an extension of time for payment is granted, the amount the time for payment of which is so extended shall be paid on or before the expiration of the period of the extension without the necessity of notice and demand. The granting of an extension of the time for payment of the tax or deficiency does not relieve the taxpayer from liability for the payment of interest thereon during the period of the extension. See section 6601 and § 301.6601-1 of this chapter (Regulations on Procedure and Administration). Further, the granting of an extension of the time for payment of one installment of the tax does not extend the time for payment of subsequent installments.

(e) Cross reference. For extensions of time for payment of estimated tax, see §§ 1.6073-4 and 1.6074-3.

* * *

Sec. 1.6662-2. Accuracy-related penalty.

(a) In general. Section 6662(a) imposes an accuracy-related penalty on any portion of an underpayment of tax (as defined in section 6664(a) and § 1.6664-2) required to be shown on a return if such portion is attributable to one or more of the following types of misconduct:

(1) Negligence or disregard of rules or regulations (see § 1.6662-3);

(2) Any substantial understatement of income tax (see § 1.6662-4); or

(3) Any substantial (or gross) valuation misstatement under chapter 1 ("substantial valuation misstatement" or "gross valuation misstatement"), provided the applicable dollar limitation set forth in section 6662(e)(2) is satisfied (see § 1.6662-5).

The accuracy-related penalty applies only in cases in which a return of tax is filed, except that the penalty does not apply in the case of a return prepared by the Secretary under the authority of section 6020(b). The accuracy-related penalty under section 6662 and the penalty under section 6651 for failure to timely file a return of tax may both be imposed on the same portion of an underpayment if a return is filed, but is filed late. The fact that a return is filed late, however, is not taken into account in determining whether an accuracy-related penalty should be imposed.

No accuracy-related penalty may be imposed on any portion of an underpayment of tax on which the fraud penalty set forth in section 6663 is imposed.

(b) Amount of penalty – (1) In general. The amount of the accuracy-related penalty is 20 percent of the portion of an underpayment of tax required to be shown on a return that is attributable to any of the types of misconduct listed in paragraphs (a)(1) through (a)(3) of this section, except as provided in paragraph (b)(2) of this section.

(2) Increase in penalty for gross valuation misstatement. In the case of a gross valuation misstatement, as defined in section 6662(h)(2) and § 1.6662-5(e)(2), the amount of the accuracy-related penalty is 40 percent of the portion of an underpayment of tax required to be shown on a return that is attributable to the gross valuation misstatement, provided the applicable dollar limitation set forth in section 6662(e)(2) is satisfied.

(c) No stacking of accuracy-related penalty components. The maximum accuracy-related penalty imposed on a portion of an underpayment may not exceed 20 percent of such portion (40 percent of the portion attributable to a gross valuation misstatement), notwithstanding that such portion is attributable to more than one of the types of misconduct described in paragraph (a) of this section. For example, if a portion of an underpayment of tax required to be shown on a return is attributable both to negligence and a substantial understatement of income tax, the maximum accuracy-related penalty is 20 percent of such portion. Similarly, the maximum accuracy-related penalty imposed on any portion of an underpayment that is attributable both to negligence and a gross valuation misstatement is 40 percent of such portion.

* * *

Sec. 1.6662-3. Negligence or disregard of rules or regulations.

(a) In general. If any portion of an underpayment, as defined in section 6664(a) and § 1.6664-2, of any income tax imposed under subtitle A of the Internal Revenue Code that is required to be shown on a return is attributable to negligence or disregard of rules or regulations, there is added to the tax an amount equal to 20 percent of such portion. The penalty for disregarding rules or regulations does not apply, however, if the requirements of paragraph (c)(1) of this section are satisfied and the position in question is adequately disclosed as provided in paragraph (c)(2) of this section (and, if the position relates to a reportable transaction as defined in § 1.6011-4(b) (or § 1.6011-4T(b), as applicable), the transaction is disclosed in accordance with § 1.6011-4 (or § 1.6011-4T, as applicable)), or to the extent that the reasonable cause and good faith exception to this penalty set forth in § 1.6664-4 applies. In addition, if a position with respect to an item (other than with respect to a reportable transaction, as defined in § 1.6011-4(b) or § 1.6011-4T(b), as applicable) is contrary to a revenue ruling or notice (other than a notice of proposed rulemaking) issued by the Internal Revenue Service and published in the Internal Revenue Bulletin (see § 601.601(d)(2) of this chapter), this penalty does not apply if the position has a realistic possibility of being sustained on its merits. See § 1.6694-2(b) of the income tax return preparer penalty regulations for a description of the realistic possibility standard.

(b) Definitions and rules — (1) Negligence. The term negligence includes any failure to make a reasonable attempt to comply with the provisions of the internal revenue laws or to exercise ordinary and reasonable care in the preparation of a tax return. "Negligence" also includes any failure by the taxpayer to keep adequate books and records or to substantiate items properly. A return position that has a reasonable basis as defined in paragraph (b)(3) of this section is not attributable to negligence. Negligence is strongly indicated where --

(i) A taxpayer fails to include on an income tax return an amount of income shown on an information return, as defined in section 6724(d)(1);

(ii) A taxpayer fails to make a reasonable attempt to ascertain the correctness of a deduction, credit or exclusion on a return which would seem to a reasonable and prudent person to be "too good to be true" under the circumstances;

(iii) A partner fails to comply with the requirements of section 6222, which requires that a partner treat partnership items on its return in a manner that is consistent with the treatment of such items on the partnership return (or notify the Secretary of the inconsistency); or

(iv) A shareholder fails to comply with the requirements of section 6242, which requires that an S corporation shareholder treat subchapter S items on its return in a manner that is consistent with the treatment of such items on the corporation's return (or notify the Secretary of the inconsistency).

(2) Disregard of rules or regulations. The term disregard includes any careless, reckless or intentional disregard of rules or regulations. The term "rules or regulations" includes the provisions of the Internal Revenue Code, temporary or final Treasury regulations issued under the Code, and revenue rulings or notices (other than notices of proposed rulemaking) issued by the Internal Revenue Service and published in the Internal Revenue Bulletin. A disregard of rules or regulations is "careless" if the taxpayer does not exercise reasonable diligence to determine the correctness of a return position that is contrary to the rule or regulation. A disregard is "reckless" if the taxpayer makes little or no effort to determine whether a rule or regulation exists, under circumstances which demonstrate a substantial deviation from the standard of conduct that a reasonable person would observe. A disregard is "intentional" if the taxpayer knows of the rule or regulation that is disregarded. Nevertheless, a taxpayer who takes a position (other than with respect to a reportable transaction, as defined in § 1.6011-4(b) or § 1.6011-4T(b), as applicable) contrary to a revenue ruling or notice has not disregarded the ruling or notice if the contrary position has a realistic possibility of being sustained on its merits.

(3) Reasonable basis. Reasonable basis is a relatively high standard of tax reporting, that is, significantly higher than not frivolous or not patently improper. The reasonable basis standard is not satisfied by a return position that is merely arguable or that is merely a colorable claim. If a return position is reasonably based on one or more of the authorities set forth in § 1.6662-4(d)(3)(iii) (taking into account the relevance and persuasiveness of the authorities, and subsequent developments), the return position will generally satisfy the reasonable basis standard even though it may not satisfy the substantial authority standard as defined in § 1.6662-4(d)(2). (See § 1.6662-4(d)(3)(ii) for rules with respect to relevance, persuasiveness, subsequent developments, and use of a well-reasoned construction of an applicable statutory provision for purposes of the substantial understatement penalty.) In addition, the reasonable cause and good faith exception in § 1.6664-4 may provide relief from the penalty for negligence or disregard of rules or regulations, even if a return position does not satisfy the reasonable basis standard.

(c) Exception for adequate disclosure — (1) In general. No penalty under section 6662(b)(1) may be imposed on any portion of an underpayment that is attributable to a position contrary to a rule or regulation if the position is disclosed in accordance with the rules of paragraph (c)(2) of this section (and, if the position relates to a reportable transaction as defined in § 1.6011-4(b) (or § 1.6011-4T(b), as applicable), the transaction is disclosed in accordance with § 1.6011-4 (or § 1.6011-4T, as applicable)) and, in case of a position contrary to a regulation, the position represents a good faith challenge to the validity of the regulation. This disclosure exception does not apply, however, in the case of a position that does not have a reasonable basis or where the taxpayer fails to keep adequate books and records or to substantiate items properly.

(2) Method of disclosure. Disclosure is adequate for purposes of the penalty for disregarding rules or regulations if made in accordance with the provisions of §§ 1.6662-4(f)(1), (3), (4), and (5), which permit disclosure on a properly completed and filed Form 8275 or 8275-R, as appropriate. In addition, the statutory or regulatory provision or ruling in question must be adequately identified on the Form 8275 or 8275-R, as appropriate. The provisions of § 1.6662-4(f)(2), which permit disclosure in accordance with an annual revenue procedure for purposes of the substantial understatement penalty, do not apply for purposes of this section.

* * *

Sec. 1.6662-4. Substantial understatement of income tax.

* * *

(d) Substantial authority — (1) Effect of having substantial authority. If there is substantial authority for the tax treatment of an item, the item is treated as if it were shown properly on the return for the taxable year in computing the amount of the tax shown on the return. Thus, for purposes of section 6662(d) the tax attributable to the item is not included in the understatement for that year. (For special rules relating to tax shelter items see § 1.6662-4(g).)

(2) Substantial authority standard. The substantial authority standard is an objective standard involving an analysis of the law and application of the law to relevant facts. The substantial authority standard is less stringent than the more likely than not standard (the standard that is met when there is a greater than 50-percent likelihood of the position being upheld), but more stringent than the reasonable basis standard as defined in § 1.6662-3(b)(3). The possibility that a return will not be audited or, if audited, that an item will not be raised on audit, is not relevant in determining whether the substantial authority standard (or the reasonable basis standard) is satisfied.

(3) Determination of whether substantial authority is present — (i) Evaluation of authorities. There is substantial authority for the tax treatment of an item only if the weight of the authorities supporting the treatment is substantial in relation to the weight of authorities supporting contrary treatment. All authorities relevant to the tax treatment of an item, including the authorities contrary to the treatment, are taken into account in determining whether substantial authority exists. The weight of authorities is determined in light of the pertinent facts and circumstances in the manner prescribed by paragraph (d)(3)(ii) of this section. There may be substantial authority for more than one position with respect to the same item. Because the substantial authority standard is an objective standard, the taxpayer's belief that there is substantial authority for the tax treatment of an item is not relevant in determining whether there is substantial authority for that treatment.

(ii) Nature of analysis. The weight accorded an authority depends on its relevance and persuasiveness, and the type of document providing the authority. For example, a case or revenue ruling having some facts in common with the tax treatment at issue is not particularly relevant if the authority is materially distinguishable on its facts, or is otherwise inapplicable to the tax treatment at issue. An authority that merely states a conclusion ordinarily is less persuasive than one that reaches its conclusion by cogently relating the applicable law to pertinent facts. The weight of an authority from which information has been deleted, such as a private letter ruling, is diminished to the extent that the deleted information may have affected the authority's conclusions. The type of document also must be considered. For example, a revenue ruling is accorded greater weight than a private letter ruling addressing the same issue. An older private letter ruling, technical advice memorandum, general counsel memorandum or action on decision generally must be accorded less weight than a more recent one. Any document described in the preceding sentence that is more than 10 years old generally is accorded very little weight. However, the persuasiveness and relevance of a document, viewed in light of subsequent developments, should be taken into account along with the age of the document. There may be substantial authority for the tax treatment of an item despite the absence of certain types of authority. Thus, a taxpayer may have substantial authority for a position that is supported only by a well-reasoned construction of the applicable statutory provision.

(iii) Types of authority. Except in cases described in paragraph (d)(3)(iv) of this section concerning written determinations, only the following are authority for purposes of determining whether there is substantial authority for the tax treatment of an item: Applicable provisions of the Internal Revenue Code and other statutory provisions; proposed, temporary and final regulations construing such statues; revenue rulings and revenue procedures; tax treaties and regulations thereunder, and Treasury Department and other official explanations of such treaties; court cases; congressional intent as reflected in committee reports, joint explanatory statements of managers included in conference committee reports, and floor statements made prior to enactment by one of a bill's managers; General Explanations of tax legislation prepared by the Joint Committee on Taxation (the Blue Book); private letter rulings and technical advice memoranda issued after October 31, 1976; actions on decisions and general counsel memoranda issued after March 12, 1981 (as well as general counsel memoranda published in pre-1955 volumes of the Cumulative Bulletin); Internal Revenue Service information or press releases; and notices, announcements and other administrative pronouncements published by the Service in the Internal Revenue Bulletin. Conclusions reached in treatises, legal periodicals, legal opinions or opinions rendered by tax professionals are not authority. The authorities underlying such expressions of opinion where applicable to the facts of a particular case, however, may give rise to substantial authority for the tax treatment of an item. Notwithstanding the preceding list of authorities, an authority does not continue to be an authority to the extent it is overruled or modified, implicitly or explicitly, by a body with the power to overrule or modify the earlier authority. In the case of court decisions, for example, a district court opinion on an issue is not an authority if overruled or reversed by the United States Court of Appeals for such district. However, a Tax Court opinion is not considered to be overruled or modified by a court of appeals to which a taxpayer does not have a right of appeal, unless the Tax Court adopts the holding of the court of appeals. Similarly, a private letter ruling is not authority if revoked or if inconsistent with a subsequent proposed regulation, revenue ruling or other administrative pronouncement published in the Internal Revenue Bulletin.

(iv) Special rules – (A) Written determinations. There is substantial authority for the tax treatment of an item by a taxpayer if the treatment is supported by the conclusion of a ruling or a determination letter (as defined in § 301.6110-2 (d) and (e)) issued to the taxpayer, by the conclusion of a technical advice memorandum in which the taxpayer is named, or by an affirmative statement in a revenue agent's report with respect to a prior taxable year of the taxpayer ("written determinations"). The preceding sentence does not apply, however, if –

(1) There was a misstatement or omission of a material fact or the facts that subsequently develop are materially different from the facts on which the written determination was based, or

(2) The written determination was modified or revoked after the date of issuance by –

(i) A notice to the taxpayer to whom the written determination was issued,

(ii) The enactment of legislation or ratification of a tax treaty,

(iii) A decision of the United States Supreme Court,

(iv) The issuance of temporary or final regulations, or

(v) The issuance of a revenue ruling, revenue procedure, or other statement published in the Internal Revenue Bulletin.

Except in the case of a written determination that is modified or revoked on account of § 1.6662-4(d)(3)(iv)(A)(1), a written determination that is modified or revoked as described in § 1.6662-4(d)(3)(iv)(A)(2) ceases to be authority on the date, and to the extent, it is so modified or revoked. See section 6404(f) for rules which require the Secretary to abate a penalty that is attributable to erroneous written advice furnished to a taxpayer by an officer or employee of the Internal Revenue Service.

(B) Taxpayer's jurisdiction. The applicability of court cases to the taxpayer by reason of the taxpayer's residence in a particular jurisdiction is not taken into account in determining whether there is substantial authority for the tax treatment of an item. Notwithstanding the preceding sentence, there is substantial authority for the tax treatment of an item if the treatment is supported by controlling precedent of a United States Court of Appeals to which the taxpayer has a right of appeal with respect to the item.

(C) When substantial authority determined. There is substantial authority for the tax treatment of an item if there is substantial authority at the time the return containing the item is filed or there was substantial authority on the last day of the taxable year to which the return relates.

(v) Substantial authority for tax returns due before January 1, 1990. There is substantial authority for the tax treatment of an item on a return that is due (without regard to extensions) after December 31, 1982 and before January 1, 1990, if there is substantial authority for such treatment under either the provisions of paragraph (d)(3)(iii) of this section (which set forth an expanded list of authorities) or of § 1.6661-3(b)(2) (which set forth a narrower list of authorities). Under either list of authorities, authorities both for and against the position must be taken into account.

(e) Disclosure of certain information – (1) Effect of adequate disclosure. Items for which there is adequate disclosure as provided in this paragraph (e) and in paragraph (f) of this section are treated as if such items were shown properly on the return for the taxable year in computing the amount of the tax shown on the return. Thus, for purposes of section 6662(d) the tax attributable to such items is not included in the understatement for that year.

(2) Circumstances where disclosure will not have an effect. The rules of paragraph (e)(1) of this section do not apply where the item or position on the return –

(i) Does not have a reasonable basis (as defined in § 1.6662-3(b)(3));

(ii) Is attributable to a tax shelter (as defined in section 6662(d)(2)(C)(iii) and paragraph (g)(2) of this section); or

(iii) Is not properly substantiated, or the taxpayer failed to keep adequate books and records with respect to the item or position.

(3) Restriction for corporations. For purposes of paragraph (e)(2)(i) of this section, a corporation will not be treated as having a reasonable basis for its tax treatment of an item attributable to a multi-party financing transaction entered into after August 5, 1997, if the treatment does not clearly reflect the income of the corporation.

* * *

Sec. 1.6664-4. Reasonable cause and good faith exception to section 6662 penalties.

* * *

(b) Facts and circumstances taken into account — (1) In general. The determination of whether a taxpayer acted with reasonable cause and in good faith is made on a case-by-case basis, taking into account all pertinent facts and circumstances. (See paragraph (e) of this section for certain rules relating to a substantial understatement penalty attributable to tax shelter items of corporations.) Generally, the most important factor is the extent of the taxpayer's effort to assess the taxpayer's proper tax liability. Circumstances that may indicate reasonable cause and good faith include an honest misunderstanding of fact or law that is reasonable in light of all of the facts and circumstances, including the experience, knowledge, and education of the taxpayer. An isolated computational or transcriptional error generally is not inconsistent with reasonable cause and good faith. Reliance on an information return or on the advice of a professional tax advisor or an appraiser does not necessarily demonstrate reasonable cause and good faith. Similarly, reasonable cause and good faith is not necessarily indicated by reliance on facts that, unknown to the taxpayer, are incorrect. Reliance on an information return, professional advice, or other facts, however, constitutes reasonable cause and good faith if, under all the circumstances, such reliance was reasonable and the taxpayer acted in good faith. (See paragraph

(c) of this section for certain rules relating to reliance on the advice of others.) For example, reliance on erroneous information (such as an error relating to the cost or adjusted basis of property, the date property was placed in service, or the amount of opening or closing inventory) inadvertently included in data compiled by the various divisions of a multidivisional corporation or in financial books and records prepared by those divisions generally indicates reasonable cause and good faith, provided the corporation employed internal controls and procedures, reasonable under the circumstances, that were designed to identify such factual errors. Reasonable cause and good faith ordinarily is not indicated by the mere fact that there is an appraisal of the value of property. Other factors to consider include the methodology and assumptions underlying the appraisal, the appraised value, the relationship between appraised value and purchase price, the circumstances under which the appraisal was obtained, and the appraiser's relationship to the taxpayer or to the activity in which the property is used. (See paragraph (g) of this section for certain rules relating to appraisals for charitable deduction property.) A taxpayer's reliance on erroneous information reported on a Form W-2, Form 1099, or other information return indicates reasonable cause and good faith, provided the taxpayer did not know or have reason to know that the information was incorrect. Generally, a taxpayer knows, or has reason to know, that the information on an information return is incorrect if such information is inconsistent with other information reported or otherwise furnished to the taxpayer, or with the taxpayer's knowledge of the transaction. This knowledge includes, for example, the taxpayer's knowledge of the terms of his employment relationship or of the rate of return on a payor's obligation.

(2) **Examples.** The following examples illustrate this paragraph (b). They do not involve tax shelter items. (See paragraph (e) of this section for certain rules relating to the substantial understatement penalty attributable to the tax shelter items of corporations.)

Example 1. A, an individual calendar year taxpayer, engages B, a professional tax advisor, to give A advice concerning the deductibility of certain state and local taxes. A provides B with full details concerning the taxes at issue. B advises A that the taxes are fully deductible. A, in preparing his own tax return, claims a deduction for the taxes. Absent other facts, and assuming the facts and circumstances surrounding B's advice and A's reliance on such advice satisfy the requirements of paragraph (c) of this section, A is considered to have demonstrated good faith by seeking the advice of a professional tax advisor, and to have shown reasonable cause for any underpayment attributable to the deduction claimed for the taxes. However, if A had sought advice from someone that A knew, or should have known, lacked knowledge in the relevant aspects of Federal tax law, or if other facts demonstrate that A failed to act reasonably or in good faith, A would not be considered to have shown reasonable cause or to have acted in good faith.

Example 2. C, an individual, sought advice from D, a friend who was not a tax professional, as to how C might reduce his Federal tax obligations. D advised C that, for a nominal investment in Corporation X, D had received certain tax benefits which virtually eliminated D's Federal tax liability. D also named other investors who had received similar benefits. Without further inquiry, C invested in X and claimed the benefits that he had been assured by D were due him. In this case, C did not make any good faith attempt to ascertain the correctness of what D had advised him concerning his tax matters, and is not considered to have reasonable cause for the underpayment attributable to the benefits claimed.

Example 3. E, an individual, worked for Company X doing odd jobs and filling in for other employees when necessary. E worked irregular hours and was paid by the hour. The amount of E's pay check differed from week to week. The Form W-2 furnished to E reflected wages for 1990 in the amount of $29,729. It did not, however, include compensation of $1,467 paid for some hours E worked. Relying on the Form W-2, E filed a return reporting wages of $29,729. E had no reason to know that the amount reported on the Form W-2 was incorrect. Under the circumstances, E is considered to have acted in good faith in relying on the Form W-2 and to have reasonable cause for the underpayment attributable to the unreported wages.

Example 4. H, an individual, did not enjoy preparing his tax returns and procrastinated in doing so until April 15th. On April 15th, H hurriedly gathered together his tax records and materials, prepared a return, and mailed it before midnight. The return contained numerous errors, some of which were in H's favor and some of which were not. The net result of all the adjustments, however, was an underpayment of tax by H. Under these circumstances, H is not considered to have reasonable cause for the underpayment or to have acted in good faith in attempting to file an accurate return.

(c) Reliance on opinion or advice – (1) Facts and circumstances; minimum requirements. All facts and circumstances must be taken into account in determining whether a taxpayer has reasonably relied in good faith on advice (including the opinion of a professional tax advisor) as to the treatment of the taxpayer (or any entity, plan, or arrangement) under Federal tax law. For example, the taxpayer's education, sophistication and business experience will be relevant in determining whether the taxpayer's reliance on tax advice was reasonable and made in good faith. In no event will a taxpayer be considered to have reasonably relied in good faith on advice (including an opinion) unless the requirements of this paragraph (c)(1) are satisfied. The fact that these requirements are satisfied, however, will not necessarily establish that the taxpayer reasonably relied on the advice (including the opinion of a tax advisor) in good faith. For example, reliance may not be reasonable or in good faith if the taxpayer knew, or reasonably should have known, that the advisor lacked knowledge in the relevant aspects of Federal tax law.

(i) All facts and circumstances considered. The advice must be based upon all pertinent facts and circumstances and the law as it relates to those facts and circumstances. For example, the advice must take into account the taxpayer's purposes (and the relative weight of such purposes) for entering into a transaction and for structuring a transaction in a particular manner. In addition, the requirements of this paragraph (c)(1) are not satisfied if the taxpayer fails to disclose a fact that it knows, or reasonably should know, to be relevant to the proper tax treatment of an item.

(ii) No unreasonable assumptions. The advice must not be based on unreasonable factual or legal assumptions (including assumptions as to future events) and must not unreasonably rely on the representations, statements, findings, or agreements of the taxpayer or any other person. For example, the advice must not be based upon a representation or assumption which the taxpayer knows, or has reason to know, is unlikely to be true, such as an inaccurate representation or assumption as to the taxpayer's purposes for entering into a transaction or for structuring a transaction in a particular manner.

(iii) Reliance on the invalidity of a regulation. A taxpayer may not rely on an opinion or advice that a regulation is invalid to establish that the taxpayer acted with reasonable cause and good faith unless the taxpayer adequately disclosed, in accordance with § 1.6662-3(c)(2), the position that the regulation in question is invalid.

(2) Advice defined. Advice is any communication, including the opinion of a professional tax advisor, setting forth the analysis or conclusion of a person, other than the taxpayer, provided to (or for the benefit of) the taxpayer and on which the taxpayer relies, directly or indirectly, with respect to the imposition of the section 6662 accuracy-related penalty. Advice does not have to be in any particular form.

(3) Cross-reference. For rules applicable to advisors, see e.g., §§ 1.6694-1 through 1.6694-3 (regarding preparer penalties), 31 CFR 10.22 (regarding diligence as to accuracy), 31 CFR 10.33 (regarding tax shelter opinions), and 31 CFR 10.34 (regarding standards for advising with respect to tax return positions and for preparing or signing returns).

Sec. 301.6103(k)(6)-1. Disclosure of return information by certain officers and employees for investigative purposes.

* * *

(c) Definitions. The following definitions apply to this section –

(1) Disclosure of return information to the extent necessary means a disclosure of return information which an internal revenue or TIGTA employee, based on the facts and circumstances, at the time of the disclosure, reasonably believes is necessary to obtain information to perform properly the official duties described by this section, or to accomplish properly the activities connected with carrying out those official duties. The term necessary in this context does not mean essential or indispensable, but rather appropriate and helpful in obtaining the information sought. Nor does necessary in this context refer to the necessity of conducting an investigation or the appropriateness of the means or methods chosen to conduct the investigation. Section 6103(k)(6) does not limit or restrict internal revenue or TIGTA employees with respect to the decision to initiate or the conduct of an investigation. Disclosures under this paragraph (c)(1), however, may not be made indiscriminately or solely for the benefit of the recipient or as part of a negotiated quid pro quo arrangement. This paragraph (c)(1) is illustrated by the following examples:

Example 1. A revenue agent contacts a taxpayer's customer regarding the customer's purchases made from the taxpayer during the year under investigation. The revenue agent is able to obtain the purchase information only by disclosing the taxpayer's identity and the fact of the investigation. Depending on the facts and circumstances known to the revenue agent at the time of the disclosure, such as the way the customer maintains his records, it also may be necessary for the revenue agent to inform the customer of the date of the purchases and the types of merchandise involved for the customer to find the purchase information.

Example 2. A revenue agent contacts a third party witness to obtain copies of invoices of sales made to a taxpayer under examination. The third party witness provides copies of the sales invoices in question and then asks the revenue agent for the current address of the taxpayer because the taxpayer still owes money to the third party witness. The revenue agent may not disclose that current address because this disclosure would be only for the benefit of the third party witness and not necessary to obtain information for the examination.

Example 3. A revenue agent contacts a third party witness to obtain copies of invoices of sales made to a taxpayer under examination. The third party witness agrees to provide copies of the sales invoices in question only if the revenue agent provides him with the current address of the taxpayer because the taxpayer still owes money to the third party witness. The revenue agent may not disclose that current address because this disclosure would be a negotiated quid pro quo arrangement.

(2) Disclosure of return information to accomplish properly an activity connected with official duties means a disclosure of return information to carry out a function associated with official duties generally consistent with established practices and procedures. This paragraph (c)(2) is illustrated by the following example:

Example. A taxpayer failed to file an income tax return and pay the taxes owed. After the taxes were assessed and the taxpayer was notified of the balance due, a revenue officer filed a notice of federal tax lien and then served a notice of levy on the taxpayer's bank. The notices of lien and levy contained the taxpayer's name, social security number, amount of outstanding liability, and the tax period and type of tax involved. The taxpayer's assets were levied to satisfy the tax debt, but it was determined that, prior to the levy, the revenue officer failed to issue the taxpayer a notice of intent to levy, as required by section 6331 and a notice of right to hearing before the levy, as required by section 6330. The disclosure of the taxpayer's return information in the notice of levy is authorized by section 6103(k)(6) despite the revenue officer's failure to issue the notice of intent to levy or the notice of right to hearing. The ultimate validity of the underlying levy is irrelevant to the issue of whether the disclosure was authorized by section 6103(k)(6).

(3) Information not otherwise reasonably available means information that an internal revenue or TIGTA employee reasonably believes, under the facts and circumstances, at the time of a disclosure, cannot be obtained in a sufficiently accurate or probative form, or in a timely manner, and without impairing the proper performance of the official duties described by this section, without making the disclosure. This definition does not require or create the presumption or expectation that an internal revenue or TIGTA employee must seek information from a taxpayer or authorized representative prior to contacting a third party witness in an investigation. Neither the Internal Revenue Code, IRS procedures, nor these regulations require repeated contacting of an uncooperative taxpayer. Moreover, an internal revenue or TIGTA employee may make a disclosure to a third party witness to corroborate information provided by a taxpayer. This paragraph (c)(3) is illustrated by the following examples:

Example 1. A revenue agent is conducting an examination of a taxpayer. The taxpayer refuses to cooperate or provide any information to the revenue agent. Information relating to the taxpayer's examination would be information not otherwise reasonably available because of the taxpayer's refusal to cooperate and supply any information to the revenue agent. The revenue agent may seek information from a third party witness.

Example 2. A special agent is conducting a criminal investigation of a taxpayer. The special agent has acquired certain information from the taxpayer. Although the special agent has no specific reason to disbelieve the taxpayer's information, the special agent contacts several third party witnesses to confirm the information. The special agent may contact third party witnesses to verify the correctness of the information provided by the taxpayer because the IRS is not required to rely solely on information provided by a taxpayer, and a special agent may take appropriate steps, including disclosures to third party witnesses under section 6103(k)(6), to verify independently or corroborate information obtained from a taxpayer.

(4) Internal revenue employee means, for purposes of this section, an officer or employee of the IRS or Office of Chief Counsel for the IRS, or an officer or employee of a Federal agency responsible for administering and enforcing taxes under Chapters 32 (Part III of Subchapter D), 51, 52, or 53 of the Internal Revenue Code, or investigating tax refund check fraud under 18 U.S.C. 510.

(5) TIGTA employee means an officer or employee of the Office of Treasury Inspector General for Tax Administration.

(d) Examples. The following examples illustrate the application of this section:

Example 1. A revenue agent is conducting an examination of a taxpayer. The taxpayer has been very cooperative and has supplied copies of invoices as requested. Some of the taxpayer's invoices show purchases that seem excessive in comparison to the size of the taxpayer's business. The revenue agent contacts the taxpayer's suppliers for the purpose of corroborating the invoices the taxpayer provided. In contacting the suppliers, the revenue agent discloses the taxpayer's name, the dates of purchase, and the type of merchandise at issue. These disclosures are permissible under section 6103(k)(6) because, under the facts and circumstances known to the revenue agent at the time of the disclosures, the disclosures were necessary to obtain information (corroboration of invoices) not otherwise reasonably available because suppliers would be the only source available for corroboration of this information.

Example 2. A revenue agent is conducting an examination of a taxpayer. The revenue agent asks the taxpayer for business records to document the deduction of the cost of goods sold shown on Schedule C of the taxpayer's return. The taxpayer will not provide the business records to the revenue agent, who contacts a third party witness for verification of the amount on the Schedule C. In the course of the contact, the revenue agent shows the Schedule C to the third party witness. This disclosure is not authorized under section 6103(k)(6). Section 6103(k)(6) permits disclosure only of return information, not the return (including schedules and attachments) itself. If necessary, a revenue agent may disclose return information extracted from a return when questioning a third party witness. Thus, the revenue agent could have extracted the amount of cost of goods sold from the Schedule C and disclosed that amount to the third party witness.

Example 3. A special agent is conducting a criminal investigation of a taxpayer, a doctor, for tax evasion. Notwithstanding the records provided by the taxpayer and the taxpayer's bank, the special agent decided to obtain information from the taxpayer's patients to verify amounts paid to the taxpayer for his services. Accordingly, the special agent sent letters to the taxpayer's patients to verify these amounts. In the letters, the agent disclosed that he was a special agent with IRS-CI and that he was conducting a criminal investigation of the taxpayer.

Section 6103(k)(6) permits these disclosures (including the special agent disclosing his affiliation with CI and the nature of the investigation) to confirm the taxpayer's income. The decision whether to verify information already obtained is a matter of investigative judgment and is not limited by section 6103(k)(6).

Example 4. Corporation A requests a private letter ruling (PLR) as to the tax consequences of a planned transaction. Corporation A has represented that it is in compliance with laws administered by Agency B that may relate to the tax consequences of the proposed transaction. Further information is needed from Agency B relating to possible tax consequences. Under section 6103(k)(6), the IRS may disclose Corporation A's return information to Agency B to the extent necessary to obtain information from Agency B for the purpose of properly considering the tax consequences of the proposed transaction that is the subject of the PLR.

* * *

Sec. 301.6159-1. Agreements for payment of tax liabilities in installments.

* * *

(c) Acceptance, form, and terms of installment agreements — (1) Acceptance of an installment agreement — (i) In general. A proposed installment agreement has not been accepted until the IRS notifies the taxpayer or the taxpayer's representative of the acceptance. Except as provided in paragraph (c)(1)(iii) of this section, the Commissioner has the discretion to accept or reject any proposed installment agreement.

(ii) Acceptance does not reduce liabilities. The acceptance of an installment agreement by the IRS does not reduce the amount of taxes, interest, or penalties owed. (However, penalties may continue to accrue at a reduced rate pursuant to section 6651(h).)

(iii) Guaranteed installment agreements. In the case of a liability of an individual for income tax, the Commissioner shall accept a proposed installment agreement if, as of the date the individual proposes the installment agreement—

(A) The aggregate amount of the liability (not including interest, penalties, additions to tax, and additional amounts) does not exceed $10,000;

(B) The taxpayer (and, if the liability relates to a joint return, the taxpayer's spouse) has not, during any of the preceding five taxable years—

(1) Failed to file any income tax return;

(2) Failed to pay any required income tax; or

(3) Entered into an installment agreement for the payment of any income tax;

(C) The Commissioner determines that the taxpayer is financially unable to pay the liability in full when due (and the taxpayer submits any information the Commissioner requires to make that determination);

(D) The installment agreement requires full payment of the liability within three years; and

(E) The taxpayer agrees to comply with the provisions of the Internal Revenue Code for the period the agreement is in effect.

(2) Form of installment agreements. An installment agreement must be in writing. A written installment agreement may take the form of a document signed by the taxpayer and the Commissioner or a written confirmation of an agreement entered into by the taxpayer and the Commissioner that is mailed or personally delivered to the taxpayer.

(3) Terms of installment agreements. (i) Except as otherwise provided in this section, an installment agreement is effective from the date the IRS notifies the taxpayer or the taxpayer's representative of its acceptance until the date the agreement ends by its terms or until it is superseded by a new installment agreement.

(ii) By its terms, an installment agreement may end upon the expiration of the period of limitations on collection in section 6502 and § 301.6502-1, or at some prior date.

(iii) As a condition to entering into an installment agreement with a taxpayer, the Commissioner may require that—

(A) The taxpayer agree to a reasonable extension of the period of limitations on collection; and

(B) The agreement contain terms that protect the interests of the Government.

(iv) Except as otherwise provided in an installment agreement, all payments made under the installment agreement will be applied in the best interests of the Government.

(v) While an installment agreement is in effect, the Commissioner may request, and the taxpayer must provide, a financial condition update at any time.

(vi) At any time after entering into an installment agreement, the Commissioner and the taxpayer may agree to modify or terminate an installment agreement or may agree to a new installment agreement that supercedes the existing agreement.

(d) Rejection of a proposed installment agreement — (1) When a proposed installment agreement becomes rejected. A proposed installment agreement has not been rejected until the IRS notifies the taxpayer or the taxpayer's representative of the rejection, the reason(s) for rejection, and the right to an appeal.

(2) Independent administrative review. The IRS may not notify a taxpayer or taxpayer's representative of the rejection of an installment agreement until an independent administrative review of the proposed rejection is completed.

(3) Appeal of rejection of a proposed installment agreement. The taxpayer may administratively appeal a rejection of a proposed installment agreement to the IRS Office of Appeals (Appeals) if, within the 30-day period commencing the day after the taxpayer is notified of the rejection, the taxpayer requests an appeal in the manner provided by the Commissioner.

(e) Modification or termination of installment agreements by the Internal Revenue Service — (1) Inadequate information or jeopardy. The Commissioner may terminate an installment agreement if the Commissioner determines that—

(i) Information which was provided to the IRS by the taxpayer or the taxpayer's representative in connection with the granting of the installment agreement was inaccurate or incomplete in any material respect; or

(ii) Collection of any liability to which the installment agreement applies is in jeopardy.

(2) Change in financial condition, failure to timely pay an installment or another Federal tax liability, or failure to provide requested financial information. The Commissioner may modify or terminate an installment agreement if—

(i) The Commissioner determines that the financial condition of a taxpayer that is party to the agreement has significantly changed; or

(ii) A taxpayer that is party to the installment agreement fails to—

(A) Timely pay an installment in accordance with the terms of the installment agreement;

(B) Pay any other Federal tax liability when the liability becomes due; or

(C) Provide a financial condition update requested by the Commissioner.

(3) Notice. Unless the Commissioner determines that collection of the tax is in jeopardy, the Commissioner will notify the taxpayer in writing at least 30 days prior to modifying or terminating an installment agreement pursuant to paragraph (e)(1) or (2) of this section. The notice provided pursuant to this section must briefly describe the reason for the intended modification or termination. Upon receiving notice, the taxpayer may provide information showing that the reason for the proposed modification or termination is incorrect.

(4) Appeal of modification or termination of an installment agreement. The taxpayer may administratively appeal the modification or termination of an installment agreement to Appeals if, following issuance of the notice required by paragraph (e)(3) of this section and prior to the expiration of the 30-day period commencing the day after the modification or termination is to take effect, the taxpayer requests an appeal in the manner provided by the Commissioner.

* * *

(g) Suspension of the statute of limitations on collection. The statute of limitations under section 6502 for collection of any liability shall be suspended during the period that a proposed installment agreement relating to that liability is pending with the IRS, for 30 days immediately following the rejection of a proposed installment agreement, and for 30 days immediately following the termination of an installment agreement. If, within the 30 days following the rejection or termination of an installment agreement, the taxpayer files an appeal with Appeals, the statute of limitations for collection shall be suspended while the rejection or termination is being considered by Appeals. The statute of limitations for collection shall continue to run if an exception under paragraph (f)(2) of this section applies and levy is not prohibited with respect to the taxpayer.

Sec. 301.6320-1. Notice and opportunity for hearing upon filing of notice of Federal tax lien.

* * *

(b) Entitlement to a CDP hearing — (1) In general. A taxpayer is entitled to one CDP hearing with respect to the first filing of a NFTL (on or after January 19, 1999) for a given tax period or periods with respect to the unpaid tax shown on the NFTL if the taxpayer timely requests such a hearing. The taxpayer must request such a hearing during the 30-day period that commences the day after the end of the five business day period within which the IRS is required to provide the taxpayer with notice of the filing of the NFTL.

(2) Questions and answers. The questions and answers illustrate the provisions of this paragraph (b) as follows:

Q-B1. Is a taxpayer entitled to a CDP hearing with respect to the filing of a NFTL for a type of tax and tax periods previously subject to a CDP Notice with respect to a NFTL filed in a different location on or after January 19, 1999?

A-B1. No. Although the taxpayer will receive notice of each filing of a NFTL, under section 6320(b)(2), the taxpayer is entitled to only one CDP hearing under section 6320 for the type of tax and tax periods with respect to the first filing of a NFTL that occurs on or after January 19, 1999, with respect to that unpaid tax. Accordingly, if the taxpayer does not timely request a CDP hearing with respect to the first filing of a NFTL on or after January 19, 1999, for a given tax period or periods with respect to an unpaid tax, the taxpayer forgoes the right to a CDP hearing with Appeals and judicial review of the Appeals determination with respect to the NFTL. Under such circumstances, the taxpayer may request an equivalent hearing as described in paragraph (i) of this section.

Q-B2. Is the taxpayer entitled to a CDP hearing when a NFTL for an unpaid tax is filed on or after January 19, 1999, in one recording office and a NFTL was previously filed for the same unpaid tax in another recording office prior to that date?

A-B2. Yes. Under section 6320(b)(2), the taxpayer is entitled to a CDP hearing under section 6320 for each tax period with respect to the first filing of a NFTL on or after January 19, 1999, with respect to an unpaid tax, whether or not a NFTL was filed prior to January 19, 1999, for the same unpaid tax and tax period or periods.

Q-B3. When the IRS provides the taxpayer with a substitute CDP Notice and the taxpayer timely requests a CDP hearing, is the taxpayer entitled to a CDP hearing before Appeals?

A-B3. Yes. Unless the taxpayer provides the IRS a written withdrawal of the request that Appeals conduct a CDP hearing, the taxpayer is entitled to a CDP hearing before Appeals. Following the hearing, Appeals will issue a Notice of Determination, and the taxpayer is entitled to seek judicial review of that Notice of Determination.

Q-B4. If the IRS sends a second CDP Notice under section 6320 (other than a substitute CDP Notice) for a tax period and with respect to an unpaid tax for which a section 6320 CDP Notice was previously sent, is the taxpayer entitled to a section 6320 CDP hearing based on the second CDP Notice?

A-B4. No. The taxpayer is entitled to a CDP hearing under section 6320 for each tax period only with respect to the first filing of a NFTL on or after January 19, 1999, with respect to an unpaid tax.

Q-B5. Is a nominee of, or a person holding property of, the taxpayer entitled to a CDP hearing or an equivalent hearing?

A-B5. No. Such person is not the person described in section 632 and is, therefore, not entitled to a CDP hearing or an equivalent hearing (as discussed in paragraph (i) of this section). Such person, however, may seek reconsideration by the IRS office collecting the tax or filing the NFTL, an administrative hearing before Appeals under its Collection Appeals Program, or assistance from the National Taxpayer Advocate. However, any such administrative hearing would not be a CDP hearing under section 6320 and any determination or decision resulting from the hearing would not be subject to judicial review under section 6320. Such person also may avail himself of the administrative procedure included in section 6325(b)(4) or of any other procedures to which he is entitled.

(3) Examples. The following examples illustrate the principles of this paragraph (b):

Example 1. H and W are jointly and severally liable with respect to a jointly filed income tax return for 1996. The IRS files a NFTL with respect to H and W in County X on January 26, 1999. This is the first NFTL filed on or after January 19, 1999, for their 1996 liability. H and W are each entitled to a CDP hearing with respect to the NFTL filed in County X. On June 17, 1999, a NFTL for the same tax liability is filed against H and W in County Y. The IRS will give H and W notification of the NFTL filed in County Y. H and W, however, are not entitled to a CDP hearing or an equivalent hearing with respect to the NFTL filed in County Y.

Example 2. Federal income tax liability for 1997 is assessed against individual D. D buys an asset and puts it in individual E's name. A NFTL is filed against E, as nominee of D in County X on June 5, 1999, for D's federal income tax liability for 1997. The IRS will give D a CDP Notice with respect to the NFTL filed in County X. The IRS will not notify E of the NFTL filed in County X. The IRS is not required to notify E of the filing of the NFTL in County X. Although E is named on the NFTL filed in County X, E is not the person described in section 6321 (the taxpayer) who is named on the NFTL.

(c) Requesting a CDP hearing — (1) In general. When a taxpayer is entitled to a CDP hearing under section 6320 the CDP hearing must be requested during the 30-day period that commences the day after the end of the five business day period within which the IRS is required to provide the taxpayer with a CDP Notice with respect to the filing of the NFTL.

(2) Questions and answers. The questions and answers illustrate the provisions of this paragraph (c) as follows:

Q-C1. What must a taxpayer do to obtain a CDP hearing?

A-C1. (i) The taxpayer must make a request in writing for a CDP hearing. The request for a CDP hearing shall include the information and signature specified in A-C1(ii) of this paragraph (c)(2). See A-D7 and A-D8 of paragraph (d)(2).

(ii) The written request for a CDP hearing must be dated and must include the following:

(A) The taxpayer's name, address, daytime telephone number (if any), and taxpayer identification number (e.g., SSN, ITIN or EIN).

(B) The type of tax involved.

(C) The tax period at issue.

(D) A statement that the taxpayer requests a hearing with Appeals concerning the filing of the NFTL.

(E) The reason or reasons why the taxpayer disagrees with the filing of the NFTL.

(F) The signature of the taxpayer or the taxpayer's authorized representative.

(iii) If the IRS receives a timely written request for CDP hearing that does not satisfy the requirements set forth in A-C1(ii) of this paragraph (c)(2), the IRS will make a reasonable attempt to contact the taxpayer and request that the taxpayer comply with the unsatisfied requirements. The taxpayer must perfect any timely written request for a CDP hearing that does not satisfy the requirements set forth in A-C1(ii) of this paragraph (c)(2) within a reasonable period of time after a request from the IRS.

(iv) Taxpayers are encouraged to use Form 12153, "Request for a Collection Due Process Hearing," in requesting a CDP hearing so that the request can be readily identified and forwarded to Appeals. Taxpayers may obtain a copy of Form 12153 by contacting the IRS office that issued the CDP Notice, by downloading a copy from the IRS Internet site, http://www.irs.gov/pub/[fxsp0]irs-pdf/f12153.pdf, or by calling, toll-free, 1-800-829-3676.

(v) The taxpayer must affirm any timely written request for a CDP hearing which is signed or alleged to have been signed on the taxpayer's behalf by the taxpayer's spouse or other unauthorized representative by filing, within a reasonable period of time after a request from the IRS, a signed, written affirmation that the request was originally submitted on the taxpayer's behalf. If the affirmation is filed within a reasonable period of time after a request, the timely CDP hearing request will be considered timely with respect to the non-signing taxpayer. If the affirmation is not filed within a reasonable period of time after a request, the CDP hearing request will be denied with respect to the non-signing taxpayer.

Q-C2. Must the request for the CDP hearing be in writing?

A-C2. Yes. There are several reasons why the request for a CDP hearing must be in writing. The filing of a timely request for a CDP hearing is the first step in what may result in a court proceeding. A written request will provide proof that the CDP hearing was requested and thus permit the court to verify that it has jurisdiction over any subsequent appeal of the Notice of Determination issued by Appeals. In addition, the receipt of the written request will establish the date on which the periods of limitation under section 6502 (relating to collection after assessment), section 6531 (relating to criminal prosecutions), and section 6532 (relating to suits) are suspended as a result of the CDP hearing and any judicial appeal. Moreover, because the IRS anticipates that taxpayers will contact the IRS office that issued the CDP Notice for further information or assistance in filling out Form 12153, or to attempt to resolve their liabilities prior to going through the CDP hearing process, the requirement of a written request should help prevent any misunderstanding as to whether a CDP hearing has been requested. If the information requested on Form 12153 is furnished by the taxpayer, the written request also will help to establish the issues for which the taxpayer seeks a determination by Appeals.

Q-C3. When must a taxpayer request a CDP hearing with respect to a CDP Notice issued under section 6320?

A-C3. A taxpayer must submit a written request for a CDP hearing within the 30-day period that commences the day after the end of the five business day period following the filing of the NFTL. Any request filed during the five business day period (before the beginning of the 30-day period) will be deemed to be filed on the first day of the 30-day period. The period for submitting a written request for a CDP hearing with respect to a CDP Notice issued under section 6320 is slightly different from the period for submitting a written request for a CDP hearing with respect to a CDP Notice issued under section 6330. For a CDP Notice issued under section 6330 the taxpayer must submit a written request for a CDP hearing within the 30-day period commencing the day after the date of the CDP Notice.

Q-C4. How will the timeliness of a taxpayer's written request for a CDP hearing be determined?

A-C4. The rules and regulations under section 7502 and section 7503 will apply to determine the timeliness of the taxpayer's request for a CDP hearing, if properly transmitted and addressed as provided in A-C6 of this paragraph (c)(2).

Q-C5. Is the 30-day period within which a taxpayer must make a request for a CDP hearing extended because the taxpayer resides outside the United States?

A-C5. No. Section 6320 does not make provision for such a circumstance. Accordingly, all taxpayers who want a CDP hearing under section 6320 must request such a hearing within the 30-day period that commences the day after the end of the five business day notification period.

Q-C6. Where must the written request for a CDP hearing be sent?

A-C6. The written request for a CDP hearing must be sent, or hand delivered (if permitted), to the IRS office and address as directed on the CDP Notice. If the address of that office does not appear on the CDP Notice, the taxpayer should obtain the address of the office to which the written request should be sent or hand delivered by calling, toll-free, 1-800-829-1040 and providing the taxpayer's identification number (e.g., SSN, ITIN or EIN).

Q-C7. What will happen if the taxpayer does not request a CDP hearing in writing within the 30-day period that commences the day after the end of the five business day notification period?

A-C7. If the taxpayer does not request a CDP hearing in writing within the 30-day period that commences on the day after the end of the five-business-day notification period, the taxpayer foregoes the right to a CDP hearing under section 6320 with respect to the unpaid tax and tax periods shown on the CDP Notice. A written request submitted within the 30-day period that does not satisfy the requirements set forth in A-C1(ii)(A), (B), (C), (D) or (F) of this paragraph (c)(2) is considered timely if the request is perfected within a reasonable period of time pursuant to A-C1(iii) of this paragraph (c)(2). If the request for CDP hearing is untimely, either because the request was not submitted within the 30-day period or not perfected within the reasonable period provided, the taxpayer will be notified of the untimeliness of the request and offered an equivalent hearing. In such cases, the taxpayer may obtain an equivalent hearing without submitting an additional request. See paragraph (i) of this section.

Q-C8. When must a taxpayer request a CDP hearing with respect to a substitute CDP Notice?

A-C8. A CDP hearing with respect to a substitute CDP Notice must be requested in writing by the taxpayer prior to the end of the 30-day period commencing the day after the date of the substitute CDP Notice.

Q-C9. Can taxpayers attempt to resolve the matter of the NFTL with an officer or employee of the IRS office collecting the tax or filing the NFTL either before or after requesting a CDP hearing?

A-C9. Yes. Taxpayers are encouraged to discuss their concerns with the IRS office collecting the tax or filing the NFTL, either before or after they request a CDP hearing. If such a discussion occurs before a request is made for a CDP hearing, the matter may be resolved without the need for Appeals consideration. However, these discussions do not suspend the running of the 30-day period, commencing the day after the end of the five business day notification period, within which the taxpayer is required to request a CDP hearing, nor do they extend that 30-day period. If discussions occur after the request for a CDP hearing is filed and the taxpayer resolves the matter with the IRS office collecting the tax or filing the NFTL, the taxpayer may withdraw in writing the request that a CDP hearing be conducted by Appeals. The taxpayer can also waive in writing some or all of the requirements regarding the contents of the Notice of Determination.

(3) Examples. The following examples illustrate the principles of this paragraph (c):

Example 1. A NFTL for a 1997 income tax liability assessed against individual A is filed in County X on June 17, 1999. The IRS mails a CDP Notice to individual A's last known address on June 18, 1999. Individual A has until July 26, 1999, a Monday, to request a CDP hearing. The five business day period within which the IRS is required to notify individual A of the filing of the NFTL in County X expires on June 24, 1999. The 30-day period within which individual A may request a CDP hearing begins on June 25, 1999. Because the 30-day period expires on July 24, 1999, a Saturday, individual A's written request for a CDP hearing will be considered timely if it is properly transmitted and addressed to the IRS in accordance with section 7502 and the regulations thereunder no later than July 26, 1999.

Example 2. Same facts as in Example 1, except that individual A is on vacation, outside the United States, or otherwise does not receive or read the CDP Notice until July 19, 1999. As in Example 1, individual A has until July 26, 1999, to request a CDP hearing. If individual A does not request a CDP hearing, individual A may request an equivalent hearing as to the NFTL at a later time. The taxpayer should make a request for an equivalent hearing at the earliest possible time.

Example 3. Same facts as in Example 2, except that individual A does not receive or read the CDP Notice until after July 26, 1999, and does not request a hearing by July 26, 1999. Individual A is not entitled to a CDP hearing. Individual A may request an equivalent hearing as to the NFTL at a later time. The taxpayer should make a request for an equivalent hearing at the earliest possible time.

Example 4. Same facts as in Example 1, except the IRS determines that the CDP Notice mailed on June 18, 1999, was not mailed to individual A's last known address. As soon as practicable after making this determination, the IRS will mail a substitute CDP Notice to individual A at individual A's last known address, hand deliver the substitute CDP Notice to individual A, or leave the substitute CDP Notice at individual A's dwelling or usual place of business. Individual A will have 30 days commencing on the day after the date of the substitute CDP Notice within which to request a CDP hearing.

* * *

(i) Equivalent hearing — (1) In general. A taxpayer who fails to make a timely request for a CDP hearing is not entitled to a CDP hearing. Such a taxpayer may nevertheless request an administrative hearing with Appeals, which is referred to herein as an "equivalent hearing." The equivalent hearing will be held by Appeals and generally will follow Appeals' procedures for a CDP hearing. Appeals will not, however, issue a Notice of Determination. Under such circumstances, Appeals will issue a Decision Letter.

(2) Questions and answers. The questions and answers illustrate the provisions of this paragraph (i) as follows:

Q-I1. What must a taxpayer do to obtain an equivalent hearing?

A-I1. (i) A request for an equivalent hearing must be made in writing. A written request in any form that requests an equivalent hearing will be acceptable if it includes the information and signature required in A-I1(ii) of this paragraph (i)(2).

(ii) The request must be dated and must include the following:

(A) The taxpayer's name, address, daytime telephone number (if any), and taxpayer identification number (e.g., SSN, ITIN or EIN).

(B) The type of tax involved.

(C) The tax period at issue.

(D) A statement that the taxpayer is requesting an equivalent hearing with Appeals concerning the filing of the NFTL.

(E) The reason or reasons why the taxpayer disagrees with the filing of the NFTL.

(F) The signature of the taxpayer or the taxpayer's authorized representative.

(iii) The taxpayer must perfect any timely written request for an equivalent hearing that does not satisfy the requirements set forth in A-I1(ii) of this paragraph (i)(2) within a reasonable period of time after a request from the IRS. If the requirements are not satisfied within a reasonable period of time, the taxpayer's equivalent hearing request will be denied.

(iv) The taxpayer must affirm any timely written request for an equivalent hearing that is signed or alleged to have been signed on the taxpayer's behalf by the taxpayer's spouse or other unauthorized representative, and that otherwise meets the requirements set forth in A-I1(ii) of this paragraph (i)(2), by filing, within a reasonable period of time after a request from the IRS, a signed written affirmation that the request was originally submitted on the taxpayer's behalf. If the affirmation is filed within a reasonable period of time after a request, the timely equivalent hearing request will be considered timely with respect to the non-signing taxpayer. If the affirmation is not filed within a reasonable period of time, the equivalent hearing request will be denied with respect to the non-signing taxpayer.

Q-I2. What issues will Appeals consider at an equivalent hearing?

A-I2. In an equivalent hearing, Appeals will consider the same issues that it would have considered at a CDP hearing on the same matter.

Q-I3. Are the periods of limitation under sections 6502, 6531, and 6532 suspended if the taxpayer does not timely request a CDP hearing and is subsequently given an equivalent hearing?

A-I3. No. The suspension period provided for in section 6330(e) relates only to hearings requested within the 30-day period that commences on the day after the end of the five business day period following the filing of the NFTL, that is, CDP hearings.

Q-I4. Will collection action, including the filing of additional NFTLs, be suspended if a taxpayer requests and receives an equivalent hearing?

A-I4. Collection action is not required to be suspended. Accordingly, the decision to take collection action during the pendency of an equivalent hearing will be determined on a case-by-case basis. Appeals may request the IRS office with responsibility for collecting the taxes to suspend all or some collection action or to take other appropriate action if it determines that such action is appropriate or necessary under the circumstances.

Q-I5. What will the Decision Letter state?

A-I5. The Decision Letter will generally contain the same information as a Notice of Determination.

Q-I6. Will a taxpayer be able to obtain Tax Court review of a decision made by Appeals with respect to an equivalent hearing?

A-I6. Section 6320 does not authorize a taxpayer to appeal the decision of Appeals with respect to an equivalent hearing. A taxpayer may under certain circumstances be able to seek Tax Court review of Appeals' denial of relief under section 6015. Such review must be sought within 90 days of the issuance of Appeals' determination on those issues, as provided by section 6015(e).

Q-I7. When must a taxpayer request an equivalent hearing with respect to a CDP Notice issued under section 6320?

A-I7. A taxpayer must submit a written request for an equivalent hearing within the one-year period commencing the day after the end of the five-business-day period following the filing of the NFTL. This period is slightly different from the period for submitting a written request for an equivalent hearing with respect to a CDP Notice issued under section 6330. For a CDP Notice issued under section 6330 a taxpayer must submit a written request for an equivalent hearing within the one-year period commencing the day after the date of the CDP Notice issued under section 6330.

Q-I8. How will the timeliness of a taxpayer's written request for an equivalent hearing be determined?

A-I8. The rules and regulations under section 7502 and section 7503 will apply to determine the timeliness of the taxpayer's request for an equivalent hearing, if properly transmitted and addressed as provided in A-I10 of this paragraph (i)(2).

Q-I9. Is the one-year period within which a taxpayer must make a request for an equivalent hearing extended because the taxpayer resides outside the United States?

A-I9. No. All taxpayers who want an equivalent hearing concerning the filing of the NFTL must request the hearing within the one-year period commencing the day after the end of the five-business-day period following the filing of the NFTL.

Q-I10. Where must the written request for an equivalent hearing be sent?

A-I10. The written request for an equivalent hearing must be sent, or hand delivered (if permitted), to the IRS office and address as directed on the CDP Notice. If the address of the issuing office does not appear on the CDP Notice, the taxpayer should obtain the address of the office to which the written request should be sent or hand delivered by calling, toll-free, 1-800-829-1040 and providing the taxpayer's identification number (e.g., SSN, ITIN or EIN).

Q-I11. What will happen if the taxpayer does not request an equivalent hearing in writing within the one-year period commencing the day after the end of the five-business-day period following the filing of the NFTL?

A-I11. If the taxpayer does not request an equivalent hearing with Appeals within the one-year period commencing the day after the end of the five-business-day period following the filing of the NFTL, the taxpayer foregoes the right to an equivalent hearing with respect to the unpaid tax and tax periods shown on the CDP Notice. A written request submitted within the one-year period that does not satisfy the requirements set forth in A-I1(ii) of this paragraph (i)(2) is considered timely if the request is perfected within a reasonable period of time pursuant to A-I1(iii) of this paragraph (i)(2). If a request for equivalent hearing is untimely, either because the request was not submitted within the one-year period or not perfected within the reasonable period provided, the equivalent hearing request will be denied. The taxpayer, however, may seek reconsideration by the IRS office collecting the tax, assistance from the National Taxpayer Advocate, or an administrative hearing before Appeals under its Collection Appeals Program or any successor program.

* * *

Sec. 301.6323(b)-1. Protection for certain interests even though notice filed.

(a) Securities — (1) In general. Even though a notice of a lien imposed by section 6321 is filed in accordance with § 301.6323(f)-1, the lien is not valid with respect to a security (as defined in paragraph (d) of § 301.6323(h)-1) against –

(i) A purchaser (as defined in paragraph (f) of § 301.6323(h)-1) of the security who at the time of purchase did not have actual notice or knowledge (as defined in paragraph (a) of § 301.6323(i)-1) of the existence of the lien;

(ii) A holder of a security interest (as defined in paragraph (a) of § 301.6323(h)-1) in the security who did not have actual notice or knowledge (as defined in paragraph (a) of § 301.6323(i)-1) of the existence of the lien at the time the security interest came into existence or at the time such security interest was acquired from a previous holder for a consideration in money or money's worth; or

(iii) A transferee of an interest protected under subdivision (i) or (ii) of this subparagraph to the same extent the lien is invalid against his transferor.

For purposes of subdivision (iii) of this subparagraph, no person can improve his position with respect to the lien by reacquiring the interest from an intervening purchaser or holder of a security interest against whom the lien is invalid.

(2) Examples. The application of this paragraph may be illustrated by the following examples:

Example 1. On May 1, 1969, in accordance with § 301.6323(f)-1, a notice of lien is filed with respect to A's delinquent tax liability. On May 20, 1969. A sells 100 shares of common stock in X corporation to B, who, on the date of the sale, does not have actual notice or knowledge of the existence of the lien. Because B purchased the stock without actual notice or knowledge of the lien, under subdivision (i) of subparagraph (1) of this paragraph, the stock purchased by B is not subject to the lien.

Example 2. Assume the same facts as in example 1 except that on May 30, 1969, B sells the 100 shares of common stock in X corporation to C who on May 5, 1969, had actual notice of the existence of the tax lien against A. Because the X stock when purchased by B was not subject to the lien, under subdivision (iii) of subparagraph (1) of this paragraph, the stock purchased by C is not subject to the lien. C succeeds to B's rights, even though C had actual notice of the lien before B's purchase.

Example 3. On June 1, 1970, in accordance with § 301.6323(f)-1, a notice of lien is filed with respect to D's delinquent tax liability. D owns 20 $1,000 bonds issued by the Y company. On June 10, 1970, D obtains a loan from M bank for $5,000 using the Y company bonds as collateral. At the time the loan is made M bank does not have actual notice or knowledge of the existence of the tax lien. Because M bank did not have actual notice or knowledge of the lien when the security interest came into existence, under subdivision (ii) of subparagraph (1) of this paragraph, the tax lien is not valid against M bank to the extent of its security interest.

Example 4. Assume the same facts as in example 3 except that on June 19, 1970, M bank assigns the chose in action and its security interest to N, who had actual notice or knowledge of the existence of the lien on June 1, 1970. Because the security interest was not subject to the lien to the extent of M bank's security interest, the security interest held by N is to the same extent entitled to priority over the tax lien because N succeeds to M bank's rights. See subdivision (iii) of subparagraph (1) of this paragraph.

Example 5. On July 1, 1970, in accordance with § 301.6323(f)-1, a notice of lien is filed with respect to E's delinquent tax liability. E owns ten $1,000 bonds issued by the Y company. On July 5, 1970, E borrows $4,000 from F and delivers the bonds to F as collateral for the loan. At the time the loan is made, F has actual knowledge of the existence of the tax lien and, therefore, holds the security interest subject to the lien on the bonds. On July 10, 1970, F sells the security interest to G for $4,000 and delivers the Y company bonds pledged as collateral. G does not have actual notice or knowledge of the existence of the lien on July 10, 1970. Because G did not have actual notice or knowledge of the lien at the time he purchased the security interest, under subdivision (ii) of subparagraph (1) of this paragraph, the tax lien is not valid against G to the extent of his security interest.

Example 6. Assume the same facts as in example 5 except that, instead of purchasing the security interest from F on July 10, 1970, G lends $4,000 to F and takes a security interest in F's security interest in the bonds on that date. Because G became the holder of a security interest in a security interest after notice of lien was filed and does not directly have a security interest in a security, the security interest held by G is not entitled to a priority over the tax lien under the provisions of subparagraph (1) of this paragraph.

(b) Motor vehicles — (1) In general. Even though a notice of a lien imposed by section 6321 is filed in accordance with § 301.6323(f)-1, the lien is not valid against a purchaser (as defined in paragraph (f) of § 301.6323(h)-1) of a motor vehicle (as defined in paragraph (c) of § 301.6323(h)-1) if –

(i) At the time of the purchase, the purchaser did not have actual notice or knowledge (as defined in paragraph (a) of § 301.6323(i)-1) of the existence of the lien, and

(ii) Before the purchaser obtains such notice or knowledge, he has acquired actual possession of the motor vehicle and has not thereafter relinquished actual possession to the seller or his agent.

(2) Examples. The application of this paragraph may be illustrated by the following examples:

Example (1). A, a delinquent taxpayer against whom a notice of tax lien has been filed in accordance with § 301.6323(f)-1, sells his automobile (which qualifies as a motor vehicle under paragraph (c) of § 301.6323(h)-1) to B, an automobile dealer. B takes actual possession of the automobile and does not thereafter relinquish actual possession to the seller or his agent. Subsequent to his purchase, B learns of the existence of the tax lien against A. Even though notice of lien was filed before the purchase, the lien is not valid against B, because B did not know of the existence of the lien before the purchase and before acquiring actual possession of the vehicle.

Example (2). C is a wholesaler of used automobiles. A notice of lien has been filed with respect to C's delinquent tax liability in accordance with § 301.6323(f)-1. Subsequent to such filing, D, a used automobile dealer, purchases and takes actual possession of 20 automobiles (which qualify as motor vehicles under the provisions of paragraph (c) of §

301.6323(h)-1) from C at an auction and places them on his lot for sale. C does not reacquire possession of any of the automobiles. At the time of his purchase, D does not have actual notice or knowledge of the existence of the lien against C. Even though notice of lien was filed before D's purchase, the lien was not valid against D because D did not know of the existence of the lien before the purchase and before acquiring actual possession of the vehicles.

(3) Cross reference. For provisions relating to additional circumstances in which the lien imposed by section 6321 may not be valid against the purchaser of tangible personal property (including a motor vehicle) purchased at retail, see paragraph (c) of this section.

(c) Personal property purchased at retail — (1) In general. Even though a notice of a lien imposed by section 6321 is filed in accordance with § 301.6323(f)-1, the lien is not valid against a purchaser (as defined in paragraph (f) of § 301.6323(h)-1) of tangible personal property purchased at a retail sale (as defined in subparagraph (2) of this paragraph (c)) unless at the time of purchase the purchaser intends the purchase to (or knows that the purchase will) hinder, evade, or defeat the collection of any tax imposed by the Internal Revenue Code of 1954.

(2) Definition of retail sale. For purposes of this paragraph, the term "retail sale" means a sale, made in the ordinary course of the seller's trade or business, of tangible personal property of which the seller is the owner. Such term includes a sale in customary retail quantities by a seller who is going out of business, but does not include a bulk sale or an auction sale in which goods are offered in quantities substantially greater than are customary in the ordinary course of the seller's trade or business or an auction sale of goods the owner of which is not in the business of selling such goods.

(3) Example. The application of this paragraph may be illustrated by the following example:

> **Example.** A purchases a refrigerator from the M company, a retail appliance dealer. Prior to such purchase, a notice of lien was filed with respect to M's delinquent tax liability in accordance with § 301.6323(f)-1. At the time of the purchase A knows of the existence of the lien. However, A does not intend the purchase to hinder, evade, or defeat the collection of any internal revenue tax, and A does not have any reason to believe that the purchase will affect the collection of any internal revenue tax. Even though notice of lien was filed before the purchase, the lien is not valid against A because A in good faith purchased the refrigerator at retail in the ordinary course of the M company's business.

(d) Personal property purchased in casual sale — (1) In general. Even though a notice of lien imposed by section 6321 is filed in accordance with § 301.6323(f)-1, the lien is not valid against a purchaser (as defined in § 301.6323(h)-1(f)) of household goods, personal effects, or other tangible personal property of a type described in § 301.6334-1 (which includes wearing apparel, school books, fuel, provisions, furniture, arms for personal use, livestock, and poultry (whether or not the seller is the head of a family); and books and tools of a trade, business, or profession (whether or not the trade, business, or profession of the seller)), purchased, other than for resale, in a casual sale for less than $1,380, effective for 2010 and adjusted each year based on the rate of inflation (excluding interest and expenses described in § 301.6323(e)-1).

(2) Limitation. This paragraph applies only if the purchaser does not have actual notice or knowledge (as defined in paragraph (a) of § 301.6323(i)-1) –

(i) Of the existence of the tax lien, or

(ii) That the sale is one of a series of sales.

For purposes of subdivision (ii) of this subparagraph, a sale is one of a series of sales if the seller plans to dispose of, in separate transactions, substantially all of his household goods, personal effects, and other tangible personal property described in § 301.6334-1.

(3) Examples. The application of this paragraph may be illustrated by the following examples:

Example 1. A, an attorney's widow, sells a set of law books for $200 to B, for B's own use. Prior to the sale a notice of lien was filed with respect to A's delinquent tax liability in accordance with § 301.6323(f)-1. B has no actual notice or knowledge of the tax lien. In addition, B does not know that the sale is one of a series of sales. Because the sale is a casual sale for less than $1,380 and involves books of a profession (tangible personal property of a type described in § 301.6334-1, irrespective of the fact that A has never engaged in the legal profession), the tax lien is not valid against B even though a notice of lien was filed prior to the time of B's purchase.

Example 2. Assume the same facts as in example 1 except that B purchases the books for resale in his second-hand bookstore. Because B purchased the books for resale, he purchased the books subject to the lien.

Example 3. In an advertisement appearing in a local newspaper, G indicates that he is offering for sale a lawn mower, a used television set, a desk, a refrigerator, and certain used dining room furniture. In response to the advertisement, H purchases the dining room furniture for $200. H does not receive any information which would impart notice of a lien, or that the sale is one of a series of sales, beyond the information contained in the advertisement. Prior to the sale a notice of lien was filed with respect to G's delinquent tax liability in accordance with § 301.6323(f)-1. Because H had no actual notice or knowledge that substantially all of G's household goods were being sold or that the sale is one of a series of sales, and because the sale is a casual sale for less than $1,380, H does not purchase the dining room furniture subject to the lien. The household goods are of a type described in § 301.6334-1(a)(2) irrespective of whether G is the head of a family or whether all such household goods offered for sale exceed $8,250 in value.

(e) Personal property subject to possessory liens. Even though a notice of a lien imposed by section 6321 is filed in accordance with § 301.6323(f)-1, the lien is not valid against a holder of a lien on tangible personal property which under local law secures the reasonable price of the repair or improvement of the property if the property is, and has been, continuously in the possession of the holder of the lien from the time the possessory lien arose. For example, if local law gives an automobile repairman the right to retain possession of an automobile he has repaired as security for payment of the repair bill and the repairman retains continuous possession of the automobile until his lien is satisfied, a tax line filed in accordance with section 6323(f)(1) which has attached to the automobile will not be valid to the extent of the reasonable price of the repairs. It is immaterial that the notice of tax lien was filed before the repairman undertook his work or that he knew of the lien before undertaking the work.

(f) Real property tax and special assessment liens — (1) In general. Even though a notice of a lien imposed by section 6321 is filed in accordance with § 301.6323(f)-1, the lien is not valid against the holder of another lien upon the real property (regardless of when such other lien arises), if such other lien is entitled under local law to priority over security interests in real property which are prior in time and if such other lien on real property secures payment of –

(i) A tax of general application levied by any taxing authority based upon the value of the property;

(ii) A special assessment imposed directly upon the property by any taxing authority, if the assessment is imposed for the purpose of defraying the cost of any public improvement; or

(iii) Charges for utilities or public services furnished to the property by the United States, a State or political subdivision thereof, or an instrumentality of any one or more of the foregoing.

(2) Examples. The application of this paragraph may be illustrated by the following examples:

Example 1. A owns Blackacre in the city of M. A notice of lien affecting Blackacre is filed in accordance with § 301.6323(f)-1. Subsequent to the filing of the notice of lien, the city of M acquires a lien against Blackacre to secure payment of real estate taxes. Such taxes are levied against all property in the city in proportion to the value of the property. Under local law, the holder of a lien for real property taxes is entitled to priority over a security interest in real property even though the security interest is prior in time. Because the real property tax lien held by the city of M secures payment of a tax of general application and is entitled to priority over security interests which are prior in time, the lien held by the city of M is entitled to priority over the Federal tax lien with respect to Blackacre.

Example 2. B owns Whiteacre in N county. A notice of lien affecting Whiteacre is filed in accordance with § 301.6323(f)-1. Subsequent to the filing of the notice of lien, N county constructs a sidewalk, paves the street, and installs water and sewer lines adjacent to Whiteacre. In order to defray the cost of these improvements, N county imposes upon Whiteacre a special assessment which under local law results in a lien upon Whiteacre that is entitled to priority over security interests that are prior in time. Because the special assessment lien is (i) entitled under local law to priority over security interests which are prior in time, and (ii) imposed directly upon real property to defray the cost of a public improvement, the special assessment lien has priority over the Federal tax lien with respect to Whiteacre.

Example 3. C owns Greenacre in town O. A notice of lien affecting Greenacre is filed in accordance with § 301.6323(f)-1. Town O furnishes water and electricity to Greenacre and periodically collects a fee for these services. Subsequent to the filing of the notice of lien, town O supplies water and electricity to Greenacre, and C fails to pay the charges for these services. Under local law, town O acquires a lien to secure charges for the services, and this lien has priority over security interests which are prior in time. Because the lien of town O (i) is for services furnished to the real property and (ii) has priority over earlier security interests, town O's lien has priority over the Federal tax lien with respect to Greenacre.

(g) Residential property subject to a mechanic's lien for certain repairs and improvements — (1) In general. Even though a notice of a lien imposed by section 6321 is filed in accordance with § 301.6323(f)-1, the lien is not valid against a mechanic's lienor (as defined in § 301.6323(h)-1(b)) who holds a lien for the repair or improvement of a personal residence if –

(i) The residence is occupied by the owner and contains no more than four dwelling units; and

(ii) The contract price on the prime contract with the owner for the repair or improvement (excluding interest and expenses described in § 301.6323(e)-1) is not more than $6,890, effective for 2010 and adjusted each year based on the rate of inflation.

(iii) For purposes of paragraph (g)(1)(ii) of this section, the amounts of subcontracts under the prime contract with the owner are not to be taken into consideration for purposes of computing the $6,890 prime contract price. It is immaterial that the notice of tax lien was filed before the contractor undertakes his work or that he knew of the lien before undertaking his work.

(2) Examples. The application of this paragraph may be illustrated by the following examples:

Example 1. A owns a building containing four apartments, one of which he occupies as his personal residence. A notice of lien which affects the building is filed in accordance with § 301.6323(f)-1. Thereafter, A enters into a contract with B in the amount of $800, which includes labor and materials, to repair the roof of the building. B purchases roofing shingles from C for $300. B completes the work and A fails to pay B the agreed amount. In turn, B fails to pay C for the shingles. Under local law, B and C acquire mechanic's liens on A's building. Because the contract price on the prime contract with A is not more than $6,890 and under local law B and C acquire mechanic's liens on A's building, the liens of B and C have priority over the Federal tax lien.

Example 2. Assume the same facts as in Example 1, except that the amount of the prime contract between A and B is $7,100. Because the amount of the prime contract with the owner, A, is in excess of $6,890, the tax lien has priority over the entire amount of each of the mechanic's liens of B and C, even though the amount of the contract between B and C is $300.

Example 3. Assume the same facts as in Example 1, except that A and B do not agree in advance upon the amount due under the prime contract but agree that B will perform the work for the cost of materials and labor plus 10 percent of such cost. When the work is completed, it is determined that the total amount due is $850. Because the prime contract price is not more than $6,890 and under local law B and C acquire mechanic's liens on A's residence, the liens of B and C have priority over the Federal tax lien.

(h) Attorney's liens — (1) In general. Even though notice of a lien imposed by section 6321 is filed in accordance with § 301.6323(f)-1, the lien is not valid against an attorney who, under local law, holds a lien upon, or a contract enforceable against, a judgment or other amount in settlement of a claim or of a cause of action. The priority afforded an attorney's lien under this paragraph shall not exceed the amount of the attorney's reasonable compensation for obtaining the judgment or procuring the settlement. For purposes of this paragraph, reasonable compensation means the amount customarily allowed under local law for an attorney's services for litigating or settling a similar case or administrative claim. However, reasonable compensation shall be determined on the basis of the facts and circumstances of each individual case. It is immaterial that the notice of tax lien is filed before the attorney undertakes his work or that the attorney knows of the tax lien before undertaking his work. This paragraph does not apply to an attorney's lien which may arise from the defense of a claim or cause of action against a taxpayer except to the extent such lien is held upon a judgment or other amount arising from the adjudication or settlement of a counterclaim in favor of the taxpayer. In the case of suits against the taxpayer, see § 301.6325-1(d)(2) for rules relating to the subordination of the tax lien to facilitate tax collection.

(2) Claim or cause of action against the United States. Paragraph (h)(1) of this section does not apply to an attorney's lien with respect to—

(i) Any judgment or other fund resulting from the successful litigation or settlement of an administrative claim or cause of action against the United States to the extent that the United States, under any legal or equitable right, offsets its liability under the judgment or settlement against any liability of the taxpayer to the United States, or

(ii) Any amount credited against any liability of the taxpayer in accordance with section 6402.

(3) Examples. The provisions of this paragraph may be illustrated by the following examples:

Example 1. A notice of lien is filed against A in accordance with § 301.6323(f)-1. Subsequently, A is struck by an automobile and retains B, an attorney to institute suit on A's behalf against the operator of the automobile. B knows of the tax lien before he begins his work. Under local law, B is entitled to a lien upon any recovery in order to secure payment of his fee. A is awarded damages of $10,000. B charges a fee of $3,000 which is the fee customarily allowed under local law in similar cases and which is found to be reasonable under the circumstances of this particular case. Because, under local law, B holds a lien for the amount of his reasonable compensation for obtaining the judgment, B's lien has priority over the Federal tax lien.

Example 2. Assume the same facts as in example 1, except that before suit is instituted A and the owner of the automobile settle out of court for $7,500. B charges a reasonable and customary fee of $1,800 for procuring the settlement and under local law holds a lien upon the settlement in order to secure payment of the fee. Because, under local law, B holds a lien for the amount of his reasonable compensation for obtaining the settlement, B has priority over the Federal tax lien.

Example 3. In accordance with § 301.6323(f)-1, a notice of lien in the amount of $8,000 is filed against C, a contractor. Subsequently C retains D, an attorney, to initiate legal proceedings to recover the amount allegedly due him for construction work he has performed for the United States. C and D enter into an agreement which provides that D will receive a reasonable and customary fee of $2,500 as compensation for his services. Under local law, the agreement will give rise to a lien which is enforceable by D against any amount recovered in the suit. C is successful in the suit and is awarded $10,000. D claims $2,500 of the proceeds as his fee. The United States, however, exercises its right of set-off and applies $8,000 of the $10,000 award to satisfy C's tax liability. Because the $10,000 award resulted from the successful litigation of a cause of action against the United States, B's contract for attorney's fees is not enforceable against the amount recovered to the extent the United States offsets its liability under the judgment against C's tax liability. It is immaterial that D had no notice or knowledge of the tax lien at the time he began work on the case.

(i) Certain insurance contracts — (1) In general. Even though a notice of a lien imposed by section 6321 is filed in accordance with § 301.6323(f)-1, the lien is not valid with respect to a life insurance, endowment, or annuity contract, against an organization which is the insurer under the contract, at any time –

(i) Before the insuring organization has actual notice or knowledge (as defined in paragraph (a) of § 301.6323(i)-1) of the existence of the tax lien,

(ii) After the insuring organization has actual notice or knowledge of the lien (as defined in paragraph (a) of § 301.6323(i)-1), with respect to advances (including contractual interest thereon as provided in paragraph (a) of § 301.6323(e)-1) required to be made automatically to maintain the contract in force under an agreement entered into before the insuring organization had such actual notice or knowledge, or

(iii) After the satisfaction of a levy pursuant to section 6332(b), unless and until the Internal Revenue Service delivers to the insuring organization a notice (for example, another notice of levy, a letter, etc.) executed after the date of such satisfaction, that the lien exists.

Delivery of the notice described in subdivision (iii) of this subparagraph may be made by any means, including regular mail, and delivery of the notice shall be effective only from the time of actual receipt of the notification by the insuring organization. The provisions of this paragraph are applicable to matured as well as unmatured insurance contracts.

(2) Examples. The provisions of this paragraph may be illustrated by the following examples:

Example 1. On May 1, 1964, the X insurance company issues a life insurance policy to A. On June 1, 1970, a tax assessment is made against A, and on June 2, 1970, a notice of lien with respect to the assessment is filed in accordance with § 301.6323(f)-1. On July 1, 1970, without actual notice or knowledge of the tax lien, the X company makes a "policy loan" to A. Under subparagraph (1)(i) of this paragraph, the loan, including interest (in accordance with the provisions of paragraph (a) of § 301.6323(e)-1), will have priority over the tax lien because X company did not have actual notice or knowledge of the tax lien at the time the policy loan was made.

Example 2. On May 1, 1964, B enters into a life insurance contract with the Y insurance company. Under one of the provisions of the contract, in the event a premium is not paid, Y is to advance out of the cash loan value of the policy the amount of an unpaid premium in order to maintain the contract in force. The contract also provides for interest on any advances so made. On June 1, 1971, a tax assessment is made against B, and on June 2, 1971, in accordance with section 6323(f)-1, a notice of lien is filed. On July 1, 1971, B fails to pay the premium due on that date, and Y makes an automatic premium loan to keep the policy in force. At the time the automatic premium loan is made, Y had actual knowledge of the tax lien. Under subparagraph (1)(ii) of this paragraph, the lien is not valid against Y with respect to the advance (and the contractual interest thereon), because the advance was required to be made automatically under an agreement entered into before Y had actual notice or knowledge of the tax lien.

Example 3. On May 1, 1964, C enters into a life insurance contract with the Z insurance company. On January 4, 1971, an assessment is made against C for $5,000 unpaid income taxes, and on January 11, 1971, in accordance with § 301.6323(f)-1, a notice of lien is filed. On January 29, 1971, a notice of levy with respect to C's delinquent tax is served on Z company. The amount which C could have had advanced to him from Z company under the contract on the 90th day after service of the notice of levy on Z company is $2,000. The Z company pays $2,000 pursuant to the notice of levy, thereby satisfying the levy upon the contract in accordance with § 6332(b). On February 1, 1973, Z company advances $500 to C, which is the increment in policy loan value since satisfaction of the levy of January 29, 1971. On February 5, 1973, a new notice of levy for the unpaid balance of the delinquent taxes, executed after the first levy was satisfied, is served upon Z company. Because the new notification was not received by Z company until after the policy loan was made, under paragraph (1)(iii) of this paragraph, the tax lien is not valid against Z company with respect to the policy loan (including interest thereon in accordance with paragraph (a) of § 301.6323(e)-1).

Example 4. On June 1, 1973, a tax assessment is made against D and on June 2, 1973, in accordance with § 301.6323(f)-1, a notice of lien with respect to the assessment is filed. On July 2, 1973, D executes an assignment of his rights, as the insured, under an insurance contract to M bank as security for a loan. M bank holds its security interest subject to the lien because it is not an insurer entitled to protection under section 6323(b)(9) and did not become a holder of the security interest prior to the filing of the notice of lien for purposes of section 6323(a). It is immaterial that a notice of levy had not been served upon the insurer before the assignment to M bank was made.

(j) Effective/applicability date. This section applies to any notice of Federal tax lien filed on or after April 4, 2011.

Sec. 301.6323(h)-1. Definitions.

(a) Security interest — (1) In general. The term "security interest" means any interest in property acquired by contract for the purpose of securing payment or performance of an obligation or indemnifying against loss or liability. A security interest exists at any time –

(i) If, at such time, the property is in existence and the interest has become protected under local law against a subsequent judgment lien (as provided in subparagraph (2) of this paragraph (a)) arising out of an unsecured obligation; and

(ii) To the extent that, at such time, the holder has parted with money or money's worth (as defined in subparagraph (3) of this paragraph (a)).
For purposes of this subparagraph, a contract right (as defined in paragraph (c)(2)(i) of § 301.6323(c)-1) is in existence when the contract is made. An account receivable (as defined in paragraph (c)(2)(ii) of § 301.6323(c)-1) is in existence when, and to the extent, a right to payment is earned by performance.

A security interest must be in existence, within the meaning of this paragraph, at the time as of which its priority against a tax lien is determined. For example, to be afforded priority under the provisions of paragraph (a) of § 301.6323(a)-1 a security interest must be in existence within the meaning of this paragraph before a notice of lien is filed.

(2) Protection against a subsequent judgment lien. (i) For purposes of this paragraph, a security interest is deemed to be protected against a subsequent judgment lien on –

(A) The date on which all actions required under local law to establish the priority of a security interest against a judgment lien have been taken, or

(B) If later, the date on which all required actions are deemed effective, under local law, to establish the priority of the security interest against a judgment lien. For purposes of this subdivision, the dates described in (A) and (B) of this subdivision (i) shall be determined without regard to any rule or principle of local law which permits the relation back of any requisite action to a date earlier than the date on which the action is actually performed. For purposes of this paragraph, a judgment lien is a lien held by a judgment lien creditor as defined in paragraph (g) of this section.

(ii) The following example illustrates the application of paragraph (a)(2):

Example. (i) Under the law of State X, a security interest in certificated securities, negotiable documents, or instruments may be perfected, and hence protected against a judgment lien, by filing or by the secured party taking possession of the collateral. However, a security interest in such intangible personal property is considered to be temporarily perfected for a period of 20 days from the time the security interest attaches, to the extent that it arises for new value given under an authenticated security agreement. Under the law of X, a security interest attaches to such collateral when there is an agreement between the creditor and debtor that the interest attaches, the debtor has rights in the property, and consideration is given by the creditor. Under the law of X, in the case of temporary perfection, the security interest in such property is protected during the 20-day period against a judgment lien arising, after the security interest attaches, out of an unsecured obligation. Upon expiration of the 20-day period, the holder of the security interest must perfect its security interest under local law.

(ii) Because the security interest is perfected during the 20-day period against a subsequent judgment lien arising out of an unsecured obligation, and because filing or the taking of possession before the conclusion of the period of temporary perfection is not considered, for purposes of paragraph (a)(2)(i) of this section, to be a requisite action which relates back to the beginning of such period, the requirements of this paragraph are satisfied. Because filing or taking possession is a condition precedent to continued perfection, filing or taking possession of the collateral is a requisite action to establish such priority after expiration of the period of temporary perfection. If there is a lapse of perfection for failure to file or take possession, the determination of when the security interest exists (for purposes of protection against the tax lien) is made without regard to the period of temporary perfection.

(3) Money or money's worth. For purposes of this paragraph, the term money or money's worth includes money, a security (as defined in paragraph (d) of this section), tangible or intangible property, services, and other consideration reducible to a money value. Money or money's worth also includes any consideration which otherwise would constitute money or money's worth under the preceding sentence which was parted with before the security interest would otherwise exist if, under local law, past consideration is sufficient to support an agreement giving rise to a security interest, and provided that the grant of the security interest is not a fraudulent transfer under local law or 28 U.S.C. § 3304(a)(2). A firm commitment to part with money, a security, tangible or intangible property, services, or other consideration reducible to a money value does not, in itself, constitute a consideration in money or money's worth. A relinquishing or promised relinquishment of dower, courtesy, or of a statutory estate created in lieu of dower or courtesy, or of other marital rights is not a consideration in money or money's worth. Nor is love and affection, promise of marriage, or any other consideration not reducible to a money value a consideration in money or money's worth.

(4) Holder of a security interest. For purposes of this paragraph, the holder of a security interest is the person in whose favor there is a security interest. For provisions relating to the treatment of a purchaser of commercial financing security as a holder of a security interest, see § 301.6323(c)-1(e).

(b) Mechanic's lienor — (1) In general. The term "mechanic's lienor" means any person who under local law has a lien on real property (or on the proceeds of a contract relating to real property) for services, labor, or materials furnished in connection with the construction or improvement (including demolition) of the property. A mechanic's lienor is treated as having a lien on the later of –

(i) The date on which the mechanic's lien first becomes valid under local law against subsequent purchasers of the real property without actual notice, or

(ii) The date on which the mechanic's lienor begins to furnish the services, labor, or materials.

(2) Example. The provisions of this paragraph may be illustrated by the following example:

Example. On February 1, 1968, A lets a contract for the construction of an office building on property owned by him. On March 1, 1968, in accordance with § 301.6323(f)-1, a notice of lien for delinquent Federal taxes owed by A is filed. On April 1, 1968, B, a lumber dealer, delivers lumber to A's property. On May 1, 1968, B records a mechanic's lien against the property to secure payment of the price of the lumber. Under local law, B's mechanic's lien is valid against subsequent purchasers of real property without notice from February 1, 1968, which is the date the construction contract was entered into. Because the date on which B's mechanic's lien is valid under local law against subsequent purchasers is February 1, and the date on which B begins to furnish the materials is April 1, the date on which B becomes a mechanic's lienor within the meaning of this paragraph is April 1, the later of these two dates. Under paragraph (a) of § 301.6323(a)-1, B's mechanic's lien will not have priority over the Federal tax lien, even though under local law the mechanic's lien relates back to the date of the contract.

(c) Motor vehicle. (1) The term "motor vehicle" means a self-propelled vehicle which is registered for highway use under the laws of any State, the District of Columbia, or a foreign country.

(2) A motor vehicle is "registered for highway use" at the time of a sale if immediately prior to the sale it is so registered under the laws of any State, the District of Columbia, or a foreign country. Where immediately prior to the sale of a motor vehicle by a dealer, the dealer is permitted under local law to operate it under a dealer's tag, license, or permit issued to him, the motor vehicle is considered to be registered for highway use in the name of the dealer at the time of the sale.

(d) Security. The term "security" means any bond, debenture, note, or certificate or other evidence of indebtedness, issued by a corporation or a government or political subdivision thereof, with interest coupons or in registered form, share of stock, voting trust certificate, or any certificate of interest or participation in, certificate of deposit or receipt for, temporary or interim certificate for, or warrant or right to subscribe to or purchase, any of the foregoing; negotiable instrument; or money.

(e) Tax lien filing. The term "tax lien filing" means the filing of notice of the lien imposed by section 6321 in accordance with § 301.6323(f)-1.

(f) Purchaser — (1) In general. The term "purchaser" means a person who, for adequate and full consideration in money or money's worth (as defined in subparagraph (3) of this paragraph (f)), acquires an interest (other than a lien or security interest) in property which is valid under local law against subsequent purchasers without actual notice.

(2) Interest in property. For purposes of this paragraph, each of the following interest is treated as an interest in property, if it is not a lien or security interest:

(i) A lease of property,

(ii) A written executory contract to purchase or lease property,

(iii) An option to purchase or lease property and any interest therein, or

(iv) An option to renew or extend a lease of property.

(3) Adequate and full consideration in money or money's worth. For purposes of this paragraph, the term "adequate and full consideration in money or money's worth" means a consideration in money or money's worth having a reasonable relationship to the true value of the interest in property acquired. See paragraph (a)(3) of this section for definition of the term "money or money's worth." Adequate and full consideration in money or money's worth may include the consideration in a bona fide bargain purchase. The term also includes the consideration in a transaction in which the purchaser has not completed performance of his obligation, such as the consideration in an installment purchase contract, even though the purchaser has not completed the installment payments.

(4) Examples. The provisions of this paragraph may be illustrated by the following examples:

Example 1. A enters into a contract for the purchase of a house and lot from B. Under the terms of the contract A makes a down payment and is to pay the balance of the purchase price in 120 monthly installments. After payment of the last installment, A is to receive a deed to the property. A enters into possession, which under local law protects his interest in the property against subsequent purchasers without actual notice. After A has paid five monthly installments, a notice of lien for Federal taxes is filed against B in accordance with § 301.6323(f)-1. Because the contract is an executory contract to purchase property and is valid under local law against subsequent purchasers without actual notice, A qualifies as a purchaser under this paragraph.

Example 2. C owns a residence which he leases to his son-in-law, D, for a period of 5 years commencing January 1, 1968. The lease provides for payment of $100 a year, although the fair rental value of the residence is $2,500 a year. The lease is recorded on December 31, 1967. On March 1, 1968, a notice of tax lien for unpaid Federal taxes of C is filed in accordance with § 301.6323(f)-1. Under local law, D's interest is protected against subsequent purchasers without actual notice. However, because the rental paid by D has no reasonable relationship to the value of the interest in property acquired, D does not qualify as a purchaser under this paragraph.

(g) Judgment lien creditor. The term "judgment lien creditor" means a person who has obtained a valid judgment, in a court of record and of competent jurisdiction, for the recovery of specifically designated property or for a certain sum of money. In the case of a judgment for the recovery of a certain sum of money, a judgment lien creditor is a person who has perfected a lien under the judgment on the property involved. A judgment lien is not perfected until the identity of the lienor, the property subject to the lien, and the amount of the lien are established. Accordingly, a judgment lien does not include an attachment or garnishment lien until the lien has ripened into judgment, even though under local law the lien of the judgment relates back to an earlier date. If recording or docketing is necessary under local law before a judgment becomes effective against third parties acquiring liens on real property, a judgment lien under such local law is not perfected with respect to real property until the time of such recordation or docketing. If under local law levy or seizure is necessary before a judgment lien becomes effective against third parties acquiring liens on personal property, then a judgment lien under such local law is not perfected until levy or seizure of the personal property involved. The term "judgment" does not include the determination of a quasi-judicial body or of an individual acting in a quasi-judicial capacity such as the action of State taxing authorities.

(h) Effective/applicability date. This section applies as of April 4, 2011.

* * *

Sec. 301.6330-1. Notice and opportunity for hearing prior to levy.

* * *

(d) Conduct of CDP hearing — (1) In general. If a taxpayer requests a CDP hearing under section 6330(a)(3)(B) (and does not withdraw that request), the CDP hearing will be held with Appeals. The taxpayer is entitled to only one CDP hearing under section 6330 with respect to the unpaid tax and tax periods shown on the CDP Notice. To the extent practicable, the CDP hearing requested under section 6330 will be held in conjunction with any CDP hearing the taxpayer requests under section 6320. A CDP hearing will be conducted by an employee or officer of Appeals who, prior to the first CDP hearing under section 6320 or section 6330, has had no involvement with respect to the tax for the tax periods to be covered by the hearing, unless the taxpayer waives this requirement.

(2) Questions and answers. The questions and answers illustrate the provisions of this paragraph (d) as follows:

Q-D1. Under what circumstances can a taxpayer receive more than one pre-levy CDP hearing under section 6330 with respect to a tax period?

A-D1. The taxpayer may receive more than one CDP pre-levy hearing under section 6330 with respect to a tax period where the tax involved is a different type of tax (for example, an employment tax liability, where the original CDP hearing for the tax period involved an income tax liability), or where the same type of tax for the same period is involved, but where the amount of the unpaid tax has changed as a result of an additional assessment of tax (not including interest or penalties) for that period or an additional accuracy-related or filing-delinquency penalty has been assessed. The taxpayer is not entitled to another CDP hearing under section 6330 if the additional assessment represents accruals of interest, accruals of penalties, or both.

Q-D2. Will a CDP hearing with respect to one tax period be combined with a CDP hearing with respect to another tax period?

A-D2. To the extent practicable, a CDP hearing with respect to one tax period shown on a CDP Notice will be combined with any and all other CDP hearings which the taxpayer has requested.

Q-D3. Will a CDP hearing under section 6330 be combined with a CDP hearing under section 6320?

A-D3. To the extent it is practicable, a CDP hearing under section 6330 will be held in conjunction with a CDP hearing under section 6320.

Q-D4. What is considered to be prior involvement by an employee or officer of Appeals with respect to the tax and tax period or periods involved in the hearing?

A-D4. Prior involvement by an Appeals officer or employee includes participation or involvement in a matter (other than a CDP hearing held under either section 6320 or section 6330, that the taxpayer may have had with respect to the tax and tax period shown on the CDP Notice. Prior involvement exists only when the taxpayer, the tax and the tax period at issue in the CDP hearing also were at issue in the prior non-CDP matter, and the Appeals officer or employee actually participated in the prior matter.

Q-D5. How can a taxpayer waive the requirement that the officer or employee of Appeals have no prior involvement with respect to the tax and tax period or periods involved in the CDP hearing?

A-D5. The taxpayer must sign a written waiver.

Q-D6. How are CDP hearings conducted?

A-D6. The formal hearing procedures required under the Administrative Procedure Act, 5 U.S.C. 551 et seq., do not apply to CDP hearings. CDP hearings are much like Collection Appeal Program (CAP) hearings in that they are informal in nature and do not require the Appeals officer or employee and the taxpayer, or the taxpayer's representative, to hold a face-to-face meeting. A CDP hearing may, but is not required to, consist of a face-to-face meeting, one or more written or oral communications between an Appeals officer or employee and the taxpayer or the taxpayer's representative, or some combination thereof. A transcript or recording of any face-to-face meeting or conversation between an Appeals officer or employee and the taxpayer or the taxpayer's representative is not required. The taxpayer or the taxpayer's representative does not have the right to subpoena and examine witnesses at a CDP hearing.

Q-D7. If a taxpayer wants a face-to-face CDP hearing, where will it be held?

A-D7. Except as provided in A-D8 of this paragraph (d)(2), a taxpayer who presents in the CDP hearing request relevant, non-frivolous reasons for disagreement with the proposed levy will ordinarily be offered an opportunity for a face-to-face conference at the Appeals office closest to taxpayer's residence. A business taxpayer will ordinarily be offered an opportunity for a face-to-face conference at the Appeals office closest to the taxpayer's principal place of business. If that is not satisfactory to the taxpayer, the taxpayer will be given an opportunity for a hearing by telephone or by correspondence. In all cases, the Appeals officer or employee will review the case file, as described in A-F4 of paragraph (f)(2). If no face-to-face or telephonic conference is held, or other oral communication takes place, review of the documents in the case file, as described in A-F4 of paragraph (f)(2), will constitute the CDP hearing for purposes of section 6330(b).

Q-D8. In what circumstances will a face-to-face CDP conference not be granted?

A-D8. A taxpayer is not entitled to a face-to-face CDP conference at a location other than as provided in A-D7 of this paragraph (d)(2) and this A-D8. If all Appeals officers or employees at the location provided for in A-D7 of this paragraph (d)(2) have had prior involvement with the taxpayer as provided in A-D4 of this paragraph (d)(2), the taxpayer will not be offered a face-to-face conference at that location, unless the taxpayer elects to waive the requirement of section 6330(b)(3). The taxpayer will be offered a face-to-face conference at another Appeals office if Appeals would have offered the taxpayer a face-to-face conference at the location provided in A-D7 of this paragraph (d)(2), but for the disqualification of all Appeals officers or employees at that location. A face-to-face CDP conference concerning a taxpayer's underlying liability will not be granted if the request for a hearing or other taxpayer communication indicates that the taxpayer wishes only to raise irrelevant or frivolous issues concerning that liability. A face-to-face CDP conference concerning a collection alternative, such as an installment agreement or an offer to compromise liability, will not be granted unless other taxpayers would be eligible for the alternative in similar circumstances. For example, because the IRS does not consider offers to compromise from taxpayers who have not filed required returns or have not made certain required deposits of tax, as set forth in Form 656, "Offer in Compromise," no face-to-face conference will be granted to a taxpayer who wishes to make an offer to compromise but has not fulfilled those obligations. Appeals in its discretion, however, may grant a face-to-face conference if Appeals determines that a face-to-face conference is appropriate to explain to the taxpayer the requirements for becoming eligible for a collection alternative. In all cases, a taxpayer will be given an opportunity to demonstrate eligibility for a collection alternative and to become eligible for a collection alternative, in order to obtain a face-to-face conference. For purposes of determining whether a face-to-face conference will be granted, the determination of a taxpayer's eligibility for a collection alternative is made without regard to the taxpayer's ability to pay the unpaid tax. A face-to-face conference need not be granted if the taxpayer does not provide the required information set forth in A-C1(ii)(E) of paragraph (c)(2). See also A-C1(iii) of paragraph (c)(2).

(3) Examples. The following examples illustrate the principles of this paragraph (d):

Example 1. Individual A timely requests a CDP hearing concerning a proposed levy for the 1998 income tax liability assessed against individual A. Appeals employee B previously conducted a CDP hearing regarding a NFTL filed with respect to individual A's 1998 income tax liability. Because employee B's only prior involvement with individual A's 1998 income tax liability was in connection with a section 6320 CDP hearing, employee B may conduct the CDP hearing under section 6330 involving the proposed levy for the 1998 income tax liability.

Example 2. Individual C timely requests a CDP hearing concerning a proposed levy for the 1998 income tax liability assessed against individual C. Appeals employee D previously conducted a Collection Appeals Program (CAP) hearing regarding a NFTL filed with respect to individual C's 1998 income tax liability. Because employee D's prior involvement with individual C's 1998 income tax liability was in connection with a non-CDP hearing, employee D may not conduct the CDP hearing under section 6330 unless individual C waives the requirement that the hearing will be conducted by an Appeals officer or employee who has had no prior involvement with respect to individual C's 1998 income tax liability.

Example 3. Same facts as in Example 2, except that the prior CAP hearing only involved individual C's 1997 income tax liability and employment tax liabilities for 1998 reported on Form 941, "Employer's Quarterly Federal Tax Return." Employee D would not be considered to have prior involvement because the prior CAP hearing in which she participated did not involve individual C's 1998 income tax liability.

Example 4. Appeals employee F is assigned to a CDP hearing concerning a proposed levy for a trust fund recovery penalty (TFRP) assessed pursuant to section 6672 against individual E. Appeals employee F participated in a prior CAP hearing involving individual E's 1999 income tax liability, and participated in a CAP hearing involving the employment taxes of business entity X, which incurred the employment tax liability to which the TFRP assessed against individual E relates. Appeals employee F would not be considered to have prior involvement because the prior CAP hearings in which he participated did not directly involve the TFRP assessed against individual E.

Example 5. Appeals employee G is assigned to a CDP hearing concerning a proposed levy for a TFRP assessed pursuant to section 6672 against individual H. In preparing for the CDP hearing, Appeals employee G reviews the Appeals case file concerning the prior CAP hearing involving the TFRP assessed pursuant to section 6672 against individual H. Appeals employee G is not deemed to have participated in the previous CAP hearing involving the TFRP assessed against individual H by such review.

* * *

Sec. 301.6402-2. Claims for credit or refund.

* * *

(b) Grounds set forth in claim. (1) No refund or credit will be allowed after the expiration of the statutory period of limitation applicable to the filing of a claim therefor except upon one or more of the grounds set forth in a claim filed before the expiration of such period. The claim must set forth in detail each ground upon which a credit or refund is claimed and facts sufficient to apprise the Commissioner of the exact basis thereof. The statement of the grounds and facts must be verified by a written declaration that it is made under the penalties of perjury. A claim which does not comply with this paragraph will not be considered for any purpose as a claim for refund or credit.

* * *

Sec. 301.6404-2 Abatement of interest.

(a) In general. (1) Section 6404(e)(1) provides that the Commissioner may (in the Commissioner's discretion) abate the assessment of all or any part of interest on any –

(i) Deficiency (as defined in section 6211(a), relating to income, estate, gift, generation-skipping, and certain excise taxes) attributable in whole or in part to any unreasonable error or delay by an officer or employee of the Internal Revenue Service (IRS) (acting in an official capacity) in performing a ministerial or managerial act; or

(ii) Payment of any tax described in section 6212(a) (relating to income, estate, gift, generation-skipping, and certain excise taxes) to the extent that any unreasonable error or delay in payment is attributable to an officer or employee of the IRS (acting in an official capacity) being erroneous or dilatory in performing a ministerial or managerial act.

(2) An error or delay in performing a ministerial or managerial act will be taken into account only if no significant aspect of the error or delay is attributable to the taxpayer involved or to a person related to the taxpayer within the meaning of section 267(b) or section 707(b)(1). Moreover, an error or delay in performing a ministerial or managerial act will be taken into account only if it occurs after the IRS has contacted the taxpayer in writing with respect to the deficiency or payment. For purposes of this paragraph (a)(2), no significant aspect of the error or delay is attributable to the taxpayer merely because the taxpayer consents to extend the period of limitations.

(b) Definitions — (1) Managerial act means an administrative act that occurs during the processing of a taxpayer's case involving the temporary or permanent loss of records or the exercise of judgment or discretion relating to management of personnel. A decision concerning the proper application of federal tax law (or other federal or state law) is not a managerial act. Further, a general administrative decision, such as the IRS's decision on how to organize the processing of tax returns or its delay in implementing an improved computer system, is not a managerial act for which interest can be abated under paragraph (a) of this section.

(2) Ministerial act means a procedural or mechanical act that does not involve the exercise of judgment or discretion, and that occurs during the processing of a taxpayer's case after all prerequisites to the act, such as conferences and review by supervisors, have taken place. A decision concerning the proper application of federal tax law (or other federal or state law) is not a ministerial act.

(c) Examples. The following examples illustrate the provisions of paragraphs (b) (1) and (2) of this section. Unless otherwise stated, for purposes of the examples, no significant aspect of any error or delay is attributable to the taxpayer, and the IRS has contacted the taxpayer in writing with respect to the deficiency or payment. The examples are as follows:

Example 1. A taxpayer moves from one state to another before the IRS selects the taxpayer's income tax return for examination. A letter explaining that the return has been selected for examination is sent to the taxpayer's old address and then forwarded to the new address. The taxpayer timely responds, asking that the audit be transferred to the IRS's district office that is nearest the new address. The group manager timely approves the request. After the request for transfer has been approved, the transfer of the case is a ministerial act. The Commissioner may (in the Commissioner's discretion) abate interest attributable to any unreasonable delay in transferring the case.

Example 2. An examination of a taxpayer's income tax return reveals a deficiency with respect to which a notice of deficiency will be issued. The taxpayer and the IRS identify all agreed and unagreed issues, the notice is prepared and reviewed (including review by District Counsel, if necessary), and any other relevant prerequisites are completed. The issuance of the notice of deficiency is a ministerial act. The Commissioner may (in the Commissioner's discretion) abate interest attributable to any unreasonable delay in issuing the notice.

Example 3. A revenue agent is sent to a training course for an extended period of time, and the agent's supervisor decides not to reassign the agent's cases. During the training course, no work is done on the cases assigned to the agent. The decision to send the revenue agent to the training course and the decision not to reassign the agent's cases are not ministerial acts; however, both decisions are managerial acts. The Commissioner may (in the Commissioner's discretion) abate interest attributable to any unreasonable delay resulting from these decisions.

Example 4. A taxpayer appears for an office audit and submits all necessary documentation and information. The auditor tells the taxpayer that the taxpayer will receive a copy of the audit report. However, before the report is prepared, the auditor is permanently reassigned to another group. An extended period of time passes before the auditor's cases are reassigned. The decision to reassign the auditor and the decision not to reassign the auditor's cases are not ministerial acts; however, they are managerial acts. The Commissioner may (in the Commissioner's discretion) abate interest attributable to any unreasonable delay resulting from these decisions.

Example 5. A taxpayer is notified that the IRS intends to audit the taxpayer's income tax return. The agent assigned to the case is granted sick leave for an extended period of time, and the taxpayer's case is not reassigned. The decision to grant sick leave and the decision not to reassign the taxpayer's case to another agent are not ministerial acts; however, they are managerial acts. The Commissioner may (in the Commissioner's discretion) abate interest attributable to any unreasonable delay caused by these decisions.

Example 6. A revenue agent has completed an examination of the income tax return of a taxpayer. There are issues that are not agreed upon between the taxpayer and the IRS. Before the notice of deficiency is prepared and reviewed, a clerical employee misplaces the taxpayer's case file. The act of misplacing the case file is a managerial act. The Commissioner may (in the Commissioner's discretion) abate interest attributable to any unreasonable delay resulting from the file being misplaced.

Example 7. A taxpayer invests in a tax shelter and reports a loss from the tax shelter on the taxpayer's income tax return. IRS personnel conduct an extensive examination of the tax shelter, and the processing of the taxpayer's case is delayed because of that examination. The decision to delay the processing of the taxpayer's case until the completion of the examination of the tax shelter is a decision on how to organize the processing of tax returns. This is a general administrative decision. Consequently, interest attributable to a delay caused by this decision cannot be abated under paragraph (a) of this section.

Example 8. A taxpayer claims a loss on the taxpayer's income tax return and is notified that the IRS intends to examine the return. However, a decision is made not to commence the examination of the taxpayer's return until the processing of another return, for which the statute of limitations is about to expire, is completed. The decision on how to prioritize the processing of returns based on the expiration of the statute of limitations is a general administrative decision. Consequently, interest attributable to a delay caused by this decision cannot be abated under paragraph (a) of this section.

Example 9. During the examination of an income tax return, there is disagreement between the taxpayer and the revenue agent regarding certain itemized deductions claimed by the taxpayer on the return. To resolve the issue, advice is requested in a timely manner from the Office of Chief Counsel on a substantive issue of federal tax law. The decision to request advice is a decision concerning the proper application of federal tax law; it is neither a ministerial nor a managerial act. Consequently, interest attributable to a delay resulting from the decision to request advice cannot be abated under paragraph (a) of this section.

Example 10. The facts are the same as in Example 9 except the attorney who is assigned to respond to the request for advice is granted leave for an extended period of time. The case is not reassigned during the attorney's absence. The decision to grant leave and the decision not to reassign the taxpayer's case to another attorney are not ministerial acts; however, they are managerial acts. The Commissioner may (in the Commissioner's discretion) abate interest attributable to any unreasonable delay caused by these decisions.

Example 11. A taxpayer contacts an IRS employee and requests information with respect to the amount due to satisfy the taxpayer's income tax liability for a particular taxable year. Because the employee fails to access the most recent data, the employee gives the taxpayer an incorrect amount due. As a result, the taxpayer pays less than the amount required to satisfy the tax liability. Accessing the most recent data is a ministerial act. The Commissioner may (in the Commissioner's discretion) abate interest attributable to any unreasonable error or delay arising from giving the taxpayer an incorrect amount due to satisfy the taxpayer's income tax liability.

Example 12. A taxpayer contacts an IRS employee and requests information with respect to the amount due to satisfy the taxpayer's income tax liability for a particular taxable year. To determine the current amount due, the employee must interpret complex provisions of federal tax law involving net operating loss carrybacks and foreign tax credits. Because the employee incorrectly interprets these provisions, the employee gives the taxpayer an incorrect amount due. As a result, the taxpayer pays less than the amount required to satisfy the tax liability. Interpreting complex provisions of federal tax law is neither a ministerial nor a managerial act. Consequently, interest attributable to an error or delay arising from giving the taxpayer an incorrect amount due to satisfy the taxpayer's income tax liability in this situation cannot be abated under paragraph (a) of this section.

Example 13. A taxpayer moves from one state to another after the IRS has undertaken an examination of the taxpayer's income tax return. The taxpayer asks that the audit be transferred to the IRS's district office that is nearest the new address. The group manager approves the request, and the case is transferred. Thereafter, the taxpayer moves to yet another state, and once again asks that the audit be transferred to the IRS's district office that is nearest that new address. The group manager approves the request, and the case is again transferred. The agent then assigned to the case is granted sick leave for an extended period of time, and the taxpayer's case is not reassigned. The taxpayer's repeated moves result in a delay in the completion of the examination. Under paragraph (a)(2) of this section, interest attributable to this delay cannot be abated because a significant aspect of this delay is attributable to the taxpayer. However, as in Example 5, the Commissioner may (in the Commissioner's discretion) abate interest attributable to any unreasonable delay caused by the managerial decisions to grant sick leave and not to reassign the taxpayer's case to another agent.

(d) Effective dates — (1) In general. Except as provided in paragraph (d)(2) of this section, the provisions of this section apply to interest accruing with respect to deficiencies or payments of any tax described in section 6212(a) for taxable years beginning after July 30, 1996.

(2) Special rules — (i) Estate tax. The provisions of this section apply to interest accruing with respect to deficiencies or payments of –

(A) Estate tax imposed under section 2001 on estates of decedents dying after July 30, 1996;

(B) The additional estate tax imposed under sections 2032A(c) and 2056A(b)(1)(B) in the case of taxable events occurring after July 30, 1996; and

(C) The additional estate tax imposed under section 2056A(b)(1)(A) in the case of taxable events occurring after December 31, 1996.

(ii) Gift tax. The provisions of this section apply to interest accruing with respect to deficiencies or payments of gift tax imposed under chapter 12 on gifts made after December 31, 1996.

(iii) Generation-skipping transfer tax. The provisions of this section apply to interest accruing with respect to deficiencies or payments of generation-skipping transfer tax imposed under chapter 13 –

(A) On direct skips occurring at death, if the transferor dies after July 30, 1996; and

(B) On inter vivos direct skips, and all taxable terminations and taxable distributions occurring after December 31, 1996.

Sec. 301.6404-4. Suspension of interest and certain penalties when the Internal Revenue Service does not timely contact the taxpayer.

(a) Suspension – (1) In general. Except as provided in paragraph (b) of this section, if an individual taxpayer files a return of tax imposed by subtitle A on or before the due date for the return (including extensions) and the Internal Revenue Service does not timely provide the taxpayer with a notice specifically stating the amount of any increased liability and the basis for that liability, then the IRS must suspend the imposition of any interest, penalty, addition to tax, or additional amount, with respect to any failure relating to the return that is computed by reference to the period of time the failure continues to exist and that is properly allocable to the suspension period. The notice described in this paragraph (a) is timely if provided before the close of the 18-month period (36-month period in the case of notices provided after November 25, 2007, subject to the provisions of paragraph (a)(5)) beginning on the later of the date on which the return is filed or the due date of the return without regard to extensions.

(2) Treatment of amended returns and other documents – (i) Amended returns filed on or after December 21, 2005, that show an increase in tax liability. If a taxpayer, on or after December 21, 2005, provides to the IRS an amended return or one or more other signed written documents showing an increase in tax liability, the date on which the return was filed will, for purposes of this paragraph (a), be the date on which the last of the documents was provided. Documents described in this paragraph (a)(2)(i) are provided on the date that they are received by the IRS.

(ii) Amended returns that show a decrease in tax liability. If a taxpayer provides to the IRS an amended return or other signed written document that shows a decrease in tax liability, any interest, penalty, addition to tax, or additional amount will not be suspended if the IRS at any time proposes to adjust the changed item or items on the amended return or other signed written document.

(iii) Amended returns and other documents as notice.

(A) As to the items reported, an amended return or one or more other signed written documents showing that the taxpayer owes an additional amount of tax for the taxable year serves as the notice described in paragraph (a)(1) of this section with respect to the items reported on the amended return.

(B) Example. An individual taxpayer timely files a Federal income tax return for taxable year 2008 on April 15, 2009. On January 19, 2010, the taxpayer mails to the IRS an amended return reporting an additional item of income and an increased tax liability for taxable year 2008. The IRS receives the amended return on January 21, 2010. The amended return will be treated for purposes of this paragraph (a) as filed on January 21, 2010, the date the IRS received it. Pursuant to paragraph (a)(2)(iii) of this section, the amended return serves as the notice described in paragraph (a)(1) of this section with respect to the item reported on the amended return. Accordingly, because the filing of the amended return and the provision of notice occur simultaneously, no suspension of any interest, penalty, addition to tax or additional amount will occur under this paragraph (a) with respect to the item reported on the amended return.

(iv) Joint return after filing separate return. A joint return filed under section 6013(b) is subject to the rules for amended returns described in this paragraph (a)(2). The IRS will not suspend any interest, penalty, addition to tax, or additional amount on a joint return filed under section 6013(b) after the filing of a separate return unless each spouse's separate return, if required to be filed, was timely.

(3) Separate application. This paragraph (a) shall be applied separately with respect to each item or adjustment.

(4) Duration of suspension period. The suspension period described in paragraph (a)(1) of this section begins the day after the close of the 18-month period (36-month period, in the case of notices provided after November 25, 2007, subject to the provisions of paragraph (a)(5)) beginning on the later of the date on which the return is filed or the due date of the return without regard to extensions. The suspension period ends 21 days after the earlier of the date on which the IRS mails the required notice to the taxpayer's last known address, the date on which the required notice is hand-delivered to the taxpayer, or the date on which the IRS receives an amended return or other signed written document showing an increased tax liability.

(5) Certain notices provided on or after November 26, 2007. If the IRS provides the notice described in paragraph (a)(1) of this section to a taxpayer on or after November 26, 2007, and the notice relates to an individual Federal income tax return that was timely filed before that date, the following rules will apply:

(i) Eighteen-month period has closed. If, as of November 25, 2007, the 18-month period described in paragraph (a)(1) of this section has closed and the IRS has not provided the taxpayer with the notice described in that paragraph (a)(1), the suspension described in paragraph (a)(1) of this section will begin on the day after the close of the 18-month period. The suspension will end on the date that is 21 days after the notice is provided.

(ii) All other cases. In all other cases, the suspension described in paragraph (a)(1) of this section will begin on the day after the close of the 36-month period described in that paragraph (a)(1) and end on the date that is 21 days after the notice described in paragraph (a)(1) of this section is provided.

(6) Examples. The following examples, which assume that no exceptions in section 6404(g)(2) to the general rule of suspension apply, illustrate the rules of this paragraph (a).

Example 1. An individual taxpayer timely files a Federal income tax return for taxable year 2005 on April 17, 2006. On December 11, 2007, the taxpayer mails to the IRS an amended return reporting an additional item of income and an increased tax liability for taxable year 2005. The IRS receives the amended return on December 13, 2007. On January 16, 2008, the IRS provides the taxpayer with a notice stating that the taxpayer has an additional tax liability based on the disallowance of a deduction the taxpayer claimed on his original return and did not change on his amended return. The date the amended return was received substitutes for the date that the original return was filed with respect to the additional item of tax liability reported on the amended return. Thus, the IRS will not suspend any interest, penalty, addition to tax, or additional amount with respect to the additional item of income and the increased tax liability reported on the amended return. The suspension period for the additional tax liability based on the IRS's disallowance of the deduction begins on October 17, 2007, so the IRS will suspend any interest, penalty, addition to tax, and additional amount with respect to the disallowed deduction and additional tax liability from that date through February 6, 2008, which is 21 days after the IRS provided notice of the additional tax liability and the basis for that liability. The suspension period in this example begins 18 months after filing the return (not 36 months) because, as of November 25, 2007, the 18-month period beginning on the date the return was filed had closed without the IRS giving notice of the additional liability. Thus, under the rules in paragraph (a)(5) of this section, the suspension period begins 18 months from the April 17, 2006 return filing date.

Example 2. An individual taxpayer files a Federal income tax return for taxable year 2008 on April 15, 2009. The taxpayer consents to extend the time within which the IRS may assess any tax due on the return until June 30, 2013. On December 20, 2012, the IRS provides a notice to the taxpayer specifically stating the taxpayer's liability and the basis for the liability. The suspension period for the liability identified by the IRS begins on April 15, 2012, so the IRS will suspend any interest, penalty, addition to tax, and additional amount with respect to that liability from that date through January 10, 2013, which is 21 days after the IRS provided notice of the additional tax liability and the basis for that liability.

(7) Notice of liability and the basis for the liability – (i) In general. Notice to the taxpayer must be in writing and specifically state the amount of the liability and the basis for the liability. The notice must provide the taxpayer with sufficient information to identify which items of income, deduction, loss, or credit the IRS has adjusted or proposes to adjust, and the reason for that adjustment. Notice of the reason for the adjustment does not require a detailed explanation or a citation to any Internal Revenue Code section or other legal authority. The IRS need not incorporate all of the information necessary to satisfy the notice requirement within a single document or provide all of the information at the same time. Documents that may contain information sufficient to constitute notice, either alone or in conjunction with other documents, include, but are not limited to, statutory notices of deficiency; examination reports (for example, Form 4549, Income Tax Examination Changes or Form 886-A, Explanation of Items); Form 870, Waiver of Restriction on Assessments and Collection of Deficiency in Tax and Acceptance of Overassessment; notices of proposed deficiency that allow the taxpayer an opportunity for review in the Office of Appeals (30-day letters); notices pursuant to section 6213(b) (mathematical or clerical errors); and notice and demand for payment of a jeopardy assessment under section 6861.

(ii) Tax attributable to TEFRA partnership items. Notice to the partner or the tax matters partner (TMP) of a partnership subject to the unified audit and litigation procedures of subchapter C of chapter 63 of subtitle F of the Internal Revenue Code (TEFRA partnership procedures) that provides specific information about the basis for the adjustments to partnership items is sufficient notice if a partner could reasonably compute the specific tax attributable to the partnership item based on the proposed adjustments as applied to the partner's individual tax situation. Documents provided by the IRS during a TEFRA partnership proceeding that may contain information sufficient to satisfy the notice requirements include, but are not limited to, a Notice of Final Partnership Administrative Adjustment (FPAA); examination reports (for example, Form 4605-A or Form 886-A); or a letter that allows the partners an opportunity for review in the Office of Appeals (60-day letter).

(iii) Examples. The following examples illustrate the rules of this paragraph (a)(7).

Example 1. During an audit of Taxpayer A's 2005 taxable year return, the IRS questions a charitable deduction claimed on the return. The IRS provides A with a 30-day letter that proposes to disallow the charitable contribution deduction resulting in a deficiency of $ 1,000 and informs A that A may file a written protest of the proposed disallowance with the Office of Appeals within 30 days. The letter includes as an attachment a copy of the revenue agent's report that states, "It has not been established that the amount shown on your return as a charitable contribution was paid during the tax year. Therefore, this deduction is not allowable." The information in the 30-day letter and attachment provides A with notice of the specific amount of the liability and the basis for that liability as described in this paragraph (a)(7).

Example 2. Taxpayer B is a partner in partnership P, a TEFRA partnership for taxable year 2005. B claims a distributive share of partnership income on B's Federal income tax return for 2005 timely filed on April 17, 2006. On October 1, 2007, during the course of a partnership audit of P for taxable year 2005, the IRS provides P's TMP with a 60-day letter proposing to adjust P's income by $ 10,000. The IRS previously had provided the TMP with a copy of the examination report explaining that the adjustment was based on $ 10,000 of unreported net income. On October 31, 2007, P's TMP informs B of the proposed adjustment as required by § 301.6223(g)-1(b). By accounting for B's distributive share of the $ 10,000 of unreported income from P with B's other income tax items, B can determine B's tax attributable to the $ 10,000 partnership adjustment. The information in the 60-day letter and the examination report allows B to compute the specific amount of the liability attributable to the adjustment to the partnership item and the basis for that adjustment and therefore satisfies the notice requirement of paragraph (a). Because the IRS provided that notice to the TMP, B's agent under the TEFRA partnership provisions, within 18 months of the April 17, 2006 filing date of B's return, any interest, penalty, addition to tax, or additional amount with respect to B's tax liability attributable to B's distributive share of the $ 10,000 of unreported partnership income will not be suspended under section 6404(g).

(8) Providing notice – (i) In general. The IRS may provide notice by mail or in person to the taxpayer or the taxpayer's representative. If the IRS mails the notice, it must be sent to the taxpayer's last known address under rules similar to section 6212(b), except that certified or registered mail is not required. Notice is considered provided as of the date of mailing or delivery in person.

(ii) Providing notice in TEFRA partnership proceedings. In the case of TEFRA partnership proceedings, the IRS must provide notice of final partnership administrative adjustments (FPAA) by mail to those partners specified in section 6223. Within 60 days of an FPAA being mailed, the TMP is required to forward notice of the FPAA to those partners not entitled to direct notice from the IRS under section 6223. Certain partners with small interests in partnerships with more than 100 partners may form a Notice Group and designate a partner to receive the FPAA on their behalf. The IRS may provide other information after the beginning of the partnership administrative proceeding to the TMP who, in turn, must provide that information to the partners specified in § 301.6223(g)-1 within 30 days of receipt. Pass-thru partners who receive notices and other information from the IRS or the TMP must forward that notice or information within 30 days to those holding an interest through the pass-thru partner. Information provided by the IRS to the TMP is deemed to be notice for purposes of this section to those partners specified in § 301.6223(g)-1 as of the date the IRS provides that notice to the TMP. A similar rule applies to notice provided to the designated partner of a Notice Group, and to notice provided to a pass-thru partner. In the foregoing situations, the TMP, designated partner, and pass-thru partner are agents for direct and indirect partners. Consequently, notice to these agents is deemed to be notice to the partners for whom they act.

Sec. 301.6503(a)-1. Suspension of running of period of limitation; issuance of statutory notice of deficiency.

(a) General rule. * * *

(2) This paragraph may be illustrated by the following example:

Example. A taxpayer filed a return for the calendar year 1973 on April 15, 1974; the notice of deficiency was mailed to him (at an address within the United States) on April 15, 1977; and he filed a petition with the Tax Court on July 14, 1977. The decision of the Tax Court became final on November 6, 1978. The running of the period of limitation for assessment is suspended from April 15, 1977, to January 5, 1979, which date is 60 days after the date (November 6, 1978), on which the decision became final. If in this example the taxpayer had failed to file a petition with the Tax Court, the running of the period of limitation for assessment would then be suspended from April 15, 1977 (the date of notice), to September 12, 1977 (that is, for the 90-day period in which he could file a petition with the Tax Court, and for 60 days thereafter).

* * *

Sec. 301.6601-1. Interest on underpayments. (current version with proposed amendments in *bold italics*)

(a) General rule. (1) Interest at the annual rate referred to in the regulations under section 6621 shall be paid on any unpaid amount of tax from the last date prescribed for payment of the tax (determined without regard to any extension of time for payment) to the date on which payment is received.

(2) For provisions requiring the payment of interest during the period occurring before July 1, 1975, see section 6601(a) prior to its amendment by section 7 of the Act of Jan. 3, 1975 (Pub. L. 93-625, 88 Stat. 2115).

(b) Satisfaction by credits made after December 31, 1957 – (1) In general. If any portion of a tax is satisfied by the credit of an overpayment after December 31, 1957, interest shall not be imposed under section 6601 on such portion of the tax for any period during which interest on the overpayment would have been allowable if the overpayment had been refunded.

(2) Examples. The provisions of this paragraph may be illustrated by the following examples:

Example 1. An examination of A's income tax returns for the calendar years 1955 and 1956 discloses an underpayment of $800 for 1955 and an overpayment of $500 for 1956. Interest under section 6601(a) ordinarily accrues on the underpayment of $800 from April 15, 1956, to the date of payment. However, the 1956 overpayment of $500 is credited after December 31, 1957, against the underpayment in accordance with the provisions of section 6402(a) and § 301.6402-1. Under such circumstances interest on the $800 underpayment runs from April 15, 1956, the last date prescribed for payment of the 1955 tax, to April 15,

1957, the date the overpayment of $500 was made. Since interest would have been allowed on the overpayment, if refunded, from April 15, 1957, to a date not more than 30 days prior to the date of the refund check, no interest is imposed after April 15, 1957, on $500, the portion of the underpayment satisfied by credit. Interest continues to run, however, on $300 (the $ 800 underpayment for 1955 less the $ 500 overpayment for 1956) to the date of payment.

Example 2. An examination of A's income tax returns for the calendar years 1956 and 1957 discloses an overpayment, occurring on April 15, 1957, of $700 for 1956 and an underpayment of $400 for 1957. After April 15, 1958, the last date prescribed for payment of the 1957 tax, the district director credits $400 of the overpayment against the underpayment. In such a case, interest will accrue upon the overpayment of $700 from April 15, 1957, to April 15, 1958, the due date of the amount against which the credit is taken. Interest will also accrue under section 6611 upon $ 300 ($700 overpayment less $400 underpayment) from April 15, 1958, to a date not more than 30 days prior to the date of the refund check. Since a refund of the portion of the overpayment credited against the underpayment would have resulted in interest running upon such portion from April 15, 1958, to a date not more than 30 days prior to the date of the refund check, no interest is imposed upon the underpayment.

(c) Last date prescribed for payment. (1) In determining the last date prescribed for payment, any extension of time granted for payment of tax (including any postponement elected under section 6163(a) shall be disregarded. The granting of an extension of time for the payment of tax does not relieve the taxpayer from liability for the payment of interest thereon during the period of the extension. Thus, except as provided in paragraph (b) of this section, interest at the annual rate referred to in the regulations under section 6621 is payable on any unpaid portion of the tax for the period during which such portion remains unpaid by reason of an extension of time for the payment thereof.

(2)(i) If a tax or portion thereof is payable in installments in accordance with an election made under section 6152(a) or 6156(a), the last date prescribed for payment of any installment of such tax or portion thereof shall be determined under the provisions of section 6152(b) or 6156(b), as the case may be, and interest shall run on any unpaid installment from such last date to the date on which payment is received. However, in the event installment privileges are terminated for failure to pay an installment when due as provided by section 6152(d) and the time for the payment of any remaining installment is accelerated by the issuance of a notice and demand therefor, interest shall run on such unpaid installment from the date of the notice and demand to the date on which payment is received. But see section 6601(e)(4).

(ii) If the tax shown on a return is payable in installments, interest will run on any tax not shown on the return from the last date prescribed for payment of the first installment. If a deficiency is prorated to any unpaid installments, in accordance with section 6152(c), interest shall run on such prorated amounts from the date prescribed for the payment of the first installment to the date on which payment is received.

(3) If, by reason of jeopardy, a notice and demand for payment of any tax is issued before the last date otherwise prescribed for payment, such last date shall nevertheless be used for the purpose of the interest computation, and no interest shall be imposed for the period commencing with the date of the issuance of the notice and demand and ending on such last date. If the tax is not paid on or before such last date, interest will automatically accrue from such last date to the date on which payment is received.

(4) In the case of taxes payable by stamp and in all other cases where the last date for payment of the tax is not otherwise prescribed, such last date for the purpose of the interest computation shall be deemed to be the date on which the liability for the tax arose. However, such last date shall in no event be later than the date of issuance of a notice and demand for the tax.

(d) Suspension of interest; waiver of restrictions on assessment. In the case of a deficiency determined by a district director (or an assistant regional commissioner, appellate) with respect to any income, estate, gift *tax*, or *excise tax imposed by* chapters 41, 42, 43, or 44 *and 45*, if the taxpayer files with such internal revenue officer an agreement waiving the restrictions on assessment of such deficiency, and if notice and demand for payment of such deficiency is not made within 30 days after the filing of such waiver, no interest shall be imposed on the deficiency for the period beginning immediately after such 30th day and ending on the date notice and demand is made. In the case of an agreement with respect to a portion of the deficiency, the rules as set forth in this paragraph are applicable only to that portion of the deficiency to which the agreement relates.

Sec. 301.6611-1. Interest on overpayments. [PROPOSED]

* * *

(b) Date of overpayment. (1) In general. Except as provided in section 6401(a), relating to assessment and collection after the expiration of the applicable period of limitation, there can be no overpayment of tax until the entire tax liability has been satisfied. Therefore, the dates of overpayment of any tax are the date of payment of the first amount which (when added to previous payments) is in excess of the tax liability (including any interest, addition to the tax, or additional amount) and the dates of payment of all amounts subsequently paid with respect to such tax liability. For rules relating to the determination of the date of payment in the case of an advance payment of tax, a payment of estimated tax, and a credit for income tax withholding, see paragraph (d) of this section.

(2) Period for which interest is allowable in the case of credits of overpayment — (i) General rule. If an overpayment of tax is credited, interest shall be allowed from the date of overpayment to the due date (as determined under paragraph (b)(2)(ii) of this section) of the amount against which such overpayment is credited. See paragraph (b)(4) of this section for late returns.

(ii) Determination of due date. **(A)** In general. The term "due date", as used in this section, means the last day fixed by law or regulations for the payment of the tax (determined without regard to any extension of time), and not the date on which the district director or the director of the regional service center makes demand for the payment of the tax. Therefore, the due date of a tax is the date fixed for the payment of the tax or the several installments thereof.

(B) Tax payable in installments. **(1)** In general. In the case of a credit against a tax, where the taxpayer had properly elected to pay the tax in installments, the due date is the date prescribed for the payment of the installment against which the credit is applied.

(2) Delinquent installment. If the taxpayer is delinquent in payment of an installment of tax and a notice and demand has been issued for the payment of the delinquent installment and the remaining installments, the due date of each remaining installment shall then be the date of such notice and demand.

(C) Tax or installment not yet due. If a taxpayer agrees to the crediting of an overpayment against tax or an installment of tax and the schedule of allowance is signed prior to the date on which such tax or installment would otherwise become due, then the due date of such tax or installment shall be the date on which such schedule is signed.

(D) Assessed interest. In the case of a credit against assessed interest, the due date is the date of the assessment of such interest.

(E) Additional amount, addition to the tax, or assessable penalty. In the case of a credit against an amount assessed as an additional amount, addition to the tax, or assessable penalty, the due date is the date of the assessment.

(F) Estimated income tax for succeeding year. If the taxpayer elects to have all or part of the overpayment shown by his return applied to his estimated tax for his succeeding taxable year, no interest shall be allowed on such portion of the overpayment credited and such amount shall be applied as a payment on account of the estimated tax for such year or the installments thereof.

(3) Period for which interest is allowable in the case of refunds of overpayment. If an overpayment of tax is refunded, interest shall be allowed from the date of the overpayment to a date determined by the district director or the director of the regional service center, which shall be not more than 30 days prior to the date of the refund check. The acceptance of a refund check shall not deprive the taxpayer of the right to make a claim for any additional overpayment and interest thereon, provided the claim is made within the applicable period of limitation. However, if a taxpayer does not accept a refund check, no additional interest on the amount of the overpayment included in such check shall be allowed. See paragraph (b)(4) of this section for late returns.

(4) Late returns. For the purpose of paragraphs (b)(2), (b)(3) and (f) of this section, if, after October 3, 1982, a return is filed after the last date prescribed for filing such return (including any extension of time for filing the return), no interest shall be allowed or paid for any day before the date on which the return is filed. A return will not be treated as filed until it is filed in processible form. For rules relating to the processible form requirement, see paragraph (h)(1) of this section.

(c) Examples. The provisions of paragraph (b) of this section may be illustrated by the following examples:

Example (1). Corporation X files an income tax return on March 15, 1955, for the calendar year 1954 disclosing a tax liability of $1,000 and elects to pay the tax in installments. Subsequent to payment of the final installment, the correct tax liability is determined to be $900.

Tax Liability

Assessed	$1,000
Correct liability	$ 900
Overassessment	$ 100

Record of Payments

Mar. 15, 1955	$ 500
June 15, 1955	$ 500

Since the correct liability in this case is $900, the payment of $500 made on March 15, 1955, and $400 of the payment made on June 15, 1955, are applied in satisfaction of the tax liability. The balance of the payment made on June 15, 1955 ($100) constitutes the amount of the overpayment, and the date on which such payment was made would be the date of the overpayment from which interest would be computed.

Example (2). Corporation Y files an income tax return for the calendar year 1954 on March 15, 1955, disclosing a tax liability of $50,000, and elects to pay the tax in installments. On October 15, 1956, a deficiency in the amount of $10,000 is assessed and is paid in equal amounts on November 15 and November 26, 1956. On April 15, 1957, it is determined that the correct tax liability of the taxpayer for 1954 is only $35,000.

Tax Liability

Original assessment	$50,000
Deficiency assessment	$10,000
Total assessed	$60,000
Correct liability	$35,000
Overassessment	$25,000

Record of Payments

Mar. 15, 1955	$25,000
June 15, 1955	$25,000
Nov. 15, 1956	$ 5,000
Nov. 26, 1956	$ 5,000

Since the correct liability in this case is $35,000, the entire payment of $25,000 made on March 15, 1955, and $10,000 of the payment made on June 15, 1955, are applied in satisfaction of the tax liability. The balance of the payment made on June 15, 1955 ($15,000), plus the amounts paid on November 15 ($5,000), and November 26, 1956 ($5,000), constitute the amount of the overpayment. The dates of the overpayments from which interest would be computed are as follows:

Date	Amount of over payment
June 15, 1955	$15,000
Nov. 15, 1956	$ 5,000
Nov. 26, 1956	$ 5,000

The amount of any interest paid with respect to the deficiency of $10,000 is also an overpayment.

Example (3). Corporation Z failed to file a timely income tax return for the calendar year 1982. Z filed the 1982 return on November 20, 1983, disclosing a tax liability of $50,000 which was paid in full on March 15,1983. on October 15, 1984, a deficiency in the amount of $10,000 is assessed and is paid on November 15, 1984. On April 15, 1985, it is determined that the correct tax liability of the taxpayer for 1982 is only $35,000.

Tax Liability
Original assessment	$50,000
Deficiency assessment	$10,000
Total assessed	$60,000
Correct liability	$35,000
Overassessment	$25,000

Record of Payments
March 15, 1983	$50,000
Nov. 15, 1984	$10,000

Since the correct liability in this case is $35,000, only $35,000 of the $50,000 payment made on March 15, 1983 is applied in satisfaction of the tax liability. The balance of the payment made on March 15, 1983 (15,000), plus the amount paid on November 15, 1984 (10,000), constitute the amount of the overpayment. The dates of the overpayment from which interest would be computed are as follows:

Date	Amount of over payment
Nov. 20, 1983	$15,000
Nov. 15, 1984	$10,000

The amount of any interest paid with respect to the deficiency of $10,000 is also an overpayment.

(d) Advance payment of tax, payment of estimated tax, and credit for income tax withholding. In the case of an advance payment of tax, a payment of estimated income tax, or a credit for income tax withholding, the provisions of section 6513 (except the provisions of subsection (c) thereof), applicable in determining the date of payment of tax for purposes of the period of limitations on credit or refund, shall apply in determining the date of overpayment for purposes of computing interest thereon.

* * *

Sec. 301.6621-3. Higher interest rate payable on large corporate underpayments.

* * *

(b) Large corporate underpayment — (1) Defined. For purposes of section 6621(c) and this section, "large corporate underpayment" means any underpayment of a tax by a C corporation for any taxable period if the amount of the threshold underpayment of the tax (as defined in paragraph (b)(2)(ii) of this section) for that taxable period exceeds $100,000.

* * *

Sec. 301.6651-1. Failure to file tax return or to pay tax.

(a) Addition to the tax — (1) Failure to file tax return. In case of failure to file a return required under authority of –

    (i) Subchapter A, chapter 61 of the Code, relating to returns and records (other than sections 6015 and 6016, relating to declarations of estimated tax, and part III thereof, relating to information returns);

    (ii) Subchapter A, chapter 51 of the Code, relating to distilled spirits, wines, and beer;

    (iii) Subchapter A, chapter 52 of the Code, relating to cigars, cigarettes, and cigarette papers and tubes; or

    (iv) Subchapter A, chapter 53 of the Code, relating to machine guns, destructive devices, and certain other firearms; and

The regulations thereunder, on or before the date prescribed for filing (determined with regard to any extension of time for such filing), there shall be added to the tax required to be shown on the return the amount specified below unless the failure to file the return within the prescribed time is shown to the satisfaction of the district director or the director of the service center to be due to reasonable cause and not to willful neglect. The amount to be added to the tax is 5 percent thereof if the failure is for not more than 1 month, with an additional 5 percent for each additional month or fraction thereof during which the failure continues, but not to exceed 25 percent in the aggregate. The amount of any addition under this subparagraph shall be reduced by the amount of the addition under subparagraph (2) of this paragraph for any month to which an addition to tax applies under both subparagraphs (1) and (2) of this paragraph (a).

(2) Failure to pay tax shown on return. In case of failure to pay the amount shown as tax on any return (required to be filed after December 31, 1969, without regard to any extension of time for filing thereof) specified in subparagraph (1) of this paragraph (a), on or before the date prescribed for payment of such tax (determined with regard to any extension of time for payment), there shall be added to the tax shown on the return the amount specified below unless the failure to pay the tax within the prescribed time is shown to the satisfaction of the district director, or, as provided in paragraph (a) of this section, the Assistant Regional Commissioner (Alcohol, Tobacco and Firearms), the director of the service center, to be due to reasonable cause and not to willful neglect. Except as provided in paragraph (a)(4) of this section, the amount to be added to the tax is 0.5 percent of the amount of tax shown on the return if the failure is for not more than 1 month, with an additional 0.5 percent for each additional month or fraction thereof during which the failure continues, but not to exceed 25 percent in the aggregate.

(3) Failure to pay tax not shown on return. In the case of failure to pay any amount of any tax required to be shown on a return specified in paragraph (a)(1) of this section that is not so shown (including an assessment made pursuant to section 6213(b)) within 21 calendar days from the date of the notice and demand (10 business days if the amount assessed and shown on the notice and demand equals or exceeds $100,000) with respect to any notice and demand made after December 31, 1996, there will be added to the amount stated in the notice and demand the amount specified below unless the failure to pay the tax within the prescribed time is shown to the satisfaction of the district director or the director of the service center to be due to reasonable cause and not to willful neglect. Except as provided in paragraph (a)(4) of this section, the amount to be added to the tax is 0.5 percent of the amount stated in the notice and demand if the failure is for not more than 1 month, with an additional 0.5 percent for each additional month or fraction thereof during which the failure continues, but not to exceed 25 percent in the aggregate. For purposes of this paragraph (a)(3), see § 301.6601-1(f)(5) for the definition of calendar day and business day.

(4) Reduction of failure to pay penalty during the period an installment agreement is in effect — (i) In general. In the case of a return filed by an individual on or before the due date for the return (including extensions) –

(A) The amount added to tax for a month or fraction thereof is determined by using 0.25 percent instead of 0.5 percent under paragraph (a)(2) of this section if at any time during the month an installment agreement under section 6159 is in effect for the payment of such tax; and

(B) The amount added to tax for a month or fraction thereof is determined by using 0.25 percent instead of 0.5 percent under paragraph (a)(3) of this section if at any time during the month an installment agreement under section 6159 is in effect for the payment of such tax.

(ii) Effective date. This paragraph (a)(4) applies for purposes of determining additions to tax for months beginning after December 31, 1999.

* * *

(c) Showing of reasonable cause. (1) Except as provided in subparagraphs (3) and (4) of this paragraph (b), a taxpayer who wishes to avoid the addition to the tax for failure to file a tax return or pay tax must make an affirmative showing of all facts alleged as a reasonable cause for his failure to file such return or pay such tax on time in the form of a written statement containing a declaration that it is made under penalties of perjury. Such statement should be filed with the district director or the director of the service center with whom the return is required to be filed; Provided, That where special tax returns of liquor dealers are delivered to an alcohol, tobacco and firearms officer working under the supervision of the Regional Director, Bureau of Alcohol, Tobacco and Firearms, such statement may be delivered with the return. If the district director, the director of the service center, or, where applicable, the Regional Director, Bureau of Alcohol, Tobacco and Firearms, determines that the delinquency was due to a reasonable cause and not to willful neglect, the addition to the tax will not be assessed. If the taxpayer exercised ordinary business care and prudence and was nevertheless unable to file the return within the prescribed time, then the delay is due to a reasonable cause. A failure to pay will be considered to be due to reasonable cause to the extent that the taxpayer has made a satisfactory showing that he exercised ordinary business care and prudence in providing for payment of his tax liability and was nevertheless either unable to pay the tax or would suffer an undue hardship (as described in § 1.6161-1(b) of this chapter) if he paid on the due date. In determining whether the taxpayer was unable to pay the tax in spite of the exercise of ordinary business care and prudence in providing for payment of his tax liability, consideration will be given to all the facts and circumstances of the taxpayer's financial situation, including the amount and nature of the taxpayer's expenditures in light of the income (or other amounts) he could, at the time of such expenditures, reasonably expect to receive prior to the date prescribed for the payment of the tax. Thus, for example, a taxpayer who incurs lavish or extravagant living expenses in an amount such that the remainder of his assets and anticipated income will be insufficient to pay his tax, has not exercised ordinary business care and prudence in providing for the payment of his tax liability. Further, a taxpayer who invests funds in speculative or illiquid assets has not exercised ordinary business care and prudence in providing for the payment of his tax liability unless, at the time of the investment, the remainder of the taxpayer's assets and estimated income will be sufficient to pay his tax or it can be reasonably foreseen that the speculative or illiquid investment made by the taxpayer can be utilized (by sale or as security for a loan) to realize sufficient funds to satisfy the tax liability. A taxpayer will be considered to have exercised ordinary business care and prudence if he made reasonable efforts to conserve sufficient assets in marketable form to satisfy his tax liability and nevertheless was unable to pay all or a portion of the tax when it became due.

(2) In determining if the taxpayer exercised ordinary business care and prudence in providing for the payment of his tax liability, consideration will be given to the nature of the tax which the taxpayer has failed to pay. Thus, for example, facts and circumstances which, because of the taxpayer's efforts to conserve assets in marketable form, may constitute reasonable cause for nonpayment of income taxes may not constitute reasonable cause for failure to pay over taxes described in section 7501 that are collected or withheld from any other person.

(3) If, for a taxable year ending on or after December 31, 1995, an individual taxpayer satisfies the requirement of § 1.6081-4(a) of this chapter (relating to automatic extension of time for filing an individual income tax return), reasonable cause will be presumed, for the period of the extension of time to file, with respect to any underpayment of tax if –

(i) The excess of the amount of tax shown on the individual income tax return over the amount of tax paid on or before the regular due date of the return (by virtue of tax withheld by the employer, estimated tax payments, and any payment with an application for extension of time to file pursuant to § 1.6081-4 of this chapter) is no greater than 10 percent of the amount of tax shown on the individual income tax return; and

(ii) Any balance due shown on the individual income tax return is remitted with the return.

(4) If, for a taxable year ending on or after December 31, 1972, a corporate taxpayer satisfies the requirements of § 1.6081-3 (a) (relating to an automatic extension of time for

filing a corporation income tax return), reasonable cause shall be presumed, for the period of the extension of time to file, with respect to any underpayment of tax if

(i) The amount of tax (determined without regard to any prepayment thereof) shown on Form 7004, or the amount of tax paid on or before the regular due date of the return, is at least 90 percent of the amount of tax shown on the taxpayer's Form 1120, and

(ii) Any balance due shown on the Form 1120 is paid on, or before the due date of the return, including any extensions of time for filing.

* * *

Sec. 301.7122-1. Compromises.

* * *

(b) Grounds for compromise — (1) Doubt as to liability. Doubt as to liability exists where there is a genuine dispute as to the existence or amount of the correct tax liability under the law. Doubt as to liability does not exist where the liability has been established by a final court decision or judgment concerning the existence or amount of the liability. See paragraph (f)(4) of this section for special rules applicable to rejection of offers in cases where the Internal Revenue Service (IRS) is unable to locate the taxpayer's return or return information to verify the liability.

(2) Doubt as to collectibility. Doubt as to collectibility exists in any case where the taxpayer's assets and income are less than the full amount of the liability.

(3) Promote effective tax administration. (i) A compromise may be entered into to promote effective tax administration when the Secretary determines that, although collection in full could be achieved, collection of the full liability would cause the taxpayer economic hardship within the meaning of § 301.6343-1.

(ii) If there are no grounds for compromise under paragraphs (b)(1), (2), or (3)(i) of this section, the IRS may compromise to promote effective tax administration where compelling public policy or equity considerations identified by the taxpayer provide a sufficient basis for compromising the liability. Compromise will be justified only where, due to exceptional circumstances, collection of the full liability would undermine public confidence that the tax laws are being administered in a fair and equitable manner. A taxpayer proposing compromise under this paragraph (b)(3)(ii) will be expected to demonstrate circumstances that justify compromise even though a similarly situated taxpayer may have paid his liability in full.

(iii) No compromise to promote effective tax administration may be entered into if compromise of the liability would undermine compliance by taxpayers with the tax laws.

(c) Special rules for evaluating offers to compromise — (1) In general. Once a basis for compromise under paragraph (b) of this section has been identified, the decision to accept or reject an offer to compromise, as well as the terms and conditions agreed to, is left to the discretion of the Secretary. The determination whether to accept or reject an offer to compromise will be based upon consideration of all the facts and circumstances, including whether the circumstances of a particular case warrant acceptance of an amount that might not otherwise be acceptable under the Secretary's policies and procedures.

(2) Doubt as to collectibility — (i) Allowable expenses. A determination of doubt as to collectibility will include a determination of ability to pay. In determining ability to pay, the Secretary will permit taxpayers to retain sufficient funds to pay basic living expenses. The determination of the amount of such basic living expenses will be founded upon an evaluation of the individual facts and circumstances presented by the taxpayer's case. To guide this determination, guidelines published by the Secretary on national and local living expense standards will be taken into account.

(ii) Nonliable spouses — (A) In general. Where a taxpayer is offering to compromise a liability for which the taxpayer's spouse has no liability, the assets and income of the nonliable spouse will not be considered in determining the amount of an adequate offer. The assets and income of a nonliable spouse may be considered, however, to the extent property has been transferred by the taxpayer to the nonliable spouse under circumstances that would permit the IRS to effect collection of the taxpayer's liability from such property (e.g., property that was conveyed in fraud of creditors), property has been transferred by the taxpayer to the nonliable spouse for the purpose of removing the property from consideration by the IRS in evaluating the compromise, or as provided in paragraph (c)(2)(ii)(B) of this section. The IRS also may request information regarding the assets and income of the nonliable spouse for the purpose of verifying the amount of and responsibility for expenses claimed by the taxpayer.

(B) Exception. Where collection of the taxpayer's liability from the assets and income of the nonliable spouse is permitted by applicable state law (e.g., under state community property laws), the assets and income of the nonliable spouse will be considered in determining the amount of an adequate offer except to the extent that the taxpayer and the nonliable spouse demonstrate that collection of such assets and income would have a material and adverse impact on the standard of living of the taxpayer, the nonliable spouse, and their dependents.

(3) Compromises to promote effective tax administration — (i) Factors supporting (but not conclusive of) a determination that collection would cause economic hardship within the meaning of paragraph (b)(3)(i) of this section include, but are not limited to –

(A) Taxpayer is incapable of earning a living because of a long term illness, medical condition, or disability, and it is reasonably foreseeable that taxpayer's financial resources will be exhausted providing for care and support during the course of the condition;

(B) Although taxpayer has certain monthly income, that income is exhausted each month in providing for the care of dependents with no other means of support; and

(C) Although taxpayer has certain assets, the taxpayer is unable to borrow against the equity in those assets and liquidation of those assets to pay outstanding tax liabilities would render the taxpayer unable to meet basic living expenses.

(ii) Factors supporting (but not conclusive of) a determination that compromise would undermine compliance within the meaning of paragraph (b)(3)(iii) of this section include, but are not limited to –

(A) Taxpayer has a history of noncompliance with the filing and payment requirements of the Internal Revenue Code;

(B) Taxpayer has taken deliberate actions to avoid the payment of taxes; and

(C) Taxpayer has encouraged others to refuse to comply with the tax laws.

(iii) The following examples illustrate the types of cases that may be compromised by the Secretary, at the Secretary's discretion, under the economic hardship provisions of paragraph (b)(3)(i) of this section:

Example 1. The taxpayer has assets sufficient to satisfy the tax liability. The taxpayer provides full time care and assistance to her dependent child, who has a serious long-term illness. It is expected that the taxpayer will need to use the equity in his assets to provide for adequate basic living expenses and medical care for his child. The taxpayer's overall compliance history does not weigh against compromise.

Example 2. The taxpayer is retired and his only income is from a pension. The taxpayer's only asset is a retirement account, and the funds in the account are sufficient to satisfy the liability. Liquidation of the retirement account would leave the taxpayer without an adequate means to provide for basic living expenses. The taxpayer's overall compliance history does not weigh against compromise.

Example 3. The taxpayer is disabled and lives on a fixed income that will not, after allowance of basic living expenses, permit full payment of his liability under an installment agreement. The taxpayer also owns a modest house that has been specially equipped to accommodate his disability. The taxpayer's equity in the house is sufficient to permit payment of the liability he owes. However, because of his disability and limited earning potential, the taxpayer is unable to obtain a mortgage or otherwise borrow against this equity. In addition, because the taxpayer's home has been specially equipped to accommodate his disability, forced sale of the taxpayer's residence would create severe adverse consequences for the taxpayer. The taxpayer's overall compliance history does not weigh against compromise.

(iv) The following examples illustrate the types of cases that may be compromised by the Secretary, at the Secretary's discretion, under the public policy and equity provisions of paragraph (b)(3)(ii) of this section:

Example 1. In October of 1986, the taxpayer developed a serious illness that resulted in almost continuous hospitalizations for a number of years. The taxpayer's medical condition was such that during this period the taxpayer was unable to manage any of his financial affairs. The taxpayer has not filed tax returns since that time. The taxpayer's health has now improved and he has promptly begun to attend to his tax affairs. He discovers that the IRS prepared a substitute for return for the 1986 tax year on the basis of information returns it had received and had assessed a tax deficiency. When the taxpayer discovered the liability, with penalties and interest, the tax bill is more than three times the original tax liability. The taxpayer's overall compliance history does not weigh against compromise.

Example 2. The taxpayer is a salaried sales manager at a department store who has been able to place $2,000 in a tax-deductible IRA account for each of the last two years. The taxpayer learns that he can earn a higher rate of interest on his IRA savings by moving those savings from a money management account to a certificate of deposit at a different financial institution. Prior to transferring his savings, the taxpayer submits an email inquiry to the IRS at its Web Page, requesting information about the steps he must take to preserve the tax benefits he has enjoyed and to avoid penalties. The IRS responds in an answering e-mail that the taxpayer may withdraw his IRA savings from his neighborhood bank, but he must redeposit those savings in a new IRA account within 90 days. The taxpayer withdraws the funds and redeposits them in a new IRA account 63 days later. Upon audit, the taxpayer learns that he has been misinformed about the required rollover period and that he is liable for additional taxes, penalties and additions to tax for not having redeposited the amount within 60 days. Had it not been for the erroneous advice that is reflected in the taxpayer's retained copy of the IRS e-mail response to his inquiry, the taxpayer would have redeposited the amount within the required 60-day period. The taxpayer's overall compliance history does not weigh against compromise.

* * *

(g) Effect of offer to compromise on collection activity — (1) In general. The IRS will not levy against the property or rights to property of a taxpayer who submits an offer to compromise, to collect the liability that is the subject of the offer, during the period the offer is pending, for 30 days immediately following the rejection of the offer, and for any period when a timely filed appeal from the rejection is being considered by Appeals.

(2) Revised offers submitted following rejection. If, following the rejection of an offer to compromise, the taxpayer makes a good faith revision of that offer and submits the revised offer within 30 days after the date of rejection, the IRS will not levy to collect from the taxpayer the liability that is the subject of the revised offer to compromise while that revised offer is pending.

(3) Jeopardy. The IRS may levy to collect the liability that is the subject of an offer to compromise during the period the IRS is evaluating whether that offer will be accepted if it determines that collection of the liability is in jeopardy.

(4) Offers to compromise determined by IRS to be nonprocessable or submitted solely for purposes of delay. If the IRS determines, under paragraph (d)(2) of this section, that a pending offer did not contain sufficient information to permit evaluation of whether the offer should be accepted, that the offer was submitted solely to delay collection, or that the offer was otherwise nonprocessable, then the IRS may levy to collect the liability that is the subject of that offer at any time after it returns the offer to the taxpayer.

(5) Offsets under section 6402. Notwithstanding the evaluation and processing of an offer to compromise, the IRS may, in accordance with section 6402, credit any overpayments made by the taxpayer against a liability that is the subject of an offer to compromise and may offset such overpayments against other liabilities owed by the taxpayer to the extent authorized by section 6402.

(6) Proceedings in court. Except as otherwise provided in this paragraph (g)(6), the IRS will not refer a case to the Department of Justice for the commencement of a proceeding in court, against a person named in a pending offer to compromise, if levy to collect the liability is prohibited by paragraph (g)(1) of this section. Without regard to whether a person is named in a pending offer to compromise, however, the IRS may authorize the Department of Justice to file a counterclaim or third-party complaint in a refund action or to join that person in any other proceeding in which liability for the tax that is the subject of the pending offer to compromise may be established or disputed, including a suit against the United States under 28 U.S.C. 2410. In addition, the United States may file a claim in any bankruptcy proceeding or insolvency action brought by or against such person.

* * *

(i) Statute of limitations — (1) Suspension of the statute of limitations on collection. The statute of limitations on collection will be suspended while levy is prohibited under paragraph (g)(1) of this section.

(2) Extension of the statute of limitations on assessment. For any offer to compromise, the IRS may require, where appropriate, the extension of the statute of limitations on assessment. However, in any case where waiver of the running of the statutory period of limitations on assessment is sought, the taxpayer must be notified of the right to refuse to extend the period of limitations or to limit the extension to particular issues or particular periods of time.

* * *

Sec. 301.7430-1. Exhaustion of administrative remedies. (current version with proposed amendments in *italics*)

* * *

(b) Requirements – (1) In general. A party has not exhausted the administrative remedies available within the Internal Revenue Service with respect to any tax matter for which an Appeals office conference is available under §§ 601.105 and 601.106 of this chapter (other than a tax matter described in paragraph (c) of this section) unless --

(i) The party, prior to filing a petition in the Tax Court or a civil action for refund in a court of the United States (including the Court of Federal Claims), participates, either in person or through a qualified representative described in § 601.502 of this chapter, in an Appeals office conference; or

(ii) If no Appeals office conference is granted, the party, prior to the issuance of a statutory notice in the case of a petition in the Tax Court or the issuance of a notice of disallowance in the case of a civil action for refund in a court of the United States (including the Court of Federal Claims) –

(A) Requests an Appeals office conference in accordance with §§ 601.105 and 601.106 of this chapter *or any successor published guidance*; and

(B) Files a written protest if a written protest is required to obtain an Appeals office conference.

(2) Participates. For purposes of this section, a party or qualified representative of the party described in § 601.502 of this chapter participates in an Appeals office conference if the party or qualified representative discloses to the Appeals office all relevant information regarding the party's tax matter to the extent such information and its relevance were known or should have been known to the party or qualified representative at the time of such conference.

(3) Tax matter. For purposes of this section, "tax matter" means a matter in connection with the determination, collection or refund of any tax, interest, penalty, addition to tax or additional amount under the Internal Revenue Code.

(4) Failure to agree to extension of time for assessments. Any failure by the prevailing party to agree to an extension of the time for the assessment of any tax will not be taken into account for purposes of determining whether the prevailing party has exhausted the administrative remedies available to the party within the Internal Revenue Service.

* * *

Sec. 301.7430-2. Requirements and procedures for recovery of reasonable administrative costs. (current version with proposed amendments in *italics*)

* * *

(c) Procedure for recovering reasonable administrative costs – (1) In general. The Internal Revenue Service will not award administrative costs under section 7430 unless the taxpayer files a written request to recover reasonable administrative costs in accordance with the provisions of this section.

(2) Where request must be filed. A request required by paragraph (c)(1) of this section must be filed with the Internal Revenue Service personnel who have jurisdiction over the tax matter underlying the claim for the costs, except that requests with respect to administrative proceedings as defined by § 301.7430-8(c) should be made to the Chief, Local Insolvency Unit. However, if those persons are unknown to the taxpayer making the request, the taxpayer may send the request to the Internal Revenue Service office that considered the underlying matter.

(3) Contents of request. The request must be in writing and must contain the following statements, affidavits, documentation, and information with regard to the taxpayer's administrative proceeding –

(i) Statements.

(A) A statement that the underlying substantive issues or the issue of reasonable administrative costs are not, and have never been, before any court of the United States (including the Tax Court or United States Court of Federal Claims) with jurisdiction over those issues;

(B) A clear and concise statement of the reasons why the taxpayer alleges that the position of the Internal Revenue Service in the administrative proceeding was not substantially justified. For administrative proceedings commenced after July 30, 1996, if the taxpayer alleges that the Internal Revenue Service did not follow any applicable published guidance, the statement must identify all applicable published guidance that the taxpayer alleges that the Internal Revenue Service did not follow. For purposes of this paragraph (c)(3)(i)(B), the term applicable published guidance means final or temporary regulations, revenue rulings, revenue procedures, information releases, notices, announcements, and, if issued to the taxpayer, private letter rulings, technical advice memoranda, and determination letters. Also, for purposes of this paragraph (c)(3)(i)(B), the term administrative proceeding includes only those administrative

- 230 -

proceedings or portions of administrative proceedings occurring on or after the administrative proceeding date as defined in § 301.7430-3(c). *For costs incurred after January 18, 1999, if the taxpayer alleges that the United States has lost in courts of appeal for other circuits on substantially similar issues, the taxpayer must provide the full name of the case, volume and pages of the reporter in which the opinion appears, the circuit in which the case was decided, and the year of the opinion;*

(C) A statement sufficient to demonstrate that the taxpayer has substantially prevailed as to the amount in controversy or with respect to the most significant issue or set of issues presented in the proceeding;

(D) A statement that the taxpayer has not unreasonably protracted the portion of the administrative proceeding for which the taxpayer is requesting costs; and

(E) A statement supported by a detailed affidavit executed by the taxpayer or the taxpayer's representative that sets forth the nature and amount of each specific item of reasonable administrative costs for which the taxpayer is seeking recovery. *This statement must identify whether the representation is on a pro bono basis as defined in § 301.7430–4(d) and, if so, to whom payment should be made. Specifically, the statement must direct whether payment should be made to the taxpayer's representative or to the representative's employer.*

(ii) Affidavit or affidavits.

(A) An affidavit executed by the taxpayer stating that the taxpayer meets the net worth and size limitations of § 301.7430-5(f);

(B) An affidavit supporting the statement described in paragraph (c)(3)(i)(E) of this section; and

(C) *For costs incurred after January 18, 1999*, if more than $125 per hour as adjusted *for* increase*s* in the cost of living *pursuant to* § 301.7430-4(b)(3) is claimed for the fees of a representative in connection with the administrative proceeding, *stating that a special factor described in § 301.7430–4(b)(3) is applicable, such as the difficulty of the issues presented in the case or the lack of local availability of tax expertise. If a special factor is claimed based on specialized skills and distinctive knowledge as described in § 301.7430–4(b)(2)(ii), the affidavit must state –*

(1) Why the specialized skills and distinctive knowledge were necessary in the representation;

(2) That there is a limited availability of representatives possessing these specialized skills and distinctive knowledge; and

(3) How the education and experience qualifies the representative as someone with the necessary specialized skills and distinctive knowledge.

(iii) Documentation and information.

(A) A copy of the billing records of the representative for the requested fees; and

(B) An address at which the taxpayer wishes to receive notice of the determination of the Internal Revenue Service with regard to the request for reasonable administrative costs.

(C) In cases of pro bono representation, time records similar to billing records, detailing the time spent and work completed must be submitted for the requested fees.

(4) Form of Request. No specific form is required for the request other than one which satisfies the requirements of paragraph (c)(3) of this section. Where practicable the required statements may be included in a single document. Similarly, where practicable, the required affidavits may be combined in a single affidavit to the extent they are to be executed by the same person.

(5) Period for requesting costs from the Internal Revenue Service. To recover reasonable administrative costs pursuant to section 7430 and this section, the taxpayer must file a *written* request for costs *within* 90 days after the date the final *adverse* decision of the Internal Revenue Service with respect to all tax, additions to tax, *interest,* and penalties at issue in the administrative proceeding is mailed, or otherwise furnished, to the taxpayer. *For purposes of this section, interest means the interest that is specifically at issue in the administrative proceeding independent of the taxpayer's objections to the underlying tax imposed.* The final decision of the Internal Revenue Service for purposes of this section is the document that resolves the tax liability of the taxpayer with regard to all tax, additions to tax, *interest,* and penalties at issue in the administrative proceeding (such as a Form 870 or closing agreement), or a notice of assessment for that liability (such as the notice and demand under section 6303 whichever is earlier mailed or otherwise furnished to the taxpayer. For purposes of this section, if the 90th day falls on a Saturday, Sunday, or a legal holiday, the 90-day period shall end on the next succeeding day *that* is not a Saturday, Sunday, or a legal holiday *as defined by section 7503.* The term legal holiday means a legal holiday in the District of Columbia. If the request for costs is to be filed with the Internal Revenue Service at an office of the Internal Revenue Service located outside the District of Columbia but within an internal revenue district, the term legal holiday also means a Statewide legal holiday in the State where such office is located.

(6) Notice. The Internal Revenue Service is authorized, but not required, to notify the taxpayer of its decision to grant or deny (in whole or in part) an award for reasonable administrative costs under section 7430 and this section by certified mail or registered mail. If the Internal Revenue Service does not respond on the merits to a request by the taxpayer for an award of reasonable administrative costs filed under paragraph (c)(1) of this section within 6 months after such request is filed, the Internal Revenue Service's failure to respond may be considered by the taxpayer as a decision of the Internal Revenue Service denying an award for reasonable administrative costs.

(7) Appeal to Tax Court. A taxpayer may appeal a decision by the Internal Revenue Service denying (in whole or in part) a request for reasonable administrative costs under section 7430 and this section by filing a petition for reasonable administrative costs with the Tax Court. The petition must be in accordance with the Tax Court's Rules of Practice and Procedure and must be filed with the Tax Court after the Internal Revenue Service denies (in whole or in part) the taxpayer's request for reasonable administrative costs. *If the notice of decision denying (in whole or in part) an award for reasonable administrative costs was mailed by the Internal Revenue Service via certified mail or registered mail, a taxpayer may obtain judicial* *review of that decision by filing a petition for review with the Tax Court prior to the 91st day after the mailing of the notice of decision.*

* * *

Sec. 301.7430-4. Reasonable administrative costs. (current with proposed amendments in *italics*)

* * *

(c) Certain costs excluded – (1) Costs not incurred in an administrative proceeding. Costs that are not reasonable administrative costs for purposes of section 7430 include any costs incurred in connection with a proceeding that is not an administrative proceeding within the meaning of § 301.7430-3.

(2) Costs incurred in an administrative proceeding but not reasonable – (i) In general. Costs incurred in an administrative proceeding that are incurred on or after the administrative proceeding date, and that are otherwise described in paragraph (b) of this section, are not recoverable unless they are reasonable in both nature and amount. For example, costs normally included in the hourly rate of the representative by the custom and usage of the representative's profession, when billed separately, are not recoverable separate and apart from the representative's hourly rate. *These* costs typically include costs such as secretarial and overhead expenses. In contrast, costs *that* are normally billed separately may be reasonable administrative costs that may be recoverable in addition to the representative's hourly rate. Therefore, necessary costs incurred for travel; expedited mail delivery; messenger service; expenses while on travel; long distance telephone calls; and necessary copying fees imposed by the Internal Revenue Service, any court, bank or other third party, when normally billed separately from the representative's hourly rate, may be reasonable administrative costs.

(ii) Special Rule for Expert Witness' Fees on Issue of Prevailing Market Rates. Under paragraph (b)(3)(iii)(C) of this section, the taxpayer may initially establish a limited availability of specially qualified representatives for the proceeding by submission of an affidavit signed by the taxpayer or by the taxpayer's representative. The Internal Revenue Service may endeavor to rebut the affidavit submitted on this issue by demonstrating either that a specially qualified representative was not necessary to represent the taxpayer in the proceeding, that the taxpayer's representative is not a specially qualified representative or that the prevailing rate for specially qualified representatives does not exceed *$125* per hour (as adjusted for an increase in the cost of living). Unless the Internal Revenue Service endeavors to demonstrate that the prevailing rate for specially qualified representatives does not exceed *$125* per hour (as adjusted for an increase in the cost of living), fees for expert witnesses used to establish prevailing market rates are not included in the term reasonable administrative costs.

(3) Litigation costs. Litigation costs are not reasonable administrative costs because they are not incurred in connection with an administrative proceeding. Litigation costs include – **(i)** Costs incurred in connection with the preparation and filing of a petition with the United States Tax Court or in connection with the commencement of any other court proceeding; and

(ii) Costs incurred after the filing of a petition with the United States Tax Court or after the commencement of any other court proceeding.

(4) Examples. The provisions of this section are illustrated by the following examples:

Example 1. After incurring fees for representation during the Internal Revenue Service's examination of taxpayer A's income tax return, A receives a notice of proposed deficiency (30-day letter). A files a request for and is granted an Appeals office conference. At the conference no agreement is reached on the tax matters at issue. The Internal Revenue Service then issues a notice of deficiency. Upon receiving the notice of deficiency, A discontinues A's administrative efforts and files a petition with the Tax Court. A's costs incurred before the date of the mailing of the 30-day letter are not reasonable administrative costs because they were incurred before the administrative proceeding date. Similarly, A's costs incurred in connection with the preparation and filing of a petition with the Tax Court are litigation costs and not reasonable administrative costs.

Example 2. Assume the same facts as in Example 1 except that after A receives the notice of deficiency, A recontacts Appeals and Appeals agrees with A. If A seeks administrative costs, A may recover costs incurred after the date of the mailing of the 30-day letter, costs incurred in recontacting Appeals after the issuance of the notice of deficiency, and costs incurred up to the time the Tax Court petition was filed, as reasonable administrative costs, but only if the other requirements of section 7430 and the regulations thereunder are satisfied. The costs incurred before the date of the mailing of the 30-day letter are not reasonable administrative costs because they were incurred before the administrative proceeding date, as set forth in § 301.7430– (c)(1)(iii). A's costs incurred in connection with the filing of a petition with the Tax Court are not reasonable administrative costs because those costs are litigation costs. Similarly, A's costs incurred after the filing of the petition are not reasonable administrative costs, as they are litigation costs.

* * *

Sec. 301.7430-5. Prevailing party. (current version with proposed amendments in *italics*)

(a) In general. For purposes of an award of reasonable administrative costs under section 7430 in the case of administrative proceedings commenced after July 30, 1996, a taxpayer is a prevailing party *(other than by reason of section 7430(c)(4)(E))* only if – (1) *At least one issue (other than recovery of administrative costs) remains in dispute as of the date that the Internal Revenue Service takes a position in the administrative proceeding, as described in paragraph (b) of this section;*

(2) The position of the Internal Revenue Service was not substantially justified;

(3) The taxpayer substantially prevails as to the amount in controversy or with respect to the most significant issue or set of issues presented; and

(4) The taxpayer satisfies the net worth and size limitations referenced in paragraph (f) of this section.

(b) Position of the Internal Revenue Service. The position of the Internal Revenue Service in an administrative proceeding is the position taken by the Internal Revenue Service as of the *earlier of – (1) The date of the receipt by the taxpayer of the notice of the decision of the Internal Revenue Service Office of Appeals; or*

(2) The date of the notice of deficiency or any date thereafter.

*(c) **Examples**. The provisions of this section may be illustrated by the following examples:*

> *Example 1. Taxpayer A receives a notice of proposed deficiency (30-day letter). A pays the amount of the proposed deficiency and files a claim for refund. A's claim is considered and a notice of proposed claim disallowance is issued by the Area Director. A does not request an Appeals office conference and the Area Director issues a notice of claim disallowance. A then files suit in a United States District Court. A cannot recover reasonable administrative costs because the notice of claim disallowance is not a notice of the decision of the Internal Revenue Service Office of Appeals or a notice of deficiency. Accordingly, the Internal Revenue Service has not taken a position in the administrative proceeding pursuant to section 7430(c)(7)(B).*

> *Example 2. Taxpayer B receives a notice of proposed deficiency (30-day letter). B disputes the proposed adjustments and requests an Appeals office conference. The Appeals office determines that B has no additional tax liability. B requests administrative costs from the date of the 30-day letter. B is not the prevailing party and may not recover administrative costs because all of the proposed adjustments in the case were resolved as of the date that the Internal Revenue Service took a position in the administrative proceeding.*

(d) **Substantially justified.** *(1)* **In general.** The position of the Internal Revenue Service is substantially justified if it has a reasonable basis in both fact and law. A significant factor in determining whether the position of the Internal Revenue Service is substantially justified as of a given date is whether, on or before that date, the taxpayer has presented all relevant information under the taxpayer's control and relevant legal arguments supporting the taxpayer's position to the appropriate Internal Revenue Service personnel. The appropriate Internal Revenue Service personnel are personnel responsible for reviewing the information or arguments, or personnel who would transfer the information or arguments in the normal course of procedure and administration to the personnel who are responsible.

*(2) **Position in courts of appeal**. Whether the United States has won or lost an issue substantially similar to the one in the taxpayer's case in courts of appeal for circuits other than the one to which the taxpayer's case would be appealable should be taken into consideration in determining whether the Internal Revenue Service's position was substantially justified.*

*(3) **Example**. The provisions of this section are illustrated by the following example:*

> *Example. The Internal Revenue Service, in the conduct of a correspondence examination of taxpayer A's individual income tax return, requests substantiation from A of claimed medical expenses. A does not respond to the request and the Service issues a notice of deficiency. After receiving the notice of deficiency, A presents sufficient information and arguments to convince a revenue agent that the notice of deficiency is incorrect and that A owes no tax. The revenue agent then closes the case showing no deficiency. Although A incurred costs after the issuance of the notice of deficiency, A is unable to recover these costs because, as of the date these costs were incurred, A had not presented relevant information under A's control and relevant legal arguments supporting A's position to the appropriate Internal Revenue Service personnel. Accordingly, the*

position of the Internal Revenue Service was substantially justified at the time the costs were incurred.

(4) Included costs. (i) An award of reasonable administrative costs shall only include costs incurred on or after the earliest of—

(A) The date of the receipt by the taxpayer of the notice of decision from Appeals;

(B) The date of the notice of deficiency; or

(C) The date on which the first letter of proposed deficiency that allows the taxpayer an opportunity for administrative review in the Office of Appeals is sent.

(ii) If the Internal Revenue Service takes a position in an administrative proceeding, as defined in paragraph (b) of this section, and the position is not substantially justified, the taxpayer may be permitted to recover costs incurred before the position was taken, but not before the dates set forth in this paragraph (d)(4).

(5) Examples. The provisions of this section may be illustrated by the following examples:

Example 1. Pursuant to section 6672, taxpayer D receives from the Area Director Collection Operations (Collection) a proposed assessment of trust fund taxes (Trust Fund Recovery Penalty). D requests and is granted Appeals office consideration. Appeals considers the issues and decides to uphold Collection's recommended assessment. Appeals notifies D of this decision in writing. Collection then assesses the tax and notice and demand is made. D timely pays the minimum amount required to commence a court proceeding, files a claim for refund, and furnishes the required bond. Collection disallows the claim, but Appeals, on reconsideration, reverses its original position, thus upholding D's position. If Appeals concedes its initial determination was not substantially justified, D may recover administrative costs incurred on or after the mailing of the proposed assessment of trust fund taxes, because the proposed assessment is the first determination letter that allows the taxpayer an opportunity for administrative review in the Internal Revenue Service Office of Appeals.

Example 2. Taxpayer E receives a notice of proposed deficiency (30-day letter). E pays the amount of the proposed deficiency and files a claim for refund. E's claim is considered and a notice of proposed disallowance is issued by the Area Director. E requests and is granted Appeals office consideration. No agreement is reached with Appeals and the Office of Appeals issues a notice of claim disallowance. E does not file suit in a United States District Court but instead contacts the Appeals office to attempt to reverse the decision. E convinces the Appeals officer that the notice of claim disallowance is in error. The Appeals officer then abates the assessment. E may recover reasonable administrative costs if the position taken in the notice of claim disallowance issued by the Office of Appeals was not substantially justified and the other requirements of section 7430 and the regulations thereunder are satisfied. If so, E may recover administrative costs incurred from the mailing date of the 30-day letter because the requirements of paragraph (c)(2) of this section are met. E cannot recover the costs incurred prior to the mailing of the 30-day letter because they were incurred before the administrative proceeding date.

(6) **Exception.** If the position of the Internal Revenue Service was substantially justified with respect to some issues in the proceeding and not substantially justified with respect to the remaining issues, any award of reasonable administrative costs to the taxpayer may be limited

to only reasonable administrative costs attributable to those issues with respect to which the position of the Internal Revenue Service was not substantially justified. If the position of the Internal Revenue Service was substantially justified for only a portion of the period of the proceeding and not substantially justified for the remaining portion of the proceeding, any award of reasonable administrative costs to the taxpayer may be limited to only reasonable administrative costs attributable to that portion during which the position of the Internal Revenue Service was not substantially justified. Where an award of reasonable administrative costs is limited to that portion of the administrative proceeding during which the position of the Internal Revenue Service was not substantially justified, whether the position of the Internal Revenue Service was substantially justified is determined as of the date any cost is incurred.

(7) **Presumption.** If the Internal Revenue Service did not follow any applicable published guidance in an administrative proceeding commenced after July 30, 1996, the position of the Internal Revenue Service, on those issues to which the guidance applies and for all periods during which the guidance was not followed, will be presumed not to be substantially justified. This presumption may be rebutted. For purposes of this paragraph *(d)(7)*, the term applicable published guidance means final or temporary regulations, revenue rulings, revenue procedures, information releases, notices, *and* announcements *published in the Internal Revenue Bulletin* and, if issued to the taxpayer, private letter rulings, technical advice memoranda, and determination letters (see § 601.601(d)(2) of this chapter). Also, for purposes of this paragraph (c)(3), the term administrative proceeding includes only those administrative proceedings or portions of administrative proceedings occurring on or after the administrative proceeding date as defined in § 301.7430-3(c).

(e) **Amount in controversy.** The amount in controversy shall include the amount in issue as of the administrative proceeding date as increased by any amounts subsequently placed in issue by any party. The amount in controversy is determined without increasing or reducing the amount in controversy for amounts of loss, deduction, or credit carried over from years not in issue.

(f) **Most significant issue or set of issues presented**—*(1) In general.* Where the taxpayer has not substantially prevailed with respect to the amount in controversy the taxpayer may nonetheless be a prevailing party if the taxpayer substantially prevails with respect to the most significant issue or set of issues presented. The issues presented include those raised as of the administrative proceeding date and those raised subsequently. Only in a multiple issue proceeding can a most significant issue or set of issues presented exist. However, not all multiple issue proceedings contain a most significant issue or set of issues presented. An issue or set of issues constitutes the most significant issue or set of issues presented if, despite involving a lesser dollar amount in the proceeding than the other issue or issues, it objectively represents the most significant issue or set of issues for the taxpayer or the Internal Revenue Service. This may occur because of the effect of the issue or set of issues on other transactions or other taxable years of the taxpayer or related parties.

(2) Example. The provisions of this section may be illustrated by the following example:

Example. In the purchase of an ongoing business, Taxpayer F obtains from the previous owner of the business a covenant not to compete for a period of five years. On audit of F's individual income tax return for the year in which the business is acquired, the Internal

Revenue Service challenges the basis assigned to the covenant not to compete and a deduction taken as a business expense for a seminar attended by F. Both parties agree that the covenant not to compete is amortizable over a period of five years; however, the Internal Revenue Service asserts that the proper basis of the covenant is $2X while F asserts the basis is $4X. The deduction for the seminar attended by F was reported on the return in question in the amount of $7X. The Internal Revenue Service determines that the deduction for the seminar should be disallowed entirely. In the notice of deficiency, the Internal Revenue Service adjusts the amortization deduction to reflect the change to the basis of the covenant not to compete, and disallows the seminar expense. Thus, of the two adjustments determined for the year under audit, the adjustment attributable to the disallowance of the seminar is larger than that attributable to the covenant not to compete. Due to the impact on the next succeeding four years, however, the covenant not to compete adjustment is objectively the most significant issue to both F and the Internal Revenue Service.

(g) Net worth and size limitations – (1) Individuals. A taxpayer who is a natural person meets the net worth and size limitations of this paragraph if the taxpayer's net worth does not exceed two million dollars. The net worth limitation shall be determined for individuals using the fair market value of the individual's assets as of the administrative proceeding date. For purposes of determining net worth, individuals filing a joint return shall be treated as separate individuals. Thus, individuals filing a joint return will each be subject to a separate net worth limitation of two million dollars.

(2) Estates and trusts. An estate or a trust meets the net worth and size limitations of this paragraph if the taxpayer's net worth does not exceed two million dollars. The net worth of an estate shall be determined using the fair market value of the assets of the estate as of the date of the decedent's death provided the date of death is prior to the date the court proceeding is commenced. The net worth of a trust shall be determined using the fair market value of the assets of the trust as of the last day of the last taxable year involved in the proceeding.

(3) Others. (i) A taxpayer that is a partnership, corporation, association, unit of local government, or organization (other than an organization described in paragraph (g)(4) of this section) meets the net worth and size limitations of this paragraph if, as of the administrative proceeding date:

(A) The taxpayer's net worth does not exceed seven million dollars; and

(B) The taxpayer does not have more than 500 employees.

(ii) A taxpayer who is a natural person and owns an unincorporated business is subject to the net worth and size limitations contained in paragraph (g)(3)(i) of this section if the tax at issue (or any interest, additional amount, addition to tax, or penalty, together with any costs in addition to the tax) relates directly to the business activities of the unincorporated business.

(4) **Special rule for charitable organizations and certain cooperatives.** An organization described in section 501(c)(3) exempt from taxation under section 501(a), or a cooperative association as defined in section 15(a) of the Agricultural Marketing Act, 12 U.S.C. 1141j(a) (as in effect on October 22, 1986), meets the net worth and size limitations of this paragraph

if, as of the administrative proceeding date, the organization or cooperative association does not have more than 500 employees.

(5) *Special rule for TEFRA partnership proceedings.*

(i) In cases involving partnerships subject to the unified audit and litigation procedures of subchapter C of chapter 63 of the Internal Revenue Code (TEFRA partnership cases), the TEFRA partnership meets the net worth and size limitations requirements of this paragraph (g) if, on the administrative proceeding date –

(A) The partnership's net worth does not exceed seven million dollars; and

(B) The partnership does not have more than 500 employees.

(ii) In addition, each partner requesting fees pursuant to section 7430 must meet the appropriate net worth and size limitations set forth in paragraph (g)(1), (g)(2) or (g)(3) of this section. For example, if a partner is an individual, his or her net worth must not exceed two million dollars as of the administrative proceeding date. If the partner is a corporation, its net worth must not exceed seven million dollars and it must not have more than 500 employees.

(h) Determination of prevailing party. If the final decision with respect to the tax, interest, or penalty is made at the administrative level, the determination of whether a taxpayer is a prevailing party shall be made by agreement of the parties, or absent ~~such~~ *an* agreement, by the Internal Revenue Service. See § 301.7430-2(c)(7) regarding the right to appeal the decision of the Internal Revenue Service denying (in whole or in part) a request for reasonable administrative costs to the Tax Court.

Sec. 301.7430-7. Qualified offers.

(a) In general. Section 7430(c)(4)(E) (the qualified offer rule) provides that a party to a court proceeding satisfying the timely filing and net worth requirements of section 7430(c)(4)(A)(ii) shall be treated as the prevailing party if the liability of the taxpayer pursuant to the judgment in the proceeding (determined without regard to interest) is equal to or less than the liability of the taxpayer which would have been so determined if the United States had accepted the last qualified offer of the party as defined in section 7430(g). For purposes of this section, the term judgment means the cumulative determinations of the court concerning the adjustments at issue and litigated to a determination in the court proceeding. In making the comparison between the liability under the qualified offer and the liability under the judgment, the taxpayer's liability under the judgment is further modified by the provisions of paragraph (b)(3) of this section. The provisions of the qualified offer rule do not apply if the taxpayer's liability under the judgment, as modified by the provisions of paragraph (b)(3) of this section, is determined exclusively pursuant to a settlement, or to any proceeding in which the amount of tax liability is not in issue, including any declaratory judgment proceeding, any proceeding to enforce or quash any summons issued pursuant to the Internal Revenue Code (Code), and any action to restrain disclosure under section 6110(f). If the qualified offer rule applies to the court proceeding, the determination of whether the liability under the qualified offer would have equaled or exceeded the liability pursuant to the judgment is made by reference to the last qualified offer made with respect to the tax liability at issue in the administrative or court proceeding. An award of reasonable administrative and litigation costs under the qualified offer rule only includes those costs incurred on or after the date of the last qualified offer and is limited to those costs attributable to the adjustments at issue at the time the last qualified offer was made that were included in the court's judgment other than by reason of settlement. The qualified offer rule is inapplicable to reasonable administrative or litigation costs otherwise awarded to a taxpayer who is a prevailing party under any other provision of section 7430(c)(4). This section sets forth the requirements to be satisfied for a taxpayer to be treated as a prevailing party by reason of the taxpayer making a qualified offer, as well as the circumstances leading to the application of the exceptions, special rules, and coordination provisions of the qualified offer rule. Furthermore, this section sets forth the elements necessary for an offer to be treated as a qualified offer under section 7430(g).

(b) Requirements for treatment as a prevailing party based upon having made a qualified offer — (1) In general. In order to be treated as a prevailing party by reason of having made a qualified offer, the liability of the taxpayer for the type or types of tax and the taxable year or years at issue in the proceeding (as calculated pursuant to paragraph (b)(2) of this section), based on the last qualified offer (as defined in paragraph (c) of this section) made by the taxpayer in the court or administrative proceeding, must equal or exceed the liability of the taxpayer pursuant to the judgment by the court for the same type or types of tax and the same taxable year or years (as calculated pursuant to paragraph (b)(3) of this section). Furthermore, the taxpayer must meet the timely filing and net worth requirements of section 7430(c)(4)(A)(ii). If all of the adjustments subject to the last qualified offer are settled prior to the entry of the judgment by the court, the taxpayer is not a prevailing party by reason of having made a qualified offer. The taxpayer may, however, still qualify as a prevailing party if the requirements of section 7430(c)(4)(A) are met. If one or more adjustments covered by a qualified offer (see paragraph (c)(3)) are settled following a ruling by the court that substantially resolves those adjustments, then those adjustments will not be treated as having been settled prior to the entry of the judgment by the court and instead will be treated as amounts included in the judgment as a result of the court's determinations. For purposes of the preceding sentence, rulings relating to discovery, admissibility of evidence, and burden of proof are not rulings that substantially resolve adjustments covered by a qualified offer.

(2) Liability under the last qualified offer. For purposes of paragraph (b)(1) of this section, the taxpayer's liability under the last qualified offer is the change in the taxpayer's liability that would have resulted if the United States had accepted the taxpayer's last qualified offer on all of the adjustments that were at issue in the administrative or court proceeding at the time that the offer was made compared to the amount shown on the return or returns (or as previously adjusted). The portion of a taxpayer's liability that is attributable to adjustments raised by either party after the making of the last qualified offer is not included in the calculation of the liability under that offer. The taxpayer's liability under the last qualified offer is calculated without regard to adjustments that the parties have stipulated will be resolved in accordance with the outcome of a separate pending Federal, state, or other judicial or administrative proceeding. For example, the parties may stipulate that the taxpayer's liability will be resolved in accordance with the outcome of an alternative dispute resolution proceeding or a separate court proceeding, such as a probate, tort liability, or trademark action. Furthermore, the taxpayer's liability under the last qualified offer is calculated without regard to interest, unless the taxpayer's liability for, or entitlement to, interest is a contested issue in the administrative or court proceeding and is one of the adjustments included in the last qualified offer.

(3) Liability pursuant to the judgment. For purposes of paragraph (b)(1) of this section, the taxpayer's liability pursuant to the judgment is the change in the taxpayer's liability resulting from amounts contained in the judgment as a result of the court's determinations, and amounts contained in settlements not included in the judgment, that are attributable to all adjustments that were included in the last qualified offer compared to the amount shown on the return or returns (or as previously adjusted). This liability includes amounts attributable to adjustments included in the last qualified offer and settled by the parties prior to the entry of judgment regardless of whether those amounts are actually included in the judgment entered by the court. The taxpayer's liability pursuant to the judgment does not include amounts attributable to adjustments that are not included in the last qualified offer, even if those amounts are actually included in the judgment entered by the court. The taxpayer's liability under the judgment is calculated without regard to adjustments that the parties have stipulated will be resolved in accordance with the outcome of a separate pending Federal, state, or other judicial or administrative proceeding. Furthermore, the taxpayer's liability pursuant to the judgment is calculated without regard to interest, unless the taxpayer's liability for, or entitlement to, interest is a contested issue in the administrative or court proceeding and is one of the adjustments included in the last qualified offer. Where adjustments raised by either party subsequent to the making of the last qualified offer are included in the judgment entered by the court, or are settled prior to the court proceeding, the taxpayer's liability pursuant to the judgment is calculated by treating the subsequently raised adjustments as if they had never been raised.

(c) Qualified offer — (1) In general. A qualified offer is defined in section 7430(g) to mean a written offer which –

(i) Is made by the taxpayer to the United States during the qualified offer period;

(ii) Specifies the offered amount of the taxpayer's liability (determined without regard to interest, unless interest is a contested issue in the proceeding);

(iii) Is designated at the time it is made as a qualified offer for purposes of section 7430(g); and

(iv) By its terms, remains open during the period beginning on the date it is made and ending on the earliest of the date the offer is rejected, the date the trial begins, or the 90th day after the date the offer is made.

(2) To the United States. (i) A qualified offer is made to the United States when it is delivered to the office or personnel within the Internal Revenue Service, Office of Appeals, Office of Chief Counsel (including field personnel) or Department of Justice that has jurisdiction over the tax matter at issue in the administrative or court proceeding. If those offices or persons are unknown to the taxpayer making the qualified offer, the taxpayer may deliver the offer to the appropriate office, as follows:

(A) If the taxpayer's initial pleading in a court proceeding has been answered, the taxpayer may deliver the offer to the office that filed the answer.

(B) If the taxpayer's petition in the Tax Court has not yet been answered, the taxpayer may deliver the offer to the Office of Chief Counsel, 1111 Constitution Avenue, NW., Washington, DC 20224.

(C) If the taxpayer's initial pleading in any Federal court, other than the Tax Court, has not yet been answered, the taxpayer may deliver the offer to the Attorney General of the United States, 950 Pennsylvania Ave., NW., Washington, DC 20530-0001. For a suit brought in a United States district court, a copy of the offer should also be delivered to the United States Attorney for the district in which the suit was brought.

(D) In any other situation, the taxpayer may deliver the offer to the office that sent the taxpayer the first letter of proposed deficiency which allows the taxpayer an opportunity for administrative review in the Internal Revenue Service Office of Appeals.

(ii) Until an offer is received by the appropriate personnel or office under this paragraph (c)(2), it is not considered to have been made, with the following exception. If the offer is deposited in the United States mail, in an envelope or other appropriate wrapper, postage prepaid, properly addressed to the appropriate personnel or office under this paragraph (c)(2), the date of the United States postmark stamped on the cover in which the offer is mailed shall be deemed to be the date of receipt of that offer by the addressee. If any offer is deposited with a designated delivery service, as defined in section 7502(f)(2), in lieu of the United States mail, the provisions of section 7502(f)(1) shall apply in determining whether that offer qualifies for this exception.

(3) Specifies the offered amount. A qualified offer specifies the offered amount if it clearly specifies the amount for the liability of the taxpayer, calculated as set forth in paragraph (b)(2) of this section. The offer may be a specific dollar amount of the total liability or a percentage of the adjustments at issue in the proceeding at the time the offer is made. This amount must be with respect to all of the adjustments at issue in the administrative or court proceeding at the time the offer is made and only those adjustments. The specified amount must be an amount, the acceptance of which by the United States will fully resolve the taxpayer's liability, and only that liability (determined without regard to adjustments that the parties have stipulated will be resolved in accordance with the outcome of a separate pending Federal, state, or other judicial or administrative proceeding, or interest, unless interest is a contested issue in the proceeding) for the type or types of tax and the taxable year or years at issue in the proceeding. In cases involving multiple tax years, if adjustments in different tax years arise from separate and distinct issues such that the resolution of issues in one or more tax years will not affect the taxpayer's liability in one or more of the other tax years in the proceeding, then a qualified offer may be made for less than all of the tax years involved. A qualified offer, however, must resolve all of the issues for the tax years covered by the offer and also must cover all tax years in the proceeding affected by those issues. A tax year (affected year) is affected by an issue if the treatment of the issue in another tax year involved in the proceeding necessarily affects the treatment of the issue in the affected year.

(4) Designated at the time it is made as a qualified offer. An offer is not a qualified offer unless it designates in writing at the time it is made that it is a qualified offer for purposes of section 7430(g). An offer made at a time when one or more adjustments not included in the first letter of proposed deficiency which allows the taxpayer an opportunity for administrative review in the Internal Revenue Service Office of Appeals have been raised by the taxpayer and remain unresolved, is not considered to be a qualified offer unless contemporaneously or prior to the making of the offer, the taxpayer has provided the United States with the substantiation and legal and factual arguments necessary to allow for informed consideration of the merits of those adjustments. For example, a taxpayer will be considered to have provided the United States with the necessary substantiation and legal and factual arguments if the taxpayer (or a recognized representative of the taxpayer described in § 601.502 of this chapter) participates in an Appeals office conference, participates in an Area Counsel conference, or confers with the Department of Justice, and at that time, discloses all relevant information. All relevant information includes, but is not limited to, the legal and factual arguments supporting the taxpayer's position on any adjustments raised by the taxpayer after the issuance of the first letter of proposed deficiency which allows the taxpayer an opportunity for administrative review in the Internal Revenue Service Office of Appeals. A taxpayer has disclosed all relevant information if the taxpayer has supplied sufficient information to allow informed consideration of the taxpayer's tax matter to the extent the information and its relevance were known or should have been known to the taxpayer at the time of the conference.

(5) Remains open. A qualified offer must, by its terms, remain open for acceptance by the United States from the date it is made, as defined in paragraph (c)(2)(ii) of this section, until the earliest of the date it is rejected in writing by a person with authority to reject the offer, the date the trial begins, or the 90th day after being received by the United States. The offer, by its written terms, may remain open after the occurrence of one or more of the above-referenced events. Once made, the period during which a qualified offer remains open may be extended by the taxpayer prior to its expiration, but an extension cannot be used to make an offer meet the minimum period for remaining open required by this paragraph (c)(5).

(6) Last qualified offer. A taxpayer may make multiple qualified offers during the qualified offer period. For purposes of the comparison under paragraph (b) of this section, the making of a qualified offer supersedes any previously made qualified offers. In making the comparison described in paragraph (b) of this section, only the qualified offer made most closely in time to the end of the qualified offer period is compared to the taxpayer's liability under the judgment.

(7) Qualified offer period. To constitute a qualified offer, an offer must be made during the qualified offer period. The qualified offer period begins on the date on which the first letter of proposed deficiency which allows the taxpayer an opportunity for administrative review in the Internal Revenue Service Office of Appeals is sent to the taxpayer. For this purpose, the date of the notice of claim disallowance will begin the qualified offer period in a refund case. If there has been no notice of claim disallowance in a refund case, the qualified offer period begins on the date on which the answer or other responsive pleading is filed with the court. The qualified offer period ends on the date which is thirty days before the date the case is first set for trial. In determining when the qualified offer period ends for cases in the Tax Court and other Federal courts using calendars for trial, a case will be considered set for trial on the date scheduled for the calendar call. A case may be removed from a trial calendar at any time. Thus, a case may be removed from a trial calendar before the date that precedes by thirty days the date scheduled for that trial calendar. The qualified offer period does not end until the case remains on a trial calendar on the date that precedes by 30 days the scheduled date of the calendar call for that trial session. The qualified offer period may not be extended beyond the periods set forth in this paragraph (c)(7), although the period during which a qualified offer remains open may extend beyond the end of the qualified offer period.

* * *

Sec. 301.7502-1. Timely mailing of documents and payments treated as timely filing and paying.

* * *

(e) Delivery – (1) General rule. Except as provided in section 7502(f) [26 USCS § 7502(f)] and paragraphs (c)(3) and (d) of this section, section 7502 [26 USCS § 7502] is not applicable unless the document or payment is delivered by U.S. mail to the agency, officer, or office with which the document is required to be filed or to which payment is required to be made.

(2) Exceptions to actual delivery –

(i) Registered and certified mail. In the case of a document (but not a payment) sent by registered or certified mail, proof that the document was properly registered or that a postmarked certified mail sender's receipt was properly issued and that the envelope was properly addressed to the agency, officer, or office constitutes prima facie evidence that the document was delivered to the agency, officer, or office. Other than direct proof of actual delivery, proof of proper use of registered or certified mail, and proof of proper use of a duly designated PDS as provided for by paragraph (e)(2)(ii) of this section, are the exclusive means to establish prima facie evidence of delivery of a document to the agency, officer, or office with which the document is required to be filed. No other evidence of a postmark or of mailing will be prima facie evidence of delivery or raise a presumption that the document was delivered.

(ii) Equivalents of registered and certified mail. Under section 7502(f)(3) [26 USCS § 7502(f)(3)], the Secretary may extend the prima facie evidence of delivery rule of section 7502(c)(1)(A) [26 USCS § 7502(c)(1)(A)] to a service of a designated PDS, which is substantially equivalent to United States registered or certified mail. Thus, the Commissioner may, in guidance published in the Internal Revenue Bulletin (see § 601.601(d)(2)(ii)(b) of this chapter), prescribe procedures and additional rules to designate a service of a PDS for purposes of demonstrating prima facie evidence of delivery of a document pursuant to section 7502(c) [26 USCS § 7502(c)].

Sec. 301.7602-2. Third party contacts.

* * *

(c) Elements of third-party contact explained — (1) Initiation by an IRS employee

(i) Explanation — (A) Initiation. An IRS employee initiates a communication whenever it is the employee who first tries to communicate with a person other than the taxpayer. Returning unsolicited telephone calls or speaking with persons other than the taxpayer as part of an attempt to speak to the taxpayer are not initiations of third-party contacts.

(B) IRS employee. For purposes of this section, an IRS employee includes all officers and employees of the IRS, the Chief Counsel of the IRS and the National Taxpayer Advocate, as well as a person described in section 6103(n), an officer or employee of such person, or a person who is subject to disclosure restrictions pursuant to a written agreement in connection with the solicitation of an agreement described in section 6103(n) and its implementing regulations. No inference about the employment or contractual relationship of such other persons with the IRS may be drawn from this regulation for any purpose other than the requirements of section 7602(c).

(ii) Examples. The following examples illustrate this paragraph (c)(1):

Example 1. An IRS employee receives a message to return an unsolicited call. The employee returns the call and speaks with a person who reports information about a taxpayer who is not meeting his tax responsibilities. Later, the employee makes a second call to the person and asks for more information. The first call is not a contact initiated by an IRS employee. Just because the employee must return the call does not change the fact that it is the other person, and not the employee, who initiated the contact. The second call, however, is initiated by the employee and so meets the first element.

Example 2. An IRS employee wants to hire an appraiser to help determine the value of a taxpayer's oil and gas business. At the initial interview, the appraiser signs an agreement that prohibits him from disclosing return information of the taxpayer except as allowed by the agreement. Once hired, the appraiser initiates a contact by calling an industry expert in Houston and discusses the taxpayer's business. The IRS employee's contact with the appraiser does not meet the first element of a third-party contact because the appraiser is treated, for section 7602(c) purposes only, as an employee of the IRS. For the same reason, however, the appraiser's call to the industry expert does meet the first element of a third-party contact.

Example 3. A revenue agent trying to contact the taxpayer to discuss the taxpayer's pending examination twice calls the taxpayer's place of business. The first call is answered by a receptionist who states that the taxpayer is not available. The IRS employee leaves a message with the receptionist stating only his name and telephone number, and asks that the taxpayer call him. The second call is answered by the office answering machine, on which the IRS employee leaves the same message. Neither of these phone calls meets the first element of a third-party contact because the IRS employee is trying to initiate a communication with the taxpayer and not a person other than the taxpayer. The fact that the IRS employee must either speak with a third party (the receptionist) or leave a message on the answering machine, which may be heard by a third party, does not mean that the employee is initiating a communication with a person other than the taxpayer. Both the receptionist and the answering machine are only intermediaries in the process of reaching the taxpayer.

(2) Person other than the taxpayer — (i) Explanation. The phrases "person other than the taxpayer" and "third party" are used interchangeably in this section, and do not include –

(A) An officer or employee of the IRS, as defined in paragraph (c)(1)(i)(B) of this section, acting within the scope of his or her employment;

(B) Any computer database or website regardless of where located and by whom maintained, including databases or web sites maintained on the Internet or in county courthouses, libraries, or any other real or virtual site; or

(C) A current employee, officer, or fiduciary of a taxpayer when acting within the scope of his or her employment or relationship with the taxpayer. Such employee, officer, or fiduciary shall be conclusively presumed to be acting within the scope of his or her employment or relationship during business hours on business premises.

(ii) Examples: The following examples illustrate this paragraph (c)(2):

Example 1. A revenue agent examining a taxpayer's return speaks with another revenue agent who has previously examined the same taxpayer about a recurring issue. The revenue agent has not contacted a "person other than the taxpayer" within the meaning of section 7602(c).

Example 2. A revenue agent examining a taxpayer's return speaks with one of the taxpayer's employees on business premises during business hours. The employee is conclusively presumed to be acting within the scope of his employment and is therefore not a "person other than the taxpayer" for section 7602(c) purposes.

Example 3. A revenue agent examining a corporate taxpayer's return uses a commercial online research service to research the corporate structure of the taxpayer. The revenue agent uses an IRS account, logs on with her IRS user name and password, and uses the name of the corporate taxpayer in her search terms. The revenue agent later explores several Internet web sites that may have information relevant to the examination. The searches on the commercial online research service and Internet websites are not contacts with "persons other than the taxpayer."

(3) With respect to the determination or collection of the tax liability of such taxpayer

(i) Explanation — (A) With respect to. A contact is "with respect to" the determination or collection of the tax liability of such taxpayer when made for the purpose of either determining or collecting a particular tax liability and when directly connected to that purpose. While a contact made for the purpose of determining a particular taxpayer's tax liability may also affect the tax liability of one or more other taxpayers, such contact is not for that reason alone a contact "with respect to" the determination or collection of those other taxpayers' tax liabilities. Contacts to determine the tax status of a pension plan under chapter 1, subchapter D (Deferred Compensation) of the Internal Revenue Code, are not "with respect to" the determination of plan participants" tax liabilities. Contacts to determine the tax status of a bond issue under chapter 1, subchapter B, Part IV (Tax Exemption Requirements for State and Local Bonds) of the Internal Revenue Code, are not "with respect to" the determination of the bondholders' tax liabilities. Contacts to determine the tax status of an organization under chapter 1, subchapter F (Exempt Organizations) of the Internal Revenue Code, are not "with respect to" the determination of the contributors' liabilities, nor are any similar determinations "with respect to" any persons with similar relationships to the taxpayer whose tax liability is being determined or collected.

(B) Determination or collection. A contact is with respect to the "determination or collection" of the tax liability of such taxpayer when made during the administrative determination or collection process. For purposes of this paragraph (c) only, the administrative determination or collection process may include any administrative action to ascertain the correctness of a return, make a return when none has been filed, or determine or collect the tax liability of any person as a transferee or fiduciary under chapter 71 of Title 26.

(C) Tax liability. A tax liability means the liability for any tax imposed by Title 26 of the United States Code (including any interest, additional amount, addition to the tax, or penalty) and does not include the liability for any tax imposed by any other jurisdiction nor any liability imposed by other Federal statutes.

(D) Such taxpayer. A contact is with respect to the determination or collection of the tax liability of "such taxpayer" when made while determining or collecting the tax liability of a particular, identified taxpayer. Contacts made during an investigation of a particular, identified taxpayer are third-party contacts only as to the particular, identified taxpayer under investigation and not as to any other taxpayer whose tax liabilities might be affected by such contacts.

(ii) Examples. The following examples illustrate the operation of this paragraph (c)(3):

Example 1. As part of a compliance check on a return preparer, an IRS employee visits the preparer's office and reviews the preparer's client files to ensure that the proper forms and records have been created and maintained. This contact is not a third-party contact "with respect to" the preparer's clients because it is not for the purpose of determining the tax liability of the preparer's clients, even though the agent might discover information that would lead the agent to recommend an examination of one or more of the preparer's clients.

Example 2. A revenue agent is assigned to examine a taxpayer's return, which was prepared by a return preparer. As in all such examinations, the revenue agent asks the taxpayer routine questions about what information the taxpayer gave the preparer and what advice the preparer gave the taxpayer. As a result of the examination, the revenue agent recommends that the preparer be investigated for penalties under section 6694 or 6695. Neither the examination of the taxpayer's return nor the questions asked of the taxpayer are "with respect to" the determination of the preparer's tax liabilities within the meaning of section 7602(c) because the purpose of the contacts was to determine the taxpayer's tax liability, even though the agent discovered information that may result in a later investigation of the preparer.

Example 3. To help identify taxpayers in the florist industry who may not have filed proper returns, an IRS employee contacts a company that supplies equipment to florists and asks for a list of its customers in the past year in order to cross-check the list against filed returns. The employee later contacts the supplier for more information about one particular florist who the employee believes did not file a proper return. The first contact is not a contact with respect to the determination of the tax liability of "such taxpayer" because no particular taxpayer has been identified for investigation at the time the contact is made. The later contact, however, is with respect to the determination of the tax liability of "such taxpayer" because a particular taxpayer has been identified. The later contact is also "with respect to" the determination of that taxpayer's liability because, even though no examination has been opened on the taxpayer, the information sought could lead to an examination.

Example 4. A revenue officer, trying to collect the trust fund portion of unpaid employment taxes of a corporation, begins to investigate the liability of two corporate officers for the section 6672 Trust Fund Recovery Penalty (TFRP). The revenue officer obtains the signature cards for the corporation's bank accounts from the corporation's bank. The contact with the bank to obtain the signature cards is a contact with respect to the determination of the two identified corporate officers' tax liabilities because it is directly connected to the purpose of determining a tax liability of two identified taxpayers. It is not, however, a contact with respect to any other person not already under investigation for TFRP liability, even though the signature cards might identify other potentially liable persons.

Example 5. The IRS is asked to rule on whether a certain pension plan qualifies under section 401 so that contributions to the pension plan are excludable from the employees' incomes under section 402 and are also deductible from the employer's income under section 404. Contacts made with the plan sponsor (and with persons other than the plan sponsor) are not contacts "with respect to" the determination of the tax liabilities of the pension plan participants because the purpose of the contacts is to determine the status of the plan, even though that determination may affect the participants' tax liabilities.

Example 6(a). The IRS audits a TEFRA partnership at the partnership (entity) level pursuant to sections 6221 through 6233. The tax treatment of partnership items is at issue, but the respective tax liabilities of the partners may be affected by the results of the TEFRA partnership audit. With respect to the TEFRA partnership, contacts made with employees of the partnership acting within the scope of their duties or any partner are not section 7602(c) contacts because they are considered the equivalent of contacting the partnership. Contacts relating to the tax treatment of partnership items made with persons other than the employees of the partnership who are acting within the scope of their duties or the partners are section 7602(c) contacts with respect to the TEFRA partnership, and reasonable advance notice should be provided by sending the appropriate Letter 3164 to the partnership's tax matters partner (TMP). Individual partners who are merely affected by the partnership audit but who are not identified as subject to examination with respect to their individual tax liabilities need not be sent Letters 3164.

Example 6(b). In the course of an audit of a TEFRA partnership at the partnership (entity) level, the IRS intends to contact third parties regarding transactions between the TEFRA partnership and specific, identified partners. In addition to the partnership's TMP, the specific, identified partners should also be provided advance notice of any third-party contacts relating to such transactions.

(4) Discloses the identity of the taxpayer being investigated — (i) Explanation. An IRS employee discloses the taxpayer's identity whenever the employee knows or should know that the person being contacted can readily ascertain the taxpayer's identity from the information given by the employee.

(ii) Examples. The following examples illustrate this paragraph (c)(4):

Example 1. A revenue agent seeking to value the taxpayer's condominium calls a real estate agent and asks for a market analysis of the taxpayer's condominium, giving the unit number of the taxpayer's condominium. The revenue agent has revealed the identity of the taxpayer, regardless of whether the revenue agent discloses the name of the taxpayer, because the real estate agent can readily ascertain the taxpayer's identity from the address given.

Example 2. A revenue officer seeking to value the taxpayer's condominium calls a real estate agent and, without identifying the taxpayer's unit, asks for the sales prices of similar units recently sold and listing prices of similar units currently on the market. The revenue officer has not revealed the identity of the taxpayer because the revenue officer has not given any information from which the real estate agent can readily ascertain the taxpayer's identity.

(5) Discloses the association of the IRS employee with the IRS. An IRS employee discloses his association with the IRS whenever the employee knows or should know that the person being contacted can readily ascertain the association from the information given by the employee.

* * *

Sec. 601.601. Rules and Regulations.

* * *

(d) Publication of rules and regulations — (1) "General." All Internal Revenue Regulations and Treasury decisions are published in the Federal Register and in the Code of Federal Regulations. See paragraph (a) of § 601.702. The Treasury decisions are also published in the weekly Internal Revenue Bulletin and the semiannual Cumulative Bulletin. The Internal Revenue Bulletin is the authoritative instrument of the Commissioner for the announcement of official rulings, decisions, opinions, and procedures, and for the publication of Treasury decisions, Executive orders, tax conventions, legislation, court decisions, and other items pertaining to internal revenue matters. It is the policy of the Internal Revenue Service to publish in the Bulletin all substantive and procedural rulings of importance or general interest, the publication of which is considered necessary to promote a uniform application of the laws administered by the Service. Procedures set forth in Revenue Procedures published in the Bulletin which are of general applicability and which have continuing force and effect are incorporated as amendments to the Statement of Procedural Rules. It is also the policy to publish in the Bulletin all rulings which revoke, modify, amend, or affect any published ruling. Rules relating solely to matters of internal practices and procedures are not published; however, statements of internal practices and procedures affecting rights or duties of taxpayers, or industry regulation, which appear in internal management documents, are published in the Bulletin. No unpublished ruling or decision will be relied on, used, or cited by any officer or employee of the Internal Revenue Service as a precedent in the disposition of other cases.

(2) Objectives and standards for publication of Revenue Rulings and Revenue Procedures in the Internal Revenue Bulletin. (i) (a) A "Revenue Ruling" is an official interpretation by the Service that has been published in the Internal Revenue Bulletin. Revenue Rulings are issued only by the National Office and are published for the information and guidance of taxpayers, Internal Revenue Service officials, and others concerned.

(b) A "Revenue Procedure" is a statement of procedure that affects the rights or duties of taxpayers or other members of the public under the Code and related statutes or information that, although not necessarily affecting the rights and duties of the public, should be a matter of public knowledge.

(ii) (a) The Internal Revenue Bulletin is the authoritative instrument of the Commissioner of Internal Revenue for the publication of official rulings and procedures of the Internal Revenue Service, including all rulings and statements of procedure which supersede, revoke, modify, amend, or affect any previously published ruling or procedure. The Service also announces in the Bulletin the Commissioner's acquiescences and nonacquiescences in decisions of the U.S. Tax Court (other than decisions in memorandum opinions), and publishes Treasury decisions, Executive orders, tax conventions, legislation, court decisions, and other items considered to be of general interest. The Assistant Commissioner (Technical) administers the Bulletin program.

(b) The Bulletin is published weekly. In order to provide a permanent reference source, the contents of the Bulletin are consolidated semiannually into an indexed Cumulative Bulletin. The Bulletin Index-Digest System provides a research and reference guide to matters appearing in the Cumulative Bulletins. These materials are sold by the Superintendent of Documents, U.S. Government Printing Office, Washington, DC 20402.

(iii) The purpose of publishing revenue rulings and revenue procedures in the Internal Revenue Bulletin is to promote correct and uniform application of the tax laws by Internal Revenue Service employees and to assist taxpayers in attaining maximum voluntary compliance by informing Service personnel and the public of National Office interpretations of the internal revenue laws, related statutes, treaties, regulations, and statements of Service procedures affecting the rights and duties of taxpayers. Therefore, issues and answers involving substantive tax law under the jurisdiction of the Internal Revenue Service will be published in the Internal Revenue Bulletin, except those involving:

(a) Issues answered by statute, treaty, or regulations;

(b) Issues answered by rulings, opinions, or court decisions previously published in the Bulletin;

(c) Issues that are of insufficient importance or interest to warrant publication;

(d) Determinations of fact rather than interpretations of law;

(e) Informers and informers' rewards; or

(f) Disclosure of secret formulas, processes, business practices, and similar information.

Procedures affecting taxpayers' rights or duties that relate to matters under the jurisdiction of the Service will be published in the Bulletin.

(iv) [Reserved]

(v) (a) Rulings and other communications involving substantive tax law published in the Bulletin are published in the form of Revenue Rulings. The conclusions expressed in Revenue Rulings will be directly responsive to and limited in scope by the pivotal facts stated in the revenue ruling. Revenue Rulings arise from various sources, including rulings to taxpayers, technical advice to district offices, studies undertaken by the Office of the Assistant Commissioner (Technical), court decisions, suggestions from tax practitioner groups, publications, etc.

(b) It will be the practice of the Service to publish as much of the ruling or communication as is necessary for an understanding of the position stated. However, in order to prevent unwarranted invasions of personal privacy and to comply with statutory provisions, such as 18 U.S.C. 1905 and 26 U.S.C. 7213, dealing with disclosure of information obtained from members of the public, identifying details, including the names and addresses of persons involved, and information of a confidential nature are deleted from the ruling.

(c) Revenue Rulings, other than those relating to the qualification of pension, annuity, profit-sharing, stock bonus, and bond purchase plans, apply retroactively unless the Revenue Ruling includes a specific statement indicating, under the authority of section 7805(b) of the Internal Revenue Code of 1954, the extent to which it is to be applied without retroactive effect. Where Revenue Rulings revoke or modify rulings previously published in the Bulletin the authority of section 7805(b) of the Code ordinarily is invoked to provide that the new rulings will not be applied retroactively to the extent that the new rulings have adverse tax consequences to taxpayers. Section 7805(b) of the Code provides that the Secretary of the Treasury or his delegate may prescribe the extent to which any ruling is to be applied without retroactive effect. The exercise of this authority requires an affirmative action. For the effect of Revenue Rulings on determination letters and opinion letters issued with respect to the qualification of pension, annuity, profit-sharing, stock bonus, and bond purchase plans, see paragraph (o) of § 601.201.

(d) Revenue Rulings published in the Bulletin do not have the force and effect of Treasury Department Regulations (including Treasury decisions), but are published to provide precedents to be used in the disposition of other cases, and may be cited and relied upon for that purpose. No unpublished ruling or decision will be relied on, used, or cited, by any officer or employee of the Service as a precedent in the disposition of other cases.

(e) Taxpayers generally may rely upon Revenue Rulings published in the Bulletin in determining the tax treatment of their own transactions and need not request specific rulings applying the principles of a published Revenue Ruling to the facts of their particular cases. However, since each Revenue Ruling represents the conclusion of the Service as to the application of the law to the entire state of facts involved, taxpayers, Service personnel, and others concerned are cautioned against reaching the same conclusion in other cases unless the facts and circumstances are substantially the same. They should consider the effect of subsequent legislation, regulations, court decisions, and revenue rulings.

(f) Comments and suggestions from taxpayers or taxpayer groups on Revenue Rulings being prepared for publication in the Bulletin may be solicited, if justified by special circumstances. Conferences on Revenue Rulings being prepared for publication will not be granted except where the Service determines that such action is justified by special circumstances.

(vi) Statements of procedures which affect the rights or duties of taxpayers or other members of the public under the Code and related statutes will be published in the Bulletin in the form of Revenue Procedures. Revenue Procedures usually reflect the contents of internal management documents, but, where appropriate, they are also published to announce practices and procedures for guidance of the public. It is Service practice to publish as much of the internal management document or communication as is necessary for an understanding of the procedure. Revenue Procedures may also be based on internal management documents which should be a matter of public knowledge even though not necessarily affecting the rights or duties of the public. When publication of the substance of a Revenue Procedure in the Federal Register is required pursuant to 5 U.S.C. 552, it will usually be accomplished by an amendment of the Statement of procedural Rules (26 CFR Part 601).

(vii) (a) The Assistant Commissioner (Technical) is responsible for administering the system for the publication of Revenue Rulings and Revenue Procedures in the Bulletin, including the standards for style and format.

(b) In accordance with the standards set forth in subdivision (iv) of this subparagraph, each Assistant Commissioner is responsible for the preparation and appropriate referral for publication of Revenue Rulings reflecting interpretations of substantive tax law made by his office and communicated in writing to taxpayers or field offices. In this connection, the Chief Counsel is responsible for the referral to the appropriate Assistant Commissioner, for consideration for publication as Revenue Rulings, of interpretations of substantive tax law made by his Office.

(c) In accordance with the standards set forth in subdivision (iv) of this subparagraph, each Assistant Commissioner and the Chief Counsel is responsible for determining whether procedures established by any office under his jurisdiction should be published as Revenue Procedures and for the initiation, content, and appropriate referral for publication of such Revenue Procedures.

(e) Foreign tax law. (1) The Service will accept the interpretation placed by a foreign tax convention country on its revenue laws which do not affect the tax convention. However, when such interpretation conflicts with a provision in the tax convention, reconsideration of that interpretation may be requested.

(2) Conferences in the National Office of the Service will be granted to representatives of American firms doing business abroad and of American citizens residing abroad, in order to discuss with them foreign tax matters with respect to those countries with which we have tax treaties in effect.

* * *

Sec. 601.702. Publication, public inspection, and specific requests for records.

(a) Publication in the FEDERAL REGISTER — (1) Requirement. (i) Subject to the application of the exemptions and exclusions described in the Freedom of Information Act, 5 U.S.C. 552(b) and (c), and subject to the limitations provided in paragraph (a)(2) of this section, the IRS is required under 5 U.S.C. 552(a)(1), to state separately and publish currently in the FEDERAL REGISTER for the guidance of the public the following information –

(A) Descriptions of its central and field organization and the established places at which, the persons from whom, and the methods whereby, the public may obtain information, make submittals or requests, or obtain decisions, from the IRS;

(B) Statement of the general course and method by which its functions are channeled and determined, including the nature and requirements of all formal and informal procedures which are available;

(C) Rules of procedure, descriptions of forms available or the places at which forms may be obtained, and instructions as to the scope and contents of all papers, reports, or examinations;

(D) Substantive rules of general applicability adopted as authorized by law, and statements of general policy or interpretations of general applicability formulated and adopted by the IRS; and

(E) Each amendment, revision, or repeal of matters referred to in paragraphs (a)(1)(i)(A) through (D) of this section.

(ii) Pursuant to the foregoing requirements, the Commissioner publishes in the FEDERAL REGISTER from time to time a statement, which is not codified in this chapter, on the organization and functions of the IRS, and such amendments as are needed to keep the statement on a current basis. In addition, there are published in the FEDERAL REGISTER the rules set forth in this part 601 (Statement of Procedural Rules), such as those in paragraph E of this section, relating to conference and practice requirements of the IRS; the regulations in part 301 of this chapter (Procedure and Administration Regulations); and the various substantive regulations under the Internal Revenue Code of 1986, such as the regulations in part 1 of this chapter (Income Tax Regulations), in part 20 of this chapter (Estate Tax Regulations), and in part 31 of this chapter (Employment Tax Regulations).

(2) Limitations. (i) Incorporation by reference in the FEDERAL REGISTER. Matter which is reasonably available to the class of persons affected thereby, whether in a private or public publication, shall be deemed published in the FEDERAL REGISTER for purposes of paragraph (a)(1) of this section when it is incorporated by reference therein with the approval of the Director of the Office of the FEDERAL REGISTER. The matter which is incorporated by reference must be set forth in the private or public publication substantially in its entirety and not merely summarized or printed as a synopsis. Matter, the location and scope of which are familiar to only a few persons having a special working knowledge of the activities of the IRS, may not be incorporated in the FEDERAL REGISTER by reference. Matter may be incorporated by reference in the FEDERAL REGISTER only pursuant to the provisions of 5 U.S.C. 552(a)(1) and 1 CFR part 20.

(ii) Effect of failure to publish. Except to the extent that a person has actual and timely notice of the terms of any matter referred to in paragraph (a)(1) of this section which is required to be published in the FEDERAL REGISTER, such person is not required in any manner to resort to, or be adversely affected by, such matter if it is not so published or is not incorporated by reference therein pursuant to paragraph (a)(2)(i) of this section. Thus, for example, any such matter which imposes an obligation and which is not so published or incorporated by reference shall not adversely change or affect a person's rights.

* * *

(c) Specific requests for other records — (1) In general. (i) Subject to the application of the exemptions described in 5 U.S.C. 552(b) and the exclusions described in 5 U.S.C. 552(c), the IRS shall, in conformance with 5 U.S.C. 552(a)(3), make reasonably described records available to a person making a request for such records which conforms in every respect with the rules and procedures set forth in this section. Any request or any appeal from the initial denial of a request that does not comply with the requirements set forth in this section shall not be considered subject to the time constraints of paragraphs (c)(9), (10), and (11) of this section, unless and until the request or appeal is amended to comply. The IRS shall promptly advise the requester in what respect the request or appeal is deficient so that it may be resubmitted or amended for consideration in accordance with this section. If a requester does not resubmit a perfected request or appeal within 35 days from the date of a communication from the IRS, the request or appeal file shall be closed. When the resubmitted request or appeal conforms with the requirements of this section, the time constraints of paragraphs (c)(9), (10), and (11) of this section shall begin.

(ii) Requests for the continuing production of records created or for records created after the date of receipt of the request shall not be honored.

(iii) Specific requests under paragraph (a)(3) for material described in paragraph (a)(2)(A)through(C) and which is in the Freedom of Information Reading Room shall not be honored.

(2) Electronic format records. (i) The IRS shall provide the responsive record or records in the form or format requested if the record or records are readily reproducible by the IRS in that form or format. The IRS shall make reasonable efforts to maintain its records in forms or formats that are reproducible for the purpose of disclosure. For purposes of this paragraph, the term readily reproducible means, with respect to electronic format, a record or records that can be downloaded or transferred intact to a floppy disk, computer disk (CD), tape, or other electronic medium using equipment currently in use by the office or offices processing the request. Even though some records may initially be readily reproducible, the need to segregate exempt from nonexempt records may cause the releasable material to be not readily reproducible.

(ii) In responding to a request for records, the IRS shall make reasonable efforts to search for the records in electronic form or format, except where such efforts would significantly interfere with the operation of the agency's automated information system(s). For purposes of this paragraph (c), the term search means to locate, manually or by automated means, agency records for the purpose of identifying those records which are responsive to a request.

(iii) Searches for records maintained in electronic form or format may require the application of codes, queries, or other minor forms of programming to retrieve the requested records.

(3) Requests for records not in control of the IRS. (i) Where the request is for a record which is determined to be in the possession or under the control of a constituent unit of the Department of the Treasury other than the IRS, the request for such record shall immediately be transferred to the appropriate constituent unit and the requester notified to that effect. Such referral shall not be deemed a denial of access within the meaning of these regulations. The constituent unit of the Department to which such referral is made shall treat such request as a new request addressed to it and the time limits for response set forth in paragraphs (c)(9) and (c)(10) of this section shall commence when the referral is received by the designated office or officer of the constituent unit. Where the request is for a record which is of a type that is not maintained by any constituent unit of the Department of the Treasury, the requester shall be so advised.

(ii) Where the record requested was created by another agency or constituent unit of the Department of the Treasury and a copy thereof is in the possession of the IRS, the IRS official to whom the request is delivered shall refer the request to the agency or constituent unit which originated the record for direct reply to the requester. The requester shall be informed of such referral. This referral shall not be considered a denial of access within the meaning of these regulations. Where the record is determined to be exempt from disclosure under 5 U.S.C. 552, the referral need not be made, but the IRS shall inform the originating agency or constituent unit of its determination. Where notifying the requester of its referral may cause a harm to the originating agency or constituent unit which would enable the originating agency or constituent unit to withhold the record under 5 U.S.C. 552, then such referral need not be made. In both of these circumstances, the IRS official to whom the request is delivered shall process the request in accordance with the procedures set forth in this section.

(iii) When a request is received for a record created by the IRS (i.e., in its possession and control) that includes information originated by another agency or constituent unit of the Department of the Treasury, the record shall be referred to the originating agency or constituent unit for review, coordination, and concurrence prior to being released to a requester. The IRS official to whom the request is delivered may withhold the record without prior consultation with the originating agency or constituent unit.

(4) Form of request. (i) Requesters are advised that only requests for records which fully comply with the requirements of this section can be processed in accordance with this section. Requesters shall be notified promptly in writing of any requirements which have not been met or any additional requirements to be met. Every effort shall be made to comply with the requests as written. The initial request for records must –

(A) Be made in writing and signed by the individual making the request;

(B) State that it is made pursuant to the Freedom of Information Act, 5 U.S.C. 552, or regulations thereunder;

(C) Be addressed to and mailed to the office of the IRS official who is responsible for the control of the records requested (see paragraph (h) of this section for the responsible officials and their addresses), regardless of where such records are maintained. Generally, requests for records pertaining to the requester, or other matters of local interest, should be directed to the office servicing the requester's geographic area of residence. Requests for records maintained in the Headquarters of the IRS and its National Office of Chief Counsel, concerning matters of nationwide applicability, such as published guidance (regulations and revenue rulings), program management, operations, or policies, should be directed to the Headquarters Disclosure Office. If the person making the request does not know the official responsible for the control of the records being requested, the person making the request may contact, by telephone or in writing, the disclosure office servicing the requester's geographic area of residence to ascertain the identity of the official having control of the records being requested so that the request can be addressed, and delivered, to the appropriate responsible official. Misdirected requests that otherwise satisfy the requirements of this section shall be immediately transferred to the appropriate responsible IRS official and the requester notified to that effect. Such transfer shall not be deemed a denial of access within the meaning of these regulations. The IRS official to whom the request is redirected shall treat such request as a new request addressed to it and the time limits for response set forth in paragraphs (c)(9) and (c)(11) of this section shall commence when the transfer is received by the designated office;

(D) Reasonably describe the records in accordance with paragraph (c)(5)(i) of this section;

(E) In the case of a request for records the disclosure of which is limited by statute or regulations (as, for example, the Privacy Act of 1974 (5 U.S.C. 552a) or section 6103 and the regulations thereunder), establish the identity and the right of the person making the request to the disclosure of the records in accordance with paragraph (c)(5)(iii) of this section;

(F) Set forth the address where the person making the request desires to be notified of the determination as to whether the request shall be granted;

(G) State whether the requester wishes to inspect the records or desires to have a copy made and furnished without first inspecting them;

(H) State the firm agreement of the requester to pay the fees for search, duplication, and review ultimately determined in accordance with paragraph (f) of this section, or, in accordance with paragraph (c)(4)(ii) of this section, place an upper limit for such fees that the requester is willing to pay, or request that such fees be reduced or waived and state the justification for such request; and

(I) Identify the category of the requester and, with the exception of "other requesters," state how the records shall be used, as required by paragraph (f)(3) of this section.

(ii) As provided in paragraph (c)(4)(i)(H) of this section, rather than stating a firm agreement to pay the fee ultimately determined in accordance with paragraph (f) of this section or requesting that such fees be reduced or waived, the requester may place an upper limit on the amount the requester agrees to pay. If the requester chooses to place an upper limit and the estimated fee is deemed to be greater than the upper limit, or where the requester asks for an estimate of the fee to be charged, the requester shall be promptly advised of the estimate of the fee and asked to agree to pay such amount. Where the initial request includes a request for reduction or waiver of the fee, the IRS officials responsible for the control of the requested records (or their delegates) shall determine whether to grant the request for reduction or waiver in accordance with paragraph (f) of this section and notify the requester of their decisions and, if their decisions result in the requester being liable for all or part of the fee normally due, ask the requester to agree to pay the amount so determined. The requirements of this paragraph shall not be deemed met until the requester has explicitly agreed to pay the fee applicable to the request for records, if any, or has made payment in advance of the fee estimated to be due. If the requester has any outstanding balance of search, review, or duplication fees, the requirements of this paragraph shall not be deemed met until the requester has remitted the outstanding balance due.

(5) Reasonable description of records; identity and right of the requester. (i) The request for records must describe the records in reasonably sufficient detail to enable the IRS employees who are familiar with the subject matter of the request to locate the records without placing an unreasonable burden upon the IRS. While no specific formula for a reasonable description of a record can be established, the requirement shall generally be satisfied if the requester gives the name, taxpayer identification number (e.g., social security number or employer identification number), subject matter, location, and years at issue, of the requested records. If the request seeks records pertaining to pending litigation, the request shall indicate the title of the case, the court in which the case was filed, and the nature of the case. It is suggested that the person making the request furnish any additional information which shall more clearly identify the requested records. Where the requester does not reasonably describe the records being sought, the requester shall be afforded an opportunity to refine the request. Such opportunity may involve a conference with knowledgeable IRS personnel at the discretion of the disclosure officer. The reasonable description requirement shall not be used by officers or employees of the Internal Revenue as a device for improperly withholding records from the public.

(ii) The IRS shall make a reasonable effort to comply fully with all requests for access to records subject only to any applicable exemption set forth in 5 U.S.C. 552(b) or any exclusion described in 5 U.S.C. 552(c). In any situation in which it is determined that a request for voluminous records would unduly burden and interfere with the operations of the IRS, the person making the request shall be asked to be more specific and to narrow the request, or to agree on an orderly procedure for the production of the requested records, in order to satisfy the request without disproportionate adverse effect on IRS operations.

(iii) Statutory or regulatory restrictions — **(A)** In the case of records containing information with respect to particular persons the disclosure of which is limited by statute or regulations, persons making requests shall establish their identity and right to access to such records. Persons requesting access to such records which pertain to themselves may establish their identity by –

(1) The presentation of a single document bearing a photograph (such as a passport or identification badge), or the presentation of two items of identification which do not bear a photograph but do bear both a name and signature (such as a credit card or organization membership card), in the case of a request made in person,

(2) The submission of the requester's signature, address, and one other identifier (such as a photocopy of a driver's license) bearing the requester's signature, in the case of a request by mail, or

(3) The presentation in person or the submission by mail of a notarized statement, or a statement made under penalty of perjury in accordance with 28 U.S.C. 1746, swearing to or affirming such person's identity.

(B) Additional proof of a person's identity shall be required before the requests shall be deemed to have met the requirement of paragraph (c)(4)(i)(E) of this section if it is determined that additional proof is necessary to protect against unauthorized disclosure of information in a particular case. Persons who have identified themselves to the satisfaction of IRS officials pursuant to this paragraph (c) shall be deemed to have established their right to access records pertaining to themselves. Persons requesting records on behalf of or pertaining to another person must provide adequate proof of the legal relationship under which they assert the right to access the requested records before the requirement of paragraph (c)(4)(i)(E) of this section shall be deemed met.

(C) In the case of an attorney-in-fact, or other person requesting records on behalf of or pertaining to other persons, the requester shall furnish a properly executed power of attorney, Privacy Act consent, or tax information authorization, as appropriate. In the case of a corporation, if the requester has the authority to legally bind the corporation under applicable state law, such as its corporate president or chief executive officer, then a written statement or tax information authorization certifying as to that person's authority to make a request on behalf of the corporation shall be sufficient. If the requester is any other officer or employee of the corporation, then such requester shall furnish a written statement certifying as to that person's authority to make a request on behalf of the corporation by any principal officer and attested to by the secretary or other officer (other than the requester) that the person making the request on behalf of the corporation is properly authorized to make such a request. If the requester is other than one of the above, then such person may furnish a resolution by the corporation's board of directors or other governing body which provides that the person making the request on behalf of the corporation is properly authorized to make such a request, or shall otherwise satisfy the requirements set forth in section 6103(e). A person requesting access to records of a partnership or a subchapter S Corporation shall provide a notarized statement, or a statement made under penalty of perjury in accordance with 28 U.S.C. 1746, that the requester was a member of the partnership or subchapter S corporation for a part of each of the years included in the request.

(6) Requests for expedited processing. (i) When a requester demonstrates compelling need, a request shall be taken out of order and given expedited treatment. A compelling need involves –

(A) Circumstances in which the lack of expedited treatment could reasonably be expected to pose an imminent threat to the life or physical safety of an individual;

(B) An urgency to inform the public concerning actual or alleged Federal government activity, if made by a person primarily engaged in disseminating information. A person primarily engaged in disseminating information, if not a full-time representative of the news media, as defined in paragraph (f)(3)(ii)(B) of this section, must establish that he or she is a person whose main professional activity or occupation is information dissemination, though it need not be his or her sole occupation. A person primarily engaged in disseminating information does not include individuals who are engaged only incidentally in the dissemination of information. The standard of urgency to inform requires that the records requested pertain to a matter of current exigency to the American public, beyond the public's right to know about government activity generally, and that delaying a response to a request for records would compromise a significant recognized interest to and throughout the American general public;

(C) The loss of substantial due process rights.

(ii) A requester who seeks expedited processing must submit a statement, certified to be true and correct to the best of his or her knowledge and belief, explaining in detail why there is a compelling need for expedited processing.

(iii) A request for expedited processing may be made at the time of the initial request for records or at any later time. For a prompt determination, requests for expedited processing must be submitted to the responsible official of the IRS who maintains the records requested except that a request for expedited processing under paragraph (c)(6)(i)(B) of this section shall be submitted directly to the Director, Communications Division, whose address is Office of Media Relations, CLInternal Revenue Service, Room 7032, 1111 Constitution Avenue, NW., Washington, DC 20224.

(iv) Upon receipt by the responsible official in the IRS, a request for expedited processing shall be considered and a determination as to whether to grant or deny the request shall be made, and the requester notified, within ten days of the date of the request, provided that in no event shall the IRS have less than five days (excluding Saturdays, Sundays, and legal public holidays) from the date of the responsible official's receipt of the request for such processing. The determination to grant or deny a request for expedited processing shall be made solely on the information initially provided by the requester.

(v) An appeal of an initial determination to deny expedited processing must be made within ten days of the date of the initial determination to deny expedited processing, and must otherwise comply with the requirements of paragraph (c)(10) of this section. Both the envelope and the appeal itself shall be clearly marked, "Appeal for Expedited Processing."

(vi) IRS action to deny or affirm denial of a request for expedited processing pursuant to this paragraph, and IRS failure to respond in a timely manner to such a request shall be subject to judicial review, except that judicial review shall be based on the record before the IRS at the time of the determination. A district court of the United States shall not have jurisdiction to review the IRS's denial of expedited processing of a request for records after the IRS has provided a complete response to the request.

(7) Date of receipt of request. (i) Requests for records and any separate agreement to pay, final notification of waiver of fees, or letter transmitting payment, shall be promptly stamped with the date of delivery to or dispatch by the office of the IRS official responsible for the control of the records requested. A request for records shall be considered to have been received on the date on which a complete request containing the information required by paragraphs (c)(4)(i)(A) through (I) has been received by the IRS official responsible for the control of the records requested. A determination that a request is deficient in any respect is not a denial of access, and such determinations are not subject to administrative appeal.

(ii) The latest of such stamped dates shall be deemed for purposes of this section to be the date of receipt of the request, provided that the requirements of paragraphs (c)(4)(i)(A) through (I) of this section have been satisfied, and, where applicable –

(A) The requester has agreed in writing, by executing a separate contract or otherwise, to pay the fees for search, duplication, and review determined due in accordance with paragraph (f) of this section, or

(B) The fees have been waived in accordance with paragraph (f) of this section, or

(C) Payment in advance has been received from the requester.

(8) Search for records requested. (i) Upon the receipt of a request, search services shall be performed by IRS personnel to identify and locate the requested records. Search time includes any and all time spent looking for material responsive to the request, including page-by-page or line-by-line identification of material within records. Where duplication of an entire record would be less costly than a line-by-line identification, duplication should be substituted for this kind of search. With respect to records maintained in computerized form, a search shall include services functionally analogous to a search for records which are maintained on paper.

(ii) In determining which records are responsive to a request, the IRS official responsible for the control of the records requested shall include only those records within the official's possession and control as of the date of the receipt of the request by the appropriate disclosure officer.

(9) Initial determination. (i) Responsible official.

(A) The Associate Director, Personnel Security or delegate shall have the sole authority to make initial determinations with respect to requests for records under that office's control.

(B) The Director of the Office of Governmental Liaison and Disclosure or delegate shall have the sole authority to make initial determinations with respect to all other requests for records of the IRS maintained in the Headquarters and its National Office of the Chief Counsel. For all other records within the control of the IRS, the initial determination with respect to requests for records may be made either by the Director, Office of Governmental Liaison and Disclosure, or by the IRS officials responsible for the control of the records requested, or their delegates (see paragraph (h) of this section).

(ii) Processing of request. The appropriate responsible official or delegate shall respond in the approximate order of receipt of the requests, to the extent consistent with sound administrative practice. In any event, the initial determination shall be made and notification thereof mailed within 20 days (excepting Saturdays, Sundays, and legal public holidays) after the date of receipt of the request, as determined in accordance with paragraph (c)(7) of this section, unless the responsible official invokes an extension pursuant to paragraph (c)(11) of this section, the requester otherwise agrees to an extension of the 20 day time limitation, or the request is an expedited request.

(iii) Granting of request. If the request is granted in full or in part, and if the requester wants a copy of the records, a statement of the applicable fees, if there are any, shall be mailed to the requester either at the time of the determination or shortly thereafter. In the case of a request for inspection, the records shall be made available promptly for inspection, at the time and place stated, normally at the appropriate office where the records requested are controlled. If the person making the request has expressed a desire to inspect the records at another office of the IRS, a reasonable effort shall be made to comply with the request. Records shall be made available for inspection at such reasonable and proper times so as not to interfere with their use by the IRS or to exclude other persons from making inspections. In addition, reasonable limitations may be placed on the number of records which may be inspected by a person on any given date. The person making the request shall not be allowed to remove the records from the office where inspection is made. If, after making inspection, the person making the request desires copies of all or a portion of the requested records, copies shall be furnished upon payment of the established fees prescribed by paragraph (f) of this section.

(iv) Denial of request. If it is determined that some records shall be denied, the person making the request shall be so notified by mail. The letter of notification shall specify the city or other location where the requested records are situated, contain a brief statement of the grounds for not granting the request in full including the exemption(s) relied upon, the name and any title or position of the official responsible for the denial, and advise the person making the request of the right to appeal to the Commissioner in accordance with paragraph (c)(10) of this section.

(A) In denying a request for records, in whole or in part, the IRS shall include the date that the request was received in the appropriate disclosure office, and shall provide an estimate of the volume of the denied matter to the person making the request, unless providing such estimate would harm an interest protected by an exemption in 5 U.S.C. 552(b) or (c) pursuant to which the denial is made; and

(B) The amount of information deleted shall be indicated on the released portion of the record, unless including that indication would harm an interest protected by an exemption in 5 U.S.C. 552(b) under which the deletion is made. If technically feasible, the amount of the information deleted and the asserted exemption shall be indicated at the place in the record where such deletion is made.

(v) Inability to locate and evaluate within time limits. Where the records requested cannot be located and evaluated within the initial twenty day period or any extension thereof in accordance with paragraph (c)(11) of this section, the search for the records or evaluation shall continue, but the requester shall be notified, and advised that the requester may consider such notification a denial of the request for records. The requester shall be provided with a statement of judicial rights along with the notification letter. The requester may also be invited, in the alternative, to agree to a voluntary extension of time in which to locate and evaluate the records. Such voluntary extension of time shall not constitute a waiver of the requester's right to appeal or seek judicial review of any denial of access ultimately made or the requester's right to seek judicial review in the event of failure to comply with the time extension granted.

(10) Administrative appeal. (i) The requester may submit an administrative appeal to the Commissioner of Internal Revenue by letter that is postmarked within 35 days after the later of the date of any letter of notification described in paragraph (c)(9)(iv) of this section, the date of any letter of notification of an adverse determination of the requester's category described in paragraph (f)(3) of this section, the date of any letter of notification of an adverse determination of the requester's fee waiver or reduction request described in paragraph (f)(2) of this section, the date of any letter determining that no responsive records exist, or the date of the last transmission of the last records released. An administrative appeal for denial of a request for expedited processing must be made to the Commissioner of Internal Revenue by letter that is postmarked within 10 days after the date of any letter of notification discussed in paragraph (c)(6)(iv) of this section.

(ii) The letter of appeal shall — (A) Be made in writing and signed by the requester;

(B) Be addressed to the Commissioner and mailed to IRS Appeals, 6377A Riverside Avenue, Suite 110, Riverside, California 92506-FOIA Appeal;

(C) Reasonably describe the records requested to which the appeal pertains in accordance with paragraph (c)(5)(i) of this section;

(D) Set forth the address where the appellant desires to be notified of the determination on appeal;

(E) Specify the date of the request, the office to which the request was submitted, and where possible, enclose a copy of the initial request and the initial determination being appealed; and

(F) Ask the Commissioner to grant the request for records, fee waiver, expedited processing, or favorable fee category, as applicable, or verify that an appropriate search was conducted and the responsive records were either produced or an appropriate exemption asserted. The person submitting the appeal may submit any argument in support of the appeal in the letter of appeal.

(iii) Appeals shall be stamped promptly with the date of their receipt in the Office of Appeals, and the later of this stamped date or the stamped date of a document submitted subsequently which supplements the original appeal so that the appeal satisfies the requirements set forth in paragraphs (c)(10)(ii)(A) through (F) of this section shall be deemed by the IRS to be the date of receipt of the appeal for all purposes of this section. The Commissioner or a delegate shall acknowledge receipt of the appeal and advise the requester of the date of receipt and the date a response is due in accordance with this paragraph. If an appeal fails to satisfy any of the requirements of paragraph (c)(10)(ii)(A) through (F) of this section, the person making the request shall be advised promptly in writing of the additional requirements to be met. Except for appeals of denials of expedited processing, the determination to affirm the initial denial (in whole or in part) or to grant the request for records shall be made and notification of the determination shall be mailed within twenty days (exclusive of Saturdays, Sundays, and legal public holidays) after the date of receipt of the appeal unless extended pursuant to paragraph (c)(11)(i) of this section. Appeals of initial determinations to deny expedited processing must be made within 10 calendar days of the determination to deny the expedited processing. If it is determined that the appeal from the initial denial is to be denied (in whole or in part), the requester shall be notified in writing of the denial, the reasons therefor, the name and title or position of the official responsible for the denial on appeal, and the provisions of 5 U.S.C. 552(a)(4) for judicial review of that determination.

(11) Time extensions. (i) Unusual circumstances. (A) In unusual circumstances, the time limitations specified in paragraphs (c)(9) and (10) of this section may be extended by written notice from the official charged with the duty of making the determinations to the person making the request or appeal setting forth the reasons for this extension and the date on which the determination is expected to be sent. As used in this paragraph, the term unusual circumstances means, but only to the extent reasonably necessary to the proper processing of the particular request:

(1) The need to search for and collect the requested records from field facilities or other establishments that are separate from the office processing the request;

(2) The need to search for, collect, and appropriately examine a voluminous amount of separate and distinct records which are demanded in a single request;

(3) The need for consultation, which shall be conducted with all practicable speed, with another agency having a substantial interest in the determination of the request or among two or more constituent units of the Department of the Treasury having substantial subject matter interest therein; and

(4) The need for consultation with business submitters to determine the nature and extent of proprietary information in accordance with this section.

(B) Any extension or extensions of time for unusual circumstances shall not cumulatively total more than ten days (exclusive of Saturday, Sunday and legal public holidays). If additional time is needed to process the request, the IRS shall notify the requester and provide the requester an opportunity to limit the scope of the request or arrange for an alternative time frame for processing the request or a modified request. The requester shall retain the right to define the desired scope of the request, as long as it meets the requirements contained in this section.

(ii) Aggregation of requests. If more than one request is received from the same requester, or from a group of requesters acting in concert, and the IRS believes that such requests constitute a single request which would otherwise satisfy the unusual circumstances specified in subparagraph (c)(11)(i) of this section, and the requests involve clearly related matters, the IRS may aggregate these requests for processing purposes. Multiple requests involving unrelated matters shall not be aggregated.

(12) Failure to comply. If the IRS fails to comply with the time limitations specified in paragraphs (c)(9), (10), or paragraph (c)(11)(i) of this section, any person making a request for records satisfying the requirements of paragraphs (c)(4)(i)(A) through (I) of this section, shall be deemed to have exhausted administrative remedies with respect to such request. Accordingly, this person may initiate suit in accordance with paragraph (c)(13) of this section.

(13) Judicial review. If an administrative appeal pursuant to paragraph (c)(10) of this section for records or fee waiver or reduction is denied, or if a request for expedited processing is denied and there has been no determination as to the release of records, or if a request for a favorable fee category under paragraph (f)(3) of this section is denied, or a determination is made that there are no responsive records, or if no determination is made within the twenty day periods specified in paragraphs (c)(9) and (10) of this section, or the period of any extension pursuant to paragraph (c)(11)(i) of this section, or by grant of the requester, respectively, the person making the request may commence an action in a United States district court in the district in which the requester resides, in which the requester's principal place of business is located, in which the records are situated, or in the District of Columbia, pursuant to 5 U.S.C. 552(a)(4)(B). The statute authorizes an action only against the agency. With respect to records of the IRS, the agency is the IRS, not an officer or an employee thereof. Service of process in such an action shall be in accordance with the Federal Rules of Civil Procedure (28 U.S.C. App.) applicable to actions against an agency of the United States. Delivery of process upon the IRS shall be directed to the Commissioner of

Internal Revenue, Attention: CC1111 Constitution Avenue, NW., Washington, DC 20224. The IRS shall serve an answer or otherwise plead to any complaint made under this paragraph within 30 days after service upon it, unless the court otherwise directs for good cause shown. The district court shall determine the matter de novo, and may examine the contents of the IRS records in question in camera to determine whether such records or any part thereof shall be withheld under any of the exemptions described in 5 U.S.C. 552(b) and the exclusions described in 5 U.S.C. 552(c). The burden shall be upon the IRS to sustain its action in not making the requested records available. The court may assess against the United States reasonable attorney fees and other litigation costs reasonably incurred by the person making the request in any case in which the complainant has substantially prevailed.

(14) Preservation of records. All correspondence relating to the requests received by the IRS under this chapter, and all records processed pursuant to such requests, shall be preserved, until such time as the destruction of such correspondence and records is authorized pursuant to title 44 of the United States Code. Under no circumstances shall records be destroyed while they are the subject of a pending request, appeal, or lawsuit under 5 U.S.C. 552.

* * *

PART III

Constitution of the United States of America
(Selected Provisions)

CONSTITUTION OF THE UNITED STATES OF AMERICA

(Current through PL 112-173, approved 8/16/12)

Amend. 4 *Unreasonable searches and seizures.*

The right of the people to be secure in their persons, houses, papers, and effects, against unreasonable searches and seizures, shall not be violated, and no Warrants shall issue, but upon probable cause, supported by Oath or affirmation, and particularly describing the place to be searched, and the persons or things to be seized.

Amend. 5 *Criminal actions – Provisions concerning – Due process of law and just compensation clauses.*

No person shall be held to answer for a capital, or otherwise infamous crime, unless on a presentment or indictment of a Grand Jury, except in cases arising in the land or naval forces, or in the Militia, when in actual service in time of War or public danger; nor shall any person be subject for the same offence to be twice put in jeopardy of life or limb; nor shall be compelled in any criminal case to be a witness against himself, nor be deprived of life, liberty, or property, without due process of law; nor shall private property be taken for public use, without just compensation.

Amend. 16 *Income tax.*

The Congress shall have power to lay and collect taxes on incomes, from whatever source derived, without apportionment among the several States, and without regard to any census or enumeration.

PART IV

United States Code Other than Title 26
(Selected Sections)

5 USC § 551. Definitions.

For the purpose of this subchapter

(1) "agency" means each authority of the Government of the United States, whether or not it is within or subject to review by another agency, but does not include--

(A) the Congress;

(B) the courts of the United States;

(C) the governments of the territories or possessions of the United States;

(D) the government of the District of Columbia;

or except as to the requirements of section 552 of this title –

(E) agencies composed of representatives of the parties or of representatives of organizations of the parties to the disputes determined by them;

(F) courts martial and military commissions;

(G) military authority exercised in the field in time of war or in occupied territory; or

(H) functions conferred by sections 1738, 1739, 1743, and 1744 of title 12; subchapter II of chapter 471 of title 49; or sections 1884, 1891-1902, and former section 1641(b)(2), of title 50, appendix;

(2) "person" includes an individual, partnership, corporation, association, or public or private organization other than an agency;

(3) "party" includes a person or agency named or admitted as a party, or properly seeking and entitled as of right to be admitted as a party, in an agency proceeding, and a person or agency admitted by an agency as a party for limited purposes;

(4) "rule" means the whole or a part of an agency statement of general or particular applicability and future effect designed to implement, interpret, or prescribe law or policy or describing the organization, procedure, or practice requirements of an agency and includes the approval or prescription for the future of rates, wages, corporate or financial structures or reorganizations thereof, prices, facilities, appliances, services or allowances therefor or of valuations, costs, or accounting, or practices bearing on any of the foregoing;

(5) "rule making" means agency process for formulating, amending, or repealing a rule;

(6) "order" means the whole or a part of a final disposition, whether affirmative, negative, injunctive, or declaratory in form, of an agency in a matter other than rule-making but including licensing;

(7) "adjudication" means agency process for the formulation of an order;

(8) "license" includes the whole or a part of an agency permit, certificate, approval, registration, charter, membership, statutory exemption or other form of permission;

(9) "licensing" includes agency process respecting the grant, renewal, denial, revocation, suspension, annulment, withdrawal, limitation, amendment, modification, or conditioning of a license;

(10) "sanction" includes the whole or a part of an agency—

(A) prohibition, requirement, limitation, or other condition affecting the freedom of a person;

(B) withholding of relief;

(C) imposition of penalty or fine;

(D) destruction, taking, seizure, or withholding of property;

(E) assessment of damages, reimbursement, restitution, compensation, costs, charges, or fees;

(F) requirement, revocation, or suspension of a license; or

(G) taking other compulsory or restrictive action;

(11) "relief" includes the whole or a part of an agency—

(A) grant of money, assistance, license, authority, exemption, exception, privilege, or remedy;

(B) recognition of a claim, right, immunity, privilege, exemption, or exception; or

(C) taking of other action on the application or petition of, and beneficial to, a person;

(12) "agency proceeding" means an agency process as defined by paragraphs (5), (7), and (9) of this section;

(13) "agency action" includes the whole or a part of an agency rule, order, license, sanction, relief, or the equivalent or denial thereof, or failure to act; and

(14) "ex parte communication" means an oral or written communication not on the public record with respect to which reasonable prior notice to all parties is not given, but it shall not include requests for status reports on any matter or proceeding covered by this subchapter.

5 USC § 552. Public information; agency rules, opinions, orders, records, and proceedings.

(a) Each agency shall make available to the public information as follows:

(1) Each agency shall separately state and currently publish in the Federal Register for the guidance of the public--

(A) descriptions of its central and field organization and the established places at which, the employees (and in the case of a uniformed service, the members) from whom, and the methods whereby, the public may obtain information, make submittals or requests, or obtain decisions;

(B) statements of the general course and method by which its functions are channeled and determined, including the nature and requirements of all formal and informal procedures available;

(C) rules of procedure, descriptions of forms available or the places at which forms may be obtained, and instructions as to the scope and contents of all papers, reports, or examinations;

(D) substantive rules of general applicability adopted as authorized by law, and statements of general policy or interpretations of general applicability formulated and adopted by the agency; and

(E) each amendment, revision, or repeal of the foregoing.

Except to the extent that a person has actual and timely notice of the terms thereof, a person may not in any manner be required to resort to, or be adversely affected by, a matter required to be published in the Federal Register and not so published. For the purpose of this paragraph, matter reasonably available to the class of persons affected thereby is deemed published in the Federal Register when incorporated by reference therein with the approval of the Director of the Federal Register.

(2) Each agency, in accordance with published rules, shall make available for public inspection and copying--

(A) final opinions, including concurring and dissenting opinions, as well as orders, made in the adjudication of cases;

(B) those statements of policy and interpretations which have been adopted by the agency and are not published in the Federal Register;

(C) administrative staff manuals and instructions to staff that affect a member of the public;

(D) copies of all records, regardless of form or format, which have been released to any person under paragraph (3) and which, because of the nature of their subject matter, the agency determines have become or are likely to become the subject of subsequent requests for substantially the same records; and

(E) a general index of the records referred to under subparagraph (D); unless the materials are promptly published and copies offered for sale. For records created on or after November 1, 1996, within one year after such date, each agency shall make such records available, including by computer telecommunications or, if computer telecommunications means have not been established by the agency, by other electronic means. To the extent required to prevent a clearly unwarranted invasion of personal privacy, an agency may delete identifying details when it makes available or publishes an opinion, statement of policy, interpretation, staff manual, instruction, or copies of records referred to in subparagraph (D). However, in each case the justification for the deletion shall be explained fully in writing, and the extent of such deletion shall be indicated on the portion of the record which is made available or published, unless including that indication would harm an interest protected by the exemption in subsection (b) under which the deletion is made. If technically feasible, the extent of the deletion shall be indicated at the place in the record where the deletion was made. Each agency shall also maintain and make available for public inspection and copying current indexes providing identifying information for the public as to any matter issued, adopted, or promulgated after July 4, 1967, and required by this paragraph to be made available or published. Each agency shall make the index referred to in subparagraph (E) available by computer telecommunications by December 31, 1999. Each agency shall promptly publish, quarterly or more frequently, and distribute (by sale or otherwise) copies of each index or supplements thereto unless it determines by order published in the Federal Register that the publication would be unnecessary and impracticable, in which case the agency shall nonetheless provide copies of such index on request at a cost not to exceed the direct cost of duplication. A final order, opinion, statement of policy, interpretation, or staff manual or instruction that affects a member of the public may be relied on, used, or cited as precedent by an agency against a party other than an agency only if—

(i) it has been indexed and either made available or published as provided by this paragraph; or

(ii) the party has actual and timely notice of the terms thereof.

(3) (A) Except with respect to the records made available under paragraphs (1) and (2) of this subsection, and except as provided in subparagraph (E), each agency, upon any request for records which (i) reasonably describes such records and (ii) is made in

accordance with published rules stating the time, place, fees (if any), and procedures to be followed, shall make the records promptly available to any person.

(B) In making any record available to a person under this paragraph, an agency shall provide the record in any form or format requested by the person if the record is readily reproducible by the agency in that form or format. Each agency shall make reasonable efforts to maintain its records in forms or formats that are reproducible for purposes of this section.

(C) In responding under this paragraph to a request for records, an agency shall make reasonable efforts to search for the records in electronic form or format, except when such efforts would significantly interfere with the operation of the agency's automated information system.

(D) For purposes of this paragraph, the term "search" means to review, manually or by automated means, agency records for the purpose of locating those records which are responsive to a request.

(E) An agency, or part of an agency, that is an element of the intelligence community (as that term is defined in section 3(4) of the National Security Act of 1947 (50 U.S.C. 401a(4))) shall not make any record available under this paragraph to—

　　(i) any government entity, other than a State, territory, commonwealth, or district of the United States, or any subdivision thereof; or

　　(ii) a representative of a government entity described in clause (i).

(4) (A) (i) In order to carry out the provisions of this section, each agency shall promulgate regulations, pursuant to notice and receipt of public comment, specifying the schedule of fees applicable to the processing of requests under this section and establishing procedures and guidelines for determining when such fees should be waived or reduced. Such schedule shall conform to the guidelines which shall be promulgated, pursuant to notice and receipt of public comment, by the Director of the Office of Management and Budget and which shall provide for a uniform schedule of fees for all agencies.

* * *

　　(iii) Documents shall be furnished without any charge or at a charge reduced below the fees established under clause (ii) if disclosure of the information is in the public interest because it is likely to contribute significantly to public understanding of the operations or activities of the government and is not primarily in the commercial interest of the requester.

　　(iv) Fee schedules shall provide for the recovery of only the direct costs of search, duplication, or review. Review costs shall include only the direct costs incurred during the initial examination of a document for the purposes of determining whether the documents must be disclosed under this section and for the purposes of withholding any portions exempt from disclosure under this section. Review costs may not include any costs incurred in resolving issues of law or policy that may be raised in the course of processing a request under this section. No fee may be charged by any agency under this section--

> **(I)** if the costs of routine collection and processing of the fee are likely to equal or exceed the amount of the fee; or
>
> **(II)** for any request described in clause (ii)(II) or (III) of this subparagraph for the first two hours of search time or for the first one hundred pages of duplication.

(v) No agency may require advance payment of any fee unless the requester has previously failed to pay fees in a timely fashion, or the agency has determined that the fee will exceed $250.

(vi) Nothing in this subparagraph shall supersede fees chargeable under a statute specifically providing for setting the level of fees for particular types of records.

(vii) In any action by a requester regarding the waiver of fees under this section, the court shall determine the matter de novo: *Provided,* That the court's review of the matter shall be limited to the record before the agency.

(viii) An agency shall not assess search fees (or in the case of a requester described under clause (ii)(II), duplication fees) under this subparagraph if the agency fails to comply with any time limit under paragraph (6), if no unusual or exceptional circumstances (as those terms are defined for purposes of paragraphs (6)(B) and (C), respectively) apply to the processing of the request.

(B) On complaint, the district court of the United States in the district in which the complainant resides, or has his principal place of business, or in which the agency records are situated, or in the District of Columbia, has jurisdiction to enjoin the agency from withholding agency records and to order the production of any agency records improperly withheld from the complainant. In such a case the court shall determine the matter de novo, and may examine the contents of such agency records in camera to determine whether such records or any part thereof shall be withheld under any of the exemptions set forth in subsection (b) of this section, and the burden is on the agency to sustain its action. In addition to any other matters to which a court accords substantial weight, a court shall accord substantial weight to an affidavit of an agency concerning the agency's determination as to technical feasibility under paragraph (2)(C) and subsection (b) and reproducibility under paragraph (3)(B).

(C) Notwithstanding any other provision of law, the defendant shall serve an answer or otherwise plead to any complaint made under this subsection within thirty days after service upon the defendant of the pleading in which such complaint is made, unless the court otherwise directs for good cause shown.

(D) [Repealed]

(E) (i) The court may assess against the United States reasonable attorney fees and other litigation costs reasonably incurred in any case under this section in which the complainant has substantially prevailed.

(ii) For purposes of this subparagraph, a complainant has substantially prevailed if the complainant has obtained relief through either—

(I) a judicial order, or an enforceable written agreement or consent decree; or

(II) a voluntary or unilateral change in position by the agency, if the complainant's claim is not insubstantial.

(F) (i) Whenever the court orders the production of any agency records improperly withheld from the complainant and assesses against the United States reasonable attorney fees and other litigation costs, and the court additionally issues a written finding that the circumstances surrounding the withholding raise questions whether agency personnel acted arbitrarily or capriciously with respect to the withholding, the Special Counsel shall promptly initiate a proceeding to determine whether disciplinary action is warranted against the officer or employee who was primarily responsible for the withholding. The Special Counsel, after investigation and consideration of the evidence submitted, shall submit his findings and recommendations to the administrative authority of the agency concerned and shall send copies of the findings and recommendations to the officer or employee or his representative. The administrative authority shall take the corrective action that the Special Counsel recommends.

(ii) The Attorney General shall--

(I) notify the Special Counsel of each civil action described under the first sentence of clause (i); and

(II) annually submit a report to Congress on the number of such civil actions in the preceding year.

(iii) The Special Counsel shall annually submit a report to Congress on the actions taken by the Special Counsel under clause (i).

(G) In the event of noncompliance with the order of the court, the district court may punish for contempt the responsible employee, and in the case of a uniformed service, the responsible member.

(5) Each agency having more than one member shall maintain and make available for public inspection a record of the final votes of each member in every agency proceeding.

(6) (A) Each agency, upon any request for records made under paragraph (1), (2), or (3) of this subsection, shall--

(i) determine within 20 days (excepting Saturdays, Sundays, and legal public holidays) after the receipt of any such request whether to comply with such request and shall immediately notify the person making such request of such determination and the reasons therefor, and of the right of such person to appeal to the head of the agency any adverse determination; and

(ii) make a determination with respect to any appeal within twenty days (excepting Saturdays, Sundays, and legal public holidays) after the receipt of such appeal. If on appeal the denial of the request for records is in whole or in part upheld, the agency shall notify the person making such request of the provisions for judicial review of that determination under paragraph (4) of this subsection.

The 20-day period under clause (i) shall commence on the date on which the request is first received by the appropriate component of the agency, but in any event not later than ten days after the request is first received by any component of the agency that is designated in the agency's regulations under this section to receive requests under this section. The 20-day period shall not be tolled by the agency except--

(I) that the agency may make one request to the requester for information and toll the 20-day period while it is awaiting such information that it has reasonably requested from the requester under this section; or

(II) if necessary to clarify with the requester issues regarding fee assessment. In either case, the agency's receipt of the requester's response to the agency's request for information or clarification ends the tolling period.

(B) (i) In unusual circumstances as specified in this subparagraph, the time limits prescribed in either clause (i) or clause (ii) of subparagraph (A) may be extended by written notice to the person making such request setting forth the unusual circumstances for such extension and the date on which a determination is expected to be dispatched. No such notice shall specify a date that would result in an extension for more than ten working days, except as provided in clause (ii) of this subparagraph.

* * *

(D) (i) Each agency may promulgate regulations, pursuant to notice and receipt of public comment, providing for multitrack processing of requests for records based on the amount of work or time (or both) involved in processing requests.

(ii) Regulations under this subparagraph may provide a person making a request that does not qualify for the fastest multitrack processing an opportunity to limit the scope of the request in order to qualify for faster processing.

(iii) This subparagraph shall not be considered to affect the requirement under subparagraph (C) to exercise due diligence.

(E) (i) Each agency shall promulgate regulations, pursuant to notice and receipt of public comment, providing for expedited processing of requests for records--

(I) in cases in which the person requesting the records demonstrates a compelling need; and

(II) in other cases determined by the agency.

(ii) Notwithstanding clause (i), regulations under this subparagraph must ensure--

(I) that a determination of whether to provide expedited processing shall be made, and notice of the determination shall be provided to the person making the request, within 10 days after the date of the request; and

(II) expeditious consideration of administrative appeals of such determinations of whether to provide expedited processing.

(iii) An agency shall process as soon as practicable any request for records to which the agency has granted expedited processing under this subparagraph. Agency action to deny or affirm denial of a request for expedited processing pursuant to this subparagraph, and failure by an agency to respond in a timely manner to such a request shall be subject to judicial review under paragraph (4), except that the judicial review shall be based on the record before the agency at the time of the determination.

(iv) A district court of the United States shall not have jurisdiction to review an agency denial of expedited processing of a request for records after the agency has provided a complete response to the request.

(v) For purposes of this subparagraph, the term "compelling need" means--

(I) that a failure to obtain requested records on an expedited basis under this paragraph could reasonably be expected to pose an imminent threat to the life or physical safety of an individual; or

(II) with respect to a request made by a person primarily engaged in disseminating information, urgency to inform the public concerning actual or alleged Federal Government activity.

(vi) A demonstration of a compelling need by a person making a request for expedited processing shall be made by a statement certified by such person to be true and correct to the best of such person's knowledge and belief.

(F) In denying a request for records, in whole or in part, an agency shall make a reasonable effort to estimate the volume of any requested matter the provision of which is denied, and shall provide any such estimate to the person making the request, unless providing such estimate would harm an interest protected by the exemption in subsection (b) pursuant to which the denial is made.

(7) Each agency shall--

(A) establish a system to assign an individualized tracking number for each request received that will take longer than ten days to process and provide to each person making a request the tracking number assigned to the request; and

(B) establish a telephone line or Internet service that provides information about the status of a request to the person making the request using the assigned tracking number, including—

(i) the date on which the agency originally received the request; and

(ii) an estimated date on which the agency will complete action on the request.

(b) This section does not apply to matters that are--

(1) (A) specifically authorized under criteria established by an Executive order to be kept secret in the interest of national defense or foreign policy and (B) are in fact properly classified pursuant to such Executive order;

(2) related solely to the internal personnel rules and practices of an agency;

(3) specifically exempted from disclosure by statute (other than section 552b of this title), if that statute--

(A) (i) requires that the matters be withheld from the public in such a manner as to leave no discretion on the issue; or

(ii) establishes particular criteria for withholding or refers to particular types of matters to be withheld; and

(B) if enacted after the date of enactment of the OPEN FOIA Act of 2009, specifically cites to this paragraph.

(4) trade secrets and commercial or financial information obtained from a person and privileged or confidential;

(5) inter-agency or intra-agency memorandums or letters which would not be available by law to a party other than an agency in litigation with the agency;

(6) personnel and medical files and similar files the disclosure of which would constitute a clearly unwarranted invasion of personal privacy;

(7) records or information compiled for law enforcement purposes, but only to the extent that the production of such law enforcement records or information (A) could reasonably be expected to interfere with enforcement proceedings, (B) would deprive a person of a right to a fair trial or an impartial adjudication, (C) could reasonably be expected to constitute an unwarranted invasion of personal privacy, (D) could reasonably be expected to disclose the identity of a confidential source, including a State, local, or foreign agency or authority or any private institution which furnished information on a confidential basis, and, in the case of a record or information compiled by criminal law enforcement authority in the course of a criminal investigation or by an agency conducting a lawful national security intelligence investigation, information furnished by a confidential source, (E) would disclose techniques and procedures for law enforcement investigations or prosecutions, or would disclose guidelines for law enforcement investigations or prosecutions if such disclosure could reasonably be expected to risk circumvention of the law, or (F) could reasonably be expected to endanger the life or physical safety of any individual;

(8) contained in or related to examination, operating, or condition reports prepared by, on behalf of, or for the use of an agency responsible for the regulation or supervision of financial institutions; or

(9) geological or geophysical information and data, including maps, concerning wells. Any reasonably segregable portion of a record shall be provided to any person requesting such record after deletion of the portions which are exempt under this subsection. The amount of information deleted, and the exemption under which the deletion is made, shall be indicated on the released portion of the record, unless including that indication would harm an interest protected by the exemption in this subsection under which the deletion is made. If technically feasible, the amount of the information deleted, and the exemption under which the deletion is made, shall be indicated at the place in the record where such deletion is made.

(c) (1) Whenever a request is made which involves access to records described in subsection (b)(7)(A) and--

(A) the investigation or proceeding involves a possible violation of criminal law; and

(B) there is reason to believe that (i) the subject of the investigation or proceeding is not aware of its pendency, and (ii) disclosure of the existence of the records could reasonably be expected to interfere with enforcement proceedings, the agency may, during only such time as that circumstance continues, treat the records as not subject to the requirements of this section.

(2) Whenever informant records maintained by a criminal law enforcement agency under an informant's name or personal identifier are requested by a third party according to the informant's name or personal identifier, the agency may treat the records as not subject to the requirements of this section unless the informant's status as an informant has been officially confirmed.

(3) Whenever a request is made which involves access to records maintained by the Federal Bureau of Investigation pertaining to foreign intelligence or counterintelligence, or international terrorism, and the existence of the records is classified information as provided in subsection (b)(1), the Bureau may, as long as the existence of the records remains classified information, treat the records as not subject to the requirements of this section.

(d) This section does not authorize withholding of information or limit the availability of records to the public, except as specifically stated in this section. This section is not authority to withhold information from Congress.

* * *

(f) For purposes of this section, the term--

(1) "agency" as defined in section 551(1) of this title includes any executive department, military department, Government corporation, Government controlled corporation, or other establishment in the executive branch of the Government (including the Executive Office of the President), or any independent regulatory agency; and

(2) "record" and any other term used in this section in reference to information includes--

(A) any information that would be an agency record subject to the requirements of this section when maintained by an agency in any format, including an electronic format; and

(B) any information described under subparagraph (A) that is maintained for an agency by an entity under Government contract, for the purposes of records management.

(g) The head of each agency shall prepare and make publicly available upon request, reference material or a guide for requesting records or information from the agency, subject to the exemptions in subsection (b), including--

(1) an index of all major information systems of the agency;

(2) a description of major information and record locator systems maintained by the agency; and

(3) a handbook for obtaining various types and categories of public information from the agency pursuant to chapter 35 of title 44, and under this section.

(h) (1) There is established the Office of Government Information Services within the National Archives and Records Administration.

(2) The Office of Government Information Services shall--

(A) review policies and procedures of administrative agencies under this section;

(B) review compliance with this section by administrative agencies; and

(C) recommend policy changes to Congress and the President to improve the administration of this section.

(3) The Office of Government Information Services shall offer mediation services to resolve disputes between persons making requests under this section and administrative agencies as a non-exclusive alternative to litigation and, at the discretion of the Office, may issue advisory opinions if mediation has not resolved the dispute.

(i) The Government Accountability Office shall conduct audits of administrative agencies on the implementation of this section and issue reports detailing the results of such audits.

(j) Each agency shall designate a Chief FOIA Officer who shall be a senior official of such agency (at the Assistant Secretary or equivalent level).

(k) The Chief FOIA Officer of each agency shall, subject to the authority of the head of the agency--

(1) have agency-wide responsibility for efficient and appropriate compliance with this section;

(2) monitor implementation of this section throughout the agency and keep the head of the agency, the chief legal officer of the agency, and the Attorney General appropriately informed of the agency's performance in implementing this section;

(3) recommend to the head of the agency such adjustments to agency practices, policies, personnel, and funding as may be necessary to improve its implementation of this section;

(4) review and report to the Attorney General, through the head of the agency, at such times and in such formats as the Attorney General may direct, on the agency's performance in implementing this section;

(5) facilitate public understanding of the purposes of the statutory exemptions of this section by including concise descriptions of the exemptions in both the agency's handbook issued under subsection (g), and the agency's annual report on this section, and by providing an overview, where appropriate, of certain general categories of agency records to which those exemptions apply; and

(6) designate one or more FOIA Public Liaisons.

(l) FOIA Public Liaisons shall report to the agency Chief FOIA Officer and shall serve as supervisory officials to whom a requester under this section can raise concerns about the service the requester has received from the FOIA Requester Center, following an initial response from the FOIA Requester Center Staff. FOIA Public Liaisons shall be responsible for assisting in reducing delays, increasing transparency and understanding of the status of requests, and assisting in the resolution of disputes.

5 USC § 552a. Records maintained on individuals.

(a) Definitions. For purposes of this section--

(1) the term "agency" means agency as defined in section 552[(f)](e) of this title;

(2) the term "individual" means a citizen of the United States or an alien lawfully admitted for permanent residence;

(3) the term "maintain" includes maintain, collect, use, or disseminate;

(4) the term "record" means any item, collection, or grouping of information about an individual that is maintained by an agency, including, but not limited to, his education, financial transactions, medical history, and criminal or employment history and that contains his name, or the identifying number, symbol, or other identifying particular assigned to the individual, such as a finger or voice print or a photograph;

(5) the term "system of records" means a group of any records under the control of any agency from which information is retrieved by the name of the individual or by some identifying number, symbol, or other identifying particular assigned to the individual;

(6) the term "statistical record" means a record in a system of records maintained for statistical research or reporting purposes only and not used in whole or in part in making any determination about an identifiable individual, except as provided by section 8 of title 13;

(7) the term "routine use" means, with respect to the disclosure of a record, the use of such record for a purpose which is compatible with the purpose for which it was collected; and

(8) the term "matching program"--

(A) means any computerized comparison of--

(i) two or more automated systems of records or a system of records with non-Federal records for the purpose of--

(I) establishing or verifying the eligibility of, or continuing compliance with statutory and regulatory requirements by, applicants for, recipients or beneficiaries of, participants in, or providers of services with respect to, cash or in-kind assistance or payments under Federal benefit programs, or

(II) recouping payments or delinquent debts under such Federal benefit programs, or

(ii) two or more automated Federal personnel or payroll systems of records or a system of Federal personnel or payroll records with non-Federal records,

(B) but does not include--

(i) matches performed to produce aggregate statistical data without any personal identifiers;

(ii) matches performed to support any research or statistical project, the specific data of which may not be used to make decisions concerning the rights, benefits, or privileges of specific individuals;

(iii) matches performed, by an agency (or component thereof) which performs as its principal function any activity pertaining to the enforcement of criminal laws, subsequent to the initiation of a specific criminal or civil law enforcement investigation of a named person or persons for the purpose of gathering evidence against such person or persons;

(iv) matches of tax information (I) pursuant to section 6103(d) of the Internal Revenue Code of 1986, (II) for purposes of tax administration as defined in section 6103(b)(4) of such Code, (III) for the purpose of intercepting a tax refund due an individual under authority granted by section 404(e), 464, or 1137 of the Social Security Act; or (IV) for the purpose of intercepting a tax refund due an individual under any other tax refund intercept program authorized by statute which has been determined by the Director of the Office of Management and Budget to contain verification, notice, and hearing requirements that are substantially similar to the procedures in section 1137 of the Social Security Act;

    (v) matches--

        (I) using records predominantly relating to Federal personnel, that are performed for routine administrative purposes (subject to guidance provided by the Director of the Office of Management and Budget pursuant to subsection (v)); or

        (II) conducted by an agency using only records from systems of records maintained by that agency;

        if the purpose of the match is not to take any adverse financial, personnel, disciplinary, or other adverse action against Federal personnel;

    (vi) matches performed for foreign counterintelligence purposes or to produce background checks for security clearances of Federal personnel or Federal contractor personnel;

    (vii) matches performed incident to a levy described in section 6103(k)(8) of the Internal Revenue Code of 1986;

    (viii) matches performed pursuant to section 202(x)(3) or 1611(e)(1) of the Social Security Act (42 U.S.C. 402(x)(3), 1382(e)(1)); or

    (ix) matches performed by the Secretary of Health and Human Services or the Inspector General of the Department of Health and Human Services with respect to potential fraud, waste, and abuse, including matches of a system of records with non-Federal records;

* * *

(e) Agency requirements. Each agency that maintains a system of records shall--

    (1) maintain in its records only such information about an individual as is relevant and necessary to accomplish a purpose of the agency required to be accomplished by statute or by executive order of the President;

    (2) collect information to the greatest extent practicable directly from the subject individual when the information may result in adverse determinations about an individual's rights, benefits, and privileges under Federal programs;

    (3) inform each individual whom it asks to supply information, on the form which it uses to collect the information or on a separate form that can be retained by the individual--

        (A) the authority (whether granted by statute, or by executive order of the President) which authorizes the solicitation of the information and whether disclosure of such information is mandatory or voluntary;

        (B) the principal purpose or purposes for which the information is intended to be used;

(C) the routine uses which may be made of the information, as published pursuant to paragraph (4)(D) of this subsection; and

(D) the effects on him, if any, of not providing all or any party of the requested information;

(4) subject to the provisions of paragraph (11) of this subsection, publish in the Federal Register upon establishment or revision a notice of the existence and character of the system of records, which notice shall include—

(A) the name and location of the system;

(B) the categories of individuals on whom records are maintained in the system;

(C) the categories of records maintained in the system;

(D) each routine use of the records contained in the system, including the categories of users and the purpose of such use;

(E) the policies and practices of the agency regarding storage, retrievability, access controls, retention, and disposal of the records;

(F) the title and business address of the agency official who is responsible for the system of records;

(G) the agency procedures whereby an individual can be notified at his request if the system of records contains a record pertaining to him;

(H) the agency procedures whereby an individual can be notified at his request how he can gain access to any record pertaining to him contained in the system of records, and how he can contest its content; and

(I) the categories of sources or records in the system;

(5) maintain all records which are used by the agency in making any determination about any individual with such accuracy, relevance, timeliness, and completeness as is reasonably necessary to assure fairness to the individual in the determination;

(6) prior to disseminating any record about an individual to any person other than an agency, unless the dissemination is made pursuant to subsection (b)(2) of this section, make reasonable efforts to assure that such records are accurate, complete, timely, and relevant for agency purposes;

(7) maintain no record describing how any individual exercises rights guaranteed by the First Amendment unless expressly authorized by statute or by the individual about whom the record is maintained or unless pertinent to and within the scope of an authorized law enforcement activity;

(8) make reasonable efforts to serve notice on an individual when any record on such individual is made available to any person under compulsory legal process when such process becomes a matter of public record;

(9) establish rules of conduct for persons involved in the design, development, operation, or maintenance of any system of records, or in maintaining any record, and instruct each such person with respect to such rules and the requirements of this section, including any other rules and procedures adopted pursuant to this section and the penalties for noncompliance;

(10) establish appropriate administrative, technical, and physical safeguards to insure the security and confidentiality of records and to protect against any anticipated threats or hazards to their security or integrity which could result in substantial harm,

embarrassment, inconvenience, or unfairness to any individual on whom information is maintained;

(11) at least 30 days prior to publication of information under paragraph (4)(D) of this subsection, publish in the Federal Register notice of any new use or intended use of the information in the system, and provide an opportunity for interested persons to submit written data, views, or arguments to the agency; and

(12) if such agency is a recipient agency or a source agency in a matching program with a non-Federal agency, with respect to any establishment or revision of a matching program, at least 30 days prior to conducting such program, publish in the Federal Register notice of such establishment or revision.

(f) Agency Rules. In order to carry out the provisions of this section, each agency that maintains a system of records shall promulgate rules, in accordance with the requirements (including general notice) of section 553 of this title, which shall--

(1) establish procedures whereby an individual can be notified in response to his request if any system of records named by the individual contains a record pertaining to him;

(2) define reasonable times, places, and requirements for identifying an individual who requests his record or information pertaining to him before the agency shall make the record or information available to the individual;

(3) establish procedures for the disclosure to an individual upon his request of his record or information pertaining to him, including special procedure, if deemed necessary, for the disclosure to an individual of medical records, including psychological records, pertaining to him;

(4) establish procedures for reviewing a request from an individual concerning the amendment of any record or information pertaining to the individual, for making a determination on the request, for an appeal within the agency of an initial adverse agency determination, and for whatever additional means may be necessary for each individual to be able to exercise fully his rights under this section; and

(5) establish fees to be charged, if any, to any individual for making copies of his record, excluding the cost of any search for and review of the record.

The Office of the Federal Register shall biennially compile and publish the rules promulgated under this subsection and agency notices published under subsection (e)(4) of this section in a form available to the public at low cost.

(g) Civil remedies.

(1) Whenever any agency--

(A) makes a determination under subsection (d)(3) of this section not to amend an individual's record in accordance with his request, or fails to make such review in conformity with that subsection;

(B) refuses to comply with an individual request under subsection (d)(1) of this section;

(C) fails to maintain any record concerning any individual with such accuracy, relevance, timeliness, and completeness as is necessary to assure fairness in any determination relating to the qualifications, character, rights, or opportunities of, or benefits to the individual that may be made on the basis of such record, and consequently a determination is made which is adverse to the individual; or

(D) fails to comply with any other provision of this section, or any rule promulgated thereunder, in such a way as to have an adverse effect on an individual, the individual may bring a civil action against the agency, and the district courts of the United States shall have jurisdiction in the matters under the provisions of this subsection.

(2) (A) In any suit brought under the provisions of subsection (g)(1)(A) of this section, the court may order the agency to amend the individual's record in accordance with his request or in such other way as the court may direct. In such a case the court shall determine the matter de novo.

(B) The court may assess against the United States reasonable attorney fees and other litigation costs reasonably incurred in any case under this paragraph in which the complainant has substantially prevailed.

(3) (A) In any suit brought under the provisions of subsection (g)(1)(B) of this section, the court may enjoin the agency from withholding the records and order the production to the complainant of any agency records improperly withheld from him. In such a case the court shall determine the matter de novo, and may examine the contents of any agency records in camera to determine whether the records or any portion thereof may be withheld under any of the exemptions set forth in subsection (k) of this section, and the burden is on the agency to sustain its action.

(B) The court may assess against the United States reasonable attorney fees and other litigation costs reasonably incurred in any case under this paragraph in which the complainant has substantially prevailed.

(4) In any suit brought under the provisions of subsection (g)(1)(C) or (D) of this section in which the court determines that the agency acted in a manner which was intentional or willful, the United States shall be liable to the individual in an amount equal to the sum of--

(A) actual damages sustained by the individual as a result of the refusal or failure, but in no case shall a person entitled to recovery receive less than the sum of $1,000; and

(B) the costs of the action together with reasonable attorney fees as determined by the court.

(5) An action to enforce any liability created under this section may be brought in the district court of the United States in the district in which the complainant resides, or has his principal place of business, or in which the agency records are situated, or in the District of Columbia, without regard to the amount in controversy, within two years from the date on which the cause of action arises, except that where an agency has materially and willfully misrepresented any information required under this section to be disclosed to an individual and the information so misrepresented is material to establishment of the liability of the agency to the individual under this section, the action may be brought at any time within two years after discovery by the individual of the misrepresentation. Nothing in this section shall be construed to authorize any civil action by reason of any injury sustained as the result of a disclosure of a record prior to September 27, 1975.

(h) Rights of legal guardians. For the purposes of this section, the parent of any minor, or the legal guardian of any individual who has been declared to be incompetent due to physical or mental incapacity or age by a court of competent jurisdiction, may act on behalf of the individual.

(i) Criminal penalties.

(1) Any officer or employee of an agency, who by virtue of his employment or official position, has possession of, or access to, agency records which contain individually identifiable information the disclosure of which is prohibited by this section or by rules or regulations established thereunder, and who knowing that disclosure of the specific material is so prohibited, willfully discloses the material in any manner to any person or agency not entitled to receive it, shall be guilty of a misdemeanor and fined not more than $5,000.

(2) Any officer or employee of any agency who willfully maintains a system of records without meeting the notice requirements of subsection (e)(4) of this section shall be guilty of a misdemeanor and fined not more than $5,000.

(3) Any person who knowingly and willfully requests or obtains any record concerning an individual from an agency under false pretenses shall be guilty of a misdemeanor and fined not more than $5,000.

(j) General exemptions. The head of any agency may promulgate rules, in accordance with the requirements (including general notice) of sections 553(b)(1), (2), and (3), (c), and (e) of this title, to exempt any system of records within the agency from any part of this section except subsections (b), (c)(1) and (2), (e)(4)(A) through (F), (e)(6), (7), (9), (10), and (11), and (i) if the system of records is--

(1) maintained by the Central Intelligence Agency; or

(2) maintained by an agency or component thereof which performs as its principal function any activity pertaining to the enforcement of criminal laws, including police efforts to prevent, control, or reduce crime or to apprehend criminals, and the activities of prosecutors, courts, correctional, probation, pardon, or parole authorities, and which consists of (A) information compiled for the purpose of identifying individual criminal offenders and alleged offenders and consisting only of identifying data and notations of arrests, the nature and disposition of criminal charges, sentencing, confinement, release, and parole and probation status; (B) information compiled for the purpose of a criminal investigation, including reports of informants and investigators, and associated with an identifiable individual; or (C) reports identifiable to an individual compiled at any stage of the process of enforcement of the criminal laws from arrest or indictment through release from supervision.

At the time rules are adopted under this subsection, the agency shall include in the statement required under section 553(c) of this title, the reasons why the system of records is to be exempted from a provision of this section.

(k) Specific exemptions. The head of any agency may promulgate rules, in accordance with the requirements (including general notice) of sections 553(b)(1), (2), and (3), (c), and (e) of this title, to exempt any system of records within the agency from subsections (c)(3), (d), (e)(1), (e)(4)(G), (H), and (I) and (f) of this section if the system of records is--

(1) subject to provisions of section 552(b)(1) of this title;

(2) investigatory material compiled for law enforcement purposes, other than material within the scope of subsection (j)(2) of this section: *Provided, however,* That if any individual is denied any right, privilege, or benefit that he would otherwise be entitled by Federal law, or for which he would otherwise be eligible, as a result of the maintenance of such material, such material shall be provided to such individual, except to the extent that the disclosure of such material would reveal the identity of a source who

furnished information to the Government under an express promise that the identity of the source would be held in confidence, or, prior to the effective date of this section, under an implied promise that the identity of the source would be held in confidence;

(3) maintained in connection with providing protective services to the President of the United States or other individuals pursuant to section 3056 of title 18;

(4) required by statute to be maintained and used solely as statistical records;

(5) investigatory material compiled solely for the purpose of determining suitability, eligibility, or qualifications for Federal civilian employment, military service, Federal contracts, or access to classified information, but only to the extent that the disclosure of such material would reveal the identity of a source who furnished information to the Government under an express promise that the identity of the source would be held in confidence, or, prior to the effective date of this section, under an implied promise that the identity of the source would be held in confidence;

(6) testing or examination material used solely to determine individual qualifications for appointment or promotion in the Federal service the disclosure of which would compromise the objectivity or fairness of the testing or examination process; or

(7) evaluation material used to determine potential for promotion in the armed services, but only to the extent that the disclosure of such material would reveal the identity of a source who furnished information to the Government under an express promise that the identity of the source would be held in confidence, or, prior to the effective date of this section, under an implied promise that the identity of the source would be held in confidence.

At the time rules are adopted under this subsection, the agency shall include in the statement required under section 553(c) of this title, the reasons why the system of records is to be exempted from a provision of this section.

* * *

(m) Government contractors.

(1) When an agency provides by a contract for the operation by or on behalf of the agency of a system of records to accomplish an agency function, the agency shall, consistent with its authority, cause the requirements of this section to be applied to such system. For purposes of subsection (i) of this section any such contractor and any employee of such contractor, if such contract is agreed to on or after the effective date of this section, shall be considered to be an employee of an agency.

(2) A consumer reporting agency to which a record is disclosed under section 3711(e) of title 31 shall not be considered a contractor for the purposes of this section.

(n) Mailing lists. An individual's name and address may not be sold or rented by an agency unless such action is specifically authorized by law. This provision shall not be construed to require the withholding of names and addresses otherwise permitted to be made public.

(o) Matching agreements.

(1) No record which is contained in a system of records may be disclosed to a recipient agency or non-Federal agency for use in a computer matching program except pursuant to a written agreement between the source agency and the recipient agency or non-Federal agency specifying--

(A) the purpose and legal authority for conducting the program;

(B) the justification for the program and the anticipated results, including a specific estimate of any savings;

(C) a description of the records that will be matched, including each data element that will be used, the approximate number of records that will be matched, and the projected starting and completion dates of the matching program;

(D) procedures for providing individualized notice at the time of application, and notice periodically thereafter as directed by the Data Integrity Board of such agency (subject to guidance provided by the Director of the Office of Management and Budget pursuant to subsection (v)), to--

    (i) applicants for and recipients of financial assistance or payments under Federal benefit programs, and

    (ii) applicants for and holders of positions as Federal personnel, that any information provided by such applicants, recipients, holders and individuals may be subject to verification through matching programs;

(E) procedures for verifying information produced in such matching program as required by subsection (p);

(F) procedures for the retention and timely destruction of identifiable records created by a recipient agency or non-Federal agency in such matching program;

(G) procedures for ensuring the administrative, technical, and physical security of the records matched and the results of such programs;

(H) prohibitions on duplication and redisclosure of records provided by the source agency within or outside the recipient agency or the non-Federal agency, except where required by law or essential to the conduct of the matching program;

(I) procedures governing the use by a recipient agency or non-Federal agency of records provided in a matching program by a source agency, including procedures governing return of the records to the source agency or destruction of records used in such program;

(J) information on assessments that have been made on the accuracy of the records that will be used in such matching program; and

(K) that the Comptroller General may have access to all records of a recipient agency or a non-Federal agency that the Comptroller General deems necessary in order to monitor or verify compliance with the agreement.

(2) (A) A copy of each agreement entered into pursuant to paragraph (1) shall--

    (i) be transmitted to the Committee on Governmental Affairs of the Senate and the Committee on Government Operations of the House of Representatives; and

    (ii) be available upon request to the public.

(B) No such agreement shall be effective until 30 days after the date on which such a copy is transmitted pursuant to subparagraph (A)(i).

(C) Such an agreement shall remain in effect only for such period, not to exceed 18 months, as the Data Integrity Board of the agency determines is appropriate in light of the purposes, and length of time necessary for the conduct, of the matching program.

(D) Within 3 months prior to the expiration of such an agreement pursuant to subparagraph (C), the Data Integrity Board of the agency may, without additional review, renew the matching agreement for a current, ongoing matching program for not more than one additional year if--

(i) such program will be conducted without any change; and

(ii) each party to the agreement certifies to the Board in writing that the program has been conducted in compliance with the agreement.

(p) Verification and opportunity to contest findings.

(1) In order to protect any individual whose records are used in a matching program, no recipient agency, non-Federal agency, or source agency may suspend, terminate, reduce, or make a final denial of any financial assistance or payment under a Federal benefit program to such individual, or take other adverse action against such individual, as a result of information produced by such matching program, until--

(A) (i) the agency has independently verified the information; or

(ii) the Date Integrity Board of the agency, or in the case of a non-Federal agency the Data Integrity Board of the source agency, determines in accordance with guidance issued by the Director of the Office of Management and Budget that--

(I) the information is limited to identification and amount of benefits paid by the source agency under a Federal benefit program; and

(II) there is a high degree of confidence that the information provided to the recipient agency is accurate;

(B) the individual receives a notice from the agency containing a statement of its findings and informing the individual of the opportunity to contest such findings; and

(C) (i) the expiration of any time period established for the program by statute or regulation for the individual to respond to that notice; or

(ii) in the case of a program for which no such period is established, the end of the 30-day period beginning on the date on which notice under subparagraph (B) is mailed or otherwise provided to the individual.

(2) Independent verification referred to in paragraph (1) requires investigation and confirmation of specific information relating to an individual that is used as a basis for an adverse action against the individual, including where applicable investigation and confirmation of--

(A) the amount of any asset or income involved;

(B) whether such individual actually has or had access to such asset or income for such individual's own use; and

(C) the period or periods when the individual actually had such asset or income.

(3) Notwithstanding paragraph (1), an agency may take any appropriate action otherwise prohibited by such paragraph if the agency determines that the public health or public safety may be adversely affected or significantly threatened during any notice period required by such paragraph.

(q) Sanctions.

(1) Notwithstanding any other provision of law, no source agency may disclose any record which is contained in a system of records to a recipient agency or non-Federal agency for a matching program if such source agency has reason to believe that the requirements of subsection (p), or any matching agreement entered into pursuant to subsection (o), or both, are not being met by such recipient agency.

(2) No source agency may renew a matching agreement unless--

(A) the recipient agency or non-Federal agency has certified that it has complied with the provisions of that agreement; and

(B) the source agency has no reason to believe that the certification is inaccurate.

(r) Report on new systems and matching programs. Each agency that proposes to establish or make a significant change in a system of records or a matching program shall provide adequate advance notice of any such proposal (in duplicate) to the Committee on Government Operations of the House of Representatives, the Committee on Governmental Affairs of the Senate, and the Office of Management and Budget in order to permit an evaluation of the probable or potential effect of such proposal on the privacy or other rights of individuals.

* * *

(t) Effect of other laws.

(1) No agency shall rely on any exemption contained in section 552 of this title to withhold from an individual any record which is otherwise accessible to such individual under the provisions of this section.

(2) No agency shall rely on any exemption in this section to withhold from an individual any record which is otherwise accessible to such individual under the provisions of section 552 of this title.

(u) Data Integrity Boards.

(1) Every agency conducting or participating in a matching program shall establish a Data Integrity Board to oversee and coordinate among the various components of such agency the agency's implementation of this section.

(2) Each Data Integrity Board shall consist of senior officials designated by the head of the agency, and shall include any senior official designated by the head of the agency as responsible for implementation of this section, and the inspector general of the agency, if any. The inspector general shall not serve as chairman of the Data Integrity Board.

* * *

5 USC § 553. Rulemaking.

(a) This section applies, according to the provisions thereof, except to the extent that there is involved--

(1) a military or foreign affairs function of the United States; or

(2) a matter relating to agency management or personnel or to public property, loans, grants, benefits, or contracts.

(b) General notice of proposed rulemaking shall be published in the Federal Register, unless persons subject thereto are named and either personally served or otherwise have actual notice thereof in accordance with law. The notice shall include—

      (1) a statement of the time, place, and nature of public rule making proceedings;

      (2) reference to the legal authority under which the rule is proposed; and

      (3) either the terms or substance of the proposed rule or a description of the subjects and issues involved.

Except when notice or hearing is required by statute, this subsection does not apply--

      (A) to interpretative rules, general statements of policy, or rules of agency organization, procedure, or practice; or

      (B) when the agency for good cause finds (and incorporates the finding and a brief statement of reasons therefor in the rules issued) that notice and public procedure thereon are impracticable, unnecessary, or contrary to the public interest.

(c) After notice required by this section, the agency shall give interested persons an opportunity to participate in the rule making through submission of written data, views, or arguments with or without opportunity for oral presentation. After consideration of the relevant matter presented, the agency shall incorporate in the rules adopted a concise general statement of their basis and purpose. When rules are required by statute to be made on the record after opportunity for an agency hearing, sections 556 and 557 of this title apply instead of this subsection.

(d) The required publication or service of a substantive rule shall be made not less than 30 days before its effective date, except--

      (1) a substantive rule which grants or recognizes an exemption or relieves a restriction;

      (2) interpretative rules and statements of policy; or

      (3) as otherwise provided by the agency for good cause found and published with the rule.

(e) Each agency shall give an interested person the right to petition for the issuance, amendment, or repeal of a rule.

5 USC § 555. Ancillary matters.

    (a) This section applies, according to the provisions thereof, except as otherwise provided by this subchapter.

    (b) A person compelled to appear in person before an agency or representative thereof is entitled to be accompanied, represented, and advised by counsel or, if permitted by the agency, by other qualified representative. A party is entitled to appear in person or by or with counsel or other duly qualified representative in an agency proceeding. So far as the orderly conduct of public business permits, an interested person may appear before an agency or its responsible employees for the presentation, adjustment, or determination of an issue, request, or controversy in a proceeding, whether interlocutory, summary, or otherwise, or in connection with an agency function. With due regard for the convenience and necessity of the parties or their representatives and within a reasonable time, each agency shall proceed to conclude a matter presented to it. This subsection does not grant or deny a person who is not a lawyer the right to appear for or represent others before an agency or in an agency proceeding.

(c) Process, requirement of a report, inspection, or other investigative act or demand may not be issued, made, or enforced except as authorized by law. A person compelled to submit data or evidence is entitled to retain or, on payment of lawfully prescribed costs, procure a copy or transcript thereof, except that in a nonpublic investigatory proceeding the witness may for good cause be limited to inspection of the official transcript of his testimony.

(d) Agency subpenas authorized by law shall be issued to a party on request and, when required by rules of procedure, on a statement or showing of general relevance and reasonable scope of the evidence sought. On contest, the court shall sustain the subpena or similar process or demand to the extent that it is found to be in accordance with law. In a proceeding for enforcement, the court shall issue an order requiring the appearance of the witness or the production of the evidence or data within a reasonable time under penalty of punishment for contempt in case of contumacious failure to comply.

(e) Prompt notice shall be given of the denial in whole or in part of a written application, petition, or other request of an interested person made in connection with any agency proceeding. Except in affirming a prior denial or when the denial is self-explanatory, the notice shall be accompanied by a brief statement of the grounds for denial.

11 USC § 101. Definitions.

In this title the following definitions shall apply:

(1) The term "accountant" means accountant authorized under applicable law to practice public accounting, and includes professional accounting association, corporation, or partnership, if so authorized.

(2) The term "affiliate" means--

(A) entity that directly or indirectly owns, controls, or holds with power to vote, 20 percent or more of the outstanding voting securities of the debtor, other than an entity that holds such securities--

(i) in a fiduciary or agency capacity without sole discretionary power to vote such securities; or

(ii) solely to secure a debt, if such entity has not in fact exercised such power to vote;

(B) corporation 20 percent or more of whose outstanding voting securities are directly or indirectly owned, controlled, or held with power to vote, by the debtor, or by an entity that directly or indirectly owns, controls, or holds with power to vote, 20 percent or more of the outstanding voting securities of the debtor, other than an entity that holds such securities--

(i) in a fiduciary or agency capacity without sole discretionary power to vote such securities; or

(ii) solely to secure a debt, if such entity has not in fact exercised such power to vote;

(C) person whose business is operated under a lease or operating agreement by a debtor, or person substantially all of whose property is operated under an operating agreement with the debtor; or

(D) entity that operates the business or substantially all of the property of the debtor under a lease or operating agreement.

(3) The term "assisted person" means any person whose debts consist primarily of consumer debts and the value of whose nonexempt property is less than $175,750.

(4) The term "attorney" means attorney, professional law association, corporation, or partnership, authorized under applicable law to practice law.

(4A) The term "bankruptcy assistance" means any goods or services sold or otherwise provided to an assisted person with the express or implied purpose of providing information, advice, counsel, document preparation, or filing, or attendance at a creditors' meeting or appearing in a case or proceeding on behalf of another or providing legal representation with respect to a case or proceeding under this title.

(5) The term "claim" means--

    (A) right to payment, whether or not such right is reduced to judgment, liquidated, unliquidated, fixed, contingent, matured, unmatured, disputed, undisputed, legal, equitable, secured, or unsecured; or

    (B) right to an equitable remedy for breach of performance if such breach gives rise to a right to payment, whether or not such right to an equitable remedy is reduced to judgment, fixed, contingent, matured, unmatured, disputed, undisputed, secured, or unsecured.

* * *

(10A) The term "current monthly income"--

    (A) means the average monthly income from all sources that the debtor receives (or in a joint case the debtor and the debtor's spouse receive) without regard to whether such income is taxable income, derived during the 6-month period ending on--

        (i) the last day of the calendar month immediately preceding the date of the commencement of the case if the debtor files the schedule of current income required by section 521(a)(1)(B)(ii); or

        (ii) the date on which current income is determined by the court for purposes of this title if the debtor does not file the schedule of current income required by section 521(a)(1)(B)(ii); and

    (B) includes any amount paid by any entity other than the debtor (or in a joint case the debtor and the debtor's spouse), on a regular basis for the household expenses of the debtor or the debtor's dependents (and in a joint case the debtor's spouse if not otherwise a dependent), but excludes benefits received under the Social Security Act, payments to victims of war crimes or crimes against humanity on account of their status as victims of such crimes, and payments to victims of international terrorism (as defined in section 2331 of title 18) or domestic terrorism (as defined in section 2331 of title 18) on account of their status as victims of such terrorism.

(11) The term "custodian" means--

    (A) receiver or trustee of any of the property of the debtor, appointed in a case or proceeding not under this title;

    (B) assignee under a general assignment for the benefit of the debtor's creditors; or

    (C) trustee, receiver, or agent under applicable law, or under a contract, that is appointed or authorized to take charge of property of the debtor for the purpose of enforcing a lien against such property, or for the purpose of general administration of such property for the benefit of the debtor's creditors.

(12) The term "debt" means liability on a claim.

(12A) The term "debt relief agency" means any person who provides any bankruptcy assistance to an assisted person in return for the payment of money or other valuable consideration, or who is a bankruptcy petition preparer under section 110, but does not include--

(A) any person who is an officer, director, employee, or agent of a person who provides such assistance or of the bankruptcy petition preparer;

(B) a nonprofit organization that is exempt from taxation under section 501(c)(3) of the Internal Revenue Code of 1986;

(C) a creditor of such assisted person, to the extent that the creditor is assisting such assisted person to restructure any debt owed by such assisted person to the creditor;

(D) a depository institution (as defined in section 3 of the Federal Deposit Insurance Act) or any Federal credit union or State credit union (as those terms are defined in section 101 of the Federal Credit Union Act), or any affiliate or subsidiary of such depository institution or credit union; or

(E) an author, publisher, distributor, or seller of works subject to copyright protection under title 17, when acting in such capacity.

(13) The term "debtor" means person or municipality concerning which a case under this title has been commenced.

(13A) The term "debtor's principal residence"--

(A) means a residential structure if used as the principal residence by the debtor, including incidental property, without regard to whether that structure is attached to real property; and

(B) includes an individual condominium or cooperative unit, a mobile or manufactured home, or trailer if used as the principal residence by the debtor.

* * *

(15) The term "entity" includes person, estate, trust, governmental unit, and United States trustee.

* * *

(22) The term "financial institution" means--

(A) a Federal reserve bank, or an entity that is a commercial or savings bank, industrial savings bank, savings and loan association, trust company, federally-insured credit union, or receiver, liquidating agent, or conservator for such entity and, when any such Federal reserve bank, receiver, liquidating agent, conservator or entity is acting as agent or custodian for a customer (whether or not a "customer", as defined in section 741) in connection with a securities contract (as defined in section 741) such customer; or

(B) in connection with a securities contract (as defined in section 741) an investment company registered under the Investment Company Act of 1940.

* * *

(27) The term "governmental unit" means United States; State; Commonwealth; District; Territory; municipality; foreign state; department, agency, or instrumentality of the United States (but not a United States trustee while serving as a trustee in a case under this title), a State, a Commonwealth, a District, a Territory, a municipality, or a foreign state; or other foreign or domestic government.

* * *

(41) The term "person" includes individual, partnership, and corporation, but does not include governmental unit, except that a governmental unit that--

(A) acquires an asset from a person--

(i) as a result of the operation of a loan guarantee agreement; or

(ii) as receiver or liquidating agent of a person;

(B) is a guarantor of a pension benefit payable by or on behalf of the debtor or an affiliate of the debtor; or

(C) is the legal or beneficial owner of an asset of--

(i) an employee pension benefit plan that is a governmental plan, as defined in section 414(d) of the Internal Revenue Code of 1986; or

(ii) an eligible deferred compensation plan, as defined in section 457(b) of the Internal Revenue Code of 1986; shall be considered, for purposes of section 1102 of this title, to be a person with respect to such asset or such benefit.

* * *

(42) The term "petition" means petition filed under section 301, 302, 303, or 1504 of this title, as the case may be, commencing a case under this title.

* * *

(50) The term "security agreement" means agreement that creates or provides for a security interest.

(51) The term "security interest" means lien created by an agreement.

(51A) The term "settlement payment" means, for purposes of the forward contract provisions of this title, a preliminary settlement payment, a partial settlement payment, an interim settlement payment, a settlement payment on account, a final settlement payment, a net settlement payment, or any other similar payment commonly used in the forward contract trade.

* * *

(53) The term "statutory lien" means lien arising solely by force of a statute on specified circumstances or conditions, or lien of distress for rent, whether or not statutory, but does not include security interest or judicial lien, whether or not such interest or lien is provided by or is dependent on a statute and whether or not such interest or lien is made fully effective by statute.

(53A) The term "stockbroker" means person--

(A) with respect to which there is a customer, as defined in section 741 of this title; and

(B) that is engaged in the business of effecting transactions in securities--

(i) for the account of others; or

(ii) with members of the general public, from or for such person's own account.

* * *

(54) The term "transfer" means--

(A) the creation of a lien;

(B) the retention of title as a security interest;

(C) the foreclosure of a debtor's equity of redemption; or

(D) each mode, direct or indirect, absolute or conditional, voluntary or involuntary, of disposing of or parting with--

(i) property; or

(ii) an interest in property.

(54A) The term "uninsured State member bank" means a State member bank (as defined in section 3 of the Federal Deposit Insurance Act) the deposits of which are not insured by the Federal Deposit Insurance Corporation.

(55) "United States", when used in a geographical sense, includes all locations where the judicial jurisdiction of the United States extends, including territories and possessions of the United States.

11 USC § 102. Rules of construction.

In this title--

(1) "after notice and a hearing", or a similar phrase--

(A) means after such notice as is appropriate in the particular circumstances, and such opportunity for a hearing as is appropriate in the particular circumstances; but

(B) authorizes an act without an actual hearing if such notice is given properly and if--

(i) such a hearing is not requested timely by a party in interest; or

(ii) there is insufficient time for a hearing to be commenced before such act must be done, and the court authorizes such act;

(2) "claim against the debtor" includes claim against property of the debtor;

(3) "includes" and "including" are not limiting;

(4) "may not" is prohibitive, and not permissive;

(5) "or" is not exclusive;

(6) "order for relief" means entry of an order for relief;

(7) the singular includes the plural;

(8) a definition, contained in a section of this title that refers to another section of this title, does not, for the purpose of such reference, affect the meaning of a term used in such other section; and

(9) "United States trustee" includes a designee of the United States trustee.

11 USC § 105. Power of court.

(a) The court may issue any order, process, or judgment that is necessary or appropriate to carry out the provisions of this title. No provision of this title providing for the raising of an issue by a party in interest shall be construed to preclude the court from, sua sponte, taking any action or making any determination necessary or appropriate to enforce or implement court orders or rules, or to prevent an abuse of process.

(b) Notwithstanding subsection (a) of this section, a court may not appoint a receiver in a case under this title.

(c) The ability of any district judge or other officer or employee of a district court to exercise any of the authority or responsibilities conferred upon the court under this title shall be determined by reference to the provisions relating to such judge, officer, or employee set forth in title 28. This subsection shall not be interpreted to exclude bankruptcy judges and other officers or employees appointed pursuant to chapter 6 of title 28 from its operation.

(d) The court, on its own motion or on the request of a party in interest--

(1) shall hold such status conferences as are necessary to further the expeditious and economical resolution of the case; and

(2) unless inconsistent with another provision of this title or with applicable Federal Rules of Bankruptcy Procedure, may issue an order at any such conference prescribing such limitations and conditions as the court deems appropriate to ensure that the case is handled expeditiously and economically, including an order that--

(A) sets the date by which the trustee must assume or reject an executory contract or unexpired lease; or

(B) in a case under chapter 11 of this title--

(i) sets a date by which the debtor, or trustee if one has been appointed, shall file a disclosure statement and plan;

(ii) sets a date by which the debtor, or trustee if one has been appointed, shall solicit acceptances of a plan;

(iii) sets the date by which a party in interest other than a debtor may file a plan;

(iv) sets a date by which a proponent of a plan, other than the debtor, shall solicit acceptances of such plan;

(v) fixes the scope and format of the notice to be provided regarding the hearing on approval of the disclosure statement; or

(vi) provides that the hearing on approval of the disclosure statement may be combined with the hearing on confirmation of the plan.

11 USC § 109. Who may be a debtor.

(a) Notwithstanding any other provision of this section, only a person that resides or has a domicile, a place of business, or property in the United States, or a municipality, may be a debtor under this title.

(b) A person may be a debtor under chapter 7 of this title only if such person is not--

(1) a railroad;

(2) a domestic insurance company, bank, savings bank, cooperative bank, savings and loan association, building and loan association, homestead association, a New Markets Venture Capital company as defined in section 351 of the Small Business Investment Act of 1958, a small business investment company licensed by the Small Business Administration under section 301 of the Small Business Investment Act of 1958, credit union, or industrial bank or similar institution which is an insured bank as defined in section 3(h) of the Federal Deposit Insurance Act, except that an uninsured State member bank, or a corporation organized under section 25A of the Federal Reserve Act, which operates, or operates as, a multilateral clearing organization pursuant to section 409 of the Federal Deposit Insurance Corporation Improvement Act of 1991 may be a debtor if a petition is filed at the direction of the Board of Governors of the Federal Reserve System; or

(3) (A) a foreign insurance company, engaged in such business in the United States; or

(B) a foreign bank, savings bank, cooperative bank, savings and loan association, building and loan association, or credit union, that has a branch or agency (as defined in section 1(b) of the International Banking Act of 1978) in the United States.

(c) An entity may be a debtor under chapter 9 of this title if and only if such entity--

(1) is a municipality;

(2) is specifically authorized, in its capacity as a municipality or by name, to be a debtor under such chapter by State law, or by a governmental officer or organization empowered by State law to authorize such entity to be a debtor under such chapter;

(3) is insolvent;

(4) desires to effect a plan to adjust such debts; and

(5) (A) has obtained the agreement of creditors holding at least a majority in amount of the claims of each class that such entity intends to impair under a plan in a case under such chapter;

(B) has negotiated in good faith with creditors and has failed to obtain the agreement of creditors holding at least a majority in amount of the claims of each class that such entity intends to impair under a plan in a case under such chapter;

(C) is unable to negotiate with creditors because such negotiation is impracticable; or

(D) reasonably believes that a creditor may attempt to obtain a transfer that is avoidable under section 547 of this title.

(d) Only a railroad, a person that may be a debtor under chapter 7 of this title (except a stockbroker or a commodity broker), and an uninsured State member bank, or a corporation organized under section 25A of the Federal Reserve Act, which operates, or operates as, a multilateral clearing organization pursuant to section 409 of the Federal Deposit Insurance Corporation Improvement Act of 1991 may be a debtor under chapter 11 of this title.

(e) Only an individual with regular income that owes, on the date of the filing of the petition, noncontingent, liquidated, unsecured debts of less than $360,475 and noncontingent, liquidated, secured debts of less than $1,081,400 or an individual with regular income and such individual's spouse, except a stockbroker or a commodity broker, that owe, on the date of the filing of the petition, noncontingent, liquidated, unsecured debts that aggregate less than

$360,475 and noncontingent, liquidated, secured debts of less than $1,081,400 may be a debtor under chapter 13 of this title.

* * *

11 USC § 362. Automatic stay.

(a) Except as provided in subsection (b) of this section, a petition filed under section 301, 302, or 303 of this title, or an application filed under section 5(a)(3) of the Securities Investor Protection Act of 1970, operates as a stay, applicable to all entities, of--

(1) the commencement or continuation, including the issuance or employment of process, of a judicial, administrative, or other action or proceeding against the debtor that was or could have been commenced before the commencement of the case under this title, or to recover a claim against the debtor that arose before the commencement of the case under this title;

(2) the enforcement, against the debtor or against property of the estate, of a judgment obtained before the commencement of the case under this title;

(3) any act to obtain possession of property of the estate or of property from the estate or to exercise control over property of the estate;

(4) any act to create, perfect, or enforce any lien against property of the estate;

(5) any act to create, perfect, or enforce against property of the debtor any lien to the extent that such lien secures a claim that arose before the commencement of the case under this title;

(6) any act to collect, assess, or recover a claim against the debtor that arose before the commencement of the case under this title;

(7) the setoff of any debt owing to the debtor that arose before the commencement of the case under this title against any claim against the debtor; and

(8) the commencement or continuation of a proceeding before the United States Tax Court concerning a tax liability of a debtor that is a corporation for a taxable period the bankruptcy court may determine or concerning the tax liability of a debtor who is an individual for a taxable period ending before the date of the order for relief under this title.

(b) The filing of a petition under section 301, 302, or 303 of this title, or of an application under section 5(a)(3) of the Securities Investor Protection Act of 1970, does not operate as a stay--

(1) under subsection (a) of this section, of the commencement or continuation of a criminal action or proceeding against the debtor;

(2) under subsection (a)—

(A) of the commencement or continuation of a civil action or proceeding--

(i) for the establishment of paternity;

(ii) for the establishment or modification of an order for domestic support obligations;

(iii) concerning child custody or visitation;

(iv) for the dissolution of a marriage, except to the extent that such proceeding seeks to determine the division of property that is property of the estate; or

(v) regarding domestic violence;

(B) of the collection of a domestic support obligation from property that is not property of the estate;

(C) with respect to the withholding of income that is property of the estate or property of the debtor for payment of a domestic support obligation under a judicial or administrative order or a statute;

(D) of the withholding, suspension, or restriction of a driver's license, a professional or occupational license, or a recreational license, under State law, as specified in section 466(a)(16) of the Social Security Act;

(E) of the reporting of overdue support owed by a parent to any consumer reporting agency as specified in section 466(a)(7) of the Social Security Act;

(F) of the interception of a tax refund, as specified in sections 464 and 466(a)(3) of the Social Security Act or under an analogous State law; or

(G) of the enforcement of a medical obligation, as specified under title IV of the Social Security Act;

(3) under subsection (a) of this section, of any act to perfect, or to maintain or continue the perfection of, an interest in property to the extent that the trustee's rights and powers are subject to such perfection under section 546(b) of this title or to the extent that such act is accomplished within the period provided under section 547(e)(2)(A) of this title;

(4) under paragraph (1), (2), (3), or (6) of subsection (a) of this section, of the commencement or continuation of an action or proceeding by a governmental unit or any organization exercising authority under the Convention on the Prohibition of the Development, Production, Stockpiling and Use of Chemical Weapons and on Their Destruction, opened for signature on January 13, 1993, to enforce such governmental unit's or organization's police and regulatory power, including the enforcement of a judgment other than a money judgment, obtained in an action or proceeding by the governmental unit to enforce such governmental unit's or organization's police or regulatory power;

(5) [Deleted]

(6) under subsection (a) of this section, of the exercise by a commodity broker, forward contract merchant, stockbroker, financial institution, financial participant, or securities clearing agency of any contractual right (as defined in section 555 or 556) under any security agreement or arrangement or other credit enhancement forming a part of or related to any commodity contract, forward contract or securities contract, or of any contractual right (as defined in section 555 or 556) to offset or net out any termination value, payment amount, or other transfer obligation arising under or in connection with 1 or more such contracts, including any master agreement for such contracts;

(7) under subsection (a) of this section, of the exercise by a repo participant or financial participant of any contractual right (as defined in section 559) under any security agreement or arrangement or other credit enhancement forming a part of or related to any repurchase agreement, or of any contractual right (as defined in section 559) to offset or net out any termination value, payment amount, or other transfer obligation arising under or in connection with 1 or more such agreements, including any master agreement for such agreements;

(8) under subsection (a) of this section, of the commencement of any action by the Secretary of Housing and Urban Development to foreclose a mortgage or deed of trust in any case in which the mortgage or deed of trust held by the Secretary is insured or was formerly insured under the National Housing Act and covers property, or combinations of property, consisting of five or more living units;

(9) under subsection (a), of--

(A) an audit by a governmental unit to determine tax liability;

(B) the issuance to the debtor by a governmental unit of a notice of tax deficiency;

(C) a demand for tax returns; or

(D) the making of an assessment for any tax and issuance of a notice and demand for payment of such an assessment (but any tax lien that would otherwise attach to property of the estate by reason of such an assessment shall not take effect unless such tax is a debt of the debtor that will not be discharged in the case and such property or its proceeds are transferred out of the estate to, or otherwise revested in, the debtor).

(10) under subsection (a) of this section, of any act by a lessor to the debtor under a lease of nonresidential real property that has terminated by the expiration of the stated term of the lease before the commencement of or during a case under this title to obtain possession of such property;

(11) under subsection (a) of this section, of the presentment of a negotiable instrument and the giving of notice of and protesting dishonor of such an instrument;

(12) under subsection (a) of this section, after the date which is 90 days after the filing of such petition, of the commencement or continuation, and conclusion to the entry of final judgment, of an action which involves a debtor subject to reorganization pursuant to chapter 11 of this title and which was brought by the Secretary of Transportation under section 31325 of title 46 (including distribution of any proceeds of sale) to foreclose a preferred ship or fleet mortgage, or a security interest in or relating to a vessel or vessel under construction, held by the Secretary of Transportation under chapter 537 of title 46 or section 109(h) of title 49, or under applicable State law;

(13) under subsection (a) of this section, after the date which is 90 days after the filing of such petition, of the commencement or continuation, and conclusion to the entry of final judgment, of an action which involves a debtor subject to reorganization pursuant to chapter 11 of this title and which was brought by the Secretary of Commerce under section 31325 of title 46 (including distribution of any proceeds of sale) to foreclose a preferred ship or fleet mortgage in a vessel or a mortgage, deed of trust, or other security interest in a fishing facility held by the Secretary of Commerce under chapter 537 of title 46;

(14) under subsection (a) of this section, of any action by an accrediting agency regarding the accreditation status of the debtor as an educational institution;

(15) under subsection (a) of this section, of any action by a State licensing body regarding the licensure of the debtor as an educational institution;

(16) under subsection (a) of this section, of any action by a guaranty agency, as defined in section 435(j) of the Higher Education Act of 1965 or the Secretary of Education regarding the eligibility of the debtor to participate in programs authorized under such Act;

(17) under subsection (a) of this section, of the exercise by a swap participant or financial participant of any contractual right (as defined in section 560) under any

security agreement or arrangement or other credit enhancement forming a part of or related to any swap agreement, or of any contractual right (as defined in section 560) to offset or net out any termination value, payment amount, or other transfer obligation arising under or in connection with 1 or more such agreements, including any master agreement for such agreements;

(18) under subsection (a) of the creation or perfection of a statutory lien for an ad valorem property tax, or a special tax or special assessment on real property whether or not ad valorem, imposed by a governmental unit, if such tax or assessment comes due after the date of the filing of the petition;

(19) under subsection (a), of withholding of income from a debtor's wages and collection of amounts withheld, under the debtor's agreement authorizing that withholding and collection for the benefit of a pension, profit-sharing, stock bonus, or other plan established under section 401, 403, 408, 408A, 414, 457, or 501(c) of the Internal Revenue Code of 1986, that is sponsored by the employer of the debtor, or an affiliate, successor, or predecessor of such employer--

   (A) to the extent that the amounts withheld and collected are used solely for payments relating to a loan from a plan under section 408(b)(1) of the Employee Retirement Income Security Act of 1974 or is subject to section 72(p) of the Internal Revenue Code of 1986; or

   (B) a loan from a thrift savings plan permitted under subchapter III of chapter 84 of title 5, that satisfies the requirements of section 8433(g) of such title; but nothing in this paragraph may be construed to provide that any loan made under a governmental plan under section 414(d), or a contract or account under section 403(b), of the Internal Revenue Code of 1986 constitutes a claim or a debt under this title;

(20) under subsection (a), of any act to enforce any lien against or security interest in real property following entry of the order under subsection (d)(4) as to such real property in any prior case under this title, for a period of 2 years after the date of the entry of such an order, except that the debtor, in a subsequent case under this title, may move for relief from such order based upon changed circumstances or for other good cause shown, after notice and a hearing;

(21) under subsection (a), of any act to enforce any lien against or security interest in real property--

   (A) if the debtor is ineligible under section 109(g) to be a debtor in a case under this title; or

   (B) if the case under this title was filed in violation of a bankruptcy court order in a prior case under this title prohibiting the debtor from being a debtor in another case under this title;

* * *

(26) under subsection (a), of the setoff under applicable nonbankruptcy law of an income tax refund, by a governmental unit, with respect to a taxable period that ended before the date of the order for relief against an income tax liability for a taxable period that also ended before the date of the order for relief, except that in any case in which the setoff of an income tax refund is not permitted under applicable nonbankruptcy law because of a pending action to determine the amount or legality of a tax liability, the governmental unit may hold the refund pending the resolution of the action, unless the court, on the motion of the trustee and after notice and a hearing, grants the taxing authority adequate protection (within the meaning of section 361) for the secured claim of such authority in the setoff under section 506(a);

* * *

(e) (1) Thirty days after a request under subsection (d) of this section for relief from the stay of any act against property of the estate under subsection (a) of this section, such stay is terminated with respect to the party in interest making such request, unless the court, after notice and a hearing, orders such stay continued in effect pending the conclusion of, or as a result of, a final hearing and determination under subsection (d) of this section. A hearing under this subsection may be a preliminary hearing, or may be consolidated with the final hearing under subsection (d) of this section. The court shall order such stay continued in effect pending the conclusion of the final hearing under subsection (d) of this section if there is a reasonable likelihood that the party opposing relief from such stay will prevail at the conclusion of such final hearing. If the hearing under this subsection is a preliminary hearing, then such final hearing shall be concluded not later than thirty days after the conclusion of such preliminary hearing, unless the 30-day period is extended with the consent of the parties in interest or for a specific time which the court finds is required by compelling circumstances.

(2) Notwithstanding paragraph (1), in a case under chapter 7, 11, or 13 in which the debtor is an individual, the stay under subsection (a) shall terminate on the date that is 60 days after a request is made by a party in interest under subsection (d), unless--

(A) a final decision is rendered by the court during the 60-day period beginning on the date of the request; or

(B) such 60-day period is extended--

(i) by agreement of all parties in interest; or

(ii) by the court for such specific period of time as the court finds is required for good cause, as described in findings made by the court.

(f) Upon request of a party in interest, the court, with or without a hearing, shall grant such relief from the stay provided under subsection (a) of this section as is necessary to prevent irreparable damage to the interest of an entity in property, if such interest will suffer such damage before there is an opportunity for notice and a hearing under subsection (d) or (e) of this section.

(g) In any hearing under subsection (d) or (e) of this section concerning relief from the stay of any act under subsection (a) of this section--

(1) the party requesting such relief has the burden of proof on the issue of the debtor's equity in property; and

(2) the party opposing such relief has the burden of proof on all other issues.

* * *

11 USC § 505. Determination of tax liability.

(a) (1) Except as provided in paragraph (2) of this subsection, the court may determine the amount or legality of any tax, any fine or penalty relating to a tax, or any addition to tax, whether or not previously assessed, whether or not paid, and whether or not contested before and adjudicated by a judicial or administrative tribunal of competent jurisdiction.

(2) The court may not so determine--

(A) the amount or legality of a tax, fine, penalty, or addition to tax if such amount or legality was contested before and adjudicated by a judicial or administrative tribunal of competent jurisdiction before the commencement of the case under this title;

(B) any right of the estate to a tax refund, before the earlier of--

(i) 120 days after the trustee properly requests such refund from the governmental unit from which such refund is claimed; or

(ii) a determination by such governmental unit of such request; or

(C) the amount or legality of any amount arising in connection with an ad valorem tax on real or personal property of the estate, if the applicable period for contesting or redetermining that amount under applicable nonbankruptcy law has expired.

(b) (1) (A) The clerk shall maintain a list under which a Federal, State, or local governmental unit responsible for the collection of taxes within the district may--

(i) designate an address for service of requests under this subsection; and

(ii) describe where further information concerning additional requirements for filing such requests may be found.

(B) If such governmental unit does not designate an address and provide such address to the clerk under subparagraph (A), any request made under this subsection may be served at the address for the filing of a tax return or protest with the appropriate taxing authority of such governmental unit.

(2) A trustee may request a determination of any unpaid liability of the estate for any tax incurred during the administration of the case by submitting a tax return for such tax and a request for such a determination to the governmental unit charged with responsibility for collection or determination of such tax at the address and in the manner designated in paragraph (1). Unless such return is fraudulent, or contains a material misrepresentation, the estate, the trustee, the debtor, and any successor to the debtor are discharged from any liability for such tax--

(A) upon payment of the tax shown on such return, if--

(i) such governmental unit does not notify the trustee, within 60 days after such request, that such return has been selected for examination; or

(ii) such governmental unit does not complete such an examination and notify the trustee of any tax due, within 180 days after such request or within such additional time as the court, for cause, permits;

(B) upon payment of the tax determined by the court, after notice and a hearing, after completion by such governmental unit of such examination; or

(C) upon payment of the tax determined by such governmental unit to be due.

(c) Notwithstanding section 362 of this title, after determination by the court of a tax under this section, the governmental unit charged with responsibility for collection of such tax may assess such tax against the estate, the debtor, or a successor to the debtor, as the case may be, subject to any otherwise applicable law.

11 USC § 506. Determination of secured status.

(a) (1) An allowed claim of a creditor secured by a lien on property in which the estate has an interest, or that is subject to setoff under section 553 of this title, is a secured claim to the extent of the value of such creditor's interest in the estate's interest in such property, or to the extent of the amount subject to setoff, as the case may be, and is an unsecured claim to the extent that the value of such creditor's interest or the amount so subject to set off is less than the amount of such allowed claim. Such value shall be determined in light of the purpose of the valuation and of the proposed disposition or use of such property, and in conjunction with any hearing on such disposition or use or on a plan affecting such creditor's interest.

(2) If the debtor is an individual in a case under chapter 7 or 13, such value with respect to personal property securing an allowed claim shall be determined based on the replacement value of such property as of the date of the filing of the petition without deduction for costs of sale or marketing. With respect to property acquired for personal, family, or household purposes, replacement value shall mean the price a retail merchant would charge for property of that kind considering the age and condition of the property at the time value is determined.

(b) To the extent that an allowed secured claim is secured by property the value of which, after any recovery under subsection (c) of this section, is greater than the amount of such claim, there shall be allowed to the holder of such claim, interest on such claim, and any reasonable fees, costs, or charges provided for under the agreement or State statute under which such claim arose.

(c) The trustee may recover from property securing an allowed secured claim the reasonable, necessary costs and expenses of preserving, or disposing of, such property to the extent of any benefit to the holder of such claim, including the payment of all ad valorem property taxes with respect to the property.

(d) To the extent that a lien secures a claim against the debtor that is not an allowed secured claim, such lien is void, unless--

(1) such claim was disallowed only under section 502(b)(5) or 502(e) of this title; or

(2) such claim is not an allowed secured claim due only to the failure of any entity to file a proof of such claim under section 501 of this title.

11 USC § 507. Priorities.

(a) The following expenses and claims have priority in the following order:

(1) First:

(A) Allowed unsecured claims for domestic support obligations that, as of the date of the filing of the petition in a case under this title, are owed to or recoverable by a spouse, former spouse, or child of the debtor, or such child's parent, legal guardian, or responsible relative, without regard to whether the claim is filed by such person or is filed by a governmental unit on behalf of such person, on the condition that funds received under this paragraph by a governmental unit under this title after the date of the filing of the petition shall be applied and distributed in accordance with applicable nonbankruptcy law.

(B) Subject to claims under subparagraph (A), allowed unsecured claims for domestic support obligations that, as of the date of the filing of the petition, are assigned by a spouse, former spouse, child of the debtor, or such child's parent, legal guardian, or responsible relative to a governmental unit (unless such obligation is assigned voluntarily by the spouse, former spouse, child, parent, legal guardian, or responsible relative of the child for the purpose of collecting the debt) or are owed directly to or recoverable by a governmental unit under applicable nonbankruptcy law, on the condition that funds received under this paragraph by a governmental unit under this title after the date of the filing of the petition be applied and distributed in accordance with applicable nonbankruptcy law.

(C) If a trustee is appointed or elected under section 701, 702, 703, 1104, 1202, or 1302, the administrative expenses of the trustee allowed under paragraphs (1)(A), (2), and (6) of section 503(b) shall be paid before payment of claims under subparagraphs (A) and (B), to the extent that the trustee administers assets that are otherwise available for the payment of such claims.

(2) Second, administrative expenses allowed under section 503(b) of this title, unsecured claims of any Federal reserve bank related to loans made through programs or facilities authorized under section 13(3) of the Federal Reserve Act (12 U.S.C. 343), and any fees and charges assessed against the estate under chapter 123 of title 28.

(3) Third, unsecured claims allowed under section 502(f) of this title.

(4) Fourth, allowed unsecured claims, but only to the extent of $11,725 for each individual or corporation, as the case may be, earned within 180 days before the date of the filing of the petition or the date of the cessation of the debtor's business, whichever occurs first, for--

(A) wages, salaries, or commissions, including vacation, severance, and sick leave pay earned by an individual; or

(B) sales commissions earned by an individual or by a corporation with only 1 employee, acting as an independent contractor in the sale of goods or services for the debtor in the ordinary course of the debtor's business if, and only if, during the 12 months preceding that date, at least 75 percent of the amount that the individual or corporation earned by acting as an independent contractor in the sale of goods or services was earned from the debtor.

(5) Fifth, allowed unsecured claims for contributions to an employee benefit plan--

(A) arising from services rendered within 180 days before the date of the filing of the petition or the date of the cessation of the debtor's business, whichever occurs first; but only

(B) for each such plan, to the extent of--

(i) the number of employees covered by each such plan multiplied by $11,725; less

(ii) the aggregate amount paid to such employees under paragraph (4) of this subsection, plus the aggregate amount paid by the estate on behalf of such employees to any other employee benefit plan.

(6) Sixth, allowed unsecured claims of persons--

(A) engaged in the production or raising of grain, as defined in section 557(b) of this title, against a debtor who owns or operates a grain storage facility, as defined in section 557(b) of this title, for grain or the proceeds of grain, or

(B) engaged as a United States fisherman against a debtor who has acquired fish or fish produce from a fisherman through a sale or conversion, and who is engaged in operating a fish produce storage or processing facility--

but only to the extent of $5,775 for each such individual.

(7) Seventh, allowed unsecured claims of individuals, to the extent of $2,600 for each such individual, arising from the deposit, before the commencement of the case, of money in connection with the purchase, lease, or rental of property, or the purchase of services, for the personal, family, or household use of such individuals, that were not delivered or provided.

(8) Eighth, allowed unsecured claims of governmental units, only to the extent that such claims are for--

(A) a tax on or measured by income or gross receipts for a taxable year ending on or before the date of the filing of the petition--

(i) for which a return, if required, is last due, including extensions, after three years before the date of the filing of the petition;

(ii) assessed within 240 days before the date of the filing of the petition, exclusive of--

(I) any time during which an offer in compromise with respect to that tax was pending or in effect during that 240-day period, plus 30 days; and

(II) any time during which a stay of proceedings against collections was in effect in a prior case under this title during that 240-day period, plus 90 days; or

(iii) other than a tax of a kind specified in section 523(a)(1)(B) or 523(a)(1)(C) of this title, not assessed before, but assessable, under applicable law or by agreement, after, the commencement of the case;

(B) a property tax incurred before the commencement of the case and last payable without penalty after one year before the date of the filing of the petition;

(C) a tax required to be collected or withheld and for which the debtor is liable in whatever capacity;

(D) an employment tax on a wage, salary, or commission of a kind specified in paragraph (4) of this subsection earned from the debtor before the date of the filing of the petition, whether or not actually paid before such date, for which a return is last due, under applicable law or under any extension, after three years before the date of the filing of the petition;

* * *

(9) Ninth, allowed unsecured claims based upon any commitment by the debtor to a Federal depository institutions regulatory agency (or predecessor to such agency) to maintain the capital of an insured depository institution.

(10) Tenth, allowed claims for death or personal injury resulting from the operation of a motor vehicle or vessel if such operation was unlawful because the debtor was intoxicated from using alcohol, a drug, or another substance.

(b) If the trustee, under section 362, 363, or 364 of this title, provides adequate protection of the interest of a holder of a claim secured by a lien on property of the debtor and if, notwithstanding such protection, such creditor has a claim allowable under subsection (a)(2) of this section arising from the stay of action against such property under section 362 of this title, from the use, sale, or lease of such property under section 363 of this title, or from the granting of a lien under section 364(d) of this title, then such creditor's claim under such subsection shall have priority over every other claim allowable under such subsection.

(c) For the purpose of subsection (a) of this section, a claim of a governmental unit arising from an erroneous refund or credit of a tax has the same priority as a claim for the tax to which such refund or credit relates.

(d) An entity that is subrogated to the rights of a holder of a claim of a kind specified in subsection (a)(1), (a)(4), (a)(5), (a)(6), (a)(7), (a)(8), or (a)(9) of this section is not subrogated to the right of the holder of such claim to priority under such subsection.

11 USC § 511. Rate of interest on tax claims.

(a) If any provision of this title requires the payment of interest on a tax claim or on an administrative expense tax, or the payment of interest to enable a creditor to receive the present value of the allowed amount of a tax claim, the rate of interest shall be the rate determined under applicable nonbankruptcy law.

(b) In the case of taxes paid under a confirmed plan under this title, the rate of interest shall be determined as of the calendar month in which the plan is confirmed.

11 USC § 521. Debtor's duties.

(a) The debtor shall--
    (1) file--
        (A) a list of creditors; and
        (B) unless the court orders otherwise--
            (i) a schedule of assets and liabilities;
            (ii) a schedule of current income and current expenditures;
            (iii) a statement of the debtor's financial affairs and, if section 342(b) applies, a certificate--
                (I) of an attorney whose name is indicated on the petition as the attorney for the debtor, or a bankruptcy petition preparer signing the petition under section 110(b)(1), indicating that such attorney or the bankruptcy petition preparer delivered to the debtor the notice required by section 342(b); or
                (II) if no attorney is so indicated, and no bankruptcy petition preparer signed the petition, of the debtor that such notice was received and read by the debtor;
            (iv) copies of all payment advices or other evidence of payment received within 60 days before the date of the filing of the petition, by the debtor from any employer of the debtor;

(v) a statement of the amount of monthly net income, itemized to show how the amount is calculated; and

(vi) a statement disclosing any reasonably anticipated increase in income or expenditures over the 12-month period following the date of the filing of the petition;

(2) if an individual debtor's schedule of assets and liabilities includes debts which are secured by property of the estate--

(A) within thirty days after the date of the filing of a petition under chapter 7 of this title or on or before the date of the meeting of creditors, whichever is earlier, or within such additional time as the court, for cause, within such period fixes, file with the clerk a statement of his intention with respect to the retention or surrender of such property and, if applicable, specifying that such property is claimed as exempt, that the debtor intends to redeem such property, or that the debtor intends to reaffirm debts secured by such property; and

(B) within 30 days after the first date set for the meeting of creditors under section 341(a), or within such additional time as the court, for cause, within such 30-day period fixes, perform his intention with respect to such property, as specified by subparagraph (A) of this paragraph; except that nothing in subparagraphs (A) and (B) of this paragraph shall alter the debtor's or the trustee's rights with regard to such property under this title, except as provided in section 362(h);

(3) if a trustee is serving in the case or an auditor is serving under section 586(f) of title 28, cooperate with the trustee as necessary to enable the trustee to perform the trustee's duties under this title;

(4) if a trustee is serving in the case or an auditor is serving under section 586(f) of title 28, surrender to the trustee all property of the estate and any recorded information, including books, documents, records, and papers, relating to property of the estate, whether or not immunity is granted under section 344 of this title;

(5) appear at the hearing required under section 524(d) of this title;

(6) in a case under chapter 7 of this title in which the debtor is an individual, not retain possession of personal property as to which a creditor has an allowed claim for the purchase price secured in whole or in part by an interest in such personal property unless the debtor, not later than 45 days after the first meeting of creditors under section 341(a), either--

(A) enters into an agreement with the creditor pursuant to section 524(c) with respect to the claim secured by such property; or

(B) redeems such property from the security interest pursuant to section 722.

If the debtor fails to so act within the 45-day period referred to in paragraph (6), the stay under section 362(a) is terminated with respect to the personal property of the estate or of the debtor which is affected, such property shall no longer be property of the estate, and the creditor may take whatever action as to such property as is permitted by applicable nonbankruptcy law, unless the court determines on the motion of the trustee filed before the expiration of such 45-day period, and after notice and a hearing, that such property is of consequential value or benefit to the estate, orders appropriate adequate protection of the creditor's interest, and orders the debtor to deliver any collateral in the debtor's possession to the trustee; and

(7) unless a trustee is serving in the case, continue to perform the obligations required of the administrator (as defined in section 3 of the Employee Retirement Income Security Act of 1974) of an employee benefit plan if at the time of the commencement of the case the debtor (or any entity designated by the debtor) served as such administrator.

* * *

11 USC § 522. Exemptions.

(a) In this section--

(1) "dependent" includes spouse, whether or not actually dependent; and

(2) "value" means fair market value as of the date of the filing of the petition or, with respect to property that becomes property of the estate after such date, as of the date such property becomes property of the estate.

(b) (1) Notwithstanding section 541 of this title, an individual debtor may exempt from property of the estate the property listed in either paragraph (2) or, in the alternative, paragraph (3) of this subsection. In joint cases filed under section 302 of this title and individual cases filed under section 301 or 303 of this title by or against debtors who are husband and wife, and whose estates are ordered to be jointly administered under Rule 1015(b) of the Federal Rules of Bankruptcy Procedure, one debtor may not elect to exempt property listed in paragraph (2) and the other debtor elect to exempt property listed in paragraph (3) of this subsection. If the parties cannot agree on the alternative to be elected, they shall be deemed to elect paragraph (2), where such election is permitted under the law of the jurisdiction where the case is filed.

(2) Property listed in this paragraph is property that is specified under subsection (d), unless the State law that is applicable to the debtor under paragraph (3)(A) specifically does not so authorize.

(3) Property listed in this paragraph is--

(A) subject to subsections (o) and (p), any property that is exempt under Federal law, other than subsection (d) of this section, or State or local law that is applicable on the date of the filing of the petition to the place in which the debtor's domicile has been located for the 730 days immediately preceding the date of the filing of the petition or if the debtor's domicile has not been located in a single State for such 730-day period, the place in which the debtor's domicile was located for 180 days immediately preceding the 730-day period or for a longer portion of such 180-day period than in any other place;

(B) any interest in property in which the debtor had, immediately before the commencement of the case, an interest as a tenant by the entirety or joint tenant to the extent that such interest as a tenant by the entirety or joint tenant is exempt from process under applicable nonbankruptcy law; and

(C) retirement funds to the extent that those funds are in a fund or account that is exempt from taxation under section 401, 403, 408, 408A, 414, 457, or 501(a) of the Internal Revenue Code of 1986.

If the effect of the domiciliary requirement under subparagraph (A) is to render the debtor ineligible for any exemption, the debtor may elect to exempt property that is specified under subsection (d).

(4) For purposes of paragraph (3)(C) and subsection (d)(12), the following shall apply:

(A) If the retirement funds are in a retirement fund that has received a favorable determination under section 7805 of the Internal Revenue Code of 1986, and that determination is in effect as of the date of the filing of the petition in a case under this title, those funds shall be presumed to be exempt from the estate.

(B) If the retirement funds are in a retirement fund that has not received a favorable determination under such section 7805, those funds are exempt from the estate if the debtor demonstrates that--

(i) no prior determination to the contrary has been made by a court or the Internal Revenue Service; and

(ii) (I) the retirement fund is in substantial compliance with the applicable requirements of the Internal Revenue Code of 1986; or

(II) the retirement fund fails to be in substantial compliance with the applicable requirements of the Internal Revenue Code of 1986 and the debtor is not materially responsible for that failure.

(C) A direct transfer of retirement funds from 1 fund or account that is exempt from taxation under section 401, 403, 408, 408A, 414, 457, or 501(a) of the Internal Revenue Code of 1986, under section 401(a)(31) of the Internal Revenue Code of 1986, or otherwise, shall not cease to qualify for exemption under paragraph (3)(C) or subsection (d)(12) by reason of such direct transfer.

(D) (i) Any distribution that qualifies as an eligible rollover distribution within the meaning of section 402(c) of the Internal Revenue Code of 1986 or that is described in clause (ii) shall not cease to qualify for exemption under paragraph (3)(C) or subsection (d)(12) by reason of such distribution.

(ii) A distribution described in this clause is an amount that--

(I) has been distributed from a fund or account that is exempt from taxation under section 401, 403, 408, 408A, 414, 457, or 501(a) of the Internal Revenue Code of 1986; and

(II) to the extent allowed by law, is deposited in such a fund or account not later than 60 days after the distribution of such amount.

(c) Unless the case is dismissed, property exempted under this section is not liable during or after the case for any debt of the debtor that arose, or that is determined under section 502 of this title as if such debt had arisen, before the commencement of the case, except--

(1) a debt of a kind specified in paragraph (1) or (5) of section 523(a) (in which case, notwithstanding any provision of applicable nonbankruptcy law to the contrary, such property shall be liable for a debt of a kind specified in such paragraph);

(2) a debt secured by a lien that is--

(A) (i) not avoided under subsection (f) or (g) of this section or under section 544, 545, 547, 548, 549, or 724(a) of this title; and

(ii) not void under section 506(d) of this title; or

(B) a tax lien, notice of which is properly filed;

(3) a debt of a kind specified in section 523(a)(4) or 523(a)(6) of this title owed by an institution-affiliated party of an insured depository institution to a Federal depository institutions regulatory agency acting in its capacity as conservator, receiver, or liquidating agent for such institution; or

(4) a debt in connection with fraud in the obtaining or providing of any scholarship, grant, loan, tuition, discount, award, or other financial assistance for purposes of financing an education at an institution of higher education (as that term is defined in section 101 of the Higher Education Act of 1965 (20 U.S.C. 1001)).

(d) The following property may be exempted under subsection (b)(2) of this section:

(1) The debtor's aggregate interest, not to exceed $21,625 in value, in real property or personal property that the debtor or a dependent of the debtor uses as a residence, in a cooperative that owns property that the debtor or a dependent of the debtor uses as a residence, or in a burial plot for the debtor or a dependent of the debtor.

(2) The debtor's interest, not to exceed $3,450 in value, in one motor vehicle.

(3) The debtor's interest, not to exceed $550 in value in any particular item or $11,525 in aggregate value, in household furnishings, household goods, wearing apparel, appliances, books, animals, crops, or musical instruments, that are held primarily for the personal, family, or household use of the debtor or a dependent of the debtor.

(4) The debtor's aggregate interest, not to exceed $1,450 in value, in jewelry held primarily for the personal, family, or household use of the debtor or a dependent of the debtor.

(5) The debtor's aggregate interest in any property, not to exceed in value $1,150 plus up to $10,825 of any unused amount of the exemption provided under paragraph (1) of this subsection.

(6) The debtor's aggregate interest, not to exceed $2,175 in value, in any implements, professional books, or tools, of the trade of the debtor or the trade of a dependent of the debtor.

(7) Any unmatured life insurance contract owned by the debtor, other than a credit life insurance contract.

(8) The debtor's aggregate interest, not to exceed in value $11,525 less any amount of property of the estate transferred in the manner specified in section 542(d) of this title, in any accrued dividend or interest under, or loan value of, any unmatured life insurance contract owned by the debtor under which the insured is the debtor or an individual of whom the debtor is a dependent.

(9) Professionally prescribed health aids for the debtor or a dependent of the debtor.

(10) The debtor's right to receive--

(A) a social security benefit, unemployment compensation, or a local public assistance benefit;

(B) a veterans' benefit;

(C) a disability, illness, or unemployment benefit;

(D) alimony, support, or separate maintenance, to the extent reasonably necessary for the support of the debtor and any dependent of the debtor;

(E) a payment under a stock bonus, pension, profitsharing, annuity, or similar plan or contract on account of illness, disability, death, age, or length of service, to the extent reasonably necessary for the support of the debtor and any dependent of the debtor, unless—

(i) such plan or contract was established by or under the auspices of an insider that employed the debtor at the time the debtor's rights under such plan or contract arose;

(ii) such payment is on account of age or length of service; and

(iii) such plan or contract does not qualify under section 401(a), 403(a), 403(b), or 408 of the Internal Revenue Code of 1986.

(11) The debtor's right to receive, or property that is traceable to--

(A) an award under a crime victim's reparation law;

(B) a payment on account of the wrongful death of an individual of whom the debtor was a dependent, to the extent reasonably necessary for the support of the debtor and any dependent of the debtor;

(C) a payment under a life insurance contract that insured the life of an individual of whom the debtor was a dependent on the date of such individual's death, to the extent reasonably necessary for the support of the debtor and any dependent of the debtor;

(D) a payment, not to exceed $21,625, on account of personal bodily injury, not including pain and suffering or compensation for actual pecuniary loss, of the debtor or an individual of whom the debtor is a dependent; or

(E) a payment in compensation of loss of future earnings of the debtor or an individual of whom the debtor is or was a dependent, to the extent reasonably necessary for the support of the debtor and any dependent of the debtor.

(12) Retirement funds to the extent that those funds are in a fund or account that is exempt from taxation under section 401, 403, 408, 408A, 414, 457, or 501(a) of the Internal Revenue Code of 1986.

(e) A waiver of an exemption executed in favor of a creditor that holds an unsecured claim against the debtor is unenforceable in a case under this title with respect to such claim against property that the debtor may exempt under subsection (b) of this section. A waiver by the debtor of a power under subsection (f) or (h) of this section to avoid a transfer, under subsection (g) or (i) of this section to exempt property, or under subsection (i) of this section to recover property or to preserve a transfer, is unenforceable in a case under this title.

* * *

(k) Property that the debtor exempts under this section is not liable for payment of any administrative expense except--

(1) the aliquot share of the costs and expenses of avoiding a transfer of property that the debtor exempts under subsection (g) of this section, or of recovery of such property, that is attributable to the value of the portion of such property exempted in relation to the value of the property recovered; and

(2) any costs and expenses of avoiding a transfer under subsection (f) or (h) of this section, or of recovery of property under subsection (i)(1) of this section, that the debtor has not paid.

(l) The debtor shall file a list of property that the debtor claims as exempt under subsection (b) of this section. If the debtor does not file such a list, a dependent of the debtor may file such a list, or may claim property as exempt from property of the estate on behalf of the debtor. Unless a party in interest objects, the property claimed as exempt on such list is exempt.

(m) Subject to the limitation in subsection (b), this section shall apply separately with respect to each debtor in a joint case.

* * *

11 USC § 523. Exceptions to discharge.

(a) A discharge under section 727, 1141, 1228(a), 1228(b), or 1328(b) of this title does not discharge an individual debtor from any debt--

(1) for a tax or a customs duty--

(A) of the kind and for the periods specified in section 507(a)(3) or 507(a)(8) of this title, whether or not a claim for such tax was filed or allowed;

(B) with respect to which a return, or equivalent report or notice, if required--

(i) was not filed or given; or

(ii) was filed or given after the date on which such return, report, or notice was last due, under applicable law or under any extension, and after two years before the date of the filing of the petition; or

(C) with respect to which the debtor made a fraudulent return or willfully attempted in any manner to evade or defeat such tax;

(2) for money, property, services, or an extension, renewal, or refinancing of credit, to the extent obtained, by--

(A) false pretenses, a false representation, or actual fraud, other than a statement respecting the debtor's or an insider's financial condition;

(B) use of a statement in writing--

(i) that is materially false;

(ii) respecting the debtor's or an insider's financial condition;

(iii) on which the creditor to whom the debtor is liable for such money, property, services, or credit reasonably relied; and

(iv) that the debtor caused to be made or published with intent to deceive; or

(C) (i) for purposes of subparagraph (A)--

(I) consumer debts owed to a single creditor and aggregating more than $600 for luxury goods or services incurred by an individual debtor on or within 90 days before the order for relief under this title are presumed to be nondischargeable; and

(II) cash advances aggregating more than $875 that are extensions of consumer credit under an open end credit plan obtained by an individual debtor on or within 70 days before the order for relief under this title, are presumed to be nondischargeable; and

(ii) for purposes of this subparagraph--

(I) the terms "consumer", "credit", and "open end credit plan" have the same meanings as in section 103 of the Truth in Lending Act; and

(II) the term "luxury goods or services" does not include goods or services reasonably necessary for the support or maintenance of the debtor or a dependent of the debtor;

* * *

(b) Notwithstanding subsection (a) of this section, a debt that was excepted from discharge under subsection (a)(1), (a)(3), or (a)(8) of this section, under section 17a(1), 17a(3), or 17a(5) of the Bankruptcy Act, under section 439A of the Higher Education Act of 1965, or under section 733(g) of the Public Health Service Act in a prior case concerning the debtor under this title or under the Bankruptcy Act, is dischargeable in a case under this title unless, by the terms of subsection (a) of this section, such debt is not dischargeable in the case under this title.

* * *

11 USC § 524. Effect of discharge.
    (a) A discharge in a case under this title--
        (1) voids any judgment at any time obtained, to the extent that such judgment is a determination of the personal liability of the debtor with respect to any debt discharged under section 727, 944, 1141, 1228, or 1328 of this title, whether or not discharge of such debt is waived;
        (2) operates as an injunction against the commencement or continuation of an action, the employment of process, or an act, to collect, recover or offset any such debt as a personal liability of the debtor, whether or not discharge of such debt is waived; and
        (3) operates as an injunction against the commencement or continuation of an action, the employment of process, or an act, to collect or recover from, or offset against, property of the debtor of the kind specified in section 541(a)(2) of this title that is acquired after the commencement of the case, on account of any allowable community claim, except a community claim that is excepted from discharge under section 523, 1228(a)(1), or 1328(a)(1), or that would be so excepted, determined in accordance with the provisions of sections 523(c) and 523(d) of this title, in a case concerning the debtor's spouse commenced on the date of the filing of the petition in the case concerning the debtor, whether or not discharge of the debt based on such community claim is waived.
    (b) Subsection (a)(3) of this section does not apply if--
        (1) (A) the debtor's spouse is a debtor in a case under this title, or a bankrupt or a debtor in a case under the Bankruptcy Act, commenced within six years of the date of the filing of the petition in the case concerning the debtor; and
            (B) the court does not grant the debtor's spouse a discharge in such case concerning the debtor's spouse; or
        (2) (A) the court would not grant the debtor's spouse a discharge in a case under chapter 7 of this title concerning such spouse commenced on the date of the filing of the petition in the case concerning the debtor; and
            (B) a determination that the court would not so grant such discharge is made by the bankruptcy court within the time and in the manner provided for a determination under section 727 of this title of whether a debtor is granted a discharge.

* * *

(e) Except as provided in subsection (a)(3) of this section, discharge of a debt of the debtor does not affect the liability of any other entity on, or the property of any other entity for, such debt.

(f) Nothing contained in subsection (c) or (d) of this section prevents a debtor from voluntarily repaying any debt.

* * *

11 USC § 547. Preferences.

(a) In this section--

(1) "inventory" means personal property leased or furnished, held for sale or lease, or to be furnished under a contract for service, raw materials, work in process, or materials used or consumed in a business, including farm products such as crops or livestock, held for sale or lease;

(2) "new value" means money or money's worth in goods, services, or new credit, or release by a transferee of property previously transferred to such transferee in a transaction that is neither void nor voidable by the debtor or the trustee under any applicable law, including proceeds of such property, but does not include an obligation substituted for an existing obligation;

(3) "receivable" means right to payment, whether or not such right has been earned by performance; and

(4) a debt for a tax is incurred on the day when such tax is last payable without penalty, including any extension.

(b) Except as provided in subsections (c) and (i) of this section, the trustee may avoid any transfer of an interest of the debtor in property--

(1) to or for the benefit of a creditor;

(2) for or on account of an antecedent debt owed by the debtor before such transfer was made;

(3) made while the debtor was insolvent;

(4) made--

(A) on or within 90 days before the date of the filing of the petition; or

(B) between ninety days and one year before the date of the filing of the petition, if such creditor at the time of such transfer was an insider; and

(5) that enables such creditor to receive more than such creditor would receive if--

(A) the case were a case under chapter 7 of this title;

(B) the transfer had not been made; and

(C) such creditor received payment of such debt to the extent provided by the provisions of this title.

(c) The trustee may not avoid under this section a transfer--

(1) to the extent that such transfer was--

(A) intended by the debtor and the creditor to or for whose benefit such transfer was made to be a contemporaneous exchange for new value given to the debtor; and

(B) in fact a substantially contemporaneous exchange;

(2) to the extent that such transfer was in payment of a debt incurred by the debtor in the ordinary course of business or financial affairs of the debtor and the transferee, and such transfer was--

    (A) made in the ordinary course of business or financial affairs of the debtor and the transferee; or

    (B) made according to ordinary business terms;

(3) that creates a security interest in property acquired by the debtor--

    (A) to the extent such security interest secures new value that was--

        (i) given at or after the signing of a security agreement that contains a description of such property as collateral;

        (ii) given by or on behalf of the secured party under such agreement;

        (iii) given to enable the debtor to acquire such property; and

        (iv) in fact used by the debtor to acquire such property; and

    (B) that is perfected on or before 30 days after the debtor receives possession of such property;

(4) to or for the benefit of a creditor, to the extent that, after such transfer, such creditor gave new value to or for the benefit of the debtor--

    (A) not secured by an otherwise unavoidable security interest; and

    (B) on account of which new value the debtor did not make an otherwise unavoidable transfer to or for the benefit of such creditor;

(5) that creates a perfected security interest in inventory or a receivable or the proceeds of either, except to the extent that the aggregate of all such transfers to the transferee caused a reduction, as of the date of the filing of the petition and to the prejudice of other creditors holding unsecured claims, of any amount by which the debt secured by such security interest exceeded the value of all security interests for such debt on the later of--

    (A) (i) with respect to a transfer to which subsection (b)(4)(A) of this section applies, 90 days before the date of the filing of the petition; or

        (ii) with respect to a transfer to which subsection (b)(4)(B) of this section applies, one year before the date of the filing of the petition; or

    (B) the date on which new value was first given under the security agreement creating such security interest;

(6) that is the fixing of a statutory lien that is not avoidable under section 545 of this title;

(7) to the extent such transfer was a bona fide payment of a debt for a domestic support obligation;

(8) if, in a case filed by an individual debtor whose debts are primarily consumer debts, the aggregate value of all property that constitutes or is affected by such transfer is less than $600; or

(9) if, in a case filed by a debtor whose debts are not primarily consumer debts, the aggregate value of all property that constitutes or is affected by such transfer is less than $5,850.

(d) The trustee may avoid a transfer of an interest in property of the debtor transferred to or for the benefit of a surety to secure reimbursement of such a surety that furnished a bond or other obligation to dissolve a judicial lien that would have been avoidable by the trustee under subsection (b) of this section. The liability of such surety under such bond or obligation shall be discharged to the extent of the value of such property recovered by the trustee or the amount paid to the trustee.

(e) (1) For the purposes of this section--

(A) a transfer of real property other than fixtures, but including the interest of a seller or purchaser under a contract for the sale of real property, is perfected when a bona fide purchaser of such property from the debtor against whom applicable law permits such transfer to be perfected cannot acquire an interest that is superior to the interest of the transferee; and

(B) a transfer of a fixture or property other than real property is perfected when a creditor on a simple contract cannot acquire a judicial lien that is superior to the interest of the transferee.

(2) For the purposes of this section, except as provided in paragraph (3) of this subsection, a transfer is made--

(A) at the time such transfer takes effect between the transferor and the transferee, if such transfer is perfected at, or within 30 days after, such time, except as provided in subsection (c)(3)(B);

(B) at the time such transfer is perfected, if such transfer is perfected after such 30 days; or

(C) immediately before the date of the filing of the petition, if such transfer is not perfected at the later of--

(i) the commencement of the case; or

(ii) 30 days after such transfer takes effect between the transferor and the transferee.

(3) For the purposes of this section, a transfer is not made until the debtor has acquired rights in the property transferred.

(f) For the purposes of this section, the debtor is presumed to have been insolvent on and during the 90 days immediately preceding the date of the filing of the petition.

(g) For the purposes of this section, the trustee has the burden of proving the avoidability of a transfer under subsection (b) of this section, and the creditor or party in interest against whom recovery or avoidance is sought has the burden of proving the nonavoidability of a transfer under subsection (c) of this section.

(h) The trustee may not avoid a transfer if such transfer was made as a part of an alternative repayment schedule between the debtor and any creditor of the debtor created by an approved nonprofit budget and credit counseling agency.

(i) If the trustee avoids under subsection (b) a transfer made between 90 days and 1 year before the date of the filing of the petition, by the debtor to an entity that is not an insider for the benefit of a creditor that is an insider, such transfer shall be considered to be avoided under this section only with respect to the creditor that is an insider.

11 USC § 724. Treatment of certain liens.

(a) The trustee may avoid a lien that secures a claim of a kind specified in section 726(a)(4) of this title.

(b) Property in which the estate has an interest and that is subject to a lien that is not avoidable under this title (other than to the extent that there is a properly perfected unavoidable tax lien arising in connection with an ad valorem tax on real or personal property of the estate) and that secures an allowed claim for a tax, or proceeds of such property, shall be distributed--

　　(1) first, to any holder of an allowed claim secured by a lien on such property that is not avoidable under this title and that is senior to such tax lien;

　　(2) second, to any holder of a claim of a kind specified in section 507(a)(1)(C) or 507(a)(2) (except that such expenses under each such section, other than claims for wages, salaries, or commissions that arise after the date of the filing of the petition, shall be limited to expenses incurred under this chapter and shall not include expenses incurred under chapter 11 of this title), 507(a)(1)(A), 507(a)(1)(B), 507(a)(3), 507(a)(4), 507(a)(5), 507(a)(6), or 507(a)(7) of this title, to the extent of the amount of such allowed tax claim that is secured by such tax lien;

　　(3) third, to the holder of such tax lien, to any extent that such holder's allowed tax claim that is secured by such tax lien exceeds any amount distributed under paragraph (2) of this subsection;

　　(4) fourth, to any holder of an allowed claim secured by a lien on such property that is not avoidable under this title and that is junior to such tax lien;

　　(5) fifth, to the holder of such tax lien, to the extent that such holder's allowed claim secured by such tax lien is not paid under paragraph (3) of this subsection; and

　　(6) sixth, to the estate.

　(c) If more than one holder of a claim is entitled to distribution under a particular paragraph of subsection (b) of this section, distribution to such holders under such paragraph shall be in the same order as distribution to such holders would have been other than under this section.

　(d) A statutory lien the priority of which is determined in the same manner as the priority of a tax lien under section 6323 of the Internal Revenue Code of 1986 shall be treated under subsection (b) of this section the same as if such lien were a tax lien.

　(e) Before subordinating a tax lien on real or personal property of the estate, the trustee shall--

　　(1) exhaust the unencumbered assets of the estate; and

　　(2) in a manner consistent with section 506(c), recover from property securing an allowed secured claim the reasonable, necessary costs and expenses of preserving or disposing of such property.

　(f) Notwithstanding the exclusion of ad valorem tax liens under this section and subject to the requirements of subsection (e), the following may be paid from property of the estate which secures a tax lien, or the proceeds of such property:

　　(1) Claims for wages, salaries, and commissions that are entitled to priority under section 507(a)(4).

　　(2) Claims for contributions to an employee benefit plan entitled to priority under section 507(a)(5).

11 USC § 727. Discharge.

　(a) The court shall grant the debtor a discharge, unless--

　　(1) the debtor is not an individual;

　　(2) the debtor, with intent to hinder, delay, or defraud a creditor or an officer of the estate charged with custody of property under this title, has transferred, removed, destroyed, mutilated, or concealed, or has permitted to be transferred, removed, destroyed, mutilated, or concealed--

    (A) property of the debtor, within one year before the date of the filing of the petition; or

    (B) property of the estate, after the date of the filing of the petition;

(3) the debtor has concealed, destroyed, mutilated, falsified, or failed to keep or preserve any recorded information, including books, documents, records, and papers, from which the debtor's financial condition or business transactions might be ascertained, unless such act or failure to act was justified under all of the circumstances of the case;

(4) the debtor knowingly and fraudulently, in or in connection with the case--

    (A) made a false oath or account;

    (B) presented or used a false claim;

    (C) gave, offered, received, or attempted to obtain money, property, or advantage, or a promise of money, property, or advantage, for acting or forbearing to act; or

    (D) withheld from an officer of the estate entitled to possession under this title, any recorded information, including books, documents, records, and papers, relating to the debtor's property or financial affairs;

(5) the debtor has failed to explain satisfactorily, before determination of denial of discharge under this paragraph, any loss of assets or deficiency of assets to meet the debtor's liabilities;

(6) the debtor has refused, in the case--

    (A) to obey any lawful order of the court, other than an order to respond to a material question or to testify;

    (B) on the ground of privilege against self-incrimination, to respond to a material question approved by the court or to testify, after the debtor has been granted immunity with respect to the matter concerning which such privilege was invoked; or

    (C) on a ground other than the properly invoked privilege against self-incrimination, to respond to a material question approved by the court or to testify;

(7) the debtor has committed any act specified in paragraph (2), (3), (4), (5), or (6) of this subsection, on or within one year before the date of the filing of the petition, or during the case, in connection with another case, under this title or under the Bankruptcy Act, concerning an insider;

(8) the debtor has been granted a discharge under this section, under section 1141 of this title, or under section 14, 371, or 476 of the Bankruptcy Act, in a case commenced within 8 years before the date of the filing of the petition;

(9) the debtor has been granted a discharge under section 1228 or 1328 of this title, or under section 660 or 661 of the Bankruptcy Act, in a case commenced within six years before the date of the filing of the petition, unless payments under the plan in such case totaled at least--

    (A) 100 percent of the allowed unsecured claims in such case; or

    (B) (i) 70 percent of such claims; and

        (ii) the plan was proposed by the debtor in good faith, and was the debtor's best effort;

(10) the court approves a written waiver of discharge executed by the debtor after the order for relief under this chapter;

(11) after filing the petition, the debtor failed to complete an instructional course concerning personal financial management described in section 111, except that this paragraph shall not apply with respect to a debtor who is a person described in section 109(h)(4) or who resides in a district for which the United States trustee (or the bankruptcy administrator, if any) determines that the approved instructional courses are not adequate to service the additional individuals who would otherwise be required to complete such instructional courses under this section (The United States trustee (or the bankruptcy administrator, if any) who makes a determination described in this paragraph shall review such determination not later than 1 year after the date of such determination, and not less frequently than annually thereafter.); or

(12) the court after notice and a hearing held not more than 10 days before the date of the entry of the order granting the discharge finds that there is reasonable cause to believe that--

(A) section 522(q)(1) may be applicable to the debtor; and

(B) there is pending any proceeding in which the debtor may be found guilty of a felony of the kind described in section 522(q)(1)(A) or liable for a debt of the kind described in section 522(q)(1)(B).

11 USC § 1328. Discharge.

(a) Subject to subsection (d), as soon as practicable after completion by the debtor of all payments under the plan, and in the case of a debtor who is required by a judicial or administrative order, or by statute, to pay a domestic support obligation, after such debtor certifies that all amounts payable under such order or such statute that are due on or before the date of the certification (including amounts due before the petition was filed, but only to the extent provided for by the plan) have been paid, unless the court approves a written waiver of discharge executed by the debtor after the order for relief under this chapter, the court shall grant the debtor a discharge of all debts provided for by the plan or disallowed under section 502 of this title, except any debt--

(1) provided for under section 1322(b)(5);

(2) of the kind specified in section 507(a)(8)(C) or in paragraph (1)(B), (1)(C), (2), (3), (4), (5), (8), or (9) of section 523(a);

(3) for restitution, or a criminal fine, included in a sentence on the debtor's conviction of a crime; or

(4) for restitution, or damages, awarded in a civil action against the debtor as a result of willful or malicious injury by the debtor that caused personal injury to an individual or the death of an individual.

(b) Subject to subsection (d), at any time after the confirmation of the plan and after notice and a hearing, the court may grant a discharge to a debtor that has not completed payments under the plan only if--

(1) the debtor's failure to complete such payments is due to circumstances for which the debtor should not justly be held accountable;

(2) the value, as of the effective date of the plan, of property actually distributed under the plan on account of each allowed unsecured claim is not less than the amount

that would have been paid on such claim if the estate of the debtor had been liquidated under chapter 7 of this title on such date; and

    (3) modification of the plan under section 1329 of this title is not practicable.

(c) A discharge granted under subsection (b) of this section discharges the debtor from all unsecured debts provided for by the plan or disallowed under section 502 of this title, except any debt--

    (1) provided for under section 1322(b)(5) of this title; or

    (2) of a kind specified in section 523(a) of this title.

(d) Notwithstanding any other provision of this section, a discharge granted under this section does not discharge the debtor from any debt based on an allowed claim filed under section 1305(a)(2) of this title if prior approval by the trustee of the debtor's incurring such debt was practicable and was not obtained.

(e) On request of a party in interest before one year after a discharge under this section is granted, and after notice and a hearing, the court may revoke such discharge only if—

    (1) such discharge was obtained by the debtor through fraud; and

    (2) the requesting party did not know of such fraud until after such discharge was granted.

(f) Notwithstanding subsections (a) and (b), the court shall not grant a discharge of all debts provided for in the plan or disallowed under section 502, if the debtor has received a discharge--

    (1) in a case filed under chapter 7, 11, or 12 of this title during the 4-year period preceding the date of the order for relief under this chapter, or

    (2) in a case filed under chapter 13 of this title during the 2-year period preceding the date of such order.

(g) (1) The court shall not grant a discharge under this section to a debtor unless after filing a petition the debtor has completed an instructional course concerning personal financial management described in section 111.

    (2) Paragraph (1) shall not apply with respect to a debtor who is a person described in section 109(h)(4) or who resides in a district for which the United States trustee (or the bankruptcy administrator, if any) determines that the approved instructional courses are not adequate to service the additional individuals who would otherwise be required to complete such instructional course by reason of the requirements of paragraph (1).

    (3) The United States trustee (or the bankruptcy administrator, if any) who makes a determination described in paragraph (2) shall review such determination not later than 1 year after the date of such determination, and not less frequently than annually thereafter.

(h) The court may not grant a discharge under this chapter unless the court after notice and a hearing held not more than 10 days before the date of the entry of the order granting the discharge finds that there is no reasonable cause to believe that--

    (1) section 522(q)(1) may be applicable to the debtor; and

    (2) there is pending any proceeding in which the debtor may be found guilty of a felony of the kind described in section 522(q)(1)(A) or liable for a debt of the kind described in section 522(q)(1)(B).

15 USC § 1692. Congressional findings and declaration of purpose.

(a) Abusive practices. There is abundant evidence of the use of abusive, deceptive, and unfair debt collection practices by many debt collectors. Abusive debt collection practices contribute to the number of personal bankruptcies, to marital instability, to the loss of jobs, and to invasions of individual privacy.

(b) Inadequacy of laws. Existing laws and procedures for redressing these injuries are inadequate to protect consumers.

(c) Available non-abusive collection methods. Means other than misrepresentation or other abusive debt collection practices are available for the effective collection of debts.

(d) Interstate commerce. Abusive debt collection practices are carried on to a substantial extent in interstate commerce and through means and instrumentalities of such commerce. Even where abusive debt collection practices are purely intrastate in character, they nevertheless directly affect interstate commerce.

(e) Purposes. It is the purpose of this title to eliminate abusive debt collection practices by debt collectors, to insure that those debt collectors who refrain from using abusive debt collection practices are not competitively disadvantaged, and to promote consistent State action to protect consumers against debt collection abuses.

18 USC § 1503. Influencing or injuring officer or juror generally.

(a) Whoever corruptly, or by threats or force, or by any threatening letter or communication, endeavors to influence, intimidate, or impede any grand or petit juror, or officer in or of any court of the United States, or officer who may be serving at any examination or other proceeding before any United States magistrate judge or other committing magistrate, in the discharge of his duty, or injures any such grand or petit juror in his person or property on account of any verdict or indictment assented to by him, or on account of his being or having been such juror, or injures any such officer, magistrate judge, or other committing magistrate in his person or property on account of the performance of his official duties, or corruptly or by threats or force, or by any threatening letter or communication, influences, obstructs, or impedes, or endeavors to influence, obstruct, or impede, the due administration of justice, shall be punished as provided in subsection (b). If the offense under this section occurs in connection with a trial of a criminal case, and the act in violation of this section involves the threat of physical force or physical force, the maximum term of imprisonment which may be imposed for the offense shall be the higher of that otherwise provided by law or the maximum term that could have been imposed for any offense charged in such case.

(b) The punishment for an offense under this section is--

　　(1) in the case of a killing, the punishment provided in sections 1111 and 1112;

　　(2) in the case of an attempted killing, or a case in which the offense was committed against a petit juror and in which a class A or B felony was charged, imprisonment for not more than 20 years, a fine under this title, or both; and

　　(3) in any other case, imprisonment for not more than 10 years, a fine under this title, or both.

28 USC § 41. Number and composition of circuits.

The thirteen judicial circuits of the United States are constituted as follows:

```
Circuits                    Composition
District of Columbia .....   District of Columbia.
First ...................    Maine, Massachusetts, New Hampshire, Puerto Rico,
                             Rhode Island.
Second ..................    Connecticut, New York, Vermont.
Third ...................    Delaware, New Jersey, Pennsylvania, Virgin
                             Islands.
Fourth ..................    Maryland, North Carolina, South Carolina,
                             Virginia, West Virginia.
Fifth ...................    District of the Canal Zone, Louisiana,
                             Mississippi, Texas.
Sixth ...................    Kentucky, Michigan, Ohio, Tennessee.
Seventh .................    Illinois, Indiana, Wisconsin.
Eighth ..................    Arkansas, Iowa, Minnesota, Missouri, Nebraska,
                             North Dakota, South Dakota.
Ninth ...................    Alaska, Arizona, California, Idaho, Montana,
                             Nevada, Oregon, Washington, Guam, Hawaii.
Tenth ...................    Colorado, Kansas, New Mexico, Oklahoma, Utah,
                             Wyoming.
Eleventh ................    Alabama, Florida, Georgia.
Federal .................    All Federal judicial districts.
```

28 USC § 171. Appointment and number of judges; character of court; designation of chief judge.

(a) The President shall appoint, by and with the advice and consent of the Senate, sixteen judges who shall constitute a court of record known as the United States Court of Federal Claims. The court is declared to be a court established under article I of the Constitution of the United States [USCS Constitution, Art. I].

(b) The President shall designate one of the judges of the Court of Federal Claims who is less than seventy years of age to serve as chief judge. The chief judge may continue to serve as such until he reaches the age of seventy years or until another judge is designated as chief judge by the President. After the designation of another judge to serve as chief judge, the former chief judge may continue to serve as a judge of the court for the balance of the term to which appointed.

28 USC § 172. Tenure and salaries of judges.

(a) Each judge of the United States Court of Federal Claims shall be appointed for a term of fifteen years.

(b) Each judge shall receive a salary at the rate of pay, and in the same manner, as judges of the district courts of the United States.

28 USC § 173. Times and places of holding court.

The principal office of the United States Court of Federal Claims shall be in the District of Columbia, but the Court of Federal Claims may hold court at such times and in such places as it may fix by rule of court. The times and places of the sessions of the Court of Federal Claims shall be prescribed with a view to securing reasonable opportunity to citizens to appear before the Court of Federal Claims with as little inconvenience and expense to citizens as is practicable.

28 USC § 1254. Courts of appeals; certiorari; certified questions.

Cases in the courts of appeals may be reviewed by the Supreme Court by the following methods:

(1) By writ of certiorari granted upon the petition of any party to any civil or criminal case, before or after rendition of judgment or decree;

(2) By certification at any time by a court of appeals of any question of law in any civil or criminal case as to which instructions are desired, and upon such certification the Supreme Court may give binding instructions or require the entire record to be sent up for decision of the entire matter in controversy.

28 USC § 1291. Final decisions of district courts.

The courts of appeals (other than the United States Court of Appeals for the Federal Circuit) shall have jurisdiction of appeals from all final decisions of the district courts of the United States, the United States District Court for the District of the Canal Zone, the District Court of Guam, and the District Court of the Virgin Islands, except where a direct review may be had in the Supreme Court. The jurisdiction of the United States Court of Appeals for the Federal Circuit shall be limited to the jurisdiction described in sections 1292(c) and (d) and 1295 of this title.

28 USC § 1295. Jurisdiction of the United States Court of Appeals for the Federal Circuit.

(a) The United States Court of Appeals for the Federal Circuit shall have exclusive jurisdiction--

(1) of an appeal from a final decision of a district court of the United States, the District Court of Guam, the District Court of the Virgin Islands, or the District Court of the Northern Mariana Islands, in any civil action arising under, or in any civil action in which a party has asserted a compulsory counterclaim arising under, any Act of Congress relating to patents or plant variety protection;

(2) of an appeal from a final decision of a district court of the United States, the United States District Court for the District of the Canal Zone, the District Court of Guam, the District Court of the Virgin Islands, or the District Court for the Northern Mariana Islands, if the jurisdiction of that court was based, in whole or in part, on section 1346 of this title, except that jurisdiction of an appeal in a case brought in a district court under section 1346(a)(1), 1346(b), 1346(e), or 1346(f) of this title or under section 1346(a)(2) when the claim is founded upon an Act of Congress or a regulation of an executive department providing for internal revenue shall be governed by sections 1291, 1292, and 1294 of this title;

(3) of an appeal from a final decision of the United States Claims Court [United States Court of Federal Claims];

(4) of an appeal from a decision of--

(A) the Board of Patent Appeals and Interferences of the United States Patent and Trademark Office with respect to patent applications and interferences, at the instance of an applicant for a patent or any party to a patent interference, and any such appeal shall waive the right of such applicant or party to proceed under section 145 or 146 of title 35;

(B) the Under Secretary of Commerce for Intellectual Property and Director of the United States Patent and Trademark Office or the Trademark Trial and Appeal Board with respect to applications for registration of marks and other proceedings as provided in section 21 of the Trademark Act of 1946 (15 U.S.C. 1071); or

(C) a district court to which a case was directed pursuant to section 145, 146, or 154(b) of title 35;

(5) of an appeal from a final decision of the United States Court of International Trade;

(6) to review the final determinations of the United States International Trade Commission relating to unfair practices in import trade, made under section 337 of the Tariff Act of 1930 (19 U.S.C. 1337);

(7) to review, by appeal on questions of law only, findings of the Secretary of Commerce under U.S. note 6 to subchapter X of chapter 98 of the Harmonized Tariff Schedule of the United States (relating to importation of instruments or apparatus);

(8) of an appeal under section 71 of the Plant Variety Protection Act (7 U.S.C. 2461);

(9) of an appeal from a final order or final decision of the Merit Systems Protection Board, pursuant to sections 7703(b)(1) and 7703(d) of title 5;

(10) of an appeal from a final decision of an agency board of contract appeals pursuant to section 7107(a)(1) of title 41;

(11) of an appeal under section 211 of the Economic Stabilization Act of 1970;

(12) of an appeal under section 5 of the Emergency Petroleum Allocation Act of 1973;

(13) of an appeal under section 506(c) of the Natural Gas Policy Act of 1978; and

(14) of an appeal under section 523 of the Energy Policy and Conservation Act.

(b) The head of any executive department or agency may, with the approval of the Attorney General, refer to the Court of Appeals for the Federal Circuit for judicial review any final decision rendered by a board of contract appeals pursuant to the terms of any contract with the United States awarded by that department or agency which the head of such department or agency has concluded is not entitled to finality pursuant to the review standards specified in section 7017(b) of title 41. The head of each executive department or agency shall make any referral under this section within one hundred and twenty days after the receipt of a copy of the final appeal decision.

(c) The Court of Appeals for the Federal Circuit shall review the matter referred in accordance with the standards specified in section 7107(b) of title 41. The court shall proceed with judicial review on the administrative record made before the board of contract appeals on matters so referred as in other cases pending in such court, shall determine the issue of finality of the appeal decision, and shall, if appropriate, render judgment thereon, or remand the matter to any administrative or executive body or official with such direction as it may deem proper and just.

28 USC § 1391. Venue generally.

(a) Applicability of section. Except as otherwise provided by law--

(1) this section shall govern the venue of all civil actions brought in district courts of the United States; and

(2) the proper venue for a civil action shall be determined without regard to whether the action is local or transitory in nature.

(b) Venue in general. A civil action may be brought in--

(1) a judicial district in which any defendant resides, if all defendants are residents of the State in which the district is located;

(2) a judicial district in which a substantial part of the events or omissions giving rise to the claim occurred, or a substantial part of property that is the subject of the action is situated; or

(3) if there is no district in which an action may otherwise be brought as provided in this section, any judicial district in which any defendant is subject to the court's personal jurisdiction with respect to such action.

(c) Residency. For all venue purposes--

(1) a natural person, including an alien lawfully admitted for permanent residence in the United States, shall be deemed to reside in the judicial district in which that person is domiciled;

(2) an entity with the capacity to sue and be sued in its common name under applicable law, whether or not incorporated, shall be deemed to reside, if a defendant, in any judicial district in which such defendant is subject to the court's personal jurisdiction with respect to the civil action in question and, if a plaintiff, only in the judicial district in which it maintains its principal place of business; and

(3) a defendant not resident in the United States may be sued in any judicial district, and the joinder of such a defendant shall be disregarded in determining where the action may be brought with respect to other defendants.

(d) Residency of corporations in States with multiple districts. For purposes of venue under this chapter, in a State which has more than one judicial district and in which a defendant that is a corporation is subject to personal jurisdiction at the time an action is commenced, such corporation shall be deemed to reside in any district in that State within which its contacts would be sufficient to subject it to personal jurisdiction if that district were a separate State, and, if there is no such district, the corporation shall be deemed to reside in the district within which it has the most significant contacts.

(e) Actions where defendant is officer or employee of the United States.

(1) In general. A civil action in which a defendant is an officer or employee of the United States or any agency thereof acting in his official capacity or under color of legal authority, or an agency of the United States, or the United States, may, except as otherwise provided by law, be brought in any judicial district in which (A) a defendant in the action resides, (B) a substantial part of the events or omissions giving rise to the claim occurred, or a substantial part of property that is the subject of the action is situated, or (C) the plaintiff resides if no real property is involved in the action. Additional persons may be joined as parties to any such action in accordance with the Federal Rules of Civil Procedure and with such other venue requirements as would be applicable if the United States or one of its officers, employees, or agencies were not a party.

(2) Service. The summons and complaint in such an action shall be served as provided by the Federal Rules of Civil Procedure except that the delivery of the summons and complaint to the officer or agency as required by the rules may be made by certified mail beyond the territorial limits of the district in which the action is brought.

(f) Civil actions against a foreign state. A civil action against a foreign state as defined in section 1603(a) of this title may be brought--

    (1) in any judicial district in which a substantial part of the events or omissions giving rise to the claim occurred, or a substantial part of property that is the subject of the action is situated;

    (2) in any judicial district in which the vessel or cargo of a foreign state is situated, if the claim is asserted under section 1605(b) of this title;

    (3) in any judicial district in which the agency or instrumentality is licensed to do business or is doing business, if the action is brought against an agency or instrumentality of a foreign state as defined in section 1603(b) of this title; or

    (4) in the United States District Court for the District of Columbia if the action is brought against a foreign state or political subdivision thereof.

(g) Multiparty, multiforum litigation. A civil action in which jurisdiction of the district court is based upon section 1369 of this title may be brought in any district in which any defendant resides or in which a substantial part of the accident giving rise to the action took place.

28 USC § 2401.   Time for commencing action against United States.

(a) Except as provided by chapter 71 of title 41, every civil action commenced against the United States shall be barred unless the complaint is filed within six years after the right of action first accrues. The action of any person under legal disability or beyond the seas at the time the claim accrues may be commenced within three years after the disability ceases.

(b) A tort claim against the United States shall be forever barred unless it is presented in writing to the appropriate Federal agency within two years after such claim accrues or unless action is begun within six months after the date of mailing, by certified or registered mail, of notice of final denial of the claim by the agency to which it was presented.

28 USC § 2501.   Time for filing suit.

Every claim of which the United States Court of Federal Claims has jurisdiction shall be barred unless the petition thereon is filed within six years after such claim first accrues.

Every claim under section 1497 of this title shall be barred unless the petition thereon is filed within two years after the termination of the river and harbor improvements operations on which the claim is based.

A petition on the claim of a person under legal disability or beyond the seas at the time the claim accrues may be filed within three years after the disability ceases.

A suit for the fees of an officer of the United States shall not be filed until his account for such fees has been finally acted upon, unless the General Accounting Office [Government Accountability Office] fails to act within six months after receiving the account.

PART V

Rules of Practice and Procedure of the United States Tax Court
(Selected Provisions)

RULES OF PRACTICE AND PROCEDURE OF THE UNITED STATES TAX COURT

Rule 1. Rulemaking Authority; Scope of Rules; Publication of Rules and Amendments; Construction. (a) *Rulemaking authority.* The United States Tax Court, after giving appropriate public notice and an opportunity for comment, may make and amend rules governing its practice and procedure.

(b) *Scope of Rules.* These Rules govern the practice and procedure in all cases and proceedings before the Court. Where in any instance there is no applicable rule of procedure, the Court or the Judge before whom the matter is pending may prescribe the procedure, giving particular weight to the Federal Rules of Civil Procedure to the extent that they are suitably adaptable to govern the matter at hand.

(c) *Publication of Rules and Amendments.* When new rules or amendments to these rules are proposed by the Court, notice of such proposals and the ability of the public to comment shall be provided to the bar and to the general public and shall be posted on the Court's Internet Web site. If the Court determines that there is an immediate need for a particular rule or amendment to an existing rule, it may proceed without public notice and opportunity for comment, but the Court shall promptly thereafter afford such notice and opportunity for comment.

(d) *Construction.* The Court's Rules shall be construed to secure the just, speedy, and inexpensive determination of every case.

Rule 3. Definitions. (a) *Division.* The Chief Judge may from time to time divide the Court into Divisions of one or more Judges and, in case of a Division of more than one Judge, designate the chief thereof.

(b) *Clerk.* Reference to the Clerk in these Rules means the Clerk of the United States Tax Court.

(c) *Commissioner.* Reference to the Commissioner in these Rules means the Commissioner of Internal Revenue.

(d) *Special Trial Judge.* The term Special Trial Judge as used in these Rules refers to a judicial officer appointed pursuant to Code Section 7443A(a). See Rule 180.

(e) *Time.* As provided in these Rules and in orders and notices of the Court, time means standard time in the location mentioned except when advanced time is substituted therefor by law. For computation of time, see Rule 25.

(f) *Business Hours.* As to the Court's business hours, see Rule 10(d).

(g) *Filing.* For requirements as to filing with the Court, see Rule 22.

(h) *Code.* Any reference or citation to the Code relates to the Internal Revenue Code of 1986, as in effect for the relevant period or the relevant time.

Rule 10. Name, Office, and Sessions. (a) *Name.* The name of the Court is the United States Tax Court.

(b) *Office of Court.* The principal office of the Court shall be in the District of Columbia, but the Court or any of its Divisions may sit at any place within the United States. See Code Sections 7445 and 7701(a)(9).

(c) *Sessions.* The time and place of sessions of the Court shall be prescribed by the Chief Judge.

(d) *Business Hours.* The office of the Clerk at Washington, D.C., shall be open during business hours on all days, except Saturdays, Sundays, and Federal holidays, for the purpose of receiving petitions, pleadings, motions, and other papers. Business hours are from 8 a.m. to 4:30 p.m.

(e) *Mailing Address.* Mail to the Court should be addressed to the United States Tax Court, 400 Second Street, N. W., Washington, D. C. 20217. Other addresses, such as locations at which the Court may be in session, should not be used, unless the Court directs otherwise.

Rule 11. Payments to the Court. All payments to the Court for fees or charges of the Court shall be made either in cash or by check, money order, or other draft made payable to the order of "Clerk, United States Tax Court", and shall be mailed or delivered to the Clerk of the Court at Washington, D.C. The Court may also permit specified fees or charges to be paid by credit card. For the Court's address, see Rule 10(e). For particular payments, see Rules 12(c) (copies of Court records), 20(c) (filing of petition), 173(a)(2) (small tax cases), 200(a) (application to practice before Court), 200(g) (periodic registration fee), 271(c) (filing of petition for administrative costs), 281(c) (filing of petition for review of failure to abate interest), 291(d) (filing of petition for redetermination of employment status), 311(c) (filing of petition for declaratory judgment relating to treatment of items other than partnership items with respect to an oversheltered return), 321(d) (filing of petition for determination of relief from joint and several liability on a joint return), 331(d) (filing of petition for lien and levy action), and 341(c) (filing of petition for whistleblower action). For fees and charges payable to the Court, see Appendix II.

Rule 12. Court Records. (a) *Removal of Records.* No original record, paper, document, or exhibit filed with the Court shall be taken from the courtroom, from the offices of the Court, or from the custody of a Judge, a Special Trial Judge, or an employee of the Court, except as authorized by a Judge or Special Trial Judge of the Court or except as may be necessary for the Clerk to furnish copies or to transmit the same to other courts for appeal or other official purposes. With respect to return of exhibits after a decision of the Court becomes final, see Rule 143(e)(2).

(b) *Copies of Records.* After the Court renders its decision in a case, a plain or certified copy of any document, record, entry, or other paper, pertaining to the case and still in the custody of the Court, may be obtained upon application to the Court's Copywork Office and payment of the required fee. Unless otherwise permitted by the Court, no copy of any exhibit or original document in the files of the Court shall be furnished to other than the parties until the Court renders its decision. With respect to protective orders that may restrict the availability of exhibits and documents, see Code section 7461 and Rule 103(a).

(c) *Fees.* The fees to be charged and collected for any copies will be determined in accordance with Code section 7474. See Appendix II.

Rule 13. Jurisdiction. (a) *Notice of Deficiency or of Transferee or Fiduciary Liability Required.* Except in actions for declaratory judgment, for disclosure, for readjustment or adjustment of partnership items, for administrative costs, for review of failure to abate interest, for redetermination of employment status, for determination of relief from joint and several liability, for lien and levy, or for review of whistleblower awards (see Titles XXI, XXII, XXIV, and XXVI through XXXIII), the jurisdiction of the Court depends (1) in a case commenced in the Court by a taxpayer, upon the issuance by the Commissioner of a notice of deficiency in income, gift, or estate tax or, in the taxes under Code Chapter 41, 42, 43, or 44 (relating to the excise taxes on certain organizations and persons dealing with them), or in the tax under Code Chapter 45 (relating to the windfall profit tax), or in any other taxes which are the subject of the issuance of a notice of deficiency by the Commissioner; and (2) in a case commenced in the

Court by a transferee or fiduciary, upon the issuance by the Commissioner of a notice of liability to the transferee or fiduciary. See Code secs. 6212, 6213, and 6901.

(b) *Declaratory Judgment, Disclosure, Partnership, Administrative Costs, Review of Failure To Abate Interest, Redetermination of Employment Status, Determination of Relief From Joint and Several Liability, Lien and Levy, or Whistleblower Actions.* For the jurisdictional requirements in an action for declaratory judgment, for disclosure, for readjustment or adjustment of partnership items, for administrative costs, for review of failure to abate interest, for redetermination of employment status, for determination of relief from joint and several liability, for lien and levy, or for review of whistleblower awards, see Rules 210(c), 220(c), 240(c), 270(c), 280(b), 290(b), 300(c), 310(c), 320(b), 330(b), and 340(b).

(c) *Timely Petition Required.* In all cases, the jurisdiction of the Court also depends on the timely filing of a petition. See Code sections 6213, 7502; with respect to administrative costs actions, see Code section 7430(f); with respect to declaratory judgment actions, see Code sections 6234, 7428, 7476, 7477, 7478, and 7479; with respect to determination of relief from joint and liability actions, see Code section 6015(e); with respect to disclosure actions, see Code section 6110; with respect to lien and levy actions, see Code sections 6320 and 6330; with respect to partnership actions, see Code sections 6226, 6228, and 6247; with respect to redetermination of employment status actions, see Code section 7436; with respect to review of failure to abate interest actions, see Code section 6404(h); and with respect to whistleblower actions, see Code section 7623(b)(4).

(d) *Contempt of Court.* Contempt of Court may be punished by fine or imprisonment within the scope of Code section 7456(c).

(e) *Bankruptcy and Receivership.* With respect to the filing of a petition or the continuation of proceedings in this Court after the filing of a bankruptcy petition, see 11 U.S.C. section 362(a)(8) and Code section 6213(f)(1). With respect to the filing of a petition in this Court after the appointment of a receiver in a receivership proceeding, see Code section 6871(c)(2).

Rule 20. Commencement of Case. (a) *General.* A case is commenced in the Court by filing a petition with the Court, inter alia, to redetermine a deficiency set forth in a notice of deficiency issued by the Commissioner, or to redetermine the liability of a transferee or fiduciary set forth in a notice of liability issued by the Commissioner to the transferee or fiduciary, or to obtain a declaratory judgment, or to obtain or restrain a disclosure, or to adjust or readjust partnership items, or to obtain an award for reasonable administrative costs, or to obtain a review of the Commissioner's failure to abate interest. See Rule 13, Jurisdiction.

(b) *Statement of Taxpayer Identification Number.* The petitioner shall submit with the petition a statement of the petitioner's taxpayer identification number (e.g., Social Security number or employer identification number), or lack thereof. The statement shall be substantially in accordance with Form 4 shown in Appendix I.

(c) *Disclosure Statement.* A nongovernmental corporation, large partnership, or limited liability company, or a tax matters partner or partner other than the tax matters partner of a nongovernmental partnership filing a petition with the Court shall file with the petition a separate disclosure statement. In the case of a nongovernmental corporation, the disclosure statement shall identify any parent corporation and any publicly held entity owning 10 percent or more of petitioner's stock or state that there is no such entity. In the case of a nongovernmental large partnership or limited liability company, or a tax matters partner or partner other than a tax matters partner of a nongovernmental partnership, the disclosure statement shall identify any publicly held entity owning an interest in the large partnership, the limited liability company, or the partnership, or state that there is no such entity. A petitioner shall promptly file a supplemental statement if there is any change in the information required under this rule. For the form of such disclosure statement, see Form 6, Appendix I. For the definition of a large partnership, see Rule 300(b)(1). For the definitions of a partnership and a tax matters partner, see Rule 240(b)(1), (4). A partner other than a tax matters partner is a notice partner or a 5-percent group as defined in Rule 240(b)(8) and (9).

(d) *Filing Fee.* At the time of filing a petition, a fee of $60 shall be paid. The payment of any fee under this paragraph may be waived if the petitioner establishes to the satisfaction of the Court by an affidavit containing specific financial information the inability to make such payment.

Rule 21. Service of Papers. (a) *When Required.* Except as otherwise required by these Rules or directed by the Court, all pleadings, motions, orders, decisions, notices, demands, briefs, appearances, or other similar documents or papers relating to a case, including a disciplinary matter under Rule 202, also referred to as the papers in a case, shall be served on each of the parties or other persons involved in the matter to which the paper relates other than the party who filed the paper.

(b) *Manner of Service.* (1) *General.* All petitions shall be served by the Clerk. Unless otherwise provided in these Rules or directed by the Court, all other papers required to be served on a party shall be served by the party filing the paper, and the original paper shall be filed with a certificate by a party or a party's counsel that service of that paper has been made on the party to be served or such party's counsel. For the form of such certificate of service, see Form 9, Appendix I. Such service may be made by:

(A) Mail directed to the party or the party's counsel at such person's last known address. Service by mail is complete upon mailing, and the date of such mailing shall be the date of such service.

(B) Delivery to a party, or a party's counsel or authorized representative in the case of a party other than an individual (see Rule 24(b)).

(C) Mail directed or delivery to the Commissioner's counsel at the office address shown in the Commissioner's answer filed in the case or a motion filed in lieu of an answer. If no answer or motion in lieu of an answer has been filed, then mail shall be directed or delivered to the Chief Counsel, Internal Revenue Service, Washington, D.C. 20224.

(D) Electronic means if the person served consented in writing, in which event service is complete upon transmission, but is not effective if the serving party learns that it did not reach the person to be served.

Service on a person other than a party shall be made in the same manner as service on a party, except as otherwise provided in these Rules or directed by the Court. In cases consolidated pursuant to Rule 141, a party making service of a paper shall serve each of the other parties or counsel for each of the other parties, and the original and copies thereof required to be filed with the Court shall each have a certificate of service attached.

(2) *Counsel of Record.* Whenever under these Rules service is required or permitted to be made upon a party represented by counsel who has entered an appearance, service shall be made upon such counsel unless service upon the party is directed by the Court. Where more than one counsel appear for a party, service is required to be made only on that counsel whose appearance was first entered of record, unless that counsel notifies the Court, by a designation of counsel to

receive service filed with the Court, that other counsel of record is to receive service, in which event service is required to be made only on the person so designated.

(3) *Writs and Process.* Service and execution of writs, process, or similar directives of the Court may be made by a United States marshal, by a deputy marshal, or by a person specially appointed by the Court for that purpose, except that a subpoena may be served as provided in Rule 147(c). The person making service shall make proof thereof to the Court promptly and in any event within the time in which the person served must respond. Failure to make proof of service does not affect the validity of the service.

(4) *Change of Address.* The Court shall be promptly notified, by a notice of change of address filed with the Court, of the change of mailing address of any party, any party's counsel, or any party's duly authorized representative in the case of a party other than an individual (see Rule 24(a)(2), (a)(3), (b), and (d)). A separate notice of change of address shall be filed for each docket number. For the form of such notice of change of address, see Form 10 in Appendix I.

(5) *Using Court Transmission Facilities.* A party may make service under Rule 21(b)(1)(D) through the Court's transmission facilities pursuant to electronic service procedures prescribed by the Court.

Rule 22. Filing. Any pleadings or other papers to be filed with the Court must be filed with the Clerk in Washington, D.C., during business hours, except that the Judge or Special Trial Judge presiding at any trial or hearing may permit or require documents pertaining thereto to be filed at that particular session of the Court, or except as otherwise directed by the Court. For the circumstances under which timely mailed papers will be treated as having been timely filed, see Code section 7502.

Rule 23. Form and Style of Papers. (a) *Caption, Date, and Signature Required.* All papers filed with the Court shall have a caption, shall be dated, and shall be signed as follows:

(1) *Caption.* A proper caption shall be placed on all papers filed with the Court, and the requirements provided in Rule 32(a) shall be satisfied with respect to all such papers. All prefixes and titles, such as "Mr.", "Ms.", or "Dr.", shall be omitted from the caption. The full name and surname of each individual petitioner shall be set forth in the caption. The name of an estate or trust or other person for whom a fiduciary acts shall precede the fiduciary's name and title, as for example "Estate of Mary Doe, deceased, Richard Roe, Executor".

(2) *Date.* The date of signature shall be placed on all papers filed with the Court.

(3) *Signature.* The original signature, either of the party or the party's counsel, shall be subscribed in writing to the original of every paper filed by or for that party with the Court, except as otherwise provided by these Rules. An individual rather than a firm name shall be used, except that the signature of a petitioner corporation or unincorporated association shall be in the name of the corporation or association by one of its active and authorized officers or members, as for example "Mary Doe, Inc., by Richard Roe, President". The name, mailing address, and telephone number of the party or the party's counsel, as well as counsel's Tax Court bar number, shall be typed or printed immediately beneath the written signature. The mailing address of a signatory shall include a firm name if it is an essential part of the accurate mailing address.

(b) *Number Filed.* For each paper filed in Court, there shall be filed four conformed copies together with the signed original thereof, except as otherwise provided in these Rules. Where filing is in more than one case (as a motion to consolidate, or in cases already consolidated), the number filed shall include one additional copy for each docket number in excess of one. If service of a paper is to be made by the Clerk, copies of any attachments to the original of such paper shall be attached to each copy to be served by the Clerk. As to stipulations, see Rule 91(b).

(c) *Legible Papers Required.* Papers filed with the Court may be prepared by any process, but only if all papers, including copies, filed with the Court are clear and legible.

(d) *Size and Style.* Typewritten or printed papers shall be typed or printed only on one side, on opaque, unglazed paper, 8 1/2 inches wide by 11 inches long. All such papers shall have margins on both sides of each page that are no less than 1 inch wide, and margins on the top and bottom of each page that are no less than 3/4 inch wide. Text and footnotes shall appear in consistent typeface no smaller than 12 characters per inch produced by a typewriting element or 12-point type produced by a nonproportional print font (e. g., Courier), with double spacing between each line of text and single spacing between each line of indented quotations and footnotes. Quotations in excess of five lines shall be set off from the surrounding text and indented. Double-spaced lines shall be no more than three lines to the vertical inch, and single-spaced lines shall be no more than six lines to the vertical inch.

(e) *Binding and Covers.* All papers shall be bound together on the upper left-hand side only and shall have no backs or covers.

(f) *Citations.* All citations of case names shall be underscored when typewritten, and shall be in italics when printed.

(g) *Acceptance by the Clerk.* Except as otherwise directed by the Court, the Clerk must not refuse to file a paper solely because it is not in the form prescribed by these Rules.

Rule 24. Appearance and Representation. (a) *Appearance.* (1) *General.* Counsel may enter an appearance either by subscribing the petition or other initial pleading or document in accordance with subparagraph (2) hereof, or thereafter by filing an entry of appearance in accordance with subparagraph (3) hereof or, in a case not calendared for trial or hearing, a substitution of counsel in accordance with paragraph (d) hereof.

(2) *Appearance in Initial Pleading.* If (A) the petition or other paper initiating the participation of a party in a case is subscribed by counsel admitted to practice before the Court, and (B) such initial paper contains the mailing address and Tax Court bar number of counsel and other information required for entry of appearance (see subparagraph (3)), then (C) that counsel shall be recognized as representing that party and no separate entry of appearance shall be necessary. Thereafter counsel shall be required to notify the Clerk of any changes in applicable information to the same extent as if counsel had filed a separate entry of appearance.

(3) *Subsequent Appearance.* Where counsel has not previously appeared, counsel shall file an entry of appearance in duplicate, signed by counsel individually, containing the name and docket number of the case, the name, mailing address, telephone number, and Tax Court bar number of counsel so appearing, and a statement that counsel is admitted to practice before the Court. A separate entry of appearance, in duplicate, shall be filed for each additional docket number in which counsel shall appear. The entry of appearance shall be substantially in the form set forth in Appendix I. The Clerk shall be given prompt written notice, filed in duplicate for each docket number, of any change in the foregoing information.

(4) *Counsel Not Admitted to Practice.* No entry of appearance by counsel not admitted to practice before this Court will be effective until counsel shall have been admitted, but counsel may be recognized as counsel in a pending case to the extent permitted by the Court and then only where it appears that counsel can and will be promptly admitted. For the procedure for

admission to practice before the Court, see Rule 200.

(5) *Law Student Assistance.* With the permission of the presiding Judge or Special Trial Judge, and under the direct supervision of counsel in a case, a law student may assist such counsel by presenting all or any part of the party's case at a hearing or trial. In addition, a law student may assist counsel in a case in drafting a pleading or other document to be filed with the Court. A law student may not, however, enter an appearance in any case, be recognized as counsel in a case, or sign a pleading or other document filed with the Court. The Court may acknowledge the law student assistance.

(b) *Personal Representation Without Counsel.* In the absence of appearance by counsel, a party will be deemed to appear on the party's own behalf. An individual party may represent himself or herself. A corporation or an unincorporated association may be represented by an authorized officer of the corporation or by an authorized member of the association. An estate or trust may be represented by a fiduciary thereof. Any such person shall state, in the initial pleading or other paper filed by or for the party, such person's name, address, and telephone number, and thereafter shall promptly notify the Clerk in writing, in duplicate for each docket number involving that party, of any change in that information.

(c) *Withdrawal of Counsel.* Counsel of record desiring to withdraw such counsel's appearance, or any party desiring to withdraw the appearance of counsel of record for such party, must file a motion with the Court requesting leave therefor, showing that prior notice of the motion has been given by such counsel to such counsel's client, or such party's counsel, as the case may be, and to each of the other parties to the case or their counsel, and stating whether there is any objection to the motion. A motion to withdraw as counsel and a motion to withdraw counsel shall each also state the then current mailing address and telephone number of the party in respect of whom or by whom the motion is filed. The Court may, in its discretion, deny such motion.

(d) *Substitution of Counsel.* In a case not calendared for trial or hearing, counsel of record for a party may withdraw such counsel's appearance, and counsel who has not previously appeared may enter an appearance, by filing a substitution of counsel, showing that prior notice of the substitution has been given by counsel of record to such counsel's client, and to each of the other parties to the case or their counsel, and that there is no objection to the substitution. The substitution of counsel shall be signed by counsel of record and substituted counsel individually, and shall contain the information required by subparagraph (3) of paragraph (a). The substitution of counsel shall be substantially in the form set forth in Appendix I. Thereafter substituted counsel shall be required to notify the Clerk of any changes in applicable information to the same extent as if such counsel had filed a separate entry of appearance.

(e) *Death of Counsel.* If counsel of record dies, the Court shall be so notified, and other counsel may enter an appearance in accordance with this Rule.

(f) *Change in Party or Authorized Representative or Fiduciary.* Where (1) a party other than an individual participates in a case through an authorized representative (such as an officer of a corporation or a member of an association) or through a fiduciary, and there is a change in such representative or fiduciary, or (2) there is a substitution of parties in a pending case, counsel subscribing the motion resulting in the Court's approval of the change or substitution shall thereafter be deemed first counsel of record for the representative, fiduciary, or party. Counsel of record for the former representative, fiduciary, or party, desiring to withdraw such counsel's appearance shall file a motion in accordance with paragraph (c).

(g) *Conflict of Interest.* If any counsel of record (1) was involved in planning or promoting a transaction or operating an entity that is connected to any issue in a case, (2) represents more than one person with differing interests with respect to any issue in a case, or (3) is a potential witness in a case, then such counsel must either secure the informed consent of the client (but only as to items (1) and (2)); withdraw from the case; or take whatever other steps are necessary to obviate a conflict of interest or other violation of the ABA Model Rules of Professional Conduct, and particularly Rules 1.7, 1.8, and 3.7 thereof. The Court may inquire into the circumstances of counsel's employment in order to deter such violations. See Rule 201.

Rule 25. Computation of Time. (a) *Computation.* (1) *General.* In computing any period of time prescribed or allowed by these Rules or by direction of the Court or by any applicable statute which does not provide otherwise, the day of the act, event, or default from which a designated period of time begins to run shall not be included, and (except as provided in subparagraph (2)) the last day of the period so computed shall be included. If service is made by mail, then a period of time computed with respect to the service shall begin on the day after the date of mailing.

(2) *Saturdays, Sundays, and Holidays.* Saturdays, Sundays, and all legal holidays shall be counted, except that, (A) if the period prescribed or allowed is less than 7 days, then intermediate Saturdays, Sundays, and legal holidays in the District of Columbia shall be excluded in the computation; (B) if the last day of the period so computed is a Saturday, Sunday, or a legal holiday in the District of Columbia, then that day shall not be included and the period shall run until the end of the next day which is not a Saturday, Sunday, or such a legal holiday; and (C) if any act is required to be taken or completed no later than (or at least) a specified number of days before a date certain, then the earliest day of the period so specified shall not be included if it is a Saturday, Sunday, or a legal holiday in the District of Columbia, and the earliest such day shall be the next preceding day which is not a Saturday, Sunday, or such a legal holiday. When such a legal holiday falls on a Sunday, the next day shall be considered a holiday; and, when such a legal holiday falls on a Saturday, the preceding day shall be considered a holiday.

(3) *Cross-references.* For computation of the period within which to file a petition with the Court to redetermine a deficiency or liability, see Code section 6213; for the period within which to file a petition in a declaratory judgment action, see Code sections 7428, 7476, and 7478; for the period within which to file a petition in a disclosure action, see Code section 6110; for the period within which to file a petition in a partnership action, see Code sections 6226 and 6228; and for the period within which to file a petition in a review of failure to abate interest action, see Code section 6404(h). See also Code sec. 7502.

(b) *District of Columbia Legal Holidays.* The legal holidays within the District of Columbia, in addition to any other day appointed as a holiday by the President or the Congress of the United States, are as follows:

New Year's Day--January 1
Birthday of Martin Luther King, Jr.--Third Monday in January
Inauguration Day--Every fourth year
Washington's Birthday--Third Monday in February
District of Columbia Emancipation Day--April 16
Memorial Day--Last Monday in May
Independence Day--July 4
Labor Day--First Monday in September

Columbus Day--Second Monday in October
Veterans Day--November 11
Thanksgiving Day--Fourth Thursday in November
Christmas Day--December 25

(c) *Enlargement or Reduction of Time.* Unless precluded by statute, the Court in its discretion may make longer or shorter any period provided by these Rules. As to continuances, see Rule 133. Where a motion is made concerning jurisdiction or the sufficiency of a pleading, the time for filing a response to that pleading shall begin to run from the date of service of the order disposing of the motion by the Court, unless the Court shall direct otherwise. Where the dates for filing briefs are fixed, an extension of time for filing a brief or the granting of leave to file a brief after the due date shall correspondingly extend the time for filing any other brief due at the same time and for filing succeeding briefs, unless the Court shall order otherwise. The period fixed by statute, within which to file a petition with the Court, cannot be extended by the Court.

(d) *Miscellaneous.* With respect to the computation of time, see also Rule 3(e) (definition), Rule 10(d) (business hours of the Court), Rule 13(c) (filing of petition), and Rule 133 (continuances).

Rule 26. Electronic Filing. (a) *General.* The Court will accept for filing papers submitted, signed, or verified by electronic means that comply with procedures established by the Court. A paper filed electronically in compliance with the Court's electronic filing procedures is a written paper for purposes of these Rules.

(b) *Electronic Filing Requirement.* Electronic filing is required for all papers filed by parties represented by counsel in open cases. Mandatory electronic filing does not apply to:

(1) Petitions and other papers not eligible for electronic filing in the Court (for a complete list of those papers, see the Court's eFiling Instructions on the Court's Web site at www.ustaxcourt.gov);

(2) Self-represented petitioners, including petitioners assisted by low-income taxpayer clinics and Bar-sponsored pro bono programs; and

(3) Any counsel in a case who, upon motion filed in paper form and for good cause shown, is granted an exception from the electronic filing requirement. Because a motion for exception does not extend any period provided by these Rules, the motion shall be accompanied by any document sought to be filed in paper form.

Rule 27. Privacy Protection for Filings Made With the Court. (a) *Redacted Filings.* Except as otherwise required by these Rules or directed by the Court, in an electronic or paper filing with the Court, a party or nonparty making the filing should refrain from including or should take appropriate steps to redact the following information:

(1) *Taxpayer identification numbers* (e.g., Social Security numbers or employer identification numbers);

(2) *Dates of birth.* If a date of birth is provided, only the year should appear;

(3) *Names of minor children.* If a minor child is identified, only the minor child's initials should appear; and

(4) *Financial account numbers.* If a financial account number is provided, only the last four digits of the number should appear.

(b) *Limitations on Remote Access to Electronic Files.* Except as otherwise directed by the Court, access to an electronic file is authorized as follows:

(1) The parties and their counsel may have remote electronic access to any part of the case file maintained by the Court in electronic form; and

(2) Any other person may have electronic access at the courthouse to the public record maintained by the Court in electronic form, but may have remote electronic access only to:

(A) the docket record maintained by the Court; and

(B) any opinion, order, or decision of the Court, but not any other part of the case file.

(c) *Filings Made Under Seal.* The Court may order that a filing containing any of the information described in paragraph (a) of this Rule be made under seal without redaction. The Court may later unseal the filing or order the person who made the filing to file a redacted version for the public record.

(d) *Protective Orders.* For good cause, the Court may by order in a case:

(1) Require redaction of additional information; or

(2) Issue a protective order as provided by Rule 103(a).

(e) *Option for Additional Unredacted Filing Under Seal.* A person making a redacted filing may also file an unredacted copy under seal. The Court must retain the unredacted copy as part of the record.

(f) *Option for Filing a Reference List.* A document that contains redacted information may be filed together with a reference list that identifies each item of redacted information and specifies an appropriate identifier that uniquely corresponds to each item listed. The list must be filed with a motion to seal and may be amended as of right. Any reference in the case to a listed identifier will be construed to refer to the corresponding item of information.

(g) *Waiver of Protection of Identifiers.* A person waives the protection of this Rule as to the person's own information by filing it without redaction and not under seal. The Clerk of the Court is not required to review documents filed with the Court for compliance with this Rule. The responsibility to redact a filing rests with the party or nonparty making the filing.

(h) *Inadvertent Waiver.* A party may correct an inadvertent disclosure of identifying information in a prior filing by submitting a properly redacted substitute filing within 60 days of the original filing without leave of Court, and thereafter only by leave of Court.

Rule 30. Pleadings Allowed. There shall be a petition and an answer, and, where required under these Rules, a reply. No other pleading shall be allowed, except that the Court may permit or direct some other responsive pleading. (See Rule 173 as to small tax cases.)

Rule 31. General Rules of Pleading. (a) *Purpose.* The purpose of the pleadings is to give the parties and the Court fair notice of the matters in controversy and the basis for their respective positions.

(b) *Pleading to be Concise and Direct.* Each averment of a pleading shall be simple, concise, and direct. No technical forms of pleading are required.

(c) *Consistency.* A party may set forth two or more statements of a claim or defense alternatively or hypothetically. When two or more statements are made in the alternative and one of them would be sufficient if made independently, the pleading is not made insufficient by the insufficiency of one or more of the alternative statements. A party may state as many separate claims or defenses as the party has regardless of consistency or the grounds on which based. All statements shall be made subject to the signature requirements of Rules 23(a)(3) and 33.

(d) *Construction of Pleadings.* All pleadings shall be so construed as to do substantial justice.

Rule 32. Form of Pleadings. (a) *Caption; Names of Parties.* Every pleading shall contain a caption setting forth the name of the Court (United States Tax Court), the title of the case, the docket number after it becomes available (see Rule 35), and a designation to show the nature of the pleading. In the petition, the title of the case shall include the names of all parties, but shall not include as a party-petitioner the name of any person other than the person or persons by or on whose behalf the petition is filed. In other pleadings, it is sufficient to state the name of the first party with an appropriate indication of other parties.

(b) *Separate Statement.* All averments of claim or defense, and all statements in support thereof, shall be made in separately designated paragraphs, the contents of each of which shall be limited as far as practicable to a statement of a single item or a single set of circumstances. Such paragraph may be referred to by that designation in all succeeding pleadings. Each claim and defense shall be stated separately whenever a separation facilitates the clear presentation of the matters set forth.

(c) *Adoption by Reference; Exhibits.* Statements in a pleading may be adopted by reference in a different part of the same pleading or in another pleading or in any motion. A copy of any written instrument which is an exhibit to a pleading is a part thereof for all purposes.

(d) *Other Provisions.* With respect to other provisions relating to the form and style of papers filed with the Court, see Rules 23, 56(a), 57(a), 210(d), 220(d), 240(d), 300(d), and 320(c).

Rule 33. Signing of Pleadings. (a) *Signature.* Each pleading shall be signed in the manner provided in Rule 23. Where there is more than one attorney of record, the signature of only one is required. Except when otherwise specifically directed by the Court, pleadings need not be verified or accompanied by affidavit or declaration.

(b) *Effect of Signature.* The signature of counsel or a party constitutes a certificate by the signer that the signer has read the pleading, that, to the best of the signer's knowledge, information, and belief formed after reasonable inquiry, it is well grounded in fact and is warranted by existing law or a good faith argument for the extension, modification, or reversal of existing law, and that it is not interposed for any improper purpose, such as to harass or to cause unnecessary delay or needless increase in the cost of litigation. The signature of counsel also constitutes a representation by counsel that counsel is authorized to represent the party or parties on whose behalf the pleading is filed. If a pleading is not signed, it shall be stricken, unless it is signed promptly after the omission is called to the attention of the pleader. If a pleading is signed in violation of this Rule, the Court, upon motion or upon its own initiative, may impose upon the person who signed it, a represented party, or both, an appropriate sanction, which may include an order to pay to the other party or parties the amount of the reasonable expenses incurred because of the filing of the pleading, including reasonable counsel's fees.

Rule 34. Petition. (a) *General.* (1) *Deficiency or Liability Actions.* The petition with respect to a notice of deficiency or a notice of liability shall be substantially in accordance with Form 1 shown in Appendix I, and shall comply with the requirements of these Rules relating to pleadings. Ordinarily, a separate petition shall be filed with respect to each notice of deficiency or each notice of liability. However, a single petition may be filed seeking a redetermination with respect to all notices of deficiency or liability directed to one person alone or to such person and one or more other persons or to a husband and a wife individually, except that the Court may require a severance and a separate case to be maintained with respect to one or more of such notices. Where the notice of deficiency or liability is directed to more than one person, each such person desiring to contest it shall file a petition, either separately or jointly with any such other person, and each such person must satisfy all the requirements of this Rule in order for the petition to be treated as filed by or for such person. The petition shall be complete, so as to enable ascertainment of the issues intended to be presented. No telegram, cablegram, radiogram, telephone call, electronically transmitted copy, or similar communication will be recognized as a petition. Failure of the petition to satisfy applicable requirements may be ground for dismissal of the case. As to the joinder of parties, see Rule 61; and as to the effect of misjoinder of parties, see Rule 62. For the circumstances under which a timely mailed petition will be treated as having been timely filed, see Code section 7502.

(2) *Other Actions.* For the requirements relating to the petitions in other actions, see the following Rules: Declaratory judgment actions, Rules 211(b), 311(b); disclosure actions, Rule 221(b); partnership actions, Rules 241(b), 301(b); administrative costs actions, Rule 271(b); abatement of interest actions, Rule 281(b); redetermination of employment status actions, Rule 291(b); determination of relief from joint and several liability on a joint return actions, Rule 321(b); lien and levy actions, Rule 331(b); and whistleblower actions, Rule 341(b). As to joinder of parties in declaratory judgment actions, in disclosure actions, and in partnership actions, see Rules 215, 226, and 241(h) and 301(f), respectively.

(b) *Content of Petition in Deficiency or Liability Actions.* The petition in a deficiency or liability action shall contain (see Form 1, Appendix I):

(1) In the case of a petitioner who is an individual, the petitioner's name and State of legal residence; in the case of a petitioner other than an individual, the petitioner's name and principal place of business or principal office or agency; and, in all cases, the petitioner's mailing address and the office of the Internal Revenue Service with which the tax return for the period in controversy was filed. The mailing address, State of legal residence, principal place of business, or principal office or agency shall be stated as of the date of filing the petition. In the event of a variance between the name set forth in the notice of deficiency or liability and the correct name, a statement of the reasons for such variance shall be set forth in the petition.

(2) The date of the notice of deficiency or liability, or other proper allegations showing jurisdiction in the Court, and the city and State of the office of the Internal Revenue Service which issued the notice.

(3) The amount of the deficiency or liability, as the case may be, determined by the Commissioner, the nature of the tax, the year or years or other periods for which the determination was made; and, if different from the Commissioner's determination, the approximate amount of taxes in controversy.

(4) Clear and concise assignments of each and every error which the petitioner alleges to have been committed by the Commissioner in the determination of the deficiency or liability. The assignments of error shall include issues in respect of which the burden of proof is on the Commissioner. Any issue not raised in the assignments of error shall be deemed to be conceded. Each assignment of error shall be separately lettered.

(5) Clear and concise lettered statements of the facts on which the petitioner bases the assignments of error, except with respect to those assignments of error as to which the burden of proof is on the Commissioner.

(6) A prayer setting forth relief sought by the petitioner.

(7) The signature, mailing address, and telephone number of each petitioner or each petitioner's counsel, as well as counsel's Tax Court bar number.

(8) A copy of the notice of deficiency or liability, as the case may be, which shall be

appended to the petition, and with which there shall be included so much of any statement accompanying the notice as is material to the issues raised by the assignments of error. If the notice of deficiency or liability or accompanying statement incorporates by reference any prior notices, or other material furnished by the Internal Revenue Service, such parts thereof as are material to the issues raised by the assignments of error likewise shall be appended to the petition. A claim for reasonable litigation or administrative costs shall not be included in the petition in a deficiency or liability action. For the requirements as to claims for reasonable litigation or administrative costs, see Rule 231.

(c) *Content of Petition in Other Actions.* For the requirements as to the content of the petition in a small tax case, see Rule 173(a). For the requirements as to the content of the petition in other actions, see Rule 211(c), (d), (e), (f), and (g), Rule 221(c), (d), and (e), Rule 241(c), (d), and (e), Rule 271(b), Rule 281(b), Rule 291(b), Rule 301(b), Rule 311(b), Rule 321(b), Rule 331(b), and Rule 341(b).

(d) *Use of Form 2 Petition.* The use of a properly completed Form 2 petition satisfies the requirements of this Rule.

(e) *Original Required.* Notwithstanding Rule 23(b), only the signed original of each petition is required to be filed.

Rule 35. Entry on Docket. Upon receipt of the petition by the Clerk, the case will be entered upon the docket and assigned a number, and the parties will be notified thereof by the Clerk. The docket number shall be placed by the parties on all papers thereafter filed in the case, and shall be referred to in all correspondence with the Court.

Rule 36. Answer. (a) *Time to Answer or Move.* The Commissioner shall have 60 days from the date of service of the petition within which to file an answer, or 45 days from that date within which to move with respect to the petition. With respect to an amended petition or amendments to the petition, the Commissioner shall have like periods from the date of service of those papers within which to answer or move in response thereto, except as the Court may otherwise direct.

(b) *Form and Content.* The answer shall be drawn so that it will advise the petitioner and the Court fully of the nature of the defense. It shall contain a specific admission or denial of each material allegation in the petition; however, if the Commissioner shall be without knowledge or information sufficient to form a belief as to the truth of an allegation, then the Commissioner shall so state, and such statement shall have the effect of a denial. If the Commissioner intends to qualify or to deny only a part of an allegation, then the Commissioner shall specify so much of it as is true and shall qualify or deny only the remainder. In addition, the answer shall contain a clear and concise statement of every ground, together with the facts in support thereof on which the Commissioner relies and has the burden of proof. Paragraphs of the answer shall be designated to correspond to those of the petition to which they relate.

(c) *Effect of Answer.* Every material allegation set out in the petition and not expressly admitted or denied in the answer shall be deemed to be admitted.

(d) *Declaratory Judgment, Disclosure, and Administrative Costs Actions.* For the requirements applicable to the answer in declaratory judgment actions, in disclosure actions, and in administrative costs actions, see Rules 213(a), 223(a), and 272(a), respectively.

Rule 37. Reply. (a) *Time to Reply or Move.* The petitioner shall have 45 days from the date of service of the answer within which to file a reply, or 30 days from that date within which to move with respect to the answer. With respect to an amended answer or amendments to the answer the petitioner shall have like periods from the date of service of those papers within which to reply or move in response thereto, except as the Court may otherwise direct.

(b) *Form and Content.* In response to each material allegation in the answer and the facts in support thereof on which the Commissioner has the burden of proof, the reply shall contain a specific admission or denial; however, if the petitioner shall be without knowledge or information sufficient to form a belief as to the truth of an allegation, then the petitioner shall so state, and such statement shall have the effect of a denial. In addition, the reply shall contain a clear and concise statement of every ground, together with the facts in support thereof, on which the petitioner relies affirmatively or in avoidance of any matter in the answer on which the Commissioner has the burden of proof. In other respects the requirements of pleading applicable to the answer provided in Rule 36(b) shall apply to the reply. The paragraphs of the reply shall be designated to correspond to those of the answer to which they relate.

(c) *Effect of Reply or Failure Thereof.* Where a reply is filed, every affirmative allegation set out in the answer and not expressly admitted or denied in the reply shall be deemed to be admitted. Where a reply is not filed, the affirmative allegations in the answer will be deemed denied unless the Commissioner, within 45 days after expiration of the time for filing the reply, files a motion that specified allegations in the answer be deemed admitted. That motion may be granted unless the required reply is filed within the time directed by the Court.

(d) *New Material.* Any new material contained in the reply shall be deemed to be denied.

(e) *Declaratory Judgment, Disclosure, and Administrative Costs Actions.* For the requirements applicable to the reply in declaratory judgment actions and in disclosure actions, see Rules 213(b) and 223(b), respectively. See Rule 272(b) with respect to replies in actions for administrative costs.

Rule 38. Joinder of Issue. A case shall be deemed at issue upon the filing of the answer, unless a reply is required under Rule 37, in which event it shall be deemed at issue upon the filing of a reply or the entry of an order disposing of a motion under Rule 37(c) or the expiration of the period specified in Rule 37(c) in case the Commissioner fails to move. With respect to declaratory judgment actions, disclosure actions, partnership actions, administrative costs actions, and actions for determination of relief from joint and several liability on a joint return, see Rules 214, 224, 244, 273, and 324, respectively.

Rule 39. Pleading Special Matters. A party shall set forth in the party's pleading any matter constituting an avoidance or affirmative defense, including res judicata, collateral estoppel, estoppel, waiver, duress, fraud, and the statute of limitations. A mere denial in a responsive pleading will not be sufficient to raise any such issue.

Rule 40. Defenses and Objections Made by Pleading or Motion. Every defense, in law or fact, to a claim for relief in any pleading shall be asserted in the responsive pleading thereto if one is required, except that the following defenses may, at the option of the pleader, be made by motion: (a) lack of jurisdiction, and (b) failure to state a claim upon which relief can be granted. If a pleading sets forth a claim for relief to which the adverse party is not required to file a responsive pleading, then such party may assert at the trial any defense in law or fact to that claim for relief. If, on a motion asserting failure to state a claim on which relief can be granted, matters outside the pleading are to be presented, then the motion shall be treated as one for summary judgment and disposed of as provided in Rule 121, and the parties shall be given an opportunity to present all material made pertinent to a motion under Rule 121.

Rule 41. Amended and Supplemental Pleadings. (a) *Amendments.* A party may amend a pleading once as a matter of course at any time before a responsive pleading is served. If the pleading is one to which no responsive pleading is permitted and the case has not been placed on a trial calendar, then a party may so amend it at any time within 30 days after it is served. Otherwise a party may amend a pleading only by leave of Court or by written consent of the adverse party, and leave shall be given freely when justice so requires. No amendment shall be allowed after expiration of the time for filing the petition, however, which would involve conferring jurisdiction on the Court over a matter which otherwise would not come within its jurisdiction under the petition as then on file. A motion for leave to amend a pleading shall state the reasons for the amendment and shall be accompanied by the proposed amendment. The amendment to the pleading shall not be incorporated into the motion but rather shall be separately set forth and consistent with the requirements of Rule 23 regarding form and style of papers filed with the Court. See Rules 36(a) and 37(a) for time for responding to amended pleadings.

(b) *Amendments to Conform to the Evidence.* (1) *Issues Tried by Consent.* When issues not raised by the pleadings are tried by express or implied consent of the parties, they shall be treated in all respects as if they had been raised in the pleadings. The Court, upon motion of any party at any time, may allow such amendment of the pleadings as may be necessary to cause them to conform to the evidence and to raise these issues, but failure to amend does not affect the result of the trial of these issues.

(2) *Other Evidence.* If evidence is objected to at the trial on the ground that it is not within the issues raised by pleadings, then the Court may receive the evidence and at any time allow the pleadings to be amended to conform to the proof, and shall do so freely when justice so requires and the objecting party fails to satisfy the Court that the admission of such evidence would prejudice such party in maintaining such party's position on the merits.

(3) *Filing.* The amendment or amended pleadings permitted under this paragraph (b) shall be filed with the Court at the trial or shall be filed with the Clerk at Washington, D. C., within such time as the Court may fix.

(c) *Supplemental Pleadings.* Upon motion of a party, the Court may, upon such terms as are just, permit a party to file a supplemental pleading setting forth transactions or occurrences or events which have happened since the date of the pleading sought to be supplemented. Permission may be granted even though the original pleading is defective in its statements of a claim for relief or defense. If the Court deems it advisable that the adverse party plead to the supplemental pleading, then it shall so direct, specifying the time therefor.

(d) *Relation Back of Amendments.* When an amendment of a pleading is permitted, it shall relate back to the time of filing of that pleading, unless the Court shall order otherwise either on motion of a party or on its own initiative.

Rule 50. General Requirements. (a) *Form and Content of Motion.* An application to the Court for an order shall be by motion in writing, which shall state with particularity the grounds therefor and shall set forth the relief or order sought. The motion shall show that prior notice thereof has been given to each other party or counsel for each other party and shall state whether there is any objection to the motion. If a motion does not include such a statement, the Court will assume that there is an objection to the motion. Unless the Court directs otherwise, motions made during a hearing or trial need not be in writing. The rules applicable to captions, signing, and other matters of form and style of pleadings apply to all written motions. See Rules 23, 32, and 33(a). The effect of a signature on a motion shall be as set forth in Rule 33(b).

(b) *Disposition of Motions.* A motion may be disposed of in one or more of the following ways, in the discretion of the Court:

(1) The Court may take action after directing that a written response be filed. In that event, the opposing party shall file such response within such period as the Court may direct. Written response to a motion shall conform to the same requirements of form and style as apply to motions.

(2) The Court may take action after directing a hearing, which may be held in Washington, D.C. The Court may, on its own motion or upon the written request of any party to the motion, direct that the hearing be held at some other location which serves the convenience of the parties and the Court.

(3) The Court may take such action as the Court in its discretion deems appropriate, on such prior notice, if any, which the Court may consider reasonable. The action of the Court may be taken with or without written response, hearing, or attendance of a party to the motion at the hearing.

(c) *Attendance at Hearings.* If a motion is noticed for hearing, then a party to the motion may, prior to or at the time for such hearing, submit a written statement of such party's position together with any supporting documents. Such statement may be submitted in lieu of or in addition to attendance at the hearing.

(d) *Defects in Pleading.* Where the motion or order is directed to defects in a pleading, prompt filing of a proper pleading correcting the defects may obviate the necessity of a hearing thereon.

(e) *Postponement of Trial.* The filing of a motion shall not constitute cause for postponement of a trial. With respect to motions for continuance, see Rule 133.

(f) *Effect of Orders.* Orders shall not be treated as precedent, except as may be relevant for purposes of establishing the law of the case, res judicata, collateral estoppel, or other similar doctrine.

Rule 53. Motion to Dismiss. A case may be dismissed for cause upon motion of a party or upon the Court's initiative.

Rule 60. Proper Parties; Capacity. (a) *Petitioner.* (1) *Deficiency or Liability Actions.* A case shall be brought by and in the name of the person against whom the Commissioner determined the deficiency (in the case of a notice of deficiency) or liability (in the case of a notice of liability), or by and with the full descriptive name of the fiduciary entitled to institute a case on behalf of such person. See Rule 23(a)(1). A case timely brought shall not be dismissed on the ground that it is not properly brought on behalf of a party until a reasonable time has been allowed after objection for ratification by such party of the bringing of the case; and such ratification shall have the same effect as if the case had been properly brought by such party. Where the deficiency or liability is determined against more than one person in the notice by the Commissioner, only such of those persons who shall duly act to bring a case shall be deemed a party or parties.

(2) *Other Actions.* For the person who may bring a case as a petitioner in a declaratory judgment action, see Rules 210(b)(13), 211, and 216. For the person who may bring a case as a petitioner in a disclosure action, see Rules 220(b)(5), 221, and 225. For the person who may bring a case as a petitioner in a partnership action, see Rules 240(c)(1)(B), 240(c)(2)(B), 241, 245, 300(c)(1)(B), 300(c)(2)(B), and 301. For the person who may bring a case as a petitioner in an action for redetermination of employment status, see Rule 290(b)(2).

(b) *Respondent.* The Commissioner shall be named the respondent.

(c) *Capacity.* The capacity of an individual, other than one acting in a fiduciary or other representative capacity, to engage in litigation in the Court shall be determined by the law of the individual's domicile. The capacity of a corporation to engage in such litigation shall be determined by the law under which it was organized. The capacity of a fiduciary or other representative to litigate in the Court shall be determined in accordance with the law of the jurisdiction from which such person's authority is derived.

(d) *Infants or Incompetent Persons.* Whenever an infant or incompetent person has a representative, such as a general guardian, committee, conservator, or other like fiduciary, the representative may bring a case or defend in the Court on behalf of the infant or incompetent person. An infant or incompetent person who does not have a duly appointed representative may act by a next friend or by a guardian ad litem. Where a party attempts to represent himself or herself and, in the opinion of the Court there is a serious question as to such party's competence to do so, the Court, if it deems justice so requires, may continue the case until appropriate steps have been taken to obtain an adjudication of the question by a court having jurisdiction to do so, or may take such other action as it deems proper.

Rule 61. Permissive Joinder of Parties. (a) *Permissive Joinder.* No person, to whom a notice of deficiency or notice of liability has been issued, may join with any other such person in filing a petition in the Court, except as may be permitted by Rule 34(a)(1). With respect to the joinder of parties in declaratory judgment actions, see Rule 215; in disclosure actions, see Rule 226; and in partnership actions, see Rules 241(h) and 301(f).

(b) *Severance or Other Orders.* The Court may make such orders as will prevent a party from being embarrassed, delayed, or put to expense by the inclusion of a party, or may order separate trials or make other orders to prevent delay or prejudice; or may limit the trial to the claims of one or more parties, either dropping other parties from the case on such terms as are just or holding in abeyance the proceedings with respect to them. Any claim by or against a party may be severed and proceeded with separately. See also Rule 141(b).

Rule 63. Substitution of Parties; Change or Correction in Name. (a) *Death.* If a petitioner dies, the Court, on motion of a party or the decedent's successor or representative or on its own initiative, may order substitution of the proper parties.

(b) *Incompetency.* If a party becomes incompetent, the Court on motion of a party or the incompetent's representative or on its own initiative, may order the representative to proceed with the case.

(c) *Successor Fiduciaries or Representatives.* On motion made where a fiduciary or representative is changed, the Court may order substitution of the proper successors.

(d) *Other Cause.* The Court, on motion of a party or on its own initiative, may order the substitution of proper parties for other cause.

(e) *Change or Correction in Name.* On motion of a party or on its own initiative, the Court may order a change of or correction in the name or title of a party.

Rule 70. General Provisions. (a) *General.* (1) *Methods and Limitations of Discovery.* In conformity with these Rules, a party may obtain discovery by written interrogatories (Rule 71), by production of documents, electronically stored information, or things (Rules 72 and 73), by depositions upon consent of the parties (Rule 74(b)), or by depositions without consent of the parties in certain cases (Rule 74(c)). However, the Court expects the parties to attempt to attain the objectives of discovery through informal consultation or communication before utilizing the discovery procedures provided in these Rules. Discovery is not available under these Rules through depositions except to the limited extent provided in Rule 74. See Rules 91(a) and 100 regarding relationship of discovery to stipulations.

(2) *Time for Discovery.* Discovery shall not be commenced, without leave of Court, before the expiration of 30 days after joinder of issue (see Rule 38). Discovery shall be completed and any motion to compel or any other motion with respect to such discovery shall be filed, unless otherwise authorized by the Court, no later than 45 days prior to the date set for call of the case from a trial calendar. Discovery by a deposition under Rule 74(c) may not be commenced before a notice of trial has been issued or the case has been assigned to a Judge or Special Trial Judge and any motion to compel or any other motion with respect to such discovery shall be filed within the time provided by the preceding sentence. Discovery of matters which are relevant only to the issue of a party's entitlement to reasonable litigation or administrative costs shall not be commenced, without leave of Court, before a motion for reasonable litigation or administrative costs has been noticed for a hearing, and discovery shall be completed and any motion to compel or any other motion with respect to such discovery shall be filed, unless otherwise authorized by the Court, no later than 45 days prior to the date set for hearing.

(3) *Cases Consolidated for Trial.* With respect to a common matter in cases consolidated for trial, discovery may be had by any party to such a case to the extent provided by these Rules, and, for that purpose, the reference to a "party" in this Title VII, in Title VIII, or in Title X, shall mean any party to any of the consolidated cases involving such common matter.
Rule 70. General Provisions

(b) *Scope of Discovery.* The information or response sought through discovery may concern any matter not privileged and which is relevant to the subject matter involved in the pending case. It is not ground for objection that the information or response sought will be inadmissible at the trial, if that information or response appears reasonably calculated to lead to discovery of admissible evidence, regardless of the burden of proof involved. If the information or response sought is otherwise proper, it is not objectionable merely because the information or response involves an opinion or contention that relates to fact or to the application of law to fact. But the Court may order that the information or response sought need not be furnished or made until some designated time or a particular stage has been reached in the case or until a specified step has been taken by a party.

(c) *Limitations on Discovery.* (1) *General.* The frequency or extent of use of the discovery methods set forth in paragraph (a) shall be limited by the Court if it determines that: (A) The discovery sought is unreasonably cumulative or duplicative, or is obtainable from some other source that is more convenient, less burdensome, or less expensive;

(B) the party seeking discovery has had ample opportunity by discovery in the action to obtain the information sought; or

(C) the discovery is unduly burdensome or expensive, taking into account the needs of the case, the amount in controversy, limitations on the parties' resources, and the importance of the issues at stake in the litigation. The Court may act upon its own initiative after reasonable notice or pursuant to a motion under Rule 103.

(2) *Electronically Stored Information.* A party need not provide discovery of electronically stored information from sources that the party identifies as not reasonably accessible because of undue burden or cost. On motion to compel discovery or for a protective order, the party from whom discovery is sought must show that the information is not reasonably accessible because of undue burden or cost. If that showing is made, the Court may nonetheless order discovery from such sources if the requesting party shows good cause, considering the limitations of Rule 70(c)(1). The Court may specify conditions for the discovery.

(3) *Documents and Tangible Things.* (A) A party generally may not discover documents and tangible things that are prepared in anticipation of litigation or for trial by or for another party or its representative (including the other party's attorney, consultant, surety, indemnitor, insurer, or agent), unless, subject to Rule 70(c)(4), (i) they are otherwise discoverable under Rule 70(b); and

(ii) the party shows that it has substantial need for the materials to prepare its case and cannot, without undue hardship, obtain their substantial equivalent by other means.

(B) If the Court orders discovery of those materials, it must protect against disclosure of mental impressions, conclusions, opinions, or legal theories of a party's counsel or other representative concerning the litigation.

(4) *Experts.* (A) Rule 70(c)(3) protects drafts of any expert witness report required under Rule 143(g), regardless of the form in which the draft is recorded.

(B) Rule 70(c)(3) protects communications between a party's counsel and any witness required to provide a report under Rule 143(g), regardless of the form of the communications, except to the extent the communications: (i) relate to compensation for the expert's study or testimony;

(ii) identify facts or data that the party's counsel provided and that the expert considered in forming the opinions to be expressed; or

(iii) identify assumptions that the party's counsel provided and that the expert relied on in forming the opinions to be expressed.

(C) A party generally may not, by interrogatories or depositions, discover facts known or opinions held by an expert who has been retained or specially employed by another party in anticipation of litigation or to prepare for trial and who is not expected to be called as a witness at trial, except on a showing of exceptional circumstances under which it is impracticable for the party to obtain facts or opinions on the same subject by other means.

(d) *Party's Statements.* The answers to interrogatories, things produced in response to a request, or other information or responses obtained under Rules 71, 72, 73, and 74 may be used at trial or in any proceeding in the case prior or subsequent to trial to the extent permitted by the rules of evidence. Such answers or information or responses will not be considered as evidence until offered and received as evidence. No objections to interrogatories or the answers thereto, or to a request to produce or the response thereto, will be considered unless made within the time prescribed, except that the objection that an interrogatory or answer would be inadmissible at trial is preserved even though not made prior to trial.

(e) *Use In Case.* (1) Every request for discovery or response or objection thereto made by a party represented by counsel shall be signed by at least one counsel of record. A party who is not represented by counsel shall sign the request, response, or objection. The signature shall conform to the requirements of Rule 23(a)(3). The signature of counsel or a party constitutes a certification that the signer has read the request, response, or objection, and that to the best of the signer's knowledge, information, and belief formed after a reasonable inquiry, it is: (A) Consistent with these Rules and warranted by existing law or a good faith argument for the extension, modification, or reversal of existing law,

(B) not interposed for any improper purpose, such as to harass or to cause unnecessary delay or needless increase in the cost of litigation, and

(C) not unreasonable or unduly burdensome or expensive, given the needs of the case, the discovery already had in the case, the amount in controversy, and the importance of the issues at stake in the litigation. If a request, response, or objection is not signed, then it shall be stricken, unless it is signed promptly after the omission is called to the attention of the party making the request, response, or objection, and a party shall not be obligated to take any action with respect to it until it is signed.

(2) If a certification is made in violation of this Rule, then the Court upon motion or upon its own initiative, may impose upon the person who made the certification, the party on whose behalf the request, response, or objection is made, or both, an appropriate sanction, which may include an order to pay the amount of the reasonable expenses incurred because of the violation, including reasonable counsel's fees.

(f) *Other Applicable Rules.* For Rules concerned with the frequency and timing of discovery in relation to other procedures, supplementation of answers, protective orders, effect of evasive or incomplete answers or responses, and sanctions and enforcement action, see Title X.

Rule 71. Interrogatories. (a) *Availability.* Unless otherwise stipulated or ordered by the Court, a party may serve upon any other party no more than 25 written interrogatories, including all discrete subparts but excluding interrogatories described in paragraph (d) of this Rule, to be answered by the party served or, if the party served is a public or private corporation or a partnership or association or governmental agency, by an officer or agent who shall furnish such information as is available to the party. A motion for leave to serve additional interrogatories may be granted by the Court to the extent consistent with Rule 70(c)(1).

(b) *Answers.* All answers shall be made in good faith and as completely as the answering party's information shall permit. However, the answering party is required to make reasonable inquiry and ascertain readily obtainable information. An answering party may not give lack of information or knowledge as an answer or as a reason for failure to answer, unless such party states that such party has made reasonable inquiry and that information known or readily obtainable by such party is insufficient to enable such party to answer the substance of the interrogatory.

(c) *Procedure.* Each interrogatory shall be answered separately and fully under oath, unless it is objected to, in which event the reasons for the objection shall be stated in lieu of the answer. The answers are to be signed by the person making them and the objections shall be signed by the party or the party's counsel. The party on whom the interrogatories have been served shall serve a copy of the answers, and objections if any, upon the propounding party within 30 days after service of the interrogatories. The Court may allow a shorter or longer time. The burden shall be on the party submitting the interrogatories to move for an order with respect to any objection or other failure to answer an interrogatory, and in that connection the moving party shall annex the interrogatories to the motion, with proof of service on the other party, together with the answers and objections, if any. Prior to a motion for such an order, neither the interrogatories nor the response shall be filed with the Court.

(d) *Experts.* (1) By means of written interrogatories in conformity with this Rule, a party may require any other party: (A) To identify each person whom the other party expects to call as an expert witness at the trial of the case, giving the witness's name, address, vocation or occupation, and a statement of the witness's qualifications, and (B) to state the subject matter and the substance of the facts and opinions to which the expert is expected to testify, and give a summary of the grounds for each such opinion, or, in lieu of such statement to furnish a copy of a report of such expert presenting the foregoing information.

(2) For provisions regarding the submission and exchange of expert witness reports, see Rule 143(g). That Rule shall not serve to extend the period of time under paragraph (c) of this Rule within which a party must answer any interrogatory directed at discovering: (A) The identity and qualifications of each person whom such party expects to call as an expert witness at the trial of the case and (B) the subject matter with respect to which the expert is expected to testify.

(e) *Option to Produce Business Records.* If the answer to an interrogatory may be derived or ascertained from the business records (including electronically stored information) of the party upon whom the interrogatory has been served, or from an examination, audit, or inspection of such records, or from a compilation, abstract, or summary based thereon, and the burden of deriving or ascertaining the answer is substantially the same for the party serving the interrogatory as for the party served, it is sufficient answer to such interrogatory to specify the records from which the answer may be derived or ascertained and to afford to the party serving the interrogatory reasonable opportunity to examine, audit, or inspect such records and to make copies, compilations, abstracts, or summaries.

Rule 72. Production of Documents, Electronically Stored Information, and Things.

(a) *Scope.* Any party may, without leave of Court, serve on any other party a request to:

(1) Produce and permit the party making the request, or someone acting on such party's behalf, to inspect and copy, test, or sample any designated documents or electronically stored information (including writings, drawings, graphs, charts, photographs, sound recordings, images, and other data compilations stored in any medium from which information can be obtained, either directly or translated, if necessary, by the responding party into a reasonably usable form), or to inspect and copy, test, or sample any tangible thing, to the extent that any of the foregoing items are in the possession, custody, or control of the party on whom the request is served; or

(2) Permit entry upon designated land or other property in the possession or control of the party upon whom the request is served for the purpose of inspection and measuring, surveying, photographing, testing, or sampling the property or any designated object or operation thereon.

(b) *Procedure.* (1) *Contents of the Request.* The request shall set forth the items to be inspected, either by individual item or category, describe each item and category with reasonable particularity, and may specify the form or forms in which electronically stored information is to be produced. It shall specify a reasonable time, place, and manner of making the inspection and performing the related acts.

(2) *Responses and Objections.* The party upon whom the request is served shall serve a written response within 30 days after service of the request. The Court may allow a shorter or longer time. The response shall state, with respect to each item or category, that inspection and related activities will be permitted as requested, unless the request is objected to in whole or in part, in which event the reasons for objection shall be stated. If objection is made to part of an item or category, then that part shall be specified. The response may state an objection to a requested form for producing electronically stored information. If the responding party objects to a requested form--or if no form was specified in the request--the party shall state the form or forms it intends to use. To obtain a ruling on an objection by the responding party, on a failure to respond, or on a failure to produce or permit inspection, the requesting party shall file an appropriate motion with the Court and shall annex thereto the request, with proof of service on the other party, together with the response and objections if any. Prior to a motion for such a ruling, neither the request nor the response shall be filed with the Court.

(3) *Producing Documents or Electronically Stored Information.* Unless otherwise stipulated or ordered by the Court, these procedures apply to producing documents or electronically stored information: (A) A party shall produce documents as they are kept in the usual course of business or shall organize and label them to correspond to the categories in the request; (B) If a request does not specify a form for producing electronically stored information, a party shall produce it in a form or forms in which it is ordinarily maintained or in a reasonably usable form or forms; and (C) A party need not produce the same electronically stored information in more than one form.

(c) *Foreign Petitioners.* For production of records by foreign petitioners, see Code Section 7456(b).

Rule 73. Examination by Transferees. (a) *General.* Upon application to the Court and subject to these Rules, a transferee of property of a taxpayer shall be entitled to examine before trial the books, papers, documents, correspondence, electronically stored information, and other evidence of the taxpayer or of a preceding transferee of the taxpayer's property, but only if the transferee making the application is a petitioner seeking redetermination of such transferee's liability in respect of the taxpayer's tax liability (including interest, additional amounts, and additions provided by law). Such books, papers, documents, correspondence, electronically stored information, and other evidence may be made available to the extent that the same shall be within the United States, will not result in undue hardship to the taxpayer or preceding transferee, and in the opinion of the Court are necessary in order to enable the transferee to ascertain the liability of the taxpayer or preceding transferee.

(b) *Procedure.* A petitioner desiring an examination permitted under paragraph (a) shall file an application with the Court, showing that such petitioner is entitled to such an examination, describing the documents, electronically stored information, and other materials sought to be examined, giving the names and addresses of the persons to produce the same, and stating a reasonable time and place where the examination is to be made. If the Court shall determine that the applicable requirements are satisfied, then it shall issue a subpoena, signed by a Judge, directed to the appropriate person and ordering the production at a designated time and place of the documents, electronically stored information, and other materials involved. If the person to whom the subpoena is directed shall object thereto or to the production involved, then such person shall file the objections and the reasons therefor in writing with the Court, and serve a copy thereof upon the applicant, within 10 days after service of the subpoena or on or before such earlier time as may be specified in the subpoena for compliance. To obtain a ruling on such objections, the applicant for the subpoena shall file an appropriate motion with the Court. In all respects not inconsistent with the provisions of this Rule, the provisions of Rule 72(b) shall apply where appropriate.

(c) *Scope of Examination.* The scope of the examination authorized under this Rule shall be as broad as is authorized under Rule 72(a), including, for example, the copying of such documents, electronically stored information, and materials.

Rule 74. Depositions for Discovery Purposes. (a) *General.* In conformity with this Rule, a party may obtain discovery by depositions with the consent of the parties under paragraph (b) and without the consent of the parties under paragraph (c). Paragraph (d) describes additional uses for depositions of expert witnesses, and paragraphs (e) and (f) set forth general provisions governing the taking of all depositions for discovery purposes. An application for an order to take a deposition is required only with respect to depositions to perpetuate evidence. See Rules 80 through 84.

(b) *Depositions Upon Consent of the Parties.* (1) *When Deposition May Be Taken.* Upon consent of all the parties to a case, and within the time limits provided in Rule 70(a)(2), a deposition for discovery purposes may be taken of either a party, a nonparty witness, or an expert witness. Such consent shall be set forth in a stipulation filed in duplicate with the Court, which shall contain the information required in Rule 81(d) and which otherwise shall be subject to the procedure provided in Rule 81(d).

(2) *Notice to Nonparty Witness or Expert Witness.* A notice of deposition shall be served on a nonparty witness or an expert witness. The notice shall state that the deposition is to be taken under Rule 74(b) and shall set forth the name of the party or parties seeking the deposition; the name and address of the person to be deposed; the time and place proposed for the deposition; the name of the officer before whom the deposition is to be taken; a statement describing any books, papers, documents, electronically stored information, or tangible things to be produced at the deposition; and a statement of the issues in controversy to which the expected testimony of the witness, or the document, electronically stored information, or thing relates, and the reasons for deposing the witness. With respect to the deposition of an organization described in Rule 81(c), the notice shall also set forth the information required under that Rule, and the organization shall make the designation authorized by that Rule.

(3) *Objection by Nonparty Witness or Expert Witness.* Within 15 days after service of the notice of deposition, a nonparty witness or expert witness shall serve on the parties seeking the deposition any objections to the deposition. The burden shall be upon a party seeking the deposition to move for an order with respect to such objection or other failure of the nonparty witness or expert witness, and such party shall annex to any such motion the notice of deposition with proof of service thereof, together with a copy of the response and objections, if any.

(c) *Depositions Without Consent of the Parties.* (1) *In General.*

(A) *When Depositions May Be Taken.* After a notice of trial has been issued or after a case has been assigned to a Judge or Special Trial Judge of the Court, and within the time for completion of discovery under Rule 70(a)(2), any party may take a deposition for discovery purposes of a party, a nonparty witness, or an expert witness in the circumstances described in this paragraph.

(B) *Availability.* The taking of a deposition of a party, a nonparty witness, or an expert witness under this paragraph is an extraordinary method of discovery and may be used only where a party, a nonparty witness, or an expert witness can give testimony or possesses documents, electronically stored information, or things which are discoverable within the meaning of Rule 70(b) and where such testimony, documents, electronically stored information, or things practically cannot be obtained through informal consultation or communication (Rule 70(a)(1)), interrogatories (Rule 71), a request for production of documents, electronically stored information, or things (Rule 72), or by a deposition taken with consent of the parties (Rule 74(b)). If such requirements are satisfied, then a deposition of a witness may be taken under this paragraph, for example, where a party is a member of a partnership and an issue in the case involves an adjustment with respect to such partnership, or a party is a shareholder of an S corporation (as described in Code section 1361(a)), and an issue in the case involves an adjustment with respect to such S corporation. See Title XXIV, relating to partnership actions, brought under provisions first enacted by the Tax Equity and Fiscal Responsibility Act of 1982.

(2) *Nonparty Witnesses.* A party may take the deposition of a nonparty witness without leave of court and without the consent of all the parties as follows:

(A) *Notice.* A party desiring to take a deposition under this subparagraph shall give notice in writing to every other party to the case and to the nonparty witness to be deposed. The notice shall state that the deposition is to be taken under Rule 74(c)(2) and shall set forth the name of the party seeking the deposition; the name and address of the person to be deposed; the time and place proposed for the deposition; the officer before whom the deposition is to be taken; a statement describing any books, papers, documents, electronically stored information, or tangible things to be produced at the deposition; and a statement of the issues in controversy to which the expected testimony of the witness, or the document, electronically stored information, or thing relates, and the reasons for deposing the witness. With respect to the deposition of an organization described in Rule 81(c), the notice shall also set forth the information required under that Rule, and the organization shall make the designation authorized by that Rule.

(B) *Objections.* Within 15 days after service of the notice of deposition, a party or a nonparty witness shall serve on the party seeking the deposition any objections to the deposition. The burden shall be upon the party seeking the deposition to move for an order with respect to any such objections or any failure of the nonparty witness, and such party shall annex to any such motion the notice of deposition with proof of service thereof, together with a copy of any responses and objections. Prior to a motion for such an order, neither the notice nor the responses shall be filed with the Court.

(3) *Party Witnesses.* A party may take the deposition of another party without the consent of all the parties as follows:

(A) *Motion.* A party desiring to depose another party shall file a written motion which shall state that the deposition is to be taken under Rule 74(c)(3) and shall set forth the name of the person to be deposed, the time and place of the deposition, and the officer before whom the deposition is to be taken. With respect to the deposition of an organization described in Rule 81(c), the motion shall also set forth the information required under that Rule, and the organization shall make the designation authorized by that Rule.

(B) *Objection.* Upon the filing of a motion to take the deposition of a party, the Court shall issue an order directing each non-moving party to file a written objection or response thereto.

(C) *Action by the Court Sue Sponte.* In the exercise of its discretion the Court may on its own motion order the taking of a deposition of a party witness and may in its order allocate the cost therefor as it deems appropriate.

(4) *Expert Witnesses.* A party may take the deposition of an expert witness without the consent of all the parties as follows:

(A) *Scope of Deposition.* The deposition of an expert witness under this subparagraph shall be limited to: (i) The knowledge, skill, experience, training, or education that qualifies the witness to testify as an expert in respect of the issue or issues in dispute, (ii) the opinion of the witness in respect of which the witness's expert testimony is relevant to the issue or issues in dispute, (iii) the facts or data that underlie that opinion, and (iv) the witness's analysis, showing how the witness proceeded from the facts or data to draw the conclusion that represents the opinion of the witness.

(B) *Procedure.* (i) *In General.* A party desiring to depose an expert witness under this subparagraph (4) shall file a written motion and shall set forth therein the matters specified below:

(a) The name and address of the witness to be examined;

(b) a statement describing any books, papers, documents, electronically stored information, or tangible things to be produced at the deposition of the witness to be examined;

(c) a statement of issues in controversy to which the expected testimony of the expert witness, or the document, electronically stored information, or thing relates, and the reasons for deposing the witness;

(d) the time and place proposed for the deposition;

(e) the officer before whom the deposition is to be taken;

(f) any provision desired with respect to the payment of the costs, expenses, fees, and charges relating to the deposition (see paragraph (c)(4)(D)); and

(g) if the movant proposes to video record the deposition, then a statement to that effect and the name and address of the video recorder operator and the operator's employer. (The video recorder operator and the officer before whom the deposition is to be taken may be the same person.)

The movant shall also show that prior notice of the motion has been given to the expert witness whose deposition is sought and to each other party, or counsel for each other party, and shall state the position of each of these persons with respect to the motion, in accordance with Rule 50(a).

(ii) *Disposition of Motion.* Any objection or other response to the motion for order to depose an expert witness under this subparagraph shall be filed with the Court within 15 days after service of the motion. If the Court approves the taking of a deposition, then it will issue an order as described in paragraph (e)(4) of this Rule. If the deposition is to be video recorded, then the Court's order will so state.

(C) *Action by the Court Sua Sponte.* In the exercise of its discretion the Court may on its own motion order the taking of a deposition of an expert witness and may in its order allocate the cost therefor as it deems appropriate.

(D) *Expenses.* (i) *In General.* By stipulation among the parties and the expert witness to be deposed, or on order of the Court, provision may be made for any costs, expenses, fees, or charges relating to the deposition. If there is not such a stipulation or order, then the costs, expenses, fees, and charges relating to the deposition shall be borne by the parties as set forth in paragraph (c)(4)(D)(ii).

(ii) *Allocation of Costs, etc.* The party taking the deposition shall pay the following costs, expenses, fees, and charges:

(a) A reasonable fee for the expert witness, with regard to the usual and customary charge of the witness, for the time spent in preparing for and attending the deposition;

(b) reasonable charges of the expert witness for models, samples, or other like matters that may be required in the deposition of the witness;

(c) such amounts as are allowable under Rule 148(a) for transportation and subsistence for the expert witness;

(d) any charges of the officer presiding at or recording the deposition (other than for copies of the deposition transcript);

(e) any expenses involved in providing a place for the deposition; and

(f) the cost for the original of the deposition transcript as well as for any copies thereof that the party taking the deposition might order.

The other parties and the expert witness shall pay the cost for any copies of the deposition transcript that they might order.

(iii) *Failure to Attend.* If the party authorized to take the deposition of the expert witness fails to attend or to proceed therewith, then the Court may order that party to pay the witness such fees, charges, and expenses that the witness would otherwise be entitled to under paragraph (c)(4)(D)(ii) and to pay any other party such expenses, including attorney's fees, that the Court deems reasonable under the circumstances.

(d) *Use of Deposition of an Expert Witness for Other Than Discovery Purposes.* (1) *Use as Expert Witness Report.* Upon written motion by the proponent of the expert witness and in appropriate cases, the Court may order that the deposition transcript serve as the expert witness report required by Rule 143(g)(1). Unless the Court shall determine otherwise for good cause shown, the taking of a deposition of an expert witness will not serve to extend the date under Rule 143(g)(1) by which a party is required to furnish to each other party and to submit to the Court a copy of all expert witness reports prepared pursuant to that Rule.

(2) *Other Use.* Any other use of a deposition of an expert witness shall be governed by the provisions of Rule 81(i).

(e) *General Provisions.* Depositions taken under this Rule are subject to the following provisions.

(1) *Transcript:* A transcript shall be made of every deposition upon oral examination taken under this Rule, but the transcript and exhibits introduced in connection with the deposition generally shall not be filed with the Court. See Rule 81(h)(3).

(2) *Depositions Upon Written Questions:* Depositions under this Rule may be taken upon written questions rather than upon oral examination. If the deposition is to be taken on written questions, a copy of the written questions shall be annexed to the notice of deposition or motion to take deposition. The use of such written questions is not favored, and the deposition should not be taken in this manner in the absence of a special reason. See Rule 84(a). There shall be an opportunity for cross-questions and redirect questions to the same extent and within the same time periods as provided in Rule 84(b) (starting with service of a notice of or motion to take deposition rather than service of an application). With respect to taking the deposition, the procedure of Rule 84(c) shall apply.

(3) *Hearing:* A hearing on a motion for an order regarding a deposition under this Rule will be held only if directed by the Court. A motion for an order regarding a deposition may be granted by the Court to the extent consistent with Rule 70(c)(1).

(4) *Orders:* If the Court approves the taking of a deposition under this Rule, then it will issue an order which includes in its terms the name of the person to be examined, the time and

place of the deposition, and the officer before whom it is to be taken.

(5) *Continuances:* Unless the Court shall determine otherwise for good cause shown, the taking of a deposition under this Rule will not be regarded as sufficient ground for granting a continuance from a date or place of trial theretofore set.

(f) *Other Applicable Rules.* Unless otherwise provided in this Rule, the depositions described in this Rule generally shall be governed by the provisions of the following Rules with respect to the matters to which they apply: Rule 81(c) (designation of person to testify), 81(e) (person before whom deposition taken), 81(f) (taking of deposition), 81(g) (expenses), 81(h) (execution, form, and return of deposition), 81(i) (use of deposition), and Rule 85 (objections, errors, and irregularities). For Rules concerned with the timing and frequency of depositions, supplementation of answers, protective orders, effect of evasive or incomplete answers or responses, and sanctions and enforcement action, see Title X. For provisions governing the issuance of subpoenas, see Rule 147(d).

Rule 90. Requests for Admission. (a) *Scope and Time of Request.* A party may serve upon any other party a written request for the admission, for purposes of the pending action only, of the truth of any matters which are not privileged and are relevant to the subject matter involved in the pending action, but only if such matters are set forth in the request and relate to statements or opinions of fact or of the application of law to fact, including the genuineness of any documents described in the request. However, the Court expects the parties to attempt to attain the objectives of such a request through informal consultation or communication before utilizing the procedures provided in this Rule. Requests for admission shall not be commenced, without leave of Court, before the expiration of 30 days after joinder of issue (see Rule 38). Requests for admission shall be completed and any motion to review under paragraph (e) hereof shall be filed, unless otherwise authorized by the Court, no later than 45 days prior to the date set for call of the case from a trial calendar.

(b) *The Request.* The request may, without leave of Court, be served by any party to a pending case. The request shall separately set forth each matter of which an admission is requested and shall advise the party to whom the request is directed of the consequences of failing to respond as provided by paragraph (c). Copies of documents shall be served with the request unless they have been or are otherwise furnished or made available for inspection and copying. The party making the request shall simultaneously serve a copy thereof on the other party and file the original with proof of service with the Court.

(c) *Response to Request.* Each matter is deemed admitted unless, within 30 days after service of the request or within such shorter or longer time as the Court may allow, the party to whom the request is directed serves upon the requesting party (1) a written answer specifically admitting or denying the matter involved in whole or in part, or asserting that it cannot be truthfully admitted or denied and setting forth in detail the reasons why this is so, or (2) an objection, stating in detail the reasons therefor. The response shall be signed by the party or the party's counsel, and the original thereof, with proof of service on the other party, shall be filed with the Court. A denial shall fairly meet the substance of the requested admission, and, when good faith requires that a party qualify an answer or deny only a part of a matter, such party shall specify so much of it as is true and deny or qualify the remainder. An answering party may not give lack of information or knowledge as a reason for failure to admit or deny unless such party states that such party has made reasonable inquiry and that the information known or readily obtainable by such party is insufficient to enable such party to admit or deny. A party who considers that a matter, of which an admission has been requested, presents a genuine issue for trial may not, on that ground alone, object to the request; such party may, subject to the provisions of paragraph (g) of this Rule, deny the matter or set forth reasons why such party cannot admit or deny it. An objection on the ground of relevance may be noted by any party but it is not to be regarded as just cause for refusal to admit or deny.

(d) *Effect of Signature.* (1) The signature of counsel or a party constitutes a certification that the signer has read the request for admission or response or objection, and that to the best of the signer's knowledge, information, and belief formed after a reasonable inquiry, it is (A) consistent with these Rules and warranted by existing law or a good faith argument for the extension, modification, or reversal of existing law; (B) not interposed for any improper purpose, such as to harass or to cause unnecessary delay or needless increase in the cost of litigation; and (C) not unreasonable or unduly burdensome or expensive, given the needs of the case, the discovery already had in the case, the amount in controversy, and the importance of the issues at stake in the litigation. If a request, response, or objection is not signed, it shall be stricken, unless it is signed promptly after the omission is called to the attention of the party making the request, response, or objection, and a party shall not be obligated to take any action with respect to it until it is signed.

(2) If a certification is made in violation of this Rule, the Court, upon motion or upon its own initiative, may impose upon the person who made the certification, the party on whose behalf the request, response, or objection is made, or both, an appropriate sanction, which may include an order to pay the amount of the reasonable expenses incurred because of the violation, including reasonable counsel's fees.

(e) *Motion to Review.* The party who has requested the admissions may move to determine the sufficiency of the answers or objections. Unless the Court determines that an objection is justified, it shall order that an answer be served. If the Court determines that an answer does not comply with the requirements of this Rule, then it may order either that the matter is admitted or that an amended answer be served. In lieu of any such order, the Court may determine that final disposition of the request shall be made at some later time which may be more appropriate for disposing of the question involved.

(f) *Effect of Admission.* Any matter admitted under this Rule is conclusively established unless the Court on motion permits withdrawal or modification of the admission. Subject to any other orders made in the case by the Court, withdrawal or modification may be permitted when the presentation of the merits of the case will be subserved thereby, and the party who obtained the admission fails to satisfy the Court that the withdrawal or modification will prejudice such party in prosecuting such party's case or defense on the merits. Any admission made by a party under this Rule is for the purpose of the pending action only and is not an admission by such party for any other purpose, nor may it be used against such party in any other proceeding.

(g) *Sanctions.* If any party unjustifiably fails to admit the genuineness of any document or the truth of any matter as requested in accordance with this Rule, the party requesting the admission may apply to the Court for an order imposing such sanction on the other party or the other party's counsel as the Court may find appropriate in the circumstances, including but not limited to the sanctions provided in Title X. The failure to admit may be found unjustifiable unless the Court finds that (1) the request was held objectionable pursuant to this Rule, or (2) the admission sought was of no substantial importance, or (3) the party failing to admit had reasonable ground to doubt the truth of the matter or the genuineness of the document in respect of which the admission was sought, or (4) there was other good reason for failure to admit.

(h) *Other Applicable Rules.* For Rules concerned with frequency and timing of requests for admission in relation to other procedures, supplementation of answers, effect of evasive or incomplete answers or responses, protective orders, and sanctions and enforcement action, see Title X.

Rule 91. Stipulations for Trial. (a) *Stipulations Required.* (1) *General.* The parties are required to stipulate, to the fullest extent to which complete or qualified agreement can or fairly should be reached, all matters not privileged which are relevant to the pending case, regardless of whether such matters involve fact or opinion or the application of law to fact. Included in matters required to be stipulated are all facts, all documents and papers or contents or aspects thereof, and all evidence which fairly should not be in dispute. Where the truth or authenticity of facts or evidence claimed to be relevant by one party is not disputed, an objection on the ground of materiality or relevance may be noted by any other party but is not to be regarded as just cause for refusal to stipulate. The requirement of stipulation applies under this Rule without regard to where the burden of proof may lie with respect to the matters involved. Documents or papers or other exhibits annexed to or filed with the stipulation shall be considered to be part of the stipulation.

(2) *Stipulations to be Comprehensive.* The fact that any matter may have been obtained through discovery or requests for admission or through any other authorized procedure is not grounds for omitting such matter from the stipulation. Such procedures should be regarded as aids to stipulation, and matter obtained through them which is within the scope of subparagraph (1) must be set forth comprehensively in the stipulation, in logical order in the context of all other provisions of the stipulation. A failure to include in the stipulation a matter admitted under Rule 90(f) does not affect the Court's ability to consider such admitted matter.

(b) *Form.* Stipulations required under this Rule shall be in writing, signed by the parties thereto or by their counsel, and shall observe the requirements of Rule 23 as to form and style of papers, except that the stipulation shall be filed with the Court in duplicate and only one set of exhibits shall be required. Documents or other papers, which are the subject of stipulation in any respect and which the parties intend to place before the Court, shall be annexed to or filed with the stipulation. The stipulation shall be clear and concise. Separate items shall be stated in separate paragraphs, and shall be appropriately lettered or numbered. Exhibits attached to a stipulation shall be numbered serially; i.e., 1, 2, 3, etc. The exhibit number shall be followed by "P" if offered by the petitioner, e.g., 1-P; "R" if offered by the respondent, e.g., 2- R; or "J" if joint, e.g., 3-J.

(c) *Filing.* Executed stipulations prepared pursuant to this Rule, and related exhibits, shall be filed by the parties at or before commencement of the trial of the case, unless the Court in the particular case shall otherwise specify. A stipulation when filed need not be offered formally to be considered in evidence.

(d) *Objections.* Any objection to all or any part of a stipulation should be noted in the stipulation, but the Court will consider any objection to a stipulated matter made at the commencement of the trial or for good cause shown made during the trial.

(e) *Binding Effect.* A stipulation shall be treated, to the extent of its terms, as a conclusive admission by the parties to the stipulation, unless otherwise permitted by the Court or agreed upon by those parties. The Court will not permit a party to a stipulation to qualify, change, or contradict a stipulation in whole or in part, except that it may do so where justice requires. A stipulation and the admissions therein shall be binding and have effect only in the pending case and not for any other purpose, and cannot be used against any of the parties thereto in any other case or proceeding.

(f) *Noncompliance by a Party*. (1) *Motion to Compel Stipulation*. If, after the date of issuance of trial notice in a case, a party has refused or failed to confer with an adversary with respect to entering into a stipulation in accordance with this Rule, or a party has refused or failed to make such a stipulation of any matter within the terms of this Rule, the party proposing to stipulate may, at a time not later than 45 days prior to the date set for call of the case from a trial calendar, file a motion with the Court for an order directing the delinquent party to show cause why the matters covered in the motion should not be deemed admitted for the purposes of the case. The motion shall: (A) Show with particularity and by separately numbered paragraphs each matter which is claimed for stipulation; (B) set forth in express language the specific stipulation which the moving party proposes with respect to each such matter and annex thereto or make available to the Court and the other parties each document or other paper as to which the moving party desires a stipulation; (C) set forth the sources, reasons, and basis for claiming, with respect to each such matter, that it should be stipulated; and (D) show that opposing counsel or the other parties have had reasonable access to those sources or basis for stipulation and have been informed of the reasons for stipulation.

(2) *Procedure*. Upon the filing of such a motion, an order to show cause as moved shall be issued forthwith, unless the Court shall direct otherwise. The order to show cause will be served by the Clerk, with a copy thereof sent to the moving party. Within 20 days of the service of the order to show cause, the party to whom the order is directed shall file a response with the Court, with proof of service of a copy thereof on opposing counsel or the other parties, showing why the matters set forth in the motion papers should not be deemed admitted for purposes of the pending case. The response shall list each matter involved on which there is no dispute, referring specifically to the numbered paragraphs in the motion to which the admissions relate. Where a matter is disputed only in part, the response shall show the part admitted and the part disputed. Where the responding party is willing to stipulate in whole or in part with respect to any matter in the motion by varying or qualifying a matter in the proposed stipulation, the response shall set forth the variance or qualification and the admission which the responding party is willing to make. Where the response claims that there is a dispute as to any matter in part or in whole, or where the response presents a variance or qualification with respect to any matter in the motion, the response shall show the sources, reasons, and basis on which the responding party relies for that purpose. The Court, where it is found appropriate, may set the order to show cause for a hearing or conference at such time as the Court shall determine.

(3) *Failure of Response*. If no response is filed within the period specified with respect to any matter or portion thereof, or if the response is evasive or not fairly directed to the proposed stipulation or portion thereof, that matter or portion thereof will be deemed stipulated for purposes of the pending case, and an order will be issued accordingly.

(4) *Matters Considered*. Opposing claims of evidence will not be weighed under this Rule unless such evidence is patently incredible. Nor will a genuinely controverted or doubtful issue of fact be determined in advance of trial. The Court will determine whether a genuine dispute exists, or whether in the interests of justice a matter ought not be deemed stipulated.

Rule 103. Protective Orders. (a) *Authorized Orders*. Upon motion by a party or any other affected person, and for good cause shown, the Court may make any order which justice requires to protect a party or other person from annoyance, embarrassment, oppression, or undue burden or expense, including but not limited to one or more of the following:

(1) That the particular method or procedure not be used.

(2) That the method or procedure be used only on specified terms and conditions, including a designation of the time or place.

(3) That a method or procedure be used other than the one selected by the party.

(4) That certain matters not be inquired into, or that the method be limited to certain matters or to any other extent.

(5) That the method or procedure be conducted with no one present except persons designated by the Court.

(6) That a deposition or other written materials, after being sealed, be opened only by order of the Court.

(7) That a trade secret or other information not be disclosed or be disclosed only in a designated way.

(8) That the parties simultaneously file specified documents or information enclosed in sealed envelopes to be opened as directed by the Court.

(9) That expense involved in a method or procedure be borne in a particular manner or by specified person or persons.

(10) That documents or records (including electronically stored information) be impounded by the Court to ensure their availability for purpose of review by the parties prior to trial and use at the trial.

If a discovery request has been made, then the movant shall attach as an exhibit to a motion for a protective order under this Rule a copy of any discovery request in respect of which the motion is filed.

(b) *Denials*. If a motion for a protective order is denied in whole or in part, then the Court may, on such terms or conditions it deems just, order any party or person to comply or to respond in accordance with the procedure involved.

Rule 110. Pretrial Conferences. (a) *General*. In appropriate cases, the Court will undertake to confer with the parties in pretrial conferences with a view to narrowing issues, stipulating facts, simplifying the presentation of evidence, or otherwise assisting in the preparation for trial or possible disposition of the case in whole or in part without trial.

(b) *Cases Calendared*. Either party in a case listed on any trial calendar may request of the Court, or the Court on its own motion may order, a pretrial conference. The Court may, in its discretion, set the case for a pretrial conference during the trial session. If sufficient reason appears therefor, a pretrial conference will be scheduled prior to the call of the calendar at such time and place as may be practicable and appropriate.

(c) *Cases Not Calendared*. If a case is not listed on a trial calendar, the Chief Judge, in the exercise of discretion, upon motion of either party or sua sponte, may list such case for a pretrial conference upon a calendar in the place requested for trial, or may assign the case for a pretrial conference either in Washington, D.C., or in any other convenient place.

(d) *Conditions*. A request or motion for a pretrial conference shall include a statement of the reasons therefor. Pretrial conferences will in no circumstances be held as a substitute for the conferences required between the parties in order to comply with the provisions of Rule 91, but a pretrial conference, for the purpose of assisting the parties in entering into the stipulations called for by Rule 91, will be held by the Court where the party requesting such pretrial conference has in good faith attempted without success to obtain such stipulation from such party's adversary. Nor will any pretrial conference be held where the Court is satisfied that the request therefor is frivolous or is made for purposes of delay.

(e) *Order*. The Court may, in its discretion, issue appropriate pretrial orders.

Rule 120. Judgment on the Pleadings. (a) *General*. After the pleadings are closed but within such time as not to delay the trial, any party may move for judgment on the pleadings. The motion shall be filed and served in accordance with the requirements otherwise applicable. See Rules 50 and 54. Such motion shall be disposed of before trial unless the Court determines otherwise.

(b) *Matters Outside Pleadings*. If, on a motion for judgment on the pleadings, matters outside the pleadings are presented to and not excluded by the Court, the motion shall be treated as one for summary judgment and shall be disposed of as provided in Rule 121, and all parties shall be given reasonable opportunity to present all material made pertinent to such a motion by Rule 121.

Rule 121. Summary Judgment. (a) *General*. Either party may move, with or without supporting affidavits, for a summary adjudication in the moving party's favor upon all or any part of the legal issues in controversy. Such motion may be made at any time commencing 30 days after the pleadings are closed but within such time as not to delay the trial, and in any event no later than 60 days before the first day of the Court's session at which the case is calendared for trial, unless otherwise permitted by the Court.

(b) *Motion and Proceedings Thereon*. The motion shall be filed and served in accordance with the requirements otherwise applicable. See Rules 50 and 54. An opposing written response, with or without supporting affidavits or declarations, shall be filed within such period as the Court may direct. A decision shall thereafter be rendered if the pleadings, answers to interrogatories, depositions, admissions, and any other acceptable materials, together with the affidavits or declarations, if any, show that there is no genuine dispute as to any material fact and that a decision may be rendered as a matter of law. A partial summary adjudication may be made which does not dispose of all the issues in the case.

(c) *Case Not Fully Adjudicated on Motion*. If, on motion under this Rule, decision is not rendered upon the whole case or for all the relief asked and a trial is necessary, the Court may ascertain, by examining the pleadings and the evidence before it and by interrogating counsel, what material facts exist without substantial controversy and what material facts are actually and in good faith controverted. It may thereupon make an order specifying the facts that appear to be without substantial controversy, including the extent to which the relief sought is not in controversy, and directing such further proceedings in the case as are just. Upon the trial of the case, the facts so specified shall be deemed established, and the trial shall be concluded accordingly.

(d) *Form of Affidavits; Further Testimony; Defense Required*. Supporting and opposing affidavits or declarations shall be made on personal knowledge, shall set forth such facts as would be admissible in evidence, and shall show affirmatively that the affiant or declarant is competent to testify to the matters stated therein. Sworn or certified copies of all papers or parts thereof referred to in an affidavit or a declaration shall be attached thereto or filed therewith. The Court may permit affidavits or declarations to be supplemented or opposed by answers to interrogatories, depositions, further affidavits or declarations, or other acceptable materials, to the extent that other applicable conditions in these Rules are satisfied for utilizing such procedure. When a motion for summary judgment is made and supported as provided in this Rule, an adverse party may not rest upon the mere allegations or denials of such party's pleading, but such party's response, by affidavits or declarations or as otherwise provided in this Rule, must set forth specific facts showing that there is a genuine issue for trial. If the adverse party does not so respond, then a decision, if appropriate, may be entered against such party.

(e) *When Affidavits or Declarations Are Unavailable.* If it appears from the affidavits or declarations of a party opposing the motion that such party cannot for reasons stated present by affidavit or declaration facts essential to justify such party's opposition, then the Court may deny the motion or may order a continuance to permit affidavits or declarations to be obtained or other steps to be taken or may make such other order as is just. If it appears from the affidavits or declarations of a party opposing the motion that such party's only legally available method of contravening the facts set forth in the supporting affidavits or declarations of the moving party is through cross-examination of such affiants or declarants or the testimony of third parties from whom affidavits or declarations cannot be secured, then such a showing may be deemed sufficient to establish that the facts set forth in such supporting affidavits or declarations are genuinely disputed.

(f) *Affidavits or Declarations Made in Bad Faith.* If it appears to the satisfaction of the Court at any time that any of the affidavits or declarations presented pursuant to this Rule are presented in bad faith or for the purpose of delay, then the Court may order the party employing them to pay to the other party the amount of the reasonable expenses which the filing of the affidavits or declarations caused the other party to incur, including reasonable counsel's fees, and any offending party or counsel may be adjudged guilty of contempt or otherwise disciplined by the Court.

Rule 122. Submission Without Trial. (a) *General.* Any case not requiring a trial for the submission of evidence (as, for example, where sufficient facts have been admitted, stipulated, established by deposition, or included in the record in some other way) may be submitted at any time after joinder of issue (see Rule 38) by motion of the parties filed with the Court. The parties need not wait for the case to be calendared for trial and need not appear in Court.

(b) *Burden of Proof.* The fact of submission of a case, under paragraph (a) of this Rule, does not alter the burden of proof, or the requirements otherwise applicable with respect to adducing proof, or the effect of failure of proof.

Rule 123. Default and Dismissal. (a) *Default.* If any party has failed to plead or otherwise proceed as provided by these Rules or as required by the Court, then such party may be held in default by the Court either on motion of another party or on the initiative of the Court. Thereafter, the Court may enter a decision against the defaulting party, upon such terms and conditions as the Court may deem proper, or may impose such sanctions (see, e. g., Rule 104) as the Court may deem appropriate. The Court may, in its discretion, conduct hearings to ascertain whether a default has been committed, to determine the decision to be entered or the sanctions to be imposed, or to ascertain the truth of any matter.

(b) *Dismissal.* For failure of a petitioner properly to prosecute or to comply with these Rules or any order of the Court or for other cause which the Court deems sufficient, the Court may dismiss a case at any time and enter a decision against the petitioner. The Court may, for similar reasons, decide against any party any issue as to which such party has the burden of proof, and such decision shall be treated as a dismissal for purposes of paragraphs (c) and (d) of this Rule.

(c) *Setting Aside Default or Dismissal.* For reasons deemed sufficient by the Court and upon motion expeditiously made, the Court may set aside a default or dismissal or the decision rendered thereon.

(d) *Effect of Decision on Default or Dismissal.* A decision rendered upon a default or in consequence of a dismissal, other than a dismissal for lack of jurisdiction, shall operate as an adjudication on the merits.

Rule 130. Motions and Other Matters. (a) *Calendars.* If a hearing is to be held on a motion or other matter, apart from a trial on the merits, then such hearing may be held on a motion calendar in Washington, D.C., unless the Court, on its own motion or on the motion of a party, shall direct otherwise. As to hearings at other places, see Rule 50(b)(2). The parties will be given notice of the place and time of hearing.

(b) *Failure to Attend.* The Court may hear a matter ex parte where a party fails to appear at such a hearing. With respect to attendance at such hearings, see Rule 50(c).

Rule 131. Trial Calendars. (a) *General.* Each case, when at issue, will be placed upon a calendar for trial in accordance with Rule 140. The Clerk shall notify the parties of the place and time for which the calendar is set.

(b) *Standing Pretrial Order.* In order to facilitate the orderly and efficient disposition of all cases on a trial calendar, at the direction of the trial judge, the Clerk shall include with the notice of trial a Standing Pretrial Order or other instructions for trial preparation. Unexcused failure to comply with any such order may subject a party or a party's counsel to sanctions. See, e. g., Rules 104, 123, and 202.

(c) *Calendar Call.* Each case appearing on a trial calendar will be called at the time and place scheduled. At the call, counsel or the parties shall indicate their estimate of the time required for trial. The cases for trial will thereupon be tried in due course, but not necessarily in the order listed.

Rule 133. Continuances. A case or matter scheduled on a calendar may be continued by the Court upon motion or at its own initiative. A motion for continuance shall inform the Court of the position of the other parties with respect thereto, either by endorsement thereon by the other parties or by a representation of the moving party. A motion for continuance based upon the pendency in a court of a related case or cases shall include the name and docket number of any such related case, the names of counsel for the parties in such case, and the status of such case, and shall identify all issues common to any such related case. Continuances will be granted only in exceptional circumstances. Conflicting engagements of counsel or employment of new counsel ordinarily will not be regarded as ground for continuance. A motion for continuance, filed 30 days or less prior to the date to which it is directed, may be set for hearing on that date, but ordinarily will be deemed dilatory and will be denied unless the ground therefor arose during that period or there was good reason for not making the motion sooner. As to extensions of time, see Rule 25(c).

Rule 140. Place of Trial. (a) *Request for Place of Trial.* The petitioner, at the time of filing the petition, shall file a request for place of trial showing the place at which the petitioner would prefer the trial to be held. If the petitioner has not filed such a request, then the Commissioner, at the time the answer is filed, shall file a request showing the place of trial preferred by the Commissioner. The Court will make reasonable efforts to conduct the trial at the location most convenient to that requested where suitable facilities are available. The parties shall be notified of the place at which the trial will be held.

(b) *Form.* Such request shall be set forth on a paper separate from the petition or answer. See Form 5, Appendix I.

(c) *Motion to Change Place of Trial.* If a party desires a change in the place of trial, then such party shall file a motion to that effect, stating fully the reasons therefor. Such motions, made after the notice of the time of trial has been issued, may be deemed dilatory and may be denied unless the ground therefor arose during that period or there was good reason for not making the motion sooner.

Rule 141. Consolidation; Separate Trials. (a) *Consolidation.* When cases involving a common question of law or fact are pending before the Court, it may order a joint hearing or trial of any or all the matters in issue, it may order all the cases consolidated, and it may make such orders concerning proceedings therein as may tend to avoid unnecessary costs or delay or duplication. Similar action may be taken where cases involve different tax liabilities of the same parties, notwithstanding the absence of a common issue. Unless otherwise permitted by the Court for good cause shown, a motion to consolidate cases may be filed only after all the cases sought to be consolidated have become at issue. The caption of a motion to consolidate shall include all of the names and docket numbers of the cases sought to be consolidated arranged in chronological order (i.e., the oldest case first). Unless otherwise ordered, the caption of all documents subsequently filed in consolidated cases shall include all of the docket numbers arranged in chronological order, but may include only the name of the oldest case with an appropriate indication of other parties.

(b) *Separate Trials.* The Court, in furtherance of convenience or to avoid prejudice, or when separate trials will be conducive to expedition or economy, may order a separate trial of any one or more claims or defenses or issues, or of the tax liability of any party or parties. The Court may enter appropriate orders or decisions with respect to any such claims, defenses, issues, or parties that are tried separately. As to severance of parties or claims, see Rule 61 (b).

Rule 142. Burden of Proof. (a) *General.* (1) The burden of proof shall be upon the petitioner, except as otherwise provided by statute or determined by the Court; and except that, in respect of any new matter, increases in deficiency, and affirmative defenses, pleaded in the answer, it shall be upon the respondent. As to affirmative defenses, see Rule 39.

(2) See Code section 7491 where credible evidence is introduced by the taxpayer, or any item of income is reconstructed by the Commissioner solely through the use of statistical information on unrelated taxpayers, or any penalty, addition to tax, or additional amount is determined by the Commissioner.

(b) *Fraud.* In any case involving the issue of fraud with intent to evade tax, the burden of proof in respect of that issue is on the respondent, and that burden of proof is to be carried by clear and convincing evidence. Code sec. 7454(a).

(c) *Foundation Managers; Trustees; Organization Managers.* In any case involving the issue of the knowing conduct of a foundation manager as set forth in the provisions of Code section 4941, 4944, or 4945, or the knowing conduct of a trustee as set forth in the provisions of Code section 4951 or 4952, or the knowing conduct of an organization manager as set forth in the provisions of Code section 4912 or 4955, the burden of proof in respect of such issue is on the respondent, and such burden of proof is to be carried by clear and convincing evidence. Code sec. 7454(b).

(d) *Transferee Liability*. The burden of proof is on the respondent to show that a petitioner is liable as a transferee of property of a taxpayer, but not to show that the taxpayer was liable for the tax. Code sec. 6902(a).

(e) *Accumulated Earnings Tax*. Where the notice of deficiency is based in whole or in part on an allegation of accumulation of corporate earnings and profits beyond the reasonable needs of the business, the burden of proof with respect to such allegation is determined in accordance with Code section 534. If the petitioner has submitted to the respondent a statement which is claimed to satisfy the requirements of Code section 534(c), the Court will ordinarily, on timely motion filed after the case has been calendared for trial, rule prior to the trial on whether such statement is sufficient to shift the burden of proof to the respondent to the limited extent set forth in Code section 534(a)(2).

Rule 143. Evidence. (a) *General*. Trials before the Court will be conducted in accordance with the rules of evidence applicable in trials without a jury in the United States District Court for the District of Columbia. See Code sec. 7453. To the extent applicable to such trials, those rules include the rules of evidence in the Federal Rules of Civil Procedure and any rules of evidence generally applicable in the Federal courts (including the United States District Court for the District of Columbia). Evidence which is relevant only to the issue of a party's entitlement to reasonable litigation or administrative costs shall not be introduced during the trial of the case (other than a case commenced under Title XXVI of these Rules, relating to actions for administrative costs). As to claims for reasonable litigation or administrative costs and their disposition, see Rules 231 and 232. As to evidence in an action for administrative costs, see Rule 274 (and that Rule's incorporation of the provisions of Rule 174(b)).

(b) *Testimony*. The testimony of a witness generally must be taken in open court except as otherwise provided by the Court or these Rules. For good cause in compelling circumstances and with appropriate safeguards, the Court may permit testimony in open court by contemporaneous transmission from a different location.

(c) *Ex Parte Statements*. Ex parte affidavits or declarations, statements in briefs, and unadmitted allegations in pleadings do not constitute evidence. As to allegations in pleadings not denied, see Rules 36(c) and 37(c) and (d).

(d) *Depositions*. Testimony taken by deposition shall not be treated as evidence in a case until offered and received in evidence. Error in the transcript of a deposition may be corrected by agreement of the parties, or by the Court on proof it deems satisfactory to show an error exists and the correction to be made, subject to the requirements of Rules 81(h)(1) and 85(e). As to the use of a deposition, see Rule 81(i).

(e) *Documentary Evidence*. (1) *Copies*. A copy is admissible to the same extent as an original unless a genuine question is raised as to the authenticity of the original or in the circumstances it would be unfair to admit the copy in lieu of the original. Where the original is admitted in evidence, a clearly legible copy may be substituted later for the original or such part thereof as may be material or relevant, upon leave granted in the discretion of the Court.

(2) *Return of Exhibits*. Exhibits may be disposed of as the Court deems advisable. A party desiring the return at such party's expense of any exhibit belonging to such party, shall, within 90 days after the decision of the case by the Court has become final, make written application to the

Clerk, suggesting a practical manner of delivery. If such application is not timely made, the exhibits in the case will be destroyed.

(f) *Interpreters.* The parties ordinarily will be expected to make their own arrangements for obtaining and compensating interpreters. However, the Court may appoint an interpreter of its own selection and may fix the interpreter's reasonable compensation, which compensation shall be paid by one or more of the parties or otherwise as the Court may direct.

(g) *Expert Witness Reports.* (1) Unless otherwise permitted by the Court upon timely request, any party who calls an expert witness shall cause that witness to prepare a written report for submission to the Court and to the opposing party if the witness is one retained or specially employed to provide expert testimony in the case or one whose duties as the party's employee regularly involve giving expert testimony. The report, prepared and signed by the witness, shall contain: (A) a complete statement of all opinions the witness expresses and the basis and reasons for them;

(B) the facts or data considered by the witness in forming them;

(C) any exhibits used to summarize or support them;

(D) the witness's qualifications, including a list of all publications authored in the previous 10 years;

(E) a list of all other cases in which, during the previous 4 years, the witness testified as an expert at trial or by deposition; and

(F) a statement of the compensation to be paid for the study and testimony in the case.

(2) The report will be marked as an exhibit, identified by the witness, and received in evidence as the direct testimony of the expert witness, unless the Court determines that the witness is not qualified as an expert. Additional direct testimony with respect to the report may be allowed to clarify or emphasize matters in the report, to cover matters arising after the preparation of the report, or otherwise at the discretion of the Court. After the case is calendared for trial or assigned to a Judge or Special Trial Judge, each party who calls any expert witness shall serve on each other party, and shall submit to the Court, not later than 30 days before the call of the trial calendar on which the case shall appear, a copy of all expert witness reports prepared pursuant to this subparagraph. An expert witness's testimony will be excluded altogether for failure to comply with the provisions of this paragraph, unless the failure is shown to be due to good cause and unless the failure does not unduly prejudice the opposing party, such as by significantly impairing the opposing party's ability to cross-examine the expert witness or by denying the opposing party the reasonable opportunity to obtain evidence in rebuttal to the expert witness's testimony.

(3) The Court ordinarily will not grant a request to permit an expert witness to testify without a written report where the expert witness's testimony is based on third-party contacts, comparable sales, statistical data, or other detailed, technical information. The Court may grant such a request, for example, where the expert witness testifies only with respect to industry practice or only in rebuttal to another expert witness.

(4) For circumstances under which the transcript of the deposition of an expert witness may serve as the written report required by subparagraph (1), see Rule 74(d).

Rule 144. Exceptions Unnecessary. Formal exceptions to rulings or orders of the Court are unnecessary. It is sufficient that a party at the time the ruling or order of the Court is made or sought, makes known to the Court the action which such party desires the Court to take or such party's objection to the action of the Court and the grounds therefor; and, if a party has no opportunity to object to a ruling or order at the time it is made, the absence of an objection does not thereafter prejudice such party.

Rule 145. Exclusion of Proposed Witnesses. (a) *Exclusion.* At the request of a party, the Court shall order witnesses excluded so that they cannot hear the testimony of other witnesses and it may make the order on its own motion. This Rule does not authorize exclusion of (1) a party who is a natural person, or (2) an officer or employee of a party which is not a natural person designated as its representative by its attorney, or (3) a person whose presence is shown by a party to be essential to the presentation of such party's cause.

(b) *Contempt.* Among other measures which the Court may take in the circumstances, it may punish as for a contempt (1) any witness who remains within hearing of the proceedings after such exclusion has been directed, that fact being noted in the record; and (2) any person (witness, counsel, or party) who willfully violates instructions issued by the Court with respect to such exclusion.

Rule 147. Subpoenas. (a) *Attendance of Witnesses; Form; Issuance.* Every subpoena shall be issued under the seal of the Court, shall state the name of the Court and the caption of the case, and shall command each person to whom it is directed to attend and give testimony at a time and place therein specified. A subpoena, including a subpoena for the production of documentary evidence or electronically stored information, signed and sealed but otherwise blank, shall be issued to a party requesting it, who shall fill it in before service. Subpoenas may be obtained at the Office of the Clerk in Washington, D.C., or from a trial clerk at a trial session. See Code sec. 7456(a).

(b) *Production of Documentary Evidence and Electronically Stored Information.* A subpoena may also command the person to whom it is directed to produce the books, papers, documents, electronically stored information, or tangible things designated therein, and may specify the form or forms in which electronically stored information is to be produced. The Court, upon motion made promptly and in any event at or before the time specified in the subpoena for compliance therewith, may (1) quash or modify the subpoena if it is unreasonable and oppressive, or (2) condition denial of the motion upon the advancement by the person in whose behalf the subpoena is issued of the reasonable cost of producing the books, papers, documents, electronically stored information, or tangible things.

(c) *Service.* A subpoena may be served by a United States marshal, or by a deputy marshal, or by any other person who is not a party and is not less than 18 years of age. Service of a subpoena upon a person named therein shall be made by delivering a copy thereof to such person and by tendering to such person the fees for one day's attendance and the mileage allowed by law. When the subpoena is issued on behalf of the Commissioner, fees and mileage need not be tendered. See Rule 148 for fees and mileage payable. The person making service of a subpoena shall make the return thereon in accordance with the form appearing in the subpoena.

(d) *Subpoena for Taking Depositions.* (1) *Issuance and Response.* The order of the Court approving the taking of a deposition pursuant to Rule 81(b)(2), the executed stipulation pursuant to Rule 81(d), or the service of the notice of deposition pursuant to Rule 74(b)(2) or (c)(2), constitutes authorization for issuance of subpoenas for the persons named or described therein. The subpoena may command the person to whom it is directed to produce and permit inspection and copying of designated books, papers, documents, electronically stored information, or tangible things, which come within the scope of the order or stipulation pursuant to which the deposition is taken. Within 15 days after service of the subpoena or such earlier time designated therein for compliance, the person to whom the subpoena is directed may serve upon the party on whose behalf the subpoena has been issued written objections to compliance with the subpoena in any or all respects. Such objections should not include objections made, or which might have been made, to the application to take the deposition pursuant to Rule 81(b)(2) or to the notice of deposition under Rule 74(b)(2) or (c)(2). If an objection is made, the party serving the subpoena shall not be entitled to compliance therewith to the extent of such objection, except as the Court may order otherwise upon application to it. Such application for an order may be made, with notice to the other party and to any other objecting persons, at any time before or during the taking of the deposition, subject to the time requirements of Rule 70(a)(2) or 81(b)(2). As to availability of protective orders, see Rule 103; and, as to enforcement of such subpoenas, see Rule 104.

(2) *Place of Examination.* The place designated in the subpoena for examination of the deponent shall be the place specified in the notice of deposition served pursuant to Rule 74(b)(2) or (c)(2), in a motion to take deposition under Rule 74(c)(3) or (4), in the order of the Court referred to in Rule 81(b)(2), or in the executed stipulation referred to in Rule 81(d). With respect to a deposition to be taken in a foreign country, see Rules 74(e)(2), 81(e)(2), and 84(a).

(e) *Contempt.* Failure by any person without adequate excuse to obey a subpoena served upon any such person may be deemed a contempt of the Court.

Rule 150. Record of Proceedings. (a) *General.* Hearings and trials before the Court shall be recorded or otherwise reported, and a transcript thereof shall be made if, in the opinion of the Court or the Judge or Special Trial Judge presiding at a hearing or trial, a permanent record is deemed appropriate. Transcripts shall be supplied to the parties and other persons at such charges as may be fixed or approved by the Court.

(b) *Transcript as Evidence.* Whenever the testimony of a witness at a trial or hearing which was recorded or otherwise reported is admissible in evidence at a later trial or hearing, it may be proved by the transcript thereof duly certified by the person who reported the testimony.

Rule 151. Briefs. (a) *General.* Briefs shall be filed after trial or submission of a case, except as otherwise directed by the presiding Judge or Special Trial Judge. In addition to or in lieu of briefs, the presiding Judge or Special Trial Judge may permit or direct the parties to make oral argument or file memoranda or statements of authorities. The Court may return without filing any brief that does not conform to the requirements of this Rule.

(b) *Time for Filing Briefs.* Briefs may be filed simultaneously or seriatim, as the presiding Judge or Special Trial Judge directs. The following times for filing briefs shall prevail in the absence of any different direction by the presiding Judge or Special Trial Judge:

(1) *Simultaneous Briefs.* Opening briefs within 75 days after the conclusion of the trial, and answering briefs 45 days thereafter.

(2) *Seriatim Briefs.* Opening brief within 75 days after the conclusion of the trial, answering brief within 45 days thereafter, and reply brief within 30 days after the due date of the answering brief.

A party who fails to file an opening brief is not permitted to file an answering or reply brief except on leave granted by the Court. A motion for extension of time for filing any brief shall be made prior to the due date and shall recite that the moving party has advised such party's adversary and whether or not such adversary objects to the motion. As to the effect of extensions of time, see Rule 25(c).

(c) *Service.* Each brief shall be served upon the opposite party when it is filed, except that, in the event of simultaneous briefs, such brief shall be served by the Clerk after the corresponding brief of the other party has been filed, unless the Court directs otherwise. Delinquent briefs will not be accepted unless accompanied by a motion setting forth reasons deemed sufficient by the Court to account for the delay. In the case of simultaneous briefs, the Court may return without filing a delinquent brief from a party after such party's adversary's brief has been served upon such party.

(d) *Number of Copies.* A signed original and two copies of each brief, plus an additional copy for each person to be served, shall be filed.

(e) *Form and Content.* All briefs shall conform to the requirements of Rule 23 and shall contain the following in the order indicated:

(1) On the first page, a table of contents with page references, followed by a list of all citations arranged alphabetically as to cited cases and stating the pages in the brief at which cited. Citations shall be in italics when printed and underscored when typewritten.

(2) A statement of the nature of the controversy, the tax involved, and the issues to be decided.

(3) Proposed findings of fact (in the opening brief or briefs), based on the evidence, in the form of numbered statements, each of which shall be complete and shall consist of a concise statement of essential fact and not a recital of testimony nor a discussion or argument relating to the evidence or the law. In each such numbered statement, there shall be inserted references to the pages of the transcript or the exhibits or other sources relied upon to support the statement. In an answering or reply brief, the party shall set forth any objections, together with the reasons therefor, to any proposed findings of any other party, showing the numbers of the statements to which the objections are directed; in addition, the party may set forth alternative proposed findings of fact.

(4) A concise statement of the points on which the party relies.

(5) The argument, which sets forth and discusses the points of law involved and any disputed questions of fact.

(6) The signature of counsel or the party submitting the brief. As to signature, see Rule 23(a)(3).

Rule 152. Oral Findings of Fact or Opinion. (a) *General.* Except in actions for declaratory judgment or for disclosure (see Titles XXI and XXII), the Judge, or the Special Trial Judge in any case in which the Special Trial Judge is authorized to make the decision of the Court pursuant to Code section 7436(c) or 7443A(b)(2), (3), (4), or (5), and (c), may, in the exercise of discretion, orally state the findings of fact or opinion if the Judge or Special Trial Judge is satisfied as to the factual conclusions to be reached in the case and that the law to be applied thereto is clear.

(b) *Transcript.* Oral findings of fact or opinion shall be recorded in the transcript of the hearing or trial. The pages of the transcript that contain such findings of fact or opinion (or a written summary thereof) shall be served by the Clerk upon all parties.

(c) *Nonprecedential Effect.* Opinions stated orally in accordance with paragraph (a) of this Rule shall not be relied upon as precedent, except as may be relevant for purposes of establishing the law of the case, res judicata, collateral estoppel, or other similar doctrine.

Rule 155. Computation by Parties For Entry of Decision. (a) *Agreed Computations*. Where the Court has filed or stated its opinion or issued a dispositive order determining the issues in a case, it may withhold entry of its decision for the purpose of permitting the parties to submit computations pursuant to the Court's determination of the issues, showing the correct amount to be included in the decision. Unless otherwise directed by the Court, if the parties are in agreement as to the amount to be included in the decision pursuant to the findings and conclusions of the Court, then they, or either of them, shall file with the Court within 90 days of service of the opinion or order an original and one copy of a computation showing the amount and that there is no disagreement that the figures shown are in accordance with the findings and conclusions of the Court. In the case of an overpayment, the computation shall also include the amount and date of each payment made by the petitioner. The Court will then enter its decision.

(b) *Procedure in Absence of Agreement*. If the parties are not in agreement as to the amount to be included in the decision in accordance with the findings and conclusions of the Court, then each party shall file with the Court a computation of the amount believed by such party to be in accordance with the Court's findings and conclusions. In the case of an overpayment, the computation shall also include the amount and date of each payment made by the petitioner. A party shall file such party's computation within 90 days of service of the opinion or order, unless otherwise directed by the Court. The Clerk will serve upon the opposite party a notice of such filing and if, on or before a date specified in the Clerk's notice, the opposite party fails to file an objection or an alternative computation, then the Court may enter decision in accordance with the computation already submitted. If in accordance with this Rule computations are submitted by the parties which differ as to the amount to be entered as the decision of the Court, then the parties may, at the Court's discretion, be afforded an opportunity to be heard in argument thereon and the Court will determine the correct amount and will enter its decision accordingly.

(c) *Limit on Argument*. Any argument under this Rule will be confined strictly to consideration of the correct computation of the amount to be included in the decision resulting from the findings and conclusions made by the Court, and no argument will be heard upon or consideration given to the issues or matters disposed of by the Court's findings and conclusions or to any new issues. This Rule is not to be regarded as affording an opportunity for retrial or reconsideration.

Rule 160. Harmless Error. No error in either the admission or exclusion of evidence, and no error or defect in any ruling or order or in anything done or omitted by the Court or by any of the parties, is ground for granting a new trial or for vacating, modifying, or otherwise disturbing a decision or order, unless refusal to take such action appears to the Court inconsistent with substantial justice. The Court at every stage of a case will disregard any error or defect which does not affect the substantial rights of the parties.

Rule 161. Motion for Reconsideration of Findings or Opinion. Any motion for reconsideration of an opinion or findings of fact, with or without a new or further trial, shall be filed within 30 days after a written opinion or the pages of the transcript that contain findings of fact or opinion stated orally pursuant to Rule 152 (or a written summary thereof) have been served, unless the Court shall otherwise permit.

Rule 162. Motion to Vacate or Revise Decision. Any motion to vacate or revise a decision, with or without a new or further trial, shall be filed within 30 days after the decision has been entered, unless the Court shall otherwise permit.

Rule 163. No Joinder of Motions Under Rules 161 and 162. Motions under Rules 161 and 162 shall be made separately from each other and not joined to or made part of any other motion.

Rule 170. General. The Rules of this Title XVII, referred to herein as the "Small Tax Case Rules", set forth the special provisions which are to be applied to small tax cases. The term "small tax case" means a case in which the amount in dispute is $50,000 or less (within the meaning of the Internal Revenue Code) and the Court has concurred in the petitioner's election. See Code secs. 7436(c) and 7463. Except as otherwise provided in these Small Tax Case Rules, the other Rules of practice of the Court are applicable to such cases.

Rule 171. Election of Small Tax Case Procedure. With respect to classification of a case as a small tax case, the following shall apply:

(a) A petitioner who wishes to have the proceedings in the case conducted as a small tax case may so request at the time the petition is filed. See Rule 173.

(b) If the Commissioner opposes the petitioner's request to have the proceedings conducted as a small tax case, then the Commissioner shall file with the answer a motion that the proceedings not be conducted as a small tax case.

(c) A petitioner may, at any time after the petition is filed and before the trial commences, request that the proceedings be conducted as a small tax case. If such request is made after the answer is filed, then the Commissioner may move without leave of the Court that the proceedings not be conducted as a small tax case.

(d) If such request is made in accordance with the provisions of this Rule 171, then the case will be docketed as a small tax case. The Court, on its own motion or on the motion of a party to the case, may, at any time before the trial commences, issue an order directing that the small tax case designation be removed and that the proceedings not be conducted as a small tax case. If no such order is issued, then the petitioner will be considered to have exercised the petitioner's option and the Court shall be deemed to have concurred therein.

Rule 172. Representation. A petitioner in a small tax case may appear without representation or may be represented by any person admitted to practice before the Court. As to representation, see Rule 24.

Rule 173. Pleadings. (a) *Petition:* (1) *Form and Content:* The petition in a small tax case shall be substantially in accordance with Form 2 shown in Appendix I.

(2) *Filing Fee:* The fee for filing a petition shall be $60, payable at the time of filing. The payment of any fee under this paragraph may be waived if the petitioner establishes to the satisfaction of the Court by an affidavit or declaration containing specific financial information the inability to make such payment.

(b) *Answer:* The Commission shall file an answer or shall move with respect to the petition within the periods specified in, and in accordance with the provisions of, Rule 36.

(c) *Reply:* A reply to the answer shall not be filed unless the Court otherwise directs. Any reply shall conform to the requirements of Rule 37(b). In the absence of a requirement of a reply, the provisions of the second sentence of Rule 37(c) shall not apply and the affirmative allegations of the answer shall be deemed denied.

Rule 174. Trial. (a) *Place of Trial*: At the time of filing the petition, the petitioner may, in accordance with Form 5 in Appendix I or by other separate writing, request the place where the petitioner would prefer the trial to be held. If the petitioner has not filed such a request, then the Commissioner, at the time the answer is filed, shall file a request showing the place of trial preferred by the Commissioner. The Court will make reasonable efforts to conduct the trial at the location most convenient to that requested where suitable facilities are available.

(b) *Conduct of Trial and Evidence*: Trials of small tax cases will be conducted as informally as possible consistent with orderly procedure, and any evidence deemed by the Court to have probative value shall be admissible.

(c) *Briefs*: Neither briefs nor oral arguments will be required in small tax cases unless the Court otherwise directs.

Rule 180. Assignment. The Chief Judge may from time to time designate a Special Trial Judge (see Rule 3(d)) to deal with any matter pending before the Court in accordance with these Rules and such directions as may be prescribed by the Chief Judge.

Rule 181. Powers and Duties. Subject to the specifications and limitations in orders designating Special Trial Judges and in accordance with the applicable provisions of these Rules, Special Trial Judges have and shall exercise the power to regulate all proceedings in any matter before them, including the conduct of trials, pretrial conferences, and hearings on motions, and to do all acts and take all measures necessary or proper for the efficient performance of their duties. They may require the production before them of evidence upon all matters embraced within their assignment, including the production of all books, papers, vouchers, documents, electronically stored information, and writings applicable thereto, and they have the authority to put witnesses on oath and to examine them. Special Trial Judges may rule upon the admissibility of evidence, in accordance with the provisions of Code sections 7453 and 7463, and may exercise such further and incidental authority, including ordering the issuance of subpoenas, as may be necessary for the conduct of trials or other proceedings.

Rule 182. Cases in Which the Special Trial Judge is Authorized to Make the Decision. Except as otherwise directed by the Chief Judge, the following procedure shall be observed in small tax cases (as defined in Rule 170); in cases where neither the amount of the deficiency placed in dispute (within the meaning of Code section 7463), nor the amount of any claimed overpayment, exceeds $50,000; in declaratory judgment actions; in lien or levy actions; and in whistleblower actions:

(a) *Small Tax Cases*. Except in cases where findings of fact or opinion are stated orally pursuant to Rule 152, a Special Trial Judge who conducts the trial of a small tax case shall, as soon after such trial as shall be practicable, prepare a summary of the facts and reasons for the proposed disposition of the case, which then shall be submitted promptly to the Chief Judge, or, if the Chief Judge shall so direct, to a Judge or Division of the Court.

(b) *Other Cases Involving $50,000 or Less*. Except in cases where findings of fact or opinion are stated orally pursuant to Rule 152, a Special Trial Judge who conducts the trial of a case (other than a small tax case) where neither the amount of the deficiency placed in dispute (within the meaning of Code section 7463), nor the amount of any claimed overpayment, exceeds $50,000 shall, as soon after such trial as shall be practicable, prepare proposed findings of fact and opinion, which shall then be submitted promptly to the Chief Judge.

(c) *Declaratory Judgment, Lien or Levy, and Whistleblower Actions.* A Special Trial Judge who conducts the trial of a declaratory judgment action or, except in cases where findings of fact or opinion are stated orally pursuant to Rule 152, a lien or levy or a whistleblower action, or to whom such a case is submitted for decision, shall, as soon after such trial or submission as shall be practicable, prepare proposed findings of fact and opinion, which shall then be submitted promptly to the Chief Judge.

(d) *Decision.* The Chief Judge may authorize the Special Trial Judge to make the decision of the Court in any small tax case (as defined in Rule 170); in any case where neither the amount of the deficiency placed in dispute (within the meaning of Code section 7463), nor the amount of any claimed overpayment, exceeds $50,000; in any declaratory judgment action; in any lien or levy action; and in any whistleblower action, subject to such conditions and review as the Chief Judge may provide.

(e) *Procedure in Event of Assignment to a Judge.* In the event the Chief Judge decides to assign a case (other than a small tax case) to a Judge to prepare a report in accordance with Code section 7460 and to make the decision of the Court, the proposed findings of fact and opinion previously submitted to the Chief Judge shall be filed as the Special Trial Judge's recommended findings of fact and conclusions of law. Thereafter, the procedures of Rule 183(b), (c), and (d) shall apply.

Rule 183. Other Cases. Except in cases subject to the provisions of Rule 182 or as otherwise provided, the following procedure shall be observed in cases tried before a Special Trial Judge:

(a) *Trial and Briefs.* A Special Trial Judge shall conduct the trial of any assigned case. After such trial, the parties shall submit their briefs in accordance with the provisions of Rule 151. Unless otherwise directed, no further briefs shall be filed.

(b) *Special Trial Judge's Recommendations.* After all the briefs have been filed by all the parties or the time for doing so has expired, the Special Trial Judge shall file recommended findings of fact and conclusions of law and a copy of the recommended findings of fact and conclusions of law shall be served in accordance with Rule 21.

(c) *Objections.* Within 45 days after the service of the recommended findings of fact and conclusions of law, a party may serve and file specific, written objections to the recommended findings of fact and conclusions of law. A party may respond to another party's objections within 30 days after being served with a copy thereof. The above time periods may be extended by the Special Trial Judge. After the time for objections and responses has passed, the Chief Judge shall assign the case to a Judge for preparation of a report in accordance with Code section 7460. Unless a party shall have proposed a particular finding of fact, or unless the party shall have objected to another party's proposed finding of fact, the Judge may refuse to consider the party's objection to the Special Trial Judge's recommended findings of fact and conclusions of law for failure to make such a finding or for inclusion of such finding proposed by the other party, as the case may be.

(d) *Action on the Recommendation.* The Judge to whom the case is assigned may adopt the Special Trial Judge's recommended findings of fact and conclusions of law, or may modify or reject them in whole or in part, or may direct the filing of additional briefs, or may receive further evidence, or may direct oral argument, or may recommit the recommended findings of fact and conclusions of law with instructions. The Judge's action on the Special Trial Judge's recommended findings of fact and conclusions of law shall be reflected in the record by an appropriate order or report. Due regard shall be given to the circumstance that the Special Trial Judge had the opportunity to evaluate the credibility of witnesses, and the findings of fact recommended presumed to be correct.

Rule 190. How Appeal Taken. (a) *General.* Review of a decision of the Court by a United States Court of Appeals is obtained by filing a notice of appeal and the required filing fee with the Clerk of the Tax Court within 90 days after the decision is entered. If a timely notice of appeal is filed by one party, then any other party may take an appeal by filing a notice of appeal within 120 days after the Court's decision is entered. Code Section 7483. For other requirements governing such an appeal, see rules 13 and 14 of the Federal Rules of Appellate Procedure. A suggested form of the notice of appeal is contained in Appendix I. See Code Section 7482(a).

(b) *Dispositive Orders.* (1) *Entry and Appeal.* A dispositive order, including (A) an order granting or denying a motion to restrain assessment or collection, made pursuant to Code Section 6213(a), and (B) an order granting or denying a motion for review of a proposed sale of seized property, made pursuant to Code Section 6863(b)(3)(C), shall be entered upon the record of the Court and served forthwith by the Clerk. Such an order shall be treated as a decision of the Court for purposes of appeal.

(2) *Stay of Proceedings.* Unless so ordered, proceedings in the Tax Court shall not be stayed by virtue of any order entered under Code Section 6213(a) that is or may be the subject of an appeal pursuant to Code Section 7482(a)(3) or any order entered under Code Section 6863(b)(3)(C) that is or may be the subject of an appeal.

(c) *Venue.* For the circuit of the Court of Appeals to which the appeal is to be taken, see Code Section 7482(b).

(d) *Interlocutory Orders.* For provisions governing appeals from interlocutory orders, see Rule 193.

Rule 200. Admission to Practice and Periodic Registration Fee. (a) *Qualifications.* (1) *General.* An applicant for admission to practice before the Court must establish to the satisfaction of the Court that the applicant is of good moral and professional character and possesses the requisite qualifications to provide competent representation before the Court. In addition, the applicant must satisfy the other requirements of this Rule. If the applicant fails to satisfy the requirements of this Rule, then the Court may deny such applicant admission to practice before the Court.

(2) *Attorney Applicants.* An applicant who is an attorney at law must, as a condition of being admitted to practice, file with the Admissions Clerk at the address listed in paragraph (b) of this Rule a completed application accompanied by a fee to be established by the Court, see Appendix II, and a current certificate from the Clerk of the appropriate court, showing that the applicant has been admitted to practice before and is a member in good standing of the Bar of the Supreme Court of the United States, or of the highest or appropriate court of any State or of the District of Columbia, or any commonwealth, territory, or possession of the United States. A current court certificate is one executed within 90 calendar days preceding the date of the filing of the application.

(3) *Nonattorney Applicants.* An applicant who is not an attorney at law must, as a condition of being admitted to practice, file with the Admissions Clerk at the address listed in

paragraph (b) of this Rule, a completed application accompanied by a fee to be established by the Court. See Appendix II. In addition, such an applicant must, as a condition of being admitted to practice, satisfy the Court, by means of a written examination given by the Court, that the applicant possesses the requisite qualifications to provide competent representation before the Court. Written examinations for applicants who are not attorneys at law will be held no less often than every 2 years. By public announcement at least 6 months prior to the date of each examination, the Court will announce the date and the time of such examination. The Court will notify each applicant, whose application for admission is in order, of the time and the place at which the applicant is to be present for such examination, and the applicant must present that notice to the examiner as authority for taking such examination.

(b) *Applications for Admission.* An application for admission to practice before the Court must be on the form provided by the Court. Application forms and other necessary information will be furnished upon request addressed to the Admissions Clerk, United States Tax Court, 400 Second St., N.W., Washington, D.C. 20217. As to forms of payment for application fees, see Rule 11.

(c) *Sponsorship.* An applicant for admission by examination must be sponsored by at least two persons theretofore admitted to practice before this Court, and each sponsor must send a letter of recommendation directly to the Admissions Clerk at the address listed in paragraph (b) of this Rule, where it will be treated as a confidential communication. The sponsor shall send this letter promptly after the applicant has been notified that he or she has passed the written examination required by paragraph (a)(3) of this Rule. The sponsor shall state fully and frankly the extent of the sponsor's acquaintance with the applicant, the sponsor's opinion of the moral character and repute of the applicant, and the sponsor's opinion of the qualifications of the applicant to practice before this Court. The Court may in its discretion accept such an applicant with less than two such sponsors.

(d) *Admission.* Upon the Court's approval of an application for admission in which an applicant has subscribed to the oath or affirmation and upon an applicant's satisfaction of the other applicable requirements of this Rule, such applicant will be admitted to practice before the Court and be entitled to a certificate of admission.

(e) *Change of Address.* Each person admitted to practice before the Court shall promptly notify the Admissions Clerk at the address listed in paragraph (b) of this Rule of any change in office address for mailing purposes. See Form 10 in Appendix I regarding a form for and methods of providing the notification required by this paragraph (e). See also Rule 21(b)(4) regarding the filing of a separate notice of change of address for each docket number in which such person has entered an appearance.

(f) *Corporations and Firms Not Eligible.* Corporations and firms will not be admitted to practice or recognized before the Court.

(g) *Periodic Registration Fee.* (1) Each person admitted to practice before the Court shall pay a periodic registration fee. The frequency and the amount of such fee shall be determined by the Court, except that such amount shall not exceed $30 per calendar year. The Clerk shall maintain an Ineligible List containing the names of all persons admitted to practice before the Court who have failed to comply with the provisions of this paragraph (g)(1). No such person shall be permitted to commence a case in the Court or enter an appearance in a pending case while on the Ineligible List. The name of any person appearing on the Ineligible List shall not be removed from the List until the currently due registration fee has been paid and arrearages have been made current. Each person admitted to practice before the Court, whether or not engaged in private practice, must pay the periodic registration fee. As to forms of payment, see Rule 11.

(2) The fees described in paragraph (g)(1) of this Rule shall be used by the Court to compensate independent counsel appointed by the Court to assist it with respect to disciplinary matters. See Rule 202(h).

Rule 201. Conduct of Practice Before the Court. (a) *General.* Practitioners before the Court shall carry on their practice in accordance with the letter and spirit of the Model Rules of Professional Conduct of the American Bar Association.

(b) *Statement of Employment.* The Court may require any practitioner before it to furnish a statement, under oath, of the terms and circumstances of his or her employment in any case.

Rule 202. Disciplinary Matters. (a) *General.* A member of the Bar of this Court may be disciplined by this Court as a result of:

(1) Conviction in any court of the United States, or of the District of Columbia, or of any State, territory, commonwealth, or possession of the United States of any felony or of any lesser crime involving false swearing, misrepresentation, fraud, criminal violation of any provision of the Internal Revenue Code, bribery, extortion, misappropriation, theft, or moral turpitude;

(2) Imposition of discipline by any other court of whose bar an attorney is a member, or an attorney's disbarment or suspension by consent or resignation from the bar of such court while an investigation into allegations of misconduct is pending;

(3) Conduct with respect to the Court which violates the letter and spirit of the Model Rules of Professional Conduct of the American Bar Association, the Rules of the Court, or orders or other instructions of the Court; or

(4) Any other conduct unbecoming a member of the Bar of the Court.

(b) *Reporting Convictions and Discipline.* A member of the Bar of this Court who has been convicted of any felony or of any lesser crime described in paragraph (a)(1), who has been disciplined as described in paragraph (a)(2), or who has been disbarred or suspended from practice before an agency of the United States Government exercising professional disciplinary jurisdiction, shall inform the Chair of the Court's Committee on Admissions, Ethics, and Discipline of such action in writing no later than 30 days after entry of the judgment of conviction or order of discipline.

(c) *Disciplinary Actions.* Discipline may consist of disbarment, suspension from practice before the Court, reprimand, admonition, or any other sanction that the Court may deem appropriate. The Court may, in the exercise of its discretion, immediately suspend a practitioner from practice before the Court until further order of the Court. Except as provided in paragraph (d), no person shall be suspended for more than 60 days or disbarred until such person has been afforded an opportunity to be heard. A Judge of the Court may immediately suspend any person for not more than 60 days for contempt or misconduct during the course of any trial or hearing.

(d) *Interim Suspension Pending Final Disposition of Disciplinary Proceedings.* If a member of the Bar of this Court is convicted in any court of the United States, or of the District of Columbia, or of any State, territory, commonwealth, or possession of the United States of any felony or of any lesser crime described in paragraph (a)(1), then, notwithstanding the pendency of an appeal of the conviction, if any, the Court may, in the exercise of its discretion, immediately suspend such practitioner from practice before the Court pending final disposition of the disciplinary proceedings described in paragraph (e).

(e) *Disciplinary Proceedings.* Upon the occurrence or allegation of any event described in paragraph (a)(1) through (a)(4), except for any suspension imposed for 60 days or less pursuant to paragraph (c), the Court shall issue to the practitioner an order to show cause why the practitioner should not be disciplined or shall otherwise take appropriate action. The order to show cause shall direct that a written response be filed within such period as the Court may direct and shall set a prompt hearing on the matter before one or more Judges of the Court. If the disciplinary proceeding is predicated upon the complaint of a Judge of the Court, the hearing shall be conducted before a panel of three other Judges of the Court.

(f) *Reinstatement.* (1) A practitioner suspended for 60 days or less pursuant to paragraph (c) shall be automatically reinstated at the end of the period of suspension.

(2) A practitioner suspended for more than 60 days or disbarred pursuant to this Rule may not resume practice before the Court until reinstated by order of the Court.

(A) A disbarred practitioner or a practitioner suspended for more than 60 days who wishes to be reinstated to practice before the Court must file a petition for reinstatement. Upon receipt of the petition for reinstatement, the Court may set the matter for prompt hearing before one or more Judges of the Court. If the disbarment or suspension for more than 60 days was predicated upon the complaint of a Judge of the Court, any such hearing shall be conducted before a panel of three other Judges of the Court.

(B) In order to be reinstated before the Court, the practitioner must demonstrate by clear and convincing evidence in the petition for reinstatement and at any hearing that such practitioner's reinstatement will not be detrimental to the integrity and standing of the Court's Bar or to the administration of justice, or subversive of the public interest.

(C) No petition for reinstatement under this Rule shall be filed within 1 year following an adverse decision upon a petition for reinstatement filed by or on behalf of the same person.

(g) *Right to Counsel.* In all proceedings conducted under the provisions of this Rule, the practitioner shall have the right to be represented by counsel.

(h) *Appointment of Court Counsel.* The Court, in its discretion, may appoint counsel to the Court to assist it with respect to any disciplinary matters.

(i) *Jurisdiction.* Nothing contained in this Rule shall be construed to deny to the Court such powers as are necessary for the Court to maintain control over proceedings conducted before it, such as proceedings for contempt under Code Section 7456 or for costs under Code Section 6673(a)(2).

Rule 220. General. (a) *Applicability.* The Rules of this Title XXII set forth the special provisions which apply to the three types of disclosure actions relating to written determinations by the Internal Revenue Service and their background file documents, as authorized by Code Section 6110. They consist of (1) actions to restrain disclosure, (2) actions to obtain additional disclosure, and (3) actions to obtain disclosure of identity in the case of third party contacts. Except as otherwise provided in this Title, the other Rules of Practice and Procedure of the Court, to the extent pertinent, are applicable to such disclosure actions.

(b) *Definitions.* As used in the Rules in this Title--

(1) A "written determination" means a ruling, determination letter, or technical advice memorandum. See Code Section 6110(b)(1).

(2) A "prior written determination" is a written determination issued pursuant to a request made before November 1, 1976.

(3) A "background file document" has the meaning provided in Code Section 6110(b)(2).

(4) A "notice of intention to disclose" is the notice described in Code Section 6110(f)(1).

(5) "Party" includes a petitioner, the respondent Commissioner of Internal Revenue, and any intervenor under Rule 225.

(6) A "disclosure action" is either an "additional disclosure action", an "action to restrain disclosure", or a "third party contact action", as follows:

(A) An "additional disclosure action" is an action to obtain disclosure within Code Section 6110(f)(4).

(B) An "action to restrain disclosure" is an action within Code Section 6110(f)(3) or (h)(4) to prevent any part or all of a written determination, prior written determination, or background file document from being opened to public inspection.

(C) A "third party contact action" is an action to obtain disclosure of the identity of a person to whom a written determination pertains in accordance with Code Section 6110(d)(3).

(7) "Third party contact" means the person described in Code Section 6110(d)(1) who has communicated with the Internal Revenue Service.

(c) *Jurisdictional Requirements.* The Court does not have jurisdiction of a disclosure action under this Title unless the following conditions are satisfied:

(1) In an additional disclosure action, the petitioner has exhausted all administrative remedies available within the Internal Revenue Service. See Code Section 6110(f)(2)(A) and (4)(A).

(2) In an action to restrain disclosure--

(A) The Commissioner has issued a notice of intention to disclose or, in the case of a prior written determination, the Commissioner has issued public notice in the Federal Register that the determination is to be opened to public inspection.

(B) In the case of a written determination, the petition is filed with the Court within 60 days after mailing by the Commissioner of a notice of intention to disclose, or, in the case of a prior written determination, the petition is filed with the Court within 75 days after the date of publication of the notice in the Federal Register.

(C) The petitioner has exhausted all administrative remedies available within the Internal Revenue Service. See Code Section 6110(f)(2)(B) and (3)(A)(iii).

(3) In a third party contact action--

(A) The Commissioner was required to make a notation on the written determination in accordance with Code Section 6110(d)(1).

(B) A petition is filed within 36 months after the first date on which the written determination is open to public inspection.

(d) *Form and Style of Papers.* All papers filed in a disclosure action shall be prepared in the form and style set forth in Rule 23, except that whenever any party joins or intervenes in the action, then thereafter, in addition to the number of copies required to be filed under such Rule, an additional copy shall be filed for each party who joins or intervenes in the action. In the case of anonymous parties, see Rule 227.

Rule 221. Commencement of Disclosure Action. (a) *Commencement of Action.* A disclosure action shall be commenced by filing a petition with the Court. See Rule 22, relating to the place and manner of filing the petition, and Rule 32, relating to the form of pleadings.

(b) *Contents of Petition.* Every petition shall be entitled "Petition for Additional Disclosure" or "Petition To Restrain Disclosure" or "Petition To Disclose Identity". Subject to the provisions of Rule 227, dealing with anonymity, each petition shall contain the petitioner's name and State of legal residence, an appropriate prayer for relief, and the signature, mailing address, and telephone number of the petitioner or the petitioner's counsel, as well as counsel's Tax Court bar number. In addition, each petition shall contain the allegations described in paragraph (c), (d), or (e) of this Rule.

(c) *Petition in Additional Disclosure Action.* The petition in an additional disclosure action shall contain:

(1) A brief description (including any identifying number or symbol) of the written determination, prior written determination, or background file document, as to which petitioner seeks additional disclosure. A copy of any such determination or document, as it is then available to the public, shall be appended.

(2) The date of the petitioner's request to the Internal Revenue Service for additional disclosure, with a copy of such request appended.

(3) A statement of the Commissioner's disposition of the request, with a copy of the disposition appended.

(4) A statement that the petitioner has exhausted all administrative remedies available within the Internal Revenue Service.

(5) In separate lettered subparagraphs, a clear and concise statement identifying each portion of the written determination, prior written determination, or background file document as to which petitioner seeks additional disclosure together with any facts and reasons to support disclosure. See Rule 229 with respect to the burden of proof in an additional disclosure action.

(d) *Petition in Action to Restrain Disclosure.* The petition in an action to restrain disclosure shall contain:

(1) A statement that the petitioner is (A) a person to whom the written determination pertains, or (B) a successor in interest, executor, or other person authorized by law to act for or on behalf of such person, or (C) a person who has a direct interest in maintaining the confidentiality of the written determination or background file document or portion thereof, or (D) in the case of a prior written determination, the person who received such prior written determination.

(2) A statement that the Commissioner has issued a notice of intention to disclose with respect to a written determination or a background file document, stating the date of mailing of the notice of intention to disclose and appending a copy of it to the petition, or, in the case of a prior written determination, a statement that the Commissioner has issued public notice in the Federal Register that the determination is to be opened to public inspection, and stating the date and citation of such publication in the Federal Register.

(3) A brief description (including any identifying number or symbol) of the written determination, prior written determination, or background file document, as to which petitioner seeks to restrain disclosure.

(4) The date of petitioner's request to the Internal Revenue Service to refrain from disclosure, with a copy of such request appended.

(5) A statement of the Commissioner's disposition of the request, with a copy of such disposition appended.

(6) A statement that petitioner has exhausted all administrative remedies available within

the Internal Revenue Service.

(7) In separate lettered subparagraphs, a clear and concise statement identifying each portion of the written determination, prior written determination, or background file document as to which the petitioner seeks to restrain disclosure, together with any facts and reasons to support the petitioner's position. See Rule 229 with respect to the burden of proof in an action to restrain disclosure.

(e) *Petition in Third Party Contact Action.* The petition in a third party contact action shall contain:

(1) A brief description (including any identifying number or symbol) of the written determination to which the action pertains. There shall be appended a copy of such determination, and the background file document (if any) reflecting the third party contact, as then available to the public.

(2) The date of the first day that the written determination was open to public inspection.

(3) A statement of the disclosure sought by the petitioner.

(4) A clear and concise statement of the impropriety alleged to have occurred or the undue influence alleged to have been exercised with respect to the written determination or on behalf of the person whose identity is sought, and the public interest supporting any other disclosure. See Rule 229 with respect to the burden of proof in a third party contact action.

(f) *Service.* For the provisions relating to service of the petition and other papers, see Rule 21.

(g) *Anonymity.* With respect to anonymous pleading, see Rule 227.

Rule 222. Request for Place of Hearing. At the time of filing a petition in a disclosure action, a request for a place of hearing shall be filed in accordance with Rule 140. In addition, the petitioner shall include the date on which the petitioner believes the action will be ready for submission to the Court and the petitioner's estimate of the time required therefor. The Commissioner shall, at the time the answer is filed, also set forth in a separate statement the date on which the Commissioner expects the action will be ready for submission to the Court and an estimate of the time required therefor. An intervenor shall likewise furnish such information to the Court in a separate statement filed with the intervenor's first pleading in the case. After the action is at issue (see Rule 224), it will ordinarily, without any further request by the Court for information as to readiness for submission, be placed on a calendar for submission to the Court. See also Rule 229.

Rule 223. Other Pleadings. (a) *Answer.* (1) *Time to Answer or Move.* The Commissioner shall have 30 days from the date of service of the petition within which to file an answer or move with respect to the petition, or, in an action for additional disclosure, to file an election not to defend pursuant to Code Section 6110(f)(4)(B), in which event the Commissioner shall be relieved of the obligation of filing an answer or any subsequent pleading. With respect to intervention when the Commissioner elects not to defend, see Rule 225.

(2) *Form and Content.* The answer shall be drawn so that it will advise the petitioner and the Court fully of the nature of the defense. It shall contain a specific admission or denial of each material allegation in the petition. If the Commissioner shall be without knowledge or information sufficient to form a belief as to the truth of an allegation, then the Commissioner shall so state, and such statement shall have the effect of a denial. If the Commissioner intends to qualify or to deny only a part of an allegation, then the Commissioner shall specify so much of it as is true and shall qualify or deny only the remainder. In addition, the answer shall contain a

clear and concise statement of every ground, together with the facts in support thereof on which the Commissioner relies and has the burden of proof. Paragraphs of the answer shall be designated to correspond to those of the petition to which they relate.

(3) *Effect of Answer.* Every material allegation set out in the petition and not expressly admitted or denied in the answer shall be deemed to be admitted.

(b) *Reply.* Each petitioner may file a reply or move with respect to the answer within 20 days from the date of service of the answer. Where a reply is filed, every affirmative allegation set out in the answer and not expressly admitted or denied in the reply, shall be deemed to be admitted. Where a reply is not filed, the affirmative allegations in the answer will be deemed denied. Any new material contained in the reply shall be deemed denied.

Rule 224. Joinder of Issue. A disclosure action shall be deemed at issue upon the filing of the reply or at the expiration of the time for doing so.

Rule 225. Intervention. (a) *Who May Intervene.* The persons to whom notice is required to be given by the Commissioner pursuant to Code Section 6110(d)(3), (f)(3)(B), or (f)(4)(B) shall have the right to intervene in the action as to which the notice was given. The Commissioner shall append a copy of the petition to any such notice.

(b) *Procedure.* If a person desires to intervene, then such person shall file an initial pleading, which shall be a petition in intervention or an answer in intervention, not later than 30 days after mailing by the Commissioner of the notice referred to in paragraph (a) of this Rule. In an action for additional disclosure where the Commissioner elects not to defend pursuant to Code Section 6110(f)(4)(B), the Commissioner shall mail to each person, to whom the Commissioner has mailed the notice referred to in paragraph (a) of this Rule, a notice of the Commissioner's election not to defend, and any such person desiring to intervene shall have 30 days after such mailing within which to file a petition in intervention or an answer in intervention. The initial pleading of an intervenor, whether a petition or answer, shall show the basis for the right to intervene and shall include, to the extent appropriate, the same elements as are required for a petition under Rule 221 or an answer under Rule 223. An intervenor shall otherwise be subject to the same rules of procedure as apply to other parties. With respect to anonymous intervention, see Rule 227.

Rule 226. Joinder of Parties. The joinder of parties in a disclosure action shall be subject to the following requirements:

(a) *Commencement of Action.* Any person who meets the requirements for commencing such an action may join with any other such person in filing a petition with respect to the same written determination, prior written determination, or background file document. But see Code Section 6110(f)(3)(B) and (h)(4).

(b) *Consolidation of Actions.* If more than one petition is filed with respect to the same written determination, prior written determination, or background file document, then see Rule 141 with respect to the consolidation of the actions.

Rule 227. Anonymous Parties. (a) *Petitioners.* A petitioner in an action to restrain disclosure relating to either a written determination or a prior written determination may file the petition anonymously, if appropriate.

(b) *Intervenors.* An intervenor may proceed anonymously, if appropriate, in any disclosure action.

(c) *Procedure*. A party who proceeds pursuant to this Rule shall be designated as "Anonymous". In all cases where a party proceeds anonymously pursuant to paragraph (a) or (b) of this Rule, such party shall set forth in a separate paper such party's name and address and the reasons why such party seeks to proceed anonymously. Such separate paper shall be filed with such party's initial pleading. Anonymity, where appropriate, shall be preserved to the maximum extent consistent with the proper conduct of the action. See Rule 13(d), relating to contempt of Court. With respect to confidential treatment of pleadings and other papers, see Rule 228.

Rule 228. Confidentiality. (a) *Confidentiality*. The petition and all other papers submitted to the Court in any disclosure action shall be placed and retained by the Court in a confidential file and shall not be open to inspection unless otherwise permitted by the Court.

(b) *Publicity of Court Proceedings*. On order of the Court portions or all of the hearings, testimony, evidence, and reports in any action under this Title may be closed to the public or to inspection by the public, to the extent deemed by the Court to be appropriate in order to preserve the anonymity, privacy, or confidentiality of any person involved in an action within Code Section 6110. See Code Section 6110(f)(6).

Rule 229. Burden of Proof. The burden of proof shall be upon the petitioner as to the jurisdictional requirements described in Rule 220(c). As to other matters, the burden of proof shall be determined consistently with Rule 142(a), subject to the following:

(a) In an action for additional disclosure, the burden of proof as to the issue of whether disclosure should be made shall be on the Commissioner and on any other person seeking to deny disclosure. See Code Section 6110(f)(4)(A).

(b) In an action to restrain disclosure, the burden of proof as to the issue of whether disclosure should be made shall be upon the petitioner.

(c) In a third party contact action, the burden of proof shall be on the petitioner to establish that one could reasonably conclude that an impropriety occurred or undue influence was exercised with respect to the written determination by or on behalf of the person whose identity is sought.

Rule 229A. Procedure in Actions Heard by a Special Trial Judge of the Court. (a) Where Special Trial Judge Is to Make the Decision. If a disclosure action is assigned to a Special Trial Judge who is authorized in the order of assignment to make the decision, then the opinion and proposed decision of the Special Trial Judge shall be submitted to and approved by the Chief Judge, or by another Judge designated by the Chief Judge for that purpose, prior to service of the opinion and decision upon the parties.

(b) Where Special Trial Judge Is Not to Make the Decision. If a disclosure action is assigned to a Special Trial Judge who is not authorized in the order of assignment to make the decision, then the procedure provided in Rule 183 shall be followed.

Rule 230. General. (a) *Applicability*. The Rules of this Title XXIII set forth the special provisions which apply to claims for reasonable litigation and administrative costs authorized by Code section 7430. Except as otherwise provided in this Title, the other Rules of Practice and Procedure of the Court, to the extent pertinent, are applicable to such claims for reasonable litigation and administrative costs. See Title XXVI for Rules relating to separate actions for administrative costs, authorized by Code section 7430(f)(2).

(b) *Definitions.* As used in the Rules in this Title--

(1) "Reasonable litigation costs" include the items described in Code Section 7430(c)(1).

(2) "Reasonable administrative costs" include the items described in Code section 7430(c)(2).

(3) "Court proceeding" means any action brought in this Court in connection with the determination, collection, or refund of tax, interest, or penalty.

(4) "Administrative proceeding" means any procedure or other action within the Internal Revenue Service in connection with the determination, collection, or refund of tax, interest, or penalty.

(5) In the case of a partnership action, the term "party" includes the partner who filed the petition, the tax matters partner, and each person who satisfies the requirements of Code section 6226(c) and (d) or 6228(a)(4). See Rule 247(a).

(6) "Attorney's fees" include fees for the services of an individual (whether or not an attorney) who is authorized to practice before the Court or before the Internal Revenue Service. For the procedure for admission to practice before the Court, see Rule 200.

Rule 231. Claims for Litigation and Administrative Costs. (a) *Time and Manner of Claim.*

(1) *Agreed Cases.* Where the parties have reached a settlement which disposes of all issues in the case including litigation and administrative costs, an award of reasonable litigation and administrative costs, if any, shall be included in the stipulated decision submitted by the parties for entry by the Court.

(2) *Unagreed Cases.* Where a party has substantially prevailed or is treated as the prevailing party in the case of a qualified offer made as described in Code section 7430(g), and wishes to claim reasonable litigation or administrative costs, and there is no agreement as to that party's entitlement to such costs, a claim shall be made by motion filed--

(A) Within 30 days after the service of a written opinion determining the issues in the case;

(B) Within 30 days after the service of the pages of the transcript that contain findings of fact or opinion stated orally pursuant to Rule 152 (or a written summary thereof); or

(C) After the parties have settled all issues in the case other than litigation and administrative costs. See paragraphs (b)(3) and (c) of this Rule regarding the filing of a stipulation of settlement with the motion in such cases.

(b) *Content of Motion.* A motion for an award of reasonable litigation or administrative costs shall be in writing and shall contain the following:

(1) A statement that the moving party is a party to a Court proceeding that was commenced after February 28, 1983;

(2) If the claim includes a claim for administrative costs, a statement that the administrative proceeding was commenced after November 10, 1988;

(3) A statement sufficient to demonstrate that the moving party has substantially prevailed with respect to either the amount in controversy or the most significant issue or set of issues presented, or is treated as the prevailing party in the case of a qualified offer made as described in Code section 7430(g), either in the Court proceeding or, if the claim includes a claim for administrative costs, in the administrative proceeding, including a stipulation in the form prescribed by paragraph (c) of this Rule as to any settled issues;

(4) a statement that the moving party meets the net worth requirements, if applicable, of section 2412(d)(2)(B) of title 28, United States Code (as in effect on October 22, 1986), which

statement shall be supported by an affidavit or a declaration executed by the moving party and not by counsel for the moving party;

(5) A statement that the moving party has exhausted the administrative remedies available to such party within the Internal Revenue Service;

(6) A statement that the moving party has not unreasonably protracted the Court proceeding and, if the claim includes a claim for administrative costs, the administrative proceeding;

(7) A statement of the specific litigation and administrative costs for which the moving party claims an award, supported by an affidavit or a declaration in the form prescribed in paragraph (d) of this Rule;

(8) If the moving party requests a hearing on the motion, a statement of the reasons why the motion cannot be disposed of by the Court without a hearing (see Rule 232(a)(2) regarding the circumstances in which the Court will direct a hearing); and

(9) An appropriate prayer for relief.

(c) *Stipulation as to Settled Issues.* If some or all of the issues in a case (other than litigation and administrative costs) have been settled by the parties, then a motion for an award of reasonable litigation or administrative costs shall be accompanied by a stipulation, signed by the parties or by their counsel, setting forth the terms of the settlement as to each such issue (including the amount of tax involved). A stipulation of settlement shall be binding upon the parties unless otherwise permitted by the Court or agreed upon by those parties.

(d) *Affidavit or Declaration in Support of Costs Claimed.* A motion for an award of reasonable litigation or administrative costs shall be accompanied by a detailed affidavit or declaration by the moving party or counsel for the moving party which sets forth distinctly the nature and amount of each item of costs for which an award is claimed.

(e) *Qualified Offer.* If a qualified offer was made by the moving party as described in Code section 7430(g), then a motion for award of reasonable litigation or administrative costs shall be accompanied by a copy of such offer.

Rule 232. Disposition of Claims for Litigation and Administrative Costs. (a) *General.* A motion for reasonable litigation or administrative costs may be disposed of in one or more of the following ways, in the discretion of the Court:

(1) The Court may take action after the Commissioner's written response to the motion is filed. (See paragraph (b)).

(2) After the Commissioner's response is filed, the Court may direct that the moving party file a reply to the Commissioner's response. Additionally, the Court may direct a hearing, which will be held at a location that serves the convenience of the parties and the Court. A motion for reasonable litigation or administrative costs ordinarily will be disposed of without a hearing unless it is clear from the motion, the Commissioner's written response, and the moving party's reply that there is a bona fide factual dispute that cannot be resolved without an evidentiary hearing.

(3) [Deleted]

(b) *Response by the Commissioner.* The Commissioner shall file a written response within 60 days after service of the motion. The Commissioner's response shall contain the following: (1) A clear and concise statement of each reason why the Commissioner alleges that the position of the Commissioner in the Court proceeding and, if the claim includes a claim for administrative costs, in the administrative proceeding, was substantially justified, and a statement of the facts on which the Commissioner relies to support each of such reasons;

(2) A statement whether the Commissioner agrees that the moving party has substantially prevailed with respect to either the amount in controversy or the most significant issue or set of issues presented, or is treated as the prevailing party in the case of a qualified offer made as described in Code section 7430(g), either in the Court proceeding or, if the claim includes a claim for administrative costs, in the administrative proceeding;

(3) A statement whether the Commissioner agrees that the moving party meets the net worth requirements, if applicable, as provided by law;

(4) A statement whether the Commissioner agrees that the moving party has exhausted the administrative remedies available to such party within the Internal Revenue Service;

(5) A statement whether the Commissioner agrees that the moving party has not unreasonably protracted the Court proceeding and, if the claim includes a claim for administrative costs, the administrative proceeding;

(6) A statement whether the Commissioner agrees that the amounts of costs claimed are reasonable; and

(7) The basis for the Commissioner's disagreeing with any such allegations by the moving party.

If the Commissioner agrees with the moving party's request for a hearing, or if the Commissioner requests a hearing, then such response shall include a statement of the Commissioner's reasons why the motion cannot be disposed of without a hearing.

(c) *Conference Required.* After the date for filing the Commissioner's written response and prior to the date for filing a reply, if one is required by the Court, counsel for the Commissioner and the moving party or counsel for the moving party shall confer and attempt to reach an agreement as to each of the allegations by the parties. The Court expects that, at such conference, the moving party or counsel for the moving party shall make available to counsel for the Commissioner substantially the same information relating to any claim for attorney's fees which, in the absence of an agreement, the moving party would be required to file with the Court pursuant to paragraph (d) of this Rule.

(d) *Additional Affidavit.* Where the Commissioner's response indicates that the Commissioner and the moving party are unable to agree as to the amount of attorney's fees that is reasonable, counsel for the moving party shall, within 30 days after service of the Commissioner's response, file an additional affidavit or declaration which shall include:

(1) A detailed summary of the time expended by each individual for whom fees are sought, including a description of the nature of the services performed during each period of time summarized. Each such individual is expected to maintain contemporaneous, complete, and standardized time records which accurately reflect the work done by such individual. Where the reasonableness of the hours claimed becomes an issue, counsel is expected to make such time records available for inspection by the Court or by counsel for the Commissioner upon request.

(2) The customary fee for the type of work involved. Counsel shall provide specific evidence of the prevailing community rate for the type of work involved as well as specific evidence of counsel's actual billing practice during the time period involved. Counsel may establish the prevailing community rate by affidavits or declarations of other counsel with similar qualifications reciting the precise fees they have received from clients in comparable cases, by evidence of recent fees awarded by the courts or through settlement to counsel of comparable reputation and experience performing similar work, or by reliable legal publications.

(3) A description of the fee arrangement with the client. If any part of the fee is payable only on condition that the Court award such fee, the description shall specifically so state.

(4) The preclusion of other employment by counsel, if any, due to acceptance of the case.

(5) Any time limitations imposed by the client or by the circumstances.

(6) Any other problems resulting from the acceptance of the case.

(7) The professional qualifications and experience of each individual for whom fees are sought.

(8) The nature and length of the professional relationship with the client.

(9) Awards in similar cases, if any.

(10) A statement whether there is a special factor, such as the limited availability of qualified attorneys for the case, the difficulty of the issues presented in the case, or the local availability of tax expertise, to justify a rate in excess of the rate otherwise permitted for the services of attorneys under Code section 7430(c)(1).

(11) Any other information counsel believes will assist the Court in evaluating counsel's claim, which may include, but shall not be limited to, information relating to the novelty and difficulty of the questions presented, the skill required to perform the legal services properly, and any efforts to settle the case.

Where there are several counsel of record, all of whom are members of or associated with the same firm, an affidavit or a declaration filed by first counsel of record or that counsel's designee (see Rule 21(b)(2)) shall satisfy the requirements of this paragraph, and an affidavit or a declaration by each counsel of record shall not be required.

(e) *Burden of Proof.* The moving party shall have the burden of proving that the moving party has substantially prevailed or is treated as the prevailing party in the case of a qualified offer made as described in Code section 7430(g), that the moving party has exhausted the administrative remedies available to the moving party within the Internal Revenue Service, that the moving party has not unreasonably protracted the Court proceeding or, if the claim includes a claim for administrative costs, the administrative proceeding, that the moving party meets the net worth requirements, if applicable, as provided by law, that the amount of costs claimed is reasonable, and that the moving party has substantially prevailed with respect to either the amount in controversy or the most significant issue or set of issues presented either in the Court proceeding or, if the claim includes a claim for administrative costs, in the administrative proceeding; except that the moving party shall not be treated as the prevailing party if the Commissioner establishes that the position of the Commissioner was substantially justified. See Code sec. 7430(c)(4)(B).

(f) *Disposition.* The Court's disposition of a motion for reasonable litigation or administrative costs shall be included in the decision entered in the case. Where the Court in its opinion states that the decision will be entered under Rule 155, or where the parties have settled all of the issues other than litigation and administrative costs, the Court will issue an order granting or denying the motion and determining the amount of reasonable litigation and administrative costs, if any, to be awarded. The parties, or either of them, shall thereafter submit a proposed decision including an award of any such costs, or a denial thereof, for entry by the Court.

Rule 301. Commencement of Large Partnership Action. (a) *Commencement of Action.* A large partnership action shall be commenced by filing a petition with the Court. See Rule 20, relating to commencement of case; Rule 22, relating to the place and manner of filing the petition; Rule 32, relating to form of pleadings; Rule 34(e), relating to number of copies to be filed; and Rule 300(d), relating to caption of papers.

(b) *Content of Petition.* Each petition shall be entitled either "Petition for Readjustment of Partnership Items of a Large Partnership Under Code Section 6247" or "Petition for Adjustment of Partnership Items of a Large Partnership Under Code Section 6252". Each such petition shall contain the allegations described in paragraph (c) of this Rule, and the allegations described in either paragraph (d) or (e) of this Rule.

(c) *All Petitions.* All petitions in large partnership actions shall contain the following:

(1) The name and principal place of business of the large partnership at the time the petition is filed.

(2) The city and State of the office of the Internal Revenue Service with which the large partnership's return for the period in controversy was filed.

(3) A separate numbered paragraph setting forth the name and current address of the designated partner.

A claim for reasonable litigation or administrative costs shall not be included in the petition in a large partnership action. For the requirements as to claims for reasonable litigation or administrative costs, see Rule 231.

(d) *Petition for Readjustment of Partnership Items of a Large Partnership.* In addition to including the information specified in paragraph (c) of this Rule, a petition for readjustment of partnership items of a large partnership shall also contain:

(1) The date of the notice of partnership adjustment and the city and State of the office of the Internal Revenue Service that issued the notice.

(2) The year or years or other periods for which the notice of partnership adjustment was issued.

(3) Clear and concise statements of each and every error which the petitioner alleges to have been committed by the Commissioner in the notice of partnership adjustment. The assignments of error shall include issues in respect of which the burden of proof is on the Commissioner. Any issues not raised in the assignments of error, or in the assignments of error in any amendment to the petition, shall be deemed to be conceded. Each assignment of error shall be set forth in a separate lettered subparagraph.

(4) Clear and concise lettered statements of the facts on which the petitioner bases the assignments of error, except with respect to those assignments of error as to which the burden of proof is on the Commissioner.

(5) A prayer setting forth relief sought by the petitioner.

(6) The signature, mailing address, and telephone number of the petitioner's designated partner or the petitioner's counsel, as well as counsel's Tax Court bar number.

(7) A copy of the notice of partnership adjustment, which shall be appended to the petition, and with which there shall be included so much of any statement accompanying the notice as is material to the issues raised by the assignments of error. If the notice of partnership adjustment or any accompanying statement incorporates by reference any prior notices, or other material furnished by the Internal Revenue Service, such parts thereof as are material to the assignments of error likewise shall be appended to the petition.

(e) *Petition for Adjustment of Partnership Items of a Large Partnership.* In addition to including the information specified in paragraph (c) of this Rule, a petition for adjustment of partnership items of a large partnership shall also contain:

(1) The date that the administrative adjustment request was filed and other proper allegations showing jurisdiction in the Court in accordance with the requirements of Code Section 6252(b) and (c).

(2) The year or years or other periods to which the administrative adjustment request relates.

(3) The city and State of the office of the Internal Revenue Service with which the administrative adjustment request was filed.

(4) A clear and concise statement describing each partnership item on the large partnership return that is sought to be changed, and the basis for each such requested change. Each such statement shall be set forth in a separately lettered subparagraph.

(5) Clear and concise lettered statements of the facts on which the petitioner relies in support of such requested changes in treatment of partnership items.

(6) A prayer setting forth relief sought by the petitioner.

(7) The signature, mailing address, and telephone number of the petitioner's designated partner or the petitioner's counsel, as well as counsel's Tax Court bar number.

(8) A copy of the administrative adjustment request shall be appended to the petition.

(f) *Joinder of Parties.* (1) *Permissive Joinder.* A separate petition shall be filed with respect to each notice of partnership adjustment issued to separate large partnerships. However, a single petition for readjustment of partnership items of a large partnership or petition for adjustment of partnership items of a large partnership may be filed seeking readjustments or adjustments of partnership items with respect to more than one notice of partnership adjustment or administrative adjustment request if the notices or requests pertain to the same large partnership.

(2) *Severance or Other Orders.* With respect to a case based upon multiple notices of partnership adjustment or administrative adjustment requests, the Court may order a severance and a separate case may be maintained with respect to one or more of such notices or requests whenever it appears to the Court that proceeding separately is in furtherance of convenience, or to avoid prejudice, or when separate trials will be conducive to expedition or economy.

Rule 320. General. (a) *Applicability.* The Rules of this Title XXXI set forth the provisions that apply to actions for the determination of relief from joint and several liability on a joint return pursuant to Code section 6015(e). Except as otherwise provided in this Title, the other Rules of Practice and Procedure of the Court, to the extent pertinent, are applicable to such actions.

(b) *Jurisdiction.* The Court shall have jurisdiction of an action for determination of relief from joint and several liability on a joint return under this Title when the conditions of Code section 6015(e) have been satisfied.

(c) *Form and Style of Papers.* All papers filed in an action for determination of relief from joint and several liability on a joint return shall be prepared in the form and style set forth in Rule 23.

Rule 321. Commencement of Action for Determination of Relief from Joint and Several Liability on a Joint Return. (a) *Commencement of Action.* An action for determination of relief from joint and several liability on a joint return is commenced by filing a petition with the Court. See Rule 20, relating to commencement of case; Rule 22, relating to the place and manner of filing the petition; and Rule 32, relating to the form of pleadings.

(b) *Content of Petition.* A petition filed pursuant to this Rule shall be entitled "Petition for Determination of Relief from Joint and Several Liability on a Joint Return" and shall contain the following:

(1) The petitioner's name, State of legal residence, and mailing address.

(2) A statement of the facts upon which the petitioner relies to support the jurisdiction of the Court and, as an attachment, a copy of the Commissioner's notice of determination of the relief available pursuant to Code section 6015 or, if the Commissioner has not issued to the petitioner a notice of determination of the relief available pursuant to Code section 6015, a copy of the election for relief filed by the petitioner.

(3) A statement of the facts upon which the petitioner relies in support of the relief requested.

(4) A prayer setting forth the relief sought by the petitioner.

(5) The name and mailing address of the other individual filing the joint return, if available.

(6) The signature, mailing address, and telephone number of the petitioner or the petitioner's counsel, as well as counsel's Tax Court bar number.

A claim for reasonable litigation or administrative costs shall not be included in the petition in an action for determination of relief from joint and several liability on a joint return. For the requirements as to claims for reasonable litigation or administrative costs, see Rule 231.

(c) *Small Tax Case Under Code Section 7463(f)(1).* For provisions regarding the content of a petition in a small tax case under Code section 7463(f)(1), see Rules 170 through 175.

(d) *Filing Fee.* The fee for filing a petition for determination of relief from joint and several liability on a joint return shall be $60, payable at the time of filing.

Rule 322. Request for Place of Trial. At the time of filing a petition for determination of relief from joint and several liability on a joint return, the petitioner shall file a request for place of trial in accordance with Rule 140.

Rule 323. Other Pleadings. (a) *Answer.* The Commissioner shall file an answer or shall move with respect to the petition within the periods specified in and in accordance with the provisions of Rule 36.

(b) *Reply.* For provisions relating to the filing of a reply, see Rule 37.

Rule 324. Joinder of Issue in an Action for Determination of Relief From Joint and Several Liability on a Joint Return. An action for determination of relief from joint and several liability on a joint return shall be deemed at issue upon the later of:

(1) the time provided by Rule 38, or

(2) the expiration of the period within which a notice of intervention may be filed under Rule 325(b).

Rule 325. Notice and Intervention. (a) *Notice.* On or before 60 days from the date of the service of the petition, the Commissioner shall serve notice of the filing of the petition on the other individual filing the joint return and shall simultaneously file with the Court a copy of the notice with an attached certificate of service. The notice shall advise the other individual of the right to intervene by filing a notice of intervention with the Court not later than 60 days after the date of service on the other individual.

(b) *Intervention.* If the other individual filing the joint return desires to intervene, then such individual shall file a notice of intervention with the Court not later than 60 days after service of the notice by the Commissioner of the filing of the petition, unless the Court directs otherwise. All new matters of claim or defense in a notice of intervention shall be deemed denied. As to the form and content of a notice of intervention, see Appendix I, Form 13.

Rule 330. General. (a) *Applicability.* The Rules of this Title XXXII set forth the provisions that apply to lien and levy actions under Code sections 6320(c) and 6330(d). Except as otherwise provided in this Title, the other Rules of Practice and Procedure of the Court, to the extent pertinent, are applicable to such actions.

(b) *Jurisdiction.* The Court shall have jurisdiction of a lien or levy action under this Title when the conditions of Code section 6320(c) or 6330(d), as applicable, have been satisfied.

Rule 331. Commencement of Lien and Levy Action. (a) *Commencement of Action.* A lien and levy action under Code Sections 6320(c) and 6330(d) shall be commenced by filing a petition with the Court. See Rule 20, relating to commencement of case; Rule 22, relating to the place and manner of filing the petition; and Rule 32, regarding the form of pleadings.

(b) *Content of Petition.* A petition filed pursuant to this Rule shall be entitled "Petition for Lien or Levy Action Under Code Section 6320(c) or 6330(d)", as applicable, and shall contain the following:

(1) In the case of a petitioner who is an individual, the petitioner's name and State of legal residence; in the case of a petitioner other than an individual, the petitioner's name and principal place of business or principal office or agency; and, in all cases, the petitioner's mailing address. The mailing address, State of legal residence, and principal place of business, or principal office or agency, shall be stated as of the date that the petition is filed.

(2) The date of the notice of determination concerning collection action(s) under Code section 6320 and/or 6330 by the Internal Revenue Service Office of Appeals (hereinafter the "notice of determination"), and the city and State of the Office which made such determination.

(3) The amount or amounts and type of underlying tax liability, and the year or years or other periods to which the notice of determination relates.

(4) Clear and concise assignments of each and every error which the petitioner alleges to have been committed in the notice of determination. Any issue not raised in the assignments of error shall be deemed to be conceded. Each assignment of error shall be separately lettered.

(5) Clear and concise lettered statements of the facts on which the petitioner bases each assignment of error.

(6) A prayer setting forth the relief sought by the petitioner.

(7) The signature, mailing address, and telephone number of each petitioner or each petitioner's counsel, as well as counsel's Tax Court bar number.

(8) As an attachment, a copy of the notice of determination.

A claim for reasonable litigation or administrative costs shall not be included in the petition in a lien and levy action. For the requirements as to claims for reasonable litigation or administrative costs, see Rule 231.

(c) *Small Tax Case Under Code Section 7463(f)(2).* For provisions regarding the content of a petition in a small tax case under Code section 7463(f)(2), see Rules 170 through 175.

(d) *Filing Fee.* The fee for filing a petition for a lien and levy action shall be $60, payable at the time of filing.

Rule 332.　Request for Place of Trial.　At the time of filing a petition for a lien and levy action, a request for place of trial shall be filed in accordance with Rule 140.

Rule 333.　Other Pleadings.　(a) *Answer.* The Commissioner shall file an answer or shall move with respect to the petition within the periods specified in and in accordance with the provisions of Rule 36.

　　(b) *Reply.* For provisions relating to the filing of a reply, see Rule 37.

Rule 334.　Joinder of Issue in Lien and Levy Actions.　A lien and levy action under Code sections 6230(c) and 6330(d) shall be deemed at issue as provided by Rule 38.

Tax Court Forms

FORM 1

PETITION (Sample Format)[*]
(See Rules 30 through 34)
www.ustaxcourt.gov

UNITED STATES TAX COURT

Petitioner(s)

v.   } Docket No.

COMMISSIONER OF INTERNAL REVENUE,

Respondent

PETITION

Petitioner hereby petitions for a redetermination of the deficiency (or liability) set forth by the Commissioner of Internal Revenue in the Commissioner's notice of deficiency (or liability) dated ...., and as the basis for petitioner's case alleges as follows:

1. Petitioner is [set forth whether an individual, corporation, etc., as provided in Rule 60] with mailing address now at

....
Street (or P.O. Box)   City   State   ZIP Code

and with the State of legal residence (or principal office) now in (if different from the mailing address)

....

The return for the period here involved was filed with the Office of the Internal Revenue Service at

....
City   State

2. The notice of deficiency (or liability) was mailed to petitioner on ...., and was issued by the Office of the Internal Revenue Service at ....
City   State

---

*Form 1 provides a sample format that is especially appropriate for use by counsel in complex deficiency and liability cases. See Rule 34(a)(1), (b)(1). To adapt Form 1 for use in the following types of actions, see also the applicable Rules, as indicated: Declaratory judgment actions (Rule 211); disclosure actions (Rule 221); partnership actions (Rules 241, 301); interest abatement actions (Rule 281); employment status actions (Rule 291); actions for determination of relief from joint and several liability (Rule 321); lien and levy actions (Rule 331); and whistleblower actions (Rule 341). See Form 2 for a fillable form that may be useful for self-represented petitioners and may also be used by counsel in simple cases with limited issues. See Form 3 for a fillable form that may be used for administrative costs actions.

A copy of the notice of deficiency (or liability), including so much of the statement and schedules accompanying the notice as is material, should be redacted as provided by Rule 27 and attached to the petition as Exhibit A. Petitioner must submit with the petition a Form 4, Statement of Taxpayer Identification Number.

3. The deficiencies (or liabilities) as determined by the Commissioner are in income (estate, gift, or certain excise) taxes for the calendar (or fiscal) year ...., in the amount of $ ...., of which $ .... is in dispute.

4. The determination of the tax set forth in the said notice of deficiency (or liability) is based upon the following errors: [Here set forth specifically in lettered subparagraphs the assignments of error in a concise manner. Do not plead facts, which properly belong in the succeeding paragraph.]

5. The facts upon which petitioner relies, as the basis of petitioner's case, are as follows: [Here set forth allegations of fact, but not the evidence, sufficient to inform the Court and the Commissioner of the positions taken and the bases therefor. Set forth the allegations in orderly and logical sequence, with subparagraphs lettered, so as to enable the Commissioner to admit or deny each allegation. See Rules 31(a) and 34(b)(5).]

WHEREFORE, petitioner prays that [here set forth the relief desired].

(Signed) ....

Petitioner or Counsel

....

Present Address City, State, ZIP Code

Dated: ....

....

(Area code) Telephone No.

....

Counsel's Tax Court Bar Number

FORM 2
PETITION (Simplified Form)

UNITED STATES TAX COURT
www.ustaxcourt.gov

(FIRST)   (MIDDLE)   (LAST)

_____

(PLEASE TYPE OR PRINT)   Petitioner(s)
                    v.

COMMISSIONER OF INTERNAL REVENUE,
                    Respondent

Docket No.

PETITION

1. Please check the appropriate box(es) to show which IRS NOTICE(s) you dispute:

☐ Notice of Deficiency

☐ Notice of Determination
   Concerning Collection Action

☐ Notice of Determination Concerning Your Request for Relief
   From Joint and Several Liability. (If you requested relief from joint and
   several liability but the IRS has not made a determination, please see the
   Information for Persons Representing Themselves
   Before the U. S. Tax Court booklet or the Tax Court's Web site.)

☐ Notice of Determination of Worker Classification

2. Provide the date(s) the IRS issued the NOTICE(S) checked above and the city and State of the IRS office(s)
issuing the NOTICE(S):

_____

3. Provide the year(s) or period(s) for which the NOTICE(S) was/were issued:

_____

4. SELECT ONE OF THE FOLLOWING:

   If you want your case conducted under small tax case procedures, check here: ☐   **(CHECK**
   If you want your case conducted under regular tax case procedures, check here: ☐   **ONE BOX)**

      NOTE: A decision in a "small tax case" cannot be appealed to a Court of Appeals by the taxpayer or
      the IRS. If you do not check either box, the Court will file your case as a regular tax case.

5. Explain why you disagree with the IRS determination in this case (please list each point separately):

_____

_____

_____

_____

_____

_____

_____

_____

_____

6. State the facts upon which you rely (please list each point separately):

_____

_____

_____

_____

_____

_____

_____

You may use additional pages to explain why you disagree with the IRS determination or to state additional facts. Please do not submit tax forms, receipts, or other types of evidence with this petition.

ENCLOSURES:

Please check the appropriate boxes to show that you have enclosed the following items with this petition:

☐ A copy of the NOTICE(S) the IRS issued to you

☐ Statement of Taxpayer Identification Number (Form 4) (See PRIVACY NOTICE below)

☐ The Request for Place of Trial (Form 5)   ☐ The filing fee

PRIVACY NOTICE: Form 4 (Statement of Taxpayer Identification Number) will **not** be part of the Court's public files. All other documents filed with the Court, including this Petition and any IRS Notice that you enclose with this Petition, will become part of the Court's public files. To protect your privacy, you are <u>strongly</u> encouraged to omit or remove from this Petition, from any enclosed IRS Notice, and from any other document (other than Form 4) your taxpayer identification number (e.g., your Social Security number) and certain other confidential information as specified in the Tax Court's "Notice Regarding Privacy and Public Access to Case Files", available at www.ustaxcourt.gov.

_____   _____
Signature of Petitioner   Date   (Area Code) Telephone No.

_____   _____
Mailing Address   City, State, ZIP Code
State of legal residence (if different from the mailing address): _____

_____   _____
Signature of Additional Petitioner (e.g.,Spouse) Date   (Area Code) Telephone No.

_____   _____
Mailing Address   City, State, ZIP Code
State of legal residence (if different from the mailing address): _____

_____
Signature, Name, Address, Telephone No., and Tax Court Bar No. of Counsel, if retained by Petitioner(s)

SAMPLE

Information About Filing a Case in the United States Tax Court

Attached are the forms to use in filing your case in the United States Tax Court.

It is very important that you take time to carefully read the information on this page and that you properly complete and submit these forms to the United States Tax Court, 400 Second Street, N.W., Washington, D.C. 20217.

Small Tax Case or Regular Tax Case

If you seek review of one of the four types of IRS Notices listed in paragraph 1 of the petition form (Form 2), you may file your petition as a "small tax case" if your dispute meets certain dollar limits (described below). "Small tax cases" are handled under simpler, less formal procedures than regular cases. However, the Tax Court's decision in a small tax case cannot be appealed to a Court of Appeals by the IRS or by the taxpayer(s).

You can choose to have your case conducted as either a small tax case or a regular case by checking the appropriate box in paragraph 4 of the petition form (Form 2). If you check neither box, the Court will file your case as a regular case.

Dollar Limits: Dollar limits for a small tax case vary slightly depending on the type of IRS action you seek to have the Tax Court review:
(1) If you seek review of an IRS Notice of Deficiency, the amount of the deficiency (including any additions to tax or penalties) that you dispute cannot exceed $50,000 for any year.
(2) If you seek review of an IRS Notice of Determination Concerning Collection Action, the total amount of unpaid tax cannot exceed $50,000 for all years combined.
(3) If you seek review of an IRS Notice of Determination Concerning Your Request for Relief From Joint and Several Liability (or if the IRS failed to send you any Notice of Determination with respect to a request for spousal relief that you submitted to the IRS at least 6 months ago), the amount of spousal relief sought cannot exceed $50,000 for all years combined.
(4) If you seek review of an IRS Notice of Determination of Worker Classification, the amount in dispute cannot exceed $50,000 for any calendar quarter.

Enclosures

To help ensure that your case is properly processed, please enclose the following items when you mail your petition to the Tax Court:

1.   A copy of the Notice of Deficiency or Notice of Determination the IRS sent you;
2.   Your Statement of Taxpayer Identification Number (Form 4);
3.   The Request for Place of Trial (Form 5); and
4.   The $60 filing fee, payable by check, money order, or other draft, to the "Clerk, United States Tax Court"; or, if applicable, the fee waiver form.

For further important information, see the Court's Web site at www.ustaxcourt.gov or the "Information for Persons Representing Themselves Before the U.S. Tax Court" booklet available from the Tax Court.

FORM 3

PETITION FOR ADMINISTRATIVE COSTS (SEC. 7430(f)(2))

(See Rules 270 through 274.)

www.ustaxcourt.gov

UNITED STATES TAX COURT

....

Petitioner(s)

v.

COMMISSIONER OF INTERNAL REVENUE,

Respondent

}   Docket No.

PETITION FOR ADMINISTRATIVE COSTS
(Sec. 7430(f)(2))

1. Petitioner(s) appeal(s) the DECISION dated .... denying (in whole or in part) an award for reasonable administrative costs by the Internal Revenue Service. A copy of the DECISION should be redacted as provided by Rule 27 and attached to the petition. You must submit with the petition a Form 4, Statement of Taxpayer Identification Number.

2. Set forth in the appropriate column the AMOUNT of administrative costs (a) claimed in the administrative proceeding, (b) denied by the Internal Revenue Service, and (c) now claimed in this Court proceeding (if different from the amount claimed in the administrative proceeding).

(a) Claimed	(b) Denied	(c) Now claimed
$	$	$

3. Explain briefly why you disagree with the DECISION denying an award for reasonable administrative costs by the Internal Revenue Service.

....

....

....

....

4. Petitioner(s)' present net worth (does) (does not) exceed $2,000,000. [Strike through as appropriate.]

....

Signature of Petitioner   Date   Signature of Petitioner (Spouse)   Date

....

Present address—City, State, ZIP Code, telephone No. (including area code)

....

Signature of counsel (if retained by petitioners)   Date

....

Name, address, telephone No. (including area code), and Tax Court Bar No. of counsel

210   (1/1/10)

FORM 4

STATEMENT OF TAXPAYER IDENTIFICATION NUMBER

(See Rule 20(b).)

www.ustaxcourt.gov

UNITED STATES TAX COURT

....

Petitioner(s)

v.

COMMISSIONER OF INTERNAL REVENUE,

Respondent

} Docket No.

STATEMENT OF TAXPAYER IDENTIFICATION NUMBER

(E.g., Social Security number(s), employer identification number(s))

Name of Petitioner ....

Petitioner's Taxpayer Identification Number ....

Name of Additional Petitioner ....

Additional Petitioner's Taxpayer Identification Number ....

If either petitioner is seeking relief from joint and several liability on a joint return pursuant to Section 6015, I.R.C. 1986, and Rules 320 through 325, name of the other individual with whom petitioner filed a joint return ....
Taxpayer Identification Number of the other individual, if available ....

....
Signature of Petitioner or Counsel   Date

....
Signature of Additional Petitioner   Date

FORM 5

REQUEST FOR PLACE OF TRIAL
(See Rule 140.)
www.ustaxcourt.gov
UNITED STATES TAX COURT

....
        Petitioner(s)
            v.   } Docket No.
COMMISSIONER OF INTERNAL REVENUE,
                    Respondent

PLACE AN X IN ONE BOX. REQUEST A CITY MARKED * ONLY IF YOU ELECTED SMALL TAX CASE STATUS ON FORM 2. ANY OTHER CITY MAY BE REQUESTED FOR ANY CASE, INCLUDING A SMALL TAX CASE.

ALABAMA
  ☐ Birmingham
  ☐ Mobile
ALASKA
  ☐ Anchorage
ARIZONA
  ☐ Phoenix
ARKANSAS
  ☐ Little Rock
CALIFORNIA
  ☐ Fresno*
  ☐ Los Angeles
  ☐ San Diego
  ☐ San Francisco
COLORADO
  ☐ Denver
CONNECTICUT
  ☐ Hartford
DISTRICT OF
    COLUMBIA
  ☐ Washington
FLORIDA
  ☐ Jacksonville
  ☐ Miami
  ☐ Tallahassee*
  ☐ Tampa
GEORGIA
  ☐ Atlanta
HAWAII
  ☐ Honolulu
IDAHO
  ☐ Boise
  ☐ Pocatello*
ILLINOIS
  ☐ Chicago
  ☐ Peoria*
INDIANA
  ☐ Indianapolis
IOWA
  ☐ Des Moines

KANSAS
  ☐ Wichita*
KENTUCKY
  ☐ Louisville
LOUISIANA
  ☐ New Orleans
  ☐ Shreveport*
MAINE
  ☐ Portland*
MARYLAND
  ☐ Baltimore
MASSACHUSETTS
  ☐ Boston
MICHIGAN
  ☐ Detroit
MINNESOTA
  ☐ St. Paul
MISSISSIPPI
  ☐ Jackson
MISSOURI
  ☐ Kansas City
  ☐ St. Louis
MONTANA
  ☐ Billings*
  ☐ Helena
NEBRASKA
  ☐ Omaha
NEVADA
  ☐ Las Vegas
  ☐ Reno
NEW MEXICO
  ☐ Albuquerque
NEW YORK
  ☐ Albany*
  ☐ Buffalo
  ☐ New York City
  ☐ Syracuse*
NORTH CAROLINA
  ☐ Winston-Salem
NORTH DAKOTA
  ☐ Bismarck*

OHIO
  ☐ Cincinnati
  ☐ Cleveland
  ☐ Columbus
OKLAHOMA
  ☐ Oklahoma City
OREGON
  ☐ Portland
PENNSYLVANIA
  ☐ Philadelphia
  ☐ Pittsburgh
SOUTH CAROLINA
  ☐ Columbia
SOUTH DAKOTA
  ☐ Aberdeen*
TENNESSEE
  ☐ Knoxville
  ☐ Memphis
  ☐ Nashville
TEXAS
  ☐ Dallas
  ☐ El Paso
  ☐ Houston
  ☐ Lubbock
  ☐ San Antonio
UTAH
  ☐ Salt Lake City
VERMONT
  ☐ Burlington*
VIRGINIA
  ☐ Richmond
  ☐ Roanoke*
WASHINGTON
  ☐ Seattle
  ☐ Spokane
WEST VIRGINIA
  ☐ Charleston
WISCONSIN
  ☐ Milwaukee
WYOMING
  ☐ Cheyenne*

....
Signature of Petitioner(s) or Counsel   Date

APPENDIX IV. PLACES OF TRIAL

(See Rules 140 and 177)

Appendix.

A list of cities in which regular sessions of the Court are held appears below. * This list is published to assist parties in making designations under Rules 140 and 177. If sufficient cases are not ready for trial in a city designated by a taxpayer, or if suitable courtroom facilities are not available in that city, the Court may find it necessary to calendar cases for trial in some other city within reasonable proximity of the designated place.

* The Court sits in about 15 other cities to hear Small Tax Cases. A list of such cities is contained in a pamphlet entitled "Election of Small Tax Case Procedure and Preparation of Petitions", a copy of which may be obtained from the Clerk of the Court.

ALABAMA:
 Birmingham
 Mobile
ALASKA:
 Anchorage
ARIZONA:
 Phoenix
ARKANSAS:
 Little Rock
CALIFORNIA:
 Los Angeles
 San Diego
 San Francisco
COLORADO:
 Denver
CONNECTICUT:
 Hartford
DISTRICT OF
COLUMBIA:
 Washington
FLORIDA:
 Jacksonville
 Miami
 Tampa
GEORGIA:
 Atlanta
HAWAII:
 Honolulu
IDAHO:
 Boise
ILLINOIS:
 Chicago
INDIANA:
 Indianapolis

IOWA:
 Des Moines
KENTUCKY:
 Louisville
LOUISIANA:
 New Orleans
MARYLAND:
 Baltimore
MASSACHUSETTS:
 Boston
MICHIGAN:
 Detroit
MINNESOTA:
 St. Paul
MISSISSIPPI:
 Biloxi
 Jackson
MISSOURI:
 Kansas City
 St. Louis
MONTANA:
 Helena
NEBRASKA:
 Omaha
NEVADA:
 Las Vegas
 Reno
NEW MEXICO:
 Albuquerque
NEW YORK:
 Buffalo
 New York City
NORTH CAROLINA:
 Winston-Salem

OHIO:
 Cincinnati
 Cleveland
 Columbus
OKLAHOMA:
 Oklahoma City
OREGON:
 Portland
PENNSYLVANIA:
 Philadelphia
 Pittsburgh
SOUTH CAROLINA:
 Columbia
TENNESSEE:
 Knoxville
 Memphis
 Nashville
TEXAS:
 Dallas
 El Paso
 Houston
 Lubbock
 San Antonio
UTAH:
 Salk Lake City
VIRGINIA:
 Richmond
WASHINGTON:
 Seattle
 Spokane
WEST VIRGINIA:
 Charleston/Huntington
WISCONSIN:
 Milwaukee

PART VI

Rules of the United States Court of Federal Claims
(Selected Provisions)

COURT OF FEDERAL CLAIMS RULES

Rules of United States Court of Federal Claims (RCFC)

Rule 1. Scope and Purpose of Rules. These rules govern the procedure in the United States Court of Federal Claims in all suits. They should be construed and administered to secure the just, speedy, and inexpensive determination of every action and proceeding.

Rule 2. One Form of Action. There is one form of action--the civil action.

Rule 3. Commencing an Action. A civil action is commenced by filing a complaint with the court.

Rule 5.2. Privacy Protection For Filings Made with the Court. (a) *Redacted Filings.* Unless the court orders otherwise, in an electronic or paper filing with the court that contains an individual's social-security number, taxpayer-identification number, or birth date, the name of an individual known to be a minor, or a financial-account number, a party or nonparty making the filing may include only:

(1) the last four digits of the social-security number and taxpayer-identification number;

(2) the year of the individual's birth;

(3) the minor's initials; and

(4) the last four digits of the financial-account number.

(b) *Exemptions from the Redaction Requirement.* The redaction requirement does not apply to the following:

(1) a financial-account number that identifies the property allegedly subject to forfeiture in a forfeiture proceeding;

(2) the record of an administrative or agency proceeding;

(3) the official record of a state-court proceeding;

(4) the record of a court or tribunal, if that record was not subject to the redaction requirement when originally filed; and

(5) a filing covered by RCFC 5.2(d).

(c) [Not used.]

(d) *Filings Made Under Seal.* The court may order that a filing be made under seal without redaction. The court may later unseal the filing or order the person who made the filing to file a redacted version for the public record.

(e) *Protective Orders.* For good cause, the court may by order in a case:

(1) require redaction of additional information; or

(2) limit or prohibit a nonparty's remote electronic access to a document filed with the court.

(f) *Option for Additional Unredacted Filing Under Seal.* A person making a redacted filing may also file an unredacted copy under seal. The court must retain the unredacted copy as part of the record.

(g) *Option for Filing a Reference List.* A filing that contains redacted information may be filed together with a reference list that identifies each item of redacted information and specifies an appropriate identifier that uniquely corresponds to each item listed. The list must be filed under seal and may be amended as of right. Any reference in the case to a listed identifier will be construed to refer to the corresponding item of information.

(h) *Waiver of Protection of Identifiers.* A person waives the protection of RCFC 5.2(a) as to the person's own information by filing it without redaction and not under seal.

Rule 5.3. Proof of Service. (a) *In General.* Service is made by the party, attorney of record, or any other person acting under the attorney of record's direction by executing a certificate of service containing the following information:

(1) the day and manner of service;

(2) the person or entity served; and

(3) the method of service employed, e.g., in person, by mail, or by electronic or other means.

(b) *Attaching the Certificate of Service.* The certificate of service must be attached to the end of any original document, including an appendix, and to any copies of that document.

(c) *Amending the Certificate of Service.* The certificate of service may be amended or supplied to the court at any time unless doing so would result in material prejudice to the substantial rights of any party.

Rule 7. Pleadings Allowed; Form of Motions and Other Papers. (a) *Pleadings.* Only these pleadings are allowed:

(1) a complaint;

(2) an answer to a complaint;

(3) an answer to a counterclaim designated as a counterclaim;

(4) a reply to any offset or plea of fraud contained in the answer;

(5) a third-party pleading permitted under RCFC 14; and

(6) if the court orders one, a reply to an answer.

(b) *Motions and Other Papers.* (1) *In General* A request for a court order must be made by motion. Any motion, objection, or response may be accompanied by a brief or memorandum and, if necessary, affidavits supporting the motion. The motion must:

(A) be in writing unless made during a hearing or trial;

(B) state with particularity the grounds for seeking the order; and

(C) state the relief sought.

(2) *Form.* The rules governing captions and other matters of form in pleadings apply to motions and other papers.

Rule 8. General Rules of Pleading. (a) *Claims for Relief.* A pleading that states a claim for relief must contain: (1) a short and plain statement of the grounds for the court's jurisdiction, unless the court already has jurisdiction and the claim needs no new jurisdictional support, (2) a short and plain statement of the claim showing that the pleader is entitled to relief, and (3) a demand for the relief sought, which may include relief in the alternative or different types of relief.

(b) *Defenses; Admissions and Denials.* (1) *In General.* In responding to a pleading, a party must:

(A) state in short and plain terms its defenses to each claim asserted against it; and

(B) admit or deny the allegations asserted against it by an opposing party.

(2) *Denials--Responding to the Substance.* A denial must fairly respond to the substance of the allegation.

(3) *General and Specific Denials.* A party that intends in good faith to deny all the allegations of a pleading--including the jurisdictional grounds--may do so by a general denial. A party that does not intend to deny all the allegations must either specifically deny designated allegations or generally deny all except those specifically admitted.

(4) *Denying Part of an Allegation.* A party that intends in good faith to deny only part of an allegation must admit the part that is true and deny the rest.

(5) *Lacking Knowledge or Information.* A party that lacks knowledge or information sufficient to form a belief about the truth of an allegation must so state, and the statement has the effect of a denial.

(6) *Effect of Failing to Deny.* An allegation--other than one relating to the amount of damages--is admitted if a responsive pleading is required and the allegation is not denied. If a responsive pleading is not required, an allegation is considered denied or avoided.

(c) *Affirmative Defenses.* (1) *In General.* In responding to a pleading, a party must affirmatively state any avoidance or affirmative defense, including:

. accord and satisfaction;
. arbitration and award;
. assumption of risk;
. contributory negligence;
. duress;
. estoppel;
. failure of consideration;
. fraud;
. illegality;
. laches;
. license;
. payment;
. release;
. res judicata;
. statute of frauds;
. statute of limitations; and
. waiver.

(2) *Mistaken Designation.* If a party mistakenly designates a defense as a counterclaim, or a counterclaim as a defense, the court must, if justice requires, treat the pleading as though it were correctly designated, and may impose terms for doing so.

(d) *Pleading to Be Concise and Direct; Alternative Statements; Inconsistency.* (1) *In General.* Each allegation must be simple, concise, and direct. No technical form is required.

(2) *Alternative Statements of a Claim or Defense.* A party may set out 2 or more statements of a claim or defense alternatively or hypothetically, either in a single count or defense or in separate ones. If a party makes alternative statements, the pleading is sufficient if any one of them is sufficient.

(3) *Inconsistent Claims or Defenses.* A party may state as many separate claims or defenses as it has, regardless of consistency.

(e) *Construing Pleadings.* Pleadings must be construed so as to do justice.

Rule 15. Amended and Supplemental Pleadings. (a) *Amendments Before Trial.* (1) *Amending as a Matter of Course.* A party may amend its pleadings once as a matter of course within:

(A) 21 days after service of the pleading; or

(B) if the pleading is one to which a responsive pleading is required, 21 days after service of a responsive pleading or 21 days after service of a motion under RCFC 12(b), (e), or (f), whichever is earlier.

(2) *Other Amendments.* In all other cases, a party may amend its pleading only with the opposing party's written consent or the court's leave. The court should freely give leave when justice so requires.

(3) *Time to Respond.* Unless the court orders otherwise, any required response to an amended pleading must be made within the time remaining to respond to the original pleading or within 10 days after service of the amended pleading, whichever is later.

(b) *Amendments During and After Trial.* (1) *Based on an Objection at Trial.* If, at trial, a party objects that evidence is not within the issues raised in the pleadings, the court may permit the pleadings to be amended. The court should freely permit an amendment when doing so will aid in presenting the merits and the objecting party fails to satisfy the court that the evidence would prejudice that party's action or defense on the merits. The court may grant a continuance to enable the objecting party to meet the evidence.

(2) *For Issues Tried by Consent.* When an issue not raised by the pleadings is tried by the parties' express or implied consent, it must be treated in all respects as if raised in the pleadings. A party may move--at any time, even after judgment--to amend the pleadings to conform them to the evidence and to raise an unpleaded issue. But failure to amend does not affect the result of the trial of that issue.

(c) *Relation Back of Amendments.* (1) *When an Amendment Relates Back.* An amendment to a pleading relates back to the date of the original pleading when:

(A) the law that provides the applicable statute of limitations allows relation back;

(B) the amendment asserts a claim or defense that arose out of the conduct, transaction, or occurrence set out--or attempted to be set out--in the original pleading; or

(C) the amendment changes the party or the naming of the party against whom a claim is asserted, if RCFC 15(c)(1)(B) is satisfied and if the party to be brought in by amendment:

(i) received such notice of the action that it will not be prejudiced in defending on the merits; and

(ii) knew or should have known that the action would have been brought against it, but for a mistake concerning the proper party's identity.

(2) *Notice to the United States.* [Not Used.]

(d) *Supplemental Pleadings.* On motion and reasonable notice, the court may, on just terms, permit a party to serve a supplemental pleading setting out any transaction, occurrence, or event that happened after the date of the pleading to be supplemented. The court may permit supplementation even though the original pleading is defective in stating a claim or defense. The court may order that the opposing party plead to the supplemental pleading within a specified time.

Rule 16. Pretrial Conferences; Scheduling; Management. (a) *Purposes of a Pretrial Conference.* In any action, the court may order the attorneys and any unrepresented parties to appear for one or more pretrial conferences for such purposes as:

(1) expediting disposition of the action;

(2) establishing early and continuing control so that the case will not be protracted because of lack of management;

(3) discouraging wasteful pretrial activities;

(4) improving the quality of the trial through more thorough preparation;

(5) facilitating settlement; and

(6) assessing the utility of dispositive motions.

(b) *Scheduling.*

(1) *Scheduling Order.* The court will issue a scheduling order:

(A) after receiving the parties' Joint Preliminary Status Report under Appendix A ¶ 3; or

(B) after consulting with the parties' attorneys and any unrepresented parties at a scheduling conference or by telephone, mail, or other means.

(2) *Time to Issue.* The court will issue the scheduling order as soon as practicable after the filing of the Joint Preliminary Status Report, but in any event within 14 days after any preliminary scheduling conference.

(3) *Contents of the Order.*

(A) Required Contents. The scheduling order must limit the time to join other parties, amend the pleadings, complete discovery, and file motions.

(B) Permitted Contents. The scheduling order may:

(i) modify the timing of disclosures under RCFC 26(a) and 26(e)(1);

(ii) modify the extent of discovery;

(iii) provide for disclosure or discovery of electronically stored information;

(iv) include any agreements the parties reach for asserting claims of privilege or of protection as trial-preparation material after information is produced;

(v) set dates for pretrial conferences and for trial;

(vi) direct that the parties file any of the submissions set out in Appendix A ¶ ¶ 14, 15, 16, or 17; and

(vii) include other appropriate matters.

(4) *Modifying a Schedule.* A schedule may be modified only for good cause and with the judge's consent.

(c) *Attendance and Matters for Consideration at a Pretrial Conference.* (1) *Attendance.* A represented party must authorize at least one of its attorneys to make stipulations and admissions about all matters that can reasonably be anticipated for discussion at a pretrial conference. If appropriate, the court may require that a party or its representative be present or reasonably available by other means to consider possible settlement.

(2) *Matters for Consideration.* At any pretrial conference, the court may consider and take appropriate action on the following matters:

(A) formulating and simplifying the issues, and eliminating frivolous claims or defenses;

(B) amending the pleadings if necessary or desirable;

(C) obtaining admissions and stipulations about facts and documents to avoid unnecessary proof, and ruling in advance on the admissibility of evidence;

(D) avoiding unnecessary proof and cumulative evidence, and limiting the use of testimony under Federal Rule of Evidence 702;

(E) determining the appropriateness and timing of summary adjudication under RCFC 52.1 and 56;

(F) controlling and scheduling discovery, including orders affecting disclosures and discovery under RCFC 26 and RCFC 29 through 37;

(G) identifying witnesses and documents, scheduling the filing and exchange of any pretrial briefs, and setting dates for further conferences and for trial;

(H) referring matters to a master;

(I) settling the case and using special procedures to assist in resolving the dispute;

(J) determining the form and content of the pretrial order;

(K) disposing of pending motions;

(L) adopting special procedures for managing potentially difficult or protracted actions that may involve complex issues, multiple parties, difficult legal questions, or unusual proof problems;

(M) ordering a separate trial under RCFC 42(b) of a claim, counterclaim, third-party claim, or particular issue;

(N) ordering the presentation of evidence early in the trial on a manageable issue that might, on the evidence, be the basis for a judgment as a matter of law or a judgment on partial findings under RCFC 52(c);

(O) establishing a reasonable time limit on the time allowed to present evidence; and

(P) facilitating in other ways the just, speedy, and inexpensive disposition of the action.

(d) *Pretrial Orders.* After any conference under this rule, the court should issue an order reciting the action taken. This order controls the course of the action unless the court modifies it.

(e) *Final Pretrial Conference and Orders.* The court may hold a final pretrial conference to formulate a trial plan, including a plan to facilitate the admission of evidence. The conference must be held as close to the start of trial as is reasonable, and must be attended by at least one attorney who will conduct the trial for each party and by any unrepresented party. The court may modify the order issued after a final pretrial conference only to prevent manifest injustice.

(f) *Sanctions.* (1) *In General.* On motion or on its own, the court may issue any just orders, including those authorized by RCFC 37(b)(2)(A)(ii)-(vii), if a party or its attorney:

(A) fails to appear at a scheduling or other pretrial conference;

(B) is substantially unprepared to participate--or does not participate in good faith--in the conference; or

(C) fails to obey a scheduling or other pretrial order.

(2) *Imposing Fees and Costs.* Instead of or in addition to any other sanction, the court must order the party, its attorney, or both to pay the reasonable expenses--including attorney's fees--incurred because of any noncompliance with this rule, unless the noncompliance was substantially justified or other circumstances make an award of expenses unjust.

(g) *Additional Pretrial Procedures.* See Appendix A to these rules ("Case Management Procedure") for additional provisions controlling pretrial procedures.

Rule 26. Duty to Disclose; General Provisions Governing Discovery. (a) *Required Disclosures.* (1) *Initial Disclosure.*

(A) In General. Except as exempted by RCFC 26(a)(1)(B) or as otherwise stipulated or ordered by the court, a party must, without awaiting a discovery request, provide to the other parties:

(i) the name and, if known, the address and telephone number of each individual likely to have discoverable information--along with the subjects of that information--that the disclosing party may use to support its claims or defenses, unless the use would be solely for impeachment;

(ii) a copy--or a description by category and location--of all documents, electronically stored information, and tangible things that the disclosing party has in its possession, custody, or control and may use to support its claims or defenses, unless the use would be solely for impeachment;

(iii) a computation of each category of damages claimed by the disclosing party-- who must also make available for inspection and copying as under RCFC 34 the documents or other evidentiary material, unless privileged or protected from disclosure, on which each computation is based, including materials bearing on the nature and extent of injuries suffered; and

(iv) [not used].

(B) Proceedings Exempt from Initial Disclosure. The following proceedings are exempt from initial disclosure:

(i) an action for review on an administrative record, including procurement protest and military pay cases;

(ii) [not used];

(iii) [not used];

(iv) an action brought without an attorney by a person in the custody of the United States, a state, or a state subdivision;

(v) [not used];

(vi) [not used];

(vii) [not used];

(viii)

(ix) an action to enforce an arbitration award; and

(x) an action under the National Childhood Vaccine Injury Act.

(C) Time for Initial Disclosures--In General. A party must make the initial disclosures at or within 14 days after the Early Meeting of Counsel (see Appendix A ¶ 3) unless a different time is set by stipulation or court order, or unless a party objects during the conference that initial disclosures are not appropriate in this action and states the objection in the Joint Preliminary Status Report. In ruling on the objection, the court must determine what disclosures, if any, are to be made and must set the time for disclosure.

(D) Time for Initial Disclosures--For Parties Served or Joined Later. A party that is first served or otherwise joined after the Early Meeting of Counsel (see Appendix A ¶ 3) must make the initial disclosures within 30 days after being served or joined, unless a different time is set by stipulation or court order.

(E) Basis for Initial Disclosure; Unacceptable Excuses. A party must make its initial disclosures based on the information then reasonably available to it. A party is not excused from making its disclosures because it has not fully investigated the case or because it challenges the sufficiency of another party's disclosures or because another party has not made its disclosures.

(2) *Disclosure of Expert Testimony.*

(A) In General. In addition to the disclosures required by RCFC 26(a)(1), a party must disclose to the other parties the identity of any witness it may use at trial to present evidence under Federal Rule of Evidence 702, 703, or 705.

(B) Written Report. Unless otherwise stipulated or ordered by the court, this disclosure must be accompanied by a written report--prepared and signed by the witness--if the witness is one retained or specially employed to provide expert testimony in the case or one whose duties as the party's employee regularly involve giving expert testimony. The report must contain:

(i) a complete statement of all opinions the witness will express and the basis and reasons for them;

(ii) the facts or data considered by the witness in forming them;

(iii) any exhibits that will be used to summarize or support them;

(iv) the witness's qualifications, including a list of all publications authored in the previous 10 years;

(v) a list of all other cases in which, during the previous 4 years, the witness testified as an expert at trial or by deposition; and

(vi) a statement of the compensation to be paid for the study and testimony in the case.

(C) *Witnesses Who Do Not Provide a Written Report.* Unless otherwise stipulated or ordered by the court, if the witness is not required to provide a written report, this disclosure must state:

(i) the subject matter on which the witness is expected to present evidence under Federal Rule of Evidence 702, 703, or 705; and

(ii) a summary of the facts and opinions to which the witness is expected to testify.

(D) *Time to Disclose Expert Testimony.* A party must make these disclosures at the times and in the sequence that the court orders. Absent a stipulation or a court order (see Appendix A ¶¶ 5 and 8), the disclosures must be made:

(i) at least 90 days before the date set for trial or for the case to be ready for trial; or

(ii) if the evidence is intended solely to contradict or rebut evidence on the same subject matter identified by another party under RCFC 26(a)(2)(B) or (C), within 30 days after the other party's disclosure.

(E) *Supplementing the Disclosure.* The parties must supplement these disclosures when required under RCFC 26(e).

(3) *Pretrial Disclosures.* [Not used; see Appendix A ¶¶ 13, 15, and 16.]

(4) *Form of Disclosures.* Unless the court orders otherwise, all disclosures under RCFC 26(a) must be in writing, signed, and served.

(b) *Discovery Scope and Limits.*

(1) *Scope in General.* Unless otherwise limited by court order, the scope of discovery is as follows: Parties may obtain discovery regarding any nonprivileged matter that is relevant to any party's claim or defense--including the existence, description, nature, custody, condition, and location of any documents or other tangible things and the identity and location of persons who know of any discoverable matter. For good cause, the court may order discovery of any matter relevant to the subject matter involved in the action. Relevant information need not be admissible at the trial if the discovery appears reasonably calculated to lead to the discovery of admissible evidence. All discovery is subject to the limitations imposed by RCFC 26(b)(2)(C).

(2) *Limitations on Frequency and Extent.*

(A) *When Permitted.* By order, the court may alter the limits in these rules on the number of depositions and interrogatories or on the length of depositions under RCFC 30. By order, the court may also limit the number of requests under RCFC 36.

(B) Specific Limitations on Electronically Stored Information. A party need not provide discovery of electronically stored information from sources that the party identifies as not reasonably accessible because of undue burden or cost. On motion to compel discovery or for a protective order, the party from whom discovery is sought must show that the information is not reasonably accessible because of undue burden or cost. If that showing is made, the court may nonetheless order discovery from such sources if the requesting party shows good cause, considering the limitations of RCFC 26(b)(2)(C). The court may specify conditions for the discovery.

(C) When Required. On motion or on its own, the court must limit the frequency or extent of discovery otherwise allowed by these rules if it determines that:

(i) the discovery sought is unreasonably cumulative or duplicative, or can be obtained from some other source that is more convenient, less burdensome, or less expensive;

(ii) the party seeking discovery has had ample opportunity to obtain the information by discovery in the action; or

(iii) the burden or expense of the proposed discovery outweighs its likely benefit, considering the needs of the case, the amount in controversy, the parties' resources, the importance of the issues at stake in the action, and the importance of the discovery in resolving the issues.

(3) *Trial Preparation: Materials.*

(A) Documents and Tangible Things. Ordinarily, a party may not discover documents and tangible things that are prepared in anticipation of litigation or for trial by or for another party or its representative (including the other party's attorney, consultant, surety, indemnitor, insurer, or agent). But, subject to RCFC 26(b)(4), those materials may be discovered if:

(i) they are otherwise discoverable under RCFC 26(b)(1); and

(ii) the party shows that it has substantial need for the materials to prepare its case and cannot, without undue hardship, obtain their substantial equivalent by other means.

(B) Protection Against Disclosure. If the court orders discovery of those materials, it must protect against disclosure of the mental impressions, conclusions, opinions, or legal theories of a party's attorney or other representative concerning the litigation.

(C) Previous Statement. Any party or other person may, on request and without the required showing, obtain the person's own previous statement about the action or its subject matter. If the request is refused, the person may move for a court order, and RCFC 37(a)(5) applies to the award of expenses. A previous statement is either:

(i) a written statement that the person has signed or otherwise adopted or approved; or

(ii) a contemporaneous stenographic, mechanical, electrical, or other recording-- or a transcription of it--that recites substantially verbatim the person's oral statement.

(4) *Trial Preparation: Experts.*

(A) Deposition of an Expert Who May Testify. A party may depose any person who has been identified as an expert whose opinions may be presented at trial. If RCFC 26(a)(2)(B) requires a report from the expert, the deposition may be conducted only after the report is provided.

(B) Trial-Preparation Protection for Draft Reports or Disclosures. RCFC 26(b)(3)(A) and (B) protect drafts of any report or disclosure required under RCFC 26(a)(2), regardless of the form in which the draft is recorded.

(C) Trial-Preparation Protection for Communications Between a Party's Attorney and Expert Witnesses. RCFC 26(b)(3)(A) and (B) protect communications between the party's attorney and any witness required to provide a report under RCFC 26(a)(2)(B), regardless of the form of the communications, except to the extent that the communications:

(i) relate to compensation for the expert's study or testimony;

(ii) identify facts or data that the party's attorney provided and that the expert considered in forming the opinions to be expressed; or

(iii) identify assumptions that the party's attorney provided and that the expert relied on in forming the opinions to be expressed.

(D) Expert Employed Only for Trial Preparation. Ordinarily, a party may not, by interrogatories or deposition, discover facts known or opinions held by an expert who has been retained or specially employed by another party in anticipation of litigation or to prepare for trial and who is not expected to be called as a witness at trial. But a party may do so only:

(i) as provided in RCFC 35(b); or

(ii) on showing exceptional circumstances under which it is impracticable for the party to obtain facts or opinions on the same subject by other means.

(E) Payment. Unless manifest injustice would result, the court must require that the party seeking discovery:

(i) pay the expert a reasonable fee for time spent in responding to discovery under RCFC 26(b)(4)(A) or (D); and

(ii) for discovery under (D), also pay the other party a fair portion of the fees and expenses it reasonably incurred in obtaining the expert's facts and opinions.

(5) *Claiming Privilege or Protecting Trial-Preparation Materials.*

(A) Information Withheld. When a party withholds information otherwise discoverable by claiming that the information is privileged or subject to protection as trial-preparation material, the party must:

(i) expressly make the claim; and

(ii) describe the nature of the documents, communications, or tangible things not produced or disclosed--and do so in a manner that, without revealing information itself privileged or protected, will enable other parties to assess the claim.

(B) Information Produced. If information produced in discovery is subject to a claim of privilege or of protection as trial-preparation material, the party making the claim may notify any party that received the information of the claim and the basis for it. After being notified, a party must promptly return, sequester, or destroy the specified information and any copies it has; must not use or disclose the information until the claim is resolved; must take reasonable steps to retrieve the information if the party disclosed it before being notified; and may promptly present the information to the court under seal for a determination of the claim. The producing party must preserve the information until the claim is resolved.

(c) *Protective Orders.* (1) *In General.* A party or any person from whom discovery is sought may move for a protective order. The motion must include a certification that the movant has in good faith conferred or attempted to confer with other affected parties in an effort to resolve the dispute without court action. The court may, for good cause, issue an order to protect a party or person from annoyance, embarrassment, oppression, or undue burden or expense, including one or more of the following:

(A) forbidding the disclosure or discovery;

(B) specifying terms, including time and place, for the disclosure or discovery;

       (C) prescribing a discovery method other than the one selected by the party seeking discovery;

       (D) forbidding inquiry into certain matters, or limiting the scope of disclosure or discovery to certain matters;

       (E) designating the persons who may be present while the discovery is conducted;

       (F) requiring that a deposition be sealed and opened only on court order;

       (G) requiring that a trade secret or other confidential research, development, or commercial information not be revealed or be revealed only in a specified way; and

       (H) requiring that the parties simultaneously file specified documents or information in sealed envelopes, to be opened as the court directs.

       (2) *Ordering Discovery.* If a motion for a protective order is wholly or partly denied, the court may, on just terms, order that any party or person provide or permit discovery.

       (3) *Awarding Expenses.* RCFC 37(a)(5) applies to the award of expenses.

      (d) *Timing and Sequence of Discovery.* (1) *Timing.* A party may not seek discovery from any source before the parties have conferred as required by Appendix A ¶ 3, except in a proceeding exempted from initial disclosure under RCFC 26(a)(1)(B), or when authorized by these rules, by stipulation, or by court order.

       (2) *Sequence.* Unless, on motion, the court orders otherwise for the parties' and witnesses' convenience and in the interests of justice:

       (A) methods of discovery may be used in any sequence; and

       (B) discovery by one party does not require any other party to delay its discovery.

      (e) *Supplementing Disclosures and Responses.* (1) *In General.* A party who has made a disclosure under RCFC 26(a)--or who has responded to an interrogatory, request for production, or request for admission--must supplement or correct its disclosure or response:

       (A) in a timely manner if the party learns that in some material respect the disclosure or response is incomplete or incorrect, and if the additional or corrective information has not otherwise been made known to the other parties during the discovery process or in writing; or

       (B) as ordered by the court.

       (2) *Expert Witness.* For an expert whose report must be disclosed under RCFC 26(a)(2)(B), the party's duty to supplement extends both to information included in the report and to information given during the expert's deposition. Any additions or changes to this information must be disclosed by the time the party's pretrial disclosures under RCFC 26(a)(3) are due.

      (f) *Conference of the Parties; Planning for Discovery.* [Not used; see Appendix A ¶ 3.]

      (g) *Signing Disclosures and Discovery Requests, Responses, and Objections.* (1) *Signature Required; Effect of Signature.* Every disclosure under RCFC 26(a)(1) or Appendix A ¶¶ 13, 15, and 16, and every discovery request, response, or objection must be signed by the attorney of record in the attorney's own name--or by the party personally, if unrepresented--and must state the signer's address, e-mail address, and telephone number. By signing, an attorney or party certifies that to the best of the person's knowledge, information, and belief formed after a reasonable inquiry:

       (A) with respect to a disclosure, it is complete and correct as of the time it is made; and

       (B) with respect to a discovery request, response, or objection, it is:

       (i) consistent with these rules and warranted by existing law or by a nonfrivolous argument for extending, modifying, or reversing existing law, or for establishing new law;

(ii) not interposed for any improper purpose, such as to harass, cause unnecessary delay, or needlessly increase the cost of litigation; and

(iii) neither unreasonable nor unduly burdensome or expensive, considering the needs of the case, prior discovery in the case, the amount in controversy, and the importance of the issues at stake in the action.

(2) *Failure to Sign.* Other parties have no duty to act on an unsigned disclosure, request, response, or objection until it is signed, and the court must strike it unless a signature is promptly supplied after the omission is called to the attorney's or party's attention.

(3) *Sanction for Improper Certification.* If a certification violates this rule without substantial justification, the court, on motion or on its own, must impose an appropriate sanction on the signer, the party on whose behalf the signer was acting, or both. The sanction may include an order to pay the reasonable expenses, including attorney's fees, caused by the violation.

Rule 30. Depositions by Oral Examination. (a) *When a Deposition May Be Taken.* (1) *Without Leave.* A party may, by oral questions, depose any person, including a party, without leave of court except as provided in RCFC 30(a)(2). The deponent's attendance may be compelled by subpoena under RCFC 45.

(2) *With Leave.* A party must obtain leave of court, and the court must grant leave to the extent consistent with RCFC 26(b)(2):

(A) if the parties have not stipulated to the deposition and:

(i) the deposition would result in more than 10 depositions being taken under this rule or RCFC 31 by the plaintiffs, or by the defendant, or by the third-party defendants;

(ii) the deponent has already been deposed in the case; or

(iii) the party seeks to take the deposition before the time specified in RCFC 26(d), unless the party certifies in the notice, with supporting facts, that the deponent is expected to leave the United States and be unavailable for examination in this country after that time; or

(B) if the deponent is confined in prison.

(b) *Notice of the Deposition; Other Formal Requirements.* (1) *Notice in General.* A party who wants to depose a person by oral questions must give reasonable written notice to every other party. The notice must state the time and place of the deposition and, if known, the deponent's name and address. If the name is unknown, the notice must provide a general description sufficient to identify the person or the particular class or group to which the person belongs.

(2) *Producing Documents.* If a subpoena duces tecum is to be served on the deponent, the materials designated for production, as set out in the subpoena, must be listed in the notice or in an attachment. The notice to a party deponent may be accompanied by a request under RCFC 34 to produce documents and tangible things at the deposition.

(3) *Method of Recording.*

(A) Method Stated in the Notice. The party who notices the deposition must state in the notice the method for recording the testimony. Unless the court orders otherwise, testimony may be recorded by audio, audiovisual, or stenographic means. The noticing party bears the recording costs. Any party may arrange to transcribe a deposition.

(B) Additional Method. With prior notice to the deponent and other parties, any party may designate another method for recording the testimony in addition to that specified in the original notice. That party bears the expense of the additional record or transcript unless the court orders otherwise.

(4) *By Remote Means.* The parties may stipulate--or the court may on motion order--that a deposition be taken by telephone or other remote means. For the purpose of this rule and RCFC 28(a) and 37(b)(1), the deposition takes place where the deponent answers the questions.

(5) *Officer's Duties.*

(A) Before the Deposition. Unless the parties stipulate otherwise, a deposition must be conducted before an officer appointed or designated under RCFC 28. The officer must begin the deposition with an on-the-record statement that includes:

(i) the officer's name and business address;

(ii) the date, time, and place of the deposition;

(iii) the deponent's name;

(iv) the officer's administration of the oath or affirmation to the deponent; and

(v) the identity of all persons present.

(B) Conducting the Deposition; Avoiding Distortion. If the deposition is recorded nonstenographically, the officer must repeat the items in RCFC 30(b)(5)(A)(i)-(iii) at the beginning of each unit of the recording medium. The deponent's and attorneys' appearance or demeanor must not be distorted through recording techniques.

(C) After the Deposition. At the end of a deposition, the officer must state on the record that the deposition is complete and must set out any stipulations made by the attorneys about custody of the transcript or recording and of the exhibits, or about any other pertinent matters.

(6) *Notice or Subpoena Directed to an Organization.* In its notice or subpoena, a party may name as the deponent a public or private corporation, a partnership, an association, a governmental agency, or other entity and must describe with reasonable particularity the matters for examination. The named organization must then designate one or more officers, directors, or managing agents, or designate other persons who consent to testify on its behalf; and it may set out the matters on which each person designated will testify. A subpoena must advise a nonparty organization of its duty to make this designation. The persons designated must testify about information known or reasonably available to the organization. This paragraph (6) does not preclude a deposition by any other procedure allowed by these rules.

(c) *Examination and Cross-Examination; Record of the Examination; Objections; Written Questions.* (1) *Examination and Cross-Examination.* The examination and cross-examination of a deponent proceed as they would at trial under the Federal Rules of Evidence, except Rules 103 and 615. After putting the deponent under oath or affirmation, the officer must record the testimony by the method designated under RCFC 30(b)(3)(A). The testimony must be recorded by the officer personally or by a person acting in the presence and under the direction of the office.

(2) *Objections.* An objection at the time of the examination--whether to evidence, to a party's conduct, to the officer's qualifications, to the manner of taking the deposition, or to any other aspect of the deposition--must be noted on the record, but the examination still proceeds; the testimony is taken subject to any objection. An objection must be stated concisely in a nonargumentative and nonsuggestive manner. A person may instruct a deponent not to answer only when necessary to preserve a privilege, to enforce a limitation ordered by the court, or to present a motion under RCFC 30(d)(3).

(3) *Participating Through Written Questions.* Instead of participating in the oral examination, a party may serve written questions in a sealed envelope on the party noticing the deposition, who must deliver them to the officer. The officer must ask the deponent those

questions and record the answers verbatim.

(d) *Duration; Sanction; Motion to Terminate or Limit.* (1) *Duration.* Unless otherwise stipulated or ordered by the court, a deposition is limited to 1 day of 7 hours. The court must allow additional time consistent with RCFC 26(b)(2) if needed to fairly examine the deponent or if the deponent, another person, or any other circumstance impedes or delays the examination.

(2) *Sanction.* The court may impose an appropriate sanction--including the reasonable expenses and attorney's fees incurred by any party--on a person who impedes, delays, or frustrates the fair examination of the deponent.

(3) *Motion to Terminate or Limit.*

(A) Grounds. At any time during a deposition, the deponent or a party may move to terminate or limit it on the ground that it is being conducted in bad faith or in a manner that unreasonably annoys, embarrasses, or oppresses the deponent or party. If the objecting deponent or party so demands, the deposition must be suspended for the time necessary to obtain an order.

(B) Order. The court may order that the deposition be terminated or may limit its scope and manner as provided in RCFC 26(c). If terminated, the deposition may be resumed only by order of the court.

(C) Award of Expenses. RCFC 37(a)(5) applies to the award of expenses.

(e) *Review by the Witness; Changes.* (1) *Review; Statement of Changes.* On request by the deponent or a party before the deposition is completed, the deponent must be allowed 30 days after being notified by the officer that the transcript or recording is available in which:

(A) to review the transcript or recording; and

(B) if there are changes in form or substance, to sign a statement listing the changes and the reasons for making them.

(2) *Changes Indicated in the Officer's Certificate.* The officer must note in the certificate prescribed by RCFC 30(f)(1) whether a review was requested and, if so, must attach any changes the deponent makes during the 30-day period.

(f) *Certification and Delivery; Exhibits; Copies of the Transcript or Recording; Filing.* (1) *Certification and Delivery.* The officer must certify in writing that the witness was duly sworn and that the deposition accurately records the witness's testimony. The certificate must accompany the record of the deposition. Unless the court orders otherwise, the officer must seal the deposition in an envelope or package bearing the title of the action and marked "Deposition of [witness's name]" and must promptly send it to the attorney who arranged for the transcript or recording. The attorney must store it under conditions that will protect it against loss, destruction, tampering, or deterioration.

(2) *Documents and Tangible Things.*

(A) Originals and Copies. Documents and tangible things produced for inspection during a deposition must, on a party's request, be marked for identification and attached to the deposition. Any party may inspect and copy them. But if the person who produced them wants to keep the originals, the person may:

(i) offer copies to be marked, attached to the deposition, and then used as originals--after giving all parties a fair opportunity to verify the copies by comparing them with the originals; or

(ii) give all parties a fair opportunity to inspect and copy the originals after they are marked--in which event the originals may be used as if attached to the deposition.

(B) Order Regarding the Originals. Any party may move for an order that the originals be attached to the deposition pending final disposition of the case.

(3) *Copies of the Transcript or Recording.* Unless otherwise stipulated or ordered by the court, the officer must retain the stenographic notes of a deposition taken stenographically or a copy of the recording of a deposition taken by another method. When paid reasonable charges, the officer must furnish a copy of the transcript or recording to any party or the deponent.

(4) *Notice of Filing.* [Not used.]

(g) *Failure to Attend a Deposition or Serve a Subpoena; Expenses.* A party who, expecting a deposition to be taken, attends in person or by an attorney may recover reasonable expenses for attending, including attorney's fees, if the noticing party failed to:

(1) attend and proceed with the deposition; or

(2) serve a subpoena on a nonparty deponent, who consequently did not attend.

Rule 31. Depositions by Written Questions. (a) *When a Deposition May Be Taken.* (1) *Without Leave.* A party may, by written questions, depose any person, including a party, without leave of court except as provided in RCFC 31(a)(2). The deponent's attendance may be compelled by subpoena under RCFC 45.

(2) *With Leave.* A party must obtain leave of court, and the court must grant leave to the extent consistent with RCFC 26(b)(2):

(A) if the parties have not stipulated to the deposition and:

(i) the deposition would result in more than 10 depositions being taken under this rule or RCFC 30 by the plaintiffs, or by the defendant, or by the third-party defendants;

(ii) the deponent has already been deposed in the case; or

(iii) the party seeks to take a deposition before the time specified in RCFC 26(d); or

(B) if the deponent is confined in prison.

(3) *Service; Required Notice.* A party who wants to depose a person by written questions must serve them on every other party, with a notice stating, if known, the deponent's name and address. If the name is unknown, the notice must provide a general description sufficient to identify the person or the particular class or group to which the person belongs. The notice must also state the name or descriptive title and the address of the officer before whom the deposition will be taken.

(4) *Questions Directed to an Organization.* A public or private corporation, a partnership, an association, or a governmental agency may be deposed by written questions in accordance with RCFC 30(b)(6).

(5) *Questions from Other Parties.* Any questions to the deponent from other parties must be served on all parties as follows: cross-questions, within 14 days after being served with the notice and direct questions; redirect questions, within 7 days after being served with cross-questions; and recross-questions, within 7 days after being served with redirect questions. The court may, for good cause, extend or shorten these times.

(b) *Delivery to the Officer; Officer's Duties.* The party who noticed the deposition must deliver to the officer a copy of all questions served and of the notice. The officer must promptly proceed in the manner provided in RCFC 30(c), (e), and (f) to:

(1) take the deponent's testimony in response to the questions;

(2) prepare and certify the deposition; and

(3) send it to the party, attaching a copy of the questions and of the notice.

(c) Notice of Completion or Filing. (1) *Completion.* The party who noticed the deposition must notify all other parties when it is completed.

(2) *Filing.* [Not used.]

Rule 32. Using Depositions in Court Proceedings. (a) *Using Depositions.* (1) *In General.* At a hearing or trial, all or part of a deposition may be used against a party on these conditions:

(A) the party was present or represented at the taking of the deposition or had reasonable notice of it;

(B) it is used to the extent it would be admissible under the Federal Rules of Evidence if the deponent were present and testifying; and

(C) the use is allowed by RCFC 32(a)(2) through (8).

(2) *Impeachment and Other Uses.* Any party may use a deposition to contradict or impeach the testimony given by the deponent as a witness, or for any other purpose allowed by the Federal Rules of Evidence.

(3) *Deposition of Party, Agent, or Designee.* An adverse party may use for any purpose the deposition of a party or anyone who, when deposed, was the party's officer, director, managing agent, or designee under RCFC 30(b)(6) or 31(a)(4).

(4) *Unavailable Witness.* A party may use for any purpose the deposition of a witness, whether or not a party, if the court finds:

(A) that the witness is dead;

(B) that the witness is outside the United States, unless it appears that the witness's absence was procured by the party offering the deposition;

(C) that the witness cannot attend or testify because of age, illness, infirmity, or imprisonment;

(D) that the party offering the deposition could not procure the witness's attendance by subpoena; or

(E) on motion and notice, that exceptional circumstances make it desirable--in the interest of justice and with due regard to the importance of live testimony in open court--to permit the deposition to be used.

(5) *Limitations on Use.*

(A) Deposition Taken on Short Notice. A deposition must not be used against a party who, having received less than 11 days' notice of the deposition, promptly moved for a protective order under RCFC 26(c)(1)((B) requesting that it not be taken or be taken at a different time or place--and this motion was still pending when the deposition was taken.

(B) Unavailable Deponent; Party Could Not Obtain an Attorney. A deposition taken without leave of court under the unavailability provision of RCFC 30(a)(2)(A)(iii) must not be used against a party who shows that, when served with the notice, it could not, despite diligent efforts, obtain an attorney to represent it at the deposition.

(6) *Using Part of a Deposition.* If a party offers in evidence only part of a deposition, an adverse party may require the offeror to introduce other parts that in fairness should be considered with the part introduced, and any party may itself introduce any other parts.

(7) *Substituting a Party.* Substituting a party under RCFC 25 does not affect the right to use a deposition previously taken.

(8) *Deposition Taken in an Earlier Action.* A deposition lawfully taken and, if required, filed in any federal- or state-court action may be used in a later action involving the same subject matter between the same parties, or their representatives or successors in interest, to the same

extent as if taken in the later action. A deposition previously taken may also be used as allowed by the Federal Rules of Evidence.

(b) *Objections to Admissibility.* Subject to RCFC 28(b) and 32(d)(3), an objection may be made at a hearing or trial to the admission of any deposition testimony that would be inadmissable if the witness were present and testifying.

(c) *Form of Presentation.* Unless the court orders otherwise, a party must provide a transcript of any deposition testimony the party offers, but may provide the court with the testimony in nontranscript form as well.

(d) *Waiver of Objections.* (1) *To the Notice.* An objection to an error or irregularity in a deposition notice is waived unless promptly served in writing on the party giving the notice.

(2) *To the Officer's Qualification.* An objection based on disqualification of the officer before whom a deposition is to be taken is waived if not made:

(A) before the deposition begins; or

(B) promptly after the basis for disqualification becomes known or, with reasonable diligence, could have been known.

(3) *To the Taking of the Deposition.*

(A) Objection to Competence, Relevance, or Materiality. An objection to a deponent's competence--or to the competence, relevance, or materiality of testimony--is not waived by a failure to make the objection before or during the deposition, unless the ground for it might have been corrected at that time.

(B) Objection to an Error or Irregularity. An objection to an error or irregularity at an oral examination is waived if:

(i) it relates to the manner of taking the deposition, the form of a question or answer, the oath or affirmation, a party's conduct, or other matters that might have been corrected at that time; and

(ii) it is not timely made during the deposition.

(C) Objection to a Written Question. An objection to the form of a written question under RCFC 31 is waived if not served in writing on the party submitting the question within the time for serving responsive questions or, if the question is a recross-question, within 5 days after being served with it.

(4) *To Completing and Returning the Deposition.* An objection to how the officer transcribed the testimony--or prepared, signed, certified, sealed, endorsed, sent, or otherwise dealt with the deposition--is waived unless a motion to suppress is made promptly after the error or irregularity becomes known or, with reasonable diligence, could have been known.

Rule 33. Interrogatories to Parties. (a) *In General.* (1) *Number.* Unless otherwise stipulated or ordered by the court, a party may serve on any other party no more than 25 written interrogatories, including all discrete subparts. Leave to serve additional interrogatories may be granted to the extent consistent with RCFC 26(b)(2).

(2) *Scope.* An interrogatory may relate to any matter that may be inquired into under RCFC 26(b). An interrogatory is not objectionable merely because it asks for an opinion or contention that relates to fact or the application of law to fact, but the court may order that the interrogatory need not be answered until designated discovery is complete, or until a pretrial conference or some other time.

(b) *Answers and Objections.* (1) *Responding Party.* The interrogatories must be answered:

(A) by the party to whom they are directed; or

(B) if that party is a public or private corporation, a partnership, an association, or a governmental agency, by any officer or agent, who must furnish the information available to the party.

(2) *Time to Respond.* The responding party must serve its answers and any objections within 30 days after being served with the interrogatories. A shorter or longer time may be stipulated to under RCFC 29 or be ordered by the court.

(3) *Answering Each Interrogatory.* Each interrogatory must, to the extent it is not objected to, be answered separately and fully in writing under oath.

(4) *Objections.* The grounds for objecting to an interrogatory must be stated with specificity. Any ground not stated in a timely objection is waived unless the court, for good cause, excuses the failure.

(5) *Signature.* The person who makes the answers must sign them, and the attorney who objects must sign any objections.

(c) *Use.* An answer to an interrogatory may be used to the extent allowed by the Federal Rules of Evidence.

(d) *Option to Produce Business Records.* If the answer to an interrogatory may be determined by examining, auditing, compiling, abstracting, or summarizing a party's business records (including electronically stored information), and if the burden of deriving or ascertaining the answer will be substantially the same for either party, the responding party may answer by:

(1) specifying the records that must be reviewed, in sufficient detail to enable the interrogating party to locate and identify them as readily as the responding party could; and

(2) giving the interrogating party a reasonable opportunity to examine and audit the records and to make copies, compilations, abstracts, or summaries.

Rule 34. Producing Documents, Electronically Stored Information, and Tangible Things, or Entering onto Land, for Inspection and Other Purposes. (a) *In General.* A party may serve on any other party a request within the scope of RCFC 26(b):

(1) to produce and permit the requesting party or its representative to inspect, copy, test, or sample the following items in the responding party's possession, custody, or control:

(A) any designated documents or electronically stored information--including writings, drawings, graphs, charts, photographs, sound recordings, images, and other data or data compilations--stored in any medium from which information can be obtained either directly or, if necessary, after translation by the responding party into a reasonably usable form; or

(B) any designated tangible things; or

(2) to permit entry onto designated land or other property possessed or controlled by the responding party, so that the requesting party may inspect, measure, survey, photograph, test, or sample the property or any designated object or operation on it.

(b) *Procedure.*

(1) *Contents of the Request.* The request:

(A) must describe with reasonable particularity each item or category of items to be inspected;

(B) must specify a reasonable time, place, and manner for the inspection and for performing the related acts; and

(C) may specify the form or forms in which electronically stored information is to be produced.

(2) *Responses and Objections.*

(A) Time to Respond. The party to whom the request is directed must respond in writing within 30 days after being served. A shorter or longer time may be stipulated to under RCFC 29 or be ordered by the court.

(B) Responding to Each Item. For each item or category, the response must either state that inspection and related activities will be permitted as requested or state an objection to the request, including the reasons.

(C) Objections. An objection to part of a request must specify the part and permit inspection of the rest.

(D) Responding to a Request for Production of Electronically Stored Information. The response may state an objection to a requested form for producing electronically stored information. If the responding party objects to a requested form--or if no form was specified in the request--the party must state the form or forms it intends to use.

(E) Producing the Documents or Electronically Stored Information. Unless otherwise stipulated or ordered by the court, these procedures apply to producing documents or electronically stored information:

(i) A party must produce documents as they are kept in the usual course of business or must organize and label them to correspond to the categories in the request;

(ii) If a request does not specify a form for producing electronically stored information, a party must produce it in a form or forms in which it is ordinarily maintained or in a reasonably usable form or forms; and

(iii) A party need not produce the same electronically stored information in more than one form.

(c) *Nonparties.* As provided in RCFC 45, a nonparty may be compelled to produce documents and tangible things or to permit an inspection.

Rule 35. Physical and Mental Examinations. (a) *Order for an Examination.* (1) *In General.* The court may order a party whose mental or physical condition--including blood group--is in controversy to submit to a physical or mental examination by a suitably licensed or certified examiner. The court has the same authority to order a party to produce for examination a person who is in its custody or under its legal control.

(2) *Motion and Notice; Contents of the Order.* The order:

(A) may be made only on motion for good cause and on notice to all parties and the person to be examined; and

(B) must specify the time, place, manner, conditions, and scope of the examination, as well as the person or persons who will perform it.

(b) *Examiner's Report.*

(1) *Request by the Party or Person Examined.* The party who moved for the examination must, on request, deliver to the requester a copy of the examiner's report, together with like reports of all earlier examinations of the same condition. The request may be made by the party against whom the examination order was issued or by the person examined.

(2) *Contents.* The examiner's report must be in writing and must set out in detail the examiner's findings, including diagnoses, conclusions, and the results of any tests.

(3) *Request by the Moving Party.* After delivering the reports, the party who moved for the examination may request--and is entitled to receive--from the party against whom the examination order was issued like reports of all earlier or later examinations of the same

condition. But those reports need not be delivered by the party with custody or control of the person examined if the party shows that it could not obtain them.

(4) *Waiver of Privilege.* By requesting and obtaining the examiner's report, or by depositing the examiner, the party examined waives any privilege it may have--in that action or any other action involving the same controversy--concerning testimony about all examinations of the same condition.

(5) *Failure to Deliver a Report.* The court on motion may order--on just terms--that a party deliver the report of an examination. If the report is not provided, the court may exclude the examiner's testimony at trial.

(6) *Scope.* This subdivision (b) applies also to an examination made by the parties' agreement, unless the agreement states otherwise. This subdivision does not preclude obtaining an examiner's report or deposing an examiner under other rules.

Rule 36. Requests for Admission. (a) *Scope and Procedure.* (1) *Scope.* A party may serve on any other party a written request to admit, for purposes of the pending action only, the truth of any matters within the scope of RCFC 26(b)(1) relating to:

(A) facts, the application of law to fact, or opinions about either; and

(B) the genuineness of any described documents.

(2) *Form; Copy of a Document.* Each matter must be separately stated. A request to admit the genuineness of a document must be accompanied by a copy of the document unless it is, or has been, otherwise furnished or made available for inspection and copying.

(3) *Time to Respond; Effect of Not Responding.* A matter is admitted unless, within 30 days after being served, the party to whom the request is directed serves on the requesting party a written answer or objection addressed to the matter and signed by the party or its attorney. A shorter or longer time for responding may be stipulated to under RCFC 29 or be ordered by the court.

(4) *Answer.* If a matter is not admitted, the answer must specifically deny it or state in detail why the answering party cannot truthfully admit or deny it. A denial must fairly respond to the substance of the matter; and when good faith requires that a party qualify an answer or deny only a part of a matter, the answer must specify the part admitted and qualify or deny the rest. The answering party may assert lack of knowledge or information as a reason for failing to admit or deny only if the party states that it has made reasonable inquiry and that the information it knows or can readily obtain is insufficient to enable it to admit or deny.

(5) *Objections.* The grounds for objecting to a request must be stated. A party must not object solely on the ground that the request presents a genuine issue for trial.

(6) *Motion Regarding the Sufficiency of an Answer or Objection.* The requesting party may move to determine the sufficiency of an answer or objection. Unless the court finds an objection justified, it must order that an answer be served. On finding that an answer does not comply with this rule, the court may order either that the matter is admitted or that an amended answer be served. The court may defer its final decision until a pretrial conference or a specified time before trial. RCFC 37(a)(5) applies to an award of expenses.

(b) *Effect of an Admission; Withdrawing or Amending It.* A matter admitted under this rule is conclusively established unless the court, on motion, permits the admission to be withdrawn or amended. Subject to RCFC 16(e), the court may permit withdrawal or amendment if it would promote the presentation of the merits of the action and if the court is not persuaded that it would prejudice the requesting party in maintaining or defending the action on the merits. An admission under this rule is not an admission for any other purpose and cannot be used against the party in any other proceeding.

Rule 37. Failure to Make Disclosures or Cooperate in Discovery; Sanctions. (a) *Motion for an Order Compelling Disclosure or Discovery.* (1) *In General.* On notice to other parties and all affected persons, a party may move for an order compelling disclosure or discovery. The motion must include a certification that the movant has in good faith conferred or attempted to confer with the person or party failing to make disclosure or discovery in an effort to obtain it without court action.

(2) *Appropriate Court.* [Not used.]

(3) *Specific Motions.*

(A) To Compel Disclosure. If a party fails to make a disclosure required by RCFC 26(a), any other party may move to compel disclosure and for appropriate sanctions.

(B) To Compel a Discovery Response. A party seeking discovery may move for an order compelling an answer, designation, production, or inspection. This motion may be made if:

(i) a deponent fails to answer a question asked under RCFC 30 or 31;

(ii) a corporation or other entity fails to make a designation under RCFC 30(b)(6) or 31(a)(4);

(iii) a party fails to answer an interrogatory submitted under RCFC 33; or

(iv) a party fails to respond that inspection will be permitted--or fails to permit inspection--as requested under RCFC 34.

(C) Related to a Deposition. When taking an oral deposition, the party asking a question may complete or adjourn the examination before moving for an order.

(4) *Evasive or Incomplete Disclosure, Answer, or Response.* For purposes of this subdivision (a), an evasive or incomplete disclosure, answer, or response must be treated as a failure to disclose, answer, or respond.

(5) *Payment of Expenses; Protective Orders.*

(A) If the Motion Is Granted (or Disclosure or Discovery Is Provided After Filing). If the motion is granted--or if the disclosure or requested discovery is provided after the motion was filed--the court must, after giving an opportunity to be heard, require the party or deponent whose conduct necessitated the motion, the party or attorney advising that conduct, or both to pay the movant's reasonable expenses incurred in making the motion, including attorney's fees. But the court must not order this payment if:

(i) the movant filed the motion before attempting in good faith to obtain the disclosure or discovery without court action;

(ii) the opposing party's nondisclosure, response, or objection was substantially justified; or

(iii) other circumstances make an award of expenses unjust.

(B) If the Motion Is Denied. If the motion is denied, the court may issue any protective order authorized under RCFC 26(c) and must, after giving an opportunity to be heard, require the movant, the attorney filing the motion, or both to pay the party or deponent who opposed the motion its reasonable expenses incurred in opposing the motion, including attorney's fees. But the court must not order this payment if the motion was substantially justified or other circumstances make an award of expenses unjust.

(C) If the Motion Is Granted in Part and Denied in Part. If the motion is granted in part and denied in part, the court may issue any protective order authorized under RCFC 26(c) and may, after giving an opportunity to be heard, apportion the reasonable expenses for the motion.

(b) *Failure to Comply with a Court Order.*

(1) *Sanctions Concerning Deponents.* If the court orders a deponent to be sworn or to answer a question and the deponent fails to obey, the failure may be treated as contempt of court.

(2) *Sanctions Concerning Parties.*

(A) For Not Obeying a Discovery Order. If a party or a party's officer, director, or managing agent--or a witness designated under RCFC 30(b)(6) or 31(a)(4)--fails to obey an order to provide or permit discovery, including an order under RCFC 16(b), 35, or 37(a), the court may issue further just orders. They may include the following:

(i) directing that the matters embraced in the order or other designated facts be taken as established for purposes of the action, as the prevailing party claims;

(ii) prohibiting the disobedient party from supporting or opposing designated claims or defenses, or from introducing designated matters in evidence;

(iii) striking pleadings in whole or in part;

(iv) staying further proceedings until the order is obeyed;

(v) dismissing the action or proceeding in whole or in part;

(vi) rendering a default judgment against the disobedient party; or

(vii) treating as contempt of court the failure to obey any order except an order to submit to a physical or mental examination.

(B) For Not Producing a Person for Examination. If a party fails to comply with an order under RCFC 35(a) requiring it to produce another person for examination, the court may issue any of the orders listed in RCFC 37(b)(2)(A)(i)-(vi), unless the disobedient party shows that it cannot produce the other person.

(C) Payment of Expenses. Instead of or in addition to the orders above, the court must order the disobedient party, the attorney advising that party, or both to pay the reasonable expenses, including attorney's fees, caused by the failure, unless the failure was substantially justified or other circumstances make an award of expenses unjust.

(c) *Failure to Disclose, to Supplement an Earlier Response, or to Admit.*

(1) *Failure to Disclose or Supplement.* If a party fails to provide information or identify a witness as required by RCFC 26(a) or (e), the party is not allowed to use that information or witness to supply evidence on a motion, at a hearing, or at a trial, unless the failure was substantially justified or is harmless. In addition to or instead of this sanction, the court, on motion and after giving an opportunity to be heard:

(A) may order payment of the reasonable expenses, including attorney's fees, caused by the failure;

(B) [not used]; and

(C) may impose other appropriate sanctions, including any of the orders listed in RCFC 37(b)(2)(A)(i)-(vi).

(2) *Failure to Admit.* If a party fails to admit what is requested under RCFC 36 and if the requesting party later proves a document to be genuine or the matter true, the requesting party may move that the party who failed to admit pay the reasonable expenses, including attorney's fees, incurred in making that proof. The court must so order unless:

(A) the request was held objectionable under RCFC 36(a);

(B) the admission sought was of no substantial importance;

(C) the party failing to admit had a reasonable ground to believe that it might prevail on the matter; or

(D) there was other good reason for the failure to admit.

(d) *Party's Failure to Attend Its Own Deposition, Serve Answers to Interrogatories, or Respond to a Request for Inspection.* (1) *In General.* (A) Motion; Grounds for Sanctions. The court may, on motion, order sanctions if:

(i) a party or a party's officer, director, or managing agent--or a person designated under RCFC 30(b)(6) or 31(a)(4)--fails, after being served with proper notice, to appear for that person's deposition; or

(ii) a party, after being properly served with interrogatories under RCFC 33 or a request for inspection under RCFC 34, fails to serve its answers, objections, or written response.

(B) Certification. A motion for sanctions for failing to answer or respond must include a certification that the movant has in good faith conferred or attempted to confer with the party failing to act in an effort to obtain the answer or response without court action.

(2) *Unacceptable Excuse for Failing to Act.* A failure described in RCFC 37(d)(1)(A) is not excused on the ground that the discovery sought was objectionable, unless the party failing to act has a pending motion for a protective order under RCFC 26(c).

(3) *Types of Sanctions.* Sanctions may include any of the orders listed in RCFC 37(b)(2)(A)(i)-(vi). Instead of or in addition to these sanctions, the court must require the party failing to act, the attorney advising that party, or both to pay the reasonable expenses, including attorney's fees, caused by the failure, unless the failure was substantially justified or other circumstances make an award of expenses unjust.

(e) *Failure to Provide Electronically Stored Information.* Absent exceptional circumstances, a court may not impose sanctions under these rules on a party for failing to provide electronically stored information lost as a result of the routine, good-faith operation of an electronic information system.

(f) *Failure to Participate in Framing a Discovery Plan.* If a party or its attorney fails to participate in good faith in developing and submitting a proposed discovery plan as required by Appendix A ¶ 3, the court may, after giving an opportunity to be heard, require that party or attorney to pay to any other party the reasonable expenses, including attorney's fees, caused by the failure.

Rule 40. Scheduling Cases for Trial. The judge to whom a case is assigned is responsible for setting the case for trial by filing an order with the clerk. The court must give priority to actions entitled to priority by a federal statute.

Rule 40.1. Assigning and Transferring Cases. (a) *Random Assignment.* After a complaint is served on the United States, or after recusal or disqualification of a judge to whom the case is assigned, the case will be assigned (or reassigned) to a judge at random.

(b) *Transfer.* To promote docket efficiency, to conform to the requirements of any case management plan, or for the efficient administration of justice, the assigned judge, either on a party's motion or on the court's own initiative, may order the transfer of a case to another judge upon the agreement of both judges.

(c) *Transfer by the Chief Judge.* The chief judge may reassign any case upon a finding that the transfer is necessary for the efficient administration of justice.

Rule 41. Dismissal of Actions. (a) *Voluntary Dismissal.* (1) *By the Plaintiff.*

(A) Without a Court Order. Subject to RCFC 23(e) and 23.1(c) and any applicable federal statute, the plaintiff may dismiss an action without a court order by filing:

       (i) a notice of dismissal before the opposing party serves an answer, a motion for summary judgment, or a motion for judgment on the administrative record; or

       (ii) a stipulation of dismissal signed by all parties who have appeared.

    (B) Effect. Unless the notice or stipulation states otherwise, the dismissal is without prejudice. But if the plaintiff previously dismissed any federal- or state-court action based on or including the same claim, a notice of dismissal operates as an adjudication on the merits.

   (2) By Court Order; Effect. Except as provided in RCFC 41(a)(1), an action may be dismissed at the plaintiff's request only by court order, on terms that the court considers proper. If the defendant has pleaded a counterclaim before being served with the plaintiff's motion to dismiss, the action may be dismissed over the defendant's objection only if the counterclaim can remain pending for independent adjudication. Unless the order states otherwise, a dismissal under this paragraph (2) is without prejudice.

  (b) Involuntary Dismissal; Effect. If the plaintiff fails to prosecute or to comply with these rules or a court order, the court may dismiss on its own motion or the defendant may move to dismiss the action or any claim against it. Unless the dismissal order states otherwise, a dismissal under this subdivision (b) and any dismissal not under this rule--except one for lack of jurisdiction or failure to join a party under RCFC 19--operates as an adjudication on the merits.

  (c) Dismissing a Counterclaim or Third-Party Claim. This rule applies to a dismissal of any counterclaim or third-party claim. A claimant's voluntary dismissal under RCFC 41(a)(1)(A)(i) must be made:

    (1) before a responsive pleading is served; or

    (2) if there is no responsive pleading, before evidence is introduced at a hearing or trial.

  (d) Costs of a Previously Dismissed Action. If a plaintiff who previously dismissed an action in any court files an action based on or including the same claim against the defendant, the court:

    (1) may order the plaintiff to pay all or part of the costs of that previous action; and

    (2) may stay the proceedings until the plaintiff has complied.

Rule 54. Judgment; Costs. (a) Definition; Form. "Judgment" as used in these rules includes a decree and any order from which an appeal lies. A judgment should not include recitals of pleadings, a master's report, or a record of prior proceedings.

  (b) Judgment on Multiple Claims or Involving Multiple Parties. When an action presents more than one claim for relief--whether as a claim, counterclaim, or third-party claim--or when multiple parties are involved, the court may direct entry of a final judgment as to one or more, but fewer than all, claims or parties only if the court expressly determines that there is no just reason for delay. Otherwise, any order or other decision, however designated, that adjudicates fewer than all the claims or the rights and liabilities of fewer than all the parties does not end the action as to any of the claims or parties and may be revised at any time before the entry of a judgment adjudicating all the claims and all the parties' rights and liabilities.

  (c) Demand for Judgment; Relief to Be Granted. A default judgment must not differ in kind from, or exceed in amount, what is demanded in the pleadings. Every other final judgment should grant the relief to which each party is entitled, even if the party has not demanded that relief in its pleadings.

  (d) Costs; Attorney's Fees. (1) Costs Other Than Attorney's Fees. Costs--other than attorney's fees--should be allowed to the prevailing party to the extent permitted by law. See 28 U.S.C. § 2412(a).

(A) Filing a Bill of Costs. A claim for allowable costs must be made by filing a Bill of Costs with the clerk. See Appendix of Forms, Form 4.

(B) Timing and Contents of a Bill of Costs. A Bill of Costs must:

(i) be filed within 30 days after the date of final judgment, as defined in 28 U.S.C. § 2412(d)(2)(G);

(ii) be accompanied by an affidavit and a memorandum setting forth the grounds and authorities supporting all costs other than the filing fee; and

(iii) include as exhibits any vouchers, receipts, or invoices supporting the requested costs.

(C) Procedures Applicable to a Bill of Costs.

(i) Objection. An objection to some or all of the requested costs may be filed within 28 days after service of the Bill of Costs.

(ii) Reply. A reply to an objection may be filed within 7 days after service of the objection.

(iii) Action by the Clerk. Unless a conference is scheduled by the clerk, the taxation or disallowance of costs will be made by the clerk on the existing record.

(iv) Court Review. A motion for review of the clerk's action may be filed with the court within 14 days after action by the clerk. Unless the court orders otherwise, the review will be made on the existing record.

(D) Settlement Agreement. A settlement agreement should, by its own terms, resolve any issue relating to costs and in the absence of special agreement, each party must bear its own costs. The clerk may not tax costs on any action terminated by settlement.

(2) *Attorney's Fees.*

(A) Claim to Be by Motion. A claim for attorney's fees and related nontaxable expenses must be made by motion unless the substantive law requires those fees to be proved at trial as an element of damages. See Appendix of Forms, Form 5.

(B) Timing and Contents of the Motion. Unless a statute or a court order provides otherwise, the motion must:

(i) be filed within 30 days after the date of final judgment, as defined in 28 U.S.C. § 2412(d)(2)(G);

(ii) specify the judgment and the statute, rule, or other grounds entitling the movant to the award;

(iii) state the amount sought; and

(iv) disclose, if the court so orders, the terms of any agreement about fees for the services for which the claim is made.

(C) Proceedings. The court may decide issues of liability for fees before receiving submissions on the value of services. The court must find the facts and state its conclusions of law as provided in RCFC 52(a).

(D) Procedures Applicable to a Motion for Attorney's Fees.

(i) Response. A response to a motion for attorney's fees may be filed within 28 days after service of the motion.

(ii) Reply. A reply to a response may be filed within 14 days after service of the response.

(iii) Subsequent Procedures. After the filing of a response and a reply to a motion for attorney's fees, the court will enter an order prescribing the procedures to be followed.

(E) Exceptions. Subparagraphs (A)-(D) do not apply to claims for fees and expenses as sanctions for violating these rules or as sanctions under 28 U.S.C. § 1927.

Rule 59. New Trial; Reconsideration; Altering or Amending a Judgment. (a) *In General.* (1) *Grounds for New Trial or Reconsideration.* The court may, on motion, grant a new trial or a motion for reconsideration on all or some of the issues--and to any party--as follows:

(A) for any reason for which a new trial has heretofore been granted in an action at law in federal court;

(B) for any reason for which a rehearing has heretofore been granted in a suit in equity in federal court; or

(C) upon the showing of satisfactory evidence, cumulative or otherwise, that any fraud, wrong, or injustice has been done to the United States.

(2) *Further Action After a Trial.* The court may, on motion under this rule, open the judgment if one has been entered, take additional testimony, amend findings of fact and conclusions of law or make new ones, and direct the entry of a new judgment.

(b) *Time to File a Motion for a New Trial or for Reconsideration.* (1) A motion for a new trial under RCFC 59(a)(1)(A) or (B) must be filed no later than 28 days after the entry of judgment.

(2) A motion for a new trial under RCFC 59(a)(1)(C) may be filed--and the payment of judgment stayed--at any time while the suit is pending, after review proceedings have been initiated, or within 2 years after the final disposition of the suit.

(c) *Relying on Affidavits.* When a motion for a new trial is based on affidavits, they must be filed with the motion.

(d) *New Trial on the Court's Initiative or for Reasons Not in the Motion.* No later than 28 days after the entry of judgment, the court, on its own, may order a new trial for any reason that would justify granting one on a party's motion. After giving the parties notice and an opportunity to be heard, the court may grant a timely motion for a new trial for a reason not stated in the motion. In either event, the court must specify the reasons in its order.

(e) *Motion to Alter or Amend a Judgment.* A motion to alter or amend a judgment must be filed no later than 28 days after the entry of the judgment.

(f) *Response.* A response to any motion under this rule may be filed only at the court's request and within the time specified by the court. The court may not rule in favor of a motion under this rule without first requesting a response to the motion.

Rule 77. Conducting Business; Clerk's Authority; Notice of an Order or Judgment. (a) *When Court Is Open.* The court is considered always open for filing any paper, issuing and returning process, making a motion, or entering an order.

(b) *Place for Trial and Other Proceedings.* (1) *In General.* Every trial on the merits must be conducted in open court and, so far as convenient, in a regular courtroom. Any other act or proceeding may be done or conducted by a judge in chambers, without the attendance of the clerk or other court official, or at any other place designated by order.

(2) *A Trial or Hearing in a Foreign Country.* On motion or on the judge's own initiative, and upon a determination by the judge to whom the case is assigned that the interests of economy, efficiency, and justice will be served, the chief judge may issue an order authorizing the judge to conduct proceedings, including evidentiary hearings and trials, in a foreign country whose laws do not prohibit such proceedings.

(c) *Clerk's Office Hours; Clerk's Orders.* (1) *Hours.* The clerk's office--with a clerk or deputy on duty--must be open during business hours every day except Saturdays, Sundays, and legal holidays as defined in RCFC 6(a)(4).

(2) *Orders.* Subject to the court's power to suspend, alter, or rescind the clerk's action for good cause, the clerk may:

(A) issue process;

(B) enter a default;

(C) enter a default judgment under RCFC 55(b)(1); and

(D) act on any other matter that does not require the court's action.

(d) *Serving Notice of an Order or Judgment.* (1) *Service.* Immediately after entering an order or judgment, the clerk must serve notice of the entry, as provided in RCFC 5(b), on each party who is not in default for failing to appear. The clerk must record the service on the docket. A party also may serve notice of the entry as provided in RCFC 5(b).

(2) *Time to Appeal Not Affected by Lack of Notice.* Lack of notice of the entry does not affect the time for appeal or relieve--or authorize the court to relieve--a party for failing to appeal within the time allowed, except as allowed by Federal Rule of Appellate Procedure 4(a).

Rule 77.1. Business Hours, Scheduling, and Court Fees. (a) *Business Hours.* The clerk's office is open from 8:45 a.m. to 5:15 p.m. on business days. A night box is provided for filing with the clerk's office between 5:15 p.m. and 12:00 midnight on any business day for any paper due that day. The night box is located inside the gate at the garage entrance on H Street. Counsel are advised to telephone the clerk's office, (202) 357-6400, by 9:30 a.m. the following business day to confirm receipt.

(b) *Scheduling.* The clerk will schedule the use of courtrooms in Washington, DC, and will be responsible for all arrangements for courtrooms and other facilities required by the court at locations outside Washington, DC. All conferences, oral arguments, trials, and other recorded court proceedings will be scheduled by the assigned judge by filing an order with the clerk.

(c) *Court Fees.* (1) *In General.* Court fees are prescribed by the Judicial Conference of the United States pursuant to 28 U.S.C. § 1926(a), as adjusted in the case of the fee for admission in accordance with RCFC 83.1(b)(4).

(2) *Fee Schedule.* A copy of the applicable schedule of fees is available on the court's website at www.uscfc.uscourts.gov or may be obtained by contacting the office of the Clerk of the United States Court of Federal Claims, 717 Madison Place, NW, Washington, DC 20005.

(3) *Method of Payment.* Fees for services rendered by the clerk must be paid in advance; all checks should be made payable to "Clerk, United States Court of Federal Claims."

Rule 77.2. Authorization to Act on Certain Motions. (a) *Authority of the Clerk.* The clerk may act on any motion for an enlargement of time to answer or respond to a complaint or for substitution of counsel if:

(1) the motion states that opposing counsel has no objection;

(2) no opposition to the motion has been timely filed; or

(3) opposing counsel files a consent. The clerk may not allow enlargements that exceed 60 days in total.

(b) *Signing an Order for an Absent Judge.* If an order is required and the assigned judge is unavailable, an order may be presented to the chief judge or to another judge designated by the assigned judge for signature.

Rule 83.1. Attorneys. (a) *Eligibility to Practice.* (1) *In General.* An attorney is eligible to practice before this court if the attorney:

(A) is a member in good standing of the bar of the highest court of any U.S. state, territory, or possession or the District of Columbia; and

(B) is a member in good standing of the bar of this court; or

(C) was a member in good standing of the bar of this court's predecessor, the United States Court of Claims.

(2) *Pro Hac Vice.* An attorney may participate *pro hac vice* in any proceeding before this court if:

(A) the attorney is admitted to practice before the highest court of any U.S. state, territory, or possession or the District of Columbia; and

(B) the attorney of record for any party has requested and is present for such participation and has received the court's approval.

(3) *Pro Se Litigants.* An individual who is not an attorney may represent oneself or a member of one's immediate family, but may not represent a corporation, an entity, or any other person in any proceeding before this court. The terms counsel, attorney, and attorney of record include such individuals appearing *pro se.*

(b) *Admission to Practice.* (1) *Qualifications.* Any person of good moral character who is a member in good standing of the bar of the highest court of any U.S. state, territory, or possession or the District of Columbia may be admitted to practice before this court.

(2) *Procedures.*

(A) In General. An attorney may be admitted to practice before this court by oral motion or by verified application.

(i) By Oral Motion in an Admissions Proceeding. A member of the bar of this court may make an oral motion to admit an applicant to the bar during the monthly attorney admissions proceeding held at the Howard T. Markey National Courts Building, 717 Madison Place, NW, Washington, DC 20005, at the times posted on the court's website at www.uscfc.uscourts.gov (generally 10:00 a.m. on Thursday of the first full week in every month). Motions will be heard in a courtroom posted in the lobby of the courthouse on the day of the proceeding. Applicants for admission must appear in the clerk's office no later than 9:30 a.m. to:

(I) pay the admission fee set forth in RCFC 83.1(b)(4);

(II) complete a "Form for Admission via Motion in Open Court" (available on the court's website); and

(III) present a certificate of the clerk of the highest court of any U.S. state, territory, or possession or the District of Columbia which has been issued within 30 days and states that the applicant is a member in good standing of the bar of such court.

Applicants who for special reasons are unable to appear for admission on one of the posted dates should contact the clerk's office to make alternate arrangements.

(ii) By Oral Motion in a Proceeding Outside Washington, DC. A member of the bar of this court may make an oral motion to admit an applicant to the bar during a court proceeding before any judge of this court so long as the applicant:

(I) provides the judge with a completed copy of a verified application for admission (see Appendix of Forms, Form 1); or

(II) advises the judge of the applicant's qualifications as set forth in RCFC 83.1(b)(1), and represents that the applicant will promptly apply to the clerk for admission by verified application as provided in RCFC 83.1(b)(2)(A)(iii).

(iii) By Verified Application. An attorney may seek admission to practice before this court without appearing in person by presenting the clerk with a verified application for admission (see Appendix of Forms, Form 1) along with the following documentation:

(I) a certificate of the clerk of the highest court of any U.S. state, territory, or possession or the District of Columbia which has been issued within 30 days and states that the applicant is a member in good standing of the bar of such court;

(II) two letters or signed statements of members of the bar of this court or of the Supreme Court of the United States, not related to the applicant, affirming that the applicant is personally known to them, that the applicant possesses all of the qualifications required for admission to the bar of this court, that they have examined the application, and that the applicant's personal and professional character and standing are good; and

(III) an oath in the form prescribed in RCFC 83.1(b)(3) signed by the applicant and administered by an officer authorized to administer oaths in the U.S. state, territory, or possession or the District of Columbia where the oath is given, or as permitted by 28 U.S.C. § 1746.

(3) *Oath.* An applicant for admission to practice before this court must take the following oath, to be administered by the presiding judge or by the clerk: I, --------------, do solemnly swear (or affirm) that I will support the Constitution of the United States and that I will conduct myself in an upright manner as an attorney of this court.

(4) *Fee.* Unless the applicant is employed by this court or is an attorney representing the United States before this court, the applicant must pay the admission fee in accordance with the fee schedule posted on the court's website at www.uscfc.uscourts.gov. The admission fee includes $ 100.00 above the amount prescribed by the Judicial Conference of the United States pursuant to 28 U.S.C. § 1926(a). The clerk will deposit this additional sum in a fund to be used by the court for the benefit of the members of the bench and the bar in the administration of justice.

(5) *Notice to the Court.* An attorney admitted to the bar of this court must provide the clerk with timely notice of:

(A) any change in the attorney's address; and

(B) any change in the status of the attorney's membership in the bar of the jurisdiction upon which the attorney's admission to the bar of this court was based.

(6) *Foreign Attorneys.*

(A) In General. Any person qualified to practice in the highest court of any foreign state may be specially admitted to practice before this court but only for purposes limited to a particular case; such person may not serve as the attorney of record.

(B) Procedures. A member of the bar of this court must file with the clerk a written motion to admit the applicant at least 7 days prior to the court's consideration of the motion. In the case of such an admission, an oath and fee are not required.

(c) *Attorney of Record.* (1) *In General.* A party may have only one attorney of record in a case at any one time and, with the exception of a pro se litigant appearing under RCFC 83.1(a)(3), must be represented by an attorney (not a firm) admitted to practice before this court. Any attorney assisting the attorney of record must be designated "of counsel."

(2) *Signing Filings.* All filings must be signed in the attorney of record's name. Any attorney who is admitted to practice before this court may sign a filing in the attorney of record's name by adding the following after the name of the attorney of record: "by [the signing attorney's

full name]." Such authorization to sign filings does not relieve the attorney of record from the provisions of RCFC 11.

(3) *Entering an Appearance.*

(A) By Parties Other Than the United States. The attorney of record for any party other than the United States must include on the initial pleading or paper the attorney's name, address, electronic mail address, telephone number, and facsimile number.

(B) By the United States. After service of the complaint, the attorney of record for the United States must promptly file with the clerk and serve on all other parties a notice of appearance setting forth the attorney's name, address, electronic mail address, telephone number, and facsimile number.

(C) Changes in Contact Information. An attorney of record must promptly file with the clerk and serve on all other parties a notice of any change in the attorney's contact information.

(4) *Substituting Counsel.*

(A) By Parties Other Than the United States.

(i) In General. Any party other than the United States may seek leave of the court to substitute its attorney of record at any time by filing a motion signed by the party or by the newly designated attorney along with an affidavit of appointment by such attorney.

(I) With the Consent of the Previous Attorney. If the previous attorney's consent is annexed to or indicated in the motion, the clerk will automatically enter the substitution on the docket.

(II) Without the Consent of the Previous Attorney. If the motion is filed without the consent of the previous attorney, the previous attorney must be served with the motion and will have 14 days to show cause why the motion should not be allowed.

(ii) Death of the Previous Attorney. In the event of the death of the attorney of record, the party must promptly notify the court and move to substitute another attorney admitted to practice before this court.

(B) By the United States. The United States may substitute its attorney of record at any time by filing with the clerk and serving on all other parties a notice of appearance of the new attorney.

(5) *Withdrawing Counsel.* An attorney of record for a party other than the United States may not withdraw the attorney's appearance except by leave of the court on motion and after notice is served on the attorney's client.

(d) *Honorary Bar Membership.* Upon nomination by the chief judge and with the approval of the other judges, the court may present an honorary membership in the bar of this court to a distinguished professional of the United States or of another nation who is knowledgeable in the affairs of law and government in his or her respective country. The candidate for honorary membership will be presented at the bar in person and will receive a certificate of honorary bar membership.

PART VII

Federal Rules of Procedure and Evidence
(Selected Provisions)

Fed. Rule Crim. Proc. 6. The Grand Jury

* * *

(e) Recording and Disclosing the Proceedings. (1) *Recording the Proceedings.* Except while the grand jury is deliberating or voting, all proceedings must be recorded by a court reporter or by a suitable recording device. But the validity of a prosecution is not affected by the unintentional failure to make a recording. Unless the court orders otherwise, an attorney for the government will retain control of the recording, the reporter's notes, and any transcript prepared from those notes.

(2) *Secrecy.*

(A) No obligation of secrecy may be imposed on any person except in accordance with Rule 6(e)(2)(B).

(B) Unless these rules provide otherwise, the following persons must not disclose a matter occurring before the grand jury:

(i) a grand juror;

(ii) an interpreter;

(iii) a court reporter;

(iv) an operator of a recording device;

(v) a person who transcribes recorded testimony;

(vi) an attorney for the government; or

(vii) a person to whom disclosure is made under Rule 6(e)(3)(A)(ii) or (iii);

(3) *Exceptions.*

(A) Disclosure of a grand-jury matter--other than the grand jury's deliberations or any grand juror's vote--may be made to:

(i) an attorney for the government for use in performing that attorney's duty;

(ii) any government personnel--including those of a state, state subdivision, Indian tribe, or foreign government--that an attorney for the government considers necessary to assist in performing that attorney's duty to enforce federal criminal law; or

(iii) a person authorized by 18 U.S.C. § 3322.

(B) A person to whom information is disclosed under Rule 6(e)(3)(A)(ii) may use that information only to assist an attorney for the government in performing that attorney's duty to enforce federal criminal law. An attorney for the government must promptly provide the court that impaneled the grand jury with the names of all persons to whom a disclosure has been made, and must certify that the attorney has advised those persons of their obligation of secrecy under this rule.

(C) An attorney for the government may disclose any grand-jury matter to another federal grand jury.

(D) An attorney for the government may disclose any grand-jury matter involving foreign intelligence, counterintelligence (as defined in 50 U.S.C. § 401(a), or foreign intelligence information (as defined in Rule 6(e)(3)(D)(iii)) to any federal law enforcement, intelligence, protective, immigration, national defense, or national security official to assist the official receiving the information in the performance of that official's duties. An attorney for the government may also disclose any grand-jury matter involving, within the United States or elsewhere, a threat of attack or other grave hostile acts of a foreign power or its agent, a threat of domestic or international sabotage or terrorism, or clandestine intelligence gathering activities by an intelligence service or network of a foreign power or by its agent, to any appropriate federal, state, state subdivision, Indian tribal, or foreign government official, for the purpose of preventing or responding to such threat or activities.

(i) Any official who receives information under Rule 6(e)(3)(D) may use the information only as necessary in the conduct of that person's official duties subject to any limitations on the unauthorized disclosure of such information. Any state, state subdivision, Indian tribal, or foreign government official who receives information under Rule 6(e)(3)(D) may use the information only in a manner consistent with any guidelines issued by the Attorney General and the Director of National Intelligence.

(ii) Within a reasonable time after disclosure is made under Rule 6(e)(3)(D), an attorney for the government must file, under seal, a notice with the court in the district where the grand jury convened stating that such information was disclosed and the departments, agencies, or entities to which the disclosure was made.

(iii) As used in Rule 6(e)(3)(D), the term "foreign intelligence information" means:

(a) information, whether or not it concerns a United States person, that relates to the ability of the United States to protect against—

. actual or potential attack or other grave hostile acts of a foreign power or its agent;

. sabotage or international terrorism by a foreign power or its agent; or

. clandestine intelligence activities by an intelligence service or network of a foreign power or by its agent; or

(b) information, whether or not it concerns a United States person, with respect to a foreign power or foreign territory that relates to—

. the national defense or the security of the United States; or

. the conduct of the foreign affairs of the United States.

(E) The court may authorize disclosure--at a time, in a manner, and subject to any other conditions that it directs--of a grand-jury matter:

(i) preliminarily to or in connection with a judicial proceeding;

(ii) at the request of a defendant who shows that a ground may exist to dismiss the indictment because of a matter that occurred before the grand jury;

(iii) at the request of the government, when sought by a foreign court or prosecutor for use in an official criminal investigation;

(iv) at the request of the government if it shows that the matter may disclose a violation of State, Indian tribal, or foreign criminal law, as long as the disclosure is to an appropriate state, state subdivision, Indian tribal, or foreign government official for the purpose of enforcing that law; or

(v) at the request of the government if it shows that the matter may disclose a violation of military criminal law under the Uniform Code of Military Justice, as long as the disclosure is to an appropriate military official for the purpose of enforcing that law.

(F) A petition to disclose a grand-jury matter under Rule 6(e)(3)(E)(i) must be filed in the district where the grand jury convened. Unless the hearing is ex parte--as it may be when the government is the petitioner--the petitioner must serve the petition on, and the court must afford a reasonable opportunity to appear and be heard to:

(i) an attorney for the government;

(ii) the parties to the judicial proceeding; and

(iii) any other person whom the court may designate.

(G) If the petition to disclose arises out of a judicial proceeding in another district, the petitioned court must transfer the petition to the other court unless the petitioned court can reasonably determine whether disclosure is proper. If the petitioned court decides to transfer, it must send to the transferee court the material sought to be disclosed, if feasible, and a written evaluation of the need for continued grand jury secrecy. The transferee court must afford those persons identified in Rule 6(e)(3)(F) a reasonable opportunity to appear and be heard.

(4) *Sealed Indictment.* The magistrate judge to whom an indictment is returned may direct that the indictment be kept secret until the defendant is in custody or has been released pending trial. The clerk must then seal the indictment, and no person may disclose the indictment's existence except as necessary to issue or execute a warrant or summons.

(5) *Closed Hearing.* Subject to any right to an open hearing in a contempt proceeding, the court must close any hearing to the extent necessary to prevent disclosure of a matter occurring before a grand jury.

(6) *Sealed Records.* Records, orders, and subpoenas relating to grand-jury proceedings must be kept under seal to the extent and as long as necessary to prevent the unauthorized disclosure of a matter occurring before a grand jury.

(7) *Contempt.* A knowing violation of Rule 6, or of any guidelines jointly issued by the Attorney General and the Director of National Intelligence under Rule 6, may be punished as a contempt of court.

* * *

Fed. Rule Crim. Proc. 11. Pleas. (a) *Entering a Plea.* (1) *In general.* A defendant may plead not guilty, guilty, or (with the court's consent) nolo contendere.

(2) *Conditional Plea.* With the consent of the court and the government, a defendant may enter a conditional plea of guilty or nolo contendere, reserving in writing the right to have an appellate court review an adverse determination of a specified pretrial motion. A defendant who prevails on appeal may then withdraw the plea.

(3) *Nolo Contendere Plea.* Before accepting a plea of nolo contendere, the court must consider the parties' views and the public interest in the effective administration of justice.

(4) *Failure to Enter a Plea.* If a defendant refuses to enter a plea or if a defendant organization fails to appear, the court must enter a plea of not guilty.

(b) *Considering and Accepting a Guilty or Nolo Contendere Plea.* (1) *Advising and Questioning the Defendant.* Before the court accepts a plea of guilty or nolo contendere, the defendant may be placed under oath, and the court must address the defendant personally in open court. During this address, the court must inform the defendant of, and determine that the defendant understands, the following:

(A) the government's right, in a prosecution for perjury or false statement, to use against the defendant any statement that the defendant gives under oath;

(B) the right to plead not guilty, or having already so pleaded, to persist in that plea;

(C) the right to a jury trial;

(D) the right to be represented by counsel--and if necessary have the court appoint counsel--at trial and at every other stage of the proceeding;

(E) the right at trial to confront and cross-examine adverse witnesses, to be protected from compelled self-incrimination, to testify and present evidence, and to compel the attendance of witnesses;

(F) the defendant's waiver of these trial rights if the court accepts a plea of guilty or nolo contendere;

(G) the nature of each charge to which the defendant is pleading;

(H) any maximum possible penalty, including imprisonment, fine, and term of supervised release;

(I) any mandatory minimum penalty;

(J) any applicable forfeiture;

(K) the court's authority to order restitution;

(L) the court's obligation to impose a special assessment;

(M) in determining a sentence, the court's obligation to calculate the applicable sentencing-guideline range and to consider that range, possible departures under the Sentencing Guidelines, and other sentencing factors under 18 U.S.C. § 3553(a); and

(N) the terms of any plea-agreement provision waiving the right to appeal or to collaterally attack the sentence.

(2) *Ensuring That a Plea Is Voluntary.* Before accepting a plea of guilty or nolo contendere, the court must address the defendant personally in open court and determine that the plea is voluntary and did not result from force, threats, or promises (other than promises in a plea agreement).

(3) *Determining the Factual Basis for a Plea.* Before entering judgment on a guilty plea, the court must determine that there is a factual basis for the plea.

(c) *Plea Agreement Procedure.* (1) *In General.* An attorney for the government and the defendant's attorney, or the defendant when proceeding pro se, may discuss and reach a plea agreement. The court must not participate in these discussions. If the defendant pleads guilty or nolo contendere to either a charged offense or a lesser or related offense, the plea agreement may specify that an attorney for the government will:

(A) not bring, or will move to dismiss, other charges;

(B) recommend, or agree not to oppose the defendant's request, that a particular sentence or sentencing range is appropriate or that a particular provision of the Sentencing Guidelines, or policy statement, or sentencing factor does or does not apply (such a recommendation or request does not bind the court); or

(C) agree that a specific sentence or sentencing range is the appropriate disposition of the case, or that a particular provision of the Sentencing Guidelines, or policy statement, or sentencing factor does or does not apply (such a recommendation or request binds the court once the court accepts the plea agreement).

(2) *Disclosing a Plea Agreement.* The parties must disclose the plea agreement in open court when the plea is offered, unless the court for good cause allows the parties to disclose the plea agreement in camera.

(3) *Judicial Consideration of a Plea Agreement.*

(A) To the extent the plea agreement is of the type specified in Rule 11(c)(1)(A) or (C), the court may accept the agreement, reject it, or defer a decision until the court has reviewed the presentence report.

(B) To the extent the plea agreement is of the type specified in Rule 11(c)(1)(B), the court must advise the defendant that the defendant has no right to withdraw the plea if the court does not follow the recommendation or request.

(4) *Accepting a Plea Agreement.* If the court accepts the plea agreement, it must inform the defendant that to the extent the plea agreement is of the type specified in Rule 11(c)(1)(A) or (C), the agreed disposition will be included in the judgment.

(5) *Rejecting a Plea Agreement.* If the court rejects a plea agreement containing provisions of the type specified in Rule 11(c)(1)(A) or (C), the court must do the following on the record and in open court (or, for good cause, in camera):

(A) inform the parties that the court rejects the plea agreement;

(B) advise the defendant personally that the court is not required to follow the plea agreement and give the defendant an opportunity to withdraw the plea; and

(C) advise the defendant personally that if the plea is not withdrawn, the court may dispose of the case less favorably toward the defendant than the plea agreement contemplated.

(d) *Withdrawing a Guilty or Nolo Contendere Plea.* A defendant may withdraw a plea of guilty or nolo contendere: (1) before the court accepts the plea, for any reason or no reason; or

(2) after the court accepts the plea, but before it imposes sentence if:

(A) the court rejects a plea agreement under Rule 11(c)(5); or

(B) the defendant can show a fair and just reason for requesting the withdrawal.

(e) *Finality of a Guilty or Nolo Contendere Plea.* After the court imposes sentence, the defendant may not withdraw a plea of guilty or nolo contendere, and the plea may be set aside only on direct appeal or collateral attack.

(f) *Admissibility or Inadmissibility of a Plea, Plea Discussions, and Related Statements.* The admissibility or inadmissibility of a plea, a plea discussion, and any related statement is governed by Federal Rule of Evidence 410.

(g) *Recording the Proceedings.* The proceedings during which the defendant enters a plea must be recorded by a court reporter or by a suitable recording device. If there is a guilty plea or a nolo contendere plea, the record must include the inquiries and advice to the defendant required under Rule 11(b) and (c).

(h) *Harmless Error.* A variance from the requirements of this rule is harmless error if it does not affect substantial rights.

Fed. Rule Crim. Proc. 16. Discovery and Inspection. (a) *Government's Disclosure.* (1) *Information Subject to Disclosure.*

(A) *Defendant's Oral Statement.* Upon a defendant's request, the government must disclose to the defendant the substance of any relevant oral statement made by the defendant, before or after arrest, in response to interrogation by a person the defendant knew was a government agent if the government intends to use the statement at trial.

(B) *Defendant's Written or Recorded Statement.* Upon a defendant's request, the government must disclose to the defendant, and make available for inspection, copying, or photographing, all of the following:

(i) any relevant written or recorded statement by the defendant if:

. the statement is within the government's possession, custody, or control; and

. the attorney for the government knows--or through due diligence could know--that the statement exists;

(ii) the portion of any written record containing the substance of any relevant oral statement made before or after arrest if the defendant made the statement in response to interrogation by a person the defendant knew was a government agent; and

(iii) the defendant's recorded testimony before a grand jury relating to the charged offense.

(C) *Organizational Defendant.* Upon a defendant's request, if the defendant is an organization, the government must disclose to the defendant any statement described in Rule 16(a)(1)(A) and (B) if the government contends that the person making the statement:

(i) was legally able to bind the defendant regarding the subject of the statement because of that person's position as the defendant's director, officer, employee, or agent; or

(ii) was personally involved in the alleged conduct constituting the offense and was legally able to bind the defendant regarding that conduct because of that person's position as the defendant's director, officer, employee, or agent.

(D) *Defendant's Prior Record.* Upon a defendant's request, the government must furnish the defendant with a copy of the defendant's prior criminal record that is within the government's possession, custody, or control if the attorney for the government knows--or through due diligence could know--that the record exists.

(E) *Documents and Objects.* Upon a defendant's request, the government must permit the defendant to inspect and to copy or photograph books, papers, documents, data, photographs, tangible objects, buildings or places, or copies or portions of any of these items, if the item is within the government's possession, custody, or control and:

(i) the item is material to preparing the defense;

(ii) the government intends to use the item in its case-in-chief at trial; or

(iii) the item was obtained from or belongs to the defendant.

(F) *Reports of Examinations and Tests.* Upon a defendant's request, the government must permit a defendant to inspect and to copy or photograph the results or reports of any physical or mental examination and of any scientific test or experiment if:

(i) the item is within the government's possession, custody, or control;

(ii) the attorney for the government knows--or through due diligence could know--that the item exists; and

(iii) the item is material to preparing the defense or the government intends to use the item in its case-in-chief at trial.

(G) *Expert witnesses.* At the defendant's request, the government must give to the defendant a written summary of any testimony that the government intends to use under Rules 702, 703, or 705 of the Federal Rules of Evidence during its case-in-chief at trial. If the government requests discovery under subdivision (b)(1)(C)(ii) and the defendant complies, the government must, at the defendant's request, give to the defendant a written summary of testimony that the government intends to use under Rules 702, 703, or 705 of the Federal Rules of Evidence as evidence at trial on the issue of the defendant's mental condition. The summary provided under this subparagraph must describe the witness's opinions, the bases and reasons for those opinions, and the witness's qualifications.

(2) *Information Not Subject to Disclosure.* Except as Rule 16(a)(1) provides otherwise, this rule does not authorize the discovery or inspection of reports, memoranda, or other internal government documents made by an attorney for the government or other government agent in connection with investigating or prosecuting the case. Nor does this rule authorize the discovery or inspection of statements made by prospective government witnesses except as provided in 18 U.S.C. § 3500.

(3) *Grand Jury Transcripts.* This rule does not apply to the discovery or inspection of a grand jury's recorded proceedings, except as provided in Rules 6, 12(h), 16(a)(1), and 26.2.

(b) *Defendant's Disclosure.* (1) *Information Subject to Disclosure.*

(A) *Documents and Objects.* If a defendant requests disclosure under Rule 16(a)(1)(E) and the government complies, then the defendant must permit the government, upon request, to inspect and to copy or photograph books, papers, documents, data, photographs, tangible objects, buildings or places, or copies or portions of any of these items if:

(i) the item is within the defendant's possession, custody, or control; and

(ii) the defendant intends to use the item in the defendant's case-in-chief at trial.

(B) *Reports of Examinations and Tests.* If a defendant requests disclosure under Rule 16(a)(1)(F) and the government complies, the defendant must permit the government, upon request, to inspect and to copy or photograph the results or reports of any physical or mental examination and of any scientific test or experiment if:

(i) the item is within the defendant's possession, custody, or control; and

(ii) the defendant intends to use the item in the defendant's case-in-chief at trial, or intends to call the witness who prepared the report and the report relates to the witness's testimony.

(C) *Expert witnesses.* The defendant must, at the government's request, give to the government a written summary of any testimony that the defendant intends to use under Rules 702, 703, or 705 of the Federal Rules of Evidence as evidence at trial, if—

(i) the defendant requests disclosure under subdivision (a)(1)(G) and the government complies; or

(ii) the defendant has given notice under Rule 12.2(b) of an intent to present expert testimony on the defendant's mental condition.

This summary must describe the witness's opinions, the bases and reasons for those opinions, and the witness's qualifications.

(2) *Information Not Subject to Disclosure.* Except for scientific or medical reports, Rule 16(b)(1) does not authorize discovery or inspection of:

(A) reports, memoranda, or other documents made by the defendant, or the defendant's attorney or agent, during the case's investigation or defense; or

(B) a statement made to the defendant, or the defendant's attorney or agent, by:

(i) the defendant;

(ii) a government or defense witness; or

(iii) a prospective government or defense witness.

(c) *Continuing Duty to Disclose.* A party who discovers additional evidence or material before or during trial must promptly disclose its existence to the other party or the court if: (1) the evidence or material is subject to discovery or inspection under this rule; and

(2) the other party previously requested, or the court ordered, its production.

(d) *Regulating Discovery.* (1) *Protective and Modifying Orders.* At any time the court may, for good cause, deny, restrict, or defer discovery or inspection, or grant other appropriate relief. The court may permit a party to show good cause by a written statement that the court will inspect ex parte. If relief is granted, the court must preserve the entire text of the party's statement under seal.

(2) *Failure to Comply.* If a party fails to comply with this rule, the court may:

(A) order that party to permit the discovery or inspection; specify its time, place, and manner; and prescribe other just terms and conditions;

(B) grant a continuance;

(C) prohibit that party from introducing the undisclosed evidence; or

(D) enter any other order that is just under the circumstances.

Fed. Rule Crim. Proc. 41. Search and Seizure. (a) *Scope and Definitions.* (1) *Scope.* This rule does not modify any statute regulating search or seizure, or the issuance and execution of a search warrant in special circumstances.

(2) *Definitions.* The following definitions apply under this rule:

(A) "Property" includes documents, books, papers, any other tangible objects, and information.

(B) "Daytime" means the hours between 6:00 a.m. and 10:00 p.m. according to local time.

(C) "Federal law enforcement officer" means a government agent (other than an attorney for the government) who is engaged in enforcing the criminal laws and is within any category of officers authorized by the Attorney General to request a search warrant.

(D) "Domestic terrorism" and "international terrorism" have the meanings set out in 18 U.S.C. § 2331.

(E) "Tracking device" has the meaning set out in 18 U.S.C. § 3117(b).

(b) *Authority to Issue a Warrant.* At the request of a federal law enforcement officer or an attorney for the government: (1) a magistrate judge with authority in the district--or if none is reasonably available, a judge of a state court of record in the district--has authority to issue a warrant to search for and seize a person or property located within the district;

(2) a magistrate judge with authority in the district has authority to issue a warrant for a person or property outside the district if the person or property is located within the district when the warrant is issued but might move or be moved outside the district before the warrant is executed;

(3) a magistrate judge -- in an investigation of domestic terrorism or international terrorism -- with authority in any district in which activities related to the terrorism may have occurred has authority to issue a warrant for a person or property within or outside that district;

(4) a magistrate judge with authority in the district has authority to issue a warrant to install within the district a tracking device; the warrant may authorize use of the device to track the movement of a person or property located within the district, outside the district, or both; and

(5) a magistrate judge having authority in any district where activities related to the crime may have occurred, or in the District of Columbia, may issue a warrant for property that is located outside the jurisdiction of any state or district, but within any of the following:

(A) a United States territory, possession, or commonwealth;

(B) the premises -- no matter who owns them -- of a United States diplomatic or consular mission in a foreign state, including any appurtenant building, part of a building, or land used for the mission's purposes; or

(C) a residence and any appurtenant land owned or leased by the United States and used by United States personnel assigned to a United States diplomatic or consular mission in a foreign state.

(c) *Persons or Property Subject to Search or Seizure.* A warrant may be issued for any of the following: (1) *evidence of a crime*;

(2) contraband, fruits of crime, or other items illegally possessed;

(3) property designed for use, intended for use, or used in committing a crime; or

(4) a person to be arrested or a person who is unlawfully restrained.

(d) *Obtaining a Warrant.* (1) *In General.* After receiving an affidavit or other information, a magistrate judge--or if authorized by Rule 41(b), a judge of a state court of record--must issue the warrant if there is probable cause to search for and seize a person or property or to install and use a tracking device.

(2) *Requesting a Warrant in the Presence of a Judge.*

(A) *Warrant on an Affidavit.* When a federal law enforcement officer or an attorney for the government presents an affidavit in support of a warrant, the judge may require the affiant to appear personally and may examine under oath the affiant and any witness the affiant produces.

(B) *Warrant on Sworn Testimony.* The judge may wholly or partially dispense with a written affidavit and base a warrant on sworn testimony if doing so is reasonable under the circumstances.

(C) *Recording Testimony.* Testimony taken in support of a warrant must be recorded by a court reporter or by a suitable recording device, and the judge must file the transcript or recording with the clerk, along with any affidavit.

(3) *Requesting a Warrant by Telephonic or Other Means.* In accordance with Rule 4.1, a magistrate judge may issue a warrant based on information communicated by telephone or other reliable electronic means.

(e) *Issuing the Warrant.* (1) *In General.* The magistrate judge or a judge of a state court of record must issue the warrant to an officer authorized to execute it.

(2) *Contents of the Warrant.*

(A) *Warrant to Search for and Seize a Person or Property.* Except for a tracking-device warrant, the warrant must identify the person or property to be searched, identify any person or property to be seized, and designate the magistrate judge to whom it must be returned. The warrant must command the officer to:

(i) execute the warrant within a specified time no longer than 14 days;

(ii) execute the warrant during the daytime, unless the judge for good cause expressly authorizes execution at another time; and

(iii) return the warrant to the magistrate judge designated in the warrant.

(B) *Warrant Seeking Electronically Stored Information.* A warrant under Rule 41(e)(2)(A) may authorize the seizure of electronic storage media or the seizure or copying of electronically stored information. Unless otherwise specified, the warrant authorizes a later review of the media or information consistent with the warrant. The time for executing the warrant in Rule 41(e)(2)(A) and (f)(1)(A) refers to the seizure or on-site copying of the media or information, and not to any later off-site copying or review.

(C) *Warrant for a Tracking Device.* A tracking-device warrant must identify the person or property to be tracked, designate the magistrate judge to whom it must be returned, and specify a reasonable length of time that the device may be used. The time must not exceed 45 days from the date the warrant was issued. The court may, for good cause, grant one or more extensions for a reasonable period not to exceed 45 days each. The warrant must command the officer to:

(i) complete any installation authorized by the warrant within a specified time no longer than 10 days;

(ii) perform any installation authorized by the warrant during the daytime, unless the judge for good cause expressly authorizes installation at another time; and

(iii) return the warrant to the judge designated in the warrant.

(3) *Warrant by Telephonic or Other Means.* If a magistrate judge decides to proceed under Rule 41(d)(3)(A), the following additional procedures apply:

(A) *Preparing a Proposed Duplicate Original Warrant.* The applicant must prepare a "proposed duplicate original warrant" and must read or otherwise transmit the contents of that document verbatim to the magistrate judge.

(B) *Preparing an Original Warrant.* If the applicant reads the contents of the proposed duplicate original warrant, the magistrate judge must enter those contents into an original warrant. If the applicant transmits the contents by reliable electronic means, that transmission may serve as the original warrant.

(C) *Modification.* The magistrate judge may modify the original warrant. The judge must transmit any modified warrant to the applicant by reliable electronic means under Rule 41(e)(3)(D) or direct the applicant to modify the proposed duplicate original warrant accordingly.

(D) *Signing the Warrant.* Upon determining to issue the warrant, the magistrate judge must immediately sign the original warrant, enter on its face the exact date and time it is issued, and transmit it by reliable electronic means to the applicant or direct the applicant to sign the judge's name on the duplicate original warrant.

(f) *Executing and Returning the Warrant.* (1) *Warrant to Search for and Seize a Person or Property.*

(A) *Noting the Time.* The officer executing the warrant must enter on it the exact date and time it was executed.

(B) *Inventory.* An officer present during the execution of the warrant must prepare and verify an inventory of any property seized. The officer must do so in the presence of another officer and the person from whom, or from whose premises, the property was taken. If either one is not present, the officer must prepare and verify the inventory in the presence of at least one other credible person. In a case involving the seizure of electronic storage media or the seizure or copying of electronically stored information, the inventory may be limited to describing the physical storage media that were seized or copied. The officer may retain a copy of the electronically stored information that was seized or copied.

(C) *Receipt.* The officer executing the warrant must give a copy of the warrant and a receipt for the property taken to the person from whom, or from whose premises, the property was taken or leave a copy of the warrant and receipt at the place where the officer took the property.

(D) *Return.* The officer executing the warrant must promptly return it--together with a copy of the inventory--to the magistrate judge designated on the warrant. The officer may do so by reliable electronic means. The judge must, on request, give a copy of the inventory to the person from whom, or from whose premises, the property was taken and to the applicant for the warrant.

(2) *Warrant for a Tracking Device.*

(A) *Noting the Time.* The officer executing a tracking-device warrant must enter on it the exact date and time the device was installed and the period during which it was used.

(B) *Return.* Within 10 days after the use of the tracking device has ended, the officer executing the warrant must return it to the judge designated in the warrant. The officer may do so by reliable electronic means.

(C) *Service.* Within 10 days after the use of the tracking device has ended, the officer executing a tracking-device warrant must serve a copy of the warrant on the person who was tracked or whose property was tracked. Service may be accomplished by delivering a copy to the person who, or whose property, was tracked; or by leaving a copy at the person's residence or usual place of abode with an individual of suitable age and discretion who resides at that location and by mailing a copy to the person's last known address. Upon request of the government, the judge may delay notice as provided in Rule 41(f)(3).

(3) *Delayed Notice.* Upon the government's request, a magistrate judge--or if authorized by Rule 41(b), a judge of a state court of record--may delay any notice required by this rule if the delay is authorized by statute.

(4) *Return.* The officer executing the warrant must promptly return it--together with a copy of the inventory--to the magistrate judge designated on the warrant. The judge must, on request, give a copy of the inventory to the person from whom, or from whose premises, the property was taken and to the applicant for the warrant.

(g) *Motion to Return Property.* A person aggrieved by an unlawful search and seizure of property or by the deprivation of property may move for the property's return. The motion must be filed in the district where the property was seized. The court must receive evidence on any factual issue necessary to decide the motion. If it grants the motion, the court must return the property to the movant, but may impose reasonable conditions to protect access to the property and its use in later proceedings.

(h) *Motion to Suppress.* A defendant may move to suppress evidence in the court where the trial will occur, as Rule 12 provides.

(i) *Forwarding Papers to the Clerk.* The magistrate judge to whom the warrant is returned must attach to the warrant a copy of the return, of the inventory, and of all other related papers and must deliver them to the clerk in the district where the property was seized.

Federal Rules of Evidence

Fed. Rule Evid. 408. Compromise Offers and Negotiations. (a) *Prohibited Uses.* Evidence of the following is not admissible--on behalf of any party--either to prove or disprove the validity or amount of a disputed claim or to impeach by a prior inconsistent statement or a contradiction:

(1) furnishing, promising, or offering--or accepting, promising to accept, or offering to accept--a valuable consideration in compromising or attempting to compromise the claim; and

(2) conduct or a statement made during compromise negotiations about the claim--except when offered in a criminal case and when the negotiations related to a claim by a public office in the exercise of its regulatory, investigative, or enforcement authority.

(b) *Exceptions*. The court may admit this evidence for another purpose, such as proving a witness's bias or prejudice, negating a contention of undue delay, or proving an effort to obstruct a criminal investigation or prosecution.

Federal Rules of Civil Procedure

Fed. Rule Civ. Proc. 4. Summons. (a) *Contents; Amendments.* (1) *Contents.* A summons must:

(A) name the court and the parties;

(B) be directed to the defendant;

(C) state the name and address of the plaintiff's attorney or--if unrepresented--of the plaintiff;

(D) state the time within which the defendant must appear and defend;

(E) notify the defendant that a failure to appear and defend will result in a default judgment against the defendant for the relief demanded in the complaint;

(F) be signed by the clerk; and

(G) bear the court's seal.

(2) *Amendments.* The court may permit a summons to be amended.

(b) *Issuance.* On or after filing the complaint, the plaintiff may present a summons to the clerk for signature and seal. If the summons is properly completed, the clerk must sign, seal, and issue it to the plaintiff for service on the defendant. A summons--or a copy of a summons that is addressed to multiple defendants--must be issued for each defendant to be served.

(c) *Service.* (1) *In General.* A summons must be served with a copy of the complaint. The plaintiff is responsible for having the summons and complaint served within the time allowed by Rule 4(m) and must furnish the necessary copies to the person who makes service.

(2) *By Whom.* Any person who is at least 18 years old and not a party may serve a summons and complaint.

(3) *By a Marshal or Someone Specially Appointed.* At the plaintiff's request, the court may order that service be made by a United States marshal or deputy marshal or by a person specially appointed by the court. The court must so order if the plaintiff is authorized to proceed in forma pauperis under 28 U.S.C. § 1915 or as a seaman under 28 U.S.C. § 1916.

(d) *Waiving Service.* (1) *Requesting a Waiver.* An individual, corporation, or association that is subject to service under Rule 4(e), (f), or (h) has a duty to avoid unnecessary expenses of serving the summons. The plaintiff may notify such a defendant that an action has been commenced and request that the defendant waive service of a summons. The notice and request must:

(A) be in writing and be addressed:

(i) to the individual defendant; or

(ii) for a defendant subject to service under Rule 4(h), to an officer, a managing or general agent, or any other agent authorized by appointment or by law to receive service of process;

(B) name the court where the complaint was filed;

(C) be accompanied by a copy of the complaint, two copies of a waiver form, and a prepaid means for returning the form;

(D) inform the defendant, using text prescribed in Form 5, of the consequences of waiving and not waiving service;

(E) state the date when the request is sent;

(F) give the defendant a reasonable time of at least 30 days after the request was sent--or at least 60 days if sent to the defendant outside any judicial district of the United States--to return the waiver; and

(G) be sent by first-class mail or other reliable means.

(2) *Failure to Waive.* If a defendant located within the United States fails, without good cause, to sign and return a waiver requested by a plaintiff located within the United States, the court must impose on the defendant:

(A) the expenses later incurred in making service; and

(B) the reasonable expenses, including attorney's fees, of any motion required to collect those service expenses.

(3) *Time to Answer After a Waiver.* A defendant who, before being served with process, timely returns a waiver need not serve an answer to the complaint until 60 days after the request was sent--or until 90 days after it was sent to the defendant outside any judicial district of the United States.

(4) *Results of Filing a Waiver.* When the plaintiff files a waiver, proof of service is not required and these rules apply as if a summons and complaint had been served at the time of filing the waiver.

(5) *Jurisdiction and Venue Not Waived.* Waiving service of a summons does not waive any objection to personal jurisdiction or to venue.

(e) *Serving an Individual Within a Judicial District of the United States.* Unless federal law provides otherwise, an individual--other than a minor, an incompetent person, or a person whose waiver has been filed--may be served in a judicial district of the United States by: (1) following state law for serving a summons in an action brought in courts of general jurisdiction in the state where the district court is located or where service is made; or

(2) doing any of the following:

(A) delivering a copy of the summons and of the complaint to the individual personally;

(B) leaving a copy of each at the individual's dwelling or usual place of abode with someone of suitable age and discretion who resides there; or

(C) delivering a copy of each to an agent authorized by appointment or by law to receive service of process.

(f) *Serving an Individual in a Foreign Country.* Unless federal law provides otherwise, an individual--other than a minor, an incompetent person, or a person whose waiver has been filed--may be served at a place not within any judicial district of the United States: (1) by any internationally agreed means of service that is reasonably calculated to give notice, such as those authorized by the Hague Convention on the Service Abroad of Judicial and Extrajudicial Documents;

(2) if there is no internationally agreed means, or if an international agreement allows but does not specify other means, by a method that is reasonably calculated to give notice:

(A) as prescribed by the foreign country's law for service in that country in an action in its courts of general jurisdiction;

(B) as the foreign authority directs in response to a letter rogatory or letter of request; or

(C) unless prohibited by the foreign country's law, by:

(i) delivering a copy of the summons and of the complaint to the individual personally; or

(ii) using any form of mail that the clerk addresses and sends to the individual and that requires a signed receipt; or

(3) by other means not prohibited by international agreement, as the court orders.

(g) *Serving a Minor or an Incompetent Person.* A minor or an incompetent person in a judicial district of the United States must be served by following state law for serving a summons or like process on such a defendant in an action brought in the courts of general jurisdiction of the state where service is made. A minor or an incompetent person who is not within any judicial district of the United States must be served in the manner prescribed by Rule 4(f)(2)(A), (f)(2)(B), or (f)(3).

(h) *Serving a Corporation, Partnership, or Association.* Unless federal law provides otherwise or the defendant's waiver has been filed, a domestic or foreign corporation, or a partnership or other unincorporated association that is subject to suit under a common name, must be served: (1) in a judicial district of the United States:

(A) in the manner prescribed by Rule 4(e)(1) for serving an individual; or

(B) by delivering a copy of the summons and of the complaint to an officer, a managing or general agent, or any other agent authorized by appointment or by law to receive service of process and--if the agent is one authorized by statute and the statute so requires--by also mailing a copy of each to the defendant; or

(2) at a place not within any judicial district of the United States, in any manner prescribed by Rule 4(f) for serving an individual, except personal delivery under (f)(2)(C)(i).

(i) *Serving the United States and Its Agencies, Corporations, Officers, or Employees.* (1) *United States.* To serve the United States, a party must:

(A)(i) deliver a copy of the summons and of the complaint to the United States attorney for the district where the action is brought--or to an assistant United States attorney or clerical employee whom the United States attorney designates in a writing filed with the court clerk—or

(ii) send a copy of each by registered or certified mail to the civil-process clerk at the United States attorney's office;

(B) send a copy of each by registered or certified mail to the Attorney General of the United States at Washington, D.C.; and

(C) if the action challenges an order of a nonparty agency or officer of the United States, send a copy of each by registered or certified mail to the agency or officer.

(2) *Agency; Corporation; Officer or Employee Sued in an Official Capacity.* To serve a United States agency or corporation, or a United States officer or employee sued only in an official capacity, a party must serve the United States and also send a copy of the summons and of the complaint by registered or certified mail to the agency, corporation, officer, or employee.

(3) *Officer or Employee Sued Individually.* To serve a United States officer or employee sued in an individual capacity for an act or omission occurring in connection with duties performed on the United States' behalf (whether or not the officer or employee is also sued in an official capacity), a party must serve the United States and also serve the officer or employee under Rule 4(e), (f), or (g).

(4) *Extending Time.* The court must allow a party a reasonable time to cure its failure to:

(A) serve a person required to be served under Rule 4(i)(2), if the party has served either the United States attorney or the Attorney General of the United States; or

(B) serve the United States under Rule 4(i)(3), if the party has served the United States officer or employee.

(j) *Serving a Foreign, State, or Local Government.* (1) *Foreign State.* A foreign state or its political subdivision, agency, or instrumentality must be served in accordance with 28 U.S.C. § 1608.

(2) *State or Local Government.* A state, a municipal corporation, or any other state-created governmental organization that is subject to suit must be served by:

(A) delivering a copy of the summons and of the complaint to its chief executive officer; or

(B) serving a copy of each in the manner prescribed by that state's law for serving a summons or like process on such a defendant.

(k) *Territorial Limits of Effective Service.* (1) *In General.* Serving a summons or filing a waiver of service establishes personal jurisdiction over a defendant:

(A) who is subject to the jurisdiction of a court of general jurisdiction in the state where the district court is located;

(B) who is a party joined under Rule 14 or 19 and is served within a judicial district of the United States and not more than 100 miles from where the summons was issued; or

(C) when authorized by a federal statute.

(2) *Federal Claim Outside State-Court Jurisdiction.* For a claim that arises under federal law, serving a summons or filing a waiver of service establishes personal jurisdiction over a defendant if:

(A) the defendant is not subject to jurisdiction in any state's courts of general jurisdiction; and

(B) exercising jurisdiction is consistent with the United States Constitution and laws.

(l) *Proving Service.* (1) *Affidavit Required.* Unless service is waived, proof of service must be made to the court. Except for service by a United States marshal or deputy marshal, proof must be by the server's affidavit.

(2) *Service Outside the United States.* Service not within any judicial district of the United States must be proved as follows:

(A) if made under Rule 4(f)(1), as provided in the applicable treaty or convention; or

(B) if made under Rule 4(f)(2) or (f)(3), by a receipt signed by the addressee, or by other evidence satisfying the court that the summons and complaint were delivered to the addressee.

(3) *Validity of Service; Amending Proof.* Failure to prove service does not affect the validity of service. The court may permit proof of service to be amended.

(m) *Time Limit for Service.* If a defendant is not served within 120 days after the complaint is filed, the court--on motion or on its own after notice to the plaintiff--must dismiss the action without prejudice against that defendant or order that service be made within a specified time.

But if the plaintiff shows good cause for the failure, the court must extend the time for service for an appropriate period. This subdivision (m) does not apply to service in a foreign country under Rule 4(f) or 4(j)(1).

(n) *Asserting Jurisdiction over Property or Assets.* (1) *Federal Law.* The court may assert jurisdiction over property if authorized by a federal statute. Notice to claimants of the property must be given as provided in the statute or by serving a summons under this rule.

(2) *State Law.* On a showing that personal jurisdiction over a defendant cannot be obtained in the district where the action is brought by reasonable efforts to serve a summons under this rule, the court may assert jurisdiction over the defendant's assets found in the district. Jurisdiction is acquired by seizing the assets under the circumstances and in the manner provided by state law in that district.

Fed. Rule Civ. Proc. 4.1. Serving Other Process. (a) *In General.* Process--other than a summons under Rule 4 or a subpoena under Rule 45--must be served by a United States marshal or deputy marshal or by a person specially appointed for that purpose. It may be served anywhere within the territorial limits of the state where the district court is located and, if authorized by a federal statute, beyond those limits. Proof of service must be made under Rule 4(l).

(b) *Enforcing Orders: Committing for Civil Contempt.* An order committing a person for civil contempt of a decree or injunction issued to enforce federal law may be served and enforced in any district. Any other order in a civil-contempt proceeding may be served only in the state where the issuing court is located or elsewhere in the United States within 100 miles from where the order was issued.

Fed. Rule Civ. Proc. 8. General Rules of Pleading. (a) *Claim for Relief.* A pleading that states a claim for relief must contain: (1) a short and plain statement of the grounds for the court's jurisdiction, unless the court already has jurisdiction and the claim needs no new jurisdictional support;

(2) a short and plain statement of the claim showing that the pleader is entitled to relief; and

(3) a demand for the relief sought, which may include relief in the alternative or different types of relief.

(b) *Defenses; Admissions and Denials.* (1) *In General.* In responding to a pleading, a party must:

(A) state in short and plain terms its defenses to each claim asserted against it; and

(B) admit or deny the allegations asserted against it by an opposing party.

(2) *Denials--Responding to the Substance.* A denial must fairly respond to the substance of the allegation.

(3) *General and Specific Denials.* A party that intends in good faith to deny all the allegations of a pleading--including the jurisdictional grounds--may do so by a general denial. A party that does not intend to deny all the allegations must either specifically deny designated allegations or generally deny all except those specifically admitted.

(4) *Denying Part of an Allegation.* A party that intends in good faith to deny only part of an allegation must admit the part that is true and deny the rest.

(5) *Lacking Knowledge or Information.* A party that lacks knowledge or information sufficient to form a belief about the truth of an allegation must so state, and the statement has the effect of a denial.

(6) *Effect of Failing to Deny.* An allegation--other than one relating to the amount of damages--is admitted if a responsive pleading is required and the allegation is not denied. If a responsive pleading is not required, an allegation is considered denied or avoided.

(c) *Affirmative Defenses.* (1) *In General.* In responding to a pleading, a party must affirmatively state any avoidance or affirmative defense, including:

. accord and satisfaction;

. arbitration and award;

. assumption of risk;

. contributory negligence;

. duress;

. estoppel;

. failure of consideration;

. fraud;

. illegality;

. injury by fellow servant;

. laches;

. license;

. payment;

. release;. res judicata;

. statute of frauds;

. statute of limitations; and

. waiver.

(2) *Mistaken Designation.* If a party mistakenly designates a defense as a counterclaim, or a counterclaim as a defense, the court must, if justice requires, treat the pleading as though it were correctly designated, and may impose terms for doing so.

(d) *Pleading to Be Concise and Direct; Alternative Statements; Inconsistency.* (1) *In General.* Each allegation must be simple, concise, and direct. No technical form is required.

(2) *Alternative Statements of a Claim or Defense.* A party may set out two or more statements of a claim or defense alternatively or hypothetically, either in a single count or defense or in separate ones. If a party makes alternative statements, the pleading is sufficient if any one of them is sufficient.

(3) *Inconsistent Claims or Defenses.* A party may state as many separate claims or defenses as it has, regardless of consistency.

(e) *Construing Pleadings.* Pleadings must be construed so as to do justice.

Fed. Rule Civ. Proc. 11. Signing Pleadings, Motions, and Other Papers; Representations to the Court; Sanctions. (a) *Signature.* Every pleading, written motion, and other paper must be signed by at least one attorney of record in the attorney's name--or by a party personally if the party is unrepresented. The paper must state the signer's address, e-mail address, and telephone number. Unless a rule or statute specifically states otherwise, a pleading need not be verified or accompanied by an affidavit. The court must strike an unsigned paper unless the omission is promptly corrected after being called to the attorney's or party's attention.

(b) *Representations to the Court.* By presenting to the court a pleading, written motion, or other paper--whether by signing, filing, submitting, or later advocating it--an attorney or unrepresented party certifies that to the best of the person's knowledge, information, and belief, formed after an inquiry reasonable under the circumstances: (1) it is not being presented for any improper purpose, such as to harass, cause unnecessary delay, or needlessly increase the cost of litigation;

(2) the claims, defenses, and other legal contentions are warranted by existing law or by a nonfrivolous argument for extending, modifying, or reversing existing law or for establishing new law;

(3) the factual contentions have evidentiary support or, if specifically so identified, will likely have evidentiary support after a reasonable opportunity for further investigation or discovery; and

(4) the denials of factual contentions are warranted on the evidence or, if specifically so identified, are reasonably based on belief or a lack of information.

(c) *Sanctions.* (1) *In General.* If, after notice and a reasonable opportunity to respond, the court determines that Rule 11(b) has been violated, the court may impose an appropriate sanction on any attorney, law firm, or party that violated the rule or is responsible for the violation. Absent exceptional circumstances, a law firm must be held jointly responsible for a violation committed by its partner, associate, or employee.

(2) *Motion for Sanctions.* A motion for sanctions must be made separately from any other motion and must describe the specific conduct that allegedly violates Rule 11(b). The motion must be served under Rule 5, but it must not be filed or be presented to the court if the challenged paper, claim, defense, contention, or denial is withdrawn or appropriately corrected within 21 days after service or within another time the court sets. If warranted, the court may award to the prevailing party the reasonable expenses, including attorney's fees, incurred for the motion.

(3) *On the Court's Initiative.* On its own, the court may order an attorney, law firm, or party to show cause why conduct specifically described in the order has not violated Rule 11(b).

(4) *Nature of a Sanction.* A sanction imposed under this rule must be limited to what suffices to deter repetition of the conduct or comparable conduct by others similarly situated. The sanction may include nonmonetary directives; an order to pay a penalty into court; or, if imposed on motion and warranted for effective deterrence, an order directing payment to the movant of part or all of the reasonable attorney's fees and other expenses directly resulting from the violation.

(5) *Limitations on Monetary Sanctions.* The court must not impose a monetary sanction:

(A) against a represented party for violating Rule 11(b)(2); or

(B) on its own, unless it issued the show-cause order under Rule 11(c)(3) before voluntary dismissal or settlement of the claims made by or against the party that is, or whose attorneys are, to be sanctioned.

(6) *Requirements for an Order.* An order imposing a sanction must describe the sanctioned conduct and explain the basis for the sanction.

(d) *Inapplicability to Discovery.* This rule does not apply to disclosures and discovery requests, responses, objections, and motions under Rules 26 through 37.

Fed. Rule Civ. Proc. 22. Interpleader. (a) *Grounds.* (1) *By a Plaintiff.* Persons with claims that may expose a plaintiff to double or multiple liability may be joined as defendants and required to interplead. Joinder for interpleader is proper even though:

(A) the claims of the several claimants, or the titles on which their claims depend, lack a common origin or are adverse and independent rather than identical; or

(B) the plaintiff denies liability in whole or in part to any or all of the claimants.

(2) *By a Defendant.* A defendant exposed to similar liability may seek interpleader through a crossclaim or counterclaim.

(b) *Relation to Other Rules and Statutes.* This rule supplements--and does not limit--the joinder of parties allowed by Rule 20. The remedy it provides is in addition to--and does not supersede or limit--the remedy provided by 28 U.S.C. §§ 1335, 1397, and 2361. An action under those statutes must be conducted under these rules.

Fed. Rule Civ. Proc. 24. Intervention. (a) *Intervention of Right.* On timely motion, the court must permit anyone to intervene who:

(1) is given an unconditional right to intervene by a federal statute; or

(2) claims an interest relating to the property or transaction that is the subject of the action, and is so situated that disposing of the action may as a practical matter impair or impede the movant's ability to protect its interest, unless existing parties adequately represent that interest.

(b) *Permissive Intervention.* (1) *In General.* On timely motion, the court may permit anyone to intervene who:

(A) is given a conditional right to intervene by a federal statute; or

(B) has a claim or defense that shares with the main action a common question of law or fact.

(2) *By a Government Officer or Agency.* On timely motion, the court may permit a federal or state governmental officer or agency to intervene if a party's claim or defense is based on:

(A) a statute or executive order administered by the officer or agency; or

(B) any regulation, order, requirement, or agreement issued or made under the statute or executive order.

(3) *Delay or Prejudice.* In exercising its discretion, the court must consider whether the intervention will unduly delay or prejudice the adjudication of the original parties' rights.

(c) *Notice and Pleading Required.* A motion to intervene must be served on the parties as provided in Rule 5. The motion must state the grounds for intervention and be accompanied by a pleading that sets out the claim or defense for which intervention is sought.

Fed. Rule Civ. Proc. 26. Duty to Disclose; General Provisions Governing Discovery. (a) *Required Disclosures.* (1) *Initial Disclosure.* (A) *In General.* Except as exempted by Rule 26(a)(1)(B) or as otherwise stipulated or ordered by the court, a party must, without awaiting a discovery request, provide to the other parties:

(i) the name and, if known, the address and telephone number of each individual likely to have discoverable information--along with the subjects of that information-- that the disclosing party may use to support its claims or defenses, unless the use would be solely for impeachment;

(ii) a copy--or a description by category and location--of all documents, electrically stored information, and tangible things that the disclosing party has in its possession, custody, or control and may use to support its claims or defenses, unless the use would be solely for impeachment;

(iii) a computation of each category of damages claimed by the disclosing party-- who must also make available for inspection and copying as under Rule 34 the documents or other evidentiary material, unless privileged or protected from disclosure, on which each computation is based, including materials bearing on the nature and extent of injuries suffered; and

(iv) for inspection and copying as under Rule 34, any insurance agreement under which an insurance business may be liable to satisfy all or part of a possible judgment in the action or to indemnify or reimburse for payments made to satisfy the judgment.

(B) *Proceedings Exempt from Initial Disclosure*. The following proceedings are exempt from initial disclosure:

(i) an action for review on an administrative record;

(ii) a forfeiture action in rem arising from a federal statute;

(iii) a petition for habeas corpus or any other proceeding to challenge a criminal conviction or sentence;

(iv) an action brought without an attorney by a person in the custody of the United States, a state, or a state subdivision;

(v) an action to enforce or quash an administrative summons or subpoena;

(vi) an action by the United States to recover benefit payments;

(vii) an action by the United States to collect on a student loan guaranteed by the United States;

(viii) a proceeding ancillary to a proceeding in another court; and

(ix) an action to enforce an arbitration award.

(C) *Time for Initial Disclosures--In General*. A party must make the initial disclosures at or within 14 days after the parties' Rule 26(f) conference unless a different time is set by stipulation or court order, or unless a party objects during the conference that initial disclosures are not appropriate in this action and states the objection in the proposed discovery plan. In ruling on the objection, the court must determine what disclosures, if any, are to be made and must set the time for disclosure.

(D) *Time for Initial Disclosures--For Parties Served or Joined Later*. A party that is first served or otherwise joined after the Rule 26(f) conference must make the initial disclosures within 30 days after being served or joined, unless a different time is set by stipulation or court order.

(E) *Basis for Initial Disclosure; Unacceptable Excuses*. A party must make its initial disclosures based on the information then reasonably available to it. A party is not excused from making its disclosures because it has not fully investigated the case or because it challenges the sufficiency of another party's disclosures or because another party has not made its disclosures.

(2) *Disclosure of Expert Testimony.*

(A) *In General*. In addition to the disclosures required by Rule 26(a)(1), a party must disclose to the other parties the identity of any witness it may use at trial to present evidence under Federal Rule of Evidence 702, 703, or 705.

(B) *Witnesses Who Must Provide a Written Report.* Unless otherwise stipulated or ordered by the court, this disclosure must be accompanied by a written report--prepared and signed by the witness--if the witness is one retained or specially employed to provide expert testimony in the case or one whose duties as the party's employee regularly involve giving expert testimony. The report must contain:

(i) a complete statement of all opinions the witness will express and the basis and reasons for them;

(ii) the facts or data considered by the witness in forming them;

(iii) any exhibits that will be used to summarize or support them;

(iv) the witness's qualifications, including a list of all publications authored in the previous 10 years;

(v) a list of all other cases in which, during the previous 4 years, the witness testified as an expert at trial or by deposition; and

(vi) a statement of the compensation to be paid for the study and testimony in the case.

(C) *Witnesses Who Do Not Provide a Written Report.* Unless otherwise stipulated or ordered by the court, if the witness is not required to provide a written report, this disclosure must state:

(i) the subject matter on which the witness is expected to present evidence under Federal Rule of Evidence 702, 703, or 705; and

(ii) a summary of the facts and opinions to which the witness is expected to testify.

(D) *Time to Disclose Expert Testimony.* A party must make these disclosures at the times and in the sequence that the court orders. Absent a stipulation or a court order, the disclosures must be made:

(i) at least 90 days before the date set for trial or for the case to be ready for trial; or

(ii) if the evidence is intended solely to contradict or rebut evidence on the same subject matter identified by another party under Rule 26(a)(2)(B) or (C), within 30 days after the other party's disclosure.

(E) *Supplementing the Disclosure.* The parties must supplement these disclosures when required under Rule 26(e).

(3) *Pretrial Disclosures.*

(A) *In General.* In addition to the disclosures required by Rule 26(a)(1) and (2), a party must provide to the other parties and promptly file the following information about the evidence that it may present at trial other than solely for impeachment:

(i) the name and, if not previously provided, the address and telephone number of each witness--separately identifying those the party expects to present and those it may call if the need arises;

(ii) the designation of those witnesses whose testimony the party expects to present by deposition and, if not taken stenographically, a transcript of the pertinent parts of the deposition; and

(iii) an identification of each document or other exhibit, including summaries of other evidence--separately identifying those items the party expects to offer and those it may offer if the need arises.

(B) *Time for Pretrial Disclosures; Objections.* Unless the court orders otherwise, these disclosures must be made at least 30 days before trial. Within 14 days after they are made, unless the court sets a different time, a party may serve and promptly file a list of the following objections: any objections to the use under Rule 32(a) of a deposition designated by another party under Rule 26(a)(3)(A)(ii); and any objection, together with the grounds for it, that may be made to the admissibility of materials identified under Rule 26(a)(3)(A)(iii). An objection not so made--except for one under Federal Rule of Evidence 402 or 403--is waived unless excused by the court for good cause.

(4) *Form of Disclosures.* Unless the court orders otherwise, all disclosures under Rule 26(a) must be in writing, signed, and served.

(b) *Discovery Scope and Limits.* (1) *Scope in General.* Unless otherwise limited by court order, the scope of discovery is as follows: Parties may obtain discovery regarding any nonprivileged matter that is relevant to any party's claim or defense--including the existence, description, nature, custody, condition, and location of any documents or other tangible things and the identity and location of persons who know of any discoverable matter. For good cause, the court may order discovery of any matter relevant to the subject matter involved in the action. Relevant information need not be admissible at the trial if the discovery appears reasonably calculated to lead to the discovery of admissible evidence. All discovery is subject to the limitations imposed by Rule 26(b)(2)(C).

(2) *Limitations on Frequency and Extent.*

(A) *When Permitted.* By order, the court may alter the limits in these rules on the number of depositions and interrogatories or on the length of depositions under Rule 30. By order or local rule, the court may also limit the number of requests under Rule 36.

(B) *Specific Limitations on Electronically Stored Information.* A party need not provide discovery of electronically stored information from sources that the party identifies as not reasonably accessible because of undue burden or cost. On motion to compel discovery or for a protective order, the party from whom discovery is sought must show that the information is not reasonably accessible because of undue burden or cost. If that showing is made, the court may nonetheless order discovery from such sources if the requesting party shows good cause, considering the limitations of Rule 26(b)(2)(C). The court may specify conditions for the discovery.

(C) *When Required.* On motion or on its own, the court must limit the frequency or extent of discovery otherwise allowed by these rules or by local rule if it determines that:

(i) the discovery sought is unreasonably cumulative or duplicative, or can be obtained from some other source that is more convenient, less burdensome, or less expensive;

(ii) the party seeking discovery has had ample opportunity to obtain the information by discovery in the action; or

(iii) the burden or expense of the proposed discovery outweighs its likely benefit, considering the needs of the case, the amount in controversy, the parties' resources, the importance of the issues at stake in the action, and the importance of the discovery in resolving the issues.

(3) *Trial Preparation: Materials.*

(A) *Documents and Tangible Things.* Ordinarily, a party may not discover documents and tangible things that are prepared in anticipation of litigation or for trial by or for another party or its representative (including the other party's attorney, consultant, surety, indemnitor, insurer, or agent). But, subject to Rule 26(b)(4), those materials may be discovered if:

(i) they are otherwise discoverable under Rule 26(b)(1); and

(ii) the party shows that it has substantial need for the materials to prepare its case and cannot, without undue hardship, obtain their substantial equivalent by other means.

(B) *Protection Against Disclosure.* If the court orders discovery of those materials, it must protect against disclosure of the mental impressions, conclusions, opinions, or legal theories of a party's attorney or other representative concerning the litigation.

(C) *Previous Statement.* Any party or other person may, on request and without the required showing, obtain the person's own previous statement about the action or its subject matter. If the request is refused, the person may move for a court order, and Rule 37(a)(5) applies to the award of expenses. A previous statement is either:

(i) a written statement that the person has signed or otherwise adopted or approved; or

(ii) a contemporaneous stenographic, mechanical, electrical, or other recording--or a transcription of it--that recites substantially verbatim the person's oral statement.

(4) *Trial Preparation: Experts.*

(A) *Deposition of an Expert Who May Testify.* A party may depose any person who has been identified as an expert whose opinions may be presented at trial. If Rule 26(a)(2)(B) requires a report from the expert, the deposition may be conducted only after the report is provided.

(B) *Trial-Preparation Protection for Draft Reports or Disclosures.* Rules 26(b)(3)(A) and (B) protect drafts of any report or disclosure required under Rule 26(a)(2), regardless of the form in which the draft is recorded.

(C) *Trial-Preparation Protection for Communications Between a Party's Attorney and Expert Witnesses.* Rules 26(b)(3)(A) and (B) protect communications between the party's attorney and any witness required to provide a report under Rule 26(a)(2)(B), regardless of the form of the communications, except to the extent that the communications:

(i) relate to compensation for the expert's study or testimony;

(ii) identify facts or data that the party's attorney provided and that the expert considered in forming the opinions to be expressed; or

(iii) identify assumptions that the party's attorney provided and that the expert relied on in forming the opinions to be expressed.

(D) *Expert Employed Only for Trial Preparation.* Ordinarily, a party may not, by interrogatories or deposition, discover facts known or opinions held by an expert who has been retained or specially employed by another party in anticipation of litigation or to prepare for trial and who is not expected to be called as a witness at trial. But a party may do so only:

(i) as provided in Rule 35(b); or

(ii) on showing exceptional circumstances under which it is impracticable for the party to obtain facts or opinions on the same subject by other means.

(E) *Payment.* Unless manifest injustice would result, the court must require that the party seeking discovery:

(i) pay the expert a reasonable fee for time spent in responding to discovery under Rule 26(b)(4)(A) or (D); and

(ii) for discovery under (D), also pay the other party a fair portion of the fees and expenses it reasonably incurred in obtaining the expert's facts and opinions.

(5) *Claiming Privilege or Protecting Trial-Preparation Materials.*

(A) *Information Withheld.* When a party withholds information otherwise discoverable by claiming that the information is privileged or subject to protection as trial-preparation material, the party must:

(i) expressly make the claim; and

(ii) describe the nature of the documents, communications, or tangible things not produced or disclosed--and do so in a manner that, without revealing information itself privileged or protected, will enable other parties to assess the claim.

(B) *Information Produced.* If information produced in discovery is subject to a claim of privilege or of protection as trial-preparation material, the party making the claim may notify any party that received the information of the claim and the basis for it. After being notified, a party must promptly return, sequester, or destroy the specified information and any copies it has; must not use or disclose the information until the claim is resolved; must take reasonable steps to retrieve the information if the party disclosed it before being notified; and may promptly present the information to the court under seal for a determination of the claim. The producing party must preserve the information until the claim is resolved.

(c) *Protective Orders.* (1) *In General.* A party or any person from whom discovery is sought may move for a protective order in the court where the action is pending--or as an alternative on matters relating to a deposition, in the court for the district where the deposition will be taken. The motion must include a certification that the movant has in good faith conferred or attempted to confer with other affected parties in an effort to resolve the dispute without court action. The court may, for good cause, issue an order to protect a party or person from annoyance, embarrassment, oppression, or undue burden or expense, including one or more of the following:

(A) forbidding the disclosure or discovery;

(B) specifying terms, including time and place, for the disclosure or discovery;

(C) prescribing a discovery method other than the one selected by the party seeking discovery;

(D) forbidding inquiry into certain matters, or limiting the scope of disclosure or discovery to certain matters;

(E) designating the persons who may be present while the discovery is conducted;

(F) requiring that a deposition be sealed and opened only on court order;

(G) requiring that a trade secret or other confidential research, development, or commercial information not be revealed or be revealed only in a specified way; and

(H) requiring that the parties simultaneously file specified documents or information in sealed envelopes, to be opened as the court directs.

(2) *Ordering Discovery.* If a motion for a protective order is wholly or partly denied, the court may, on just terms, order that any party or person provide or permit discovery.

(3) *Awarding Expenses.* Rule 37(a)(5) applies to the award of expenses.

(d) *Timing and Sequence of Discovery.* (1) *Timing.* A party may not seek discovery from any source before the parties have conferred as required by Rule 26(f), except in a proceeding exempted from initial disclosure under Rule 26(a)(1)(B), or when authorized by these rules, by stipulation, or by court order.

(2) *Sequence.* Unless, on motion, the court orders otherwise for the parties' and witnesses' convenience and in the interests of justice:

(A) methods of discovery may be used in any sequence; and

(B) discovery by one party does not require any other party to delay its discovery.

(e) *Supplementing Disclosures and Responses.* (1) *In General.* A party who has made a disclosure under Rule 26(a)--or who has responded to an interrogatory, request for production, or request for admission--must supplement or correct its disclosure or response:

(A) in a timely manner if the party learns that in some material respect the disclosure or response is incomplete or incorrect, and if the additional or corrective information has not otherwise been made known to the other parties during the discovery process or in writing; or

(B) as ordered by the court.

(2) *Expert Witness.* For an expert whose report must be disclosed under Rule 26(a)(2)(B), the party's duty to supplement extends both to information included in the report and to information given during the expert's deposition. Any additions or changes to this information must be disclosed by the time the party's pretrial disclosures under Rule 26(a)(3) are due.

(f) *Conference of the Parties; Planning for Discovery.* (1) *Conference Timing.* Except in a proceeding exempted from initial disclosure under Rule 26(a)(1)(B) or when the court orders otherwise, the parties must confer as soon as practicable--and in any event at least 21 days before a scheduling conference is held or a scheduling order is due under Rule 16(b).

(2) *Conference Content; Parties' Responsibilities.* In conferring, the parties must consider the nature and basis of their claims and defenses and the possibilities for promptly settling or resolving the case; make or arrange for the disclosures required by Rule 26(a)(1); discuss any issues about preserving discoverable information; and develop a proposed discovery plan. The attorneys of record and all unrepresented parties that have appeared in the case are jointly responsible for arranging the conference, for attempting in good faith to agree on the proposed discovery plan, and for submitting to the court within 14 days after the conference a written report outlining the plan. The court may order the parties or attorneys to attend the conference in person.

(3) *Discovery Plan.* A discovery plan must state the parties' views and proposals on:

(A) what changes should be made in the timing, form, or requirement for disclosures under Rule 26(a), including a statement of when initial disclosures were made or will be made;

(B) the subjects on which discovery may be needed, when discovery should be completed, and whether discovery should be conducted in phases or be limited to or focused on particular issues;

(C) any issues about disclosure or discovery of electronically stored information, including the form or forms in which it should be produced;

(D) any issues about claims of privilege or of protection as trial-preparation materials, including--if the parties agree on a procedure to assert these claims after production-- whether to ask the court to include their agreement in an order;

(E) what changes should be made in the limitations on discovery imposed under these rules or by local rule, and what other limitations should be imposed; and

(F) any other orders that the court should issue under Rule 26(c) or under Rule 16(b) and (c).

(4) *Expedited Schedule.* If necessary to comply with its expedited schedule for Rule 16(b) conferences, a court may by local rule:

(A) require the parties' conference to occur less than 21 days before the scheduling conference is held or a scheduling order is due under Rule 16(b); and

(B) require the written report outlining the discovery plan to be filed less than 14 days after the parties' conference, or excuse the parties from submitting a written report and permit them to report orally on their discovery plan at the Rule 16(b) conference.

(g) *Signing Disclosures and Discovery Requests, Responses, and Objections.* (1) *Signature Required; Effect of Signature.* Every disclosure under Rule 26(a)(1) or (a)(3) and every discovery request, response, or objection must be signed by at least one attorney of record in the attorney's own name--or by the party personally, if unrepresented--and must state the signer's address, e-mail address, and telephone number. By signing, an attorney or party certifies that to the best of the person's knowledge, information, and belief formed after a reasonable inquiry:

(A) with respect to a disclosure, it is complete and correct as of the time it is made; and

(B) with respect to a discovery request, response, or objection, it is:

(i) consistent with these rules and warranted by existing law or by a nonfrivolous argument for extending, modifying, or reversing existing law, or for establishing new law;

(ii) not interposed for any improper purpose, such as to harass, cause unnecessary delay, or needlessly increase the cost of litigation; and

(iii) neither unreasonable nor unduly burdensome or expensive, considering the needs of the case, prior discovery in the case, the amount in controversy, and the importance of the issues at stake in the action.

(2) *Failure to Sign.* Other parties have no duty to act on an unsigned disclosure, request, response, or objection until it is signed, and the court must strike it unless a signature is promptly supplied after the omission is called to the attorney's or party's attention.

(3) *Sanction for Improper Certification.* If a certification violates this rule without substantial justification, the court, on motion or on its own, must impose an appropriate sanction on the signer, the party on whose behalf the signer was acting, or both. The sanction may include an order to pay the reasonable expenses, including attorney's fees, caused by the violation.

Fed. Rule Civ. Proc. 54. Judgments; Costs. (a) *Definition; Form.* "Judgment" as used in these rules includes a decree and any order from which an appeal lies. A judgment must not include recitals of pleadings, a master's report, or a record of prior proceedings.

(b) *Judgment on Multiple Claims or Involving Multiple Parties.* When an action presents more than one claim for relief--whether as a claim, counterclaim, crossclaim, or third-party claim--or when multiple parties are involved, the court may direct entry of a final judgment as to one or more, but fewer than all, claims or parties only if the court expressly determines that there is no just reason for delay. Otherwise, any order or other decision, however designated, that adjudicates fewer than all the claims or the rights and liabilities of fewer than all the parties does not end the action as to any of the claims or parties and may be revised at any time before the entry of a judgment adjudicating all the claims and all the parties' rights and liabilities.

(c) *Demand for Judgment; Relief to Be Granted*. A default judgment must not differ in kind from, or exceed in amount, what is demanded in the pleadings. Every other final judgment should grant the relief to which each party is entitled, even if the party has not demanded that relief in its pleadings.

(d) *Costs; Attorney's Fees*. (1) *Costs Other Than Attorney's Fees*. Unless a federal statute, these rules, or a court order provides otherwise, costs--other than attorney's fees--should be allowed to the prevailing party. But costs against the United States, its officers, and its agencies may be imposed only to the extent allowed by law. The clerk may tax costs on 14 days' notice. On motion served within the next 7 days, the court may review the clerk's action.

(2) *Attorney's Fees*.

(A) *Claim to Be by Motion*. A claim for attorney's fees and related nontaxable expenses must be made by motion unless the substantive law requires those fees to be proved at trial as an element of damages.

(B) *Timing and Contents of the Motion*. Unless a statute or a court order provides otherwise, the motion must:

(i) be filed no later than 14 days after the entry of judgment;

(ii) specify the judgment and the statute, rule, or other grounds entitling the movant to the award;

(iii) state the amount sought or provide a fair estimate of it; and

(iv) disclose, if the court so orders, the terms of any agreement about fees for the services for which the claim is made.

(C) *Proceedings*. Subject to Rule 23(h), the court must, on a party's request, give an opportunity for adversary submissions on the motion in accordance with Rule 43(c) or 78. The court may decide issues of liability for fees before receiving submissions on the value of services. The court must find the facts and state its conclusions of law as provided in Rule 52(a).

(D) *Special Procedures by Local Rule; Reference to a Master or a Magistrate Judge*. By local rule, the court may establish special procedures to resolve fee-related issues without extensive evidentiary hearings. Also, the court may refer issues concerning the value of services to a special master under Rule 53 without regard to the limitations of Rule 53(a)(1), and may refer a motion for attorney's fees to a magistrate judge under Rule 72(b) as if it were a dispositive pretrial matter.

(E) *Exceptions*. Subparagraphs (A)-(D) do not apply to claims for fees and expenses as sanctions for violating these rules or as sanctions under 28 U.S.C. § 1927.

Federal Rules of Appellate Procedure

Fed. Rule App. Proc. 4. Appeal as of Right – When Taken. (a) *Appeal in a Civil Case*. (1) *Time for Filing a Notice of Appeal*.

(A) In a civil case, except as provided in Rules 4(a)(1)(B), 4(a)(4), and 4(c), the notice of appeal required by Rule 3 must be filed with the district clerk within 30 days after entry of the judgment or order appealed from.

(B) The notice of appeal may be filed by any party within 60 days after entry of the judgment or order appealed from if one of the parties is:

(i) the United States;

(ii) a United States agency;

(iii) a United States officer or employee sued in an official capacity; or

(iv) a current or former United States officer or employee sued in an individual capacity for an act or omission occurring in connection with duties performed on the United States' behalf--including all instances in which the United States represents that person when the judgment or order is entered or files the appeal for that person.

(C) An appeal from an order granting or denying an application for a writ of error *coram nobis* is an appeal in a civil case for purposes of Rule 4(a).

(2) *Filing Before Entry of Judgment.* A notice of appeal filed after the court announces a decision or order -- but before the entry of the judgment or order -- is treated as filed on the date of and after the entry.

(3) *Multiple Appeals.* If one party timely files a notice of appeal, any other party may file a notice of appeal within 14 days after the date when the first notice was filed, or within the time otherwise prescribed by this Rule 4(a), whichever period ends later.

(4) *Effect of a Motion on a Notice of Appeal.*

(A) If a party timely files in the district court any of the following motions under the Federal Rules of Civil Procedure, the time to file an appeal runs for all parties from the entry of the order disposing of the last such remaining motion:

(i) for judgment under Rule 50(b);

(ii) to amend or make additional factual findings under Rule 52(b), whether or not granting the motion would alter the judgment;

(iii) for attorney's fees under Rule 54 if the district court extends the time to appeal under Rule 58;

(iv) to alter or amend the judgment under Rule 59;

(v) for a new trial under Rule 59; or

(vi) for relief under Rule 60 if the motion is filed no later than 28 days after the judgment is entered.

(B)(i) If a party files a notice of appeal after the court announces or enters a judgment -- but before it disposes of any motion listed in Rule 4(a)(4)(A) -- the notice becomes effective to appeal a judgment or order, in whole or in part, when the order disposing of the last such remaining motion is entered.

(ii) A party intending to challenge an order disposing of any motion listed in Rule 4(a)(4)(A), or a judgment's alteration or amendment upon such a motion, must file a notice of appeal, or an amended notice of appeal -- in compliance with Rule 3(c) -- within the time prescribed by this Rule measured from the entry of the order disposing of the last such remaining motion.

(iii) No additional fee is required to file an amended notice.

(5) *Motion for Extension of Time.* (A) The district court may extend the time to file a notice of appeal if:

(i) a party so moves no later than 30 days after the time prescribed by this Rule 4(a) expires; and

(ii) regardless of whether its motion is filed before or during the 30 days after the time prescribed by this Rule 4(a) expires, that party shows excusable neglect or good cause.

(B) A motion filed before the expiration of the time prescribed in Rule 4(a)(1) or (3) may be ex parte unless the court requires otherwise. If the motion is filed after the expiration of the prescribed time, notice must be given to the other parties in accordance with local rules.

(C) No extension under this Rule 4(a)(5) may exceed 30 days after the prescribed time or 14 days after the date when the order granting the motion is entered, whichever is later.

(6) *Reopening the Time to File an Appeal.* The district court may reopen the time to file an appeal for a period of 14 days after the date when its order to reopen is entered, but only if all the following conditions are satisfied:

(A) the court finds that the moving party did not receive notice under Federal Rule of Civil Procedure 77(d) of the entry of the judgment or order sought to be appealed within 21 days after entry;

(B) the motion is filed within 180 days after the judgment or order is entered or within 14 days after the moving party receives notice under Federal Rule of Civil Procedure 77(d) of the entry, whichever is earlier; and

(C) the court finds that no party would be prejudiced.

(7) *Entry Defined.* (A) A judgment or order is entered for purposes of this Rule 4(a):

(i) if Federal Rule of Civil Procedure 58(a) does not require a separate document, when the judgment or order is entered in the civil docket under Federal Rule of Civil Procedure 79(a); or

(ii) if Federal Rule of Civil Procedure 58(a) requires a separate document, when the judgment or order is entered in the civil docket under Federal Rule of Civil Procedure 79(a) and when the earlier of these events occurs:

. the judgment or order is set forth on a separate document, or

. 150 days have run from entry of the judgment or order in the civil docket under Federal Rule of Civil Procedure 79(a).

(B) A failure to set forth a judgment or order on a separate document when required by Federal Rule of Civil Procedure 58(a) does not affect the validity of an appeal from that judgment or order.

Fed. Rule App. Proc. 13. Review of a Decision of the Tax Court. (a) *How Obtained; Time for Filing Notice of Appeal.* (1) Review of a decision of the United States Tax Court is commenced by filing a notice of appeal with the Tax Court clerk within 90 days after the entry of the Tax Court's decision. At the time of filing, the appellant must furnish the clerk with enough copies of the notice to enable the clerk to comply with Rule 3(d). If one party files a timely notice of appeal, any other party may file a notice of appeal within 120 days after the Tax Court's decision is entered.

(2) If, under Tax Court rules, a party makes a timely motion to vacate or revise the Tax Court's decision, the time to file a notice of appeal runs from the entry of the order disposing of the motion or from the entry of a new decision, whichever is later.

* * *

Fed. Rule App. Proc. 15. Review or Enforcement of an Agency Order--How Obtained; Intervention. (a) *Petition for Review; Joint Petition.* (1) Review of an agency order is commenced by filing, within the time prescribed by law, a petition for review with the clerk of a court of appeals authorized to review the agency order. If their interests make joinder practicable, two or more persons may join in a petition to the same court to review the same order.

(2) The petition must:

(A) name each party seeking review either in the caption or the body of the petition -- using such terms as "et al.," "petitioners," or "respondents" does not effectively name the parties;

(B) name the agency as a respondent (even though not named in the petition, the United States is a respondent if required by statute); and

(C) specify the order or part thereof to be reviewed.

(3) Form 3 in the Appendix of Forms is a suggested form of a petition for review.

(4) In this rule "agency" includes an agency, board, commission, or officer; "petition for review" includes a petition to enjoin, suspend, modify, or otherwise review, or a notice of appeal, whichever form is indicated by the applicable statute.

* * *

Fed. Rule App. Proc. 16. The Record on Review or Enforcement. (a) *Composition of the Record.* The record on review or enforcement of an agency order consists of:

(1) the order involved;

(2) any findings or report on which it is based; and

(3) the pleadings, evidence, and other parts of the proceedings before the agency.

* * *

Fed. Rule App. Proc. 32.1. Citing Judicial Dispositions. (a) *Citation Permitted.* A court may not prohibit or restrict the citation of federal judicial opinions, orders, judgments, or other written dispositions that have been:

(i) designated as "unpublished," "not for publication," "non-precedential," "not precedent," or the like; and

(ii) issued on or after January 1, 2007.

(b) *Copies Required.* If a party cites a federal judicial opinion, order, judgment, or other written disposition that is not available in a publicly accessible electronic database, the party must file and serve a copy of that opinion, order, judgment, or disposition with the brief or other paper in which it is cited.

PART VIII

Miscellaneous Materials

SECTION 1. PURPOSE AND SCOPE

.01 Purpose. This revenue procedure provides guidance for a taxpayer seeking equitable relief from income tax liability under section 66(c) or section 6015(f) of the Internal Revenue Code (a "requesting spouse"). Section 4.01 of this revenue procedure provides the threshold requirements for any request for equitable relief. Section 4.02 of this revenue procedure sets forth the conditions under which the Internal Revenue Service will make streamlined relief determinations granting equitable relief under section 6015(f) from an understatement of income tax or an underpayment of income tax reported on a joint return. Section 4.03 of this revenue procedure provides a nonexclusive list of factors for consideration in determining whether relief should be granted under section 6015(f) because it would be inequitable to hold a requesting spouse jointly and severally liable when the conditions of section 4.02 are not met. The factors in section 4.03 also will apply in determining whether to relieve a spouse from income tax liability resulting from the operation of community property law under the equitable relief provision of section 66(c).

.02 Scope. This revenue procedure applies to spouses who request either equitable relief from joint and several liability under section 6015(f), or equitable relief under section 66(c) from income tax liability resulting from the operation of community property law.

SECTION 2. BACKGROUND

.01 Section 6013(d)(3) provides that married taxpayers who file a joint return under section 6013 will be jointly and severally liable for the income tax arising from that joint return. For purposes of section 6013(d)(3) and this revenue procedure, the term "tax" includes penalties, additions to tax, and interest. See sections 6601(e)(1) and 6665(a)(2).

.02 Section 3201(a) of the Internal Revenue Service Restructuring and Reform Act of 1998, Pub. L. No. 105-206, 112 Stat. 685, 734 (RRA), enacted section 6015, which provides relief in certain circumstances from the joint and several liability imposed by section 6013(d)(3). Section 6015(b) and (c) specify two sets of circumstances under which relief from joint and several liability is available in cases involving understatements of tax. Section 6015(b) is modeled after former section 6015(e), the prior innocent spouse statute, and section 6015(c) provides for separation of liability. If relief is not available under section 6015(b) or (c), section 6015(f) authorizes the Secretary to grant equitable relief if, taking into account all the facts and circumstances, the Secretary determines that it is inequitable to hold a requesting spouse liable for any unpaid tax or any deficiency (or any portion of either). Section 66(c) provides relief from income tax liability resulting from the operation of community property law to taxpayers domiciled in a community property state who do not file a joint return. Section 3201(b) of RRA amended section 66(c) to add an equitable relief provision similar to section 6015(f).

.03 Section 6015 provides relief only from joint and several liability arising from a joint return. If an individual signs a joint return under duress, the election to file jointly is not valid and there is no valid joint return. The individual is not jointly and severally liable for any income tax liabilities arising from that return. Therefore, section 6015 does not apply and is not necessary for obtaining relief.

.04 Under section 6015(b) and (c), relief is available only from an understatement or a deficiency. Section 6015(b) and (c) do not authorize relief from an underpayment of income tax reported on a joint return. Section 66(c) and section 6015(f) permit equitable relief from an underpayment of income tax or from a deficiency. The legislative history of section 6015 provides that Congress intended for the Secretary to exercise discretion in granting equitable relief from an underpayment of income tax if a requesting spouse "does not know, and had no reason to know, that funds intended for the payment of tax were instead taken by the other spouse for such other spouse's benefit." H.R. Conf. Rep. No. 105-599, at 254 (1998). Congress also intended for the Secretary to exercise the equitable relief authority under section 6015(f) in other situations if, "taking into account all the facts and circumstances, it is inequitable to hold an individual liable for all or part of any unpaid tax or deficiency arising from a joint return." *Id.*

SECTION 3. SIGNIFICANT CHANGES

This revenue procedure supersedes Revenue Procedure 2003-61, changing the following:

.01 Section 4.01(3) of this revenue procedure provides that a request for equitable relief under section 6015(f) or section 66(c) must be filed before the expiration of the period of limitation for collection under section 6502, or, if applicable, the period of limitation for credit or refund under section 6511. This is a significant change to the requirement in Revenue Procedure 2003-61, section 4.01(3) and Treas. Reg. § 1.6015-5(b)(1) (TD 9003), that the requesting spouse's claim for equitable relief must be filed no later than two years after the date of the Service's first collection activity. See Notice 2011-70.

.02 Section 4.01(7)(e) of this revenue procedure adds a new exception to the threshold condition in section 4.01(7) that the income tax liability must be attributable to an item of the nonrequesting spouse, when the nonrequesting spouse's fraud gave rise to the understatement of tax or deficiency.

.03 Section 4.02 of this revenue procedure has been revised to apply to understatements of income tax in addition to underpayments. Section 4.02 has also been revised to apply to claims for equitable relief under section 66(c).

.04 Section 4.03(2) is revised to clarify that no one factor or a majority of factors necessarily controls the determination. Therefore, depending on the facts and circumstances of the case, relief may still be appropriate if the number of factors weighing against relief exceeds the number of factors weighing in favor of relief, or a denial of relief may still be appropriate if the number of factors weighing in favor of relief exceeds the number of factors weighing against relief.

.05 Section 4.03(2)(b) of this revenue procedure revises the economic hardship equitable factor to provide minimum standards based on income, expenses, and assets, for determining whether the requesting spouse would suffer economic hardship if relief is not granted. Section 4.03(2)(b) is also revised to provide that the lack of a finding of economic hardship does not weigh against relief.

.06 Section 4.03(2)(c)(i) of this revenue procedure provides that actual knowledge of the item giving rise to an understatement or deficiency will no longer be weighed more heavily than other factors. Further, section 4.03(2)(c)(ii) clarifies that, for purposes of this factor, if the nonrequesting spouse abused the requesting spouse or maintained control over the household finances by restricting the requesting spouse's access to financial information, and, therefore, because of the abuse or financial control the requesting spouse was not able to challenge the treatment of any items on the joint return for fear of the nonrequesting spouse's retaliation, then that abuse or financial control will result in this factor weighing in favor of relief even if the requesting spouse had knowledge or reason to know of the items giving rise to the understatement or deficiency.

.07 Section 4.03(2)(c)(ii) of this revenue procedure provides that, in determining whether the requesting spouse had knowledge or reason to know that the nonrequesting spouse would not pay the tax reported as due, the Service will consider whether the requesting spouse reasonably expected that the nonrequesting spouse would pay the tax liability within a reasonably prompt time. Further, section 4.03(2)(c)(ii) clarifies that for purposes of this factor, if the nonrequesting spouse abused the requesting spouse or maintained control over the household finances by restricting the requesting spouse's access to financial information, and, therefore, because of the abuse or financial control the requesting spouse was not able to question the payment of the taxes reported as due on the joint return or challenge the nonrequesting spouse's assurance regarding payment of the taxes for fear of the nonrequesting spouse's retaliation, then that abuse or financial control will result in this factor weighing in favor of relief even if the requesting spouse had knowledge or reason to know that the nonrequesting spouse would not pay the tax liability.

.08 Section 4.03(2)(d) of this revenue procedure clarifies that a requesting spouse's legal obligation to pay outstanding tax liabilities is a factor to consider in determining whether equitable relief should be granted, in addition to whether the nonrequesting spouse has a legal obligation to pay the tax liabilities.

.09 Section 4.03(2)(f) of this revenue procedure is revised to provide that the fact that a requesting spouse is subsequently compliant with all Federal income tax laws is a factor that may weigh in favor of relief.

.10 Section 4.04 of this revenue procedure broadens the availability of refunds in cases involving deficiencies by eliminating the rule in section 4.04(1) of Rev. Proc. 2003-61 that limited refunds in cases involving deficiencies to payments made by the requesting spouse pursuant to an installment agreement.

SECTION 4. GENERAL CONDITIONS FOR RELIEF

.01 Eligibility for equitable relief. A requesting spouse must satisfy all of the following threshold conditions to be eligible to submit a request for equitable relief under section 6015(f).

With the exception of conditions (1) and (2), a requesting spouse must satisfy all of the following threshold conditions to be eligible to submit a request for equitable relief under section 66(c). The Service may relieve a requesting spouse who satisfies all the applicable threshold conditions set forth below of all or part of the income tax liability under section 66(c) or section 6015(f) if, taking into account all the facts and circumstances, the Service determines that it would be inequitable to hold the requesting spouse liable for the income tax liability. The threshold conditions are as follows:

(1) The requesting spouse filed a joint return for the taxable year for which he or she seeks relief.

(2) Relief is not available to the requesting spouse under section 6015(b) or (c).

(3) Time for filing claim for relief:

(a) If the requesting spouse is applying for relief from a liability or a portion of a liability that remains unpaid, the request for relief must be made before the expiration of the period of limitation on collection of the income tax liability, as provided in section 6502. Generally, that period expires 10 years after the assessment of tax. Section 6502.

(b) Claims for credit or refund of amounts paid must be made before the expiration of the period of limitation on credit or refund, as provided in section 6511. Generally, that period expires three years from the time the return was filed or two years from the time the tax was paid, whichever is later.

(4) No assets were transferred between the spouses as part of a fraudulent scheme by the spouses.

(5) The nonrequesting spouse did not transfer disqualified assets to the requesting spouse. For this purpose, the term "disqualified asset" has the meaning given the term by section 6015(c)(4)(B). If the nonrequesting spouse transferred disqualified assets to the requesting spouse, relief will be available only to the extent that the income tax liability exceeds the value of the disqualified assets. This condition will not result in the requesting spouse being ineligible for relief if the nonrequesting spouse abused the requesting spouse or maintained control over the household finances by restricting the requesting spouse's access to financial information, or the requesting spouse did not have actual knowledge that disqualified assets were transferred.

(6) The requesting spouse did not knowingly participate in the filing of a fraudulent joint return.

(7) The income tax liability from which the requesting spouse seeks relief is attributable (either in full or in part) to an item of the nonrequesting spouse or an underpayment resulting from the nonrequesting spouse's income. If the liability is partially attributable to the requesting spouse, then relief can only be considered for the portion of the liability attributable to the nonrequesting spouse. Nonetheless, the Service will consider granting relief regardless of whether the understatement, deficiency, or underpayment is attributable (in full or in part) to the requesting spouse if any of the following exceptions applies:

(a) Attribution solely due to the operation of community property law. If an item is attributable or partially attributable to the requesting spouse solely due to the operation of community property law, then for purposes of this revenue procedure, that item (or portion thereof) will be considered to be attributable to the nonrequesting spouse.

(b) Nominal ownership. If the item is titled in the name of the requesting spouse, the item is presumptively attributable to the requesting spouse. This presumption is rebuttable. For example, H opens an individual retirement account (IRA) in W's name and forges W's signature on the IRA in 2006. Thereafter, H makes contributions to the IRA and in 2008 takes a taxable distribution from the IRA. H and W file a joint return for the 2008 taxable year, but do not report the taxable distribution on their joint return. The Service later determines a deficiency relating to the taxable IRA distribution. W requests relief from joint and several liability under section 6015. W establishes that W did not contribute to the IRA, sign paperwork relating to the IRA, or otherwise act as if W were the owner of the IRA. W thereby rebutted the presumption that the IRA is attributable to W.

(c) Misappropriation of funds. If the requesting spouse did not know, and had no reason to know, that funds intended for the payment of tax were misappropriated by the nonrequesting spouse for the nonrequesting spouse's benefit, the Service will consider granting equitable relief although the underpayment may be attributable in part or in full to an item of the requesting spouse. The Service will consider granting relief in the case only to the extent that the funds intended for the payment of tax were taken by the nonrequesting spouse.

(d) Abuse not amounting to duress. If the requesting spouse establishes that he or she was the victim of abuse prior to the time the return was signed, and that, as a result of the prior abuse, the requesting spouse did not challenge the treatment of any items on the return, or question the payment of any balance due reported on the return, for fear of the nonrequesting spouse's retaliation, the Service will consider granting equitable relief even though the deficiency or underpayment may be attributable in part or in full to an item of the requesting spouse.

(e) Fraud committed by nonrequesting spouse. The Service will consider granting relief notwithstanding that the item giving rise to the understatement or deficiency is attributable to the requesting spouse, if the requesting spouse establishes that the nonrequesting spouse's fraud is the reason for the erroneous item. For example, W fraudulently accesses H's brokerage account to sell stock that H had separately received from an inheritance. W deposits the funds from the sale in a separate bank account to which H does not have access. H and W file a joint Federal income tax return for the year, which does not report the income from the sale of the stock. The Service determines a deficiency based on the omission of the income from the sale of the stock. H requests relief from the deficiency under section 6015(f). The income from the sale of the stock normally would be attributable to H. Because W committed fraud with respect to H, however, and because this fraud was the reason for the erroneous item, the liability is properly attributable to W.

.02 Circumstances under which the Service will make streamlined determinations granting equitable relief under sections 66(c) and 6015(f). If a requesting spouse who filed a joint return, or a requesting spouse who filed a separate return in a community property state, satisfies the threshold conditions of section 4.01, the Service will consider whether the requesting spouse is entitled to a streamlined determination of equitable relief under section 66(c) or section 6015(f) under section 4.02. If a requesting spouse is not entitled to a streamlined determination because the requesting spouse does not satisfy all the elements in section 4.02, the requesting spouse is still entitled to be considered for relief under the equitable factors in section 4.03. The Service will make streamlined determinations granting equitable relief under sections 66(c) and 6015(f), in cases in which the requesting spouse establishes that the requesting spouse:

(1) Is no longer married to the nonrequesting spouse as set forth in section 4.03(2)(a);

(2) Would suffer economic hardship if relief were not granted as set forth in section 4.03(2)(b); and

(3) Did not know or have reason to know that there was an understatement or deficiency on the joint return, as set forth in section 4.03(2)(c)(i), or did not know or have reason to know that the nonrequesting spouse would not or could not pay the underpayment of tax reported on the joint income tax return, as set forth in section 4.03(2)(c)(ii). If the nonrequesting spouse abused the requesting spouse or maintained control over the household finances by restricting the requesting spouse's access to financial information, and therefore, because of the abuse or financial control the requesting spouse was not able to challenge the treatment of any items on the joint return, or to question the payment of the taxes reported as due on the joint return or challenge the nonrequesting spouse's assurance regarding payment of the taxes, for fear of the nonrequesting spouse's retaliation, then the abuse or financial control will result in this factor being satisfied even if the requesting spouse had knowledge or reason to know of the items giving rise to the understatement or deficiency or had knowledge or reason to know that the nonrequesting spouse would not pay the tax liability.

.03 Factors for determining whether to grant equitable relief.

(1) Applicability. This section 4.03 applies to requesting spouses who request relief under section 66(c) or section 6015(f), and satisfy the threshold conditions of section 4.01, but do not qualify for streamlined determinations granting relief under section 4.02.

(2) Factors. In determining whether it is inequitable to hold the requesting spouse liable for all or part of the unpaid income tax liability or deficiency, and full or partial equitable relief under section 66(c) or section 6015(f) should be granted, all the facts and circumstances of the case are to be taken into account. The degree of importance of each factor varies depending on the circumstances of the requesting spouse and the factual context surrounding the marriage. The factors are designed as guides. It is not intended that only the factors described in this paragraph are to be taken into account in making the determination. No one factor or a majority of factors necessarily determines the outcome. Factors to consider include the following:

(a) Marital status. Whether the requesting spouse is no longer married to the nonrequesting spouse as of the date the Service makes its determination. If the requesting spouse is still married to the nonrequesting spouse, this factor is neutral. If the requesting spouse is no longer married to the nonrequesting spouse, this factor will weigh in favor of relief. For purposes of this section, a requesting spouse will be treated as being no longer married to the nonrequesting spouse only in the following situations:

> **(i)** The requesting spouse is divorced from the nonrequesting spouse,

> **(ii)** The requesting spouse is legally separated from the nonrequesting spouse under applicable state law,

> **(iii)** The requesting spouse is a widow or widower and is not an heir to the nonrequesting spouse's estate which would have sufficient assets to pay the tax liability, or

> **(iv)** The requesting spouse has not been a member of the same household as the nonrequesting spouse at any time during the 12-month period ending on the date relief was requested. For these purposes, a temporary absence (*e.g.*, due to incarceration, illness, business, military service, or education) is not considered separation if the absent spouse is expected to return to the household. See Treas. Reg. § 1.6015-3(b)(3)(i). A requesting spouse is a member of the same household as the nonrequesting spouse for any period in which the spouses maintain the same residence.

(b) Economic hardship. Whether the requesting spouse will suffer economic hardship if relief is not granted. For purposes of this factor, an economic hardship exists if satisfaction of the tax liability in whole or in part will cause the requesting spouse to be unable to pay reasonable basic living expenses. Whether the requesting spouse will suffer economic hardship is determined based on rules similar to those provided in §301.6343-1(b)(4), and will take into consideration a requesting spouse's current income and expenses and the requesting spouse's assets. In determining the requesting spouse's reasonable basic living expenses, the Service will consider whether the requesting spouse shares expenses or has expenses paid by another individual (such as a spouse). If denying relief from the joint and several liability will cause the requesting spouse to suffer economic hardship, this factor will weigh in favor of relief. If denying relief from the joint and several liability will not cause the requesting spouse to suffer economic hardship, this factor will be neutral.

In determining whether the requesting spouse would suffer economic hardship if relief is not granted, the Service will compare the requesting spouse's income to the Federal poverty guidelines (as updated periodically in the Federal Register by the U.S. Department of Health and

Human Services under the authority of 42 U.S.C. § 9902(2)) for the requesting spouse's family size and will determine by how much, if at all, the requesting spouse's monthly income exceeds the spouse's reasonable basic monthly living expenses. If the requesting spouse's income is below 250% of the Federal poverty guidelines, or if the requesting spouse's monthly income exceeds the requesting spouse's reasonable basic monthly living expenses by $300 or less, then this factor will weigh in favor of relief unless the requesting spouse has assets out of which the requesting spouse can make payments towards the tax liability and still adequately meet the requesting spouse's reasonable basic living expenses. If the requesting spouse's income exceeds these standards, the Service will consider all facts and circumstances in determining whether the requesting spouse would suffer economic hardship if relief is not granted. If the requesting spouse is deceased, this factor is neutral.

(c) Knowledge or reason to know.

(i) Understatement cases. Whether the requesting spouse knew or had reason to know of the item giving rise to the understatement or deficiency at the time the requesting spouse signed the joint return (including a joint amended return). In the case of an income tax liability that arose from an understatement or a deficiency, this factor will weigh in favor of relief if the requesting spouse did not know and had no reason to know of the item giving rise to the understatement. If the requesting spouse knew or had reason to know of the item giving rise to the understatement, this factor will weigh against relief. Actual knowledge of the item giving rise to the understatement or deficiency will not be weighed more heavily than any other factor. Depending on the facts and circumstances, if the requesting spouse was abused by the nonrequesting spouse (as described in section 4.03(2)(c)(iv)), or the nonrequesting spouse maintained control of the household finances by restricting the requesting spouse's access to financial information and, therefore, the requesting spouse was not able to challenge the treatment of any items on the joint return for fear of the nonrequesting spouse's retaliation, this factor will weigh in favor of relief even if the requesting spouse had knowledge or reason to know of the items giving rise to the understatement or deficiency.

(ii) Underpayment cases. In the case of an income tax liability that was properly reported on a joint return (including a joint amended return) but not paid, whether the requesting spouse knew or had reason to know at the time the requesting spouse signed the joint return that the nonrequesting spouse would not or could not pay the tax liability at the time the joint return was filed or within a reasonably prompt time after the filing of the joint return. This factor will weigh in favor of relief if the requesting spouse reasonably expected the nonrequesting spouse to pay the tax liability reported on the joint return. This factor will weigh against relief if, based on the facts and circumstances of the case, it was not reasonable for the requesting spouse to believe that the nonrequesting spouse would or could pay the tax liability shown on the joint return within a reasonably prompt time after filing of the return. For example, if prior to signing the return, the requesting spouse knew of the nonrequesting spouse's prior bankruptcies, financial difficulties, or other issues with the IRS or other creditors, or was otherwise aware of difficulties in timely paying bills, then this factor will generally weigh against relief. Depending on the facts and circumstances, if the requesting spouse was abused by the nonrequesting spouse (as described in section 4.03(2)(c)(iv)), or the nonrequesting spouse maintained control of the household finances by restricting the requesting spouse's access to financial information and, therefore, the requesting spouse was not able to question the payment of the taxes reported as due on the joint return or challenge the nonrequesting spouse's assurance regarding payment of the taxes for fear of the nonrequesting spouse's retaliation, this factor will weigh in favor of relief even if the requesting spouse had knowledge or reason to know regarding the nonrequesting spouse's intent or ability to pay the taxes due.

(iii) Reason to know. The facts and circumstances that are considered in determining whether the requesting spouse had reason to know of an understatement, or reason to know the nonrequesting spouse could not or would pay the reported tax liability, include, but are not limited to, the requesting spouse's level of education, any deceit or evasiveness of the nonrequesting spouse, the requesting spouse's degree of involvement in the activity generating the income tax liability, the requesting spouse's involvement in business and household financial matters, the requesting spouse's business or financial expertise, and any lavish or unusual expenditures compared with past spending levels.

(iv) Abuse by the nonrequesting spouse. For purposes of this revenue procedure, if the requesting spouse establishes that he or she was the victim of abuse (not amounting to duress, see Treas. Reg. § 1.6015-1(b)), then depending on the facts and circumstances of the requesting spouse's situation, the abuse may result in certain factors weighing in favor of relief when otherwise the factor may have weighed against relief. Abuse comes in many forms and can include physical, psychological, sexual, or emotional abuse, including efforts to control, isolate, humiliate and intimidate the requesting spouse, or to undermine the requesting spouse's ability to reason independently and be able to do what is required under the tax laws. All the facts and circumstances are considered in determining whether a requesting spouse was abused. The impact of a nonrequesting spouse's alcohol or drug abuse is also considered in determining whether a requesting spouse was abused.

(d) Legal obligation. Whether the requesting spouse or the nonrequesting spouse has a legal obligation to pay the outstanding Federal income tax liability. For purposes of this factor, a legal obligation is an obligation arising from a divorce decree or other legally binding agreement. This factor will weigh in favor of relief if the nonrequesting spouse has the sole legal obligation to pay the outstanding income tax liability pursuant to a divorce decree or agreement. This factor, however, will be neutral if the requesting spouse knew or had reason to know, when entering into the divorce decree or agreement, that the nonrequesting spouse would not pay the income tax liability. This factor will weigh against relief if the requesting spouse has the sole legal obligation. The fact that the nonrequesting spouse has been relieved of liability for the taxes at issue as a result of a discharge in bankruptcy is disregarded in determining whether the requesting spouse has the sole legal obligation. If, based on an agreement or consent order, both spouses have a legal obligation to pay the outstanding income tax liability, the spouses are not separated or divorced, or the divorce decree or agreement is silent as to any obligation to pay the outstanding income tax liability, this factor is neutral.

(e) Significant benefit. Whether the requesting spouse received significant benefit (beyond normal support) from the unpaid income tax liability or item giving rise to the deficiency. See Treas. Reg. § 1.6015-2(d). If the requesting spouse enjoyed the benefits of a lavish lifestyle, such as owning luxury assets and taking expensive vacations, this factor will weigh against relief. If the nonrequesting spouse controlled the household and business finances or there was abuse (as described in section 4.03(2)(c)(iv)) such that the nonrequesting spouse made the decision on spending funds for a lavish lifestyle, then this mitigates this factor so that it is neutral. If only the nonrequesting spouse significantly benefitted from the unpaid tax or item giving rise to an understatement or deficiency, and the requesting spouse had little or no benefit, or the nonrequesting spouse enjoyed the benefit to the requesting spouse's detriment, this factor will weigh in favor of relief. If the amount of unpaid tax or understated tax was small such that neither spouse received a significant benefit, then this factor is neutral.

(f) Compliance with income tax laws. Whether the requesting spouse has made a good faith effort to comply with the income tax laws in the taxable years following the taxable year or years to which the request for relief relates.

(1) If the requesting spouse is compliant for taxable years after being divorced from the nonrequesting spouse, then this factor will weigh in favor of relief. If the requesting spouse is not compliant, then this factor will weigh against relief. If the requesting spouse made a good faith effort to comply with the tax laws but was unable to fully comply, then this factor will be neutral. For example, if the requesting spouse timely filed an income tax return but was unable to fully pay the tax liability due to spouse's poor financial or economic situation after the divorce, then this factor will be neutral.

(2) If the requesting spouse remains married to the nonrequesting spouse, whether or not legally separated or living apart, and continues to file joint returns with the nonrequesting spouse after requesting relief, then this factor will be neutral if the joint returns are compliant with the tax laws, but will weigh against relief if the returns are not compliant.

(3) If the requesting spouse remains married to the nonrequesting spouse but files separate returns, this factor will weigh in favor of relief if the requesting spouse is compliant with the tax laws and will weigh against relief if the requesting spouse is not compliant with the tax laws. If the requesting spouse made a good faith effort to comply with the tax laws but was unable to fully comply, then this factor will be neutral. For example, if the requesting spouse timely filed an income tax return but was unable to fully pay the tax liability due to the requesting spouse's poor financial or economic situation as a result of being separated or living apart from the nonrequesting spouse, then this factor will be neutral.

(g) Mental or physical health. Whether the requesting spouse was in poor physical or mental health. This factor will weigh in favor of relief if the requesting spouse was in poor mental or physical health at the time the requesting spouse signed the return or returns for which the request for relief relates or at the time the requesting spouse requested relief. The Service will consider the nature, extent, and duration of the condition. If the requesting spouse was in neither poor physical nor poor mental health, this factor is neutral.

.04 Refunds.

In both understatement and underpayment cases, a requesting spouse is eligible for a refund of separate payments made by the requesting spouse after July 22, 1998, and the requesting spouse establishes that the funds used to make the payment for which a refund is sought were provided by the requesting spouse. A requesting spouse is not eligible for refunds of payments made with the joint return, joint payments, or payments that the nonrequesting spouse made. A requesting spouse, however, may be eligible for a refund of the requesting spouse's portion of the requesting and nonrequesting spouse's joint overpayment from another tax year that was applied to the joint income tax liability to the extent that the requesting spouse can establish that the requesting spouse provided the funds for the overpayment. The availability of refunds is subject to the refund limitations of section 6511.

SECTION 5. PROCEDURE

A requesting spouse seeking equitable relief under section 66(c) or section 6015(f) must file Form 8857, Request for Innocent Spouse Relief (and Separation of Liability, and Equitable Relief), or other similar statement signed under penalties of perjury, within the applicable period of limitation as set forth in section 4.01(3) of this revenue procedure.

SECTION 6. EFFECT ON OTHER DOCUMENTS

Revenue Procedure 2003-61, 2003-2 C.B. 296, is superseded.

SECTION 7. EFFECTIVE DATE

This revenue procedure is effective for requests for relief filed on or after **[INSERT DATE REVENUE PROCEDURE IS RELEASED TO THE PUBLIC]**. In addition, this revenue procedure is effective for requests for equitable relief pending on **[INSERT DATE REVENUE PROCEDURE IS RELEASED TO THE PUBLIC]**, whether with the Service, the Office of Appeals, or in a case docketed with a Federal court.

Subpart A – Rules Governing Authority to Practice

§ 10.0. Scope of part.

(a) This part contains rules governing the recognition of attorneys, certified public accountants, enrolled agents, enrolled retirement plan agents, registered tax return preparers, and other persons representing taxpayers before the Internal Revenue Service. Subpart A of this part sets forth rules relating to the authority to practice before the Internal Revenue Service; subpart B of this part prescribes the duties and restrictions relating to such practice; subpart C of this part prescribes the sanctions for violating the regulations; subpart D of this part contains the rules applicable to disciplinary proceedings; and subpart E of this part contains general provisions relating to the availability of official records.

(b) Effective/applicability date. This section is applicable beginning August 2, 2011.

§ 10.1. Offices.

(a) Establishment of office(s). The Commissioner shall establish the Office of Professional Responsibility and any other office(s) within the Internal Revenue Service necessary to administer and enforce this part. The Commissioner shall appoint the Director of the Office of Professional Responsibility and any other Internal Revenue official(s) to manage and direct any office(s) established to administer or enforce this part. Offices established under this part include, but are not limited to:

(1) The Office of Professional Responsibility, which shall generally have responsibility for matters related to practitioner conduct and discipline, including disciplinary proceedings and sanctions; and

(2) An office with responsibility for matters related to authority to practice before the Internal Revenue Service, including acting on applications for enrollment to practice before the Internal Revenue Service and administering competency testing and continuing education.

(b) Officers and employees within any office established under this part may perform acts necessary or appropriate to carry out the responsibilities of their office(s) under this part or as otherwise prescribed by the Commissioner.

(c) Acting. The Commissioner will designate an officer or employee of the Internal Revenue Service to perform the duties of an individual appointed under paragraph (a) of this section in the absence of that officer or employee or during a vacancy in that office.

(d) Effective/applicability date. This section is applicable beginning August 2, 2011.

Proposed Amendment (September 17, 2012)

§ 10.1. Offices.

(a)   * * *

(1) The Office of Professional Responsibility, which shall generally have responsibility for matters related to practitioner conduct and shall have exclusive responsibility for discipline, including disciplinary proceedings and sanctions; and

* * *

(d) Effective/applicability date. This section is applicable beginning after the date that final regulations are published in the Federal Register.

§ 10.2. Definitions.

(a) As used in this part, except where the text provides otherwise—

(1) Attorney means any person who is a member in good standing of the bar of the highest court of any state, territory, or possession of the United States, including a Commonwealth, or the District of Columbia.

(2) Certified public accountant means any person who is duly qualified to practice as a certified public accountant in any state, territory, or possession of the United States, including a Commonwealth, or the District of Columbia.

(3) Commissioner refers to the Commissioner of Internal Revenue.

(4) Practice before the Internal Revenue Service comprehends all matters connected with a presentation to the Internal Revenue Service or any of its officers or employees relating to a taxpayer's rights, privileges, or liabilities under laws or regulations administered by the Internal Revenue Service. Such presentations include, but are not limited to, preparing documents; filing documents; corresponding and communicating with the Internal Revenue Service; rendering written advice with respect to any entity, transaction, plan or arrangement, or other plan or arrangement having a potential for tax avoidance or evasion; and representing a client at conferences, hearings, and meetings.

(5) Practitioner means any individual described in paragraphs (a), (b), (c), (d), (e), or (f) of § 10.3.

(6) A tax return includes an amended tax return and a claim for refund.

(7) Service means the Internal Revenue Service.

(8) Tax return preparer means any individual within the meaning of section 7701(a)(36) and 26 CFR 301.7701-15.

(b) Effective/applicability date. This section is applicable beginning August 2, 2011.

§ 10.3. Who may practice.

(a) Attorneys. Any attorney who is not currently under suspension or disbarment from practice before the Internal Revenue Service may practice before the Internal Revenue Service by filing with the Internal Revenue Service a written declaration that the attorney is currently qualified as an attorney and is authorized to represent the party or parties. Notwithstanding the preceding sentence, attorneys who are not currently under suspension or disbarment from practice before the Internal Revenue Service are not required to file a written declaration with the IRS before rendering written advice covered under § 10.35 or § 10.37, but their rendering of this advice is practice before the Internal Revenue Service.

(b) Certified public accountants. Any certified public accountant who is not currently under suspension or disbarment from practice before the Internal Revenue Service may practice before the Internal Revenue Service by filing with the Internal Revenue Service a written declaration that the certified public accountant is currently qualified as a certified public accountant and is authorized to represent the party or parties. Notwithstanding the preceding sentence, certified public accountants who are not currently under suspension or disbarment from practice before the Internal Revenue Service are not required to file a written declaration with the IRS before rendering written advice covered under § 10.35 or § 10.37, but their rendering of this advice is practice before the Internal Revenue Service.

(c) Enrolled agents. Any individual enrolled as an agent pursuant to this part who is not currently under suspension or disbarment from practice before the Internal Revenue Service may practice before the Internal Revenue Service.

(d) Enrolled actuaries. (1) Any individual who is enrolled as an actuary by the Joint Board for the Enrollment of Actuaries pursuant to 29 U.S.C. 1242 who is not currently under suspension or disbarment from practice before the Internal Revenue Service may practice before the Internal Revenue Service by filing with the Internal Revenue Service a written declaration stating that he or she is currently qualified as an enrolled actuary and is authorized to represent the party or parties on whose behalf he or she acts.

(2) Practice as an enrolled actuary is limited to representation with respect to issues involving the following statutory provisions in title 26 of the United States Code: sections 401 (relating to qualification of employee plans), 403(a) (relating to whether an annuity plan meets the requirements of section 404(a)(2)), 404 (relating to deductibility of employer contributions), 405 (relating to qualification of bond purchase plans), 412 (relating to funding requirements for certain employee plans), 413 (relating to application of qualification requirements to collectively bargained plans and to plans maintained by more than one employer), 414 (relating to definitions and special rules with respect to the employee plan area), 419 (relating to treatment of funded welfare benefits), 419A (relating to qualified asset accounts), 420 (relating to transfers of excess pension assets to retiree health accounts), 4971 (relating to excise taxes payable as a result of an accumulated funding deficiency under section 412), 4972 (relating to tax on nondeductible contributions to qualified employer plans), 4976 (relating to taxes with respect to funded welfare benefit plans), 4980 (relating to tax on reversion of qualified plan assets to employer), 6057 (relating to annual registration of plans), 6058 (relating to information required in connection with certain plans of deferred compensation), 6059 (relating to periodic report of actuary), 6652(e) (relating to the failure to file annual registration and other notifications by pension plan), 6652(f) (relating to the failure to file information required in connection with certain plans of deferred compensation), 6692 (relating to the failure to file actuarial report), 7805(b) (relating to the extent to which an Internal Revenue Service ruling or determination letter coming under the statutory provisions listed here will be applied without retroactive effect); and 29 U.S.C. 1083 (relating to the waiver of funding for nonqualified plans).

(3) An individual who practices before the Internal Revenue Service pursuant to paragraph (d)(1) of this section is subject to the provisions of this part in the same manner as attorneys, certified public accountants, enrolled agents, enrolled retirement plan agents, and registered tax return preparers.

(e) Enrolled Retirement Plan Agents – (1) Any individual enrolled as a retirement plan agent pursuant to this part who is not currently under suspension or disbarment from practice before the Internal Revenue Service may practice before the Internal Revenue Service.

(2) Practice as an enrolled retirement plan agent is limited to representation with respect to issues involving the following programs: Employee Plans Determination Letter program; Employee Plans Compliance Resolution System; and Employee Plans Master and Prototype and Volume Submitter program. In addition, enrolled retirement plan agents are generally permitted to represent taxpayers with respect to IRS forms under the 5300 and 5500 series which are filed by retirement plans and plan sponsors, but not with respect to actuarial forms or schedules.

(3) An individual who practices before the Internal Revenue Service pursuant to paragraph (e)(1) of this section is subject to the provisions of this part in the same manner as attorneys, certified public accountants, enrolled agents, enrolled actuaries, and registered tax return preparers.

(f) Registered tax return preparers. (1) Any individual who is designated as a registered tax return preparer pursuant to § 10.4(c) of this part who is not currently under suspension or disbarment from practice before the Internal Revenue Service may practice before the Internal Revenue Service.

(2) Practice as a registered tax return preparer is limited to preparing and signing tax returns and claims for refund, and other documents for submission to the Internal Revenue Service. A registered tax return preparer may prepare all or substantially all of a tax return or claim for refund of tax. The Internal Revenue Service will prescribe by forms, instructions, or other appropriate guidance the tax returns and claims for refund that a registered tax return preparer may prepare and sign.

(3) A registered tax return preparer may represent taxpayers before revenue agents, customer service representatives, or similar officers and employees of the Internal Revenue Service (including the Taxpayer Advocate Service) during an examination if the registered tax return preparer signed the tax return or claim for refund for the taxable year or period under examination. Unless otherwise prescribed by regulation or notice, this right does not permit such individual to represent the taxpayer, regardless of the circumstances requiring representation, before appeals officers, revenue officers, Counsel or similar officers or employees of the Internal Revenue Service or the Treasury Department. A registered tax return preparer's authorization to practice under this part also does not include the authority to provide tax advice to a client or another person except as necessary to prepare a tax return, claim for refund, or other document intended to be submitted to the Internal Revenue Service.

(4) An individual who practices before the Internal Revenue Service pursuant to paragraph (f)(1) of this section is subject to the provisions of this part in the same manner as attorneys, certified public accountants, enrolled agents, enrolled retirement plan agents, and enrolled actuaries.

(g) Others. Any individual qualifying under paragraph (d) of § 10.5 or § 10.7 is eligible to practice before the Internal Revenue Service to the extent provided in those sections.

(h) Government officers and employees, and others. An individual, who is an officer or employee of the executive, legislative, or judicial branch of the United States Government; an officer or employee of the District of Columbia; a Member of Congress; or a Resident Commissioner may not practice before the Internal Revenue Service if such practice violates 18 U.S.C. 203 or 205.

(i) State officers and employees. No officer or employee of any State, or subdivision of any State, whose duties require him or her to pass upon, investigate, or deal with tax matters for such State or subdivision, may practice before the Internal Revenue Service, if such employment may disclose facts or information applicable to Federal tax matters.

(j) Effective/applicability date. This section is generally applicable beginning August 2, 2011.

Proposed Amendment (February 17, 2012)

§ 10.3. Who may practice.

(a) Attorneys. Any attorney who is not currently under suspension or disbarment from practice before the Internal Revenue Service may practice before the Internal Revenue Service by filing with the Internal Revenue Service a written declaration that the attorney is currently qualified as an attorney and is authorized to represent the party or parties. Notwithstanding the preceding sentence, attorneys who are not currently under suspension or disbarment from practice before the Internal Revenue Service are not required to file a written declaration with the IRS before rendering written advice covered under § 10.37, but their rendering of this advice is practice before the Internal Revenue Service.

(b) Certified public accountants. Any certified public accountant who is not currently under suspension or disbarment from practice before the Internal Revenue Service may practice before the Internal Revenue Service by filing with the Internal Revenue Service a written declaration that the certified public accountant is currently qualified as a certified public accountant and is authorized to represent the party or parties. Notwithstanding the preceding sentence, certified public accountants who are not currently under suspension or disbarment from practice before the Internal Revenue Service are not required to file a written declaration with the IRS before rendering written advice covered under § 10.37, but their rendering of this advice is practice before the Internal Revenue Service.

* * *

(g) Others. Any individual qualifying under § 10.5(e) or § 10.7 is eligible to practice before the Internal Revenue Service to the extent provided in those sections.

* * *

(j) **Effective/applicability date.** This section is applicable beginning after the date that final regulations

§ 10.4. Eligibility to become an enrolled agent, enrolled retirement plan agent, or registered tax return preparer.

(a) **Enrollment as an enrolled agent upon examination.** The Commissioner, or delegate, will grant enrollment as an enrolled agent to an applicant eighteen years of age or older who demonstrates special competence in tax matters by written examination administered by, or administered under the oversight of, the Internal Revenue Service, who possesses a current or otherwise valid preparer tax identification number or other prescribed identifying number, and who has not engaged in any conduct that would justify the suspension or disbarment of any practitioner under the provisions of this part.

(b) **Enrollment as a retirement plan agent upon examination**. The Commissioner, or delegate, will grant enrollment as an enrolled retirement plan agent to an applicant eighteen years of age or older who demonstrates special competence in qualified retirement plan matters by written examination administered by, or administered under the oversight of, the Internal Revenue Service, who possesses a current or otherwise valid preparer tax identification number or other prescribed identifying number, and who has not engaged in any conduct that would justify the suspension or disbarment of any practitioner under the provisions of this part.

(c) **Designation as a registered tax return preparer.** The Commissioner, or delegate, may designate an individual eighteen years of age or older as a registered tax return preparer provided an applicant demonstrates competence in Federal tax return preparation matters by written examination administered by, or administered under the oversight of, the Internal Revenue Service, or otherwise meets the requisite standards prescribed by the Internal Revenue Service, possesses a current or otherwise valid preparer tax identification number or other prescribed identifying number, and has not engaged in any conduct that would justify the suspension or disbarment of any practitioner under the provisions of this part.

(d) **Enrollment of former Internal Revenue Service employees.** The Commissioner, or delegate, may grant enrollment as an enrolled agent or enrolled retirement plan agent to an applicant who, by virtue of past service and technical experience in the Internal Revenue Service, has qualified for such enrollment and who has not engaged in any conduct that would justify the suspension or disbarment of any practitioner under the provisions of this part, under the following circumstances:

(1) The former employee applies for enrollment on an Internal Revenue Service form and supplies the information requested on the form and such other information regarding the experience and training of the applicant as may be relevant.

(2) The appropriate office of the Internal Revenue Service provides a detailed report of the nature and rating of the applicant's work while employed by the Internal Revenue Service and a recommendation whether such employment qualifies the applicant technically or otherwise for the desired authorization.

(3) Enrollment as an enrolled agent based on an applicant's former employment with the Internal Revenue Service may be of unlimited scope or it may be limited to permit the presentation of matters only of the particular specialty or only before the particular unit or division of the Internal Revenue Service for which the applicant's former employment has qualified the applicant. Enrollment as an enrolled retirement plan agent based on an applicant's former employment with the Internal Revenue Service will be limited to permit the presentation of matters only with respect to qualified retirement plan matters.

(4) Application for enrollment as an enrolled agent or enrolled retirement plan agent based on an applicant's former employment with the Internal Revenue Service must be made within three years from the date of separation from such employment.

(5) An applicant for enrollment as an enrolled agent who is requesting such enrollment based on former employment with the Internal Revenue Service must have had a minimum of five years continuous employment with the Internal Revenue Service during which the applicant must have been regularly engaged in applying and interpreting the provisions of the Internal Revenue Code and the regulations relating to income, estate, gift, employment, or excise taxes.

(6) An applicant for enrollment as an enrolled retirement plan agent who is requesting such enrollment based on former employment with the Internal Revenue Service must have had a minimum of five years continuous employment with the Internal Revenue Service during which the applicant must have been regularly engaged in applying and interpreting the provisions of the Internal Revenue Code and the regulations relating to qualified retirement plan matters.

(7) For the purposes of paragraphs (d)(5) and (6) of this section, an aggregate of 10 or more years of employment in positions involving the application and interpretation of the provisions of the Internal Revenue Code, at least three of which occurred within the five years preceding the date of application, is the equivalent of five years continuous employment.

(e) Natural persons. Enrollment or authorization to practice may be granted only to natural persons.

(f) Effective/applicability date. This section is applicable beginning August 2, 2011.

§ 10.5. Application to become an enrolled agent, enrolled retirement plan agent, or registered tax return preparer.

(a) Form; address. An applicant to become an enrolled agent, enrolled retirement plan agent, or registered tax return preparer must apply as required by forms or procedures established and published by the Internal Revenue Service, including proper execution of required forms under oath or affirmation. The address on the application will be the address under which a successful applicant is enrolled or registered and is the address to which all correspondence concerning enrollment or registration will be sent.

(b) Fee. A reasonable nonrefundable fee may be charged for each application to become an enrolled agent, enrolled retirement plan agent, or registered tax return preparer. See 26 CFR part 300.

(c) Additional information; examination. The Internal Revenue Service may require the applicant, as a condition to consideration of an application, to file additional information and to submit to any written or oral examination under oath or otherwise. Upon the applicant's written request, the Internal Revenue Service will afford the applicant the opportunity to be heard with respect to the application.

(d) Compliance and suitability checks. (1) As a condition to consideration of an application, the Internal Revenue Service may conduct a Federal tax compliance check and suitability check. The tax compliance check will be limited to an inquiry regarding whether an applicant has filed all required individual or business tax returns and whether the applicant has failed to pay, or make proper arrangements with the Internal Revenue Service for payment of, any Federal tax debts. The suitability check will be limited to an inquiry regarding whether an applicant has engaged in any conduct that would justify suspension or disbarment of any practitioner under the provisions of this part on the date the application is submitted, including whether the applicant has engaged in disreputable conduct as defined in § 10.51. The application will be denied only if the results of the compliance or suitability check are sufficient to establish that the practitioner engaged in conduct subject to sanctions under §§ 10.51 and 10.52.

(2) If the applicant does not pass the tax compliance or suitability check, the applicant will not be issued an enrollment or registration card or certificate pursuant to § 10.6(b) of this part. An applicant who is initially denied enrollment or registration for failure to pass a tax compliance check may reapply after the initial denial if the applicant becomes current with respect to the applicant's tax liabilities.

(e) Temporary recognition. On receipt of a properly executed application, the Commissioner, or delegate, may grant the applicant temporary recognition to practice pending a determination as to whether status as an enrolled agent, enrolled retirement plan agent, or registered tax return preparer should be granted. Temporary recognition will be granted only in unusual circumstances and it will not be granted, in any circumstance, if the application is not regular on its face, if the information stated in the application, if true, is not sufficient to warrant granting the application to practice, or the Commissioner, or delegate, has information indicating that the statements in the application are untrue or that the applicant would not otherwise qualify to become an enrolled agent, enrolled retirement plan agent, or registered tax return preparer. Issuance of temporary recognition does not constitute either a designation or a finding of eligibility as an enrolled agent, enrolled retirement plan agent, or registered tax return preparer, and the temporary recognition may be withdrawn at any time.

(f) Protest of application denial. The applicant will be informed in writing as to the reason(s) for any denial of an application. The applicant may, within 30 days after receipt of the notice of denial of the application, file a written protest of the denial as prescribed by the Internal Revenue Service in forms, guidance, or other appropriate guidance. A protest under this section is not governed by subpart D of this part.

(g) Effective/applicability date. This section is applicable to applications received on or after August 2, 2011.

§ 10.6. Term and renewal of status as an enrolled agent, enrolled retirement plan agent, or registered tax return preparer.

(a) Term. Each individual authorized to practice before the Internal Revenue Service as an enrolled agent, enrolled retirement plan agent, or registered tax return preparer will be accorded active enrollment or registration status subject to renewal of enrollment or registration as provided in this part.

(b) Enrollment or registration card or certificate. The Internal Revenue Service will issue an enrollment or registration card or certificate to each individual whose application to practice before the Internal Revenue Service is approved. Each card or certificate will be valid for the period stated on the card or certificate. An enrolled agent, enrolled retirement plan agent, or registered tax return preparer may not practice before the Internal Revenue Service if the card or certificate is not current or otherwise valid. The card or certificate is in addition to any notification that may be provided to each individual who obtains a preparer tax identification number.

(c) Change of address. An enrolled agent, enrolled retirement plan agent, or registered tax return preparer must send notification of any change of address to the address specified by the Internal Revenue Service within 60 days of the change of address. This notification must include the enrolled agent's, enrolled retirement plan agent's, or registered tax return preparer's name, prior address, new address, tax identification number(s) (including preparer tax identification number), and the date the change of address is effective. Unless this notification is sent, the address for purposes of any correspondence from the appropriate Internal Revenue Service office responsible for administering this part shall be the address reflected on the practitioner's most recent application for enrollment or registration, or application for renewal of enrollment or registration. A practitioner's change of address notification under this part will not constitute a change of the practitioner's last known address for purposes of section 6212 of the Internal Revenue Code and regulations thereunder.

(d) Renewal – (1) In general. Enrolled agents, enrolled retirement plan agents, and registered tax return preparers must renew their status with the Internal Revenue Service to maintain eligibility to practice before the Internal Revenue Service. Failure to receive notification from the Internal Revenue Service of the renewal requirement will not be justification for the individual's failure to satisfy this requirement.

(2) Renewal period for enrolled agents. (i) All enrolled agents must renew their preparer tax identification number as prescribed by forms, instructions, or other appropriate guidance.

(ii) Enrolled agents who have a Social Security number or tax identification number that ends with the numbers 0, 1, 2, or 3, except for those individuals who received their initial enrollment after November 1, 2003, must apply for renewal between November 1, 2003, and January 31, 2004. The renewal will be effective April 1, 2004.

(iii) Enrolled agents who have a social security number or tax identification number that ends with the numbers 4, 5, or 6, except for those individuals who received their initial enrollment after November 1, 2004, must apply for renewal between November 1, 2004, and January 31, 2005. The renewal will be effective April 1, 2005.

(iv) Enrolled agents who have a social security number or tax identification number that ends with the numbers 7, 8, or 9, except for those individuals who received their initial enrollment after November 1, 2005, must apply for renewal between November 1, 2005, and January 31, 2006. The renewal will be effective April 1, 2006.

(v) Thereafter, applications for renewal as an enrolled agent will be required between November 1 and January 31 of every subsequent third year as specified in paragraph (d)(2)(i), (d)(2)(ii), or (d)(2)(iii) of this section according to the last number of the individual's Social Security number or tax identification number. Those individuals who receive initial enrollment as an enrolled agent after November 1 and before April 2 of the applicable renewal period will not be required to renew their enrollment before the first full renewal period following the receipt of their initial enrollment.

(3) Renewal period for enrolled retirement plan agents. (i) All enrolled retirement plan agents must renew their preparer tax identification number as prescribed by the Internal Revenue Service in forms, instructions, or other appropriate guidance.

(ii) Enrolled retirement plan agents will be required to renew their status as enrolled retirement plan agents between April 1 and June 30 of every third year subsequent to their initial enrollment.

(4) Renewal period for registered tax return preparers. Registered tax return preparers must renew their preparer tax identification number and their status as a registered tax return preparer as prescribed by the Internal Revenue Service in forms, instructions, or other appropriate guidance.

(5) Notification of renewal. After review and approval, the Internal Revenue Service will notify the individual of the renewal and will issue the individual a card or certificate evidencing current status as an enrolled agent, enrolled retirement plan agent, or registered tax return preparer.

(6) Fee. A reasonable nonrefundable fee may be charged for each application for renewal filed. See 26 CFR part 300.

(7) Forms. Forms required for renewal may be obtained by sending a written request to the address specified by the Internal Revenue Service or from such other source as the Internal Revenue Service will publish in the Internal Revenue Bulletin (see 26 CFR 601.601(d)(2)(ii)(b)) and on the Internal Revenue Service webpage (http://www.irs.gov).

(e) Condition for renewal: continuing education. In order to qualify for renewal as an enrolled agent, enrolled retirement plan agent, or registered tax return preparer, an individual must certify, in the manner prescribed by the Internal Revenue Service, that the individual has satisfied the requisite number of continuing education hours.

(1) Definitions. For purposes of this section –

(i) Enrollment year means January 1 to December 31 of each year of an enrollment cycle.

(ii) Enrollment cycle means the three successive enrollment years preceding the effective date of renewal.

(iii) Registration year means each 12-month period the registered tax return preparer is authorized to practice before the Internal Revenue Service.

(iv) The effective date of renewal is the first day of the fourth month following the close of the period for renewal described in paragraph (d) of this section.

(2) For renewed enrollment as an enrolled agent or enrolled retirement plan agent – (i) Requirements for enrollment cycle. A minimum of 72 hours of continuing education credit, including six hours of ethics or professional conduct, must be completed during each enrollment cycle.

(ii) Requirements for enrollment year. A minimum of 16 hours of continuing education credit, including two hours of ethics or professional conduct, must be completed during each enrollment year of an enrollment cycle.

(iii) Enrollment during enrollment cycle – (A) In general. Subject to paragraph (e)(2)(iii)(B) of this section, an individual who receives initial enrollment during an enrollment cycle must complete two hours of qualifying continuing education credit for each month enrolled during the enrollment cycle. Enrollment for any part of a month is considered enrollment for the entire month.

(B) Ethics. An individual who receives initial enrollment during an enrollment cycle must complete two hours of ethics or professional conduct for each enrollment year during the enrollment cycle. Enrollment for any part of an enrollment year is considered enrollment for the entire year.

(3) Requirements for renewal as a registered tax return preparer. A minimum of 15 hours of continuing education credit, including two hours of ethics or professional conduct, three hours of Federal tax law updates, and 10 hours of Federal tax law topics, must be completed during each registration year.

(f) Qualifying continuing education – (1) General – (i) Enrolled agents. To qualify for continuing education credit for an enrolled agent, a course of learning must –

(A) Be a qualifying continuing education program designed to enhance professional knowledge in Federal taxation or Federal tax related matters (programs comprised of current subject matter in Federal taxation or Federal tax related matters, including accounting, tax return preparation software, taxation, or ethics); and

(B) Be a qualifying continuing education program consistent with the Internal Revenue Code and effective tax administration.

(ii) Enrolled retirement plan agents. To qualify for continuing education credit for an enrolled retirement plan agent, a course of learning must –

(A) Be a qualifying continuing education program designed to enhance professional knowledge in qualified retirement plan matters; and

(B) Be a qualifying continuing education program consistent with the Internal Revenue Code and effective tax administration.

(iii) Registered tax return preparers. To qualify for continuing education credit for a registered tax return preparer, a course of learning must –

(A) Be a qualifying continuing education program designed to enhance professional knowledge in Federal taxation or Federal tax related matters (programs comprised of current subject matter in Federal taxation or Federal tax related matters, including accounting, tax return preparation software, taxation, or ethics); and

(B) Be a qualifying continuing education program consistent with the Internal Revenue Code and effective tax administration.

(2) Qualifying programs – (i) Formal programs. A formal program qualifies as a continuing education program if it –

(A) Requires attendance and provides each attendee with a certificate of attendance;

(B) Is conducted by a qualified instructor, discussion leader, or speaker (in other words, a person whose background, training, education, and experience is appropriate for instructing or leading a discussion on the subject matter of the particular program);

(C) Provides or requires a written outline, textbook, or suitable electronic educational materials; and

(D) Satisfies the requirements established for a qualified continuing education program pursuant to § 10.9.

(ii) Correspondence or individual study programs (including taped programs). Qualifying continuing education programs include correspondence or individual study programs that are conducted by continuing education providers and completed on an individual basis by the enrolled individual. The allowable credit hours for such programs will be measured on a basis comparable to the measurement of a seminar or course for credit in an accredited educational institution. Such programs qualify as continuing education programs only if they –

(A) Require registration of the participants by the continuing education provider;

(B) Provide a means for measuring successful completion by the participants (for example, a written examination), including the issuance of a certificate of completion by the continuing education provider;

(C) Provide a written outline, textbook, or suitable electronic educational materials; and

(D) Satisfy the requirements established for a qualified continuing education program pursuant to § 10.9.

(iii) Serving as an instructor, discussion leader or speaker. (A) One hour of continuing education credit will be awarded for each contact hour completed as an instructor, discussion leader, or speaker at an educational program that meets the continuing education requirements of paragraph (f) of this section.

(B) A maximum of two hours of continuing education credit will be awarded for actual subject preparation time for each contact hour completed as an instructor, discussion leader, or speaker at such programs. It is the responsibility of the individual claiming such credit to maintain records to verify preparation time.

(C) The maximum continuing education credit for instruction and preparation may not exceed four hours annually for registered tax return preparers and six hours annually for enrolled agents and enrolled retirement plan agents.

(D) An instructor, discussion leader, or speaker who makes more than one presentation on the same subject matter during an enrollment cycle or registration year will receive continuing education credit for only one such presentation for the enrollment cycle or registration year.

(3) Periodic examination. Enrolled Agents and Enrolled Retirement Plan Agents may establish eligibility for renewal of enrollment for any enrollment cycle by –

(i) Achieving a passing score on each part of the Special Enrollment Examination administered under this part during the three year period prior to renewal; and

(ii) Completing a minimum of 16 hours of qualifying continuing education during the last year of an enrollment cycle.

(g) Measurement of continuing education coursework. (1) All continuing education programs will be measured in terms of contact hours. The shortest recognized program will be one contact hour.

(2) A contact hour is 50 minutes of continuous participation in a program. Credit is granted only for a full contact hour, which is 50 minutes or multiples thereof. For example, a program lasting more than 50 minutes but less than 100 minutes will count as only one contact hour.

(3) Individual segments at continuous conferences, conventions and the like will be considered one total program. For example, two 90-minute segments (180 minutes) at a continuous conference will count as three contact hours.

(4) For university or college courses, each semester hour credit will equal 15 contact hours and a quarter hour credit will equal 10 contact hours.

* * *

(j) Failure to comply. (1) Compliance by an individual with the requirements of this part is determined by the Internal Revenue Service. The Internal Revenue Service will provide notice to any individual who fails to meet the continuing education and fee requirements of eligibility for renewal. The notice will state the basis for the determination of noncompliance and will provide the individual an opportunity to furnish the requested information in writing relating to the matter within 60 days of the date of the notice. Such information will be considered in making a final determination as to eligibility for renewal. The individual must be informed of the reason(s) for any denial of a renewal. The individual may, within 30 days after receipt of the notice of denial of renewal, file a written protest of the denial as prescribed by the Internal Revenue Service in forms, instructions, or other appropriate guidance. A protest under this section is not governed by subpart D of this part.

(2) The continuing education records of an enrolled agent, enrolled retirement plan agent, or registered tax return preparer may be reviewed to determine compliance with the requirements and standards for renewal as provided in paragraph (f) of this section. As part of this review, the enrolled agent, enrolled retirement plan agent or registered tax return preparer may be required to provide the Internal Revenue Service with copies of any continuing education records required to be maintained under this part. If the enrolled agent, enrolled retirement plan agent or registered tax return preparer fails to comply with this requirement, any continuing education hours claimed may be disallowed.

(3) An individual who has not filed a timely application for renewal, who has not made a timely response to the notice of noncompliance with the renewal requirements, or who has not satisfied the requirements of eligibility for renewal will be placed on a roster of inactive enrolled individuals or inactive registered individuals. During this time, the individual will be ineligible to practice before the Internal Revenue Service.

(4) Individuals placed in inactive status and individuals ineligible to practice before the Internal Revenue Service may not state or imply that they are eligible to practice before the Internal Revenue Service, or use the terms enrolled agent, enrolled retirement plan agent, or registered tax return preparer, the designations "EA" or "ERPA" or other form of reference to eligibility to practice before the Internal Revenue Service.

(5) An individual placed in inactive status may be reinstated to an active status by filing an application for renewal and providing evidence of the completion of all required continuing education hours for the enrollment cycle or registration year. Continuing education credit under this paragraph (j)(5) may not be used to satisfy the requirements of the enrollment cycle or registration year in which the individual has been placed back on the active roster.

(6) An individual placed in inactive status must file an application for renewal and satisfy the requirements for renewal as set forth in this section within three years of being placed in inactive status. Otherwise, the name of such individual will be removed from the inactive status roster and the individual's status as an enrolled agent, enrolled retirement plan agent, or registered tax return preparer will terminate. Future eligibility for active status must then be reestablished by the individual as provided in this section.

(7) Inactive status is not available to an individual who is the subject of a pending disciplinary matter before the Internal Revenue Service.

* * *

(n) Effective/applicability date. This section is applicable to enrollment or registration effective beginning August 2, 2011.

§ 10.7. Representing oneself; participating in rulemaking; limited practice; and special appearances.

(a) Representing oneself. Individuals may appear on their own behalf before the Internal Revenue Service provided they present satisfactory identification.

(b) Participating in rulemaking. Individuals may participate in rulemaking as provided by the Administrative Procedure Act. See 5 U.S.C. 553.

(c) Limited practice – (1) In general. Subject to the limitations in paragraph (c)(2) of this section, an individual who is not a practitioner may represent a taxpayer before the Internal Revenue Service in the circumstances described in this paragraph (c)(1), even if the taxpayer is not present, provided the individual presents satisfactory identification and proof of his or her authority to represent the taxpayer. The circumstances described in this paragraph (c)(1) are as follows:

(i) An individual may represent a member of his or her immediate family.

(ii) A regular full-time employee of an individual employer may represent the employer.

(iii) A general partner or a regular full-time employee of a partnership may represent the partnership.

(iv) A bona fide officer or a regular full-time employee of a corporation (including a parent, subsidiary, or other affiliated corporation), association, or organized group may represent the corporation, association, or organized group.

(v) A regular full-time employee of a trust, receivership, guardianship, or estate may represent the trust, receivership, guardianship, or estate.

(vi) An officer or a regular employee of a governmental unit, agency, or authority may represent the governmental unit, agency, or authority in the course of his or her official duties.

(vii) An individual may represent any individual or entity, who is outside the United States, before personnel of the Internal Revenue Service when such representation takes place outside the United States.

(2) Limitations. (i) An individual who is under suspension or disbarment from practice before the Internal Revenue Service may not engage in limited practice before the Internal Revenue Service under paragraph (c)(1) of this section.

(ii) The Commissioner, or delegate, may, after notice and opportunity for a conference, deny eligibility to engage in limited practice before the Internal Revenue Service under paragraph (c)(1) of this section to any individual who has engaged in conduct that would justify a sanction under § 10.50.

(iii) An individual who represents a taxpayer under the authority of paragraph (c)(1) of this section is subject, to the extent of his or her authority, to such rules of general applicability regarding standards of conduct and other matters as prescribed by the Internal Revenue Service.

(d) Special appearances. The Commissioner, or delegate, may, subject to conditions deemed appropriate, authorize an individual who is not otherwise eligible to practice before the Internal Revenue Service to represent another person in a particular matter.

(e) Fiduciaries. For purposes of this part, a fiduciary (for example, a trustee, receiver, guardian, personal representative, administrator, or executor) is considered to be the taxpayer and not a representative of the taxpayer.

(f) Effective/applicability date. This section is applicable beginning August 2, 2011.

§ 10.8. Return preparation and application of rules to other individuals.

(a) Preparing all or substantially all of a tax return. Any individual who for compensation prepares or assists with the preparation of all or substantially all of a tax return or claim for refund must have a preparer tax identification number. Except as otherwise prescribed in forms, instructions, or other appropriate guidance, an individual must be an attorney, certified public accountant, enrolled agent, or registered tax return preparer to obtain a preparer tax identification number. Any individual who for compensation prepares or assists with the preparation of all or substantially all of a tax return or claim for refund is subject to the duties and restrictions relating to practice in subpart B, as well as subject to the sanctions for violation of the regulations in subpart C.

(b) Preparing a tax return and furnishing information. Any individual may for compensation prepare or assist with the preparation of a tax return or claim for refund (provided the individual prepares less than substantially all of the tax return or claim for refund), appear as a witness for the taxpayer before the Internal Revenue Service, or furnish information at the request of the Internal Revenue Service or any of its officers or employees.

(c) Application of rules to other individuals. Any individual who for compensation prepares, or assists in the preparation of, all or a substantial portion of a document pertaining to any taxpayer's tax liability for submission to the Internal Revenue Service is subject to the duties and restrictions relating to practice in subpart B, as well as subject to the sanctions for violation of the regulations in subpart C. Unless otherwise a practitioner, however, an individual may not for compensation prepare, or assist in the preparation of, all or substantially all of a tax return or claim for refund, or sign tax returns and claims for refund. For purposes of this paragraph, an individual described in 26 CFR 301.7701-15(f) is not treated as having prepared all or a substantial portion of the document by reason of such assistance.

(d) Effective/applicability date. This section is applicable beginning August 2, 2011.

§ 10.9. Continuing education providers and continuing education programs.

(a) Continuing education providers – (1) In general. Continuing education providers are those responsible for presenting continuing education programs. A continuing education provider must –

(i) Be an accredited educational institution;

(ii) Be recognized for continuing education purposes by the licensing body of any State, territory, or possession of the United States, including a Commonwealth, or the District of Columbia;

(iii) Be recognized and approved by a qualifying organization as a provider of continuing education on subject matters within § 10.6(f) of this part. The Internal Revenue Service may, at its discretion, identify a professional organization, society or business entity that maintains minimum education standards comparable to those set forth in this part as a qualifying organization for purposes of this part in appropriate forms, instructions, and other appropriate guidance; or

(iv) Be recognized by the Internal Revenue Service as a professional organization, society, or business whose programs include offering continuing professional education opportunities in subject matters within § 10.6(f) of this part. The Internal Revenue Service, at its discretion, may require such professional organizations, societies, or businesses to file an agreement and/or obtain Internal Revenue Service approval of each program as a qualified continuing education program in appropriate forms, instructions or other appropriate guidance.

(2) Continuing education provider numbers – (i) In general. A continuing education provider is required to obtain a continuing education provider number and pay any applicable user fee.

(ii) Renewal. A continuing education provider maintains its status as a continuing education provider during the continuing education provider cycle by renewing its continuing education provider number as prescribed by forms, instructions or other appropriate guidance and paying any applicable user fee.

* * *

(c) Effective/applicability date. This section is applicable beginning August 2, 2011.

§ 10.20. Information to be furnished.

(a) To the Internal Revenue Service. (1) A practitioner must, on a proper and lawful request by a duly authorized officer or employee of the Internal Revenue Service, promptly submit records or information in any matter before the Internal Revenue Service unless the practitioner believes in good faith and on reasonable grounds that the records or information are privileged.

(2) Where the requested records or information are not in the possession of, or subject to the control of, the practitioner or the practitioner's client, the practitioner must promptly notify the requesting Internal Revenue Service officer or employee and the practitioner must provide any information that the practitioner has regarding the identity of any person who the practitioner believes may have possession or control of the requested records or information. The practitioner must make reasonable inquiry of his or her client regarding the identity of any person who may have possession or control of the requested records or information, but the practitioner is not required to make inquiry of any other person or independently verify any information provided by the practitioner's client regarding the identity of such persons.

(3) When a proper and lawful request is made by a duly authorized officer or employee of the Internal Revenue Service, concerning an inquiry into an alleged violation of the regulations in this part, a practitioner must provide any information the practitioner has concerning the alleged violation and testify regarding this information in any proceeding instituted under this part, unless the practitioner believes in good faith and on reasonable grounds that the information is privileged.

(b) Interference with a proper and lawful request for records or information. A practitioner may not interfere, or attempt to interfere, with any proper and lawful effort by the Internal Revenue Service, its officers or employees, to obtain any record or information unless the practitioner believes in good faith and on reasonable grounds that the record or information is privileged.

(c) Effective/applicability date. This section is applicable beginning August 2, 2011.

§ 10.21. Knowledge of client's omission.

A practitioner who, having been retained by a client with respect to a matter administered by the Internal Revenue Service, knows that the client has not complied with the revenue laws of the United States or has made an error in or omission from any return, document, affidavit, or other paper which the client submitted or executed under the revenue laws of the United States, must advise the client promptly of the fact of such noncompliance, error, or omission. The practitioner must advise the client of the consequences as provided under the Code and regulations of such noncompliance, error, or omission.

§ 10.22. Diligence as to accuracy.

(a) In general. A practitioner must exercise due diligence –

(1) In preparing or assisting in the preparation of, approving, and filing tax returns, documents, affidavits, and other papers relating to Internal Revenue Service matters;

(2) In determining the correctness of oral or written representations made by the practitioner to the Department of the Treasury; and

(3) In determining the correctness of oral or written representations made by the practitioner to clients with reference to any matter administered by the Internal Revenue Service.

(b) Reliance on others. Except as provided in §§ 10.34, 10.35, and 10.37, a practitioner will be presumed to have exercised due diligence for purposes of this section if the practitioner relies on the work product of another person and the practitioner used reasonable care in engaging, supervising, training, and evaluating the person, taking proper account of the nature of the relationship between the practitioner and the person.

(c) Effective/applicability date. This section is applicable on September 26, 2007.

Proposed Amendment (September 17, 2012)

§ 10.22. Diligence as to accuracy.

* * *

(b) Reliance on others. Except as provided in §§ 10.34 and 10.37, a practitioner will be presumed to have exercised due diligence for purposes of this section if the practitioner relies on the work product of another person and the practitioner used reasonable care in engaging, supervising, training, and evaluating the person, taking proper account of the nature of the relationship between the practitioner and the person.

(c) Effective/applicability date. This section is applicable beginning after the date that final regulations are published in the Federal Register.

§ 10.23. Prompt disposition of pending matters.

A practitioner may not unreasonably delay the prompt disposition of any matter before the Internal Revenue Service.

§ 10.24. Assistance from or to disbarred or suspended persons and former Internal Revenue Service employees.

A practitioner may not, knowingly and directly or indirectly:

(a) Accept assistance from or assist any person who is under disbarment or suspension from practice before the Internal Revenue Service if the assistance relates to a matter or matters constituting practice before the Internal Revenue Service.

(b) Accept assistance from any former government employee where the provisions of § 10.25 or any Federal law would be violated.

§ 10.25. Practice by former government employees, their partners and their associates.

(a) Definitions. For purposes of this section –

(1) Assist means to act in such a way as to advise, furnish information to, or otherwise aid another person, directly, or indirectly.

(2) Government employee is an officer or employee of the United States or any agency of the United States, including a special Government employee as defined in 18 U.S.C. 202(a), or of the District of Columbia, or of any State, or a member of Congress or of any State legislature.

(3) Member of a firm is a sole practitioner or an employee or associate thereof, or a partner, stockholder, associate, affiliate or employee of a partnership, joint venture, corporation, professional association or other affiliation of two or more practitioners who represent nongovernmental parties.

(4) Particular matter involving specific parties is defined at 5 CFR 2637.201(c), or superseding post-employment regulations issued by the U.S. Office of Government Ethics.

(5) Rule includes Treasury regulations, whether issued or under preparation for issuance as notices of proposed rulemaking or as Treasury decisions, revenue rulings, and revenue procedures published in the Internal Revenue Bulletin (see 26 CFR 601.601(d)(2)(ii)(b)).

(b) General rules – (1) No former Government employee may, subsequent to Government employment, represent anyone in any matter administered by the Internal Revenue Service if the representation would violate 18 U.S.C. 207 or any other laws of the United States.

(2) No former Government employee who personally and substantially participated in a particular matter involving specific parties may, subsequent to Government employment, represent or knowingly assist, in that particular matter, any person who is or was a specific party to that particular matter.

(3) A former Government employee who within a period of one year prior to the termination of Government employment had official responsibility for a particular matter involving specific parties may not, within two years after Government employment is ended, represent in that particular matter any person who is or was a specific party to that particular matter.

(4) No former Government employee may, within one year after Government employment is ended, communicate with or appear before, with the intent to influence, any employee of the Treasury Department in connection with the publication, withdrawal, amendment, modification, or interpretation of a rule the development of which the former Government employee participated in, or for which, within a period of one year prior to the termination of Government employment, the former government employee had official responsibility. This paragraph (b)(4) does not, however, preclude any former employee from appearing on one's own behalf or from representing a taxpayer before the Internal Revenue Service in connection with a particular matter involving specific parties involving the application or interpretation of a rule with respect to that particular matter, provided that the representation is otherwise consistent with the other provisions of this section and the former employee does not utilize or disclose any confidential information acquired by the former employee in the development of the rule.

(c) Firm representation – (1) No member of a firm of which a former Government employee is a member may represent or knowingly assist a person who was or is a specific party in any particular matter with respect to which the restrictions of paragraph (b)(2) of this section apply to the former Government employee, in that particular matter, unless the firm isolates the former Government employee in such a way to ensure that the former Government employee cannot assist in the representation.

(2) When isolation of a former Government employee is required under paragraph (c)(1) of this section, a statement affirming the fact of such isolation must be executed under oath by the former Government employee and by another member of the firm acting on behalf of the firm. The statement must clearly identify the firm, the former Government employee, and the particular matter(s) requiring isolation. The statement must be retained by the firm and, upon request, provided to the office(s) of the Internal Revenue Service administering or enforcing this part.

(d) Pending representation. The provisions of this regulation will govern practice by former Government employees, their partners and associates with respect to representation in particular matters involving specific parties where actual representation commenced before the effective date of this regulation.

(e) Effective/applicability date. This section is applicable beginning August 2, 2011.

§ 10.26. Notaries.

A practitioner may not take acknowledgments, administer oaths, certify papers, or perform any official act as a notary public with respect to any matter administered by the Internal Revenue Service and for which he or she is employed as counsel, attorney, or agent, or in which he or she may be in any way interested.

§ 10.27. Fees.

(a) In general. A practitioner may not charge an unconscionable fee in connection with any matter before the Internal Revenue Service.

(b) Contingent fees – (1) Except as provided in paragraphs (b)(2), (3), and (4) of this section, a practitioner may not charge a contingent fee for services rendered in connection with any matter before the Internal Revenue Service.

(2) A practitioner may charge a contingent fee for services rendered in connection with the Service's examination of, or challenge to –

(i) An original tax return; or

(ii) An amended return or claim for refund or credit where the amended return or claim for refund or credit was filed within 120 days of the taxpayer receiving a written notice of the examination of, or a written challenge to the original tax return.

(3) A practitioner may charge a contingent fee for services rendered in connection with a claim for credit or refund filed solely in connection with the determination of statutory interest or penalties assessed by the Internal Revenue Service.

(4) A practitioner may charge a contingent fee for services rendered in connection with any judicial proceeding arising under the Internal Revenue Code.

(c) Definitions. For purposes of this section –

(1) Contingent fee is any fee that is based, in whole or in part, on whether or not a position taken on a tax return or other filing avoids challenge by the Internal Revenue Service or is sustained either by the Internal Revenue Service or in litigation. A contingent fee includes a fee that is based on a percentage of the refund reported on a return, that is based on a percentage of the taxes saved, or that otherwise depends on the specific result attained. A contingent fee also includes any fee arrangement in which the practitioner will reimburse the client for all or a portion of the client's fee in the event that a position taken on a tax return or other filing is challenged by the Internal Revenue Service or is not sustained, whether pursuant to an indemnity agreement, a guarantee, rescission rights, or any other arrangement with a similar effect.

(2) Matter before the Internal Revenue Service includes tax planning and advice, preparing or filing or assisting in preparing or filing returns or claims for refund or credit, and all matters connected with a presentation to the Internal Revenue Service or any of its officers or employees relating to a taxpayer's rights, privileges, or liabilities under laws or regulations administered by the Internal Revenue Service. Such presentations include, but are not limited to, preparing and filing documents, corresponding and communicating with the Internal Revenue Service, rendering written advice with respect to any entity, transaction, plan or arrangement, and representing a client at conferences, hearings, and meetings.

(d) Effective/applicability date. This section is applicable for fee arrangements entered into after March 26, 2008.

Proposed Amendment (July 28, 2009)

§ 10.27. Fees.

* * *

(b) Contingent fees – (1) Except as provided in paragraphs (b)(2), (3), (4), and (5) of this section, a practitioner may not charge a contingent fee for services rendered in connection with any matter before the Internal Revenue Service.

(2) A practitioner may charge a contingent fee for services rendered in connection with the Internal Revenue Service's examination of, or challenge to –

(i) An original tax return; or

(ii) An amended return or claim for refund or credit filed before the taxpayer received a written notice of examination of, or a written challenge to, the original tax return; or filed no later than 120 days after the receipt of such written notice or written challenge. The 120 days is computed from the earlier of a written notice of the examination, if any, or a written challenge to the original return.

(3) A practitioner may charge a contingent fee for services rendered in connection with a claim for credit or refund filed solely in connection with the determination of statutory interest or penalties assessed by the Internal Revenue Service.

(4) A practitioner may charge a contingent fee for services rendered in connection with a claim under section 7623 of the Internal Revenue Code.

(5) A practitioner may charge a contingent fee for services rendered in connection with any judicial proceeding arising under the Internal Revenue Code.

(c)   * * *

(1) Contingent fee is any fee that is based, in whole or in part, on whether or not a position taken on a tax return or other filing avoids challenge by the Internal Revenue Service or is sustained either by the Internal Revenue Service or in litigation. A contingent fee includes a fee that is based on a percentage of the refund reported on a return, that is based on a percentage of the taxes saved, or that otherwise depends on the specific tax result attained. A contingent fee also includes any fee arrangement in which the practitioner will reimburse the client for all or a portion of the client's fee in the event that a position taken on a tax return or other filing is challenged by the Internal Revenue Service or is not sustained, whether pursuant to an indemnity agreement, a guarantee, rescission rights, or any other arrangement with a similar effect.

(2)   * * *

(d) Applicability date. This section is applicable to fee arrangements entered into after March 26, 2008.

(e) Effective date. This section is effective on the date that the final regulations are published in the Federal Register.

§ 10.28. Return of client's records.

(a) In general, a practitioner must, at the request of a client, promptly return any and all records of the client that are necessary for the client to comply with his or her Federal tax obligations. The practitioner may retain copies of the records returned to a client. The existence of a dispute over fees generally does not relieve the practitioner of his or her responsibility under this section. Nevertheless, if applicable state law allows or permits the retention of a client's records by a practitioner in the case of a dispute over fees for services rendered, the practitioner need only return those records that must be attached to the taxpayer's return. The practitioner, however, must provide the client with reasonable access to review and copy any additional records of the client retained by the practitioner under state law that are necessary for the client to comply with his or her Federal tax obligations.

(b) For purposes of this section, Records of the client include all documents or written or electronic materials provided to the practitioner, or obtained by the practitioner in the course of the practitioner's representation of the client, that preexisted the retention of the practitioner by the client. The term also includes materials that were prepared by the client or a third party (not including an employee or agent of the practitioner) at any time and provided to the practitioner with respect to the subject matter of the representation. The term also includes any return, claim for refund, schedule, affidavit, appraisal or any other document prepared by the practitioner, or his or her employee or agent, that was presented to the client with respect to a prior representation if such document is necessary for the taxpayer to comply with his or her current Federal tax obligations. The term does not include any return, claim for refund, schedule, affidavit, appraisal or any other document prepared by the practitioner or the practitioner's firm, employees or agents if the practitioner is withholding such document pending the client's performance of its contractual obligation to pay fees with respect to such document.

§ 10.29. Conflicting interests.

(a) Except as provided by paragraph (b) of this section, a practitioner shall not represent a client before the Internal Revenue Service if the representation involves a conflict of interest. A conflict of interest exists if –

(1) The representation of one client will be directly adverse to another client; or

(2) There is a significant risk that the representation of one or more clients will be materially limited by the practitioner's responsibilities to another client, a former client or a third person, or by a personal interest of the practitioner.

(b) Notwithstanding the existence of a conflict of interest under paragraph (a) of this section, the practitioner may represent a client if –

(1) The practitioner reasonably believes that the practitioner will be able to provide competent and diligent representation to each affected client;

(2) The representation is not prohibited by law; and

(3) Each affected client waives the conflict of interest and gives informed consent, confirmed in writing by each affected client, at the time the existence of the conflict of interest is known by the practitioner. The confirmation may be made within a reasonable period after the informed consent, but in no event later than 30 days.

(c) Copies of the written consents must be retained by the practitioner for at least 36 months from the date of the conclusion of the representation of the affected clients, and the written consents must be provided to any officer or employee of the Internal Revenue Service on request.

(d) Effective/applicability date. This section is applicable on September 26, 2007.

§ 10.30. Solicitation.

(a) Advertising and solicitation restrictions. (1) A practitioner may not, with respect to any Internal Revenue Service matter, in any way use or participate in the use of any form of public communication or private solicitation containing a false, fraudulent, or coercive statement or claim; or a misleading or deceptive statement or claim. Enrolled agents, enrolled retirement plan agents, or registered tax return preparers, in describing their professional designation, may not utilize the term "certified" or imply an employer/employee relationship with the Internal Revenue Service. Examples of acceptable descriptions for enrolled agents are "enrolled to represent taxpayers before the Internal Revenue Service," "enrolled to practice before the Internal Revenue Service," and "admitted to practice before the Internal Revenue Service." Similarly, examples of acceptable descriptions for enrolled retirement plan agents are "enrolled to represent taxpayers before the Internal Revenue Service as a retirement plan agent" and "enrolled to practice before the Internal Revenue Service as a retirement plan agent." An example of an acceptable description for registered tax return preparers is "designated as a registered tax return preparer by the Internal Revenue Service."

(2) Government employee is an officer or employee of the United States or any agency of the United States, including a special Government employee as defined in 18 U.S.C. 202(a), or of the District of Columbia, or of any State, or a member of Congress or of any State legislature.

(3) Member of a firm is a sole practitioner or an employee or associate thereof, or a partner, stockholder, associate, affiliate or employee of a partnership, joint venture, corporation, professional association or other affiliation of two or more practitioners who represent nongovernmental parties.

(4) Particular matter involving specific parties is defined at 5 CFR 2637.201(c), or superseding post-employment regulations issued by the U.S. Office of Government Ethics.

(5) Rule includes Treasury regulations, whether issued or under preparation for issuance as notices of proposed rulemaking or as Treasury decisions, revenue rulings, and revenue procedures published in the Internal Revenue Bulletin (see 26 CFR 601.601(d)(2)(ii)(b)).

(b) General rules – (1) No former Government employee may, subsequent to Government employment, represent anyone in any matter administered by the Internal Revenue Service if the representation would violate 18 U.S.C. 207 or any other laws of the United States.

(2) No former Government employee who personally and substantially participated in a particular matter involving specific parties may, subsequent to Government employment, represent or knowingly assist, in that particular matter, any person who is or was a specific party to that particular matter.

(3) A former Government employee who within a period of one year prior to the termination of Government employment had official responsibility for a particular matter involving specific parties may not, within two years after Government employment is ended, represent in that particular matter any person who is or was a specific party to that particular matter.

(4) No former Government employee may, within one year after Government employment is ended, communicate with or appear before, with the intent to influence, any employee of the Treasury Department in connection with the publication, withdrawal, amendment, modification, or interpretation of a rule the development of which the former Government employee participated in, or for which, within a period of one year prior to the termination of Government employment, the former government employee had official responsibility. This paragraph (b)(4) does not, however, preclude any former employee from appearing on one's own behalf or from representing a taxpayer before the Internal Revenue Service in connection with a particular matter involving specific parties involving the application or interpretation of a rule with respect to that particular matter, provided that the representation is otherwise consistent with the other provisions of this section and the former employee does not utilize or disclose any confidential information acquired by the former employee in the development of the rule.

(c) Firm representation – (1) No member of a firm of which a former Government employee is a member may represent or knowingly assist a person who was or is a specific party in any particular matter with respect to which the restrictions of paragraph (b)(2) of this section apply to the former Government employee, in that particular matter, unless the firm isolates the former Government employee in such a way to ensure that the former Government employee cannot assist in the representation.

(2) When isolation of a former Government employee is required under paragraph (c)(1) of this section, a statement affirming the fact of such isolation must be executed under oath by the former Government employee and by another member of the firm acting on behalf of the firm. The statement must clearly identify the firm, the former Government employee, and the particular matter(s) requiring isolation. The statement must be retained by the firm and, upon request, provided to the Director of the Office of Professional Responsibility.

(d) Pending representation. The provisions of this regulation will govern practice by former Government employees, their partners and associates with respect to representation in particular matters involving specific parties where actual representation commenced before the effective date of this regulation.

(e) Effective/applicability date. This section is applicable beginning August 2, 2011.

§ 10.31. Negotiation of taxpayer checks.

A practitioner who prepares tax returns may not endorse or otherwise negotiate any check issued to a client by the government in respect of a Federal tax liability.

Proposed Amendment (September 17, 2012)

§ 10.31. Negotiation of taxpayer checks.

(a) A practitioner may not endorse or otherwise negotiate any check (including directing or accepting payment by any means, electronic or otherwise, in an account owned or controlled by the practitioner or any firm or other entity with whom the practitioner is associated) issued to a client by the government in respect of a Federal tax liability.

(b) **Effective/applicability date.** This section is applicable beginning after the date that final regulations are published in the Federal Register.

§ 10.32. Practice of law.

Nothing in the regulations in this part may be construed as authorizing persons not members of the bar to practice law.

§ 10.33. Best practices for tax advisors.

(a) **Best practices.** Tax advisors should provide clients with the highest quality representation concerning Federal tax issues by adhering to best practices in providing advice and in preparing or assisting in the preparation of a submission to the Internal Revenue Service. In addition to compliance with the standards of practice provided elsewhere in this part, best practices include the following:

(1) Communicating clearly with the client regarding the terms of the engagement. For example, the advisor should determine the client's expected purpose for and use of the advice and should have a clear understanding with the client regarding the form and scope of the advice or assistance to be rendered.

(2) Establishing the facts, determining which facts are relevant, evaluating the reasonableness of any assumptions or representations, relating the applicable law (including potentially applicable judicial doctrines) to the relevant facts, and arriving at a conclusion supported by the law and the facts.

(3) Advising the client regarding the import of the conclusions reached, including, for example, whether a taxpayer may avoid accuracy-related penalties under the Internal Revenue Code if a taxpayer acts in reliance on the advice.

(4) Acting fairly and with integrity in practice before the Internal Revenue Service.

(b) **Procedures to ensure best practices for tax advisors.** Tax advisors with responsibility for overseeing a firm's practice of providing advice concerning Federal tax issues or of preparing or assisting in the preparation of submissions to the Internal Revenue Service should take reasonable steps to ensure that the firm's procedures for all members, associates, and employees are consistent with the best practices set forth in paragraph (a) of this section.

(c) **Applicability date.** This section is effective after June 20, 2005.

§ 10.34. Standards with respect to tax returns and documents, affidavits and other papers.

(a) Tax returns. (1) A practitioner may not willfully, recklessly, or through gross incompetence –

(i) Sign a tax return or claim for refund that the practitioner knows or reasonably should know contains a position that –

(A) Lacks a reasonable basis;

(B) Is an unreasonable position as described in section 6694(a)(2) of the Internal Revenue code (Code) (including the related regulations and other published guidance); or

(C) Is a willful attempted by the practitioner to understate the liability for tax or a reckless or intentional disregard of rules or regulations by the practitioner as described in section 6694(b)(2) of the Code (including the related regulations and other published guidance).

(ii) Advise a client to take a position on a tax return or claim for refund, or prepare a portion off a tax return or claim for refund containing a position, that –

(A) Lacks a reasonable basis;

(B) Is an unreasonable position as described in section 6694(a)(2) of the Code (including the related regulations and other published guidance); or

(C) Is a willful attempt by the practitioner to understate the liability for tax or a reckless or intentional disregard of rules or regulations by the practitioner as described in section 6694(b)(2) of the Code (including the related regulations and other published guidance).

(2) A pattern of conduct is a factor that will be taken into account in determining whether a practitioner acted willfully, recklessly, or through gross incompetence.

(b) Documents, affidavits and other papers – (1) A practitioner may not advise a client to take a position on a document, affidavit or other paper submitted to the Internal Revenue Service unless the position is not frivolous.

(2) A practitioner may not advise a client to submit a document, affidavit or other paper to the Internal Revenue Service –

(i) The purpose of which is to delay or impede the administration of the Federal tax laws;

(ii) That is frivolous; or

(iii) That contains or omits information in a manner that demonstrates an intentional disregard of a rule or regulation unless the practitioner also advises the client to submit a document that evidences a good faith challenge to the rule or regulation.

(c) Advising clients on potential penalties – (1) A practitioner must inform a client of any penalties that are reasonably likely to apply to the client with respect to –

(i) A position taken on a tax return if –

(A) The practitioner advised the client with respect to the position; or

(B) The practitioner prepared or signed the tax return; and

(ii) Any document, affidavit or other paper submitted to the Internal Revenue Service.

(2) The practitioner also must inform the client of any opportunity to avoid any such penalties by disclosure, if relevant, and of the requirements for adequate disclosure.

(3) This paragraph (c) applies even if the practitioner is not subject to a penalty under the Internal Revenue Code with respect to the position or with respect to the document, affidavit or other paper submitted.

(d) Relying on information furnished by clients. A practitioner advising a client to take a position on a tax return, document, affidavit or other paper submitted to the Internal Revenue Service, or preparing or signing a tax return as a preparer, generally may rely in good faith without verification upon information furnished by the client. The practitioner may not, however, ignore the implications of information furnished to, or actually known by, the practitioner, and must make reasonable inquiries if the information as furnished appears to be incorrect, inconsistent with an important fact or another factual assumption, or incomplete.

(e) Effective/applicability date. Paragraph (a) of this section is applicable for returns or claims for refund filed, or advice provided, beginning August 2, 2011. Paragraphs (b) through (d) of this section are applicable to tax returns, documents, affidavits, and other papers filed on or after September 26, 2007.

§ 10.35. Requirements for covered opinions.

(a) A practitioner who provides a covered opinion shall comply with the standards of practice in this section.

(b) Definitions. For purposes of this subpart –

(1) A **practitioner** includes any individual described in § 10.2(a)(5).

(2) Covered opinion – (i) In general. A covered opinion is written advice (including electronic communications) by a practitioner concerning one or more Federal tax issues arising from –

(A) A transaction that is the same as or substantially similar to a transaction that, at the time the advice is rendered, the Internal Revenue Service has determined to be a tax avoidance transaction and identified by published guidance as a listed transaction under 26 CFR 1.6011-4(b)(2);

(B) Any partnership or other entity, any investment plan or arrangement, or any other plan or arrangement, the principal purpose of which is the avoidance or evasion of any tax imposed by the Internal Revenue Code; or

(C) Any partnership or other entity, any investment plan or arrangement, or any other plan or arrangement, a significant purpose of which is the avoidance or evasion of any tax imposed by the Internal Revenue Code if the written advice –

(1) Is a reliance opinion;

(2) Is a marketed opinion;

(3) Is subject to conditions of confidentiality; or

(4) Is subject to contractual protection.

(ii) Excluded advice. A covered opinion does not include –

(A) Written advice provided to a client during the course of an engagement if a practitioner is reasonably expected to provide subsequent written advice to the client that satisfies the requirements of this section;

(B) Written advice, other than advice described in paragraph (b)(2)(i)(A) of this section (concerning listed transactions) or paragraph (b)(2)(ii)(B) of this section (concerning the principal purpose of avoidance or evasion) that –

(1) Concerns the qualification of a qualified plan;

(2) Is a State or local bond opinion; or

(3) Is included in documents required to be filed with the Securities and Exchange Commission;

(C) Written advice prepared for and provided to a taxpayer, solely for use by that taxpayer, after the taxpayer has filed a tax return with the Internal Revenue Service reflecting the tax benefits of the transaction. The preceding sentence does not apply if the practitioner knows or has reason to know that the written advice will be relied upon by the taxpayer to take a position on a tax return (including for these purposes an amended return that claims tax benefits not reported on a previously filed return) filed after the date on which the advice is provided to the taxpayer;

(D) Written advice provided to an employer by a practitioner in that practitioner's capacity as an employee of that employer solely for purposes of determining the tax liability of the employer; or

(E) Written advice that does not resolve a Federal tax issue in the taxpayer's favor, unless the advice reaches a conclusion favorable to the taxpayer at any confidence level (e.g., not frivolous, realistic possibility of success, reasonable basis or substantial authority) with respect to that issue. If written advice concerns more than one Federal tax issue, the advice must comply with the requirements of paragraph (c) of this section with respect to any Federal tax issue not described in the preceding sentence.

(3) A Federal tax issue is a question concerning the Federal tax treatment of an item of income, gain, loss, deduction, or credit, the existence or absence of a taxable transfer of property, or the value of property for Federal tax purposes. For purposes of this subpart, a Federal tax issue is significant if the Internal Revenue Service has a reasonable basis for a successful challenge and its resolution could have a significant impact, whether beneficial or adverse and under any reasonably foreseeable circumstance, on the overall Federal tax treatment of the transaction(s) or matter(s) addressed in the opinion.

(4) Reliance opinion – (i) Written advice is a reliance opinion if the advice concludes at a confidence level of at least more likely than not (a greater than 50 percent likelihood) that one or more significant Federal tax issues would be resolved in the taxpayer's favor.

(ii) For purposes of this section, written advice, other than advice described in paragraph (b)(2)(i)(A) of this section (concerning listed transactions) or paragraph (b)(2)(i)(B) of this section (concerning the principal purpose of avoidance or evasion), is not treated as a reliance opinion if the practitioner prominently discloses in the written advice that it was not intended or written by the practitioner to be used, and that it cannot be used by the taxpayer, for the purpose of avoiding penalties that may be imposed on the taxpayer.

(5) Marketed opinion – (i) Written advice is a marketed opinion if the practitioner knows or has reason to know that the written advice will be used or referred to by a person other than the practitioner (or a person who is a member of, associated with, or employed by the practitioner's firm) in promoting, marketing or recommending a partnership or other entity, investment plan or arrangement to one or more taxpayer(s).

(ii) For purposes of this section, written advice, other than advice described in paragraph (b)(2)(i)(A) of this section (concerning listed transactions) or paragraph (b)(2)(i)(B) of this section (concerning the principal purpose of avoidance or evasion), is not treated as a marketed opinion if the practitioner prominently discloses in the written advice that –

(A) The advice was not intended or written by the practitioner to be used, and that it cannot be used by any taxpayer, for the purpose of avoiding penalties that may be imposed on the taxpayer;

(B) The advice was written to support the promotion or marketing of the transaction(s) or matter(s) addressed by the written advice; and

(C) The taxpayer should seek advice based on the taxpayer's particular circumstances from an independent tax advisor.

(6) Conditions of confidentiality. Written advice is subject to conditions of confidentiality if the practitioner imposes on one or more recipients of the written advice a limitation on disclosure of the tax treatment or tax structure of the transaction and the limitation on disclosure protects the confidentiality of that practitioner's tax strategies, regardless of whether the limitation on disclosure is legally binding. A claim that a transaction is proprietary or exclusive is not a limitation on disclosure if the practitioner confirms to all recipients of the written advice that there is no limitation on disclosure of the tax treatment or tax structure of the transaction that is the subject of the written advice.

(7) Contractual protection. Written advice is subject to contractual protection if the taxpayer has the right to a full or partial refund of fees paid to the practitioner (or a person who is a member of, associated with, or employed by the practitioner's firm) if all or a part of the intended tax consequences from the matters addressed in the written advice are not sustained, or if the fees paid to the practitioner (or a person who is a member of, associated with, or employed by the practitioner's firm) are contingent on the taxpayer's realization of tax benefits from the transaction. All the facts and circumstances relating to the matters addressed in the written advice will be considered when determining whether a fee is refundable or contingent, including the right to reimbursements of amounts that the parties to a transaction have not designated as fees or any agreement to provide services without reasonable compensation.

(8) Prominently disclosed. An item is prominently disclosed if it is readily apparent to a reader of the written advice. Whether an item is readily apparent will depend on the facts and circumstances surrounding the written advice including, but not limited to, the sophistication of the taxpayer and the length of the written advice. At a minimum, to be prominently disclosed an item must be set forth in a separate section (and not in a footnote) in a typeface that is the same size or larger than the typeface of any discussion of the facts or law in the written advice.

(9) State or local bond opinion. A State or local bond opinion is written advice with respect to a Federal tax issue included in any materials delivered to a purchaser of a State or local bond in connection with the issuance of the bond in a public or private offering, including an official statement (if one is prepared), that concerns only the excludability of interest on a State or local bond from gross income under section 103 of the Internal Revenue Code, the application of section 55 of the Internal Revenue Code to a State or local bond, the status of a State or local bond as a qualified tax-exempt obligation under section 265(b)(3) of the Internal Revenue Code, the status of a State or local bond as a qualified zone academy bond under section 1397E of the Internal Revenue Code, or any combination of the above.

(10) The principal purpose. For purposes of this section, the principal purpose of a partnership or other entity, investment plan or arrangement, or other plan or arrangement is the avoidance or evasion of any tax imposed by the Internal Revenue Code if that purpose exceeds any other purpose. The principal purpose of a partnership or other entity, investment plan or arrangement, or other plan or arrangement is not to avoid or evade Federal tax if that partnership, entity, plan or arrangement has as its purpose the claiming of tax benefits in a manner consistent with the statute and Congressional purpose. A partnership, entity, plan or arrangement may have a significant purpose of avoidance or evasion even though it does not have the principal purpose of avoidance or evasion under this paragraph (b)(10).

(c) Requirements for covered opinions. A practitioner providing a covered opinion must comply with each of the following requirements.

(1) Factual matters. (i) The practitioner must use reasonable efforts to identify and ascertain the facts, which may relate to future events if a transaction is prospective or proposed, and to determine which facts are relevant. The opinion must identify and consider all facts that the practitioner determines to be relevant.

(ii) The practitioner must not base the opinion on any unreasonable factual assumptions (including assumptions as to future events). An unreasonable factual assumption includes a factual assumption that the practitioner knows or should know is incorrect or incomplete. For example, it is unreasonable to assume that a transaction has a business purpose or that a transaction is potentially profitable apart from tax benefits. A factual assumption includes reliance on a projection, financial forecast or appraisal. It is unreasonable for a practitioner to rely on a projection, financial forecast or appraisal if the practitioner knows or should know that the projection, financial forecast or appraisal is incorrect or incomplete or was prepared by a person lacking the skills or qualifications necessary to prepare such projection, financial forecast or appraisal. The opinion must identify in a separate section all factual assumptions relied upon by the practitioner.

(iii) The practitioner must not base the opinion on any unreasonable factual representations, statements or findings of the taxpayer or any other person. An unreasonable factual representation includes a factual representation that the practitioner knows or should know is incorrect or incomplete. For example, a practitioner may not rely on a factual representation that a transaction has a business purpose if the representation does not include a specific description of the business purpose or the practitioner knows or should know that the representation is incorrect or incomplete. The opinion must identify in a separate section all factual representations, statements or findings of the taxpayer relied upon by the practitioner.

(2) Relate law to facts. (i) The opinion must relate the applicable law (including potentially applicable judicial doctrines) to the relevant facts.

(ii) The practitioner must not assume the favorable resolution of any significant Federal tax issue except as provided in paragraphs (c)(3)(v) and (d) of this section, or otherwise base an opinion on any unreasonable legal assumptions, representations, or conclusions.

(iii) The opinion must not contain internally inconsistent legal analyses or conclusions.

(3) Evaluation of significant Federal tax issues – (i) In general. The opinion must consider all significant Federal tax issues except as provided in paragraphs (c)(3)(v) and (d) of this section.

(ii) Conclusion as to each significant Federal tax issue. The opinion must provide the practitioner's conclusion as to the likelihood that the taxpayer will prevail on the merits with respect to each significant Federal tax issue considered in the opinion. If the practitioner is unable to reach a conclusion with respect to one or more of those issues, the opinion must state that the practitioner is unable to reach a conclusion with respect to those issues. The opinion must describe the reasons for the conclusions, including the facts and analysis supporting the conclusions, or describe the reasons that the practitioner is unable to reach a conclusion as to one or more issues. If the practitioner fails to reach a conclusion at a confidence level of at least more likely than not with respect to one or more significant Federal tax issues considered, the opinion must include the appropriate disclosure(s) required under paragraph (e) of this section.

(iii) Evaluation based on chances of success on the merits. In evaluating the significant Federal tax issues addressed in the opinion, the practitioner must not take into account the possibility that a tax return will not be audited, that an issue will not be raised on audit, or that an issue will be resolved through settlement if raised.

(iv) Marketed opinions. In the case of a marketed opinion, the opinion must provide the practitioner's conclusion that the taxpayer will prevail on the merits at a confidence level of at least more likely than not with respect to each significant Federal tax issue. If the practitioner is unable to reach a more likely than not conclusion with respect to each significant Federal tax issue, the practitioner must not provide the marketed opinion, but may provide written advice that satisfies the requirements in paragraph (b)(5)(ii) of this section.

(v) Limited scope opinions. (A) The practitioner may provide an opinion that considers less than all of the significant Federal tax issues if –

(1) The practitioner and the taxpayer agree that the scope of the opinion and the taxpayer's potential reliance on the opinion for purposes of avoiding penalties that may be imposed on the taxpayer are limited to the Federal tax issue(s) addressed in the opinion;

(2) The opinion is not advice described in paragraph (b)(2)(i)(A) of this section (concerning listed transactions), paragraph (b)(2)(i)(B) of this section (concerning the principal purpose of avoidance or evasion) or paragraph (b)(5) of this section (a marketed opinion); and

(3) The opinion includes the appropriate disclosure(s) required under paragraph (e) of this section.

(B) A practitioner may make reasonable assumptions regarding the favorable resolution of a Federal tax issue (an assumed issue) for purposes of providing an opinion on less than all of the significant Federal tax issues as provided in this paragraph (c)(3)(v). The opinion must identify in a separate section all issues for which the practitioner assumed a favorable resolution.

(4) Overall conclusion. (i) The opinion must provide the practitioner's overall conclusion as to the likelihood that the Federal tax treatment of the transaction or matter that is the subject of the opinion is the proper treatment and the reasons for that conclusion. If the practitioner is unable to reach an overall conclusion, the opinion must state that the practitioner is unable to reach an overall conclusion and describe the reasons for the practitioner's inability to reach a conclusion.

(ii) In the case of a marketed opinion, the opinion must provide the practitioner's overall conclusion that the Federal tax treatment of the transaction or matter that is the subject of the opinion is the proper treatment at a confidence level of at least more likely than not.

(d) Competence to provide opinion; reliance on opinions of others. (1) The practitioner must be knowledgeable in all of the aspects of Federal tax law relevant to the opinion being rendered, except that the practitioner may rely on the opinion of another practitioner with respect to one or more significant Federal tax issues, unless the practitioner knows or should know that the opinion of the other practitioner should not be relied on. If a practitioner relies on the opinion of another practitioner, the relying practitioner's opinion must identify the other opinion and set forth the conclusions reached in the other opinion.

(2) The practitioner must be satisfied that the combined analysis of the opinions, taken as a whole, and the overall conclusion, if any, satisfy the requirements of this section.

(e) Required disclosures. A covered opinion must contain all of the following disclosures that apply –

(1) Relationship between promoter and practitioner. An opinion must prominently disclose the existence of –

(i) Any compensation arrangement, such as a referral fee or a fee-sharing arrangement, between the practitioner (or the practitioner's firm or any person who is a member of, associated with, or employed by the practitioner's firm) and any person (other than the client for whom the opinion is prepared) with respect to promoting, marketing or recommending the entity, plan, or arrangement (or a substantially similar arrangement) that is the subject of the opinion; or

(ii) Any referral agreement between the practitioner (or the practitioner's firm or any person who is a member of, associated with, or employed by the practitioner's firm) and a person (other than the client for whom the opinion is prepared) engaged in promoting, marketing or recommending the entity, plan, or arrangement (or a substantially similar arrangement) that is the subject of the opinion.

(2) Marketed opinions. A marketed opinion must prominently disclose that –

(i) The opinion was written to support the promotion or marketing of the transaction(s) or matter(s) addressed in the opinion; and

(ii) The taxpayer should seek advice based on the taxpayer's particular circumstances from an independent tax advisor.

(3) Limited scope opinions. A limited scope opinion must prominently disclose that –

(i) The opinion is limited to the one or more Federal tax issues addressed in the opinion;

(ii) Additional issues may exist that could affect the Federal tax treatment of the transaction or matter that is the subject of the opinion and the opinion does not consider or provide a conclusion with respect to any additional issues; and

(iii) With respect to any significant Federal tax issues outside the limited scope of the opinion, the opinion was not written, and cannot be used by the taxpayer, for the purpose of avoiding penalties that may be imposed on the taxpayer.

(4) Opinions that fail to reach a more likely than not conclusion. An opinion that does not reach a conclusion at a confidence level of at least more likely than not with respect to a significant Federal tax issue must prominently disclose that –

(i) The opinion does not reach a conclusion at a confidence level of at least more likely than not with respect to one or more significant Federal tax issues addressed by the opinion; and

(ii) With respect to those significant Federal tax issues, the opinion was not written, and cannot be used by the taxpayer, for the purpose of avoiding penalties that may be imposed on the taxpayer.

(5) Advice regarding required disclosures. In the case of any disclosure required under this section, the practitioner may not provide advice to any person that is contrary to or inconsistent with the required disclosure.

(f) Effect of opinion that meets these standards – (1) In general. An opinion that meets the requirements of this section satisfies the practitioner's responsibilities under this section, but the persuasiveness of the opinion with regard to the tax issues in question and the taxpayer's good faith reliance on the opinion will be determined separately under applicable provisions of the law and regulations.

(2) Standards for other written advice. A practitioner who provides written advice that is not a covered opinion for purposes of this section is subject to the requirements of § 10.37.

(g) Effective date. This section applies to written advice that is rendered after June 20, 2005.

Proposed Amendment (September 17, 2012)

§ 10.35. Competence.

(a) A practitioner must possess the necessary competence to engage in practice before the Internal Revenue. Competent practice requires the knowledge, skill, thoroughness, and preparation necessary for the matter for which the practitioner is engaged.

(b) Effective/applicability date. This section is applicable beginning after the date that final regulations are published in the Federal Register.

§ 10.36. Procedures to ensure compliance.

(a) Requirements for covered opinions. Any practitioner who has (or practitioners who have or share) principal authority and responsibility for overseeing a firm's practice of providing advice concerning Federal tax issues must take reasonable steps to ensure that the firm has adequate procedures in effect for all members, associates, and employees for purposes of complying with § 10.35. Any such practitioner will be subject to discipline for failing to comply with the requirements of this paragraph if –

(1) The practitioner through willfulness, recklessness, or gross incompetence does not take reasonable steps to ensure that the firm has adequate procedures to comply with § 10.35, and one or more individuals who are members of, associated with, or employed by, the firm are, or have, engaged in a pattern or practice, in connection with their practice with the firm, of failing to comply with § 10.35; or

(2) The practitioner knows or should know that one or more individuals who are members of, associated with, or employed by, the firm are, or have, engaged in a pattern or practice, in connection with their practice with the firm, that does not comply with § 10.35 and the practitioner, through willfulness, recklessness, or gross incompetence, fails to take prompt action to correct the noncompliance.

(b) Requirements for tax returns and other documents. Any practitioner who has (or practitioners who have or share) principal authority and responsibility for overseeing a firm's practice of preparing tax returns, claims for refunds, or other documents for submission to the Internal Revenue Service must take reasonable steps to ensure that the firm has adequate procedures in effect for all members, associates, and employees for purposes of complying with Circular 230. Any practitioner who has (or practitioners who have or share) this principal authority will be subject to discipline for failing to comply with the requirements of this paragraph if –

(1) The practitioner through willfulness, recklessness, or gross incompetence does not take reasonable steps to ensure that the firm has adequate procedures to comply with Circular 230, and one or more individuals who are members of, associated with, or employed by, the firm are, or have, engaged in a pattern or practice, in connection with their practice with the firm, of failing to comply with Circular 230; or

(2) The practitioner knows or should know that one or more individuals who are members of, associated with, or employed by, the firm are, or have, engaged in a pattern or practice, in connection with their practice with the firm, that does not comply with Circular 230, and the practitioner, through willfulness, recklessness, or gross incompetence fails to take prompt action to correct the noncompliance.

(c) Effective/applicability date. This section is applicable beginning August 2, 2011.

Proposed Amendment (September 17, 2012)

§ 10.36. Procedures to ensure compliance.

(a) Any practitioner who has (or practitioners who have or share) principal authority and responsibility for overseeing a firm's practice governed by this part, including the provision of advice concerning Federal tax matters and preparation of tax returns, claims for refund, or other documents for submission to the Internal Revenue Service, must take reasonable steps to ensure that the firm has adequate procedures in effect for all members, associates, and employees for purposes of complying with this part, as applicable. Any practitioner who has (or practitioners who have or share) this principal authority will be subject to discipline for failing to comply with the requirements of this paragraph (a) if –

(1) The practitioner through willfulness, recklessness, or gross incompetence does not take reasonable steps to ensure that the firm has adequate procedures to comply with this part, as applicable, and one or more individuals who are members of, associated with, or employed by, the firm are, or have, engaged in a pattern or practice, in connection with their practice with the firm, of failing to comply with this part, as applicable; or

(2) The practitioner knows or should know that one or more individuals who are members of, associated with, or employed by, the firm are, or have, engaged in a pattern or practice, in connection with their practice with the firm, that does not comply with this part, as applicable, and the practitioner, through willfulness, recklessness, or gross incompetence fails to take prompt action to correct the noncompliance.

(b) Effective/applicability date. This section is applicable beginning after the date that final regulations are published in the Federal Register.

§ 10.37 Requirements for other written advice.

(a) Requirements. A practitioner must not give written advice (including electronic communications) concerning one or more Federal tax issues if the practitioner bases the written advice on unreasonable factual or legal assumptions (including assumptions as to future events), unreasonably relies upon representations, statements, findings or agreements of the taxpayer or any other person, does not consider all relevant facts that the practitioner knows or should know, or, in evaluating a Federal tax issue, takes into account the possibility that a tax return will not be audited, that an issue will not be raised on audit, or that an issue will be resolved through settlement if raised. All facts and circumstances, including the scope of the engagement and the type and specificity of the advice sought by the client will be considered in determining whether a practitioner has failed to comply with this section. In the case of an opinion the practitioner knows or has reason to know will be used or referred to by a person other than the practitioner (or a person who is a member of, associated with, or employed by the practitioner's firm) in promoting, marketing or recommending to one or more taxpayers a partnership or other entity, investment plan or arrangement a significant purpose of which is the avoidance or evasion of any tax imposed by the Internal Revenue Code, the determination of whether a practitioner has failed to comply with this section will be made on the basis of a heightened standard of care because of the greater risk caused by the practitioner's lack of knowledge of the taxpayer's particular circumstances.

(b) **Effective date.** This section applies to written advice that is rendered after June 20, 2005.

Proposed Amendment (September 17, 2012)

§ 10.37. Requirements for written advice.

(a) **Requirements. (1)** A practitioner may give written advice (including by means of electronic communication) concerning one or more Federal tax matters subject to the requirements in paragraph (a)(2) of this section.

(2) **The practitioner must –**

(i) Base the written advice on reasonable factual and legal assumptions (including assumptions as to future events);

(ii) Reasonably consider all relevant facts that the practitioner knows or should know;

(iii) Use reasonable efforts to identify and ascertain the facts relevant to written advice on each Federal tax matter;

(iv) Not rely upon representations, statements, findings, or agreements (including projections, financial forecasts, or appraisals) of the taxpayer or any other person if reliance on them would be unreasonable; and

(v) Not, in evaluating a Federal tax matter, take into account the possibility that a tax return will not be audited or that a matter will not be raised on audit.

(3) Reliance on representations, statements, findings, or agreements is unreasonable if the practitioner knows or should know that one or more representations or assumptions on which any representation is based are incorrect or incomplete.

(b) Reliance on advice of others. A practitioner may only rely on the advice of another practitioner if the advice was reasonable and the reliance is in good faith considering all the facts and circumstances. Reliance is not reasonable when –

(1) The practitioner knows or should know that the opinion of the other practitioner should not be relied on;

(2) The practitioner knows or should know that the other practitioner is not competent or lacks the necessary qualifications to provide the advice; or

(3) The practitioner knows or should know that the other practitioner has a conflict of interest as described in this part.

(c) Standard of review. (1) In evaluating whether a practitioner giving written advice concerning one or more Federal tax matters complied with the requirements of this section, the Commissioner, or delegate, will apply a reasonableness standard, considering all facts and circumstances, including, but not limited to, the scope of the engagement and the type and specificity of the advice sought by the client.

(2) In the case of an opinion the practitioner knows or has reason to know will be used or referred to by a person other than the practitioner (or a person who is a member of, associated with, or employed by the practitioner's firm) in promoting, marketing, or recommending to one or more taxpayers a partnership or other entity, investment plan or arrangement a significant purpose of which is the avoidance or evasion of any tax imposed by the Internal Revenue Code, the determination of whether a practitioner has failed to comply with this section will be made on the basis of a heightened standard of review because of the greater risk caused by the practitioner's lack of knowledge of the taxpayer's particular circumstances.

(d) Effective/applicability date. The rules of this section will apply to written advice that is rendered after the date of publication of the Treasury decision adopting these rules as final regulations in the Federal Register.

§ 10.38. Establishment of advisory committees.

(a) Advisory committees. To promote and maintain the public's confidence in tax advisors, the Internal Revenue Service is authorized to establish one or more advisory committees composed of at least six individuals authorized to practice before the Internal Revenue Service. Membership of an advisory committee must be balanced among those who practice as attorneys, accountants, enrolled agents, enrolled actuaries, enrolled retirement plan agents, and registered tax return preparers. Under procedures prescribed by the Internal Revenue Service, an advisory committee may review and make general recommendations regarding the practices, procedures, and policies of the offices described in § 10.1.

(b) Effective/applicability date. This section is applicable beginning August 2, 2011.

§ 10.50 Sanctions.

(a) Authority to censure, suspend, or disbar. The Secretary of the Treasury, or delegate, after notice and an opportunity for a proceeding, may censure, suspend, or disbar any practitioner from practice before the Internal Revenue Service if the practitioner is shown to be incompetent or disreputable (within the meaning of § 10.51), fails to comply with any regulation in this part (under the prohibited conduct standards of § 10.52), or with intent to defraud, willfully and knowingly misleads or threatens a client or prospective client. Censure is a public reprimand.

(b) Authority to disqualify. The Secretary of the Treasury, or delegate, after due notice and opportunity for hearing, may disqualify any appraiser for a violation of these rules as applicable to appraisers.

(1) If any appraiser is disqualified pursuant to this subpart C, the appraiser is barred from presenting evidence or testimony in any administrative proceeding before the Department of Treasury or the Internal Revenue Service, unless and until authorized to do so by the Internal Revenue Service pursuant to § 10.81, regardless of whether the evidence or testimony would pertain to an appraisal made prior to or after the effective date of disqualification.

(2) Any appraisal made by a disqualified appraiser after the effective date of disqualification will not have any probative effect in any administrative proceeding before the Department of the Treasury or the Internal Revenue Service. An appraisal otherwise barred from admission into evidence pursuant to this section may be admitted into evidence solely for the purpose of determining the taxpayer's reliance in good faith on such appraisal.

(c) Authority to impose monetary penalty – (1) In general. (i) The Secretary of the Treasury, or delegate, after notice and an opportunity for a proceeding, may impose a monetary penalty on any practitioner who engages in conduct subject to sanction under paragraph (a) of this section.

(ii) If the practitioner described in paragraph (c)(1)(i) of this section was acting on behalf of an employer or any firm or other entity in connection with the conduct giving rise to the penalty, the Secretary of the Treasury, or delegate, may impose a monetary penalty on the employer, firm, or entity if it knew, or reasonably should have known, of such conduct.

(2) Amount of penalty. The amount of the penalty shall not exceed the gross income derived (or to be derived) from the conduct giving rise to the penalty.

(3) Coordination with other sanctions. Subject to paragraph (c)(2) of this section –

(i) Any monetary penalty imposed on a practitioner under this paragraph (c) may be in addition to or in lieu of any suspension, disbarment or censure and may be in addition to a penalty imposed on an employer, firm or other entity under paragraph (c)(1)(ii) of this section.

(ii) Any monetary penalty imposed on an employer, firm or other entity may be in addition to or in lieu of penalties imposed under paragraph (c)(1)(i) of this section.

(d) Authority to accept a practitioner's consent to sanction. The Internal Revenue Service may accept a practitioner's offer of consent to be sanctioned under § 10.50 in lieu of instituting or continuing a proceeding under § 10.60(a).

(e) Sanctions to be imposed. The sanctions imposed by this section shall take into account all relevant facts and circumstances.

(f) Effective/applicability date. This section is applicable to conduct occurring on or after August 2, 2011, except that paragraphs (a), (b)(2), and (e) apply to conduct occurring on or after September 26, 2007, and paragraph (c) applies to prohibited conduct that occurs after October 22, 2004.

§ 10.51. Incompetence and disreputable conduct.

(a) Incompetence and disreputable conduct. Incompetence and disreputable conduct for which a practitioner may be sanctioned under § 10.50 includes, but is not limited to –

(1) Conviction of any criminal offense under the Federal tax laws.

(2) Conviction of any criminal offense involving dishonesty or breach of trust.

(3) Conviction of any felony under Federal or State law for which the conduct involved renders the practitioner unfit to practice before the Internal Revenue Service.

(4) Giving false or misleading information, or participating in any way in the giving of false or misleading information to the Department of the Treasury or any officer or employee thereof, or to any tribunal authorized to pass upon Federal tax matters, in connection with any matter pending or likely to be pending before them, knowing the information to be false or misleading. Facts or other matters contained in testimony, Federal tax returns, financial statements, applications for enrollment, affidavits, declarations, and any other document or statement, written or oral, are included in the term "information."

(5) Solicitation of employment as prohibited under § 10.30, the use of false or misleading representations with intent to deceive a client or prospective client in order to procure employment, or intimating that the practitioner is able improperly to obtain special consideration or action from the Internal Revenue Service or any officer or employee thereof.

(6) Willfully failing to make a Federal tax return in violation of the Federal tax laws, or willfully evading, attempting to evade, or participating in any way in evading or attempting to evade any assessment or payment of any Federal tax.

(7) Willfully assisting, counseling, encouraging a client or prospective client in violating, or suggesting to a client or prospective client to violate, any Federal tax law, or knowingly counseling or suggesting to a client or prospective client an illegal plan to evade Federal taxes or payment thereof.

(8) Misappropriation of, or failure properly or promptly to remit, funds received from a client for the purpose of payment of taxes or other obligations due the United States.

(9) Directly or indirectly attempting to influence, or offering or agreeing to attempt to influence, the official action of any officer or employee of the Internal Revenue Service by the use of threats, false accusations, duress or coercion, by the offer of any special inducement or promise of an advantage, or by the bestowing of any gift, favor or thing of value.

(10) Disbarment or suspension from practice as an attorney, certified public accountant, public accountant or actuary by any duly constituted authority of any State, territory, or possession of the United States, including a Commonwealth, or the District of Columbia, any Federal court of record or any Federal agency, body or board.

(11) Knowingly aiding and abetting another person to practice before the Internal Revenue Service during a period of suspension, disbarment or ineligibility of such other person.

(12) Contemptuous conduct in connection with practice before the Internal Revenue Service, including the use of abusive language, making false accusations or statements, knowing them to be false or circulating or publishing malicious or libelous matter.

(13) Giving a false opinion, knowingly, recklessly, or through gross incompetence, including an opinion which is intentionally or recklessly misleading, or engaging in a pattern of providing incompetent opinions on questions arising under the Federal tax laws. False opinions described in this paragraph (a)(13) include those which reflect or result from a knowing misstatement of fact or law, from an assertion of a position known to be unwarranted under existing law, from counseling or assisting in conduct known to be illegal or fraudulent, from concealing matters required by law to be revealed, or from consciously disregarding information indicating that material facts expressed in the opinion or offering material are false or misleading. For purposes of this paragraph (a)(13), reckless conduct is a highly unreasonable omission or misrepresentation involving an extreme departure from the standards of ordinary care that a practitioner should observe under the circumstances. A pattern of conduct is a factor that will be taken into account in determining whether a practitioner acted knowingly, recklessly, or through gross incompetence. Gross incompetence includes conduct that reflects gross indifference, preparation which is grossly inadequate under the circumstances, and a consistent failure to perform obligations to the client.

(14) Willfully failing to sign a tax return prepared by the practitioner when the practitioner's signature is required by the Federal tax laws unless the failure is due to reasonable cause and not due to willful neglect.

(15) Willfully disclosing or otherwise using a tax return or tax return information in a manner not authorized by the Internal Revenue Code, contrary to the order of a court of competent jurisdiction, or contrary to the order of an administrative law judge in a proceeding instituted under § 10.60.

(16) Willfully failing to file on magnetic or other electronic media a tax return prepared by the practitioner when the practitioner is required to do so by the Federal tax laws unless the failure is due to reasonable cause and not due to willful neglect.

(17) Willfully preparing all or substantially all of, or signing, a tax return or claim for refund when the practitioner does not possess a current or otherwise valid preparer tax identification number or other prescribed identifying number.

(18) Willfully representing a taxpayer before an officer or employee of the Internal Revenue Service unless the practitioner is authorized to do so pursuant to this part.

(b) Effective/applicability date. This section is applicable beginning August 2, 2011.

§ 10.52 Violations subject to sanction.

(a) A practitioner may be sanctioned under § 10.50 if the practitioner –

(1) Willfully violates any of the regulations (other than § 10.33) contained in this part; or

(2) Recklessly or through gross incompetence (within the meaning of § 10.51(a)(13)) violates §§ 10.34, 10.35, 10.36 or 10.37.

(b) Effective/applicability date. This section is applicable to conduct occurring on or after September 26, 2007.

Proposed Amendment (September17, 2012)

§ 10.52. Violations subject to sanction.

(a) A practitioner may be sanctioned under § 10.50 if the practitioner –

(1) Willfully violates any of the regulations (other than § 10.33) contained in this part; or

(2) Recklessly or through gross incompetence (within the meaning of § 10.51(a)(13)) violates §§ 10.34, 10.36, or 10.37.

(b) Effective/applicability date. This section is applicable to conduct occurring on or after the date final regulations are published in the Federal Register.

§ 10.53. Receipt of information concerning practitioner.

(a) Officer or employee of the Internal Revenue Service. If an officer or employee of the Internal Revenue Service has reason to believe a practitioner has violated any provision of this part, the officer or employee will promptly make a written report of the suspected violation. The report will explain the facts and reasons upon which the officer's or employee's belief rests and must be submitted to the office(s) of the Internal Revenue Service responsible for administering or enforcing this part.

(b) Other persons. Any person other than an officer or employee of the Internal Revenue Service having information of a violation of any provision of this part may make an oral or written report of the alleged violation to the office(s) of the Internal Revenue Service responsible for administering or enforcing this part or any officer or employee of the Internal Revenue Service. If the report is made to an officer or employee of the Internal Revenue Service, the officer or employee will make a written report of the suspected violation and submit the report to the office(s) of the Internal Revenue Service responsible for administering or enforcing this part.

(c) Destruction of report. No report made under paragraph (a) or (b) of this section shall be maintained unless retention of the report is permissible under the applicable records control schedule as approved by the National Archives and Records Administration and designated in the Internal Revenue Manual. Reports must be destroyed as soon as permissible under the applicable records control schedule.

(d) Effect on proceedings under subpart D. The destruction of any report will not bar any proceeding under subpart D of this part, but will preclude the use of a copy of the report in a proceeding under subpart D of this part.

(e) Effective/applicability date. This section is applicable beginning August 2, 2011.

§ 10.60. Institution of proceeding.

(a) Whenever it is determined that a practitioner (or employer, firm or other entity, if applicable) violated any provision of the laws governing practice before the Internal Revenue Service or the regulations in this part, the practitioner may be reprimanded or, in accordance with § 10.62, subject to a proceeding for sanctions described in § 10.50.

(b) Whenever a penalty has been assessed against an appraiser under the Internal Revenue Code and an appropriate officer or employee in an office established to enforce this part determines that the appraiser acted willfully, recklessly, or through gross incompetence with respect to the proscribed conduct, the appraiser may be reprimanded or, in accordance with § 10.62, subject to a proceeding for disqualification. A proceeding for disqualification of an appraiser is instituted by the filing of a complaint, the contents of which are more fully described in § 10.62.

(c) Except as provided in § 10.82, a proceeding will not be instituted under this section unless the proposed respondent previously has been advised in writing of the law, facts and conduct warranting such action and has been accorded an opportunity to dispute facts, assert additional facts, and make arguments (including an explanation or description of mitigating circumstances).

(d) Effective/applicability date. This section is applicable beginning August 2, 2011.

§ 10.61. Conferences.

(a) In general. The Commissioner, or delegate, may confer with a practitioner, employer, firm or other entity, or an appraiser concerning allegations of misconduct irrespective of whether a proceeding has been instituted. If the conference results in a stipulation in connection with an ongoing proceeding in which the practitioner, employer, firm or other entity, or appraiser is the respondent, the stipulation may be entered in the record by either party to the proceeding.

(b) Voluntary sanction – (1) In general. In lieu of a proceeding being instituted or continued under § 10.60(a), a practitioner or appraiser (or employer, firm or other entity, if applicable) may offer a consent to be sanctioned under § 10.50.

(2) Discretion; acceptance or declination. The Commissioner, or delegate, may accept or decline the offer described in paragraph (b)(1) of this section. When the decision is to decline the offer, the written notice of declination may state that the offer described in paragraph (b)(1) of this section would be accepted if it contained different terms. The Commissioner, or delegate, has the discretion to accept or reject a revised offer submitted in response to the declination or may counteroffer and act upon any accepted counteroffer.

(c) Effective/applicability date. This section is applicable beginning August 2, 2011.

§ 10.62. Contents of complaint.

(a) Charges. A complaint must name the respondent, provide a clear and concise description of the facts and law that constitute the basis for the proceeding, and be signed by an authorized representative of the Internal Revenue Service under § 10.69(a)(1). A complaint is sufficient if it fairly informs the respondent of the charges brought so that the respondent is able to prepare a defense.

(b) Specification of sanction. The complaint must specify the sanction sought against the practitioner or appraiser. If the sanction sought is a suspension, the duration of the suspension sought must be specified.

(c) Demand for answer. The respondent must be notified in the complaint or in a separate paper attached to the complaint of the time for answering the complaint, which may not be less than 30 days from the date of service of the complaint, the name and address of the Administrative Law Judge with whom the answer must be filed, the name and address of the person representing the Internal Revenue Service to whom a copy of the answer must be served, and that a decision by default may be rendered against the respondent in the event an answer is not filed as required.

(d) Effective/applicability date. This section is applicable beginning August 2, 2011.

§ 10.63. Service of complaint; service of other papers; service of evidence in support of complaint; filing of papers.

(a) Service of complaint – (1) In general. The complaint or a copy of the complaint must be served on the respondent by any manner described in paragraphs (a)(2) or (3) of this section.

(2) Service by certified or first class mail. (i) Service of the complaint may be made on the respondent by mailing the complaint by certified mail to the last known address (as determined under section 6212 of the Internal Revenue Code and the regulations thereunder) of the respondent. Where service is by certified mail, the returned post office receipt duly signed by the respondent will be proof of service.

(ii) If the certified mail is not claimed or accepted by the respondent, or is returned undelivered, service may be made on the respondent, by mailing the complaint to the respondent by first class mail. Service by this method will be considered complete upon mailing, provided the complaint is addressed to the respondent at the respondent's last known address as determined under section 6212 of the Internal Revenue Code and the regulations thereunder.

(3) Service by other than certified or first class mail. (i) Service of the complaint may be made on the respondent by delivery by a private delivery service designated pursuant to section 7502(f) of the Internal Revenue Code to the last known address (as determined under section 6212 of the Internal Revenue Code and the regulations thereunder) of the respondent. Service by this method will be considered complete, provided the complaint is addressed to the respondent at the respondent's last known address as determined under section 6212 of the Internal Revenue Code and the regulations thereunder.

(ii) Service of the complaint may be made in person on, or by leaving the complaint at the office or place of business of, the respondent. Service by this method will be considered complete and proof of service will be a written statement, sworn or affirmed by the person who served the complaint, identifying the manner of service, including the recipient, relationship of recipient to respondent, place, date and time of service.

(iii) Service may be made by any other means agreed to by the respondent. Proof of service will be a written statement, sworn or affirmed by the person who served the complaint, identifying the manner of service, including the recipient, relationship of recipient to respondent, place, date and time of service.

(4) For purposes of this section, respondent means the practitioner, employer, firm or other entity, or appraiser named in the complaint or any other person having the authority to accept mail on behalf of the practitioner, employer, firm or other entity, or appraiser.

(b) Service of papers other than complaint. Any paper other than the complaint may be served on the respondent, or his or her authorized representative under § 10.69(a)(2) by:

(1) Mailing the paper by first class mail to the last known address (as determined under section 6212 of the Internal Revenue Code and the regulations thereunder) of the respondent or the respondent's authorized representative,

(2) Delivery by a private delivery service designated pursuant to section 7502(f) of the Internal Revenue Code to the last known address (as determined under section 6212 of the Internal Revenue Code and the regulations thereunder) of the respondent or the respondent's authorized representative, or

(3) As provided in paragraphs (a)(3)(ii) and (a)(3)(iii) of this section.

(c) Service of papers on the Internal Revenue Service. Whenever a paper is required or permitted to be served on the Internal Revenue Service in connection with a proceeding under this part, the paper will be served on the Internal Revenue Service's authorized representative under § 10.69(a)(1) at the address designated in the complaint, or at an address provided in a notice of appearance. If no address is designated in the complaint or provided in a notice of appearance, service will be made on the office(s) established to enforce this part under the authority of § 10.1, Internal Revenue Service, 1111 Constitution Avenue, NW., Washington, DC 20224.

(d) Service of evidence in support of complaint. Within 10 days of serving the complaint, copies of the evidence in support of the complaint must be served on the respondent in any manner described in paragraphs (a)(2) and (3) of this section.

(e) Filing of papers. Whenever the filing of a paper is required or permitted in connection with a proceeding under this part, the original paper, plus one additional copy, must be filed with the Administrative Law Judge at the address specified in the complaint or at an address otherwise specified by the Administrative Law Judge. All papers filed in connection with a proceeding under this part must be served on the other party, unless the Administrative Law Judge directs otherwise. A certificate evidencing such must be attached to the original paper filed with the Administrative Law Judge.

(f) Effective/applicability date. This section is applicable beginning August 2, 2011.

§ 10.64. Answer; default.

(a) Filing. The respondent's answer must be filed with the Administrative Law Judge, and served on the Internal Revenue Service, within the time specified in the complaint unless, on request or application of the respondent, the time is extended by the Administrative Law Judge.

(b) Contents. The answer must be written and contain a statement of facts that constitute the respondent's grounds of defense. General denials are not permitted. The respondent must specifically admit or deny each allegation set forth in the complaint, except that the respondent may state that the respondent is without sufficient information to admit or deny a specific allegation. The respondent, nevertheless, may not deny a material allegation in the complaint that the respondent knows to be true, or state that the respondent is without sufficient information to form a belief, when the respondent possesses the required information. The respondent also must state affirmatively any special matters of defense on which he or she relies.

(c) Failure to deny or answer allegations in the complaint. Every allegation in the complaint that is not denied in the answer is deemed admitted and will be considered proved; no further evidence in respect of such allegation need be adduced at a hearing.

(d) Default. Failure to file an answer within the time prescribed (or within the time for answer as extended by the Administrative Law Judge), constitutes an admission of the allegations of the complaint and a waiver of hearing, and the Administrative Law Judge may make the decision by default without a hearing or further procedure. A decision by default constitutes a decision under § 10.76.

(e) Signature. The answer must be signed by the respondent or the respondent's authorized representative under § 10.69(a)(2) and must include a statement directly above the signature acknowledging that the statements made in the answer are true and correct and that knowing and willful false statements may be punishable under 18 U.S.C. 1001.

(f) Effective/applicability date. This section is applicable beginning August 2, 2011.

§ 10.65. Supplemental charges.

(a) In general. Supplemental charges may be filed against the respondent by amending the complaint with the permission of the Administrative Law Judge if, for example –

(1) It appears that the respondent, in the answer, falsely and in bad faith, denies a material allegation of fact in the complaint or states that the respondent has insufficient knowledge to form a belief, when the respondent possesses such information; or

(2) It appears that the respondent has knowingly introduced false testimony during the proceedings against the respondent.

(b) Hearing. The supplemental charges may be heard with other charges in the case, provided the respondent is given due notice of the charges and is afforded a reasonable opportunity to prepare a defense to the supplemental charges.

(c) Effective/applicability date. This section is applicable beginning August 2, 2011.

§ 10.66. Reply to answer.

(a) The Internal Revenue Service may file a reply to the respondent's answer, but unless otherwise ordered by the Administrative Law Judge, no reply to the respondent's answer is required. If a reply is not filed, new matter in the answer is deemed denied.

(b) Effective/applicability date. This section is applicable beginning August 2, 2011.

§ 10.67. Proof; variance; amendment of pleadings.

In the case of a variance between the allegations in pleadings and the evidence adduced in support of the pleadings, the Administrative Law Judge, at any time before decision, may order or authorize amendment of the pleadings to conform to the evidence. The party who would otherwise be prejudiced by the amendment must be given a reasonable opportunity to address the allegations of the pleadings as amended and the Administrative Law Judge must make findings on any issue presented by the pleadings as amended.

§ 10.68. Motions and requests.

(a) Motions – (1) In general. At any time after the filing of the complaint, any party may file a motion with the Administrative Law Judge. Unless otherwise ordered by the Administrative Law Judge, motions must be in writing and must be served on the opposing party as provided in § 10.63(b). A motion must concisely specify its grounds and the relief sought, and, if appropriate, must contain a memorandum of facts and law in support.

(2) Summary adjudication. Either party may move for a summary adjudication upon all or any part of the legal issues in controversy. If the non-moving party opposes summary adjudication in the moving party's favor, the non-moving party must file a written response within 30 days unless ordered otherwise by the Administrative Law Judge.

(3) Good Faith. A party filing a motion for extension of time, a motion for postponement of a hearing, or any other non-dispositive or procedural motion must first contact the other party to determine whether there is any objection to the motion, and must state in the motion whether the other party has an objection.

(b) Response. Unless otherwise ordered by the Administrative Law Judge, the nonmoving party is not required to file a response to a motion. If the Administrative Law Judge does not order the nonmoving party to file a response, and the nonmoving party files no response, the nonmoving party is deemed to oppose the motion. If a nonmoving party does not respond within 30 days of the filing of a motion for decision by default for failure to file a timely answer or for failure to prosecute, the nonmoving party is deemed not to oppose the motion.

(c) Oral motions; oral argument – (1) The Administrative Law Judge may, for good cause and with notice to the parties, permit oral motions and oral opposition to motions.

(2) The Administrative Law Judge may, within his or her discretion, permit oral argument on any motion.

(d) Orders. The Administrative Law Judge should issue written orders disposing of any motion or request and any response thereto.

(e) Effective/applicability date. This section is applicable on September 26, 2007.

§ 10.69. Representation; ex parte communication.

(a) Representation. (1) The Internal Revenue Service may be represented in proceedings under this part by an attorney or other employee of the Internal Revenue Service. An attorney or an employee of the Internal Revenue Service representing the Internal Revenue Service in a proceeding under this part may sign the complaint or any document required to be filed in the proceeding on behalf of the Internal Revenue Service.

(2) A respondent may appear in person, be represented by a practitioner, or be represented by an attorney who has not filed a declaration with the Internal Revenue Service pursuant to § 10.3. A practitioner or an attorney representing a respondent or proposed respondent may sign the answer or any document required to be filed in the proceeding on behalf of the respondent.

(b) Ex parte communication. The Internal Revenue Service, the respondent, and any representatives of either party, may not attempt to initiate or participate in ex parte discussions concerning a proceeding or potential proceeding with the Administrative Law Judge (or any person who is likely to advise the Administrative Law Judge on a ruling or decision) in the proceeding before or during the pendency of the proceeding. Any memorandum, letter or other communication concerning the merits of the proceeding, addressed to the Administrative Law Judge, by or on behalf of any party shall be regarded as an argument in the proceeding and shall be served on the other party.

(c) Effective/applicability date. This section is applicable beginning August 2, 2011.

§ 10.70. Administrative Law Judge.

(a) Appointment. Proceedings on complaints for the sanction (as described in § 10.50) of a practitioner, employer, firm or other entity, or appraiser will be conducted by an Administrative Law Judge appointed as provided by 5 U.S.C. 3105.

(b) Powers of the Administrative Law Judge. The Administrative Law Judge, among other powers, has the authority, in connection with any proceeding under § 10.60 assigned or referred to him or her, to do the following:

(1) Administer oaths and affirmations;

(2) Make rulings on motions and requests, which rulings may not be appealed prior to the close of a hearing except in extraordinary circumstances and at the discretion of the Administrative Law Judge;

(3) Determine the time and place of hearing and regulate its course and conduct;

(4) Adopt rules of procedure and modify the same from time to time as needed for the orderly disposition of proceedings;

(5) Rule on offers of proof, receive relevant evidence, and examine witnesses;

(6) Take or authorize the taking of depositions or answers to requests for admission;

(7) Receive and consider oral or written argument on facts or law;

(8) Hold or provide for the holding of conferences for the settlement or simplification of the issues with the consent of the parties;

(9) Perform such acts and take such measures as are necessary or appropriate to the efficient conduct of any proceeding; and

(10) Make decisions.

(c) Effective/applicability date. This section is applicable on September 26, 2007.

§ 10.72. Hearings.

(a) In general – (1) Presiding officer. An Administrative Law Judge will preside at the hearing on a complaint filed under § 10.60 for the sanction of a practitioner, employer, firm or other entity, or appraiser.

(2) Time for hearing. Absent a determination by the Administrative Law Judge that, in the interest of justice, a hearing must be held at a later time, the Administrative Law Judge should, on notice sufficient to allow proper preparation, schedule the hearing to occur no later than 180 days after the time for filing the answer.

(3) Procedural requirements. (i) Hearings will be stenographically recorded and transcribed and the testimony of witnesses will be taken under oath or affirmation.

(ii) Hearings will be conducted pursuant to 5 U.S.C. 556.

(iii) A hearing in a proceeding requested under § 10.82(g) will be conducted de novo.

(iv) An evidentiary hearing must be held in all proceedings prior to the issuance of a decision by the Administrative Law Judge unless –

(A) The Internal Revenue Service withdraws the complaint;

(B) A decision is issued by default pursuant to § 10.64(d);

(C) A decision is issued under § 10.82(e);

(D) The respondent requests a decision on the written record without a hearing; or

(E) The Administrative Law Judge issues a decision under § 10.68(d) or rules on another motion that disposes of the case prior to the hearing.

(b) Cross-examination. A party is entitled to present his or her case or defense by oral or documentary evidence, to submit rebuttal evidence, and to conduct cross-examination, in the presence of the Administrative Law Judge, as may be required for a full and true disclosure of the facts. This paragraph (b) does not limit a party from presenting evidence contained within a deposition when the Administrative Law Judge determines that the deposition has been obtained in compliance with the rules of this subpart D.

(c) Prehearing memorandum. Unless otherwise ordered by the Administrative Law Judge, each party shall file, and serve on the opposing party or the opposing party's representative, prior to any hearing, a prehearing memorandum containing –

(1) A list (together with a copy) of all proposed exhibits to be used in the party's case in chief;

(2) A list of proposed witnesses, including a synopsis of their expected testimony, or a statement that no witnesses will be called;

(3) Identification of any proposed expert witnesses, including a synopsis of their expected testimony and a copy of any report prepared by the expert or at his or her direction; and

(4) A list of undisputed facts.

(d) Publicity – (1) In general. All reports and decisions of the Secretary of the Treasury, or delegate, including any reports and decisions of the Administrative Law Judge, under this subpart D are, subject to the protective measures in paragraph (d)(4) of this section, public and open to inspection within 30 days after the agency's decision becomes final.

(2) Request for additional publicity. The Administrative Law Judge may grant a request by a practitioner or appraiser that all the pleadings and evidence of the disciplinary proceeding be made available for inspection where the parties stipulate in advance to adopt the protective measures in paragraph (d)(4) of this section.

(3) Returns and return information – (i) Disclosure to practitioner or appraiser. Pursuant to section 6103(l)(4) of the Internal Revenue Code, the Secretary of the Treasury, or delegate, may disclose returns and return information to any practitioner or appraiser, or to the authorized representative of the practitioner or appraiser, whose rights are or may be affected by an administrative action or proceeding under this subpart D, but solely for use in the action or proceeding and only to the extent that the Secretary of the Treasury, or delegate, determines that the returns or return information are or may be relevant and material to the action or proceeding.

(ii) Disclosure to officers and employees of the Department of the Treasury. Pursuant to section 6103(l)(4)(B) of the Internal Revenue Code, the Secretary of the Treasury, or delegate, may disclose returns and return information to officers and employees of the Department of the Treasury for use in any action or proceeding under this subpart D, to the extent necessary to advance or protect the interests of the United States.

(iii) Use of returns and return information. Recipients of returns and return information under this paragraph (d)(3) may use the returns or return information solely in the action or proceeding, or in preparation for the action or proceeding, with respect to which the disclosure was made.

(iv) Procedures for disclosure of returns and return information. When providing returns or return information to the practitioner or appraiser, or authorized representative, the Secretary of the Treasury, or delegate, will –

(A) Redact identifying information of any third party taxpayers and replace it with a code;

(B) Provide a key to the coded information; and

(C) Notify the practitioner or appraiser, or authorized representative, of the restrictions on the use and disclosure of the returns and return information, the applicable damages remedy under section 7431 of the Internal Revenue Code, and that unauthorized disclosure of information provided by the Internal Revenue Service under this paragraph (d)(3) is also a violation of this part.

(4) Protective measures – (i) Mandatory protective order. If redaction of names, addresses, and other identifying information of third party taxpayers may still permit indirect identification of any third party taxpayer, the Administrative Law Judge will issue a protective order to ensure that the identifying information is available to the parties and the Administrative Law Judge for purposes of the proceeding, but is not disclosed to, or open to inspection by, the public.

(ii) Authorized orders. (A) Upon motion by a party or any other affected person, and for good cause shown, the Administrative Law Judge may make any order which justice requires to protect any person in the event disclosure of information is prohibited by law, privileged, confidential, or sensitive in some other way, including, but not limited to, one or more of the following –

(1) That disclosure of information be made only on specified terms and conditions, including a designation of the time or place;

(2) That a trade secret or other information not be disclosed, or be disclosed only in a designated way.

(iii) Denials. If a motion for a protective order is denied in whole or in part, the Administrative Law Judge may, on such terms or conditions as the Administrative Law Judge deems just, order any party or person to comply with, or respond in accordance with, the procedure involved.

(iv) Public inspection of documents. The Secretary of the Treasury, or delegate, shall ensure that all names, addresses or other identifying details of third party taxpayers are redacted and replaced with the code assigned to the corresponding taxpayer in all documents prior to public inspection of such documents.

(e) Location. The location of the hearing will be determined by the agreement of the parties with the approval of the Administrative Law Judge, but, in the absence of such agreement and approval, the hearing will be held in Washington, D.C.

(f) Failure to appear. If either party to the proceeding fails to appear at the hearing, after notice of the proceeding has been sent to him or her, the party will be deemed to have waived the right to a hearing and the Administrative Law Judge may make his or her decision against the absent party by default.

(g) Effective/applicability date. This section is applicable beginning August 2, 2011.

§ 10.73. Evidence.

(a) In general. The rules of evidence prevailing in courts of law and equity are not controlling in hearings or proceedings conducted under this part. The Administrative Law Judge may, however, exclude evidence that is irrelevant, immaterial, or unduly repetitious,

(b) Depositions. The deposition of any witness taken pursuant to § 10.71 may be admitted into evidence in any proceeding instituted under § 10.60.

(c) Requests for admission. Any matter admitted in response to a request for admission under § 10.71 is conclusively established unless the Administrative Law Judge on motion permits withdrawal or modification of the admission. Any admission made by a party is for the purposes of the pending action only and is not an admission by a party for any other purpose, nor may it be used against a party in any other proceeding.

(d) Proof of documents. Official documents, records, and papers of the Internal Revenue Service and the Office of Professional Responsibility are admissible in evidence without the production of an officer or employee to authenticate them. Any documents, records, and papers may be evidenced by a copy attested to or identified by an officer or employee of the Internal Revenue Service or the Treasury Department, as the case may be.

(e) Withdrawal of exhibits. If any document, record, or other paper is introduced in evidence as an exhibit, the Administrative Law Judge may authorize the withdrawal of the exhibit subject to any conditions that he or she deems proper.

(f) Objections. Objections to evidence are to be made in short form, stating the grounds for the objection. Except as ordered by the Administrative Law Judge, argument on objections will not be recorded or transcribed. Rulings on objections are to be a part of the record, but no exception to a ruling is necessary to preserve the rights of the parties.

(g) Effective/applicability date. This section is applicable on September 26, 2007.

§ 10.74. Transcript.

In cases where the hearing is stenographically reported by a Government contract reporter, copies of the transcript may be obtained from the reporter at rates not to exceed the maximum rates fixed by contract between the Government and the reporter. Where the hearing is stenographically reported by a regular employee of the Internal Revenue Service, a copy will be supplied to the respondent either without charge or upon the payment of a reasonable fee. Copies of exhibits introduced at the hearing or at the taking of depositions will be supplied to the parties upon the payment of a reasonable fee (Sec. 501, Public Law 82-137)(65 Stat. 290)(31 U.S.C. 483a).

§ 10.75. Proposed findings and conclusions.

Except in cases where the respondent has failed to answer the complaint or where a party has failed to appear at the hearing, the parties must be afforded a reasonable opportunity to submit proposed findings and conclusions and their supporting reasons to the Administrative Law Judge.

§ 10.76. Decision of Administrative Law Judge.

(a) In general – (1) Hearings. Within 180 days after the conclusion of a hearing and the receipt of any proposed findings and conclusions timely submitted by the parties, the Administrative Law Judge should enter a decision in the case. The decision must include a statement of findings and conclusions, as well as the reasons or basis for making such findings and conclusions, and an order of censure, suspension, disbarment, monetary penalty, disqualification, or dismissal of the complaint.

(2) Summary adjudication. In the event that a motion for summary adjudication is filed, the Administrative Law Judge should rule on the motion for summary adjudication within 60 days after the party in opposition files a written response, or if no written response is filed, within 90 days after the motion for summary adjudication is filed. A decision shall thereafter be rendered if the pleadings, depositions, admissions, and any other admissible evidence show that there is no genuine issue of material fact and that a decision may be rendered as a matter of law. The decision must include a statement of conclusions, as well as the reasons or basis for making such conclusions, and an order of censure, suspension, disbarment, monetary penalty, disqualification, or dismissal of the complaint.

(3) Returns and return information. In the decision, the Administrative Law Judge should use the code assigned to third party taxpayers (described in § 10.72(d)).

(b) Standard of proof. If the sanction is censure or a suspension of less than six months' duration, the Administrative Law Judge, in rendering findings and conclusions, will consider an allegation of fact to be proven if it is established by the party who is alleging the fact by a preponderance of the evidence in the record. If the sanction is a monetary penalty, disbarment or a suspension of six months or longer duration, an allegation of fact that is necessary for a finding against the practitioner must be proven by clear and convincing evidence in the record. An allegation of fact that is necessary for a finding of disqualification against an appraiser must be proven by clear and convincing evidence in the record.

(c) Copy of decision. The Administrative Law Judge will provide the decision to the Internal Revenue Service's authorized representative, and a copy of the decision to the respondent or the respondent's authorized representative.

(d) When final. In the absence of an appeal to the Secretary of the Treasury or delegate, the decision of the Administrative Law Judge will, without further proceedings, become the decision of the agency 30 days after the date of the Administrative Law Judge's decision.

(e) Effective/applicability date. This section is applicable beginning August 2, 2011.

§ 10.77. Appeal of decision of Administrative Law Judge.

(a) Appeal. Any party to the proceeding under this subpart D may appeal the decision of the Administrative Law Judge by filing a notice of appeal with the Secretary of the Treasury, or delegate deciding appeals. The notice of appeal must include a brief that states exceptions to the decision of Administrative Law Judge and supporting reasons for such exceptions.

(b) Time and place for filing of appeal. The notice of appeal and brief must be filed, in duplicate, with the Secretary of the Treasury, or delegate deciding appeals, at an address for appeals that is identified to the parties with the decision of the Administrative Law Judge. The notice of appeal and brief must be filed within 30 days of the date that the decision of the Administrative Law Judge is served on the parties. The appealing party must serve a copy of the notice of appeal and the brief to any non-appealing party or, if the party is represented, the non-appealing party's representative.

(c) Response. Within 30 days of receiving the copy of the appellant's brief, the other party may file a response brief with the Secretary of the Treasury, or delegate deciding appeals, using the address identified for appeals. A copy of the response brief must be served at the same time on the opposing party or, if the party is represented, the opposing party's representative.

(d) No other briefs, responses or motions as of right. Other than the appeal brief and response brief, the parties are not permitted to file any other briefs, responses or motions, except on a grant of leave to do so after a motion demonstrating sufficient cause, or unless otherwise ordered by the Secretary of the Treasury, or delegate deciding appeals.

(e) Additional time for briefs and responses. Notwithstanding the time for filing briefs and responses provided in paragraphs (b) and (c) of this section, the Secretary of the Treasury, or delegate deciding appeals, may, for good cause, authorize additional time for filing briefs and responses upon a motion of a party or upon the initiative of the Secretary of the Treasury, or delegate deciding appeals.

(f) Effective/applicability date. This section is applicable beginning August 2, 2011.

§ 10.78. Decision on review.

(a) Decision on review. On appeal from or review of the decision of the Administrative Law Judge, the Secretary of the Treasury, or delegate, will make the agency decision. The Secretary of the Treasury, or delegate, should make the agency decision within 180 days after receipt of the appeal.

(b) Standard of review. The decision of the Administrative Law Judge will not be reversed unless the appellant establishes that the decision is clearly erroneous in light of the evidence in the record and applicable law. Issues that are exclusively matters of law will be reviewed de novo. In the event that the Secretary of the Treasury, or delegate, determines that there are unresolved issues raised by the record, the case may be remanded to the Administrative Law Judge to elicit additional testimony or evidence.

(c) Copy of decision on review. The Secretary of the Treasury, or delegate, will provide copies of the agency decision to the authorized representative of the Internal Revenue Service and the respondent or the respondent's authorized representative.

(d) Effective/applicability date. This section is applicable beginning August 2, 2011.

§ 10.79. Effect of disbarment, suspension, or censure.

(a) Disbarment. When the final decision in a case is against the respondent (or the respondent has offered his or her consent and such consent has been accepted by the Internal Revenue Service) and such decision is for disbarment, the respondent will not be permitted to practice before the Internal Revenue Service unless and until authorized to do so by the Internal Revenue Service pursuant to § 10.81.

(b) Suspension. When the final decision in a case is against the respondent (or the respondent has offered his or her consent and such consent has been accepted by the Internal Revenue Service) and such decision is for suspension, the respondent will not be permitted to practice before the Internal Revenue Service during the period of suspension. For periods after the suspension, the practitioner's future representations may be subject to conditions as authorized by paragraph (d) of this section.

(c) Censure. When the final decision in the case is against the respondent (or the Internal Revenue Service has accepted the respondent's offer to consent, if such offer was made) and such decision is for censure, the respondent will be permitted to practice before the Internal Revenue Service, but the respondent's future representations may be subject to conditions as authorized by paragraph (d) of this section.

(d) Conditions. After being subject to the sanction of either suspension or censure, the future representations of a practitioner so sanctioned shall be subject to specified conditions designed to promote high standards of conduct. These conditions can be imposed for a reasonable period in light of the gravity of the practitioner's violations. For example, where a practitioner is censured because the practitioner failed to advise the practitioner's clients about a potential conflict of interest or failed to obtain the clients' written consents, the practitioner may be required to provide the Internal Revenue Service with a copy of all consents obtained by the practitioner for an appropriate period following censure, whether or not such consents are specifically requested.

(e) Effective/applicability date. This section is applicable beginning August 2, 2011.

§ 10.80. Notice of disbarment, suspension, censure, or disqualification.

(a) In general. On the issuance of a final order censuring, suspending, or disbarring a practitioner or a final order disqualifying an appraiser, notification of the censure, suspension, disbarment or disqualification will be given to appropriate officers and employees of the Internal Revenue Service and interested departments and agencies of the Federal government. The Internal Revenue Service may determine the manner of giving notice to the proper authorities of the State by which the censured, suspended, or disbarred person was licensed to practice.

(b) Effective/applicability date. This section is applicable beginning August 2, 2011.

§ 10.90. Records.

(a) Roster. The Internal Revenue Service will maintain and make available for public inspection in the time and manner prescribed by the Secretary, or delegate, the following rosters —

(1) Individuals (and employers, firms, or other entities, if applicable) censured, suspended, or disbarred from practice before the Internal Revenue Service or upon whom a monetary penalty was imposed.

(2) Enrolled agents, including individuals —

(i) Granted active enrollment to practice;

(ii) Whose enrollment has been placed in inactive status for failure to meet the requirements for renewal of enrollment;

(iii) Whose enrollment has been placed in inactive retirement status; and

(iv) Whose offer of consent to resign from enrollment has been accepted by the Internal Revenue Service under § 10.61.

(3) Enrolled retirement plan agents, including individuals –

(i) Granted active enrollment to practice;

(ii) Whose enrollment has been placed in inactive status for failure to meet the requirements for renewal of enrollment;

(iii) Whose enrollment has been placed in inactive retirement status; and

(iv) Whose offer of consent to resign from enrollment has been accepted under § 10.61.

(4) Registered tax return preparers, including individuals –

(i) Authorized to prepare all or substantially all of a tax return or claim for refund;

(ii) Who have been placed in inactive status for failure to meet the requirements for renewal;

(iii) Who have been placed in inactive retirement status; and

(iv) Whose offer of consent to resign from their status as a registered tax return preparer has been accepted by the Internal Revenue Service under § 10.61.

(5) Disqualified appraisers.

(6) Qualified continuing education providers, including providers –

(i) Who have obtained a qualifying continuing education provider number; and

(ii) Whose qualifying continuing education number has been revoked for failure to comply with the requirements of this part.

(b) Other records. Other records of the Director of the Office of Professional Responsibility may be disclosed upon specific request, in accordance with the applicable law.

(c) Effective/applicability date. This section is applicable beginning August 2, 2011.

UNITED STATES CODE

TITLE 26 – INTERNAL REVENUE CODE

SUBTITLE A – INCOME TAXES

Chapter 1 – Normal Taxes and Surtaxes

SUBCHAPTER A – DETERMINATION OF TAX LIABILITY

SUBCHAPTER B – COMPUTATION OF TAXABLE INCOME

SUBCHAPTER C – CORPORATE DISTRIBUTIONS AND ADJUSTMENTS

SUBCHAPTER D – DEFERRED COMPENSATION, ETC.

SUBCHAPTER E – ACCOUNTING PERIODS AND METHODS OF ACCOUNTING

SUBCHAPTER F – EXEMPT ORGANIZATIONS

SUBCHAPTER G – CORPORATIONS USED TO AVOID INCOME TAX ON SHAREHOLDERS

SUBCHAPTER H – BANKING INSTITUTIONS

SUBCHAPTER I – NATURAL RESOURCES

SUBCHAPTER J – ESTATES, TRUSTS, BENEFICIARIES, AND DECEDENTS

SUBCHAPTER K – PARTNERS AND PARTNERSHIPS

SUBCHAPTER L – INSURANCE COMPANIES

SUBCHAPTER M – REGULATED INVESTMENT COMPANIES AND REAL ESTATE INVESTMENT TRUSTS

SUBCHAPTER N – TAX BASED ON INCOME FROM SOURCES WITHIN OR WITHOUT THE UNITED STATES

SUBCHAPTER O – GAIN OR LOSS ON DISPOSITION OF PROPERTY

SUBCHAPTER P – CAPITAL GAINS AND LOSSES

SUBCHAPTER Q – READJUSTMENTS OF TAX BETWEEN YEARS AND SPECIAL LIMITATIONS

Chapter 33 – Facilities and Services

Chapter 34 – Policies Issued by Foreign Insurers

Chapter 35 – Taxes on Wagering

Chapter 36 – Certain Other Excise Taxes

Chapter 37 – Repealed – Sugar

Chapter 38 – Environmental Taxes

Chapter 39 – Registration-Required Obligations

Chapter 40 – General Provisions Relating to Occupational Taxes

Chapter 41 – Public Charities

Chapter 42 – Private Foundations and Certain Other
Tax-Exempt Organizations

Chapter 43 – Qualified Pension, Etc., Plans

Chapter 44 – Qualified Investment Entities

Chapter 45 – Provisions Relating to Expatriation Entities

Chapter 46 – Golden Parachute Payments

Chapter 47 – Certain Group Health Plans

* * *

SUBTITLE E – ALCOHOL, TOBACCO, AND CERTAIN
OTHER EXCISE TAXES

Chapter 51 – Distilled Spirits, Wines, and Beer

Chapter 52 – Tobacco Products and Cigarette Papers and Tubes

Chapter 53 – Machine Guns, Destructive Devices, and
Certain Other Firearms

Chapter 54 – Greenmail

SUBPART B – INFORMATION CONCERNING TRANSACTIONS WITH OTHER PERSONS

Chapter 62 – Time and Place for Paying Tax

SUBCHAPTER A. PLACE AND DUE DATE FOR PAYMENT OF TAX

Chapter 63 – Assessment

SUBCHAPTER A. IN GENERAL

SUBCHAPTER B. DEFICIENCY PROCEDURES IN THE CASE OF INCOME, ESTATE, GIFT, AND CERTAIN EXCISE TAXES

SUBCHAPTER C. TAX TREATMENT OF PARTNERSHIP ITEMS

SUBCHAPTER D. TREATMENT OF ELECTING LARGE PARTNERSHIPS

PART I – TREATMENT OF PARTNERSHIP ITEMS AND ADJUSTMENTS

PART II – PARTNERSHIP LEVEL ADJUSTMENTS

SUBPART A – ADJUSTMENTS BY SECRETARY

SUBPART B – CLAIMS FOR ADJUSTMENTS BY PARTNERSHIP

PART III – DEFINITIONS AND SPECIAL RULES

Chapter 64 – Collection

SUBCHAPTER A. GENERAL PROVISIONS

SUBCHAPTER E. COLLECTION OF STATE INDIVIDUAL INCOME TAXES –
[REPEALED]

Chapter 65 – Abatements, Credits, and Refunds

SUBCHAPTER A. PROCEDURE IN GENERAL

SUBCHAPTER B. RULES OF SPECIAL APPLICATION

Chapter 66 – Limitations

SUBCHAPTER A. LIMITATIONS ON ASSESSMENT AND COLLECTION

SUBCHAPTER B. LIMITATIONS ON CREDIT OR REFUND

SUBCHAPTER C. MITIGATION OF EFFECT OF PERIOD OF LIMITATIONS

SUBCHAPTER D. PERIODS OF LIMITATION IN JUDICIAL PROCEEDINGS

Chapter 67 – Interest

SUBCHAPTER A. INTEREST ON UNDERPAYMENTS

SUBCHAPTER B. INTEREST ON OVERPAYMENTS

SUBCHAPTER C. DETERMINATION OF INTEREST RATE; COMPOUNDING OF INTEREST

Chapter 68 – Additions to the Tax, Additional Amounts, and Assessable Penalties

SUBCHAPTER A. ADDITIONS TO THE TAX AND ADDITIONAL AMOUNTS

PART I – GENERAL PROVISIONS

PART II – ACCURACY-RELATED AND FRAUD PENALTIES

PART III – APPLICABLE RULES

SUBCHAPTER B. ASSESSABLE PENALTIES

PART I – GENERAL PROVISIONS

Chapter 75 – Crimes, Other Offenses, and Forfeitures

SUBCHAPTER A. CRIMES

Part I – General Provisions

Part II – Penalties Applicable to Certain Taxes

SUBCHAPTER B. OTHER OFFENSES

SUBCHAPTER C. FORFEITURES

PART I – PROPERTY SUBJECT TO FORFEITURE

PART II – PROVISIONS COMMON TO FORFEITURES

SUBCHAPTER D. MISCELLANEOUS PENALTY AND FORFEITURE PROVISIONS

Chapter 76 – Judicial Proceedings

SUBCHAPTER A. CIVIL ACTIONS BY THE UNITED STATES

SUBCHAPTER B. PROCEEDINGS BY TAXPAYERS AND THIRD PARTIES

SUBCHAPTER C. THE TAX COURT

PART I – ORGANIZATION AND JURISDICTION

PART II – PROCEDURE

PART III – MISCELLANEOUS PROVISIONS

PART IV – DECLARATORY JUDGMENTS

SUBCHAPTER D. COURT REVIEW OF TAX COURT DECISIONS

SUBCHAPTER E. BURDEN OF PROOF

Chapter 77 – Miscellaneous Provisions

Chapter 78 – Discovery of Liability and Enforcement of Title

SUBCHAPTER A. EXAMINATION AND INSPECTION

PUBLIC LAW 100-647 [H. R. 4333]
102 STAT. 3342, 3730

OMNIBUS TAXPAYER BILL OF RIGHTS
PART OF THE TECHNICAL AND MISCELLANEOUS REVENUE ACT OF 1988

(d) Table of Contents.

* * *

Subtitle J -- Taxpayer Rights and Procedures

Part I -- Taxpayer Rights

Part II -- Levy and Lien Provisions

Part III -- Proceedings by Taxpayers

Part IV -- Tax Court Jurisdiction

PUBLIC LAW 104-168 [H.R. 2337]
110 STAT. 1452

TAXPAYER BILL OF RIGHTS 2

(a) Short Title. This Act may be cited as the "Taxpayer Bill of Rights 2".

* * *

(c) Table of Contents.

* * *

TITLE XIII--REVENUE OFFSETS

Subtitle A. Application of Failure-to-Pay Penalty to Substitute Returns

Subtitle B--Excise Taxes on Amounts of Private Excess Benefits

PUBLIC LAW 105-206 [H.R. 2676]
112 STAT. 685

TAXPAYER BILL OF RIGHTS 3
PART OF THE INTERNAL REVENUE SERVICE
RESTRUCTURING AND REFORM ACT OF1998

(a)   Short Title.--This Act may be cited as the "Internal Revenue Service Restructuring and Reform Act of 1998".

* * *

(d)   Table of Contents.--The table of contents for this Act is as follows:

* * *

TITLE III--TAXPAYER PROTECTION AND RIGHTS

* * *

UNITED STATES TAX COURT
WASHINGTON, DC
www.ustaxcourt.gov

STANDING PRETRIAL ORDER

The attached Notice Setting Case for Trial notifies the parties that this case is calendared for trial at the trial session beginning on [day, date]

Communication Between the Parties. The parties shall begin discussing settlement and/or preparation of a stipulation of facts as soon as practicable. Valuation cases and reasonable compensation cases are generally susceptible of settlement, and the Court expects the parties to negotiate in good faith with this goal in mind. All minor issues should be settled so that the Court can focus on the issue(s) needing a Court decision. If a party has trouble communicating with another party or complying with this Order, the affected party should promptly advise the Court in writing, with a copy to each other party, or request a conference call for the parties and the trial Judge.

Continuances. Continuances (i.e., postponements of trial) will be granted only in exceptional circumstances. See Rule 133, Tax Court Rules of Practice and Procedure. (The Court's Rules are available at www.ustaxcourt.gov.) Even joint motions for continuance are not granted automatically.

Sanctions. The Court may impose appropriate sanctions, including dismissal, for any unexcused failure to comply with this Order. See Rule 131(b). Such failure may also be considered in relation to sanctions against and disciplinary proceedings involving counsel. See Rule 202(a).

Electronic Filing (eFiling). eFiling is required for most documents **(except the petition)** filed by parties represented by counsel in cases in which the petition is filed on or after July 1, 2010. Petitioners not represented by counsel may, but are not required to, eFile. For more information about eFiling and the Court's other electronic services, see www.ustaxcourt.gov.

To help the efficient disposition of all cases on the trial calendar:

1. **Stipulation.** It is ORDERED that all facts shall be stipulated (agreed upon in writing) to the maximum extent possible. All documents and written evidence shall be marked and stipulated in accordance with Rule 91(b), unless the evidence is to be used only to impeach (discredit) a witness. Either party may preserve objections by noting them in the stipulation. If a complete stipulation of facts is not ready for submission at the start of the trial or when otherwise ordered by the Court, and if the Court determines that this is due to lack of cooperation by either party, the Court may order sanctions against the uncooperative party.

2. **Trial Exhibits**. It is ORDERED that any documents or materials which a party expects to use (except solely for impeachment) if the case is tried, but which are not stipulated, shall be identified in writing and exchanged by the parties at least 14 days before the first day of the trial session. The Court may refuse to receive in evidence any document or material that is not so stipulated or exchanged, unless the parties have agreed otherwise or the Court so allows for good cause shown.

3. **Pretrial Memoranda.** It is ORDERED that, unless a basis of settlement (resolution of the issues) has been reached, each party shall prepare a Pretrial Memorandum containing the information in the attached form. Each party shall serve on the other party and file the Pretrial Memorandum not less than 14 days before the first day of the trial session.

4. **Final Status Reports.** It is ORDERED that, if the status of the case changes from that reported in a party's Pretrial Memorandum, the party shall submit to the undersigned and to the other party a Final Status Report containing the information in the attached form. A Final Status Report may be submitted to the Court in paper format, electronically by following the procedures in the "Final Status Report" tab on the Court's Web site or by fax sent to 202-521-3378. (Only the Final Status Report may be sent to this fax number; any other documents will be discarded.) The report must be received by the Court no later than 3 p.m. eastern time on the last business day (normally Friday) before the calendar call. The Final Status Report must be promptly submitted to the opposing party by mail, email, or fax, and a copy of the report must be given to the opposing party at the calendar call if the opposing party is present.

5. **Witnesses.** It is ORDERED that witnesses shall be identified in the Pretrial Memorandum with a brief summary of their anticipated testimony. Witnesses who are not identified will not be permitted to testify at the trial without a showing of good cause.

6. **Expert Witnesses.** It is ORDERED that unless otherwise permitted by the Court, expert witnesses shall prepare a written report which shall be submitted directly to the undersigned and served upon each other party at least 30 days before the first day of the trial session. An expert witness's testimony may be excluded for failure to comply with this Order and Rule 143(g).

7. **Settlements.** It is ORDERED that if the parties have reached a basis of settlement, a stipulated decision shall be submitted to the Court prior to or at the call of the calendar on the first day of the trial session. Additional time for submitting a stipulated decision will be granted only where it is clear that all parties have approved the settlement. The parties shall be prepared to state for the record the basis of settlement and the reasons for delay. The Court will specify the date by which the stipulated decision and any related settlement documents will be due.

8. **Time of Trial.** It is ORDERED that all parties shall be prepared for trial at any time during the trial session unless a specific date has been previously set by the Court. Your case may or may not be tried on the same date as the calendar call, and you may need to return to Court on a later date during the trial session. Thus, it may be beneficial to contact the Court in advance. Within 2 weeks before the start of the trial session, the parties may jointly contact the Judge's chambers to request a time and date certain for the trial. If practicable, the Court will attempt to accommodate the request, keeping in mind other scheduling requirements and the anticipated length of the session. Parties should jointly inform the Judge as early as possible if they expect trial to require 3 days or more.

9. **Service of Documents.** It is ORDERED that every pleading, motion, letter, or other document (with the exception of the petition and the posttrial briefs, see Rule 151(c)) submitted to the Court shall contain a certificate of service as specified in Rule 21(b), which shows that the party has given a copy of that pleading, motion, letter or other document to all other parties.

[Judge's name]
Judge

Dated:

PRETRIAL MEMORANDUM FOR   (Petitioner/Respondent)
Please type or print legibly
(This form may be expanded as necessary)

NAME OF CASE: **DOCKET NO(S).:**

ATTORNEYS:
  Petitioner: _____   Respondent: _____
  Tel. No.: _____   Tel. No.: _____

AMOUNTS IN DISPUTE:
  Year(s)/Period(s)   Deficiencies/Liabilities   Additions/Penalties

STATUS OF CASE:
  Probable Settlement_____   Probable Trial_____   Definite Trial_____

CURRENT ESTIMATE OF TRIAL TIME: _____

MOTIONS YOU EXPECT TO MAKE: (Title and brief description)

STATUS OF STIPULATION OF FACTS: Completed _____   In Process _____

ISSUES:

WITNESS(ES) YOU EXPECT TO CALL:
(Name and brief summary of expected testimony)

SUMMARY OF FACTS:
(Attach separate pages, if necessary, to inform the Court of facts in chronological narrative form)

BRIEF SYNOPSIS OF LEGAL AUTHORITIES:
(Attach separate pages, if necessary, to discuss fully your legal position)

EVIDENTIARY PROBLEMS:

DATE: _____   _____

                                                            Petitioner/Respondent

Trial Judge: **[Judge's name]**
                        United States Tax Court, [room no.]
                        400 Second Street, N.W.
                        Washington, D.C. 20217
                        [Judge's chambers phone no.]

1994 Tax Rate Tables.[1]

The following adjusted tax rate tables are prescribed in lieu of the tables in subsections (a), (b), (c), (d), and (e) of section 1 of the Code with respect to tax years beginning in 1994.

MARRIED INDIVIDUALS FILING JOINT RETURNS AND SURVIVING SPOUSES

If Taxable Income Is:	The Tax Is:
Not Over $ 38,000	15% of the taxable income
Over $ 38,000 but not over $ 91,850	$ 5,700 plus 28% of the excess over $ 38,000
Over $ 91,850 but not over $ 140,000	$ 20,778 plus 31% of the excess over $ 91,850
Over $ 140,000 but not over $250,000	$ 35,704.50 plus 36% of the excess over $ 140,000
Over $ 250,000	$ 75,304.50 plus 39.6% of the excess over $ 250,000

UNMARRIED INDIVIDUALS (OTHER THAN SURVIVING SPOUSES AND HEADS OF HOUSEHOLDS)

If Taxable Income Is:	The Tax Is:
Not Over $ 22,750	15% of the taxable income
Over $ 22,750 but not over $ 55,100	$ 3,412.50 plus 28% of the excess over $ 22,750
Over $ 55,100 but not over $ 115,000	$ 12,470.50 plus 31% of the excess over $ 55,100
Over $ 115,000 but not over $ 250,000	$ 31,039.50 plus 36% of the excess over $ 115,000
Over $ 250,000	$ 79,639.50 plus 39.6% of the excess over $ 250,000

MARRIED INDIVIDUALS FILING SEPARATE RETURNS

If Taxable Income Is:	The Tax Is:
Not Over $ 19,000	15% of the taxable income
Over $ 19,000 but not over $ 45,925	$ 2,850 plus 28% of the excess over $ 19,000
Over $ 45,925 but not over $ 70,000	$ 10,389 plus 31% of the excess over $ 45,925
Over $ 70,000 but not over $ 125,000	$ 17,852.25 plus 36% of the excess over $ 70,000
Over $ 125,000	$ 37,652.25 plus 39.6% of the excess over $ 125,000

---

[1] Rev. Proc. 93-49, 1993-2 C.B. 581.

1995 Tax Rate Tables[2]

The following adjusted tax rate tables are prescribed in lieu of the tables in subsections (a), (b), (c), (d), and (c) of *§ 1 of the Internal Revenue Code* with respect to tax years beginning in 1995.

MARRIED INDIVIDUALS FILING JOINT RETURNS AND SURVIVING SPOUSES

If Taxable Income Is:	The Tax Is:
Not Over $ 39,000	15% of the taxable income
Over $ 39,000 but not over $ 94,250	$ 5,850 plus 28% of the excess over $ 39,000
Over $ 94,250 but not over $ 143,600	$ 21,320 plus 31% of the excess over $ 94,250
Over $ 143,600 but not over $ 256,500	$ 36,618.50 plus 36% of the excess over $ 143,600
Over $ 256,500	$ 77,262.50 plus 39.6% of the excess over $ 256,500

UNMARRIED INDIVIDUALS (OTHER THAN SURVIVING SPOUSES AND HEADS OF HOUSEHOLDS)

If Taxable Income Is:	The Tax Is:
Not Over $ 23,350	15% of the taxable income
Over $ 23.350 but not over $ 56,550	$ 3,502.50 plus 28% of the excess over $ 23,350
Over $ 56,550 but not over $ 117,950	$ 12,798.50 plus 31% of the excess over $ 56,550
Over $ 117,950 but not over $ 256,500	$ 31,832.50 plus 36% of the excess over $ 117,950
Over $ 256,500	$ 81,710.50 plus 39.6% of the excess over $ 256,500

MARRIED INDIVIDUALS FILING SEPARATE RETURNS

If Taxable Income Is:	The Tax Is:
Not Over $ 19,500	15% of the taxable income
Over $ 19,500 but not over $ 47,125	$ 2,925 plus 28% of the excess over $ 19,500
Over $ 47,125 but not over $ 71,800	$ 10,660 plus 31% of the excess over $ 47,125
Over $ 71,800 but not over $ 128,250	$ 18,309.25 plus 36% of the excess over $ 71,800
Over $ 128,250	$ 38,631.25 plus 39.6% of the excess over $ 128,250

---

[2] Rev. Proc. 94-72, 1994-2 C.B. 811.

1996 Tax Rate Tables[3]

The following adjusted tax rate tables are prescribed in lieu of the tables in subsections (a), (b), (c), (d), and (e) of § 1 of the Code with respect to tax years beginning in 1996.

MARRIED INDIVIDUALS FILING JOINT RETURNS AND SURVIVING SPOUSES

If Taxable Income Is:	The Tax Is:
Not Over $ 40,100	15% of the taxable income
Over $ 40,100 but not over $ 96,900	$ 6,015 plus 28% of the excess over $ 40,100
Over $ 96,900 but not over $ 147,700	$ 21,919 plus 31% of the excess over $ 96,900
Over $ 147,700 but not over $ 236,750	$ 37,667 plus 36% of the excess over $ 147,700
Over $ 263,750	$ 79,445 plus 39.6% of the excess over $ 263,750

UNMARRIED INDIVIDUALS (OTHER THAN SURVIVING SPOUSES AND HEADS OF HOUSEHOLDS)

If Taxable Income Is:	The Tax Is:
Not Over $ 24,000	15% of the taxable income
Over $ 24,000 but not over $ 58,150	$ 3,600 plus 28% of the excess over $ 24,000
Over $ 58,150 but not over $ 121,300	$ 13,162 plus 31% of the excess over $ 58,150
Over $ 121,300 but not over $ 263,750	$ 32,738.50 plus 36% of the excess over $ 121,300
Over $ 263,750	$ 84,020.50 plus 39.6% of the excess over $ 263,750

MARRIED INDIVIDUALS FILING SEPARATE RETURNS

If Taxable Income Is:	The Tax Is:
Not Over $ 20,050	15% of the taxable income
Over $ 20,050 but not over $ 48,450	$ 3,007.50 plus 28% of the excess over $ 20,050
Over $ 48,450 but not over $ 73,850	$ 10,959.50 plus 31% of the excess over $ 48,450
Over $ 73,850 but not over $ 131,875	$ 18,833.50 plus 36% of the excess over $ 73,850
Over $ 131,875	$ 39,722.50 plus 39.6% of the excess over $ 131,875

---

[3] Rev. Proc. 95-53, 1995-2 C.B. 445.

1997 Tax Rate Tables[4]

The following adjusted tax rate tables are prescribed in lieu of the tables in subsections (a), (b), (c), (d), and (e) of § 1 of the Code with respect to tax years beginning in 1997.

MARRIED INDIVIDUALS FILING JOINT RETURNS AND SURVIVING SPOUSES

If Taxable Income Is:	The Tax Is:
Not Over $ 41,200	15% of the taxable income
Over $ 41,200 but not over $ 99,600	$ 6,180 plus 28% of the excess over $ 41,200
Over $ 99,600 but not over $ 151,750	$ 22,532 plus 31% of the excess over $ 99,600
Over $ 151,750 but not over $ 271,050	$ 38,698.50 plus 36% of the excess over $ 151,750
Over $ 271,050	$ 81,646.50 plus 39.6% of the excess over $ 271,050

UNMARRIED INDIVIDUALS (OTHER THAN SURVIVING SPOUSES AND HEADS OF HOUSEHOLDS)

If Taxable Income Is:	The Tax Is:
Not Over $ 24,650	15% of the taxable income
Over $ 24,650 but not over $ 59,750	$ 3,697.50 plus 28% of the excess over $ 24,650
Over $ 59,750 but not over $ 124,650	$ 13,525.50 plus 31% of the excess over $ 59,750
Over $ 124,650 but not over $ 271,050	$ 33,644.50 plus 36% of the excess over $ 124,650
Over $ 271,050	$ 86,348.50 plus 39.6% of the excess over $ 271,050

MARRIED INDIVIDUALS FILING SEPARATE RETURNS

If Taxable Income Is:	The Tax Is:
Not Over $ 20,600	15% of the taxable income
Over $ 20,600 but not over $ 49,800	$ 3,090 plus 28% of the excess over $ 20,600
Over $ 49,800 but not over $ 75,875	$ 11,266 plus 31% of the excess over $ 49,800
Over $ 75,875 but not over $ 135,525	$ 19,349.25 plus 36% of the excess over $ 75,875
Over $ 135,525	$ 40,823.25 plus 39.6% of the excess over $ 135,525

---

[4] Rev. Proc. 96-59, 1996-2 C.B. 392.

1998 Tax Rate Tables[5]

For tax years beginning in 1998, the tax rate tables under section 1 are as follows:

MARRIED INDIVIDUALS FILING JOINT RETURNS AND SURVIVING SPOUSES

If Taxable Income Is:	The Tax Is:
Not Over $ 42,350	15% of the taxable income
Over $ 42,350 but not over $ 102,300	$ 6,352.50 plus 28% of the excess over $ 42,350
Over $ 102,300 but not over $ 155,950	$23,138.50 plus 31% of the excess over $ 102,300
Over $ 155,950 but not over $ 278,450	$39,770 plus 36% of the excess over $ 155,950
Over $ 278,450	$83,870 plus 39.6% of the excess over $ 278,450

UNMARRIED INDIVIDUALS (OTHER THAN SURVIVING SPOUSES AND HEAD OF HOUSEHOLDS)

If Taxable Income Is:	The Tax Is:
Not Over $ 25,350	15% of the taxable income
Over $ 25,350 but not over $ 61,400	$ 3,802.50 plus 28% of the excess over $ 25,350
Over $ 61,400 but not over $ 128,100	$ 13,896.50 plus 31% of the excess over $ 61,400
Over $ 128,100 but not over $ 278,450	$ 34,573.50 plus 36% of the excess over $ 128,100
Over $ 278,450	$ 88,699.50 plus 39.6% of the excess over $278,450

MARRIED INDIVIDUALS FILING SEPARATE RETURNS

If Taxable Income Is:	The Tax Is:
Not Over $ 21,175	15% if the taxable income
Over $ 21,175 but not over $ 51,150	$ 3,176.25 plus 28% of the excess over $ 21,175
Over $ 51,150 but not over $ 77,975	$11,569.25 plus 31% of the excess over $ 51,150
Over $ 77,975 but not over $ 139,225	$ 19,885 plus 36% of the excess over $ 77,975
Over $ 139,225	$41,935 plus 39.6% of the excess over $139,225

---

[5] Rev. Proc. 97-57, 1997-2 C.B. 584.

1999 Tax Rate Tables[6]

For tax years beginning in 1999, the tax rate tables under § 1 are as follows:

MARRIED INDIVIDUALS FILING JOINT RETURNS AND SURVIVING SPOUSES

If Taxable Income Is:	The Tax Is:
Not Over $ 43,050	15% of the taxable income
Over $ 43,050 but not over $ 104,050	$ 6,457.50 plus 28% of the excess over $ 43,050
Over $ 104,050 but not over $ 158,550	$ 23,537.50 plus 31% of the excess over $ 104,050
Over $ 158,550 but not over $ 283,150	$ 40,432.50 plus 36% of the excess over $ 158,550
Over $ 283,150	$ 85,288.50 plus 39.6% of the excess over $ 283,150

UNMARRIED INDIVIDUALS (OTHER THAN SURVIVING SPOUSES AND HEADS OF HOUSEHOLDS)

If Taxable Income Is:	The Tax Is:
Not Over $ 25,750	15% of the taxable income
Over $ 25,750 but not over $ 62,450	$ 3,862.50 plus 28% of the excess over $ 25,750
Over $ 62,450 but not over $ 130,250	$ 14,138.50 plus 31% of the excess over $ 62,450
Over $ 130,250 but not over $ 283,150	$ 35,156.50 plus 36% of the excess over $ 130,250
Over $ 283,150	$ 90,200.50 plus 39.6% of the excess over $ 283,150

MARRIED INDIVIDUALS FILING SEPARATE RETURNS

If Taxable Income Is:	The Tax Is:
Not Over $ 21,525	15% of the taxable income
Over $ 21,525 but not over $ 52,025	$ 3,228.75 plus 28% of the excess over $ 21,525
Over $ 52,025 but not over $ 79,275	$ 11,768.75 plus 31% of the excess over $ 52,025
Over $ 79,275 but not over $ 141,575	$ 20,216.25 plus 36% of the excess over $ 79,275
Over $ 141,575	$ 42,644.25 plus 39.6% of the excess over $ 141,575

---

[6] Rev. Proc. 98-61, 1998-2 C.B. 811.

2000 Tax Rate Tables[7]

For tax years beginning in 2000, the tax rate tables under § 1 are as follows:

MARRIED INDIVIDUALS FILING JOINT RETURNS AND SURVIVING SPOUSES

If Taxable Income Is:	The Tax Is:
Not Over $ 43,850	15% of the taxable income
Over $ 43,850 but not over $ 105,950	$ 6,577.50 plus 28% of the excess over $ 43,850
Over $ 105,950 but not over $ 161,450	$ 23,965.50 plus 31% of the excess over $ 105,950
Over $ 161,450 but not over $ 288,350	$ 41,170.50 plus 36% of the excess over $ 161,450
Over $ 288,350	$ 86,854.50 plus 39.6% of the excess over $ 288,350

UNMARRIED INDIVIDUALS (OTHER THAN SURVIVING SPOUSES AND HEADS OF HOUSEHOLDS)

If Taxable Income Is:	The Tax Is:
Not Over $ 26,250	15% of the taxable income
Over $ 26,250 but not over $ 63,550	$ 3,937.50 plus 28% of the excess over $ 26,250
Over $ 63,550 but not over $ 132,600	$ 14,381.50 plus 31% of the excess over $ 63,550
Over $ 132,600 but not over $ 288,350	$ 35,787 plus 36% of the excess over $ 132,600
Over $ 288,350	$ 91,857 plus 39.6% of the excess over $ 288,350

MARRIED INDIVIDUALS FILING SEPARATE RETURNS

If Taxable Income Is:	The Tax Is:
Not Over $ 21,925	15% of the taxable income
Over $ 21,925 but not over $ 52,975	$ 3,288.75 plus 28% of the excess over $ 21,925
Over $ 52,975 but not over $ 80,725	$ 11,982.75 plus 31% of the excess over $ 52,975
Over $ 80,725 but not over $ 144,175	$ 20,585.25 plus 36% of the excess over $ 80,725
Over $ 144,175	$ 43,427.25 plus 39.6% of the excess over $ 144,175

---

[7] Rev. Proc. 99-42, 1999-46 I.R.B. 568.

2001 Tax Rate Tables[8]

For tax years beginning in 2001, the tax rate tables under § 1 are as follows:

MARRIED INDIVIDUALS FILING JOINT RETURNS AND SURVIVING SPOUSES

If Taxable Income Is	The Tax Is:
Not Over $45,200	15% of the taxable income
Over $45,200 but not over $105,950	$6,577.50 plus 28% of the excess over $43,850
Over $105,950 but not over $161,450	$23,965.50 plus 31% of the excess over $105,950
Over $161,450 but not over $288,350	$41,170.50 plus 36% of the excess over $161,450
Over $288,350	$86,854.50 plus 39.6% of the excess over $288,350

UNMARRIED INDIVIDUALS (OTHER THAN SURVIVING SPOUSE AND HEADS OF HOUSEHOLDS)

If Taxable Income Is	The Tax Is:
Not Over $26,250	15% of the taxable income
Over $26,250 but not over $63,550	$3,937.50 plus 28% of the excess over $26,250
Over $63,550 but not over $132,600	$14,381.50 plus 31% of the excess over $63,550
Over $132,600 but not over $288,350	$35,787 plus 36% of the excess over $132,600
Over $288,350	$91,857 plus 39.6% of the excess over $288,350

MARRIED INDIVIDUALS FILING SEPARATE RETURNS

If Taxable Income Is:	The Tax Is:
Not Over $21,925	15% of the taxable income
Over $21,925 but not over $52,975	$3,288.75 plus 28% of the excess over $21,925
Over $52,975 but not over $80,725	$11,982.75 plus 31% of the excess over $52,975
Over $80,725 but not over $144,175	$20,585.25 plus 36% of the excess over $80,725
Over $144,175	$43,427.25 plus 39.6% of the excess over $144,175

---

[8] Rev. Proc. 2001-13, 2001-1 C.B. 337.

2002 Tax Rate Tables[9]

For tax years beginning in 2002, the tax rate tables under § 1 are as follows:

MARRIED INDIVIDUALS FILING JOINT RETURNS AND SURVIVING SPOUSES

If Taxable Income Is:	The Tax Is:
Not Over $12,000	10% of the taxable income
Over $12,000 but not over $46,700	$1,200 plus 15% of excess over $12,000
Over $46,700 but not over $112,850	$6,405 plus 27% of excess over $46,700
Over $112,850 but not over $171,950	$24,265.50 plus 30% of excess over $112,850
Over $171,950 but not over $307,050	$41,995.50 plus 35% of excess over $171,950
Over $307,050	$89,280.50 plus 38.6% of excess over $307,050

UNMARRIED INDIVIDUALS (OTHER THAN SURVIVING SPOUSE AND HEADS OF HOUSEHOLDS)

If Taxable Income Is:	The Tax Is:
Not over $6,000	10% of the taxable income
Over $6,000 but not over $27,950	$600 plus 15% of the excess over $6,000
Over $27,950 but not over $67,700	$3,892.50 plus 27% of the excess over $27,950
Over $67,700 but not over $141,250	$14,625 plus 30% of the excess over $67,700
Over $141,250 but not over $307,050	$36,690 plus 35% of the excess over $141,250
Over $307,050	$94,720 plus 38.6% of the excess over $307,050

MARRIED INDIVIDUALS FILING SEPARATE RETURNS

If Taxable Income Is:	The Tax Is:
Not Over $6,000	10% of the taxable income
Over $6,000 but not over $23,350	$600.00 plus 15% of the excess over $6,000
Over $23,350 but not over $56,425	$3,202.50 plus 27% of the excess over $23,350
Over $56,425 but not over $85,975	$12,132.75 plus 30% of the excess over $56,425
Over $85,975 but not over $153,525	$20,997.75 plus 35% of the excess over $85,975
Over $153,525	$44,640.25 plus 38.6% of the excess over $153,525

---

[9] Rev. Proc. 2001-59, 2001-2 C.B. 623.

2003 Tax Rate Tables[10]

For taxable years beginning in 2003, the tax rate tables under § 1 are as follows:

MARRIED INDIVIDUALS FILING JOINT RETURNS AND SURVIVING SPOUSES

If Taxable Income Is:	The Tax Is:
Not Over $12,000	10% of the taxable income
Over $12,000 but not over $47,450	$1,200 plus 15% of excess over $12,000
Over $47,450 but not over $114,650	$6,517.50 plus 27% of excess over $47,450
Over $114,650 but not over $174,700	$24,661.50 plus 30% of excess over $114,650
Over $174,700 but not over $311,950	$42,676.50 plus 35% of excess over $174,700
Over $311,950	$90,714 plus 38.6% of excess over $311,950

UNMARRIED INDIVIDUALS (OTHER THAN SURVIVING SPOUSE AND HEADS OF HOUSEHOLDS)

If Taxable Income Is:	The Tax Is:
Not over $6,000	10% of the taxable income
Over $6,000 but not over $28,400	$600 plus 15% of the excess over $6,000
Over $28,400 but not over $68,800	$3,960 plus 27% of the excess over $28,400
Over $68,800 but not over $143,500	$14,868 plus 30% of the excess over $68,800
Over $143,500 but not over $311,950	$37,278 plus 35% of the excess over $143,500
Over $311,950	$96,235.50 plus 38.6% of the excess over $311,950

MARRIED INDIVIDUALS FILING SEPARATE RETURNS

If Taxable Income Is:	The Tax Is:
Not Over $6,000	10% of the taxable income
Over $6,000 but not over $23,725	$600 plus 15% of the excess over $6,000
Over $23,725 but not over $57,325	$3,258.75 plus 27% of the excess over $23,725
Over $57,325 but not over $87,350	$12,330.75 plus 30% of the excess over $57,325
Over $87,350 but not over $155,975	$21,338.25 plus 35% of the excess over $87,350
Over $155,975	$45,357 plus 38.6% of the excess over $155,975

---

[10] Rev. Proc. 2002-70, 2002-2 C.B. 845.

2004 Tax Rate Tables[11]

For taxable years beginning in 2004, the tax rate tables under § 1 are as follows:

MARRIED INDIVIDUALS FILING JOINT RETURNS AND SURVIVING SPOUSES

If Taxable Income Is:	The Tax Is:
Not Over $14,300	10% of the taxable income
Over $14,300 but not over $58,100	$1,430 plus 15% of excess over $14,300
Over $58,100 but not over $117,250	$8,000 plus 25% of excess over $58,100
Over $117,250 but not over $178,650	$22,787.50 plus 28% of excess over $117,250
Over $178,650 but not over $319,100	$39,979.50 plus 33% of excess over $178,650
Over $319,100	$86,328 plus 35% of excess over $319,100

UNMARRIED INDIVIDUALS (OTHER THAN SURVIVING SPOUSE AND HEADS OF HOUSEHOLDS)

If Taxable Income Is:	The Tax Is:
Not over $7,150	10% of the taxable income
Over $7,150 but not over $29,050	$715 plus 15% of the excess over $7,150
Over $29,050 but not over $70,350	$4,000 plus 25% of the excess over $29,050
Over $70,350 but not over $146,750	$14,325 plus 28% of the excess over $70,350
Over $146,750 but not over $319,100	$35,717 plus 33% of the excess over $146,750
Over $319,100	$92,592.50 plus 35% of the excess over $319,100

MARRIED INDIVIDUALS FILING SEPARATE RETURNS

If Taxable Income Is:	The Tax Is:
Not Over $7,150	10% of the taxable income
Over $7,150 but not over $29,050	$715 plus 15% of the excess over $7,150
Over $29,050 but not over $58,625	$4,000 plus 25% of the excess over $29,050
Over $58,625 but not over $89,325	$11,393.75 plus 28% of the excess over $58,625
Over $89,325 but not over $159,550	$19,989.75 plus 33% of the excess over $89,325
Over $159,550	$43,164 plus 35% of the excess over $159,550

---

[11] Rev. Proc. 2003-58, 2003-2 C.B. 1184.

2005 Tax Rate Tables[12]

For taxable years beginning in 2005, the tax rate tables under § 1 are as follows:

MARRIED INDIVIDUALS FILING JOINT RETURNS AND SURVIVING SPOUSES

If Taxable Income Is:	The Tax Is:
Not Over $14,600	10% of the taxable income
Over $14,600 but not over $59,400	$1,460 plus 15% of the excess over $14,600
Over $59,400 but not over $119,950	$8,180 plus 25% of the excess over $59,400
Over $119,950 but not over $182,800	$23,317.50 plus 28% of the excess over $119,950
Over $182,800 but not over $326,450	$40,915.50 plus 33% of the excess over $182,800
Over $326,450	$88,320 plus 35% of the excess over $326,450

UNMARRIED INDIVIDUALS (OTHER THAN SURVIVING SPOUSE AND HEADS OF HOUSEHOLDS).

If Taxable Income Is:	The Tax Is:
Not Over $7,300	10% of the taxable income
Over $7,300 but not over $29,700	$730 plus 15% of the excess over $7,300
Over $29,700 but not over $71,950	$4,090 plus 25% of the excess over $29,700
Over $71,950 but not over $150,150	$14,652.50 plus 28% of the excess over $71,950
Over $150,150 but not over $326,450	$36,548.50 plus 33% of the excess over $150,150
Over $326,450	$94,727.50 plus 35% of the excess over $326,450

MARRIED INDIVIDUALS FILING SEPARATE RETURNS

If Taxable Income Is:	The Tax Is:
Not Over $7,300	10% of the taxable income
Over $7,300 but not over $29,700	$730 plus 15% of the excess over $7,300
Over $29,700 but not over $59,975	$4,090 plus 25% of the excess over $29,700
Over $59,975 but not over $91,400	$11,658.75 plus 28% of the excess over $59,975
Over $91,400 but not over $163,225	$20,457.75 plus 33% of the excess over $91,400
Over $163,225	$44,160 plus 35% of the excess over $163,225

---

[12] Rev. Proc. 2004-71, 2004-2 C.B. 970.

2006 Tax Rate Tables[13]

For taxable years beginning in 2006, the tax rate tables under § 1 are as follows:

MARRIED INDIVIDUALS FILING JOINT RETURNS AND SURVIVING SPOUSES

If Taxable Income Is:	The Tax Is:
Not Over $15,100	10% of the taxable income
Over $15,100 but not over $61,300	$1,510 plus 15% of the excess over $15,100
Over $61,300 but not over $123,700	$8,440 plus 25% of the excess over $61,300
Over $123,700 but not over $188,450	$24,040 plus 28% of the excess over $123,700
Over $188,450 but not over $336,550	$42,170 plus 33% of the excess over $188,450
Over $336,550	$91,043 plus 35% of the excess over $336,550

UNMARRIED INDIVIDUALS (OTHER THAN SURVIVING SPOUSE AND HEADS OF HOUSEHOLDS).

If Taxable Income Is:	The Tax Is:
Not Over $7,550	10% of the taxable income
Over $7,550 but not over $30,650	$755 plus 15% of the excess over $7,550
Over $30,650 but not over $74,200	$4,220 plus 25% of the excess over $30,650
Over $74,200 but not over $154,800	$15,107.50 plus 28% of the excess over $74,200
Over $154,800 but not over $336,550	$37,675.50 plus 33% of the excess over $154,800
Over $336,550	$97,653 plus 35% of the excess over $336,550

MARRIED INDIVIDUALS FILING SEPARATE RETURNS

If Taxable Income Is:	The Tax Is:
Not Over $7,550	10% of the taxable income
Over $7,550 but not over $30,650	$755 plus 15% of the excess over $7,550
Over $30,650 but not over $61,850	$4,220 plus 25% of the excess over $30,650
Over $61,850 but not over $94,225	$12,020 plus 28% of the excess over $61,850
Over $94,225 but not over $168,275	$21,085 plus 33% of the excess over $94,225
Over $168,275	$45,521.50 plus 35% of the excess over $168,275

---

[13] Rev. Proc. 2005-70, 2005-2 C.B. 979.

2007 Tax Rate Tables[14]

For taxable years beginning in 2007, the tax rate tables under § 1 are as follows:

MARRIED INDIVIDUALS FILING JOINT RETURNS AND SURVIVING SPOUSES

If Taxable Income Is:	The Tax Is:
Not Over $15,650	10% of the taxable income
Over $15,650 but not over $63,700	$1,565 plus 15% of the excess over $15,650
Over $63,700 but not over $128,500	$8,772.50 plus 25% of the excess over $63,700
Over $128,500 but not over $195,850	$24,972.50 plus 28% of the excess over $128,500
Over $195,850 but not over $349,700	$43,830.50 plus 33% of the excess over $195,850
Over $349,700	$94,601 plus 35% of the excess over $349,700

UNMARRIED INDIVIDUALS (OTHER THAN SURVIVING SPOUSES AND HEADS OF HOUSEHOLDS).

If Taxable Income Is:	The Tax Is:
Not Over $7,825	10% of the taxable income
Over $7,825 but not over $31,850	$782.50 plus 15% of the excess over $7,825
Over $31,850 but not over $77,100	$4,386.25 plus 25% of the excess over $31,850
Over $77,100 but not over $160,850	$15,698.75 plus 28% of the excess over $77,100
Over $160,850 but not over $349,700	$39,148.75 plus 33% of the excess over $160,850
Over $349,700	$101,469.25 plus 35% of the excess over $349,700

MARRIED INDIVIDUALS FILING SEPARATE RETURNS

If Taxable Income Is:	The Tax Is:
Not Over $7,825	10% of the taxable income
Over $7,825 but not over $31,850	$782.50 plus 15% of the excess over $7,825
Over $31,850 but not over $64,250	$4,386.25 plus 25% of the excess over $31,850
Over $64,250 but not over $97,925	$12,486.25 plus 28% of the excess over $64,250
Over $97,925 but not over $174,850	$21,915.25 plus 33% of the excess over $97,925
Over $174,850	$47,300.50 plus 35% of the excess over $174,850

---

[14] Rev. Proc. 2006-53, 2006-2 C.B. 996.

2008 Tax Rate Tables[15]

For taxable years beginning in 2008, the tax rate tables under § 1 are as follows:

MARRIED INDIVIDUALS FILING JOINT RETURNS AND SURVIVING SPOUSES.

If Taxable Income Is:	The Tax Is:
Not over $16,050	10% of the taxable income
Over $16,050 but not over $65,100	$1,605 plus 15% of the excess over $16,050
Over $65,100 but not over $131,450	$8,962.50 plus 25% of the excess over $65,100
Over $131,450 but not over $200,300	$25,550 plus 28% of the excess over $131,450
Over $200,300 but not over $357,700	$44,828 plus 33% of the excess over $200,300
Over $357,700	$96,770 plus 35% of the excess over $357,700

UNMARRIED INDIVIDUALS (OTHER THAN SURVIVING SPOUSES AND HEADS OF HOUSEHOLDS).

If Taxable Income Is:	The Tax Is:
Not over $8,025	10% of the taxable income
Over $8,025 but not over $32,550	$802.50 plus 15% of the excess over $8,025
Over $32,550 but not over $78,850	$4,481.25 plus 25% of the excess over $32,550
Over $78,850 but not over $164,550	$16,056.25 plus 28% of the excess over $78,850
Over $164,550 but not over $357,700	$40,052.25 plus 33% of the excess over $164,550
Over $357,700	$103,791.75 plus 35% of the excess over $357,700

MARRIED INDIVIDUALS FILING SEPARATE RETURNS.

If Taxable Income Is:	The Tax Is:
Not over $8,025	10% of the taxable income
Over $8,025 but not over $32,550	$802.50 plus 15% of the excess over $8,025
Over $32,550 but not over $65,725	$4,481.25 plus 25% of the excess over $32,550
Over $65,725 but not over $100,150	$12,775 plus 28% of the excess over $65,725
Over $100,150 but not over $178,850	$22,414 plus 33% of the excess over $100,150
Over $178,850	$48,385 plus 35% of the excess over $178,850

---

[15] Rev. Proc. 2007-66, 2007-2 C.B. 970.

2009 Tax Rate Tables[16]

For taxable years beginning in 2009, the tax rate tables under § 1 are as follows:

MARRIED INDIVIDUALS FILING JOINT RETURNS AND SURVIVING SPOUSES.

If Taxable Income Is:	The Tax Is:
Not over $16,700	10% of the taxable income
Over $16,700 but not over $67,900	$1,670 plus 15% of the excess over $16,700
Over $67,900 but not over $137,050	$9,350 plus 25% of the excess over $67,900
Over $137,050 but not over $208,850	$26,637.50 plus 28% of the excess over $137,050
Over $208,850 but not over $372,950	$46,741.50 plus 33% of the excess over $208,850
Over $372,950	$100,894.50 plus 35% of the excess over $372,950

UNMARRIED INDIVIDUALS (OTHER THAN SURVIVING SPOUSES AND HEADS OF HOUSEHOLDS).

If Taxable Income Is:	The Tax Is:
Not over $8,350	10% of the taxable income
Over $8,350 but not over $33,950	$835 plus 15% of the excess over $8,350
Over $33,950 but not over $82,250	$4,675 plus 25% of the excess over $33,950
Over $82,250 but not over $171,550	$16,750 plus 28% of the excess over $82,250
Over $171,550 but not over $372,950	$41,754 plus 33% of the excess over $171,550
Over $372,950	$108,216 plus 35% of the excess over $372,950

MARRIED INDIVIDUALS FILING SEPARATE RETURNS.

If Taxable Income Is:	The Tax Is:
Not over $8,350	10% of the taxable income
Over $8,350 but not over $33,950	$835 plus 15% of the excess over $8,350
Over $33,950 but not over $68,525	$4,675 plus 25% of the excess over $33,950
Over $68,525 but not over $104,425	$13,318.75 plus 28% of the excess over $68,525
Over $104,425 but not over $186,475	$23,370.75 plus 33% of the excess over $104,425
Over $186,475	$50,447.25 plus 35% of the excess over $186,475

---

[16] Rev. Proc. 2008-66, 2008-2 C.B. 1107.

2010 Tax Rate Tables[17]

For taxable years beginning in 2010, the tax rate tables under § 1 are as follows:

MARRIED INDIVIDUALS FILING JOINT RETURNS AND SURVIVING SPOUSES

If Taxable Income Is:	The Tax Is:
Not over $16,750	10% of the taxable income
Over $16,750 but not over $68,000	$1,675 plus 15% of the excess over $16,750
Over $68,000 but not over $137,300	$9,362.50 plus 25% of the excess over $68,000
Over $137,300 but not over $209,250	$26,687.50 plus 28% of the excess over $137,300
Over $209,250 but not over $373,650	$46,833.50 plus 33% of the excess over $209,250
Over $373,650	$101,085.50 plus 35% of the excess over $373,650

UNMARRIED INDIVIDUALS (OTHER THAN SURVIVING SPOUSES AND HEADS OF HOUSEHOLDS)

If Taxable Income Is:	The Tax Is:
Not over $8,375	10% of the taxable income
Over $8,375 but not over $34,000	$837.50 plus 15% of the excess over $8,375
Over $34,000 but not over $82,400	$4,681.25 plus 25% of the excess over $34,000
Over $82,400 but not over $171,850	$16,781.25 plus 28% of the excess over $82,400
Over $171,850 but not over $373,650	$41,827.25 plus 33% of the excess over $171,85
Over $373,650	$108,421.25 plus 35% of the excess over $373,650

MARRIED INDIVIDUALS FILING SEPARATE RETURNS

If Taxable Income Is:	The Tax Is:
Not over $8,375	10% of the taxable income
Over $8,375 but not over $34,000	$837.50 plus 15% of the excess over $8,375
Over $34,000 but not over $68,650	$4,681.25 plus 25% of the excess over $34,000
Over $68,650 but not over $104,625	$13,343.75 plus 28% of the excess over $68,650
Over $104,625 but not over $186,825	$23,416.75 plus 33% of the excess over $104,625
Over $186,825	$50,542.75 plus 35% of the excess over $186,825

---

[17] Rev. Proc. 2009-50, 2009-2 C.B. 617.

2011 Tax Rate Tables[18]

For taxable years beginning in 2011, the tax rate tables under § 1 are as follows:

SECTION 1(A) — MARRIED INDIVIDUALS FILING JOINT RETURNS AND SURVIVING SPOUSES

If Taxable Income Is:	The Tax Is:
Not over $17,000	10% of the taxable income
Over $17,000 but not over $69,000	$1,700 plus 15% of the excess over $17,000
Over $69,000 but not over $139,350	$9,500 plus 25% of the excess over $69,000
Over $139,350 but not over $212,300	$27,087.50 plus 28% of the excess over $139,350
Over $212,300 but not over $379,150	$47,513.50 plus 33% of the excess over $212,300
Over $379,150	$102,574 plus 35% of the excess over $379,150

SECTION 1(C) — UNMARRIED INDIVIDUALS (OTHER THAN SURVIVING SPOUSES AND HEADS OF HOUSEHOLDS)

If Taxable Income Is:	The Tax Is:
Not over $8,500	10% of the taxable income
Over $8,500 but not over $34,500	$850 plus 15% of the excess over $8,500
Over $34,500 but not over $83,600	$4,750 plus 25% of the excess over $34,500
Over $83,600 but not over $174,400	$17,025 plus 28% of the excess over $83,600
Over $174,400 but not over $379,150	$42,449 plus 33% of the excess over $174,400
Over $379,150	$110,016.50 plus 35% of the excess over $379,150

SECTION 1(D) — MARRIED INDIVIDUALS FILING SEPARATE RETURNS

If Taxable Income Is:	The Tax Is:
Not over $8,500	10% of the taxable income
Over $8,500 but not over $34,500	$850 plus 15% of the excess over $8,500
Over $34,500 but not over $69,675	$4,750 plus 25% of the excess over $34,500
Over $69,675 but not over $106,150	$13,543.75 plus 28% of the excess over $69,675
Over $106,150 but not over $189,575	$23,756.75 plus 33% of the excess over $106,150
Over $189,575	$51,287 plus 35% of the excess over $189,575

---

[18] Rev. Proc.

2012 Tax Rate Tables[19]

For taxable years beginning in 2012, the tax rate tables under § 1 are as follows:

MARRIED INDIVIDUALS FILING JOINT RETURNS AND SURVIVING SPOUSES

If Taxable Income Is:	The Tax Is:
Not over $17,400	10% of the taxable income
Over $17,400 but not over $70,700	$1,740 plus 15% of the excess over $17,400
Over $70,700 but not over $142,700	$9,735 plus 25% of the excess over $70,700
Over $142,700 but not over $217,450	$27,735 plus 28% of the excess over $142,700
Over $217,450 but not over $388,350	$48,665 plus 33% of the excess over $217,450
Over $388,350	$105,062 plus 35% of the excess over $388,350

UNMARRIED INDIVIDUALS (OTHER THAN SURVIVING SPOUSES AND HEADS OF HOUSEHOLDS)

If Taxable Income Is:	The Tax Is:
Not over $8,700	10% of the taxable income
Over $8,700 but not over $35,350	$870 plus 15% of the excess over $8,700
Over $35,350 but not over $85,650	$4,867.50 plus 25% of the excess over $35,350
Over $85,650 but not over $178,650	$17,442.50 plus 28% of the excess over $85,650
Over $178,650 but not over $388,350	$43,482.50 plus 33% of the excess over $178,650
Over $388,350	$112,683.50 plus 35% of the excess over $388,350

MARRIED INDIVIDUALS FILING SEPARATE RETURNS

If Taxable Income Is:	The Tax Is:
Not over $8,700	10% of the taxable income
Over $8,700 but not over $35,350	$870 plus 15% of the excess over $8,700
Over $35,350 but not over $71,350	$4,867.50 plus 25% of the excess over $35,350
Over $71,350 but not over $108,725	$13,867.50 plus 28% of the excess over $71,350
Over $108,725 but not over $194,175	$24,332.50 plus 33% of the excess over $108,725
Over $194,175	$52,531 plus 35% of the excess over $194,175

---

[19] Rev. Proc. 2011-12, 2011-1 C.B. 297.

Allowable Living Expense National Standards - effective 04/02/2012

Expense	One Person	Two Persons	Three Persons	Four Persons
Food	$301	$537	$639	$765
Housekeeping supplies	$30	$66	$65	$74
Apparel & services	$86	$162	$209	$244
Personal care products & services	$32	$55	$63	$67
Miscellaneous	$116	$209	$251	$300
Total	$565	$1,029	$1,227	$1,450

More than four persons	Additional Persons Amount
For each additional person, add to four-person total allowance:	$281

Please note that the standards change.
We recommend you check the irs.gov website periodically to assure you have the latest version.

Allowable Living Expense Health Care Standards   - effective 04/02/2012

	Out of Pocket Costs
Under 65	$60
65 and Older	$144

Please note that the standards change.
We recommend you check the irs.gov website periodically to assure you have the latest version.

Housing and Utilities Standards - effective 04/02/2012

State Name	County	Housing and Utilities for a Family of 1	Housing and Utilities for a Family of 2	Housing and Utilities for a Family of 3	Housing and Utilities for a Family of 4	Housing and Utilities for a Family of 5 or more
Alabama	Autauga County	1,196	1,405	1,480	1,650	1,677
Alabama	Baldwin County	1,321	1,552	1,635	1,824	1,853
Alabama	Barbour County	961	1,129	1,190	1,327	1,348
Alabama	Bibb County	1,063	1,249	1,316	1,467	1,491
Alabama	Blount County	1,090	1,280	1,349	1,504	1,529
Alabama	Bullock County	966	1,134	1,195	1,333	1,354
Alabama	Butler County	975	1,145	1,207	1,345	1,367
Alabama	Calhoun County	1,044	1,227	1,293	1,441	1,465
Alabama	Chambers County	989	1,162	1,224	1,365	1,387
Alabama	Cherokee County	1,004	1,179	1,242	1,385	1,407
Alabama	Chilton County	1,045	1,228	1,294	1,442	1,466
Alabama	Choctaw County	959	1,126	1,187	1,323	1,345
Alabama	Clarke County	1,057	1,242	1,308	1,459	1,482
Alabama	Clay County	917	1,077	1,135	1,266	1,286
Alabama	Cleburne County	974	1,144	1,206	1,344	1,366
Alabama	Coffee County	1,073	1,260	1,328	1,481	1,505
Alabama	Colbert County	1,063	1,249	1,316	1,467	1,491
Alabama	Conecuh County	857	1,006	1,060	1,182	1,201
Alabama	Coosa County	928	1,090	1,149	1,281	1,302
Alabama	Covington County	967	1,136	1,197	1,335	1,356
Alabama	Crenshaw County	1,036	1,217	1,282	1,430	1,453
Alabama	Cullman County	998	1,172	1,235	1,377	1,399
Alabama	Dale County	990	1,163	1,225	1,366	1,388
Alabama	Dallas County	984	1,156	1,218	1,358	1,380
Alabama	DeKalb County	897	1,054	1,110	1,238	1,258
Alabama	Elmore County	1,194	1,402	1,477	1,647	1,674
Alabama	Escambia County	951	1,117	1,177	1,313	1,334
Alabama	Etowah County	1,055	1,240	1,306	1,456	1,480
Alabama	Fayette County	944	1,109	1,169	1,303	1,324

Please note that the standards change.

We recommend you check the irs.gov website periodically to assure you have the latest version.

Housing and Utilities Standards - effective 04/02/2012

State Name	County	Housing and Utilities for a Family of 1	Housing and Utilities for a Family of 2	Housing and Utilities for a Family of 3	Housing and Utilities for a Family of 4	Housing and Utilities for a Family of 5 or more
Alabama	Franklin County	939	1,102	1,162	1,295	1,316
Alabama	Geneva County	907	1,065	1,123	1,252	1,272
Alabama	Greene County	922	1,083	1,142	1,273	1,293
Alabama	Hale County	903	1,061	1,117	1,246	1,266
Alabama	Henry County	1,016	1,194	1,258	1,403	1,425
Alabama	Houston County	1,063	1,249	1,316	1,467	1,491
Alabama	Jackson County	936	1,099	1,158	1,292	1,312
Alabama	Jefferson County	1,267	1,488	1,568	1,749	1,777
Alabama	Lamar County	868	1,020	1,074	1,198	1,217
Alabama	Lauderdale County	1,038	1,220	1,285	1,433	1,456
Alabama	Lawrence County	1,014	1,191	1,255	1,399	1,422
Alabama	Lee County	1,199	1,409	1,484	1,655	1,682
Alabama	Limestone County	1,143	1,342	1,414	1,577	1,602
Alabama	Lowndes County	1,010	1,186	1,250	1,393	1,416
Alabama	Macon County	1,004	1,179	1,242	1,385	1,407
Alabama	Madison County	1,222	1,436	1,513	1,687	1,714
Alabama	Marengo County	984	1,156	1,218	1,358	1,380
Alabama	Marion County	874	1,027	1,082	1,206	1,226
Alabama	Marshall County	984	1,156	1,218	1,358	1,380
Alabama	Mobile County	1,155	1,356	1,429	1,593	1,619
Alabama	Monroe County	970	1,139	1,200	1,338	1,360
Alabama	Montgomery County	1,171	1,376	1,450	1,617	1,643
Alabama	Morgan County	1,078	1,266	1,335	1,488	1,512
Alabama	Perry County	935	1,098	1,157	1,290	1,311
Alabama	Pickens County	942	1,106	1,166	1,300	1,321
Alabama	Pike County	1,081	1,269	1,338	1,492	1,516
Alabama	Randolph County	991	1,164	1,227	1,368	1,390
Alabama	Russell County	1,022	1,201	1,265	1,411	1,434
Alabama	Shelby County	1,443	1,695	1,786	1,992	2,024

Please note that the standards change.

We recommend you check the irs.gov website periodically to assure you have the latest version.

Housing and Utilities Standards - effective 04/02/2012

State Name	County	Housing and Utilities for a Family of 1	Housing and Utilities for a Family of 2	Housing and Utilities for a Family of 3	Housing and Utilities for a Family of 4	Housing and Utilities for a Family of 5 or more
Alabama	St. Clair County	1,118	1,313	1,384	1,543	1,568
Alabama	Sumter County	916	1,075	1,133	1,264	1,284
Alabama	Talladega County	1,028	1,208	1,273	1,419	1,442
Alabama	Tallapoosa County	1,018	1,196	1,260	1,405	1,428
Alabama	Tuscaloosa County	1,216	1,428	1,504	1,677	1,704
Alabama	Walker County	963	1,131	1,192	1,329	1,350
Alabama	Washington County	1,080	1,268	1,337	1,490	1,514
Alabama	Wilcox County	987	1,159	1,221	1,362	1,384
Alabama	Winston County	944	1,108	1,168	1,302	1,323
Alaska	Aleutians East Borough	1,119	1,315	1,385	1,545	1,569
Alaska	Aleutians West Census Area	1,658	1,947	2,052	2,287	2,324
Alaska	Anchorage Municipality	1,841	2,163	2,279	2,541	2,582
Alaska	Bethel Census Area	1,198	1,408	1,483	1,654	1,680
Alaska	Bristol Bay Borough	1,519	1,784	1,880	2,097	2,130
Alaska	Denali Borough	1,398	1,642	1,731	1,930	1,961
Alaska	Dillingham Census Area	1,406	1,651	1,740	1,940	1,971
Alaska	Fairbanks North Star Borough	1,711	2,010	2,118	2,362	2,400
Alaska	Haines Borough	1,268	1,490	1,570	1,750	1,778
Alaska	Hoonah-Angoon Census Area	1,270	1,492	1,572	1,753	1,781
Alaska	Juneau City and Borough	1,928	2,264	2,386	2,660	2,703
Alaska	Kenai Peninsula Borough	1,384	1,625	1,712	1,909	1,940
Alaska	Ketchikan Gateway Borough	1,643	1,930	2,034	2,267	2,304
Alaska	Kodiak Island Borough	1,774	2,084	2,196	2,449	2,488
Alaska	Lake and Peninsula Borough	1,575	1,850	1,949	2,174	2,209
Alaska	Matanuska-Susitna Borough	1,578	1,854	1,953	2,178	2,213
Alaska	Nome Census Area	1,225	1,439	1,516	1,691	1,718
Alaska	North Slope Borough	1,247	1,465	1,544	1,721	1,749
Alaska	Northwest Arctic Borough	1,263	1,483	1,563	1,743	1,771
Alaska	Petersburg Census Area	1,464	1,719	1,812	2,020	2,053

Please note that the standards change.

We recommend you check the irs.gov website periodically to assure you have the latest version.

Allowable Living Expense Transportation Standards - effective 04/02/2012

Public Transportation	
National	$182

Ownership Costs	One Car	Two Cars
National	$517	$1,034

Operating Costs	One Car	Two Cars
Northeast Region	$278	$556
Boston	$277	$554
New York	$342	$684
Philadelphia	$299	$598
Midwest Region	$212	$424
Chicago	$262	$524
Cleveland	$226	$452
Detroit	$295	$590
Minneapolis-St. Paul	$216	$432
South Region	$244	$488
Atlanta	$256	$512
Baltimore	$250	$500
Dallas-Ft. Worth	$277	$554
Houston	$312	$624
Miami	$346	$692
Washington, D.C.	$270	$540
West Region	$236	$472
Los Angeles	$295	$590
Phoenix	$291	$582
San Diego	$301	$602
San Francisco	$306	$612
Seattle	$192	$384

Please note that the standards change.
We recommend you check the irs.gov website periodically to assure you have the latest version.

PERPETUAL CALENDAR (from 1583 AD)

by **Ronald W. Mallen**, Adelaide (Astronomical Society of South Australia)

email: rwmallen@chariot.net.au   updated: September 2007

> PRINT this document for greater CLARITY

To find the calendar for a particular year:
- Find the first 2 digits of the year (e.g. the "19" in 1997) at the left of the INDEX
- Follow that row across to the year letter (A to G) under the last 2 digits of the year (e.g. the "97" in 1997)
- This letter (e.g. "D" for 1997) shows the days of the week in the CALENDAR for that year.
Leap years have 2 letters. Use the first letter for January and February, and the second for March to December

INDEX

LAST 2 DIGITS OF YEAR

FIRST 2 DIGITS OF YEAR

Group	FIRST 2 DIGITS
B	15 19 23 27 31 35
GA	16 20 24 28 32 36
F	17 21 25 29 33 37
D	18 22 26 30 34 38

Block 1 (last 2 digits 00–28):

	00	01	02	03	04	05	06	07	08	09	10	11	12	13	14	15	16	17	18	19	20	21	22	23	24	25	26	27	28
B	B	C	D	E	FG	A	B	C	DE	F	G	A	BC	D	E	F	GA	B	C	D	EF	G	A	B	CD	E	F	G	AB
GA	GA	B	C	D	EF	G	A	B	CD	E	F	G	AB	C	D	E	FG	A	B	C	DE	F	G	A	BC	D	E	F	GA
F	F	G	A	B	CD	E	F	G	AB	C	D	E	FG	A	B	C	DE	F	G	A	BC	D	E	F	GA	B	C	D	EF
D	D	E	F	G	AB	C	D	E	FG	A	B	C	DE	F	G	A	BC	D	E	F	GA	B	C	D	EF	G	A	B	CD

Block 2 (last 2 digits 29–56):

	29	30	31	32	33	34	35	36	37	38	39	40	41	42	43	44	45	46	47	48	49	50	51	52	53	54	55	56
B	C	D	E	FG	A	B	C	DE	F	G	A	BC	D	E	F	GA	B	C	D	EF	G	A	B	CD	E	F	G	AB
GA	B	C	D	EF	G	A	B	CD	E	F	G	AB	C	D	E	FG	A	B	C	DE	F	G	A	BC	D	E	F	GA
F	G	A	B	CD	E	F	G	AB	C	D	E	FG	A	B	C	DE	F	G	A	BC	D	E	F	GA	B	C	D	EF
D	E	F	G	AB	C	D	E	FG	A	B	C	DE	F	G	A	BC	D	E	F	GA	B	C	D	EF	G	A	B	CD

Block 3 (last 2 digits 57–84):

	57	58	59	60	61	62	63	64	65	66	67	68	69	70	71	72	73	74	75	76	77	78	79	80	81	82	83	84
B	C	D	E	FG	A	B	C	DE	F	G	A	BC	D	E	F	GA	B	C	D	EF	G	A	B	CD	E	F	G	AB
GA	B	C	D	EF	G	A	B	CD	E	F	G	AB	C	D	E	FG	A	B	C	DE	F	G	A	BC	D	E	F	GA
F	G	A	B	CD	E	F	G	AB	C	D	E	FG	A	B	C	DE	F	G	A	BC	D	E	F	GA	B	C	D	EF
D	E	F	G	AB	C	D	E	FG	A	B	C	DE	F	G	A	BC	D	E	F	GA	B	C	D	EF	G	A	B	CD

Block 4 (last 2 digits 85–99):

	85	86	87	88	89	90	91	92	93	94	95	96	97	98	99
B	C	D	E	FG	A	B	C	DE	F	G	A	BC	D	E	F
GA	B	C	D	EF	G	A	B	CD	E	F	G	AB	C	D	E
F	G	A	B	CD	E	F	G	AB	C	D	E	FG	A	B	C
D	E	F	G	AB	C	D	E	FG	A	B	C	DE	F	G	A

CALENDAR

(single letter years have no February 29)

January to June:

row	A	B	C	D	E	F	G	January	February	March	April	May	June
1	Sun	Mon	Tue	Wed	Thu	Fri	Sat	1 8 15 22 29	5 12 19 26	5 12 19 26	2 9 16 23 30	7 14 21 28	4 11 18 25
2	Mon	Tue	Wed	Thu	Fri	Sat	Sun	2 9 16 23 30	6 13 20 27	6 13 20 27	3 10 17 24	1 8 15 22 29	5 12 19 26
3	Tue	Wed	Thu	Fri	Sat	Sun	Mon	3 10 17 24 31	7 14 21 28	7 14 21 28	4 11 18 25	2 9 16 23 30	6 13 20 27
4	Wed	Thu	Fri	Sat	Sun	Mon	Tue	4 11 18 25	1 8 15 22 29	1 8 15 22 29	5 12 19 26	3 10 17 24 31	7 14 21 28
5	Thu	Fri	Sat	Sun	Mon	Tue	Wed	5 12 19 26	2 9 16 23	2 9 16 23 30	6 13 20 27	4 11 18 25	1 8 15 22 29
6	Fri	Sat	Sun	Mon	Tue	Wed	Thu	6 13 20 27	3 10 17 24	3 10 17 24 31	7 14 21 28	5 12 19 26	2 9 16 23 30
7	Sat	Sun	Mon	Tue	Wed	Thu	Fri	7 14 21 28	4 11 18 25	4 11 18 25	1 8 15 22 29	6 13 20 27	3 10 17 24

July to December:

row	A	B	C	D	E	F	G	July	August	September	October	November	December
1	Sun	Mon	Tue	Wed	Thu	Fri	Sat	2 9 16 23 30	6 13 20 27	3 10 17 24	1 8 15 22 29	5 12 19 26	3 10 17 24 31
2	Mon	Tue	Wed	Thu	Fri	Sat	Sun	3 10 17 24 31	7 14 21 28	4 11 18 25	2 9 16 23 30	6 13 20 27	4 11 18 25
3	Tue	Wed	Thu	Fri	Sat	Sun	Mon	4 11 18 25	1 8 15 22 29	5 12 19 26	3 10 17 24 31	7 14 21 28	5 12 19 26
4	Wed	Thu	Fri	Sat	Sun	Mon	Tue	5 12 19 26	2 9 16 23 30	6 13 20 27	4 11 18 25	1 8 15 22 29	6 13 20 27
5	Thu	Fri	Sat	Sun	Mon	Tue	Wed	6 13 20 27	3 10 17 24 31	7 14 21 28	5 12 19 26	2 9 16 23 30	7 14 21 28
6	Fri	Sat	Sun	Mon	Tue	Wed	Thu	7 14 21 28	4 11 18 25	1 8 15 22 29	6 13 20 27	3 10 17 24	1 8 15 22 29
7	Sat	Sun	Mon	Tue	Wed	Thu	Fri	1 8 15 22 29	5 12 19 26	2 9 16 23 30	7 14 21 28	4 11 18 25	2 9 16 23 30

Examples:

The calendar for 1969 is found by obtaining the letter "D" from the INDEX, then using the days of the week in column D of the CALENDAR.

Hence, July 21st 1969, when man first walked on the Moon, was a Monday.

For leap years 1944, 1972, 2372 use year letters "GA". The days of the week for each of these years appear in the CALENDAR in column "G" for January 1st to February 29th, and in column "A" for March 1st to December 31st.

PART IX

Internal Revenue Service Forms (Selected)

Form **SS-8**

(Rev. August 2011)

Department of the Treasury
Internal Revenue Service

Determination of Worker Status for Purposes of Federal Employment Taxes and Income Tax Withholding

OMB. No. 1545-0004

For IRS Use Only:
Case Number:

Earliest Receipt Date:

Name of firm (or person) for whom the worker performed services	Worker's name

Firm's mailing address (include street address, apt. or suite no., city, state, and ZIP code)	Worker's mailing address (include street address, apt. or suite no., city, state, and ZIP code)

Trade name	Firm's email address	Worker's daytime telephone number	Worker's email address
Firm's fax number	Firm's website	Worker's alternate telephone number	Worker's fax number
Firm's telephone number (include area code)	Firm's employer identification number	Worker's social security number	Worker's employer identification number (if any)

Note. If the worker is paid for these services by a firm other than the one listed on this form, enter the name, address, and employer identification number of the payer. ▶

Disclosure of Information

The information provided on Form SS-8 may be disclosed to the firm, worker, or payer named above to assist the IRS in the determination process. For example, if you are a worker, we may disclose the information you provide on Form SS-8 to the firm or payer named above. The information can only be disclosed to assist with the determination process. If you provide incomplete information, we may not be able to process your request. See *Privacy Act and Paperwork Reduction Act Notice* on page 6 for more information. **If you do not want this information disclosed to other parties, do not file Form SS-8.**

Parts I–V. All filers of Form SS-8 must complete all questions in Parts I–IV. Part V must be completed if the worker provides a service directly to customers or is a salesperson. If you cannot answer a question, enter "Unknown" or "Does not apply." If you need more space for a question, attach another sheet with the part and question number clearly identified. Write your firm's name (or workers' name) and employer identification number (or social security number) at the top of each additional sheet attached to this form.

Part I   General Information

1   This form is being completed by: ☐ Firm ☐ Worker; for services performed _____ to _____ .
   (beginning date)   (ending date)

2   Explain your reason(s) for filing this form (for example, you received a bill from the IRS, you believe you erroneously received a Form 1099 or Form W-2, you are unable to get worker's compensation benefits, or you were audited or are being audited by the IRS).

3   Total number of workers who performed or are performing the same or similar services: _____ .

4   How did the worker obtain the job? ☐ Application ☐ Bid ☐ Employment Agency ☐ Other (specify) _____

5   **Attach copies of all supporting documentation (for example, contracts, invoices, memos, Forms W-2 or Forms 1099-MISC issued or received, IRS closing agreements or IRS rulings).** In addition, please inform us of any current or past litigation concerning the worker's status. If no income reporting forms (Form 1099-MISC or W-2) were furnished to the worker, enter the amount of income earned for the year(s) at issue $ _____ .

   If both Form W-2 and Form 1099-MISC were issued or received, explain why. _____

6   Describe the firm's business. _____

Part I   **General Information** (continued)

7   If the worker received pay from more than one entity because of an event such as the sale, merger, acquisition, or reorganization of the firm for whom the services are performed, provide the following: Name of the firm's previous owner: _____

Previous owner's taxpayer identification number: _____ Change was a: ☐ Sale ☐ Merger ☐ Acquisition ☐ Reorganization

☐ Other (specify) _____

Description of above change: _____

Date of change (MM/DD/YY): _____

8   Describe the work done by the worker and provide the worker's job title. _____

9   Explain why you believe the worker is an employee or an independent contractor. _____

10   Did the worker perform services for the firm in any capacity before providing the services that are the subject of this determination request?

☐ Yes   ☐ No   ☐ N/A

If "Yes," what were the dates of the prior service? _____

If "Yes," explain the differences, if any, between the current and prior service. _____

11   If the work is done under a written agreement between the firm and the worker, attach a copy (preferably signed by both parties). Describe the terms and conditions of the work arrangement. _____

Part II   **Behavioral Control** (Provide names and titles of specific individuals, if applicable.)

1   What specific training and/or instruction is the worker given by the firm? _____

2   How does the worker receive work assignments? _____

3   Who determines the methods by which the assignments are performed? _____

4   Who is the worker required to contact if problems or complaints arise and who is responsible for their resolution? _____

5   What types of reports are required from the worker? Attach examples. _____

6   Describe the worker's daily routine such as his or her schedule or hours. _____

7   At what location(s) does the worker perform services (for example, firm's premises, own shop or office, home, customer's location)? Indicate the appropriate percentage of time the worker spends in each location, if more than one. _____

8   Describe any meetings the worker is required to attend and any penalties for not attending (for example, sales meetings, monthly meetings, staff meetings). _____

9   Is the worker required to provide the services personally? . . . . ☐ Yes   ☐ No

10   If substitutes or helpers are needed, who hires them? _____

11   If the worker hires the substitutes or helpers, is approval required? . . . . ☐ Yes   ☐ No

If "Yes," by whom? _____

12   Who pays the substitutes or helpers? _____

13   Is the worker reimbursed if the worker pays the substitutes or helpers? . . . . ☐ Yes   ☐ No

If "Yes," by whom? _____

Form **SS-8** (Rev. 8-2011)

Part III   Financial Control (Provide names and titles of specific individuals, if applicable.)

1   List the supplies, equipment, materials, and property provided by each party:

The firm: _____

The worker: _____

Other party: _____

2   Does the worker lease equipment, space, or a facility? . . . .   ☐ **Yes**   ☐ **No**

If "Yes," what are the terms of the lease? (Attach a copy or explanatory statement.) _____

_____

3   What expenses are incurred by the worker in the performance of services for the firm? _____

_____

4   Specify which, if any, expenses are reimbursed by:

The firm: _____

Other party: _____

5   Type of pay the worker receives: ☐ Salary   ☐ Commission   ☐ Hourly Wage   ☐ Piece Work

☐ Lump Sum   ☐ Other (specify) _____

If type of pay is commission, and the firm guarantees a minimum amount of pay, specify amount. $ _____

6   Is the worker allowed a drawing account for advances? . . . .   ☐ **Yes**   ☐ **No**

If "Yes," how often? _____

Specify any restrictions. _____

7   Whom does the customer pay? . . . .   ☐ Firm   ☐ Worker

If worker, does the worker pay the total amount to the firm?   ☐ **Yes**   ☐ **No**   If "No," explain. _____

8   Does the firm carry workers' compensation insurance on the worker? . . . .   ☐ **Yes**   ☐ **No**

9   What economic loss or financial risk, if any, can the worker incur beyond the normal loss of salary (for example, loss or damage of equipment, material)? _____

_____

_____

10   Does the worker establish the level of payment for the services provided or the products sold? . . . .   ☐ **Yes**   ☐ **No**

If "No," who does? _____

Part IV   Relationship of the Worker and Firm

1   Please check the benefits available to the worker: ☐ Paid vacations   ☐ Sick pay   ☐ Paid holidays

☐ Personal days   ☐ Pensions   ☐ Insurance benefits   ☐ Bonuses

☐ Other (specify) _____

2   Can the relationship be terminated by either party without incurring liability or penalty? . . . .   ☐ **Yes**   ☐ **No**

If "No," explain your answer. _____

3   Did the worker perform similar services for others during the time period entered in Part I, line 1? . . . .   ☐ **Yes**   ☐ **No**

If "Yes," is the worker required to get approval from the firm? . . . .   ☐ **Yes**   ☐ **No**

4   Describe any agreements prohibiting competition between the worker and the firm while the worker is performing services or during any later period. Attach any available documentation. _____

_____

5   Is the worker a member of a union? . . . .   ☐ **Yes**   ☐ **No**

6   What type of advertising, if any, does the worker do (for example, a business listing in a directory or business cards)? Provide copies, if applicable. _____

7   If the worker assembles or processes a product at home, who provides the materials and instructions or pattern? _____

_____

8   What does the worker do with the finished product (for example, return it to the firm, provide it to another party, or sell it)? _____

_____

9   How does the firm represent the worker to its customers (for example, employee, partner, representative, or contractor), and under whose business name does the worker perform these services? _____

_____

10   If the worker no longer performs services for the firm, how did the relationship end (for example, worker quit or was fired, job completed, contract ended, firm or worker went out of business)? _____

_____

Part V	For Service Providers or Salespersons. Complete this part if the worker provided a service directly to customers or is a salesperson.

1 What are the worker's responsibilities in soliciting new customers? _____

2 Who provides the worker with leads to prospective customers? _____

3 Describe any reporting requirements pertaining to the leads. _____

4 What terms and conditions of sale, if any, are required by the firm? _____

5 Are orders submitted to and subject to approval by the firm? . . . . ☐ Yes ☐ No

6 Who determines the worker's territory? _____

7 Did the worker pay for the privilege of serving customers on the route or in the territory? . . . . ☐ Yes ☐ No

If "Yes," whom did the worker pay? _____

If "Yes," how much did the worker pay? . . . . $ _____

8 Where does the worker sell the product (for example, in a home, retail establishment)? _____

9 List the product and/or services distributed by the worker (for example, meat, vegetables, fruit, bakery products, beverages, or laundry or dry cleaning services). If more than one type of product and/or service is distributed, specify the principal one. _____

10 Does the worker sell life insurance full time? . . . . ☐ Yes ☐ No

11 Does the worker sell other types of insurance for the firm? . . . . ☐ Yes ☐ No

If "Yes," enter the percentage of the worker's total working time spent in selling other types of insurance . . . . . _____ %

12 If the worker solicits orders from wholesalers, retailers, contractors, or operators of hotels, restaurants, or other similar establishments, enter the percentage of the worker's time spent in the solicitation . . . . _____ %

13 Is the merchandise purchased by the customers for resale or use in their business operations? . . . . ☐ Yes ☐ No

Describe the merchandise and state whether it is equipment installed on the customers' premises. _____

Sign Here	Under penalties of perjury, I declare that I have examined this request, including accompanying documents, and to the best of my knowledge and belief, the facts presented are true, correct, and complete.

▶ _____ Title ▶ _____ Date ▶ _____

Type or print name below signature.

Form **SS-8** (Rev. 8-2011)

Form 211 (Rev. December 2007)	Department of the Treasury - Internal Revenue Service **Application for Award for** **Original Information**	OMB No. 1545-0409
		Date Claim Received:
		Claim No. (completed by IRS)

1. Name of individual claimant	2. Claimant's Date of Birth Month　Day　Year	3. Claimant's SSN or ITIN
4. Name of spouse *(if applicable)*	5. Spouse's Date of Birth Month　Day　Year	6. Spouse's SSN or ITIN

7. Address of claimant, including zip code, and telephone number

8. Name & Title of IRS employee to whom violation was reported	9. Date violation reported:
10. Name of taxpayer (include aliases) and any related taxpayers who committed the violation:	11. Taxpayer Identification Number(s) (e.g., SSN, ITIN, or EIN):
12. Taxpayer's address, including zip code:	13. Taxpayer's date of birth or approximate age:

14. State the facts pertinent to the alleged violation. (Attach a detailed explanation and all supporting information in your possession and describe the availability and location of any additional supporting information not in your possession.) Explain why you believe the act described constitutes a violation of the tax laws.

15. Describe how you learned about and/or obtained the information that supports this claim and describe your present or former relationship to the alleged noncompliant taxpayer(s). (Attach sheet if needed.)

16. Describe the amount owed by the taxpayer(s). Please provide a summary of the information you have that supports your claim as to the amount owed. (Attach sheet if needed.)

Declaration under Penalty of Perjury
I declare under penalty of perjury that I have examined this application, my accompanying statement, and supporting documentation and aver that such application is true, correct, and complete, to the best of my knowledge.

17. Signature of Claimant	18. Date

MAIL THE COMPLETED FORM TO THE ADDRESS SHOWN ON THE BACK

Form **211** (Rev. 12-2007)　　Catalog Number 16571S　　publish.no.irs.gov　　Department of the Treasury-Internal Revenue Service

- 615 -

General Information:

On December 20, 2006, Congress made provision for the establishment of a Whistleblower Office within the IRS. This office has responsibility for the administration of the informant award program under section 7623 of the Internal Revenue Code. Section 7623 authorizes the payment of awards from the proceeds of amounts the Government collects by reason of the information provided by the claimant. Payment of awards under 7623(a) is made at the discretion of the IRS. To be eligible for an award under Section 7623(b), the amount in dispute (including tax, penalties, interest, additions to tax, and additional amounts) must exceed $2,000,000.00; if the taxpayer is an individual, the individual's gross income must exceed $200,000.00 for any taxable year at issue.

Send completed form along with any supporting information to:

Internal Revenue Service
Whistleblower Office
SE: WO
1111 Constitution Ave., NW
Washington, DC 20224

Instructions for Completion of Form 211:

Questions 1 - 7

Information regarding Claimant (informant): Name, Date of Birth, Social Security Number (SSN) or Individual Taxpayer Identification Number (ITIN), address including zip code, and telephone number (telephone number is optional).

Questions 8 - 9

If you reported the violation to an IRS employee, provide the employee's name and title and the date the violation was reported.

Questions 10 - 13

Information about Taxpayer - Provide specific and credible information regarding the taxpayer or entities that you believe have failed to comply with tax laws and that will lead to the collection of unpaid taxes.

Question 14

Attach all supporting documentation (for example, books and records) to substantiate the claim. If documents or supporting evidence are not in your possession, describe these documents and their location.

Question 15

Describe how the information which forms the basis of the claim came to your attention, including the date(s) on which this information was acquired, and a complete description of your relationship to the taxpayer.

Question 16

Describe the facts supporting the amount you claim is owed by the taxpayer.

Question 17

Information provided in connection with a claim submitted under this provision of law must be made under an original signed Declaration under Penalty of Perjury. Joint claims must be signed by each claimant.

Form **211** (Rev. 12-2007)   Catalog Number 16571S   publish.no.irs.gov   Department of the Treasury-**Internal Revenue Service**

Collection Information Statement for Wage Earners and Self-Employed Individuals

Wage Earners Complete Sections 1, 2, 3, and 4, including signature line on page 4. *Answer all questions or write N/A.*
Self-Employed Individuals Complete Sections 1, 2, 3, 4, 5 and 6 and signature line on page 4. *Answer all questions or write N/A.*
For Additional Information, refer to Publication 1854, "How To Prepare a Collection Information Statement"
Include attachments if additional space is needed to respond completely to any question.

Name on Internal Revenue Service (IRS) Account	Social Security Number SSN on IRS Account	Employer Identification Number EIN

Section 1: Personal Information

1a Full Name of Taxpayer and Spouse (if applicable)	1c Home Phone ( ) 1d Cell Phone ( )
1b Address (Street, City, State, ZIP code) (County of Residence)	1e Business Phone ( ) 1f Business Cell Phone ( )
	2b Name, Age, and Relationship of dependent(s)

2a Marital Status: ☐ Married ☐ Unmarried (Single, Divorced, Widowed)

	Social Security No. (SSN)	Date of Birth (mmddyyyy)	Driver's License Number and State
3a Taxpayer			
3b Spouse			

Section 2: Employment Information

If the taxpayer or spouse is self-employed or has self-employment income, also complete Business Information in Sections 5 and 6.

Taxpayer	Spouse
4a Taxpayer's Employer Name	5a Spouse's Employer Name
4b Address (Street, City, State, ZIP code)	5b Address (Street, City, State, ZIP code)
4c Work Telephone Number ( ) 4d Does employer allow contact at work ☐ Yes ☐ No	5c Work Telephone Number ( ) 5d Does employer allow contact at work ☐ Yes ☐ No
4e How long with this employer (years) (months) 4f Occupation	5e How long with this employer (years) (months) 5f Occupation
4g Number of exemptions claimed on Form W-4 4h Pay Period: ☐ Weekly ☐ Bi-weekly ☐ Monthly ☐ Other	5g Number of exemptions claimed on Form W-4 5h Pay Period: ☐ Weekly ☐ Bi-weekly ☐ Monthly ☐ Other

Section 3: Other Financial Information *(Attach copies of applicable documentation.)*

6   Is the individual or sole proprietorship party to a lawsuit *(If yes, answer the following)*   Yes ☐   No ☐

☐ Plaintiff ☐ Defendant	Location of Filing	Represented by	Docket/Case No.
Amount of Suit $	Possible Completion Date (mmddyyyy)	Subject of Suit	

7   Has the individual or sole proprietorship ever filed bankruptcy *(If yes, answer the following)*   Yes ☐   No ☐

Date Filed (mmddyyyy)	Date Dismissed or Discharged (mmddyyyy)	Petition No.	Location

8   Any increase/decrease in income anticipated *(business or personal)* *(If yes, answer the following)*   Yes ☐   No ☐

Explain. (Use attachment if needed)	How much will it increase/decrease $	When will it increase/decrease

9   Is the individual or sole proprietorship a beneficiary of a trust, estate, or life insurance policy
(If yes, answer the following)   Yes ☐   No ☐

Place where recorded:	EIN:
Name of the trust, estate, or policy	Anticipated amount to be received $ When will the amount be received

10   In the past 10 years, has the individual resided outside of the United States for periods of 6 months or longer
(If yes, answer the following)   Yes ☐   No ☐

Dates lived abroad: from (mmddyyyy)	To (mmddyyyy)

Section 4: Personal Asset Information for All Individuals

11   **Cash on Hand.** Include cash that is not in a bank.   **Total Cash on Hand** | $

Personal Bank Accounts. Include all checking, online bank accounts, money market accounts, savings accounts, stored value cards (e.g., payroll cards, government benefit cards, etc.) List safe deposit boxes including location and contents.

Type of Account	Full Name & Address *(Street, City, State, ZIP code)* of Bank, Savings & Loan, Credit Union, or Financial Institution.	Account Number	Account Balance As of _____ mmddyyyy
12a			
			$
12b			
			$

12c Total Cash *(Add lines 12a, 12b, and amounts from any attachments)* | $

Investments. Include stocks, bonds, mutual funds, stock options, certificates of deposit, and retirement assets such as IRAs, Keogh, and 401(k) plans. **Include all corporations, partnerships, limited liability companies or other business entities in which the individual is an officer, director, owner, member, or otherwise has a financial interest.**

Type of Investment or Financial Interest	Full Name & Address *(Street, City, State, ZIP code)* of Company	Current Value	Loan Balance (if applicable) As of _____ mmddyyyy	**Equity** Value Minus Loan
13a				
	Phone	$	$	$
13b				
	Phone	$	$	$
13c				
	Phone	$	$	$

13d Total Equity *(Add lines 13a through 13c and amounts from any attachments)* | $

Available Credit. List bank issued credit cards with available credit. Full Name & Address *(Street, City, State, ZIP code)* of Credit Institution	Credit Limit	Amount Owed As of _____ mmddyyyy	**Available Credit** As of _____ mmddyyyy
14a			
Acct No.:	$	$	$
14b			
Acct No.:	$	$	$

14c Total Available Credit *(Add lines 14a, 14b and amounts from any attachments)* | $

15a Life Insurance. Does the individual have life insurance with a cash value (Term Life insurance does not have a cash value.)
☐ **Yes** ☐ **No**   If **Yes** complete blocks 15b through 15f for each policy:

15b Name and Address of Insurance Company(ies):			
15c Policy Number(s)			
15d Owner of Policy			
15e Current Cash Value	$	$	$
15f Outstanding Loan Balance	$	$	$

15g Total Available Cash. *(Subtract amounts on line 15f from line 15e and include amounts from any attachments)* | $

Form **433-A** (Rev. 1-2008)

16 **In the past 10 years, have any assets been transferred by the individual for less than full value**
(If yes, answer the following. If no, skip to 17a)　　　　　　　　　　　　　　　　Yes ☐　　No ☐

List Asset	Value at Time of Transfer	Date Transferred *(mmddyyyy)*	To Whom or Where was it Transferred
	$		

Real Property Owned, Rented, and Leased. Include all real property and land contracts.

	Purchase/Lease Date *(mmddyyyy)*	Current Fair Market Value (FMV)	Current Loan Balance	Amount of Monthly Payment	Date of Final Payment *(mmddyyyy)*	Equity FMV Minus Loan
17a Property Description		$	$	$		$
Location *(Street, City, State, ZIP code)* and County			Lender/Lessor/Landlord Name, Address, *(Street, City, State, ZIP code)* and Phone			
17b Property Description		$	$	$		$
Location *(Street, City, State, ZIP code)* and County			Lender/Lessor/Landlord Name, Address, *(Street, City, State, ZIP code)* and Phone			

17c **Total Equity** *(Add lines 17a, 17b and amounts from any attachments)* 　　　　　　　　　　$

Personal Vehicles Leased and Purchased. Include boats, RVs, motorcycles, trailers, etc.

Description *(Year, Mileage, Make, Model)*		Purchase/Lease Date *(mmddyyyy)*	Current Fair Market Value (FMV)	Current Loan Balance	Amount of Monthly Payment	Date of Final Payment *(mmddyyyy)*	Equity FMV Minus Loan
18a Year	Mileage		$	$	$		$
Make	Model	Lender/Lessor Name, Address, *(Street, City, State, ZIP code)* and Phone					
18b Year	Mileage		$	$	$		$
Make	Model	Lender/Lessor Name, Address, *(Street, City, State, ZIP code)* and Phone					

18c **Total Equity** *(Add lines 18a, 18b and amounts from any attachments)* 　　　　　　　　$

Personal Assets. Include all furniture, personal effects, artwork, jewelry, collections *(coins, guns, etc.)*, antiques or other assets.

	Purchase/Lease Date *(mmddyyyy)*	Current Fair Market Value (FMV)	Current Loan Balance	Amount of Monthly Payment	Date of Final Payment *(mmddyyyy)*	Equity FMV Minus Loan
19a Property Description		$	$	$		$
Location *(Street, City, State, ZIP code)* and County			Lender/Lessor Name, Address, *(Street, City, State, ZIP code)* and Phone			
19b Property Description		$	$	$		$
Location *(Street, City, State, ZIP code)* and County			Lender/Lessor Name, Address, *(Street, City, State, ZIP code)* and Phone			

19c **Total Equity** *(Add lines 19a, 19b and amounts from any attachments)* 　　　　　　　$

Form **433-A** (Rev. 1-2008)

If the taxpayer is self-employed, sections 5 and 6 must be completed before continuing.

Monthly Income/Expense Statement *(For additional information, refer to Publication 1854.)*

Total Income			Total Living Expenses			IRS USE ONLY
	Source	Gross Monthly		Expense Items [5]	Actual Monthly	Allowable Expenses
20	Wages *(Taxpayer)* [1]	$	33	Food, Clothing, and Misc. [6]	$	
21	Wages *(Spouse)* [1]	$	34	Housing and Utilities [7]	$	
22	Interest - Dividends	$	35	Vehicle Ownership Costs [8]	$	
23	Net Business Income [2]	$	36	Vehicle Operating Costs [9]	$	
24	Net Rental Income [3]	$	37	Public Transportation [10]	$	
25	Distributions [4]	$	38	Health Insurance	$	
26	Pension/Social Security *(Taxpayer)*	$	39	Out of Pocket Health Care Costs [11]	$	
27	Pension/Social Security *(Spouse)*	$	40	Court Ordered Payments	$	
28	Child Support	$	41	Child/Dependent Care	$	
29	Alimony	$	42	Life insurance	$	
30	Other (Rent subsidy, Oil credit, etc.)	$	43	Taxes *(Income and FICA)*	$	
31	Other	$	44	Other Secured Debts (Attach list)	$	
32	**Total Income** *(add lines 20-31)*	$	45	**Total Living Expenses** *(add lines 33-44)*	$	

1 **Wages, salaries, pensions, and social security:** Enter gross monthly wages and/or salaries. Do not deduct withholding or allotments taken out of pay, such as insurance payments, credit union deductions, car payments, etc. To calculate the gross monthly wages and/or salaries:

If paid weekly - multiply weekly gross wages by 4.3. Example: $425.89 x 4.3 = $1,831.33

If paid biweekly (every 2 weeks) - multiply biweekly gross wages by 2.17. Example: $972.45 x 2.17 = $2,110.22

If paid semimonthly (twice each month) - multiply semimonthly gross wages by 2. Example: $856.23 x 2 = $1,712.46

2 **Net Income from Business:** Enter monthly net business income. This is the amount earned after ordinary and necessary monthly business expenses are paid. **This figure is the amount from page 6, line 82.** If the net business income is a loss, enter "0". Do not enter a negative number. If this amount is more or less than previous years, attach an explanation.

3 **Net Rental Income:** Enter monthly net rental income. This is the amount earned after ordinary and necessary monthly rental expenses are paid. Do not include deductions for depreciation or depletion. If the net rental income is a loss, enter "0". Do not enter a negative number.

4 **Distributions:** Enter the total distributions from partnerships and subchapter S corporations reported on Schedule K-1, and from limited liability companies reported on Form 1040, Schedule C, D or E.

5 **Expenses not generally allowed:** We generally do not allow tuition for private schools, public or private college expenses, charitable contributions, voluntary retirement contributions, payments on unsecured debts such as credit card bills, cable television and other similar expenses. However, we may allow these expenses if it is proven that they are necessary for the health and welfare of the individual or family or for the production of income.

6 **Food, Clothing, and Misc.:** Total of clothing, food, housekeeping supplies, and personal care products for one month.

7 **Housing and Utilities:** For principal residence: Total of rent or mortgage payment. Add the average monthly expenses for the following: property taxes, home owner's or renter's insurance, maintenance, dues, fees, and utilities. Utilities include gas, electricity, water, fuel, oil, other fuels, trash collection, telephone, and cell phone.

8 **Vehicle Ownership Costs:** Total of monthly lease or purchase/loan payments.

9 **Vehicle Operating Costs:** Total of maintenance, repairs, insurance, fuel, registrations, licenses, inspections, parking, and tolls for one month.

10 **Public Transportation:** Total of monthly fares for mass transit (e.g., bus, train, ferry, taxi, etc.)

11 **Out of Pocket Health Care Costs:** Monthly total of medical services, prescription drugs and medical supplies (e.g., eyeglasses, hearing aids, etc.)

Certification: *Under penalties of perjury, I declare that to the best of my knowledge and belief this statement of assets, liabilities, and other information is true, correct, and complete.*

Taxpayer's Signature	Spouse's Signature	Date

Attachments Required for Wage Earners and Self-Employed Individuals:
Copies of the following items for the last 3 months from the date this form is submitted (check all attached items):

☐ Income - Earnings statements, pay stubs, etc. from each employer, pension/social security/other income, self employment income (commissions, invoices, sales records, etc.).

☐ Banks, Investments, and Life Insurance - Statements for all money market, brokerage, checking and savings accounts, certificates of deposit, IRA, stocks/bonds, and life insurance policies with a cash value.

☐ Assets - Statements from lenders on loans, monthly payments, payoffs, and balances for all personal and business assets. Include copies of UCC financing statements and accountant's depreciation schedules.

☐ Expenses - Bills or statements for monthly recurring expenses of utilities, rent, insurance, property taxes, phone and cell phone, insurance premiums, court orders requiring payments (child support, alimony, etc.), other out of pocket expenses.

☐ Other - credit card statements, profit and loss statements, all loan payoffs, etc.

☐ A copy of last year's Form 1040 with all attachments. Include all Schedules K-1 from Form 1120S or Form 1065, as applicable.

Form **433-A** (Rev. 1-2008)

Sections 5 and 6 must be completed only if the taxpayer is SELF-EMPLOYED.

Section 5: Business Information

46   Is the business a sole proprietorship (filing Schedule C)   ☐ Yes, Continue with Sections 5 and 6.   ☐ No, Complete Form 433-B.
All other business entities, including limited liability companies, partnerships or corporations, must complete Form 433-B.

47 Business Name	**48** Employer Identification Number	**49** Type of Business
		Federal Contractor ☐ Yes ☐ No
50 Business Website	**51** Total Number of Employees	**52a** Average Gross Monthly Payroll
		52b Frequency of Tax Deposits

53   Does the business engage in e-Commerce (Internet sales)   ☐ Yes ☐ No

Payment Processor (e.g., PayPal, Authorize.net, Google Checkout, etc.) Name & Address *(Street, City, State, ZIP code)*	Payment Processor Account Number
54a	
54b	

Credit Cards Accepted by the Business.

Credit Card	Merchant Account Number	Merchant Account Provider, Name & Address *(Street, City, State, ZIP code)*
55a		
55b		
55c		

56   **Business Cash on Hand.** Include cash that is not in a bank.   **Total Cash on Hand** $

Business Bank Accounts. Include checking accounts, online bank accounts, money market accounts, savings accounts, and stored value cards (e.g. payroll cards, government benefit cards, etc.) *Report Personal Accounts in Section 4.*

Type of Account	Full name & Address *(Street, City, State, ZIP code)* of Bank, Savings & Loan, Credit Union or Financial Institution.	Account Number	Account Balance As of _____ mmddyyyy
57a			$
57b			$
57c Total Cash in Banks *(Add lines 57a, 57b and amounts from any attachments)*			$

Accounts/Notes Receivable. Include e-payment accounts receivable and factoring companies, and any bartering or online auction accounts. *(List all contracts separately, including contracts awarded, but not started.)* **Include Federal Government Contracts.**

Accounts/Notes Receivable & Address *(Street, City, State, ZIP code)*	Status *(e.g., age, factored, other)*	Date Due *(mmddyyyy)*	Invoice Number or Federal Government Contract Number	Amount Due
58a				$
58b				$
58c				$
58d				$
58e Total Outstanding Balance *(Add lines 58a through 58d and amounts from any attachments)*				$

Form **433-A** (Rev. 1-2008)

Business Assets. Include all tools, books, machinery, equipment, inventory or other assets used in trade or business. Include Uniform Commercial Code *(UCC)* filings. Include Vehicles and Real Property owned/leased/rented by the business, if not shown in Section 4.

	Purchase/Lease/Rental Date *(mmddyyyy)*	Current Fair Market Value (FMV)	Current Loan Balance	Amount of Monthly Payment	Date of Final Payment *(mmddyyyy)*	**Equity** FMV Minus Loan
59a Property Description		$	$	$		$
Location *(Street, City, State, ZIP code) and County*			Lender/Lessor/Landlord Name, Address *(Street, City, State, ZIP code) and Phone*			
59b Property Description		$	$	$		$
Location *(Street, City, State, ZIP code) and County*			Lender/Lessor/Landlord Name, Address *(Street, City, State, ZIP code) and Phone*			

59c Total Equity *(Add lines 59a, 59b and amounts from any attachments)* $

Section 6 should be completed only if the taxpayer is SELF-EMPLOYED

Section 6: Sole Proprietorship Information *(lines 60 through 81 should reconcile with business Profit and Loss Statement)*

Accounting Method Used: ☐ Cash ☐ Accrual

Income and Expenses during the period *(mmddyyyy)* _____ to *(mmddyyyy)* _____ .

Total Monthly Business Income			Total Monthly Business Expenses *(Use attachments as needed.)*	
Source	Gross Monthly		Expense Items	Actual Monthly
60 Gross Receipts	$	**70**	Materials Purchased [1]	$
61 Gross Rental Income	$	**71**	Inventory Purchased [2]	$
62 Interest	$	**72**	Gross Wages & Salaries	$
63 Dividends	$	**73**	Rent	$
64 Cash	$	**74**	Supplies [3]	$
Other Income *(Specify below)*		**75**	Utilities/Telephone [4]	$
65	$	**76**	Vehicle Gasoline/Oil	$
66	$	**77**	Repairs & Maintenance	$
67	$	**78**	Insurance	$
68	$	**79**	Current Taxes [5]	$
		80	Other Expenses, including installment payments *(Specify)*	$
69 **Total Income** *(Add lines 60 through 68)*	$	**81**	**Total Expenses** *(Add lines 70 through 80)*	$
		82	**Net Business Income** *(Line 69 minus 81)* [6]	$

Enter the amount from line 82 on line 23, section 4. If line 82 is a loss, enter "0" on line 23, section 4.

Self-employed taxpayers must return to page 4 to sign the certification and include all applicable attachments.

[1] **Materials Purchased:** Materials are items directly related to the production of a product or service.

[2] **Inventory Purchased:** Goods bought for resale.

[3] **Supplies:** Supplies are items used in the business that are consumed or used up within one year. This could be the cost of books, office supplies, professional equipment, etc.

[4] **Utilities/Telephone:** Utilities include gas, electricity, water, oil, other fuels, trash collection, telephone and cell phone.

[5] **Current Taxes:** Real estate, excise, franchise, occupational, personal property, sales and employer's portion of employment taxes.

[6] **Net Business Income:** Net profit from Form 1040, Schedule C may be used if duplicated deductions are eliminated (e.g., expenses for business use of home already included in housing and utility expenses on page 4). Deductions for depreciation and depletion on Schedule C are not cash expenses and must be added back to the net income figure. In addition, interest cannot be deducted if it is already included in any other installment payments allowed.

FINANCIAL ANALYSIS OF COLLECTION POTENTIAL FOR INDIVIDUAL WAGE EARNERS AND SELF-EMPLOYED INDIVIDUALS		(IRS USE ONLY)
Cash Available (Lines 11, 12c, 13d, 14c, 15g, 56, 57c and 58e)	Total Cash	$
Distrainable Asset Summary (Lines 17c, 18c, 19c, and 59c)	Total Equity	$
Monthly Total Positive Income minus Expenses (Line 32 minus Line 45)	Monthly Available Cash	$

Privacy Act: The information requested on this Form is covered under Privacy Acts and Paperwork Reduction Notices which have already been provided to the taxpayer.

Form **433-A** *(Rev. 1-2008)*

Collection Information Statement for Businesses

Note: *Complete all entry spaces with the current data available or "N/A" (not applicable). Failure to complete all entry spaces may result in rejection of your request or significant delay in account resolution.* **Include attachments if additional space is needed to respond completely to any question.**

Section 1: Business Information

1a Business Name _____

1b Business Street Address _____
Mailing Address _____
City _____
State _____ ZIP _____

1c County _____

1d Business Telephone (____) _____

1e Type of Business _____

1f Business Website _____

2a Employer Identification No. (EIN) _____

2b Type of Entity *(Check appropriate box below)*
☐ Partnership ☐ Corporation ☐ Other _____
☐ Limited Liability Company (LLC) classified as a corporation
☐ Other LLC – Include number of members _____

2c Date Incorporated/Established _____
mmddyyyy

3a Number of Employees _____

3b Monthly Gross Payroll _____

3c Frequency of Tax Deposits _____

3d Is the business enrolled in Electronic Federal Tax Payment System (EFTPS) ☐ Yes ☐ No

4 Does the business engage in e-Commerce (Internet sales) ☐ Yes ☐ No

Payment Processor (e.g., PayPal, Authorize.net, Google Checkout, etc.), Name and Address *(Street, Cty, State, ZIP code)*	Payment Processor Account Number
5a	
5b	

Credit cards accepted by the business

Type of Credit Card (e.g., Visa, MasterCard, etc.)	Merchant Account Number	Merchant Account Provider Name and Address *(Street, Cty, State, ZIP code)*
6a		Phone
6b		Phone
6c		Phone

Section 2: Business Personnel and Contacts

Partners, Officers, LLC Members, Major Shareholders, Etc.

7a Full Name _____
Title _____
Home Address _____
City _____ State _____ ZIP _____
Responsible for Depositing Payroll Taxes ☐ Yes ☐ No
Social Security Number _____
Home Telephone (____) _____
Work/Cell Phone (____) _____
Ownership Percentage & Shares or Interest
_____

7b Full Name _____
Title _____
Home Address _____
City _____ State _____ ZIP _____
Responsible for Depositing Payroll Taxes ☐ Yes ☐ No
Social Security Number _____
Home Telephone (____) _____
Work/Cell Phone (____) _____
Ownership Percentage & Shares or Interest
_____

7c Full Name _____
Title _____
Home Address _____
City _____ State _____ ZIP _____
Responsible for Depositing Payroll Taxes ☐ Yes ☐ No
Social Security Number _____
Home Telephone (____) _____
Work/Cell Phone (____) _____
Ownership Percentage & Shares or Interest
_____

7d Full Name _____
Title _____
Home Address _____
City _____ State _____ ZIP _____
Responsible for Depositing Payroll Taxes ☐ Yes ☐ No
Social Security Number _____
Home Telephone (____) _____
Work/Cell Phone (____) _____
Ownership Percentage & Shares or Interest
_____

Section 3: Other Financial Information *(Attach copies of all applicable documentation.)*

8   **Does the business use a Payroll Service Provider or Reporting Agent** *(If yes, answer the following)*   ☐ **Yes** ☐ **No**

Name and Address *(Street, City, State, ZIP code)*	Effective dates *(mmddyyyy)*

9   **Is the business a party to a lawsuit** *(If yes, answer the following)*   ☐ **Yes** ☐ **No**

☐ Plaintiff ☐ Defendant	Location of Filing	Represented by	Docket/Case No.
Amount of Suit $	Possible Completion Date *(mmddyyyy)*	Subject of Suit	

10   **Has the business ever filed bankruptcy** *(If yes, answer the following)*   ☐ **Yes** ☐ **No**

Date Filed *(mmddyyyy)*	Date Dismissed or Discharged *(mmddyyyy)*	Petition No.	Location

11   **Do any related parties (e.g., officers, partners, employees) have outstanding amounts owed to the business** *(If yes, answer the following)*   ☐ **Yes** ☐ **No**

Name and Address *(Street, City, State, ZIP code)*	Date of Loan	Current Balance As of _____ mmddyyyy	Payment Date	Payment Amount
		$		$

12   **Have any assets been transferred, in the last 10 years, from this business for less than full value** *(If yes, answer the following)*   ☐ **Yes** ☐ **No**

List Asset	Value at Time of Transfer	Date Transferred *(mmddyyyy)*	To Whom or Where Transferred
	$		

13   **Does this business have other business affiliations (e.g., subsidiary or parent companies)** *(If yes, answer the following)*   ☐ **Yes** ☐ **No**

Related Business Name and Address *(Street, City, State, ZIP code)*	Related Business EIN:

14   **Any increase/decrease in income anticipated** *(If yes, answer the following)*   ☐ **Yes** ☐ **No**

Explain *(use attachment if needed)*	How much will it increase/decrease	When will it increase/decrease
	$	

Section 4: Business Asset and Liability Information

15   **Cash on Hand.** *Include cash that is not in the bank*   **Total Cash on Hand** $

Business Bank Accounts. Include online bank accounts, money market accounts, savings accounts, checking accounts, and stored value cards (e.g., payroll cards, government benefit cards, etc.)
List safe deposit boxes including location and contents.

	Type of Account	Full Name and Address *(Street, City, State, ZIP code)* of Bank, Savings & Loan, Credit Union or Financial Institution.	Account Number	Account Balance As of _____ mmddyyyy
16a				$
16b				$
16c				$
16d	**Total Cash in Banks** *(Add lines 16a through 16c and amounts from any attachments)*			$

Accounts/Notes Receivable. Include e-payment accounts receivable and factoring companies, and any bartering or online auction accounts. *(List all contracts separately, including contracts awarded, but not started.)*

17   **Is the business a Federal Government Contractor**   ☐ **Yes** ☐ **No**   *(Include Federal Government contracts below)*

Accounts/Notes Receivable & Address *(Street, City, State, ZIP code)*	Status *(e.g., age, factored, other)*	Date Due *(mmddyyyy)*	Invoice Number or Federal Government Contract Number	**Amount Due**
18a Contact Name: Phone:				$
18b Contact Name: Phone:				$
18c Contact Name: Phone:				$
18d Contact Name: Phone:				$
18e Contact Name: Phone:				$
18f **Outstanding Balance** *(Add lines 18a through 18e and amounts from any attachments)*				$

Investments. List all investment assets below. Include stocks, bonds, mutual funds, stock options, and certificates of deposit.

Name of Company & Address *(Street, City, State, ZIP code)*	Used as collateral on loan	Current Value	Loan Balance	**Equity** Value Minus Loan
19a Phone:	☐ Yes ☐ No	$	$	$
19b Phone:	☐ Yes ☐ No	$	$	$
19c **Total Investments** *(Add lines 19a, 19b, and amounts from any attachments)*				$

Available Credit. Include all lines of credit and credit cards. Full Name & Address *(Street, City, State, ZIP code)* of Credit Institution	Credit Limit	Amount Owed As of _____ mmddyyyy	**Available Credit** As of _____ mmddyyyy
20a Account No.	$	$	$
20b Account No.	$	$	$
20c **Total Credit Available** *(Add lines 20a, 20b, and amounts from any attachments)*			$

Form **433-B** (Rev. 1-2008)

Real Property. Include all real property and land contracts the business owns/leases/rents.

	Purchase/Lease Date (mmddyyyy)	Current Fair Market Value (FMV)	Current Loan Balance	Amount of Monthly Payment	Date of Final Payment (mmddyyyy)	**Equity** FMV Minus Loan
21a Property Description		$	$	$		$
Location *(Street, City, State, ZIP code)* and County			Lender/Lessor/Landlord Name, Address *(Street, City, State, ZIP code)*, and Phone			
21b Property Description		$	$	$		$
Location *(Street, City, State, ZIP code)* and County			Lender/Lessor/Landlord Name, Address *(Street, City, State, ZIP code)*, and Phone			
21c Property Description		$	$	$		$
Location *(Street, City, State, ZIP code)* and County			Lender/Lessor/Landlord Name, Address *(Street, City, State, ZIP code)*, and Phone			
21d Property Description		$	$	$		$
Location *(Street, City, State, ZIP code)* and County			Lender/Lessor/Landlord Name, Address *(Street, City, State, ZIP code)*, and Phone			

21e Total Equity *(Add lines 21a through 21d and amounts from any attachments)* $

Vehicles, Leased and Purchased. Include boats, RVs, motorcycles, trailers, mobile homes, etc.

		Purchase/Lease Date (mmddyyyy)	Current Fair Market Value (FMV)	Current Loan Balance	Amount of Monthly Payment	Date of Final Payment (mmddyyyy)	**Equity** FMV Minus Loan
22a Year	Mileage		$	$	$		$
Make	Model	Lender/Lessor Name, Address, *(Street, City, State, ZIP code)* and Phone					
22b Year	Mileage		$	$	$		$
Make	Model	Lender/Lessor Name, Address, *(Street, City, State, ZIP code)* and Phone					
22c Year	Mileage		$	$	$		$
Make	Model	Lender/Lessor Name, Address, *(Street, City, State, ZIP code)* and Phone					
22d Year	Mileage		$	$	$		$
Make	Model	Lender/Lessor Name, Address, *(Street, City, State, ZIP code)* and Phone					

22e Total Equity *(Add lines 22a through 22d and amounts from any attachments)* $

Form **433-B** (Rev. 1-2008)

Business Equipment. Include all machinery, equipment, merchandise inventory, and/or other assets.
Include Uniform Commercial Code (UCC) filings.

	Purchase/Lease Date *(mmddyyyy)*	Current Fair Market Value (FMV)	Current Loan Balance	Amount of Monthly Payment	Date of Final Payment *(mmddyyyy)*	**Equity** FMV Minus Loan
23a Asset Description		$	$	$		$
Location of asset *(Street, City, State, ZIP code)* and County			Lender/Lessor Name, Address, *(Street, City, State, ZIP code)* and Phone			
23b Asset Description		$	$	$		$
Location of asset *(Street, City, State, ZIP code)* and County			Lender/Lessor Name, Address, *(Street, City, State, ZIP code)* and Phone			
23c Asset Description		$	$	$		$
Location of asset *(Street, City, State, ZIP code)* and County			Lender/Lessor Name, Address, *(Street, City, State, ZIP code)* and Phone			
23d Asset Description		$	$	$		$
Location of asset *(Street, City, State, ZIP code)* and County			Lender/Lessor Name, Address, *(Street, City, State, ZIP code)* and Phone			

23e Total Equity *(Add lines 23a through 23d and amounts from any attachments)* $

Business Liabilities. Include notes and judgments below.

Business Liabilities	Secured/ Unsecured	Date Pledged (mmddyyyy)	Balance Owed	Date of Final Payment (mmddyyyy)	Payment Amount
24a Description:	☐ Secured ☐ Unsecured		$		$
Name _____ Street Address _____ City/State/ZIP code _____				Phone:	
24b Description:	☐ Secured ☐ Unsecured		$		$
Name _____ Street Address _____ City/State/ZIP code _____				Phone:	
24c Description:	☐ Secured ☐ Unsecured		$		$
Name _____ Street Address _____ City/State/ZIP code _____				Phone:	

24d Total Payments *(Add lines 24a through 24c and amounts from any attachments)* $

Form **433-B** (Rev. 1-2008)

Section 5: Monthly Income/Expense Statement for Business

Accounting Method Used: ☐ Cash ☐ Accrual

Income and Expenses during the period *(mmddyyyy)*   to *(mmddyyyy)*

	Total Monthly Business Income			Total Monthly Business Expenses	
	Source	Gross Monthly		Expense Items	Actual Monthly
25	Gross Receipts from Sales/Services	$	36	Materials Purchased[1]	$
26	Gross Rental Income	$	37	Inventory Purchased[2]	$
27	Interest Income	$	38	Gross Wages & Salaries	$
28	Dividends	$	39	Rent	$
29	Cash	$	40	Supplies[3]	$
	Other Income *(Specify below)*		41	Utilities/Telephone[4]	$
30		$	42	Vehicle Gasoline/Oil	$
31		$	43	Repairs & Maintenance	$
32		$	44	Insurance	$
33		$	45	Current Taxes[5]	$
34		$	46	Other Expenses *(Specify)*	$
35	**Total Income** *(Add lines 25 through 34)*	$	47	IRS Use Only Allowable Installment Payments	$
			48	**Total Expenses** *(Add lines 36 through 47)*	$

1 Materials Purchased: Materials are items directly related to the production of a product or service.

2 Inventory Purchased: Goods bought for resale.

3 Supplies: Supplies are items used to conduct business and are consumed or used up within one year. This could be the cost of books, office supplies, professional equipment, etc.

4 Utilities/Telephone: Utilities include gas, electricity, water, oil, other fuels, trash collection, telephone and cell phone.

5 Current Taxes: Real estate, state, and local income tax, excise, franchise, occupational, personal property, sales and the employer's portion of employment taxes.

Certification: *Under penalties of perjury, I declare that to the best of my knowledge and belief this statement of assets, liabilities, and other information is true, correct, and complete.*

Signature	Title	Date

Print Name of Officer, Partner or LLC Member

Attachments Required: Copies of the following items for the last 3 months from the date this form is submitted (check all attached items):

☐ Banks and Investments - Statements for all money market, brokerage, checking/savings accounts, certificates of deposit, stocks/bonds.

☐ Assets - Statements from lenders on loans, monthly payments, payoffs, and balances, for all assets. Include copies of UCC financing statements and accountant's depreciation schedules.

☐ Expenses - Bills or statements for monthly recurring expenses of utilities, rent, insurance, property taxes, telephone and cell phone, insurance premiums, court orders requiring payments, other expenses.

☐ Other - credit card statements, profit and loss statements, all loan payoffs, etc.

☐ Copy of the last income tax return filed; Form 1120, 1120S, 1065, 1040, 990, etc.

Additional information or proof may be subsequently requested.

FINANCIAL ANALYSIS OF COLLECTION POTENTIAL FOR BUSINESSES		(IRS USE ONLY)
Cash Available (Lines 15, 16d, 18f, 19c, and 20c)	Total Cash	$
Distrainable Asset Summary (Lines 21e, 22e, and 23e)	Total Equity	$
Monthly Income Minus Expenses (Line 35 Minus Line 48)	Monthly Available Cash	$

Privacy Act: The information requested on this Form is covered under Privacy Acts and Paperwork Reduction Notices which have already been provided to the taxpayer.

Form **433-B** (Rev. 1-2008)

Form 656 Booklet

Offer in Compromise

CONTENTS

IRS contact information
If you have questions regarding qualifications for an offer in compromise, please call our toll-free number at 1-800-829-1040. You can get forms and publications by calling 1-800-TAX-FORM (1-800-829-3676), or by visiting your local IRS office or our website at www.irs.gov.

Taxpayer resources
You may also seek assistance from a professional tax assistant at a Low Income Taxpayer Clinic, if you qualify. These clinics provide help to qualified taxpayers at little or no charge. IRS Publication 4134, Low Income Taxpayer Clinic List, provides information on clinics in your area and is available through the IRS website at www.irs.gov, by phone at 1-800-TAX-FORM (1-800-829-3676), or at your local IRS office.

WHAT YOU NEED TO KNOW

What is an offer?

An offer in compromise (offer) is an agreement between you (the taxpayer) and the IRS that settles a tax debt for less than the full amount owed. The offer program provides eligible taxpayers with a path toward paying off their debt and getting a "fresh start." The ultimate goal is a compromise that suits the best interest of both the taxpayer and the IRS. To be considered, generally you must make an appropriate offer based on what the IRS considers your true ability to pay.

Submitting an offer application does not ensure that the IRS will accept your offer. It begins a process of evaluation and verification by the IRS, taking into consideration any special circumstances that might affect your ability to pay. Generally, the IRS will not accept an offer if you can pay your tax debt in full via an installment agreement or a lump sum.

This booklet will lead you through a series of steps to help you calculate an appropriate offer based on your assets, income, expenses, and future earning potential. The application requires you to describe your financial situation in detail, so before you begin, make sure you have the necessary information and documentation.

Are you eligible?

Before you submit your offer, you must (1) file all tax returns you are legally required to file, (2) make all required estimated tax payments for the current year, and (3) make all required federal tax deposits for the current quarter if you are a business owner with employees.

Bankruptcy

If you or your business is currently in an open bankruptcy proceeding, you are not eligible to apply for an offer. Any resolution of your outstanding tax debts generally must take place within the context of your bankruptcy proceeding.

If you are not sure of your bankruptcy status, contact the Centralized Insolvency Operation at 1-800-973-0424. Be prepared to provide your bankruptcy case number and/or Taxpayer Identification Number.

Doubt as to Liability

If you have a legitimate doubt that you owe part or all of the tax debt, you will need to complete a **Form 656-L Offer in Compromise (Doubt as to Liability)**. The Form 656-L is not included as part of this package. To submit a Doubt as to Liability offer, you may request a form by calling the toll free number 1-800-829-1040, by visiting a local IRS office, or at www.irs.gov.

Other important facts

Penalties and interest will continue to accrue during the offer evaluation process.

You cannot submit an offer that is only for a tax year or tax period that has not been assessed.

The law requires the IRS to make certain information from accepted offers available for public inspection and review. These public inspection files are located in designated IRS Area Offices.

A Notice of Federal Tax Lien (lien) gives the IRS a legal claim to your property as security for payment of your tax debt. The IRS may file a Notice of Federal Tax Lien during the offer investigation. However, unless a jeopardy situation exists, a request for a Notice of Federal Tax Lien will usually not be made until a final determination has been made on the offer.

If your business owes trust fund taxes, and responsible individuals may be held liable for the trust fund portion of the tax, you are not eligible to submit

1

an offer unless the trust fund portion of the tax is paid **or** the Trust Fund Recovery Penalty determinations have been made on all potentially responsible individual(s). Trust fund taxes are the money withheld from an employee's wages, such as income tax, Social Security, and Medicare taxes.

The IRS will keep any refund, including interest, for tax periods extending through the calendar year that the IRS accepts the offer. For example, if your offer is accepted in 2012 and you file your 2012 Form 1040 showing a refund, IRS will apply your refund to your tax debt.

The IRS may keep any proceeds from a levy served prior to you submitting an offer. The IRS may levy your **assets up to the time that the IRS official signs** and accepts your offer as pending. If your assets are levied after your offer is pending, immediately contact the IRS person whose name and phone number is listed on the levy.

If you currently have an approved installment agreement with IRS and are making installment payments, then you may stop making those installment agreement payments when you submit an offer. If your offer is returned for any reason, your installment agreement with IRS will be reinstated with no additional fee.

PAYING FOR YOUR OFFER

Application fee

Offers require a $150 application fee.

EXCEPTION: If you are submitting an individual offer and meet the Low Income Certification guidelines (see page 2 of Form 656, Offer in Compromise), you will not be required to send the application fee.

Payment options

Submitting an offer requires the selection of a payment option as well as sending an initial payment with your application. The amount of the initial payment and subsequent payments will depend on the total amount of your offer and which of the following payment options you choose.

Lump Sum Cash: This option requires 20% of the total offer amount to be paid with the offer and the remaining balance paid in five or fewer payments within 24 months of the date your offer is accepted.

Periodic Payment: This option requires the first payment with the offer and the remaining balance paid, within 24 months, in accordance with your proposed offer terms. Under this option, **you must continue to make all subsequent payments while the IRS is evaluating your offer. Failure to make these payments will cause your offer to be returned.**

The length of the payment option you choose may affect the amount of the offer we will accept. Generally, an offer paid within five months of acceptance will require a lesser amount. In all cases, your offer amount must be paid within 24 months of the date the offer is accepted. Your offer amount cannot include a refund we owe you.

If you meet the Low Income Certification guidelines, you will not be required to send the initial payment, or make the monthly payments during the evaluation of your offer but you will still need to choose one of the payment options.

If your offer is returned or not accepted, any required payment(s) made with the filing of your offer and thereafter, will not be refunded. Your payment(s) will **be** applied to your tax debt.

2

If you do not have sufficient cash to pay for your offer, you may need to consider borrowing money from a bank, friends, and/or family. Other options may include borrowing against or selling other assets. NOTE: If retirement savings from an IRA or 401k plan are cashed out, there will be future tax liabilities owed as a result. Contact the IRS or your tax advisor before taking this action.

Future tax obligations

If your offer is accepted, you must continue to file and pay your tax obligations that become due in the future. If you fail to file and pay any tax obligations that become due within the five years after your offer is accepted, your offer may be defaulted. If your offer is defaulted, all compromised tax debts, including penalties and interest, will be reinstated.

HOW TO APPLY

Application process

The application involves **sending**:

- Form 656 (Offer in Compromise)
- **Completed** Form 433-A (OIC), Collection Information Statement for Wages Earners and Self-Employed Individuals, if applicable
- **Completed** Form 433-B(OIC), Collection Information Statement for Businesses, if applicable
- **$150** application fee, unless **you meet** low income certification
- Initial offer payment, unless **you meet** low income certification

If you and your spouse owe joint and separate tax debts

If you have joint tax debt(s) with your spouse and also have an individual tax debt(s), you and your spouse will send in one Form 656 with all of the joint tax debt(s) and a second Form 656 with your individual tax debt(s), for a total of two Forms 656.

If you and your spouse have joint tax debt(s) and you are also each responsible for an individual tax debt(s), you will each need to send in a separate Form 656. You will complete one Form 656 for yourself listing all your joint and separate tax debts and your spouse will complete one Form 656 listing all his or her joint and individual tax debts, for a total of two Forms 656.

If you and your spouse/ex-spouse have a joint tax debt and your spouse/ex-spouse does not want to submit a Form 656, you on your own may submit a Form 656 to compromise your responsibility for the joint debt.

Each Form 656 will require the $150 application fee and initial down payment unless your household meets the Low Income Certification guidelines (See page 2 of Form 656, Offer in Compromise).

COMPLETING THE APPLICATION PACKAGE

<u>Step 1</u> – Gather your information

To calculate an offer amount, you will need to gather information about your financial situation, including cash, investments, available credit, assets, income, and debt.

You will also need to gather information about your average gross monthly household income and expenses. The entire household includes spouse, significant other, children, and others that reside in the household. This is necessary for the IRS to accurately evaluate your offer. **In general, the IRS will not accept expenses for tuition for private schools, college expenses, charitable contributions, and other unsecured debt payments as part of the expenses calculation.**

3

Step 2 – Fill out the Form 433-A (OIC), Collection Information Statement for Wage Earners and Self-Employed Individuals

Fill out the Form 433-A(OIC) if you are an individual wage earner and/or a self-employed individual. This will be used to calculate an appropriate offer amount based on your assets, income, expenses, and future earning potential. You will have the opportunity to provide a written explanation of any special circumstances that affect your financial situation.

Step 3 – Fill out Form 433-B(OIC), Collection Information Statement for Businesses

Fill out the Form 433-B(OIC) if your business is a Corporation, Partnership, Limited Liability Company (LLC) classified as a corporation, single member LLC, or other multi-owner/multi-member LLC. This will be used to calculate an appropriate offer amount based on your business assets, income, expenses, and future earning potential. If you have assets that are used to produce income (for example, a tow truck used in your business for towing vehicles), you may be allowed to exclude equity in these assets.

Step 4 – Attach required documentation

You will need to attach supporting documentation with Form(s) 433-A(OIC) and 433-B(OIC). A list of the documents required will be found at the end of each form. Include copies of all required attachments, as needed. Do not send original documents.

Note: A completed Form 433-A(OIC) and/or Form 433-B(OIC) must be included with the Form 656 application.

Step 5 – Fill out Form 656, Offer in Compromise

Fill out Form 656. The Form 656 identifies the tax years and type of tax you would like to compromise. It also identifies your offer amount and the payment terms.

The Low Income Certification guidelines are included on Form 656. If you are an individual and meet the guidelines, check the Low Income Certification box in Section 4, on Form 656.

Step 6 – Include initial payment and $150 application fee

Include a check, cashier's check, or money order for your initial payment based on the payment option you selected (20% of offer amount or first month's installment).

Include a separate check, cashier's check, or money order for the application fee ($150).

Make both payments payable to the "United States Treasury." All payments must be made in U.S. dollars.

If you meet the Low Income Certification guidelines, the initial payment and application fee are not required.

Make a copy of your application package and keep it for your records.

Step 7 – Mail the application package

Mail the application package to the appropriate IRS facility. See page 23, Application Checklist, for details.

IMPORTANT INFORMATION

After you mail your application, continue to:

File all federal tax returns you are legally required to file.

Make all required federal estimated tax payments and tax deposits that are due for current taxes, and make all required periodic offer payments.

Reply to IRS requests for additional information within the timeframe specified. Failure to reply timely to requests for additional information could result in the return of your offer without appeal rights.

4

Department of the Treasury — Internal Revenue Service

Collection Information Statement for Wage Earners and Self-Employed Individuals

Use this form if you are

- An individual who owes income tax on a Form 1040, U.S. Individual Income Tax Return
- An individual with a personal liability for Excise Tax
- An individual responsible for a Trust Fund Recovery Penalty

- An individual who is personally responsible for a partnership liability
- An individual who is self-employed or has self-employment income. You are considered to be self-employed if you are in business for yourself, or carry on a trade or business.

Wage earners Complete sections 1, 3, 4 (Box 1), 6, and 7 including signature line on page 7.
Self-employed individuals Complete all sections and signature line on page 7

Note: Include attachments if additional space is needed to respond completely to any question.

Section 1	Personal and Household Information

Last Name	First Name	Date of Birth (mm/dd/yyyy)	Social Security Number − −

Marital status ☐ Married ☐ Unmarried	Home Address (Street, City, State, ZIP Code)	Do you: ☐ Own your home ☐ Rent ☐ Other (specify e.g., share rent, live with relative, etc.)

County of Residence	Primary Phone ( ) -	Mailing Address (if different from above or Post Office Box number)
Secondary Phone ( ) -	Fax Number ( ) -	
Employer's Name		Employer's Address (Street, City, State, ZIP Code)
Occupation	How Long?	

Provide information about your spouse.

Spouse's Last Name	First Name	Date of Birth (mm/dd/yyyy)	Social Security Number − −
Occupation		Employer's Address (Street, City, State, ZIP Code)	
Employer's Name			

Provide information for all other persons in the household or claimed as a dependent.

Name	Age	Relationship	Claimed as a dependent on your Form 1040?	Contributes to household income?
			☐ Yes ☐ No	☐ Yes ☐ No
			☐ Yes ☐ No	☐ Yes ☐ No
			☐ Yes ☐ No	☐ Yes ☐ No
			☐ Yes ☐ No	☐ Yes ☐ No

Section 2	Self-employed Information

If you or your spouse is self-employed, complete this section.

Is your business a sole proprietorship (filing Schedule C)? ☐ Yes ☐ No	Address of Business (If other than personal residence)
Name of Business	

Business Telephone Number ( ) -	Employer Identification Number	Business Website	Trade Name or dba
Description of Business	Total Number of Employees	Frequency of Tax Deposits	Average Gross Monthly Payroll $

Section 2 *(Continued)* — Self-employed Information

Do you or your spouse have any other business interests?

☐ Yes *(Percentage of ownership:*   *)*   ☐ No

Business Address *(Street, City, State, ZIP code)*

Business Name

Business Telephone Number	Business Identification Number
( ) -	

Type of business *(Select one)*

☐ Partnership   ☐ LLC   ☐ Corporation   ☐ Other

Section 3 — Personal Asset Information

Cash and Investments (domestic and foreign)

Use the **most current** statement for each type of account, such as checking, savings, money market and online accounts, stored value cards *(such as, a payroll card from an employer)*, investment and retirement accounts *(IRAs, Keogh, 401(k) plans, stocks, bonds, mutual funds, certificates of deposit)*, life insurance policies that have a cash value, and safe deposit boxes. Asset value is subject to adjustment by IRS based on individual circumstances. Enter the total amount available for each of the following *(if additional space is needed include attachments)*.

If any line item is zero or less, enter "0". Do not enter negative numbers on this form.

☐ Cash ☐ Checking ☐ Savings ☐ Money Market ☐ Online Account ☐ Stored Value Card

Bank Name	Account Number

(1a) $ _____

☐ Checking ☐ Savings ☐ Money Market ☐ Online Account ☐ Stored Value Card

Bank Name	Account Number

(1b) $ _____

Total value of bank accounts from attachment   (1c) $ _____

Add lines (1a) through (1c) =   **(1) $ _____**

Investment Account: ☐ Stocks ☐ Bonds ☐ Other

Name of Financial Institution	Account Number

Current Market Value   Less Loan Balance

$ _____ X .8 = $ _____ − $ _____ = (2a) $ _____

Investment Account: ☐ Stocks ☐ Bonds ☐ Other

Name of Financial Institution	Account Number

Current Market Value   Less Loan Balance

$ _____ X .8 = $ _____ − $ _____ = (2b) $ _____

Total of investment accounts from attachment. [current market value X.8 less loan balance(s)]   (2c) $ _____

Add lines (2a) through (2c) =   **(2) $ _____**

Retirement Account: ☐ 401k ☐ IRA ☐ Other

Name of Financial Institution	Account Number

Current Market Value   Less Loan Balance

$ _____ X .7 = $ _____ − $ _____ = (3a) $ _____

Retirement Account: ☐ 401k ☐ IRA ☐ Other

Name of Financial Institution	Account Number

Current Market Value   Less Loan Balance

$ _____ X .7 = $ _____ − $ _____ = (3b) $ _____

Total of investment accounts from attachment. [current market value X .7 less loan balance(s)]   (3c) $ _____

Add lines (3a) through (3c) =   **(3) $ _____**

Section 3 (Continued) — Personal Asset Information

Cash value of life insurance policies

Name of Insurance Company	Policy Number

Current Cash Value	Less Loan Balance	
$ _____	– $ _____	= (4a) $

Total of life insurance policies from attachment.	Less Any Loan Balance(s)	
$ _____	– $ _____	= (4b) $

Add lines (4a) through (4b) = (4) $

Real Estate (Enter information about any house, condo, co-op, time share, etc. that you own or are buying)

Property Address (Street Address, City, State, ZIP Code)	Primary Residence ☐ Yes ☐ No
	Date Purchased _____
	County and Country

How is property titled? (joint tenancy, etc.)?	Description of Property

Current Market Value	Less Loan Balance (Mortgages, etc.)	
$ _____ X .8 = $ _____	– $ _____ Total Value of Real Estate =	(5a) $

Property Address (Street Address, City, State, ZIP Code)	Primary Residence ☐ Yes ☐ No
	Date Purchased _____
	County and Country

How is property titled? (joint tenancy, etc.)?	Description of Property

Current Market Value	Less Loan Balance (Mortgages, etc.)	
$ _____ X .8 = $ _____	– $ _____ Total Value of Real Estate =	(5b) $

Property Address (Street Address, City, State, ZIP Code)	Primary Residence ☐ Yes ☐ No
	Date Purchased _____
	County and Country

How is property titled? (joint tenancy, etc.)?	Description of Property

Current Market Value	Less Loan Balance (Mortgages, etc.)	
$ _____ X .8 = $ _____	– $ _____ Total Value of Real Estate =	(5c) $

Total value of property(s) from attachment [current market value X .8 less any loan balance(s)]	(5d) $

Add lines (5a) through (5d) = (5) $

Vehicles (Enter information about any cars, boats, motorcycles, etc. that you own or lease)

Vehicle Make & Model	Year	Date Purchased	Mileage	☐ Lease ☐ Loan	Monthly Lease/Loan Amount $

Current Market Value	Less Loan Balance		
$ _____ X .8 = $ _____	– $ _____	Total value of vehicle (if the vehicle is leased, enter 0 as the total value) =	(6a) $

Vehicle Make & Model	Year	Date Purchased	Mileage	☐ Lease ☐ Loan	Monthly Lease/Loan Amount $

Current Market Value	Less Loan Balance		
$ _____ X .8 = $ _____	– $ _____	Total value of vehicle (if the vehicle is leased, enter 0 as the total value) =	(6b) $

Vehicle Make & Model	Year	Date Purchased	Mileage	☐ Lease ☐ Loan	Monthly Lease/Loan Amount $

Current Market Value	Less Loan Balance		
$ _____ X .8 = $ _____	– $ _____	Total value of vehicle (if the vehicle is leased, enter 0 as the total value) =	(6c) $

Catalog Number 55896Q   www.irs.gov   Form **433-A (OIC)** (Rev. 5-2012)

Section 3 (Continued)	Personal Asset Information		
Total value of vehicles listed from attachment [current market value X .8 less any loan balance(s)]		(6d) $	
	Add lines (6a) through (6d) =	(6) $	

Other valuable items *(artwork, collections, jewelry, items of value in safe deposit boxes, etc).*

Description of asset:		
Current Market Value	Less Loan Balance	
$_____ X .8 = $_____ – $_____ =		(7a) $
Description of asset:		
Current Market Value	Less Loan Balance	
$_____ X .8 = $_____ – $_____ =		(7b) $
Total value of valuable items listed from attachment [current market value X .8 less any loan balance(s)]		(7c) $
Add lines (7a) through (7c) =		(7) $

Section 4	Business Asset Information *(for Self-Employed)*

List business assets such as bank accounts, tools, books, machinery, equipment, business vehicles and real property that is owned/leased/rented. If additional space is needed, attach a list of items. Do not enter a number less than zero.

☐ Cash ☐ Checking ☐ Savings ☐ Money Market ☐ Online Account ☐ Stored Value Card	
Bank Name Account Number	(8a) $
☐ Checking ☐ Savings ☐ Money Market ☐ Online Account ☐ Stored Value Card	
Bank Name Account Number	(8b) $
Total value of bank accounts from attachment	(8c) $
Add lines (8a) through (8c) for total bank account(s) =	(8) $

Description of asset:		
Current Market Value	Less Loan Balance	
$_____ X .8 = $_____ – $_____ =		(9a) $
Description of asset:		
Current Market Value	Less Loan Balance	
$_____ X .8 = $_____ – $_____ =		(9b) $
Total value of assets listed from attachment [current market value X .8 less any loan balance(s)]		(9c) $
Add lines (9a) through (9c) =		(9) $
IRS allowed deduction for professional books and tools of trade –		(10) $ [4,290]
Enter the value of line (9) minus line (10). If less than zero enter zero. =		(11) $

Notes Receivable
Do you have notes receivable? ☐ Yes ☐ No
If yes, attach current listing which includes name and amount of note(s) receivable.

Accounts Receivable
Do you have accounts receivable? ☐ Yes ☐ No
If yes, you may be asked to provide a list of the Account(s) Receivable.

Do not include amount on the lines with a letter beside the number. **Add lines (1) through (8), and line (11) and enter the amount in Box 1 =**	**Box 1 Available Equity in Assets** $

Section 5	Business Income and Expense Information *(for Self-Employed)*

Note: If you provide a current profit and loss (P&L) statement for the information below, enter the total gross monthly income on line 18 and your monthly expenses on line 30 below. Do not complete lines (13) - (17) and (19) - (29). You may use the amounts claimed for income and expenses on your most recent Schedule C; however, if the amount has changed significantly within the past year, a current P&L should be submitted to substantiate the claim.

Business Income *(You may average 6-12 months income/receipts to determine your Gross monthly income/receipts.)*

Gross receipts	(13)	$
Gross rental income	(14)	$
Interest income	(15)	$
Dividends	(16)	$
Other income	(17)	$
Gross Monthly Business Income - Add lines (13) through (17) =	(18)	$

Business Expenses *(You may average 6-12 months expenses to determine your average expenses.)*

Materials purchased *(e.g., items directly related to the production of a product or service)*	(19)	$
Inventory purchased *(e.g., goods bought for resale)*	(20)	$
Gross wages and salaries	(21)	$
Rent	(22)	$
Supplies *(items used to conduct business and used up within one year, e.g., books, office supplies, professional equipment, etc.)*	(23)	$
Utilities/telephones	(24)	$
Vehicle costs *(gas, oil, repairs, maintenance)*	(25)	$
Business Insurance	(26)	$
Current Business Taxes *(e.g., Real estate, excise, franchise, occupational, personal property, sales and employer's portion of employment taxes)*	(27)	$
Other secured debts *(not credit cards)*	(28)	$
Other business expenses *(include a list)*	(29)	$
Total Monthly Business Expenses - Add lines (19) through (29) =	(30)	$
Subtract line (30) from line (18) and enter the amount in Box 2 =	**Box 2 Net Business Income** $

Section 6	Monthly Household Income and Expense Information

Enter your household's gross monthly income. The information below is for yourself, your spouse, and anyone else who contributes to your household's income. The entire household includes spouse, significant other, children, and others who contribute to the household. This is necessary for the IRS to accurately evaluate your offer.

Monthly household income

Primary taxpayer

Wages	Social Security	Pension(s)		Total primary taxpayer income	
$_____	+ $_____	+ $_____	=		(31) $

Spouse

Wages	Social Security	Pension(s)		Total spouse income	
$_____	+ $_____	+ $_____	=		(32) $

Interest and dividends	(33)	$
Distributions *(such as, income from partnerships, sub-S Corporations, etc.)*	(34)	$
Net rental income	(35)	$
Net business income from Box 2	(36)	$
Child support received	(37)	$
Alimony received	(38)	$
Add lines (31) through (38) and enter the amount in Box 3 =	**Box 3 Total Household Income** $

Are there additional sources of income used to support the household, e.g. non-liable spouse, roommate, etc. ☐ Yes ☐ No

Catalog Number 55896Q

Form **433-A (OIC)** (Rev. 5-2012)

Section 6 - *(Continued)*   Monthly Household Income and Expense Information

Monthly Household Expenses

Enter your average monthly expenses.   **Note: Expenses may be adjusted based on IRS Collection Financial Standards. The standards may be found at irs.gov.**

Food, clothing, and miscellaneous *(e.g., housekeeping supplies, personal care products , minimum payment on credit card).* *A reasonable estimate of these expenses may be used.*	(41) $
Housing and utilities *(e.g., rent or mortgage payment and average monthly cost of property taxes, home insurance, maintenance, dues, fees and utilities including electricity, gas, other fuels, trash collection, water, cable television and internet, telephone, and cell phone).*	(42) $
Vehicle loan and/or lease payment(s)	(43) $
Vehicle operating costs *(e.g., average monthly cost of maintenance, repairs, insurance, fuel, registrations, licenses, inspections, parking, tolls, etc.).* *A reasonable estimate of these expenses may be used.*	(44) $
Public transportation costs *(e.g., average monthly cost of fares for mass transit such as bus, train, ferry, taxi, etc.). A reasonable estimate of these expenses may be used.*	(45) $
Health insurance premiums	(46) $
Out-of-pocket health care costs *(e.g. average monthly cost of prescription drugs, medical services, and medical supplies like eyeglasses, hearing aids, etc.)*	(47) $
Court-ordered payments *(e.g., monthly cost of any alimony, child support, etc.)*	(48) $
Child/dependent care payments *(e.g., daycare, etc.)*	(49) $
Life insurance premiums	(50) $
Current taxes *(e.g., monthly cost of federal, state, and local tax, personal property tax, etc.)*	(51) $
Other secured debts *(e.g., any loan where you pledged an asset as collateral not previously listed, government guaranteed Student Loan).*	(52) $
Delinquent State and Local Taxes	(53) $
Add lines (41) through (53) and enter the amount in Box 4 =	**Box 4 Household Expenses** $
Subtract Box 4 from Box 3 and enter the amount in Box 5 =	**Box 5 Remaining Monthly Income** $

Section 7   Calculate Your Minimum Offer Amount

The next steps calculate your minimum offer amount. The amount of time you take to pay your offer in full will affect your minimum offer amount. Paying over a shorter period of time will result in a smaller minimum offer amount.

If you will pay your offer in 5 months or less, multiply "Remaining Monthly Income" *(Box 5)* by 12 to get "Future Remaining Income" *(Box 6).*

Enter the total from Box 5 here $	**X 12 =**	**Box 6 Future Remaining Income** $

If you will pay your offer in more than 5 months, multiply "Remaining Monthly Income" *(Box 5)* by 24 to get "Future Remaining Income" (Box 7).

Enter the total from Box 5 here $	**X 24 =**	**Box 7 Future Remaining Income** $

Determine your minimum offer amount by adding the total available assets from Box 1 to amount in either Box 6 or Box 7.

Enter the amount from Box 1 here **Do Not Enter a Number Less Than Zero** $	**+**	**Enter the amount from either Box 6 or Box 7** $	**=**	**Offer Amount** **Must be more than zero** $ _____

If you have special circumstances that would hinder you from paying this amount, explain them on Form 656, Offer in Compromise, page 2, "Explanation of Circumstances."

Section 8	Other Information

Additional information IRS needs to consider settlement of your tax debt. If you or your business are currently in a bankruptcy proceeding, you are not eligible to apply for an offer.	Are you the beneficiary of a trust, estate, or life insurance policy? ☐ Yes ☐ No

Are you currently in bankruptcy? ☐ Yes ☐ No | Have you filed bankruptcy in the past 10 years? ☐ Yes ☐ No

Discharge/Dismissal Date *(mm/dd/yyyy)* | Location Filed

Are you or have you been party to a lawsuit?

☐ Yes ☐ No

If applicable, date the lawsuit was resolved: *(mm/dd/yyyy)*

In the past 10 years, have you transferred any assets for less than their full value?

☐ Yes ☐ No

If applicable, date the asset was transferred: *(mm/dd/yyyy)*

Have you lived outside the U.S. for 6 months or longer in the past 10 years?

☐ Yes ☐ No

Do you have any funds being held in trust by a third party?

☐ Yes ☐ No **If yes,** how much $ Where:

Section 9	Signatures

Under penalties of perjury, I declare that I have examined this offer, including accompanying documents, and to the best of my knowledge it is true, correct, and complete.

► **Signature of Taxpayer**	Date *(mm/dd/yyyy)*
► **Signature of Taxpayer**	Date *(mm/dd/yyyy)*

Remember to include all applicable attachments listed below.

☐ Copies of the most recent pay stub, earnings statement, etc., from each employer

☐ Copies of bank statements for the three most recent months

☐ Copies of the most recent statement, etc., from all other sources of income such as pensions, Social Security, rental income, interest and dividends, court order for child support, alimony, and rent subsidies

☐ Copies of the most recent statement for each investment and retirement account

☐ Copies of the most recent statement from lender(s) on loans such as mortgages, second mortgages, vehicles, etc., showing monthly payments, loan payoffs, and balances

☐ List of Notes Receivable, if applicable

☐ Verification of State/Local Tax Liability, if applicable

☐ Documentation to support any special circumstances described in the "Explain special circumstances" section on page 2 of Form 656, if applicable

☐ Attach a Form 2848, *Power of Attorney*, if you would like your attorney, CPA, or enrolled agent to represent you and you do not have a current form on file with the IRS.

Privacy Act Statement

The information requested on this Form is covered under Privacy Act and Paperwork Reduction Act Notices which have already been provided to the taxpayer.

| |

Form **433-B (OIC)**
(Rev. May 2012)

Collection Information Statement for Businesses

Complete this form if your business is a

- Corporation
- Partnership
- Limited Liability Company (LLC) classified as a corporation
- Other multi-owner/multi-member LLC
- Single member LLC

If your business is a sole proprietorship (filing Schedule C), do not use this form. Instead, complete Form 433-A (OIC) Collection Information Statement for Wage Earners and Self-Employed Individuals.

Include attachments if additional space is needed to respond completely to any question.

Section 1	Business Information

Business Name	Employer Identification Number

Business address (street, city, state, zip code)	County of Business Location
	Description of Business and dba or "Trade Name"

Primary Phone	Secondary Phone	Mailing address (if different from above or Post Office Box number)
( ) -	( ) -	
Business website address		

Fax Number	Does the business outsource its payroll processing and tax return preparation for a fee?
( ) -	☐ Yes ☐ No If yes, list provider name and address in box below (Street, City, State, ZIP Code)

Federal Contractor	Total Number of Employees	
☐ Yes ☐ No		
Frequency of tax deposits	Average gross monthly payroll $	

Provide information about all partners, officers, LLC members, major shareholders (foreign and domestic), etc., associated with the business. Include attachments if additional space is needed.

Last Name	First Name	Title

Percent of Ownership and annual salary	Social Security Number — —	Home address (Street, City, State, ZIP Code)

Primary Phone	Secondary Phone	
( ) -	( ) -	

Last Name	First Name	Title

Percent of Ownership and annual salary	Social Security Number — —	Home address (Street, City, State, ZIP Code)

Primary Phone	Secondary Phone	
( ) -	( ) -	

Last Name	First Name	Title

Percent of Ownership and annual salary	Social Security Number — —	Home address (Street, City, State, ZIP Code)

Primary Phone	Secondary Phone	
( ) -	( ) -	

Section 2	Business Asset Information

Gather the **most current** statement from banks, lenders on loans, mortgages *(including second mortgages)*, monthly payments, loan balances, and accountant's depreciation schedules, if applicable. Also, include make/model/year/mileage of vehicles and current value of business assets. To estimate the current value, you may consult resources like Kelley Blue Book *(www.kbb.com)*, NADA *(www.nada.com)*, local real estate postings of properties similar to yours, and any other websites or publications that show what the business assets would be worth if you were to sell them. Asset value is subject to adjustment by IRS. Enter the total amount available for each of the following *(if additional space is needed, please include attachments)*.

If any line item is zero or less, enter "0". Do not enter negative numbers on this form.

☐ Cash ☐ Checking ☐ Savings ☐ Money Market ☐ Online Account ☐ Stored Value Card

Bank Name	Account Number	
		(1a) $

☐ Checking ☐ Savings ☐ Money Market ☐ Online Account ☐ Stored Value Card

Bank Name	Account Number	
		(1b) $

☐ Checking ☐ Savings ☐ Money Market ☐ Online Account ☐ Stored Value Card

Bank Name	Account Number	
		(1c) $

Total value of bank accounts from attachment	(1d) $
Add lines (1a) through (1d) =	**(1)** $

Investment Account: ☐ Stocks ☐ Bonds ☐ Other

Name of Financial Institution	Account Number

Current Market Value	Less Loan Balance	
$ _____ X .8 = $ _____	− $ _____ =	(2a) $

Investment Account: ☐ Stocks ☐ Bonds ☐ Other

Name of Financial Institution	Account Number

Current Market Value	Less Loan Balance	
$ _____ X .8 = $ _____	− $ _____ =	(2b) $

Total of investment accounts from attachment. [current market value X.8 less loan balance(s)]	(2c) $
Add lines (2a) through (2c) =	**(2)** $

Notes receivable

Do you have notes receivable? ☐ Yes ☐ No

If yes, attach current listing which includes name and amount of note(s) receivable.

Accounts Receivable

Do you have accounts receivable? ☐ Yes ☐ No

If yes, you may be asked to provide a list of name and amount of the Account(s) Receivable.

Section 2 *(Continued)* — **Business Asset Information**

If the business owns more properties, vehicles, or equipment than shown in this form, please list on an attachment.

Real Estate *(Buildings, Lots, Commercial Property, etc.)*

Do not use negative numbers.

Property Address *(Street Address, City, State, ZIP Code)* — Property Description — Date Purchased

County and Country

Current Market Value	Less Loan Balance *(Mortgages, etc.)*	
$ _____ X .8 = $ _____	– $ _____ Total Value of Real Estate =	(3a) $

Property Address *(Street Address, City, State, ZIP Code)* — Property Description — Date Purchased

County and Country

Current Market Value	Less Loan Balance *(Mortgages, etc.)*	
$ _____ X .8 = $ _____	– $ _____ Total Value of Real Estate =	(3b) $

Total value of property(s) listed from attachment [current market value X .8 less any loan balance(s)]	(3c) $

Add lines (3a) through (3c) =	**(3)** $

Business Vehicles *(cars, boats, motorcycles, trailers, etc.).* If additional space is needed, list on an attachment.

Vehicle Make & Model — Year — Date Purchased — Mileage or Use Hours

☐ Lease ☐ Loan — Monthly Lease/Loan Amount $

Current Market Value	Less Loan Balance	
$ _____ X .8 = $ _____	– $ _____	Total value of vehicle *(if the vehicle is leased, enter 0 as the total value)* = (4a) $

Vehicle Make & Model — Year — Date Purchased — Mileage or Use Hours

☐ Lease ☐ Loan — Monthly Lease/Loan Amount $

Current Market Value	Less Loan Balance	
$ _____ X .8 = $ _____	– $ _____	Total value of vehicle *(if the vehicle is leased, enter 0 as the total value)* = (4b) $

Vehicle Make & Model — Year — Date Purchased — Mileage or Use Hours

☐ Lease ☐ Loan — Monthly Lease/Loan Amount $

Current Market Value	Less Loan Balance	
$ _____ X .8 = $ _____	– $ _____	Total value of vehicle *(if the vehicle is leased, enter 0 as the total value)* = (4c) $

Total value of vehicles listed from attachment [current market value X .8 less any loan balance(s)]	(4d) $

Add lines (4a) through (4d) =	**(4)** $

Other Business Equipment

Current Market Value	Less Loan Balance	
$ _____ X .8 = $ _____	– $ _____	Total value of equipment *(if leased, enter 0 as the total value)* = (5a) $

Total value of equipment listed from attachment [current market value X .8 less any loan balance(s)]	(5b) $

IRS allowed exemption for professional books and tools of trade -	(5c) $ [4,290]

Total value of all business equipment = **Add lines (5a) and (5b) minus line (5c), if number is less than zero, enter zero =**	**(5)** $

Do not include the amount on lines with a letter beside the number. **Add lines (1) through (5) and enter the amount in Box 1 =**	**Box 1 Available Equity in Assets** $

Section 3 — Business Income Information

Enter the **average** gross monthly income of your business. To determine your gross monthly income use the most recent 6-12 months documentation of commissions, invoices, gross receipts from sales/services, etc.; most recent 6-12 months earnings statements, etc., from every other source of income (such as rental income, interest and dividends, or subsidies); or you may use a most recent 6-12 months Profit and Loss (P&L) to provide the information of income and expenses.

Note: If you provide a current profit and loss statement for the information below, enter the total gross monthly income in Box 2 below. Do not complete lines (6) - (10).

Gross receipts	(6)	$
Gross rental income	(7)	$
Interest income	(8)	$
Dividends	(9)	$
Other income (Specify on attachment)	(10)	$
Add lines (6) through (10) and enter the amount in Box 2 =	**Box 2 Total Business Income** $	

Section 4 — Business Expense Information

Enter the average gross monthly expenses for your business using your most recent 6-12 months statements, bills, receipts, or other documents showing monthly recurring expenses.

Note: If you provide a current profit and loss statement for the information below, enter the total monthly expenses in Box 3 below. Do not complete lines (11) - (20).

Materials purchased (e.g., items directly related to the production of a product or service)	(11)	$
Inventory purchased (e.g., goods bought for resale)	(12)	$
Gross wages and salaries	(13)	$
Rent	(14)	$
Supplies (items used to conduct business and used up within one year, e.g., books, office supplies, professional equipment, etc.)	(15)	$
Utilities/telephones	(16)	$
Vehicle costs (gas, oil, repairs, maintenance)	(17)	$
Insurance (other than life)	(18)	$
Current taxes (e.g., real estate, state, and local income tax, excise franchise, occupational, personal property, sales and employer's portion of employment taxes, etc.)	(19)	$
Other expenses (e.g., secured debt payments. Specify on attachment. Do not include credit card payments)	(20)	$
Add lines (11) through (20) and enter the amount in Box 3 =	**Box 3 Total Business Expenses** $	
Subtract Box 3 from Box 2 and enter the amount in Box 4 = If number is less than zero, enter zero.	**Box 4 Remaining Monthly Income** $	

Section 5	Calculate Your Minimum Offer Amount

The next steps calculate your minimum offer amount. The amount of time you take to pay your offer in full will affect your minimum offer amount. Paying over a shorter period of time will result in a smaller minimum offer amount.

If you will pay your offer in 5 months or less, multiply "Remaining Monthly Income" (Box 4) by 12 to get "Future Remaining Income."

Enter the amount from Box 4 here $	X 12 =	Box 5 Future Remaining Income $

If you will pay your offer in more than 5 months, multiply "Remaining Monthly Income" (from Box 4) by 24 to get "Future Remaining Income."

Enter the amount from Box 4 here $	X 24 =	Box 6 Future Remaining Income $

Determine your minimum offer amount by adding the total available assets from Box 1 to amount in either Box 5 or Box 6.

Enter the amount from Box 1 here* Do not enter a number less than zero $	+	Enter the amount from either Box 5 or Box 6 $	=	Offer Amount Must be more than zero $ _____

If you have special circumstances that would hinder you from paying this amount, explain them on Form 656, Offer in Compromise, Page 2, "Explanation of Circumstances."

*You may exclude any equity in income producing assets shown in Section 2 of this form.

Section 6	Other Information

Additional information IRS needs to consider settlement of your tax debt. If this business is currently in a bankruptcy proceeding, the business is not eligible to apply for an offer.

Is the business currently in bankruptcy?
☐ Yes ☐ No

Has the business ever filed bankruptcy?
☐ Yes ☐ No

If yes, provide:

Date Filed (mm/dd/yyyy) _____   Date Dismissed or Discharged (mm/dd/yyyy) _____

Petition No. _____   Location Filed _____

Does this business have other business affiliations (e.g., subsidiary or parent companies)?
☐ Yes ☐ No

If yes, list the Name and Employer Identification Number:

Do any related parties (e.g., partners, officers, employees) owe money to the business?
☐ Yes ☐ No

Is the business currently, or in the past, a party to a lawsuit?
☐ Yes ☐ No **If applicable**, date the lawsuit was resolved: _____

In the past 10 years, has the business transferred any assets for less than their full value?
☐ Yes ☐ No **If applicable**, provide date and type of asset transferred:

Has the business been located outside the U.S. for 6 months or longer in the past 10 years?
☐ Yes ☐ No

Does the business have any funds being held in trust by a third party?
☐ Yes ☐ No **If yes**, how much $ _____   Where: _____

Does the business have any lines of credit?
☐ Yes ☐ No **If yes**, credit limit $ _____   Amount owed $ _____

What property secures the line of credit? _____

Section 7 — Signatures

Under penalties of perjury, I declare that I have examined this offer, including accompanying documents, and to the best of my knowledge it is true, correct, and complete.

Signature of Taxpayer	Title	Date (mm/dd/yyyy)

Remember to include all applicable attachments from list below.

☐ A current Profit and Loss statement covering at least the most recent 6-12 month period, if appropriate.

☐ Copies of the most recent statement for each bank, investment, and retirement account.

☐ If an asset is used as collateral on a loan, include copies of the most recent statement from lender(s) on loans, monthly payments, loan payoffs, and balances.

☐ Copies of the most recent statement of outstanding notes receivable.

☐ Copies of the most recent statements from lenders on loans, mortgages (including second mortgages), monthly payments, loan payoffs, and balances.

☐ Copies of relevant supporting documentation of the special circumstances described in the "Explain special circumstances" section on page 2 of Form 656, if applicable.

☐ Attach a Form 2848, Power of Attorney, if you would like your attorney, CPA, or enrolled agent to represent you and you do not have a current form on file with the IRS.

Privacy Act Statement

The information requested on this Form is covered under Privacy Act and Paperwork Reduction Act Notices which have already been provided to the taxpayer.

Catalog Number 55897B   www.irs.gov   Form **433-B (OIC)** (Rev. 5-2012)

Form **656** (Rev. May 2012)	Department of the Treasury — Internal Revenue Service ## Offer in Compromise

Attach Application Fee and Payment *(check or money order)* **here.**

Section 1	Your Contact Information	IRS Received Date

Your First Name, Middle Initial, Last Name

If a Joint Offer, Spouse's First Name, Middle Initial, Last Name

Your Physical Home Address *(Street, City, State, ZIP Code)*

Mailing Address *(if different from above or Post Office Box number)*

Business Name

Your Business Address *(Street, City, State, ZIP Code)*

Social Security Number (SSN)
(Primary)   *(Secondary)*

Employer Identification Number (EIN)   *(EIN not included in offer)*

Section 2	Tax Periods

▶ **To: Commissioner of Internal Revenue Service**

In the following agreement, the pronoun "we" may be assumed in place of "I" when there are joint liabilities and both parties are signing this agreement.

I submit this offer to compromise the tax liabilities plus any interest, penalties, additions to tax, and additional amounts required by law for the tax type and period(s) marked below:

☐ 1040 Income Tax-Year(s) _____

☐ 1120 Income Tax-Year(s) _____

☐ 941 Employer's Quarterly Federal Tax Return - Quarterly period(s) _____

_____

☐ 940 Employer's Annual Federal Unemployment (FUTA) Tax Return - Year(s) _____

_____

☐ Trust Fund Recovery Penalty as a responsible person of *(enter corporation name)* _____
for failure to pay withholding and Federal Insurance Contributions Act taxes (Social Security taxes), for period(s) ending

_____

_____

☐ Other Federal Tax(es) [specify type(s) and period(s)] _____

_____

Note: If you need more space, use attachment and title it "Attachment to Form 656 dated _____ ." Make sure to sign and date the attachment.

Section 3	Reason for Offer

☐ **Doubt as to Collectibility** - I have insufficient assets and income to pay the full amount.

☐ **Exceptional Circumstances (Effective Tax Administration)** - I owe this amount and have sufficient assets to pay the full amount, but due to my exceptional circumstances, requiring full payment would cause an economic hardship or would be unfair and inequitable. I am submitting a written narrative explaining my circumstances.

Section 3 *(Continued)*   **Reason for Offer**

Explanation of Circumstances *(Add additional pages, if needed)*

The IRS understands that there are unplanned events or special circumstances, such as serious illness, where paying the full amount or the minimum offer amount might impair your ability to provide for yourself and your family. If this is the case and you can provide documentation to prove your situation, then your offer may be accepted despite your financial profile. Describe your situation below and attach appropriate documents to this offer application.

_____

_____

_____

_____

_____

_____

_____

Section 4   **Low Income Certification** *(Individuals Only)*

Do you qualify for Low-Income Certification? You qualify if your gross monthly household income is less than or equal to the amount shown in the chart below based on your family size and where you live. If you qualify, you are not required to submit any payments during the consideration of your offer.

☐ **Check here if you qualify for Low-Income Certification based on the monthly income guidelines below.**

Size of family unit	48 contiguous states and D.C.	Hawaii	Alaska
1	$2,327	$2,679	$2,910
2	$3,152	$3,627	$3,942
3	$3,997	$4,575	$4,973
4	$4,802	$5,523	$6,004
5	$5,627	$6,471	$7,035
6	$6,452	$7,419	$8,067
7	$7,277	$8,367	$9,098
8	$8,102	$9,315	$10,129
For each additional person, add	$825	$948	$1,031

Section 5   **Payment Terms**

⬇   **Check one of the payment options below to indicate how long it will take you to pay your offer in full**   ⬇

Lump Sum Cash

Enter the amount of your offer $ _____

☐ **Check here if you will pay your offer in five or fewer payments:**

Enclose a check for 20% of the offer amount (waived if you are an individual and met the requirements for Low-Income certification) and fill in the amount(s) and date(s) of your future payment(s). Your offer must be fully paid 24 months from the date your offer is accepted.

Total Offer Amount	-	20% Initial Payment	=	Remaining Balance
$	-	$	=	$

You may pay the remaining balance in one payment after acceptance of the offer or up to five payments.

1) $ _____ paid on the _____ (day), _____ month(s) after acceptance.

2) $ _____ paid on the _____ (day), _____ month(s) after acceptance.

3) $ _____ paid on the _____ (day), _____ month(s) after acceptance.

4) $ _____ paid on the _____ (day), _____ month(s) after acceptance.

5) $ _____ paid on the _____ (day), _____ month(s) after acceptance.

Periodic Payment

Enter the amount of your offer $ _____

☐ **Check here if you will pay your offer in full in more than five monthly installments.**

Enclose a check for one month's installment (waived if you are an individual and met the requirements for Low-Income certification)

$ _____ is being submitted with the Form 656 and then $ _____ on the _____ (day) of each month thereafter for a

total of _____ months *(may not exceed 23)*. Total payments must equal the total Offer Amount.

You must continue to make these monthly payments while the IRS is considering the offer. Failure to make regular monthly payments will cause your offer to be returned.

Section 6 — Designation of Down Payment and Deposit *(Optional)*

If you want your payment to be applied to a specific tax year and a specific tax debt, please tell us the tax form _____ and Tax Year/Quarter _____ . If you do not designate a preference, we will apply any money you send in to the governments best interest.

If you are paying more than the required payment when you submit your offer and want any part of that payment treated as a deposit, check the box below and insert the amount.

☐ I am making a deposit of $ _____ with this offer.

Section 7 — Source of Funds and Making Your Payment

Tell us where you will obtain the funds to pay your offer. You may consider borrowing from friends and/or family, taking out a loan, or selling assets.

_____

_____

Include separate checks for the payment and application fee.

Make checks payable to the "United States Treasury" and attach to the front of your Form 656, Offer in Compromise. All payments must be in U.S. dollars. **Do not send cash.** Send a separate application fee with each offer; do not combine it with any other tax payments, as this may delay processing of your offer. Your offer will be returned to you if the application fee and the required payments are not properly remitted, or if your check is returned for insufficient funds.

Section 8 — Offer Terms

By submitting this offer, I/we have read, understand and agree to the following terms and conditions:

Terms, Conditions, and Legal Agreement

a) I request that the IRS accept the offer amount listed in this offer application as payment of my outstanding tax debt (including interest, penalties, and any additional amounts required by law) as of the date listed on this form. I authorize the IRS to amend Section 2 on page 1 in the event I failed to list any of my assessed tax debt. I understand that my offer will be accepted, by law, unless IRS notifies me otherwise, in writing, within 24 months of the date my offer was received by IRS.

IRS will keep my payments, fees, and some refunds.

b) I voluntarily submit the payments made on this offer and **understand that they are not refundable even if I withdraw the offer or the IRS rejects or returns the offer.** Unless I designated how to apply the required payment (page 3 of this application), the IRS will apply my payment in the best interest of the government, choosing which tax years and tax liabilities to pay off. The IRS will also keep my application fee unless the offer is not accepted for processing.

c) The IRS will keep **any** refund, including interest, that I might be due for tax periods extending through the calendar year in which the IRS accepts my offer. I cannot designate that the refund be applied to estimated tax payments for the following year or the accepted offer amount. If I receive a refund after I submit this offer for any tax period extending through the calendar year in which the IRS accepts my offer, I will return the refund as soon as possible.

d) The IRS will keep any monies it has collected prior to this offer and any payments that I make relating to this offer that I did not designate as a deposit. Only amounts that exceed the mandatory payments can be treated as a deposit. Such a deposit will be refundable if the offer is rejected or returned by the IRS or is withdrawn. I understand that the IRS will not pay interest on any deposit. The IRS may seize ("levy") my assets up to the time that the IRS official signs and accepts my offer as pending.

Pending status of an offer and right to appeal

e) Once an authorized IRS official signs this form, my offer is considered pending as of that signature date and it remains pending until the IRS accepts, rejects, returns, or terminates my offer or I withdraw my offer. An offer is also considered pending for 30 days after any rejection of my offer by the IRS, and during the time that any rejection of my offer is being considered by the Appeals Office. An offer will be considered withdrawn when the IRS receives my written notification of withdrawal by personal delivery or certified mail or when I inform the IRS of my withdrawal by other means and the IRS acknowledges in writing my intent to withdraw the offer.

f) I waive the right to an Appeals hearing if I do not request a hearing within 30 days of the date the IRS notifies me of the decision to reject the offer.

I must comply with my future tax obligations and understand I remain liable for the full amount of my tax debt until all terms and conditions of this offer have been met.

g) I will file tax returns and pay required taxes for the five year period beginning with the date of acceptance of this offer. If this is an offer being submitted for joint tax debt, and one of us does not comply with future obligations, only the non-compliant taxpayer will be in default of this agreement.

h) The IRS will not remove the original amount of my tax debt from its records until I have met all the terms and conditions of this offer. Penalty and interest will continue to accrue until all payment terms of the offer have been met. If I file for bankruptcy before the terms are fully met, any claim the IRS files in the bankruptcy proceedings will be a tax claim.

i) Once the IRS accepts my offer in writing, I have no right to contest, in court or otherwise, the amount of the tax debt.

I understand what will happen if I fail to meet the terms of my offer (e.g., default).

j) If I fail to meet any of the terms of this offer, the IRS may levy or sue me to collect any amount ranging from the unpaid balance of the offer to the original amount of the tax debt without further notice of any kind. The IRS will continue to add interest, as Section 6601 of the Internal Revenue Code requires, on the amount the IRS determines is due after default. The IRS will add interest from the date I default until I completely satisfy the amount owed.

I agree to waive time limits provided by law.

k) To have my offer considered, I agree to the extension of the time limit provided by law to assess my tax debt (statutory period of assessment). I agree that the date by which the IRS must assess my tax debt will now be the date by which my debt must currently be assessed plus the period of time my offer is pending plus one additional year if the IRS rejects, returns, or terminates my offer or I withdraw it. (Paragraph (e) of this section

Section 8 - *(Continued)* — Offer Terms

defines pending and withdrawal). I understand that I have the right not to waive the statutory period of assessment or to limit the waiver to a certain length or certain periods or issues. I understand, however, that the IRS may not consider my offer if I refuse to waive the statutory period of assessment or if I provide only a limited waiver. I also understand that the statutory period for collecting my tax debt will be suspended during the time my offer is pending with the IRS, for 30 days after any rejection of my offer by the IRS, and during the time that any rejection of my offer is being considered by the Appeals Office.

I understand the IRS may file a Notice of Federal Tax Lien on my property.

l) The IRS may file a Notice of Federal Tax Lien during the offer investigation. The IRS may file a Notice of Federal Tax Lien to protect the Government's interest on offers that will be paid over time. This tax lien will be released when the payment terms of the accepted offer have been satisfied.

I authorize the IRS to contact relevant third parties in order to process my offer

m) By authorizing the IRS to contact third parties including credit bureaus, I understand that I will not be notified of which third parties the IRS contacts as part of the offer application process, as stated in section 7602(c) of the Internal Revenue Code.

I am submitting an offer as an individual for a joint liability

n) I understand if the liability sought to be compromised is the joint and individual liability of myself and my co-obligor(s) and I am submitting this offer to compromise my individual liability only, then if this offer is accepted, it does not release or discharge my co-obligor(s) from liability. The United States still reserves all rights of collection against the co-obligor(s).

Section 9 — Signatures

Under penalties of perjury, I declare that I have examined this offer, including accompanying schedules and statements, and to the best of my knowledge and belief, it is true, correct and complete.

Signature of Taxpayer/Corporation Name	Phone Number	Date *(mm/dd/yyyy)*
Signature of Taxpayer/Authorized Corporate Officer	Phone Number	Date *(mm/dd/yyyy)*

Section 10 — Paid Preparer Use Only

Signature of Preparer	Phone Number	Date *(mm/dd/yyyy)*
Name of Paid Preparer	Preparer's CAF no. or PTIN	

Firm's Name, Address, and ZIP Code

Include a valid, signed Form 2848 or 8821 with this application, if one is not on file.

Section 11 — Third Party Designee

Do you want to allow another person to discuss this offer with the IRS? ☐ Yes ☐ No

If yes, provide designee's name | Telephone Number ( )

IRS Use Only

I accept the waiver of the statutory period of limitations on assessment for the Internal Revenue Service, as described in Section 8 (k).

Signature of Authorized Internal Revenue Service Official	Title	Date *(mm/dd/yyyy)*

Privacy Act Statement

We ask for the information on this form to carry out the internal revenue laws of the United States. Our authority to request this information is Section 7801 of the Internal Revenue Code.

Our purpose for requesting the information is to determine if it is in the best interests of the IRS to accept an offer. You are not required to make an offer; however, if you choose to do so, you must provide all of the taxpayer information requested. Failure to provide all of the information may prevent us from processing your request.

If you are a paid preparer and you prepared the Form 656 for the taxpayer submitting an offer, we request that you complete and sign Section 10 on Form 656, and provide identifying information. Providing this information is voluntary. This information will be used to administer and enforce the internal revenue laws of the United States and may be used to regulate practice before the Internal Revenue Service for those persons subject to Treasury Department Circular No. 230, Regulations Governing the Practice of Attorneys, Certified Public Accountants, Enrolled Agents, Enrolled Actuaries, and Appraisers before the Internal Revenue Service. Information on this form may be disclosed to the Department of Justice for civil and criminal litigation.

We may also disclose this information to cities, states and the District of Columbia for use in administering their tax laws and to combat terrorism. Providing false or fraudulent information on this form may subject you to criminal prosecution and penalties.

Catalog Number 16728N   www.irs.gov   Form **656** (Rev. 5-2012)

APPLICATION CHECKLIST
Review the entire application and verify that it is complete.

Forms 433-A (OIC), 433-B (OIC), and 656

☐ Did you complete all fields and sign all forms?

☐ Did you make an offer amount that is equal to the offer amount calculated on the Form 433-A (OIC) or Form 433-B (OIC)? If not, did you describe the special circumstances that are leading you to offer less than the minimum in the "Explanation of Circumstances" Section 3 of Form 656, and did you provide supporting documentation of the special circumstances?

☐ Did you select a payment option on Form 656?

☐ If you want to allow the IRS to discuss your offer with another person, did you complete the "Third-Party Designee" section on the Form 656?

☐ If someone other than you completed the Form 656, did they sign it?

☐ Did you sign and attach the Form 433-A (OIC) if applicable?

☐ Did you sign and attach the Form 433-B (OIC) if applicable?

☐ Did you sign and attach the Form 656?

Supporting documentation and additional forms

☐ Did you include photocopies of all required supporting documentation?

☐ If you want a third party to represent you during the offer process, did you include a Form 2848 or Form 8821 unless one is already on file?

Payment

☐ Did you include a check or money order made payable to the "United States Treasury" for the initial payment? (Waived if you meet Low Income Certification guidelines—see Form 656.)

☐ Did you include a separate check or money order made payable to the "United States Treasury" for the $150 application fee? (Waived if you meet Low Income Certification guidelines—see Form 656.)

Mail your application package to the appropriate IRS facility

Mail the Form 656, 433-A (OIC) and/or 433-B (OIC), and related financial document(s) to the appropriate IRS processing office for your state. You may wish to send it by Certified Mail so you have a record of the date it was mailed.

If you reside in:

AK, AL, AR, AZ, CO, FL, GA, HI, ID, KY, LA, MS, MT, NC, NM, NV, OK, OR, SC, TN, TX, UT, WA, WI, WY

CA, CT, DE, IA, IL, IN, KS, MA, MD, ME, MI, MN, MO, ND, NE, NH, NJ, NY, OH, PA, RI, SD, VT, VA, WV; DC, PR, or a foreign address

Mail your application to:

Memphis IRS Center COIC Unit
P.O. Box 30803, AMC
Memphis, TN 38130-0803
1-866-790-7117

Brookhaven IRS Center COIC Unit
P.O. Box 9007
Holtsville, NY 11742-9007
1-866-611-6191

| Form **668-A(c)(DO)** | Department of the Treasury – Internal Revenue Service |
| (Rev. July 2002) | **Notice of Levy** |

DATE:
REPLY TO:

TELEPHONE NUMBER
OF IRS OFFICE:

NAME AND ADDRESS OF TAXPAYER:

TO:

IDENTIFYING NUMBER(S):

THIS ISN'T A BILL FOR TAXES YOU OWE. THIS IS A NOTICE OF LEVY WE ARE USING TO COLLECT MONEY OWED BY THE TAXPAYER NAMED ABOVE.

Kind of Tax	Tax Period Ended	Unpaid Balance of Assessment	Statutory Additions	Total

THIS LEVY WON'T ATTACH FUNDS IN IRAs, SELF-EMPLOYED INDIVIDUALS' RETIREMENT PLANS, OR ANY OTHER RETIREMENT PLANS IN YOUR POSSESSION OR CONTROL, UNLESS IT IS SIGNED IN THE BLOCK TO THE RIGHT. ➤

Total Amount Due ▶

We figured the interest and late payment penalty to _____

The Internal Revenue Code provides that there is a lien for the amount that is owed. Although we have given the notice and demand required by the Code, the amount owed hasn't been paid. This levy requires you to turn over to us this person's property and rights to property *(such as money, credits, and bank deposits)* that you have or which you are already obligated to pay this person. However, don't send us more than the "Total Amount Due."

Money in banks, credit unions, savings and loans, and similar institutions described in section 408(n) of the Internal Revenue Code must be held for 21 calendar days from the day you receive this levy before you send us the money. Include any interest the person earns during the 21 days. Turn over any other money, property, credits, etc. that you have or are already obligated to pay the taxpayer, when you would have paid it if this person asked for payment.

Make a reasonable effort to identify all property and rights to property belonging to this person. At a minimum, search your records using the taxpayer's name, address, and identifying numbers(s) shown on this form. Don't offset money this person owes you without contacting us at the telephone number shown above for instructions. You may not subtract a processing fee from the amount you send us.

To respond to this levy —

1. Make your check or money order payable to **United States Treasury**.
2. Write the taxpayer's name, identifying number(s), kind of tax and tax period shown on this form, and "LEVY PROCEEDS" on your check or money order *(not on a detachable stub.)*.
3. Complete the back of Part 3 of this form and mail it to us with your payment in the enclosed envelope.
4. Keep Part 1 of this form for your records and give the taxpayer Part 2 within 2 days.

If you don't owe any money to the taxpayer, please complete the back of Part 3, and mail that part back to us in the enclosed envelope.

Signature of Service Representative	Title

Part 1— For Addressee | Catalog No. 15704T | www.irs.gov | Form **668-A(c)(DO)** (Rev. 7-2002)

SEC. 6331. LEVY AND DISTRAINT.

(b) Seizure and Sale of Property.–The term "levy" as used in this title includes the power of distraint and seizure by any means. Except as otherwise provided in subsection (e), a levy shall extend only to property possessed and obligations existing at the time thereof. In any case in which the Secretary may levy upon property or rights to property, he may seize and sell such property or rights to property (whether real or personal, tangible or intangible).

(c) Successive Seizures.–Whenever any property or right to property upon which levy has been made by virtue of subsection (a) is not sufficient to satisfy the claim of the United States for which levy is made, the Secretary may, thereafter, and as often as may be necessary, proceed to levy in like manner upon any other property liable to levy of the person against whom such claim exists, until the amount due from him, together with all expenses, is fully paid.

SEC. 6332. SURRENDER OF PROPERTY SUBJECT TO LEVY.

(a) Requirement.–Except as otherwise provided in this section, any person in possession of (or obligated with respect to) property or rights to property subject to levy upon which a levy has been made shall, upon demand of the Secretary, surrender such property or rights (or discharge such obligation) to the Secretary, except such part of the property or rights as is, at the time of such demand, subject to an attachment or execution under any judicial process.

(b) Special rule for Life Insurance and Endowment Contracts

(1) In general.–A levy on an organization with respect to a life insurance or endowment contract issued by such organization shall, without necessity for the surrender of the contract document, constitute a demand by the Secretary for payment of the amount described in paragraph (2) and the exercise of the right of the person against whom the tax is assessed to the advance of such amount. Such organization shall pay over such amount 90 days after service of notice of levy. Such notice shall include a certification by the Secretary that a copy of such notice has been mailed to the person against whom the tax is assessed at his last known address.

(2) Satisfaction of levy.–Such levy shall be deemed to be satisfied if such organization pays over to the Secretary the amount which the person against whom the tax is assessed could have had advanced to him by such organization on the date prescribed in paragraph (1) for the satisfaction of such levy, increased by the amount of any advance (including contractual interest thereon) made to such person on or after the date such organization had actual notice or knowledge (within the meaning of section 6323 (i)(1)) of the existence of the lien with respect to which such levy is made, other than an advance (including contractual interest thereon) made automatically to maintain such contract in force under an agreement entered into before such organization had such notice or knowledge.

(3) Enforcement proceedings.–The satisfaction of a levy under paragraph (2) shall be without prejudice to any civil action for the enforcement of any lien imposed by this title with respect to such contract.

(c) Special Rule for Banks.–Any bank (as defined in section 408(n)) shall surrender (subject to an attachment or execution under judicial process) any deposits (including interest thereon) in such bank only after 21 days after service of levy.

(d) Enforcement of Levy.

(1) Extent of personal liability.–Any person who fails or refuses to surrender any property or rights to property, subject to levy, upon demand by the Secretary, shall be liable in his own person and estate to the United States in a sum equal to the value of the property or rights not so surrendered, but not exceeding the amount of taxes for the collection of which such levy has been made, together with costs and interest on such sum at the underpayment rate established under section 6621 from the date of such levy (or, in the case of a levy described in section 6331 (d)(3), from the date such person would otherwise have been obligated to pay over such amounts to the taxpayer). Any amount (other than costs) recovered under this paragraph shall be credited against the tax liability for the collection of which such levy was made.

(2) Penalty for violation.–In addition to the personal liability imposed by paragraph (1), if any person required to surrender property or rights to property fails or refuses to surrender such property or rights to property without reasonable cause, such person shall be liable for a penalty equal to 50 percent of the amount recoverable under paragraph (1). No part of such penalty shall be credited against the tax liability for the collection of which such levy was made.

(e) Effect of honoring levy.–Any person in possession of (or obligated with respect to) property or rights to property subject to levy upon which a levy has been made who, upon demand by the Secretary, surrenders such property or rights to property (or discharges such obligation) to the Secretary (or who pays a liability under subsection (d)(1)), shall be discharged from any obligation or liability to the delinquent taxpayer and any other person with respect to such property or rights to property arising from such surrender or payment.

SEC. 6333. PRODUCTION OF BOOKS.

If a levy has been made or is about to be made on any property, or right to property, any person having custody or control of any books or records, containing evidence or statements relating to the property or right to property subject to levy, shall, upon demand of the Secretary, exhibit such books or records to the Secretary.

SEC. 6343. AUTHORITY TO RELEASE LEVY AND RETURN PROPERTY.

(a) Release of Levy and Notice of Release.–

(1) In general.–Under regulations prescribed by the Secretary, the Secretary shall release the levy upon all, or part of, the property or rights to property levied upon and shall promptly notify the person upon whom such levy was made (if any) that such levy has been released if–

(A) the liability for which such levy was made is satisfied or becomes unenforceable by reason of lapse of time,

(B) release of such levy will facilitate the collection of such liability,

(C) the taxpayer has entered into an agreement under section 6159 to satisfy such liability by means of installment payments, unless such agreement provides otherwise,

(D) the Secretary has determined that such levy is creating an economic hardship due to the financial condition of the taxpayer, or

(E) the fair market value of the property exceeds such liability and release of the levy on a part of such property could be made without hindering the collection of such liability.

For purposes of subparagraph (C), the Secretary is not required to release such levy if such release would jeopardize the secured creditor status of the Secretary.

(2) Expedited determination on certain business property.–In the case of any tangible personal property essential in carrying on the trade or business of the taxpayer, the Secretary shall provide for an expedited determination under paragraph (1) if levy on such tangible personal property would prevent the taxpayer from carrying on such trade or business.

(3) Subsequent levy.–The release of levy on any property under paragraph (1) shall not prevent any subsequent levy on such property.

(b) Return of Property.–If the Secretary determines that property has been wrongfully levied upon, it shall be lawful for the Secretary to return–

(1) the specific property levied upon,
(2) an amount of money equal to the amount of money levied upon, or
(3) an amount of money equal to the amount of money received by the United States from a sale of such property.

Property may be returned at any time. An amount equal to the amount of money levied upon or received from such sale may be returned at any time before the expiration of 9 months from the date of such levy. For purposes of paragraph (3), if property is declared purchased by the United States at a sale pursuant to section 6335(e) (relating to manner and conditions of sale), the United States shall be treated as having received an amount of money equal to the minimum price determined pursuant to such section or (if larger) the amount received by the United States from the resale of such property.

(d) Return of Property in Certain Cases.—If—

(1) any property has been levied upon, and
(2) the Secretary determines that—

(A) the levy on such property was premature or otherwise not in accordance with administrative procedures of the Secretary,

(B) the taxpayer has entered into an agreement under section 6159 to satisfy the tax liability for which the levy was imposed by means of installment payments, unless such agreement provides otherwise,

(C) the return of such property will facilitate the collection of the tax liability, or

(D) with the consent of the taxpayer or the National Taxpayer Advocate, the return of such property would be in the best interests of the taxpayer (as determined by the National Taxpayer Advocate) and the United States,

the provisions of subsection (b) shall apply in the same manner as if such property had been wrongly levied upon, except that no interest shall be allowed under subsection (c).

*   *   *   *   *   *   *   *   *   *

Applicable Sections of Internal Revenue Code

6321. LIEN FOR TAXES.
6322. PERIOD OF LIEN.
6325. RELEASE OF LIEN OR DISCHARGE OF PROPERTY.
6331. LEVY AND DISTRAINT.
6332. SURRENDER OF PROPERTY SUBJECT TO LEVY.
6333. PRODUCTION OF BOOKS.
6334. PROPERTY EXEMPT FROM LEVY.
6343. AUTHORITY TO RELEASE LEVY AND RETURN PROPERTY.
7426. CIVIL ACTIONS BY PERSONS OTHER THAN TAXPAYERS.
7429. REVIEW OF JEOPARDY LEVY OR ASSESSMENT PROCEDURES.

For more information about this notice, please call the phone number on the front of this form.

Form **668-A(c)(DO)** (Rev. 7-2002)

| Form **668-A(c)(DO)** | Department of the Treasury – Internal Revenue Service |
| (Rev. July 2002) | **Notice of Levy** |

DATE:

REPLY TO:

TELEPHONE NUMBER
OF IRS OFFICE:

NAME AND ADDRESS OF TAXPAYER:

TO:

IDENTIFYING NUMBER(S):

Kind of Tax	Tax Period Ended	Unpaid Balance of Assessment	Statutory Additions	Total

THIS LEVY WON'T ATTACH FUNDS IN IRAs, SELF-EMPLOYED INDIVIDUALS' RETIREMENT PLANS, OR ANY OTHER RETIREMENT PLANS IN YOUR POSSESSION OR CONTROL, UNLESS IT IS SIGNED IN THE BLOCK TO THE RIGHT. ➡️

Total Amount Due ▶

We figured the interest and late payment penalty to _____

Although we have told you to pay the amount you owe, it is still not paid. This is your copy of a notice of levy we have sent to collect this unpaid amount. We will send other levies if we don't get enough with this one.

Banks, credit unions, savings and loans, and similar Institutions described in section 408(n) of the Internal Revenue Code must hold your money for 21 calendar days before sending it to us. They must include the interest you earn during that time. Anyone else we send a levy to must turn over your money, property, credits, etc. that they have *(or are already obligated for)* when they would have paid you.

If you decide to pay the amount you owe now, please **bring** a guaranteed payment *(cash, cashier's check, certified check, or money order)* to the nearest IRS office with this form, so we can tell the person who received this levy not to send us your money. Make checks and money orders payable to **United States Treasury.** If you mail your payment instead of bringing it to us, we may not have time to stop the person who received this levy from sending us your money.

If we have erroneously levied your bank account, we may reimburse you for the fees your bank charged you for handling the levy. You must file a claim with the IRS on Form 8546 within one year after the fees are charged.

If you have any questions, or want to arrange payment before other levies are issued, please call or write us. If you write to us, please include your telephone number and the best time to call.

Signature of Service Representative

Title

Part 2— For Taxpayer

Form **668-A(c)(DO)** (Rev. 7-2002)

*   *   *   *   *   *   *   *   *   *

SEC. 6331. LEVY AND DISTRAINT.

(b) Seizure and Sale of Property.—The term "levy" as used in this title includes the power of distraint and seizure by any means. Except as otherwise provided in subsection (e), a levy shall extend only to property possessed and obligations existing at the time thereof. In any case in which the Secretary may levy upon property or rights to property, he may seize and sell such property or rights to property (whether real or personal, tangible or intangible).

(c) Successive Seizures.—Whenever any property or right to property upon which levy has been made by virtue of subsection (a) is not sufficient to satisfy the claim of the United States for which levy is made, the Secretary may, thereafter, and as often as may be necessary, proceed to levy in like manner upon any other property liable to levy of the person against whom such claim exists, until the amount due from him, together with all expenses, is fully paid.

SEC. 6332. SURRENDER OF PROPERTY SUBJECT TO LEVY.

(a) Requirement.—Except as otherwise provided in this section, any person in possession of (or obligated with respect to) property or rights to property subject to levy upon which a levy has been made shall, upon demand of the Secretary, surrender such property or rights (or discharge such obligation) to the Secretary, except such part of the property or rights as is, at the time of such demand, subject to an attachment or execution under any judicial process.

(b) Special rule for Life Insurance and Endowment Contracts

(1) In general.—A levy on an organization with respect to a life insurance or endowment contract issued by such organization shall, without necessity for the surrender of the contract document, constitute a demand by the Secretary for payment of the amount described in paragraph (2) and the exercise of the right of the person against whom the tax is assessed to the advance of such amount. Such organization shall pay over such amount 90 days after service of notice of levy. Such notice shall include a certification by the Secretary that a copy of such notice has been mailed to the person against whom the tax is assessed at his last known address.

(2) Satisfaction of levy.—Such levy shall be deemed to be satisfied if such organization pays over to the Secretary the amount which the person against whom the tax is assessed could have had advanced to him by such organization on the date prescribed in paragraph (1) for the satisfaction of such levy, increased by the amount of any advance (including contractual interest thereon) made to such person on or after the date such organization had actual notice or knowledge (within the meaning of section 6323 (i)(1)) of the existence of the lien with respect to which such levy is made, other than an advance (including contractual interest thereon) made automatically to maintain such contract in force under an agreement entered into before such organization had such notice or knowledge.

(3) Enforcement proceedings.—The satisfaction of a levy under paragraph (2) shall be without prejudice to any civil action for the enforcement of any lien imposed by this title with respect to such contract.

(c) Special Rule for Banks.—Any bank (as defined in section 408(n)) shall surrender (subject to an attachment or execution under judicial process) any deposits (including interest thereon) in such bank only after 21 days after service of levy.

(d) Enforcement of Levy.

(1) Extent of personal liability.—Any person who fails or refuses to surrender any property or rights to property, subject to levy, upon demand by the Secretary, shall be liable in his own person and estate to the United States in a sum equal to the value of the property or rights not so surrendered, but not exceeding the amount of taxes for the collection of which such levy has been made, together with costs and interest on such sum at the underpayment rate established under section 6621 from the date of such levy (or, in the case of a levy described in section 6331 (d)(3), from the date such person would otherwise have been obligated to pay over such amounts to the taxpayer). Any amount (other than costs) recovered under this paragraph shall be credited against the tax liability for the collection of which such levy was made.

(2) Penalty for violation.—In addition to the personal liability imposed by paragraph (1), if any person required to surrender property or rights to property fails or refuses to surrender such property or rights to property without reasonable cause, such person shall be liable for a penalty equal to 50 percent of the amount recoverable under paragraph (1). No part of such penalty shall be credited against the tax liability for the collection of which such levy was made.

(e) Effect of honoring levy.—Any person in possession of (or obligated with respect to) property or rights to property subject to levy upon which a levy has been made who, upon demand by the Secretary, surrenders such property or rights to property (or discharges such obligation) to the Secretary (or who pays a liability under subsection (d)(1)), shall be discharged from any obligation or liability to the delinquent taxpayer and any other person with respect to such property or rights to property arising from such surrender or payment.

SEC. 6333. PRODUCTION OF BOOKS.

If a levy has been made or is about to be made on any property, or right to property, any person having custody or control of any books or records, containing evidence or statements relating to the property or right to property subject to levy, shall, upon demand of the Secretary, exhibit such books or records to the Secretary.

SEC. 6343. AUTHORITY TO RELEASE LEVY AND RETURN PROPERTY.

(a) Release of Levy and Notice of Release.—

(1) In general.—Under regulations prescribed by the Secretary, the Secretary shall release the levy upon all, or part of, the property or rights to property levied upon and shall promptly notify the person upon whom such levy was made (if any) that such levy has been released if—

(A) the liability for which such levy was made is satisfied or becomes unenforceable by reason of lapse of time,

(B) release of such levy will facilitate the collection of such liability,

(C) the taxpayer has entered into an agreement under section 6159 to satisfy such liability by means of installment payments, unless such agreement provides otherwise,

(D) the Secretary has determined that such levy is creating an economic hardship due to the financial condition of the taxpayer, or

(E) the fair market value of the property exceeds such liability and release of the levy on a part of such property could be made without hindering the collection of such liability.

For purposes of subparagraph (C), the Secretary is not required to release such levy if such release would jeopardize the secured creditor status of the Secretary.

(2) Expedited determination on certain business property.—In the case of any tangible personal property essential in carrying on the trade or business of the taxpayer, the Secretary shall provide for an expedited determination under paragraph (1) if levy on such tangible personal property would prevent the taxpayer from carrying on such trade or business.

(3) Subsequent levy.—The release of levy on any property under paragraph (1) shall not prevent any subsequent levy on such property.

(b) Return of Property.—If the Secretary determines that property has been wrongfully levied upon, it shall be lawful for the Secretary to return—

(1) the specific property levied upon,

(2) an amount of money equal to the amount of money levied upon, or

(3) an amount of money equal to the amount of money received by the United States from a sale of such property.

Property may be returned at any time. An amount equal to the amount of money levied upon or received from such sale may be returned at any time before the expiration of 9 months from the date of such levy. For purposes of paragraph (3), if property is declared purchased by the United States at a sale pursuant to section 6335(e) (relating to manner and conditions of sale), the United States shall be treated as having received an amount of money equal to the minimum price determined pursuant to such section or (if larger) the amount received by the United States from the resale of such property.

(d) Return of Property in Certain Cases.—If—

(1) any property has been levied upon, and

(2) the Secretary determines that—

(A) the levy on such property was premature or otherwise not in accordance with administrative procedures of the Secretary,

(B) the taxpayer has entered into an agreement under section 6159 to satisfy the tax liability for which the levy was imposed by means of installment payments, unless such agreement provides otherwise,

(C) the return of such property will facilitate the collection of the tax liability, or

(D) with the consent of the taxpayer or the National Taxpayer Advocate, the return of such property would be in the best interests of the taxpayer (as determined by the National Taxpayer Advocate) and the United States,

the provisions of subsection (b) shall apply in the same manner as if such property had been wrongly levied upon, except that no interest shall be allowed under subsection (c).

*   *   *   *   *   *   *   *   *   *

Applicable Sections of Internal Revenue Code

6321. LIEN FOR TAXES.
6322. PERIOD OF LIEN.
6325. RELEASE OF LIEN OR DISCHARGE OF PROPERTY.
6331. LEVY AND DISTRAINT.
6332. SURRENDER OF PROPERTY SUBJECT TO LEVY.
6333. PRODUCTION OF BOOKS.
6334. PROPERTY EXEMPT FROM LEVY.
6343. AUTHORITY TO RELEASE LEVY AND RETURN PROPERTY.
7426. CIVIL ACTIONS BY PERSONS OTHER THAN TAXPAYERS.
7429. REVIEW OF JEOPARDY LEVY OR ASSESSMENT PROCEDURES.

For more information about this notice, please call the phone number on the front of this form.

Form **668-A(c)(DO)** (Rev. 7-2002)

Claim for Refund and Request for Abatement

▶ See separate instructions.

OMB No. 1545-0024

Use Form 843 if your claim or request involves:
- **(a)** a refund of one of the taxes (other than income taxes or an employer's claim for FICA tax, RRTA tax, or income tax withholding) or a fee, shown on line 3,
- **(b)** an abatement of FUTA tax or certain excise taxes, or
- **(c)** a refund or abatement of interest, penalties, or additions to tax for one of the reasons shown on line 5a.

Do not use Form 843 if your claim or request involves:
- **(a)** an overpayment of income taxes or an employer's claim for FICA tax, RRTA tax, or income tax withholding (use the appropriate amended tax return),
- **(b)** a refund of excise taxes based on the nontaxable use or sale of fuels, or
- **(c)** an overpayment of excise taxes reported on Form(s) 11-C, 720, 730, or 2290.

Name(s)	Your social security number
Address (number, street, and room or suite no.)	Spouse's social security number
City or town, state, and ZIP code	Employer identification number (EIN)
Name and address shown on return if different from above	Daytime telephone number

1 **Period.** Prepare a separate Form 843 for each tax period or fee year.
From _____ to _____

2 **Amount** to be refunded or abated:
$ _____

3 **Type of tax or fee.** Indicate the type of tax or fee to be refunded or abated or to which the interest, penalty, or addition to tax is related.

☐ Employment ☐ Estate ☐ Gift ☐ Excise ☐ Income ☐ Fee

4 **Type of penalty.** If the claim or request involves a penalty, enter the Internal Revenue Code section on which the penalty is based (see instructions). IRC section: _____

5a **Interest, penalties, and additions to tax.** Check the box that indicates your reason for the request for refund or abatement. (If none apply, go to line 6.)

☐ Interest was assessed as a result of IRS errors or delays.

☐ A penalty or addition to tax was the result of erroneous written advice from the IRS.

☐ Reasonable cause or other reason allowed under the law (other than erroneous written advice) can be shown for not assessing a penalty or addition to tax.

b Date(s) of payment(s) ▶ _____

6 **Original return.** Indicate the type of fee or return, if any, filed to which the tax, interest, penalty, or addition to tax relates.

☐ 706 ☐ 709 ☐ 940 ☐ 941 ☐ 943 ☐ 945
☐ 990-PF ☐ 1040 ☐ 1120 ☐ 4720 ☐ Other (specify) ▶

7 **Explanation.** Explain why you believe this claim or request should be allowed and show the computation of the amount shown on line 2. If you need more space, attach additional sheets.

Signature. If you are filing Form 843 to request a refund or abatement relating to a joint return, both you and your spouse must sign the claim. Claims filed by corporations must be signed by a corporate officer authorized to sign, and the officer's title must be shown.

Under penalties of perjury, I declare that I have examined this claim, including accompanying schedules and statements, and, to the best of my knowledge and belief, it is true, correct, and complete. Declaration of preparer (other than taxpayer) is based on all information of which preparer has any knowledge.

Signature (Title, if applicable. Claims by corporations must be signed by an officer.) _____ Date _____

Signature (spouse, if joint return) _____ Date _____

Paid Preparer Use Only	Print/Type preparer's name	Preparer's signature	Date	Check ☐ if self-employed	PTIN
	Firm's name ▶			Firm's EIN ▶	
	Firm's address ▶			Phone no.	

For Privacy Act and Paperwork Reduction Act Notice, see separate instructions.   Cat. No. 10180R   Form **843** (Rev. 8-2011)

Department of the Treasury—Internal Revenue Service

Waiver of Restrictions on Assessment and Collection of Deficiency in Tax and Acceptance of Overassessment

Date received by
Internal Revenue Service

Names and address of taxpayers *(Number, street, city or town, State, ZIP code)*

Social security or employer
identification number

Increase (Decrease) in Tax and Penalties

Tax year ended	Tax	Penalties		

(For instructions, see back of form)

Consent to Assessment and Collection

I consent to the immediate assessment and collection of any deficiencies *(increase in tax and penalties)* and accept any overassessment *(decrease in tax and penalties)* shown above, plus any interest provided by law. I understand that by signing this waiver, I will not be able to contest these years in the United States Tax Court, unless additional deficiencies are determined for these years.

		Date
YOUR SIGNATURE HERE ▶		
SPOUSE'S SIGNATURE ▶		Date
TAXPAYER'S REPRESENTATIVE HERE ▶		Date
CORPORATE NAME ▶		
CORPORATE OFFICER(S) SIGN HERE ▶	Title	Date
▶	Title	Date

Form 870 page 2   **Instructions**

General Information

If you consent to the assessment of the deficiencies shown in this waiver, please sign and return the form in order to limit any interest charge and expedite the adjustment to your account. Your consent will not prevent you from filing a claim for refund *(after you have paid the tax)* if you later believe you are so entitled. It will not prevent us from later determining, if necessary, that you owe additional tax; nor extend the time provided by law for either action.

We have agreements with State tax agencies under which information about Federal tax, including increases or decreases, is exchanged with the States. If this change affects the amount of your State income tax, you should file the required State form.

If you later file a claim and the Service disallows it, you may file suit for refund in a district court or in the United States Claims Court, but you may not file a petition with the United States Tax Court.

We will consider this waiver a valid claim for refund or credit of any overpayment due you resulting from any decrease in tax and penalties shown above, provided you sign and file it within the period established by law for making such a claim.

Who Must Sign

If you filed jointly, both you and your spouse must sign. If this waiver is for a corporation, it should be signed with the corporation name, followed by the signatures and titles of the corporate officers authorized to sign. An attorney or agent may sign this waiver provided such action is specifically authorized by a power of attorney which, if not previously filed, must accompany this form.

If this waiver is signed by a person acting in a fiduciary capacity *(for example, an* executor, *administrator, or a trustee)* Form 56, Notice Concerning Fiduciary Relationship, should, unless previously filed, accompany this form.

Form **870-AD**
ev. April 1992)

Department of the Treasury — Internal Revenue Service

Offer to Waive Restrictions on Assessment and Collection of Tax Deficiency and to Accept Overassessment

mbols	Name of Taxpayer	SSN or EIN

Under the provisions of section 6213(d) of the Internal Revenue Code of 1986 (the Code), or corresponding provisions of prior internal venue laws, the undersigned offers to waive the restrictions provided in section 6213(a) of the Code or corresponding provisions of prior ernal revenue laws, and to consent to the assessment and collection of the following deficiencies and additions to tax, if any, with interest provided by law. The undersigned offers also to accept the following overassessments, if any, as correct. Any waiver or acceptance of an erassessment is subject to any terms and conditions stated below and on the reverse side of this form.

Deficiencies (Overassessments) and Additions to Tax

Year Ended	Kind of Tax	Tax				
		$	$	$		
		$	$	$		
		$	$	$		
		$	$	$		
		$	$	$		
		$	$	$		

	Date
gnature of Taxpayer	Date
gnature of Taxpayer	Date
gnature of Taxpayer's Representative	Date
rporate Name	Date
Corporate Officer Title	Date

For Internal Revenue Use Only	Date Accepted for Commissioner	Signature
	Office	Title

t. No. 168960

- 663 -

Form **870-AD** (Rev. 4-92)

This offer must be accepted for the Commissioner of Internal Revenue and will take effect on the date it is accepted. Unless and until it is accepted, it will have no force or effect.

If this offer is accepted, the case will not be reopened by the Commissioner unless there was:

- fraud, malfeasance, concealment or misrepresentation of a material fact
- an important mistake in mathematical calculation
- a deficiency or overassessment resulting from adjustments made under Subchapters C and D of Chapter 63 concerning the tax treatment of partnership and subchapter S items determined at the partnership and corporate level
- an excessive tentative allowance of a carryback provided by law

No claim for refund or credit will be filed or prosecuted by the taxpayer for the years stated on this form, other than for amounts attributed to carrybacks provided by law.

The proper filing of this offer, when accepted, will expedite assessment and billing (or overassessment, credit or refund) by adjusting the tax liability. This offer, when executed and timely submitted, will be considered a claim for refund for the above overassessment(s), if any.

This offer may be executed by the taxpayer's attorney, certified public accountant, or agent provided this is specifically authorized by a power of attorney which, if not previously filed, must accompany this form. If this offer is signed by a person acting in a fiduciary capacity (for example: an executor, administrator, or a trustee) Form 56, Notice Concerning Fiduciary Relationship, must accompany this form, unless previously filed.

If this offer is executed for a year for which a joint return was filed, it must be signed by both spouses unless one spouse, acting under a power of attorney, signs as agent for the other.

If this offer is executed by a corporation, it must be signed with the corporate name followed by the signature and title of the officer(s) authorized to sign. If the offer is accepted, as a condition of acceptance, any signature by or for a corporate officer will be considered a representation by that person and the corporation, to induce reliance, that such signature is binding under law for the corporation to be assessed the deficiencies or receive credit or refund under this agreement. If the corporation later contests the signature as being unauthorized on its behalf, the person who signed may be subject to criminal penalties for representating that he or she had authority to sign this agreement on behalf of the corporation.

*U.S. GPO: 1992-617-018/48236

Form 870-AD (Rev. 4-92)

	Department of the Treasury-Internal Revenue Service	In reply refer to:
Form **872** (Rev. Dec. 2004)	**Consent to Extend the Time to Assess Tax**	Taxpayer Identification Number

_____
(Name(s))

taxpayer(s) of _____

_____
(Number, Street, City or Town, State, ZIP Code)

and the Commissioner of Internal Revenue consent and agree to the following:

(1) The amount of any Federal _____ tax due on any return(s) made by or
(Kind of tax)

for the above taxpayer(s) for the period(s) ended _____

_____

may be assessed at any time on or before _____ . However, if a notice of deficiency in tax for any such
(Expiration date)

period(s) is sent to the taxpayer(s) on or before that date, then the time for assessing the tax will be further extended by the number of days the assessment was previously prohibited, plus 60 days.

(2) The taxpayer(s) may file a claim for credit or refund and the Service may credit or refund the tax within 6 months after this agreement ends.

Your Rights as a Taxpayer

You have the right to refuse to extend the period of limitations or limit this extension to a mutually agreed-upon issue(s) or mutually agreed-upon period of time. **Publication 1035, *Extending the Tax Assessment Period*,** provides a more detailed explanation of your rights and the consequences of the choices you may make. If you have not already received a Publication 1035, the publication can be obtained, free of charge, from the IRS official who requested that you sign this consent or from the IRS' web site at www.irs.gov or by calling toll free at 1-800-829-3676. Signing this consent will not deprive you of any appeal rights to which you would otherwise be entitled.

YOUR SIGNATURE HERE ➤ ....
I am aware that I have the right to refuse to sign this consent or to limit the extension to mutually agreed-upon issues and/or period of time as set forth in I.R.C. § 6501(c)(4)(B). *(Date signed)*

SPOUSE'S SIGNATURE ➤ ....
I am aware that I have the right to refuse to sign this consent or to limit the extension to mutually agreed-upon issues and/or period of time as set forth in I.R.C. § 6501(c)(4)(B). *(Date signed)*

TAXPAYER'S REPRESENTATIVE

SIGN HERE ➤ ....
I am aware that I have the right to refuse to sign this consent or to limit the extension to mutually agreed-upon issues and/or period of time as set forth in I.R.C. § 6501(c)(4)(B). *(Date signed)*
In addition, the taxpayer(s) has been made aware of these rights.

CORPORATE
NAME ➤ ....

CORPORATE
OFFICER(S) ➤ ....
SIGN HERE *(Title)* *(Date signed)*
➤ ....
(Title) *(Date signed)*
I (we) am aware that I (we) have the right to refuse to sign this consent or to limit the extension to mutually agreed-upon issues and/or period of time as set forth in I.R.C. § 6501(c)(4)(B).

INTERNAL REVENUE SERVICE SIGNATURE AND TITLE

_____ _____
(Division Executive Name - See instructions.) *(Division Executive Title - see instructions)*

BY ....
(Authorized Official Signature and Title - See instructions.) *(Date signed)*

(Signature instructions are on the back of this form)   www.irs.gov   Catalog Number 20755I   Form **872** (Rev. 12-2004)

Instructions

If this consent is for income tax, self-employment tax, or FICA tax on tips and is made for any year(s) for which a joint return was filed, both husband and wife must sign the original and copy of this form unless one, acting under a power of attorney, signs as agent for the other. The signatures must match the names as they appear on the front of this form.

If this consent is for gift tax and the donor and the donor's spouse elected to have gifts to third persons considered as made one-half by each, both husband and wife must sign the original and copy of this form unless one, acting under a power of attorney, signs as agent for the other. The signatures must match the names as they appear on the front of this form.

If this consent is for Chapter 41, 42, or 43 taxes involving a partnership or is for a partnership return, only one authorized partner need sign.

If this consent is for Chapter 42 taxes, a separate Form 872 should be completed for each potential disqualified person, entity, or foundation manager that may be involved in a taxable transaction during the related tax year. See Revenue Ruling 75-391, 1975-2 C.B. 446.

If you are an attorney or agent of the taxpayer(s), you may sign this consent provided the action is specifically authorized by a power of attorney. If the power of attorney was not previously filed, you must include it with this form.

If you are acting as a fiduciary (such as executor, administrator, trustee, etc.) and you sign this consent, attach Form 56, Notice Concerning Fiduciary Relationship, unless it was previously filed. If the taxpayer is a corporation, sign this consent with the corporate name followed by the signature and title of the officer(s) authorized to sign.

Instructions for Internal Revenue Service Employees

Complete the Division Executive's name and title depending upon your division.

If you are in the Small Business /Self-Employed Division, enter the name and title for the appropriate division executive for your business unit (e.g., Area Director for your area; Director, Specialty Programs; Director, Compliance Campus Operations; Director, Fraud/BSA, etc.)

If you are in the Wage and Investment Division, enter the name and title for the appropriate division executive for your business unit (e.g., Area Director for your area; Director, Field Compliance Services).

If you are in the Large and Mid-Size Business Division, enter the name and title of the Director, Field Operations for your industry.

If you are in the Tax Exempt and Government Entities Division, enter the name and title for the appropriate division executive for your business unit (e.g., Director, Exempt Organizations; Director, Employee Plans; Director, Federal, State and Local Governments; Director, Indian Tribal Governments; Director, Tax Exempt Bonds).

If you are in Appeals, enter the name and title of the Chief, Appeals.

The signature and title line will be signed and dated by the appropriate authorized official within your division.

Department of the Treasury-Internal Revenue Service

Special Consent to Extend the Time to Assess Tax

In reply refer to

Taxpayer Identification Number

Taxpayer(s) of _____

(Name(s))

_____

(Number, street, city or town, state, zip code)

and the Commissioner of Internal Revenue consent and agree as follows:

(1) The amount of any Federal _____ tax due on any return(s) made by or for the

(Kind of tax)

above taxpayer(s) for the period(s) ended _____
may be assessed on or before the 90th (ninetieth) day after: (a) the date on which a Form 872-T, *Notice of Termination of Special Consent to Extend the Time to Assess Tax,* is received by the division operating unit of the Internal Revenue Service having jurisdiction over the taxable period(s) at the address provided in paragraph (4) below or the address designated by the division operating unit in a Form 872-U, *Change of IRS Address to Submit Notice of Termination of Special Consent to Extend the Time to Assess Tax,* which address will supersede the address provided in paragraph (4) below; or (b) the Internal Revenue Service mails Form 872-T to the last known address of the taxpayer(s); or (c) the Internal Revenue Service mails a notice of deficiency for such period(s); except that if a notice of deficiency is sent to the taxpayer(s), the time for assessing the tax for the period(s) stated in the notice of deficiency will end 60 days after the period during which the making of an assessment is prohibited. A final adverse determination subject to declaratory judgment under sections 7428, 7476, or 7477 of the Internal Revenue Code will not terminate this agreement.

(2) This agreement ends on the earlier of expiration date determined in paragraph (1) above or the assessment date of an increase in the above tax or the overassessment date of a decrease in the above tax that reflects the final determination of tax and the final administrative appeals consideration. An assessment or overassessment for one period covered by this agreement will not end this agreement for any other period it covers. Some assessments do not reflect a final determination and appeals consideration and therefore will not terminate the agreement before the expiration date. Examples are assessments of: (a) tax under a partial agreement; (b) tax in jeopardy; (c) tax to correct mathematical or clerical errors; (d) tax reported on amended returns; and (e) advance payments. In addition, unassessed payments, such as amounts treated by the Service as cash bonds and advance payments not assessed by the Service, will not terminate this agreement before the expiration date determined in (1) above. This agreement ends on the date determined in (1) above regardless of any assessment for any period includable in a report to the Joint Committee on Taxation submitted under section 6405 of the Internal Revenue Code.

(3) This agreement will not reduce the period of time otherwise provided by law for making such assessment.

(4) This agreement may be terminated by either the taxpayer or the Internal Revenue Service with the use of Form 872-T which is available from the division operating unit of the Internal Revenue Service considering the taxpayer's case. For a termination initiated by the taxpayer to be valid, the executed Form 872-T must be delivered to one of the following addresses or the address designated by the division operating unit considering the taxpayer's case in a Form 872-U, which address will supersede the address below:

If **MAILING** Form 872-T, send to: If **HAND CARRYING** Form 872-T, deliver to:

(5) The taxpayer(s) may file a claim for credit or refund and the Service may credit or refund the tax within 6 (six) months after this agreement ends.

(Signature instructions and space for signature are on the back of this form)   www.irs.gov   Catalog Number 20760B Form **872-A** (Rev. 2-2005)

Your Rights as a Taxpayer

You have the right to refuse to extend the period of limitations or limit this extension to a mutually agreed-upon issue(s) or mutually agreed-upon period of time. Publication 1035, *Extending the Tax Assessment Period,* provides a more detailed explanation of your rights and the consequences of the choices you may make. If you have not already received a Publication 1035, you can obtain one, free of charge, from the IRS official who requested that you sign this consent or from the IRS' web site at www.irs.gov or by calling toll free at **1-800-829-3676**. Signing this consent will not deprive you of any appeal rights to which you would otherwise be entitled.

	Date signed
Your signature here I am aware that I have the right to refuse to sign this consent or to limit the extension to mutually agreed-upon issues and/or period of time as set forth in I.R.C. §6501(c)(4)(B).	
Spouse's signature I am aware that I have the right to refuse to sign this consent or to limit the extension to mutually agreed-upon issues and/or period of time as set forth in I.R.C. §6501(c)(4)(B).	Date signed
Taxpayer's Representative signature I am aware that I have the right to refuse to sign this consent or to limit the extension to mutually agreed-upon issues and/or period of time as set forth in I.R.C. §6501(c)(4)(B). In addition, the taxpayer(s) has been made aware of these rights.	Date signed

(You must also attach written authorization as stated in the instructions below.)

Corporate Officer's signature
I (we) am aware that I (we) have the right to refuse to sign this consent or to limit the extension to mutually agreed-upon issues and/or period of time as set forth in I.R.C. §6501(c)(4)(B).

	Date signed
Authorized Official signature and title *(see instructions)*	
Authorized Official signature and title *(see instructions)*	Date signed

INTERNAL REVENUE SERVICE SIGNATURE AND TITLE

Division Executive name *(see instructions)*	Division Executive title *(see instructions)*

BY Authorized Official signature and title *(see instructions)*	Date signed

Instructions

If this consent is for income tax, self-employment tax, or FICA tax on tips and is made for any year(s) for which a joint return was filed, both husband and wife must sign the original and copy of this form unless one, acting under a power of attorney, signs as agent for the other. The signatures must match the names as they appear on the front of this form.

If this consent is for gift tax and the donor and the donor's spouse elected to have gifts to third persons considered as made one-half by each, both husband and wife must sign the original and copy of this form unless one, acting under a power of attorney, signs as agent for the other. The signatures must match the names as they appear on the front of this form.

If this consent is for Chapter 41, 42, or 43 taxes involving a partnership, only one authorized partner need sign.

If this consent is for Chapter 42 taxes, a separate Form 872-A should be completed for each potential disqualified person or entity that may have been involved in a taxable transaction during the related tax year. See Revenue Ruling 75-391, 1975-2 C.B. 446.

If you are an attorney or agent of the taxpayer(s), you may sign this consent provided the action is specifically authorized by a power of attorney. If the power of attorney was not previously filed, you must include it with this form.

If you are acting as a fiduciary *(such as executor, administrator, trustee, etc.)* and you sign this consent, attach Form 56, *Notice Concerning Fiduciary Relationship,* unless it was previously filed.

If the taxpayer is a corporation, sign this consent with the corporate name followed by the signature and title of the officer(s) authorized to sign.

Instructions for Internal Revenue Service Employees

Complete the Division Executive's name and title depending upon your division:

- Small Business and Self-Employed Division = Area Director; Director, Specialty Programs; Director, Compliance Campus Operations, etc.
- Wage and Investment Division = Area Director; Director, Field Compliance Services.
- Large and Mid-Size Business Division = Director, Field Operations for your industry.
- Tax Exempt and Government Entities Division = Director, Exempt Organizations; Director, Employee Plans; Director, Federal, State and Local Governments; Director, Indian Tribal Governments; Director, Tax Exempt Bonds.
- Appeals = Chief, Appeals.

The appropriate authorized official within your division must sign and date the signature and title line.

Form **872-A** (Rev. 2-2005)

Form **872-T**
(Rev. November 2011)

Department of the Treasury-Internal Revenue Service

Notice of Termination of Special Consent to Extend the Time to Assess Tax

In reply refer to

Taxpayer(s) Name(s)

Termination by
☐ Taxpayer
☐ Internal Revenue Service

Taxpayer(s) Address

Taxpayer Identification Number

Office where
Form 872-A/Form 872-IA
Originated

Kind of Tax

Tax Period(s) Covered by this Notice

IRS Center Where Return Filed

This form is written notification of termination of: *(Check the appropriate box)*

☐ Form 872-A, Special Consent to Extend the Time to Assess Tax

☐ Form 872-IA, Special Consent to Extend the Time to Assess Tax As Well As Tax Attributable to Items of a Partnership

for the kind of tax and tax period(s) indicated above. This notice of termination of consent is provided under the terms of the agreement between the taxpayer(s) named above the Commissioner of Internal Revenue dated _____.

See the back of this form for signature instructions.
Please note that signing this notice may alter the taxpayer(s) appeal rights.

YOUR SIGNATURE ▶ ....
_____
(Type or print name)

....
(Date signed)

SPOUSE'S SIGNATURE ▶ ....
_____
(Type or print name)

....
(Date signed)

TAXPAYER'S REPRESENTATIVE'S SIGNATURE
(Only needed if signing on behalf of the taxpayer.) ▶ ....
_____
(Type or print name)

....
(Date signed)

(You must also attach written authorization as stated in the instructions on the back of this form)

CORPORATE NAME

....

....

CORPORATE OFFICER(S) SIGNATURE ▶ ....
(Name) *(Title)*
_____
(Type or print name)

....
(Date signed)

▶ ....
(Name) *(Title)*
(Authorized Official Signature and Title - see instructions)
_____
(Type or print name)

....
(Date signed)

INTERNAL REVENUE SERVICE SIGNATURE AND TITLE

....
(IRS Official's Name - see instructions) *(IRS Official's Title - see instructions)*

....
(IRS Official's Signature - see instructions) *(Date signed)*

(Instructions are on the 2nd page of this form)   www.irs.gov   Catalog Number 20775A   Form **872-T** (Rev. 11-2011)

Instructions

This notice may be made by either the taxpayer(s) or the Commissioner of Internal Revenue. All requested information must be included when this form is completed.

Please enter; in the space provided on the front of this form, the date Form 872-A/Form 872-IA was signed for the Internal Revenue Service.

If this notice is for:

- Income tax, self-employment tax, or FICA tax on tips and is made for any year(s) for which a joint return was filed, both husband and wife must sign this form unless one, acting under a power of attorney, signs as agent for the other. The signatures must match the names as they appear on the Form 872-A/Form 872-IA.

- Gift tax and the donor and the donor's spouse elected to have gifts to third persons considered as made one-half by each, both husband and wife must sign this form unless one, acting under a power of attorney, signs as agent for the other. The signatures must match the names as they appear on the Form 872-A/Form 872-IA.

- Chapter 41, 42, or 43 taxes involving a partnership, only one authorized partner need sign.

If you are an attorney or agent of the taxpayer(s), you may sign this notice provided the action is specifically authorized by a power of attorney. If the power of attorney was not previously filed, you must include it with this form.

If you are acting as a fiduciary (such as executor, administrator, trustee, etc.) and you sign this notice, attach Form 56, Notice Concerning Fiduciary Relationship, unless it was previously filed.

If the taxpayer is a corporation, sign this notice with the corporate name followed by the signature and title of the officer(s) authorized to sign.

Delivery Instructions: See Form 872-A, Item (4)/Form 872-IA, Item (1) for the proper address to mail or hand carry this notice. This notice must be received by the Internal Revenue office from which the Form 872-A/Form 872-IA originated unless a Form 872-U, Change of IRS Address to Submit Notice of Termination of Special Consent to Extend the Time to Access Tax has been issued by the Commissioner of Internal Revenue changing the office and address to which this form must delivered. This notice has no force or effect until it is received by the office designated by the Commissioner of Internal Revenue.

Instructions for Internal Revenue Service Employees

Complete the delegated IRS official's name and title of the employee who is signing the form on behalf of the IRS.

An IRS official delegated authority under Delegation Order 25-2 must sign and date the consent. See IRM 1.2.52.3.

Form 906
(Rev. August 1994)

Department of the Treasury—Internal Revenue Service

Closing Agreement On Final Determination
Covering Specific Matters

Under section 7121 of the Internal Revenue Code _____

_____

(Taxpayer's name, address, and identifying number)

_____

and the Commissioner of Internal Revenue make the following closing agreement:

Instructions

This agreement must be signed and filed in triplicate. (All copies must have original signatures.) The original and copies of the agreement must be identical. The name of the taxpayer must be stated accurately. The agreement may relate to one or more years.

If an attorney or agent signs the agreement for the taxpayer, the power of attorney (or a copy) authorizing that person to sign must be attached to the agreement. If the agreement is made for a year when a joint income tax return was filed by a husband and wife, it should be signed by or for both spouses. One spouse may sign as agent for the other if the document (or a copy) specifically authorizing that spouse to sign is attached to the agreement.

If the fiduciary signs the agreement for a decedent or an estate, an attested copy of the letters testamentary or the court order authorizing the fiduciary to sign, and a certificate of recent date that the authority remains in full force and effect must be attached to the agreement. If a trustee signs, a certified copy of the trust instrument or a certified copy of extracts from that instrument must be attached showing:

(1) the date of the instrument;

(2) that it is or is not of record in any court;

(3) the names of the beneficiaries;

(4) the appointment of the trustee, the authority granted, and other information necessary to show that the authority extends to Federal tax matters; and

(5) that the trust has not been terminated, and that the trustee appointed is still acting. If a fiduciary is a party, Form 56, Notice Concerning Fiduciary Relationship, is ordinarily required.

If the taxpayer is a corporation, the agreement must be dated and signed with the name of the corporation, the signature and title of an authorized officer or officers, or the signature of an authorized attorney or agent. It is not necessary that a copy of an enabling corporate resolution be attached.

Use additional pages if necessary, and identify them as part of this agreement.

Please see Revenue Procedure 68 16, C.B. 1968 1, page 770, for a detailed description of practices and procedures applicable to most closing agreements.

This agreement is final and conclusive except:
(1) the matter it relates to may be reopened in the event of fraud, malfeasance, or misrepresentation of material fact;
(2) it is subject to the Internal Revenue Code sections that expressly provide that effect be given to their provisions (including any stated exception for Code section 7122) notwithstanding any other law or rule of law; and
(3) if it relates to a tax period ending after the date of this agreement, it is subject to any law, enacted after the agreement date, that applies to that tax period.

By signing, the above parties certify that they have read and agreed to the terms of this document.

Your signature _____ Date Signed _____

Spouse's signature (if a joint return was filed) _____ Date Signed _____

Taxpayer's representative _____ Date Signed _____

Taxpayer (other than individual) _____

        By _____ Date Signed _____

      Title _____

Commissioner of Internal Revenue

        By _____ Date Signed _____

      Title _____

I have examined the specific matters involved and recommend the acceptance of the proposed agreement.

_____   _____
(Receiving Officer)   (Date)

_____
(Title)

I have reviewed the specific matters involved and recommend approval of the proposed agreement.

_____   _____
(Reviewing Officer)   (Date)

_____
(Title)

Department of the Treasury - Internal Revenue Service

Request for Taxpayer Advocate Service Assistance
(And Application for Taxpayer Assistance Order)

Form **911**
(Rev. 5-2011)

Section I – Taxpayer Information *(See Pages 3 and 4 for Form 911 Filing Requirements and Instructions for Completing this Form.)*

1a. Your name as shown on tax return

1b. Taxpayer Identifying Number (SSN, ITIN, EIN)

2a. Spouse's name as shown on tax return *(if applicable)*

2b. Spouse's Taxpayer Identifying Number (SSN, ITIN)

3a. Your current street address *(Number, Street, & Apt. Number)*

3b. City

3c. State *(or Foreign Country)*

3d. ZIP code

4. Fax number *(if applicable)*

5. Email address

6. Tax form(s)

7. Tax period(s)

8. Person to contact

9a. Daytime phone number

9b. ☐ Check here if you consent to have confidential information about your tax issue left on your answering machine or voice message at this number.

10. Best time to call

☐ Check if Cell Phone

11. Indicate the special communication needs you require *(if applicable)*

☐ TTY/TDD Line   ☐ Interpreter - Specify language other than English *(including sign language)*

☐ Other *(please specify)*

12a. Please describe the tax issue you are experiencing and any difficulties it may be creating *(If more space is needed, attach additional sheets.)*

12b. Please describe the relief/assistance you are requesting *(If more space is needed, attach additional sheets.)*

I understand that Taxpayer Advocate Service employees may contact third parties in order to respond to this request and I authorize such contacts to be made. Further, by authorizing the Taxpayer Advocate Service to contact third parties, I understand that I will not receive notice, pursuant to section 7602(c) of the Internal Revenue Code, of third parties contacted in connection with this request.

13a. Signature of Taxpayer or Corporate Officer, and title, if applicable

13b. Date signed

14a. Signature of spouse

14b. Date signed

Section II – Representative Information *(Attach Form 2848 if not already on file with the IRS.)*

1. Name of authorized representative

2. Centralized Authorization File (CAF) number

3. Current mailing address

4. Daytime phone number

☐ Check if Cell Phone

5. Fax number

6. Signature of representative

7. Date signed

Catalog Number 16965S

www.irs.gov

Form **911** (Rev. 5-2011)

Section III – Initiating Employee Information *(Section III is to be completed by the IRS only)*

Taxpayer name			Taxpayer Identifying Number *(TIN)*	
1. Name of employee	2. Phone number	3a. Function	3b. Operating division	4. Organization code no.

5. How identified and received *(Check the appropriate box)* | **6. IRS received date**

IRS Function identified issue as meeting Taxpayer Advocate Service (TAS) criteria

☐ (r) Functional referral (Function identified taxpayer issue as meeting TAS criteria).

☐ (x) Congressional correspondence/inquiry not addressed to TAS but referred for TAS handling.

Name of Senator/Representative _____

Taxpayer or Representative requested TAS assistance

☐ (n) Taxpayer or representative called into a National Taxpayer Advocate (NTA) Toll-Free site.

☐ (s) Functional referral (taxpayer or representative specifically requested TAS assistance).

7. TAS criteria *(Check the appropriate box.* **NOTE: Checkbox 9 is for TAS Use Only***)*

☐ (1) The taxpayer is experiencing economic harm or is about to suffer economic harm.

☐ (2) The taxpayer is facing an immediate threat of adverse action.

☐ (3) The taxpayer will incur significant costs if relief is not granted (including fees for professional representation).

☐ (4) The taxpayer will suffer irreparable injury or long-term adverse impact if relief is not granted.

(if any items 1-4 are checked, complete Question 9 below)

☐ (5) The taxpayer has experienced a delay of more than 30 days to resolve a tax account problem.

☐ (6) The taxpayer did not receive a response or resolution to their problem or inquiry by the date promised.

☐ (7) A system or procedure has either failed to operate as intended, or failed to resolve the taxpayer's problem or dispute within the IRS.

☐ (8) The manner in which the tax laws are being administered raise considerations of equity, or have impaired or will impair the taxpayer's rights.

☐ (9) The NTA determines compelling public policy warrants assistance to an individual or group of taxpayers **(TAS Use Only)**

8. What action(s) did you take to help resolve the issue? *(This block MUST be completed by the initiating employee)*
If you were unable to resolve the issue, state the reason why (if applicable)

9. Provide a description of the Taxpayer's situation, and where appropriate, explain the circumstances that are creating the economic burden and how the Taxpayer could be adversely affected if the requested assistance is not provided
(This block MUST be completed by the initiating employee)

10. How did the taxpayer learn about the Taxpayer Advocate Service

☐ IRS Forms or Publications   ☐ Media   ☐ IRS Employee   ☐ Other *(please specify)* _____

Instructions for completing Form 911 (Rev. 5-2011)

Form 911 Filing Requirements

When to Use this Form: The Taxpayer Advocate Service (TAS) is your voice at the IRS. TAS may be able to help you if you're experiencing a problem with the IRS and:

- Your problem with the IRS is causing financial difficulties for you, your family or your business;
- You face (or you business is facing) an immediate threat of adverse action; or
- You have tried repeatedly to contact the IRS, but no one has responded, or the IRS has not responded by the date promised.

If an IRS office will not give you the help you've asked for or will not help you in time to avoid harm, you may submit this form. The Taxpayer Advocate Service will generally ask the IRS to stop certain activities while your request for assistance is pending (for example, lien filings, levies, and seizures).

Where to Send this Form:

- **The quickest method is Fax.** TAS has at least one office in every state, the District of Columbia, and Puerto Rico. Submit this request to the Taxpayer Advocate office in the state or city where you reside. You can find the fax number in the government listings in your local telephone directory, on our website at www.irs.gov/advocate, or in Publication 1546, Taxpayer Advocate Service - Your Voice at the IRS.
- **You also can mail this form.** You can find the mailing address and phone number (voice) of your local Taxpayer Advocate office in your phone book, on our website, and in Pub. 1546, or get this information by calling our toll-free number: 1-877-777-4778.
- **Are you sending the form from overseas?** Fax it to 1-787-622-8933 or mail it to: Taxpayer Advocate Service, Internal Revenue Service, PO Box 193479, San Juan, Puerto Rico 00919-3479.
- Please be sure to fill out the form completely and submit it to the Taxpayer Advocate office nearest you so we can work your issue as soon as possible.

What Happens Next?

If you do not hear from us within one week of submitting Form 911, please call the TAS office where you sent your request. You can find the number at www.irs.gov/advocate.

Important Notes: Please be aware that by submitting this form, you are authorizing the Taxpayer Advocate Service to contact third parties as necessary to respond to your request, and you may not receive further notice about these contacts. For more information see IRC 7602(c).

Caution: The Taxpayer Advocate Service will not consider frivolous arguments raised on this form. You can find examples of frivolous arguments in Publication 2105, Why do I have to Pay Taxes? If you use this form to raise frivolous arguments, you may be subject to a penalty of $5,000.

Paperwork Reduction Act Notice: We ask for the information on this form to carry out the Internal Revenue laws of the United States. Your response is voluntary. You are not required to provide the information requested on a form that is subject to the Paperwork Reduction Act unless the form displays a valid OMB control number. Books or records relating to a form or its instructions must be retained as long as their contents may become material in the administration of any Internal Revenue law. Generally, tax returns and return information are confidential, as required by Code section 6103. Although the time needed to complete this form may vary depending on individual circumstances, the estimated average time is 30 minutes.

Should you have comments concerning the accuracy of this time estimate or suggestions for making this form simpler, please write to: **Internal Revenue Service**, Tax Products Coordinating Committee, Room 6406, 1111 Constitution Ave. NW, Washington, DC 20224.

Instructions for Section I

1a. Enter your name as shown on the tax return that relates to this request for assistance.

1b. Enter your Taxpayer Identifying Number. If you are an individual this will be either a Social Security Number (SSN) or Individual Taxpayer Identification Number (ITIN). If you are a business entity this will be your Employer Identification Number (EIN) (e.g. a partnership, corporation, trust or self-employed individual with employees).

2a. Enter your spouse's name (if applicable) if this request relates to a jointly filed return.

2b. Enter your spouse's Taxpayer Identifying Number (SSN or ITIN) if this request relates to a jointly filed return.

3a-d. Enter your current mailing address, including street number and name, city, state, or foreign country, and zip code.

4. Enter your fax number, including the area code.

5. Enter your e-mail address. We will only use this to contact you if we are unable to reach you by telephone and your issue appears to be time sensitive. We will not, however, use your e-mail address to discuss the specifics of your case.

6. Enter the number of the Federal tax return or form that relates to this request. For example, an individual taxpayer with an income tax issue would enter Form 1040.

7. Enter the quarterly, annual, or other tax period that relates to this request. For example, if this request involves an income tax issue, enter the calendar or fiscal year, if an employment tax issue, enter the calendar quarter.

Instructions for Section I
continue on the next page

Instructions for Section I - *(Continued from Page 3)*

8.   Enter the name of the individual we should contact. For partnerships, corporations, trusts, etc., enter the name of the individual authorized to act on the entity's behalf. If the contact person is not the taxpayer or other authorized individual, please see the Instructions for Section II.

9a. Enter your daytime telephone number, including the area code. If this is a cell phone number, please check the box.

9b. If you have an answering machine or voice mail at this number and you consent to the Taxpayer Advocate Service leaving confidential information about your tax issue at this number, please check the box. You are not obligated to have information about your tax issue left at this number. If other individuals have access to the answering machine or the voice mail and you do not wish for them to receive any confidential information about your tax issue, please do not check the box.

10. Indicate the best time to call you. Please specify A.M. or P.M. hours.

11. Indicate any special communication needs you require (such as sign language). Specify any language other than English.

12a. Please describe the tax issue you are experiencing and any difficulties it may be creating. Specify the actions that the IRS has taken (or not taken) to resolve the issue. If the issue involves an IRS delay of more than 30 days in resolving your issue, indicate the date you first contacted the IRS for assistance in resolving your issue.

12b. Please describe the relief/assistance you are requesting. Specify the action that you want taken and that you believe necessary to resolve the issue. Furnish any documentation that you believe would assist us in resolving the issue.

13-14. If this is a joint assistance request, both spouses must sign in the appropriate blocks and enter the date the request was signed. If only one spouse is requesting assistance, only the requesting spouse must sign the request. If this request is being submitted for another individual, only a person authorized and empowered to act on that individual's behalf should sign the request. Requests for corporations must be signed by an officer and include the officer's title.

Note: The signing of this request allows the IRS by law to suspend any applicable statutory periods of limitation relating to the assessment or collection of taxes. However, it does not suspend any applicable periods for you to perform acts related to assessment or collection, such as petitioning the Tax Court for redetermination of a deficiency or requesting a Collection Due Process hearing.

Instructions for Section II

Taxpayers: If you wish to have a representative act on your behalf, you must give him/her power of attorney or tax information authorization for the tax return(s) and period(s) involved. For additional information see Form 2848, Power of Attorney and Declaration of Representative, or Form 8821, Tax Information Authorization, and the accompanying instructions. Information can also be found in Publication 1546, Taxpayer Advocate Service-Your Voice at the IRS.

Representatives: If you are an authorized representative submitting this request on behalf of the taxpayer identified in Section I, complete Blocks 1 through 7 of Section II. Attach a copy of Form 2848, Form 8821, or other power of attorney. Enter your Centralized Authorization File (CAF) number in Block 2 of Section II. The CAF number is the unique number that the IRS assigns to a representative after Form 2848 or Form 8821 is filed with an IRS office.

Note: Form 8821 does not authorize your appointee to advocate your position with respect to the Federal tax laws; to execute waivers, consents, or closing agreements; or to otherwise represent you before the IRS. Form 8821 does authorize anyone you designate to inspect and/or receive your confidential tax information in any office of the IRS, for the type of tax and tax periods you list on Form 8821.

Instructions for Section III   (For IRS Use Only) *Please complete this section in its entirety.*

Enter the taxpayer's name and taxpayer identification number from the first page of this form.

1.   Enter your name.

2.   Enter your phone number.

3a. Enter your Function (e.g., ACS, Collection, Examination, Customer Service, etc.).

3b. Enter your Operating Division (W&I, SB/SE, LS&I, or TE/GE).

4.   Enter the Organization code number for your office (e.g., 18 for AUSC, 95 for Los Angeles).

5.   Check the appropriate box that best reflects how the need for TAS assistance was identified. For example, did taxpayer or representative call or write to an IRS function or the Taxpayer Advocate Service (TAS).

6.   Enter the date the taxpayer or representative called or visited an IRS office to request TAS assistance. Or enter the date when the IRS received the Congressional correspondence/inquiry or a written request for TAS assistance from the taxpayer or representative. If the IRS identified the taxpayer's issue as meeting TAS criteria, enter the date this determination was made.

7.   Check the box that best describes the reason TAS assistance is requested. Box 9 is for TAS Use Only.

8.   State the action(s) you took to help resolve the taxpayer's issue. State the reason(s) that prevented you from resolving the taxpayer's issue. For example, levy proceeds cannot be returned because they were already applied to a valid liability; an overpayment cannot be refunded because the statutory period for issuing a refund expired; or current law precludes a specific interest abatement.

9.   Provide a description of the taxpayer's situation, and where appropriate, explain the circumstances that are creating the economic burden and how the taxpayer could be adversely affected if the requested assistance is not provided.

10. Ask the taxpayer how he or she learned about the Taxpayer Advocate Service and indicate the response here.

Form **1040**

Department of the Treasury—Internal Revenue Service (99)

U.S. Individual Income Tax Return

2011

OMB No. 1545-0074 | IRS Use Only—Do not write or staple in this space.

For the year Jan. 1–Dec. 31, 2011, or other tax year beginning , 2011, ending , 20 | See separate instructions.

Your first name and initial	Last name	Your social security number

If a joint return, spouse's first name and initial	Last name	Spouse's social security number

Home address (number and street). If you have a P.O. box, see instructions. | Apt. no.

▲ Make sure the SSN(s) above and on line 6c are correct.

City, town or post office, state, and ZIP code. If you have a foreign address, also complete spaces below (see instructions).

Presidential Election Campaign

Check here if you, or your spouse if filing jointly, want $3 to go to this fund. Checking a box below will not change your tax or refund. ☐ You ☐ Spouse

Foreign country name	Foreign province/county	Foreign postal code

Filing Status

Check only one box.

1 ☐ Single
2 ☐ Married filing jointly (even if only one had income)
3 ☐ Married filing separately. Enter spouse's SSN above and full name here. ▶
4 ☐ Head of household (with qualifying person). (See instructions.) If the qualifying person is a child but not your dependent, enter this child's name here. ▶
5 ☐ Qualifying widow(er) with dependent child

Exemptions

6a ☐ **Yourself.** If someone can claim you as a dependent, **do not** check box 6a . . . . .
b ☐ **Spouse** . . . .

} Boxes checked on 6a and 6b _____

c **Dependents:**

(1) First name Last name	(2) Dependent's social security number	(3) Dependent's relationship to you	(4) ✓ if child under age 17 qualifying for child tax credit (see instructions)
			☐
			☐
			☐
			☐

If more than four dependents, see instructions and check here ▶ ☐

No. of children on 6c who:
• lived with you
• did not live with you due to divorce or separation (see instructions)

Dependents on 6c not entered above

Add numbers on lines above ▶ _____

d Total number of exemptions claimed . . . .

Income

Attach Form(s) W-2 here. Also attach Forms W-2G and 1099-R if tax was withheld.

If you did not get a W-2, see instructions.

Enclose, but do not attach, any payment. Also, please use Form 1040-V.

7	Wages, salaries, tips, etc. Attach Form(s) W-2	7
8a	**Taxable** interest. Attach Schedule B if required	8a
b	**Tax-exempt** interest. **Do not** include on line 8a . . .	8b
9a	Ordinary dividends. Attach Schedule B if required	9a
b	Qualified dividends	9b
10	Taxable refunds, credits, or offsets of state and local income taxes	10
11	Alimony received	11
12	Business income or (loss). Attach Schedule C or C-EZ	12
13	Capital gain or (loss). Attach Schedule D if required. If not required, check here ▶ ☐	13
14	Other gains or (losses). Attach Form 4797	14
15a	IRA distributions . 15a	b Taxable amount . . .	15b
16a	Pensions and annuities 16a	b Taxable amount . . .	16b
17	Rental real estate, royalties, partnerships, S corporations, trusts, etc. Attach Schedule E	17
18	Farm income or (loss). Attach Schedule F	18
19	Unemployment compensation	19
20a	Social security benefits 20a	b Taxable amount . . .	20b
21	Other income. List type and amount _____	21
22	Combine the amounts in the far right column for lines 7 through 21. This is your **total income** ▶	22

Adjusted Gross Income

23	Educator expenses	23
24	Certain business expenses of reservists, performing artists, and fee-basis government officials. Attach Form 2106 or 2106-EZ	24
25	Health savings account deduction. Attach Form 8889 .	25
26	Moving expenses. Attach Form 3903	26
27	Deductible part of self-employment tax. Attach Schedule SE .	27
28	Self-employed SEP, SIMPLE, and qualified plans . .	28
29	Self-employed health insurance deduction	29
30	Penalty on early withdrawal of savings	30
31a	Alimony paid b Recipient's SSN ▶	31a
32	IRA deduction	32
33	Student loan interest deduction	33
34	Tuition and fees. Attach Form 8917	34
35	Domestic production activities deduction. Attach Form 8903	35
36	Add lines 23 through 35	36
37	Subtract line 36 from line 22. This is your **adjusted gross income** . . . . . . ▶	37

For Disclosure, Privacy Act, and Paperwork Reduction Act Notice, see separate instructions. | Cat. No. 11320B | Form **1040** (2011)

Tax and Credits

38	Amount from line 37 (adjusted gross income)	38	

39a Check if: ☐ **You** were born before January 2, 1947, ☐ Blind. ☐ **Spouse** was born before January 2, 1947, ☐ Blind. } Total boxes checked ▶ 39a

Standard Deduction for—
- People who check any box on line 39a or 39b **or** who can be claimed as a dependent, see instructions.
- All others:
Single or Married filing separately, $5,800
Married filing jointly or Qualifying widow(er), $11,600
Head of household, $8,500

b	If your spouse itemizes on a separate return or you were a dual-status alien, check here ▶ 39b☐		
40	**Itemized deductions** (from Schedule A) **or** your **standard deduction** (see left margin)	40	
41	Subtract line 40 from line 38	41	
42	**Exemptions.** Multiply $3,700 by the number on line 6d	42	
43	**Taxable income.** Subtract line 42 from line 41. If line 42 is more than line 41, enter -0-	43	
44	**Tax** (see instructions). Check if any from: a ☐ Form(s) 8814 b ☐ Form 4972 c ☐ 962 election	44	
45	**Alternative minimum tax** (see instructions). Attach Form 6251	45	
46	Add lines 44 and 45 ▶	46	
47	Foreign tax credit. Attach Form 1116 if required	47	
48	Credit for child and dependent care expenses. Attach Form 2441	48	
49	Education credits from Form 8863, line 23	49	
50	Retirement savings contributions credit. Attach Form 8880	50	
51	Child tax credit (see instructions)	51	
52	Residential energy credits. Attach Form 5695	52	
53	Other credits from Form: a ☐ 3800 b ☐ 8801 c ☐	53	
54	Add lines 47 through 53. These are your **total credits**	54	
55	Subtract line 54 from line 46. If line 54 is more than line 46, enter -0- ▶	55	

Other Taxes

56	Self-employment tax. Attach Schedule SE	56	
57	Unreported social security and Medicare tax from Form: a ☐ 4137 b ☐ 8919	57	
58	Additional tax on IRAs, other qualified retirement plans, etc. Attach Form 5329 if required	58	
59a	Household employment taxes from Schedule H	59a	
b	First-time homebuyer credit repayment. Attach Form 5405 if required	59b	
60	Other taxes. Enter code(s) from instructions	60	
61	Add lines 55 through 60. This is your **total tax** ▶	61	

Payments

If you have a qualifying child, attach Schedule EIC.

62	Federal income tax withheld from Forms W-2 and 1099	62	
63	2011 estimated tax payments and amount applied from 2010 return	63	
64a	**Earned income credit (EIC)**	64a	
b	Nontaxable combat pay election	64b	
65	Additional child tax credit. Attach Form 8812	65	
66	American opportunity credit from Form 8863, line 14	66	
67	First-time homebuyer credit from Form 5405, line 10	67	
68	Amount paid with request for extension to file	68	
69	Excess social security and tier 1 RRTA tax withheld	69	
70	Credit for federal tax on fuels. Attach Form 4136	70	
71	Credits from Form: a ☐ 2439 b ☐ 8839 c ☐ 8801 d ☐ 8885	71	
72	Add lines 62, 63, 64a, and 65 through 71. These are your **total payments** ▶	72	

Refund

Direct deposit? See instructions.

73	If line 72 is more than line 61, subtract line 61 from line 72. This is the amount you **overpaid**	73	
74a	Amount of line 73 you want **refunded to you.** If Form 8888 is attached, check here ▶ ☐	74a	
▶ b	Routing number ▶ c Type: ☐ Checking ☐ Savings		
▶ d	Account number		
75	Amount of line 73 you want **applied to your 2012 estimated tax** ▶ 75		

Amount You Owe

76	**Amount you owe.** Subtract line 72 from line 61. For details on how to pay, see instructions ▶	76	
77	Estimated tax penalty (see instructions) 77		

Third Party Designee

Do you want to allow another person to discuss this return with the IRS (see instructions)? ☐ **Yes.** Complete below. ☐ **No**

Designee's name ▶   Phone no. ▶   Personal identification number (PIN) ▶

Sign Here

Joint return? See instructions.
Keep a copy for your records.

Under penalties of perjury, I declare that I have examined this return and accompanying schedules and statements, and to the best of my knowledge and belief, they are true, correct, and complete. Declaration of preparer (other than taxpayer) is based on all information of which preparer has any knowledge.

Your signature	Date	Your occupation	Daytime phone number
Spouse's signature. If a joint return, **both** must sign.	Date	Spouse's occupation	If the IRS sent you an Identity Protection PIN, enter it here (see inst.)

Paid Preparer Use Only

Print/Type preparer's name	Preparer's signature	Date	Check ☐ if self-employed	PTIN
Firm's name ▶			Firm's EIN ▶	
Firm's address ▶			Phone no.	

Form **1040** (2011)

SCHEDULE A
(Form 1040)

Department of the Treasury
Internal Revenue Service (99)

Itemized Deductions

▶ **Attach to Form 1040.**　　▶ **See Instructions for Schedule A (Form 1040).**

OMB No. 1545-0074

2011

Attachment
Sequence No. **07**

Name(s) shown on Form 1040

Your social security number

Medical and Dental Expenses	**Caution.** Do not include expenses reimbursed or paid by others.		
	1 Medical and dental expenses (see instructions)	1	
	2 Enter amount from Form 1040, line 38 [2]		
	3 Multiply line 2 by 7.5% (.075)	3	
	4 Subtract line 3 from line 1. If line 3 is more than line 1, enter -0-		4
Taxes You Paid	5 State and local **(check only one box):** a ☐ Income taxes, **or** b ☐ General sales taxes	5	
	6 Real estate taxes (see instructions)	6	
	7 Personal property taxes	7	
	8 Other taxes. List type and amount ▶ _____ _____	8	
	9 Add lines 5 through 8		9
Interest You Paid **Note.** Your mortgage interest deduction may be limited (see instructions).	10 Home mortgage interest and points reported to you on Form 1098	10	
	11 Home mortgage interest not reported to you on Form 1098. If paid to the person from whom you bought the home, see instructions and show that person's name, identifying no., and address ▶ _____ _____	11	
	12 Points not reported to you on Form 1098. See instructions for special rules	12	
	13 Mortgage insurance premiums (see instructions)	13	
	14 Investment interest. Attach Form 4952 if required. (See instructions.)	14	
	15 Add lines 10 through 14		15
Gifts to Charity If you made a gift and got a benefit for it, see instructions.	16 Gifts by cash or check. If you made any gift of $250 or more, see instructions	16	
	17 Other than by cash or check. If any gift of $250 or more, see instructions. You **must** attach Form 8283 if over $500 . . .	17	
	18 Carryover from prior year	18	
	19 Add lines 16 through 18		19
Casualty and Theft Losses	20 Casualty or theft loss(es). Attach Form 4684. (See instructions.)		20
Job Expenses and Certain Miscellaneous Deductions	21 Unreimbursed employee expenses—job travel, union dues, job education, etc. Attach Form 2106 or 2106-EZ if required. (See instructions.) ▶ _____	21	
	22 Tax preparation fees	22	
	23 Other expenses—investment, safe deposit box, etc. List type and amount ▶ _____ _____	23	
	24 Add lines 21 through 23	24	
	25 Enter amount from Form 1040, line 38 [25]		
	26 Multiply line 25 by 2% (.02)	26	
	27 Subtract line 26 from line 24. If line 26 is more than line 24, enter -0-		27
Other Miscellaneous Deductions	28 Other—from list in instructions. List type and amount ▶ _____ _____		28
Total Itemized Deductions	29 Add the amounts in the far right column for lines 4 through 28. Also, enter this amount on Form 1040, line 40		29
	30 If you elect to itemize deductions even though they are less than your standard deduction, check here . . . . ▶ ☐		

For Paperwork Reduction Act Notice, see Form 1040 instructions.　　Cat. No. 17145C　　**Schedule A (Form 1040) 2011**

| SCHEDULE B
(Form 1040A or 1040)

Department of the Treasury
Internal Revenue Service (99) | Interest and Ordinary Dividends

▶ Attach to Form 1040A or 1040.
▶ Information about Schedule B (Form 1040A or 1040) and its instructions is at *www.irs.gov/form1040*. | OMB No. 1545-0074

20**12**
Attachment
Sequence No. **08** |

Name(s) shown on return | Your social security number

Part I

Interest

(See instructions on back and the instructions for Form 1040A, or Form 1040, line 8a.)

Note. If you received a Form 1099-INT, Form 1099-OID, or substitute statement from a brokerage firm, list the firm's name as the payer and enter the total interest shown on that form.

			Amount
1	List name of payer. If any interest is from a seller-financed mortgage and the buyer used the property as a personal residence, see instructions on back and list this interest first. Also, show that buyer's social security number and address ▶	**1**	
2	Add the amounts on line 1	**2**	
3	Excludable interest on series EE and I U.S. savings bonds issued after 1989. Attach Form 8815	**3**	
4	Subtract line 3 from line 2. Enter the result here and on Form 1040A, or Form 1040, line 8a . . . . ▶	**4**	

Note. If line 4 is over $1,500, you must complete Part III.

Part II

Ordinary Dividends

(See instructions on back and the instructions for Form 1040A, or Form 1040, line 9a.)

Note. If you received a Form 1099-DIV or substitute statement from a brokerage firm, list the firm's name as the payer and enter the ordinary dividends shown on that form.

			Amount
5	List name of payer ▶	**5**	
6	Add the amounts on line 5. Enter the total here and on Form 1040A, or Form 1040, line 9a . . . . ▶	**6**	

Note. If line 6 is over $1,500, you must complete Part III.

Part III

Foreign Accounts and Trusts

(See instructions on back.)

You must complete this part if you **(a)** had over $1,500 of taxable interest or ordinary dividends; **(b)** had a foreign account; or **(c)** received a distribution from, or were a grantor of, or a transferor to, a foreign trust.

		Yes	No
7a	At any time during 2012, did you have a financial interest in or signature authority over a financial account (such as a bank account, securities account, or brokerage account) located in a foreign country? See instructions		
	If "Yes," are you required to file Form TD F 90-22.1 to report that financial interest or signature authority? See Form TD F 90-22.1 and its instructions for filing requirements and exceptions to those requirements		
b	If you are required to file Form TD F 90-22.1, enter the name of the foreign country where the financial account is located ▶		
8	During 2012, did you receive a distribution from, or were you the grantor of, or transferor to, a foreign trust? If "Yes," you may have to file Form 3520. See instructions on back		

For Paperwork Reduction Act Notice, see your tax return instructions. | Cat. No. 17146N | **Schedule B (Form 1040A or 1040) 2012**

SCHEDULE C	**Profit or Loss From Business**	OMB No. 1545-0074
(Form 1040)	(Sole Proprietorship)	20**11**
Department of the Treasury Internal Revenue Service (99)	▶ For information on Schedule C and its instructions, go to *www.irs.gov/schedulec* ▶ Attach to Form 1040, 1040NR, or 1041; partnerships generally must file Form 1065.	Attachment Sequence No. **09**

Name of proprietor	Social security number (SSN)

A	Principal business or profession, including product or service (see instructions)	**B** Enter code from instructions ▶

C	Business name. If no separate business name, leave blank.	**D** Employer ID number (EIN), (see instr.)

E Business address (including suite or room no.) ▶ _____
City, town or post office, state, and ZIP code

F Accounting method: **(1)** ☐ Cash **(2)** ☐ Accrual **(3)** ☐ Other (specify) ▶ _____

G Did you "materially participate" in the operation of this business during 2011? If "No," see instructions for limit on losses . ☐ Yes ☐ No

H If you started or acquired this business during 2011, check here . . . . ▶ ☐

I Did you make any payments in 2011 that would require you to file Form(s) 1099? (see instructions) . . . . ☐ Yes ☐ No

J If "Yes," did you or will you file all required Forms 1099? . . . . ☐ Yes ☐ No

Part I Income

1a	Merchant card and third party payments. For 2011, enter -0- . . .	**1a**	
b	Gross receipts or sales not entered on line 1a (see instructions) . .	**1b**	
c	Income reported to you on Form W-2 if the "Statutory Employee" box on that form was checked. **Caution.** See instr. before completing this line	**1c**	
d	**Total gross receipts.** Add lines 1a through 1c	**1d**	
2	Returns and allowances plus any other adjustments (see instructions)	**2**	
3	Subtract line 2 from line 1d	**3**	
4	Cost of goods sold (from line 42)	**4**	
5	**Gross profit.** Subtract line 4 from line 3	**5**	
6	Other income, including federal and state gasoline or fuel tax credit or refund (see instructions) . . .	**6**	
7	**Gross income.** Add lines 5 and 6 . . . . ▶	**7**	

Part II Expenses Enter expenses for business use of your home only on line 30.

8	Advertising	**8**		**18**	Office expense (see instructions)	**18**	
9	Car and truck expenses (see instructions)	**9**		**19**	Pension and profit-sharing plans .	**19**	
10	Commissions and fees .	**10**		**20**	Rent or lease (see instructions):		
11	Contract labor (see instructions)	**11**		**a**	Vehicles, machinery, and equipment	**20a**	
12	Depletion	**12**		**b**	Other business property . . .	**20b**	
13	Depreciation and section 179 expense deduction (not included in Part III) (see instructions).	**13**		**21**	Repairs and maintenance . . .	**21**	
				22	Supplies (not included in Part III) .	**22**	
				23	Taxes and licenses	**23**	
				24	Travel, meals, and entertainment:		
14	Employee benefit programs (other than on line 19) . .	**14**		**a**	Travel	**24a**	
15	Insurance (other than health)	**15**		**b**	Deductible meals and entertainment (see instructions) .	**24b**	
16	Interest:			**25**	Utilities	**25**	
a	Mortgage (paid to banks, etc.)	**16a**		**26**	Wages (less employment credits) .	**26**	
b	Other	**16b**		**27a**	Other expenses (from line 48) . .	**27a**	
17	Legal and professional services	**17**		**b**	**Reserved for future use** . . .	**27b**	

28	**Total expenses** before expenses for business use of home. Add lines 8 through 27a . . . . . . ▶	**28**	
29	Tentative profit or (loss). Subtract line 28 from line 7	**29**	
30	Expenses for business use of your home. Attach **Form 8829**. Do **not** report such expenses elsewhere . .	**30**	
31	**Net profit or (loss).** Subtract line 30 from line 29.		

• If a profit, enter on both **Form 1040, line 12** (or **Form 1040NR, line 13**) and on **Schedule SE, line 2.**
If you entered an amount on line 1c, see instr. Estates and trusts, enter on **Form 1041, line 3.**   **31**

• If a loss, you **must** go to line 32.

32 If you have a loss, check the box that describes your investment in this activity (see instructions).

• If you checked 32a, enter the loss on both **Form 1040, line 12**, (or **Form 1040NR, line 13**) and on **Schedule SE, line 2.** If you entered an amount on line 1c, see the instructions for line 31. Estates and trusts, enter on **Form 1041, line 3.**

32a ☐ All investment is at risk.
32b ☐ Some investment is not at risk.

• If you checked 32b, you **must** attach **Form 6198.** Your loss may be limited.

For Paperwork Reduction Act Notice, see your tax return instructions.   Cat. No. 11334P   Schedule C (Form 1040) 2011

Part III   **Cost of Goods Sold** (see instructions)

33   Method(s) used to
value closing inventory: **a** ☐ Cost   **b** ☐ Lower of cost or market   **c** ☐ Other (attach explanation)

34   Was there any change in determining quantities, costs, or valuations between opening and closing inventory?
If "Yes," attach explanation . . . . ☐ **Yes**   ☐ **No**

35	Inventory at beginning of year. If different from last year's closing inventory, attach explanation . . .	35	
36	Purchases less cost of items withdrawn for personal use	36	
37	Cost of labor. Do not include any amounts paid to yourself	37	
38	Materials and supplies	38	
39	Other costs	39	
40	Add lines 35 through 39	40	
41	Inventory at end of year	41	
42	**Cost of goods sold.** Subtract line 41 from line 40. Enter the result here and on line 4	42	

Part IV   **Information on Your Vehicle.** Complete this part **only** if you are claiming car or truck expenses on line 9 and are not required to file Form 4562 for this business. See the instructions for line 13 to find out if you must file Form 4562.

43   When did you place your vehicle in service for business purposes? (month, day, year)   ▶ _____ / _____ / _____

44   Of the total number of miles you drove your vehicle during 2011, enter the number of miles you used your vehicle for:

   a   Business _____   **b** Commuting (see instructions) _____   **c** Other _____

45   Was your vehicle available for personal use during off-duty hours? . . . . ☐ **Yes**   ☐ **No**

46   Do you (or your spouse) have another vehicle available for personal use?. . . . . ☐ **Yes**   ☐ **No**

47a   Do you have evidence to support your deduction? . . . . ☐ **Yes**   ☐ **No**

  b   If "Yes," is the evidence written? . . . . ☐ **Yes**   ☐ **No**

Part V   **Other Expenses.** List below business expenses not included on lines 8–26 or line 30.

---	
48 **Total other expenses.** Enter here and on line 27a	48

Department of the Treasury—Internal Revenue Service

Amended U.S. Individual Income Tax Return

▶ See separate instructions.

OMB No. 1545-0074

This return is for calendar year ☐ 2011 ☐ 2010 ☐ 2009 ☐ 2008

Other year. Enter one: calendar year ☐☐☐☐☐ **or** fiscal year (month and year ended): ☐☐☐☐☐

Your first name and initial	Last name	Your social security number

If a joint return, spouse's first name and initial	Last name	Spouse's social security number

Home address (number and street). If you have a P.O. box, see instructions.	Apt. no.	Your phone number

City, town or post office, state, and ZIP code. If you have a foreign address, also complete spaces below (see instructions).

Foreign country name	Foreign province/county	Foreign postal code

Amended return filing status. You must check one box even if you are not changing your filing status.
Caution. You cannot change your filing status from joint to separate returns after the due date.

☐ Single
☐ Married filing jointly
☐ Married filing separately
☐ Qualifying widow(er)
☐ Head of household (If the qualifying person is a child but not your dependent, see instructions.)

Use Part III on the back to explain any changes

			A. Original amount or as previously adjusted (see instructions)	**B.** Net change— amount of increase or (decrease)— explain in Part III	**C.** Correct amount
Income and Deductions					
1	Adjusted gross income. If net operating loss (NOL) carryback is included, check here ▶ ☐	1			
2	Itemized deductions or standard deduction	2			
3	Subtract line 2 from line 1	3			
4	Exemptions. **If changing, complete Part I on the back and enter the amount from line 30**	4			
5	Taxable income. Subtract line 4 from line 3	5			
Tax Liability					
6	Tax. Enter method used to figure tax:	6			
7	Credits. If general business credit carryback is included, check here ▶ ☐	7			
8	Subtract line 7 from line 6. If the result is zero or less, enter -0-	8			
9	Other taxes	9			
10	Total tax. Add lines 8 and 9	10			
Payments					
11	Federal income tax withheld and excess social security and tier 1 RRTA tax withheld (**if changing,** see instructions)	11			
12	Estimated tax payments, including amount applied from prior year's return	12			
13	Earned income credit (EIC)	13			
14	Refundable credits from ☐ Schedule M or Form(s) ☐ 2439 ☐ 4136 ☐ 5405 ☐ 8801 ☐ 8812 ☐ 8839 ☐ 8863 ☐ 8885 or ☐ other (specify):	14			
15	Total amount paid with request for extension of time to file, tax paid with original return, and additional tax paid after return was filed			15	
16	Total payments. Add lines 11 through 15			16	
Refund or Amount You Owe *(Note. Allow 8–12 weeks to process Form 1040X.)*					
17	Overpayment, if any, as shown on original return or as previously adjusted by the IRS			17	
18	Subtract line 17 from line 16 (If less than zero, see instructions)			18	
19	**Amount you owe.** If line 10, column C, is more than line 18, enter the difference			19	
20	If line 10, column C, is less than line 18, enter the difference. This is the amount **overpaid** on this return			20	
21	Amount of line 20 you want **refunded to you**			21	
22	Amount of line 20 you want **applied to your** (enter year): ☐☐☐☐ estimated tax	22			

Complete and sign this form on Page 2.

For Paperwork Reduction Act Notice, see instructions.　　　Cat. No. 11360L　　　Form **1040X** (Rev. 12-2011)

Part I	Exemptions

Complete this part **only** if you are:

• Increasing or decreasing the number of exemptions (personal and dependents) claimed on line 6d of the return you are amending, or

• Increasing or decreasing the exemption amount for housing individuals displaced by a Midwestern disaster in 2008 or 2009.

See Form 1040 or Form 1040A instructions and Form 1040X instructions.

			A. Original number of exemptions or amount reported or as previously adjusted	**B. Net change**	**C. Correct number or amount**
23	Yourself and spouse. **Caution.** *If someone can claim you as a dependent, you cannot claim an exemption for yourself*	23			
24	Your dependent children who lived with you	24			
25	Your dependent children who did not live with you due to divorce or separation	25			
26	Other dependents	26			
27	Total number of exemptions. Add lines 23 through 26	27			
28	Multiply the number of exemptions claimed on line 27 by the exemption amount shown in the instructions for line 28 for the year you are amending	28			
29	If you are claiming an exemption amount for housing individuals displaced by a Midwestern disaster, enter the amount from Form 8914, line 2 for 2008, or line 6 for 2009	29			
30	Add lines 28 and 29. Enter the result here and on line 4 on page 1 of this form	30			

31 List **ALL** dependents (children and others) claimed on this amended return. If more than 4 dependents, see instructions.

(a) First name Last name	**(b)** Dependent's social security number	**(c)** Dependent's relationship to you	**(d)** Check box if qualifying child for child tax credit (see instructions)
			☐
			☐
			☐
			☐

Part II	Presidential Election Campaign Fund

Checking below will not increase your tax or reduce your refund.

☐   Check here if you did not previously want $3 to go to the fund, but now do.

☐   Check here if this is a joint return and your spouse did not previously want $3 to go to the fund, but now does.

Part III	Explanation of changes. In the space provided below, tell us why you are filing Form 1040X.

▶ Attach any supporting documents and new or changed forms and schedules.

Sign Here
Remember to keep a copy of this form for your records.

Under penalties of perjury, I declare that I have filed an original return and that I have examined this amended return, including accompanying schedules and statements, and to the best of my knowledge and belief, this amended return is true, correct, and complete. Declaration of preparer (other than taxpayer) is based on all information about which the preparer has any knowledge.

▶		▶	
Your signature	Date	Spouse's signature. If a joint return, **both** must sign.	Date

Paid Preparer Use Only

▶		
Preparer's signature	Date	Firm's name (or yours if self-employed)
Print/type preparer's name		Firm's address and ZIP code
	☐ Check if self-employed	
PTIN		Phone number EIN

For forms and publications, visit IRS.gov.   Form **1040X** (Rev. 12-2011)

Instructions for Form 1040X

(Rev. December 2011)

Amended U.S. Individual Income Tax Return

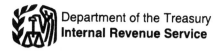

Department of the Treasury
Internal Revenue Service

Section references are to the Internal Revenue Code unless otherwise noted.

General Instructions

What's New

The IRS has created a page on IRS.gov for information about Form 1040X and its instructions at *www.irs.gov/form1040x*. Information about any future developments affecting Form 1040X (such as legislation enacted after we release it) will be posted on that page.

Form 1040X will be your new tax return, changing your original return to include new information. The entries you make on Form 1040X under the columns headed *Correct amount* and *Correct number or amount* are the entries you would have made on your original return had it been done correctly.

 Many find the easiest way to figure the entries for Form 1040X is to first make the changes in the margin of the return you are amending.

To complete Form 1040X, you will need:
• Form 1040X and these separate instructions;
• A copy of the return you are amending (for example, 2009 Form 1040), including supporting forms, schedules, and any worksheets you completed;
• Notices from the IRS on any adjustments to that return; and
• Instructions for the return you are amending. If you don't have the instructions, you can order them by calling 1-800-TAX-FORM (1-800-829-3676) or find them online at *www.irs.gov/formspubs*. If you are amending a prior year return, click on "Previous Years."

Purpose of Form

Use Form 1040X to do the following.
• Correct Forms 1040, 1040A, 1040EZ, 1040NR, or 1040NR-EZ.
• Make certain elections after the prescribed deadline (see Regulations sections 301.9100-1 through -3 for details).
• Change amounts previously adjusted by the IRS. However, do not include any interest or penalties on Form 1040X; they will be adjusted accordingly.
• Make a claim for a carryback due to a loss or unused credit. However, you may be able to use Form 1045, Application for Tentative Refund, instead of Form 1040X. For more information, see *Loss or credit carryback* on page 2 and the discussion on carryback claims on page 3.

File a separate Form 1040X for each year you are amending. If you are changing your federal return, you also may need to change your state return.

Note. Allow 8 to 12 weeks for Form 1040X to be processed.

 If you file Form 1040X claiming a refund or credit for more than the allowable amount, you may be subject to a penalty of 20% of the disallowed amount. See Penalty for erroneous refund claim or credit *on page 2.*

Do not file Form 1040X if you are requesting a refund of penalties and interest or an addition to tax that you have already paid. Instead, file Form 843, Claim for Refund and Request for Abatement.

Do not file Form 1040X for an injured spouse claim. Instead, file Form 8379, Injured Spouse Allocation. But if you are filing Form 1040X to request an additional refund after filing Form 8379, see *Injured spouse claim* on page 3.

Interest and Penalties

Interest. The IRS will charge you interest on taxes not paid by their due date, even if you had an extension of time to file. We will also charge you interest on penalties imposed for failure to file, negligence, fraud, substantial valuation misstatements, substantial understatements of tax, and reportable transaction understatements. Interest is charged on the penalty from the due date of the return (including extensions).

Penalty for late payment of tax. If you do not pay the additional tax due on Form 1040X within 21 calendar days from the date of notice and demand for payment (10 business days from that date if the amount of tax is $100,000 or more), the penalty is usually ½ of 1% of the unpaid amount for each month or part of a month the tax is not paid. The penalty can be as much as 25% of the unpaid amount and applies to any unpaid tax on the return. This penalty is in addition to interest charges on late payments. You will not have to pay the penalty if you can show reasonable cause for not paying your tax on time.

Penalty for erroneous refund claim or credit. If you file a claim for refund or credit in excess of the amount allowable, you may have to pay a penalty equal to 20% of the disallowed amount, unless you can show a reasonable basis for the way you treated an item. The penalty will not be figured on any part of the disallowed amount of the claim that relates to the earned income credit or on which accuracy-related or fraud penalties are charged.

Penalty for frivolous return. In addition to any other penalties, the law imposes a penalty of $5,000 for filing a frivolous return. A frivolous return is one that does not contain information needed to figure the correct tax or shows a substantially incorrect tax because you take a frivolous position or desire to delay or interfere with the tax laws. This includes altering or striking out the preprinted language above the space where you sign. For a list of positions identified as frivolous, see Notice 2010-33, 2010-17 I.R.B. 609, available at *www.irs.gov/irb/2010-17_IRB/ar13.html*.

Other penalties. Other penalties can be imposed for negligence, substantial understatement of tax, reportable transaction understatements, and fraud. See Pub. 17, Your Federal Income Tax, for more information.

When To File

File Form 1040X only after you have filed your original return. Generally, for a credit or refund, you must file Form 1040X within 3 years (including extensions) after the date you filed your original return or within 2 years after the date you paid the tax, whichever is later. If you filed your original return early (for example, March 1 for a calendar year return), your return is considered filed on the due date (generally April 15). However, if you had an extension to file (for example, until October 15) but you filed earlier and we received it July 1, your return is considered filed on July 1.

Note. The time limit for filing Form 1040X can be suspended for certain people who are physically or mentally unable to manage their financial affairs. For details, see Pub. 556, Examination of Returns, Appeal Rights, and Claims for Refund.

 Do not file more than one original return for the same year, even if you have not received your refund or have not heard from the IRS since you filed. Filing more than one original return for the same year, or sending in more than

one copy of the same return (unless we ask you to do so), could delay your refund.

Bad debt or worthless security. A Form 1040X based on a bad debt or worthless security generally must be filed within 7 years after the due date of the return for the tax year in which the debt or security became worthless. For more details, see section 6511.

Foreign tax credit or deduction. A Form 1040X to claim or change a foreign tax credit or deduction for foreign taxes generally must be filed within 10 years from the due date for filing the return (without regard to any extension of time to file) for the year in which the foreign taxes were actually paid or accrued. For details, see Pub. 514, Foreign Tax Credit for Individuals.

Note. This extended period for filing Form 1040X applies **only** to amounts affected by changes in your foreign tax credit or deduction.

If you are filing Form 1040X to carry back your unused foreign tax credit, follow the procedures under *Loss or credit carryback* next.

Loss or credit carryback. File **either** Form 1045 or Form 1040X to apply for a refund based on the carryback of a net operating loss, an unused general business credit, or a net section 1256 contracts loss; or an overpayment of tax due to a claim of right adjustment under section 1341(b)(1). If you use Form 1040X, see the special instructions for carryback claims on page 3 of these instructions. A Form 1040X based on a net operating loss or capital loss carryback or a credit carryback generally must be filed within 3 years (10 years for carryback of foreign tax credit or deduction) after the due date of the return (including extensions) for the tax year of the net operating loss, capital loss, or unused credit. If you use Form 1045, you must file the claim within 1 year after the end of the year in which the loss, credit, or claim of right adjustment arose. For more details, see the Instructions for Form 1045.

Reducing a casualty loss deduction after receiving hurricane-related grant. You must file Form 1040X by the due date (as extended) for filing your tax return for the tax year in which you received the grant. For more information, see *Reimbursement received for hurricane-related casualty loss* on page 4.

Retroactive determination of nontaxable disability pay. Retired members of the uniformed services whose retirement pay, in whole or in part, is retroactively determined by the Department of Veterans Affairs (VA) to be nontaxable disability pay can file claims for credits or refunds using Form 1040X. You have until the **later** of (a) 1 year after the determination date, or (b) the normal deadline for filing a claim for refund or credit. The normal deadline is the later of 3 years after filing the original return or 2 years after paying the tax. Attach a copy of an official letter from the VA granting the retroactive determination of nontaxable disability pay.

Special Situations

Many amended returns deal with situations that have special qualifications or special rules that must be followed. The items that follow give you this specialized information so your amended return can be filed and processed correctly.

⚠️ **CAUTION** *Only the special procedures are given here. Unless otherwise stated, you still must complete all appropriate lines on Form 1040X, as discussed under* Line Instructions *beginning on page 5.*

Form 1040X (Rev. December 2011)

Carryback claim—net operating loss (NOL). Enter "Carryback Claim" at the top of page 1 of Form 1040X. Attach a computation of your NOL using Schedule A (Form 1045) and a computation of any NOL carryover using Schedule B (Form 1045). A refund based on an NOL does not include a refund of self-employment tax reported on Form 1040X, line 9. For details, see Pub. 536, Net Operating Losses (NOLs) for Individuals, Estates, and Trusts.

Note. Interest will not be paid on any NOL refund shown on an amended return processed within 45 days of receipt.

Carryback claim—credits and other losses. Enter "Carryback Claim" at the top of page 1 of Form 1040X. Attach copies of the following.
• Both pages of Form 1040 and Schedules A and D, if applicable, for the year in which the loss or credit originated. Enter "Attachment to Form 1040X—Copy Only—Do Not Process" at the top of these forms.
• Any Schedules K-1 you received from any partnership, S corporation, estate, or trust for the year of the loss or credit that contributed to the loss or credit carryback.
• Any form or schedule from which the carryback results, such as Form 3800; Form 1116, Foreign Tax Credit; Form 6781, Gains and Losses From Section 1256 Contracts and Straddles; Form 4684, Casualties and Thefts; or Schedule C or F (Form 1040).
• Forms or schedules for items refigured in the carryback year, such as Form 6251, Alternative Minimum Tax—Individuals; Form 3800; or Schedule A (Form 1040).

 You must attach all appropriate forms and schedules to Form 1040X or it will be returned.

Note. If you were married and you did not have the same filing status (married filing jointly or married filing separately) for all of the years involved in figuring the loss or credit carryback, you may have to allocate income, deductions, and credits. For details, see the publication for the type of carryback you are claiming. For example, for NOL carrybacks, see Pub. 536.

Deceased taxpayer. If filing Form 1040X for a deceased taxpayer, enter "Deceased," the deceased taxpayer's name, and the date of death across the top of Form 1040X, page 1.

If you are filing a joint return as a surviving spouse, enter "Filing as surviving spouse" in the area where you sign the return. If someone else is the personal representative, he or she must also sign.

Claiming a refund for a deceased taxpayer. If you are filing a joint return as a surviving spouse, you only need to file Form 1040X to claim the refund. If you are a court-appointed personal representative or any other person claiming the refund, file Form 1040X and attach Form 1310, Statement of Person Claiming Refund Due a Deceased Taxpayer, and any other information required by its instructions. For more details, see Pub. 559, Survivors, Executors, and Administrators.

First-time homebuyer credit. If you meet the requirements for the first-time homebuyer credit, you can amend your return to take the credit in the prior year.

Homes purchased in 2009. If you purchased your home in 2009, you can choose to claim the credit on your 2008 return. To amend your 2008 return, file Form 1040X with a completed Form 5405.

For homes purchased before November 7, 2009, you can use either the 2008 or the December 2009 revision of Form 5405 to claim the credit. If you use the 2008 revision, you must check the box in Part I, line C. If you use the December 2009 revision, you must check the box in Part I, line F, and attach any required documentation (see the instructions for the appropriate revision of Form 5405).

For homes purchased after November 6, 2009, and before January 1, 2010, you must use the December 2009 revision of Form 5405.

Note. If you made this election before the 2008 Form 5405 was released, you can file Form 1040X with a new Form 5405 to claim the additional $500 credit for homes purchased in 2009.

Homes purchased in 2010. You can choose to claim the credit on your 2009 return for a home you purchase:
• After December 31, 2009, and before May 1, 2010, or
• After April 30, 2010, and before October 1, 2010, **and** you entered into a binding contract before May 1, 2010, to purchase the property before July 1, 2010.

Homes purchased in 2011. This only applies to members of the uniformed services or Foreign Service or employees of the intelligence community who meet the following conditions.
　1.　You (or your spouse if married) were a member of the uniformed services or Foreign Service or an employee of the intelligence community, and
　2.　You were on qualified official extended duty outside the United States for at least 90 days during the period beginning after December 31, 2008, and ending before May 1, 2010.

If you meet these conditions, you can choose to claim the credit on your 2010 return for a home you purchase:
• After December 31, 2010, and before May 1, 2011, or
• After April 30, 2011, and before July 1, 2011, **and** you entered into a binding contract before May 1, 2011, to purchase the property before July 1, 2011.

For the definitions of a member of the uniformed services or Foreign Service, or an employee of the intelligence community, and qualified official extended duty, see the Instructions for Form 5405, First-Time Homebuyer Credit and Repayment of the Credit.

Household employment taxes. If you are correcting the amount of employment taxes you paid to household employees, attach Schedule H (Form 1040) and include in Part III of Form 1040X the date the error was discovered. If you owe tax, pay in full with this return. If you are changing the wages paid to an employee for whom you filed Form W-2, you must also file Form W-2c, Corrected Wage and Tax Statement, and Form W-3c, Transmittal of Corrected Wage and Tax Statements, with the Social Security Administration. For more information, see Pub. 926, Household Employer's Tax Guide, for the appropriate year.

Injured spouse claim. If you file Form 1040X to request an additional refund and you do not want your portion of the overpayment to be applied (offset) against your spouse's past-due obligation(s), complete and attach another Form 8379 to allocate the additional refund.

Qualified reservist distributions. Reservists called to active duty after September 11, 2001, can claim a refund of any 10% additional tax paid on an early distribution from a qualified retirement plan.

To make this claim:
• You must have been ordered or called to active duty after September 11, 2001, for more than 179 days or for an indefinite period,
• The distribution from a qualified retirement plan must have been made on or after the date you were ordered or called to active duty and before the close of your active duty period, and
• The distribution must have been from an IRA, or from amounts attributable to elective deferrals under a section 401(k) or 403(b) plan or a similar arrangement.

Eligible reservists should enter "Active Duty Reservist" at the top of page 1 of Form 1040X. In Part III, include the date called to active duty, the amount of the retirement distribution, and the amount of the early distribution tax paid. For more information, see Pub. 590, Individual Retirement Arrangements (IRAs), for distributions from IRAs; and Pub. 575, Pension and Annuity Income, for distributions from elective deferral plans.

Form 1040X (Rev. December 2011)　　　　　　　　　**-3-**

Recovery rebate credit (2008 only). You can use Form 1040X to claim this credit if you did not claim it or if you did not claim the correct amount on your original 2008 Form 1040, 1040A, or 1040EZ. For information on how to claim the credit, see the 2008 instructions for the form you are amending.

Reimbursement received for hurricane-related casualty loss. If you claimed a casualty loss on your main home resulting from Hurricanes Katrina, Rita, or Wilma, and later received a qualified grant as reimbursement for that loss, you can file an amended return for the year the casualty loss deduction was claimed (and for any tax year to which the deduction was carried) to reduce the casualty loss deduction (but not below zero) by the amount of the reimbursement. To qualify, your grant must have been issued under Public Law 109-148, 109-234, or 110-116. Examples of qualified grants are the Louisiana Road Home Grants and the Mississippi Development Authority Hurricane Katrina Homeowner Grants.

At the top of page 1 of Form 1040X, enter "Hurricane Grant Relief" in dark, bold letters. Include the following materials with your amended return.

1. Proof of the amount of any hurricane relief grant received.

2. A completed Form 2848, Power of Attorney and Declaration of Representative, if you wish to have your designated representative speak with us. (Do not include this if a valid Form 2848 is already on file with the IRS that covers the same tax year and tax matters.)

 Do not include on Form 1040X any adjustments other than the reduction of the casualty loss deduction if the period of limitations on assessment is closed for the tax year in which you claimed the casualty loss deduction. Generally, this period is closed if it is more than 3 years after the return was filed and more than 2 years after the tax was paid. If you filed the return earlier than the due date of the return (including appropriate extensions), your return is considered filed on the due date of the return (including extensions).

Waiver of penalties and interest. If you pay the entire balance due on your amended return within 1 year of timely filing your amended return, no interest or penalties will be charged on the balance due. Payments made after you file Form 1040X should clearly designate that the payment is to be applied to reduce the balance due shown on the Form 1040X per IRS Notice 2008-95.

Special rule for previously filed amended returns. In order to receive the benefits discussed in this section, you must notify the IRS if you previously filed an amended return based on receiving one of the grants mentioned earlier. For instructions on how to notify the IRS, see Notice 2008-95, 2008-44 I.R.B. 1076, available at *www.irs.gov/irb/2008-44_IRB/ar09.html*.

Relief for homeowners with corrosive drywall. If you suffered property losses due to the effects of certain imported drywall installed in homes between 2001 and 2009, you may be able to file an amended return to claim a casualty loss for repairs made to your personal residence or household appliances. For further information on claiming this loss, see Rev. Proc. 2010-36, 2010-42 I.R.B. 439, available at *www.irs.gov/irb/2010-42_IRB/ar11.html*.

Resident and nonresident aliens. Use Form 1040X to amend Form 1040NR or Form 1040NR-EZ. Also, use Form 1040X if you should have filed Form 1040, 1040A, or 1040EZ instead of Form 1040NR or 1040NR-EZ, or vice versa.

To amend Form 1040NR or 1040NR-EZ, or to file the correct return, do the following:

• Enter your name, address, and social security number (SSN) or IRS individual taxpayer identification number (ITIN) on the front of Form 1040X.

• Do not enter any other information on page 1. Also, do not complete Parts I or II on page 2 of Form 1040X.

• Enter in Part III the reason why you are filing Form 1040X.

• Complete a new or corrected return (Form 1040, Form 1040NR, etc.).

• Attach the new or corrected return to the back of Form 1040X.

• Across the top of the new or corrected return, write "Amended."

For more information, see Pub. 519, U.S. Tax Guide for Aliens.

Signing your child's return. If your child cannot sign the return, either parent can sign the child's name in the space provided. Then, enter "By (your signature), parent for minor child."

Student loan forgiveness for health care professionals working in underserved areas. Under the Affordable Care Act of 2010, health care professionals who received student loan relief under state programs that encourage individuals to work in underserved areas may qualify for refunds on their 2009 federal income tax returns.

Before the enactment of the new law, only amounts received under the National Health Service Corps Loan Repayment Program or certain state loan repayment programs eligible for funding under the Public Health Service Act qualified for the tax exclusion. The Affordable Care Act expanded the tax exclusion to include any state loan repayment or loan forgiveness program intended to increase the availability of health care services in underserved areas or health professional shortage areas. The exclusion is retroactive to the 2009 tax year.

To claim this refund, you must file an amended return for 2009. Enter "Excluded student loan amount under 2010 Affordable Care Act" in Part III.

Tax shelters. If you are amending your return to disclose information for a reportable transaction in which you participated, attach Form 8886, Reportable Transaction Disclosure Statement.

Where To File

If you are amending your return because of any of the situations listed next, use the corresponding address.

IF you are filing Form 1040X:	THEN mail Form 1040X and attachments to:
In response to a notice you received from the IRS	The address shown in the notice
Because you received reimbursement for a hurricane-related loss	Department of the Treasury Internal Revenue Service Center Austin, TX 73301-0255
With Form 1040NR or 1040NR-EZ	Department of the Treasury Internal Revenue Service Center Austin, TX 73301-0215

If none of the situations listed above apply to you, mail your return to the Internal Revenue Service Center shown next that applies to you.

-4- **Form 1040X (Rev. December 2011)**

IF you live in:	THEN mail Form 1040X and attachments to:
Florida, Louisiana, Mississippi, Texas	Department of the Treasury Internal Revenue Service Center Austin, TX 73301
Alaska, Arizona, Arkansas, California, Colorado, Hawaii, Idaho, Illinois, Indiana, Iowa, Kansas, Michigan, Minnesota, Montana, Nebraska, Nevada, New Mexico, North Dakota, Ohio, Oklahoma, Oregon, South Dakota, Utah, Washington, Wisconsin, Wyoming	Department of the Treasury Internal Revenue Service Center Fresno, CA 93888-0422
Alabama, Connecticut, Delaware, District of Columbia, Georgia, Kentucky, Maine, Maryland, Massachusetts, Missouri, New Hampshire, New Jersey, New York, North Carolina, Pennsylvania, Rhode Island, South Carolina, Tennessee, Vermont, Virginia, West Virginia	Department of the Treasury Internal Revenue Service Center Kansas City, MO 64999
A foreign country, U.S. possession or territory;* or use an APO or FPO address, or file Form 2555, 2555-EZ, or 4563; or are a dual-status alien	Department of the Treasury Internal Revenue Service Center Austin, TX 73301-0215

*If you live in American Samoa, Puerto Rico, Guam, the U.S. Virgin Islands, or the Northern Mariana Islands, see Pub. 570.

Line Instructions

Calendar or Fiscal Year

Above your name, check the box for the calendar year or enter the other calendar year or fiscal year you are amending.

Name, Address, and Social Security Number (SSN)

If you and your spouse are amending a joint return, list your names and SSNs in the same order as shown on the original return. If you are changing from separate to a joint return and your spouse did not file an original return, enter your name and SSN first.

P.O. box. Enter your box number only if your post office does not deliver mail to your home.

Foreign address. If you have a foreign address, enter the city name on the appropriate line. Do not enter any other information on that line, but also complete the spaces below that line. Do not abbreviate the country name. Follow the country's practice for entering the postal code and the name of the province, county, or state.

Amended Return Filing Status

Check the box that corresponds to your filing status on this return. If this is a change from the filing status on your original return, the following information may apply to you.

Changing from separate to a joint return. Generally, if you file a joint return, both you and your spouse (or former spouse) have joint and several liability. This means both of you are responsible for the tax and any interest or penalties due on the return, as well as any understatement of tax that may become due later. If one spouse does not pay the tax due, the other may have to. However, you may qualify for innocent spouse relief. For details, see Form 8857 or Pub. 971 (both relating to innocent spouse relief).

Changing to head of household filing status. If the qualifying person is a child but not your dependent, enter the child's name and "QND" in Part III.

 Generally, married people cannot file as head of household. But for an exception, see Pub. 501, Exemptions, Standard Deduction, and Filing Information.

Lines 1 Through 31—Which Lines To Complete

Before looking at the instructions for specific lines, the following information may point you in the right direction for completing Form 1040X.

You need information about income, deductions, etc. If you have questions such as what income is taxable or what expenses are deductible, the instructions for the form you are amending should help. Also use those instructions to find the method you should use to figure the correct tax. To get prior year forms, schedules, and instructions, call 1-800-TAX-FORM (1-800-829-3676) or download them from *www.irs.gov/ formspubs.*

You are providing only additional information. If you are not changing any dollar amounts you originally reported, but are sending in only additional information, do the following.
• Check the box for the calendar year or enter the other calendar or fiscal year you are amending.
• Complete name, address, and SSN.
• Check a box in Part II, if applicable, for the Presidential Election Campaign Fund.
• Complete Part III, Explanation of changes

You are changing from separate to a joint return. If you and your spouse are changing from separate returns to a joint return, follow these steps.

1. Enter in column A the amounts from your return as originally filed or as previously adjusted (either by you or the IRS).

2. To determine the amounts to enter in column B, combine the amounts from your spouse's return as originally filed or as previously adjusted with any other changes you or your spouse are making. If your spouse did not file an original return, include your spouse's income, deductions, credits, other taxes, etc., in the amounts you enter in column B.

3. Read the instructions for column C on page 6 to figure the amounts to enter in that column.

4. Both of you must sign and date Form 1040X.

You are changing amounts on your original return or as previously adjusted by the IRS. Because Form 1040X can be used for so many purposes, it is sometimes difficult to know which part(s) of the form to fill out. Unless instructions elsewhere in this booklet tell you otherwise, follow the rules below.
• Always complete the top of page 1 through *Amended return filing status.*
• Complete the lines shown in the following chart according to what you are changing.

- Check a box in Part II, if applicable, for the Presidential Election Campaign Fund.
- Complete Part III, Explanation of changes.
- Sign and date the form.

IF you are changing only...*	THEN complete Form 1040X...
Filing status	Lines 1–22
Exemptions	Lines 1–31
Income 1040 lines 7–21 1040A lines 7–14b 1040EZ lines 1–3	Lines 1–22
Adjustments to income 1040 lines 23–35** 1040A lines 16–19	Lines 1–22
Itemized or standard deductions 1040 line 40 (2009 line 40a) 1040A line 24 (2009 line 24a) 1040EZ line 5	Lines 1–22
Tax before credits 1040 lines 44–45 1040A line 28 1040EZ line 11 (2011 line 10)	Lines 5–22
Nonrefundable credits 1040 lines 47–53 (2008 lines 47–54) 1040A lines 29–33	Lines 6–22
Other taxes 1040 lines 56–59** (2011 lines 56–60, 2008 lines 57–60**) 2008–2010 1040A line 36	Lines 6–22
Payments and refundable credits 1040 lines 62–71** (2010 lines 61–71**, 2009 lines 61–70**, 2008 lines 62–70**) 1040A lines 38–43** (2011 lines 36–40**, 2008 lines 38–42**) 1040EZ lines 7–9a** (2011 lines 7–8a**, 2008 lines 7–9**)	Lines 10–22

* This column gives line numbers for 2008 through 2011 returns. Where the same lines do not apply to all years, those that are different are shown in parentheses.

** Plus any write-in amounts shown on the total line for the lines indicated.

Columns A Through C

Column A. Enter the amounts from your original return. However, if you previously amended that return or it was changed by the IRS, enter the adjusted amounts.

Column B. Enter the net increase or decrease for each line you are changing.

Explain each change in Part III. If you need more space, attach a statement.

Attach any schedule or form relating to the change. For example, attach Schedule A (Form 1040) if you are amending Form 1040 to itemize deductions. If you are amending your return because you received another Form W-2, attach a copy of the new W-2. Do not attach items unless required to do so.

Column C. To figure the amounts to enter in this column:
- Add the increase in column B to the amount in column A, or
- Subtract the decrease in column B from the amount in column A.

For any item you do not change, enter the amount from column A in column C

Note. Show any negative numbers (losses or decreases) in Columns A, B, or C in parentheses.

Example. Andy originally reported $21,000 as his adjusted gross income on his 2009 Form 1040. He received another Form W-2 for $500 after he filed his return. He completes line 1 of Form 1040X as follows.

	Col. A	Col. B	Col. C
Line 1	21,000	500	21,500

He would also report any additional federal income tax withheld on line 11 in column B.

Income and Deductions

Line 1—Adjusted Gross Income

Enter your adjusted gross income (AGI), which is the total of your income minus certain deductions (adjustments). Any change to the income or adjustments on the return you are amending will be reflected on this line.

Use the following chart to find the corresponding line.

IF you are amending tax year...	THEN the corresponding line on Form...		
	1040 is:	**1040A is:**	**1040EZ is:**
2011, 2010, 2009, or 2008	37	21	4

A change you make to your AGI can cause other amounts to increase or decrease. For example, changing your AGI can change your:
- Miscellaneous itemized deductions, credit for child and dependent care expenses, child tax credit, education credits, retirement savings contributions credit, or making work pay credit;
- Allowable charitable contributions deduction or the taxable amount of social security benefits; or
- Total itemized deductions or deduction for exemptions (see the instructions for line 4 on page 7).

If you change your AGI, refigure these items—those listed above—and any other deduction or credit you are claiming that has a limit based on AGI.

Correcting your wages or other employee compensation. Attach a copy of all additional or corrected Forms W-2 you received after you filed your original return. Also attach any additional or corrected Forms 1099-R that show federal income tax withheld.

Changing your IRA deduction. In Part III of Form 1040X, enter "IRA deduction" and the amount of the increase or decrease. If changing from a deductible to a nondeductible IRA contribution, also complete and attach Form 8606, Nondeductible IRAs.

Line 2—Itemized Deductions or Standard Deduction

If you itemized your deductions, enter in column A the total from your original Schedule A (Form 1040) or your deduction as previously adjusted by the IRS. If you are now itemizing your deductions instead of using the standard deduction, or have changed the amount of any deduction, or your new AGI limitations have changed any deduction, attach a copy of the corrected Schedule A to this amended return.

If you are using the standard deduction, enter the amount for your filing status for the year you are amending. If you are amending Form 1040EZ, see *Form 1040EZ Filers—Lines 2 and 4* on the next page for the amount to enter. Remember that the standard deduction for all years can be increased for the age and/or blindness of the taxpayer(s). Also, for 2008, 2009, and 2010, the standard deduction can be increased by certain other amounts. See the form instructions for the year you are amending. None of these additions to the standard deduction appear on Form 1040EZ, so for more information see the instructions for Form 1040 or 1040A.

Line 4—Exemptions

Enter on line 4, column A, the amount from:
- The return you are amending (Form 1040, line 42, or Form 1040A, line 26), or
- The amount indicated under *Form 1040EZ Filers—Lines 2 and 4*, if the return you are amending is Form 1040EZ.

Changing the number of exemptions claimed. You must complete the *Exemptions* section on page 2 of Form 1040X if:
- You are increasing or decreasing the number of dependents you claim,
- You are claiming a personal exemption for you or your spouse that you did not previously claim, or
- You are eliminating a personal exemption for you or your spouse that you previously claimed, but were not entitled to claim.

If any of these situations apply to you, complete Form 1040X, lines 23 through 31.

Multiply the total number of exemptions claimed by the amount shown in the table below for the year you are amending. However, if the amount on line 1 of Form 1040X is more than $119,975 and you are amending a tax year beginning before 2010, first see *Who must use the Deduction for Exemptions Worksheet* below.

IF you are amending your...	THEN the amount for one exemption is...
2011 return	$3,700
2009 or 2010 return	$3,650
2008 return	$3,500

Note. Special instructions apply if you are claiming or changing a 2008 or 2009 exemption amount for housing Midwestern displaced individuals. If you are not changing the number of exemptions previously claimed, or if you are claiming or changing a Midwestern displaced individual exemption amount in addition to changing the number of exemptions previously claimed, see the line 29 instructions on page 11.

Who must use the Deduction for Exemptions Worksheet. If you increased the amount on line 1, you may not be allowed the full deduction for your exemptions. However, if you reduced the amount on line 1, you now may be allowed the full deduction. Use the following chart to find out if you must use this worksheet to figure a reduced amount to enter on line 4 and, if applicable, line 28. Be sure to use the Deductions for Exemptions Worksheet in the instructions for the form and year you are amending.

Note. In 2010 and 2011, there is no limitation on the deduction amounts claimed and no Deduction for Exemptions Worksheet to complete.

You are amending your:	You must use the Deduction for Exemptions Worksheet if—	
	And your filing status is:	And the amount on line 1 is over:
2009 return	Married filing separately	$125,100
	Married filing jointly or Qualifying widow(er)	250,200
	Single	166,800
	Head of household	208,500
2008 return	Married filing separately	$119,975
	Married filing jointly or Qualifying widow(er)	239,950
	Single	159,950
	Head of household	199,950

Form 1040EZ Filers—Lines 2 and 4

Did someone claim you as a dependent on his or her return? (If yes, one or both boxes on line 5 of Form 1040EZ will be checked.)

☐ **Yes.** On Form 1040X, **line 2, column A**, enter the amount from line E of the worksheet on the back of Form 1040EZ. On Form 1040X, **line 4, column A**, enter -0- (or, if married filing jointly, the amount from line F of the 1040EZ worksheet).

☐ **No.** Use the chart below to find the amounts to enter on lines 2 and 4.

IF you are amending your...	AND your filing status is...	THEN enter on Form 1040X, line 2...	line 4...
2011 return	Single	$ 5,800	$3,700
	Married filing jointly	11,600	7,400
2009 or 2010 return	Single	$ 5,700	$3,650
	Married filing jointly	11,400	7,300
2008 return	Single	$ 5,450	$3,500
	Married filing jointly	10,900	7,000

Line 5—Taxable Income

If the taxable income on the return you are amending is $0 and you have made changes on Form 1040X, line 1, 2, or 4, enter on line 5, column A, the actual taxable income instead of $0. Enclose a negative amount in parentheses.

Example. Margaret showed $0 taxable income on her original return, even though she actually had a loss of $1,000. She later discovered she had additional income of $2,000. Her Form 1040X, line 5, would show ($1,000) in column A, $2,000 in column B, and $1,000 in column C. If she failed to take into account the loss she actually had on her original return, she would report $2,000 in column C and possibly overstate her tax liability.

Tax Liability

Line 6—Tax

Figure the tax on your taxable income shown on line 5, column C. Generally, you will use the tax table or other method you used to figure the tax on your original return. However, you may need to change to a different method if, for example, you amend your return to include or change the amount of certain types of income, such as capital gains or qualified dividends.

See the instructions for the income tax return you are amending to find the appropriate method, tax table, and worksheet, if necessary. Indicate the method you used to figure the tax entered on line 6, as shown in the chart below.

IF you figured the corrected tax using...	THEN enter in the blank area on line 6...
Tax Table	Table
Tax Computation Worksheet	TCW
Schedule D Tax Worksheet	Sch D
Schedule J (Form 1040)	Sch J
Qualified Dividends and Capital Gain Tax Worksheet	QDCGTW
Foreign Earned Income Tax Worksheet	FEITW
Form 8615, Tax for Certain Children Who Have Investment Income of More Than $1,900 (for 2008, Form 8615, Tax for Certain Children Who Have Investment Income of More Than $1,800)	F8615

Example. The taxable income on your original 2008 Form 1040A was $49,650. You used the Tax Table in the 2008 Instructions for Form 1040A to find the tax, $8,763. You are amending your 2008 Form 1040A to add $160 of interest income, which you add in on line 1 of Form 1040X. There are no other changes. According to the 2008 Form 1040A instructions for line 28 (Tax), you should use the Tax Table to look up the tax on your corrected taxable income ($49,810). The revised tax shown in the Tax Table is $8,800. Below is your completed Form 1040X, line 6.

6	Tax (see page 8 of instructions). Enter method used to figure tax: Table	6	8,763	37	8,800

Once you have figured the tax on the line 5 amount, add to it any additional taxes from Form 4972, Tax on Lump-Sum Distributions; Form 8814, Parents' Election To Report Child's Interest and Dividends; and any recapture of education credits.

Also include any alternative minimum tax from Form 6251, Alternative Minimum Tax—Individuals, or the Alternative Minimum Tax Worksheet in the Form 1040A instructions.

 Any changes you made to Form 1040X, lines 1 through 4, may affect the amount of or cause you to owe alternative minimum tax. See the instructions for the form and year you are amending.

Attach the schedule or form(s), if any, that you used to figure your revised tax. Do not attach worksheets.

Line 7—Credits

Enter your total nonrefundable credits in column A. Nonrefundable credits are those that reduce your tax, but any excess is not refunded to you. Use the chart below to find the corresponding lines.

IF you are amending tax year...	THEN the corresponding lines on Form...		
	1040 are:	1040A are:	1040EZ are:
2009– 2011	47–53	29–33	N/A
2008	47–54	29–33	N/A

If you made any changes to Form 1040X, lines 1 through 6, be sure to refigure your original credits. Attach the appropriate forms for the credits you are adding or changing.

Line 9—Other Taxes

Enter other taxes you paid in column A. Use the chart below to find the corresponding lines.

IF you are amending tax year...	THEN the corresponding line(s) on Form...		
	1040 are:	1040A is:	1040EZ is:
2011	56–60	N/A	N/A
2009 and 2010	56–59 (plus any write-in amounts shown on line 60)	36	N/A
2008	57–60 (plus any write-in amounts shown on line 61)	36	N/A

If you made any changes to Form 1040X, lines 1 through 6, you may need to refigure other taxes that were included in the same section on your original return.

Payments

Line 11—Withholding

In column A, enter from the return you are amending any federal income tax withheld and any excess social security and tier 1 RRTA tax withheld (SS/RRTA). Use the chart that follows to find the corresponding lines.

If you are changing your withholding or excess SS/RRTA, attach to the front of Form 1040X a copy of all additional or corrected Forms W-2 you received after you filed your original return. Also attach additional or corrected Forms 1099-R that showed any federal income tax withheld.

IF you are amending tax year...	THEN the corresponding line(s) on Form...		
	1040 are:	1040A are:	1040EZ is:
2011	62, 69	36 (plus any write-in for excess SS/RRTA on line 41)	7
2009 or 2010	61, 69	38 (plus any write-in for excess SS/RRTA on line 44)	7
2008	62, 65	38 (plus any write-in for excess SS/RRTA on line 43)	7

Line 12—Estimated Tax Payments

In column A, enter the estimated tax payments you claimed on your original return. If you filed Form 1040-C, U.S. Departing Alien Income Tax Return, include on this line the amount you paid as the balance due with that return. Also include any of your prior year's overpayment that you elected to apply to estimated tax payments for the year you are amending.

IF you are amending tax year...	THEN the corresponding line on Form...		
	1040 is:	1040A is:	1040EZ is:
2011	63	37	N/A
2009 or 2010	62	39	N/A
2008	63	39	N/A

Line 13—Earned Income Credit (EIC)

If you are amending your return to claim the EIC and you have a qualifying child, attach Schedule EIC (Form 1040A or 1040).

If you changed the amount on line 1 or line 5, the amount of any EIC you claimed on your original return may change. Use the following chart to find the correct line on your original return.

If you are amending your EIC based on a nontaxable combat pay election, enter "nontaxable combat pay" and the amount in Part III of Form 1040X. If you are amending your 2008 EIC to elect to use your 2007 earned income instead of your 2008 earned income, enter "PYEI" and the amount of your 2007 earned income in Part III of Form 1040X.

 If your EIC was reduced or disallowed for the tax year you are amending, see the Instructions for Form 8862, Information To Claim Earned Income Credit After Disallowance, to find out if you must also file that form to claim the credit.

IF you are amending tax year...	THEN the corresponding line on Form...		
	1040 is:	1040A is:	1040EZ is:
2011	64a	38a	8a
2009 or 2010	64a	41a	9a
2008	64a	40a	8a

Line 14—Refundable Credits

A refundable credit can give you a refund for any part of a credit that is more than your total tax.

If you are amending your return to claim or change a refundable credit, attach the appropriate form(s).

In addition to the credits listed on this line, refundable credits also include the recovery rebate credit. Specify this credit in the blank area after "other (specify):" and include this amount in the line 14 total.

IF you are amending tax year...	THEN the corresponding line(s) on Form...		
	1040 are:	1040A are:	1040EZ is:
2011	65–67, 70, 71	39, 40	N/A
2010	63, 65–67, 70, 71	40, 42, 43	8
2009	63, 65–67, 70	40, 42, 43	8
2008	66, 68–70	41, 42	9

Line 15—Amount Paid With Extension or Tax Return

On this line enter the total of the following amounts.

- Any amount paid with your request for an extension on Form 4868 or 2350 (use the following chart to find the corresponding line). Also include any amount paid with a credit or debit card or the Electronic Federal Tax Payment System (EFTPS) used to get an extension of time to file, but do not include the convenience fee you were charged. Also include any amount paid by electronic funds withdrawal.

- The amount of the check or money order you sent with your original return, the amount paid with a credit or debit card or the EFTPS, or by electronic funds withdrawal. Also include any additional payments you made after it was filed. However, do not include payments of interest or penalties, or the convenience fee you were charged for paying with a credit or debit card.

IF you are amending tax year...	THEN the corresponding line on Form...		
	1040 is:	1040A is:	1040EZ is:
2011	68	41 (write–in amount)	9 (write-in amount)
2009 and 2010	68	44 (write-in amount)	10 (write-in amount)
2008	67	43 (write-in amount)	10 (write-in amount)

Line 16—Total Payments

Include in the total on this line any payments shown on Form 8689, Allocation of Individual Income Tax to the U.S. Virgin Islands, lines 40 and 44. Enter "USVI" and the amount on the dotted line to the left of line 16.

Refund or Amount You Owe

The purpose of this section is to figure the additional tax you owe or excess amount you have paid (overpayment). All of your payments (for the tax year you are amending) received up to the date of this amended return are taken into account, as well as any overpayment on your original return or after adjustment by the IRS. It is as if you were using the new information to complete your original return. If the results show a larger overpayment than before, the difference between the two becomes your new overpayment. You can choose to receive the refund or apply it to your estimated tax for the following year. In either case, it can be used by the IRS to pay other federal or state debts that still exist. If the results show that you owe, it is because you do not have enough additional withholding or because filing your original return with the information you have now would have resulted in a smaller overpayment or a balance due.

Line 17—Overpayment

Enter the overpayment from your original return. Use the following chart to find the corresponding line.

IF you are amending tax year...	THEN the corresponding line on Form...		
	1040 is:	1040A is:	1040EZ is:
2011	73	42	11a
2010	73	45	12a
2009	72	45	12a
2008	72	44	12a

If your original return was changed by the IRS and the result was an additional overpayment of tax, also include that amount on line 17. Do not include interest you received on any refund.

Any additional refund you are entitled to on Form 1040X will be sent separately from any refund you have not yet received from your original return.

Line 18—Amount Available To Pay Additional Tax

If line 17 is larger than line 16, line 18 will be negative. You will owe additional tax. To figure the amount owed, treat the amount on line 18 as positive and add it to the amount on line 10. Enter the result on line 19.

Line 19—Amount You Owe

You can pay by check, money order, credit or debit card or the EFTPS.

To pay by check or money order. Send your signed Form 1040X with a check or money order for the full amount payable to the "United States Treasury." Do not send cash. Do not attach your payment to Form 1040X. Instead, enclose it in the envelope with your amended return.

On your payment, put your name, address, daytime phone number, and SSN. If you are filing a joint Form 1040X, enter the SSN shown first on the return. Also, enter the tax year and type of return you are amending (for example, "2011 Form 1040"). The IRS will figure any interest due and send you a bill.

To help process your payment, enter the amount on the right side of the check like this: $ XXX.XX. Do not use dashes or lines (for example, do not enter "$ XXX—" or "$ XXX $\frac{XX}{100}$").

To pay by credit or debit card or the EFTPS. For information on paying your taxes electronically, including by credit or debit card or the EFTPS, go to *www.irs.gov/e-pay*.

What if you cannot pay. If you cannot pay the full amount shown on line 19, you can ask to make monthly installment payments. Generally, you can have up to 72 months to pay.

To ask for an installment agreement, apply online or use Form 9465, Installment Agreement Request. To apply online, go to IRS.gov, click on "Tools" and then "Online Payment Agreement." If you use Form 9465, see its instructions.

 If the total amount you owe is greater than $25,000, see Form 9465-FS and its instructions.

Note. If you elected to apply any part of an overpayment on your original return to your next year's estimated tax, you cannot reverse that election on your amended return.

Line 21—Overpayment Received as Refund

If the IRS does not use your overpayment to pay past due federal or state debts, the refund amount on line 21 will be sent separately from any refund you claimed on your original return (see the instructions for line 17). We will figure any interest and include it in your refund.

Note. You will receive a check for any refund due to you. A refund on an amended return **cannot** be deposited directly to your bank account.

Line 22—Overpayment Applied to Estimated Tax

Enter on line 22 the amount, if any, from line 20 you want applied to your estimated tax for next year. Also, enter that tax year in the box indicated. No interest will be paid on this amount.

You will be notified if any of your overpayment was used to pay past due federal or state debts so that you will know how much was applied to your estimated tax.

 *You **cannot** change your election to apply part or all of the overpayment on line 20 to next year's estimated tax.*

Part I—Exemptions

If you are changing the number of exemptions claimed on your return, complete lines 23 through 30, and line 31, if necessary. Enter the new exemption amount on line 30 and line 4, column C.

Line 28—Exemption Amount

To figure the amount to enter on line 28, you may need to use the Deduction for Exemptions Worksheet in the Form 1040 or Form 1040A instructions for the year you are amending. To find out if you do, see *Who must use the Deduction for Exemptions Worksheet* on page 7. If you do not have to use that worksheet, multiply the applicable dollar amount shown in the following table by the number of exemptions on line 27.

IF you are amending your...	THEN the amount for one exemption is...
2011	$3,700
2009 or 2010 return	$3,650
2008 return	$3,500

Line 29—Additional Exemption Amount for Housing Midwestern Displaced Individuals

If you are claiming or changing a 2008 or 2009 exemption amount for housing Midwestern displaced individuals, complete lines 1 and 2 of the 2008 Form 8914 (or lines 1 through 6 of the 2009 Form 8914), Exemption Amount for Taxpayers Housing Midwestern Displaced Individuals. Enter the amount from Form 8914, line 2 for 2008 (line 6 for 2009), on Form 1040X, line 29. Complete line 30. Be sure to attach Form 8914 to Form 1040X.

Line 31—Dependents

List **all** dependents claimed on this amended return. This includes:
• Dependents claimed on your original return who are still being claimed on this return, and
• Dependents not claimed on your original return who are being added to this return.

If you are now claiming more than four dependents, attach a separate statement with the required information.

Column (b). You must enter each dependent's social security number (SSN). If your dependent child was born and died in the tax year you are amending and you do not have an SSN for the child, enter "Died" in column (b), and attach a copy of the child's birth certificate, death certificate, or hospital medical records. The document must show the child was born alive.

Be sure the name and SSN entered agree with the dependent's social security card. Otherwise, at the time we process your return, we may disallow the exemption claimed for the dependent and reduce or disallow any other tax benefits (such as the child tax credit) based on that dependent.

Note. For details on how to get an SSN or correct a name or number, see the 2011 Form 1040, 1040A, or 1040EZ instructions.

Column (d). Check the box in column (d) if your dependent is also a qualifying child for the child tax credit. See the Form 1040 or 1040A instructions for the year you are amending to find out who is a qualifying child.

Children who did not live with you due to divorce or separation. If you are claiming a child who did not live with you under the rules for children of divorced or separated parents, you must attach certain forms or statements to Form 1040X. For more information, see Pub. 501 or the instructions for Form 1040 or 1040A for the tax year you are amending.

Part II—Presidential Election Campaign Fund

You can use Form 1040X to have $3 go to the Presidential Election Campaign Fund if you (or your spouse on a joint return) did not do so on your original return. This must be done within 20½ months after the original due date for filing the return. For calendar year 2011, this period ends on January 2, 2014. A previous designation of $3 to the fund cannot be changed.

Part III—Explanation of Changes

The IRS needs to know **why** you are filing Form 1040X. For example, you:
• Received another Form W-2 after you filed your return,
• Forgot to claim the child tax credit,
• Discovered you could claim a tuition and fees deduction for 2009,
• Changed your filing status from qualifying widow(er) to head of household,
• Did not add the sales tax on your new car to your 2009 standard deduction, or
• Are carrying an unused NOL or credit to an earlier year.

Paid Preparer

Generally, anyone you pay to prepare your return must sign it and include their Preparer Tax Identification Number (PTIN) in the space provided. The preparer must give you a copy of the return for your records. Someone who prepares your return but does not charge you should not sign.

Assembling Your Return

Assemble any schedules and forms behind Form 1040X in order of the "Attachment Sequence No." shown in the upper right corner of the schedule or form. If you have supporting statements, arrange them in the same order as the schedules or forms they support and attach them last. Do not attach correspondence or other items unless required to do so, including a copy of your original return.

Attach to the front of Form 1040X:
• A copy of any Forms W-2, W-2c (a corrected Form W-2), and 2439 that support changes made on this return;
• A copy of any Form W-2G and 1099-R that support changes made on this return, but only if tax was withheld; and
• A copy of any Forms 1042S, SSA-1042S, RRB-1042S, and 8288-A that support changes made on this return.

Attach to the back of Form 1040X any Form 8805 that supports changes made on this return.

If you owe tax, enclose (do not attach) your check or money order in the envelope with your amended return. See the instructions for line 19 on page 10.

Paperwork Reduction Act Notice

We ask for the information on this form to carry out the Internal Revenue laws of the United States. You are required to give us the information. We need it to ensure that you are complying with these laws and to allow us to figure and collect the right amount of tax.

You are not required to provide the information requested on a form that is subject to the Paperwork Reduction Act unless the form displays a valid OMB control number. Books or records relating to a form or its instructions must be retained as long as their contents may become material in the administration of any Internal Revenue law. Generally, tax returns and return information are confidential, as required by section 6103.

We welcome comments on forms. If you have comments or suggestions for making this form simpler, we would be happy to hear from you. You can email us at *taxforms@irs.gov*. Enter "Forms Comment" on the subject line. Or you can write to the Internal Revenue Service, Individual and Specialty Forms and Publications Branch, SE:W:CAR:MP:T:I, 1111 Constitution Ave. NW, IR-6526, Washington, DC 20224. Do not send the form to this address. Instead, see *Where To File* on page 4.

Estimates of Taxpayer Burden

The table below shows burden estimates as of November 15, 2010, for taxpayers filing a 2010 Form 1040X tax return. Time spent and out-of-pocket costs are presented separately. Out-of-pocket costs include any expenses incurred by taxpayers to prepare and submit their tax returns. Examples include tax return preparation and submission fees, postage and photocopying costs, and tax preparation software costs. While these estimates do not include burden associated with post-filing activities, IRS operational data indicate that electronically prepared and filed returns have fewer arithmetic errors, implying lower post-filing burden.

Reported time and cost burden is a national average and does not necessarily reflect a "typical" case. The estimated average time burden for all taxpayers filing a Form 1040X is 7 hours, with an average cost of $100 per return. This average includes all associated forms and schedules, across all preparation methods and taxpayer activities. There is significant variation in taxpayer activity within this estimate. Similarly, tax preparation fees vary extensively depending on the tax situation of the taxpayer, the type of professional preparer, and the geographic area.

If you have comments concerning the time and cost estimates below, you can contact us at either one of the addresses shown under *We welcome comments on forms* earlier.

	Average Time Burden (Hours)	Average Cost (Dollars)
All 1040X Taxpayers	7	$100

Form **1127**
(Rev. December 2011)
Department of the Treasury
Internal Revenue Service

Application for Extension of Time for Payment of Tax Due to Undue Hardship

OMB No. 1545-2131

Before you begin: Use the chart on page 3 to see if you should file this form.

Name(s) shown on return

Identifying number

Number, street, and apt., room, or suite no. If you have a P.O. box, see instructions.

City, town, or post office, state, and ZIP code. If you have a foreign address, see instructions.

Part I — Request for Extension

I request an extension from _____ , 20 _____ , to _____ , 20 _____ , to pay tax of $ _____ .

This request is for (check only one box):

☐ The tax shown or required to be shown on Form _____ .

☐ An amount determined as a deficiency on Form _____ .

This request is for calendar year 20 _____ , or fiscal year ending _____ , 20 _____ .

Part II — Reason for Extension

Undue hardship. Enter below a detailed explanation of the undue hardship that will result if your application is denied. (If more space is required, please attach a separate sheet.) To establish undue hardship, you must show that you would sustain a substantial financial loss if forced to pay a tax or deficiency on the due date. For a complete definition of "undue hardship," see the instructions on page 3 under *Who Should File.*

Part III — Supporting Documentation

To support my application, I certify that I have attached (you must check both boxes or your application will not be accepted):

☐ A statement of my assets and liabilities at the end of last month (showing book and market values of assets and whether securities are listed or unlisted), and

☐ An itemized list of my income and expenses for each of the 3 months prior to the due date of the tax.

Signature and Verification

Under penalties of perjury, I declare that I have examined this application, including any accompanying schedules and statements, and to the best of my knowledge and belief, it is true, correct, and complete; and, if prepared by someone other than the taxpayer, that I am authorized to prepare this form.

Signature of taxpayer ▶ _____   Date ▶ _____

Signature of spouse ▶ _____   Date ▶ _____

Signature of preparer
other than taxpayer ▶ _____   Date ▶ _____

FOR IRS USE ONLY (Do not detach)

This application is   ☐ Approved   ☐ Denied   ☐ Returned:

Reason(s): _____

Signature of authorized official _____   Date _____

For Privacy Act and Paperwork Reduction Act Notice, see instructions.   Cat. No. 172380   Form **1127** (Rev. 12-2011)

Section references are to the Internal Revenue Code.

General Instructions

What's New

The IRS has created a page on IRS.gov for information about Form 1127 and its instructions at *www.irs.gov/form1127*. Information about any recent developments affecting Form 1127 will be posted on that page.

Purpose of Form

Use Form 1127 to request an extension of time under section 6161 for payment of the following amounts.

• The tax shown or required to be shown on a return.

• An amount determined as a deficiency (an amount you owe after an examination of your return).

Determination Chart

Use this chart to determine if Form 1127 is the correct form for you to file.

IF you . . .	THEN . . .
Are seeking an extension of time to file your income tax return	File Form 4868, Application for Automatic Extension of Time To File U.S. Individual Income Tax Return, or Form 2350, Application for Extension of Time To File U.S. Income Tax Return. **Do not file Form 1127.**
Are seeking an extension of time to pay estate tax	File Form 4768, Application for Extension of Time To File a Return and/or Pay U.S. Estate (and Generation-Skipping Transfer) Taxes. **Do not file Form 1127.**
Are requesting a monthly installment payment plan	See Form 9465, Installment Agreement Request. **Do not file Form 1127.**
Are requesting to postpone payment of the full amount of tax shown on your return or any amount determined as a deficiency	File Form 1127 by the due date of your return or by the due date for the amount determined as a deficiency.
Owe any tax and are not requesting, or do not qualify for, either a monthly installment payment plan or an extension of time to pay the full amount	Call, write, or visit your local IRS office to discuss your situation. For more information, see Pub. 594, The IRS Collection Process. **Do not file Form 1127.**

Who Should File

You can file Form 1127 if you will owe any of the following, and paying the tax at the time it is due will cause an undue hardship.

• Income taxes.

• Self-employment income taxes.

• Withheld taxes on nonresident aliens and foreign corporations.

• Taxes on private foundations and certain other tax-exempt organizations.

• Taxes on qualified investment entities.

• Taxes on greenmail.

• Taxes on structured settlement factoring transactions.

• Gift taxes.

Form 1127 can also be filed if you receive a notice and demand for payment (or tax bill) for any of the taxes shown below and paying them at the time they are due will cause an undue hardship.

• Normal taxes and surtaxes.

• Taxes on private foundations and certain other tax-exempt organizations.

• Taxes on qualified investments.

• Gift taxes.

Undue hardship. The term "undue hardship" means more than an inconvenience. You must show you will have a substantial financial loss (such as selling property at a sacrifice price) if you pay your tax on the date it is due.

Note. If you need an extension to pay estate tax, file Form 4768.

When To File

Form 1127, and its supporting documentation, should be filed as soon as you are aware of a tax liability or a tax deficiency you cannot pay without causing undue hardship.

If you are requesting an extension of time to pay the tax due on an upcoming return, Form 1127 must be received on or before the due date of that return, not including extensions.

If you are requesting an extension of time to pay an amount determined as a deficiency, Form 1127 must be received on or before the due date for payment indicated in the tax bill.

Where To File

File Form 1127 with the Internal Revenue Service (Attn: Advisory Group Manager), for the area where you maintain your legal residence or principal place of business. See Pub. 4235, Collection Advisory Group Addresses, to find the address for your local advisory group.

However, if the tax due is a gift tax reportable on Form 709, send Form 1127 to:

Department of the Treasury
Internal Revenue Service Center
Cincinnati, OH 45999

Extension Period

An extension of more than 6 months generally will not be granted to pay the tax shown on a return. However, except for taxes due under sections 4981, 4982, and 5881, an extension for more than 6 months may be granted if you are out of the country.

An extension to pay an amount determined as a deficiency is generally limited to 18 months from the date payment is due. However, in exceptional circumstances, an additional 12 months may be granted.

Note. An extension to pay a deficiency will not be granted if the deficiency is due to negligence, intentional disregard of rules and regulations, or fraud with intent to evade tax.

Payment Due Date

You must pay the tax before the extension runs out. **Do not** wait to receive a bill from the IRS.

Interest. You will owe interest on any tax not paid by the due date of the return, or the due date of any amount determined to be a deficiency, regardless of whether an extension of time to pay the tax has been obtained. The interest runs until you pay the tax.

Penalties. Penalties may be imposed if you fail to pay the tax within the extension period granted.

Specific Instructions

Name, Address, and Identification Number

Individuals. Enter your name, address, and social security number (SSN) or individual taxpayer identification number (ITIN). If this application is for the tax shown on a joint return or a joint tax liability for an amount determined as a deficiency, include both spouses' names in the order in which they appear or will appear on your return, and enter the SSN or ITIN of the spouse whose name appears first.

Corporations. Enter your company's name, address, and employer identification number.

P.O. box. Enter your box number only if your post office does not deliver to your street address.

Foreign address. Enter the information in the following order: city, province or state, and country. Follow the country's practice for entering the postal code. Do not abbreviate the country name.

Part I

Request for extension. Enter the due date of your return (not including extensions) or the due date for paying the amount determined as a deficiency. Enter the date you propose to pay the tax and the amount of tax you owe. The date you propose to pay the tax can be up to:

• 6 months from the due date of your return (not including extensions), if your request is for payment of the tax shown on your return (the date you propose can be more than 6 months if you are out of the country), or

• 18 months from the date payment is due, if your request is for payment of an amount determined as a deficiency (an additional 12 months can be requested for a deficiency in exceptional circumstances).

Check the applicable box and enter the form number to which the tax you owe relates. Enter the tax year, if the tax you owe is figured on a calendar year; if the tax you owe is figured on a fiscal year, enter the ending month, day, and year.

Part II

Reason for extension. In order for your application to be considered, you must provide a detailed explanation of the undue hardship that will result if you pay the tax on or before the due date. An extension will not be granted if you provide only a general statement of hardship.

Part III

Supporting documentation. You must attach:

• A statement(s) of your assets and liabilities, and

• An itemized list of your income and expenses for each of the 3 months prior to the due date of the tax.

Note. Once your request has been reviewed, additional conditions may have to be met.

Signature and Verification

This form must be signed and dated.

Individuals. If this application is for the tax shown on a joint return or a joint tax liability for an amount determined as a deficiency, both you and your spouse must sign and date this form. If your spouse cannot sign, see Pub. 501, Exemptions, Standard Deduction, and Filing Information.

Privacy Act and Paperwork Reduction Act Notice. We ask for the information on this form to carry out the Internal Revenue laws of the United States. We need this information to ensure compliance with these laws and to properly grant extensions of time to pay tax. Applying for an extension of time for the payment of tax is voluntary. However, providing the requested information is mandatory if you apply for the extension. Our legal right to ask for the information requested on this form is based in sections 6001, 6011, 6109, and 6161 and their regulations. If you fail to provide all or part of the information requested, your application may be denied. If you provide false or fraudulent information, you may be subject to penalties.

You are not required to provide the information requested on a form that is subject to the Paperwork Reduction Act unless the form displays a valid OMB control number. Books or records relating to a form or its instructions must be retained as long as their contents may become material in the administration of any Internal Revenue law. Generally, tax returns and return information are confidential, as required by section 6103. However, section 6103 allows or requires the Internal Revenue Service to disclose the information to others as described in the Code. For example, we may disclose this information to the Department of Justice for enforcement of civil or criminal tax laws; to cities, states, the District of Columbia, and U.S. commonwealths or possessions to administer their tax laws; to other countries under a tax treaty; to federal and state agencies to enforce non-tax criminal laws; or to federal law enforcement and intelligence agencies to combat terrorism.

The time needed to complete and file this form will vary depending on individual circumstances. The estimated burden for individual taxpayers filing this form is approved under OMB control number 1545-0074 and is included in the estimates shown in the instructions for their individual income tax return. The estimated burden for all other taxpayers who file this form is shown below.

Recordkeeping	3 hr., 6 min.
Learning about the law or the form	55 min.
Preparing and sending the form to the IRS	3 hr., 25 min.

If you have comments concerning the accuracy of these time estimates or suggestions for making this form simpler, we would be happy to hear from you. See the instructions for the tax return for which this form is filed.

Form **2688**

Department of the Treasury
Internal Revenue Service

Application for Additional Extension of Time To File
U.S. Individual Income Tax Return

▶ See instructions on back.
▶ You must complete all items that apply to you.

OMB No. 1545-0066

2004

Please type or print.	Your first name and initial	Last name	Your social security number
File by the due date for filing your return.	If a joint return, spouse's first name and initial	Last name	Spouse's social security number
	Home address (number and street)		
	City, town or post office, state, and ZIP code		

Please fill in the Return Label at the bottom of this page.

1 I request an extension of time until.. , to file Form 1040EZ, Form 1040A, Form 1040, Form 1040NR-EZ, or Form 1040NR for the calendar year 2004, or other tax year ending ....

2 Explain why you need an extension. You must give an adequate explanation ▶ ....
....
....
....
....

3 Have you filed Form 4868 to request an automatic extension of time to file for this tax year? . . . . ☐ **Yes** ☐ **No**
If you checked "No," we will grant your extension only for undue hardship. Fully explain the hardship in item 2. Attach any information you have that helps explain the hardship.

Signature and Verification

Under penalties of perjury, I declare that I have examined this form, including accompanying schedules and statements, and to the best of my knowledge and belief, it is true, correct, and complete; and, if prepared by someone other than the taxpayer, that I am authorized to prepare this form.

Signature of taxpayer ▶ _____ Date ▶ _____

Signature of spouse ▶ _____ Date ▶ _____
(If filing jointly, **both** must sign even if only one had income.)

Signature of preparer
other than taxpayer ▶ _____ Date ▶ _____

Please fill in the **Return Label** below with your name, address, and social security number. The IRS will complete the **Notice to Applicant** and return it to you. If you want it sent to another address or to an agent acting for you, enter the other address and add the agent's name.

....
(Do not detach)

| Notice to Applicant

To Be Completed by the IRS	☐ We **have** approved your application.
	☐ We **have not** approved your application. However, we have granted a 10-day grace period to .... This grace period is considered a valid extension of time for elections otherwise required to be made on a timely return.
	☐ We **have not** approved your application. After considering the information you provided in item 2 above, we cannot grant your request for an extension of time to file. We are not granting a 10-day grace period.
	☐ We cannot consider your application because it was filed after the due date of your return.
	☐ Other..

_____   _____
Director   Date

Return Label (Please type or print)	**Taxpayer's name** (and agent's name, if applicable). If a joint return, also give spouse's name.	Taxpayer's social security number
	Number and street (include suite, room, or apt. no.) or P.O. box number	Spouse's social security number
	City, town or post office, state, and ZIP code	Agents: Always include taxpayer's name on Return Label.

For Privacy Act and Paperwork Reduction Act Notice, see back of form.   Cat. No. 11958F   Form **2688** (2004)

What's New

Form 2688 no longer contains entries for a gift or GST tax payment. See *Gift or generation-skipping transfer (GST) tax return (Form 709)* below for details on paying gift or GST tax.

General Instructions

 It's Convenient, Safe, and Secure

IRS *e-file* is the IRS's electronic filing program. You can get an additional extension of time to file your tax return by filing Form 2688 electronically. You will receive an electronic acknowledgment once you complete the transaction. Keep it with your records. Do not send in Form 2688 if you file electronically.

E-file using your personal computer or through a tax professional. Refer to your software package or tax preparer for ways to file electronically. Be sure to have a copy of last year's tax return—you will be asked to provide information from the return for taxpayer verification.

Purpose of Form

Use Form 2688 to ask for more time to file Form 1040EZ, Form 1040A, Form 1040, Form 1040NR-EZ, or Form 1040NR. Generally, use it only if you already asked for more time on Form 4868 (the "automatic" extension form) and that time was not enough. We will make an exception only for undue hardship. Generally, the maximum extension of time allowed by law is 6 months.

To get the extra time, you must (a) complete and file Form 2688 on time and (b) have a good reason why the first 4 months were not enough. Explain this on line 2.

Generally, we will not give you more time to file just for the convenience of your tax return preparer. But if the reasons for being late are beyond his or her control or, despite a good effort, you cannot get professional help in time to file, we will usually give you the extra time.

 If we give you more time to file and later find that the statements made on this form are false or misleading, the extension is null and void. You will owe the late filing penalty explained on this page.

You cannot have the IRS figure your tax if you file after the regular due date of your return.

Gift or generation-skipping transfer (GST) tax return (Form 709). An extension of time to file your 2004 calendar year income tax return also extends the time to file Form 709 for 2004. However, it does not extend the time to pay any gift or GST tax you may owe for 2004. To make a payment of gift or GST tax, see Form 8892.

If you live abroad. U.S. citizens or resident aliens living abroad may qualify for special tax treatment if they meet the foreign residence or presence tests. If you do not expect to meet either of those tests by the due date of your return, request an extension to a date after you expect to qualify, using Form 2350, Application for Extension of Time To File U.S. Income Tax Return. See Pub. 54, Tax Guide for U.S. Citizens and Resident Aliens Abroad.

Total Time Allowed

Generally, we cannot extend the due date of your return for more than 6 months. This includes the 4 extra months allowed by Form 4868. There may be an exception if you live abroad. See the previous discussion.

When To File

If you filed Form 4868, file Form 2688 by the extended due date of your return. For most people, this is August 15, 2005. If you did not file Form 4868 first because you need more than a 4-month extension due to an undue hardship, file Form 2688 as early as possible, but no later than the due date of your return. The due date is April 15, 2005, for a calendar year return. Be sure to fully explain on line 2 why you are filing Form 2688 first. Also, file Form 2688 early so that if your request is not approved, you can still file your return on time.

If you are a U.S. citizen or resident out of the country (defined on this page) on the regular due date of your return, you are allowed 2 extra months to file your return. For a calendar year return, this is June 15, 2005. If you need an additional 2 months (until August 15, 2005, for most calendar year taxpayers), file Form 4868. Then, if you need another 2 months, file Form 2688 by the extended due date.

Out of the country means either (a) you live outside the United States and Puerto Rico and your main place of work is outside the United States and Puerto Rico or (b) you are in military or naval service outside the United States and Puerto Rico. If you qualify as being "out of the country," you will still be eligible for the extension, even if you are physically present in the United States or Puerto Rico on the regular due date of the return.

Where To File

Mail Form 2688 to the Internal Revenue Service Center where you will file your return.

Filing Your Tax Return

You may file your tax return any time before the extension expires. Do not attach Form 2688 to your tax return.

Form 2688 does not extend the time to pay taxes. If you do not pay the amount due by the regular due date, you will owe interest and may also be charged penalties.

Interest. You will owe interest on any tax not paid by the regular due date of your return even if you had a good reason for not paying on time. The interest runs until you pay the tax.

Penalties. The late payment penalty is usually ½ of 1% of any tax (other than estimated tax) not paid by the regular due date. It is charged for each month or part of a month the tax is unpaid. The maximum penalty is 25%.

The late filing penalty is usually charged if your return is filed after the due date (including extensions). The penalty is usually 5% of the amount due for each month or part of a month your return is late. Generally, the maximum penalty is 25%. If your return is more than 60 days late, the minimum penalty is $100 or the balance of tax due on your return, whichever is smaller.

You might not owe these penalties if you have a good reason for paying and/or filing late. Attach a statement to your return, not Form 2688, explaining the reason.

How to claim credit for payment made with this form. The instructions for the following line of your tax return will tell you how to report any payment you sent with Form 2688.

- Form 1040, line 68; Form 1040A, line 43; or Form 1040EZ, line 9.
- Form 1040NR, line 62; or Form 1040NR-EZ, line 21.

If you and your spouse each filed a separate Form 2688 but later file a joint return for 2004, enter the total paid with both Forms 2688 on the appropriate line of your joint return.

If you and your spouse jointly filed Form 2688 but later file separate returns for 2004, you may enter the total amount paid with Form 2688 on either of your separate returns. Or you and your spouse may divide the payment in any agreed amounts. Be sure each separate return has the social security numbers of both spouses.

Specific Instructions

Name, address, and social security number (SSN). If you plan to file a joint return, include your spouse's name and SSN in the same order they will appear on your return.

If you are filing Form 1040NR-EZ or Form 1040NR, and do not have (and are not eligible to obtain) an SSN, enter your IRS-issued individual taxpayer identification number (ITIN). For information on obtaining an ITIN, see Form W-7, Application for IRS Individual Taxpayer Identification Number.

Line 2. Clearly describe the reasons that will delay your return. We cannot accept incomplete reasons, such as "illness" or "practitioner too busy," without adequate explanations. If it is clear that you have no important reason but only want more time, we will deny your request. The 10-day grace period will also be denied.

Signature and verification. This form must be signed. If you plan to file a joint return, both of you should sign. If there is a good reason why one of you cannot, the other spouse may sign for both. Attach a statement explaining why the other spouse cannot sign.

Others who can sign for you. Anyone with a power of attorney can sign. Attorneys, CPAs, and enrolled agents can sign for you without a power of attorney. Also, a person in a close personal or business relationship to you can sign without a power of attorney if you cannot sign. There must be a good reason why you cannot sign, such as illness or absence. Attach an explanation.

Notice to Applicant and Return Label. You must complete the Return Label to receive the Notice to Applicant. We will use it to tell you if your application is approved. Do not attach it to your return—keep it for your records.

If the post office does not deliver mail to your street address, enter your P.O. box number instead.

Note. If you changed your mailing address after you filed your last return, use Form 8822, Change of Address, to notify the IRS of the change. Showing a new address on Form 2688 will not update your record. You can get Form 8822 by calling 1-800-829-3676.

Privacy Act and Paperwork Reduction Act Notice. We ask for the information on this form to carry out the Internal Revenue laws of the United States. We need this information to determine your eligibility for an additional extension of time to file your individual income tax return. If you choose to apply for an additional extension of time to file, you are required by Internal Revenue Code sections 6001, 6011(a), and 6081 to provide the information requested on this form. Under section 6109 you must disclose your social security number (SSN) or individual taxpayer identification number (ITIN). Routine uses of this information include giving it to the Department of Justice for civil and criminal litigation, and to cities, states, and the District of Columbia for use in administering their tax laws. We may also disclose this information to other countries under a tax treaty, or to federal and state agencies to enforce federal nontax criminal laws and to combat terrorism. If you fail to provide this information in a timely manner, or provide incomplete or false information, you may be liable for interest and penalties.

You are not required to provide the information requested on a form that is subject to the Paperwork Reduction Act unless the form displays a valid OMB control number. Books or records relating to a form or its instructions must be retained as long as their contents may become material in the administration of any Internal Revenue law. Generally, tax returns and return information are confidential, as required by section 6103.

The time needed to complete and file this form will vary depending on individual circumstances. The estimated average time is: **Learning about the law or the form,** 12 min.; **Preparing the form,** 15 min.; and **Copying, assembling, and sending the form to the IRS,** 16 min.

If you have comments concerning the accuracy of these time estimates or suggestions for making this form simpler, we would be happy to hear from you. You can write to us at the following address: Internal Revenue Service, Tax Products Coordinating Committee, SE:W:CAR:MP:T:T:SP, 1111 Constitution Ave. NW, Washington, DC 20224. Do not send the form to this address. Instead, see *Where To File* on this page.

 Printed on recycled paper

Form 2848
(Rev. March 2012)
Department of the Treasury
Internal Revenue Service

Power of Attorney
and Declaration of Representative

▶ Type or print. ▶ See the separate instructions.

OMB No. 1545-0150

For IRS Use Only

Received by:

Name _____

Telephone _____

Function _____

Date ___ / ___ / ___

Part I Power of Attorney

Caution: *A separate Form 2848 should be completed for each taxpayer. Form 2848 will not be honored for any purpose other than representation before the IRS.*

1 Taxpayer information. Taxpayer must sign and date this form on page 2, line 7.

Taxpayer name and address	Taxpayer identification number(s)	
	Daytime telephone number	Plan number (if applicable)

hereby appoints the following representative(s) as attorney(s)-in-fact:

2 Representative(s) must sign and date this form on page 2, Part II.

Name and address	CAF No. _____
	PTIN _____
	Telephone No. _____
	Fax No. _____
Check if to be sent notices and communications ☐	Check if new: Address ☐ Telephone No. ☐ Fax No. ☐
Name and address	CAF No. _____
	PTIN _____
	Telephone No. _____
	Fax No. _____
Check if to be sent notices and communications ☐	Check if new: Address ☐ Telephone No. ☐ Fax No. ☐
Name and address	CAF No. _____
	PTIN _____
	Telephone No. _____
	Fax No. _____
	Check if new: Address ☐ Telephone No. ☐ Fax No. ☐

to represent the taxpayer before the Internal Revenue Service for the following matters:

3 Matters

Description of Matter (Income, Employment, Payroll, Excise, Estate, Gift, Whistleblower, Practitioner Discipline, PLR, FOIA, Civil Penalty, etc.) (see instructions for line 3)	Tax Form Number (1040, 941, 720, etc.) (if applicable)	Year(s) or Period(s) (if applicable) (see instructions for line 3)

4 Specific use not recorded on Centralized Authorization File (CAF). If the power of attorney is for a specific use not recorded on CAF, check this box. See the instructions for Line 4. **Specific Uses Not Recorded on CAF** . . . . ▶ ☐

5 Acts authorized. Unless otherwise provided below, the representatives generally are authorized to receive and inspect confidential tax information and to perform any and all acts that I can perform with respect to the tax matters described on line 3, for example, the authority to sign any agreements, consents, or other documents. The representative(s), however, is (are) not authorized to receive or negotiate any amounts paid to the client in connection with this representation (including refunds by either electronic means or paper checks). Additionally, unless the appropriate box(es) below are checked, the representative(s) is (are) not authorized to execute a request for disclosure of tax returns or return information to a third party, substitute another representative or add additional representatives, or sign certain tax returns.

☐ Disclosure to third parties;   ☐ Substitute or add representative(s);   ☐ Signing a return; _____

☐ Other acts authorized: _____

_____ (see instructions for more information)

Exceptions. An unenrolled return preparer cannot sign any document for a taxpayer and may only represent taxpayers in limited situations. An enrolled actuary may only represent taxpayers to the extent provided in section 10.3(d) of Treasury Department Circular No. 230 (Circular 230). An enrolled retirement plan agent may only represent taxpayers to the extent provided in section 10.3(e) of Circular 230. A registered tax return preparer may only represent taxpayers to the extent provided in section 10.3(f) of Circular 230. See the line 5 instructions for restrictions on tax matters partners. In most cases, the student practitioner's (level k) authority is limited (for example, they may only practice under the supervision of another practitioner).

List any specific deletions to the acts otherwise authorized in this power of attorney: _____

_____

_____

_____

For Privacy Act and Paperwork Reduction Act Notice, see the instructions.   Cat. No. 11980J   Form **2848** (Rev. 3-2012)

- 705 -

6 Retention/revocation of prior power(s) of attorney. The filing of this power of attorney automatically revokes all earlier power(s) of attorney on file with the Internal Revenue Service for the same matters and years or periods covered by this document. If you **do not** want to revoke a prior power of attorney, check here . . . . ▶ ☐

YOU MUST ATTACH A COPY OF ANY POWER OF ATTORNEY YOU WANT TO REMAIN IN EFFECT.

7 Signature of taxpayer. If a tax matter concerns a year in which a joint return was filed, the husband and wife must each file a separate power of attorney even if the same representative(s) is (are) being appointed. If signed by a corporate officer, partner, guardian, tax matters partner, executor, receiver, administrator, or trustee on behalf of the taxpayer, I certify that I have the authority to execute this form on behalf of the taxpayer.

▶ **IF NOT SIGNED AND DATED, THIS POWER OF ATTORNEY WILL BE RETURNED TO THE TAXPAYER.**

Signature	Date	Title (if applicable)
Print Name	☐☐☐☐☐ PIN Number	Print name of taxpayer from line 1 if other than individual

---

Part II   Declaration of Representative

Under penalties of perjury, I declare that:

- I am not currently under suspension or disbarment from practice before the Internal Revenue Service;
- I am aware of regulations contained in Circular 230 (31 CFR, Part 10), as amended, concerning practice before the Internal Revenue Service;
- I am authorized to represent the taxpayer identified in Part I for the matter(s) specified there; and
- I am one of the following:

  a Attorney—a member in good standing of the bar of the highest court of the jurisdiction shown below.

  b Certified Public Accountant—duly qualified to practice as a certified public accountant in the jurisdiction shown below.

  c Enrolled Agent—enrolled as an agent under the requirements of Circular 230.

  d Officer—a bona fide officer of the taxpayer's organization.

  e Full-Time Employee—a full-time employee of the taxpayer.

  f Family Member—a member of the taxpayer's immediate family (for example, spouse, parent, child, grandparent, grandchild, step-parent, step-child, brother, or sister).

  g Enrolled Actuary—enrolled as an actuary by the Joint Board for the Enrollment of Actuaries under 29 U.S.C. 1242 (the authority to practice before the Internal Revenue Service is limited by section 10.3(d) of Circular 230).

  h Unenrolled Return Preparer—Your authority to practice before the Internal Revenue Service is limited. You must have been eligible to sign the return under examination and have signed the return. **See Notice 2011-6 and Special rules for registered tax return preparers and unenrolled return preparers in the instructions.**

  i Registered Tax Return Preparer—registered as a tax return preparer under the requirements of section 10.4 of Circular 230. Your authority to practice before the Internal Revenue Service is limited. You must have been eligible to sign the return under examination and have signed the return. **See Notice 2011-6 and Special rules for registered tax return preparers and unenrolled return preparers in the instructions.**

  k Student Attorney or CPA—receives permission to practice before the IRS by virtue of his/her status as a law, business, or accounting student working in LITC or STCP under section 10.7(d) of Circular 230. See instructions for Part II for additional information and requirements.

  r Enrolled Retirement Plan Agent—enrolled as a retirement plan agent under the requirements of Circular 230 (the authority to practice before the Internal Revenue Service is limited by section 10.3(e)).

  ▶ **IF THIS DECLARATION OF REPRESENTATIVE IS NOT SIGNED AND DATED, THE POWER OF ATTORNEY WILL BE RETURNED. REPRESENTATIVES MUST SIGN IN THE ORDER LISTED IN LINE 2 ABOVE.** See the instructions for Part II.

Note: For designations d-f, enter your title, position, or relationship to the taxpayer in the "Licensing jurisdiction" column. See the instructions for Part II for more information.

Designation—Insert above letter **(a–r)**	Licensing jurisdiction (state) or other licensing authority (if applicable)	Bar, license, certification, registration, or enrollment number (if applicable). See instructions for Part II for more information.	Signature	Date

Instructions for Form 2848

Department of the Treasury
Internal Revenue Service

(Rev. March 2012)
Power of Attorney and Declaration of Representative

Section references are to the Internal Revenue Code unless otherwise noted.

General Instructions

What's New

Joint returns. Joint filers must now complete and submit separate Forms 2848 to have the power of attorney recorded on the IRS's Centralized Authorization File (CAF).

Copies of notices and communications. You must check the box next to your representative's name and address if you want to authorize the IRS to send copies of all notices and communications to your representative.

Acts authorized. Check boxes have been added to assist you in identifying certain specific acts that your representative may perform. The CAF no longer records authorizations allowing your representative to receive but not endorse your refund check; the check box authorizing this act has been eliminated.

Representative designations. A new designation (i) has been added for registered tax return preparers. Also, the designations for student attorneys and student certified public accountants (CPA) have been combined into one designation (k). See the instructions for Part II.

Future developments. The IRS has created a page on IRS.gov for Form 2848 and its instructions, at *www.irs.gov/form2848*. Information about any future developments affecting Form 2848 (such as legislation enacted after we release it) will be posted on that page.

Purpose of Form

Use Form 2848 to authorize an individual to represent you before the IRS. See "Substitute Form 2848" for information about using a power of attorney other than a Form 2848 to authorize an individual to represent you before the IRS. The individual you authorize must

be an individual eligible to practice before the IRS. Eligible individuals are listed in Part II, Declaration of Representative, items a-r. You may authorize a student who works in a qualified Low Income Taxpayer Clinic (LITC) or Student Tax Clinic Program (STCP) to represent you under a special order issued by the Office of Professional Responsibility, see the instructions for Part II, later. Your authorization of an eligible representative will also allow that individual to receive and inspect your confidential tax information. See the instructions for line 7.

Use Form 8821, Tax Information Authorization, if you want to authorize an individual or organization to receive or inspect confidential tax return information, but do not want to authorize an individual to represent you before the IRS. Use Form 4506T, Request for Transcript of Tax Return, if you want to authorize an individual or organization to receive or inspect transcripts of your confidential return information, but do not want to authorize an individual to represent you before the IRS. This form is often used by third parties to verify your tax compliance.

Use Form 56, Notice Concerning Fiduciary Relationship, to notify the IRS of the existence of a fiduciary relationship. A fiduciary (trustee, executor, administrator, receiver, or guardian) stands in the position of a taxpayer and acts as the taxpayer, not as a representative. If a fiduciary wishes to authorize an individual to represent or perform certain acts on behalf of the entity, the fiduciary must file a power of attorney that names the eligible individual(s) as representative(s) for the entity. Because the fiduciary stands in the position of the entity, the fiduciary signs the power of attorney on behalf of the entity.

Note. Authorizing someone to represent you does not relieve you of your tax obligations.

Where To File

Except as provided in this paragraph, completed Forms 2848 should be mailed or faxed directly to the IRS office identified in the *Where To File Chart* below. The exceptions are listed as follows:

Where To File Chart

IF you live in...	THEN use this address...	Fax number*
Alabama, Arkansas, Connecticut, Delaware, District of Columbia, Florida, Georgia, Illinois, Indiana, Kentucky, Louisiana, Maine, Maryland, Massachusetts, Michigan, Mississippi, New Hampshire, New Jersey, New York, North Carolina, Ohio, Pennsylvania, Rhode Island, South Carolina, Tennessee, Vermont, Virginia, or West Virginia	Internal Revenue Service P.O. Box 268, Stop 8423 Memphis, TN 38101-0268	901-546-4115
Alaska, Arizona, California, Colorado, Hawaii, Idaho, Iowa, Kansas, Minnesota, Missouri, Montana, Nebraska, Nevada, New Mexico, North Dakota, Oklahoma, Oregon, South Dakota, Texas, Utah, Washington, Wisconsin, or Wyoming	Internal Revenue Service 1973 N. Rulon White Blvd. MS 6737 Ogden, UT 84404	801-620-4249
All APO and FPO addresses, American Samoa, nonpermanent residents of Guam or the U.S. Virgin Islands**, Puerto Rico (or if excluding income under Internal Revenue Code section 933), a foreign country: U.S. citizens and those filing Form 2555, 2555-EZ, or 4563.	Internal Revenue Service International CAF Team 2970 Market Street MS:3-E08.123. Philadelphia, PA 19104	267-941-1017

* These numbers may change without notice.

**Permanent residents of Guam should use Department of Taxation, Government of Guam, P.O. Box 23607, GMF, GU 96921; permanent residents of the U.S. Virgin Islands should use: V.I. Bureau of Internal Revenue, 6115 Estate Smith Bay, Suite 225, St. Thomas, V.I. 00802.

- If Form 2848 is for a specific use, mail or fax it to the office handling the specific matter. For more information on specific use, see the instructions for line 4.
- Your representative may be able to file Form 2848 electronically via the IRS website. For more information, go to *IRS.gov* and under the *Tax Professionals* tab, click on *e-services — for Tax Pros*. If you complete Form 2848 for electronic signature authorization, do not file Form 2848 with the IRS. Instead, give it to your representative, who will retain the document. When a power of attorney is mailed or faxed to the IRS using the *Where To File Chart*, the power of attorney will be recorded on the CAF. Unless when the power of attorney is revoked or withdrawn earlier, a power of attorney recorded on the CAF generally will be deleted from the CAF seven years after it is first recorded. However, you may re-establish the record of the authorization for representation by resubmitting the power of attorney to the IRS using the *Where To File Chart*. In the case of a power of attorney held by a student of an LITC or an STCP, the CAF record will be deleted 130 days after it is received and you generally must submit a new power of attorney to the IRS if you want to authorize the same student or another student of an LITC or an STCP to represent you.

Authority Granted

Except as specified below or in other IRS guidance, this power of attorney authorizes the listed representative(s) to receive and inspect confidential tax information and to perform all acts (that is, sign agreements, consents, waivers or other documents) that you can perform with respect to matters described in the power of attorney. However, this authorization, does not include the power to receive a check issued in connection with any liability for tax or any act specifically excluded on line 5 of the power of the attorney. Additionally, unless specifically provided in the power of attorney, this authorization does not include the power to substitute another representative or add another representative, the power to sign certain returns or the power to execute a request for disclosure of tax returns or return information to a third party. See instructions to line 5 for more information regarding specific authorities.

Note. The power to sign tax returns only may be granted in limited situations. See instructions to line 5 for more information.

Special rules for registered tax return preparers and unenrolled return preparers

Registered tax return preparers and unenrolled return preparers may only represent taxpayers before revenue agents, customer service representatives, or similar officers and employees of the Internal Revenue Service (including the Taxpayer Advocate Service) during an examination of the taxable period covered by the tax return they prepared and signed. Registered tax return preparers and unenrolled return preparers cannot represent taxpayers, regardless of the circumstances requiring representation, before appeals officers, revenue officers, counsel or similar officers or employees of the Internal Revenue Service or the Department of Treasury. Registered tax return preparers and unenrolled return preparers cannot execute closing agreements, extend the statutory period for tax assessments or collection of tax, execute waivers, execute claims for refund, or sign any document on behalf of a taxpayer.

A registered tax return preparer is an individual who has passed an IRS competency test. A registered tax return preparer may prepare and sign Form 1040 series tax returns as a paid return preparer. An unenrolled return preparer is an individual other than an attorney, CPA, enrolled agent, enrolled retirement plan agent, enrolled actuary, or registered tax return preparer who prepares and signs a taxpayer's return as the preparer, or who prepares a return but is not required (by the instructions to the return or regulations) to sign the return.

If a registered tax return preparer or an unenrolled return preparer does not meet the requirements for limited representation, you may authorize the unenrolled return preparer to inspect and/or receive your taxpayer information, by filing Form 8821. Completing the Form 8821 will not authorize the unenrolled return preparer to represent you. See Form 8821.

Revocation of Power of Attorney/ Withdrawal of Representative

If you want to revoke an existing power of attorney and do not want to name a new representative, or if a representative wants to withdraw from representation, mail or fax a copy of the previously executed power of attorney to the IRS, using the *Where To File Chart*, or if the power of attorney is for a specific matter, to the IRS office handling the matter. If the taxpayer is revoking the power of attorney, the taxpayer must write "REVOKE " across the top of the first page with a current signature and date below this annotation. If the representative is withdrawing from the representation, the representative must write "WITHDRAW " across the top of the first page with a current signature and date below this annotation. If you do not have a copy of the power of attorney you want to revoke or withdraw, send a statement to the IRS. The statement of revocation or withdrawal must indicate that the authority of the power of attorney is revoked, list the matters and periods, and must be signed and dated by the taxpayer or representative as applicable. If the taxpayer is revoking, list the name and address of each recognized representative whose authority is revoked. When the taxpayer is completely revoking authority, the form should state "remove all years/periods" instead of listing the specific tax matter, years, or periods. If the representative is withdrawing, list the name, TIN, and address (if known) of the taxpayer.

Substitute Form 2848

The IRS will accept a power of attorney other than Form 2848 provided the document satisfies the requirements for a power of attorney. See Pub. 216, Conference and Practice Requirements, section 601.503(a). These alternative powers of attorney cannot, however, be recorded on the CAF unless a completed Form 2848 is attached. See Instruction to Line 4 for more information. You are not required to sign the Form 2848 when it is attached to an alternative power of attorney that has been signed by you, but your representative must sign the Declaration of Representative on the Form 2848. See Pub. 216, Conference and Practice Requirements, section 601.503(b)(2).

Representative Address Change

If the representative's address has changed, a new Form 2848 is not required. The representative can send a written notification that includes the new information and the representative's signature to the location where the Form 2848 was filed.

Additional Information

Additional information concerning practice before the IRS may be found in:
- Treasury Department Circular No. 230, Regulations Governing the Practice before the Internal Revenue Service (Circular 230), and
- Pub. 216, Conference and Practice Requirements.

For general information about taxpayer rights, see Pub. 1, Your Rights as a Taxpayer.

Specific Instructions

Part I. Power of Attorney

Line 1. Taxpayer Information

Enter the information requested about you. Do not enter information about any other person, including your spouse, except as stated in the specific instructions below.

Individuals. Enter your name, social security number (SSN), individual taxpayer identification number (ITIN), and/or employer identification number (EIN), if applicable, and your street address or post office box. Do not use your representative's address or post office box for your own. If you file a tax return that includes a sole proprietorship business (Schedule C) and the matters that you are authorizing the listed representative(s) to represent you include your individual and business tax matters, including employment tax liabilities, enter both your SSN (or ITIN) and your business EIN as your taxpayer identification numbers. If you, your spouse, or former spouse are submitting powers of attorney to the CAF in connection with a joint return that you filed, you must submit separate Forms 2848 even if you are authorizing the same representative(s) to represent you.

Corporations, partnerships, or associations. Enter the name, EIN, and business address. If this form is being prepared for corporations filing a consolidated tax return (Form 1120) and the representation concerns matters related to the consolidated return, do not attach a list of subsidiaries to this form. Only the parent corporation information is required on line 1. Also, for line 3 only list Form 1120 in the Tax Form Number column. A subsidiary must file its own Form 2848 for returns that must be filed separately from the consolidated return, such as Form 720, Quarterly Federal Excise Tax Return, Form 940, Employer's Annual Federal Unemployment (FUTA) Tax Return, and Form 941, Employer's QUARTERLY Federal Tax Return.

Exempt organization. Enter the name, address, and EIN of the exempt organization.

Trust. Enter the name, title, and address of the trustee, and the name and EIN of the trust.

Deceased Individual. For Form 1040: Enter the name and SSN (or ITIN) of the decedent as well as the name, title, and address of the decedent's executor or personal representative.

Estate. Enter the name of the decedent as well as the name, title, and address of the decedent's executor or personal representative. For Forms 706: Enter the decedent's SSN (or ITIN) for the taxpayer identification number. For all other IRS forms: Enter the estate's EIN for the taxpayer identification number, or, if the estate does not have an EIN, enter the decedent's SSN (or ITIN).

Gifts. Enter the name, address, and SSN (or ITIN) of the donor.

Employee plan. Enter the name, address, and EIN or SSN of the plan sponsor. Also, enter the three-digit plan number. If the plan's trust is under examination, see the instructions relating to trust above. If both the plan and trust are being represented by the same representative, separate Forms 2848 are required.

Line 2. Representative(s)

Enter your representative's full name. Only individuals who are eligible to practice before the IRS may be named as representatives. Use the identical full name on all submissions and correspondence. If you want to name more than three representatives, indicate so on this line and attach an additional Form(s) 2848.

Enter the nine-digit CAF number for each representative. If a CAF number has not been assigned, enter "None," and the IRS will issue one directly to your representative. The CAF number is a unique nine-digit identification number (not the SSN, EIN, PTIN, or enrollment card number) that the IRS assigns to representatives. The CAF number is not an indication of authority to practice. The representative should use the assigned CAF number on all future powers of attorney. CAF numbers will not be assigned for employee plans and exempt organizations application requests.

Enter the PTIN, if applicable, for each representative. If a PTIN has not been assigned, but one has been applied for, then write "applied for" on the line.

Check the appropriate box to indicate if either the address, telephone number, or fax number is new since a CAF number was assigned.

Check the box on the line for up to two representatives to indicate that you want original and other written correspondence to be sent to you and a copy to the indicated representative(s). You must check the box next to a representative's name and address if you want to authorize this representative to receive copies of all notices and communications sent to you by the IRS. If you do not want any notices sent to your representative(s) then do not check the box. By checking this box you are not changing your last known address with the IRS. To change your last known address, use Form 8822 for your home address and use Form 8822-B to change your business address. Both forms are available at *IRS.gov*. Also, by checking this box, you are replacing any prior designation of a different representative to receive copies of written correspondence related to the matters designated on line 3.

Note. Representatives will not receive forms, publications, and other related materials with the notices.

If the representative is a former employee of the federal government, he or she must be aware of the postemployment restrictions contained in 18 U.S.C. 207 and in Circular 230, section 10.25. Criminal penalties are provided for violation of the statutory restrictions, and the Office of Professional Responsibility is authorized to take disciplinary action against the practitioner.

Students in LITCs and the STCP. The lead attorney or CPA must be listed as a representative. List the lead attorney or CPA first on line 2, then the student on the next line. Also see *Declaration of Representative* later, to complete *Part II*.

Line 3. Description of Matters

Enter the description of the matter, and where applicable, the tax form number, and the year(s) or period(s) in order for the power of attorney to be valid. For example, you may list "Income, 1040" for calendar year "2010" and "Excise, 720" for "2010" (this covers all quarters in 2010). For multiple years or a series of inclusive periods, including quarterly periods, you may list 2008 through (thru or a hyphen) 2010. For example, "2008 thru 2010" or "2nd 2009 - 3rd 2010." For fiscal years, enter the ending year and month, using the YYYYMM format. Do not use a general reference such as "All years," "All periods," or "All taxes." Any power of attorney with a general reference will be returned. Representation only applies for the years or periods listed on line 3. Only tax forms directly related to the taxpayer may be listed on line 3.

You may list the current year/period and any tax years or periods that have already ended as of the date you sign the power of attorney. However, you may include on a power of attorney only future tax periods that end no later than 3 years after the date the power of attorney is received by the IRS. The 3 future periods are determined starting after December 31 of the year the power of attorney is received by the IRS. You must enter the description of the matter, the tax form number, and the future year(s) or period(s). If the matter relates to estate tax, enter the date of the decedent's death instead of the year or period. If the matter relates to an employee plan, include the plan number in the description of the matter.

If the matter is not a tax matter, or if the tax form number, or years or periods does not apply to the matter (for example, representation for a penalty or filing a ruling request or a determination letter, or Application for Award for Original Information under section 7623, Closing Agreement on Final Determination Covering Specific Classification Settlement Program (CSP), Form 8952, Application for Voluntary Classification Settlement Program (VSCP), or FOIA) specifically describe the matter to which the power of attorney pertains (including, if applicable, the name of the employee benefit plan) and enter "Not Applicable" in the appropriate column(s).

Civil penalty representation (including the trust fund recovery penalty). Unless you specifically provide otherwise on line 5, representation for return-related penalties and interest is presumed to be included when representation is authorized for the related tax return on line 3. However, if the penalty is not related to a return, you must reference "civil penalties" or the specific penalties for which representation is authorized on line 3. For example, Joann prepares Form 2848 authorizing Margaret to represent her before the IRS in connection with the examination of her 2009 and 2010 Forms 1040. Margaret is authorized to represent Joann with respect to the accuracy-related penalty that the revenue agent is proposing for the 2009 tax year. Similarly, if Diana authorizes John to represent her in connection with his Forms 941 and W-2 for 2010, John is authorized to represent in connection with the failure to file Forms W-2 penalty that the revenue agent is considering imposing for 2010. However, if Diana only authorizes John to represent her in connection with her Form 1040 for 2010, he is not authorized to represent her when the revenue agent proposes to impose a trust fund recovery penalty against her in connection with the employment taxes owed by the Schedule C business she owns.

How to complete line 3. If you are authorizing this representative to represent you *only with respect to penalties and interest* due on the penalties, enter "civil penalties" on line 3. The description of matter column and the year(s) to which the penalty applies in the year(s) or period(s) column. Enter "Not Applicable" in the tax form number column. You do not have to enter the specific penalty.

Note. If the taxpayer is subject to penalties related to an individual retirement account (IRA) (for example, a penalty for excess contributions), enter "IRA civil penalty" on line 3.

Line 4. Specific Uses Not Recorded on CAF

Generally, the IRS records powers of attorney on the CAF system. The CAF system is a computer file system containing information regarding the authority of individuals appointed under powers of attorney. The system gives IRS personnel quicker access to authorization information without requesting the original document from the taxpayer or representative. However, a specific-use power of attorney is a one-time or specific-issue grant of authority to a representative or is a power of attorney that does not relate to a specific tax period (except for civil penalties) that is not recorded in the CAF. Examples of specific issues include but are not limited to the following:
- Requests for a private letter ruling or technical advice,
- Applications for an EIN,
- Claims filed on Form 843, Claim for Refund and Request for Abatement,
- Corporate dissolutions,
- Circular 230 Disciplinary Investigations and Proceedings,
- Requests to change accounting methods or periods,
- Applications for recognition of exemption under sections 501(c)(3), 501(a), or 521 (Forms 1023, 1024, or 1028),
- Request for a determination of the qualified status of an employee benefit plan (Forms 5300, 5307, 5316, or 5310),
- Application for Award for Original Information under section 7623,
- Voluntary submissions under the Employee Plans Compliance Resolution System (EPCRS), and
- Freedom of Information Act requests.

Check the box on line 4 if the power of attorney is for a use that will not be listed on the CAF. If the box on line 4 is checked, the representative should mail or fax the power of attorney to the IRS office handling the matter. Otherwise, the representative should bring a copy of the power of attorney to each meeting with the IRS.

A specific-use power of attorney will not revoke any prior powers of attorney recorded on the CAF or provided to the IRS in connection with an unrelated specific matter.

Line 5. Acts Authorized

Use line 5 to modify the acts that your named representative(s) can perform. Check the box for the acts authorized that you intend to authorize or specifically not authorize your representative to perform on your behalf. In the space provided, describe any specific additions or deletions.

Substituting or adding a representative . Your representative cannot substitute or add another representative without your written permission unless this authority is specifically delegated to your representative on line 5. If you authorize your representative to substitute another representative, the new representative can send in a new Form 2848 with a copy of the Form 2848 you are now signing attached and you do not need to sign the new Form 2848.

Disclosure of returns to a third party. A representative cannot execute consents that will allow the IRS to disclose your tax return or return information to a third party unless this authority is specifically delegated to the representative on line 5.

Authority to sign your return. Treasury regulations section 1.6012-1(a)(5) permits another person to sign a return for you only in the following circumstances:
(a) Disease or injury,
(b) Continuous absence from the United States (including Puerto Rico), for a period of at least 60 days prior to the date required by law for filing the return, or
(c) Specific permission is requested of and granted by the IRS for other good cause.
Authority to sign your income tax return may be granted to (1) your representative or (2) an agent (a person other than your representative).

Authorizing your representative. Check the box on line 5 authorizing your representative to sign your income tax return and include the following statement on the line provided: "This power of

attorney is being filed pursuant to Treasury regulations section 1.6012-1(a)(5), which requires a power of attorney to be attached to a return if a return is signed by an agent by reason of *[enter the specific reason listed under (a), (b), or (c) under* Authority to sign your return, *earlier]*. No other acts on behalf of the taxpayer are authorized."

Authorizing an agent. To authorize an agent you must do all four of the following:
1. Complete lines 1-3.
2. Check the box on line 4.
3. Write the following statement on line 5:
"This power of attorney is being filed pursuant to Treasury regulations section 1.6012-1(a)(5), which requires a power of attorney to be attached to a return if a return is signed by an agent by reason of *[enter the specific reason listed under (a), (b), or (c) under* Authority to sign your return, *earlier]*. No other acts on behalf of the taxpayer are authorized."
4. Sign and date the form. If your return is electronically filed, your representative should attach Form 2848 to Form 8453, U.S. Individual Income Tax Transmittal for an IRS *e-file* Return, and send to the address listed in the instructions for Form 8453. If you file a paper return, Form 2848 should be attached to your return. See the instructions for line 7 for more information on signatures. The agent does not complete Part II of Form 2848.

Other. List any other acts you want your representative to be able to perform on your behalf.

Tax matters partner. The tax matters partner (TMP) (as defined in section 6231(a)(7)) is authorized to perform various acts on behalf of the partnership. The following are examples of acts performed by the TMP that cannot be delegated to the representative:
- Binding nonnotice partners to a settlement agreement under section 6224 and, under certain circumstances, binding all partners to a settlement agreement under Tax Court Rule 248 and
- Filing a request for administrative adjustment on behalf of the partnership under section 6227.

Check the box for deletions and list the act or acts you do not want your representative to perform on your behalf.

Line 6. Retention/Revocation of Prior Power(s) of Attorney

If this power of attorney is filed on the CAF system, it generally will revoke any earlier power of attorney previously recorded on the system for the same matter. If this power of attorney is for a specific use or is not filed on the CAF, this power of attorney only will revoke an earlier power of attorney that is on file with the same office and for the same matters. For example, you previously provided the IRS's Office of Chief Counsel with a power of attorney authorizing Attorney A to represent you in a PLR matter. Now, several months later you decide you want to have Attorney B handle this matter for you. By providing the IRS' Office of Chief Counsel with a power of attorney designating Attorney B to handle the same PLR matter, you are revoking the earlier power of attorney given to Attorney A. If you do not want to revoke any existing power(s) of attorney check the box on this line and attach a copy of the power(s) of attorney. The filing of a Form 2848 will not revoke any Form 8821 that is in effect.

Line 7. Signature of Taxpayer(s)

Individuals. You must sign and date the power of attorney. If a joint return has been filed, your spouse must execute his or her own power of attorney on a separate Form 2848 to designate a representative.

Corporations or associations. An officer having authority to bind the taxpayer must sign.

Partnerships. All partners must sign unless one partner is authorized to act in the name of the partnership. A partner is authorized to act in the name of the partnership if, under state law, the partner has authority to bind the partnership. A copy of such authorization must be attached. For purposes of executing Form 2848, the TMP is authorized to act in the name of the partnership. However, see *Tax matters partner,* earlier. For dissolved partnerships, see 26 CFR 601.503(c)(6).

Estate. If there is more than one executor, only one co-executor having the authority to bind the estate is required to sign. See 26 CFR 601.503(d).

Employee plan. If the plan is listed as the taxpayer on line 1, a duly authorized individual having authority to bind the taxpayer must sign and that individual's exact title must be entered. If the trust is the taxpayer listed on line 1, a trustee having the authority to bind the trust must sign with the title of trustee entered. A Form 56, Notice Concerning Fiduciary Relationship, must also be completed to identify the current trustee.

All others. If the taxpayer is a dissolved corporation, decedent, insolvent, or a person for whom or by whom a fiduciary (a trustee, guarantor, receiver, executor, or administrator) has been appointed, see 26 CFR 601.503(d).

Note. Generally the taxpayer signs first, granting the authority and then the representative signs, accepting the authority granted. The date between when the taxpayer signs and when the representative subsequently signs must be within 45 days for domestic authorizations and within 60 days for authorization from taxpayers residing abroad. If the taxpayer signs after the representative signs, there is no time requirement.

PIN number. If you are submitting this form electronically through the IRS's e-services portal, enter the PIN number you used to sign the form you submitted electronically on the copy of the form you retain. You should not provide your PIN number to your representative(s) or include it on the copy of the form your representative(s) will retain.

Part II. Declaration of Representative

The representative(s) you name must sign and date this declaration and enter the designation (for example, items a-r) under which he or she is authorized to practice before the IRS. Representatives must sign in the order listed in line 2 earlier. In addition, the representative(s) must list the following in the "Licensing jurisdiction (state) or other licensing authority" and "Bar, license, certification, registration, or enrollment number" columns:

a Attorney—Enter the two-letter abbreviation for the state (for example, "NY" for New York) in which admitted to practice and associated bar or license number, if any.

b Certified Public Accountant—Enter the two-letter abbreviation for the state (for example, "CA" for California) in which licensed to practice and associated certification or license number, if any.

c Enrolled Agent—Enter the enrollment card number issued by the Office of Professional Responsibility.

d Officer—Enter the title of the officer (for example, President, Vice President, or Secretary).

e Full-Time Employee—Enter title or position (for example, Comptroller or Accountant).

f Family Member—Enter the relationship to taxpayer (generally, must be a spouse, parent, child, brother, sister, grandparent, grandchild, step-parent, step-child, step-brother, or step-sister).

g Enrolled Actuary—Enter the enrollment card number issued by the Joint Board for the Enrollment of Actuaries.

h Unenrolled Return Preparer—Enter your PTIN.

i Registered Tax Return Preparer —Enter your PTIN.

k Student—Enter LITC or STCP.

r Enrolled Retirement Plan Agent—Enter the enrollment card number issued by the Office of Professional Responsibility.

Students in LITCs and the STCP. You must receive permission to practice before the IRS by virtue of your status as a law, business, or accounting student working in a Low Income Taxpayer Clinic or the Student Tax Clinic Program under section 10.7(d) of Circular 230. Be sure to attach a copy of the letter from the Office of Professional Responsibility authorizing practice before the IRS.

Note. In many cases, the student practitioner's authority is limited (for example, they may only practice under the supervision of another practitioner). At the end of 130 days after input to the CAF, they are automatically purged from the CAF.

 Any individual may represent an individual or entity before personnel of the IRS when such representation occurs outside the United States. Individuals acting as representatives must sign and date the declaration; leave the Licensing jurisdiction (state) or other licensing authority column blank. See section 10.7(c)(1)(vii) of Circular 230.

Privacy Act and Paperwork Reduction Act Notice. We ask for the information on this form to carry out the Internal Revenue laws. Form 2848 is provided by the IRS for your convenience and its use is voluntary. If you choose to designate a representative to act on your behalf, you must provide the requested information. Section 6109 requires you to provide your identifying number; section 7803 authorizes us to collect the other information. We use this information to properly identify you and your designated representative and determine the extent of the representative's authority. Failure to provide the information requested may delay or prevent honoring your Power of Attorney designation.

The IRS may provide this information to the Department of Justice for civil and criminal litigation, and to cities, states, the District of Columbia, and U.S. possessions to carry out their tax laws. We may also disclose this information to other countries under a tax treaty, to federal and state agencies to enforce federal nontax criminal laws, or to federal law enforcement and intelligence agencies to combat terrorism.

You are not required to provide the information requested on a form that is subject to the Paperwork Reduction Act unless the form displays a valid OMB control number. Books or records relating to a form or its instructions must be retained as long as their contents may become material in the administration of any Internal Revenue law.

The time needed to complete and file Form 2848 will vary depending on individual circumstances. The estimated average time is: **Recordkeeping,** 11 min.; **Learning about the law or the form,** 53 min.; **Preparing the form,** 77 min.; **Copying and sending the form to the IRS,** 58 min.

If you have comments concerning the accuracy of these time estimates or suggestions for making Form 2848 simpler, we would be happy to hear from you. You can write to the Internal Revenue Service, Individual and Specialty Forms and Publications Branch, SE:W:CAR:MP:T:I, 1111 Constitution Ave. NW, IR-6526, Washington, DC 20224. Do not send Form 2848 to this address. Instead, see the *Where To File Chart.*

Form **4506**

(Rev. January 2012)

Department of the Treasury
Internal Revenue Service

Request for Copy of Tax Return

OMB No. 1545-0429

▶ **Request may be rejected if the form is incomplete or illegible.**

Tip. You may be able to get your tax return or return information from other sources. If you had your tax return completed by a paid preparer, they should be able to provide you a copy of the return. The IRS can provide a **Tax Return Transcript** for many returns free of charge. The transcript provides most of the line entries from the original tax return and usually contains the information that a third party (such as a mortgage company) requires. See **Form 4506-T, Request for Transcript of Tax Return,** or you can quickly request transcripts by using our automated self-help service tools. Please visit us at IRS.gov and click on "Order a Transcript" or call 1-800-908-9946.

1a Name shown on tax return. If a joint return, enter the name shown first.	**1b** First social security number on tax return, individual taxpayer identification number, or employer identification number (see instructions)
2a If a joint return, enter spouse's name shown on tax return.	**2b** Second social security number or individual taxpayer identification number if joint tax return

3 Current name, address (including apt., room, or suite no.), city, state, and ZIP code (see instructions)

4 Previous address shown on the last return filed if different from line 3 (see instructions)

5 If the tax return is to be mailed to a third party (such as a mortgage company), enter the third party's name, address, and telephone number.

Caution. *If the tax return is being mailed to a third party, ensure that you have filled in lines 6 and 7 before signing. Sign and date the form once you have filled in these lines. Completing these steps helps to protect your privacy. Once the IRS discloses your IRS return to the third party listed on line 5, the IRS has no control over what the third party does with the information. If you would like to limit the third party's authority to disclose your return information, you can specify this limitation in your written agreement with the third party.*

6 **Tax return requested.** Form 1040, 1120, 941, etc. and all attachments as originally submitted to the IRS, including Form(s) W-2, schedules, or amended returns. Copies of Forms 1040, 1040A, and 1040EZ are generally available for 7 years from filing before they are destroyed by law. Other returns may be available for a longer period of time. Enter only one return number. If you need more than one type of return, you must complete another Form 4506. ▶ _____

Note. *If the copies must be certified for court or administrative proceedings, check here* . . . . ☐

7 **Year or period requested.** Enter the ending date of the year or period, using the mm/dd/yyyy format. If you are requesting more than eight years or periods, you must attach another Form 4506.

_____ _____ _____ _____

_____ _____ _____ _____

8 **Fee.** There is a $57 fee for each return requested. **Full payment must be included with your request or it will be rejected. Make your check or money order payable to "United States Treasury." Enter your SSN or EIN and "Form 4506 request" on your check or money order.**

a	Cost for each return	$	**$57.00**
b	Number of returns requested on line 7		
c	Total cost. Multiply line 8a by line 8b	$	

9 If we cannot find the tax return, we will refund the fee. If the refund should go to the third party listed on line 5, check here . . . . . ☐

Caution. Do not sign this form unless all applicable lines have been completed.

Signature of taxpayer(s). I declare that I am either the taxpayer whose name is shown on line 1a or 2a, or a person authorized to obtain the tax return requested. If the request applies to a joint return, **either** husband or wife must sign. If signed by a corporate officer, partner, guardian, tax matters partner, executor, receiver, administrator, trustee, or party other than the taxpayer, I certify that I have the authority to execute Form 4506 on behalf of the taxpayer. **Note.** *For tax returns being sent to a third party, this form must be received within 120 days of the signature date.*

Phone number of taxpayer on line 1a or 2a

Sign Here

▶ Signature (see instructions)   Date

▶ Title (if line 1a above is a corporation, partnership, estate, or trust)

▶ Spouse's signature   Date

For Privacy Act and Paperwork Reduction Act Notice, see page 2.   Cat. No. 41721E   Form **4506** (Rev. 1-2012)

Section references are to the Internal Revenue Code unless otherwise noted.

What's New

The IRS has created a page on IRS.gov for information about Form 4506 and its instructions, at *www.irs.gov/form4506*. Information about any recent developments affecting Form 4506, Form 4506T and Form 4506T-EZ will be posted on that page.

General Instructions

Caution. Do not sign this form unless all applicable lines have been completed.

Purpose of form. Use Form 4506 to request a copy of your tax return. You can also designate (on line 5) a third party to receive the tax return.

How long will it take? It may take up to 60 calendar days for us to process your request.

Tip. Use Form 4506-T, Request for Transcript of Tax Return, to request tax return transcripts, tax account information, W-2 information, 1099 information, verification of non-filing, and record of account.

Automated transcript request. You can quickly request transcripts by using our automated self-help service tools. Please visit us at IRS.gov and click on "Order a Transcript" or call 1-800-908-9946.

Where to file. Attach payment and mail Form 4506 to the address below for the state you lived in, or the state your business was in, when that return was filed. There are two address charts: one for individual returns (Form 1040 series) and one for all other returns.

If you are requesting a return for more than one year and the chart below shows two different addresses, send your request to the address based on the address of your most recent return.

Chart for individual returns (Form 1040 series)

If you filed an individual return and lived in:	Mail to the "Internal Revenue Service" at:
Alabama, Kentucky, Louisiana, Mississippi, Tennessee, Texas, a foreign country, American Samoa, Puerto Rico, Guam, the Commonwealth of the Northern Mariana Islands, the U.S. Virgin Islands, or A.P.O. or F.P.O. address	RAIVS Team Stop 6716 AUSC Austin, TX 73301
Alaska, Arizona, Arkansas, California, Colorado, Hawaii, Idaho, Illinois, Indiana, Iowa, Kansas, Michigan, Minnesota, Montana, Nebraska, Nevada, New Mexico, North Dakota, Oklahoma, Oregon, South Dakota, Utah, Washington, Wisconsin, Wyoming	RAIVS Team Stop 37106 Fresno, CA 93888
Connecticut, Delaware, District of Columbia, Florida, Georgia, Maine, Maryland, Massachusetts, Missouri, New Hampshire, New Jersey, New York, North Carolina, Ohio, Pennsylvania, Rhode Island, South Carolina, Vermont, Virginia, West Virginia	RAIVS Team Stop 6705 P-6 Kansas City, MO 64999

Chart for all other returns

If you lived in or your business was in:	Mail to the "Internal Revenue Service" at:
Alabama, Alaska, Arizona, Arkansas, California, Colorado, Florida, Hawaii, Idaho, Iowa, Kansas, Louisiana, Minnesota, Mississippi, Missouri, Montana, Nebraska, Nevada, New Mexico, North Dakota, Oklahoma, Oregon, South Dakota, Texas, Utah, Washington, Wyoming, a foreign country, or A.P.O. or F.P.O. address	RAIVS Team P.O. Box 9941 Mail Stop 6734 Ogden, UT 84409
Connecticut, Delaware, District of Columbia, Georgia, Illinois, Indiana, Kentucky, Maine, Maryland, Massachusetts, Michigan, New Hampshire, New Jersey, New York, North Carolina, Ohio, Pennsylvania, Rhode Island, South Carolina, Tennessee, Vermont, Virginia, West Virginia, Wisconsin	RAIVS Team P.O. Box 145500 Stop 2800 F Cincinnati, OH 45250

Specific Instructions

Line 1b. Enter your employer identification number (EIN) if you are requesting a copy of a business return. Otherwise, enter the first social security number (SSN) or your individual taxpayer identification number (ITIN) shown on the return. For example, if you are requesting Form 1040 that includes Schedule C (Form 1040), enter your SSN.

Line 3. Enter your current address. If you use a P.O. box, please include it on this line 3.

Line 4. Enter the address shown on the last return filed if different from the address entered on line 3.

Note. If the address on Lines 3 and 4 are different and you have not changed your address with the IRS, file Form 8822, Change of Address.

Signature and date. Form 4506 must be signed and dated by the taxpayer listed on line 1a or 2a. If you completed line 5 requesting the return be sent to a third party, the IRS must receive Form 4506 within 120 days of the date signed by the taxpayer or it will be rejected. Ensure that all applicable lines are completed before signing.

Individuals. Copies of jointly filed tax returns may be furnished to either spouse. Only one signature is required. Sign Form 4506 exactly as your name appeared on the original return. If you changed your name, also sign your current name.

Corporations. Generally, Form 4506 can be signed by: (1) an officer having legal authority to bind the corporation, (2) any person designated by the board of directors or other governing body, or (3) any officer or employee on written request by any principal officer and attested to by the secretary or other officer.

Partnerships. Generally, Form 4506 can be signed by any person who was a member of the partnership during any part of the tax period requested on line 7.

All others. See section 6103(e) if the taxpayer has died, is insolvent, is a dissolved corporation, or if a trustee, guardian, executor, receiver, or administrator is acting for the taxpayer.

Documentation. For entities other than individuals, you must attach the authorization document. For example, this could be the letter from the principal officer authorizing an employee of the corporation or the letters testamentary authorizing an individual to act for an estate.

Signature by a representative. A representative can sign Form 4506 for a taxpayer only if this authority has been specifically delegated to the representative on Form 2848, line 5. Form 2848 showing the delegation must be attached to Form 4506.

Privacy Act and Paperwork Reduction Act Notice. We ask for the information on this form to establish your right to gain access to the requested return(s) under the Internal Revenue Code. We need this information to properly identify the return(s) and respond to your request. If you request a copy of a tax return, sections 6103 and 6109 require you to provide this information, including your SSN or EIN, to process your request. If you do not provide this information, we may not be able to process your request. Providing false or fraudulent information may subject you to penalties.

Routine uses of this information include giving it to the Department of Justice for civil and criminal litigation, and cities, states, the District of Columbia, and U.S. commonwealths and possessions for use in administering their tax laws. We may also disclose this information to other countries under a tax treaty, to federal and state agencies to enforce federal nontax criminal laws, or to federal law enforcement and intelligence agencies to combat terrorism.

You are not required to provide the information requested on a form that is subject to the Paperwork Reduction Act unless the form displays a valid OMB control number. Books or records relating to a form or its instructions must be retained as long as their contents may become material in the administration of any Internal Revenue law. Generally, tax returns and return information are confidential, as required by section 6103.

The time needed to complete and file Form 4506 will vary depending on individual circumstances. The estimated average time is: **Learning about the law or the form,** 10 min.; **Preparing the form,** 16 min.; and **Copying, assembling, and sending the form to the IRS,** 20 min.

If you have comments concerning the accuracy of these time estimates or suggestions for making Form 4506 simpler, we would be happy to hear from you. You can write to:

Internal Revenue Service
Tax Products Coordinating Committee
SE:W:CAR:MP:T:M:S
1111 Constitution Ave. NW, IR-6526
Washington, DC 20224.

Do not send the form to this address. Instead, see *Where to file* on this page.

<table>
<tr><td>Form **4564**
(Rev. September 2006)</td><td colspan="2">Department of the Treasury — Internal Revenue Service
Information Document Request</td><td>Request Number</td></tr>
<tr><td colspan="2" rowspan="3">To: *(Name of Taxpayer and Company Division or Branch)*</td><td colspan="2">Subject</td></tr>
<tr><td>SAIN number</td><td>Submitted to:</td></tr>
<tr><td colspan="2">Dates of Previous Requests *(mmddyyyy)*</td></tr>
</table>

Please return Part 2 with listed documents to requester identified below

Description of documents requested

Information Due By _____ At Next Appointment ☐　　Mail in ☐

<table>
<tr><td rowspan="2">**From:**</td><td>Name and Title of Requester</td><td>Employee ID number</td><td>Date *(mmddyyyy)*</td></tr>
<tr><td>Office Location</td><td colspan="2">Telephone Number
(　　)</td></tr>
</table>

Catalog Number 23145K　　　www.irs.gov　　　Part 1 - Taxpayer's File Copy　　　Form **4564** (Rev. 9-2006)

Application for Automatic Extension of Time To File U.S. Individual Income Tax Return

OMB No. 1545-0074

20**11**

There are three ways to request an automatic extension of time to file a U.S. individual income tax return.

1. You can file Form 4868 electronically by accessing IRS *e-file* using your home computer or by using a tax professional who uses *e-file.*
2. You can pay all or part of your estimate of income tax due using a credit or debit card or by using the Electronic Federal Tax Payment System (EFTPS).
3. You can file a paper Form 4868.

 **It's Convenient, Safe, and Secure**

IRS *e-file* is the IRS's electronic filing program. You can get an automatic extension of time to file your tax return by filing Form 4868 electronically. You will receive an electronic acknowledgment once you complete the transaction. Keep it with your records. Do not send in Form 4868 if you file electronically, unless you are making a payment with a check or money order (see page 3).

Complete Form 4868 to use as a worksheet. If you think you may owe tax when you file your return, you will need to estimate your total tax liability and subtract how much you have already paid (lines 4, 5, and 6 below).

Several companies offer free e-filing of Form 4868 through the Free File program. For more details, go to IRS.gov and click on *freefile.*

 ***E-file* Using Your Personal Computer or Through a Tax Professional**

Refer to your tax software package or tax preparer for ways to file electronically. Be sure to have a copy of your 2010 tax return—you will be asked to provide information from the return for taxpayer verification. If you wish to make a payment, you can pay by electronic funds withdrawal or send your check or money order to the address shown in the middle column under *Where To File a Paper Form 4868* (see page 4).

 Pay by Credit or Debit Card or EFTPS

You can get an extension if you pay part or all of your estimate of income tax due by using a credit or debit card. Your payment must be at least $1. You can also get an extension when you pay part or all of your estimate of income tax due using EFTPS. You can pay by phone or over the Internet (see page 3).

 File a Paper Form 4868

If you wish to file on paper instead of electronically, fill in the Form 4868 below and mail it to the address shown on page 4.

For information on using a private delivery service, see page 4.

Note. If you are a fiscal year taxpayer, you must file a paper Form 4868.

General Instructions

Purpose of Form

Use Form 4868 to apply for 6 more months (4 if "out of the country" (defined on page 2) and a U.S. citizen or resident) to file Form 1040, 1040A, 1040EZ, 1040NR, 1040NR-EZ, 1040-PR, or 1040-SS.

Gift and generation–skipping transfer (GST) tax return (Form 709). An extension of time to file your 2011 calendar year income tax return also extends the time to file Form 709 for 2011. However, it does not extend the time to pay any gift and GST tax you may owe for 2011. To make a payment of gift and GST tax, see Form 8892. If you do not pay the amount due by the regular due date for Form 709, you will owe interest and may also be charged penalties. If the donor died during 2011, see the instructions for Forms 709 and 8892.

Qualifying for the Extension

To get the extra time you must:

1. Properly estimate your 2011 tax liability using the information available to you,
2. Enter your total tax liability on line 4 of Form 4868, and
3. File Form 4868 by the regular due date of your return.

 Although you are not required to make a payment of the tax you estimate as due, Form 4868 does not extend the time to pay taxes. If you do not pay the amount due by the regular due date, you will owe interest. You may also be charged penalties. For more details, see Interest *and* Late Payment Penalty *on page 2. Any remittance you make with your application for extension will be treated as a payment of tax.*

You do not have to explain why you are asking for the extension. We will contact you only if your request is denied.

Do not file Form 4868 if you want the IRS to figure your tax or you are under a court order to file your return by the regular due date.

▼ DETACH HERE ▼

Form **4868**

Department of the Treasury
Internal Revenue Service (99)

Application for Automatic Extension of Time To File U.S. Individual Income Tax Return

OMB No. 1545-0074

20**11**

For calendar year 2011, or other tax year beginning   , 2011, ending   , 20   .

Part I Identification	**Part II** Individual Income Tax
1 Your name(s) (see instructions)	**4** Estimate of total tax liability for 2011 . . $ _____
	5 Total 2011 payments . . . . _____
Address (see instructions)	**6** **Balance due.** Subtract line 5 from line 4 (see instructions) . . . . . . _____
	7 Amount you are paying (see instructions) ▶ _____
City, town, or post office | State | ZIP Code	**8** Check here if you are "out of the country" and a U.S. citizen or resident (see instructions) . . . . . . ▶ ☐
2 Your social security number | **3** Spouse's social security number	**9** Check here if you file Form 1040NR or 1040NR-EZ and did not receive wages as an employee subject to U.S. income tax withholding. . . . . ▶ ☐

For Privacy Act and Paperwork Reduction Act Notice, see page 4.   Cat. No. 13141W   Form **4868** (2011)

When To File Form 4868

File Form 4868 by April 17, 2012. Fiscal year taxpayers, file Form 4868 by the regular due date of the return.

Taxpayers who are out of the country. If, on the regular due date of your return, you are out of the country and a U.S. citizen or resident, you are allowed 2 extra months to file your return and pay any amount due without requesting an extension. For a calendar year return, this is June 15, 2012. File this form and be sure to check the box on line 8 if you need an additional 4 months to file your return.

If you are out of the country and a U.S. citizen or resident, you may qualify for special tax treatment if you meet the foreign residence or physical presence tests. If you do not expect to meet either of those tests by the due date of your return, request an extension to a date after you expect to qualify using Form 2350, Application for Extension of Time To File U.S. Income Tax Return.

You are out of the country if:

• You live outside the United States and Puerto Rico and your main place of work is outside the United States and Puerto Rico, or

• You are in military or naval service outside the United States and Puerto Rico.

If you qualify as being out of the country, you will still be eligible for the extension even if you are physically present in the United States or Puerto Rico on the regular due date of the return.

For more information on extensions for taxpayers out of the country, see Pub. 54, Tax Guide for U.S. Citizens and Resident Aliens Abroad.

Form 1040NR or 1040NR-EZ filers. If you cannot file your return by the due date, you should file Form 4868. You must file Form 4868 by the regular due date of the return.

If you did not receive wages as an employee subject to U.S. income tax withholding, and your return is due June 15, 2012, check the box on line 9.

Total Time Allowed

Generally, we cannot extend the due date of your return for more than 6 months (October 15, 2012, for most calendar year taxpayers). However, there may be an exception if you are living out of the country. See Pub. 54 for more information.

Filing Your Tax Return

You can file your tax return any time before the extension expires.

Do not attach a copy of Form 4868 to your return.

Interest

You will owe interest on any tax not paid by the regular due date of your return, even if you qualify for the 2-month extension because you were out of the country. The interest runs until you pay the tax. Even if you had a good reason for not paying on time, you will still owe interest.

Late Payment Penalty

The late payment penalty is usually ½ of 1% of any tax (other than estimated tax) not paid by April 17, 2012. It is charged for each month or part of a month the tax is unpaid. The maximum penalty is 25%.

The late payment penalty will not be charged if you can show reasonable cause for not paying on time. Attach a statement to your return fully explaining the reason. Do not attach the statement to Form 4868.

You are considered to have reasonable cause for the period covered by this automatic extension if at least 90% of your actual 2011 tax liability is paid before the regular due date of your return through withholding, estimated tax payments, or payments made with Form 4868.

Late Filing Penalty

A late filing penalty is usually charged if your return is filed after the due date (including extensions). The penalty is usually 5% of the amount due for each month or part of a month your return is late. The maximum penalty is 25%. If your return is more than 60 days late, the minimum penalty is $135 or the balance of the tax due on your return, whichever is smaller. You might not owe the penalty if you have a reasonable explanation for filing late. Attach a statement to your return fully explaining the reason. Do not attach the statement to Form 4868.

How To Claim Credit for Payment Made With This Form

When you file your 2011 return, include the amount of any payment you made with Form 4868 on the appropriate line of your tax return.

The instructions for the following line of your tax return will tell you how to report the payment.

• Form 1040, line 68.
• Form 1040A, line 41.
• Form 1040EZ, line 9.
• Form 1040NR, line 64.
• Form 1040NR-EZ, line 21.
• Form 1040-PR, line 10.
• Form 1040-SS, line 10.

If you and your spouse each filed a separate Form 4868 but later file a joint return for 2011, enter the total paid with both Forms 4868 on the appropriate line of your joint return.

If you and your spouse jointly file Form 4868 but later file separate returns for 2011, you can enter the total amount paid with Form 4868 on either of your separate returns. Or you and your spouse can divide the payment in any agreed amounts. Be sure each separate return has the social security numbers of both spouses.

Specific Instructions

How To Complete Form 4868

Part I—Identification

Enter your name(s) and address. If you plan to file a joint return, include both spouses' names in the order in which they will appear on the return.

If you want correspondence regarding this extension to be sent to you at an address other than your own, enter that address. If you want the correspondence sent to an agent acting for you, include the agent's name (as well as your own) and the agent's address.

If you changed your name after you filed your last return because of marriage, divorce, etc., be sure to report this to the Social Security Administration before filing Form 4868. This prevents delays in processing your extension request.

If you changed your mailing address after you filed your last return, you should use Form 8822, Change of Address, to notify the IRS of the change. Showing a new address on Form 4868 will not update your record. You can get IRS forms by calling 1-800-TAX-FORM (1-800-829-3676). You can also download forms at IRS.gov.

If you plan to file a joint return, enter on line 2 the social security number (SSN) that you will show first on your return. Enter on line 3 the other SSN to be shown on the joint return.

IRS individual taxpayer identification numbers (ITINs) for aliens. If you are a nonresident or resident alien and you do not have and are not eligible to get an SSN, you must apply for an ITIN. Although an ITIN is not required to file Form 4868, you will need one to file your income tax return. For details on how to apply for an ITIN, see Form W-7 and its instructions. If you already have an ITIN, enter it wherever your SSN is requested. If you do not have an ITIN, enter "ITIN TO BE REQUESTED" wherever your SSN is requested.

 An ITIN is for tax use only. It does not entitle you to social security benefits or change your employment or immigration status under U.S. law.

Part II—Individual Income Tax

Rounding off to whole dollars. You can round off cents to whole dollars on Form 4868. If you do round to whole dollars, you must round all amounts. To round, drop amounts under 50 cents and increase amounts from 50 to 99 cents to the next dollar. For example, $1.39 becomes $1 and $2.50 becomes $3. If you have to add two or more amounts to figure the amount to enter on a line, include cents when adding the amounts and round off only the total.

Line 4—Estimate of Total Tax Liability for 2011

Enter on line 4 the total tax liability you expect to report on your 2011:

- Form 1040, line 61.
- Form 1040A, line 35.
- Form 1040EZ, line 10.
- Form 1040NR, line 60.
- Form 1040NR-EZ, line 17.
- Form 1040-PR, line 5.
- Form 1040-SS, line 5.

　If you expect this amount to be zero, enter -0-.

 Make your estimate as accurate as you can with the information you have. If we later find that the estimate was not reasonable, the extension will be null and void.

Line 5—Estimate of Total Payments for 2011

Enter on line 5 the total payments you expect to report on your 2011:

- Form 1040, line 72 (excluding line 68).
- Form 1040A, line 41.
- Form 1040EZ, line 9.
- Form 1040NR, line 69 (excluding line 64).
- Form 1040NR-EZ, line 21.
- Form 1040-PR, line 10.
- Form 1040-SS, line 10.

 For Forms 1040A, 1040EZ, 1040NR-EZ, 1040-PR, and 1040-SS, do not include on line 5 the amount you are paying with this Form 4868.

Line 6—Balance Due

Subtract line 5 from line 4. If line 5 is more than line 4, enter -0-.

Line 7—Amount You Are Paying

If you find you cannot pay the amount shown on line 6, you can still get the extension. But you should pay as much as you can to limit the amount of interest you will owe. Also, you may be charged the late payment penalty on the unpaid tax from the regular due date of your return. See *Late Payment Penalty* on page 2.

Line 8—Out of the Country

If you are out of the country on the regular due date of your return, check the box on line 8. "Out of the country" is defined on page 2.

Line 9—Form 1040NR or 1040NR-EZ Filers

If you did not receive wages subject to U.S. income tax withholding, and your return is due June 15, 2012, check the box on line 9.

How To Make a Payment With Your Application

Making Payments Electronically

For information on paying your taxes electronically, including by credit card, debit card, or EFTPS, go to *www.irs.gov/e-pay*. You must enroll in EFTPS before you can use it. Go to *www.eftps.gov* for details.

Confirmation number. You will receive a confirmation number when you pay by credit card, debit card, or EFTPS. Enter the confirmation number below and keep for your records.

Enter confirmation number here　▶ -------------------------------

Do not file a paper Form 4868.

Pay by Check or Money Order

- When paying by check or money order with Form 4868, use the appropriate address in the middle column under *Where To File a Paper Form 4868* on page 4.
- Make your check or money order payable to the "United States Treasury." Do not send cash.
- Write your social security number, daytime phone number, and "2011 Form 4868" on your check or money order.
- Do not staple or attach your payment to Form 4868.

Note. If you e-file Form 4868 and mail a check or money order to the IRS for payment, use a completed paper Form 4868 as a voucher.

Where To File a Paper Form 4868

If you live in:	And you are making a payment, send Form 4868 with your payment to Internal Revenue Service:	And you are not making a payment, send Form 4868 to Department of the Treasury, Internal Revenue Service Center:
Alabama, Georgia, North Carolina, South Carolina	P.O. Box 105050 Atlanta, GA 30348-5050	Kansas City, MO 64999-0045
Connecticut, Delaware, District of Columbia, Maine, Maryland, Massachusetts, New Hampshire, New York, Pennsylvania, Rhode Island, Vermont	P.O. Box 37009 Hartford, CT 06176-0009	Kansas City, MO 64999-0045
Florida, Louisiana, Mississippi, Texas	P.O. Box 1302 Charlotte, NC 28201-1302	Austin, TX 73301-0045
Alaska, Arizona, California, Colorado, Hawaii, Nevada, Oregon, Washington	P.O. Box 7122 San Francisco, CA 94120-7122	Fresno, CA 93888-0045
Arkansas, Idaho, Illinois, Indiana, Iowa, Kansas, Michigan, Minnesota, Montana, Nebraska, New Mexico, North Dakota, Ohio, Oklahoma, South Dakota, Utah, Wisconsin, Wyoming	P.O. Box 802503 Cincinnati, OH 45280-2503	Fresno, CA 93888-0045
Kentucky, Missouri, New Jersey, Tennessee, Virginia, West Virginia	P.O. Box 970028 St. Louis, MO 63197-0028	Kansas City, MO 64999-0045
A foreign country, U.S. possession or territory*, or use an APO or FPO address, or file Form 2555, 2555-EZ, or 4563, or are a dual-status alien.	P.O. Box 1302 Charlotte, NC 28201-1302 USA	Austin, TX 73301-0215 USA
All Form 1040NR, 1040NR-EZ, 1040-SS, and 1040-PR filers	P.O. Box 1302 Charlotte, NC 28201-1302 USA	Austin, TX 73301-0045 USA

*If you live in American Samoa, Puerto Rico, Guam, the U.S. Virgin Islands, or the Northern Mariana Islands, see Pub. 570.

Private Delivery Services

You can use certain private delivery services designated by the IRS to meet the "timely mailing as timely filing/paying" rule for tax returns and payments. These private delivery services include only the following.

• DHL Express (DHL): DHL Same Day Service.

• Federal Express (FedEx): FedEx Priority Overnight, FedEx Standard Overnight, FedEx 2 Day, FedEx International Priority, and FedEx International First.

• United Parcel Service (UPS): UPS Next Day Air, UPS Next Day Air Saver, UPS 2nd Day Air, UPS 2nd Day Air A.M., UPS Worldwide Express Plus, and UPS Worldwide Express.

The private delivery service can tell you how to get written proof of the mailing date.

 Private delivery services cannot deliver items to P.O. boxes. You must use the U.S. Postal Service to mail any item to an IRS P.O. box address.

Privacy Act and Paperwork Reduction Act Notice. We ask for the information on this form to carry out the Internal Revenue laws of the United States. We need this information so that our records will reflect your intention to file your individual income tax return within 6 months after the regular due date. If you choose to apply for an automatic extension of time to file, you are required by Internal Revenue Code section 6081 to provide the information requested on this form. Under section 6109, you must disclose your social security number or individual taxpayer identification number. Routine uses of this information include giving it to the Department of Justice for civil and criminal litigation, and to cities, states, the District of Columbia, and U.S. Commonwealths and possessions for use in administering their tax laws. We may also disclose this information to other countries under a tax treaty, to federal and state agencies to enforce federal nontax criminal laws, or to federal law enforcement and intelligence agencies to combat terrorism. If you fail to provide this information in a timely manner or provide incomplete or false information, you may be liable for penalties and interest.

You are not required to provide the information requested on a form that is subject to the Paperwork Reduction Act unless the form displays a valid OMB control number. Books or records relating to a form or its instructions must be retained as long as their contents may become material in the administration of any Internal Revenue law. Generally, tax returns and return information are confidential, as required by Internal Revenue Code section 6103.

The average time and expenses required to complete and file this form will vary depending on individual circumstances. For the estimated averages, see the instructions for your income tax return.

If you have suggestions for making this form simpler, we would be happy to hear from you. See the instructions for your income tax return.

 Printed on recycled paper

Form 7004
(Rev. November 2011)
Department of the Treasury
Internal Revenue Service

Application for Automatic Extension of Time To File Certain Business Income Tax, Information, and Other Returns

▶ File a separate application for each return.
▶ See separate instructions.

OMB No. 1545-0233

Print or Type	Name		Identifying number
	Number, street, and room or suite no. (If P.O. box, see instructions.)		
	City, town, state, and ZIP code (If a foreign address, enter city, province or state, and country (follow the country's practice for entering postal code)).		

Note. *File request for extension by the due date of the return for which the extension is granted. See instructions before completing this form.*

Part I Automatic 5-Month Extension

1a Enter the form code for the return that this application is for (see below) . . . . ☐☐

Application Is For:	Form Code	Application Is For:	Form Code
Form 1065	09	Form 1041 (estate other than a bankruptcy estate)	04
Form 8804	31	Form 1041 (trust)	05

Part II Automatic 6-Month Extension

b Enter the form code for the return that this application is for (see below) . . . . ☐☐

Application Is For:	Form Code	Application Is For:	Form Code
Form 706-GS(D)	01	Form 1120-ND (section 4951 taxes)	20
Form 706-GS(T)	02	Form 1120-PC	21
Form 1041 (bankruptcy estate only)	03	Form 1120-POL	22
Form 1041-N	06	Form 1120-REIT	23
Form 1041-QFT	07	Form 1120-RIC	24
Form 1042	08	Form 1120S	25
Form 1065-B	10	Form 1120-SF	26
Form 1066	11	Form 3520-A	27
Form 1120	12	Form 8612	28
Form 1120-C	34	Form 8613	29
Form 1120-F	15	Form 8725	30
Form 1120-FSC	16	Form 8831	32
Form 1120-H	17	Form 8876	33
Form 1120-L	18	Form 8924	35
Form 1120-ND	19	Form 8928	36

2 If the organization is a foreign corporation that does not have an office or place of business in the United States, check here . . . . ▶ ☐

3 If the organization is a corporation and is the common parent of a group that intends to file a consolidated return, check here . . . . ▶ ☐

If checked, attach a schedule, listing the name, address, and Employer Identification Number (EIN) for each member covered by this application.

Part III All Filers Must Complete This Part

4 If the organization is a corporation or partnership that qualifies under Regulations section 1.6081-5, check here . ▶ ☐

5a The application is for calendar year 20___, or tax year beginning _____, 20___, and ending _____, 20___

b **Short tax year.** If this tax year is less than 12 months, check the reason:

☐ Initial return   ☐ Final return   ☐ Change in accounting period   ☐ Consolidated return to be filed

6	Tentative total tax	**6**	
7	**Total** payments and credits (see instructions)	**7**	
8	**Balance due.** Subtract line 7 from line 6 (see instructions)	**8**	

For Privacy Act and Paperwork Reduction Act Notice, see separate Instructions.   Cat. No. 13804A   Form **7004** (Rev. 11-2011)

Form **8275**
(Rev. August 2008)

Department of the Treasury
Internal Revenue Service

Disclosure Statement

Do not use this form to disclose items or positions that are contrary to Treasury regulations. Instead, use Form 8275-R, Regulation Disclosure Statement. See separate instructions.

▶ Attach to your tax return.

OMB No. 1545-0889

Attachment
Sequence No. **92**

Name(s) shown on return

Identifying number shown on return

Part I General Information (see instructions)

	(a) Rev. Rul., Rev. Proc., etc.	(b) Item or Group of Items	(c) Detailed Description of Items	(d) Form or Schedule	(e) Line No.	(f) Amount
1						
2						
3						
4						
5						
6						

Part II Detailed Explanation (see instructions)

1 _____

2 _____

3 _____

4 _____

5 _____

6 _____

Part III Information About Pass-Through Entity. To be completed by partners, shareholders, beneficiaries, or residual interest holders.

Complete this part only if you are making adequate disclosure for a pass-through item.

Note: *A pass-through entity is a partnership, S corporation, estate, trust, regulated investment company (RIC), real estate investment trust (REIT), or real estate mortgage investment conduit (REMIC).*

1 Name, address, and ZIP code of pass-through entity	2 Identifying number of pass-through entity
	3 Tax year of pass-through entity / / to / /
	4 Internal Revenue Service Center where the pass-through entity filed its return

For Paperwork Reduction Act Notice, see separate instructions.

Cat. No. 61935M

Form **8275** (Rev. 8-2008)

Part IV **Explanations** *(continued from Parts I and/or II)*

Form **8275-R**

(Rev. August 2008)

Department of the Treasury
Internal Revenue Service

Regulation Disclosure Statement

Use this form only to disclose items or positions that are contrary to Treasury regulations. For other disclosures, use Form 8275, Disclosure Statement.
See separate instructions.

▶ Attach to your tax return.

OMB No. 1545-0889

Attachment
Sequence No. **92A**

Name(s) shown on return

Identifying number shown on return

Part I General Information (see instructions)

(a) Regulation Section	(b) Item or Group of Items	(c) Detailed Description of Items	(d) Form or Schedule	(e) Line No.	(f) Amount
1					
2					
3					
4					
5					
6					

Part II Detailed Explanation (see instructions)

1

2

3

4

5

6

Part III Information About Pass-Through Entity. To be completed by partners, shareholders, beneficiaries, or residual interest holders.

Complete this part only if you are making adequate disclosure for a pass-through item.

Note: *A pass-through entity is a partnership, S corporation, estate, trust, regulated investment company (RIC), real estate investment trust (REIT), or real estate mortgage investment conduit (REMIC).*

1 Name, address, and ZIP code of pass-through entity	2 Identifying number of pass-through entity
	3 Tax year of pass-through entity / / to / /
	4 Internal Revenue Service Center where the pass-through entity filed its return

For Paperwork Reduction Act Notice, see separate instructions.

Cat. No. 14594X

Form **8275-R** (Rev. 8-2008)

Part IV   **Explanations** *(continued from Parts I and/or II)*

Form 8379

(Rev. December 2010)
Department of the Treasury
Internal Revenue Service

Injured Spouse Allocation

▶ **See instructions.**

OMB No. 1545-0074

Attachment
Sequence No. **104**

Part I **Should you file this form?** You must complete this part.

1 Enter the tax year for which you are filing this form. ▶ _____ Answer the following questions for that year.

2 Did you (or will you) file a joint return?
   ☐ **Yes.** Go to line 3.
   ☐ **No. Stop here.** Do not file this form. You are not an injured spouse.

3 Did (or will) the IRS use the joint overpayment to pay any of the following legally enforceable past-due debt(s) owed only by your spouse? (see instructions)
   • Federal tax • State income tax • Child support • Spousal support • Federal nontax debt (such as a student loan)
   ☐ **Yes.** Go to line 4.
   ☐ **No. Stop here.** Do not file this form. You are not an injured spouse.
   Note. If the past-due amount is for a joint federal tax, you may qualify for innocent spouse relief for the year to which the overpayment was applied. See *Innocent Spouse Relief*, in the instructions for more information.

4 Are you legally obligated to pay this past-due amount?
   ☐ **Yes. Stop here.** Do not file this form. You are not an injured spouse.
   Note. If the past-due amount is for a joint federal tax, you may qualify for innocent spouse relief for the year to which the overpayment was applied. See *Innocent Spouse Relief*, in the instructions for more information.
   ☐ **No.** Go to line 5.

5 Were you a resident of a community property state (Arizona, California, Idaho, Louisiana, Nevada, New Mexico, Texas, Washington, or Wisconsin) at any time during the tax year entered on line 1? (see instructions)
   ☐ **Yes.** Enter name(s) of community property states(s) _____ .
   Skip lines 6 through 9 and **go to Part II** and complete the rest of this form.
   ☐ **No.** Go to line 6.

6 Did you make and report payments, such as federal income tax withholding or estimated tax payments?
   ☐ **Yes.** Skip lines 7 through 9 and **go to Part II** and complete the rest of this form.
   ☐ **No.** Go to line 7.

7 Did you have earned income, such as wages, salaries, or self-employment income?
   ☐ **Yes.** Go to line 8.
   ☐ **No.** Skip line 8 and go to line 9.

8 Did (or will) you claim the earned income credit or additional child tax credit?
   ☐ **Yes.** Skip line 9 and **go to Part II** and complete the rest of this form.
   ☐ **No.** Go to line 9.

9 Did (or will) you claim a refundable tax credit (see instructions)?
   ☐ **Yes. Go to Part II** and complete the rest of this form.
   ☐ **No. Stop here.** Do not file this form. You are not an injured spouse.

Part II **Information About the Joint Tax Return for Which This Form Is Filed**

10 Enter the following information exactly as it is shown on the tax return for which you are filing this form.
    The spouse's name and social security number shown first on that tax return must also be shown first below.

First name, initial, and last name shown first on the return	Social security number shown first	If Injured Spouse, check here ▶ ☐
First name, initial, and last name shown second on the return	Social security number shown second	If Injured Spouse, check here ▶ ☐

11 Check this box only if you are divorced or legally separated from the spouse with whom you filed the joint return and you want your refund issued in your name only . . . . ☐

12 Do you want any injured spouse refund mailed to an address different from the one on your joint return?   ☐ Yes   ☐ No
    If "Yes," enter the address. _____

    Number and street   City, town, or post office, state, and ZIP code

For Privacy Act and Paperwork Reduction Act Notice, see separate instructions.   Cat. No. 62474Q   Form **8379** (Rev. 12-2010)

Part III	Allocation Between Spouses of Items on the Joint Tax Return (see instructions)			
	Allocated Items	**(a)** Amount shown on joint return	**(b)** Allocated to injured spouse	**(c)** Allocated to other spouse
13	Income: **a.** Wages			
	b. All other income			
14	Adjustments to income			
15	Standard deduction or Itemized deductions			
16	Number of exemptions			
17	Credits (**do not** include any earned income credit)			
18	Other taxes			
19	Federal income tax withheld			
20	Payments			

Part IV	Signature. Complete this part only if you are filing Form 8379 by itself and not with your tax return.

Under penalties of perjury, I declare that I have examined this form and any accompanying schedules or statements and to the best of my knowledge and belief, they are true, correct, and complete. Declaration of preparer (other than taxpayer) is based on all information of which preparer has any knowledge.

Keep a copy of this form for your records	Injured spouse's signature		Date	Phone number (optional)
Paid Preparer Use Only	Print/Type preparer's name	Preparer's signature	Date	Check ☐ if self-employed / PTIN
	Firm's name ▶		Firm's EIN ▶	
	Firm's Address ▶		Phone no.	

Form **8379** (Rev. 12-2010)

Declaration Control Number (DCN)

0 0 - ☐☐☐☐☐☐ - ☐☐☐☐☐ - 2

IRS Use Only—Do not write or staple in this space.

Form **8453**

Department of the Treasury
Internal Revenue Service

U.S. Individual Income Tax Transmittal for an IRS _e-file_ Return

For the year January 1–December 31, 2011
▶ See instructions on back.

OMB No. 1545-0074

2011

Please print or type.

P R I N T   C L E A R L Y

Your first name and initial	Last name	Your social security number
If a joint return, spouse's first name and initial	Last name	Spouse's social security number
Home address (number and street). If you have a P.O. box, see instructions.	Apt. no.	▲ **Important!** ▲ You **must** enter your SSN(s) above.
City, town or post office, state, and ZIP code (If a foreign address also complete spaces below.)		
Foreign country name	Foreign province/county	Foreign postal code

---

**FILE THIS FORM ONLY IF YOU ARE ATTACHING ONE OR MORE
OF THE FOLLOWING FORMS OR SUPPORTING DOCUMENTS.**

Check the applicable box(es) to identify the attachments.

☐ Appendix A, Statement by Taxpayer Using the Procedures in Rev. Proc. 2009-20 to Determine a Theft Loss Deduction Related to a Fraudulent Investment Arrangement

☐ Form 1098-C, Contributions of Motor Vehicles, Boats, and Airplanes (or equivalent contemporaneous written acknowledgement)

☐ Form 2848, Power of Attorney and Declaration of Representative (or POA that states the agent is granted authority to sign the return)

☐ Form 3115, Application for Change in Accounting Method

☐ Form 3468 - attach a copy of the first page of NPS Form 10-168a, Historic Preservation Certification Application (Part 2— Description of Rehabilitation), with an indication that it was received by the Department of the Interior or the State Historic Preservation Officer, together with proof that the building is a certified historic structure (or that such status has been requested)

☐ Form 4136 - attach the Certificate for Biodiesel and, if applicable, Statement of Biodiesel Reseller or a certificate from the provider identifying the product as renewable diesel and, if applicable, a statement from the reseller

☐ Form 5713, International Boycott Report

☐ Form 8283, Noncash Charitable Contributions, Section A, (if any statement or qualified appraisal is required) or Section B, Donated Property, and any related attachments (including any qualified appraisal or partnership Form 8283)

☐ Form 8332, Release / Revocation of Release of Claim to Exemption for Child by Custodial Parent (or certain pages from a divorce decree or separation agreement, that went into effect after 1984 and before 2009) (see instructions)

☐ Form 8858, Information Return of U.S. Persons With Respect to Foreign Disregarded Entities

☐ Form 8864 - attach the Certificate for Biodiesel and, if applicable, Statement of Biodiesel Reseller or a certificate from the provider identifying the product as renewable diesel and, if applicable, a statement from the reseller

☐ Form 8885, Health Coverage Tax Credit, and all required attachments

☐ Form 8949, Sales and Other Dispositions of Capital Assets, (or a statement with the same information), if you elect not to report your transactions electronically on Form 8949

DO NOT SIGN THIS FORM.

For Paperwork Reduction Act Notice, see your tax return instructions.   Cat. No. 62766T   Form **8453** (2011)

General Instructions

Purpose of Form

Use Form 8453 to send any required paper forms or supporting documentation listed next to the checkboxes on Form 8453 (do not send Forms W-2, W-2G, or 1099-R).

 Do not attach any form or document that is not shown on Form 8453 next to the **CAUTION** *checkboxes. If you are required to mail in any documentation not listed on Form 8453, you cannot file the tax return electronically.*

Note. Do not mail a copy of an electronically filed Form 1040, 1040A, 1040EZ, or 1040-SS to the Internal Revenue Service (IRS).

When and Where To File

If you are an ERO, you must mail Form 8453 to the IRS within 3 business days after receiving acknowledgement that the IRS has accepted the electronically filed tax return.

If you are filing your tax return using an online provider, mail Form 8453 to the IRS within 3 business days after you have received acknowledgement from your intermediate service provider and/or transmitter that the IRS has accepted your electronically filed tax return. If you do not receive an acknowledgement, you must contact your intermediate service provider and/or transmitter.

Mail Form 8453 to:

Internal Revenue Service
Attn: Shipping and Receiving, 0254
Receipt and Control Branch
Austin, TX 73344-0254

Line Instructions

Declaration control number (DCN). The DCN is a 14-digit number assigned to each tax return. It should be included in your acknowledgement message. Clearly print or type the DCN in the top left corner of each Form 8453 after the IRS has acknowledged receipt of the electronic tax return. The first two digits are the file identification number and are always "00." The next six digits are the electronic filer identification number (EFIN). The next five digits are the batch number and the serial number. The last digit is the year digit (for returns filed in 2012, the year digit is "2").

Example. The EFIN is 509325. The batch and serial numbers are 00056. The DCN is 00-509325-00056-2.

Name and address. Print or type the information in the spaces provided. If using a foreign address, do not abbreviate the country name.

P.O. box. Enter the box number only if the post office does not deliver mail to the home address.

Note. The address must match the address shown on the electronically filed tax return.

Social security number (SSN). Be sure to enter the taxpayer's SSN in the space provided on Form 8453. If a joint tax return, list the SSNs in the same order as the first names.

Payments

Do not attach a payment to Form 8453. Instead, mail it by April 17, 2012, with Form 1040-V to the IRS at the applicable address shown on that form. If a Form 1040-V is not available, see the instructions for your tax return for other ways to get forms or you can go to IRS.gov.

Form 2848. An electronically transmitted return signed by an agent must have a power of attorney attached to Form 8453 that specifically authorizes the agent to sign the return.

Divorce decree or separation agreement. If the divorce decree or separation agreement went into effect after 1984 and before 2009, the noncustodial parent can attach certain pages from the decree or agreement instead of Form 8332. To be able to do this, the decree or agreement must state all three of the following.

1. The noncustodial parent can claim the child as a dependent without regard to any condition (such as payment of support).

2. The other parent will not claim the child as a dependent.

3. The years for which the claim is released.

The noncustodial parent must attach all of the following pages from the decree or agreement.

• Cover page (include the other parent's SSN on that page).

• The pages that include all of the information identified in (1) through (3) above.

• Signature page with the other parent's signature and date of agreement.

Note. The noncustodial parent must attach the required information even if it was filed with a return in an earlier year.

Form **8822**
(Rev. January 2012)

Department of the Treasury
Internal Revenue Service

Change of Address

(For Individual, Gift, Estate, or Generation-Skipping Transfer Tax Returns)

▶ Please type or print.
▶ See instructions on back.   ▶ Do not attach this form to your return.

OMB No. 1545-1163

Part I   **Complete This Part To Change Your Home Mailing Address**

Check **all** boxes this change affects:

1 ☐ Individual income tax returns (Forms 1040, 1040A, 1040EZ, 1040NR, etc.)
   ▶ If your last return was a joint return and you are now establishing a residence separate from the spouse with whom you filed that return, check here . . . . ▶ ☐

2 ☐ Gift, estate, or generation-skipping transfer tax returns (Forms 706, 709, etc.)
   ▶ For Forms 706 and 706-NA, enter the decedent's name and social security number below.

   ▶ Decedent's name   ▶ Social security number

3a Your name (first name, initial, and last name)	**3b** Your social security number
4a Spouse's name (first name, initial, and last name)	**4b** Spouse's social security number

5a Your prior name(s). See instructions.

5b Spouse's prior name(s). See instructions.

6a Your old address (no., street, apt. no., city or town, state, and ZIP code). If a P.O. box, see instructions. If foreign address, also complete spaces below, see instructions.

Foreign country name	Foreign province/county	Foreign postal code

6b Spouse's old address, if different from line 6a (no., street, apt. no., city or town, state, and ZIP code). If a P.O. box, see instructions. If foreign address, also complete spaces below, see instructions.

Foreign country name	Foreign province/county	Foreign postal code

7 New address (no., street, apt. no., city or town, state, and ZIP code). If a P.O. box, see instructions. If foreign address, also complete spaces below, see instructions.

Foreign country name	Foreign province/county	Foreign postal code

Part II   **Signature**

Daytime telephone number of person to contact (optional) ▶ _____

Sign Here

▶ Your signature	Date	▶ Signature of representative, executor, administrator/if applicable	Date
▶ If joint return, spouse's signature	Date	▶ Title	

For Privacy Act and Paperwork Reduction Act Notice, see back of form.   Cat. No. 12081V   Form **8822** (Rev. 1-2012)

Purpose of Form

You can use Form 8822 to notify the Internal Revenue Service if you changed your home mailing address. If this change also affects the mailing address for your children who filed income tax returns, complete and file a separate Form 8822 for each child. If you are a representative signing for the taxpayer, attach to Form 8822 a copy of your power of attorney.

Changing both home and business addresses? Use Form 8822-B to change your business address.

Future developments. The IRS has created a page on IRS.gov for information about Form 8822 and its instructions, at *www.irs.gov/form8822*. Information about any future developments affecting Form 8822 (such as legislation enacted after we release it) will be posted on that page.

Prior Name(s)

If you or your spouse changed your name because of marriage, divorce, etc., complete line 5. Also, be sure to notify the Social Security Administration of your new name so that it has the same name in its records that you have on your tax return. This prevents delays in processing your return and issuing refunds. It also safeguards your future social security benefits.

Addresses

Be sure to include any apartment, room, or suite number in the space provided.

P.O. Box

Enter your box number instead of your street address only if your post office does not deliver mail to your street address.

Foreign Address

Follow the country's practice for entering the postal code. Please do not abbreviate the country.

"In Care of" Address

If you receive your mail in care of a third party (such as an accountant or attorney), enter "C/O" followed by the third party's name and street address or P.O. box.

Signature

The taxpayer, executor, donor, or an authorized representative must sign. If your last return was a joint return, your spouse must also sign (unless you have indicated by checking the box on line 1 that you are establishing a separate residence).

 If you are a representative signing on behalf of the taxpayer, you must attach to Form 8822 a copy of your power of attorney. To do this, you can use Form 2848. The Internal Revenue Service will not complete an address change from an "unauthorized" third party.

Where To File

Send this form to the Department of the Treasury, Internal Revenue Service Center, and the address shown next that applies to you. Generally, it takes 4 to 6 weeks to process your change of address.

Note. If you checked the box on line 2, or you checked the box on both lines 1 and 2, send this form to: Cincinnati, OH 45999-0023.

IF your old home mailing address was in . . .	THEN use this address . . .
Alabama, Connecticut, Delaware, District of Columbia, Georgia, Kentucky, Maine, Maryland, Massachusetts, Missouri, New Hampshire, New Jersey, New York, North Carolina, Pennsylvania, Rhode Island, South Carolina, Tennessee, Vermont, Virginia, West Virginia	Department of the Treasury Internal Revenue Service Kansas City, MO 64999-0023
Florida, Louisiana, Mississippi, Texas	Department of the Treasury Internal Revenue Service Austin, TX 73301-0023
Alaska, Arizona, Arkansas, California, Colorado, Hawaii, Idaho, Illinois, Indiana, Iowa, Kansas, Michigan, Minnesota, Montana, Nebraska, Nevada, New Mexico, North Dakota, Ohio, Oklahoma, Oregon, South Dakota, Utah, Washington, Wisconsin, Wyoming	Department of the Treasury Internal Revenue Service Fresno, CA 93888-0023
A foreign country, American Samoa, or Puerto Rico (or are excluding income under Internal Revenue Code section 933), or use an APO or FPO address, or file Form 2555, 2555-EZ, or 4563, or are a dual-status alien or non bona fide resident of Guam or the Virgin Islands.	Department of the Treasury Internal Revenue Service Austin, TX 73301-0023
Guam: bona fide residents	Department of Revenue and Taxation Government of Guam P.O. Box 23607 GMF, GU 96921
Virgin Islands: bona fide residents	V.I. Bureau of Internal Revenue 6115 Estate Smith Bay Suite 225 St. Thomas, VI 00802

Privacy Act and Paperwork Reduction Act Notice. We ask for the information on this form to carry out the Internal Revenue laws of the United States. Our legal right to ask for information is Internal Revenue Code sections 6001 and 6011, which require you to file a statement with us for any tax for which you are liable. Section 6109 requires that you provide your social security number on what you file. This is so we know who you are, and can process your form and other papers.

Generally, tax returns and return information are confidential, as required by section 6103. However, we may give the information to the Department of Justice and to other federal agencies, as provided by law. We may give it to cities, states, the District of Columbia, and U.S. commonwealths or possessions to carry out their tax laws. We may also disclose this information to other countries under a tax treaty, to federal and state agencies to enforce federal nontax criminal laws, or to federal law enforcement and intelligence agencies to combat terrorism.

The use of this form is voluntary. However, if you fail to provide the Internal Revenue Service with your current mailing address, you may not receive a notice of deficiency or a notice and demand for tax. Despite the failure to receive such notices, penalties and interest will continue to accrue on the tax deficiencies.

You are not required to provide the information requested on a form that is subject to the Paperwork Reduction Act unless the form displays a valid OMB control number. Books or records relating to a form or its instructions must be retained as long as their contents may become material in the administration of any Internal Revenue law.

The time needed to complete and file this form will vary depending on individual circumstances. The estimated average time is 16 minutes.

If you have comments concerning the accuracy of this time estimate or suggestions for making this form simpler, we would be happy to hear from you. You can write to the

Internal Revenue Service
Individual and Specialty Forms and Publications Branch
SE:W:CAR:MP:T:I
1111 Constitution Ave. NW
IR-6526
Washington, DC 20224

Do not send the form to this address. Instead, see *Where To File* on this page.

Form **8857**

(Rev. September 2010)

Department of the Treasury
Internal Revenue Service (99)

Request for Innocent Spouse Relief

▶ **See separate instructions.**

OMB No. 1545-1596

Important things you should know

- **Do not file this form with your tax return.** See *Where To File* in the instructions.
- Answer all the questions on this form that apply, attach any necessary documentation, and sign on page 4. Do not delay filing this form because of missing documentation. See instructions.
- By law, the IRS must contact the person who was your spouse for the years you want relief. There are no exceptions, even for victims of spousal abuse or domestic violence. Your personal information (such as your current name, address, and employer) will be protected. However, if you petition the Tax Court, your personal information may be released, unless you ask the Tax Court to withhold it. See instructions for details.
- If you need help, see *How To Get Help* in the instructions.

Part I   **Should you file this form?** You **must** complete this part for each tax year.

		Tax Year 1		Tax Year 2		Tax Year 3*	
1	Enter each tax year you want relief. It is important to enter the correct year. For example, if the IRS used your 2009 income tax refund to pay a 2007 tax amount you jointly owed, enter tax year 2007, not tax year 2009 ▶ **1**						

Caution. The IRS generally cannot collect the amount you owe until your request for each year is resolved. However, the time the IRS has to collect is extended. See *Collection Statute of Limitations* on page 3 of the instructions.

2	Check the box for each year you would like a refund if you qualify for relief. You may be required to provide proof of payment. See instructions ▶ **2**	☐		☐		☐	

		Yes	No	Yes	No	Yes	No
3	Did the IRS use your share of the joint refund to pay any of the following past-due debts of your spouse: federal tax, state income tax, child support, spousal support, or federal non-tax debt such as a student loan? • If "Yes," **stop here;** do not file this form for that tax year. Instead, file Form 8379, Injured Spouse Allocation. See instructions. • If "No," go to line 4 ▶ **3**	☐	☐	☐	☐	☐	☐
4	Was a return claiming married filing jointly status filed for the tax year listed on line 1? **See instructions.** • If "Yes," skip line 5 and go to line 6. • If "No," go to line 5 ▶ **4**	☐	☐	☐	☐	☐	☐
5	If a joint return for that tax year was not filed, were you a resident of Arizona, California, Idaho, Louisiana, Nevada, New Mexico, Texas, Washington, or Wisconsin? • If "Yes," see *Community Property Laws* on page 2 of the instructions. • If "No" on both lines 4 and 5, **stop here.** Do not file this form for that tax year ▶ **5**	☐	☐	☐	☐	☐	☐

*If you want relief for more than 3 years, fill out an additional form.

Part II   **Tell us about yourself**

6 Your current name (see instructions)	**Your social security number**

Your current mailing address (number and street).	Apt. no.	**County**

City, town or post office, state, and ZIP code. If a foreign address, see instructions.	Best daytime phone number

---

Part III   **Tell us about you and your spouse for the tax years you want relief**

7   **Who was your spouse for the tax years you want relief?** File a separate Form 8857 for tax years involving different spouses or former spouses.

That person's current name	**Social security number** (if known)

Current home address (number and street) (if known). If a P.O. box, see instructions.	Apt. no.

City, town or post office, state, and ZIP code. If a foreign address, see instructions.	Best daytime phone number

---

   Cat. No. 24647V   Form **8857** (Rev. 9-2010)

Note. If you need more room to write your answer for any question, attach more pages. Be sure to write your name and social security number on the top of all pages you attach.

Part III	(Continued)

8   **What is the current marital status between you and the person on line 7?**

☐ Married and still living together

☐ Married and living apart since _____
    MM   DD   YYYY

☐ Widowed since _____   Attach a photocopy of the death certificate and will (if one exists).
    MM   DD   YYYY

☐ Legally separated since _____   Attach a photocopy of your entire separation agreement.
    MM   DD   YYYY

☐ Divorced since _____   Attach a photocopy of your entire divorce decree.
    MM   DD   YYYY

Note. A divorce decree stating that your former spouse must pay all taxes does not necessarily mean you qualify for relief.

9   **What was the highest level of education you had completed when the return(s) were filed?** If the answers are **not** the same for all tax years, explain.

☐ High school diploma, equivalent, or less
☐ Some college
☐ College degree or higher. List any degrees you have ▶ --

List any college-level business or tax-related courses you completed ▶ ---

Explain ▶ ---

10   **Were you a victim of spousal abuse or domestic violence during any of the tax years you want relief?** If the answers are **not** the same for all tax years, explain.

☐ Yes. **Attach a statement** to explain the situation and **when** it started. Provide photocopies of any documentation, such as police reports, a restraining order, a doctor's report or letter, or a notarized statement from someone who was aware of the situation.

☐ No.

11   **Did you (or the person on line 7) incur any large expenses, such as trips, home improvements, or private schooling, or make any large purchases, such as automobiles, appliances, or jewelry, during any of the years you want relief or any later years?**

☐ Yes. **Attach a statement** describing (a) the types and amounts of the expenses and purchases and (b) the years they were incurred or made.

☐ No.

12   **Did you sign the return(s)?** If the answers are **not** the same for all tax years, explain.

☐ Yes. If you were forced to sign under duress (threat of harm or other form of coercion), check here ▶ ☐ . See instructions.
☐ No. Your signature was forged. See instructions.

13   **When any of the returns were signed, did you have a mental or physical health problem or do you have a mental or physical health problem now?** If the answers are **not** the same for all tax years, explain.

☐ Yes. **Attach a statement** to explain the problem and **when** it started. Provide photocopies of any documentation, such as medical bills or a doctor's report or letter.

☐ No.

Part IV	Tell us how you were involved with finances and preparing returns for those tax years

14   **How were you involved with preparing the returns?** Check all that apply and explain, if necessary. If the answers are **not** the same for all tax years, explain.

☐ You filled out or helped fill out the returns.
☐ You gathered receipts and cancelled checks.
☐ You gave tax documents (such as Forms W-2, 1099, etc.) to the person who prepared the returns.
☐ You reviewed the returns before they were signed.
☐ You did not review the returns before they were signed. Explain below.
☐ You were not involved in preparing the returns.
☐ Other ▶ --

Explain how you were involved ▶ --

Note. If you need more room to write your answer for any question, attach more pages. Be sure to write your name and social security number on the top of all pages you attach.

| Part IV | (Continued) |

15 When the returns were signed, what did you know about any incorrect or missing information? Check all that apply and explain, if necessary. If the answers are **not** the same for all tax years, explain.

☐ You knew something was incorrect or missing, but you said nothing.

☐ You knew something was incorrect or missing and asked about it.

☐ You did not know anything was incorrect or missing.

Explain ▶ --

16 When any of the returns were signed, what did you know about the income of the person on line 7? Check all that apply and explain, if necessary. If the answers are **not** the same for all tax years, explain.

☐ You knew that person had income.

List each type of income on a separate line. (Examples are wages, social security, gambling winnings, or self-employment business income.) Enter each tax year and the amount of income for each type you listed. If you do not know any details, enter "I don't know."

Type of income	Who paid it to that person	Tax Year 1	Tax Year 2	Tax Year 3
		$	$	$
		$	$	$
		$	$	$

☐ You knew that person was self-employed and you helped with the books and records.

☐ You knew that person was self-employed and you did not help with the books and records.

☐ You knew that person had no income.

☐ You did not know if that person had income.

Explain ▶ --

17 When the returns were signed, did you know any amount was owed to the IRS for those tax years? If the answers are **not** the same for all tax years, explain.

☐ Yes. Explain when and how you thought the amount of tax reported on the return would be paid ▶ ------------------------------------

☐ No.

Explain ▶ --

18 When any of the returns were signed, were you having financial problems (for example, bankruptcy or bills you could not pay)? If the answers are **not** the same for all tax years, explain.

☐ Yes. Explain ▶ --

☐ No.

☐ Did not know.

Explain ▶ --

19 For the years you want relief, how were you involved in the household finances? Check all that apply. If the answers are **not** the same for all tax years, explain.

☐ You knew the person on line 7 had separate accounts.

☐ You had joint accounts but you had limited use of them or did not use them. Explain below.

☐ You used joint accounts. You made deposits, paid bills, balanced the checkbook, or reviewed the monthly bank statements.

☐ You made decisions about how money was spent. For example, you paid bills or made decisions about household purchases.

☐ You were not involved in handling money for the household.

☐ Other ▶

Explain anything else you want to tell us about your household finances ▶ --

20 Has the person on line 7 ever transferred assets (money or property) to you? (Property includes real estate, stocks, bonds, or other property that you own.) See instructions.

☐ Yes. List the assets, the dates they were transferred, and their fair market values on the dates transferred. Explain why the assets were transferred ▶ --

☐ No.

Form **8857** (Rev. 9-2010)

Part V   **Tell us about your current financial situation**

21   **Tell us the number of people currently in your household.**   Adults _____   Children _____

22   **Tell us your current average monthly income and expenses for your entire household.** If family or friends are helping to support you, include the amount of support as gifts under **Monthly income.** Under **Monthly expenses,** enter all expenses, including expenses paid with income from gifts.

Monthly income	Amount	Monthly expenses	Amount
Gifts		Federal, state, and local taxes deducted from your paycheck	
Wages (Gross pay)		Rent or mortgage	
Pensions		Utilities	
Unemployment		Telephone	
Social security			
Government assistance, such as housing, food stamps, grants		Food	
		Car expenses, payments, insurance, etc.	
Alimony		Medical expenses, including medical insurance	
Child support		Life insurance	
Self-employment business income . .		Clothing	
Rental income		Child care	
Interest and dividends		Public transportation	
Other income, such as disability payments, gambling winnings, etc. List the type below:		Other expenses, such as real estate taxes, child support, etc. List the type below:	
Type _____		Type _____	
Type _____		Type _____	
Type _____		Type _____	
Total . . . . ▶		Total . . . . ▶	

23   **Tell us about your assets.** Your assets are your money and property. Property includes real estate, motor vehicles, stocks, bonds, and other property that you own. Tell us the amount of cash you have on hand and in your bank accounts. Also give a description of each item of property, the fair market value of each item, and the balance of any outstanding loans you used to acquire each item. Do not list any money or property you listed on line 20. If you need more room, attach more pages. Write your name and social security number on the top of all pages you attach.

----

24   **Please provide any other information you want us to consider in determining whether it would be unfair to hold you liable for the tax.** If you need more room, attach more pages. Write your name and social security number on the top of all pages you attach.

Caution

By signing this form, you understand that, by law, we must contact the person on line 7. See instructions for details.

Sign Here

Keep a copy for your records.

Under penalties of perjury, I declare that I have examined this form and any accompanying schedules and statements, and to the best of my knowledge and belief, they are true, correct, and complete. Declaration of preparer (other than taxpayer) is based on all information of which preparer has any knowledge.

Your signature		Date

Paid Preparer's Use Only

Preparer's signature ▶	Date	Check if self-employed ☐	Preparer's SSN or PTIN
Firm's name (or yours if self-employed), address, and ZIP code ▶		EIN	
		Phone no.	

Form **8857** (Rev. 9-2010)

Instructions for Form 8857

Department of the Treasury
Internal Revenue Service

(Rev. September 2011)

Request for Innocent Spouse Relief
For use with Form 8857 (Rev. September 2010)

Section references are to the Internal Revenue Code unless otherwise noted.

General Instructions

Note. In these instructions, the term "your spouse or former spouse" means the person who was your spouse for the year(s) you want relief. This is the person whose name you enter on line 7.

What's New

Expanded filing deadline for equitable relief. The period of time in which you may request equitable relief has been expanded. See *When To File* on this page.

More information. For more information about the latest developments on Form 8857 and its instructions, go to *www.irs. gov/form8857*.

Purpose of Form

When you file a joint income tax return, the law makes both you and your spouse responsible for the entire tax liability. This is called joint and several liability. Joint and several liability applies not only to the tax liability you show on the return but also to any additional tax liability the IRS determines to be due, even if the additional tax is due to the income, deductions, or credits of your spouse or former spouse. You remain jointly and severally liable for taxes, and the IRS can still collect them from you, even if you later divorce and the divorce decree states that your former spouse will be solely responsible for the tax.

If you believe that only your spouse or former spouse should be held responsible for all or part of the tax, you can request relief from the tax liability, plus related penalties and interest. To request relief, you must file Form 8857. The IRS will use the information you provide on the form and any attachments to determine if you are eligible for relief. If the IRS needs additional information, you will be contacted.

Married people who did not file joint returns, but who live in community property states may also request relief. Community property states are Arizona, California, Idaho, Louisiana, Nevada, New Mexico, Texas, Washington, and Wisconsin. See *Community Property Laws* later.

Note. We recognize that some of the questions on the form involve sensitive subjects. However, we need this information to evaluate the circumstances of your case and properly determine whether you qualify for relief.

Situations in Which You Should Not File Form 8857

Do not file Form 8857 for any tax year to which the following situations apply. Do not file the form even if you check "Yes" on line 4 or 5 for that year.
- In a final decision dated after July 22, 1998, a court considered whether to grant you relief from joint liability and decided not to do so.
- In a final decision dated after July 22, 1998, a court did not consider whether to grant you relief from joint liability, but you meaningfully participated in the proceeding and could have asked for relief.
- You entered into an offer in compromise with the IRS.
- You entered into a closing agreement with the IRS that disposed of the same liability for which you want to seek relief. However, see Pub. 971, Innocent Spouse Relief, for an exception that applies to TEFRA partnership proceedings.

- You check "Yes" on line 3. See the instructions for line 3 later.

When To File

You should file Form 8857 as soon as you become aware of a tax liability for which you believe only your spouse or former spouse should be held responsible. The following are some of the ways you may become aware of such a liability.
- The IRS is examining your tax return and proposing to increase your tax liability.
- The IRS sends you a notice.

However, you generally must file Form 8857 no later than 2 years after the first IRS attempt to collect the tax from you that occurs after July 22, 1998. (But see the **exceptions** below for different filing deadlines that apply.) For this reason, do not delay filing because you do not have all the required documentation.

Collection activities that may start the 2-year period are:
- The IRS offset your income tax refund against an amount you owed on a joint return for another year and the IRS informed you about your right to file Form 8857.
- The filing of a claim by the IRS in a court proceeding in which you were a party or the filing of a claim in a proceeding that involves your property. This includes the filing of a proof of claim in a bankruptcy proceeding.
- The filing of a suit by the United States against you to collect the joint liability.
- The issuance of a section 6330 notice, which notifies you of the IRS' intent to levy and your right to a collection due process (CDP) hearing. The collection-related notices include but are not limited to Letter 11 and Letter 1058.

Exception for equitable relief. On July 25, 2011, the IRS issued Notice 2011-70 (available at *www.irs.gov/irb/ 2011-32_IRB/ar11.html*) expanding the amount of time to request equitable relief. The amount of time to request equitable relief depends on whether you are seeking relief from a balance due, seeking a credit or refund, or both:
- Balance Due – Generally, you must file your request within the time period the IRS has to collect the tax. Generally, the IRS has 10 years from the date the tax liability was assessed to collect the tax. In certain cases, the 10-year period is suspended. The amount of time the suspension is in effect will extend the time the IRS has to collect the tax. See Pub. 594, The IRS Collection Process, for details.
- Credit or Refund – Generally, you must file your request within 3 years after the date the original return was filed or within 2 years after the date the tax was paid, whichever is later. But you may have more time to file if you live in a federally declared disaster area or you are physically or mentally unable to manage your financial affairs. See Pub. 556, Examination of Returns, Appeal Rights, and Claims for Refund, for details.
- Both a Balance Due and a Credit or Refund – If you are seeking a refund of amounts you paid and relief from a balance due over and above what you have paid, the time period for credit or refund will apply to any payments you have made, and the time period for collection of a balance due amount will apply to any unpaid liability.

Exception for relief based on community property laws. If you are requesting relief based on community property laws, a different filing deadline applies. See *Relief from liability arising from community property law* discussed later under *Community Property Laws*.

Where To File

Do not file Form 8857 with your tax return or the Tax Court. Instead, send it to:

Internal Revenue Service
Stop 840F, P.O. Box 120053
Covington, KY 41012

OR

Fax the form and attachments to the IRS at (859) 669-5256 or (859) 669-7187.

Write your name and social security number on any attachments.

Send it to the above address or fax it to the above number even if you are communicating with an IRS employee because of an examination, examination appeal, or collection.

If you received an IRS notice of deficiency, you also should file a petition with the Tax Court before the end of the 90-day period, as explained in the notice. In your petition, you should raise innocent spouse relief as a defense to the deficiency. By doing so, you preserve your rights if the IRS is unable to properly consider your request before the end of the 90-day period. Include the information that supports your position, including when and why you filed Form 8857 with the IRS, in your petition to the Tax Court. The time for filing with the Tax Court is not extended while the IRS is considering your request.

The IRS Must Contact Your Spouse or Former Spouse

By law, the IRS must contact your spouse or former spouse. There are **no** exceptions, even for victims of spousal abuse or domestic violence.

We will inform your spouse or former spouse that you filed Form 8857 and will allow him or her to participate in the process. If you are requesting relief from joint and several liability on a joint return, the IRS must also inform him or her of its preliminary and final determinations regarding your request for relief.

However, to protect your privacy, the IRS will not disclose your personal information (for example, your current name, address, phone number(s), information about your employer, your income or assets) or any other information that does not relate to making a determination about your request for relief from liability.

 If you petition the Tax Court (explained later under What Happens After You File Form 8857*), your spouse or former spouse may see your personal information, unless you ask the Tax Court to withhold it.*

Types of Relief

Four types of relief are available. They are:
1. Innocent spouse relief.
2. Separation of liability relief.
3. Equitable relief.
4. Relief from liability arising from community property law. (See *Community Property Laws* later).

Innocent Spouse Relief

You may be allowed innocent spouse relief only if all of the following apply.
- You filed a joint return for the year(s) entered on line 1.
- There is an understated tax on the return(s) that is due to erroneous items (defined below) of the person with whom you filed the joint return.
- You can show that when you signed the return(s) you did not know and had no reason to know that the understated tax existed (or the extent to which the understated tax existed).
- Taking into account all the facts and circumstances, it would be unfair to hold you liable for the understated tax.

Understated tax. You have an understated tax if the IRS determined that your total tax should be more than the amount actually shown on the return.

Example. You and your former spouse filed a joint return showing $5,000 of tax, which was fully paid. The IRS later examines the return and finds $10,000 of income that your former spouse earned but did not report. With the additional income, the total tax becomes $6,500. The understated tax is $1,500, for which you and your former spouse are both liable.

Erroneous items. Any income, deduction, credit, or basis is an erroneous item if it is omitted from or incorrectly reported on the joint return.

Partial innocent spouse relief. If you knew about any of the erroneous items, but not the full extent of the item(s), you may be allowed relief for the part of the understatement you did not know about.

Additional information. For additional information on innocent spouse relief, see Pub. 971.

Separation of Liability Relief

You may be allowed separation of liability relief for any understated tax (defined above) shown on the joint return(s) if the person with whom you filed the joint return is deceased or you and that person:
- Are now divorced,
- Are now legally separated, or
- Have lived apart at all times during the 12-month period prior to the date you file Form 8857.

See Pub. 504, Divorced or Separated Individuals, for details on divorce and separation.

Exception. If, at the time you signed the joint return, you knew about any item that resulted in part or all of the understated tax, then your request will not apply to that part of the understated tax.

Additional information. For additional information on separation of liability relief, see Pub. 971.

Equitable Relief

You may be allowed equitable relief if both of the following conditions are met.
- You have an understated tax (defined earlier) or underpaid tax (defined next), and
- Taking into account all the facts and circumstances, the IRS determines it would be unfair to hold you liable for the understated or underpaid tax.

Equitable relief is the only type of relief available for an underpaid tax.

Underpaid tax. An underpaid tax is tax that is properly shown on your return but has not been paid.

Example. You and your former spouse filed a joint return that properly reflects your income and deductions but showed an unpaid balance due of $5,000. The underpaid tax is $5,000. You gave your former spouse $2,500 and he or she promised to pay the full $5,000, but paid nothing. There is still an underpaid tax of $5,000, for which you and your former spouse are both liable.

Additional information. For additional information on equitable relief, see Pub. 971 and Rev. Proc. 2003-61. You can find Rev. Proc. 2003-61 on page 296 of Internal Revenue Bulletin 2003-32 at *www.irs.gov/irb/2003-32_IRB/ar16.html*.

Community Property Laws

Generally, you must follow community property laws when filing a tax return if you are married and live in a community property state. Community property states are: Arizona, California, Idaho, Louisiana, Nevada, New Mexico, Texas, Washington, and Wisconsin. Generally, community property laws provide that you and your spouse are both entitled to one-half of your total community income and expenses. If you and your spouse filed a joint return in a community property state, you are both jointly and severally liable for the total liability on the return. If you request relief from joint and several liability, state community property laws are not taken into account in determining whether an item belongs to you or your spouse or former spouse.

If you were a married resident of a community property state, but did not file a joint return and are now liable for an underpaid

-2-

or understated tax, check "Yes" on line 5; you have the following two ways to get relief.

1. Relief from liability arising from community property law. You are not responsible for the tax related to an item of community income if **all** of the following conditions exist.
- You did not file a joint return for the tax year.
- You did not include the item in gross income on your separate return.
- Under section 879(a), the item was income that belonged to your spouse or former spouse. For details, see *Community Property Laws* in Pub. 971.
- You establish that you did not know of, and had no reason to know of, that item.
- Under all facts and circumstances, it would not be fair to include the item in your gross income.

If you meet the above conditions, complete this form.

You must file Form 8857 no later than 6 months before the expiration of the period of limitations on assessment (including extensions) against your spouse or former spouse for the tax year for which you are requesting relief. However, if the IRS begins an examination of your return during that 6-month period, the latest time for requesting relief is 30 days after the date of the IRS' initial contact letter to you. The period of limitations on assessment is the amount of time, generally 3 years, that the IRS has from the date you filed the return to assess taxes that you owe.

2. Equitable relief. If you do not qualify for the relief described above and are now liable for an underpaid or understated tax you believe should be paid only by your spouse or former spouse, you may request equitable relief. See *Equitable Relief*, earlier.

What Happens After You File Form 8857

We will review your form for completeness and contact your spouse or former spouse to ask if he or she wants to participate in the process. Generally, once we have all of the necessary information to make a decision, we will send a preliminary determination letter to you and your spouse or former spouse. If neither of you appeals the decision, we will issue a final determination letter to both of you. If either or both of you appeal to the IRS Office of Appeals, Appeals will issue a final determination letter to both of you after consideration of your appeal.

Note. If you did not file a joint return for the year you are requesting relief, we will send the determination letters only to you.

Tax Court review of request. You may be able to petition (ask) the Tax Court to review your request for relief if:
- The IRS sends you a final determination letter regarding your request for relief, or
- You do not receive a final determination letter from the IRS within 6 months from the date you filed Form 8857.

 If you seek equitable relief for an underpayment of tax, you will be able to get Tax Court review of your claim only if the tax arose or remained unpaid on or after December 20, 2006.

The petition must be filed **no later than the 90th day after** the date the IRS mails you a final determination letter. If you do not file a petition, or if you file it late, the Tax Court cannot review your request for relief. See Pub. 971 for details on petitioning the Tax Court.

How To Get Help

See Pub. 971, Innocent Spouse Relief. To get Pub. 971 and other IRS forms and publications go to IRS.gov or call 1-800-TAX-FORM (1-800-829-3676).

 The IRS can help you with your request. If you are working with an IRS employee, you can ask that employee, or you can call 1-866-897-4270.

 You can use the Innocent Spouse Tax Relief Eligibility Explorer by going to IRS.gov and entering "Innocent Spouse" in the search box.

Contacting your Taxpayer Advocate. The Taxpayer Advocate Service is an independent organization within the IRS. We help taxpayers who are experiencing economic harm, such as not being able to provide necessities like housing, transportation, or food; taxpayers who are seeking help in resolving tax problems with the IRS; and those who believe that an IRS system or procedure is not working as it should.

You can contact the Taxpayer Advocate Service by calling your local advocate, whose number is in your phone book, in Pub. 1546, Taxpayer Advocate Service - Your Voice at the IRS, and at *www.IRS.gov/advocate*. You can also call toll-free 1-877-777-4778 or TTY/TDD 1-800-829-4059. You can file Form 911, Request for Taxpayer Advocate Service Assistance (And Application for Taxpayer Assistance Order), or ask an IRS employee to complete it on your behalf. For more information, go to *www.IRS.gov/advocate*.

Low Income Taxpayer Clinics (LITCs). The Low Income Taxpayer Clinic program serves individuals who have a problem with the IRS and whose income is below a certain level. LITCs are independent from the IRS. Most LITCs can provide representation before the IRS or in court on audits, tax collection disputes, and other issues for free or a small fee. If an individual's native language is not English, some clinics can provide multilingual information about taxpayer rights and responsibilities. For more information, see Publication 4134, Low Income Taxpayer Clinic List. This publication is available at IRS.gov, by calling 1-800-TAX-FORM (1-800-829-3676), or at your local IRS office.

Representation. You may either represent yourself or, with proper written authorization, have someone else represent you. Your representative must be someone who is allowed to practice before the IRS, such as an attorney, certified public accountant, or enrolled agent (a person enrolled to practice before the IRS). Use Form 2848, Power of Attorney and Declaration of Representative, to authorize someone else to represent you before the IRS.

Specific Instructions

Note. If you need more room to write your answer for any question, attach more pages. Be sure to write your name and social security number on the top of all pages you attach.

Also write your name and social security number on the top of the documents and statements required by lines 2, 8, 10, 11, 12, and 13.

Lines 1 through 5

You **must** complete lines 1 through 5 to determine if you should file Form 8857.

Collection Statute of Limitations

Generally, the IRS has 10 years to collect an amount you owe. This is the collection statute of limitations. By law, the IRS is not allowed to collect from you after the 10-year period ends.

If you request relief for any tax year, the IRS cannot collect from you for that year while your request is pending. But interest and penalties continue to accrue. Your request is generally considered pending from the date the IRS receives your Form 8857 until the date your request is resolved. This includes the time the Tax Court is considering your request.

After your case is resolved, the IRS can begin or resume collecting from you. The 10-year period will be increased by the amount of time your request for relief was pending plus 60 days.

Line 2

You must indicate that you want a refund in order for the IRS to consider whether you are entitled to it. If you are granted relief, refunds are:
- Permitted under innocent spouse relief as explained later under *Limit on Amount of Refund*.
- Not permitted under separation of liability relief.
- Permitted in limited circumstances under equitable relief, as explained under *Refunds Under Equitable Relief* later.

Proof Required

The IRS will only refund payments you made with your own money. However, you must provide proof that you made the payments with your own money. Examples of proof are a copy of your bank statement or a canceled check. No proof is required if your individual refund was used by the IRS to pay a tax you owed on a joint tax return for another year.

Refunds Under Equitable Relief

In the following situations, you are eligible to receive a refund of certain payments you made.

Underpaid tax. If you are granted relief for an underpaid tax, you are eligible for a refund of separate payments that you made after July 22, 1998. However, you are not eligible for refunds of payments made with the joint return, joint payments, or payments that your spouse (or former spouse) made. For example, withholding tax and estimated tax payments cannot be refunded because they are considered made with the joint return.

The amount of the refund is subject to the limit discussed later under *Limit on Amount of Refund.*

Understated tax. If you are granted relief for an understated tax, you are eligible for a refund of certain payments made under an installment agreement that you entered into with the IRS, if you have not defaulted on the installment agreement. You are not in default if the IRS did not issue you a notice of default or take any action to end the installment agreement. Only installment payments made after the date you filed Form 8857 are eligible for a refund.

The amount of the refund is subject to the limit discussed next.

Limit on Amount of Refund

The amount of your refund is limited. Read the following chart to find out the limit.

IF you file Form 8857 . . .	THEN the refund cannot be more than . . .
Within 3 years after filing your return	The part of the tax paid within the 3 years (plus any extension of time for filing your return) before you filed Form 8857.
After the 3-year period, but within 2 years from the time you paid the tax	The tax you paid within the 2 years immediately before you filed Form 8857.

Line 3

Check "Yes" for any tax year to which all of the following apply.
• You filed a joint return for the year listed on line 1.
• At the time you filed the joint return, your spouse owed past-due federal tax, state income tax, child support, spousal support, or federal nontax debt, such as a student loan.
• The IRS used (offset) the refund to pay your spouse's past-due amount.
If all three of the above apply, do not file Form 8857 for that tax year. However, you may be able to get back your share of the refund for that tax year if you file Form 8379, Injured Spouse Allocation.

If all three of the above do not apply, check "No" and go to line 4.

Line 4

Check "Yes" if a return claiming married filing jointly status was filed for the tax year listed on line 1. Check "Yes" even if you signed the return under duress or your signature was forged.

Line 6

Enter your current name, social security number, current mailing address, and best daytime phone number to call you if we need more information. Also enter your county.

If your current name is different from your name as shown on your tax return for any year for which you are requesting

relief, enter your former name in parentheses after your current name. For example, enter "Jane Maple (formerly Jane Oak)."

Foreign address. Enter the information in the following order: City, province or state, and country. Follow the country's practice for entering the postal code. **Do not** abbreviate the country name.

Change of address. If you move after you file Form 8857, please use Form 8822, Change of Address, to notify the IRS of your new address.

Line 7

Enter the current name and SSN (if known) of the person to whom you were married at the end of the year(s) listed on line 1.

P.O. box. Enter the box number **only** if:
• You do not know the street address, or
• The post office does not deliver mail to the street address.

Foreign address. See the instructions for line 6 above.

Line 12

By law, if a person's name is signed to a return, it is presumed to be signed by that person. You must prove that your signature on the joint return was forged or that you signed under duress (threat of harm or other form of coercion). Attach a statement explaining why you believe your signature was forged or you signed under duress.

Forged signature. Your signature on the joint return is considered to be forged if it was not signed by you and you did not authorize (give tacit consent) the signing of your name to the return.

Tacit consent. Tacit consent means that, based on your actions at the time the joint return was filed, you agreed to the filing of the joint return even if you now claim the signature on the return is not yours. Whether you have tacitly consented to the filing of the joint return is based on an examination of all the facts of your case. Factors that may support a finding that you consented to the filing of the joint return include the following.
• You gave tax information (such as Forms W-2 and 1099) to your spouse.
• You did not object to the filing.
• There was an apparent advantage to you in filing a joint return.
• You filed joint returns with your spouse or former spouse in prior years.
• You failed to file a married filing separate return and you had a filing requirement.

Sign under duress. You are considered to have signed under duress (threat of harm or other form of coercion) if you were unable to resist demands to sign the return and you would not have signed the return except for the constraint applied by your spouse or former spouse. The duress must be directly connected with the signing of the joint return.

Line 20

You may not be entitled to relief if either of the following applies.
• Your spouse (or former spouse) transferred property (or the right to property) to you for the main purpose of avoiding tax or payment of tax. A transfer will be presumed to meet this condition if the transfer is made after the date that is 1 year before the date on which the IRS sent its first letter of proposed deficiency.
• The IRS proves that you and your spouse (or former spouse) transferred property to one another as part of a fraudulent scheme. A fraudulent scheme includes a scheme to defraud the IRS or another third party such as a creditor, former spouse, or business partner.
For more information about transfers of property, see Pub. 971.

Fair market value. Fair market value is the price at which property would change hands between a willing buyer and a willing seller when both have reasonable knowledge of the relevant facts and neither has to buy or sell.

Line 23

See the instructions for line 20 for the definition of fair market value.

Sign Form 8857

If you do not sign Form 8857, the IRS cannot consider your request and will return it to you. Also be sure to date it.

Keep a copy of the completed form for your records.

Paid Preparer Must Sign

Generally, anyone you pay to prepare Form 8857 must sign it in the space provided. The preparer must give you a copy of Form 8857 for your records. Someone who prepares Form 8857 but does not charge you should not sign it.

Privacy Act and Paperwork Reduction Act Notice. We ask for the information on this form to carry out the Internal Revenue laws of the United States. We need it to determine the amount of liability, if any, of which you may be relieved. Internal Revenue Code sections 66(c) and 6015 allow relief from liability. Requesting relief from liability is voluntary. If you request relief of liability, you must give us the information requested on this form. Code section 6109 requires you to provide your social security number. Routine uses of this information include giving it to the Department of Justice for civil and criminal litigation, and to cities, states, the District of Columbia, and U.S. commonwealths and possessions for use in administering their tax laws. We may also disclose this information to other countries under a tax treaty, to federal and state agencies to enforce federal nontax criminal laws, or to federal law enforcement and intelligence agencies to combat terrorism. If you do not provide all the information in a timely manner, we may not be able to process your request.

You are not required to provide the information requested on a form that is subject to the Paperwork Reduction Act unless the form displays a valid OMB control number. Books or records relating to a form or its instructions must be retained as long as their contents may become material in the administration of any Internal Revenue law. Generally, tax returns and return information are confidential, as required by Code section 6103.

The time needed to complete and file this form will vary depending on individual circumstances. The estimated average time is:

Learning about the law or the form, 1 hr., 9 min; **Preparing the form,** 2 hr., 36 min; and **Copying, assembling, and sending the form to the IRS,** 1 hr., 3 min.

If you have comments concerning the accuracy of this time estimate or suggestions for making this form simpler, we would be happy to hear from you. You can email us at *taxforms@irs. gov.* Enter "Forms Comment" on the subject line. Or you can write to the Internal Revenue Service, Tax Products Coordinating Committee, SE:W:CAR:MP:T:M:S, 1111 Constitution Ave. NW, IR-6526, Washington, DC 20224. **Do not** send the form to this address. Instead, see *Where To File* earlier.

Installment Agreement Request

▶ **If you are filing this form with your tax return, attach it to the front of the return.**
▶ **See separate instructions.**

OMB No. 1545-0074

Caution: *Do not file this form if you are currently making payments on an installment agreement or can pay your balance in full within 120 days. Instead, call 1-800-829-1040. If you are in bankruptcy or we have accepted your offer-in-compromise, see* **Bankruptcy or offer-in-compromise,** *in the instructions.*

This request is for Form(s) (for example, Form 1040 or Form 1040EZ) ▶ _____ and for tax year(s) (for example, 2010 and 2011) ▶ _____

1	Your first name and initial	Last name	Your social security number
	If a joint return, spouse's first name and initial	Last name	Spouse's social security number

Current address (number and street). If you have a P.O. box and no home delivery, enter your box number.	Apt. number

City, town or post office, state, and ZIP code. If a foreign address, enter city, province or state, and country. Follow the country's practice for entering the postal code.

2	If this address is new since you filed your last tax return, check here . . . . ▶ ☐

3		4	
	Your home phone number Best time for us to call		Your work phone number Ext. Best time for us to call
5	Name of your bank or other financial institution:	6	Your employer's name:
	Address		Address
	City, state, and ZIP code		City, state, and ZIP code

7	Enter the total amount you owe as shown on your tax return(s) (or notice(s))	7	
8	Enter the amount of any payment you are making with your tax return(s) (or notice(s)). See instructions	8	
9	Enter the amount you can pay each month. **Make your payments as large as possible to limit interest and penalty charges.** The charges will continue until you pay in full	9	

10   Enter the date you want to make your payment each month. **Do not** enter a date later than the 28th ▶ _____

11   If you want to make your payments by electronic funds withdrawal from your checking account, see the instructions and fill in lines 11a and 11b. This is the most convenient way to make your payments and it will ensure that they are made on time.

▶ **a**   Routing number   ☐☐☐☐☐☐☐☐☐

▶ **b**   Account number   ☐☐☐☐☐☐☐☐☐☐☐☐☐☐☐☐☐

I authorize the U.S. Treasury and its designated Financial Agent to initiate a monthly ACH debit (electronic withdrawal) entry to the financial institution account indicated for payments of my Federal taxes owed, and the financial institution to debit the entry to this account. This authorization is to remain in full force and effect until I notify the U.S. Treasury Financial Agent to terminate the authorization. To revoke payment, I must contact the U.S. Treasury Financial Agent at **1-800-829-1040** no later than 14 business days prior to the payment (settlement) date. I also authorize the financial institutions involved in the processing of the electronic payments of taxes to receive confidential information necessary to answer inquiries and resolve issues related to the payments.

Your signature	Date	Spouse's signature. If a joint return, **both** must sign.	Date

For Privacy Act and Paperwork Reduction Act Notice, see instructions.   Cat. No. 14842Y   Form **9465** (Rev. 12-2011)

Instructions for Form 9465

Department of the Treasury
Internal Revenue Service

(Rev. December 2011)
Installment Agreement Request

Section references are to the Internal Revenue Code unless otherwise noted.

General Instructions

What's New

The IRS has created a page on IRS.gov for information about Form 9465 and its instructions at www.irs.gov/form9465. Information about any future developments affecting Form 9465 (such as legislation enacted after we release it) will be posted on that page.

Purpose of Form

Use Form 9465 to request a monthly installment plan if you cannot pay the full amount you owe shown on your tax return (or on a notice we sent you). Generally, you can have up to 72 months to pay. In certain circumstances, you can have longer to pay or your agreement can be approved for an amount that is less than the amount of tax you owe. However, before requesting an installment agreement, you should consider other less costly alternatives, such as getting a bank loan or using available credit on a credit card. If you have any questions about this request, call 1-800-829-1040.

Use Form 9465 if you are an individual:
- Who owes income tax in the amount of $25,000 or less on Form 1040,
- Who may be responsible for a Trust Fund Recovery Penalty,
- Who was self-employed and owes self-employment or unemployment taxes and is no longer operating the business,
- Who is personally responsible for a partnership liability and the partnership is no longer operating, or
- Owner who is personally responsible for taxes in the name of a limited liability company (LLC) and the LLC is no longer operating.

Do not use Form 9465 if:
- You can pay the full amount you owe within 120 days (see *Can you pay in full within 120 days?*),
- You want to request an online payment agreement (see *Applying online for a payment agreement*), or
- The amount you owe is greater than $25,000. Instead, you may be able to use Form 9465-FS.

Guaranteed installment agreement. Your request for an installment agreement cannot be turned down if the tax you owe is not more than $10,000 and all three of the following apply.
- During the past 5 tax years, you (and your spouse if filing a joint return) have timely filed all income tax returns and paid any income tax due, and have not entered into an installment agreement for payment of income tax.
- The IRS determines that you cannot pay the tax owed in full when it is due and you give the IRS any information needed to make that determination.
- You agree to pay the full amount you owe within 3 years and to comply with the tax laws while the agreement is in effect.

 A Notice of Federal Tax Lien may be filed to protect the government's interests until you pay in full.

Can you pay in full within 120 days? If you can pay the full amount you owe within 120 days, call 1-800-829-1040 to establish your request to pay in full. If you can do this, you can avoid paying the fee to set up an installment agreement. Instead of calling, you can apply online.

Applying online for a payment agreement. Instead of filing Form 9465, you can apply online for a payment agreement. To do that, go to IRS.gov and click on "More..." under *Tools*.

Bankruptcy or offer-in-compromise. If you are in bankruptcy or we have accepted your offer-in-compromise, do not file this form. Instead, call 1-800-829-1040 to get the number of your local IRS Insolvency function for bankruptcy or Technical Support function for offer-in-compromise.

How the Installment Agreement Works

We will usually let you know within 30 days after we receive your request whether it is approved or denied. However, if this request is for tax due on a return you filed after March 31, it may take us longer than 30 days to reply. If we approve your request, we will send you a notice detailing the terms of your agreement and requesting a fee of $105 ($52 if you make your payments by electronic funds withdrawal). However, you may qualify to pay a reduced fee of $43 if your income is below a certain level. The IRS will let you know whether you qualify for the reduced fee. If the IRS does not say you qualify for the reduced fee, you can request the reduced fee using Form 13844, Application For Reduced User Fee For Installment Agreements.

You will also be charged interest and may be charged a late payment penalty on any tax not paid by its due date, even if your request to pay in installments is granted. Interest and any applicable penalties will be charged until the balance is paid in full. To limit interest and penalty charges, file your return on time and pay as much of the tax as possible with your return (or notice). All payments received will be applied to your account in the best interests of the United States.

By approving your request, we agree to let you pay the tax you owe in monthly installments instead of immediately paying the amount in full. In return, you agree to make your monthly payments on time. You also agree to meet all your future tax liabilities. This means that you must have enough withholding or estimated tax payments so that your tax liability for future years is paid in full when you timely file your return. Your request for an installment agreement will be denied if all required tax returns have not been filed. Any refund due you in a future year will be applied against the amount you owe. If your refund is applied to your balance, you are still required to make your regular monthly installment payment.

Payment methods. You can make your payments by check, money order, credit card, or one of the other payment methods shown next. The fee for each payment method is also shown.

Payment method	Applicable fee
Check, money order, or credit card	$105
Electronic funds withdrawal	$ 52
Payroll deduction installment agreement	$105

For details on how to pay, see your tax return instructions, visit IRS.gov, or call 1-800-829-1040.

After we receive each payment, we will send you a notice showing the remaining amount you owe, and the due date and amount of your next payment. But if you choose to have your payments automatically withdrawn from your checking account, you will not receive a notice. Your bank statement is your record of payment. We will also send you an annual statement showing the amount you owed at the beginning of the year, all payments made during the year, and the amount you owe at the end of the year.

If you do not make your payments on time or do not pay any balance due on a return you file later, you will be in default on your agreement and we may take enforcement actions, such as the filing of a Notice of Federal Tax Lien or an IRS levy action, to collect the entire amount you owe. To ensure that your payments are made timely, you should consider making them by electronic funds withdrawal (see the instructions for lines 11a and 11b, later).

Requests to modify or terminate an installment agreement. After an installment agreement is approved, you may submit a request to modify or terminate an installment agreement. This request will not suspend the statute of limitations on collection. While the IRS considers your request to modify or terminate the installment agreement, you must comply with the existing agreement.

 An installment agreement may be terminated if you provide materially incomplete or inaccurate information in response to an IRS request for a financial update.

For additional information on the IRS collection process, see Pub. 594, The IRS Collection Process.

Where To File

Attach Form 9465 to the front of your return and send it to the address shown in your tax return booklet. If you have already filed your return or you are filing this form in response to a notice, file Form 9465 by itself with the Internal Revenue Service Center using the address in the table below that applies to you.

For all taxpayers except those filing Form 1040 with Schedule(s) C, E, or F for any tax year for which this installment agreement is being requested.

IF you live in . . .	THEN use this address . . .
Alabama, Florida, Georgia, Kentucky, Louisiana, Mississippi, North Carolina, South Carolina, Texas, Virginia	Department of the Treasury Internal Revenue Service P.O. Box 47421 Stop 74 Doraville, GA 30362
Alaska, Arizona, Colorado, Connecticut, Delaware, District of Columbia, Hawaii, Idaho, Illinois, Maine, Maryland, Massachusetts, Montana, Nevada, New Hampshire, New Jersey, New Mexico, North Dakota, Oregon, Rhode Island, South Dakota, Tennessee, Utah, Vermont, Washington, Wisconsin, Wyoming	Department of the Treasury Internal Revenue Service 310 Lowell St. Stop 830 Andover, MA 01810
Arkansas, California, Indiana, Iowa, Kansas, Michigan, Minnesota, Missouri, Nebraska, New York, Ohio, Oklahoma, Pennsylvania, West Virginia	Department of the Treasury Internal Revenue Service Stop P-4 5000 Kansas City, MO 64999-0250
A foreign country, American Samoa, or Puerto Rico (or are excluding income under Internal Revenue Code section 933), or use an APO or FPO address, or file Form 2555, 2555-EZ, or 4563, or are a dual-status alien or nonpermanent resident of Guam or the Virgin Islands*	Department of the Treasury Internal Revenue Service 3651 South I-H 35, 5501AUSC Austin, TX 78741

* Permanent residents of Guam or the Virgin Islands cannot use Form 9465.

For taxpayers filing Form 1040 with Schedule(s) C, E, or F for any tax year for which this installment agreement is being requested.

IF you live in . . .	THEN use this address . . .
Alabama, Arkansas, Georgia, Illinois, Indiana, Iowa, Kansas, Kentucky, Louisiana, Michigan, Minnesota, Mississippi, Missouri, Nebraska, New Jersey, North Dakota, Ohio, Oklahoma, Pennsylvania, South Dakota, Tennessee, Texas, West Virginia, Wisconsin	Department of the Treasury Internal Revenue Service P.O. Box 69 Stop 811 Memphis, TN 38101-0069
Alaska, Arizona, California, Colorado, Hawaii, Idaho, Montana, Nevada, New Mexico, Oregon, Utah, Washington, Wyoming	Department of the Treasury Internal Revenue Service P.O. Box 9941 Stop 5500 Ogden, UT 84409
Connecticut, Maine, Massachusetts, New Hampshire, New York, Rhode Island, Vermont	Department of the Treasury Internal Revenue Service P.O. Box 480 Stop 660 Holtsville, NY 11742-0480
Delaware, Florida, Maryland, District of Columbia, North Carolina, South Carolina, Virginia	Department of the Treasury Internal Revenue Service Stop 4-N31.142 Philadelphia, PA 19255–0030
A foreign country, American Samoa, or Puerto Rico (or are excluding income under Internal Revenue Code section 933), or use an APO or FPO address, or file Form 2555, 2555-EZ, or 4563, or are a dual-status alien or nonpermanent resident of Guam or the Virgin Islands*	Department of the Treasury Internal Revenue Service 3651 South I-H 35, 5501AUSC Austin, TX 78741

* Permanent residents of Guam or the Virgin Islands cannot use Form 9465.

Specific Instructions

Line 1

If you are making this request for a joint tax return, show the names and social security numbers (SSNs) in the same order as on your tax return.

Line 7

Enter the total amount you owe as shown on your tax return (or notice).

 If the total amount you owe is more than $25,000 (including any amounts you owe from prior years), see Form 9465-FS.

Line 8

Even if you cannot pay the full amount you owe now, you should pay as much as possible to limit penalty and interest charges. If you are filing this form with your tax return, make the payment with your return. For details on how to pay, see your tax return instructions.

If you are filing this form by itself, such as in response to a notice, attach a check or money order payable to the "United States Treasury." Do not send cash. Be sure to include:
• Your name, address, SSN, and daytime phone number.
• The tax year and tax return (for example," 2009 Form 1040") for which you are making this request.

-2-

Line 9

You should try to make your payments large enough so that your balance due will be paid off as quickly as possible without causing you a financial burden.

Line 10

You can choose the day of each month your payment is due. This can be on or after the 1st of the month, but no later than the 28th of the month. For example, if your rent or mortgage payment is due on the 1st of the month, you may want to make your installment payments on the 15th. When we approve your request, we will tell you the month and day that your first payment is due.

If we have not replied by the date you chose for your first payment, you can send the first payment to the Internal Revenue Service Center at the address shown earlier that applies to you. See the instructions for line 8 above for details on what to write on your payment.

Lines 11a and 11b

 Making your payments by electronic funds withdrawal will help ensure that your payments are made timely and that you are not in default of this agreement.

To pay by electronic funds withdrawal from your checking account at a bank or other financial institution (such as mutual fund, brokerage firm, or credit union), fill in lines 11a and 11b. Check with your financial institution to make sure that an electronic funds withdrawal is allowed and to get the correct routing and account numbers.

Line 11a. The routing number must be nine digits. The first two digits of the routing number must be 01 through 12 or 21 through 32. Use a check to verify the routing number. On the sample check on this page, the routing number is 250250025. But if your check is payable through a financial institution different from the one at which you have your checking account, do not use the routing number on that check. Instead, contact your financial institution for the correct routing number.

Line 11b. The account number can be up to 17 characters (both numbers and letters). Include hyphens but omit spaces and special symbols. Enter the number from left to right and leave any unused boxes blank. On the sample check below, the account number is 20202086. Do not include the check number.

Note. We may have filed a notice of federal tax lien against your property. If so, you may be able to get the notice of lien withdrawn if you choose to make payments by direct debit. To see if you qualify and to learn more about lien withdrawals, visit IRS.gov and enter "lien withdrawal" in the search box.

 The electronic funds withdrawal from your checking account will not be approved unless you (and your spouse if filing a joint return) sign Form 9465.

Sample Check—Lines 11a and 11b

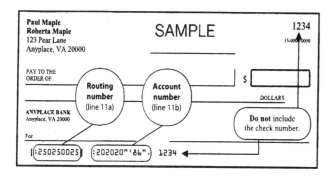

 The routing and account numbers may be in different places on your check.

Privacy Act and Paperwork Reduction Act Notice. Our legal right to ask for the information on this form is sections 6001, 6011, 6012(a), 6109, and 6159 and their regulations. We will use the information to process your request for an installment agreement. The reason we need your name and social security number is to secure proper identification. We require this information to gain access to the tax information in our files and properly respond to your request. You are not required to request an installment agreement. If you do request an installment agreement, you are required to provide the information requested on this form. Failure to provide this information may prevent processing your request; providing false information may subject you to fines or penalties.

You are not required to provide the information requested on a form that is subject to the Paperwork Reduction Act unless the form displays a valid OMB control number. Books or records relating to a form or its instructions must be retained as long as their contents may become material in the administration of any Internal Revenue law. Generally, tax returns and return information are confidential, as required by section 6103. However, we may give this information to the Department of Justice for civil and criminal litigation, and to cities, states, the District of Columbia, and U.S. commonwealths and possessions to carry out their tax laws. We may also disclose this information to other countries under a tax treaty, to federal and state agencies to enforce federal nontax criminal laws, or to federal law enforcement and intelligence agencies to combat terrorism.

The average time and expenses required to complete and file this form will vary depending on individual circumstances. For the estimated averages, see the instructions for your income tax return.

If you have suggestions for making this form simpler, we would be happy to hear from you. See the instructions for your income tax return.

-3-

Request for a Collection Due Process or Equivalent Hearing

Use this form to request a Collection Due Process (CDP) or equivalent hearing with the IRS Office of Appeals if you have been issued one of the following lien or levy notices:

- Notice of Federal Tax Lien Filing and Your Right to a Hearing under IRC 6320,
- Notice of Intent to Levy and Notice of Your Right to a Hearing,
- Notice of Jeopardy Levy and Right of Appeal,
- Notice of Levy on Your State Tax Refund,
- Notice of Levy and Notice of Your Right to a Hearing.

Complete this form and send it to the address shown on your lien or levy notice. Include a copy of your lien or levy notice to ensure proper handling of your request.

Call the phone number on the notice or 1-800-829-1040 if you are not sure about the correct address or if you want to fax your request.

You can find a section explaining the deadline for requesting a Collection Due Process hearing in this form's instructions. If you've missed the deadline for requesting a CDP hearing, you must check line 6 (Equivalent Hearing) to request an equivalent hearing.

1. Taxpayer Name: (Taxpayer 1) _____

   Taxpayer Identification Number _____

   Current Address _____

   City _____ State _____ Zip Code _____

2. Telephone Number and Best Time to Call During Normal Business Hours

   Home ( ) ___ - _____ _____ ☐ am. ☐ pm.
   Work ( ) ___ - _____ _____ ☐ am. ☐ pm.
   Cell ( ) _____ ☐ am. ☐ pm.

3. Taxpayer Name: (Taxpayer 2) _____

   Taxpayer Identification Number _____

   Current Address _____
   (If Different from Address Above) City _____ State _____ Zip Code _____

4. Telephone Number and Best Time to Call During Normal Business Hours

   Home ( ) ___ - _____ _____ ☐ am. ☐ pm.
   Work ( ) ___ - _____ _____ ☐ am. ☐ pm.
   Cell ( ) - ☐ am. ☐ pm.

5. Tax Information as Shown on the Lien or Levy Notice (*If possible, attach a copy of the notice*)

Type of Tax (Income, Employment, Excise, etc. or Civil Penalty)	Tax Form Number (1040, 941, 720, etc)	Tax Period or Periods

Form **12153** (Rev. 3-2011)   Catalog Number 26685D   www.irs.gov   Department of the Treasury - **Internal Revenue Service**

Request for a Collection Due Process or Equivalent Hearing

6. Basis for Hearing Request (Both boxes can be checked if you have received both a lien and levy notice)

☐ Filed Notice of Federal Tax Lien   ☐ Proposed Levy or Actual Levy

7. Equivalent Hearing (See the instructions for more information on Equivalent Hearings)

☐ I would like an Equivalent Hearing - I would like a hearing equivalent to a CDP Hearing if my request for a CDP hearing does not meet the requirements for a timely CDP Hearing.

8. Check the most appropriate box for the reason you disagree with the filing of the lien or the levy. **See page 4 of this form for examples.** You can add more pages if you don't have enough space.

If, during your CDP Hearing, you think you would like to discuss a Collection Alternative to the action proposed by the Collection function it is recommended you submit a completed Form 433A (Individual) and/or Form 433B (Business), as appropriate, with this form. See www.irs.gov for copies of the forms.

Collection Alternative ☐ Installment Agreement   ☐ Offer in Compromise   ☐ I Cannot Pay Balance

Lien   ☐ Subordination   ☐ Discharge   ☐ Withdrawal

Please explain:

My Spouse Is Responsible   ☐ Innocent Spouse Relief (Please attach Form 8857, *Request for Innocent Spouse Relief,* to your request.)

Other (*For examples, see page 4*)   ☐

Reason (*You must provide a reason for the dispute or your request for a CDP hearing will not be honored. Use as much space as you need to explain the reason for your request. Attach extra pages if necessary.*):

9. Signatures

I understand the CDP hearing and any subsequent judicial review will suspend the statutory period of limitations for collection action. I also understand my representative or I must sign and date this request before the IRS Office of Appeals can accept it. If you are signing as an officer of a company add your title (*president, secretary, etc.*) behind your signature.

SIGN HERE

Taxpayer 1's Signature	Date

Taxpayer 2's Signature (*if a joint request, both must sign*)	Date

☐ I request my CDP hearing be held with my authorized representative (*attach a copy of Form 2848*)

Authorized Representative's Signature	Authorized Representative's Name	Telephone Number

IRS Use Only

IRS Employee (Print)	Employee Telephone Number	IRS Received Date

Form **12153** (Rev. 3-2011)   Catalog Number 26685D   www.irs.gov   Department of the Treasury - **Internal Revenue Service**

Information You Need To Know When Requesting A Collection Due Process Hearing

What Is the Deadline for Requesting a Timely Collection Due Process (CDP) Hearing?

- Your request for a CDP hearing about a Federal Tax Lien filing must be postmarked by the date indicated in the *Notice of Federal Tax Lien Filing and Your Right to a Hearing under IRC 6320* (lien notice).

- Your request for a CDP hearing about a levy must be postmarked within 30 days after the date of the *Notice of Intent to Levy and Notice of Your Right to a Hearing* (levy notice) or Notice of Your Right to a Hearing After an Actual Levy.

Your timely request for a CDP hearing will prohibit levy action in most cases. A timely request for CDP hearing will also suspend the 10-year period we have, by law, to collect your taxes. Both the prohibition on levy and the suspension of the 10-year period will last until the determination the IRS Office of Appeals makes about your disagreement is final. The amount of time the suspension is in effect will be added to the time remaining in the 10-year period. For example, if the 10-year period is suspended for six months, the time left in the period we have to collect taxes will be extended by six months.

You can go to court to appeal the CDP determination the IRS Office of Appeals makes about your disagreement.

What Is an Equivalent Hearing?

If you still want a hearing with the IRS Office of Appeals after the deadline for requesting a timely CDP hearing has passed, you can use this form to request an equivalent hearing. You must check the Equivalent Hearing box on line 6 of the form to request an equivalent hearing. **An equivalent hearing request does not prohibit levy or suspend the 10-year period for collecting your taxes; also, you cannot go to court to appeal the IRS Office of Appeals' decision about your disagreement.** You must request an equivalent hearing within the following timeframe:

- Lien Notice-- one year plus five business days from the filing date of the Notice of Federal Tax Lien.

- Levy Notice-- one year from the date of the levy notice.

- Your request for a CDP levy hearing, whether timely or Equivalent, does not prohibit the Service from filing a Notice of Federal Tax Lien.

Where Should You File Your CDP or Equivalent Hearing Request?

File your request by mail at the address on your lien notice or levy notice. You may also fax your request. Call the telephone number on the lien or levy notice to ask for the fax number. **Do not send your CDP or equivalent hearing request directly to the IRS Office of Appeals, it must be sent to the address on the lien or levy notice. If you send your request directly to Appeals it may result in your request not being considered a timely request. Depending upon your issue the originating function may contact you in an attempt to resolve the issue(s) raised in your request prior to forwarding your request to Appeals.**

Where Can You Get Help?

You can call the telephone number on the lien or levy notice with your questions about requesting a hearing. The contact person listed on the notice or other representative can access your tax information and answer your questions.

In addition, you may qualify for representation by a low-income taxpayer clinic for free or nominal charge. Our Publication 4134, Low Income Taxpayer Clinic List, provides information on clinics in your area.

If you are experiencing economic harm, the Taxpayer Advocate Service (TAS) may be able to help you resolve your problems with the IRS. TAS cannot extend the time you have to request a CDP or equivalent hearing. See Publication 594, *The IRS Collection Process*, or visit www.irs.gov/advocate/index-html. You also can call 1-877-777-4778 for TAS assistance.

Note– The IRS Office of Appeals will not consider frivolous requests. You can find examples of frivolous reasons for requesting a hearing or disagreeing with a tax assessment in Publication 2105, *Why do I have to Pay Taxes?*, or at www.irs.gov by typing "frivolous" into the search engine.

> **You can get copies of tax forms, schedules, instructions, publications, and notices at www.irs.gov, at your local IRS office, or by calling toll-free *1-800-TAX-FORM (829-3676)*.**

Form **12153** (Rev. 3-2011)   Catalog Number 26685D   www.irs.gov   Department of the Treasury - **Internal Revenue Service**

Information You Need To Know When Requesting A Collection Due Process Hearing

What Are Examples of Reasons for Requesting a Hearing?

You will have to explain your reason for requesting a hearinq when you make your request. Below are examples of reasons for requesting a hearing.

You want a collection alternative-- "I would like to propose a different way to pay the money I owe." Common collection alternatives include:

- Full payment-- you pay your taxes by personal check, cashier's check, money order, or credit card.
- Installment Agreement-- you pay your taxes fully or partially by making monthly payments.
- Offer in Compromise-- you offer to make a payment or payments to settle your tax liability for less than the full amount you owe.

"I cannot pay my taxes." Some possible reasons why you cannot pay your taxes are: (1) you have a terminal illness or excessive medical bills; (2) your only source of income is Social Security payments, welfare payments, or unemployment benefit payments; (3) you are unemployed with little or no income; (4) you have reasonable expenses exceeding your income; or (5) you have some other hardship condition. The IRS Office of Appeals may consider freezing collection action until your circumstances improve. Penalty and interest will continue to accrue on the unpaid balance.

You want action taken about the filing of the tax lien against your property-- You can get a Federal Tax Lien released if you pay your taxes in full. You also may request a lien subordination, discharge, or withdrawal. See www.irs.gov for more information.

When you request **lien subordination**, you are asking the IRS to make a Federal Tax Lien secondary to a non-IRS lien. For example, you may ask for a subordination of the Federal Tax Lien to get a refinancing mortgage on your house or other real property you own. You would ask to make the Federal Tax Lien secondary to the mortgage, even though the mortgage came after the tax lien filing. The IRS Office of Appeals would consider lien subordination, in this example, if you used the mortgage proceeds to pay your taxes.

When you request a **lien discharge**, you are asking the IRS to remove a Federal Tax Lien from a specific property. For example, you may ask for a discharge of the Federal Tax Lien in order to sell your house if you use all of the sale proceeds to pay your taxes even though the sale proceeds will not fully pay all of the tax you owe.

When you request a **lien withdrawal**, you are asking the IRS to remove the Notice of Federal Tax Lien (NFTL) information from public records because you believe the NFTL should not have been filed. For example, you may ask for a withdrawal of the filing of the NFTL if you believe the IRS filed the NFTL prematurely or did not follow procedures, or you have entered into an installment agreement and the installment agreement does not provide for the filing of the NFTL. A withdrawal does not remove the lien from your IRS records.

Your spouse is responsible-- "My spouse (or former spouse) is responsible for all or part of the tax liability." You may believe that your spouse or former spouse is the only one responsible for all or a part of the tax liability. If this is the case, you are requesting a hearing so you can receive relief as an innocent spouse. You should complete and attach Form 8857, *Request for Innocent Spouse Relief*, to your hearing request.

Other Reasons-- "I am not liable for (I don't owe) all or part of the taxes." You can raise a disagreement about the amount you owe only if you did not receive a deficiency notice for the liability (a notice explaining why you owe taxes-it gives you the right to challenge in court, within a specific timeframe, the additional tax the IRS says you owe), or if you have not had another prior opportunity to disagree with the amount you owe.

"I do not believe I should be responsible for penalties." The IRS Office of Appeals may remove all or part of the penalties if you have a reasonable cause for not paying or not filing on time. See Notice 746, Information About Your Notice, Penalty and Interest for what is reasonable cause for removing penalties.

"I have already paid all or part of my taxes." You disagree with the amount the IRS says you haven't paid if you think you have not received credit for payments you have already made.

> **See Publication 594, *The IRS Collection Process*, for more information on the following topics: Installment Agreements and Offers in Compromise; Lien Subordination, Discharge, and Withdrawal; Innocent Spouse Relief; Temporarily Delay Collection; and belief that tax bill is wrong.**

Form **12153** (Rev. 3-2011)   Catalog Number 26685D   www.irs.gov   Department of the Treasury - Internal Revenue Service

Form 12510	**Questionnaire for Requesting Spouse**
(March 2005)	(Used in Conjunction with Form 8857, Request for Innocent Spouse Relief)

Name	Tax Year(s)	Social Security Number

We recognize that some of these questions involve sensitive subjects. However, we need this information to evaluate the circumstances of your case and properly determine whether you qualify for relief. If this form is not completed and returned your claim may be denied.

This form is divided into 4 parts.
- **Part 1 must be completed by everyone seeking relief.**
- **Parts 2 and 4 must be completed by everyone seeking relief from a balance due shown on your return when filed but not paid.**
- **Part 3 must be completed and it is recommended that you complete Part 4 if you are seeking relief from a tax liability that was determined as a result of an examination of the joint return.**

Please answer all the questions for those parts that must be completed. If more space is needed you may attach additional pages. Attach any documents you have that support your answers.

Part 1 – Complete this part for **all** requests for relief.

If you qualify for relief, you may also be entitled to a refund of your individual payments or credits previously applied to the balance due. If we previously applied a tax refund belonging to you individually or if you made individual payments whether voluntary or involuntary, which includes lien or levy payments, and you want us to consider the payment(s) for refund, please check yes to the following question and provide the type, date and amount of payment. If the payment(s) previously applied to the account were made in the form of check or money order, it is your responsibility to provide us with a copy of the front and back of the document(s).

1. Are you requesting a refund of any payments **you individually** made? [ ] Yes [ ] No

2. What is the **current** relationship between you and your (former) spouse with whom you filed the joint return(s) for the year(s) you are requesting relief:

[ ] Married and living together
[ ] Married living apart   Provide date (month, day, year) _____/_/____
[ ] Legally Separated   Provide date (month, day, year) _____/_/____
[ ] Divorced   Provide date (month, day, year) _____/_/____
[ ] Widowed   Provide date (month, day, year) _____/_/____

> **(Enclose a complete copy of the separation agreement, divorce decree, death certificate and will if applicable. If you are still married but living apart, provide documentation to verify the date of your separation such as copies of your lease agreement or utility bills in your individual name.)**

2a. During the year(s) in question, did you and your (former) spouse live together the full year?
    If no, please list dates of separation.

3. Why did you file a joint return instead of your own separate return?

4. What was your involvement in the preparation of the return(s)? For example, did you gather the receipts and cancelled checks, or just provide your W-2(s), etc.

5. Did you review the tax return(s) before signing?   [ ] Yes   [ ] No

5a. If no, explain why not.

5b. Did you ask your (former) spouse or the return preparer any questions about the return(s)?
    Please list the questions you asked, who responded and the response given.

6. During the year(s) in question did you have **your own separate** bank account(s)? [ ] Yes [ ] No
   If yes, indicate the type of account(s).
   [ ] Checking [ ] Savings [ ] Other

6a. What funds were deposited to the account(s)?

6b. What bills were paid out of the account(s)?

7. During the year(s) in question did you and your (former) spouse have any **joint** bank account(s)? [ ] Yes [ ] No
   If yes, indicate the type of account(s).
   [ ] Checking [ ] Savings [ ] Other

7a. What access did you have to the account(s)? (For example, were you able to make deposits, write checks and withdraw funds?)

7b. What funds were deposited to the account(s)?

7c. Who made the deposits?

7d. What bills were paid out of the account(s)?

7e. Who wrote the checks?

7f. Did you review the monthly bank statements? [ ] Yes [ ] No

7g. Did you balance the checkbook to the bank statements? [ ] Yes [ ] No

8. Did you pick up and/or open the household mail? [ ] Yes [ ] No

9. Please complete the following **for the year(s) you are requesting relief:**

Average Monthly Household Income and Expenses

Income	Amount	Expenses	Amount
Wages		Rent or Mortgage	
Pensions		Food	
Unemployment		Utilities	
Social Security		Telephone	
State, Local and Federal Support		Auto Payments	
Alimony		Auto Insurance	
Child Support		Auto - Gasoline & Repairs	
Self-Employment		Medical - Insurance & Other	
Rental Income		Life Insurance	
Interest and Dividends		Clothing	
Other(Gov't Assistance, Food Stamps, etc)		Child Care	
		Public Transportation	
		Other (please explain)	
Less deductions for W/H, Medicare, state Taxes, etc	( )		
TOTAL		TOTAL	

10. Were you abused by your (former) spouse during year(s) in question? Please describe the nature and extent of the abuse.

> **Since we do not request information of this nature from third parties, it is your responsibility to provide dates and any documentation such as police reports, doctor's statements or an affidavit from someone aware of the abuse.**

11. On the date you signed the return or at the time you requested relief were you suffering from mental or physical health problems?

> If yes, Please describe the nature and extent of your mental or physical health problem. Since we do not request information of this nature from third parties, it is your responsibility to provide dates and any documentation such as doctor statements or affidavits from someone aware of the problem.

12. What was your highest level of education during the year(s) you are requesting relief? Note any business or tax related courses you completed by that time.

13. What was your (former) spouse's highest level of education during the year(s) you are requesting relief? Note any business or tax related courses he or she completed by that time.

14. Have any assets been transferred from your (former) spouse to you?   [ ] Yes   [ ] No
If yes, list the assets and the date of transfer. Explain why they were transferred to you.

15. How was the money from the unpaid taxes spent?

16. Explain any other factors you feel should be considered for granting relief.

Part 2 – Complete this part if you are requesting relief for a **balance due** shown on your return when filed, but not paid.

1. At the time you signed the return(s) did you know there was a balance due? [ ] Yes   [ ] No

1a. If no, explain why you did not know.

1b. If yes, Who was responsible for paying the tax?

1c. Did you and your (former) spouse discuss when and how the underpayment would be paid?

2. At the time you signed the return, did you know about any financial problems you and your (former) spouse were having such as a bankruptcy, high credit card debt or difficulty in paying monthly living expenses?   [ ] Yes   [ ] No
If yes, please describe them.

3. After the return(s) was filed, what efforts were made by you and your (former) spouse to pay the tax?

Part 3 – Complete this part if you are requesting relief for **additional tax as a result of an IRS examination.**

1. List all places of employment of your (former) spouse and the income received for the year(s) in question.
   a. $_____
   b. $_____
   c. $_____
   d. $_____

2. Was your (former) spouse self-employed?   [ ] Yes   [ ] No
If so, please indicate the type of self-employment.

2a. If your (former) spouse was self-employed, did you assist him/her with the business?　[ ] Yes　[ ] No

2b. If yes, what were your duties or responsibilities?

3. At the time of signing the tax return(s), were you concerned about any item(s) omitted from or reported incorrectly on the return(s)?　[ ] Yes　[ ] No

3a. If yes, did you inquire of your (former) spouse about your concerns and what were you told?

3b. If no, when and how did you first become aware of the incorrect item(s)?

3c. At the time you signed the return, how much did you know about each of the incorrect items? (Example: the dollar amount, type of income, deduction, expense, credit, etc.)

4. If a refund was due/issued when the return was filed, how was the money used?

Part 4 – Complete this part if you completed Part 2. Completing this part is <u>optional</u> if you completed Part 3. However, doing so now may expedite consideration of your claim.

1. Please list the total number of adults and children in the household.

2. Please complete the following based on your **current** average monthly household income and expenses. Household includes a spouse or another person living with you:

Current Average Monthly Household Income and Expenses

Income	Amount	Expenses	Amount
Wages		Rent or Mortgage	
Pensions		Food	
Unemployment		Utilities	
Social Security		Telephone	
State, Local and Federal Support		Auto Payments	
Alimony		Auto Insurance	
Child Support		Auto - Gasoline & Repairs	
Self-Employment		Medical - Insurance & Other	
Rental Income		Life Insurance	
Interest and Dividends		Clothing	
Other(Gov't Assistance, Food Stamps, etc)		Child Care	
		Public Transportation	
		Other (please explain)	
Less deductions for W/H, Medicare, state Taxes, etc	(　　　)		
TOTAL		**TOTAL**	

Under penalties of perjury, I declare that I have examined this statement and to the best of my knowledge it is true, correct, and complete.

_____　　_____　　_____
Signature　　　　　　　　　　　SSN　　　　　　　　　　　　　　Date

_____　　_____
Daytime Phone #　　　　　　　Best Time to Call

Form **12510** (Rev. 3-2005)　　　Catalog Number 28752D　　　Page 4 of 4　　　Department of the Treasury **Internal Revenue Service**

PART X

Internal Revenue Service Publications (Selected)

Department of the Treasury
Internal Revenue Service

Publication 1

(Rev. May 2005)

Catalog Number 64731W

www.irs.gov

Your Rights as a Taxpayer

The first part of this publication explains some of your most important rights as a taxpayer. The second part explains the examination, appeal, collection, and refund processes. This publication is also available in Spanish.

Declaration of Taxpayer Rights

I. Protection of Your Rights

IRS employees will explain and protect your rights as a taxpayer throughout your contact with us.

II. Privacy and Confidentiality

The IRS will not disclose to anyone the information you give us, except as authorized by law. You have the right to know why we are asking you for information, how we will use it, and what happens if you do not provide requested information.

III. Professional and Courteous Service

If you believe that an IRS employee has not treated you in a professional, fair, and courteous manner, you should tell that employee's supervisor. If the supervisor's response is not satisfactory, you should write to the IRS director for your area or the center where you file your return.

IV. Representation

You may either represent yourself or, with proper written authorization, have someone else represent you in your place. Your representative must be a person allowed to practice before the IRS, such as an attorney, certified public accountant, or enrolled agent. If you are in an interview and ask to consult such a person, then we must stop and reschedule the interview in most cases.

You can have someone accompany you at an interview. You may make sound recordings of any meetings with our examination, appeal, or collection personnel, provided you tell us in writing 10 days before the meeting.

V. Payment of Only the Correct Amount of Tax

You are responsible for paying only the correct amount of tax due under the law—no more, no less. If you cannot pay all of your tax when it is due, you may be able to make monthly installment payments.

VI. Help With Unresolved Tax Problems

The Taxpayer Advocate Service can help you if you have tried unsuccessfully to resolve a problem with the IRS. Your local Taxpayer Advocate can offer you special help if you have a significant hardship as a result of a tax problem. For more information, call toll free 1–877–777–4778 (1–800–829–4059 for TTY/TDD) or write to the Taxpayer Advocate at the IRS office that last contacted you.

VII. Appeals and Judicial Review

If you disagree with us about the amount of your tax liability or certain collection actions, you have the right to ask the Appeals Office to review your case. You may also ask a court to review your case.

VIII. Relief From Certain Penalties and Interest

The IRS will waive penalties when allowed by law if you can show you acted reasonably and in good faith or relied on the incorrect advice of an IRS employee. We will waive interest that is the result of certain errors or delays caused by an IRS employee.

THE IRS MISSION

PROVIDE AMERICA'S TAXPAYERS TOP QUALITY SERVICE BY HELPING THEM UNDERSTAND AND MEET THEIR TAX RESPONSIBILITIES AND BY APPLYING THE TAX LAW WITH INTEGRITY AND FAIRNESS TO ALL.

Examinations, Appeals, Collections, and Refunds

Examinations (Audits)

We accept most taxpayers' returns as filed. If we inquire about your return or select it for examination, it does not suggest that you are dishonest. The inquiry or examination may or may not result in more tax. We may close your case without change; or, you may receive a refund.

The process of selecting a return for examination usually begins in one of two ways. First, we use computer programs to identify returns that may have incorrect amounts. These programs may be based on information returns, such as Forms 1099 and W-2, on studies of past examinations, or on certain issues identified by compliance projects. Second, we use information from outside sources that indicates that a return may have incorrect amounts. These sources may include newspapers, public records, and individuals. If we determine that the information is accurate and reliable, we may use it to select a return for examination.

Publication 556, Examination of Returns, Appeal Rights, and Claims for Refund, explains the rules and procedures that we follow in examinations. The following sections give an overview of how we conduct examinations.

By Mail

We handle many examinations and inquiries by mail. We will send you a letter with either a request for more information or a reason why we believe a change to your return may be needed. You can respond by mail or you can request a personal interview with an examiner. If you mail us the requested information or provide an explanation, we may or may not agree with you, and we will explain the reasons for any changes. Please do not hesitate to write to us about anything you do not understand.

By Interview

If we notify you that we will conduct your examination through a personal interview, or you request such an interview, you have the right to ask that the examination take place at a reasonable time and place that is convenient for both you and the IRS. If our examiner proposes any changes to your return, he or she will explain the reasons for the changes. If you do not agree with these changes, you can meet with the examiner's supervisor.

Repeat Examinations

If we examined your return for the same items in either of the 2 previous years and proposed no change to your tax liability, please contact us as soon as possible so we can see if we should discontinue the examination.

Appeals

If you do not agree with the examiner's proposed changes, you can appeal them to the Appeals Office of IRS. Most differences can be settled without expensive and time-consuming court trials. Your appeal rights are explained in detail in both Publication 5, Your Appeal Rights and How To Prepare a Protest If You Don't Agree, and Publication 556, Examination of Returns, Appeal Rights, and Claims for Refund.

If you do not wish to use the Appeals Office or disagree with its findings, you may be able to take your case to the U.S. Tax Court, U.S. Court of Federal Claims, or the U.S. District Court where you live. If you take your case to court, the IRS will have the burden of proving certain facts if you kept adequate records to show your tax liability, cooperated with the IRS, and meet certain other conditions. If the court agrees with you on most issues in your case and finds that our position was largely unjustified, you may be able to recover some of your administrative and litigation costs. You will not be eligible to recover these costs unless you tried to resolve your case administratively, including going through the appeals system, and you gave us the information necessary to resolve the case.

Collections

Publication 594, The IRS Collection Process, explains your rights and responsibilities regarding payment of federal taxes. It describes:

- What to do when you owe taxes. It describes what to do if you get a tax bill and what to do if you think your bill is wrong. It also covers making installment payments, delaying collection action, and submitting an offer in compromise.

- IRS collection actions. It covers liens, releasing a lien, levies, releasing a levy, seizures and sales, and release of property.

Your collection appeal rights are explained in detail in Publication 1660, Collection Appeal Rights.

Innocent Spouse Relief

Generally, both you and your spouse are each responsible for paying the full amount of tax, interest, and penalties due on your joint return. However, if you qualify for innocent spouse relief, you may be relieved of part or all of the joint liability. To request relief, you must file Form 8857, Request for Innocent Spouse Relief no later than 2 years after the date on which the IRS first attempted to collect the tax from you. For example, the two-year period for filing your claim may start if the IRS applies your tax refund from one year to the taxes that you and your spouse owe for another year. For more information on innocent spouse relief, see Publication 971, Innocent Spouse Relief, and Form 8857.

Potential Third Party Contacts

Generally, the IRS will deal directly with you or your duly authorized representative. However, we sometimes talk with other persons if we need information that you have been unable to provide, or to verify information we have received. If we do contact other persons, such as a neighbor, bank, employer, or employees, we will generally need to tell them limited information, such as your name. The law prohibits us from disclosing any more information than is necessary to obtain or verify the information we are seeking. Our need to contact other persons may continue as long as there is activity in your case. If we do contact other persons, you have a right to request a list of those contacted.

Refunds

You may file a claim for refund if you think you paid too much tax. You must generally file the claim within 3 years from the date you filed your original return or 2 years from the date you paid the tax, whichever is later. The law generally provides for interest on your refund if it is not paid within 45 days of the date you filed your return or claim for refund. Publication 556, Examination of Returns, Appeal Rights, and Claims for Refund, has more information on refunds.

If you were due a refund but you did not file a return, you generally must file your return within 3 years from the date the return was due (including extensions) to get that refund.

Tax Information

The IRS provides the following sources for forms, publications, and additional information.

- **Tax Questions:** 1–800–829–1040 (1–800–829–4059 for TTY/TDD)

- **Forms and Publications:** 1–800–829–3676 (1–800–829–4059 for TTY/TDD)

- **Internet:** www.irs.gov

- **Small Business Ombudsman:** A small business entity can participate in the regulatory process and comment on enforcement actions of IRS by calling 1-888-REG-FAIR.

- **Treasury Inspector General for Tax Administration:** You can confidentially report misconduct, waste, fraud, or abuse by an IRS employee by calling 1–800–366–4484 (1–800–877–8339 for TTY/TDD). You can remain anonymous.

 Printed on recycled paper

Your Appeal Rights and How To Prepare a Protest If You Don't Agree

Department of the Treasury
Internal Revenue Service

www.irs.ustreas.gov

Publication 5 **(Rev. 01-1999)**
Catalog Number **46074I**

Introduction

This Publication tells you how to appeal your tax case if you don't agree with the Internal Revenue Service (IRS) findings.

If You Don't Agree

If you don't agree with any or all of the IRS findings given you, you may request a meeting or a telephone conference with the supervisor of the person who issued the findings. If you still don't agree, you may appeal your case to the Appeals Office of IRS.

If you decide to do nothing and your case involves an examination of your income, estate, gift, and certain excise taxes or penalties, you will receive a formal Notice of Deficiency. The Notice of Deficiency allows you to go to the Tax Court and tells you the procedure to follow. If you do not go to the Tax Court, we will send you a bill for the amount due.

If you decide to do nothing and your case involves a trust fund recovery penalty, or certain employment tax liabilities, the IRS will send you a bill for the penalty. If you do not appeal a denial of an offer in compromise or a denial of a penalty abatement, the IRS will continue collection action.

If you don't agree, we urge you to appeal your case to the Appeals Office of IRS. The Office of Appeals can settle most differences without expensive and time-consuming court trials. [Note: Appeals can not consider your reasons for not agreeing if they don't come within the scope of the tax laws (for example, if you disagree solely on moral, religious, political, constitutional, conscientious, or similar grounds.)]

The following general rules tell you how to appeal your case.

Appeals Within the IRS

Appeals is the administrative appeals office for the IRS. You may appeal most IRS decisions with your local Appeals Office. The Appeals Office is separate from - and independent of - the IRS Office taking the action you disagree with. The Appeals Office is the only level of administrative appeal within the IRS.

Conferences with Appeals Office personnel are held in an informal manner by correspondence, by telephone or at a personal conference. There is no need for you to have representation for an Appeals conference, but if you choose to have a representative, see the requirements under **Representation.**

If you want an Appeals conference, follow the instructions in our letter to you. Your request will be sent to the Appeals Office to arrange a conference at a convenient time and place. You or your representative should prepare to discuss all issues you don't agree with at the conference. Most differences are settled at this level.

In most instances, you may be eligible to take your case to court if you don't reach an agreement at your Appeals conference, or if you don't want to appeal your case to the IRS Office of Appeals. See the later section *Appeals To The Courts.*

Protests

When you request an appeals conference, you may also need to file a formal written protest or a small case request with the office named in our letter to you. Also, see the special appeal request procedures in Publication 1660, Collection Appeal Rights, if you disagree with lien, levy, seizure, or denial or termination of an installment agreement.

You need to file a written protest:

- In all employee plan and exempt organization cases without regard to the dollar amount at issue.

- In all partnership and S corporation cases without regard to the dollar amount at issue.

- In all other cases, unless you qualify for the small case request procedure, or other special appeal procedures such as requesting Appeals consideration of liens, levies, seizures, or installment agreements. See Publication 1660.

How to prepare a protest:

When a protest is required, **send it within the time limit specified in the letter you received.** Include in your protest:

1) Your name and address, and a daytime telephone number,

2) A statement that you want to appeal the IRS findings to the Appeals Office,

3) A copy of the letter showing the proposed changes and findings you don't agree with (or the date and symbols from the letter),

4) The tax periods or years involved,

5) A list of the changes that you don't agree with, and why you don't agree.

6) The facts supporting your position on any issue that you don't agree with,

7) The law or authority, if any, on which you are relying.

8) You must sign the written protest, stating that it is true, under the penalties of perjury as follows:

"Under the penalties of perjury, I declare that I examined the facts stated in this protest, including any accompanying documents, and, to the best of my knowledge and belief, they are true, correct, and complete."

If your representative prepares and signs the protest for you, he or she must substitute a declaration stating:

1) That he or she submitted the protest and accompanying documents and

2) Whether he or she knows personally that the facts stated in the protest and accompanying documents are true and correct.

We urge you to provide as much information as you can, as this will help us speed up your appeal. This will save you both time and money.

Small Case Request:

If the total amount for any tax period is not more than $25,000, you may make a small case request instead of filing a formal written protest. In computing the total amount, include a proposed increase or decrease in tax (including penalties), or claimed refund. For an offer in compromise, in calculating the total amount, include total unpaid tax, penalty and interest due. For a small case request, follow the instructions in our letter to you by: sending a letter requesting Appeals consideration, indicating the changes you don't agree with, and the reasons why you don't agree.

Representation

You may represent yourself at your appeals conference, or you may have an attorney, certified public accountant, or an individual enrolled to practice before the IRS represent you. Your representative must be qualified to practice before the IRS. If you want your representative to appear without you, you must provide a properly completed power of attorney to the IRS before the representative can receive or inspect confidential information. Form 2848, Power of Attorney and Declaration of Representative, or any other properly written power of attorney or authorization may be used for this purpose. You can get copies of Form 2848 from an IRS office, or by calling 1-800-TAX-FORM (1-800-829-3676).

You may also bring another person(s) with you to support your position.

Appeals To The Courts

If you and Appeals don't agree on some or all of the issues after your Appeals conference, or if you skipped our appeals system, you may take your case to the United States Tax Court, the United States Court of Federal Claims, or your United States District Court, after satisfying certain procedural and jurisdictional requirements as described below under each court. (However, if you are a nonresident alien, you cannot take your case to a United States District Court.) These courts are independent judicial bodies and have no connection with the IRS.

Tax Court

If your disagreement with the IRS is over whether you owe additional income tax, estate tax, gift tax, certain excise taxes or penalties related to these proposed liabilities, you can go to the United States Tax Court. (Other types of tax controversies, such as those involving some employment tax issues or manufacturers' excise taxes, cannot be heard by the Tax Court.) You can do this after the IRS issues a formal letter, stating the amounts that the IRS believes you owe. This letter is called a notice of deficiency. You have 90 days from the date this notice is mailed to you to file a petition with the Tax Court (or 150 days if the notice is addressed to you outside the United States). The last date to file your petition will be entered on the notice of deficiency issued to you by the IRS. If you don't file the petition within the 90-day period (or 150 days, as the case may be), we will assess the proposed liability and send you a bill. You may also have the right to take your case to the Tax Court in some other situations, for example, following collection action by the IRS in certain cases. See Publication 1660.

If you discuss your case with the IRS during the 90-day period (150-day period), the discussion will not extend the period in which you may file a petition with the Tax Court.

The court will schedule your case for trial at a location convenient to you. You may represent yourself before the Tax Court, or you may be represented by anyone permitted to practice before that court.

Note: If you don't choose to go to the IRS Appeals Office before going to court, normally you will have an opportunity to attempt settlement with Appeals before your trial date.

If you dispute not more than $50,000 for any one tax year, there are simplified procedures. You can get information about these procedures and

other matters from the Clerk of the Tax Court, 400 Second St. NW, Washington, DC 20217.

Frivolous Filing Penalty

Caution: If the Tax Court determines that your case is intended primarily to cause a delay, or that your position is frivolous or groundless, the Tax Court may award a penalty of up to $25,000 to the United States in its decision.

District Court and Court of Federal Claims

If your claim is for a refund of any type of tax, you may take your case to your United States District Court or to the United States Court of Federal Claims. Certain types of cases, such as those involving some employment tax issues or manufacturers' excise taxes, can be heard only by these courts.

Generally, your District Court and the Court of Federal Claims hear tax cases only after you have paid the tax and filed a claim for refund with the IRS. You can get information about procedures for filing suit in either court by contacting the Clerk of your District Court or the Clerk of the Court of Federal Claims.

If you file a formal refund claim with the IRS, and we haven't responded to you on your claim within 6 months from the date you filed it, you may file suit for a refund immediately in your District Court or the Court of Federal Claims. If we send you a letter that proposes disallowing or disallows your claim, you may request Appeals review of the disallowance. If you wish to file a refund suit, you must file your suit no later than 2 years from the date of our notice of claim disallowance letter.

Note: Appeals review of a disallowed claim doesn't extend the 2 year period for filing suit. However, it may be extended by mutual agreement.

Recovering Administrative and Litigation Costs

You may be able to recover your reasonable litigation and administrative costs if you are the prevailing party, and if you meet the other requirements. You must exhaust your administrative remedies within the IRS to receive reasonable litigation costs. You must not unreasonably delay the administrative or court proceedings.

Administrative costs include costs incurred on or after the date you receive the Appeals decision letter, the date of the first letter of proposed deficiency, or the date of the notice of deficiency, whichever is earliest.

Recoverable litigation or administrative costs may include:

- Attorney fees that generally do not exceed $125 per hour. This amount will be indexed for a cost of living adjustment.

- Reasonable amounts for court costs or any administrative fees or similar charges by the IRS.

- Reasonable expenses of expert witnesses.

- Reasonable costs of studies, analyses, tests, or engineering reports that are necessary to prepare your case.

You are the prevailing party if you meet all the following requirements:

- You substantially prevailed on the amount in controversy, or on the most significant tax issue or issues in question.

- You meet the net worth requirement. For individuals or estates, the net worth cannot exceed $2,000,000 on the date from which costs are recoverable. Charities and certain cooperatives must not have more than 500 employees on the date from which costs are recoverable. And taxpayers other than the two categories listed above must not have net worth exceeding $7,000,000 and cannot have more than 500 employees on the date from which costs are recoverable.

You are not the prevailing party if:

- The United States establishes that its position was substantially justified. If the IRS does not follow applicable published guidance, the United States is presumed to not be substantially justified. This presumption is rebuttable. Applicable published guidance means regulations, revenue rulings, revenue procedures, information releases, notices, announcements, and, if they are issued to you, private letter rulings, technical advice memoranda and determination letters. The court will also take into account whether the Government has won or lost in the courts of appeals for other circuits on substantially similar issues, in determining if the United States is substantially justified.

You are also the prevailing party if:

- The final judgment on your case is less than or equal to a "qualified offer" which the IRS rejected, and if you meet the net worth requirements referred to above.

A court will generally decide who is the prevailing party, but the IRS makes a final determination of liability at the administrative level. This means you may receive administrative costs from the IRS without going to court. You must file your claim for administrative costs no later than the 90th day after the final determination of tax, penalty or interest is mailed to you. The Appeals Office makes determinations for the IRS on administrative costs. A denial of administrative costs may be appealed to the Tax Court no later than the 90th day after the denial.

Department of the Treasury
Internal Revenue Service

Publication 556
(Rev. May 2008)
Cat. No. 15104N

Examination of Returns, Appeal Rights, and Claims for Refund

Get forms and other information faster and easier by:

Internet • www.irs.gov

Contents

The IRS Mission

Provide America's taxpayers top quality service by helping them understand and meet their tax responsibilities and by applying the tax law with integrity and fairness to all.

What's New

Penalty for filing erroneous claim for refund or credit. You may have to pay a penalty if you file an erroneous claim for refund or credit. See *Penalty for erroneous claim for refund*, later under *Claims for Refund*.

Interest and penalties suspended if notice not mailed within 36 months. If you file your return timely (including extensions), interest and certain penalties will be suspended if the IRS does not mail a notice to you within 36 months. See *Suspension of interest and penalties*, later under *Examination of Returns*.

Important Reminder

Fast track mediation. The IRS offers fast track mediation services to help taxpayers resolve many disputes resulting from:

- Examinations (audits),
- Offers in compromise,
- Trust fund recovery penalties, and
- Other collection actions.

See *Fast track mediation* under *If You Do Not Agree*.

Introduction

The Internal Revenue Service (IRS) accepts most federal tax returns as filed. However, the IRS examines (or audits) some returns to determine if income, expenses, and credits are being reported accurately.

If your return is selected for examination, it does not suggest that you made an error or are dishonest. Returns are chosen by computerized screening, by random sample, or by an income document matching program. See *Examination selection criteria*, later. You should also know that many examinations result in a refund or acceptance of the tax return without change.

This publication discusses general rules and procedures that the IRS follows in examinations. It explains what happens during an examination and your appeal rights, both within the IRS and in the federal court system. It also explains how to file a claim for refund of tax you already paid.

As a taxpayer, you have the right to be treated fairly, professionally, promptly, and courteously by IRS employees. Publication 1, Your Rights as a Taxpayer, explains your rights when dealing with the IRS.

Comments and suggestions. We welcome your comments about this publication and your suggestions for future editions.

You can write to us at the following address:

Internal Revenue Service
Individual Forms and Publications Branch
SE:W:CAR:MP:T:I
1111 Constitution Ave. NW, IR-6526
Washington, DC 20224

We respond to many letters by telephone. Therefore, it would be helpful if you would include your daytime phone number, including the area code, in your correspondence.

You can email us at *taxforms@irs.gov. (The asterisk must be included in the address.) Please put "Publications Comment" on the subject line. Although we cannot respond individually to each email, we do appreciate your feedback and will consider your comments as we revise our tax products.

Ordering forms and publications. Visit *www.irs.gov/formspubs* to download forms and publications, call 1-800-829-3676, or write to the address below and receive a response within 10 days after your request is received.

Internal Revenue Service
1201 N. Mitsubishi Motorway
Bloomington, IL 61704-6613

Tax questions. If you have a tax question, check the information available on *www.irs.gov* or call 1-800-829-1040. We cannot answer tax questions sent to either of the above addresses.

Useful Items

You may want to see:

Publication

- ❏ **1** Your Rights as a Taxpayer
- ❏ **5** Your Appeal Rights and How To Prepare a Protest If You Don't Agree
- ❏ **547** Casualties, Disasters, and Thefts
- ❏ **594** The IRS Collection Process
- ❏ **910** Guide to Free Tax Services
- ❏ **971** Innocent Spouse Relief
- ❏ **1546** Taxpayer Advocate Service–Your Voice at the IRS
- ❏ **1660** Collection Appeal Rights
- ❏ **3605** Fast Track Mediation
- ❏ **3920** Tax Relief for Victims of Terrorist Attacks

Form (and Instructions)

- ❏ **843** Claim for Refund and Request for Abatement
- ❏ **1040X** Amended U.S. Individual Income Tax Return
- ❏ **2848** Power of Attorney and Declaration of Representative
- ❏ **4506** Request for Copy of Tax Return
- ❏ **4506-T** Request for Transcript of Tax Return
- ❏ **8379** Injured Spouse Allocation
- ❏ **8857** Request for Innocent Spouse Relief

See *How To Get Tax Help*, near the end of this publication, for information about getting these publications and forms.

Examination of Returns

Your return may be examined for a variety of reasons, and the examination may take place in any one of several ways. After the examination, if any changes to your tax are proposed, you can either agree with those changes and pay any additional tax you may owe, or you can disagree with the changes and appeal the decision.

Examination selection criteria. Your return may be selected for examination on the basis of computer scoring. A computer program called the Discriminant Inventory Function System (DIF) assigns a numeric score to each individual and some corporate tax returns after they have been processed. If your return is selected because of a high score under the DIF system, the potential is high that an examination of your return will result in a change to your income tax liability.

Your return may also be selected for examination on the basis of information received from third-party documentation, such as Forms 1099 and W-2, that does not match the information reported on your return. Or, your return may be selected to address both the questionable treatment of an item and to study the behavior of similar taxpayers (a market segment) in handling a tax issue.

In addition, your return may be selected as a result of information received from other sources on potential non-compliance with the tax laws or inaccurate filing. This information can come from a number of sources, including newspapers, public records, and individuals. The information is evaluated for reliability and accuracy before it is used as the basis of an examination or investigation.

Notice of IRS contact of third parties. The IRS must give you reasonable notice before contacting other persons about your tax matters. You must be given reasonable notice in advance that, in examining or collecting your tax liability, the IRS may contact third parties such as your neighbors, banks, employers, or employees. The IRS must also give you notice of specific contacts by providing you with a record of persons contacted on both a periodic basis and upon your request.

 This provision does not apply:

- *To any pending criminal investigation,*
- *When providing notice would jeopardize collection of any tax liability,*
- *Where providing notice may result in reprisal against any person, or*
- *When you authorized the contact.*

Taxpayer Advocate Service. The Taxpayer Advocate Service is an independent organization within the IRS whose goal is to help taxpayers resolve problems with the IRS. If you have an ongoing issue with the IRS that has not been resolved through normal processes, or you have suffered, or are about to suffer a significant hardship as a result of the administration of the tax laws, contact the Taxpayer Advocate Service.

 Before contacting the Taxpayer Advocate, you should first discuss any problem with a supervisor. Your local Taxpayer Advocate will assist you if you are unable to resolve the problem with the supervisor.

For more information, see Publication 1546. See *How To Get Tax Help*, near the end of this publication, for more information about contacting the Taxpayer Advocate Service.

Comments from small business. The Small Business and Agricultural Regulatory Enforcement Ombudsman and 10 Regional Fairness Boards have been established to receive comments from small business about federal agency enforcement actions. The Ombudsman will annually evaluate the enforcement activities of each agency and rate their responsiveness to small business. If you

wish to comment on the enforcement actions of the IRS, you can take any of the following steps.

- Fax your comments to 1-202-481-5719.

- Write to the following address:
  Office of the National Ombudsman
  U.S. Small Business Administration
  409 3rd Street, SW
  Washington, DC 20416

- Call 1-888-734-3247.

- Send an email to *ombudsman@sba.gov*.

- File a comment or complaint online at *www.sba.gov/ombudsman*.

If Your Return Is Examined

Some examinations are handled entirely by mail. Examinations not handled by mail can take place in your home, your place of business, an Internal Revenue office, or the office of your attorney, accountant, or enrolled agent. If the time, place, or method is not convenient for you, the examiner will try to work out something more suitable. However, the IRS makes the final determination of when, where, and how the examination will take place.

Throughout the examination, you can act on your own behalf or have someone represent you or accompany you. If you filed a joint return, either you or your spouse, or both, can meet with the IRS. You can have someone represent or accompany you. This person can be any federally authorized practitioner, including an attorney, a certified public accountant, an enrolled agent (a person enrolled to practice before the IRS), an enrolled actuary, or the person who prepared the return and signed it as the preparer.

If you want someone to represent you in your absence, you must furnish that person with proper written authorization. You can use Form 2848 or any other properly written authorization. If you want to consult with an attorney, a certified public accountant, an enrolled agent, or any other person permitted to represent a taxpayer during an interview for examining a tax return or collecting tax, you should make arrangements with that person to be available for the interview. In most cases, the IRS must suspend the interview and reschedule it. The IRS cannot suspend the interview if you are there because of an administrative summons.

Third party authorization. If you checked the box in the signature area of your income tax return (Form 1040, Form 1040A, or Form 1040EZ) to allow the IRS to discuss your return with another person (a third party designee), this authorization does not replace Form 2848. The box you checked on your return only authorizes the other person to receive information about the processing of your return and the status of your refund during the period your return is being processed. For more information, see the instructions for your return.

Confidentiality privilege. Generally, the same confidentiality protection that you have with an attorney also applies to certain communications that you have with federally authorized practitioners.

Confidential communications are those that:

- Advise you on tax matters within the scope of the practitioner's authority to practice before the IRS,

- Would be confidential between an attorney and you, and

- Relate to noncriminal tax matters before the IRS, or

- Relate to noncriminal tax proceedings brought in federal court by or against the United States.

In the case of communications in connection with the promotion of a person's participation in a tax shelter, the confidentiality privilege does not apply to written communications between a federally authorized practitioner and that person, any director, officer, employee, agent, or representative of that person, or any other person holding a capital or profits interest in that person.

A tax shelter is any entity, plan, or arrangement, a significant purpose of which is the avoidance or evasion of income tax.

Recordings. You can make an audio recording of the examination interview. Your request to record the interview should be made in writing. You must notify the examiner 10 days in advance and bring your own recording equipment. The IRS also can record an interview. If the IRS initiates the recording, you must be notified 10 days in advance and you can get a copy of the recording at your expense.

Transfers to another area. Generally, your return is examined in the area where you live. But if your return can be examined more quickly and conveniently in another area, such as where your books and records are located, you can ask to have the case transferred to that area.

Repeat examinations. The IRS tries to avoid repeat examinations of the same items, but sometimes this happens. If your tax return was examined for the same items in either of the 2 previous years and no change was proposed to your tax liability, please contact the IRS as soon as possible to see if the examination should be discontinued.

The Examination

An examination usually begins when you are notified that your return has been selected. The IRS will tell you which records you will need. The examination can proceed more easily if you gather your records before any interview.

Any proposed changes to your return will be explained to you or your authorized representative. It is important that you understand the reasons for any proposed changes. You should not hesitate to ask about anything that is unclear to you.

The IRS must follow the tax laws set forth by Congress in the Internal Revenue Code. The IRS also follows Treasury Regulations, other rules, and procedures that were written to administer the tax laws. The IRS also follows court decisions. However, the IRS can lose cases that involve taxpayers with the same issue and still apply its interpretation of the law to your situation.

Most taxpayers agree to changes proposed by examiners, and the examinations are closed at this level. If you do not agree, you can appeal any proposed change by following the procedures provided to you by the IRS. A more complete discussion of appeal rights is found later under *Appeal Rights*.

If You Agree

If you agree with the proposed changes, you can sign an agreement form and pay any additional tax you may owe. You must pay interest on any additional tax. If you pay when you sign the agreement, the interest is generally figured from the due date of your return to the date of your payment.

If you do not pay the additional tax when you sign the agreement, you will receive a bill that includes interest. If you pay the amount due within 10 business days of the billing date, you will not have to pay more interest or penalties. This period is extended to 21 calendar days if the amount due is less than $100,000.

If you are due a refund, you will receive it sooner if you sign the agreement form. You will be paid interest on the refund.

If the IRS accepts your tax return as filed, you will receive a letter in a few weeks stating that the examiner proposed no changes to your return. You should keep this letter with your tax records.

If You Do Not Agree

If you do not agree with the proposed changes, the examiner will explain your appeal rights. If your examination takes place in an IRS office, you can request an immediate meeting with the examiner's supervisor to explain your position. If an agreement is reached, your case will be closed.

If you cannot reach an agreement with the supervisor at this meeting, or if the examination took place outside of an IRS office, the examiner will write up your case explaining your position and the IRS' position. The examiner will forward your case for processing.

Fast track mediation. The IRS offers fast track mediation services to help taxpayers resolve many disputes resulting from:

- Examinations (audits),

- Offers in compromise,

- Trust fund recovery penalties, and

- Other collection actions.

Most cases that are not docketed in any court qualify for fast track mediation. Mediation can take place at a conference you request with a supervisor, or later. The process involves an Appeals Officer who has been trained in mediation. You may represent yourself at the mediation session, or someone else can act as your representative. For more information, see Publication 3605.

30-day letter and 90-day letter. Within a few weeks after your closing conference with the examiner and/or supervisor, you will receive a package with:

- A letter (known as a 30-day letter) notifying you of your right to appeal the proposed changes within 30 days,

- A copy of the examination report explaining the examiner's proposed changes,

- An agreement or waiver form, and

- A copy of Publication 5.

You generally have 30 days from the date of the 30-day letter to tell the IRS whether you will accept or appeal the proposed changes. The letter will explain what steps you should take, depending on which action you choose. Be sure to follow the instructions carefully. *Appeal Rights* are explained later.

90-day letter. If you do not respond to the 30-day letter, or if you later do not reach an agreement with an Appeals Officer, the IRS will send you a 90-day letter, which is also known as a notice of deficiency.

You will have 90 days (150 days if it is addressed to you outside the United States) from the date of this notice to file a petition with the Tax Court. Filing a petition with the Tax Court is discussed later under *Appeals to the Courts* and *Tax Court.*

 The notice will show the 90th (and 150th) day by which you must file your petition with the Tax Court.

Suspension of interest and penalties. Generally, the IRS has 3 years from the date you filed your return (or the date the return was due, if later) to assess any additional tax. However, if you file your return timely (including extensions), interest and certain penalties will be suspended if the IRS does not mail a notice to you, stating your liability and the basis for that liability, within a 36-month period beginning on the later of:

- The date on which you filed your tax return, or

- The due date (without extensions) of your tax return.

If the IRS mails a notice after the 36-month period, interest and certain penalties applicable to the suspension period will be suspended.

The suspension period begins the day after the close of the 36-month period and ends 21 days after the IRS mails a notice to you stating your liability and the basis for that liability. Also, the suspension period applies separately to each notice stating your liability and the basis for that liability received by you.

 The suspension does not apply to a:

- *Failure-to-pay penalty,*

- *Fraudulent tax return,*

- *Penalty, interest, addition to tax, or additional amount with respect to any tax liability shown on your return or with respect to any gross misstatement,*

- *Penalty, interest, addition to tax, or additional amount with respect to any reportable transaction that is not adequately disclosed or any listed transaction, or*

- *Criminal penalty.*

Seeking relief from improperly assessed interest. You can seek relief if interest is assessed for periods during which interest should have been suspended because the IRS did not mail a notice to you in a timely manner.

If you believe that interest was assessed with respect to a period during which interest should have been suspended, submit Form 843, writing "Section 6404(g) Notification" at the top of the form, with the IRS Service Center where you filed your return. The IRS will review the Form 843 and notify you whether interest will be abated. If the IRS does not abate interest, you can pay the disputed interest assessment and file a claim for refund. If your claim is denied or not acted upon within 6 months from the date you filed it, you can file suit for a refund in your United States District Court or in the United States Court of Federal Claims.

If you believe that an IRS officer or employee has made an unreasonable error or delay in performing a ministerial or managerial act (discussed later under *Abatement of Interest Due to Error or Delay by the IRS*), file Form 843 with the IRS Service Center where you filed the tax return. If the Service denies your claim, the Tax Court may be able to review that determination. See *Tax Court can review failure to abate interest,* later under *Abatement of Interest Due to Error or Delay by the IRS.*

If you later agree. If you agree with the examiner's changes after receiving the examination report or the 30-day letter, sign and return either the examination report or the waiver form. Keep a copy for your records. You can pay any additional amount you owe without waiting for a bill. Include interest on the additional tax at the applicable rate. This interest rate is usually for the period from the due date of the return to the date of payment. The examiner can tell you the interest rate(s) or help you figure the amount.

You must pay interest on penalties and on additional tax for failing to file returns, for overstating valuations, for understating valuations on estate and gift tax returns, and for substantially understating tax liability. Interest is generally figured from the date (including extensions) the tax return is required to be filed to the date you pay the penalty and/or additional tax.

If you pay the amount due within 10 business days after the date of notice and demand for immediate payment, you will not have to pay any additional penalties and interest. This period is extended to 21 calendar days if the amount due is less than $100,000.

How To Stop Interest From Accruing

If you think that you will owe additional tax at the end of the examination, you can stop the further accrual of interest by sending money to the IRS to cover all or part of the amount you think you will owe. Interest on part or all of any amount you owe will stop accruing on the date the IRS receives your money.

You can send an amount either in the form of a deposit in the nature of a cash bond or as a payment of tax. Both a deposit and a payment stop any further accrual of interest. However, making a deposit or payment will stop the accrual of interest on only the amount you sent. Because of compounding rules, interest will continue to accrue on accrued interest, even though you have paid the underlying tax.

 To stop the accrual of interest on both tax and interest, you must make a deposit or payment for both the tax and interest that has accrued as of the date of deposit or payment.

Payment or Deposit

Deposits differ from payments in two ways:

1. You can have all or part of your deposit returned to you without filing for a refund. However, if you request and receive your deposit and the IRS later assesses a deficiency for that period and type of tax, interest will be figured as if the funds were never on deposit. Also, your deposit will not be returned if one of the following situations applies:

   a. The IRS assesses a tax liability.

   b. The IRS determines that, by returning the deposit, it may not be able to collect a future deficiency.

   c. The IRS determines that the deposit should be applied against another tax liability.

2. Deposits returned to you will include interest based on the Federal short-term rate determined under section 6621(b).

The deposit returned will be treated as a tax payment to the extent of the disputed tax. A disputed tax means the amount of tax specified at the time of deposit as a reasonable estimate of the maximum amount of any tax owed by you, such as the deficiency proposed in the 30-day letter.

Notice not mailed. If you send money before the IRS mails you a notice of deficiency, you can ask the IRS to treat it as a deposit. You must make your request in writing.

If, after being notified of a proposed liability but before the IRS mails you a notice of deficiency, you send an amount large enough to cover the proposed liability, it will be considered a payment unless you request in writing that it be treated as a deposit.

If the amount you send is at least as much as the proposed liability and you do not request that it be treated as a deposit, the IRS will not send you a notice of deficiency. If you do not receive a notice of deficiency, you cannot take your case to the Tax Court. See *Tax Court,* later under *Appeal Rights.*

Notice mailed. If, after the IRS mails the notice of deficiency, you send money without written instructions, it will be treated as a payment. You will still be able to petition the Tax Court.

If you send money after receiving a notice of deficiency and you have specified in writing that it is a "deposit in the nature of a cash bond," the IRS will treat it as a deposit if you send it before either:

- The close of the 90-day or 150-day period for filing a petition with the Tax Court to appeal the deficiency, or

- The date the Tax Court decision is final, if you have filed a petition.

Using a Deposit To Pay the Tax

If you agree with the examiner's proposed changes after the examination, your deposit will be applied against any amount you may owe. The IRS will not mail you a notice of deficiency and you will not have the right to take your case to the Tax Court.

If you do not agree to the full amount of the deficiency after the examination, the IRS will mail you a notice of deficiency. Your deposit will be applied against the proposed deficiency unless you write to the IRS before the end of the 90-day or 150-day period stating that you still want the money to be treated as a deposit. You will still have the right to take your case to the Tax Court.

Installment Agreement Request

You can request a monthly installment plan if you cannot pay the full amount you owe. To be valid, your request must be approved by the IRS. However, if you owe $10,000 or less in tax and you meet certain other criteria, the IRS must accept your request.

 Before you request an installment agreement, you should consider other less costly alternatives, such as a bank loan. You will continue to be charged interest and penalties on the amount you owe until it is paid in full.

Unless your income is below a certain level, the fee for an approved installment agreement has increased to $105

($52 if you make your payments by electronic funds withdrawal). If your income is below a certain level, you may qualify to pay a reduced fee of $43.

For more information about installment agreements, see Form 9465, Installment Agreement Request.

Interest Netting

If you owe interest to the IRS on an underpayment for the same period the IRS owes you interest on an overpayment, the IRS will figure interest on the underpayment and overpayment at the same interest rate (up to the amount of the overpayment). As a result, the net rate is zero for that period.

Abatement of Interest Due to Error or Delay by the IRS

The IRS may abate (reduce) the amount of interest you owe if the interest is due to an unreasonable error or delay by an IRS officer or employee in performing a ministerial or managerial act (discussed later). Only the amount of interest on income, estate, gift, generation-skipping, and certain excise taxes can be reduced.

The amount of interest will not be reduced if you or anyone related to you contributed significantly to the error or delay. Also, the interest will be reduced only if the error or delay happened after the IRS contacted you in writing about the deficiency or payment on which the interest is based. An audit notification letter is such a contact.

The IRS cannot reduce the amount of interest due to a general administrative decision, such as a decision on how to organize the processing of tax returns.

Ministerial act. This is a procedural or mechanical act, not involving the exercise of judgment or discretion, during the processing of a case after all prerequisites (for example, conferences and review by supervisors) have taken place. A decision concerning the proper application of federal tax law (or other federal or state law) is not a ministerial act.

Example 1. You move from one state to another before the IRS selects your tax return for examination. A letter stating that your return has been selected is sent to your old address and then forwarded to your new address. When you get the letter, you respond with a request that the examination be transferred to the area office closest to your new address. The examination group manager approves your request. After your request has been approved, the transfer is a ministerial act. The IRS can reduce the interest because of any unreasonable delay in transferring the case.

Example 2. An examination of your return reveals tax due for which a notice of deficiency (90-day letter) will be issued. After you and the IRS discuss the issues, the notice is prepared and reviewed. After the review process, issuing the notice of deficiency is a ministerial act. If there is an unreasonable delay in sending the notice of deficiency to you, the IRS can reduce the interest resulting from the delay.

Managerial act. This is an administrative act during the processing of a case that involves the loss of records or the exercise of judgment or discretion concerning the management of personnel. A decision concerning the proper application of federal tax law (or other federal or state law) is not a managerial act.

Example. A revenue agent is examining your tax return. During the middle of the examination, the agent is sent to an extended training course. The agent's supervisor decides not to reassign your case, so the work is unreasonably delayed until the agent returns. Interest from the unreasonable delay can be abated since both the decision to send the agent to the training class and not to reassign the case are managerial acts.

How to request abatement of interest. You request an abatement (reduction) of interest on Form 843. You should file the claim with the IRS service center where you filed the tax return that was affected by the error or delay.

If you have already paid the interest and you would like a credit or refund of interest paid, you must file Form 843 within 3 years from the date you filed your original return or 2 years from the date you paid the interest, whichever is later. If you have not paid any of the interest, these time limitations for filing Form 843 do not apply.

Generally, you should file a separate Form 843 for each tax period and each type of tax. However, complete only one Form 843 if the interest is from an IRS error or delay that affected your tax for more than one tax period or for more than one type of tax (for example, where 2 or more tax years were being examined).

If your request for abatement of interest is denied, you can appeal the decision to the IRS Appeals Office.

Tax Court can review failure to abate interest. The Tax Court can review the IRS' refusal to abate (reduce) interest if all of the following requirements are met.

- You filed a request for abatement of interest (Form 843) with the IRS after July 30, 1996.

- The IRS has mailed you a notice of final determination or a notice of disallowance.

- You file a petition with the Tax Court within 180 days of the mailing of the notice of final determination or the notice of disallowance.

The following requirements must also be met.

- For individual and estate taxpayers — your net worth must not exceed $2 million as of the filing date of your petition for review. For this purpose, individuals filing a joint return shall be treated as separate individuals.

- For charities and certain cooperatives — you must not have more than 500 employees as of the filing date of your petition for review.

- For all other taxpayers — your net worth must not exceed $7 million, and you must not have more than 500 employees as of the filing date of your petition for review.

Abatement of Interest for Individuals Affected by Presidentially Declared Disasters or Military or Terrorist Actions

If you are (or were) affected by a Presidentially declared disaster occurring after 1996 or a terrorist or military action occurring after September 10, 2001, the IRS may abate (reduce) the amount of interest you owe on certain taxes. The IRS may abate interest for the period of any additional time to file or pay that the IRS provides on account of the disaster or the terrorist or military action. The IRS will issue a notice or news release indicating who are affected taxpayers and stating the period of relief.

If you are eligible for relief from interest, but were charged interest for the period of relief, the IRS may retroactively abate your interest. To the extent possible, the IRS can take the following actions.

- Make appropriate adjustments to your account.

- Notify you when the adjustments are made.

- Refund any interest paid by you where appropriate.

For more information on disaster area losses, see *Disaster Area Losses* in Publication 547. For more information on other tax relief for victims of terrorist attacks, see Publication 3920.

Offer in Compromise

In certain circumstances, the IRS will allow you to pay less than the full amount you owe. If you think you may qualify, you should submit your offer by filing Form 656, Offer in Compromise. The IRS may accept your offer for any of the following reasons.

- There is doubt about the amount you owe (or whether you owe it).

- There is doubt as to whether you can pay the amount you owe based on your financial situation.

- An economic hardship would result if you had to pay the full amount owed.

- Your case presents compelling reasons that the IRS determines are a sufficient basis for compromise.

If your offer is rejected, you have 30 days to ask the Appeals Office of the IRS to reconsider your offer.

 The IRS offers fast track mediation services to help taxpayers resolve many issues including a dispute regarding an offer in compromise. For more information, see Publication 3605.

Generally, if you submit an offer in compromise, the IRS will delay certain collection activities. The IRS usually will not levy (take) your property to settle your tax bill during the following periods.

- While the IRS is evaluating your offer in compromise.

- The 30 days immediately after the offer is rejected.

- While your timely-filed appeal is being considered by Appeals.

Also, if the IRS rejects your original offer and you submit a revised offer within 30 days of the rejection, the IRS generally will not levy your property while it considers your revised offer.

For more information about submitting an offer in compromise, see Form 656.

Appeal Rights

Because people sometimes disagree on tax matters, the Service has an appeals system. Most differences can be settled within this system without expensive and time-consuming court trials.

However, your reasons for disagreeing must come within the scope of the tax laws. For example, you cannot appeal your case based only on moral, religious, political, constitutional, conscientious, or similar grounds.

In most instances, you may be eligible to take your case to court if you do not reach an agreement at your appeals conference, or if you do not want to appeal your case to the IRS Office of Appeals. See *Appeals to the Courts*, later, for more information.

Appeal Within the IRS

You can appeal an IRS tax decision to a local Appeals Office, which is separate from and independent of the IRS office taking the action you disagree with. The Appeals Office is the only level of appeal within the IRS. Conferences with Appeals Office personnel are held in an informal manner by correspondence, by telephone, or at a personal conference.

If you want an appeals conference, follow the instructions in the letter you received. Your request will be sent to the Appeals Office to arrange a conference at a convenient time and place. You or your representative should be prepared to discuss all disputed issues at the conference. Most differences are settled at this level.

If agreement is not reached at your appeals conference, you may be eligible to take your case to court. See *Appeals to the Courts*, later.

Protests and Small Case Requests

When you request an Appeals conference, you may also need to file either a formal written protest or a small case request with the office named in the letter you received.

Also, see the special appeal request procedures in Publication 1660. In addition, for the appeal procedures for a spouse or former spouse of a taxpayer seeking relief from joint and several liability on a joint return, see Rev. Proc. 2003-19, which is on page 371 of the Internal Revenue Bulletin 2003-5 at *www.irs.gov/pub/irs-irbs/irb03-05.pdf*.

Written protest. You need to file a written protest in the following cases.

- All employee plan and exempt organization cases without regard to the dollar amount at issue.

- All partnership and S corporation cases without regard to the dollar amount at issue.

- All other cases, unless you qualify for the small case request procedure, or other special appeal procedures such as requesting Appeals consideration of liens, levies, seizures, or installment agreements.

If you must submit a written protest, see the instructions in Publication 5 about the information you need to provide. The IRS urges you to provide as much information as you can, as it will help speed up your appeal. That will save you both time and money.

 Be sure to send the protest within the time limit specified in the letter you received.

Small case request. If the total amount for any tax period is not more than $25,000, you may make a small case request instead of filing a formal written protest. In figuring the total amount, include a proposed increase or decrease in tax (including penalties), or claimed refund. If you are making an offer in compromise, include total unpaid tax, penalty, and interest due. For a small case request, follow the instructions in our letter to you by sending a letter:

- Requesting Appeals consideration,

- Indicating the changes you do not agree with, and

- Indicating the reasons why you do not agree.

Representation

You can represent yourself at your appeals conference, or you can be represented by any federally authorized practitioner, including an attorney, a certified public accountant, an enrolled actuary, or an enrolled agent.

If your representative attends a conference without you, he or she can receive or inspect confidential information only if you have filed a power of attorney or a tax information authorization. You can use a Form 2848 or any other properly written power of attorney or authorization.

You can also bring witnesses to support your position.

Confidentiality privilege. Generally, the same confidentiality protection that you have with an attorney also applies to certain communications that you have with federally authorized practitioners. See *Confidentiality privilege* under *If Your Return Is Examined*, earlier.

Appeals to the Courts

If you and the IRS still disagree after the appeals conference, you may be entitled to take your case to the United States Tax Court, the United States Court of Federal Claims, or the United States District Court. These courts are independent of the IRS.

If you elect to bypass the IRS' appeals system, you may be able to take your case to one of the courts listed above. However, a case petitioned to the United States Tax Court will normally be considered for settlement by an Appeals Office before the Tax Court hears the case.

 If you unreasonably fail to pursue the IRS' appeals system, or if your case is intended primarily to cause a delay, or your position is frivolous or groundless, the Tax Court may impose a penalty of up to $25,000. See Appeal Within the IRS, *earlier.*

Prohibition on requests to taxpayers to give up rights to bring civil action. The Government cannot ask you to waive your right to sue the United States or a Government officer or employee for any action taken in connection with the tax laws. However, your right to sue can be waived if:

- You knowingly and voluntarily waive that right,

- The request to waive that right is made in writing to your attorney or other federally authorized practitioner, or

- The request is made in person and your attorney or other representative is present.

Burden of proof. For court proceedings resulting from examinations started after July 22, 1998, the IRS generally has the burden of proof for any factual issue if you have met the following requirements.

- You introduced credible evidence relating to the issue.

- You complied with all substantiation requirements of the Internal Revenue Code.

- You maintained all records required by the Internal Revenue Code.

- You cooperated with all reasonable requests by the IRS for information regarding the preparation and related tax treatment of any item reported on your tax return.

- You had a net worth of $7 million or less and not more than 500 employees at the time your tax liability is contested in any court proceeding if your tax return is for a corporation, partnership, or trust.

 The burden of proof does not change on an issue when another provision of the tax laws requires a specific burden of proof with respect to that issue.

Use of statistical information. In the case of an individual, the IRS has the burden of proof in court proceedings based on any IRS reconstruction of income solely through the use of statistical information on unrelated taxpayers.

Penalties. The IRS has the burden of initially producing evidence in court proceedings with respect to the liability of any individual taxpayer for any penalty, addition to tax, or additional amount imposed by the tax laws.

Recovering litigation or administrative costs. These are the expenses that you pay to defend your position to the IRS or the courts. You may be able to recover reasonable litigation or administrative costs if all of the following conditions apply.

- You are the prevailing party.

- You exhaust all administrative remedies within the IRS.

- Your net worth is below a certain limit (see *Net worth requirements*, later).

- You do not unreasonably delay the proceeding.

- You apply for administrative costs within 90 days of the date on which the final decision of the IRS Office of Appeals as to the determination of the tax, interest, or penalty was mailed to you.

- You apply for litigation costs within the time frames provided by Tax Court Rule 231.

Prevailing party, reasonable litigation costs, and reasonable administrative costs are explained later.

Note. If the IRS denies your award of administrative costs, and you want to appeal, you must petition the Tax Court within 90 days of the date on which the IRS mails the denial notice.

Prevailing party. Generally, you are the prevailing party if:

- You substantially prevail with respect to the amount in controversy or on the most significant tax issue or set of issues in question, and

- You meet the net worth requirements, discussed later.

You will not be treated as the prevailing party if the United States establishes that its position was substantially justified. The position of the United States is presumed not to be substantially justified if the IRS:

- Did not follow its applicable published guidance (such as regulations, revenue rulings, notices, announcements, private letter rulings, technical advice memoranda, and determination letters issued to the taxpayer) in the proceeding (This presumption can be overcome by evidence.), or

- Has lost in courts of appeal for other circuits on substantially similar issues.

The court will generally decide who is the prevailing party.

Reasonable litigation costs. These include the following costs.

- Reasonable court costs.

- The reasonable costs of studies, analyses, engineering reports, tests, or projects found by the court to be necessary for the preparation of your case.

- The reasonable costs of expert witnesses.

- Attorney fees that generally may not exceed $170 per hour for calendar year 2007. The hourly rate is indexed for inflation. See *Attorney fees*, later.

Reasonable administrative costs. These include the following costs.

- Any administrative fees or similar charges imposed by the IRS.

- The reasonable costs of studies, analyses, engineering reports, tests, or projects.

- The reasonable costs of expert witnesses.

- Attorney fees that generally may not exceed $170 per hour for calendar year 2007. See *Attorney fees*, later.

Timing of costs. Administrative costs can be awarded for costs incurred after the earliest of:

- The date the first letter of proposed deficiency is sent that allows you an opportunity to request administrative review in the IRS Office of Appeals,

- The date you receive notice of the IRS Office of Appeals' decision, or

- The date of the notice of deficiency.

Net worth requirements. An individual taxpayer may be able to recover litigation or administrative costs if the following requirements are met.

- For individuals — your net worth does not exceed $2 million as of the filing date of your petition for review. For this purpose, individuals filing a joint return are treated as separate individuals.

- For estates — your net worth does not exceed $2 million as of the date of the decedent's death.

- For charities and certain cooperatives — you do not have more than 500 employees as of the filing date of your petition for review.

- For all other taxpayers — as of the filing date of your petition for review, your net worth does not exceed $7 million, and you must not have more than 500 employees.

Qualified offer rule. You can also receive reasonable costs and fees and be treated as a prevailing party in a civil action or proceeding if:

- You make a qualified offer to the IRS to settle your case,

- The IRS does not accept that offer, and

- The tax liability (not including interest, unless interest is at issue) later determined by the court is equal to or less than the amount of your qualified offer.

You must also meet the remaining requirements, including the exhaustion of administrative remedies and the net worth requirement, discussed earlier, to get the benefit of the qualified offer rule.

Qualified offer. This is a written offer made by you during the qualified offer period. It must specify both the offered amount of your liability (not including interest) and that it is a qualified offer.

To be a qualified offer, it must remain open from the date it is made until the earliest of:

- The date it is rejected,

- The date the trial begins, or

- 90 days from the date it is made.

Qualified offer period. This period begins on the day the IRS mails you the first letter of proposed deficiency that allows you to request review by the IRS Office of Appeals. It ends 30 days before your case is first set for trial.

Attorney fees. For the calendar year 2007, the basic rate for attorney fees is $170 per hour and can be higher in certain limited circumstances. Those circumstances include the level of difficulty of the issues in the case and the local availability of tax expertise. The basic rate will be subject to a cost-of-living adjustment each year.

 Attorney fees include the fees paid by a taxpayer for the services of anyone who is authorized to practice before the Tax Court or before the IRS. In addition, attorney fees can be awarded in civil actions for unauthorized inspection or disclosure of a taxpayer's return or return information.

Fees can be awarded in excess of the actual amount charged if:

- You are represented for no fee, or for a nominal fee, as a pro bono service, and

- The award is paid to your representative or to your representative's employer.

Jurisdiction for determination of employment status. The Tax Court can review IRS employment status determinations (for example, whether individuals hired by you are in fact your employees or independent contractors) and the amount of employment tax under such determinations. Tax Court review can take place only if, in connection with an audit of any person, there is an actual controversy involving a determination by the IRS as part of an examination that either:

- One or more individuals performing services for that person are employees of that person, or

- That person is not entitled to relief under *Section 530(a) of the Revenue Act of 1978* (discussed later).

The following rules also apply to a Tax Court review of employment status.

- A Tax Court petition to review these determinations can be filed only by the person for whom the services are performed,

- If you receive a Notice of Determination by certified or registered mail, you must file a petition for Tax Court review within 90 days of the date of mailing that notice (150 days if the notice is addressed to you outside the United States),

- If during the Tax Court proceeding, you begin to treat as an employee an individual whose employment status is at issue, the Tax Court will not consider that change in its decision,

- Assessment and collection of tax is suspended while the Tax Court review is taking place,

- There can be a *de novo* review by the Tax Court (a review which does not consider IRS administrative findings), and

- At your request and with the Tax Court's agreement, small tax case procedures (discussed later) are available to simplify the case resolution process when the amount at issue (including additions to tax and penalties) is $50,000 or less for each tax period involved.

For further information, see Publication 3953, Questions and Answers About Tax Court Proceedings for Determination of Employment Status Under IRC Section 7436.

Section 530(a) of the Revenue Act of 1978. This section relieves an employer of certain employment tax responsibilities for individuals not treated as employees. It also provides relief to taxpayers under audit or involved in administrative or judicial proceedings.

Tax Court review of request for relief from joint and several liability on a joint return. As discussed later, at *Relief from joint and several liability on a joint return* under *Claims for Refund*, you can request relief from liability for tax you owe, plus related penalties and interest, that you believe should be paid by your spouse (or former spouse). You also can petition (ask) the Tax Court to review your request for innocent spouse relief or separation of liability if either:

- The IRS sends you a determination notice denying, in whole or in part, your request, or

- You do not receive a determination notice from the IRS within 6 months from the date you file Form 8857.

If you receive a determination notice, you must petition the Tax Court to review your request during the 90-day period that begins on the date the IRS mails the notice. See Publication 971 for more information.

Note. Your spouse or former spouse may file a written protest and request an Appeals conference to protest your claim of innocent spouse relief or separation of liability.

Tax Court

You can take your case to the United States Tax Court if you disagree with the IRS over:

- Income tax,
- Estate tax,
- Gift tax, or
- Certain excise taxes of private foundations, public charities, qualified pension and other retirement plans, or real estate investment trusts.

For information on Tax Court review of a determination of employment status, see *Jurisdiction for determination of employment status*, earlier.

For information on Tax Court review of an IRS refusal to abate interest, see *Tax Court can review failure to abate interest*, earlier under *Examination of Returns*.

For information on Tax Court review of Appeals determinations with respect to lien notices and proposed levies, see Publication 1660.

You cannot take your case to the Tax Court before the IRS sends you a notice of deficiency. You can only appeal your case if you file a petition within 90 days from the date the notice is mailed to you (150 days if it is addressed to you outside the United States).

 The notice will show the 90th (and 150th) day by which you must file your petition with the Tax Court.

Note. If you consent, the IRS can withdraw a notice of deficiency. Once withdrawn, the limits on credits, refunds, and assessments concerning the notice are void, and you and the IRS have the rights and obligations that you had before the notice was issued. The suspension of any time limitation while the notice of deficiency was issued will not change when the notice is withdrawn.

 After the notice is withdrawn, you cannot file a petition with the Tax Court based on the notice. Also, the IRS can later issue a notice of deficiency in a greater or lesser amount than the amount in the withdrawn deficiency.

Generally, the Tax Court hears cases before any tax has been assessed and paid; however, you can pay the tax after the notice of deficiency has been issued and still petition the Tax Court for review. If you do not file your petition on time, the proposed tax will be assessed, a bill will be sent, and you will not be able to take your case to the Tax Court. Under the law, you must pay the tax within 21 days (10 business days if the amount is $100,000 or more). Collection can proceed even if you think that the amount is excessive. Publication 594 explains IRS collection procedures.

If you filed your petition on time, the court will schedule your case for trial at a location convenient to you. You can represent yourself before the Tax Court or you can be represented by anyone admitted to practice before that court.

Small tax case procedure. If the amount in your case is $50,000 or less for any 1 tax year or period, you can request that your case be handled under the small tax case procedure. If the Tax Court approves, you can present your case to the Tax Court for a decision that is final and that you cannot appeal. You can get more information regarding the small tax case procedure and other Tax Court matters from the United States Tax Court, 400 Second Street, N.W., Washington, DC 20217. More information can be found on the Tax Court's website at *www. ustaxcourt.gov*.

Motion to request redetermination of interest. In certain cases, you can file a motion asking the Tax Court to redetermine the amount of interest on either an underpayment or an overpayment. You can do this only in a situation that meets all of the following requirements.

- The IRS has assessed a deficiency that was determined by the Tax Court.
- The assessment included interest.
- You have paid the entire amount of the deficiency plus the interest claimed by the IRS.
- The Tax Court has found that you made an overpayment.

You must file the motion within one year after the decision of the Tax Court becomes final.

District Court and Court of Federal Claims

Generally, the District Court and the Court of Federal Claims hear tax cases only after you have paid the tax and filed a claim for a credit or refund. As explained later under *Claims for Refund*, you can file a claim with the IRS for a credit or refund if you think that the tax you paid is incorrect or excessive. If your claim is totally or partially disallowed by the IRS, you should receive a notice of claim disallowance. If the IRS does not act on your claim within 6 months from the date you filed it, you can then file suit for a refund.

You generally must file suit for a credit or refund no later than 2 years after the IRS informs you that your claim has been rejected. However, you can file suit if it has been 6 months since you filed your claim and the IRS has not yet delivered a decision.

You can file suit for a credit or refund in your United States District Court or in the United States Court of Federal Claims. However, you cannot appeal to the United States Court of Federal Claims if your claim is for credit or refund of a penalty that relates to promoting an abusive tax shelter or to aiding and abetting the understatement of tax liability on someone else's return.

For information about procedures for filing suit in either court, contact the Clerk of your District Court or of the United States Court of Federal Claims. For information on

District Court review of Appeals determinations with respect to lien notices and proposed levies, see Publication 1660.

Refund or Credit of Overpayments Before Final Determination

Any court with proper jurisdiction, including the Tax Court, can order the IRS to refund any part of a tax deficiency that the IRS collects from you during a period when the IRS is not permitted to assess that deficiency, or to levy or engage in any court proceeding to collect that deficiency. In addition, the court can order a refund of any part of an overpayment determined by the Tax Court that is not at issue on appeal to a higher court. The court can order these refunds before its decision on the case is final.

Generally, the IRS is not permitted to take action on a tax deficiency during:

- The 90-day (or 150-day if outside the United States) period that you have to petition a notice of deficiency to the Tax Court, or

- The period that the case is under appeal if a bond is provided.

Claims for Refund

If you believe you have overpaid your tax, you have a limited amount of time in which to file a claim for a credit or refund. You can claim a credit or refund by filing Form 1040X. See *Time for Filing a Claim for Refund*, later.

File your claim by mailing it to the Internal Revenue Service Center where you filed your original return. File a separate form for each year or period involved. Include an explanation of each item of income, deduction, or credit on which you are basing your claim.

Corporations should file Form 1120X, Amended U.S. Corporation Income Tax Return, or other form appropriate to the type of credit or refund claimed.

 See Publication 3920 for information on filing claims for tax forgiveness for individuals affected by terrorist attacks.

Requesting a copy of your tax return. You can obtain a copy of the actual return and all attachments you filed with the IRS for an earlier year. This includes a copy of the Form W-2 or Form 1099 filed with your return. Use Form 4506 to make your request. You will be charged a fee, which you must pay when you submit Form 4506.

Requesting a copy of your tax account information. Use Form 4506-T, Request for Transcript of Tax Return, to request free copies of your tax return transcript, tax account transcript, record of account, verification of nonfiling, or Form W-2, Form 1099 series, Form 1098 series, or Form 5498 series transcript. The tax return transcript contains most of the line items of a tax return. A tax account transcript contains information on the financial status of the account, such as payments, penalty assessments, and adjustments. A record of account is a combination of line item information and later adjustments to the account. Form W-2, Form 1099 series, Form 1098 series, or Form 5498 series transcript contains data from these information returns.

Penalty for erroneous claim for refund. If you claim an excessive amount of tax refund or credit relating to income tax (other than a claim relating to the earned income credit), you may be liable for a penalty of 20% of the amount that is determined to be excessive. An excessive amount is the amount of the claim for refund or credit that is more than the amount of claim allowable for the tax year. The penalty may be waived if you can show that you had a reasonable basis for making the claim.

Time for Filing a Claim for Refund

Generally, you must file a claim for a credit or refund within 3 years from the date you filed your original return or 2 years from the date you paid the tax, whichever is later. If you do not file a claim within this period, you may no longer be entitled to a credit or a refund.

If the due date to file a return or a claim for a credit or refund is a Saturday, Sunday, or legal holiday, it is filed on time if it is filed on the next business day. Returns you filed before the due date are considered filed on the due date. This is true even when the due date is a Saturday, Sunday, or legal holiday.

Disaster area claims for refund. If you live in a Presidentially declared disaster area or are affected by terroristic or military action, the deadline to file a claim for a refund may be postponed. This section discusses the special rules that apply to Presidentially declared disaster area refunds.

A Presidentially declared disaster is a disaster that occurred in an area declared by the President to be eligible for federal assistance under the Disaster Relief and Emergency Assistance Act.

Postponed refund deadlines. The IRS may postpone for up to 1 year the deadlines for filing a claim for refund. The postponement can be used by taxpayers who are affected by a Presidentially declared disaster. The IRS may also postpone deadlines for filing income and employment tax returns, paying income and employment taxes, and making contributions to a traditional IRA or Roth IRA. For more information, see Publication 547.

If any deadline is postponed, the IRS will publicize the postponement in your area and publish a news release, revenue ruling, revenue procedure, notice, announcement, or other guidance in the Internal Revenue Bulletin.

 A list of the areas eligible for assistance under the Disaster Relief and Emergency Assistance Act is available at the Federal Emergency Management Agency (FEMA) website at www.fema.gov and at the IRS website at www.irs.gov.

Nonfilers can get refund of overpayments paid within 3-year period. The Tax Court can consider taxes paid during the 3-year period preceding the date of a notice of deficiency for determining any refund due to a nonfiler.

This means that if you do not file your return, and you receive a notice of deficiency in the third year after the due date (with extensions) of your return and file suit with the Tax Court to contest the notice of deficiency, you may be able to receive a refund of excessive amounts paid within the 3-year period preceding the date of the notice of deficiency.

 The IRS may postpone for up to 1 year certain tax deadlines, including the time for filing claims for refund, for taxpayers who are affected by a terrorist attack occurring after September 10, 2001. For more information, see Publication 3920.

Claim for refund by estates electing the installment method of payment. In certain cases where an estate has elected to make tax payments through the installment method, the executor can file a suit for refund with a Federal District Court or the U.S. Court of Federal Claims before all the installment payments have been made. However, all the following must be true before a suit can be filed.

- The estate consists largely of an interest in a closely-held business.

- All installment payments due on or before the date the suit is filed have been made.

- No accelerated installment payments have been made.

- No Tax Court case is pending with respect to any estate tax liability.

- If a notice of deficiency was issued to the estate regarding its liability for estate tax, the time for petitioning the Tax Court has passed.

- No proceeding is pending for a declaratory judgment by the Tax Court on whether the estate is eligible to pay tax in installments.

- The executor has not included any previously litigated issues in the current suit for refund.

- The executor does not discontinue making installment payments timely, while the court considers the suit for refund.

 If in its final decision on the suit for refund the court redetermines the estate's tax liability, the IRS must refund any part of the estate tax amount that is disallowed. This includes any part of the disallowed amount previously collected by the IRS.

Protective claim for refund. If your right to a refund is contingent on future events and may not be determinable until after the time period for filing a claim for refund expires, you can file a protective claim for refund. A protective claim can be either a formal claim or an amended return for credit or refund. Protective claims are often based on current litigation or expected changes in the tax law, other legislation, or regulations. A protective claim preserves your right to claim a refund when the contingency is resolved. A protective claim does not have to state a particular dollar amount or demand an immediate refund. However, to be valid, a protective claim must:

- Be in writing and be signed,

- Include your name, address, social security number or individual taxpayer identification number, and other contact information,

- Identify and describe the contingencies affecting the claim,

- Clearly alert the IRS to the essential nature of the claim, and

- Identify the specific year(s) for which a refund is sought.

Generally, the IRS will delay action on the protective claim until the contingency is resolved. Once the contingency is resolved, the IRS may obtain additional information necessary to process the claim and then either allow or disallow the claim.

Mail your protective claim for refund to the address listed in the instructions for Form 1040X, under *Where To File.*

Exceptions

The limits on your claim for refund can be affected by the type of item that forms the basis of your claim.

Special refunds. If you file a claim for refund based on one of the items listed below, the limits discussed earlier under *Time for Filing a Claim for Refund* may not apply. These special items are:

- A bad debt,

- A worthless security,

- A payment or accrual of foreign tax,

- A net operating loss carryback, and

- A carryback of certain tax credits.

The limits discussed earlier also may not apply if you have signed an agreement to extend the period of assessment of tax.

 For information on special rules on filing claims for an individual affected by a terrorist attack, see Publication 3920.

Periods of financial disability. If you are an individual (not a corporation or other taxpaying entity), the period of limitations on credits and refunds can be suspended during periods when you cannot manage your financial affairs because of physical or mental impairment that is medically determinable and either:

- Has lasted or can be expected to last continuously for at least 12 months, or

- Can be expected to result in death.

The period for filing a claim for refund will not be suspended for any time that someone else, such as your spouse or guardian, was authorized to act for you in financial matters.

To claim financial disability, you generally must submit the following statements with your claim for credit or refund:

1. A written statement signed by a physician, qualified to make the determination, that sets forth:

   a. The name and a description of your physical or mental impairment,

   b. The physician's medical opinion that your physical or mental impairment prevented you from managing your financial affairs,

   c. The physician's medical opinion that your physical or mental impairment was or can be expected to result in death, or that it has lasted (or can be expected to last) for a continuous period of not less than 12 months, and

   d. To the best of the physician's knowledge, the specific time period during which you were prevented by such physical or mental impairment from managing your financial affairs, and

2. A written statement by the person signing the claim for credit or refund that no person, including your spouse, was authorized to act on your behalf in financial matters during the period described in paragraph (1)(d) of the physician's statement. Alternatively, if a person was authorized to act on your behalf in financial matters during any part of the period described in that paragraph, the beginning and ending dates of the period of time the person was so authorized.

 The period of limitations will not be suspended on any claim for refund that (without regard to this provision) was barred as of July 22, 1998.

Limit on Amount of Refund

If you file your claim within 3 years after filing your return, the credit or refund cannot be more than the part of the tax paid within the 3 years (plus the length of any extension of time granted for filing your return) before you filed the claim.

Example 1. You made estimated tax payments of $1,000 and got an automatic extension of time from April 15, 2003, to August 15, 2003, to file your 2002 income tax return. When you filed your return on that date, you paid an additional $200 tax. Three years later, on August 15, 2006, you file an amended return and claim a refund of $700. Because you filed within 3 years after filing your return, you could get a refund of any tax paid after April 15, 2003.

Example 2. The situation is the same as in Example 1, except that you filed your return on October 31, 2003, 2½

months after the extension period ended. You paid an additional $200 on that date. Three years later, on October 27, 2006, you file an amended return and claim a refund of $700. Although you filed your claim within 3 years from the date you filed your original return, the refund is limited to $200. The estimated tax of $1,000 was paid before the 3 years plus the 4-month extension period.

Claim filed after the 3-year period. If you file a claim after the 3-year period, but within 2 years from the time you paid the tax, the credit or refund cannot be more than the tax you paid within the 2 years immediately before you filed the claim.

Example. You filed your 2002 tax return on April 15, 2003. You paid $500 in tax. On November 2, 2004, after an examination of your 2002 return, you had to pay $200 in additional tax. On May 2, 2006, you file a claim for a refund of $300. Your refund will be limited to the $200 you paid during the 2 years immediately before you filed your claim.

Processing Claims for Refund

Claims are usually processed shortly after they are filed. Your claim may be denied, accepted as filed, or it may be examined. If a claim is examined, the procedures are almost the same as in the examination of a tax return.

However, if you are filing a claim for credit or refund based only on contested income tax or on estate tax or gift tax issues considered in previously examined returns and you do not want to appeal within the IRS, you should request in writing that the claim be immediately rejected. A notice of claim disallowance will then be promptly sent to you. You have 2 years from the date of mailing of the notice of disallowance to file a refund suit in the United States District Court or in the United States Court of Federal Claims.

Explanation of Any Claim for Refund Disallowance

The IRS must explain to you the specific reasons why your claim for refund is disallowed or partially disallowed. Claims for refund are disallowed based on a preliminary review or on further examination. Some of the reasons your claim may be disallowed include the following.

- It was filed late.
- It was based solely on the unconstitutionality of the revenue acts.
- It was waived as part of a settlement.
- It covered a tax year or issues which were part of a closing agreement or an offer in compromise.
- It was related to a return closed by a final court order.

If your claim is disallowed for these reasons, or any other reason, the IRS must send you an explanation.

Reduced Refund

Your refund may be reduced by an additional tax liability. Also, your refund may be reduced by amounts you owe for past-due child support, debts you owe to another federal agency, or past-due legally enforceable state income tax obligations. You will be notified if this happens. For those reductions, you cannot use the appeal and refund procedures discussed in this publication. However, you may be able to take action against the other agency.

Offset of past-due state income tax obligations against overpayments. Federal tax overpayments can be used to offset past-due, legally enforceable state income tax obligations. For the offset procedure to apply, your federal income tax return must show an address in the state that requests the offset. In addition, the state must first:

- Notify you by certified mail with return receipt that the state plans to ask for an offset against your federal income tax overpayment,

- Give you at least 60 days to show that some or all of the state income tax is not past due or not legally enforceable,

- Consider any evidence from you in determining that income tax is past due and legally enforceable,

- Satisfy any other requirements to ensure that there is a valid past-due, legally enforceable state income tax obligation, and

- Show that all reasonable efforts to obtain payment have been made before requesting the offset.

Past-due, legally enforceable state income tax obligation. This is an obligation (debt):

- Established by a court decision or administrative hearing and no longer subject to judicial review, or

- That is assessed, uncollected, can no longer be redetermined, and is less than 10 years overdue.

Offset priorities. Overpayments are offset in the following order.

1. Federal income tax owed.

2. Past-due child support.

3. Past-due, legally enforceable debt owed to a federal agency.

4. Past-due, legally enforceable state income tax debt.

5. Future federal income tax liability.

Note. If more than one state agency requests an offset for separate debts, the offsets apply against your overpayment in the order in which the debts accrued. In addition, state income tax includes any local income tax administered by the chief tax administration agency of a state.

Note. The Tax Court cannot decide the validity or merits of the credits or offsets (for example, collection of delinquent child support or student loan payments) made that reduce or eliminate a refund to which you were otherwise entitled.

Injured spouse exception. When a joint return is filed and the refund is used to pay one spouse's past-due child support, spousal support, or a federal debt, the other spouse can be considered an injured spouse. An injured spouse can get a refund for his or her share of the overpayment that would otherwise be used to pay the past-due amount.

You are considered an injured spouse if:

1. You are not legally obligated to pay the past-due amount and

2. You meet any of the following conditions:

   a. You made and reported tax payments (such as federal income tax withheld from wages or estimated tax payments).

   b. You had earned income (such as wages, salaries, or self-employment income) and claimed the earned income credit or the additional child tax credit.

   c. You claimed a refundable credit, such as the health coverage tax credit or the refundable credit for prior year minimum tax.

Note. If your residence was in a community property state at any time during the year, you can file Form 8379 even if only item (1) above applies.

If you are an injured spouse, you can obtain your portion of the joint refund by completing Form 8379. Follow the instructions on the form.

Relief from joint and several liability on a joint return. Generally, joint and several liability applies to all joint returns. This means that both you and your spouse (or former spouse) are liable for any tax shown on a joint return plus any understatement of tax that may become due later. This is true even if a divorce decree states that a former spouse will be responsible for any amounts due on previously filed joint returns.

In some cases, a spouse will be relieved of the tax, interest, and penalties on a joint tax return. Three types of relief are available.

- Innocent spouse relief.

- Separation of liability.

- Equitable relief.

Form 8857. Each kind of relief is different and has different requirements. You must file Form 8857, Request for Innocent Spouse Relief, to request relief. Form 8857 must be filed no later than 2 years after the date on which the IRS first attempted to collect the tax from you. See the instructions for Form 8857 and Publication 971 for more information on these kinds of relief and who may qualify for them.

How To Get Tax Help

You can get help with unresolved tax issues, order free publications and forms, ask tax questions, and get information from the IRS in several ways. By selecting the method that is best for you, you will have quick and easy access to tax help.

Contacting your Taxpayer Advocate. The Taxpayer Advocate Service (TAS) is an independent organization within the IRS whose employees assist taxpayers who are experiencing economic harm, who are seeking help in resolving tax problems that have not been resolved through normal channels, or who believe that an IRS system or procedure is not working as it should.

You can contact the TAS by calling the TAS toll-free case intake line at 1-877-777-4778 or TTY/TDD 1-800-829-4059 to see if you are eligible for assistance. You can also call or write to your local taxpayer advocate, whose phone number and address are listed in your local telephone directory and in Publication 1546, Taxpayer Advocate Service — Your Voice at the IRS. You can file Form 911, Request for Taxpayer Advocate Service Assistance (And Application for Taxpayer Assistance Order), or ask an IRS employee to complete it on your behalf. For more information, go to *www.irs.gov/advocate*.

Taxpayer Advocacy Panel (TAP). The TAP listens to taxpayers, identifies taxpayer issues, and makes suggestions for improving IRS services and customer satisfaction. If you have suggestions for improvements, contact the TAP, toll free at 1-888-912-1227 or go to *www.improveirs.org*.

Low Income Taxpayer Clinics (LITCs). LITCs are independent organizations that provide low income taxpayers with representation in federal tax controversies with the IRS for free or for a nominal charge. The clinics also provide tax education and outreach for taxpayers with limited English proficiency or who speak English as a second language. Publication 4134, Low Income Taxpayer Clinic List, provides information on clinics in your area. It is available at *www.irs.gov* or at your local IRS office.

Free tax services. To find out what services are available, get Publication 910, IRS Guide to Free Tax Services. It contains a list of free tax publications and describes other free tax information services, including tax education and assistance programs and a list of TeleTax topics.

Accessible versions of IRS published products are available on request in a variety of alternative formats for people with disabilities.

 Internet. You can access the IRS website at *www.irs.gov* 24 hours a day, 7 days a week to:

- *E-file* your return. Find out about commercial tax preparation and *e-file* services available free to eligible taxpayers.

- Check the status of your 2007 refund. Click on *Where's My Refund*. Wait at least 6 weeks from the date you filed your return (3 weeks if you filed electronically). Have your 2007 tax return available because you will need to know your social security number, your filing status, and the exact whole dollar amount of your refund.

- Download forms, instructions, and publications.

- Order IRS products online.

- Research your tax questions online.

- Search publications online by topic or keyword.

- View Internal Revenue Bulletins (IRBs) published in the last few years.

- Figure your withholding allowances using the withholding calculator online at *www.irs.gov/individuals*.

- Determine if Form 6251 must be filed using our Alternative Minimum Tax (AMT) Assistant.

- Sign up to receive local and national tax news by email.

- Get information on starting and operating a small business.

 Phone. Many services are available by phone.

- *Ordering forms, instructions, and publications.* Call 1-800-829-3676 to order current-year forms, instructions, and publications, and prior-year forms and instructions. You should receive your order within 10 days.

- *Asking tax questions.* Call the IRS with your tax questions at 1-800-829-1040.

- *Solving problems.* You can get face-to-face help solving tax problems every business day in IRS Taxpayer Assistance Centers. An employee can explain IRS letters, request adjustments to your account, or help you set up a payment plan. Call your local Taxpayer Assistance Center for an appointment. To find the number, go to *www.irs.gov/localcontacts* or look in the phone book under *United States Government, Internal Revenue Service*.

- *TTY/TDD equipment.* If you have access to TTY/TDD equipment, call 1-800-829-4059 to ask tax questions or to order forms and publications.

- *TeleTax topics.* Call 1-800-829-4477 to listen to pre-recorded messages covering various tax topics.

- *Refund information.* To check the status of your 2007 refund, call 1-800-829-4477 and press 1 for automated refund information or call 1-800-829-1954. Be sure to wait at least 6 weeks from the date you filed your return (3 weeks if you filed electronically). Have your 2007 tax return available because you will need to know your social security number, your filing status, and the exact whole dollar amount of your refund.

Evaluating the quality of our telephone services. To ensure IRS representatives give accurate, courteous, and professional answers, we use several methods to evaluate the quality of our telephone services. One method is for a second IRS representative to listen in on or record random telephone calls. Another is to ask some callers to complete a short survey at the end of the call.

 Walk-in. Many products and services are available on a walk-in basis.

- *Products.* You can walk in to many post offices, libraries, and IRS offices to pick up certain forms, instructions, and publications. Some IRS offices, libraries, grocery stores, copy centers, city and county government offices, credit unions, and office supply stores have a collection of products available to print from a CD or photocopy from reproducible proofs. Also, some IRS offices and libraries have the Internal Revenue Code, regulations, Internal Revenue Bulletins, and Cumulative Bulletins available for research purposes.

- *Services.* You can walk in to your local Taxpayer Assistance Center every business day for personal, face-to-face tax help. An employee can explain IRS letters, request adjustments to your tax account, or help you set up a payment plan. If you need to resolve a tax problem, have questions about how the tax law applies to your individual tax return, or you're more comfortable talking with someone in person, visit your local Taxpayer Assistance Center where you can spread out your records and talk with an IRS representative face-to-face. No appointment is necessary, but if you prefer, you can call your local Center and leave a message requesting an appointment to resolve a tax account issue. A representative will call you back within 2 business days to schedule an in-person appointment at your convenience. To find the number, go to *www.irs.gov/localcontacts* or look in the phone book under *United States Government, Internal Revenue Service.*

 Mail. You can send your order for forms, instructions, and publications to the address below. You should receive a response within 10 days after your request is received.

Internal Revenue Service
1201 N. Mitsubishi Motorway
Bloomington, IL 61704-6613

 CD/DVD for tax products. You can order Publication 1796, IRS Tax Products CD/DVD, and obtain:

- Current-year forms, instructions, and publications.

- Prior-year forms, instructions, and publications.

- Bonus: Historical Tax Products DVD - Ships with the final release.

- Tax Map: an electronic research tool and finding aid.

- Tax law frequently asked questions.

- Tax Topics from the IRS telephone response system.

- Fill-in, print, and save features for most tax forms.

- Internal Revenue Bulletins.

- Toll-free and email technical support.

- The CD which is released twice during the year.
  – The first release will ship the beginning of January 2008.
  – The final release will ship the beginning of March 2008.

Purchase the CD/DVD from National Technical Information Service (NTIS) at *www.irs.gov/cdorders* for $35 (no handling fee) or call 1-877-CDFORMS (1-877-233-6767) toll free to buy the CD/DVD for $35 (plus a $5 handling fee). Price is subject to change.

 CD for small businesses. Publication 3207, The Small Business Resource Guide CD for 2007, is a must for every small business owner or any taxpayer about to start a business. This year's CD includes:

- Helpful information, such as how to prepare a business plan, find financing for your business, and much more.

- All the business tax forms, instructions, and publications needed to successfully manage a business.

- Tax law changes for 2007.

- Tax Map: an electronic research tool and finding aid.

- Web links to various government agencies, business associations, and IRS organizations.

- "Rate the Product" survey—your opportunity to suggest changes for future editions.

- A site map of the CD to help you navigate the pages of the CD with ease.

- An interactive "Teens in Biz" module that gives practical tips for teens about starting their own business, creating a business plan, and filing taxes.

An updated version of this CD is available each year in early April. You can get a free copy by calling 1-800-829-3676 or by visiting *www.irs.gov/smallbiz*.

Index

To help us develop a more useful index, please let us know if you have ideas for index entries. See "Comments and Suggestions" in the "Introduction" for the ways you can reach us.

The IRS Collection Process
Publication 594

This publication provides a general description of the IRS collection process. The collection process is a series of actions that the IRS can take against you to collect the taxes you owe if you don't voluntarily pay them. The collection process will begin if you don't make your required payments in full and on time, after receiving your bill.

Please keep in mind that this publication is for information only, and may not account for every tax collection scenario. It's also not a technical analysis of tax law.

If you have questions or need help
Please visit www.irs.gov/formspubs/ to find all the IRS tax forms and publications mentioned here, or to do a keyword search on any topic.

You can also visit your local IRS office, or call the number on your bill. If you don't have a bill, please call:
- 1-800-829-1040 (individuals)
- 1-800-829-4933 (businesses)

Overview:
Filing a tax return, billing, and collection

After you file your tax return, we'll determine if you owe taxes. If you owe, we'll send a bill for the amount due, including any penalties and interest. You're required to pay this, so if you avoid payment, we can take collection actions to recover your debt. Our goal is always to work with you to resolve your case before we have to take collection actions.

General steps from billing to collection

You file your tax return. Most returns are filed annually (by April 15th) or quarterly.

1. If you owe taxes, we'll send you a bill. This is your first bill for tax due. Based on your return, we'll calculate how much tax you owe, plus any interest and penalties.

2. If you don't pay your first bill, we'll send you at least one more bill. Remember, interest and penalties continue to accrue until you've paid your full amount due.

3. If you still don't pay after you receive your final bill, we'll begin collection actions. Collection actions can range from applying your previous tax year's refund to tax due to seizing your property and assets.

What you should do when you get an IRS bill

If you agree with the information on the bill, pay the full amount before the due date. If you can't pay the full amount due, pay as much as you can, and immediately contact us to explain your situation. Based on your ability to pay, we may provide you with alternate payment options.

If you disagree with the information on the bill, call the number on the bill, or visit your local IRS office. Be sure to have a copy of the bill and any tax returns, cancelled checks, or other records that will help us understand why you believe your bill is wrong. If we find that you're right, we'll adjust your account and, if necessary, send a revised bill.

If you don't pay the amount due or tell us why you disagree with it, we may take collection actions.

If you're involved in bankruptcy proceedings, please notify us immediately. The bankruptcy may not eliminate your tax debt, but we may temporarily stop collection. Call the number on your bill or 1-800-973-0424.

Who to contact for help

The Internal Revenue Service (IRS)
Please don't hesitate to contact us with any questions you may have. Call the number on your bill or 1-800-829-1040. You can also visit your local IRS office to speak with an IRS representative in person.

Taxpayer Advocate Service (TAS)
The Taxpayer Advocate Service is your voice at the IRS. It helps taxpayers whose problems with the IRS are causing financial difficulties, who have tried but haven't been able to resolve their problems with the IRS, and those who believe an IRS system or procedure is not working as it should. If you believe you're eligible for Taxpayer Advocate Service assistance, call the toll-free number at 1-877-777-4778 or TTY/TDD 1-800-829-4059. For more information, go to www.irs.gov/advocate.

Low Income Taxpayer Clinics (LITCs)
Low Income Taxpayer Clinics are independent from the IRS. Some clinics serve individuals whose income is below a certain level and who need to resolve a tax problem. These clinics provide professional representation before the IRS or in court on audits, appeals, tax collection disputes, and other issues for free or for a small fee. Some clinics can provide information about taxpayer rights and responsibilities in many different languages for individuals who speak English as a second language. For more information and to find a clinic near you, see the Low Income Taxpayer Clinics page on www.taxpayeradvocate.irs.gov or Publication 4134, Low Income Taxpayer Clinic List. This publication is also available by calling 1-800-829-3676 or at your local IRS office.

Ways to pay your taxes

To minimize interest and penalties, we recommend paying your taxes in full. However, if you're unable to pay in full, you can request an Installment Agreement or Offer in Compromise. These payment plans allow you to pay your taxes in installments over time, to pay less than you owe, or both. Keep in mind it's also important to stay current on your payments for future taxes. This means making your estimated tax payments, withholding payments, or federal tax deposits as necessary.

Options for paying in full

Pay with electronic funds transfer
For a convenient, secure way to pay, you can use the Electronic Federal Tax Payment System (EFTPS). To enroll, visit www.eftps.com or call 1-800-555-4477. For more information, see Publication 966, Electronic Choices to Pay All Your Federal Taxes.

Pay with your credit or debit card
For a fee, you can pay by credit or debit card by using an electronic payment service provider. For more information on making a payment using a credit or debit card, visit www.irs.gov/e-pay.

Pay by mail or in person at a local IRS office

You can mail a check to us at the address listed on your bill or bring it to your local IRS office. For a listing of offices near you, please visit www.irs.gov/localcontacts/index.html.

Options if you can't pay in full now

Apply for an Installment Agreement

An Installment Agreement with the IRS means that we'll allow you to make smaller periodic payments over time if you can't pay the full amount at once. There are several ways to apply for an Installment Agreement:

- **Online** at www.irs.gov/individuals/article/0,,id=149373,00.html. Only individuals who owe $50,000 or less can apply online.
- **By phone** Please call the number on your bill or 1-800-829-1040.
- **By mail** Please complete Form 9465, Installment Agreement Request, if you owe $25,000 or less. Complete Form 9465-FS, Installment Agreement Request, if you owe more than $25,000. Or you can use Form 2159, Payroll Deduction Agreement. Mail your form to the address on your bill.
- **In person** at your local IRS office.

If you request a payment plan, you can reduce penalties and interest by making voluntary payments according to the proposed plan's terms until you're notified whether we've accepted your payment plan request. Keep in mind that our acceptance of your interim payments doesn't mean we've approved your request. We'll notify you in writing once we've made our decision.

With an Installment Agreement, you can pay by check, direct debit, through payroll deductions, or electronic funds transfer. Keep in mind there's a user fee for Installment Agreements. However, if you meet our low-income guidelines, you can pay a reduced user fee. For more information, see Form 13844, Application for Reduced User Fee for Installment Agreements.

To be eligible for an Installment Agreement, you must file all required tax returns. Prior to approving your Installment Agreement request, we may ask you to complete a Collection Information Statement (Form 433-F, 433-A and/or Form 433-B) and provide proof of your financial status. Please have your financial information available if you apply over the phone or at an IRS office. For more information, see Publication 1854, How to Complete a Collection Information Statement (Form 433-A).

If we approve your request, we'll still charge applicable interest and penalties until you pay the amount or balance due in full, and may file a Notice of Federal Tax Lien (see page 4.) If we reject your Installment Agreement request, you may request that the Office of Appeals review your case. For more information, see Publication 1660, Collection Appeal Rights.

If you're unable to meet the terms of your approved Installment Agreement, please contact us immediately.

Apply for an Offer in Compromise (OIC)

You may be eligible for an Offer in Compromise if you can't pay the amount you owe in full or through installments. By requesting an Offer in Compromise, you're asking to settle unpaid taxes for less than the full amount you owe. We may accept an Offer in Compromise if:

- We agree that your tax debt may not be accurate,
- You have insufficient assets and income to pay the amount due, or
- Because of your exceptional circumstances, paying the amount due would cause an economic hardship or would be unjust.

For an Offer in Compromise to be considered, you must pay an application fee and make an initial or periodic payment. However, low income taxpayers may qualify for a waiver of the application fee and initial or periodic payment.

For more information, please see the Low Income Certification on Form 656, Offer in Compromise.

To apply for an Offer in Compromise, complete one of the following forms:

- **Form 656-L, Offer in Compromise (Doubt as to Liability)** Complete this if you think your tax debt isn't accurate.
- **Form 656, Offer in Compromise** Complete this if you're unable to pay the amount due, have an economic hardship, or other special circumstance that would cause paying the amount due to be unjust.

For more information, see Form 656-B, Offer in Compromise Booklet or visit www.irs.gov/individuals/article/0,,id=243822,00.html.

If you need more time to pay

Ask that we delay collection

If you can't pay any of the amount due, you can request that we delay collection until you're able to pay. Prior to approving your request, we may ask you to complete a Collection Information Statement and provide proof of your financial status. Please remember that even if we delay collection, we'll still charge applicable penalties and interest until you pay the full amount, and we may file a Notice of Federal Tax Lien (see page 4). We may also request updated financial information during this temporary delay to review your ability to pay.

How long we have to collect taxes

We can attempt to collect your taxes up to 10 years from the date they were assessed. However, there are exceptions to this time frame. For example, by law, we'll suspend and extend collection while:

- We're considering your request for an Installment Agreement or Offer in Compromise. If your request is rejected, we'll suspend collection for another 30 days, and during any period the Appeals Office is considering your appeal request.
- You live outside the U.S. continuously for at least 6 months. Collection is suspended while you're outside the U.S. and, if at the time of your return the normal collection period would expire before 6 months from the date of your return, the extended period won't expire before the expiration of the 6 months after your return.

- The tax periods we're collecting on are included in a bankruptcy with an automatic stay. We'll suspend collection for the time period we can't collect because of the automatic stay, plus 6 months.
- You request a Collection Due Process hearing. Collection will be suspended from the date of your request until a Notice of Determination is issued or the Tax Court's decision is final.
- We're considering your request for Innocent Spouse Relief. Collection will be suspended from the date of your request until 90 days after a Notice of Determination is issued, or if you file a timely petition to the Tax Court, until 60 days after the Tax Court's final decision. If you appeal the Tax Court's decision to a U.S. Court of Appeals, the collection period will begin 60 days after the appeal is filed, unless a bond is posted.

How to appeal an IRS decision

You can appeal most collection actions. Your main options for appeals are the following:

Collection Due Process (CDP)

The purpose of a Collection Due Process hearing is to review collection actions that were taken or have been proposed. You can request a Collection Due Process hearing if you receive any of the following notices:

- Notice of Federal Tax Lien Filing and Your Right to a Hearing
- Final Notice—Notice of Intent to Levy and Notice of Your Right to a Hearing
- Notice of Jeopardy Levy and Right of Appeal
- Notice of Levy on Your State Tax Refund—Notice of Your Right to a Hearing
- Notice of Levy and of Your Right to a Hearing

To request a Collection Due Process hearing, complete Form 12153, Request for a Collection Due Process or Equivalent Hearing, and send it to the address on your notice. You have 30 days from the date of the notice to request a Collection Due Process hearing. You can also request an Equivalent Hearing within one year from the date of the notice.

Collection Appeals Program (CAP)

Under the Collections Appeals Program, if you disagree with an IRS employee's decision and want to appeal it, you can ask their manager to review your case. If you then disagree with the manager's decision, you may continue with the Collection Appeals Program as outlined in Publication 1660. Instances in which you can pursue the Collection Appeals Program include, but aren't limited to:

- Before or after we file a Notice of Federal Tax Lien
- Before or after we seize ("levy") your property
- After we reject, terminate, or propose to terminate your Installment Agreement (a conference with the manager is recommended, but not required)

For more information about the Collection Due Process and Collection Appeals Program, please see Publication 1660, Collection Appeal Rights.

If you don't pay on time: Understanding collection actions

There are several words and phrases particular to the collection process. Here, we've defined some of the most commonly used collection terms:

Federal tax lien: A legal claim against all your current and future property, such as a house or car, and rights to property, such as wages and bank accounts. The lien automatically comes into existence if you don't pay your amount due after receiving your first bill.

Notice of Federal Tax Lien (NFTL): A public notice to creditors. It notifies them that there is a federal tax lien that attaches to all your current and future property and rights to property.

Levy: A legal seizure of property or rights to property to satisfy a tax debt. When property is seized ("levied"), it will be sold to help pay your tax debt. If wages or bank accounts are seized, the money will be applied to your tax debt.

Seizure: There is no legal difference between a seizure and a levy. Throughout this publication, we'll use both terms interchangeably.

Notice of Intent to Levy and Notice of Your Right to a Hearing: Generally, before property is seized, we have to send you this notice. If you don't pay your overdue taxes, make other arrangements to satisfy the tax debt, or request a hearing within 30 days of the date of this notice, we may seize your property.

Summons: A summons legally compels you or a third party to meet with the IRS and provide information, documents, or testimony.

Collection actions in detail

Federal tax lien: A legal claim against property

A lien is a legal claim against all your current and future property. When you don't pay your first bill for taxes due, a lien is created by law and attaches to your property. It applies to property (such as your home and car) and to any current and future rights you have to property.

Notice of Federal Tax Lien: Provides public notice to creditors that a lien exists

A Notice of Federal Tax Lien gives public notice to creditors. We file the Notice of Federal Tax Lien so we can establish the priority of our claim versus the claims of other creditors. The Notice of Federal Tax Lien is filed with local or state authorities, such as county registers of deeds or the Secretary of State offices.

If a Notice of Federal Tax Lien is filed against you, it's often reported by consumer credit reporting agencies. This can have a negative effect on your credit rating and make it difficult for you to receive credit (such as a loan or credit card). Employers, landlords, and others may also use this information and not favorably view the fact that a Notice of Federal Tax Lien has been filed against you.

What to do if a Notice of Federal Tax Lien is filed against you

You should pay the full amount you owe immediately. Keep in mind the Notice of Federal Tax Lien only shows your assessed balance as of the date of the notice. It doesn't show your payoff balance or include our charges for filing and releasing the lien. To find out the full amount you must pay to have the lien released, call 1-800-913-6050. If you have questions, call the number on your lien notice or 1-800-829-1040 or visit www.irs.gov/businesses/small/article/0,,id=108339,00.html.

How to appeal a Notice of Federal Tax Lien

Within 5 business days of filing the Notice of Federal Tax Lien, we'll send you a Notice of Your Right to a Collection Due Process Hearing. You'll have until the date shown on the notice to request a Collection Due Process hearing with the Office of Appeals. Send your Collection Due Process hearing request to the address on the notice. For more information, see Form 12153, Request for a Collection Due Process or Equivalent Hearing.

After your Collection Due Process hearing, the Office of Appeals will issue a determination on whether the Notice of Federal Tax Lien should remain filed, or whether it should be withdrawn, released, discharged, or subordinated. If you disagree with the determination, you have 30 days after it's made to seek a review in the U.S. Tax Court.

If you don't file a hearing request within 30 days, you aren't entitled to a Collection Due Process hearing, but you may be entitled to an equivalent hearing. The request for an equivalent hearing; however, doesn't prohibit us from seizing and doesn't suspend the 10-year period for collecting tax. In addition, you aren't entitled to a judicial review of the decision from the Equivalent Hearing.

In addition to any Collection Due Process rights you may have, you may also appeal a proposed or actual filing of a Notice of Federal Tax Lien under the Collection Appeals Program.

Reasons we'll "release" a federal tax lien

A "release" of a federal tax lien means that we have cleared both the lien for your debt and the public Notice of Federal Tax Lien. We do this by filing a Certificate of Release of Federal Tax Lien with the same state and local authorities with whom we filed your Notice of Federal Tax Lien. We'll release your lien if:

- Your debt is fully paid,
- Payment of your debt is guaranteed by a bond, or
- The period for collection has ended. (In this case, the release is automatic.)

For more information, see Publication 1450, Instructions on How to Request a Certificate of Release of Federal Tax Lien.

Reasons we may "withdraw" a Notice of Federal Tax Lien

A "withdrawal" removes the Notice of Federal Tax Lien from public record. The withdrawal tells other creditors that we're abandoning our lien priority. This doesn't mean that the federal tax lien is released, or that you're no longer liable for the amount due.

We may withdraw a Notice of Federal Tax Lien if:

- You've entered into an Installment Agreement to satisfy the tax liability, unless the Agreement provides otherwise. For certain types of taxes, we'll routinely withdraw a Notice of Federal Tax Lien if you've entered into a direct debit installment agreement and meet certain other conditions,
- It will help you pay your taxes more quickly,
- We didn't follow IRS procedures,
- It was filed during a bankruptcy automatic stay period, or
- It's in your best interest (as determined by the Taxpayer Advocate) and in the best interest of the government. For example, this could include when your debt has been satisfied and you request a withdrawal.

For more information, see Form 12277, Application for Withdrawal of Filed Notice of Federal Tax Lien.

How to apply for a "discharge" of a federal tax lien from property

A "discharge" removes the lien from specific property. There are several circumstances under which the federal tax lien can be discharged. For example, we may issue a Certificate of Discharge if you're selling property and a Notice of Federal Tax Lien has been filed; you may be able to remove or discharge the lien from that property through the sale. For more information on whether you qualify for a discharge, see Publication 783, Instructions on How to Apply for a Certificate of Discharge of Property from Federal Tax Lien. To watch an instructional video about Publication 783, visit www.irsvideos.gov/Individual/IRSLiens.

How to make the federal tax lien secondary to other creditors ("subordination")

A "subordination" is where a creditor is allowed to move ahead of the government's priority position. For example, if you're trying to refinance a mortgage on your home, but aren't able to because the federal tax lien has priority over the new mortgage, you may request that we subordinate our lien to the new mortgage. For more information on whether you qualify for a subordination, see Publication 784, How to Prepare an Application for a Certificate of Subordination of Federal Tax Lien. To watch an instructional video about Publication 784, visit www.irsvideos.gov/Individual/IRSLiens.

Appeal rights for withdrawal, discharge, or subordination

If we deny your request for a withdrawal, discharge, or subordination, you may appeal under Collections Appeals Program.

Levy: A seizure of property

While a federal tax lien is a legal claim against your property, a levy is a legal seizure that actually takes your property (such as your house or car) or your rights to property (such as your income, bank account, or Social Security payments) to satisfy your tax debt.

Keep in mind that we can't seize your property if you have a current or pending Installment Agreement, Offer in Compromise, or if we agree that you're unable to pay due to economic hardship, meaning seizing your property would result in your inability to meet basic, reasonable living expenses.

Reasons we may seize ("levy") your property or rights to property

If you don't pay your taxes (or make arrangements to settle your debt), we could seize and sell your property. We usually seize only after the following things have occurred:

- We assessed the tax and sent you a bill,
- You neglected or refused to pay the tax, and
- We sent you a Final Notice of Intent to Levy and Notice of Your Right to a Hearing at least 30 days before the seizure.

However, there are exceptions for when we don't have to provide a 30-day notice before seizing your property. These include situations when:

- The collection of the tax is in jeopardy,
- A levy is served to collect tax from a state tax refund,
- A levy is served to collect the tax debt of a federal contractor, or
- A Disqualified Employment Tax Levy (DETL) is served. A Disqualified Employment Tax Levy is the seizure of unpaid employment taxes and can be served when a taxpayer previously requested a Collection Due Process appeal on employment taxes for other periods within the past 2 years.

If we serve a levy under one of these exceptions, we'll send you a letter explaining the seizure and your appeal rights after the levy is issued.

What you should do if your property is seized ("levied")

If your property or federal payments are seized, call the number on your levy notice or 1-800-829-1040. If you're already working with an IRS employee, call him or her for assistance.

Examples of property we can seize ("levy")

- **Wages, salary, or commission held by someone else** If we seize your rights to wages, salary, commissions, or similar payments that are held by someone else, we'll serve a levy once, not each time you're paid. The one levy continues until your debt is fully paid, other arrangements are made, or the collection period ends.

  Other payments you receive, such as dividends and payments on promissory notes, are also subject to seizure. However, the seizure only reaches the payments due or the right to future payments as of the date of the levy.

- **Your bank account** Seizure of the funds in your bank account will include funds available for withdrawal up to the amount of the seizure. After the levy is issued, the bank will hold the available funds and give you 21 days to resolve any disputes about who owns the account before sending us the money. After 21 days, the bank will send us your money, plus any interest earned on that amount, unless you have resolved the issue in another way.

- **Your federal payments** As an alternative to the levy procedure used for other payments such as dividends and promissory notes, certain federal payments may be systemically seized through the Federal Payment Levy Program in order to pay your tax debt.

  Under this program, we can generally seize up to 15% of your federal payments (up to 100% of payments due to a vendor for goods or services sold or leased to the federal government). We'll serve the levy once, not each time you are paid. The one levy continues until your debt is fully paid, other arrangements are made, the collection period ends, or the IRS releases the levy.

The federal payments that can be seized in this program include, but aren't limited to, federal retirement annuity income from the Office of Personnel Management, Social Security benefits under Title II of the Social Security Act (OASDI), and federal contractor/vendor payments.

- **Your house, car, or other property** If we seize your house or other property, we'll sell your interest in the property and apply the proceeds (after the costs of the sale) to your tax debt.

  Prior to selling your property, we'll calculate a minimum bid price. We'll also provide you with a copy of the calculation and give you an opportunity to challenge the fair market value determination. We'll then provide you with the notice of sale and announce the pending sale to the public, usually through local newspapers or flyers posted in public places.

  After giving public notice, we'll generally wait 10 days before selling your property. Money from the sale pays for the cost of seizing and selling the property and, finally, your tax debt. If there's money left over from the sale after paying off your tax debt, we'll tell you how to get a refund.

Property that can't be seized ("levied")

Certain property is exempt from seizure. For example, we can't seize the following: unemployment benefits, certain annuity and pension benefits, certain service-connected disability payments, workers compensation, certain public assistance payments, minimum weekly exempt income, assistance under the Job Training Partnership Act, and income for court-ordered child support payments.

We also can't seize necessary schoolbooks and clothing, undelivered mail, certain amounts worth of fuel, provisions, furniture, personal effects for a household, and certain amounts worth of books and tools for trade, business, or professions. There are also limitations on our ability to seize a primary residence and certain business assets.

Lastly, we can't seize your property unless we expect net proceeds to help pay off your tax debt.

How to appeal a proposed seizure ("levy")

You can request a Collection Due Process hearing within 30 days from the date of your Notice of Intent to Levy and Notice of Your Right to a Hearing. Send your request to the address on your notice. For more information, see Form 12153, Request for a Collection Due Process or Equivalent Hearing. At the conclusion of your hearing, the Office of Appeals will provide a determination. You'll have 30 days after the determination to challenge it in the U.S. Tax Court.

If you don't file a hearing request within 30 days, you're not entitled to a Collection Due Process hearing, but you may be entitled to an Equivalent Hearing. The request for an Equivalent Hearing, however, doesn't prohibit us from seizing and doesn't suspend the 10-year period for collecting tax. In addition, you're not entitled to a judicial review of the decision from the Equivalent Hearing.

If Collection Due Process rights aren't available for your case, you may have other appeal options, such as the Collection Appeals Program.

Reasons we "release" a levy

The Internal Revenue Code (IRC) specifically provides that we must release a levy if we determine that:

- You paid the amount you owe,
- The period for collection ended prior to the levy being issued,
- It will help you pay your taxes,
- You enter into an Installment Agreement and the terms of the agreement don't allow for the levy to continue,
- The levy creates an economic hardship on you, meaning we've determined that you're unable to meet basic, reasonable living expenses, or
- The value of the property is more than the amount owed and releasing the levy won't hinder our ability to collect the amount owed.

In addition, a levy on wages or salary must be released as soon as possible if we determine that your tax isn't collectible.

We'll also release a levy if it was issued improperly. For example, we'll release a levy if it was issued:

- Against property exempt from seizure,
- Prematurely,
- Before we sent you the required notice,
- While you're in bankruptcy and an automatic stay is in effect,
- Where the expenses of seizing and selling the levied property would be greater than the fair market value of the property,
- While an Installment Agreement request, Innocent Spouse Relief request, or Offer in Compromise is being considered or had been accepted and is in effect, or
- While the Office of Appeals or Tax Court is considering certain appeals and the levy wasn't a Disqualified Employment Tax Levy to collect employment taxes, a state refund, or jeopardy levy.

Reasons we may return seized ("levied") property

We may return your property if:

- Its seizure was premature,
- Its seizure was in violation of the law,
- Returning the seized property will help our collection of your debt,
- You enter into an Installment Agreement that doesn't allow a levy,
- We didn't follow IRS procedures, or
- It's in your best interest (as determined by the Taxpayer Advocate) and in the best interest of the government.

If we decide to return your property but it's already been sold, we'll give you the money we received from the sale. You can file a request for seized property to be returned, or we can return seized property on our own initiative, generally up to 9 months after the seizure.

How to recover seized ("levied") property that's been sold

To recover your real estate, you (and anyone with interest in the property) may recoup it within 180 days of the sale by paying the purchaser what they paid, plus interest at 20% annually.

If your property has been seized ("levied") to collect tax owed by someone else, you may appeal under the Collection Appeals Program or (within the time prescribed by law), file a claim under Internal Revenue Code section 6343(b), or you may (within the time prescribed by law) file a suit under Internal Revenue Code section 7426 for the return of the wrongfully seized property. For more information, see Publication 4528, Making an Administrative Wrongful Levy Claim under Internal Revenue Code section 6343(b).

How to recover economic damages

If our seizure was in error, your payment was lost or misplaced, or there was a direct debit Installment Agreement processing error and you incurred bank charges, we may reimburse you for charges you paid. For more information, see Form 8546, Claim for Reimbursement of Bank Charges. If your claim is denied, you can sue the federal government for economic damages.

If we intentionally or negligently didn't follow Internal Revenue law while collecting your taxes, or you're not the taxpayer and we wrongfully seized your property, you may be entitled to recover economic damages. Mail your written administrative claim to the attention of the Advisory Group Manager for your area at the address listed in Publication 4235, Collection Advisory Group Addresses. If you've filed a claim and your claim is denied, you can sue the federal government, but not the IRS employee, for economic damages.

Summons: Used to secure information

If we're having trouble gathering information to determine or collect taxes you owe, we may serve a summons. A summons legally compels you or a third party to meet with an officer of the IRS and provide information, documents, and/or testimony.

If you're responsible for a tax liability and we serve a summons on you, you may be required to:

- Testify,
- Bring books and records to prepare a tax return, and/or
- Produce documents to prepare a Collection Information Statement, Form 433-A or Form 433-B.

If you can't make your summons appointment, immediately call the number listed on your notice. If you don't call us and don't attend your appointment, serious legal action may be taken against you.

If we serve a third-party summons to determine tax liability, you'll receive a notice indicating that we're contacting a third party. Third parties can be financial institutions, record keepers, or people with relevant information to your case. We won't review their information or receive testimony until the end of the 23rd day after the notice was given. You also have the right to:

- Petition to reject ("quash") the summons before the end of the 20th day after the date of the notice, or
- Petition to intervene in a suit to enforce a summons to which the third party didn't comply.

If we issue a third-party summons to collect taxes you already owe, you won't receive notice or be able to petition to reject or intervene in a suit to enforce the summons.

Information for employers: Collection of employment tax

About employment taxes

Employment taxes are the amount you must withhold from your employees for their income tax and Social Security/Medicare tax, plus the amount of Social Security/Medicare tax you pay for each employee. Federal unemployment taxes are also considered employment taxes.

What we'll do if you don't pay your employment taxes:

- Assess a failure to deposit penalty, up to 15% of the amount not deposited in a timely manner.
- We may propose a Trust Fund Recovery Penalty assessment against the individuals responsible for failing to pay the trust fund taxes.

About trust fund taxes

Trust fund taxes are the income tax, Social Security tax, and Medicare tax withheld from the employee's wages. They are called trust fund taxes because the employer holds these funds "in trust" for the government until it submits them in a federal tax deposit. Certain excise taxes are also considered trust fund taxes because they are collected and held in trust for the government until submitted in a federal tax deposit. For more information, see Publication 510, Excise Taxes.

To encourage prompt payment of withheld employment taxes and collected excise taxes, Congress has passed a law that provides for the Trust Fund Recovery Penalty. For more information, see Publication 15, Circular E, Employer's Tax Guide.

Trust Fund Recovery Penalty

The Trust Fund Recovery Penalty is a penalty that is assessed personally against the individual or individuals who are responsible for paying the trust fund taxes but willfully did not do so. The amount of the penalty is equal to the amount of the unpaid trust fund taxes. For additional information, please see Notice 784, Could You be Personally Liable for Certain Unpaid Federal Taxes?, or visit www.irs.gov/businesses/small/article/0,,id=108357,00.html.

If the Trust Fund Recovery Penalty is proposed against you

You'll receive a letter and Form 2751, Proposed Assessment of Trust Fund Recovery Penalty.

If you agree with the penalty, sign and return Form 2751 within 60 days from the date of the letter. To avoid the assessment of the Trust Fund Recovery Penalty, you may also pay the trust fund taxes personally.

If you disagree with the penalty, you have 10 days from the date of the letter to let us know that you don't agree with the proposed assessment, have additional information to support your case, or want to try to resolve the matter informally. If you can't resolve the disagreement with us, you have 60 days from the date of the letter to appeal with the Office of Appeals. For more information, see Publication 5, Your Appeal Rights and How to Prepare a Protest if You Don't Agree.

If you don't respond to the letter, we'll assess the penalty amount against you personally and begin the collection process to collect it. We may assess this penalty against a responsible person regardless of whether the company is still in business.

Additional information

Innocent Spouse Relief

Generally, both you and your spouse are responsible, jointly and individually, for paying any tax, interest, or penalties on your joint return. If you believe your current or former spouse should be solely responsible for an incorrect item or an underpayment of tax on your joint tax return, you may be eligible for Innocent Spouse Relief. This could change the amount you owe, or you may be entitled to a refund. Keep in mind you generally must submit Form 8857, Request for Innocent Spouse Relief, no later than two years from the date of our first attempt to collect the outstanding debt, except for requests for equitable relief under Internal Revenue Code section 6015(f). For additional information, see Publication 971, Innocent Spouse Relief.

Representation during the collection process

During the collection process, a hearing, or an appeal, you can be represented by yourself, an attorney, a certified public accountant, an enrolled agent, an immediate family member, or any person enrolled to practice before the IRS. If you're a business, you can also be represented by full-time employees, general partners, or bona fide officers.

To have your representative appear before us, contact us on your behalf, and/or receive your confidential material, file Form 2848, Power of Attorney and Declaration of Representative.

To authorize someone to receive or inspect confidential material, file Form 8821, Tax Information Authorization.

Sharing your tax information

During the collection process, we're authorized to share your tax information in some cases with city and state tax agencies, the Department of Justice, federal agencies, people you authorize to represent you, and certain foreign governments (under tax treaty provisions).

We may contact a third party

The law allows us to contact others (such as neighbors, banks, employers, or employees) to investigate your case. You have the right to request a list of third parties contacted about your case.

Department of the Treasury
Internal Revenue Service

Publication 947
(Rev. May 2012)

Cat. No. 13392P

Practice Before the IRS and Power of Attorney

Get forms and other information faster and easier by:

Internet IRS.gov

Contents

What's New

Registered tax return preparers. Registered tax return preparers may prepare and sign as the preparer tax returns and claims for refund and other documents for submission to the IRS. They may also represent taxpayers before revenue agents, customer service representatives, and similar IRS employees during an examination if they signed the return or claim for refund for the tax year or period under examination.

Future developments. The IRS has created a page on IRS.gov for information about Publication 947 at www.irs.gov/pub947. Information about any future developments (such as legislation enacted after we release it) will be posted on that page.

Practitioners' Hotline

The Practitioner Priority Service® is a nationwide, toll-free hotline that provides professional support to practitioners with account-related questions. The toll-free number for this service is 1-866-860-4259.

Introduction

This publication discusses who can represent a taxpayer before the IRS and what forms or documents are used to authorize a person to represent a taxpayer. Usually, attorneys, certified public accountants (CPAs), enrolled agents, enrolled retirement plan agents, and enrolled actuaries can represent taxpayers before the IRS. Under special circumstances, other individuals, including registered tax return preparers, unenrolled return preparers, and students can represent taxpayers before the IRS. For details regarding taxpayer representation, see *Who Can Practice Before the IRS*, later.

Definitions. Many of the terms used in this publication, such as "enrolled agent" and "practitioner" are defined in the *Glossary* at the back of this publication.

Comments and suggestions. We welcome your comments about this publication and your suggestions for future editions.

You can write to us at the following address:

Internal Revenue Service
Individual Forms and Publications Branch
SE:W:CAR:MP:T:I
1111 Constitution Ave. NW, IR-6526
Washington, DC 20224

We respond to many letters by telephone. Therefore, it would be helpful if you would include your daytime phone number, including the area code, in your correspondence.

You can email us at *taxforms@irs.gov*. Please put "Publications Comment" on the subject line. You can also send us comments from www.irs.gov/formspubs/, select "Comment on Tax Forms and Publications" under "Information About."

Ordering forms and publications. Visit www.irs.gov/formspubs/ to download forms and publications, call 1-800-829-3676, or write to the address below and receive a response within 10 days after your request is received.

Internal Revenue Service
1201 N. Mitsubishi Motorway
Bloomington, IL 61705-6613

Tax questions. If you have a tax question, check the information available on IRS.gov or call 1-800-829-1040. We cannot answer tax questions sent to either of the above addresses.

Useful Items

You may want to see:

Publications

- ❏ **1** Your Rights as a Taxpayer
- ❏ **470** Limited Practice Without Enrollment
- ❏ **Circular No. 230** Regulations Governing Practice before the Internal Revenue Service

Forms and Instructions

- ❏ **2848** Power of Attorney and Declaration of Representative
- ❏ **8821** Tax Information Authorization

Practice Before the IRS

Terms you may need to know (see Glossary):

Attorney-in-fact

CAF number

Centralized Authorization File (CAF) System

Commissioner

Durable power of attorney

Enrolled agent

Fiduciary

General power of attorney

Government officer or employee

Limited power of attorney

Practitioner

Recognized representative

Registered tax return preparer

Unenrolled tax return preparer

The Office of Professional Responsibility and the Return Preparer Office generally are responsible for administering and enforcing the regulations governing practice before the IRS. The Office of Professional Responsibility generally has responsibility for matters related to practitioner conduct and exclusive responsibility for discipline, including disciplinary proceedings and sanctions. The Return Preparer Office is responsible for matters related to the authority to practice, including acting on applications for enrollment and administering competency testing and continuing education.

What Is Practice Before the IRS?

Practice before the IRS covers all matters relating to any of the following.

- 792 -

- Communicating with the IRS for a taxpayer regarding the taxpayer's rights, privileges, or liabilities under laws and regulations administered by the IRS.

- Representing a taxpayer at conferences, hearings, or meetings with the IRS.

- Preparing and filing documents, including tax returns, with the IRS for a taxpayer.

- Providing a client with written advice which has a potential for tax avoidance or evasion.

Furnishing information at the request of the IRS or appearing as a witness for the taxpayer is not practice before the IRS.

Who Can Practice Before the IRS?

The following individuals can practice before the IRS. However, any individual who is recognized to practice (a recognized representative) must be designated as the taxpayer's representative and file a written declaration with the IRS stating that he or she is authorized and qualified to represent a particular taxpayer. Form 2848 can be used for this purpose.

Attorneys. Any attorney who is not currently under suspension or disbarment from practice before the IRS and who is a member in good standing of the bar of the highest court of any state, possession, territory, commonwealth, or the District of Columbia may practice before the IRS.

Certified public accountants (CPAs). Any CPA who is not currently under suspension or disbarment from practice before the IRS and who is duly qualified to practice as a CPA in any state, possession, territory, commonwealth, or the District of Columbia may practice before the IRS.

Enrolled agents. Any enrolled agent in active status who is not currently under suspension or disbarment from practice before the IRS may practice before the IRS.

Enrolled retirement plan agents. Any enrolled retirement plan agent in active status who is not currently under suspension or disbarment from practice before the IRS may practice before the IRS. The practice of enrolled retirement plan agents is limited to certain Internal Revenue Code sections that relate to their area of expertise, principally those sections governing employee retirement plans.

Enrolled actuaries. Any individual who is enrolled as an actuary by the Joint Board for the Enrollment of Actuaries who is not currently under suspension or disbarment from practice before the IRS may practice before the IRS. The practice of enrolled actuaries is limited to certain Internal Revenue Code sections that relate to their area of expertise, principally those sections governing employee retirement plans.

Student. Under certain circumstances, a student who is supervised by a practitioner may request permission to represent another person before the IRS. For more information, see *Authorization for special appearances*, later.

Registered tax return preparers and unenrolled return preparers. A registered tax return preparer is an individual who has passed an IRS competency test and is authorized to prepare and sign tax returns as the preparer. An unenrolled return preparer is an individual other than an attorney, CPA, enrolled agent, enrolled retirement plan agent, or enrolled actuary who prepares and signs a taxpayer's return as the preparer, or who prepares a return but is not required (by the instructions to the return or regulations) to sign the return.

Registered tax return preparers and unenrolled return preparers may only represent taxpayers before revenue agents, customer service representatives, or similar officers and employees of the Internal Revenue Service (including the Taxpayer Advocate Service) during an examination of the taxable year or period covered by the tax return they prepared and signed. Registered tax return preparers and unenrolled return preparers cannot represent taxpayers, regardless of the circumstances requiring representation, before appeals officers, revenue officers, counsel or similar officers or employees of the Internal Revenue Service or the Department of Treasury. Registered tax return preparers and unenrolled return preparers cannot execute closing agreements, extend the statutory period for tax assessments or collection of tax, execute waivers, execute claims for refund, or sign any document on behalf of a taxpayer.

If the unenrolled return preparer does not meet the requirements for limited representation, you may file Form 8821 to allow the preparer to inspect your tax information and receive copies of notices sent to you by the IRS. See Form 8821.

Practice denied. Any individual engaged in limited practice before the IRS who is involved in disreputable conduct is subject to disciplinary action. Disreputable conduct includes, but is not limited to, the list of items under *Incompetence and Disreputable Conduct* shown later under *What Are the Rules of Practice.*

Other individuals who may serve as representatives. Because of their special relationship with a taxpayer, the following individuals can represent the specified taxpayers before the IRS, provided they present satisfactory identification and, except in the case of an individual described in (1) below, proof of authority to represent the taxpayer.

1. *An individual.* An individual can represent himself or herself before the IRS and does not have to file a written declaration of qualification and authority.

2. *A family member.* An individual can represent members of his or her immediate family. Immediate family includes a spouse, child, parent, brother, or sister of the individual.

3. *An officer.* A bona fide officer of a corporation (including a parent, subsidiary, or other affiliated corporation), association, or organized group can represent the corporation, association, or organized group. An officer of a governmental unit, agency, or authority, in the course of his or her official duties, can represent the organization before the IRS.

4. *A partner.* A general partner may represent the partnership before the IRS.

5. *An employee.* A regular full-time employee can represent his or her employer. An employer can be, but is not limited to, an individual, partnership, corporation (including a parent, subsidiary, or other affiliated corporation), association, trust, receivership, guardianship, estate, organized group, governmental unit, agency, or authority.

6. *A fiduciary.* A fiduciary (trustee, executor, personal representative, administrator, receiver, or guardian) stands in the position of a taxpayer and acts as the taxpayer, not as a representative. See *Fiduciary* under *When Is a Power of Attorney Not Required*, later.

Representation Outside the United States

Any individual may represent an individual or entity, who is outside the United States, before personnel of the IRS when such representation occurs outside the United States. See section 10.7(c)(1)(vii) of Circular 230.

Authorization for Special Appearances

The Commissioner of Internal Revenue, or delegate, can authorize an individual who is not otherwise eligible to practice before the IRS to represent another person for a particular matter. The prospective representative must request this authorization in writing from the Office of Professional Responsibility. However, it is granted only when extremely compelling circumstances exist. If granted, the Commissioner, or delegate, will issue a letter that details the conditions related to the appearance and the particular tax matter for which the authorization is granted.

The authorization letter should not be confused with a letter from an IRS center advising an individual that he or she has been assigned a Centralized Authorization File (CAF) number. The issuance of a CAF number does not indicate that an individual is either recognized or authorized to practice before the IRS. It merely confirms that a centralized file for authorizations has been established for the individual under that number.

Students in LITCs and the STCP. A student who works in a Low Income Taxpayer Clinic (LITC) or Student Tax Clinic Program (STCP) who is supervised by a practitioner may request permission to represent another person before the IRS. Authorization requests must be made to the Office of Professional Responsibility. If granted, a letter authorizing the student's special appearance and detailing any conditions related to the appearance will be issued. Students receiving an authorization letter generally can represent taxpayers before any IRS function or office subject to any conditions in the authorization letter. If you intend to have a student represent you, review the authorization letter and ask your student, your student's supervisor, or the Office of Professional Responsibility if you have questions about the terms of the authorization.

Who Cannot Practice Before the IRS?

In general, individuals who are not eligible or who have lost the privilege as a result of certain actions cannot practice before the IRS. If an individual loses eligibility to practice, the IRS will not recognize a power of attorney that names the individual as a representative.

Corporations, associations, partnerships, and other persons that are not individuals. These organizations (or persons) are not eligible to practice before the IRS.

Loss of Eligibility

Generally, individuals lose their eligibility to practice before the IRS in the following ways.

- Not meeting the requirements for renewal of enrollment (such as continuing professional education).
- Requesting to be placed in inactive retirement status.
- Being suspended or disbarred by the Office of Professional Responsibility for violating the regulations governing practice before the IRS.

Failure to meet requirements. Individuals who fail to comply with the requirements for eligibility for renewal of enrollment will be notified by the IRS. The notice will explain the reason for noncompliance and provide the individual with an opportunity to furnish information for reconsideration. The individual has 60 days from the date of the notice to respond.

Inactive roster. An individual will be placed on the roster of inactive individuals for a period of three years, if he or she:

- Fails to respond timely to the notice of noncompliance with the renewal requirements,
- Fails to file timely the application for renewal, or
- Does not satisfy the requirements of eligibility for renewal.

The individual must file an application for renewal **and** satisfy all requirements for renewal after being placed in inactive status. Otherwise, at the conclusion of the next renewal cycle, he or she will be removed from the roster and the enrollment or registration terminated.

Inactive retirement status. Individuals who request to be placed in an inactive retirement status will be ineligible to practice before the IRS. They must continue to adhere to all renewal requirements. They can be reinstated to an active enrollment status by filing an application for renewal **and** providing evidence that they have completed the required continuing professional education hours for the enrollment cycle or registration year.

Suspension and disbarment. Individuals authorized to practice before the IRS are subject to disciplinary proceedings and may be suspended or disbarred for violating any regulation governing practice before the IRS. This includes engaging in acts of disreputable conduct. For more information, see *Incompetence and Disreputable Conduct* under *What are the Rules of Practice*, later.

Practitioners who are suspended in a disciplinary proceeding are not allowed to practice before the IRS during the period of suspension. See *What Is Practice Before the IRS*, earlier.

Practitioners who are disbarred in a disciplinary proceeding are not allowed to practice before the IRS. However, a practitioner can seek reinstatement from the Office of Professional Responsibility five years after disbarment.

If the practitioner seeks reinstatement, he or she may not practice before the IRS until the Office of Professional Responsibility authorizes reinstatement. The Office of Professional Responsibility may reinstate the practitioner if it is determined that:

- The practitioner's future conduct is not likely to be in violation of the regulations, and

- Granting the reinstatement would not be contrary to the public interest.

How Does an Individual Become Enrolled?

The Return Preparer Office can grant enrollment to practice before the IRS to an applicant who demonstrates special competence in tax matters by passing a written examination administered by the IRS. Enrollment also can be granted to an applicant who qualifies because of past service and technical experience in the IRS. In either case, certain application forms, discussed next, must be filed.

Additionally, an applicant must not have engaged in any conduct that would justify suspension or disbarment from practice before the IRS. See *Incompetence and Disreputable Conduct,* later.

Form 2587. Applicants can apply to take the special enrollment examination by filing Form 2587, *Application for Special Enrollment Examination.* Form 2587 can be filed online, by mail, or by fax. For more information, see instructions and fees listed on the form. To get Form 2587, see *How To Get Tax Help*, later.

Form 23 and Form 23-EP. Individuals who have passed the examination or are applying on the basis of past service and technical experience with the IRS can apply for enrollment by filing Form 23, *Application for Enrollment to Practice Before the Internal Revenue Service,* or Form 23-EP, *Application for Enrollment to Practice Before the Internal Revenue Service as an Enrolled Retirement Plan Agent.* The application must include a check or money order in the amount of the fee shown on Form 23 or Form 23-EP. Alternatively, payment may be made electronically pursuant to instructions on the forms. To get Form 23 or Form 23-EP, see *How To Get Tax Help*, later.

Form 5434. An individual may apply as an enrolled actuary on the basis of past employment with the IRS and technical experience by filing Form 5434, *Application for Enrollment,* with the Joint Board for the Enrollment of Actuaries. The application must include a check or money

order in the amount of the fee shown on Form 5434. To get Form 5434, see *How To Get Tax Help*, later.

Period of enrollment. An enrollment card will be issued to each individual whose enrollment application is approved. The individual is enrolled until the expiration date shown on the enrollment card or certificate. To continue practicing beyond the expiration date, the individual must request renewal of the enrollment by filing Form 8554, *Application for Renewal of Enrollment to Practice Before the Internal Revenue Service,* or Form 8554-EP, *Application for Renewal of Enrollment to Practice Before the Internal Revenue Service as an Enrolled Retirement Plan Agent (ERPA).*

What Are the Rules of Practice?

The rules governing practice before the IRS are published in the Code of Federal Regulations at 31 C.F.R. part 10 and reprinted in Treasury Department Circular No. 230 (Circular 230). An attorney, CPA, enrolled agent, enrolled retirement plan agent, registered tax return preparer, or enrolled actuary authorized to practice before the IRS (referred to hereafter as a practitioner) has the duty to perform certain acts and is restricted from performing other acts. In addition, a practitioner cannot engage in disreputable conduct (discussed later). Any practitioner who does not comply with the rules of practice or engages in disreputable conduct is subject to disciplinary action. Also, unenrolled preparers must comply with the rules of practice and conduct to exercise the privilege of limited practice before the IRS. See Publication 470 for a discussion of the special rules for limited practice by unenrolled preparers.

Duties

Practitioners must promptly submit records or information requested by officers or employees of the IRS, except when the practitioner believes on reasonable belief and good faith that the information is privileged. Communications with respect to tax advice between a federally authorized tax practitioner and a taxpayer generally are confidential to the same extent that communication would be privileged if it were between a taxpayer and an attorney if the advice relates to:

- Noncriminal tax matters before the IRS, or

- Noncriminal tax proceedings brought in federal court by or against the United States.

Communications regarding corporate tax shelters. This protection of tax advice communications does not apply to any written communications between a federally authorized tax practitioner and any person, including a director, shareholder, officer, employee, agent, or representative of a corporation if the communication involves the promotion of the direct or indirect participation of the corporation in any tax shelter.

Duty to advise. A practitioner who knows that his or her client has not complied with the revenue laws or has made an error or omission in any return, document, affidavit, or other required paper, has the responsibility to advise the client promptly of the noncompliance, error, or omission, and the consequences of the noncompliance, error, or omission.

Due diligence. A practitioner must exercise due diligence when performing the following duties.

- Preparing or assisting in the preparing, approving, and filing of returns, documents, affidavits, and other papers relating to IRS matters.

- Determining the correctness of oral or written representations made by him or her to the Department of the Treasury.

- Determining the correctness of oral or written representations made by him or her to clients with reference to any matter administered by the IRS.

Restrictions

Practitioners are restricted from engaging in certain practices. The following paragraphs discuss some of these restricted practices.

Delays. A practitioner must not unreasonably delay the prompt disposition of any matter before the IRS.

Assistance from disbarred or suspended persons and former IRS employees. A practitioner must not knowingly, directly or indirectly, do the following.

- Accept assistance from, or assist, any person who is under disbarment or suspension from practice before the IRS if the assistance relates to matters considered practice before the IRS.

- Accept assistance from any former government employee where provisions of Circular 230 or any federal law would be violated.

Performance as a notary. A practitioner who is a notary public and is employed as counsel, attorney, or agent in a matter before the IRS, or has a material interest in the matter, cannot engage in any notary activities related to that matter.

Negotiations of taxpayer refund checks. Practitioners must not endorse or otherwise negotiate (cash) any refund check (including directing or accepting payment by any means, electronic or otherwise, in an account owned or controlled by the practitioner or any firm or other entity with whom the practitioner is associated) issued to the taxpayer.

Incompetence and Disreputable Conduct

Any practitioner or unenrolled return preparer may be disbarred or suspended from practice before the IRS, or censured, for incompetence or disreputable conduct. The following list contains examples of conduct that is considered disreputable.

- Being convicted of any criminal offense under the revenue laws or of any offense involving dishonesty or breach of trust.

- Knowingly giving false or misleading information in connection with federal tax matters, or participating in such activity.

- Soliciting employment by prohibited means as discussed in section 10.30 of Circular 230.

- Willfully failing to file a federal tax return, evading or attempting to evade any federal tax or payment, or participating in such actions.

- Misappropriating, or failing to properly and promptly remit, funds received from clients for payment of taxes or other obligations due the United States.

- Directly or indirectly attempting to influence the official action of IRS employees by the use of threats, false accusations, duress, or coercion, or by offering gifts, favors, or any special inducements.

- Being disbarred or suspended from practice as an attorney, CPA, public accountant, or actuary, by the District of Columbia or any state, possession, territory, commonwealth, or any federal court, or any federal agency, body, or board.

- Knowingly aiding and abetting another person to practice before the IRS during a period of suspension, disbarment, or ineligibility of that other person.

- Using abusive language, making false accusations and statements knowing them to be false, circulating or publishing malicious or libelous matter, or engaging in any contemptuous conduct in connection with practice before the IRS.

- Giving a false opinion knowingly, recklessly, or through gross incompetence; or following a pattern of providing incompetent opinions in questions arising under the federal tax laws.

Censure, Disbarments, and Suspensions

The Office of Professional Responsibility may censure or institute proceedings to censure, suspend or disbar any attorney, CPA, or enrolled agent who has violated Circular 230. A practitioner will be given the opportunity to demonstrate compliance with the rules before any disciplinary action is taken.

Authorizing a Representative

You may either represent yourself, or you may authorize an individual to represent you before the IRS. If you chose to have someone represent you, your representative must be a person eligible to practice before the IRS. See *Who Can Practice Before the IRS*, earlier.

What Is a Power of Attorney?

A power of attorney is your written authorization for an individual to act on your behalf. If the authorization is not limited, the individual generally can perform all acts that you can perform. The authority granted to a registered tax return preparer or an unenrolled preparer is limited. For information on the limits regarding registered tax return preparers, see Circular 230 §10.3(f). For information on the limits regarding unenrolled preparers, see Publication 470.

Acts performed. Any representative, other than a registered tax return preparer or an unenrolled return preparer, can usually perform the following acts.

1. Represent you before any office of the IRS.

2. Sign an offer or a waiver of restriction on assessment or collection of a tax deficiency, or a waiver of notice of disallowance of claim for credit or refund.

3. Sign a consent to extend the statutory time period for assessment or collection of a tax.

4. Sign a closing agreement.

Signing your return. The representative named under a power of attorney is not permitted to sign your income tax return unless:

1. The signature is permitted under the Internal Revenue Code and the related regulations (see Regulations section 1.6012-1(a)(5)).

2. You specifically authorize this in your power of attorney.

For example, the regulation permits a representative to sign your return if you are unable to sign the return due to:

- Disease or injury.

- Continuous absence from the United States (including Puerto Rico) for a period of at least 60 days prior to the date required by law for filing the return.

- Other good cause if specific permission is requested of and granted by the IRS.

When a return is signed by a representative, it must be accompanied by a power of attorney (or copy) authorizing the representative to sign the return. For more information, see the Form 2848 instructions.

Limitation on substitution or delegation. A recognized representative can substitute or delegate authority under the power of attorney to another recognized representative only if the act is specifically authorized by you on the power of attorney.

After a substitution has been made, only the newly recognized representative will be recognized as the taxpayer's representative. If a delegation of power has been made, both the original and the delegated representative will be recognized by the IRS to represent you.

Disclosure of returns to a third party. Your representative cannot execute consents that will allow the IRS to disclose tax return or return information to a third party unless you specifically delegate this authority to your representative on line 5 of Form 2848.

Incapacity or incompetency. A power of attorney is generally terminated if you become incapacitated or incompetent.

The power of attorney can continue, however, in the case of your incapacity or incompetency if you authorize this on line 5 "Other" of the Form 2848 and if your non-IRS durable power of attorney meets all the requirements for acceptance by the IRS. See *Non-IRS powers of attorney*, later.

When Is a Power of Attorney Required?

Submit a power of attorney when you want to authorize an individual to represent you before the IRS, whether or not the representative performs any of the other acts cited earlier under *What Is a Power of Attorney*.

A power of attorney is most often required when you want to authorize another individual to perform at least one of the following acts on your behalf.

1. Represent you at a meeting with the IRS.

2. Prepare and file a written response to the IRS.

Form Required

Use Form 2848 to appoint a recognized representative to act on your behalf before the IRS. Individuals recognized to practice before the IRS are listed under *Part II, Declaration of Representative*, of Form 2848. Your representative must complete that part of the form.

Non-IRS powers of attorney. The IRS will accept a non-IRS power of attorney, but a completed Form 2848 must be attached in order for the power of attorney to be entered on the Centralized Authorization File (CAF) system. For more information, see *Processing a non-IRS power of attorney*, later.

If you want to use a power of attorney document other than Form 2848, it must contain the following information.

- Your name and mailing address.

- Your social security number and/or employer identification number.

- Your employee plan number, if applicable.

- The name and mailing address of your representative(s).

- The types of tax involved.

- The federal tax form number.

- The specific year(s) or period(s) involved.

- For estate tax matters, the decedent's date of death.

- A clear expression of your intention concerning the scope of authority granted to your representative(s).

- Your signature and date.

You also must attach to the non-IRS power of attorney a signed and dated statement made by your representative. This statement, which is referred to as the Declaration of Representative, is contained in Part II of Form 2848. The statement should read:

1. I am not currently under suspension or disbarment from practice before the Internal Revenue Service or other practice of my profession by any other authority,

2. I am aware of the regulations contained in Circular 230,

3. I am authorized to represent the taxpayer(s) identified in the power of attorney, and

4. I am an individual described in 26 CFR 601.502(b).

Required information missing. The IRS will not accept your non-IRS power of attorney if it does not contain all the information listed above. You can sign and submit a completed Form 2848 or a new non-IRS power of attorney that contains all the information. If you cannot sign an acceptable replacement document, your attorney-in-fact may be able to perfect (make acceptable to the IRS) your non-IRS power of attorney by using the procedure described next.

Procedure for perfecting a non-IRS power of attorney. Under the following conditions, the attorney-in-fact named in your non-IRS power of attorney can sign a Form 2848 on your behalf.

1. The original non-IRS power of attorney grants authority to handle federal tax matters (for example, general authority to perform any acts).

2. The attorney-in-fact attaches a statement (signed under penalty of perjury) to the Form 2848 stating that the original non-IRS power of attorney is valid under the laws of the governing jurisdiction.

Example. John Elm, a taxpayer, signs a non-IRS durable power of attorney that names his neighbor and CPA, Ed Larch, as his attorney-in-fact. The power of attorney grants Ed the authority to perform any and all acts on John's behalf. However, it does not list specific tax-related information such as types of tax or tax form numbers.

Shortly after John signs the power of attorney, he is declared incompetent. Later, a federal tax matter arises concerning a prior year return filed by John. Ed attempts to represent John before the IRS but is rejected because the durable power of attorney does not contain required information.

If Ed attaches a statement (signed under the penalty of perjury) that the durable power of attorney is valid under the laws of the governing jurisdiction, he can sign a completed Form 2848 and submit it on John's behalf. If Ed can practice before the IRS (see *Who Can Practice Before the IRS,* earlier), he can name himself as representative on Form 2848. Otherwise, he must name another individual who can practice before the IRS.

Processing a non-IRS power of attorney. The IRS has a centralized computer database system called the CAF system. This system contains information on the authority of taxpayer representatives. Generally, when you submit a power of attorney document to the IRS, it is processed for inclusion on the CAF system. Entry of your power of attorney on the CAF system enables IRS personnel, who do not have a copy of your power of attorney, to

verify the authority of your representative by accessing the CAF. It also enables the IRS to automatically send copies of notices and other IRS communications to your representative if you specify that your representative should receive those communications.

You can have your non-IRS power of attorney entered on the CAF system by attaching it to a completed Form 2848 and submitting it to the IRS. Your signature is not required; however, your attorney-in-fact must sign the *Declaration of Representative* (see Part II of Form 2848).

Preparation of Form — Helpful Hints

The preparation of Form 2848 is illustrated by an example, later under *How Do I Fill Out Form 2848.* However, the following will also assist you in preparing the form.

Line-by-line hints. The following hints are summaries of some of the line-by-line instructions for Form 2848.

Line 1—Taxpayer information. If a joint return is involved, the husband and wife each file a separate Form 2848 if they both want to be represented. If only one spouse wants to be represented in the matter, that spouse files a Form 2848.

Line 2—Representative(s). Only individuals may be named as representatives. If your representative has not been assigned a CAF number, enter "None" on that line and the IRS will issue one to your representative. If the representative's address or phone number has changed since the CAF number was issued, you should check the appropriate box. Enter your representative's fax number if available.

If you want to name more than three representatives, attach additional Form(s) 2848. The IRS can send copies of notices and communications to two of your representatives. You **must**, however, check the boxes on line 2 of the Form 2848 if you want the IRS to routinely send copies of notices and communications to your representatives. If you do not check the boxes, your representatives will not routinely receive copies of notices and communications.

Line 3—Tax matters. You may list any tax years or periods that have already ended as of the date you sign the power of attorney. However, you may include on a power of attorney only future tax periods that end no later than 3 years after the date the power of attorney is received by the IRS. The 3 future periods are determined starting after December 31 of the year the power of attorney is received by the IRS. However, avoid general references such as "all years" or "all taxes." Any Form 2848 with general references will be returned.

Line 4—Specific use not recorded on Centralized Authorization File (CAF). Certain matters cannot be recorded on the CAF system. Examples of such matters include, but are not limited to, the following.

- Requests for a private letter ruling or technical advice.

- Applications for an employer identification number (EIN).

- Claims filed on Form 843, Claim for Refund and Request for Abatement.
- Corporate dissolutions.
- Requests for change of accounting method.
- Requests for change of accounting period.
- Applications for recognition of exemption under sections 501(c)(3), 501(a), or 521 (Forms 1023, 1034, or 1028).
- Request for a determination of the qualified status of an employee benefit plan (Forms 5300, 5307, or 5310).
- Application for Award for Original Information under section 7623.
- Voluntary submissions under the Employee Plans Compliance Resolution System (EPCRS).
- Freedom of Information Act requests.

If the tax matter described on line 3 of Form 2848 concerns one of these matters specifically, check the box on line 4. If this box is checked, the representative should mail or fax the power of attorney to the IRS office handling the matter. Otherwise, the representative should bring a copy of the power of attorney to each meeting with the IRS.

Where To File a Power of Attorney

Generally, you can mail or fax a paper Form 2848 directly to the IRS. To determine where you should file Form 2848, see *Where To File* in the instructions for Form 2848.

If Form 2848 is for a specific use, mail or fax it to the office handling that matter. For more information on specific use, see the *Instructions for Form 2848*, line 4.

FAX copies. The IRS will accept a copy of a power of attorney that is submitted by facsimile transmission (fax). If you choose to file a power of attorney by fax, be sure the appropriate IRS office is equipped to accept this type of transmission.

 Your representative may be able to file Form 2848 electronically via the IRS website. For more information, your representative can go to www. irs.gov and under the Tax Professionals tab, click on e-services–Online Tools for Tax Professionals. If you complete Form 2848 for electronic signature authorization, do not file Form 2848 with the IRS. Instead, give it to your representative, who will retain the document.

Updating a power of attorney. Submit any update or modification to an existing power of attorney in writing. Your signature (or the signature of the individual(s) authorized to sign on your behalf) is required. Do this by sending the updated Form 2848 or non-IRS power of attorney to the IRS office(s) where you previously sent the original(s), including the center where the related return was, or will be filed.

A recognized representative may substitute or delegate authority if you specifically authorize your representative to substitute or delegate representation in the original power of attorney. To make a substitution or delegation, the representative must file the following items with the IRS office(s) where the power of attorney was filed.

1. A written notice of substitution or delegation signed by the recognized representative.
2. A written declaration of representative made by the new representative.
3. A copy of the power of attorney that specifically authorizes the substitution or delegation.

Retention/Revocation of Prior Power(s) of Attorney

A newly filed power of attorney concerning the same matter will revoke a previously filed power of attorney. However, the new power of attorney will not revoke the prior power of attorney if it specifically states it does not revoke such prior power of attorney and either of the following are attached to the new power of attorney.

- A copy of the unrevoked prior power of attorney, or
- A statement signed by the taxpayer listing the name and address of each representative authorized under the prior unrevoked power of attorney.

Note. The filing of Form 2848 will not revoke any Form 8821 that is in effect.

Revocation of Power of Attorney/Withdrawal of Representative

If you want to revoke an existing power of attorney and do not want to name a new representative, or if a representative wants to withdraw from representation, mail or fax a copy of the previously executed power of attorney to the IRS, or if the power of attorney is for a specific matter, to the IRS office handling the matter. If the taxpayer is revoking the power of attorney, the taxpayer must write "REVOKE" across the top of the first page with a current signature and date below this annotation. If the representative is withdrawing from the representation, the representative must write "WITHDRAW" across the top of the first page with a current signature and date below this annotation. If you do not have a copy of the power of attorney you want to revoke or withdraw, send a statement to the IRS. The statement of revocation or withdrawal must indicate that the authority of the power of attorney is revoked or withdrawn, list the matters and periods, and must be signed and dated by the taxpayer or representative as applicable. If the taxpayer is revoking, list the name and address of each recognized representative whose authority is revoked. When the taxpayer is completely revoking authority, the form should state "remove all years/periods" instead of listing the specific tax matter, years, or periods. If the representative is withdrawing, list the name, TIN, and address (if known) of the taxpayer.

To revoke a specific use power of attorney, send the power of attorney or statement of revocation to the IRS office handling your case, using the above instructions.

A power of attorney held by a student will be recorded on the CAF system for 130 days from the receipt date. If you are authorizing a student to represent you after that time, you will need to submit a current and valid Form 2848.

When Is a Power of Attorney Not Required?

A power of attorney is not required when the third party is not dealing with the IRS as your representative. The following situations do not require a power of attorney.

- Providing information to the IRS.

- Authorizing the disclosure of tax return information through Form 8821, *Tax Information Authorization,* or other written or oral disclosure consent.

- Allowing the IRS to discuss return information with a third party via the checkbox provided on a tax return or other document.

- Allowing a tax matters partner or person (TMP) to perform acts for the partnership.

- Allowing the IRS to discuss return information with a fiduciary.

How Do I Fill Out Form 2848?

The following example illustrates how to complete Form 2848. The two completed forms for this example are shown on the next pages.

Example. Stan and Mary Doe have been notified that their joint tax returns (Forms 1040) for 2009, 2010, and 2011 are being examined. They have decided to appoint Jim Smith, an enrolled agent, to represent them in this matter and any future matters concerning these returns. Jim, who has prepared returns at the same location for years, already has a Centralized Authorization File (CAF) number assigned to him. Mary does not want Jim to sign any agreements on her behalf, but Stan is willing to have Jim do so. They want copies of all notices and written communications sent to Jim. This is the first time Stan and Mary have given power of attorney to anyone. They should each complete a Form 2848 as follows.

Line 1—Taxpayer information. Stan and Mary must each file a separate Form 2848. On his separate Form 2848, Stan enters his name, street address, and social security number in the spaces provided. Mary does likewise on her separate Form 2848.

Line 2—Representative(s). On their separate Forms 2848, Stan and Mary each enters the name and current address of their chosen representative, Jim Smith. Both Stan and Mary want Jim Smith to receive notices and communications concerning the matters identified in line 3, so on their separate Forms 2848, Stan and Mary each checks the box in the first column of line 2. They also enter

Mr. Smith's CAF number, his telephone number, and his fax number. Mr. Smith's address, telephone number, and fax number have not changed since the IRS issued his CAF number, so Stan and Mary do not check the boxes in the second column.

Line 3—Tax Matters. On their separate Forms 2848, Stan and Mary each enters "income" for the type of tax, "1040" for the form number, and "2009, 2010, and 2011" for the tax years.

Line 4—Specific use not recorded on Centralized Authorization File (CAF). On their separate Forms 2848, Stan and Mary make no entry on this line because they do not want to restrict the use of their powers of attorney to a specific use that is not recorded on the CAF. See *Preparation of Form — Helpful Hints,* earlier.

Line 5—Acts authorized. Mary wants to sign any agreement that reflects changes to her and Stan's joint 2009, 2010, and 2011 income tax liability, so she writes "Taxpayer must sign any agreement form" on line 5 of her Form 2848. Stan does not wish to restrict the authority of Jim Smith in this regard, so he leaves line 5 of his Form 2848 blank. If either Mary or Stan had chosen, they could have listed other restrictions on line 5 of their separate Forms 2848.

Line 6—Retention/revocation of prior power(s) of attorney. Stan and Mary are each filing their first powers of attorney, so they make no entry on this line. However, if they had filed prior powers of attorney, the filing of this current power would revoke any earlier ones for the same tax matter(s) unless they checked the box on line 6 and attached a copy of the prior power of attorney that they wanted to remain in effect.

If Mary later decides that she can handle the examination on her own, she can revoke her power of attorney even though Stan does not revoke his power of attorney. (See *Revocation of Power of Attorney/Withdrawal of Representative,* earlier, for the special rules that apply.)

Line 7—Signature of taxpayer. Stan and Mary each signs and dates his or her Form 2848. If a taxpayer does not sign, the IRS cannot accept the form.

Part II—Declaration of Representative. Jim Smith must complete this part of Form 2848. If he does not sign this part, the IRS cannot accept the form.

What Happens to the Power of Attorney When Filed?

A power of attorney will be recognized after it is received, reviewed, and determined by the IRS to contain the required information. However, until a power of attorney is entered on the CAF system, IRS personnel may be unaware of the authority of the person you have named to represent you. Therefore, during this interim period, IRS personnel may request that you or your representative bring a copy to any meeting with the IRS.

Form **2848**

(Rev. March 2012)
Department of the Treasury
Internal Revenue Service

Power of Attorney
and Declaration of Representative

▶ Type or print. ▶ See the separate instructions.

OMB No. 1545-0150

For IRS Use Only

Received by:

Name _____
Telephone _____
Function _____
Date ___/___/___

Part I	**Power of Attorney**

Caution: *A separate Form 2848 should be completed for each taxpayer. Form 2848 will not be honored for any purpose other than representation before the IRS.*

1   Taxpayer information. Taxpayer must sign and date this form on page 2, line 7.

Taxpayer name and address	Taxpayer identification number(s)
Stan Doe	000-00-0000
1040 Any Street	
Anytown, VA 22000	Daytime telephone number · Plan number (if applicable)
	703-555-1212

hereby appoints the following representative(s) as attorney(s)-in-fact:

2   Representative(s) must sign and date this form on page 2, Part II.

Name and address	
Jim Smith	CAF No. __6800-06530R__
1065 Any Street	PTIN _____
Anytown, VA 22000	Telephone No. __703 555-4321__
	Fax No. __703 555-5432__
Check if to be sent notices and communications ☑	Check if new: Address ☐ Telephone No. ☐ Fax No. ☐

Name and address	
	CAF No. _____
	PTIN _____
	Telephone No. _____
	Fax No. _____
Check if to be sent notices and communications ☐	Check if new: Address ☐ Telephone No. ☐ Fax No. ☐

Name and address	
	CAF No. _____
	PTIN _____
	Telephone No. _____
	Fax No. _____
	Check if new: Address ☐ Telephone No. ☐ Fax No. ☐

to represent the taxpayer before the Internal Revenue Service for the following matters:

3   Matters

Description of Matter (Income, Employment, Payroll, Excise, Estate, Gift, Whistleblower, Practitioner Discipline, PLR, FOIA, Civil Penalty, etc.) (see instructions for line 3)	Tax Form Number (1040, 941, 720, etc.) (if applicable)	Year(s) or Period(s) (if applicable) (see instructions for line 3)
Income Tax	1040	2009, 2010, 2011

4   Specific use not recorded on Centralized Authorization File (CAF). If the power of attorney is for a specific use not recorded on CAF, check this box. See the instructions for Line 4. **Specific Uses Not Recorded on CAF** . . . . ▶ ☐

5   Acts authorized. Unless otherwise provided below, the representatives generally are authorized to receive and inspect confidential tax information and to perform any and all acts that I can perform with respect to the tax matters described on line 3, for example, the authority to sign any agreements, consents, or other documents. The representative(s), however, is (are) not authorized to receive or negotiate any amounts paid to the client in connection with this representation (including refunds by either electronic means or paper checks). Additionally, unless the appropriate box(es) below are checked, the representative(s) is (are) not authorized to execute a request for disclosure of tax returns or return information to a third party, substitute another representative or add additional representatives, or sign certain tax returns.

☐ Disclosure to third parties;   ☐ Substitute or add representative(s);   ☐ Signing a return; _____

☐ Other acts authorized: _____

_____ (see instructions for more information)

Exceptions. An unenrolled return preparer cannot sign any document for a taxpayer and may only represent taxpayers in limited situations. An enrolled actuary may only represent taxpayers to the extent provided in section 10.3(d) of Treasury Department Circular No. 230 (Circular 230). An enrolled retirement plan agent may only represent taxpayers to the extent provided in section 10.3(e) of Circular 230. A registered tax return preparer may only represent taxpayers to the extent provided in section 10.3(f) of Circular 230. See the line 5 instructions for restrictions on tax matters partners. In most cases, the student practitioner's (level k) authority is limited (for example, they may only practice under the supervision of another practitioner).

List any specific deletions to the acts otherwise authorized in this power of attorney:

_____
_____
_____
_____

For Privacy Act and Paperwork Reduction Act Notice, see the instructions.   Cat. No. 11980J   Form **2848** (Rev. 3-2012)

6 **Retention/revocation of prior power(s) of attorney.** The filing of this power of attorney automatically revokes all earlier power(s) of attorney on file with the Internal Revenue Service for the same matters and years or periods covered by this document. If you **do not** want to revoke a prior power of attorney, check here . . . . ▶ ☐
   YOU MUST ATTACH A COPY OF ANY POWER OF ATTORNEY YOU WANT TO REMAIN IN EFFECT.

7 **Signature of taxpayer.** If a tax matter concerns a year in which a joint return was filed, the husband and wife must each file a separate power of attorney even if the same representative(s) is (are) being appointed. If signed by a corporate officer, partner, guardian, tax matters partner, executor, receiver, administrator, or trustee on behalf of the taxpayer, I certify that I have the authority to execute this form on behalf of the taxpayer.

   ▶ **IF NOT SIGNED AND DATED, THIS POWER OF ATTORNEY WILL BE RETURNED TO THE TAXPAYER.**

Stan Doe	*12/21/2012*	
Signature	Date	Title (if applicable)

Stan Doe	☐☐☐☐☐	
Print Name	PIN Number	Print name of taxpayer from line 1 if other than individual

---

Part II   **Declaration of Representative**

Under penalties of perjury, I declare that:

• I am not currently under suspension or disbarment from practice before the Internal Revenue Service;

• I am aware of regulations contained in Circular 230 (31 CFR, Part 10), as amended, concerning practice before the Internal Revenue Service;

• I am authorized to represent the taxpayer identified in Part I for the matter(s) specified there; and

• I am one of the following:

   a Attorney—a member in good standing of the bar of the highest court of the jurisdiction shown below.

   b Certified Public Accountant—duly qualified to practice as a certified public accountant in the jurisdiction shown below.

   c Enrolled Agent—enrolled as an agent under the requirements of Circular 230.

   d Officer—a bona fide officer of the taxpayer's organization.

   e Full-Time Employee—a full-time employee of the taxpayer.

   f Family Member—a member of the taxpayer's immediate family (for example, spouse, parent, child, grandparent, grandchild, step-parent, step-child, brother, or sister).

   g Enrolled Actuary—enrolled as an actuary by the Joint Board for the Enrollment of Actuaries under 29 U.S.C. 1242 (the authority to practice before the Internal Revenue Service is limited by section 10.3(d) of Circular 230).

   h Unenrolled Return Preparer—Your authority to practice before the Internal Revenue Service is limited. You must have been eligible to sign the return under examination and have signed the return. **See Notice 2011-6 and Special rules for registered tax return preparers and unenrolled return preparers in the instructions.**

   i Registered Tax Return Preparer—registered as a tax return preparer under the requirements of section 10.4 of Circular 230. Your authority to practice before the Internal Revenue Service is limited. You must have been eligible to sign the return under examination and have signed the return. **See Notice 2011-6 and Special rules for registered tax return preparers and unenrolled return preparers in the instructions.**

   k Student Attorney or CPA—receives permission to practice before the IRS by virtue of his/her status as a law, business, or accounting student working in LITC or STCP under section 10.7(d) of Circular 230. See instructions for Part II for additional information and requirements.

   r Enrolled Retirement Plan Agent—enrolled as a retirement plan agent under the requirements of Circular 230 (the authority to practice before the Internal Revenue Service is limited by section 10.3(e)).

   ▶ **IF THIS DECLARATION OF REPRESENTATIVE IS NOT SIGNED AND DATED, THE POWER OF ATTORNEY WILL BE RETURNED. REPRESENTATIVES MUST SIGN IN THE ORDER LISTED IN LINE 2 ABOVE.** See the instructions for Part II.

Note: For designations d-f, enter your title, position, or relationship to the taxpayer in the "Licensing jurisdiction" column. See the instructions for Part II for more information.

Designation—Insert above letter (a–r)	Licensing jurisdiction (state) or other licensing authority (if applicable)	Bar, license, certification, registration, or enrollment number (if applicable). See instructions for Part II for more information.	Signature	Date
c	VA	90-99999	*Jim Smith*	*12/21/2012*

Form **2848** (Rev. 3-2012)

Power of Attorney
and Declaration of Representative

▶ Type or print.   ▶ See the separate instructions.

OMB No. 1545-0150

For IRS Use Only

Received by:

Name _____

Telephone _____

Function _____

Date ____ / ____ / ____

Part I	Power of Attorney

Caution: *A separate Form 2848 should be completed for each taxpayer. Form 2848 will not be honored for any purpose other than representation before the IRS.*

1 Taxpayer information. Taxpayer must sign and date this form on page 2, line 7.

Taxpayer name and address	Taxpayer identification number(s)
Mary Doe	000-00-0001
1040 Any Street	
Anytown, VA 22000	Daytime telephone number / Plan number (if applicable)
	703-555-1212

hereby appoints the following representative(s) as attorney(s)-in-fact:

2   Representative(s) must sign and date this form on page 2, Part II.

Name and address	
Jim Smith	CAF No. .... 6800-06530R ....
1065 Any Street	PTIN ---
Anytown, VA 22000	Telephone No. .... 703 555-4321 ....
	Fax No. ------------- 703 555-5432 -------------
Check if to be sent notices and communications ☑	Check if new: Address ☐ Telephone No. ☐ Fax No. ☐

Name and address	
	CAF No. ---
	PTIN ---
	Telephone No. ---
	Fax No. ---
Check if to be sent notices and communications ☐	Check if new: Address ☐ Telephone No. ☐ Fax No. ☐

Name and address	
	CAF No. ---
	PTIN ---
	Telephone No. ---
	Fax No. ---
	Check if new: Address ☐ Telephone No. ☐ Fax No. ☐

to represent the taxpayer before the Internal Revenue Service for the following matters:

3   Matters

Description of Matter (Income, Employment, Payroll, Excise, Estate, Gift, Whistleblower, Practitioner Discipline, PLR, FOIA, Civil Penalty, etc.) (see instructions for line 3)	Tax Form Number (1040, 941, 720, etc.) (if applicable)	Year(s) or Period(s) (if applicable) (see instructions for line 3)
Income Tax	1040	2009, 2010, 2011

4   Specific use not recorded on Centralized Authorization File (CAF). If the power of attorney is for a specific use not recorded on CAF, check this box. See the instructions for Line 4. **Specific Uses Not Recorded on CAF** . . . . ▶ ☐

5   Acts authorized. Unless otherwise provided below, the representatives generally are authorized to receive and inspect confidential tax information and to perform any and all acts that I can perform with respect to the tax matters described on line 3, for example, the authority to sign any agreements, consents, or other documents. The representative(s), however, is (are) not authorized to receive or negotiate any amounts paid to the client in connection with this representation (including refunds by either electronic means or paper checks). Additionally, unless the appropriate box(es) below are checked, the representative(s) is (are) not authorized to execute a request for disclosure of tax returns or return information to a third party, substitute another representative or add additional representatives, or sign certain tax returns.

☐ Disclosure to third parties;   ☐ Substitute or add representative(s);   ☐ Signing a return; _____

☐ Other acts authorized: _____

_____ (see instructions for more information)

Exceptions. An unenrolled return preparer cannot sign any document for a taxpayer and may only represent taxpayers in limited situations. An enrolled actuary may only represent taxpayers to the extent provided in section 10.3(d) of Treasury Department Circular No. 230 (Circular 230). An enrolled retirement plan agent may only represent taxpayers to the extent provided in section 10.3(e) of Circular 230. A registered tax return preparer may only represent taxpayers to the extent provided in section 10.3(f) of Circular 230. See the line 5 instructions for restrictions on tax matters partners. In most cases, the student practitioner's (level k) authority is limited (for example, they may only practice under the supervision of another practitioner).

List any specific deletions to the acts otherwise authorized in this power of attorney:

Taxpayer must sign any agreement form. --

For Privacy Act and Paperwork Reduction Act Notice, see the instructions.   Cat. No. 11980J   Form **2848** (Rev. 3-2012)

6   **Retention/revocation of prior power(s) of attorney.** The filing of this power of attorney automatically revokes all earlier power(s) of attorney on file with the Internal Revenue Service for the same matters and years or periods covered by this document. If you **do not** want to revoke a prior power of attorney, check here . . . . ▶ ☐

            YOU MUST ATTACH A COPY OF ANY POWER OF ATTORNEY YOU WANT TO REMAIN IN EFFECT.

7   **Signature of taxpayer.** If a tax matter concerns a year in which a joint return was filed, the husband and wife must each file a separate power of attorney even if the same representative(s) is (are) being appointed. If signed by a corporate officer, partner, guardian, tax matters partner, executor, receiver, administrator, or trustee on behalf of the taxpayer, I certify that I have the authority to execute this form on behalf of the taxpayer.

         ▶ **IF NOT SIGNED AND DATED, THIS POWER OF ATTORNEY WILL BE RETURNED TO THE TAXPAYER.**

Mary Doe	12/21/2012	
Signature	Date	Title (if applicable)

Mary Doe	☐☐☐☐☐	
Print Name	PIN Number	Print name of taxpayer from line 1 if other than individual

---

Part II	**Declaration of Representative**

Under penalties of perjury, I declare that:

- I am not currently under suspension or disbarment from practice before the Internal Revenue Service;

- I am aware of regulations contained in Circular 230 (31 CFR, Part 10), as amended, concerning practice before the Internal Revenue Service;

- I am authorized to represent the taxpayer identified in Part I for the matter(s) specified there; and

- I am one of the following:

  a Attorney—a member in good standing of the bar of the highest court of the jurisdiction shown below.

  b Certified Public Accountant—duly qualified to practice as a certified public accountant in the jurisdiction shown below.

  c Enrolled Agent—enrolled as an agent under the requirements of Circular 230.

  d Officer—a bona fide officer of the taxpayer's organization.

  e Full-Time Employee—a full-time employee of the taxpayer.

  f Family Member—a member of the taxpayer's immediate family (for example, spouse, parent, child, grandparent, grandchild, step-parent, step-child, brother, or sister).

  g Enrolled Actuary—enrolled as an actuary by the Joint Board for the Enrollment of Actuaries under 29 U.S.C. 1242 (the authority to practice before the Internal Revenue Service is limited by section 10.3(d) of Circular 230).

  h Unenrolled Return Preparer—Your authority to practice before the Internal Revenue Service is limited. You must have been eligible to sign the return under examination and have signed the return. **See Notice 2011-6 and Special rules for registered tax return preparers and unenrolled return preparers in the instructions.**

  i Registered Tax Return Preparer—registered as a tax return preparer under the requirements of section 10.4 of Circular 230. Your authority to practice before the Internal Revenue Service is limited. You must have been eligible to sign the return under examination and have signed the return. **See Notice 2011-6 and Special rules for registered tax return preparers and unenrolled return preparers in the instructions.**

  k Student Attorney or CPA—receives permission to practice before the IRS by virtue of his/her status as a law, business, or accounting student working in LITC or STCP under section 10.7(d) of Circular 230. See instructions for Part II for additional information and requirements.

  r Enrolled Retirement Plan Agent—enrolled as a retirement plan agent under the requirements of Circular 230 (the authority to practice before the Internal Revenue Service is limited by section 10.3(e)).

    ▶ **IF THIS DECLARATION OF REPRESENTATIVE IS NOT SIGNED AND DATED, THE POWER OF ATTORNEY WILL BE RETURNED. REPRESENTATIVES MUST SIGN IN THE ORDER LISTED IN LINE 2 ABOVE.** See the instructions for Part II.

Note: For designations d-f, enter your title, position, or relationship to the taxpayer in the "Licensing jurisdiction" column. See the instructions for Part II for more information.

Designation—Insert above letter **(a–r)**	Licensing jurisdiction (state) or other licensing authority (if applicable)	Bar, license, certification, registration, or enrollment number (if applicable). See instructions for Part II for more information.	Signature	Date
c	VA	90-99999	Jim Smith	12/21/2012

                                                   Form **2848** (Rev. 3-2012)

Processing and Handling

How the power of attorney is processed and handled depends on whether it is a complete or incomplete document.

Incomplete document. If Form 2848 is incomplete, the IRS will attempt to secure the missing information either by writing or telephoning you or your representative. For example, if your signature or signature date is missing, the IRS will contact you. If information concerning your representative is missing and information sufficient to make a contact (such as an address and/or a telephone number) is on the document, the IRS will try to contact your representative.

In either case, the power of attorney is not considered valid until all required information is entered on the document. The individual(s) named as representative(s) will not be recognized to practice before the IRS, on your behalf, until the document is complete and accepted by the IRS.

Complete document. If the power of attorney is complete and valid, the IRS will take action to recognize the representative. In most instances, this includes processing the document on the CAF system. Recording the data on the CAF system enables the IRS to direct copies of mailings to authorized representatives and to readily recognize the scope of authority granted.

Documents not processed on CAF. Specific-use powers of attorney are not processed on the CAF system (see *Preparation of Form – Helpful Hints*, earlier). For example, a power of attorney that is a one-time or specific-issue grant of authority is not processed on the CAF system. These documents remain with the related case files. In this situation, you should check the box on line 4 of Form 2848. In these situations, the representative should bring a copy of the power of attorney to each meeting with the IRS.

Dealing With the Representative

After a valid power of attorney is filed, the IRS will recognize your representative. However, if it appears the representative is responsible for unreasonably delaying or hindering the prompt disposition of an IRS matter by failing to furnish, after repeated requests, nonprivileged information, the IRS can contact you directly. For example, in most instances in which a power of attorney is recognized, the IRS will contact the representative to set up appointments and to provide lists of required items. However, if the representative is unavailable, does not respond to repeated requests, and does not provide required items (other than items considered privileged), the IRS can bypass your representative and contact you directly.

If a representative engages in conduct described above, the matter can be referred to the Office of Professional Responsibility for consideration of possible disciplinary action.

Notices and other correspondence. If you have a recognized representative, you and the representative will routinely receive notices and other correspondence from the IRS (either the original or a copy) if you checked the box in the left column of line 2 of Form 2848. If the power of attorney is processed on the CAF system, the IRS will send your representative(s) a duplicate of all computer-generated correspondence that is sent to you. This includes notices and letters produced either at the Martinsburg Computing Center, or other IRS centers. The IRS employee handling the case is responsible for ensuring that the original and any requested copies of each manually-generated correspondence are sent to you and your representative(s) in accordance with your authorization.

How To Get Tax Help

You can get help with unresolved tax issues, order free publications and forms, ask tax questions, and get information from the IRS in several ways. By selecting the method that is best for you, you will have quick and easy access to tax help.

Free help with your return. Free help in preparing your return is available nationwide from IRS-certified volunteers. The Volunteer Income Tax Assistance (VITA) program is designed to help low and moderate income taxpayers and the Tax Counseling for the Elderly (TCE) program is designed to assist taxpayers age 60 and older with their tax returns. Most VITA and TCE sites offer free electronic filing and all volunteers will let you know about credits and deductions you may be entitled to claim. To find the nearest VITA or TCE site, visit IRS.gov or call 1-800-906-9887 or 1-800-829-1040.

As part of the TCE program, AARP offers the Tax-Aide counseling program. To find the nearest AARP Tax-Aide site, call 1-888-227-7669 or visit AARP's website at *www.aarp.org/money/taxaide*.

For more information on these programs, go to IRS.gov and enter keyword "VITA" in the upper right-hand corner.

 Internet. You can access the IRS website at IRS.gov 24 hours a day, 7 days a week to:

- *E-file* your return. Find out about commercial tax preparation and *e-file* services available free to eligible taxpayers.

- Check the status of your refund. Go to IRS.gov and click on *Where's My Refund*. Wait at least 72 hours after the IRS acknowledges receipt of your e-filed return, or 3 to 4 weeks after mailing a paper return. If you filed Form 8379 with your return, wait 14 weeks (11 weeks if you filed electronically). Have your tax return available so you can provide your social security number, your filing status, and the exact whole dollar amount of your refund.

- Download forms, including talking tax forms, instructions, and publications.

- Order IRS products online.

- Research your tax questions online.

- Search publications online by topic or keyword.

- Use the online Internal Revenue Code, regulations, or other official guidance.

- View Internal Revenue Bulletins (IRBs) published in the last few years.

- Figure your withholding allowances using the withholding calculator online at *www.irs.gov/individuals*.

- Determine if Form 6251 must be filed by using our Alternative Minimum Tax (AMT) Assistant available online at *www.irs.gov/individuals*.

- Sign up to receive local and national tax news by email.

- Get information on starting and operating a small business.

 Phone. Many services are available by phone.

- *Ordering forms, instructions, and publications.* Call 1-800-TAX -FORM (1-800-829-3676) to order current-year forms, instructions, and publications, and prior-year forms and instructions. You should receive your order within 10 days.

- *Asking tax questions.* Call the IRS with your tax questions at 1-800-829-1040.

- *Solving problems.* You can get face-to-face help solving tax problems every business day in IRS Taxpayer Assistance Centers. An employee can explain IRS letters, request adjustments to your account, or help you set up a payment plan. Call your local Taxpayer Assistance Center for an appointment. To find the number, go to *www.irs.gov/localcontacts* or look in the phone book under *United States Government, Internal Revenue Service.*

- *TTY/TDD equipment.* If you have access to TTY/TDD equipment, call 1-800-829-4059 to ask tax questions or to order forms and publications.

- *TeleTax topics.* Call 1-800-829-4477 to listen to pre-recorded messages covering various tax topics.

- *Refund information.* To check the status of your refund, call 1-800-829-1954 or 1-800-829-4477 (automated refund information 24 hours a day, 7 days a week). Wait at least 72 hours after the IRS acknowledges receipt of your e-filed return, or 3 to 4 weeks after mailing a paper return. If you filed Form 8379 with your return, wait 14 weeks (11 weeks if you filed electronically). Have your tax return available so you can provide your social security number, your filing status, and the exact whole dollar amount of your refund. If you check the status of your refund and are not given the date it will be issued, please wait until the next week before checking back.

- *Other refund information.* To check the status of a prior-year refund or amended return refund, call 1-800-829-1040.

Evaluating the quality of our telephone services. To ensure IRS representatives give accurate, courteous, and professional answers, we use several methods to evaluate the quality of our telephone services. One method is for a second IRS representative to listen in on or record random telephone calls. Another is to ask some callers to complete a short survey at the end of the call.

 Walk-in. Many products and services are available on a walk-in basis.

- *Products.* You can walk in to many post offices, libraries, and IRS offices to pick up certain forms, instructions, and publications. Some IRS offices, libraries, grocery stores, copy centers, city and county government offices, credit unions, and office supply stores have a collection of products available to print from a CD or photocopy from reproducible proofs. Also, some IRS offices and libraries have the Internal Revenue Code, regulations, Internal Revenue Bulletins, and Cumulative Bulletins available for research purposes.

- *Services.* You can walk in to your local Taxpayer Assistance Center every business day for personal, face-to-face tax help. An employee can explain IRS letters, request adjustments to your tax account, or help you set up a payment plan. If you need to resolve a tax problem, have questions about how the tax law applies to your individual tax return, or you are more comfortable talking with someone in person, visit your local Taxpayer Assistance Center where you can spread out your records and talk with an IRS representative face-to-face. No appointment is necessary—just walk in. If you prefer, you can call your local Center and leave a message requesting an appointment to resolve a tax account issue. A representative will call you back within 2 business days to schedule an in-person appointment at your convenience. If you have an ongoing, complex tax account problem or a special need, such as a disability, an appointment can be requested. All other issues will be handled without an appointment. To find the number of your local office, go to *www.irs.gov/localcontacts* or look in the phone book under *United States Government, Internal Revenue Service.*

 Mail. You can send your order for forms, instructions, and publications to the address below. You should receive a response within 10 days after your request is received.

Internal Revenue Service
1201 N. Mitsubishi Motorway
Bloomington, IL 61705-6613

Taxpayer Advocate Service. The Taxpayer Advocate Service (TAS) is your voice at the IRS. Our job is to ensure that every taxpayer is treated fairly, and that you know and understand your rights. We offer free help to guide you through the often-confusing process of resolving tax problems that you haven't been able to solve on your own. Remember, the worst thing you can do is nothing at all.

TAS can help if you can't resolve your problem with the IRS and:

- Your problem is causing financial difficulties for you, your family, or your business.
- You face (or your business is facing) an immediate threat of adverse action.
- You have tried repeatedly to contact the IRS but no one has responded, or the IRS has not responded to you by the date promised.

If you qualify for our help, we'll do everything we can to get your problem resolved. You will be assigned to one advocate who will be with you at every turn. We have offices in every state, the District of Columbia, and Puerto Rico. Although TAS is independent within the IRS, our advocates know how to work with the IRS to get your problems resolved. And our services are always free.

As a taxpayer, you have rights that the IRS must abide by in its dealings with you. Our tax toolkit at *www. TaxpayerAdvocate.irs.gov* can help you understand these rights.

If you think TAS might be able to help you, call your local advocate, whose number is in your phone book and on our website at *www.irs.gov/advocate*. You can also call our toll-free number at 1-877-777-4778 or TTY/TDD 1-800-829-4059.

TAS also handles large-scale or systemic problems that affect many taxpayers. If you know of one of these broad issues, please report it to us through our Systemic Advocacy Management System at *www.irs.gov/advocate*.

Low Income Taxpayer Clinics (LITCs). Low Income Taxpayer Clinics (LITCs) are independent from the IRS. Some clinics serve individuals whose income is below a certain level and who need to resolve a tax problem. These clinics provide professional representation before the IRS or in court on audits, appeals, tax collection disputes, and other issues for free or for a small fee. Some clinics can provide information about taxpayer rights and responsibilities in many different languages for individuals who speak English as a second language. For more information and to find a clinic near you, see the LITC page on *www.irs.gov/ advocate* or IRS Publication 4134, *Low Income Taxpayer Clinic List*. This publication is also available by calling 1-800-829-3676 or at your local IRS office.

Free tax services. Publication 910, IRS Guide to Free Tax Services, is your guide to IRS services and resources. Learn about free tax information from the IRS, including publications, services, and education and assistance programs. The publication also has an index of over 100 TeleTax topics (recorded tax information) you can listen to on the telephone. The majority of the information and services listed in this publication are available to you free of charge. If there is a fee associated with a resource or service, it is listed in the publication.

Accessible versions of IRS published products are available on request in a variety of alternative formats for people with disabilities.

 DVD for tax products. You can order Publication 1796, IRS Tax Products DVD, and obtain:

- Current-year forms, instructions, and publications.
- Prior-year forms, instructions, and publications.
- Tax Map: an electronic research tool and finding aid.
- Tax law frequently asked questions.
- Tax Topics from the IRS telephone response system.
- Internal Revenue Code—Title 26 of the U.S. Code.
- Links to other Internet based Tax Research Materials.
- Fill-in, print, and save features for most tax forms.
- Internal Revenue Bulletins.
- Toll-free and email technical support.
- Two releases during the year.
  – The first release will ship the beginning of January.
  – The final release will ship the beginning of March.

Purchase the DVD from National Technical Information Service (NTIS) at *www.irs.gov/cdorders* for $30 (no handling fee) or call 1-877-233-6767 toll free to buy the DVD for $30 (plus a $6 handling fee).

Glossary

The definitions in this glossary are the meanings of the terms as used in this publication. The same term used in another publication may have a slightly different meaning.

Attorney-in-fact: An agent authorized by a person under a power of attorney to perform certain act(s) or kind(s) of acts for that person.

CAF number: The Centralized Authorization File number issued by the IRS to each representative whose power of attorney, and each designee whose tax information authorization, has been recorded on the CAF system.

Centralized Authorization File (CAF) System: The computer file system containing information regarding the authority of individuals appointed under powers of attorney or persons designated under the tax information authorization system. This system gives IRS personnel quicker access to authorization information.

Commissioner: The Commissioner of the Internal Revenue Service.

Durable power of attorney: A power of attorney that is not subject to a time limit and that will continue in force after the incapacitation or incompetency of the principal (the taxpayer).

Enrolled agent: Any individual who is enrolled under the provisions of Treasury Department Circular No. 230 to practice before the IRS.

Fiduciary: Any trustee, executor, administrator, receiver, or guardian that stands in the position of a taxpayer and acts as the taxpayer, not as a representative.

General power of attorney: A power of attorney that authorizes the attorney-in-fact to perform any and all acts the taxpayer can perform.

Government officer or employee: An individual who is an officer or employee of the executive, legislative, or judicial branch of a state or of the United States Government; an officer or employee of the District of Columbia; a Member of Congress.

Limited power of attorney: A power of attorney that limits the attorney-in-fact to perform only certain specified act(s).

Practitioner: Generally, an attorney, CPA, enrolled agent, enrolled retirement plan agent, registered return preparer, or enrolled actuary authorized to practice before the IRS. Other individuals may qualify to practice temporarily or engage in limited practice before the IRS; however, they are not referred to as practitioners.

Recognized representative: An individual who is recognized to practice before the IRS.

Registered tax return preparer: An individual who has passed an IRS competency test and is authorized to prepare and sign tax returns.

Unenrolled return preparer: An individual other than an attorney, CPA, enrolled agent, enrolled retirement plan agent, registered tax return preparer, or enrolled actuary who prepares and signs a taxpayer's return as the preparer, or who prepares a return but is not required (by the instructions to the return or regulations) to sign the return.

■

Index

∎

Department of the Treasury
Internal Revenue Service

Publication 971
(Rev. September 2011)

Cat. No. 25757C

Innocent Spouse Relief

Get forms and other information faster and easier by:

Internet IRS.gov

Contents

What's New

Expanded filing deadline for equitable relief. The period of time in which you may request equitable relief has been expanded. See *How To Request Relief* later.

More information. For more information about the latest developments on Publication 971, go to *www.irs.gov/pub971*.

Introduction

When you file a joint income tax return, the law makes both you and your spouse responsible for the entire tax liability. This is called joint and several liability. Joint and several liability applies not only to the tax liability you show on the return but also to any additional tax liability the IRS determines to be due, even if the additional tax is due to income, deductions, or credits of your spouse or former spouse. You remain jointly and severally liable for the taxes, and the IRS still can collect from you, even if you later divorce and the divorce decree states that your former spouse will be solely responsible for the tax.

In some cases, a spouse (or former spouse) will be relieved of the tax, interest, and penalties on a joint tax return. Three types of relief are available to married persons who filed joint returns.

1. Innocent spouse relief.

2. Separation of liability relief.

3. Equitable relief.

Oct 07, 2011

- 811 -

Married persons who did not file joint returns, but who live in community property states, may also qualify for relief. See *Community Property Laws*, later.

This publication explains these types of relief, who may qualify for them, and how to get them. You can also use the Innocent Spouse Tax Relief Eligibility Explorer at *IRS.gov* by entering "Innocent Spouse" in the search box.

What this publication does not cover. This publication does *not* discuss *injured spouse relief*. You are an injured spouse if your share of the overpayment shown on your joint return was, or is expected to be, applied (offset) against your spouse's legally enforceable past-due federal taxes, state income taxes, state unemployment compensation debts, child or spousal support payments, or a federal nontax debt, such as a student loan. If you are an injured spouse, you may be entitled to receive a refund of your share of the overpayment. For more information, see *Form 8379, Injured Spouse Allocation*.

Comments and suggestions. We welcome your comments about this publication and your suggestions for future editions.

You can write to us at the following address:

Internal Revenue Service
Individual Forms and Publications Branch
SE:W:CAR:MP:T:I
1111 Constitution Ave. NW, IR-6526
Washington, DC 20224

We respond to many letters by telephone. Therefore, it would be helpful if you would include your daytime phone number, including the area code, in your correspondence.

You can email us at *taxforms@irs.gov*. Please put "Publications Comment" on the subject line. You can also send us comments from *www.irs.gov/formspubs/*, select "Comment on Tax Forms and Publications" under "Information about."

Although we cannot respond individually to each email, we do appreciate your feedback and will consider your comments as we revise our tax products.

Ordering forms and publications. Visit *www.irs.gov/formspubs* to download forms and publications, call 1-800-829-3676, or write to the address below and receive a response within 10 days after your request is received.

Internal Revenue Service
1201 N. Mitsubishi Motorway
Bloomington, IL 61705-6613

Questions about innocent spouse relief.

 The IRS can help you with your request for innocent spouse relief. If you are working with an IRS employee, you can ask that employee, or you can call 866-897-4270.

Useful Items

You may want to see:

Publications

- ❑ **504** Divorced or Separated Individuals
- ❑ **555** Community Property
- ❑ **556** Examination of Returns, Appeal Rights, and Claims for Refund
- ❑ **594** The IRS Collection Process

Forms (and Instructions)

- ❑ **8857** Request for Innocent Spouse Relief

How To Request Relief

File Form 8857 to ask the IRS for the types of relief discussed in this publication. If you are requesting relief for more than three tax years, you must file an additional Form 8857.

The IRS will review your Form 8857 and let you know if you qualify.

A completed Form 8857 is shown later.

When to file Form 8857. You should file Form 8857 as soon as you become aware of a tax liability for which you believe only your spouse or former spouse should be held responsible. The following are some of the ways you may become aware of such a liability.

- The IRS is examining your tax return and proposing to increase your tax liability.

- The IRS sends you a notice.

You must file Form 8857 no later than two years after the date on which the IRS first attempted to collect the tax from you that occurs after July 22, 1998. (But see the **exceptions** below for different filing deadlines that apply.) For this reason, do not delay filing because you do not have all the documentation.

Collection activities that may start the 2-year period are:

- The IRS offset your income tax refund against an amount you owed on a joint return for another year and the IRS informed you about your right to file Form 8857.

- The filing of a claim by the IRS in a court proceeding in which you were a party or the filing of a claim in a proceeding that involves your property. This includes the filing of a proof of claim in a bankruptcy proceeding.

- The filing of a suit by the United States against you to collect the joint liability.

- The issuance of a section 6330 notice, which notifies you of the IRS' intent to levy and your right to a collection due process (CDP) hearing. The collection-related notices include, but are not limited to, Letter 11 and Letter 1058.

Exception for equitable relief. On July 25, 2011, the IRS issued Notice 2011-70 (available at *www.irs.gov/irb/2011-32_IRB/ar11.html*) expanding the amount of time to request equitable relief. The amount of time to request equitable relief depends on whether you are seeking relief from a balance due, seeking a credit or refund, or both:

- Balance Due – Generally, you must file your request within the time period the IRS has to collect the tax. Generally, the IRS has 10 years from the date the tax liability was assessed to collect the tax. In certain cases, the 10-year period is suspended. The amount of time the suspension is in effect will extend the time the IRS has to collect the tax. See Pub. 594, The IRS Collection Process, for details.

- Credit or Refund – Generally, you must file your request within 3 years after the date the original return was filed or within 2 years after the date the tax was paid, whichever is later. But you may have more time to file if you live in a federally declared disaster area or you are physically or mentally unable to manage your financial affairs. See Pub. 556, Examination of Returns, Appeal Rights, and Claims for Refund, for details.

- Both a Balance Due and a Credit or Refund – If you are seeking a refund of amounts you paid and relief from a balance due over and above what you have paid, the time period for credit or refund will apply to any payments you have made, and the time period for collection of a balance due amount will apply to any unpaid liability.

Exception for relief based on community property laws. If you are requesting relief based on community property laws, a different filing deadline applies. See *Relief from liability arising from community property law* discussed later under *Community Property Laws*.

Form 8857 filed by or on behalf of a decedent. An executor (including any other duly appointed representative) may pursue a Form 8857 filed during the decedent's lifetime. An executor (including any other duly appointed representative) may also file Form 8857 as long as the decedent satisfied the eligibility requirements while alive. For purposes of separation of liability relief (discussed later), the decedent's marital status is determined on the earlier of the date relief was requested or the date of death.

Situations in which you are not entitled to relief. You are not entitled to innocent spouse relief for any tax year to which the following situations apply.

1. In a final decision dated after July 22, 1998, a court considered whether to grant you relief from joint liability and decided not to do so.

2. In a final decision dated after July 22, 1998, a court did not consider whether to grant you relief from joint liability, but you meaningfully participated in the proceeding and could have asked for relief.

3. You entered into an offer in compromise with the IRS.

4. You entered into a closing agreement with the IRS that disposed of the same liability for which you want to seek relief.

Exception for agreements relating to TEFRA partnership proceedings. You may be entitled to relief, discussed in (4) earlier, if you entered into a closing agreement for both partnership items and nonpartnership items, while you were a party to a pending TEFRA partnership proceeding. (*TEFRA* is an acronym that refers to the "Tax Equity and Fiscal Responsibility Act of 1982" that prescribed the tax treatment of partnership items.) You are not entitled to relief for the nonpartnership items, but you will be entitled to relief for the partnership items (if you otherwise qualify).

Transferee liability not affected by innocent spouse relief provisions. The innocent spouse relief provisions do not affect tax liabilities that arise under federal or state transferee liability or property laws. Therefore, even if you are relieved of the tax liability under the innocent spouse relief provisions, you may remain liable for the unpaid tax, interest, and penalties to the extent provided by these laws.

Example. Herb and Wanda timely filed their 2008 joint income tax return on April 15, 2009. Herb died in March 2010, and the executor of Herb's will transferred all of the estate's assets to Wanda. In August 2010, the IRS assessed a deficiency for the 2008 return. The items causing the deficiency belong to Herb. Wanda is relieved of the deficiency under the innocent spouse relief provisions, and Herb's estate remains solely liable for it. However, the IRS may collect the deficiency from Wanda to the extent permitted under federal or state transferee liability or property laws.

The IRS Must Contact Your Spouse or Former Spouse

By law, the IRS must contact your spouse or former spouse. There are **no** exceptions, even for victims of spousal abuse or domestic violence.

We will inform your spouse or former spouse that you filed Form 8857 and will allow him or her to participate in the process. If you are requesting relief from joint and several liability on a joint return, the IRS must also inform him or her of its preliminary and final determinations regarding your request for relief.

However, to protect your privacy, the IRS will not disclose your personal information (for example, your current name, address, phone number(s), information about your employer, your income or assets) or any other information that does not relate to making a determination about your request for relief from liability.

 If you petition the Tax Court (explained below), your spouse or former spouse may see your personal information.

Tax Court Review of Request

After you file Form 8857, you may be able to petition (ask) the United States Tax Court to review your request for relief in the following two situations.

1. The IRS sends you a final determination letter regarding your request for relief.

2. You do not receive a final determination letter from the IRS within six months from the date you filed Form 8857.

 If you seek equitable relief for an underpaid tax, you will be able to get a Tax Court review of your request only if the tax arose or remained unpaid on or after December 20, 2006.

The United States Tax Court is an independent judicial body and is not part of the IRS.

You must file a petition with the United States Tax Court in order for it to review your request for relief. You must file the petition no later than the 90th day after the date the IRS mails its final determination notice to you. If you do not file a petition, or you file it late, the Tax Court cannot review your request for relief.

 You can get a copy of the rules for filing a petition by writing to the Tax Court at the following address:

United States Tax Court
400 Second Street, NW
Washington, DC 20217

Or you can visit the Tax Court's website at *www. ustaxcourt.gov*

Community Property Laws

You must generally follow community property laws when filing a tax return if you are married and live in a community property state. Community property states are Arizona, California, Idaho, Louisiana, Nevada, New Mexico, Texas, Washington, and Wisconsin. Generally, community property laws require you to allocate community income and expenses equally between both spouses. However, community property laws are not taken into account in determining whether an item belongs to you or to your spouse (or former spouse) for purposes of requesting any relief from liability.

Relief for Married Persons Who Did Not File Joint Returns

Married persons who live in community property states, but who did not file joint returns, have two ways to get relief.

Relief From Liability Arising From Community Property Law

You are not responsible for the tax relating to an item of community income if all the following conditions exist.

1. You did not file a joint return for the tax year.

2. You did not include the item of community income in gross income.

3. The item of community income you did not include is one of the following:

   a. Wages, salaries, and other compensation your spouse (or former spouse) received for services he or she performed as an employee.

   b. Income your spouse (or former spouse) derived from a trade or business he or she operated as a sole proprietor.

   c. Your spouse's (or former spouse's) distributive share of partnership income.

   d. Income from your spouse's (or former spouse's) separate property (other than income described in (a), (b), or (c)). Use the appropriate community property law to determine what is separate property.

   e. Any other income that belongs to your spouse (or former spouse) under community property law.

4. You establish that you did not know of, and had no reason to know of, that community income. See *Actual Knowledge or Reason To Know*, below.

5. Under all facts and circumstances, it would not be fair to include the item of community income in your gross income. See *Indications of unfairness for liability arising from community property law*, later.

Actual knowledge or reason to know. You knew or had reason to know of an item of community income if:

- You actually knew of the item of community income, or

- A reasonable person in similar circumstances would have known of the item of community income.

Amount of community income unknown. If you are aware of the source of the item of community income or the income-producing activity, but are unaware of the specific amount, you are considered to know or have reason to know of the item of community income. Not knowing the specific amount is not a basis for relief.

Reason to know. The IRS will consider all facts and circumstances in determining whether you had reason to know of an item of community income. The facts and circumstances include:

- The nature of the item of community income and the amount of the item relative to other income items.

- The financial situation of you and your spouse (or former spouse).

- Your educational background and business experience.

- Whether the item of community income represented a departure from a recurring pattern reflected in prior years' returns (for example, omitted income from an investment regularly reported on prior years' returns).

Indications of unfairness for liability arising from community property law. The IRS will consider all of the facts and circumstances of the case in order to determine whether it is unfair to hold you responsible for the understated tax due to the item of community income.

The following are examples of factors the IRS will consider.

- Whether you received a benefit, either directly or indirectly, from the omitted item of community income (defined below).

- Whether your spouse (or former spouse) deserted you.

- Whether you and your spouse have been divorced or separated.

For other factors see *Factors for Determining Whether To Grant Equitable Relief* later.

Benefit from omitted item of community income. A benefit includes normal support, but does not include de minimis (small) amounts. Evidence of a direct or indirect benefit may consist of transfers of property or rights to property, including transfers received several years after the filing of the return.

For example, if you receive property, including life insurance proceeds, from your spouse (or former spouse) and the property is traceable to omitted items of community income attributable to your spouse (or former spouse), you are considered to have benefitted from those omitted items of community income.

Equitable Relief

If you do not qualify for the relief described above and are now liable for an underpaid or understated tax you believe should be paid only by your spouse (or former spouse), you may request equitable relief (discussed later).

How and When To Request Relief

You request relief by filing Form 8857, as discussed earlier. Fill in Form 8857 according to the instructions.

For relief from liability arising from community property law, you must file Form 8857 no later than 6 months before the expiration of the period of limitations on assessment (including extensions) against your spouse for the tax year for which you are requesting relief. However, if the IRS

begins an examination of your return during that 6-month period, the latest time for requesting relief is 30 days after the date the IRS' initial contact letter to you. The period of limitation on assessment is the amount of time, generally three years, that the IRS has from the date you filed the return to assess taxes that you owe.

Innocent Spouse Relief

By requesting innocent spouse relief, you can be relieved of responsibility for paying tax, interest, and penalties if your spouse (or former spouse) improperly reported items or omitted items on your tax return. Generally, the tax, interest, and penalties that qualify for relief can only be collected from your spouse (or former spouse). However, you are jointly and individually responsible for any tax, interest, and penalties that do not qualify for relief. The IRS can collect these amounts from either you or your spouse (or former spouse).

You must meet all of the following conditions to qualify for innocent spouse relief.

1. You filed a joint return.

2. There is an understated tax on the return that is due to erroneous items (defined later) of your spouse (or former spouse).

3. You can show that when you signed the joint return you did not know, and had no reason to know, that the understated tax existed (or the extent to which the understated tax existed). See *Actual Knowledge or Reason To Know,* later.

4. Taking into account all the facts and circumstances, it would be unfair to hold you liable for the understated tax. See *Indications of Unfairness for Innocent Spouse Relief,* later.

Innocent spouse relief will not be granted if the IRS proves that you and your spouse (or former spouse) transferred property to one another as part of a fraudulent scheme. A fraudulent scheme includes a scheme to defraud the IRS or another third party, such as a creditor, former spouse, or business partner.

Understated Tax

You have an understated tax if the IRS determined that your total tax should be more than the amount that was actually shown on your return.

Erroneous Items

Erroneous items are either of the following.

1. **Unreported income.** This is any gross income item received by your spouse (or former spouse) that is not reported.

2. **Incorrect deduction, credit, or basis.** This is any improper deduction, credit, or property basis claimed by your spouse (or former spouse).

The following are examples of erroneous items.

- The expense for which the deduction is taken was never paid or incurred. For example, your spouse, a cash-basis taxpayer, deducted $10,000 of advertising expenses on Schedule C of your joint Form 1040, but never paid for any advertising.

- The expense does not qualify as a deductible expense. For example, your spouse claimed a business fee deduction of $10,000 that was for the payment of state fines. Fines are not deductible.

- No factual argument can be made to support the deductibility of the expense. For example, your spouse claimed $4,000 for security costs related to a home office, which were actually veterinary and food costs for your family's two dogs.

Actual Knowledge or Reason To Know

You knew or had reason to know of an understated tax if:

- You actually knew of the understated tax, or

- A reasonable person in similar circumstances would have known of the understated tax.

Actual knowledge. If you actually knew about an erroneous item that belongs to your spouse (or former spouse), the relief discussed here does not apply to any part of the understated tax due to that item. You and your spouse (or former spouse) remain jointly liable for that part of the understated tax. For information about the criteria for determining whether you actually knew about an erroneous item, see *Actual Knowledge* later under *Separation of Liability Relief*.

Reason to know. If you had reason to know about an erroneous item that belongs to your spouse (or former spouse), the relief discussed here does not apply to any part of the understated tax due to that item. You and your spouse (or former spouse) remain jointly liable for that part of the understated tax.

The IRS will consider all facts and circumstances in determining whether you had reason to know of an understated tax due to an erroneous item. The facts and circumstances include:

- The nature of the erroneous item and the amount of the erroneous item relative to other items.

- The financial situation of you and your spouse (or former spouse).

- Your educational background and business experience.

- The extent of your participation in the activity that resulted in the erroneous item.

- Whether you failed to ask, at or before the time the return was signed, about items on the return or omitted from the return that a reasonable person would question.

- Whether the erroneous item represented a departure from a recurring pattern reflected in prior years' returns (for example, omitted income from an investment regularly reported on prior years' returns).

Partial relief when a portion of erroneous item is unknown. You may qualify for partial relief if, at the time you filed your return, you had no knowledge or reason to know of only a portion of an erroneous item. You will be relieved of the understated tax due to that portion of the item if all other requirements are met for that portion.

Example. At the time you signed your joint return, you knew that your spouse did not report $5,000 of gambling winnings. The IRS examined your tax return several months after you filed it and determined that your spouse's unreported gambling winnings were actually $25,000. You established that you did not know about, and had no reason to know about, the additional $20,000 because of the way your spouse handled gambling winnings. The understated tax due to the $20,000 will qualify for innocent spouse relief if you meet the other requirements. The understated tax due to the $5,000 of gambling winnings you knew about will not qualify for relief.

Indications of Unfairness for Innocent Spouse Relief

The IRS will consider all of the facts and circumstances of the case in order to determine whether it is unfair to hold you responsible for the understated tax.

The following are examples of factors the IRS will consider.

- Whether you received a significant benefit (defined below), either directly or indirectly, from the understated tax.

- Whether your spouse (or former spouse) deserted you.

- Whether you and your spouse have been divorced or separated.

- Whether you received a benefit on the return from the understated tax.

For other factors, see *Factors for Determining Whether To Grant Equitable Relief* later under *Equitable Relief*.

Significant benefit. A significant benefit is any benefit in excess of normal support. Normal support depends on your particular circumstances. Evidence of a direct or indirect benefit may consist of transfers of property or rights to property, including transfers that may be received several years after the year of the understated tax.

Example. You receive money from your spouse that is beyond normal support. The money can be traced to your spouse's lottery winnings that were not reported on your joint return. You will be considered to have received a significant benefit from that income. This is true even if your spouse gives you the money several years after he or she received it.

Separation of Liability Relief

Under this type of relief, the understated tax (plus interest and penalties) on your joint return is allocated between you and your spouse (or former spouse). The understated tax allocated to you is generally the amount you are responsible for.

This type of relief is available only for unpaid liabilities resulting from the understated tax. Refunds are not allowed.

To request separation of liability relief, you must have filed a joint return and meet either of the following requirements at the time you file Form 8857.

- You are no longer married to, or are legally separated from, the spouse with whom you filed the joint return for which you are requesting relief. (Under this rule, you are no longer married if you are widowed.)

- You were not a member of the same household (explained below) as the spouse with whom you filed the joint return at any time during the 12-month period ending on the date you file Form 8857.

Members of the same household. You and your spouse are not members of the same household if you are living apart and are estranged. However, you and your spouse are considered members of the same household if any of the following conditions are met.

1. You and your spouse reside in the same dwelling.

2. You and your spouse reside in separate dwellings but are not estranged, and one of you is temporarily absent from the other's household as explained in (3) below.

3. Either spouse is temporarily absent from the household and it is reasonable to assume that the absent spouse will return to the household, and the household or a substantially equivalent household is maintained in anticipation of the absent spouse's return. Examples of temporary absences include absence due to imprisonment, illness, business, vacation, military service, or education.

Burden of proof. You must be able to prove that you meet all of the requirements for separation of liability relief (except actual knowledge) and that you did not transfer property to avoid tax (discussed later). You must also establish the basis for allocating the erroneous items.

Limitations on Relief

Even if you meet the requirements discussed previously, separation of liability relief will not be granted in the following situations.

- The IRS proves that you and your spouse (or former spouse) transferred assets to one another as part of a fraudulent scheme. A fraudulent scheme includes a scheme to defraud the IRS or another third party, such as a creditor, former spouse, or business partner.

- The IRS proves that at the time you signed your joint return, you had actual knowledge (explained below) of any erroneous items giving rise to the deficiency that were allocable to your spouse (or former spouse). For the definition of erroneous items, see *Erroneous Items* earlier under *Innocent Spouse Relief.*

- Your spouse (or former spouse) transferred property to you to avoid tax or the payment of tax. See *Transfers of Property To Avoid Tax*, later.

Actual Knowledge

The relief discussed here does not apply to any part of the understated tax due to your spouse's (or former spouse's) erroneous items of which you had actual knowledge. You and your spouse (or former spouse) remain jointly and severally liable for this part of the understated tax.

If you had actual knowledge of only a portion of an erroneous item, the IRS will not grant relief for that portion of the item.

You had actual knowledge of an erroneous item if:

- You knew that an item of unreported income was received. (This rule applies whether or not there was a receipt of cash.)

- You knew of the facts that made an incorrect deduction or credit unallowable.

- For a false or inflated deduction, you knew that the expense was not incurred, or not incurred to the extent shown on the tax return.

Knowledge of the source of an erroneous item is not sufficient to establish actual knowledge. Also, your actual knowledge may not be inferred when you merely had a reason to know of the erroneous item. Similarly, the IRS does not have to establish that you knew of the source of an erroneous item in order to establish that you had actual knowledge of the item itself.

Your actual knowledge of the proper tax treatment of an erroneous item is not relevant for purposes of demonstrating that you had actual knowledge of that item. Neither is your actual knowledge of how the erroneous item was treated on the tax return. For example, if you knew that your spouse received dividend income, relief is not available for that income even if you did not know it was taxable.

Example. Bill and Karen Green filed a joint return showing Karen's wages of $50,000 and Bill's self-employment income of $10,000. The IRS audited their return and found that Bill did not report $20,000 of self-employment income. The additional income resulted in a $6,000 understated tax, plus interest and penalties. After obtaining a legal separation from Bill, Karen filed Form 8857 to request separation of liability relief. The IRS proved that Karen actually knew about the $20,000 of additional income at the time she signed the joint return. Bill is liable for all of the understated tax, interest, and penalties because all of it was due to his unreported income. Karen is also liable for the understated tax, interest, and penalties due to the $20,000 of unreported income because she actually knew of the item. The IRS can collect the entire $6,000 plus interest and penalties from either Karen or Bill because they are jointly and individually liable for it.

Factors supporting actual knowledge. The IRS may rely on all facts and circumstances in determining whether you actually knew of an erroneous item at the time you signed the return. The following are examples of factors the IRS may use.

- Whether you made a deliberate effort to avoid learning about the item in order to be shielded from liability.

- Whether you and your spouse (or former spouse) jointly owned the property that resulted in the erroneous item.

Exception for spousal abuse or domestic violence. Even if you had actual knowledge, you may still qualify for relief if you establish that:

- You were the victim of spousal abuse or domestic violence before signing the return, and

- Because of that abuse, you did not challenge the treatment of any items on the return because you were afraid your spouse (or former spouse) would retaliate against you.

If you establish that you signed your joint return under duress (threat of harm or other form of coercion), then it is not a joint return, and you are not liable for any tax shown on that return or any tax deficiency for that return. However, you may be required to file a separate return for that tax year. For more information about duress, see the instructions for Form 8857.

Transfers of Property To Avoid Tax

If your spouse (or former spouse) transfers property (or the right to property) to you for the main purpose of avoiding tax or payment of tax, the tax liability allocated to you will be increased by the fair market value of the property on the date of the transfer. The increase may not be more than the entire amount of the liability. A transfer will be presumed to have as its main purpose the avoidance of tax or payment of tax if the transfer is made after the date that is 1

year before the date on which the IRS sent its first letter of proposed deficiency. This presumption will not apply if:

- The transfer was made under a divorce decree, separate maintenance agreement, or a written instrument incident to such an agreement, or

- You establish that the transfer did not have as its main purpose the avoidance of tax or payment of tax.

If the presumption does not apply, but the IRS can establish that the purpose of the transfer was the avoidance of tax or payment of tax, the tax liability allocated to you will be increased as explained above.

Equitable Relief

If you do not qualify for innocent spouse relief, separation of liability relief, or relief from liability arising from community property law, you may still be relieved of responsibility for tax, interest, and penalties through equitable relief.

Unlike innocent spouse relief or separation of liability relief, you can get equitable relief from an understated tax (defined earlier under *Innocent Spouse Relief*) or an underpaid tax. An underpaid tax is an amount of tax you properly reported on your return but you have not paid. For example, your joint 2009 return shows that you and your spouse owed $5,000. You paid $2,000 with the return. You have an underpaid tax of $3,000.

Conditions for Getting Equitable Relief

You may qualify for equitable relief if you meet all of the following conditions.

1. You are not eligible for innocent spouse relief, separation of liability relief, or relief from liability arising from community property law.

2. You have an understated tax or an underpaid tax.

3. You did not pay the tax. However, see *Refunds*, later, for situations in which you are entitled to a refund of payments you made.

4. You establish that, taking into account all the facts and circumstances, it would be unfair to hold you liable for the understated or underpaid tax. See *Factors for Determining Whether To Grant Equitable Relief*, later.

5. You and your spouse (or former spouse) did not transfer assets to one another as a part of a fraudulent scheme. A fraudulent scheme includes a scheme to defraud the IRS or another third party, such as a creditor, former spouse, or business partner.

6. Your spouse (or former spouse) did not transfer property to you for the main purpose of avoiding tax or the payment of tax. See *Transfers of Property To*

Avoid Tax, earlier, under *Separation of Liability Relief.*

7. You did not file or fail to file your return with the intent to commit fraud.

8. The income tax liability from which you seek relief must be attributable to an item of the spouse (or former spouse) with whom you filed the joint return, unless one of the following exceptions applies:

   a. The item is attributable or partially attributable to you solely due to the operation of community property law. If you meet this exception, that item will be considered attributable to your spouse (or former spouse) for purposes of equitable relief.

   b. If the item is titled in your name, the item is presumed to be attributable to you. However, you can rebut this presumption based on the facts and circumstances.

   c. You did not know, and had no reason to know, that funds intended for the payment of tax were misappropriated by your spouse (or former spouse) for his or her benefit. If you meet this exception, the IRS will consider granting equitable relief although the underpaid tax may be attributable in part or in full to your item, and only to the extent the funds intended for payment were taken by your spouse (or former spouse).

   d. You establish that you were the victim of spousal abuse or domestic violence before signing the return, and that, as a result of the prior abuse, you did not challenge the treatment of any items on the return for fear of your spouse's (or former spouse's) retaliation. If you meet this exception, relief will be considered although the understated tax or underpaid tax may be attributable in part or in full to your item.

Factors for Determining Whether To Grant Equitable Relief

The IRS will consider all of the facts and circumstances in order to determine whether it is unfair to hold you responsible for the understated or underpaid tax. The following are examples of factors that the IRS will consider to determine whether to grant equitable relief. The IRS will consider all factors and weigh them appropriately.

Relevant Factors

The following are examples of factors that may be relevant to whether the IRS will grant equitable relief.

- Whether you are separated (whether legally or not) or divorced from your spouse. A temporary absence, such as an absence due to imprisonment, illness, business, vacation, military service, or education, is

not considered separation for this purpose. A temporary absence is one where it is reasonable to assume that the absent spouse will return to the household, and the household or a substantially equivalent household is maintained in anticipation of the absent spouse's return.

- Whether you would suffer a significant economic hardship if relief is not granted. (In other words, you would not be able to pay your reasonable basic living expenses.)

- Whether you have a legal obligation under a divorce decree or agreement to pay the tax. This factor will not weigh in favor of relief if you knew or had reason to know, when entering into the divorce decree or agreement, that your former spouse would not pay the income tax liability.

- Whether you received a significant benefit (beyond normal support) from the underpaid tax or item causing the understated tax. (For a definition of significant benefit, see *Indications of Unfairness for Innocent Spouse Relief* earlier.)

- Whether you have made a good faith effort to comply with federal income tax laws for the tax year for which you are requesting relief or the following years.

- Whether you knew or had reason to know about the items causing the understated tax or that the tax would not be paid, as explained next.

Knowledge or reason to know. In the case of an underpaid tax, the IRS will consider whether you did not know and had no reason to know that your spouse (or former spouse) would not pay the income tax liability.

In the case of an income tax liability that arose from an understated tax, the IRS will consider whether you did not know and had no reason to know of the item causing the understated tax. Reason to know of the item giving rise to the understated tax will not be weighed more heavily than other factors. Actual knowledge of the item giving rise to the understated tax, however, is a strong factor weighing against relief. This strong factor may be overcome if the factors in favor of equitable relief are particularly compelling.

Reason to know. In determining whether you had reason to know, the IRS will consider your level of education, any deceit or evasiveness of your spouse (or former spouse), your degree of involvement in the activity generating the income tax liability, your involvement in business and household financial matters, your business or financial expertise, and any lavish or unusual expenditures compared with past spending levels.

Example. You and your spouse filed a joint 2009 return. That return showed you owed $10,000. You had $5,000 of your own money and you took out a loan to pay the other $5,000. You gave 2 checks for $5,000 each to your spouse to pay the $10,000 liability. Without telling you, your spouse took the $5,000 loan and spent it on himself. You and your spouse were divorced in 2010. In addition, you had no knowledge or reason to know at the time you signed the return that the tax would not be paid. These facts indicate to the IRS that it may be unfair to hold you liable for the $5,000 underpaid tax. The IRS will consider these facts, together with all of the other facts and circumstances, to determine whether to grant you equitable relief from the $5,000 underpaid tax.

Factors Weighing in Favor of Equitable Relief

The following are examples of factors that will weigh in favor of equitable relief, but will not weigh against equitable relief.

- Whether your spouse (or former spouse) abused you.
- Whether you were in poor mental or physical health on the date you signed the return or at the time you requested relief.

Refunds

If you are granted relief, refunds are:

- Permitted under innocent spouse relief as explained later under *Limit on Amount of Refund*.
- Not permitted under separation of liability relief.
- Permitted in limited circumstances under equitable relief, as explained under *Refunds Under Equitable Relief*.

Proof Required

The IRS will only refund payments you made with your own money. However, you must provide proof that you made the payments with your own money. Examples of proof are a copy of your bank statement or a canceled check. No proof is required if your individual refund was used by the IRS to pay a tax you owed on a joint tax return for another year.

Refunds Under Equitable Relief

In the following situations, you are eligible to receive a refund of certain payments you made.

Underpaid tax. If you are granted relief for an underpaid tax, you are eligible for a refund of separate payments that you made after July 22, 1998. However, you are not eligible for refunds of payments made with the joint return, joint payments, or payments that your spouse (or former spouse) made. For example, withholding tax and estimated tax payments cannot be refunded because they are considered made with the joint return.

The amount of the refund is subject to the limit discussed later under *Limit on Amount of Refund*.

Understated tax. If you are granted relief for an understated tax, you are eligible for a refund of certain payments made under an installment agreement that you entered into with the IRS, if you have not defaulted on the installment agreement. You are not in default if the IRS did not issue you a notice of default or take any action to end the installment agreement. Only installment payments made after the date you filed Form 8857 are eligible for a refund.

The amount of the refund is subject to the limit discussed next.

Limit on Amount of Refund

The amount of your refund is limited. Read the following chart to find out the limit.

IF you file Form 8857...	THEN the refund cannot be more than...
Within 3 years after filing your return	The part of the tax paid within 3 years (plus any extension of time for filing your return) before you filed Form 8857.
After the 3-year period, but within 2 years from the time you paid the tax	The tax you paid within 2 years immediately before you filed Form 8857.

Filled-in Form 8857

This part explains how Janie Boulder fills out Form 8857 to request innocent spouse relief.

Janie and Joe Boulder filed a joint tax return for 2007. They claimed one dependency exemption for their son Michael. Their return was adjusted by the IRS because Joe did not report a $5,000 award he won that year. Janie did not know about the award when the return was filed. They agreed to the adjustment but could not pay the additional amount due of $815 ($650 tax + $165 penalty and interest). Janie and Joe were divorced on May 13, 2009. In February 2010, Janie filed her 2009 federal income tax return as head of household. She expected a refund of $1,203. In May 2010, she received a notice informing her that the IRS had offset her refund against the $815 owed on her joint 2007 income tax return and that she had a right to file Form 8857.

Janie applies the conditions listed earlier under *Innocent Spouse Relief* to see if she qualifies for relief.

1. Janie meets the first and second conditions because the joint tax return they filed has an understated tax due to Joe's erroneous item.

2. Janie believes she meets the third condition. She did not know about the award and had no reason to know about it because of the secretive way Joe conducted his financial affairs.

3. Janie believes she meets the fourth condition. She believes it would be unfair to be held liable for the tax because she did not benefit from the award. Joe spent it on personal items for his use only.

Because Janie believes she qualifies for innocent spouse relief, she first completes Part I of Form 8857 to determine if she should file the form. In Part I, she makes all entries under the Tax Year 1 column because she is requesting relief for only one year.

Part I

Line 1. She enters "2007" on line 1 because this is the tax year for which she is requesting relief.

Line 2. She checks the box because she wants a refund.

Note. Because the IRS used her individual refund to pay the tax owed on the joint tax return, she does not need to provide proof of payment.

Line 3. She checks the "No" box because the IRS did not use her share of a joint refund to pay Joe's past-due debts.

Line 4. She checks the "Yes" box because she filed a joint tax return for tax year 2007.

Line 5. She skips this line because she checked the "Yes" box on line 4.

Part II

Line 6. She enters her name, address, social security number, county, and best daytime phone number.

Part III

Line 7. She enters Joe's name, address, social security number, and best daytime phone number.

Line 8. She checks the "divorced since" box and enters the date she was divorced as "05/13/2009." She attaches a copy of her entire divorce decree (not Illustrated) to the form.

Line 9. She checks the box for "High school diploma, equivalent, or less," because she had completed high school when her 2007 joint tax return was filed.

Line 10. She checks the "No" box because she was not a victim of spousal abuse or domestic violence.

Line 11. She checks the "No" box because neither she nor Joe incurred any large expenses during the year for which she wants relief.

Line 12. She checks the "Yes" box because she signed the 2007 joint tax return.

Line 13. She checks the "No" box because she did not have a mental or physical condition when the return was filed and does not have one now.

Part IV

Line 14. Because she was not involved in preparing the return, she checks the box, "You were not involved in preparing the returns."

Line 15. She checks the box, "You did not know anything was incorrect or missing" because she did not know that Joe had received a $5,000 award. She explains this in the space provided.

Line 16. She checks the box, "You knew that person had income" because she knew Joe had income from wages. She also lists Joe's income. Under "Type of Income" she enters "wages." Under "Who paid it to that person," she enters the name of Joe's employer, "Allied." Under "Tax Year 1" she enters the amount of Joe's wages, "$40,000." Because she is only requesting relief for one tax year, she leaves the entry spaces for "Tax Year 2" and "Tax Year 3" blank.

Line 17. She checks the "No" box because she did not know any amount was owed to the IRS when the 2007 return was signed.

Line 18. She checks the "No" box because, when the return was signed, she was not having financial problems.

Line 19. She checks the box, "You were not involved in handling money for the household" because Joe handled all the money for the household. She provides additional information in the space provided.

Line 20. She checks the "No" box because Joe has never transferred money or property to her.

Part V

Line 21. She enters the number "1" on both the line for "Adults" and the line for "Children" because her current household consists of herself and her son.

Line 22. She enters her average monthly income for her entire household.

Line 23. She lists her assets, which are $500 for the fair market value of a car, $450 in her checking account, and $100 in her savings account.

Signing and mailing Form 8857. Janie signs and dates the form. She attaches the copy of her divorce decree (not illustrated) required by line 8. Finally, she sends the form to the IRS address or fax number shown in the instructions for Form 8857.

Form 8857
(Rev. September 2010)
Department of the Treasury
Internal Revenue Service (99)

Request for Innocent Spouse Relief

► See separate instructions.

OMB No. 1545-1596

Important things you should know

- **Do not file this form with your tax return.** See *Where To File* in the instructions.
- Answer all the questions on this form that apply, attach any necessary documentation, and sign on page 4. Do not delay filing this form because of missing documentation. See instructions.
- By law, the IRS must contact the person who was your spouse for the years you want relief. There are no exceptions, even for victims of spousal abuse or domestic violence. Your personal information (such as your current name, address, and employer) will be protected. However, if you petition the Tax Court, your personal information may be released, unless you ask the Tax Court to withhold it. See instructions for details.
- If you need help, see *How To Get Help* in the instructions.

Part I Should you file this form? You **must** complete this part for each tax year.

		Tax Year 1		Tax Year 2		Tax Year 3*	
1	Enter each tax year you want relief. It is important to enter the correct year. For example, if the IRS used your 2009 income tax refund to pay a 2007 tax amount you jointly owed, enter tax year 2007, not tax year 2009 . . . . ► **1**	2007					
	Caution. The IRS generally cannot collect the amount you owe until your request for each year is resolved. However, the time the IRS has to collect is extended. See *Collection Statute of Limitations* on page 3 of the instructions.						
2	Check the box for each year you would like a refund if you qualify for relief. You may be required to provide proof of payment. See instructions . . . . ► **2**	☑		☐		☐	
		Yes	No	Yes	No	Yes	No
3	Did the IRS use your share of the joint refund to pay any of the following past-due debts of your spouse: federal tax, state income tax, child support, spousal support, or federal non-tax debt such as a student loan? • If "Yes," **stop here**; do not file this form for that tax year. Instead, file Form 8379, Injured Spouse Allocation. See instructions. • If "No," go to line 4 . . . . ► **3**	☐	☑	☐	☐	☐	☐
4	Was a return claiming married filing jointly status filed for the tax year listed on line 1? See instructions. • If "Yes," skip line 5 and go to line 6. • If "No," go to line 5 . . . . ► **4**	☑	☐	☐	☐	☐	☐
5	If a joint return for that tax year was not filed, were you a resident of Arizona, California, Idaho, Louisiana, Nevada, New Mexico, Texas, Washington, or Wisconsin? • If "Yes," see *Community Property Laws* on page 2 of the instructions. • If "No" on both lines 4 and 5, **stop here.** Do not file this form for that tax year . . . ► **5**	☐	☐	☐	☐	☐	☐

*If you want relief for more than 3 years, fill out an additional form.

Part II Tell us about yourself

6	Your current name (see instructions)	Your social security number
	Janie Boulder	123-00-9876

Your current mailing address (number and street).	Apt. no.	**County**
5161 Old Farm Estates		Montgomery

City, town or post office, state, and ZIP code. If a foreign address, see instructions.	Best daytime phone number
Hutchinson, IA 55555	721-555-1023

Part III Tell us about you and your spouse for the tax years you want relief

7 Who was your spouse for the tax years you want relief? File a separate Form 8857 for tax years involving different spouses or former spouses.

That person's current name	Social security number (if known)
Joe E. Boulder	234-00-8765

Current home address (number and street) (if known). If a P.O. box, see instructions.	Apt. no.
3895 Timber Way	

City, town or post office, state, and ZIP code. If a foreign address, see instructions.	Best daytime phone number
Creekbed, WY 77777	271-555-2345

For Privacy Act and Paperwork Reduction Act Notice, see instructions.   Cat. No. 24647V   Form **8857** (Rev. 9-2010)

Note. If you need more room to write your answer for any question, attach more pages. Be sure to write your name and social security number on the top of all pages you attach.

Part III (Continued)

8 **What is the current marital status between you and the person on line 7?**

☐ Married and still living together

☐ Married and living apart since _____ MM DD YYYY

☐ Widowed since _____ MM DD YYYY   Attach a photocopy of the death certificate and will (if one exists).

☐ Legally separated since _____ MM DD YYYY   Attach a photocopy of your entire separation agreement.

☑ Divorced since   05-13-2009   MM DD YYYY   Attach a photocopy of your entire divorce decree.

Note. A divorce decree stating that your former spouse must pay all taxes does not necessarily mean you qualify for relief.

9 **What was the highest level of education you had completed when the return(s) were filed?** If the answers are **not** the same for all tax years, explain.

☑ High school diploma, equivalent, or less

☐ Some college

☐ College degree or higher. List any degrees you have ▶

List any college-level business or tax-related courses you completed ▶

Explain ▶

10 **Were you a victim of spousal abuse or domestic violence during any of the tax years you want relief?** If the answers are **not** the same for all tax years, explain.

☐ **Yes. Attach a statement** to explain the situation and **when** it started. Provide photocopies of any documentation, such as police reports, a restraining order, a doctor's report or letter, or a notarized statement from someone who was aware of the situation.

☑ No.

11 **Did you (or the person on line 7) incur any large expenses, such as trips, home improvements, or private schooling, or make any large purchases, such as automobiles, appliances, or jewelry, during any of the years you want relief or any later years?**

☐ **Yes. Attach a statement** describing (a) the types and amounts of the expenses and purchases and (b) the years they were incurred or made.

☑ No.

12 **Did you sign the return(s)?** If the answers are **not** the same for all tax years, explain.

☑ Yes. If you were forced to sign under duress (threat of harm or other form of coercion), check here ▶ ☐ . See instructions.

☐ No. Your signature was forged. See instructions.

13 **When any of the returns were signed, did you have a mental or physical health problem or do you have a mental or physical health problem now?** If the answers are **not** the same for all tax years, explain.

☐ **Yes. Attach a statement** to explain the problem and **when** it started. Provide photocopies of any documentation, such as medical bills or a doctor's report or letter.

☑ No.

Part IV   Tell us how you were involved with finances and preparing returns for those tax years

14 **How were you involved with preparing the returns?** Check all that apply and explain, if necessary. If the answers are **not** the same for all tax years, explain.

☐ You filled out or helped fill out the returns.

☐ You gathered receipts and cancelled checks.

☐ You gave tax documents (such as Forms W-2, 1099, etc.) to the person who prepared the returns.

☐ You reviewed the returns before they were signed.

☐ You did not review the returns before they were signed. Explain below.

☑ You were not involved in preparing the returns.

☐ Other ▶

Explain how you were involved ▶

Form **8857** (Rev. 9-2010)

Note. If you need more room to write your answer for any question, attach more pages. Be sure to write your name and social security number on the top of all pages you attach.

Part IV *(Continued)*

15 **When the returns were signed, what did you know about any incorrect or missing information?** Check all that apply and explain, if necessary. If the answers are **not** the same for all tax years, explain.

☐ You knew something was incorrect or missing, but you said nothing.

☐ You knew something was incorrect or missing and asked about it.

☒ You did not know anything was incorrect or missing.

Explain ▶ *I did not know about the $5,000 award. My ex-husband was very secretive about the way he conducted his financial affairs.*

16 **When any of the returns were signed, what did you know about the income of the person on line 7?** Check all that apply and explain, if necessary. If the answers are **not** the same for all tax years, explain.

☒ You knew that person had income.

List each type of income on a separate line. (Examples are wages, social security, gambling winnings, or self-employment business income.) Enter each tax year and the amount of income for each type you listed. If you do not know any details, enter "I don't know."

Type of income	Who paid it to that person	Tax Year 1	Tax Year 2	Tax Year 3
Wages	Allied	$ 40,000	$	$
		$	$	$
		$	$	$

☐ You knew that person was self-employed and you helped with the books and records.

☐ You knew that person was self-employed and you did not help with the books and records.

☐ You knew that person had no income.

☐ You did not know if that person had income.

Explain ▶

17 **When the returns were signed, did you know any amount was owed to the IRS for those tax years?** If the answers are **not** the same for all tax years, explain.

☐ Yes. Explain when and how you thought the amount of tax reported on the return would be paid ▶

☒ No.

Explain ▶

18 **When any of the returns were signed, were you having financial problems** (for example, bankruptcy or bills you could not pay)? If the answers are **not** the same for all tax years, explain.

☐ Yes. Explain ▶

☒ No.

☐ Did not know.

Explain ▶

19 **For the years you want relief, how were you involved in the household finances?** Check all that apply. If the answers are **not** the same for all tax years, explain.

☐ You knew the person on line 7 had separate accounts.

☐ You had joint accounts but you had limited use of them or did not use them. Explain below.

☐ You used joint accounts. You made deposits, paid bills, balanced the checkbook, or reviewed the monthly bank statements.

☐ You made decisions about how money was spent. For example, you paid bills or made decisions about household purchases.

☒ You were not involved in handling money for the household.

☐ Other ▶

Explain anything else you want to tell us about your household finances ▶ *My ex-husband handled the household finances. He didn't want me involved. He was so secretive about it, too.*

20 **Has the person on line 7 ever transferred assets (money or property) to you?** (Property includes real estate, stocks, bonds, or other property that you own.) See instructions.

☐ Yes. List the assets, the dates they were transferred, and their fair market values on the dates transferred. Explain why the assets were transferred ▶

☒ No.

Form **8857** (Rev. 9-2010)

Part V   Tell us about your current financial situation

21   Tell us the number of people currently in your household.   Adults   1   Children   1

22   **Tell us your current average monthly income and expenses for your entire household.** If family or friends are helping to support you, include the amount of support as gifts under **Monthly income.** Under **Monthly expenses,** enter all expenses, including expenses paid with income from gifts.

Monthly income	Amount	Monthly expenses	Amount
Gifts		Federal, state, and local taxes deducted from your paycheck	250
Wages (Gross pay)	2000	Rent or mortgage	620
Pensions		Utilities	100
Unemployment		Telephone	40
Social security			
Government assistance, such as housing, food stamps, grants		Food	568
Alimony		Car expenses, payments, insurance, etc.	254
		Medical expenses, including medical insurance	200
Child support	750	Life insurance	10
Self-employment business income		Clothing	200
Rental income		Child care	455
Interest and dividends		Public transportation	
Other income, such as disability payments, gambling winnings, etc.		Other expenses, such as real estate taxes, child support, etc.	
List the type below:		List the type below:	
Type _____		Type _____	
Type _____		Type _____	
Type _____		Type _____	
Total ▶	2,750	**Total** ▶	2,697

23   **Tell us about your assets.** Your assets are your money and property. Property includes real estate, motor vehicles, stocks, bonds, and other property that you own. Tell us the amount of cash you have on hand and in your bank accounts. Also give a description of each item of property, the fair market value of each item, and the balance of any outstanding loans you used to acquire each item. Do not list any money or property you listed on line 20. If you need more room, attach more pages. Write your name and social security number on the top of all pages you attach.

I have a car with a fair market value of $500, $450 in my checking account, and $100 in a savings account.

24   **Please provide any other information you want us to consider in determining whether it would be unfair to hold you liable for the tax.** If you need more room, attach more pages. Write your name and social security number on the top of all pages you attach.

Caution

By signing this form, you understand that, by law, we must contact the person on line 7. See instructions for details.

Sign Here

Keep a copy for your records.

Under penalties of perjury, I declare that I have examined this form and any accompanying schedules and statements, and to the best of my knowledge and belief, they are true, correct, and complete. Declaration of preparer (other than taxpayer) is based on all information of which preparer has any knowledge.

Your signature *Janie Boulder*	Date 8/01/2010

Paid Preparer's Use Only

Preparer's signature	Date	Check if self-employed ☐	Preparer's SSN or PTIN
Firm's name (or yours if self-employed), address, and ZIP code		EIN	
		Phone no.	

Form **8857** (Rev. 9-2010)

Flowcharts

The following flowcharts provide a quick way for determining whether you may qualify for relief. But do not rely on these flowcharts alone. Also read the earlier discussions.

Figure A. Do You Qualify for Innocent Spouse Relief?

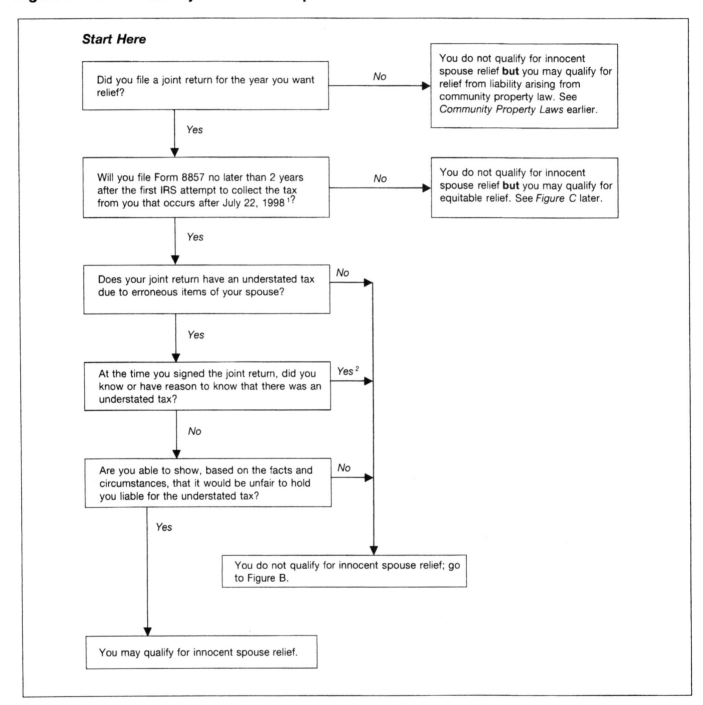

¹ Collection activities that may start the 2-year period are described earlier under *How To Request Relief*.

² You may qualify for partial relief if, at the time you filed your return, you knew or had reason to know of only a portion of an erroneous item.

Figure B. Do You Qualify for Separation of Liability Relief?

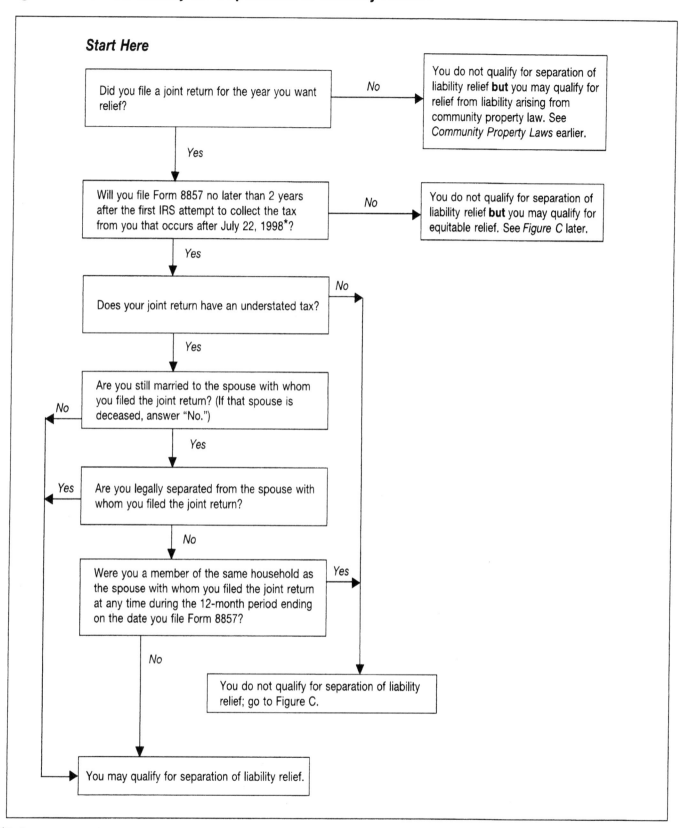

*Collection activities that may start the 2-year period are described earlier under *How To Request Relief.*

Figure C. Do You Qualify for Equitable Relief?

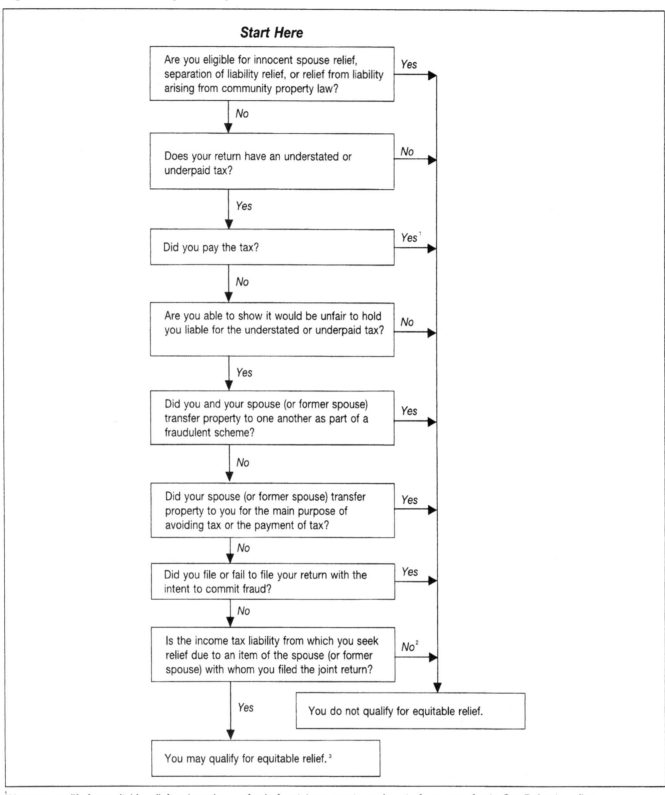

Start Here

Are you eligible for innocent spouse relief, separation of liability relief, or relief from liability arising from community property law? — **Yes** →

↓ **No**

Does your return have an understated or underpaid tax? — **No** →

↓ **Yes**

Did you pay the tax? — **Yes** [1] →

↓ **No**

Are you able to show it would be unfair to hold you liable for the understated or underpaid tax? — **No** →

↓ **Yes**

Did you and your spouse (or former spouse) transfer property to one another as part of a fraudulent scheme? — **Yes** →

↓ **No**

Did your spouse (or former spouse) transfer property to you for the main purpose of avoiding tax or the payment of tax? — **Yes** →

↓ **No**

Did you file or fail to file your return with the intent to commit fraud? — **Yes** →

↓ **No**

Is the income tax liability from which you seek relief due to an item of the spouse (or former spouse) with whom you filed the joint return? — **No** [2] →

↓ **Yes**

You do not qualify for equitable relief.

You may qualify for equitable relief. [3]

[1] You may qualify for equitable relief and receive a refund of certain payments made out of your own funds. See *Refunds* earlier.

[2] You may qualify for equitable relief if you meet any of the exceptions to condition (8) discussed earlier under *Conditions for Getting Equitable Relief.*

[3] You must file Form 8857 by the filing deadlines explained earlier in *Exception for equitable relief* under *How To Request Relief.*

Questions & Answers

This section answers questions commonly asked by taxpayers about innocent spouse relief.

What is joint and several liability?

When you file a joint income tax return, the law makes both you and your spouse responsible for the entire tax liability. This is called joint and several liability. Joint and several liability applies not only to the tax liability you show on the return but also to any additional tax liability the IRS determines to be due, even if the additional tax is due to the income, deductions, or credits of your spouse or former spouse. You remain jointly and severally liable for taxes, and the IRS still can collect from you, even if you later divorce and the divorce decree states that your former spouse will be solely responsible for the tax.

How can I get relief from joint and several liability?

There are three types of relief for filers of joint returns: "innocent spouse relief," "separation of liability relief," and "equitable relief." Each type has different requirements. They are explained separately below.

What are the rules for innocent spouse relief?

To qualify for innocent spouse relief, you must meet all of the following conditions.

- You must have filed a joint return which has an understated tax.

- The understated tax must be due to erroneous items of your spouse (or former spouse).

- You must establish that at the time you signed the joint return, you did not know, and had no reason to know, that there was an understated tax.

- Taking into account all of the facts and circumstances, it would be unfair to hold you liable for the understated tax.

- You must request relief within 2 years after the date on which the

IRS first began collection activity against you after July 22, 1998.

What are "erroneous items"?

Erroneous items are any deductions, credits, or bases that are incorrectly stated on the return, and any income that is not properly reported on the return.

What is an "understated tax"?

You have an understated tax if the IRS determined that your total tax should be more than the amount actually shown on your return. For example, you reported total tax on your 2008 return of $2,500. IRS determined in an audit of your 2008 return that the total tax should be $3,000. You have a $500 understated tax.

Will I qualify for innocent spouse relief in any situation where there is an understated tax?

No. There are many situations in which you may owe tax that is related to your spouse (or former spouse), but not be eligible for innocent spouse relief. For example, you and your spouse file a joint return on which you report $10,000 of income and deductions, but you knew that your spouse was not reporting $5,000 of dividends. You are not eligible for innocent spouse relief because you have knowledge of the understated tax.

What are the rules for separation of liability relief?

Under this type of relief, you allocate (separate) the understated tax (plus interest and penalties) on your joint return between you and your spouse (or former spouse). The understated tax allocated to you is generally the amount you are responsible for. To qualify for separation of liability relief, you must have filed a joint return and meet either of the following requirements at the time you file Form 8857.

- You are no longer married to, or are legally separated from, the spouse with whom you filed the

joint return for which you are requesting relief. (Under this rule, you are no longer married if you are widowed.)

- You were not a member of the same household as the spouse with whom you filed the joint return at any time during the 12-month period ending on the date you file Form 8857.

In addition to the above requirements, you must file a Form 8857 within 2 years after the date on which the IRS first began collection activity against you after July 22, 1998.

Why would a request for separation of liability relief be denied?

Even if you meet the requirements listed earlier, a request for separation of liability relief will not be granted in the following situations.

- The IRS proves that you and your spouse (or former spouse) transferred assets to one another as part of a fraudulent scheme.

- The IRS proves that at the time you signed your joint return, you had actual knowledge of any erroneous items giving rise to the deficiency that are allocable to your spouse (or former spouse).

- Your spouse (or former spouse) transferred property to you to avoid tax or the payment of tax.

What are the rules for equitable relief?

Equitable relief is only available if you meet all of the following conditions.

- You do not qualify for innocent spouse relief, separation of liability relief, or relief from liability arising from community property law.

- You have an understated tax or underpaid tax. See *Note* later.

- You did not pay the tax. However, see *Refunds*, earlier, for exceptions.

- The IRS determines that it is unfair to hold you liable for the understated or underpaid tax taking into account all the facts and circumstances.

- You and your spouse (or former spouse) did not transfer assets to one another as a part of a fraudulent scheme.

- Your spouse (or former spouse) did not transfer property to you for the main purpose of avoiding tax or the payment of tax.

- You did not file or fail to file your return with the intent to commit fraud.

- The income tax liability for which you seek relief is attributable to your spouse (or former spouse) with whom you filed the joint return. For exceptions to this condition, see item (8) under *Conditions for Getting Equitable Relief,* earlier.

- You timely file Form 8857 as explained earlier in *Exception for equitable relief* under *How To Request Relief.*

Note. Unlike innocent spouse relief or separation of liability relief, if you qualify for equitable relief, you can also get relief from an underpaid tax. (An underpaid tax is tax that is properly shown on the return, but has not been paid.)

How do state community property laws affect my ability to qualify for relief?

Community property states are Arizona, California, Idaho, Louisiana, Nevada, New Mexico, Texas, Washington, and Wisconsin. Generally, community property laws require you to allocate community income and expenses equally between both spouses. However, community property laws are not taken into account in determining whether an item belongs to you or to your spouse (or former spouse) for purposes of requesting any relief from liability.

How do I request relief?

File Form 8857, *Request for Innocent Spouse Relief,* to ask the IRS for relief. You must file an additional Form 8857 if you are requesting relief for more than three years.

When should I file Form 8857?

If you are requesting innocent spouse relief or separation of liability relief, file Form 8857 no later than two years after the date on which the IRS first began collection activities against you after July 22, 1998.

If you are requesting equitable relief, see *Exception for equitable relief.* under *How To Request Relief,* earlier, for when to file Form 8857.

If you are requesting relief from liability arising from community property law, see *How and When To Request Relief* under *Community Property Laws,* earlier, for when to file Form 8857.

Where should I file Form 8857?

Use the address or fax number shown in the Instructions for Form 8857.

I am currently undergoing an examination of my return. How do I request innocent spouse relief?

File Form 8857 at the address or send it to the fax number shown in the Instructions for Form 8857. Do not file it with the employee assigned to examine your return.

What if the IRS has given me notice that it will levy my account for the tax liability and I decide to request relief?

Generally, the IRS has 10 years to collect an amount you owe. This is the collection statute of limitations. By law, the IRS is not allowed to collect from you after the 10-year period ends.

If you request relief for any tax year, the IRS cannot collect from you for that year while your request is pending. But interest and penalties continue to accrue. Your request is generally considered pending from the date the IRS receives your Form 8857 until the date your request is resolved. This includes the time the Tax Court is considering your request.

After your case is resolved, the IRS can begin or resume collecting from you. The 10-year period will be increased by the amount of time your request for relief was pending plus 60 days. See Publication 594 for more information.

What is "injured spouse relief"?

Injured spouse relief is different from innocent spouse relief. When a joint return is filed and the refund is used to pay one spouse's past-due federal tax, state income tax, state unemployment compensation debts, child support, spousal support, or federal non-tax debt, such as a student loan, the other spouse may be considered an injured spouse. The injured spouse can get back his or her share of the joint overpayment using *Form 8379, Injured Spouse Allocation.*

You are considered an injured spouse if:

1. You are not legally obligated to pay the past-due amount, and

2. You meet any of the following conditions:

   a. You made and reported tax payments (such as federal income tax withholding or estimated tax payments).

   b. You had earned income (such as wages, salaries, or self-employment income) and claimed the earned income credit or the additional child tax credit.

   c. You claimed a refundable tax credit, such as the health coverage tax credit or the refundable credit for prior year minimum tax.

Note. If your residence was in a community property state at any time during the year, you may file Form 8379 even if only item (1) above applies.

How To Get Tax Help

You can get help with unresolved tax issues, order free publications and forms, ask tax questions, and get information from the IRS in several ways. By selecting the method that is best for you, you will have quick and easy access to tax help.

Free help with your return. Free help in preparing your return is available nationwide from IRS-certified volunteers. The Volunteer Income Tax Assistance (VITA) program is designed to help low-moderate income taxpayers and the Tax Counseling for the Elderly (TCE) program is designed to assist taxpayers age 60 and older with their tax returns. Most VITA and TCE sites offer free electronic filing and all volunteers will let you know about credits and deductions you may be entitled to claim. To find the nearest VITA or TCE site, visit IRS.gov or call 1-800-906-9887 or 1-800-829-1040.

As part of the TCE program, AARP offers the Tax-Aide counseling program. To find the nearest AARP Tax-Aide site, call 1-888-227-7669 or visit AARP's website at www.aarp.org/money/taxaide.

For more information on these programs, go to IRS.gov and enter keyword "VITA" in the upper right-hand corner.

 Internet. You can access the IRS website at IRS.gov 24 hours a day, 7 days a week to:

- *E-file* your return. Find out about commercial tax preparation and *e-file* services available free to eligible taxpayers.

- Check the status of your 2011 refund. Go to IRS.gov and click on *Where's My Refund.* Wait at least 72 hours after the IRS acknowledges receipt of your e-filed return, or 3 to 4 weeks after mailing a paper return. If you filed Form 8379 with your return, wait 14 weeks (11 weeks if you filed electronically). Have your 2011 tax return available so you can provide your social security number, your filing status, and the exact whole dollar amount of your refund.

- Download forms, including talking tax forms, instructions, and publications.

- Order IRS products online.

- Research your tax questions online.

- Search publications online by topic or keyword.

- Use the online Internal Revenue Code, regulations, or other official guidance.

- View Internal Revenue Bulletins (IRBs) published in the last few years.

- Figure your withholding allowances using the withholding calculator online at www.irs.gov/individuals.

- Determine if Form 6251 must be filed by using our Alternative Minimum Tax (AMT) Assistant available online at www.irs.gov/individuals.

- Sign up to receive local and national tax news by email.

- Get information on starting and operating a small business.

 Phone. Many services are available by phone.

- *Ordering forms, instructions, and publications.* Call 1-800-TAX-FORM (1-800-829-3676) to order current-year forms, instructions, and publications, and prior-year forms and instructions. You should receive your order within 10 days.

- *Asking tax questions.* Call the IRS with your tax questions at 1-800-829-1040.

- *Solving problems.* You can get face-to-face help solving tax problems every business day in IRS Taxpayer Assistance Centers. An employee can explain IRS letters, request adjustments to your account, or help you set up a payment plan. Call your local Taxpayer Assistance Center

for an appointment. To find the number, go to www.irs.gov/localcontacts or look in the phone book under *United States Government, Internal Revenue Service.*

- *TTY/TDD equipment.* If you have access to TTY/TDD equipment, call 1-800-829-4059 to ask tax questions or to order forms and publications.

- *TeleTax topics.* Call 1-800-829-4477 to listen to pre-recorded messages covering various tax topics.

- *Refund information.* To check the status of your 2011 refund, call 1-800-829-1954 or 1-800-829-4477 (automated refund information 24 hours a day, 7 days a week). Wait at least 72 hours after the IRS acknowledges receipt of your e-filed return, or 3 to 4 weeks after mailing a paper return. If you filed Form 8379 with your return, wait 14 weeks (11 weeks if you filed electronically). Have your 2011 tax return available so you can provide your social security number, your filing status, and the exact whole dollar amount of your refund. If you check the status of your refund and are not given the date it will be issued, please wait until the next week before checking back.

- *Other refund information.* To check the status of a prior-year refund or amended return refund, call 1-800-829-1040.

Evaluating the quality of our telephone services. To ensure IRS representatives give accurate, courteous, and professional answers, we use several methods to evaluate the quality of our telephone services. One method is for a second IRS representative to listen in on or record random telephone calls. Another is to ask some callers to complete a short survey at the end of the call.

Walk-in. Many products and services are available on a walk-in basis.

- *Products.* You can walk in to many post offices, libraries, and IRS offices to pick up certain forms, instructions, and publications. Some IRS offices, libraries, grocery stores, copy centers, city and county government offices, credit unions, and office supply stores have a collection of products available to print from a CD or photocopy from reproducible proofs. Also, some IRS offices and libraries have the Internal Revenue Code, regulations, Internal Revenue Bulletins, and Cumulative Bulletins available for research purposes.

- *Services.* You can walk in to your local Taxpayer Assistance Center every business day for personal, face-to-face tax help. An employee can explain IRS letters, request adjustments to your tax account, or help you set up a payment plan. If you need to resolve a tax problem, have questions about how the tax law applies to your individual tax return, or you are more comfortable talking with someone in person, visit your local Taxpayer Assistance Center where you can spread out your records and talk with an IRS representative face-to-face. No appointment is necessary—just walk in. If you prefer, you can call your local Center and leave a message requesting an appointment to resolve a tax account issue. A representative will call you back within 2 business days to schedule an in-person appointment at your convenience. If you have an ongoing, complex tax account problem or a special need, such as a disability, an appointment can be requested. All other issues will be handled without an appointment. To find the number of your local office, go to *www.irs.gov/localcontacts* or look in the phone book under *United States Government, Internal Revenue Service.*

 Mail. You can send your order for forms, instructions, and publications to the address below. You should receive a response within 10 days after your request is received.

Internal Revenue Service
1201 N. Mitsubishi Motorway
Bloomington, IL 61705-6613

Taxpayer Advocate Service. The Taxpayer Advocate Service (TAS) is your voice at the IRS. Our job is to ensure that every taxpayer is treated fairly, and that you know and understand your rights. We offer free help to guide you through the often-confusing process of resolving tax problems that you haven't been able to solve on your own. Remember, the worst thing you can do is nothing at all.

TAS can help if you can't resolve your problem with the IRS and:

- Your problem is causing financial difficulties for you, your family, or your business.

- You face (or your business is facing) an immediate threat of adverse action.

- You have tried repeatedly to contact the IRS but no one has responded, or the IRS has not responded to you by the date promised.

If you qualify for our help, we'll do everything we can to get your problem resolved. You will be assigned to one advocate who will be with you at every turn. We have offices in every state, the District of Columbia, and Puerto Rico. Although TAS is independent within the IRS, our advocates know how to work with the IRS to get your problems resolved. And our services are always free.

As a taxpayer, you have rights that the IRS must abide by in its dealings with you. Our tax toolkit at *www. TaxpayerAdvocate.irs.gov* can help you understand these rights.

If you think TAS might be able to help you, call your local advocate, whose number is in your phone book and on our website at *www.irs.gov/ advocate.* You can also call our toll-free number at 1-877-777-4778 or TTY/TDD 1-800-829-4059.

TAS also handles large-scale or systemic problems that affect many taxpayers. If you know of one of these broad issues, please report it to us through our Systemic Advocacy Management System at *www.irs.gov/advocate.*

Low Income Taxpayer Clinics (LITCs). Low Income Taxpayer Clinics (LITCs) are independent from the IRS. Some clinics serve individuals whose income is below a certain level and who need to resolve a tax problem. These clinics provide professional representation before the IRS or in court on audits, appeals, tax collection disputes, and other issues for free or for a small fee. Some clinics can provide information about taxpayer rights and responsibilities in many different languages for individuals who speak English as a second language. For more information and to find a clinic near you, see the LITC page on *www.irs.gov/advocate* or IRS Publication 4134, *Low Income Taxpayer Clinic List.* This publication is also available by calling 1-800-829-3676 or at your local IRS office.

Free tax services. Publication 910, IRS Guide to Free Tax Services, is your guide to IRS services and resources. Learn about free tax information from the IRS, including publications, services, and education and assistance programs. The publication also has an index of over 100 TeleTax topics (recorded tax information) you can listen to on the telephone. The majority of the information and services listed in this publication are available to you free of charge. If there is a fee associated with a resource or service, it is listed in the publication.

Accessible versions of IRS published products are available on request in a variety of alternative formats for people with disabilities.

 DVD for tax products. You can order Publication 1796, IRS Tax Products DVD, and obtain:

- Current-year forms, instructions, and publications.

- Prior-year forms, instructions, and publications.

- Tax Map: an electronic research tool and finding aid.
- Tax law frequently asked questions.
- Tax Topics from the IRS telephone response system.
- Internal Revenue Code—Title 26 of the U.S. Code.
- Links to other Internet based Tax Research Materials.

- Fill-in, print, and save features for most tax forms.
- Internal Revenue Bulletins.
- Toll-free and email technical support.
- Two releases during the year.
  – The first release will ship the beginning of January 2012.
  – The final release will ship the beginning of March 2012.

Purchase the DVD from National Technical Information Service (NTIS) at *www.irs.gov/cdorders* for $30 (no handling fee) or call 1-877-233-6767 toll free to buy the DVD for $30 (plus a $6 handling fee).

Index

 To help us develop a more useful index, please let us know if you have ideas for index entries. See "Comments and Suggestions" in the "Introduction" for the ways you can reach us.

The IRS Mission

Provide America's taxpayers top quality service by helping them understand and meet their tax responsibilities and by applying the tax law with integrity and fairness to all.

The Examination Process

Introduction

The Internal Revenue Service (IRS) accepts most federal returns as filed. Some returns, however, are examined, or audited, to determine if income, expenses, and credits are reported accurately.

This publication discusses general rules and procedures we follow in examinations. It explains what happens before, during, and after an examination. It also explains appeal and payment procedures.

As a taxpayer, you have the right to fair, professional, prompt, and courteous service from IRS employees, as outlined in the Declaration of Taxpayer Rights found on page 3.

We must follow the tax rules set forth by Congress in the Internal Revenue Code. We also follow Treasury Regulations, court decisions, and other rules and procedures written to administer the tax laws.

If the examination results in a change to your tax liability, you may ask us to reconsider your case. Some reasons why we may reconsider your case include:

- You are submitting additional information that could result in a change to the additional amount we have determined that you owe;

- You are filing an original delinquent return after we have determined that you owe an additional amount, or;

- You are identifying a mathematical or processing error we made.

You must request reconsideration in writing and submit it to your local IRS office.

Department of the Treasury
Internal Revenue Service

www.irs.gov

Publication 3498 (Rev. 11-2004)
Catalog Number 73074S

What's *Inside* . . .

Introduction

Do you have questions or need help right away? Call us. We are here to help you.

For General Information:

For information about a specific examination please contact the person named on the appointment letter.

For tax information and help:

Call the number on the bill you received or call us toll free at:

1-800-829-1040 *(for 1040 filers)*
1-800-829-4933 *(for business filers)*
1-800-829-4059 /TDD

For tax forms and publications:

1-800-829-3676

1-800-829-4059 /TDD

1-703-368-9694-Forms by Fax

Internet: www.irs.gov

FTP - ftp.fedworld.gov/pub/

TELENET-iris.irs.gov

You'll find answers to frequently asked tax questions, tax forms on-line, searchable publications, hot tax issues, news, and help through e-mail.

If you prefer to write to us . .

Enclose a copy of your tax bill. Print your name, social security number or taxpayer identification number, and the tax form and period shown on your bill. Write to us at the address shown on your tax bill.

You may also visit your nearest IRS Office.

You'll find the exact address in your local phone book under *U.S. Government*

Declaration of Taxpayer Rights

I. Protection of Your Rights

IRS employees will explain and protect your rights as a taxpayer throughout your contact with us.

II. Privacy and Confidentiality

The IRS will not disclose to anyone the information you give us, except as authorized by law. You have the right to know why we are asking you for information, how we will use it, and what happens if you do not provide requested information.

III. Professional and Courteous Service

If you believe that an IRS employee has not treated you in a professional, fair, and courteous manner, you should tell that employee's supervisor. If the supervisor's response is not satisfactory, you should write to the IRS Director for your Area or the Center where you file your return.

IV. Representation

You may either represent yourself or, with proper written authorization, have someone else represent you. Your representative must be a person allowed to practice before the IRS, such as an attorney, certified public accountant, or enrolled agent (a person enrolled to practice before the IRS). If you are in an interview and ask to consult such a person, then we must stop and reschedule the interview in most cases.

You can have someone accompany you at an interview. You may make sound recordings of any meetings with our examination, appeal, or collection personnel, provided you tell us in writing 10 days before the meeting.

V. Payment of Only the Correct Amount of Tax

You are responsible for paying only the correct amount of tax due under the law—no more, no less. If you cannot pay all of your tax when it is due, you may be able to make monthly payments.

VI. Help with Unresolved Tax Problems

The Taxpayer Advocate Service can help you if you have tried unsuccessfully to resolve a problem with the IRS. Your local Taxpayer Advocate can offer you special help if you have a significant hardship as a result of a tax problem. For more information, call toll-free, 1-877-777-4778 (1-800-829-4059 for TTY/TDD) or write to the Taxpayer Advocate at the IRS office that last contacted you.

VII. Appeals and Judicial Review

If you disagree with us about the amount of your tax liability or certain collection actions, you have the right to ask the Appeals Office to review your case. You may also ask a court to review your case.

VIII. Relief from Certain Penalties and Interest

The IRS will waive penalties when allowed by law if you can show you acted reasonably and in good faith or relied on the incorrect advice of an IRS employee. We will waive interest that is the result of certain errors or delays caused by an IRS employee.

Your Return Is Going To Be Examined.

Before the Examination

We accept most taxpayers' returns as filed. If we inquire about your return or select it for examination, it does not suggest that you are dishonest. The inquiry or examination may or may not result in more tax. We may close your case without change or you may receive a refund.

The process of selecting a return for examination usually begins in one of two ways. One way is to use computer programs to identify returns that may have incorrect amounts. The programs may be based on information returns, such as Forms 1099 or W-2, on studies of past examinations, or on certain issues identified by other special projects. Another way is to use information from compliance projects that indicates a return may have incorrect amounts. These sources may include newspapers, public records, and individuals. If we determine the information is accurate and reliable, we may use it to select a return for examination.

Publication 556, *Examination of Returns, Appeal Rights, and Claims for Refund,* explains the rules and procedures that we follow in examinations. The following sections give an overview of how we conduct examinations.

During the Examination

Examinations by Mail

Some examinations are conducted entirely by mail. If the examination is conducted by mail, you'll receive a letter from us asking for additional information about certain items shown on your return, such as income, expenses, and itemized deductions.

If the examination is conducted by mail, you can:

1. Act on your own behalf. *(In the case of a jointly filed return, either spouse can respond or both spouses can send a joint response.)*

2. Have someone represent you in correspondence with us. This person must be an attorney, accountant, enrolled agent, an enrolled actuary, or the person who prepared the return and signed it as the preparer. If you choose to have someone represent you, you must furnish us with written authorization. Make this authorization on Form 2848, *Power of Attorney and Declaration of Representative.*

   Note: *You may obtain any of the forms and publications referenced in this publication by calling 1-800-829-3676.*

Examinations in Person

An examination conducted in person begins when we notify you that your return has been selected. We will tell you what information you need to provide at that time. If you gather the information before the examination, we may be able to complete it more easily and in a shorter time.

If the examination is conducted in person, it can take place in your home, your place of business, an IRS office, or the office of your attorney, accountant, or enrolled agent *(a person enrolled to practice before the IRS).* If the time or place is not convenient for you, the examiner will try to work out something more suitable.

If the examination is conducted in person, you can:

1. Act on your own behalf. _(In the case of a jointly filed return, either spouse or both can attend the interview.)_ If you are acting on your own behalf, you may leave to consult with your representative. We will suspend the interview and reschedule the examination. We cannot suspend the interview if we are conducting it as a result of your receiving an administrative summons.

2. Have someone accompany you, either to support your position or to witness to the proceedings.

3. Accompany someone who will represent you. This person must be an attorney, accountant, enrolled agent, an enrolled actuary, or the person who prepared the return and signed it as the preparer.

4. Have your representative act for you and not be present at the audit yourself. If you choose to have someone represent you in your absence, you must furnish us with written authorization. Make this authorization on **Form 2848**, _Power of Attorney and Declaration of Representative._

How to Stop Interest from Accumulating

During your examination, if you think you will owe additional tax at the end of the examination, you can stop interest from accumulating by paying all or part of the amount you think you will owe. Interest will stop accumulating on the part you pay when the IRS receives your money. Interest will only be charged on the tax, penalties, and interest that are unpaid on the date they are assessed.

Consents to Extend the Statute of Limitations

We try to examine tax returns as soon as possible after they are filed, but occasionally we may request that you extend the statute of limitations of your tax return.

A return's statute of limitation generally limits the time we have to examine it and assess tax. Assessments of tax must be made within 3 years after a return is due or filed, whichever is later. We can't assess additional tax or make a refund or credit _(unless you filed a timely claim)_ after the statute of limitations has expired. Also, if you disagree with the results of the examination, you can't appeal the items you disagree with unless sufficient time remains on the statute. Because of these restrictions, if there isn't much time remaining to examine your return, assess additional taxes, and/or exercise your appeal rights, you have the opportunity to extend the statute of limitations. This will allow you additional time to provide further documentation to support your position, request an appeal if you do not agree with our findings, or to claim a tax refund or credit. It also allows the Service time to complete the examination, make any additional assessment, if necessary, and provide sufficient time for processing.

A written agreement between you and the Service to extend the statutory period of a tax return is called a "consent." Consents can be used for all types of tax except estate tax.

There are two basic kinds of consent forms. One sets a specific expiration date for the extension, and the other for an indefinite period of time. Either type of consent may be limited by restrictive conditions. The use of a restricted consent is to allow the statute to expire with regard to all items on the return except those covered by the restrictive language.

If the statute of limitations for your tax return is approaching, you may be asked to sign a consent. You may:

1. Refuse to extend the statute of limitations;

2. Limit or restrict the consent to particular issues, or

3. Limit the extension to a particular period of time.

The consent will be sent or presented to you with a letter explaining this process and **Publication 1035**, _Extending the Tax Assessment Period._ For further information, refer to this publication.

Results of the Examination

If we accept your return as filed, you will receive a letter stating that the examiner proposed no changes to your return. You should keep this letter with your tax records.

If we don't accept your return as filed, we will explain any proposed changes to you and your authorized representative. It is important that you understand the reasons for any proposed changes; don't hesitate to ask about anything that is unclear to you.

What to Do When You Receive a Bill from the IRS

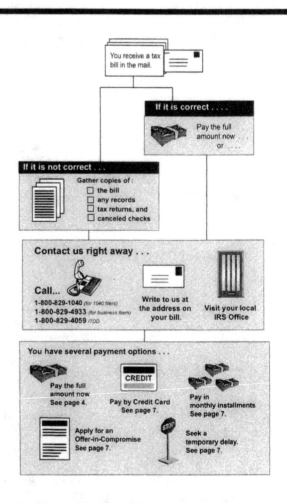

What To Do If You Agree or Disagree with the Examination Results

If You Agree

If you agree with a proposed *increase* to tax, you can sign an agreement form and pay any additional tax you may owe. You must pay interest and applicable penalties on any additional balance due. If you pay when you sign the agreement, interest is generally figured from the due date of your return to the date of your payment.

If you do not pay the additional tax and interest, you will receive a bill *(See "What To do When You Receive a Bill from the IRS" on page 4.)* If the amount due *(including interest and applicable penalties)* is less than $100,000 and you pay it within 21 business days, we will not charge more interest or penalties. If the amount is $100,000 or more, the period is reduced to 10 calendar days. If you can't pay the tax due at the end of the examination, you may pay whatever amount you can and request an installment agreement for the balance. *(See "Setting up an Installment Agreement" on page 7.)*

If you are entitled to a refund, you will receive it sooner if you sign the agreement form at the end of the examination. You will also be paid interest on the refund.

If You Do Not Agree

If you do not agree with the proposed changes, the examiner will explain your appeal rights. If your examination takes place in an IRS office, you may request an immediate meeting with the examiner's supervisor to explain your situation. You may also enter into an *Agreement to Mediate* to help resolve disputes through Fast Track Mediation services. *(See next column.)* Mediation can take place at this meeting or afterwards. If an agreement is reached, your case will be closed.

If you cannot reach an agreement with the supervisor at this meeting, or if the examination took place outside an IRS office or was conducted through correspondence with an IRS Campus employee, the examiner will prepare a report explaining your position and ours. The examiner will forward your case to the Area office for processing .

You will receive:

- A letter (known as a 30-day letter) notifying you of your rights to appeal the proposed changes within 30 days,

- A copy of the examiner's report explaining the proposed changes, and

- An agreement or a waiver form.

You generally have 30 days from the date of the 30-day letter to tell us whether you will accept the proposed changes or appeal them. The letter will explain what steps you should take, depending on what action you choose. Be sure to follow the instructions carefully. Appeal rights are explained following this section.

Caution

If you do not respond to the 30-day letter, or if you respond but do not reach an agreement with an appeals officer, we will send you a 90-day letter, also known as a *Notice of Deficiency*. This is a legal document that explains the proposed changes and the amount of the proposed tax increase. You will have 90 days (150 days if it is addressed to you outside the United States) from the date of this notice to file a petition with the Tax Court. If you do not petition the Tax Court you will receive a bill for the amount due.

Fast Track Mediation Services

If you do not agree with any or all of the IRS findings, you may request Fast Track Mediation services to help you resolve disputes resulting from the examination (audits). Fast Track Mediation offers an expedited process with a trained mediator, who will help facilitate communication, in a neutral setting. The mediator will work with you and the IRS to understand the nature of the dispute. The purpose is to help the two of you reach a mutually satisfactory resolution that is consistent with the applicable law. The mediator has no authority to require either party to accept any resolution. You may withdraw from the mediation process anytime. If any issues remain unresolved you will retain all of your usual appeal rights.

Most cases qualify for Fast Track Mediation. To begin the process, you may request the examiner or IRS representative to arrange a mediation meeting. Both you and the IRS representative must sign a simple *Agreement to Mediate* form. A mediator will then be assigned. Generally, within a week, the mediator will contact you and the IRS representative to schedule a meeting. After a brief explanation of the process, the mediator will discuss with you when and where to hold the mediation session.

For additional information, refer to Publication 3605, *Fast Track Mediation-A Process for Prompt Resolution of Tax Issues.*

How Do You Appeal a Decision?

The Appeal System

Because people sometimes disagree on tax matters, the Service has an appeal system. Most differences can be settled within this system without going to court.

Your reasons for disagreeing must come within the scope of tax laws, however. For example, you cannot appeal your case based only on moral, religious, political, constitutional, conscientious, or similar grounds.

If you do not want to appeal your case within the IRS, you may take your case directly to tax court.

Appeal Within the IRS

You may appeal our tax decision to a local appeals office, which is separate and independent of the IRS Office taking the action you disagree with. An appeals office is the only level of appeal within the IRS. Conferences with Appeals Office personnel may be conducted in person, through correspondence, or by telephone with you or your authorized representative

If you want to have a conference with an appeals officer, follow the instructions in the letter you received. We will send your conference request letter to the appeals office to arrange for a conference at a convenient time and place. You or your qualified representative should be prepared to discuss all disputed issues at the conference. Most differences are settled at this level. Only attorneys, certified public accountants or enrolled agents are allowed to represent a taxpayer before Appeals. An unenrolled preparer may be a witness at the conference, but not a representative.

If you want to have a conference with an appeals officer, you may also need to file either a **small case request** or a **formal written protest** with the contact person named in the letter you receive.

Whether you file a small case request or a formal written protest depends on several factors.

Making a Small Case Request

You may make a **small case request** if the total amount of tax, penalties, and interest for *each* tax period involved is $25,000 or less, and you do not meet one of the exceptions below for which a formal protest is required. If more than one tax period is involved and *any* tax period exceeds the $25,000 threshold, you must file a formal written protest for all periods involved. The total amount includes the proposed increase or decrease in tax and penalties or claimed refund. For an *Offer-in-Compromise*, include total unpaid tax, penalty, and interest due.

To make a small case request, follow the instructions in our letter to you by sending a brief written statement requesting an appeals conference. Indicate the changes you do not agree with and the reasons you do not agree with them.

Caution

Be sure to send the protest within the time limit specified in the letter you received.

You must file a formal written protest

- If the total amount of tax, penalties, and interest for any tax period is more than $25,000;
- In all partnership and S corporation cases, regardless of the dollar amount;
- In all employee plan and exempt organization cases, regardless of the dollar amount;
- In all other cases, unless you qualify for other special appeal procedures, such as requesting appeals consideration of liens, levies, seizures, or installment agreements. *(See Publication 1660, Collection Appeal Rights, for more information on special collection appeals procedures.)*

Filing a Formal Protest

When a **formal protest** is required, send it within the time limit specified in the letter you received. Include in your protest:

- Your name and address, and a daytime telephone number.
- A statement that you want to appeal the IRS findings to the Appeals Office.
- A copy of the letter showing the proposed changes and findings you do not agree with *(or the date and symbols from the letter.)*
- The tax periods or years involved.
- A list of the charges that you do not agree with, and why you do not agree.
- The facts supporting your position on any issue that you do not agree with.
- The law or authority, if any, on which you are relying.
- You must sign the written protest, stating that it is true, under the penalties of perjury as follows:

"Under the penalties of perjury, I declare that I examined the facts stated in this protest, including any accompanying documents, and, to the best of my knowledge and belief, they are true, correct, and complete."

If your representative prepares and signs the protest for you, he or she must substitute a declaration stating:

- That he or she submitted the protest and accompanying documents and;
- Whether he or she knows personally that the facts stated in the protest and accompanying documents are true and correct.

We urge you to provide as much information as you can, as this will help us speed up your appeal. This will save you both time and money.

Additional information about the Appeals process may be found in **Publication 5**, *Your Appeals Rights and How to Prepare a Protest if you Don't Agree.*

After the Examination

Payment Options

You cannot pay all that you owe now

If you cannot pay all your taxes now, pay as much as you can. By paying now, you reduce the amount of interest and penalty you owe. Then immediately call, write, or visit the nearest IRS office to explain your situation. After you explain your situation, we may ask you to fill out a Collection Information Statement. If you are contacting us by mail or by telephone, we will mail the statement to you to complete and return to us. This will help us compare your monthly income with your expenses so we can figure the amount you can pay. We can then help you work out a payment plan that fits your situation. This is known as an installment agreement.

Payment by credit card

Individual taxpayers may make credit *(and debit)* card payments on tax liabilities *(including installment agreement* payments) by phone or Internet. Payments may be made to the United States Treasury through authorized credit card service providers.

The service providers charge a convenience fee based on the payment amount. You will be informed of the convenience fee amount before the credit card payment is authorized. This fee is in addition to any charges, such as interest, that may be assessed by the credit card issuer. Visit www.irs.gov to obtain a list of authorized service providers and to obtain updated information on credit card payment options.

Note: *You can use debit cards issued by VISA and MasterCard when making tax payments through the participating service providers. However, the service providers and card issuers treat debit cards and credit cards equally for the purpose of processing electronic tax payments. Therefore, debit card users are charged the same fee traditionally associated with credit card transactions*

Payment by Electronic Federal Tax Payment System (EFTPS)

EFTPS is an Electronic Federal Tax Payment System developed by the Internal Revenue Service and Financial Management Service (FMS).

The system allows federal taxes to be paid electronically. The system allows the use of the Internet at www.eftps.gov or telephone to initiate tax payments directly. EFTPS payments may also be made through your local financial institution. The service is convenient, secure and saves time.

You may enroll in EFTPS through the website at www.eftps.gov or by completing a form available from EFTPS customer service at (800) 555-4477 or (800) 945-8400.

Setting up an installment agreement

Installment agreements allow you to pay your full debt in smaller, more manageable amounts. Installment agreements generally require equal monthly payments. The amount and number of your installment payments will be based on the amount you owe and your ability to pay that amount within the time we can legally collect payment from you.

You should be aware, however, that an installment agreement is more costly than paying all the taxes you owe now. Like revolving credit arrangements, we charge interest on the unpaid portion of the debt. Penalties also continue to accumulate on installment agreements.

If you want to pay off your tax debt through an installment agreement, call the number shown on your bill. If you owe:

- $25,000 or less in tax, we will tell you what you need to do to set up the agreement;

- More than $25,000, we may still be able to set up an installment agreement for you, but we may also ask for financial information to help us determine your ability to pay.

Even if you set up an installment agreement, we may still file a Notice of Federal Tax Lien to secure the government's interest until you make your final payment.

Note: *We cannot take any collection actions affecting your property while we consider your request for an installment agreement, while your agreement is in effect, for 30 days after we reject your request for an agreement, or for any period while you appeal the rejection.*

If you arrange for an installment agreement, you may pay with:

- Personal or business checks, money orders, or certified funds *(all made payable to the U.S. Treasury),*

- Credit and debit cards,

- Payroll deductions your employer takes from your salary and regularly sends to IRS, or

- Electronic transfers from your bank account or other similar means.

Apply for an Offer-in-Compromise

In some cases, we may accept an *Offer-in-Compromise* to settle an unpaid tax account, including any penalties and interest. With this kind of arrangement, we can accept less than the full amount you owe when it is doubtful we will be able to collect the entire amount due.

Offers in compromise are also possible if collection action would create an economic hardship. You may want to discuss these options with your examiner.

Temporarily Delay the Collection Process

If we determine that you can't pay *any* of your tax debt, we may temporarily delay collection until your financial condition improves. You should know that if we delay collecting from you, your debt will increase because penalties and interest are charged until you pay the full amount. During a temporary delay, we will again review your ability to pay. We may also file a *Notice of Federal Tax Lien*, to protect the government's interest in your assets. See Publication 594, *The IRS Collection Process.*

Innocent Spouse Relief

If you filed a joint tax return, you are jointly and individually responsible for the tax and any interest or penalty due on the joint return, even if you later divorce. In some cases, a spouse may be relieved of the tax, interest, and penalties on a joint return.

You can ask for relief no matter how small the liability.

Three types of relief are available.

* Innocent spouse relief - may apply to all joint filers;

* Separation of liability - may apply to joint filers who are divorced, widowed, legally separated, or have not lived together for the past 12 months;

* Equitable relief - applies to all joint filers.

Innocent spouse relief and separation of liability apply only to items incorrectly reported on the return. If a spouse does not qualify for innocent spouse relief or separation of liability, the IRS may grant equitable relief.

Each type of relief is different and each has different requirements. You must file Form 8857, *Request for Innocent Spouse Relief*, to request any of these methods of relief. Publication 971, *Innocent Spouse Relief*, explains each type of relief, who may qualify, and how to request relief.

You Must Contact Us

It is important that you contact us regarding any correspondence you receive from us. If you do not pay your bill or work out a payment plan, we are required by law to take further collection actions.

What If You Believe Your Bill is Wrong

Caution

If you believe your bill is wrong, let us know as soon as possible. Call the number on your bill, write to the IRS office that sent you the bill, call 1-800-829-1040 *(for 1040 filers)*, 1-800-829-4933 *(for business filers)*, 1-800-829-4059 */TDD,* or visit your local IRS office.

To help us correct the problem, gather a copy of the bill along with copies of any records, tax returns, and canceled checks, etc., that will help us understand why you believe your bill is wrong.

If you write to us, tell us why you believe your bill is wrong. With your letter, include copies of all the documents you gathered to explain your case. Please do not send original documents. If we find you are correct, we will adjust your account and, if necessary, send you a corrected bill.

Privacy Act Statement

The Privacy Act of 1974 says that when we ask you for information, we must first tell you our legal right to ask for the information, why we are asking for it, and how it will be used. We must also tell you what could happen if you do not provide it and whether or not you must respond under the law.

This notice applies to tax returns and any papers filed with them. It also applies to any questions we need to ask you so we can complete, correct, or process your return; figure your tax; and collect tax, interest, or penalties.

Our legal right to ask for information is found in Internal Revenue Code sections 6001, 6011, and 6012(a), and their regulations. They say that you must file a return or statement with us for any tax you are liable for. Your response is mandatory under these sections.

Code section 6109 and its regulations say that you must show your social security number or individual taxpayer identification number on what you file. You must also fill in all parts of the tax form that apply to you. This is so we know who you are, and can process your return and papers. You do not have to check the boxes for the Presidential Election Campaign Fund.

We ask for tax return information to carry out the U.S. tax laws. We need it to figure and collect the right amount of tax.

We may give the information to the Department of Justice and to other Federal agencies, as provided by law. We may also give it to cities, states, the District of Columbia, and U.S. Commonwealths or possessions to carry out their tax laws. And we may give it to certain foreign governments under tax treaties they have with the United States.

We may also disclose this information to Federal, state, or local agencies that investigate or respond to acts or threats of terrorism or participate in intelligence or counterintelligence activities concerning terrorism.

If you do not file a return, do not give us the information we ask for, or provide fraudulent information, the law says that we may have to charge you penalties and, in certain cases, subject you to criminal prosecution. We may also have to disallow the exemptions, exclusions, credits, deductions, or adjustments shown on your tax return. This could make your tax higher or delay any refund. Interest may also be charged.

Please keep this notice with your records. You may want to refer to it if we ask you for other information. If you have questions about the rules for filing and giving information, please call or visit any Internal Revenue Service office.